The Global Justice Reader

The Global Justice Reader

Edited by Thom Brooks

Blackwell
Publishing

Editorial material and organization © 2008 by Blackwell Publishing Ltd

BLACKWELL PUBLISHING
350 Main Street, Malden, MA 02148-5020, USA
9600 Garsington Road, Oxford OX4 2DQ, UK
550 Swanston Street, Carlton, Victoria 3053, Australia

The right of Thom Brooks to be identified as the author of the editorial material in this work has been asserted
in accordance with the UK Copyright, Designs, and Patents Act 1988.

First published 2008 by Blackwell Publishing Ltd

1 2008

Library of Congress Cataloging-in-Publication Data is available

ISBN: 978-1-4051-6965-3 (hardback)
ISBN: 978-1-4051-6964-6 (paperback)

A catalogue record for this title is available from the British Library.

Set in 10.5 on 12.5 pt Minion
by SNP Best-set Typesetter Ltd., Hong Kong
Printed and bound in Singapore
by Markono Print Media Pte Ltd

The publisher's policy is to use permanent paper from mills that operate a sustainable forestry policy, and
which has been manufactured from pulp processed using acid-free and elementary chlorine-free practices.
Furthermore, the publisher ensures that the text paper and cover board used have met acceptable
environmental accreditation standards.

For further information on
Blackwell Publishing, visit our website at
www.blackwellpublishing.com

Contents

Preface

I have accumulated many debts in preparing *The Global Justice Reader*. First, I must thank Fabian Freyenhagen and Peter Jones for first encouraging me to pursue this volume: it would never have been possible without their help from the start. Second, I must thank my friends at Wiley–Blackwell, principally Nick Bellorini and Kelvin Matthews, for their tireless efforts at making this project a reality. In particular, I owe a special debt of gratitude to Nick for his support from the very beginning. I cannot be more thankful.

The work on this Reader took place during a year of research leave. I gratefully acknowledge my thanks to the School of Geography, Politics and Sociology at the University of Newcastle for granting me leave, and the Arts and Humanities Research Council for helping to fund my leave.

A number of friends and colleagues gave invaluable advice on the contents for this collection. I must sincerely thank Simon Caney, Fabian Freyenhagen, Lisa Fuller, Carol Gould, Tim Hayward, Matt Lister, Graham Long, Martha C. Nussbaum, James Pattison, Thomas W. Pogge, Leif Wenar, Lenka Žemberová, and anonymous readers for the publisher for their excellent advice – although, of course, I alone assume responsibility for the Reader's contents.

Finally, I owe a very special and personal debt to my teacher, Leif Wenar. It was under his wing that my interest in global justice first began and continues to grow. His work has long been truly inspirational for me, as well as his example. I gratefully offer him my thanks for the priceless gift of opening my eyes to a new and exciting world.

T.B.

Acknowledgments

The editor and publisher gratefully acknowledge the permission granted to reproduce the copyright material in this book:

1. Thomas Hobbes, Chapters 14, 17–18, pp. 91–9, 117–29 from Richard Tuck (ed.), *Leviathan* (Cambridge: Cambridge University Press, 1996).
2. Charles R. Beitz, "A State of Nature," pp. 13–63 from *Political Theory and International Relations*, 2nd edn. (Princeton, NJ: Princeton University Press, 1999). © 1979 Princeton University Press. Afterword © paperback edition 1999 Princeton University Press. Reprinted with permission of Princeton University Press.
3. Thomas W. Pogge, "Cosmopolitanism and Sovereignty," pp. 48–75 from *Ethics* 103 (1992). © 1992 by The University of Chicago Press. Reprinted with permission.
4. Avishai Margalit and Joseph Raz, "National Self-Determination," pp. 439–61 from *The Journal of Philosophy* 87:9 (September 1990). Copyright © 1990 by The Journal of Philosophy Inc. Reprinted by permission of *The Journal of Philosophy* and the authors.
5. Allen Buchanan, "Theories of Secession," pp. 31–61 from *Philosophy & Public Affairs* 26:1 (1997). Reprinted with permission of Blackwell Publishing.
6. United Nations, *Universal Declaration of Human Rights*. Reprinted with kind permission of the United Nations.
7. Leif Wenar, "The Nature of Rights," pp. 223–52 from *Philosophy & Public Affairs* 33:3 (2005). © 2005 by Blackwell Publishing, Inc. Reprinted with permission of Blackwell Publishing.
8. Charles R. Beitz, "Human Rights as a Common Concern," pp. 269–82 from *American Political Science Review* 95:2 (June 2001). Reprinted with permission of Cambridge University Press and the author.
9. Peter Jones, "Group Rights and Group Oppression," pp. 353–77 from *The Journal of Political Philosophy* 7:4 (1999). © 1999 by Blackwell Publishers. Reprinted with permission of Blackwell Publishing.
10. David Sussman, "What's Wrong with Torture?" pp. 1–33 from *Philosophy & Public Affairs* 33:1 (2005). © 2005 by Blackwell Publishing, Inc. Reprinted with permission of Blackwell Publishing.

11. John Rawls, Parts I (§§1–4) and II (§§7–9, 11–12), pp. 3–4, 11–19, 23–43 from *The Law of Peoples* (Cambridge, MA: Harvard University Press, 1999). Copyright © 1999 by the President and Fellows of Harvard College. Reprinted by permission of the publisher.

12. Thomas W. Pogge, "An Egalitarian Law of Peoples," pp. 195–224 from *Philosophy & Public Affairs* 23 (1994). Reprinted with permission of Blackwell Publishing.

13. Robert E. Goodin, "What is so Special about our Fellow Countrymen?," pp. 663–86 from *Ethics* 98 (July 1988). © 1988 by the University of Chicago Press. Reprinted with permission.

14. David Miller, "The Ethics of Nationality," pp. 49–80 from *On Nationality* (Oxford: Oxford University Press, 1995). Reprinted with permission of Oxford University Press.

15. Martha C. Nussbaum, "Patriotism and Cosmopolitanism," pp. 2–17, 145 (notes) from Joshua Cohen (ed.), *For Love of Country? Debating the Limits of Patriotism* (Boston, MA: Beacon Press, 2002).

16. Immanuel Kant, extracts from Sections I and II, pp. 3–21, 23–34 from Lewis White Beck (ed.), *Perpetual Peace* (Indianapolis, IN: Bobbs-Merrill, 1957).

17. Jürgen Habermas, "Kant's Idea of Perpetual Peace, with the Benefit of Two Hundred Years' Hindsight," pp. 113–53 from James Bohman and Matthias Lutz-Bachmann (eds.), *Perpetual Peace: Essays on Kant's Cosmopolitan Ideal* (Cambridge, MA: MIT Press, 1997). © 1997 Massachusetts Institute of Technology, published by the MIT Press. Reprinted with permission.

18. Thomas W. Pogge, "Moral Universalism and Global Economic Justice," pp. 91–117, 230–6 (notes) from *World Poverty and Human Rights* (Cambridge: Polity, 2002). Reprinted with permission of Sage Publications.

19. Peter Singer, "Famine, Affluence, and Morality," pp. 229–43 from *Philosophy & Public Affairs* 1:3 (1972). Reprinted with permission of Blackwell Publishing.

20. Leif Wenar, "What We Owe to Distant Others," pp. 283–304 from *Politics, Philosophy & Economics* 2 (2003). © 1988 Sage Publications Ltd. Reprinted with permission of Sage Publications.

21. Thomas Nagel, "The Problem of Global Justice," pp. 113–47 from *Philosophy & Public Affairs* 33:2 (2005). © 2005 by Blackwell Publishing, Inc. Reprinted with permission of Blackwell Publishing.

22. Thomas W. Pogge, "Eradicating Systemic Poverty: Brief for a Global Resources Dividend," pp. 59–77 from *The Journal of Human Development* 2:1 (2001). Reprinted with permission of Taylor & Francis Ltd; www.informaworld.com

23. Lisa L. Fuller, "Poverty Relief, Global Institutions, and the Problem of Compliance," pp. 285–97 from *The Journal of Moral Philosophy* 2:3 (2005). © 2005 Sage Publications London. Reprinted with permission of Sage Publications.

24. St. Thomas Aquinas, "War, Sedition, and Killing," pp. 239–42, 247–8, 251–6, 261–6 from *Political Writings*, ed. R. W. Dyson (Cambridge: Cambridge University Press, 2002). Copyright © in the selection, translation, and editorial matter Cambridge University Press. Reprinted with permission of Cambridge University Press.

25. John Stuart Mill, "A Few Words on Non-Intervention," pp. 118–24 from *Collected Works of John Stuart Mill*, ed. John M. Robson, vol. XXI (Toronto: University of Toronto Press, 1984). Reprinted with permission of University of Toronto Press.

26. United Nations, Chapter VII from *Charter*, www.un.org. Reprinted with permission of United Nations, New York.

27. Thomas Nagel, "War and Massacre," pp. 123–44 from *Philosophy & Public Affairs* 1:2 (1972). Reprinted with permission of Blackwell Publishing.

28. Michael Walzer, "Anticipations," pp. 74–85, 340–1 (notes) from *Just and Unjust War: A Moral Argument with Historical Illustrations*, 3rd edn. (New York: Basic Books, 2000). Reprinted with permission of Perseus Books LLC.

29. Jeff McMahan, "Just Cause for War," pp. 55–75 from *Ethics & International Affairs* 19:3 (2005). Reprinted with permission of Blackwell Publishing.

30. Michael Walzer, "Noncombatant Immunity and Military Necessity," pp. 138–59, 343–4 (notes) from *Just and Unjust Wars: A Moral Argument with Historical Illustrations*, 3rd edn. (New York: Basic Books, 2000). Reprinted with permission of Perseus Books LLC.

31. David Rodin, "Terrorism without Intention," pp. 752–71 from *Ethics* 114 (July 2004). © 2004 the University of Chicago Press. Reprinted with permission.

32. Saul Smilansky, "Terrorism, Justification, and Illusion," pp. 790–805 from *Ethics* 114 (July 2004). © 2004 by the University of Chicago Press. Reprinted with permission.

33. Susan Moller Okin, "Is Multiculturalism Bad for Women?" pp. 9–24, 133–5 (notes) from Joshua Cohen, Matthew Howard, and Martha C. Nussbaum (eds.), *Is Multiculturalism Bad for Women?* (Princeton, NJ: Princeton University Press, 1999). © 1999 Princeton University Press. Reprinted with permission of Princeton University Press.

34. Martha C. Nussbaum, "Capabilities as Fundamental Entitlements: Sen and Social Justice," pp. 33–50, 56–9 from *Feminist Economics* 9:2–3 (2003). © 2003 IAFFE.

35. Martha C. Nussbaum, "The Role of Religion," pp. 168–212, 235–40 from *Women and Human Development: The Capabilities Approach* (Cambridge: Cambridge University Press, 2000). Reprinted with permission of Cambridge University Press.

36. Carol C. Gould, "Conceptualizing Women's Human Rights," pp. 139–55 from *Globalizing Democracy and Human Rights* (Cambridge: Cambridge University Press, 2004). Reprinted with permission of Cambridge University Press.

37. Peter Singer, "One Atmosphere," pp. 14–50, 205–8 (notes) from *One World: The Ethics of Globalization*, 2nd edn. (New Haven, CT: Yale University Press, 2002).

38. Simon Caney, "Cosmopolitan Justice, Responsibility, and Global Climate Change," pp. 747–72, 774–5 from *Leiden Journal of International Law* 18 (2005). © Foundation of the Leiden Journal of International Law. Reprinted with permission of Cambridge University Press and the author.

Every effort has been made to trace copyright holders and to obtain their permission for the use of copyright material. The publisher apologizes for any errors or omissions in the above list and would be grateful if notified of any corrections that should be incorporated in future reprints or editions of this book.

Introduction

I

The Global Justice Reader brings together the best work in the area from contemporary political philosophy and its history. The Reader is divided into thirty-eight chapters in eleven parts. These parts cover (1) "sovereignty," (2) "rights to self-determination," (3) "human rights," (4) "Rawls's *The Law of Peoples*," (5) "nationalism and patriotism," (6) "cosmopolitanism," (7) "global poverty and international distributive justice," (8) "just war," (9) "terrorism," (10) "women and global justice," and (11) "international environmental justice." The authors surveyed here include the most influential writers on global justice. In this Introduction, I will offer a brief overview of the important themes covered in this Reader.

II

The history of political philosophy has been marked by an interest in domestic justice within the state. Indeed, the vast majority of what philosophers had to say about justice did not extend to considerations of global justice outside the state. Coincidentally, the vast literature on justice and rights that has developed over the years has focussed on questions of distributive justice within a single society, rather than across several societies or states.

However, it is certainly true that many philosophers in the past had an interest in matters of international justice. For example, both St. Augustine (in his *The City of God*) and St. Thomas Aquinas (in his *Summa theologiae*) offer revealing and influential theories on what constitutes a "just war" (see chapter 24).[1] Thus, Aquinas will argue that a just war requires several elements: the legitimacy of government, a just cause, and a right intention. A government cannot wage a just war if it is illegitimate. Legitimate governments, in turn, can only wage just war with both a just cause and just intent. In other words, the offending state must have performed some act of wrongdoing, a wrong that is in need of being put right by others. Moreover, a state must not only be legitimate and wage war for a just cause, but it must also have a just intent. Our intention must be to spread good or help avert evil. We cannot wage just war if we lack righteous intentions even if the state we want to attack deserves punishment for its actions. Thus, we have two justificatory grounds for a just war: *jus ad bellum* (the justifiability of the war) and *jus in bello* (the justifiability of the way war is waged).

The body of work on just war and international affairs offered by Augustine and Aquinas was extended by others, including Hugo Grotius and Samuel Pufendorf, and continues in recent contributions to the debate over just war by Jeff McMahan, Thomas Nagel, and Michael Walzer (see Part VIII).[2] These philosophers defend very different views of what can amount to just war. For example, Nagel opts for strict "absolutist" limits on what might serve as a justification for war and its justified conduct, such as an absolute prohibition on the killing of innocent noncombatants (chapter 27). McMahan makes an argument for the view that a war that lacks a just cause cannot be fought justly (chapter 29). That is, just war theorists separate the distinctions of (a) *jus ad bellum* and (b) *jus in bello*. For McMahan, these distinctions are not equal partners. If *jus ad bellum* is not satisfied, then it does not matter how virtuously we conduct the battle because it cannot be considered a just war. Finally, Walzer queries whether a state can engage in pre-emptive self-defense (chapter 28). He argues that we can be morally justified to wage a pre-emptive war, but only if a threat is sufficiently established.

Contemporary commentators have moved in different directions and alert us to the importance of various distinctions, contributing to our understanding of just war. However, the link with the past work of Aquinas remains strong. Our work today benefits clearly from earlier work by canonical figures. However, the issue of just war theory is not unique in this respect.

Of course, just war theorists offer us various accounts of how war might be justified. This position takes for granted the possibility of war being justifiable. Some philosophers have argued against the justifiability of war. Thus, for example John Stuart Mill presents us with a distinctly unique perspective in his essay 'A Few Words on Non-Intervention' (chapter 25). We might often think that we sometimes do a favor to countries when we conquer them. After all, perhaps these states are authoritarian or worse. Perhaps they lack the know-how or political will to transform their economy and political institutions to bring benefit to their citizens and the world community. If going to war brought with it good consequences such as these, then we might think these good reasons to go to war. Mill disagrees. He argues that battles may be won, but a people's freedom is to be won only by their own toil: "No people ever was and remained free, but because it was determined to be so . . . for, unless the spirit of liberty is strong in a people, those who have the executive in their hands easily work any institutions to the purposes of despotism." Thus, freedom is something a people earn and not something they can simply be given by others. It is true that part of Mill's argument rests on more than a moral claim about legitimate justifications to invade others and, instead, on an empirical matter of fact: the political stability of a country will be undermined if its freedoms and constitution are imposed from outside and not fought for and developed by a country's own citizens. Of course, Mill is far from alone in believing history helps to prove his point. In fact, G. W. F. Hegel argues that:

> For a constitution is not simply made: it is the work of centuries, the Idea and consciousness of the [nation] . . . What Napoleon gave to the Spanish was more rational than what they had before, and yet they rejected it as something alien . . . The constitution of a nation must embody the nation's feeling for its rights and [present] condition; otherwise it will have no meaning or value.[3]

If history does prove this view of Hegel's and Mill's, then this poses a threat to just war theorists who claim war might be justified in the effort of nation-building.[4] Thus far, the sad experiences of Afghanistan and Iraq do not yet appear to correct this view even if it is unclear why history has acted with such "cunning."

There is a further powerful argument often made by those who oppose war in general. This argument is made by the Danish philosopher Søren Kierkegaard in his essay "Neither Victims Nor Executioners."[5] Kierkegaard grounds his argument on an empirical claim as well. He begins by claiming that every war entails a loss of innocent life. In other words, every military conflict will involve the deaths of *both* combatants and innocent noncombatants without exception, no matter how careful we are to avoid harm to innocents. This, in turn, raises an important consideration we tend to overlook when deciding whether or not a war is a just war. If it follows that whenever I lend my support behind a decision to go to war that innocent noncombatants will be one important casualty of the conflict, then when I support the decision to go to war I am deciding that innocent people elsewhere can be killed. Of course, I would not be choosing which innocent persons were killed during the course of any conflict: these persons would be selected randomly. Thus, I condemn innocent people selected at random when I support the decision to go to war. These innocent people will become victims of my support of a "justified" war and I become their executioner: these innocent people would live if I had not supported military conflict. Kierkegaard then makes a startling argument. If I am to ever support a decision to go to war, then I must likewise be willing to become an innocent noncombatant death during this war. For Kierkegaard, I am inconsistent at best (and immoral at worst) to support a war that will have the consequence of the innocent deaths of randomly selected civilians if I were unwilling to die similarly from such an attack. Kierkegaard importantly reminds us that the decision to go to war is more than an intellectual exercise. Innocent people die in every conflict. In supporting a conflict, we must be willing not only to support the deaths of these innocent victims, but be willing to die ourselves as an innocent victim if all innocent people share equal moral worth. Thus, pacifism is the only path where all human beings are "neither victims nor executioners" and we escape this moral problem. Whether or not we are persuaded by this argument, Kierkegaard does well to highlight an important consideration that is too often overlooked. Indeed, the main casualties of every conflict seem always to be the innocent.

Philosophers in the past have made important contributions to how we think about issues in the present and most especially on the justifiability of war. At present, politicians have argued for just war as a response to terrorism. This has offered many problems of its own. The first problem is perhaps definitional, namely, what precisely *is* terrorism? For one thing, terrorism appears to be rather similar to sedition and treason. That is, terrorism seems to be a distinctly political activity aimed at political change. The traitor is interested in betraying his country, contributing to its demise. Those engaged in sedition aspire to undermine their political leaders.

And, yet, terrorism seems much more. For one thing, "terror" seems essential to "terrorism." Indeed, an act that did not attempt to instill fear might be best categorized rather differently. If a person was involved in a random murder spree, then we would understand that person to be a murderer, not a terrorist. However, we might then think that what makes a terrorist is not simply *causing* terror but *intending to cause* terror. In other words, we might think that a person or group of persons must intend to cause terror for their act to be a terrorist act. However, David Rodin persuasively argues that what such persons intend is immaterial: we can be terrorists without intending to cause terror (chapter 31). Just as we might be found guilty of murder if we killed someone through reckless or negligent behavior, Rodin believes that terrorism is terrorism even if performed out of recklessness or negligence.

The next question concerns whether or not such activities might ever be justified. Michael Walzer has looked at the place of innocent noncombatants in war (see chapter 30). We might think that all combatants are potentially targets of justified killing and, yet, Walzer documents how often soldiers on the front line fail to see one another as potential targets unless directly engaged in a firefight. Such a view might mislead us into thinking then the number of justified targets is quite small. However, the situation is more complicated than that. For example, on the one hand, innocent combatants who provide food to all citizens and soldiers indirectly promote the war effort, but not purposefully. These innocent persons should be immune from harm in any military conflict. On the other hand, innocent persons who directly promote the war effort – perhaps responsible for transporting military equipment on the military's behalf exclusively – may become targets of a military strike.

If innocent noncombatants can become legitimate *military* targets, then we might wonder if it follows if they can become legitimate *terrorist* targets. Terrorism does not aim exclusively at spreading terror, but its victims are often innocent noncombatants. If their deaths can be justified at all, then perhaps they can become legitimate targets for terrorists. Saul Smilansky examines the major cases of terrorism in the world today, such as the activities of the Irish Republican Army, Palestinian liberation fighters, and al-Qaeda (chapter 32). In all cases, Smilansky argues these groups lack justification for their terror. This is not to say that he then believes terrorism is never justified: instead, he argues it is only justified in response to a clear and present danger. That said, a strong reason to argue against ever legitimizing terrorism is that the vast majority of what passes for terrorism is unjustified.

III

In his *Leviathan*, Thomas Hobbes makes several fundamental contributions to how we conceive international affairs (chapter 1). Hobbes introduces the idea of "a state of nature": a world without a common source of authoritative power where individuals compete against each other to further their advantage. Hobbes argues there is no justice in international affairs because there is no world body that can judge whether a state acts rightly or wrongly. Whether or not states should abide by any treaties with other states is a judgment left to individual states. Thus, the international sphere is characterized by anarchy where states compete against one another in pursuit of self-interest. This classical "realist" understanding of international politics continues to be highly influential to this day.

Moreover, Hobbes offers an important contribution to how we understand sovereignty as well. He argues that a state has legitimate authority over its members if, and only if, it has the consent of all members. This consent takes the form of a social contract where all members consent to the authority of a monarch or assembly. It is now commonplace (and perhaps modern common sense) that any legitimate government remains a sovereign power over its members only if it has the consent of its members. This fact speaks clearly to the great contribution Hobbes's work on consent and sovereignty offers us today, raising new questions about justified political authority and rights, if any, to secession and self-determination (see Part II).

In the late eighteenth century, Immanuel Kant published his *Perpetual Peace* and this remains a defining moment in the development of work on global justice (chapter 16).

Perpetual Peace marks a distinct departure from Hobbes's *Leviathan*. Whilst both agree on the importance of consent, Kant denies that the lack of world government must lead to international anarchy and the absence of international justice. Instead, Kant argues that a state needs the consent of its people in order for it to justify going to war. However, citizens will only rarely agree to engaging in war given the many costs involved. There will therefore be great pressure to avoid war and create "a league of nations," a body where states engage in diplomacy. A "perpetual peace" amongst states is possible and without a world state.

This Kantian view that we can have international justice in the absence of a world state is developed by later writers as well, such as Charles R. Beitz, Thomas W. Pogge, John Rawls, and Jürgen Habermas and remains an enduring legacy of Kant's work (see chapters 2, 3, 11, and 17). Beitz agrees with Kant against Hobbes: the international sphere may lack a political body with authority over all member states, but it is not a realm of anarchy. In fact, there are a variety of international norms that continue to govern our activities, not least with respect to the rules of war. The fact that we lack a world-state does not discredit the fact of the absence of anarchy in the international sphere: we are bound by rules that member states should recognize and uphold.

Pogge agrees with this perspective and argues that one important implication is that some states have a negative duty to assist those in severe poverty. Our world is not governed by anarchy nor a world-state, but a world order that is supported and maintained by wealthy states. This world order contributes to severe poverty in poor states. Wealthy states harm poor states in maintaining a coercive global order that contributes to severe poverty. Wealthy states have a negative duty to refrain from contributing to harm and rectifying the damage caused, eradicating severe poverty. Economic justice is not something that exists alone within a particular state, but something we can extend across borders.

Whereas Kant puts forward a picture of states in perpetual peace united in a common project, Rawls offers us a less robust, but no less philosophically complex, vision (chapter 11). Kant is often credited with presenting us with the democratic peace thesis: democratic states do not engage with war with one another. The key to perpetual peace may lie in expanding the number of representative states across the earth. For Rawls, we can have peace between states even if they are not entirely democratic. Instead, he speaks of "liberal peoples" who are democratic and "decent peoples" who are not. What is crucial is that both groups respect the rule of law and permit dissent. Together they create a "Law of Peoples" which governs the peaceful relations between them. We can enjoy a cosmopolitan, peaceful world without every state having to be democratic and respecting the right of different peoples to establish varying political constitutions within certain safeguards.

The Hobbesian and Kantian perspectives on international justice present us with two different vantage points from which to consider the international realm. The Hobbesian is largely nationalist, claiming no duties to distant others beyond a state's borders. My duties are only to my countrymen with whom I share an important relation, namely, our shared identity as citizens of our state. The Kantian is more cosmopolitan. This person argues that the individual person is the highest unity of concern, not the realm of the state. Justice for all exists beyond state borders given that people live in other states and, as people, they are entitled to equal concern and respect.

There has been an important literature springing up behind each view. Contemporary nationalists, such as David Miller, argue that we have special obligations to fellow citizens (chapter 14). If our relational attachments have special significance, then our attachment to others in our group gives fellow group members a special status for us. This does not deny that we may have obligations to all, but it is to argue that we have special obligations above and beyond this to fellow citizens of our state.

The view that we should extend a special *moral* status to compatriots above and beyond citizens of different countries is argued against by cosmopolitans. They might argue, following Robert E. Goodin, that membership in the same political state is most often a product of chance, not design (chapter 13). Arbitrary moral benefits contradict justice and it is arbitrary that we extend a special moral status to compatriots. Thus, we should extend equal status to all. Martha C. Nussbaum argues for a more "modified cosmopolitanism" (chapter 15).[6] She does not deny that we have special connections with those in relation to us, whether family or friends or fellow citizens. What she denies is that we lack any relation to humanity as a whole. Our task, for Nussbaum, is to bring these different layers of connection together so all share equal status.

What is curious about this debate is how close the two positions appear. Most nationalists do not deny that we have obligations beyond our borders. Instead, nationalism often amounts to the position that we have obligations to all and special duties to a few – namely, our fellow citizens. Most cosmopolitans, similarly, do not deny that we have special duties to people with whom we share a special connection. For example, suppose our child was drowning in one lake and someone else's child was drowning in a second lake. We stand equidistant between each drowning child and only able to rescue one of them. We may believe each child has an equal moral right to life, while also believe that, if we must choose to save but one of these lives, we ought to choose to save the life of our own child. In fact, many of us would be uneasy with someone who thought this fact made no difference and used a coin toss to decide whom to save.[7] Cosmopolitans might both choose to save their own child *and* claim all people have an equal right to life. Given these general characterizations, it can be difficult to discriminate sharply between these two views as *both* most nationalists *and* most cosmopolitans *agree* that duties exist beyond our borders and that we have a special connection with those nearest and dearest to us. The difference then only lies with how highly we prize our obligations to compatriots and how strong are our commitments to non-citizens.

If most commentators on global justice – whether nationalist or cosmopolitan – accept duties to persons elsewhere, then this raises the question of international distributive justice and our obligations to the global poor. The plight of the global poor is perhaps the leading moral problem of our times. Peter Singer argues that we have a duty to extend assistance to the global poor (chapter 19). If preventing something bad from happening to other people involves relatively minor costs, then we are obliged to act and prevent harm. Thus, wealthy nations that can alleviate global poverty are under an obligation to the poor as the costs are relatively minor. Singer's work was revolutionary at the time and heralded a new attitude to issues of global justice.

Of course, we may have a moral obligation to the global poor that requires us to contribute financial help. Leif Wenar argues (in chapter 20) that we should take a serious look at the issue of the relationship between contributing this help and its ability to provide concrete benefits to the poor. We need to know more about the effectiveness of our aid contributions in relieving poverty to best deliver on any obligations we have to the global poor. Furthermore, some argue, following Thomas Nagel, that whatever the institutions we will need to bring about greater global equality, we must recognize that these institutions will be first unjust and serve the interests of affluent states before contributing to the cause of good (chapter 21). The path to justice must lead through injustice. Once these institutions are in place (even if most likely for less justified reasons), then and only then can a global institutional order be constructed that can address global inequalities, such as global poverty.

Nevertheless, even if we have international institutions that might help facilitate our effectively providing resources to the poor, a question still remains as to how we should best choose these resources. For example, Amartya Sen argues that we should not look at development solely in terms of resources. He reminds us that a lack of resources does not explain, say, long life expectancy, literacy, and other features we expect to find only in affluent, rather than poor, communities. Instead, we can locate communities that are financially prosperous who score low on these counts, and communities who are not financially prosperous who score well. For example, the United States is wealthier and possesses more resources than either Kerala in India or China and, yet, the survival rates of African-American men fare worse than men in Kerala or China, or indeed than white men in the United States. Instead of focussing only upon resources, we should adopt a view of "poverty as a deprivation of basic capabilities, rather than merely as low income."[8] Thus, the best measure of a people's development is their ability to pursue basic capabilities: development is freedom, not merely resources. Sen's well-known and powerful example is that no democracy has ever suffered a famine.[9]

Most importantly, the use of the capabilities approach is not meant only to provide us with a better understanding of development, but of universal freedom: the capabilities of someone living in the United States are no different from those of us living in the United Kingdom, China, India or Brazil. Thus, the capability approach is universalistic in its application to all cultures as well as equally to men and women. Martha C. Nussbaum provides a useful advance on Sen's approach insofar as she sets out to define precisely what are our capabilities. She claims all human beings are entitled to capabilities to life; bodily health; bodily integrity; senses, imagination, and thought; emotions; practical reason; affiliation; other species; play; and control over one's environment (see chapter 34). Governments are under a duty to permit their citizens the opportunities to exercise their capabilities, leaving this choice to the individuals' discretion.

Thus, one view is that our assistance to others should be aimed at expanding the possibilities others have to exercise their full range of capabilities. A second view is less ambitious and more traditional: our assistance should be targeted at the protection of human rights or capabilities. Human rights are universal: they are rights that all possess in virtue of being a human being. It makes no difference whether we are rich or poor, tall or short, nor male or female. Our rights are shared in equal measure in common.

The question is then how to determine what are our human rights. One attempt to set out what are our human rights is the "Universal Declaration of Human Rights (UDHR)" (chapter 6). The UDHR enshrines a number of rights as the rights of all human beings everywhere as agreed by virtually all countries in the world, irrespective of wealth, ethnicity, religion or continent. These rights include the less controversial rights to life and employment, as well as the more controversial rights of choosing one's marriage partner. The specification of rights is, of course, itself of tremendous importance given that most of us argue that states possess legitimacy when they respect the rights of their citizens (see chapter 8). Similarly, we believe states are damaged when they use torture, as this is seen as a serious abuse of human rights (see chapter 10).

Leif Wenar examines the nature of rights and clarifies our understanding of them (chapter 7). He offers us a "several-functions theory of rights," where not all "Hohfeldian" incidents are rights but where all rights are incidents.[10] Hohfeldian incidents support one or more particular functions, such as exemption, discretion, authorization, protection, provision, and performance. Wenar's "several-functions" theory of rights is meant to overcome "single-function" theories, such as the will theory (e.g., rights are incidents that offer the rights holder specific varieties of choices) and the interest theory (e.g., rights are incidents that further the well-being of the rights holder). A several-functions theory can acknowledge that all rights must serve at least one function without claiming that all rights must serve at least one particular function.

Of course, a several-functions theory (or, indeed, a theory of capabilities) does not reject the possibility of non-individualistic rights. One importance of rights is that they capture something of significance to human beings. Part of what is of significance to us is our identity in particular groups. According to Peter Jones, if this view is correct, then rights can belong both to individuals and the groups that they belong to (chapter 9). That is, we have individual rights as well as group rights.

We might next ask that however we understand duties we have beyond our borders – whether in terms of rights or capabilities – what practical measures might we employ to satisfy these duties. Thomas Pogge argues that wealthy nations support a coercive global order that contributes to and maintains global poverty. He proposes a "global resources dividend," essentially a tax on resources, to help create a more egalitarian global order (chapters 12 and 22). All people share a stake in the earth's resources. All should become beneficiaries of the use of these resources. The global poor suffer a burden when wealthy nations exploit the earth's resources through a decreased share of resources and through suffering harm from environmental degradation. As a matter of justice, wealthy states should pay a tax on the use of their resources. This money would contribute toward alleviating global poverty. Wealthy states have a negative duty to alleviate global poverty because they contribute to its existence. Through a global resources dividend, wealthy states can heal the damage they have generated. In her contribution, Lisa L. Fuller considers the question of how we can ensure states will comply with a scheme of international distributive justice (chapter 23). Fuller argues that Pogge is too optimistic in arguing that affluent states would acceptably self-police their global resources dividend payments to the global poor. She argues instead in favor of NGO-delivered aid to the global poor, fostering a transparent and accountable system more likely to succeed.

We might believe something is missing in what has been said thus far. Global justice may demand we have duties to those in dire need. It may demand that we have a duty to protect the rights and capabilities of all. However, we must not only give special concern to the plight of the global poor who so often visibly command our attention, but also to the status of women who seem almost invisible in far too many discussions of global justice. Indeed, women make up half the world's population and yet they often only possess secondary status. For nearly every state, no woman has held top positions of power and many of the few occasions where women have so risen it is as a widow or daughter of an important male politician.

One way forward is Nussbaum's defense of the capabilities approach mentioned above (see chapter 34). In other words, the protection of the capabilities of each citizen will best help the realization of the freedoms of all persons. A different approach is offered by Carol C. Gould. She argues for the centrality of the feminist notion of care. That is, it is precisely because we *care* about the well-being of others that we defend and recognize the human rights of others. We do not only have care for those nearest and dearest, but we can easily extend this to a cosmopolitan care of all human beings whether male or female. Thus, the use of care helps us understand the value we place on the rights on all without excluding or damaging the rights of women.

We might suppose that a greater respect for women would entail a greater respect for group rights and multiculturalism. Full respect of groups, such as women and multicultural groups, may help correct the problem of a male-dominated society that has harmed the status of women and these groups. Susan Moller Okin alerts us to an important reservation we should have, namely, that the respect for multiculturalism may be harmful to women (chapter 33). Many groups perpetuate violations of the rights of women, taking the form of practices such as female genital mutilation, polygamy, forced marriages, and much worse. The fact that these practices are part of a culture is an insufficient reason to respect the right of a culture to continue such practices. We harm the rights of women if we permit these group rights. Instead, we should only respect group rights insofar as they do not violate individual rights, not least the rights of women.

In a similar vein, if we should exercise strong caution against certain cultural practices that harm the interests of women, then it might seem that we should be particularly firm against toleration of many religious practices. After all, many of the worries Okin discusses are not merely the practices of a cultural group, but practices justified by certain religious beliefs of these cultural groups. Martha Nussbaum helpfully considers distinctly feminist responses to this problem, arguing in favor of "the intrinsic value of religious capabilities" (chapter 35). She claims that the ability to participate in religious activities is a valuable human good for men and women that need not bring harm to either. Nussbaum defends broad freedoms of religious expression, while placing an important limit on their free exercise: violation of others' capabilities.

Thus, it is clearly true that philosophers have long taken a clear interest in matters of global justice. However, it remains the case that their contributions have not been of primary interest to modern-day commentators, that is, until now.

IV

Perhaps the final frontier of global justice is international environmental justice. There is an increasingly rich and diverse literature erupting in this area worthy of concern and interest. Indeed, issues of international environmental justice are certain to gain an increasing priority in our discussions of justice as the signs of environmental degradation become ever more clear.

For example, Peter Singer documents the enormous damage being inflicted on our environment through human activities (chapter 37). He argues that the atmosphere has a "sink": a certain capacity to absorb human pollution without damage. Emissions from all countries must be below this limit if we are to live in a sustainable environment without contributing to further damage. Our task is then to determine how much emission is permissible. Singer argues that states are each distributed a per capita share of the atmosphere's sink.

An alternative to Singer's solution is Andrew Dobson's defense of "the ecological footprint."[11] Singer's solution is based on how much we can pollute the planet, not how much we might use as such. Dobson's alternative is to argue that we each leave a footprint on our environment. We leave a footprint in the amount of resources we require and pollution we contribute to the environment. No one has the right to leave a footprint so large it damages others. In fact, every person has only the right to leave a stamp on the environment within a prescribed and equal limit.

Another solution we might think best is that, since those who pollute create the damage that harms us all, we should enforce an international norm that polluters should pay reparations in proportion to the damage they generate. Simon Caney argues that this "the polluter pays principle" is difficult to enforce in practice (chapter 38), as it is difficult to measure exactly how much harm each polluter contributes. Much of the damage the environment suffers from was created by previous generations. Like Singer, Caney claims we can permissibly emit greenhouse gases within a certain limit that our atmosphere can tolerate. If we exceed this limit, then we are required to provide compensation. However, this entails that the most advantaged states have a duty to create global institutions to discourage non-compliance. Caney, thus, calls his position a "hybrid" view of the "polluter pays" principle.

One criticism of all these views is that they tend to see environmental degradation as an exclusively anthropocentric problem where the only harms we consider are to human beings, not nature itself. Indeed, this may strike us as a curious position to take as surely part of the damage caused by environmental degradation is the harm caused to the earth's creatures and landscape. Moreover, it may strike us that if human activities contribute to global climate change and if this change has resulted in harm to human beings, then it does not necessarily follow that we should then pollute the planet less than we do. If the problem is the harm caused to fellow human beings through rising sea levels, higher rates of cholera, and withering crops, then one solution is to resolve these harms: we might relocate threatened coastal communities, provide free inoculations to all, and create new genetically modified crops that can survive in greater heat in more arid climates. If harm to human beings is the problem, then one solution is to stop generating harms by addressing the problem of climate change. However, a second solution is to make the planet more adaptable to climate change. If we are unsatisfied with this second approach, perhaps we believe part of the harms involved pertain to the damage we suffer to our ways of life and the damage done to our natural world. If so, then the importance of how we live and the sacredness of nature should become part of any account of environmental justice.

V

This brief discussion sets out the many issues of concern to global justice theorists. *The Global Justice Reader* brings together the best work in political philosophy concerning global justice from both antiquity and the modern day and it concludes with an extended bibliography. Any Reader must be selective and it cannot include all the best work in any area. For this reason, the bibliography has been expanded to include most of the important work in global justice in print since Plato, with a special focus on contemporary writings.

Students of global justice who become interested in the topics and contents of this Reader are encouraged to read leisurely through the bibliography to help supplement their further reading into the ever more important issue of global justice.

The area of global justice is expanding at an ever increasing rate. It is my hope that this collection makes the task of those coming to work in this area for the first time far easier by bringing together the best in the field at present. Few things in life are certain. However, one thing that is certain is that the topic of global justice will continue to remain a dominant area of concern for contemporary political philosophers for some time to come.

As our world continues to shrink, the need for clear thinking on matters of global justice become ever pressing. Let us hope that work in this area inspires us all to rise to this important challenge.

Notes

1   See St. Augustine, *The City of God Against the Pagans*, ed. R. W. Dyson (Cambridge: Cambridge University Press, 1998) and St. Thomas Aquinas, *Political Writings*, ed. R. W. Dyson (Cambridge: Cambridge University Press, 2002).

2   See Hugo Grotius, *Rights of War and Peace: Books 1–3*, ed. Richard Tuck (New York: Liberty Fund, 2005) and Samuel Pufendorf, *On the Duty of Man and Citizen According to Natural Law*, ed. James Tully (Cambridge: Cambridge University Press, 1991).

3   G. W. F. Hegel, *Elements of the Philosophy of Right*, ed. Allen W. Wood, trans. H. B. Nisbet (Cambridge: Cambridge University Press, 1991): §274 Addition. On Hegel's views on global justice, see my *Hegel's Political Philosophy: A Systematic Reading of the Philosophy of Right* (Edinburgh: Edinburgh University Press, 2007), chapter 8.

4   Or, in the words of my Newcastle colleague Martin Harrop, we might prefer the term "nation-destroying" to "nation-building."

5   See Søren Kierkegaard, *Neither Victims nor Executions*, trans. Dwight Macdonald (Philadelphia: New Society Publishers, 1986).

6   The phrase "modified cosmopolitanism" is used by Thomas W. Pogge. See his "Cosmopolitanism: a Defence," *Critical Review of International Social and Political Philosophy* 5 (2002): 86–91 and, in discussion, my "Cosmopolitanism and Distributing Responsibilities," *Critical Review of International Social and Political Philosophy* 5 (2002): 92–7.

7   Of course, this example becomes perhaps more revealing if we suppose the rescuer flips a coin, chooses to save the child that is not his own, and does rescue that child successfully. Meanwhile, emergency personnel arrive on the scene and resuscitate the rescuer's child who lives despite initially almost drowning. In this addition to the original example, we might think that not only was the rescuer wrong not to save his own child, but this wrong becomes further manifest when the rescuer tries to convince his child why he chose to save someone else – witnessed by the child – as his child is drowning. None of this is to claim that the second child has any less right to live, but only that if we must choose only one child to save it is less arbitrary (and perhaps even justified) to save someone with a closer relation or kinship to oneself than someone without such a close relationship.

8   See Amartya Sen, *Development as Freedom* (Oxford: Oxford University Press, 1999), pp. 20–4.

9   Ibid., chapter 7.

10 Wesley Hohfeld distinguishes between various rights claims, or "incidents," including the privilege, the claim, the power, and the immunity. See Wesley Hohfeld, *Fundamental Legal Conceptions as Applied in Judicial Reasoning* (New Haven, CT: Yale University Press, 1919).

11 See Andrew Dobson, *Citizenship and the Environment* (Oxford: Oxford University Press, 2003) and his *Justice and the Environment* (Oxford: Oxford University Press, 1998).

Part I

Sovereignty

Introduction

Sovereignty is a central concept in global justice, focussing on the exercise of legitimate power over others, defining the limits for the exercise of legitimate power, and the forms that legitimate power may adopt. The first selection is from Thomas Hobbes's classic *Leviathan* first published in 1651. In *Leviathan*, Hobbes speaks of a "state of nature." This is a world without political states, authority, or security. A person's rights exist only to the degree that he or she is able to exercise them through their own power. People relate to each other in a condition of war, a war of one against all. Hobbes argues that any reasonable person would choose to leave the state of nature for a political state. We would all much prefer to limit our freedom in a political state in order to make our freedoms more secure, rather than remain in a state of nature where our unlimited freedoms are insecure and constantly under threat. Thus, our movement from the state of nature to the political state is a transition from a state of war to a state of peace. The legitimacy of the state is built upon our consent to be governed. We may be less free, but our freedoms are made more permanent and secure when protected and regulated by the state. We consent to such an arrangement in a social contract. The contract transfers the right to a common power that alone has the authority to govern members of the state.

This discussion of the social contract is hypothetical. No date exists when individuals gathered together to sign an actual contract binding themselves and future generations to live under a sovereign government, waiving certain freedoms in exchange for the security and protection of a state. Instead, our contractual obligation is hypothetical, but our obligation is no less real. All that is required is that we *would* have freely agreed to such a contract. For Hobbes, no reasonable person would reject consenting to a social contract. When we come to form a state, it may take many shapes, such as a monarchy or an assembly. What makes the state sovereign is that it possesses the consent of "every one, with every one" in the community. The leaders of the political state then become authorized to legitimately act on behalf of the members of the state.

Hobbes offers us a number of incredibly useful concepts that will appear again and again in future readings, namely, the idea of a state of nature and the importance of popular consent to justify state authority. Indeed, Hobbes's views of *individual persons* in a state of nature is often discussed within the international realm as a state of nature composed of *individual states.* Whereas individual persons have reason to come together and agree to a common power through popular consent, "realist" scholars have argued that states have no common power to which to appeal, and so the international sphere remains a state of nature and a realm of anarchy.

In the second chapter, Charles R. Beitz considers the international sphere as a state of nature. Beitz argues that in a Hobbesian state of nature we may lack an obligation to adhere to moral principles in the absence of a central political authority, but this is not to say that moral principles do not exist: in fact, Hobbes claims that "laws of nature" exist in a state of nature. A common authority is necessary only to enforce compliance with these laws by threat of punishment.

Beitz provides us with a case in favor of an international morality. We live in an interdependent world. Contemporary states relate with one another more than ever, not least in terms of trade, taking part in a variety of international economic organizations, such as the International Monetary Fund and the World Bank. Our world is not a Hobbesian world of atomistic states fully independent from each other. In our interdependent world, states voluntarily comply with a variety of international norms and rules taking the form of international organization memberships, such as membership in the World Health Organization, NATO or the European Union. Moreover, a set of international norms that guide the conduct of states in the international sphere has arisen, defining the rules of war and conventions of diplomacy. Thus, Beitz presents us with a strong challenge to the Hobbesian understanding of international politics.

Finally, in chapter 3, Thomas W. Pogge argues in favor of an institutional understanding of moral cosmopolitanism. Moral cosmopolitanism is the view that a human being is the "ultimate unit of moral concern." This view is institutional for the following reason. In virtue of the fact of a global order within which we all participate, the rights of all human beings have become the concern of all human beings. Thus, our concern is not simply with regard to the protection and safeguarding of human rights for their own sake, insofar as human rights violations are created "by social institutions in which we are significant participants." Those of us in the developed world have a collective responsibility to the global poor insofar as we support a global order that contributes to human rights violations amongst the global poor. If we are responsible for harm to others in upholding the global order, then we have a duty to cease causing them harm and repair our damage.

However, we might then worry that however compelling the moral justification for this cosmopolitan perspective on harm caused to the global poor through the global institutional order, we uphold that our cosmopolitan solution violates state sovereignty and, therefore, should be abandoned. Alternatively, we might think that, if correct, Pogge's views would lead us to endorse a world-state: an effective political body that would have legitimate control over all peoples in order to protect the rights of human beings, defending the person as our ultimate unit of moral concern. On the contrary, Pogge does not defend a world-state largely on the grounds that such a body would be impractical. Instead, he favors a wide distribution of sovereignty amongst individual (democratic) states, rather than one body.

All three chapters argue for the importance of sovereignty. For Hobbes, sovereignty is best situated within the state, not the international sphere. Beitz argues that the international sphere is a place where authoritative norms arise that constrain states, driven by the interests of the states themselves. For Pogge, when we respect sovereignty, we must first respect the rights of individuals. States do not have any right to create human rights violations, but neither do they have any right to foster human rights violations through a coercive global order. The respect of state sovereignty is not merely the task of respecting the sovereignty of other states, but of respecting the relationship of states to each other within a global order. Whichever view we find most persuasive, each account offers a compelling picture of how we should consider sovereignty.

Chapter 1

*Leviathan**
Thomas Hobbes

Chapter XIV

The RIGHT OF NATURE, which Writers commonly call *Jus Naturale,* is the Liberty each man hath, to use his own powers, as he will himself, for the preservation of his own Nature; that is to say, of his own Life; and consequently, of doing any thing, which in his own Judgement, and Reason, hee shall conceive to be the aptest means thereunto.

By LIBERTY, is understood, according to the proper signification of the word, the absence of externall Impediments: which Impediments, may oft take away part of a mans power to do what hee would; but cannot hinder him from using the power left him, according as his judgement, and reason shall dictate to him.

A LAW OF NATURE (*Lex Naturalis*) is a Precept, or generall Rule, found out by Reason, by which a man is forbidden to do, that, which is destructive of his life, or taketh away the means of preserving the same; and to omit, that, by which he thinketh it may be best preserved. For though they that speak of this subject, use to confound *Jus,* and *Lex,*

Right and *Law;* yet they ought to be distinguished; because RIGHT, consisteth in liberty to do, or to forbeare; Whereas LAW, determineth, and bindeth to one of them: so that Law, and Right, differ as much, as Obligation, and Liberty; which in one and the same matter are inconsistent.

And because the condition of Man . . . is a condition of Warre of every one against every one; in which case every one is governed by his own Reason; and there is nothing he can make use of, that may not be a help unto him, in preserving his life against his enemyes; It followeth, that in such a condition, every man has a Right to every thing; even to one anothers body. And therefore, as long as this naturall Right of every man to every thing endureth, there can be no security to any man (how strong or wise soever he be) of living out the time, which Nature ordinarily alloweth men to live. And consequently it is a precept, or generall rule of Reason, *That every man, ought to endeavour Peace, as farre as he has hope of obtaining it; and when he cannot obtain it, that he may seek, and use, all helps, and advantages of Warre.* The first branch of which Rule, containeth the first, and Fundamentall Law of Nature; which is, *to seek Peace, and follow it.* The Second, the summe of the Right of

* From Thomas Hobbes, *Leviathan,* ed. Richard Tuck (Cambridge: Cambridge University Press, 1996), Chapters 14, 17–18, pp. 91–9, 117–29.

Nature; which is, *By all means we can, to defend our selves.*

From this Fundamentall Law of Nature, by which men are commanded to endeavour Peace, is derived this second Law; *That a man be willing, when others are so too, as farre-forth, as for Peace, and defence of himself he shall think it necessary, to lay down this right to all things; and be contented with so much liberty against other men, as he would allow other men against himselfe.* For as long as every man holdeth this Right, of doing any thing he liketh; so long are all men in the condition of Warre. But if other men will not lay down their Right, as well as he; then there is no Reason for any one, to devest himselfe of his: For that were to expose himselfe to Prey (which no man is bound to) rather than to dispose himselfe to Peace. This is that Law of the Gospell; *Whatsoever you require that others should do to you, that do ye to them.* And that Law of all men, *Quod tibi fieri non vis, alteri ne feceris.*

To *lay downe a mans Right* to any thing, is to *devest* himselfe of the *Liberty*, of hindring another of the benefit of his own Right to the same. For he that renounceth, or passeth away his Right, giveth not to any other man a Right which he had not before; because there is nothing to which every man had not Right by Nature: but onely standeth out of his way, that he may enjoy his own originall Right, without hindrance from him; not without hindrance from another. So that the effect which redoundeth to one man, by another mans defect of Right, is but so much diminution of impediments to the use of his own Right originall.

Right is layd aside, either by simply Renouncing it; or by Transferring it to another. By *Simply* RENOUNCING; when he cares not to whom the benefit thereof redoundeth. By TRANSFERRING; when he intendeth the benefit thereof to some certain person, or persons. And when a man hath in either manner abandoned, or granted away

his Right; then is he said to be OBLIGED, or BOUND, not to hinder those, to whom such Right is granted, or abandoned, from the benefit of it: and that he *Ought*, and it is his DUTY, not to make voyd that voluntary act of his own: and that such hindrance is INJUSTICE, and INJURY, as being *Sine Jure*; the Right being before renounced, or transferred. So that *Injury*, or *Injustice*, in the controversies of the world, is somewhat like to that, which in the disputations of Scholers is called *Absurdity*. For as it is there called an Absurdity, to contradict what one maintained in the Beginning: so in the world, it is called Injustice, and Injury, voluntarily to undo that, which from the beginning he had voluntarily done. The way by which a man either simply Renounceth, or Transferreth his Right, is a Declaration, or Signification, by some voluntary and sufficient signe, or signes, that he doth so Renounce, or Transferre; or hath so Renounced, or Transferred the same, to him that accepteth it. And these Signes are either Words onely, or Actions onely; or (as it happeneth most often) both Words, and Actions. And the same are the BONDS, by which men are bound, and obliged: Bonds, that have their strength, not from their own Nature (for nothing is more easily broken than a mans word) but from Feare of some evill consequence upon the rupture.

Whensoever a man Transferreth his Right, or Renounceth it; it is either in consideration of some Right reciprocally transferred to himselfe; or for some other good he hopeth for thereby. For it is a voluntary act: and of the voluntary acts of every man, the object is some *Good to himselfe*. And therefore there be some Rights, which no man can be understood by any words, or other signes, to have abandoned, or transferred. As first a man cannot lay down the right of resisting them, that assault him by force, to take away his life; because he cannot be understood to ayme thereby, at any Good to himself. The same may be sayd of Wounds, and Chayns, and Imprisonment; both because there is no benefit consequent to such patience; as there is to the patience of suffering another to be wounded, or imprisoned: as also because a man cannot tell, when he seeth men proceed against him by violence, whether they intend his death or not. And lastly the motive, and end for which this renouncing and transferring of Right is introduced, is nothing else but the security of a mans person, in his life, and in the means of so preserving life, as not to be weary of it. And therefore if a man by words, or other signes, seem to despoyle himselfe of the End, for which those signes were intended; he is not to be understood as if he meant it, or that it was his will; but that he was ignorant of how such words and actions were to be interpreted.

The mutuall transferring of Right, is that which men call CONTRACT.

There is difference, between transferring of Right to the Thing; and transferring, or tradition, that is, delivery of the Thing it selfe. For the Thing may be delivered together with the Translation of the Right; as in buying and selling with ready mony, or exchange of goods, or lands: and it may be delivered some time after.

Again, one of the Contractors, may deliver the Thing contracted for on his part, and leave the other to perform his part at some determinate time after, and in the mean time be trusted; and then the Contract on his part, is called PACT, or COVENANT: Or both parts may contract now, to performe hereafter: in which cases, he that is to performe in time to come, being trusted, his performance is called *Keeping of Promise,* or Faith; and the fayling of performance (if it be voluntary) *Violation of Faith.*

When the transferring of Right, is not mutuall; but one of the parties transferreth, in hope to gain thereby friendship, or service from another, or from his friends; or in hope to gain the reputation of Charity, or Magna-nimity; or to deliver his mind from the pain of compassion; or in hope of reward in heaven; This is not Contract, but GIFT, FREE–GIFT, GRACE: which words signifie one and the same thing.

Signes of Contract, are either *Expresse,* or *by Inference.* Expresse, are words spoken with understanding of what they signifie: And such words are either of the time *Present,* or *Past;* as, *I Give, I Grant, I have Given, I have Granted, I will that this be yours:* Or of the future; as, *I will Give, I will Grant:* which words of the future are called PROMISE.

Signes by Inference, are sometimes the consequence of Words; sometimes the consequence of Silence; sometimes the consequence of Actions; sometimes the consequence of Forbearing an Action: and generally a signe by Inference, of any Contract, is whatsoever sufficiently argues the will of the Contractor.

Words alone, if they be of the time to come, and contain a bare promise, are an insufficient signe of a Free-gift and therefore not obligatory. For if they be of the time to Come, as, *To morrow I will Give,* they are a signe I have not given yet, and consequently that my right is not transferred, but remaineth till I transferre it by some other Act. But if the words be of the time Present, or Past, as, *I have given, or do give to be delivered to morrow,* then is my to morrows Right given away to day; and that by the vertue of the words, though there were no other argument of my will. And there is a great difference in the signification of these words, *Volo hoc tuum esse cras,* and *Cras dabo*; that is, between *I will that this be thine to morrow,* and, *I will give it thee to morrow*: For the word *I will,* in the former manner of speech, signifies an act of the will Present; but in the later, it signifies a promise of an act of the will to Come: and therefore the former words, being of the Present, transferre a future right; the later, that be of the Future, transferre nothing. But if there be other signes of the Will to transferre a Right, besides Words; then, though the gift be Free, yet may the Right be understood to passe by words of the future: as if a man propound a Prize to him that comes first to the end of a race, The gift is Free; and though the words be of the Future, yet the Right passeth: for if he would not have his words so understood, he should not have let them runne.

In Contracts, the right passeth, not onely where the words are of the time Present, or Past; but also where they are of the Future: because all Contract is mutuall translation, or change of Right; and therefore he that promiseth onely, because he hath already received the benefit for which he promiseth, is to be understood as if he intended the Right should passe: for unlesse he had been content to have his words so understood, the other would not have performed his part first. And for that cause, in buying, and selling, and other acts of Contract, a Promise is equivalent to a Covenant; and therefore obligatory.

. . .

If a Covenant be made, wherein neither of the parties performe presently, but trust one another; in the condition of meer Nature (which is a condition of Warre of every man against every man), upon any reasonable suspition, it is Voyd: But if there be a common Power set over them both, with right and force sufficient to compell performance; it is not Voyd. For he that performeth first, has no assurance the other will performe after; because the bonds of words are too weak to bridle mens ambition, avarice, anger, and other Passions, without the feare of some coërcive Power; which in the condition of meer Nature, where all men are equall, and judges of the justnesse of their own fears, cannot possibly be supposed. And therfore he which performeth first, does but betray himselfe to his enemy; contrary to the Right

(he can never abandon) of defending his life, and means of living.

But in a civill estate, where there is a Power set up to constrain those that would otherwise violate their faith, that feare is no more reasonable; and for that cause, he which by the Covenant is to perform first, is obliged so to do.

The cause of feare, which maketh such a Covenant invalid, must be always something arising after the Covenant made; as some new fact, or other signe of the Will not to performe: else it cannot make the Covenant voyd. For that which could not hinder a man from promising, ought not to be admitted as a hindrance of performing.

He that transferreth any Right, transferreth the Means of enjoying it, as farre as lyeth in his power. As he that selleth Land, is understood to transferre the Herbage, and whatsoever growes upon it; Nor can he that sells a Mill turn away the Stream that drives it. And they that give to a man the Right of government in Soveraignty, are understood to give him the right of levying mony to maintain Souldiers; and of appointing Magistrates for the administration of Justice.

To make Covenants with bruit Beasts, is impossible; because not understanding our speech, they understand not, nor accept of any translation of Right; nor can translate any Right to another: and without mutuall acceptation, there is no Covenant.

. . .

The matter, or subject of a Covenant, is always something that falleth under deliberation (for to Covenant, is an act of the Will; that is to say an act, and the last act, of deliberation) and is therefore always understood to be something to come; and which is judged Possible for him that Covenanteth, to performe.

And therefore, to promise that which is known to be Impossible, is no Covenant. But if that prove impossible afterwards, which before was thought possible, the Covenant is valid, and bindeth (though not to the thing it selfe) yet to the value; or, if that also be impossible, to the unfeigned endeavour of performing as much as is possible: for to more no man can be obliged.

Men are freed of their Covenants two wayes; by Performing; or by being Forgiven. For Performance, is the naturall end of obligation; and Forgivenesse, the restitution of liberty; as being a re-transferring of that Right, in which the obligation consisted.

Covenants entred into by fear, in the condition of meer Nature, are obligatory. For example, if I Covenant to pay a ransome, or service for my life, to an enemy; I am bound by it. For it is a Contract, wherein one receiveth the benefit of life; the other is to receive mony, or service for it; and consequently, where no other Law (as in the condition, of meer Nature) forbiddeth the performance, the Covenant is valid. Therefore Prisoners of warre, if trusted with the payment of their Ransome, are obliged to pay it: And if a weaker Prince, make a disadvantageous peace with a stronger, for feare; he is bound to keep it; unlesse (as hath been sayd before) there ariseth some new, and just cause of feare, to renew the war. And even in Common-wealths, if I be forced to redeem my selfe from a Theefe by promising him money, I am bound to pay it, till the Civill Law discharge me. For whatsoever I may lawfully do without Obligation, the same I may lawfully Covenant to do through feare: and what I lawfully Covenant, I cannot lawfully break.

A former Covenant, makes voyd a later. For a man that hath passed away his Right to one man to day, hath it not to passe to morrow to another: and therefore the later promise passeth no Right, but is null.

A Covenant not to defend my selfe from force, by force, is alwayes voyd. For . . . no man can transferre, or lay down his Right to save himselfe from Death, Wounds, and Imprisonment (the avoyding whereof is the onely End of laying down any Right) and therefore the promise of not resisting force, in no Covenant transferreth any right; nor is obliging. For though a man may Covenant thus, *Unless I do so, or so, kill me*; he cannot Covenant, thus, *Unlesse I do so, or so, I will not resist you, when you come to kill me.* For man by nature chooseth the lesser evill, which is danger of death in resisting; rather than the greater, which is certain and present death in not resisting. And this is granted to be true by all men, in that they lead Criminals to Execution, and Prison, with armed men, notwithstanding that such Criminals have consented to the Law, by which they are condemned.

A Covenant to accuse ones selfe, without assurance of pardon, is likewise invalide. For in the condition of Nature, where every man is Judge, there is no place for Accusation: and in the Civil State, the Accusation is followed with Punishment; which being Force, a man is not obliged not to resist. The same is also true, of the Accusation of those, by whose Condemnation a man falls into misery; as of a Father, Wife, or Benefactor. For the Testimony of such an Accuser, if it be not willingly given, is praesumed to be corrupted by Nature; and therefore not to be received: and where a mans Testimony is not to be credited, he is not bound to give it. Also Accusations upon Torture, are not to be reputed as Testimonies. For Torture is to be used but as means of conjecture, and light, in the further examination, and search of truth: and what is in that case confessed, tendeth to the ease of him that is Tortured; not to the informing of the Torturers: and therefore ought not to have the credit of a sufficient Testimony: for whether he deliver himselfe by true, or false Accusation, he does it by the Right of preserving his own life.

. . .

Chapter XVII

The finall Cause, End, or Designe of men (who naturally love Liberty, and Dominion over others), in the introduction of that restraint upon themselves (in which wee see them live in Common-wealths), is the foresight of their own preservation, and of a more contented life thereby; that is to say, of getting themselves out from that miserable condition of Warre, which is necessarily consequent (as hath been shewn) to the naturall Passions of men, when there is no visible Power to keep them in awe, and tye them by feare of punishment to the performance of their Covenants, and observation of those Lawes of Nature set down in the fourteenth and fifteenth Chapters.

For the Lawes of Nature (as *Justice, Equity, Modesty, Mercy*, and (in summe) *doing to others, as wee would be done to*), of themselves, without the terrour of some Power, to cause them to be observed, are contrary to our naturall Passions, that carry us to Partiality, Pride, Revenge, and the like. And Covenants, without the Sword, are but Words, and of no strength to secure a man at all. Therefore notwithstanding the Lawes of Nature (which every one hath then kept, when he has the will to keep them, when he can do it safely), if there be no Power erected, or not great enough for our security; every man will, and may lawfully rely on his own strength and art, for caution against all other men. And in all places, where men have lived by small Families, to robbe and spoyle one another, has been a Trade, and so farre from being reputed against the Law of Nature, that the greater spoyles they gained, the greater was their honour; and men observed no other Lawes therein, but the Lawes of Honour; that is, to abstain from cruelty, leaving to men their lives, and instruments of husbandry. And as small Familyes did then; so now do Cities and Kingdomes which

are but greater Families (for their own security) enlarge their Dominions, upon all pretences of danger, and fear of Invasion, or assistance that may be given to Invaders, endeavour as much as they can, to subdue, or weaken their neighbours, by open force, and secret arts, for want of other Caution, justly; and are remembred for it in after ages with honour.

Nor is it the joyning together of a finall number of men, that gives them this security; because in small numbers, small additions on the one side or the other, make the advantage of strength so great, as is sufficient to carry the Victory; and therefore gives encouragement to an Invasion. The Multitude sufficient to confide in for our Security, is not determined by any certain number, but by comparison with the Enemy we feare; and is then sufficient, when the odds of the Enemy is not of so visible and conspicuous moment, to determine the event of warre, as to move him to attempt.

And be there never so great a Multitude; yet if their actions be directed according to their particular judgements, and particular appetites, they can expect thereby no defence, nor protection, neither against a Common enemy, nor against the injuries of one another. For being distracted in opinions concerning the best use and application of their strength, they do not help, but hinder one another; and reduce their strength by mutuall opposition to nothing: whereby they are easily, not onely subdued by a very few that agree together; but also when there is no common enemy, they make warre upon each other, for their particular interests. For if we could suppose a great Multitude of men to consent in the observation of Justice, and other Lawes of Nature, without a common Power to keep them all in awe; we might as well suppose all Mankind to do the same; and then there neither would be, nor need to be any Civill Government, or Common-wealth at all; because there would be Peace without subjection.

Nor is it enough for the security, which men desire should last all the time of their life, that they be governed, and directed by one judgement, for a limited time; as in one Battell, or one Warre. For though they obtain a Victory by their unanimous endeavour against a forraign enemy; yet afterwards, when either they have no common enemy, or he that by one part is held for an enemy, is by another part held for a friend, they must needs by the difference of their interests dissolve, and fall again into a Warre amongst themselves.

It is true, that certain living creatures, as Bees, and Ants, live sociably one with another (which are therefore by *Aristotle* numbred amongst Politicall creatures) and yet have no other direction, than their particular judgements and appetites; nor speech, whereby one of them can signifie to another, what he thinks expedient for the common benefit: and therefore some man may perhaps desire to know, why Man-kind cannot do the same. To which I answer,

First, that men are continually in competition for Honour and Dignity, which these creatures are not; and consequently amongst men there ariseth on that ground, Envy and Hatred, and finally Warre; but amongst these not so.

Secondly, that amongst these creatures, the Common good differeth not from the Private; and being by nature enclined to their private, they procure thereby the common benefit. But man, whose Joy consisteth in comparing himselfe with other men, can relish nothing but what is eminent.

Thirdly, that these creatures, having not (as man) the use of reason, do not see, nor think they see any fault, in the administrations of their common businesse: whereas amongst men, there are very many, that thinke themselves wiser, and abler to govern

the Publique, better than the rest; and these strive to reforme and innovate, one this way, another that way; and thereby bring it into Distraction and Civill warre.

Fourthly, that these creatures, though they have some use of voice, in making knowne to one another their desires, and other affections; yet they want that art of words, by which some men can represent to others, that which is Good, in the likenesse of Evill; and Evill, in the likenesse of Good; and augment, or diminish the apparent greatnesse of Good and Evill; discontenting men, and troubling their Peace at their pleasure.

Fiftly, irrationall creatures cannot distinguish betweene *Injury*, and *Dammage*; and therefore as long as they be at ease, they are not offended with their fellowes: whereas Man is then most troublesome, when he is most at ease: for then it is that he loves to shew his Wisdome, and controule the Actions of them that governe the Common-wealth.

Lastly, the agreement of these creatures is Naturall; that of men, is by Covenant only, which is Artificiall: and therefore it is no wonder if there be somwhat else required (besides Covenant) to make their Agreement constant and lasting; which is a Common Power, to keep them in awe, and to direct their actions to the Common Benefit.

The only way to erect such a Common Power, as may be able to defend them from the invasion of Forraigners, and the injuries of one another, and thereby to secure them in such sort, as that by their owne industrie, and by the fruites of the Earth, they may nourish themselves and live contentedly; is, to conferre all their power and strength upon one Man, or upon one Assembly of men, that may reduce all their Wills, by plurality of voices, unto one Will; which is as much as to say, to appoint one Man, or Assembly of men, to beare their Person, and every one to owne, and acknowledge himselfe to be Author of whatsoever he that so beareth their Person, shall Act, or cause to be Acted, in those things which concerne the Common Peace and Safetie; and therein to submit their Wills, every one to his Will, and their Judgements, to his Judgement. This is more than Consent, or Concord; it is a reall Unitie of them all, in one and the same Person, made by Covenant of every man with every man, in such manner, as if every man should say to every man, _I Authorize and give up my Right of Governing my selfe, to this Man, or to this Assembly of men, on this condition, that thou give up thy Right to him, and Authorise all his Actions in like manner._ This done, the Multitude so united in one Person, is called a COMMON-WEALTH, in latine CIVITAS. This is the Generation of that great LEVIATHAN, or rather (to speake more reverently) of that _Mortall God_, to which wee owe under the _Immortal God_, our peace and defence. For by this Authoritie, given him by every particular man in the Common-Wealth, he hath the use of so much Power and Strength conferred on him, that by terror thereof, he is inabled to conforme the wills of them all, to Peace at home, and mutuall ayd against their enemies abroad. And in him consisteth the Essence of the Common-wealth; which (to define it) is _One Person, of whose Acts a great Multitude, by mutuall Covenants one with another, have made themselves every one the Author, to the end he may use the strength and means of them all, as he shall think expedient, for their Peace and Common Defence._

And he that carryeth this Person, is called SOVERAIGNE, and said to have _Soveraigne Power; and_ every one besides, his SUBJECT.

The attaining to this Soveraigne Power, is by two wayes. One, by Naturall force; as when a man maketh his children, to submit themselves, and their children to his government, as being able to destroy them if they refuse; or by Warre subdueth his enemies to his will, giving them their lives on that condition. The other, is when men agree amongst themselves, to submit to some Man, or

Assembly of men, voluntarily, on confidence to be protected by him against all others. This later, may be called a Politicall Commonwealth, or Common-wealth by _Institution_; and the former, a Common-wealth by _Acquisition_. And first, I shall speak of a Commonwealth by Institution.

Chapter XVIII

A Common-wealth is said to be _Instituted_, when a _Multitude_ of men do Agree, and _Covenant, every one, with every one_, that to whatsoever _Man_, or _Assembly of Men_, shall be given by the major part, the _Right_ to _Present_ the Person of them all (that is to say, to be their _Representative_) every one, as well he that _Voted for it_, as he that _Voted against it_, shall _Authorise_ all the Actions and Judgements, of that Man, or Assembly of men, in the same manner, as if they were his own, to the end, to live peaceably amongst themselves, and be protected against other men.

From this Institution of a Commonwealth are derived all the _Rights_, and _Facultyes_ of him, or them, on whom the Soveraigne Power is conferred by the consent of the People assembled.

First, because they Covenant, it is to be understood, they are not obliged by former Covenant to any thing repugnant hereunto. And Consequently they that have already Instituted a Common-wealth, being thereby bound by Covenant, to own the Actions, and Judgements of one, cannot lawfully make a new Covenant, amongst themselves, to be obedient to any other, in any thing whatsoever, without his permission. And therefore, they that are subjects to a Monarch, cannot without his leave cast off Monarchy, and return to the confusion of a disunited Multitude; nor transferre their Person from him that beareth it, to another Man, or other Assembly of men: for they are bound, every man to every man, to Own, and be reputed Author of all, that he that already is their

Soveraigne, shall do, and judge fit to be done: so that any one man dissenting, all the rest should break their Covenant made to that man, which is injustice: and they have also every man given the Soveraignty to him that beareth their Person; and therefore if they depose him, they take from him that which is his own, and so again it is injustice. Besides, if he that attempteth to depose his Soveraign, be killed, or punished by him for such attempt, he is author of his own punishment, as being by the Institution, Author of all his Sovereign shall do: And because it is injustice for a man to do any thing, for which he may be punished by his own authority, he is also upon that title, unjust. And whereas some men have pretended for their disobedience to their Soveraign, a new Covenant, made, not with men, but with God; this also is unjust: for there is no Covenant with God, but by mediation of some body that representeth Gods Person; which none doth but Gods Lieutenant, who hath the Soveraignty under God. But this pretence of Covenant with God, is so evident a lye, even in the pretenders own consciences, that it is not onely an act of an unjust, but also of a vile, and unmanly disposition.

Secondly, Because the Right of bearing the Person of them all, is given to him they make Soveraigne, by Covenant onely of one to another, and not of him to any of them; there can happen no breach of Covenant on the part of the Soveraigne; and consequently none of his Subjects, by any pretence of forfeiture, can be freed from his Subjection. That he which is made Soveraigne maketh no Covenant with his Subjects before-hand, is manifest; because either he must make it with the whole multitude, as one party to the Covenant; or he must make a severall Covenant with every man. With the whole, as one party, it is impossible; because as yet they are not one Person: and if he make so many severall Covenants as there be men, those Covenants after he hath the Soveraignty are voyd, because what act soever can he pretended by any one of them for breach thereof, is the act both of himselfe, and of all the rest, because done in the Person, and by the Right of every one of them in particular. Besides, if any one, or more of them, pretend a breach of the Covenant made by the Soveraigne at his Institution; and others, or one other of his Subjects, or himselfe alone, pretend there was no such breach, there is in this case, no Judge to decide the controversie: it returns therefore to the Sword again; and every man recovereth the right of Protecting himselfe by his own strength, contrary to the designe they had in the Institution. It is therefore in vain to grant Soveraignty by way of precedent Covenant. The opinion that any Monarch receiveth his Power by Covenant, that is to say on Condition, proceedeth from want of understanding this easie truth, that Covenants being but words, and breath, have no force to oblige, contain, constrain, or protect any man, but what it has from the publique Sword; that is, from the untyed hands of that Man, or Assembly of men that hath the Soveraignty, and whose action are avouched by them all, and performed by the strength of them all, in him united. But when an Assembly of men is made Soveraigne; then no man imagineth any such Covenant to have past in the Institution; for no man is so dull as to say, for example, the People of *Rome*, made a Covenant with the Romans, to hold the Soveraignty on such or such conditions; which not performed, the Romans might lawfully depose the Roman People. That men see not the reason to be alike in a Monarchy, and in a Popular Government, proceedeth from the ambition of some, that are kinder to the government of an Assembly, whereof they may hope to participate, than of Monarchy, which they despair to enjoy.

Thirdly, because the major part hath by consenting voices declared a Soveraigne; he that dissented must now consent with the rest; that is, be contented to avow all the actions he shall do, or else justly be destroyed by the rest. For if he voluntarily entered into the Congregation of them that were assembled, he sufficiently declared thereby his will (and therefore tacitely covenanted) to stand to what the major part should ordayne: and therefore if he refuse to stand thereto, or make Protestation against any of their Decrees, he does contrary to his Covenant, and therefore unjustly. And whether he be of the Congregation, or not; and whether his consent be asked, or not, he must either submit to their decrees, or be left in the condition of warre he was in before; wherein he might without injustice be destroyed by any man whatsoever.

Fourthly, because every Subject is by this Institution Author of all the Actions, and Judgments of the Soveraigne Instituted; it followes, that whatsoever he doth, it can be no injury to any of his Subjects; nor ought he to be by any of them accused of Injustice. For he that doth any thing by authority from another, doth therein no injury to him by whose authority he acteth: But by this Institution of a Common-wealth, every particular man is Author of all the Soveraigne doth; and consequently he that complaineth of injury from his Soveraigne, complaineth of that whereof he himselfe is Author; and therefore ought not to accuse any man but himselfe; no nor himselfe of injury; because to do injury to ones selfe, is impossible. It is true that they that have Soveraigne power, may commit Iniquity; but not Injustice, or Injury in the proper signification.

Fiftly, and consequently to that which was sayd last, no man that hath Soveraigne power can justly be put to death, or otherwise in any manner by his Subjects punished. For seeing every Subject is Author of the actions of his Soveraigne; he punisheth another, for the actions committed by himselfe.

And because the End of this Institution, is the Peace and Defence of them all; and

whosoever has right to the End, has right to the Means; it belongeth of Right, to whatsoever Man, or Assembly that hath the Soveraignty, to be Judge both of the meanes of Peace and Defence; and also of the hindrances, and disturbances of the same; and to do whatsoever he shall think necessary to be done, both before hand, for the preserving of Peace and Security, by prevention of Discord at home, and Hostility from abroad; and, when Peace and Security are lost, for the recovery of the same. And therefore,

Sixtly, it is annexed to the Soveraignty, to be Judge of what Opinions and Doctrines are averse, and what conducing to Peace; and consequently, on what occasions, how farre, and what, men are to be trusted withall, in speaking to Multitudes of people; and who shall examine the Doctrines of all bookes before they be published. For the Actions of men proceed from their Opinions; and in the well governing of Opinions, consisteth the well governing of mens Actions, in order to their Peace, and Concord. And though in matter of Doctrine, nothing ought to be regarded but the Truth; yet this is not repugnant to regulating of the same by Peace. For Doctrine repugnant to Peace, can no more be True, than Peace and Concord can be against the Law of Nature. It is true, that in a Common-wealth, where by the negligence, or unskilfullnesse of Governours, and Teachers, false Doctrines are by time generally received; the contrary Truths may be generally offensive: Yet the most sudden, and rough busling in of a new Truth, that can be, does never breake the Peace, but only sometimes awake the Warre. For those men that are so remissely governed, that they dare take up Armes, to defend, or introduce an Opinion, are still in Warre; and their condition not Peace, but only a Cessation of Armes for feare of one another; and they live as it were, in the procincts of battaile continually. It belongeth therefore to him that hath the Soveraign Power, to be Judge, or constitute all Judges of Opinions and Doctrines, as a thing necessary to Peace; thereby to prevent Discord and Civill Warre.

Seventhly, is annexed to the Soveraigntie, the whole power of prescribing the Rules, whereby every man may know, what Goods he may enjoy, and what Actions he may doe, without being molested by any of his fellow Subjects: And this is it men call *Propriety*. For before constitution of Soveraign Power (as hath already been shewn) all men had right to all things; which necessarily causeth Warre: and therefore this Proprietie, being necessary to Peace, and depending on Soveraign Power, is the Act of that Power, in order to the publique peace. These Rules of Propriety (or *Meum* and *Tuum*) and of *Good*, *Evil*, *Lawfull*, and *Unlawfull* in the actions of Subjects, are the Civill Lawes; that is to say, the Lawes of each Common-wealth in particular, though the name of Civill Law be now restrained to the antient Civill Lawes of the City of *Rome*, which being the head of a great part of the World, her Lawes at that time were in these parts the Civill Law.

Eightly, is annexed to the Soveraigntie, the Right of Judicature; that is to say, of hearing and deciding all Controversies, which may arise concerning Law, either Civill, or Naturall, or concerning Fact. For without the decision of Controversies, there is no protection of one Subject, against the injuries of another; the Lawes concerning *Meum* and *Tuum* are in vaine; and to every man remaineth, from the naturall and neces-sary appetite of his own conservation, the right of protecting himselfe by his private strength, which is the condition of Warre; and contrary to the end for which every Common-wealth is instituted.

Ninthly, is annexed to the Soveraignty, the Right of making Warre, and Peace with other Nations, and Common-wealths; that is to say, of Judging when it is for the publique good, and how great forces are to be assem-bled, armed, and payd for that end; and to

levy mony upon the Subjects, to defray the expences thereof. For the Power by which the people are to be defended, consisteth in their Armies; and the strength of an Army, in the union of their strength under one Command; which Command the Soveraign Instituted, therefore hath; because the command of the *Militia*, without other Insti-tution, maketh him that hath it Soveraign. And therefore whosoever is made Generall of an Army, he that hath the Soveraign Power is alwayes Generallissimo.

Tenthly, is annexed to the Soveraignty, the choosing of all Counsellours, Ministers, Magistrates, and Officers, both in Peace, and War. For seeing the Soveraign is charged with the End, which is the common Peace and Defence; he is understood to have Power to use such Means, as he shall think most fit for his discharge.

Eleventhly, to the Soveraign is committed the Power of Rewarding with riches, or honour; and of Punishing with corporall, or pecuniary punishment, or with ignominy every Subject according to the Law he hath formerly made; or if there be no Law made, according as he shall judge most to conduce to the encouraging of men to serve the Common-wealth, or deterring of them from doing dis-service to the same.

Lastly, considering what values men are naturally apt to set upon themselves; what respect they look for from others; and how little they value other men; from whence continually arise amongst them, Emulation, Quarrells, Factions, and at last Warre, to the destroying of one another, and diminution of their strength against a Common Enemy; It is necessary that there be Lawes of Honour, and a publique rate of the worth of such men as have deserved, or are able to deserve well of the Common-wealth; and that there be force in the hands of some or other, to put those Lawes in execution. But it hath already been shewn, that not onely the whole *Militia*, or forces of the Common-wealth; but also the Judicature of all Controversies, is annexed to the Soveraignty. To the Soveraign therefore it belongeth also to give titles of Honour; and to appoint what Order of place, and dignity, each man shall hold; and what signes of respect, in publique or private meetings, they shall give to one another.

These are the Rights, which make the Essence of Soveraignty; and which are the market, whereby a man may discern in what Man, or Assembly of men, the Soveraign Power is placed, and resideth. For these are incommunicable, and inseparable. The Power to coyn Mony; to dispose of the estate and persons of Infant heires; to have praeemption in Markets; and all other Statute Praerogatives, may be transferred by the Soveraign; and yet the Power to protect his Subjects be retained. But if he transferre the *Militia,* he retains the Judicature in vain, for want of execution of the Lawes: Or if he grant away the Power of raising Mony; the *Militia* is in vain: or if he give away the government of Doctrines, men will be frighted into rebellion with the feare of Spirits. And so if we consider any one of the said Rights, we shall presently see, that the holding of all the rest, will produce no effect, in the conservation of Peace and Justice, the end for which all Common-wealths are Instituted. And this division is it, whereof it is said, a *Kingdome divided in it selfe cannot stand:* For unlesse this division precede, division into opposite Armies can never happen. If there had not first been an opinion received of the greatest part of *England,* that these Powers were divided between the King, and the Lords, and the House of Commons, the people had never been divided, and fallen into this Civill Warre; first between those that disagreed in Politiques; and after between the Dissenters about the liberty of Religion, which have so instructed men in this point of Soveraign Right, that there be few now (in *England*) that do not see, that these Rights are inseparable, and will be so

generally acknowledged, at the next return of Peace; and so continue, till their miseries are forgotten; and no longer, except the vulgar be better taught than they have hetherto been.

And because they are essentiall and inseparable Rights, it follows necessarily, that in whatsoever words any of them seem to be granted away, yet if the Soveraign Power it selfe be not in direct termes renounced, and the name of Soveraign no more given by the Grantees to him that Grants them, the Grant is voyd: for when he has granted all he can, if we grant back the Soveraignty, all is restored, as inseparably annexed thereunto.

This great Authority being Indivisible, and inseparably annexed to the Soveraignty, there is little ground for the opinion of them, that say of Soveraign Kings, though they be *singulis majores,* of greater Power than every one of their Subjects, yet they be *Universis minores,* of lesse power than them all together. For if by *all together,* they mean not the collective body as one person, then *all together,* and *every one,* signifie the same; and the speech is absurd. But if by *all together,* they understand them as one Person (which person the Soveraign bears), then the power of all together, is the same with the Soveraigns power; and so again the speech is absurd: which absurdity they see well enough, when the Soveraignty is in an Assembly of the people; but in a Monarch they see it not; and yet the power of Soveraignty is the same in whomsoever it be placed.

And as the Power, so also the Honour of the Soveraign, ought to be greater, than that of any, or all the Subjects. For in the Soveraignty is the fountain of Honour. The dignities of Lord, Earle, Duke, and Prince are his Creatures. As in the presence of the Master, the Servants are equall, and without any honour at all; So are the Subjects, in the presence of the Soveraign. And though they shine some more, some lesse, when they are out of his sight; yet in his presence, they shine no more than the Starres in presence of the Sun.

But a man may here object, that the Condition of Subjects is very miserable; as being obnoxious to the lusts, and other irregular passions of him, or them that have so unlimited a Power in their hands. And commonly they that live under a Monarch, think it the fault of Monarchy; and they that live under the government of Democracy, or other Soveraign Assembly, attribute all the inconvenience to that forme of Commonwealth; whereas the Power in all formes, if they be perfect enough to protect them, is the same; not considering that the estate of Man can never be without some incommodity or other; and that the greatest, that in any forme of Government can possibly happen to the people in generall, is scarce sensible, in respect of the miseries, and horrible calamities, that accompany a Civil Warre; or that dissolute condition of masterlesse men, without subjection to Lawes, and a coërcive Power to tye their hands from rapine, and revenge: nor considering that the greatest pressure of Soveraign Governours, proceedeth not from any delight, or profit they can expect in the dammage, or weakening of their Subjects, in whole vigor, consisteth their own strength and glory; but in the restiveness of themselves, that unwillingly contributing to their own defence, make it necessary for their Governours to draw from them what they can in time of Peace, that they may have means on any emergent occasion, or sudden need, to resist, or take advantage of their Enemies. For all men are by nature provided of notable multiplying glasses (that is their Passions and Selfe-love) through which, every little payment appeareth a great grievance; but are destitute of those prospective glasses (namely Morall and Civill Science) to see a farre off the miseries that hang over them, and cannot without such payments be avoyded.

Chapter 2

A State of Nature*
Charles R. Beitz

The state, like other institutions that can affect people's well-being and their rights, must satisfy certain moral requirements if we are to consider it legitimate. It is by these standards that we evaluate the state's claims on us and orient our efforts at political change. The normative component of political theory is the search for such standards and for the reasoning that forms their justification.

We do not often take the same attitude toward the complex structure of institutions and practices that lies beyond the state. This is in accord with the modern tradition of political theory, but it is worth asking if there are reasons of principle for following tradition in this respect. In this part, I consider whether it makes sense to look for general principles of international political theory that can supply reasons for and against particular choices in the same way that the principles of domestic political theory guide choices about alternative policies within the state. Is normative international political theory possible?

Any attempt to lay the groundwork for normative international political theory must face the fact that there is a substantial body of thought, often referred to as "political realism," that denies this possibility. Skepticism about international morality derives from a variety of sources, such as cultural relativism, apprehension about the effects of "moralism" on foreign policy, the view that rulers have an overriding obligation to follow the national interest, and the idea that there can be no moral principles of universal application in a world order of sovereign states. In the first section of this part, I argue that none of these arguments supports international moral skepticism, either because such arguments involve elementary confusions or fallacious assumptions, or because they are incomplete.

A more sophisticated argument for international skepticism is that certain structural features of an anarchical world order make international morality impossible. This argument (reconstructed in detail in section 2) characterizes international relations as a Hobbesian state of nature, that is, as an order of independent agents, each pursuing its own interests, without any common power

* From Charles R. Beitz, *Political Theory and International Relations*, 2nd edn. (Princeton, NJ: Princeton University Press, 1999), pp. 13–63.

capable of enforcing rules of cooperation. The image of international relations as a state of nature has been influential both in the modern tradition of political theory and in contemporary thought about international affairs. Moreover, it yields a plausible argument for international skepticism and so deserves close attention.

The Hobbesian argument for international skepticism combines two premises, which I examine separately in sections 3 and 4. The first is the empirical claim that the international state of nature is a state of war, in which no state has an overriding interest in following moral rules that restrain the pursuit of more immediate interests. The second is the theoretical claim that moral principles must be justified by showing that following them promotes the long-range interests of each agent to whom they apply. I shall argue that each premise is wrong: the first because it involves an inaccurate perception of the structure and dynamics of contemporary international politics, and the second because it provides an incorrect account of the basis of moral principles and of the moral character of the state. Both premises are embodied in the image of international relations as a Hobbesian state of nature, and in both respects this image is misleading.

If my argument against the Hobbesian conception of international relations is correct, a main reason for skepticism about the possibility of international political theory will have been removed. In fact, I shall argue, one cannot maintain that moral judgments about international affairs are meaningless without embracing a more far-reaching skepticism about all morality – something, I assume, that few would be willing to do. However, a successful defense of the possibility of international political theory does not say much about the content of its principles.

. . .

1 The Skepticism of the Realists

For many years, it has been impossible to make moral arguments about international relations to its American students without encountering the claim that moral judgments have no place in discussions of international affairs or foreign policy. This claim is one of the foundations of the so-called realist approach to international studies and foreign policy. On the surface, it is a most implausible view, especially in a culture conscious of itself as an attempt to realize a certain moral ideal in its domestic political life. All the more remarkable is the fact that the realists' skepticism about the possibility of international moral norms has attained the status of a professional orthodoxy in both academic and policy circles, accepted by people with strong moral commitments about other matters of public policy. Although the realists have often used arguments with deep roots in modern political theory, I believe that their skepticism can be shown to rest on fallacious reasoning and incorrect empirical assumptions.

To support this view, I shall argue that one cannot consistently maintain that there are moral restrictions on individual action but no such restrictions on the actions of states. I begin by considering the distinction (implied by this argument) between (generalized) moral skepticism and what I shall call international skepticism and show in more detail exactly what is involved in the assumption that moral skepticism is incorrect. It should be emphasized that this is indeed an assumption; I make no attempt to provide a general argument against moral skepticism.

One might be skeptical about the possibility of international morality because one is skeptical, in general, about the possibility of all kinds of morality. Perhaps one thinks that all or most people are incapable of being motivated by moral considerations, or that moral judgments are so subjective as to be useless in resolving conflicting claims and in fulfilling the other social functions usually assigned to morality. Whatever its rationale, moral skepticism, and its derivative, skepticism about political ethics, represent a refusal to accept moral arguments as sources of reasons for action. Moral skepticism might take a variety of forms, including a denial that moral judgments can be true or false, a denial that moral judgments have meaning, or a denial that the truth of moral judgments provides a reason for acting on them.

Generalized moral and political skepticism might be countered to some extent by examining the arguments that support them, Probably these arguments would turn out to contain important confusions or deep inconsistencies. But one could not thereby demonstrate the possibility of social or political ethics; other arguments for skepticism could be advanced, and at some point in the attempt to counter them one would need to rely on substantive ethical or metaethical views to demonstrate the weaknesses of the skeptical arguments. This, however, would be to assume that skepticism is wrong, rather than to argue it. Generalized moral and political skepticism can only be shown to be wrong by exhibiting an acceptable theory of ethics and of its foundation, because one of the functions of such a theory is to explain the possibility of just those features of ethics that the skeptic claims not to understand. At a minimum, such a theory must distinguish morality from egoism and explain how it can be rational to act on reasons that are (or might be) inconsistent with considerations of prudence or self-interest. Indeed, the idea that considerations of advantage are distinct from those of morality, and that it might be rational to allow the latter to override the former, seems to be at the core of our intuitions about morality.[1]

In what follows I shall have to assume without discussion that some such theory can be provided. The leading controversies in metaethics are likely to linger for a long while, and progress in normative areas ought not to await a resolution of these other problems even though they are in some sense logically prior. Obviously, one would like to offer a sufficiently complete theory to meet objections on both fronts. But this seems beyond reach at present. Instead, I shall proceed on the assumption that we share some basic ideas about the nature and requirements of morality (which I refer to as moral intuitions) and see whether international skepticism is consistent with them.

One important source of international skepticism is cultural relativism. International lawyers and cultural anthropologists have documented wide disparities in the views of rationality and of the good prevalent in the world's cultures. These differences are reflected in the structures of various legal systems and in the attitudes customarily taken by different cultures toward social rules, collective ideals, and the value of individual autonomy.[2] In some cultures, for example, autonomy is readily sacrificed to the requirements of collective goals. In general, given any consistent ranking of social goods or any plausible view of how such rankings might be morally justified, it is possible (and often likely) that a culture or society can be found in which there is dominant a divergent ranking of goods or view of moral justification. If this is the case, a skeptic might say, then there are no rational grounds for holding one social morality superior to another when their requirements conflict. Any doctrine that purports to be an international morality and that extends beyond the least common denominator of the various social moralities will be insecure in its foundations, But, typically, the least-common-denominator approach will leave most international conflicts unresolved because these have at their root conflicts over which principles are to apply to given situations or which goods should be sacrificed when several goods conflict. Since principles adequate to resolve such conflicts are fundamentally insecure, the skeptic claims, no normative international political theory is possible.[3]

This argument can be met on two levels, depending on the kind of intercultural disagreement to which it appeals. If the skeptical appeal is to disagreements over, say, the rankings of various social goods or their definitions, it may be that there is no challenge to the possibility of valid international principles but merely to the contents of particular ones. A consideration of views held in other cultures might persuade us that our assumptions ought to be altered in some ways to conform with conditions of which we had previously been insufficiently aware. This may be true of disagreements about the relative importance of individual autonomy and economic welfare. We are accustomed to defending individual rights in contexts of relative affluence, but considerations of economic development or of nonindustrial social structures might move us to recognize a dimension of relativity in these defenses. I do not mean to take a position on this issue at this point; I only mean to note one way in which cultural variations might be accommodated within an international political theory. In this case we would recognize a condition on the justification of principles of right that had previously gone unnoticed. Here, considerations of cultural diversity enter our thinking as data that may require revisions of particular principles; they do not undermine the possibility of normative theory itself.

But skeptics might say that what is at issue is something deeper; since different cultures might have radically different conceptions of what morality is, we have no right to be confident that our conception is correct. This carries the argument to a second level, but now it is difficult to say what the argument means. Perhaps it means that members of some other culture typically count as decisive certain kinds of reasons for action that we regard as utterly irrelevant from the point of view of our own morality. If so, we may ultimately have to say that the other culture's conception simply is not morality, or, at least, that claims founded on that conception do not count against our moral principles, even those that apply globally. It might seem that this attitude involves some sort of intellectual imperialism because it imposes a conception on cultures to which the conception is quite alien. But surely this is not correct. At some point, having learned what we can from the views of others, we must be prepared to acknowledge that some conception of morality is the most reasonable one available under the circumstances, and go forward to see what principles result. Notice that this does not say that everyone must be able to acknowledge the reasonableness of the same assumptions; actual agreement of everyone concerned is too stringent a requirement to place on the justification of moral principles (just as it is on epistemological ones). Notice also that the problem of relativism is not limited to international ethics; intrasocietal conflicts might involve similar disagreements over fundamental ethical assumptions. In either case, it is enough, in establishing standards for conduct, that we be able to regard them as the most rational choices available for anyone appropriately situated and that we be prepared to defend this view with arguments addressed to anyone who disagrees. In this way we reach decisions that are as likely to be morally right as any that are in our power to reach. We can do no more than this in matters of moral choice.[4]

One need not embrace cultural relativism to maintain that moral judgments are inappropriate in international relations. Indeed,

Charles R. Beitz

political realism more often starts from different premises. Some realists begin with the assertion that it is unrealistic to expect nations to behave morally in an anarchic world. For example, Hans Morgenthau, a leading realist, objects that "writers have put forward moral precepts which statesmen and diplomats ought to take to heart in order to make relations between nations more peaceful and less anarchical . . .; but they have rarely asked themselves whether and to what extent such precepts, however desirable in themselves, actually determine the actions of men."[5] While conceding the existence of some weak ethical restraints on international behavior, Morgenthau argues that international morality is largely a thing of the past and that competing national interests are now the main motives in world politics. This, he claims, is as it should be: "[T]he state has no right to let its moral disapprobation . . . get in the way of successful political action, itself inspired by the moral principle of national survival."[6]

How shall we understand this claim? One version is that we will fail to understand international behavior if we expect states to conform to moral standards appropriate to individuals. If we seek something like scientific knowledge of world politics – say, a body of lawlike generalizations with at least limited predictive power – we are unlikely to make much progress by deriving our hypotheses from moral rules appropriate to individual behavior.[7] This seems fairly obvious, but perhaps Morgenthau's emphasis on it can be understood in the perspective of the "idealist" legal approaches to the study of international relations that he sought to discredit.[8] In any event, this version of the claim does not imply that we ought not to make moral judgments about international behavior when thinking normatively rather than descriptively.

Another version of the claim, which is encountered more often, is this: we are likely to make mistaken foreign policy choices if we take an excessively "moralistic" attitude toward them.[9] This might mean either of two things. Perhaps it means that a steadfast commitment to a moral principle that is inappropriate to some situation is likely to move us to make immoral or imprudent decisions about it. Or it might mean that an idealistic or overzealous commitment even to an appropriate principle might cause us to overlook some salient facts and make bad decisions as a result. Each of these recommends reasonable circumspection in making moral judgments about international relations. But neither implies that it is wrong to make such judgments at all. What is being said is that the moral reasoning regarding some decision is flawed: either an inappropriate moral principle is being applied, or an appropriate principle is being incorrectly applied. It does not follow that it is wrong even to attempt to apply moral principles to international affairs, yet this conclusion must be proved to show that international skepticism is true, An argument is still needed to explain why it is wrong to make moral judgments about international behavior whereas it is not wrong to make them about domestic political behavior or about interpersonal behavior.

It is often thought that such an argument can be provided by appealing to the concept of the national interest. Thus, for example, Morgenthau seems to claim (in a passage already cited) that a state's pursuit of its own interests justifies disregard for moral standards that would otherwise constrain its actions.[10]

Machiavelli argues in this way. He writes, for instance, "[I]t must be understood that a prince, and especially a new prince, cannot observe all those things which are considered good in men, being often obliged, in order to maintain the state, to act against faith, against charity, against humanity, and against religion."[11] Machiavelli does not simply represent the prince as amoral and self-aggrandizing. His claim is that violation by the prince of the moral rules usually thought appropriate for individuals is warranted when necessary "to maintain the state." The prince should "not deviate from what is good, if possible, but be able to do evil if constrained."[12]

Now Machiavelli is not saying that rulers have license to behave as they please, nor is he claiming that their official actions are exempt from critical assessment. The issue is one of standards: what principles should be invoked to justify or criticize a prince's official actions? Machiavelli holds that princes are justified in breaking the moral rules that apply to ordinary citizens when they do so for reasons of state. Another statement of his view might be that rulers are subject to moral rules, but that the rules to which they are subject are not always, and perhaps not usually, the same as the rules to which ordinary citizens are bound. The private virtues – liberality, kindness, charity – are vices in the public realm because their observance is inconsistent with the promotion of the well-being of the state. The rule "preserve the state" is the first principle of the prince's morality, and it is of sufficient importance to override the requirements of other, possibly conflicting, rules which one might regard as constitutive of private morality.[13]

Is Machiavelli's position really a form of international skepticism? The view that a prince is justified in acting to promote the national interest amounts to the claim that an argument can be given that in so acting the prince is doing the (morally) right thing. But if this is true, one might say, then Machiavelli's view and its contemporary variants are not forms of international skepticism. They do not deny that moral judgments are appropriate in international relations; instead, they maintain that moral evaluations of a state's actions must be cast in terms of the relation between the state's actions and its own interests. The distinction between international skepticism and the Machiavellian view turns out to be like the distinction between general moral skepticism and ethical egoism. One pair of views denies the possibility of morality altogether, while the other pair advances a substantive moral principle. However, in both cases, the distinction is without a difference. What is distinctively *moral* about a system of rules is the possibility that the rules might require people to act in ways that do not promote their individual self-interest. The ethical egoist denies this by asserting that the first principle of his "morality" is that one should always act to advance one's own interests. To call such a view a kind of morality is at least paradoxical, since, in accepting the view, one commits oneself to abandoning the defining feature of morality. Thus, it seems better to say, as does Frankena, that "prudentialism or living wholly by the principle of enlightened self-love just is not a kind of *morality*."[14] Similarly, to say that the first principle of international morality is that states should promote their own interests denies the possibility that moral considerations might require a state to act otherwise. And this position is closer to international skepticism than to anything that could plausibly be called international morality.

If Machiavelli's view is, after all, a version of international skepticism, it does not follow that it is incorrect. Perhaps there *is* nothing that could plausibly be called international morality. At this point, we can only observe that the position as outlined provides no reason for drawing this conclusion. Why should we say that right conduct for officials of a state consists in action that promotes the state's interests? It is not obvious that the pursuit of self-interest by persons necessarily leads to morally right action, and it is no more obvious in the parallel case for officials of states. The argument involves a non sequitur. At a minimum, what is needed to vindicate the national interest view is an argument to show that following the national interest always does produce morally right action in international relations.

There is a tendency to resolve this problem by bringing in considerations regarding the responsibilities of political leaders to their constituents. Leaders should follow the national interest, it might be said, because that is their obligation as holders of the people's trust. To do otherwise would be irresponsible.[15] Leaving aside the fantasy of describing some leaders as trustees, the difficulty with this approach is that it involves an assumption that the people have a right to have done for them anything that can be described as in the national interest. But this is just as much in need of proof as international skepticism itself. In domestic affairs, few would disagree that what people have a right to have done for them is limited by what they have a right to do for themselves. For example, if people have no right to enslave ten percent of their number, their leaders have no right to do so for them. Why should the international actions of national leaders be any different? It seems that what leaders may rightfully do for their people, internationally or domestically, is limited by what the people may rightfully do for themselves. But if this is true, then the responsibility of leaders to their constituents is not necessarily to follow the national interest wherever it leads, without regard to the moral considerations that would constrain groups of individuals in their mutual interactions. The appeal to the responsibilities of leaders does not show that it is always right for leaders to pursue the national interest.

Faced with the charge that the national interest as an ultimate standard is indifferent to larger moral values (e.g., the global interest or the welfare of the disadvantaged elsewhere), realists often expand the definition of the national interest to include these larger values. For example, Morgenthau claims at some points that the national interest of a power must be constrained by its own morality.[16] Apparently he means that the calculations that enter into the identification of the national interest should include the relevant moral considerations. This maneuver seems to allow him to maintain the skeptical thesis (i.e., that the rule "follow the national interest" is the first principle of international conduct) while avoiding the non sequitur noted above. But it is hard to believe that any serious skeptic would be satisfied with such a revised national interest view. What the skeptic wants to maintain is that the definition and pursuit of the national interest is not subject to any moral conditions. In other words, it would be inappropriate to criticize leaders on moral grounds for their choices of foreign policy goals and means. Now suppose that Morgenthau's revised view were accepted, but that a leader mistakenly failed to include in his calculations identifying the national interest the relevant moral considerations. Then, apparently, the leader's conception of the national interest could be criticized on moral grounds, a possibility that the skeptic wants to avoid. Morgenthau's claim that the national interest of a power must be constrained by its own morality seems to be an ad hoc concession to a position inconsistent with his own skepticism. A consistent skepticism about international ethics must maintain that there are no moral restrictions on a state's definition of its own interests, that is, that a state is always morally justified in acting to promote its perceived interests. The problem is to explain how this position can be maintained without endorsing a general skepticism about all morality.

In response to this challenge, the international skeptic might claim that certain peculiar features of the international order make moral judgments inappropriate. National sovereignty is often claimed to be such a feature. On this view, states are not subject to international moral requirements because they represent separate and discrete political orders with no common authority among them. Jean Bodin is sometimes interpreted as arguing in this way. He writes, for example, "[T]here are none on earth, after God, greater than sovereign princes, whom God establishes as His lieutenants to command the rest of mankind."[17] The sovereign power is exercised "simply and absolutely" and "cannot be subject to the commands of another, for it is he who makes law for the subject."[18] Such a sovereign is bound by obligations to other sovereigns only if the obligations result from voluntary agreements made or endorsed by the sovereigns themselves.[19]

Bodin tempers his view with the claim that even princes ought to follow natural reason and justice.[20] He distinguishes between "true kings" and "despots" according to whether they follow the "laws of nature."[21] While the discussion in which this distinction is drawn concerns what we might call internal sovereignty – roughly, a prince's legal authority over his own subjects – one might infer that a sovereign ruler's conduct with respect to other sovereignties might be appraised on the same standard. This would give moral judgment a foothold in international relations, but such appraisals, in Bodin's view, would lack one feature that seems essential to full-fledged moral judgment. This feature emerges when a comparison is made between international and internal sovereignty. While it is possible for sovereign rulers to break the natural law, this would not justify subjects opposing their rulers because there is no superior authority to which appeal can be made to decide the issue.[22] Analogously in the international case, one might argue (although Bodin is silent on this matter) that no prince can justify opposition to the policies of another prince on the grounds that the latter has violated natural law, because there is no common authority capable of resolving the moral conflict. Notice that this is not to say that no prince can ever justify opposition to the policies of others; it merely makes *moral* (i.e., natural law) justifications inappropriate.

My interest here is in the suggestion that the absence of a common judge provides a reason for skepticism about international morality. It is clear that on some (particularly positivist) views of jurisprudence, the absence of a common judge shows that there is no positive law.[23] But, even if we grant the positivists' claim that there is no genuine international *law,* it is difficult to see why the fact of competing national sovereignties should entail there being no sense at all in *moral* evaluation of international action. We do not make such stringent demands on domestic affairs; there are many areas of interpersonal and social relations that are not subject to legal regulation but about which we feel that moral evaluation would be meaningful. Furthermore, in principle, it does not seem that the idea of a common judge plays a role in morality analogous to its role in law. Even if we do assume that there is a correct answer to every moral question, we do not assume that there is a special office or authority responsible for providing the answer.[24]

This is not enough to establish the possibility of international morality, however, for someone might say that it is not simply sovereignty, but certain special features of an order of sovereign states, that makes international morality impossible. A similar recourse is available to proponents of the view that the perceived national interest is the supreme value in international politics. In comparing international relations to the state of nature, Hobbes produced such an argument. Because it is the strongest argument available for skepticism about international normative principles, I shall consider it at length in the following sections.

2 The Hobbesian Situation

The most powerful argument that has been given for international skepticism pictures international relations as a state of nature. For example, Raymond Aron writes: "Since states have not renounced taking the law into their own hands and remaining sole judges of what their honor requires, the survival of political units depends, in the final analysis, on the balance of forces, and it is the duty of statesmen to be concerned, *first of all*, with the nation whose destiny is entrusted to them. The necessity of national egoism derives logically from what philosophers called the *state of nature* which rules among states."[25] The necessity (or "duty") to follow the national interest is dictated by a rational appreciation of the fact that other states will do the same, using force when necessary, in a manner unrestrained by a consideration of the interests of other actors or of the international community.

The idea that international relations is a state of nature is common in modern political theory, particularly in the writings of modern natural law theorists.[26] It makes a difference, as we shall see, which version of this idea one adopts as the basis for understanding the role of morality in international affairs. Since most contemporary writers (like Aron)[27] follow Hobbes's account, we shall begin there.

According to Hobbes, the state of nature is defined by the absence of a political authority sufficiently powerful to assure people security and the means to live a felicitous life. Hobbes holds that there can be no effective moral principles in the state of nature. I use "effective" to describe principles with which agents have an obligation to conform their actions; effective principles oblige, in Hobbes's phrase, "*in foro externo*" and are not merely principles that should regulate a preferred world but do not apply directly to the actual world. Principles of the latter sort oblige "*in foro interno*" and require us only to "desire, and endeavor" that the world were such that conformity with them would have a rational justification.[28]

In Hobbes's view, one has reason to do something (like adhere to moral norms) if

doing the thing is likely to promote one's interests, in particular, one's overriding interests in avoiding death and securing a felicitous life. Morality is a system of rules that promote each person's overriding interests, and hence to which each person has reason to adhere, only when everyone (or almost everyone) complies with them. In other words, a condition of the rationality of acting on moral rules is that one have adequate assurance of the compliance of others.[29] Hobbes thinks that adequate assurance of reciprocal compliance with moral rules can only be provided by a government with power to reward compliance and punish noncompliance. Where there is no such assurance – as in the state of nature, where there is no government – there is no reason to comply. Instead, there is a very good reason not to comply, namely, one's own survival, which would be threatened if, for example, one abstained from harming others while they did not observe the same restraint.

Hobbes gives two accounts of why the state of nature is sufficiently dangerous to render compliance with moral restrictions unreasonable. In the earlier works (*Human Nature* and *De Cive*) he relies heavily on the psychological assumption that people will be moved by the love of glory to contend with others for preeminence.[30] In *Leviathan*, he develops another account which relies less on substantive psychological assumptions and more on uncertainty. Here the claim is that some (perhaps only a few) people in the state of nature will be seekers after glory, but that prudent persons aware of this fact would become "diffident," distrustful, and competitive, always ready to protect themselves by all means available.[31] On both accounts the outcome is the state of war, "a tract of time, wherein the will to contend by battle is sufficiently known."[32] In such an unstable situation it would be irrational to restrict one's behavior according to moral rules, "for that were to expose himself to prey, which no man is bound to."[33] Thus, Hobbes concludes, in the state of nature "nothing can be unjust. The notions of right and wrong, justice and injustice have there no place."[34]

Some commentators have thought this conclusion too hasty. For, they point out, Hobbes allows that covenants may be made in the state of nature, and that some such covenants give rise to binding obligations to perform even when performance cannot be shown to be in the interest of the agent. In particular, Hobbes says that covenants are binding on a person not only "where there is a power to make him perform," but also "where one of the parties has performed already."[35] Since Hobbes's definition of justice is the performance of covenants, it seems that he is committed to the view that justice *does* have a place in the state of nature, at least in cases involving covenants "where one of the parties has performed already." This position receives additional textual support from Hobbes's discussion of the ransomed soldier, in which he claims that such a soldier, having been released on promise of subsequent payment of a ransom, thereby incurs an obligation to make good on the promise even though there may be no common power to enforce it.[36]

These passages have led some to think that Hobbes does not hold what might be called a prudential theory of obligation, for he seems to say that there are cases in which one has an obligation to perform as one has agreed even though supporting reasons of self-interest are absent.[37] This is a difficult position to maintain since it is in direct conflict with other portions of Hobbes's text. For example, he claims, without qualification, that "covenants without the sword, are but words, and of no strength to secure a man at all."[38] Furthermore, Hobbes's own justification of the claim about covenants where one of the

parties has performed already rests on clearly prudential arguments.[39] While I cannot argue this issue at length, I believe that these textual considerations, taken together with Hobbes's psychological egoism, support the view that his theory of obligation is purely prudential; people have no obligation to perform actions when performance cannot be shown to advance their (long-range) self-interests.[40]

To say that persons situated in the state of nature have no obligation to follow moral principles is not to say that there are no such principles. Indeed, Hobbes proposes nineteen "laws of nature" as the constitutive principles of "the true moral philosophy."[41] These principles are such that it is in the interests of each person that everyone abide by them. Hobbes argues that life in a society effectively regulated by the laws of nature would be infinitely preferable to life in the state of nature, since, in the state of nature, where no one has an obligation to restrict his actions according to moral principles, "the life of man" is "solitary, poor, nasty, brutish, and short."[42] The problem posed by Hobbes's theory is how to create conditions in which the laws of nature would be effective, that is, would oblige "*in foro externo.*" Hobbes thinks that a common power is needed to assure each person that everyone else will follow the laws of nature. The dilemma is that creating a common power seems to require cooperation in the state of nature, but cooperation, on Hobbes's account, would be irrational there. (Who could rationally justify taking the first step?) There appears to be no exit from the state of nature despite the fact that any rational person in that state could recognize the desirability of establishing a common power and bringing the state of nature to a close. Thus, while there are moral principles or laws of nature in the state of nature, they do not bind to action in the absence of a common power.

International skeptics have seized on this feature of Hobbes's theory to support the view that there are no effective moral obligations in international relations. This conclusion follows from the analogy that Hobbes himself draws between international relations and the state of nature: "But though there had never been any time, wherein particular men were in a condition of war one against another; yet in all times, kings, and persons of sovereign authority, because of their independency, are in continual jealousies, and in the state and posture of gladiators; having their weapons pointing, and their eyes fixed on one another; that is, their forts, garrisons, and guns upon the frontiers of their kingdoms; and continual spies upon their neighbors; which is a posture of war."[43] In such a situation, each state is at liberty to seek its own interest unrestrained by any higher moral requirements: "[I]n states, and commonwealths not dependent on one another, every commonwealth, not every man, has an absolute liberty, to do what it shall judge, that is to say, what that man, or assembly that representeth it, shall judge most conducing to their benefit."[44] Supposing that moral rules cannot require a man (or a nation) to do that which he (or it) has no reason to do, the argument holds that it is irrational to adhere to moral rules in the absence of a reliable expectation that others will do the same.

This seems to be the strongest argument that the skeptic can advance, because it is based on the plausible intuition that conformity to moral rules must be reasonable from the point of view of the agent in order to represent a binding requirement. When the agents are persons, the force of this intuition can be questioned on the ground that other things than self-interest can come into the definition of rationality. A successful counterargument of this kind results in the view that some sacrifices of self-interest might be

rational when necessary to achieve other goods. But this kind of counterargument is not as obviously available when the agents are states, since it can be argued that, as a matter of fact, there is far less assurance that states would sacrifice their perceived interests to achieve other goals.[45] Thus, even if Hobbesian skepticism about individual ethics in the absence of government is rejected, it might still move us to deny the possibility of effective regulative principles for the conduct of nations.[46]

It is important to be clear about the conclusion to which the skeptic is committed by this argument. The conclusion follows from applying Hobbes's theory of obligation to international relations. Accordingly, we might reformulate the conclusion as the claim that the officials of states have no obligation to conform their official actions in international affairs to moral principles. Such principles are not effective when there are no reliable expectations of reciprocal compliance. However, this is not to say that it would not be desirable for all states (or their officials) to conform their actions to certain principles, or that some such principles, analogous to Hobbes's law of nature, cannot be formulated. It is only to say, to repeat Hobbes's phrase, that whatever international principles exist apply "*in foro interno*" but not "*in foro externo*."

As I have said, the moral problem posed by Hobbes's theory is how to create conditions in which the laws of nature would be effective. Characterizing international relations as a state of nature poses a similar moral problem. If international relations is a state of nature, it follows that no state has an obligation to comply with regulative principles analogous to the laws of nature. But it also follows that widespread compliance with such principles would be desirable from the point of view of each state.[47] Carrying through the analogy with the state of nature therefore raises two further questions: what is the content of the principles it would be desirable for every state to accept? How can conditions be brought about such that it would be in the interests of each state to comply with these principles?

That such questions arise as a consequence of the characterization of international relations as a state of nature may suggest that the skeptics are inconsistent in invoking this characterization to support their view. For the first question presupposes that it would be desirable that conditions be created in which states would have reason to comply with certain normative principles, and the second question at least suggests that it is possible to create such conditions. From this one might argue that states have an obligation to do what they can to establish the requisite conditions, at least when they can do so without unacceptable risk. If this is true, then international skepticism is false, since it would not be the case that states are not subject to any moral requirements.

Hobbes does not posit an *effective* obligation to escape the interpersonal state of nature because the actions necessary to escape from it are inconsistent with the actions required for self-preservation within it. To defend international skepticism against the difficulty noted above, one would have to argue that international relations, like the state of nature, involves conditions such that the actions needed to establish an effective international morality are inconsistent with the actions required for the preservation of states. In that case it would follow that states are not subject to any binding moral requirements. And, while it would still be the case that conformity with appropriate international normative principles would be desirable, it would be academic to inquire about their content since there would be no way of rendering them effective.

3   International Relations as a State of Nature

The application of Hobbes's conception of the state of nature to international relations serves two different functions in the argument for international skepticism. First, it provides an analytical model that explains war as the result of structural properties of international relations.[48] It produces the conclusion that conflict among international actors will issue in a state of war ("a tract of time, wherein the will to contend by battle is sufficiently known") in the absence of a superior power capable of enforcing regulative rules. Second, the state of nature provides a model of the concept of moral justification that explains how normative principles for international relations should be justified. This explanation holds that since the basis of a state's compliance with moral rules is its rational self-interest, the justification of such rules must appeal to those interests states hold in common.

These two uses of the idea of an international state of nature are distinct because one leads to predictions about state behavior whereas the other leads to prescriptions. While the two uses are related in the sense that the predictions that result from the first use are taken as premises for the second, they should be separated for purposes of evaluation and criticism. In the first case, we need to ask whether the Hobbesian description of international relations is empirically acceptable: do the facts warrant application of this predictive model to international behavior? Our question in the second case is different: does Hobbes's state of nature give a correct account of the justification of moral principles for the international realm?

Let us look first at the predictive use of Hobbes's international state of nature. The description of international relations as a state of nature leads to the conclusion that a state of war will obtain among international actors in the absence of a superior power capable of enforcing regulative rules against any possible violator. As I have suggested, this conclusion is required as one premise in the argument for international skepticism, for, on a Hobbesian view, the reason that no actor has an obligation to follow rules of cooperation is the lack of assurance that other actors will do the same. Indeed, each actor has a reason not to follow such rules, since, in a state of war, an actor might rationally expect to be taken advantage of by other actors in the system if it were unilaterally to follow cooperative rules. Even if we accept Hobbes's conception of morality, for international skepticism to be a convincing position it must be the case that international relations is analogous to the state of nature in the respects relevant to the prediction that a state of nature regularly issues in a state of war.

For this analogy to be acceptable, at least four propositions must be true:

1   The actors in international relations are states.
2   States have relatively equal power (the weakest can defeat the strongest).
3   States are independent of each other in the sense that they can order their internal (i.e., nonsecurity) affairs independently of the internal policies of other actors.
4   There are no reliable expectations of reciprocal compliance by the actors with rules of cooperation in the absence of a superior power capable of enforcing these rules.

If these conditions are not met by international relations, then the analogy between international relations and the state of nature does not hold, and the prediction that international relations is a state of war does not necessarily follow.

I shall argue that contemporary international relations does not meet any of these conditions. Let us begin with the first. It establishes the analogy between the state of nature and international relations by identifying states as the actors in international relations just as individuals are the actors in the interpersonal state of nature. This may seem so obvious as not to deserve mention, but it is very important for the skeptic's argument that this condition actually obtain. The radical individualism of Hobbes's state of nature helps to make plausible the prediction of a resulting state of war because it denies the existence of any other actors (secondary associations, functional groups, economic institutions, or extended families, to name a few examples) that might mediate interpersonal conflict, coordinate individuals' actions, insulate individuals from the competition of others, share risks, or encourage the formation of less competitive attitudes. The view that states are the only actors in international relations denies the possibility of analogous international conflict-minimizing coalitions, alliances, and secondary associations. Since it is obviously true that such coalitions have existed at various times in the history of international relations, one might say flatly that international relations does not resemble the state of nature in this important respect.[49]

The difficulty with this claim is that Hobbes himself allows for the possibility of coalitions and alliances in the interpersonal state of nature.[50] However, he argues that these would not be stable. They would, if anything, increase the chances of violence among coalitions, and the shared interests that would lead to their formation would not be long lasting.[51]

One might make similar claims to defend the analogy of international relations and the state of nature, but it is not obvious that the claims would be empirically correct. Some alliances appear to confirm Hobbes's hypothesis that forming alliances increases the chances of war, despite the fact that alliances are often viewed as mechanisms for stabilizing a balance of power and making credible the threat to retaliate on attack.[52] On the other hand, several types of coalitions have produced opposite results. For example, regional political and economic organizations appear to have played significant roles in the nonviolent resolution of international conflicts. They have also made it easier for national leaders to perceive their common interests in peace and stability.[53] The same seems true, although in a more limited range of circumstances, of global international organizations like the United Nations.[54] To Hobbes's view that coalitions (and, by extension, universal organizations short of world government) are unlikely to be long lasting, it can only be replied that the important question is how long any particular conflict-minimizing coalition is likely to endure. Clearly, one should not expect such coalitions to persist forever, but it is historically demonstrable that some coalitions have enjoyed life spans sufficiently long to defeat the claim that they have made no significant contribution to peace and cooperation.

The view that states are the only actors in international relations also denies the possibility that transnational associations of persons might have common interests that would motivate them to exert pressures for cooperation on their respective national governments. The view does so by obscuring the fact that states, unlike persons, are aggregations of units (persons and secondary associations) that are capable of independent political action. These units might be grouped according to other criteria than citizenship, for example, according to interests that transcend national boundaries. When such interests exist, one would expect that transnational interest groups or their functional equivalents might exert pressures on their respective governments to favor policies that advance the groups' shared interests.

Since the second world war, the number, variety, membership, and importance of transnational groups have all increased, in some cases dramatically.[55] Early academic attention to transnational interests focused on groups of specialists (economists, labor leaders) and on functionally specific transnational organizations (the World Meteorological Organization, European Coal and Steel Community) and hypothesized that successful collaboration with respect to some functions would promote by a process of social learning collaboration with respect to other functions. The resulting progressive enlargement of areas of transnational collaboration was expected to undermine international political conflict by making clear to domestic constituencies and decision makers the extent of transnationally shared interests.[56] Subsequent experience has failed to corroborate the early functionalists' hypothesis for all cases of functional collaboration, but there are particular cases in which the hypothesized social-learning process has taken root.[57]

Although the central hypothesis of the theory of functional integration has been discredited, the insight that transnational interest groups might alter the outcomes of international politics by exerting pressures on national government policy making has not. In fact, the effectiveness of such groups in promoting their interests at the national level has been illustrated in several quite different areas. Two important examples of politically effective transnational groups are multinational corporations and informal, transnational groups of middle-level government bureaucrats. In each case, although to very different extents, it is clear that transnationally shared interests have sometimes led to substantial pressures on government foreign policy decisions.[58] As the difficulties of integration theory suggest, it should not be inferred that the effect of rapidly increasing transnational political activity is necessarily to minimize the chances of international conflict or to promote international cooperation, because a variety of other factors is involved.[59] In particular, transnational political activity is unlikely to promote international cooperation in the absence of perceptions by national decision makers of significant shared interests that would justify such cooperation.[60] The theoretical importance of the rise of transnational politics lies elsewhere. It lies in the fact that nation-states can no longer be regarded as the only, or as the ultimate, actors in international relations, since their actions may be influenced significantly by pressures from groups that represent transnational interests. Depending on the strength and extent of these interests, this new element of complexity in international relations renders problematic the Hobbesian explanation of why international relations should be regarded as a state of war.

The second condition is that the units that make up the state of nature must be of relatively equal power in the sense that the weakest can defeat the strongest.[61] The assumption of equal power is most obviously necessary for Hobbes's claim that the state of nature is a state of war because it eliminates the possibility of dictatorship (or empire) arising in the state of nature as a result of the preponderant power of any one actor or coalition. This assumption might seem unnecessarily strong, since the possibility of dictatorship within the state of nature might be ruled out with the weaker assumption that no actor is strong enough to dominate the rest. However, there is another reason for assuming equal power, and in this case nondominance will not do. The further reason is to rule out as irrationally risky, actions by any actor designed to promote the development of conditions in which moral behavior (i.e., behavior according to the laws of nature) would have a rational justification. In other words, Hobbes defines the state of nature so that both conformity to the laws of nature and action to escape the state of nature are equally irrational. The stronger assumption of equal power secures both conclusions, whereas, on the weaker assumption of nondominance, it could be argued that the relatively stronger actors may have obligations to work for changes in those background conditions that make moral behavior irrational for all. This would be because some such actions might be undertaken without undue risk to the relatively stronger actors.

Now our question is whether it is appropriate to make the relatively stronger assumption of equal power about contemporary international relations. It seems clear that this condition is not met; there are vast disparities in relative levels of national power.[62] David Gauthier has argued that the development and proliferation of nuclear weapons render these inequalities less severe and make international relations more like a Hobbesian state of nature than it had been previously.[63] But this is too simple. While the possession of nuclear weapons may increase the relative power of some states not usually considered major powers, it is not true that all or most states are developing or will develop operational nuclear arsenals. The likely result of proliferation is not a world of nuclear powers but a world divided between an expanded number of nuclear powers and a large number of states that continue to lack nuclear weapons. Gauthier suggests that it is not equal nuclear capacity but equal vulnerability to nuclear attack that secures the analogy of nuclear politics and the state of nature.[64] But this shift does not help, since states are highly unequal in this sense as well, as a result of their varying levels of retaliatory capabilities (and hence of deterrent strengths) and of nuclear defenses.[65] Also, as long as the deterrence system works, conventional-force imbalances – which are often substantial – will continue to differentiate strong states from weak ones. If this is true, then the most that can be claimed about relative levels of national power is that no state can dominate all the others. As we have seen, this alone may be enough to show that compliance with moral rules is irrational for any state, but it is not enough to show that some states (the strong ones) do not have obligations to try to change the rules of the international game so as to render compliance with moral rules more rational. As we shall see, even the relatively weaker assumption is thrown into question by some further characteristics of power in contemporary international relations.

The third condition is that the units be able to order their internal (i.e., nonsecurity) affairs independently of the internal policies of the other units. (As economists would say, the units must have independent utility functions once corrected for security considerations.)[66] If the units in the state of nature were interdependent in the way suggested, then the pursuit of self-interest by any one unit might require cooperation with other units in the system. The relations among parties in the state of nature would then resemble a game of mixed interests rather than a zero-sum game. Thus, if the units were interdependent, Hobbes's assumption that the pursuit of self-interest by the parties in the state of nature will usually lead to violent conflict would be undermined.

Again, it seems unlikely that this condition applies to international relations. It is increasingly true that the security and prosperity of any one state depends to a greater or lesser extent on that of some or all other states. In terms of security, this is reflected in the recognition that the great powers have a shared interest in avoiding a nuclear confrontation, and this justifies a measure of trust and predictability in their relations with one another.[67] The interdependence of

state interests has recently been illustrated in the broad area of economic and welfare concerns as well. Here it has been argued that the success of states in meeting domestic economic goals (e.g., full employment, control of inflation, balanced economic growth) requires substantially higher levels of cooperation among governments than has been the case in the past.[68]

Such interdependencies explain the rise of international institutions and practices that organize interstate rivalries in ways that require cooperation if the practices are to be maintained and conflicts resolved by nonviolent means. In the economic area, these include the organizational and consultative practices of the International Monetary Fund and its rules governing adjustment of currency exchange rates, and the related rules of trade formulated in the General Agreement on Tariffs and Trade. Taken together, these institutions can be seen as the constitutional structure of international finance and trade; their role is fundamental in promoting or retarding the growth of trade, the flow of investment, and the international transmission of inflation and unemployment.[69]

There is no doubt that such practices and institutions (or "regimes," as they are sometimes called)[70] have come to occupy a far more important place in international relations than previously as a result of the increasing volume and significance of transnational transactions. They are noticeable primarily in economic relations, but they are also significant in other areas (for example, regulation of the oceans and of the atmosphere, control of resource use, coordination of health policies).[71] As a result, the character of power in international relations has been transformed.[72]

Power might be defined, very roughly, as an actor's capacity to cause other actors to act (or not to act) in ways in which they would not have acted (or would have acted) otherwise. The use or threat of violence is a paradigmatic instrument of power because there are very few situations in which we can imagine violence or its threat not causing others to act. But there is nothing about power that limits its instruments to the instruments of violence. Threats of something other than violence, as well as positive inducements, might count as forms of power in appropriate circumstances. The instruments of power available to an actor are partly determined by the kinds of relationships in which the actor stands with respect to the other actors it wishes to influence. In particular, common membership in institutions or common participation in practices often constitutes nonviolent forms of power. Thus, for example, members of organizations like the United Nations can bargain their votes for desired actions by other global actors. Or, traders in some commodity (say, oil) can withhold the commodity from the market to cause others to change their behavior in prescribed ways.

It is difficult to say how the rise of these new forms of international power will affect prospects for recourse to older forms. One might expect the international role of violence or its threat to vary inversely with the density of international institutions and practices that serve important interests. Common institutions and practices of the kind described require stable environmental conditions for their operation and a measure of consensual support, at least from their more significant members. It is likely (though not necessary) that all or most participants would share an interest in minimizing the chances that continued functioning of their institutions and practices will be undermined by outbreaks of violence.[73]

On the other hand, while agreeing that new forms of power have arisen as a result of the development of new actors and relationships in international politics, one might think that this is, in fact, a reason to expect the use or threat of violence to become more rather than less common.[74] Perhaps the rise of new forms of power simply reflects the fact that states demand more from international relations now than in the past. A common example is that now, unlike, say, the eighteenth century, states are widely committed to maintaining high levels of domestic employment. Success in this commitment often depends on other international actors following particular kinds of policies. Since more is at stake in international relations now than previously, one might conclude, states have more reasons rather than fewer for using violence or its threat to protect and advance their interests.

This position, while not entirely incorrect, seems to overstate the case. First, as I have pointed out, the international mechanisms that states rely on to pursue various domestic (especially economic) goals often require stable environmental conditions and broad consensual support. Both of these might be upset if a state resorted to violence to pursue its goals. Violence, in other words, might be self-defeating in such circumstances. Furthermore, the view assumes that various forms of power in international relations are interchangeable; for example, if one cannot obtain an objective with a nonviolent form of power (say, one's influence in the decision-making structure of international finance institutions), one can still obtain it with superior military power. But it is not clear that forms of international power are so interchangeable, especially in view of the increasing diversity of objectives that states and other actors seek in international relations. The use of military power may not only be self-defeating, but its costs may be too great, or it may simply be irrelevant to the objective being pursued.[75]

The fourth condition is that there be no reliable expectations of reciprocal compliance in the absence of an authority capable of enforcing moral rules.[76] Hobbes is guilty here of formulating an overly restrictive condition. It has been pointed out that the reliability of the expectations involved is more properly understood as a function of the degree to which there is a settled habit of obedience to moral rules in the society.[77] A common power might effectively raise the level of obedience or it might not; what matters to the state-of-nature argument is that the appropriate expectations are lacking. But this does not fundamentally damage the Hobbesian position. One need only redefine the state of nature as a situation in which there are neither settled habits of obedience to moral rules nor well-established moral conventions.

This modification of Hobbes's position should be applied in the comparison with international relations as well. However, even some (like Kurt Baier) who have proposed the modification have failed to apply it to the international case. According to Baier's reconstruction of Hobbes's argument, "the doctrine of the sovereignty of nations and the absence of an effective international law and police force are a guarantee that nations live in a state of nature, without commonly accepted rules that are somehow enforced."[78] But this empirical claim hardly stands up against evidence of actual international behavior. Although there is no international police force, the international community possesses a variety of devices for promoting compliance with established norms. These range from such mild sanctions as community disapproval and censure by international organizations to coordinated national policies of economic embargoes of offending states. As international organizations grow in size and scope, exclusion from participation in the production and distribution of collective goods (for example, information and technology) is likely to become increasingly effective as an additional sanction.[79]

Regardless of the presence or absence of such machinery for enforcement, a wide variety of areas of international relations are characterized by high degrees of voluntary compliance with customary norms and institutionalized rules established by agreement. These areas are primarily associated with specific functions in which many states take an interest, but from which no state benefits without the cooperation of the other states involved. Governments participate in a wide range of specialized agencies (the Postal Union, the World Health Organization, the UN Conference on Trade and Development, etc.) and in many sectional associations like military alliances (NATO, the Warsaw Pact) and regional trade and development organizations (the European Economic Community).[80] In addition, there are rules and practices that are expressed in other than organizational forms – for example, customary international law, the conventions of diplomatic practice, and the rules of war.[81] The sphere of economic organizations and practices presents even clearer evidence of the existence of a highly articulated system of international institutions.

Evidence of areas of cooperation in which expectations of reciprocal compliance are reasonable could be multiplied, but enough has been said already to defeat the claim that the absence of a global coercive authority shows that international relations is, in the relevant sense, analogous to a Hobbesian state of nature. It is worth pausing to ask why, in the face of such fairly obvious empirical considerations, people might continue to think that the analogy holds, Perhaps, H. L. A. Hart suggests, this is the result of accepting a more fundamental analogy between the forms and conditions of interaction among individual persons and among communities organized as states. States, unlike persons, are not of such relatively equal strength as to make possible, or perhaps even desirable, machinery for coercive enforcement on the model of domestic society. There is no assurance that an offending state can be effectively coerced by a coalition of other states, while the use of sanctions even by a preponderant coalition might involve costs far in excess of the benefits to be derived from general compliance with appropriate rules.[82] It might be added that states can coordinate relatively complex activities with less reliance than individuals on centrally administered coercive threats because of their more diversified administrative and information-gathering capabilities. As a result, in a world not hierarchically ordered on the model of domestic societies, one can talk of a "horizontal" ordering which nevertheless involves substantial expectations of reciprocal compliance with rules of cooperation.[83]

This picture of international relations might seem to leave little room for war, and this might seem rather unrealistic in view of the massive violence that has marked the last hundred years. But I have not meant to argue that war is a thing of the past, nor that it is no longer in some sense the ultimate problem of international politics. The point is that the concerns of international relations have broadened considerably, with the result that competition among international actors may often take a variety of nonviolent forms, each requiring at least tacit agreement on certain rules of the game that express important common interests of the actors involved. The actors in international politics, their forms of interaction and competition, their power, and the goals the system can promote have all changed. While international relations can still be characterized as "a tract of time, wherein the will to contend by battle is sufficiently known," it has become more complex than this as well. But this new complexity, which has both analytical and normative importance, is likely to be obscured if one accepts the model of international

relations as a state of nature in which the only major problem is war.

If these empirical criticisms are correct, then, even if one holds that states are obligated to observe moral rules only when it is in their interests to do so, it seems that there are some rules of cooperation that are binding on states. This is because states have common interests, and there are reasonable grounds for expecting reciprocal compliance with some rules that advance these interests even in the absence of a higher coercive authority. Of course, a substantially more sophisticated analysis would be required to identify these rules.[84] Furthermore, when established practices are flawed (in some sense yet to be specified), or when certain kinds of actions or policies are not governed by established practices, it is still not the case that no state has an obligation to improve the system. Since states are of unequal power, it may be that some states (those that are relatively powerful) can take remedial actions without incurring substantial risks. Thus, the analogy of international relations and the state of nature fails, and as a result neither of the conclusions of the Hobbesian argument for skepticism carries over to international relations.

A final caveat should be added, if only because the point is so often obscured. My claim that it is wrong to conceptualize international relations as a Hobbesian state of nature does not imply that the international realm should be understood for all purposes on the analogy of domestic society. I have suggested . . . that the two realms are similar in several respects relevant to the justifications of principles of social justice. But there are important differences as well. The institutions and practices of international relations perform fewer tasks than their domestic counterparts, are generally less efficient, and are less capable of coordinating the performance of tasks in diverse areas. More important, from our point of view, international relations includes fewer effective procedures for peaceful political change, and those procedures that do exist are more prone to problems of noncompliance. Rather than assimilate international relations to the state of nature or to domestic society, it would be better to understand it as occupying a middle ground. As in domestic society, there are, in international relations, both shared and opposed interests, providing a basis for both cooperation and competition. But effective institutions for exploiting the bases of cooperation are insufficiently developed, and their further growth faces great obstacles. These considerations do not argue for the meaninglessness of talk about international ethics, but they do present distinctive problems for any plausible international normative theory. . . .

4   The Basis of International Morality

The second, prescriptive, use of the state of nature explains the justification of regulative principles for political or international life. It does so by showing that a principle or set of principles would be the most rational choice available for persons situated in a state of nature.

Hobbes argues that the first law of nature – that is, the first principle to which rational persons situated in the state of nature would agree – is "that every man, ought to endeavour peace, as far as he has hope of obtaining it"; this law is qualified by what Hobbes calls "the right of nature," namely, that when a man cannot obtain peace, "he may seek, and use, all helps, and advantages of war."[85] The justification of these prescriptions, as I have argued, is based on rational self-interest. The analytical use of the state of nature shows that compliance with the laws of nature in the absence of an effective agreement by others to do the same would not be in the interests of any person. The prescriptive use

of the state of nature provides the grounds for inferring that this is a reason not to comply with the laws of nature unless the compliance of everyone else can be assured. "[I]f other men will not lay down their right" of nature, "then there is no reason for any one, to divest himself of his: for that were to expose himself to prey."[86]

It is clear that the description of the state of nature, and of the persons located in it, should express the point of view from which regulative principles should be chosen. Hobbes thinks that this point of view is adequately captured by the idea of self-interest: principles for domestic or international politics must be justified, respectively, by considerations of individual or national self-interest. This view is expressed by his description of a state of nature in which the parties do what is in their own interests, and by his conception of a law of nature as a rule "by which a man is forbidden to do that, which is destructive of his life, or taketh away the means of preserving the same."[87] Our problem in assessing the prescriptive use of the international version of the state of nature is not, as it was with the analytical use considered above, to determine whether there are common interests among states that can support rules of cooperation, and whether the circumstances of international relations ever allow states to follow those rules without unacceptable risk. Instead, we must ask whether the Hobbesian account, applied to international relations, provides an acceptable theory of the justification of international moral principles. There are two questions. First, should the justification of principles for international relations appeal ultimately to considerations about states (e.g., whether general acceptance of a principle would promote each *state's* interests)? Second, should the justification of such principles appeal only to *interests*?

The argument that states should pursue their own interests in the absence of reliable expectations of reciprocal compliance with common rules depends on the analogy drawn between persons in the interpersonal state of nature and states in international relations. But this analogy is imperfect. In the interpersonal case, the idea that persons can pursue their interests unrestrained by moral rules might seem plausible because we assume that each has a right of self-preservation. Hobbes's claim that the laws of nature are not effective in the state of nature follows from the empirical claim that compliance with laws of nature in such a situation could require a person to act against his or her legitimate interest in self-preservation. But this reasoning does not obviously apply in the international case. By analogy with the interpersonal case, the argument for following the national interest when it conflicts with moral rules would be that there is a *national* right of self-preservation which states cannot be required to give up. The difficulty is that it is not clear what such a right involves or how it can be justified. States are more than aggregations of persons; at a minimum, they are characterized by territorial boundaries and a structure of political and economic institutions. How much of this – to say nothing of such other elements of statehood as cultural tradition, social structure, and so on – is covered by the presumed right of national self-preservation?

The plausibility of the claim that there is a basic right of national self-preservation seems to diminish as the idea of statehood is expanded. For example, it might seem relatively unobjectionable to say that the national interest justifies some action or policy when this is necessary to preserve the lives of the state's inhabitants against an external threat. In this case, the analogy with the interpersonal state of nature seems most acceptable, because it can be argued that the state's right of self-preservation is based directly on its individual members' rights of self-preservation. The presumed right is less acceptable

when it is not lives but a state's territorial integrity that is at stake, since there is not necessarily any threat to individual lives. Persons often survive changes in national boundaries. If we expand the idea of statehood still farther – say, another state threatens a particular government but does not threaten lives or territory – the analogy loses even more of its persuasiveness. I am not arguing that persons would not have legitimate claims against other states and persons in these cases, but rather that these claims could not be based on individual rights of self-preservation. In each case, the grounds on which pursuit of the national interest could be justified are the effects of the external threat on other rights of persons. These are not captured by the analogy with the state of nature.

This point is obscured because the skeptical position carries over the analogy of states and persons from the analytical and descriptive use of the international state of nature to the prescriptive use. I have argued that this analogy is misleading even in the analytic use. But even if this is incorrect, it would not follow that the analogy may be employed appropriately in justifying prescriptions for international behavior. It is easy to see how one might be led to carry the analogy too far. When the state of nature is used for analytical purposes and the actors are persons, there is no difficulty in using the same construct to justify principles of conduct, since these are in any event to be based on a consideration of the moral properties of persons. But when the state of nature is applied to international relations, one must recognize that analytical and prescriptive interests may require different interpretations of the state of nature. If we wish to *understand* the behavior of states, perhaps it would be helpful to view them as rational actors which respond to international circumstances on the basis of a calculation of their rational self-interest. (The analysis in section 3 suggests some doubts about the realism of rational-actor models of international politics, but that is beside the point at the moment.) But if we wish to *prescribe* principles to guide the behavior of states, we are involved in a quite different sort of question. For then our justification of normative principles must appeal ultimately to those kinds of considerations that are appropriate in a prescriptive context, namely, the rights and interests of persons. If the idea of the national interest plays any role in justifying prescriptions for state behavior, it can only be because the national interest derives its normative importance from these deeper and more ultimate concerns.

Those who wish to apply Hobbes's argument to international relations should say that the parties to the international state of nature, when it is used as a device for showing which rules of conduct are rational, are to be conceived as persons rather than as states. This state of nature is international in the sense that the parties to it are of diverse citizenship. But they are still persons, and their choice of rules for the behavior of states (on such a revised Hobbesian view) is guided by their desire to preserve themselves as persons rather than simply to preserve their states as states. The effect of redefining the international state of nature in this way is to limit the choice of international rules in accordance with the considerations advanced above. The parties would still agree to a principle that used the national interest as a guide to behavior in the absence of reliable expectations of reciprocal compliance with moral rules. But now they would limit the national interest to what is required to preserve their lives. On the other hand, where there *are* reliable expectations of reciprocal compliance, there is no need to appeal to the national interest to justify principles of international conduct at all. For in that case individual rights of self-preservation are assured by the existence of stable expectations. The

important question in identifying justifiable rules of international conduct would then be the effects of mutual compliance with the various alternative rules on the other rights of persons.[88]

The national interest is often invoked to justify disregard of moral principles that would otherwise constrain choices among alternative foreign policies. Thus, for example, Morgenthau writes that "the state has no right to let its moral disapprobation . . . get in the way of successful political action, itself inspired by the moral principle of national survival."[89] It is tempting to interpret Morgenthau as claiming that "the moral principle of national survival" should receive greater weight in deliberations concerning foreign policy than those other principles on which officials might base their "moral disapprobation." If my remarks above are correct, however, this interpretation is unhelpful because it fails to remove an important ambiguity from Morgenthau's formulation and hence fails to explain why his view is plausible at all. The ambiguity concerns the scope of "national survival." When this means "the survival of the state's citizens," the view seems prima facie acceptable, but this is because we generally assume that persons (not states) have rights of self-preservation. When "national survival" extends further (for example, to the preservation of forms of cultural life or to the defense of economic interests) the view's prima facie acceptability dissipates precisely because the survival of persons is no longer at issue. In such cases the invocation of the national interest does not necessarily justify disregard of other moral standards. What is required is a balancing of the rights and interests presumably protected by acting to further the national interest and those involved in acting on the competing principle that gives rise to moral disapprobation. While it cannot be maintained a priori that the individual rights presumably protected by the national interest would never win out in such cases, the opposite cannot be maintained either. Yet this is exactly what an uncritical acceptance of Morgenthau's view invites. Thus, to clarify the issues involved in debates regarding foreign policy choices, it would seem preferable to dispense with the idea of the national interest altogether and instead appeal directly to the rights and interests of all persons affected by the choice. Similarly, nothing is gained, and considerable clarity is lost, by attempting to justify principles of international conduct with reference to their effects on the interests of states. It is the rights and interests of persons that are of fundamental importance from the moral point of view, and it is to these considerations that the justification of principles for international relations should appeal.

The other objection to the Hobbesian state of nature as a device for justifying rules of international conduct goes deeper and requires further changes in the definition of the state of nature. This criticism is generally relevant to the view of ethics according to which moral rules oblige only when they can be shown to be in the interests of everyone to whom they apply. The view does not allow moral criticism of established practices (although it allows criticism on other, e.g., prudential, grounds) nor does it admit principles whose general observance might seem morally required but would not benefit every party. But both of these seem, intuitively, to be part of the idea of morality.

The issue raised by this objection, of course, is fundamental to ethics: how can anyone have a reason to do particular actions or subscribe to general practices that cannot be shown to work to his advantage when a more advantageous alternative is available? In other words, how is ethics possible? The question is made complex because it requires a joint solution to the problems of moral justification – in what sense is compliance with moral rules rational? – and of moral

motivation – how can these rules move us to act? These questions deserve discussion in their own right, but this would carry us far from the subject of international norms. Rather than pursue the question in any depth here, I shall assume that we share some general intuitions about the nature of ethics and try to show that the Hobbesian view falls far short of them. Then I shall return to the problem of expectations of reciprocal compliance and ask how it is relevant to the justification of principles for international relations.[90]

The view that ethics is based on enlightened self-interest is inadequate. It fails to account for certain principles that intuitively seem to impose requirements on our actions regardless of considerations of actual or possible resulting benefit to ourselves. Elementary examples of such principles are the rule not to cause unnecessary suffering or to help save a life if that can be done at acceptable cost and risk. Although, in general, we are likely to think that others would behave similarly if they were in our shoes and were called upon to comply with these rules, it does not seem that this is the reason we would give for acting on them. Indeed, we would say that there may be at least some moral obligations that impose requirements on action regardless of the presence or absence of expectations of reciprocal compliance, and, a fortiori, of conventions and enforceable rules that institutionalize these expectations and enhance their reliability. If the notion of natural moral requirements has a clear reference, it is to these sorts of obligations which do not gain their binding quality from the expectations, conventions, and institutions of particular communities.

One might agree with all of this, but claim that some other principles are based on self-interest – in particular, principles of justice that require compliance with political institutions or actions aimed at their reform. The argument would be that only self-interest provides a sufficiently strong motive for the sorts of actions required by justice, since natural moral requirements (for example, those discussed above which are, perhaps, based on such moral sentiments as altruism) are too few and too weak to support a very extensive system of social cooperation.[91] However, the Hobbesian view is inadequate here too. For it seems impossible to justify on the basis of self-interest compliance with the general rules governing participation in institutions. Consider, for example, the principle of political obligation. In one formulation, this principle holds that those who have submitted to the rules imposed by an institution, thus restricting their liberty, "have a right to a similar submission from those who have benefited by their submission."[92] Any defense of this principle based on self-interest sooner or later runs into the free-rider problem – why should someone submit to a restriction when he can benefit equally from nonsubmission? It requires truly heroic empirical assumptions to defeat such objections without giving up the claim that political obligation must be based on considerations of self-interest. But a Hobbesian view of ethics leaves no alternative.[93]

The Hobbesian position and that expressed by these intuitive reflections represent two points of view from which we might make choices about how to act. To assert that ethics is possible is to say that there are occasions when we have reason to override the demands of self-interest by taking a moral point of view toward human affairs. Speaking very roughly, the moral point of view requires us to regard the world from the perspective of one person among many rather than from that of a particular self with particular interests, and to choose courses of action, policies, rules, and institutions on grounds that would be acceptable to any agent who was impartial among the competing interests involved. Of course, this is not to say that interests are irrelevant to moral choice. The question is how interests come into the justification of such choices. From the point of view of self-interest, one chooses that action or policy that best serves one's own interests, all things considered. From the moral point of view, on the other hand, one views one's interests as one set of interests among many and weighs the entire range of interests according to some impartial scheme. Both points of view are normative in the sense that they may impose requirements on action – for example, by requiring us to subordinate some immediate desire to some other consideration: either long-range self-interest (on Hobbes's view) or the interests of everyone. But only the moral perspective allows us to explain the basis of such natural moral requirements (and perhaps some institutional ones as well) as may move us to act even when there is no assurance of reciprocal compliance, and hence no self-interested justification, available.

This conclusion may seem stronger than it is. While I have argued that the moral point of view is not irrelevant to political theory, I have not said anything about the content of the moral norms that should constitute its substance. Thus, while it follows that the putative absence of reliable expectations in international relations does not show the impossibility of international political theory, very little is obvious about the strength or extent of the theoretical principles appropriate to such an environment. In other words, there is a gap between the structure of moral choice and the content of the rules, policies, and so on that should be chosen to govern various realms of action. How the gap is filled depends on the morally relevant features of the realm in question.

This explains how it is possible, as I observed above, to reject Hobbes's general conception of the state of nature (and with it his moral skepticism) and yet persist in the conclusion that the only effective principle of international morality is that of self-preservation. The empirical situation might be such that, when it is appraised from the moral point of view, the most that can be said is that agents should each pursue his own interests. While I have argued that such an empirical situation does not exist in some important areas of contemporary international relations, it could exist, and if it did, the moral conclusions that would follow would be, so to speak, extensionally equivalent to those reached on Hobbes's view. There is an important difference, however; while these conclusions rest, for Hobbes, on considerations of enlightened self-interest, on the other view they are founded on a consideration of all affected interests, balanced by an (as yet vague) impartial process. Thus, my claim that international political theory is possible does not imply that its principles are the same as (or analogous to) those that characterize the political theory of the state. Surely one factor that one would consider in choosing international principles from the moral point of view is the relatively lower reliability of expectations of reciprocal compliance in international relations. If it turns out that this factor is morally relevant in particular contexts of justification, then it would certainly affect the strength and extent of the resulting principles.

The position I have sketched as an alternative to Hobbes's is a reconstruction of that taken by many writers of the natural law tradition. The most familiar of these is Locke. Like Hobbes, he specifically compares the relations of states to the relations of persons in the state of nature.[94] Unlike Hobbes, Locke argues that even the state of nature "has a Law of Nature to govern it, which obliges every one: And Reason, which is that Law, teaches all Mankind, who will but consult it, that being equal and independent, no one ought to harm another in his Life, Health, Liberty, or Possessions."[95] However, Locke paid little attention to the specific require-

ments of the law of nature as applied to international relations.[96]

Although less familiar to us than Locke, Samuel Pufendorf is far more instructive on the application of natural law to nations. His major work on the subject, *Of the Law of Nature and Nations* (*De jure naturae et gentium*), is especially interesting because it explicitly takes up Hobbes's arguments and attempts to defend the natural law tradition against them while producing similar conclusions regarding the weakness of moral rules in international affairs.[97] Against Hobbes, Pufendorf claims that justice and injustice were "defined by natural law and binding upon the consciences of men . . . before there were civil sovereignties."[98] Furthermore, these principles are effective even in the absence of a superior power on earth who explicitly proclaims and enforces the law; it is enough if they can be regarded as commands of God "arrived at and understood in any way whatsoever, whether by the inner dictate of the mind, from the condition of our nature, or the character of the business to be undertaken."[99]

Pufendorf has a problem with principles for nations because he wants to derive essentially Hobbesian results from a moralized (one might say Lockean) image of the state of nature. Like Hobbes, he argues that principles for nations can be derived from principles for individuals in the state of nature by regarding nations as "moral persons." Then principles for nations would be just the principles for individuals writ large.[100] Yet he also holds that the result of reinterpreting the principles in this way is a group of principles weaker in several respects than their analogues for individuals. For example, he seems to hold that pacts and treaties are binding on nations only when they serve mutual interests, whereas promises among individuals bind regardless of such considerations.[101] Also, while he holds that individuals always have a reason to combine into states to escape the state of nature, he does not believe that nations have an analogous reason to form some sort of supranational federation or world government.[102]

The explanation for these apparent inconsistencies is that Pufendorf does not view international relations as precisely analogous to the state of nature for individuals.[103] The interpersonal and international states of nature are similar insofar as both are characterized by rough equality of strength of the units and lack of a common enforcer of laws.[104] In both cases reason determines the regulative principles. But other circumstances differ, and the contents of the principles vary accordingly. There seem to be two main respects in which the analogy fails to hold. First, Pufendorf claims that states are less likely than persons to be moved by other-regarding considerations when these come into conflict with self-interest.[105] If this is generally true, then it can be argued that those forms of obligation that depend on the availability of other-regarding motivations (such as keeping promises) are correspondingly weaker. A further, and more fundamental, difference is that the safety and liberty of individuals is far less secure in the interpersonal state of nature than in a state of nature made up of independent nations. The "state or commonwealth" is "the most perfect form of society, and is that wherein is contained the greatest safety for mankind."[106] Because the "safety" of individuals is adequately assured by the organization of commonwealths, the international state of nature "lacks those inconveniences which are attendant upon a pure state of nature."[107]

Some aspects of Pufendorf's view of the international state of nature are subject to the same empirical criticisms that I have made against Hobbes's. In particular, Pufendorf seems to accept the view that states are the only actors in international relations, that they are largely noninterdependent, and

that they entertain few reliable expectations of reciprocal compliance with rules and common practices. I shall not rehearse my criticisms of these views again here. The importance of Pufendorf's system is that it gives a more acceptable account than Hobbes's of why principles for nations may sometimes fail to be analogous to those for individuals in civil society. This possibility, which seems to be a common intuition about international ethics and is clearly captured in the relative weakness of customary international law, need not force us to the extreme conclusion that morality and the normative political theory that derives from it have no place in international relations. Indeed, it is impossible to maintain this view as a matter of principle short of adopting a thoroughgoing skepticism about all morality. It is more reasonable to explain the peculiar features of international principles as the result of empirical differences between the domestic and international environments, viewed from a common perspective of moral justification. If this is true, then we can reformulate the relationship between principles for individuals in the state of nature and for nations in international relations. Rather than derive the former and reinterpret them, putting nations for persons, to obtain international principles, we might choose another procedure. We might, instead, regard the choice of international principles as a problem of political theory in its own right, which is to be solved independently of the choice of principles for persons outside of civil society. Principles for persons in the state of nature would then come into the discussion of international theory in the form of arguments by analogy. While they have no special status in the international context, they provide guidance in formulating international principles just in case the analogy between international relations and the state of nature is in the relevant respects appropriate. But the justification of international principles is independent of this comparison; it is to be sought in a return to the machinery of justification – which I have vaguely called the moral point of view – that is the common foundation of principles in both realms.

Notes

1   For a further discussion, see Thomas Nagel, *The Possibility of Altruism*, pp. 125–42.

2   For example, see F. S. C. Northrup, *The Meeting of East and West*, esp. ch. 10; and Adda B. Bozeman, *The Future of Law in a Multicultural World*, pp. ix–xvii, 14–33.

3   This construction might account for Kennan's non sequitur: "[L]et us not assume that our moral values . . . necessarily have viability for people everywhere. In particular, let us not assume that the *purposes* of states, as distinguished from their methods, are fit subjects for measurement in moral terms." *Realities of American Foreign Policy*, p. 47; emphasis in original.

4   There is a helpful discussion of some general issues of ethical relativism in Richard B. Brandt, *Ethical Theory*, pp. 271–84.

5   Hans J. Morgenthau, "The Twilight of International Morality," p. 79.

6   Hans J. Morgenthau, *Politics Among Nations*, p. 10. There is an ambiguity here regarding the moral status of the national interest as an evaluative standard. One might call this view a form of moral skepticism, or one might say that it demonstrates that there is a moral warrant for following the national interest. I argue below that the former is the more appropriate interpretation. It should be noted, however, that some realist writers – probably including Aron and Morgenthau – have clearly thought that they were arguing the latter view instead. On this ambiguity, see Hedley Bull, "Society and Anarchy in International Relations," pp. 37–8.

7   On the other hand, we may be equally misled by the research hypotheses that follow from a variety of realist assumptions. There is a useful criticism of realism as a research orientation, rather than as a skeptical doctrine about international norms, in Robert O. Keohane and Joseph S. Nye, Jr, *Power and Interdependence*, ch. 2.

8   As Charles Frankel suggests in *Morality and US Foreign Policy*, pp. 12–18. See also Kenneth W. Thompson, *Political Realism and the Crisis of World Politics*, pp. 32–8.

9   Hans J. Morgenthau, *In Defense of the National Interest*, pp. 37–8. Compare Dean Acheson, "Ethics in International Relations Today," p. 16.

10 Morgenthau, *Politics Among Nations*, p. 10; see also his *In Defense of the National Interest*, pp. 33–9.

11 Niccolò Machiavelli, *The Prince* [1532], XVIII, p. 65.

12 Ibid.; see also *Discourses* [1531], I, ix, p. 139, and II, vi, pp. 298–9.

13 Machiavelli, *Discourses*, III, xli, pp. 527–8. There is, of course, an extensive secondary literature devoted to the explication of Machiavelli's position. No doubt many would take issue with my reading of his view, but I cannot enter the debate here. On Machiavelli's notion of *virtù* and its relation to the national interest, see Sheldon S. Wolin, *Politics and Vision*, pp. 224–8 and 230–1.

14 W. K. Frankena, *Ethics*, p. 19; emphasis in original.

15 See, for example, Arthur Schlesinger, Jr, "The Necessary Amorality of Foreign Affairs," pp. 72–3.

16 Morgenthau, *In Defense of the National Interest*, pp. 36–7; see also his letter to the editor of *International Affairs*. There is a similar claim in Thompson, *Political Realism*, p. 167. In the context of policy questions, Morgenthau is more straightforward. For example, in a discussion of US policy toward Indochina, he writes that intervention is justified whenever it advances decision makers' best judgments of the national interest, notwithstanding the customary prohibition of interventionary diplomacy in international law and morality. "To Intervene or Not to Intervene," p. 430.

17 Jean Bodin, *Six Books of the Commonwealth* [1576], I, x, p. 40.

18 Ibid., viii, pp. 27–8.

19 Ibid., p. 29.

20 Ibid., pp. 33–4.

21 Ibid., II, iii, p. 59.

22 Ibid., v, p. 67.

23 For this argument applied to international law, see John Austin, *The Province of Jurisprudence Determined* [1832], lecture 6, pp. 193–4, 200–1.

24 Compare Henry Sidgwick, *The Elements of Politics* [1891], XV, sec. 1, pp. 238–41.

25 Raymond Aron, *Peace and War*, p. 580; emphasis in original.

26 See the references in Otto von Gierke, *Natural Law and the Theory of Society*, vol. 2, p. 288, note 1.

27 Aron, *Peace and War*, p. 72.

28 Thomas Hobbes, *Leviathan* [1651], ch. 15, p. 145; compare Thomas Hobbes, *Philosophical Rudiments concerning Government and Society* [*De Cive*] [1651], III, sec. 33, pp. 49–50.

29 Hobbes, *Leviathan*, ch. 11, p. 85, and ch. 14, pp. 116–17.

30 Thomas Hobbes, *Human Nature* [1650], ch. 9, pp. 40–1; *De Cive*, ch. 1, pp. 6–7.

31 Hobbes, *Leviathan*, ch. 13, p. 111. This account also appears in the earlier works, although with less emphasis. See *De Cive*, Preface, pp. xiv–xv, and ch. 1, p. 6.

32 Hobbes, *Leviathan*, ch. 13, p. 113.

33 Ibid., ch. 14, p. 118.

34 Ibid., ch. 13, p. 115.

35 Ibid., ch. 15, p. 133.

36 Ibid., ch. 14, pp. 126–7.

37 See, for example, Brian Barry, "Warrender and his Critics."

38 Hobbes, *Leviathan*, ch. 17, p. 153.

39 Ibid., ch. 15, pp. 133–4.

40 For helpful discussions, see David P. Gauthier, *The Logic of Leviathan*, pp. 57–62; and J. W. N. Watkins, *Hobbes's System of Ideas*, pp. 55–64.

41 Hobbes, *Leviathan*, ch. 15, p. 146.

42 Ibid., ch. 13, p. 113.

43 Ibid., p. 115. See also *De Cive*, Preface, p. xv; and Thomas Hobbes, *De Corpore Politico* [1650], II, ch. 10, p. 228.

44 Hobbes, *Leviathan*, ch. 21, p. 201. Compare ch. 30, p. 342: "[E]very sovereign hath the same right, in procuring the safety of his people, that any particular man can have, in procuring the safety of his own body. And the same law, that dictateth to men that have no civil government, what they ought to do, and what to avoid in regard of one another, dictateth the same to commonwealths."

45 Compare Edward Hallett Carr, *The Twenty Years' Crisis, 1919–1939*, pp. 166–9.

46 This seems to have been Rousseau's view. See "L'état de guerre" [1896; written 1753–5?], pp. 297–9. Perhaps this explains the hesitation about questions of international political theory expressed in *The Social Contract*. See J. J. Rousseau, *Du contrat social* [1762], III, xvi, p. 98, note 2, and IV, ix, p. 134.

47 Apparently Hobbes recognized that this would follow from his own characterization of international relations as a state of nature, but he did not argue for an international Leviathan. Perhaps the reason is his view that, since states in a posture of war "uphold thereby, the industry of their subjects; there does not follow from it, that misery, which accompanies the liberty of particular men" (*Leviathan*, ch. 13, p. 115). To say the least, it is not obvious that this claim is empirically accurate. Furthermore, even if it is correct, it would not follow that international agreement on regulative principles for nations is not desirable, but only that such agreement is less urgent than the analogous agreement to institute civil government.

48 In this sense, Hobbes uses the state of nature to give what Kenneth Waltz has called a "third image" account of the causes of war – that is, an account based on the image of international anarchy. See *Man, the State, and War*, pp. 159–86, in which Waltz concentrates on the third-image explanations given by Spinoza and Rousseau.

49 Oran Young, "The Actors in World Politics."

50 Hobbes, *Leviathan*, ch. 17, pp. 154–5.

51 Ibid.

52 See, for example, J. David Singer and Melvin Small, "Alliance Aggregation and the Onset of War, 1815–1914."

53 Joseph S. Nye, Jr, *Peace in Parts*, chs 4–5.

54 Ernst B. Haas, Robert L. Butterworth, and Joseph S. Nye, Jr, *Conflict Management by International Organizations*, esp. pp. 56–61.

55 The most useful survey of the growth of transnationalism is provided by the essays in Robert O. Keohane and Joseph S. Nye, Jr, eds, *Transnational Relations and World Politics*.

56 The most influential early statement of this view is David Mitrany, *A Working Peace System*. There is a revised formulation in Ernst B. Haas, *Beyond the Nation-State*, part 1. For a review of the more recent literature, see Michael Haas, "International Integration."

57 See James Patrick Sewell, *Functionalism and World Politics*, parts 1 and 3; and Ernst B. Haas, "The Study of Regional Integration."

58 See, on multinational corporations, Joseph S. Nye, Jr, "Multinational Corporations in World Politics," pp. 155–9, and the references cited there; and, on interbureaucracy contacts, Robert O. Keohane and Joseph S. Nye, Jr, "Transgovernmental Relations and International Organizations."

59 Donald P. Warwick, "Transnational Participation and International Peace," pp. 321–4.

60 As John Gerard Ruggie suggests. "Collective Goods and Future International Collaboration," p. 878.

61 Hobbes, *Leviathan*, ch. 13, p. 110.

62 It has been suggested that this is one reason Hobbes thought that the inconveniences of the international state of nature would not lead to an international Leviathan. States of unequal power and vulnerability can "secure their ends by treaties and alliances, rather than by a resignation of their sovereignty." Howard Warrender, *The Political Philosophy of Hobbes*, p. 119.

63 Gauthier, *The Logic of Leviathan*, pp. 207–8.

64 Ibid., p. 207.

65 There is a detailed discussion of these issues in Albert Legault and George Lindsey, *The Dynamics of the Nuclear Balance*, esp. chs 3–5.

66 Hobbes, *Leviathan*, ch. 13, pp. 112–13. Actually, Hobbes's assumption may be stronger than this. When men quarrel for reasons of honor and glory, one might say that their utility functions are inversely related and hence (negatively) interdependent. But the argument only requires the condition of independence given above.

67 This conclusion emerges most clearly from the debate over the application of game theoretic models of conflict and cooperation to nuclear strategy. See, for example, Anatol Rapoport, *Strategy and Conscience*, part 2. There is a thorough review of this literature in John R. Raser, "International Deterrence."

68 Edward L. Morse, "The Transformation of Foreign Policies." For a helpful discussion of the recent debate about the extent and kinds of interdependence, see Richard Rosecrance, "Interdependence: Myth or Reality."

69 Richard N. Cooper, "Prolegomena to the Choice of an International Monetary System."

70 By Keohane and Nye, for example. *Power and Interdependence*, p. 19.

71 The literature is large; see, for example, Richard N. Cooper, "Economic Interdependence and Foreign Policy in the Seventies"; Edward L. Morse, "Transnational Economic Processes"; and Alex Inkeles, "The Emerging Social Structure of the World."

72 Seyom Brown, *New Forces in World Politics*, pp. 112–17 and 186–90; and Stanley Hoffmann, "Notes on the Elusiveness of Modern Power."

73 This appears to be Kant's view in the First Supplement to *Perpetual Peace* [1795], p. 114.

74 This view derives from J. J. Rousseau, *Discours sur l'inégalité* [1755], pp. 203–6. See also Stanley Hoffmann, "Rousseau on War and Peace," *The State of War*, pp. 62–3. But see Hoffmann's more recent remarks in "Notes on the Elusiveness of Modern Power," pp. 191–5 and 205–6.

75 For a further discussion, see Keohane and Nye, *Power and Interdependence*, pp. 11–19, 27–9.

76 Hobbes, *Leviathan*, ch. 14, pp. 114–16.

77 See, for example, Kurt Baier, *The Moral Point of View*, pp. 238–9.

78 Ibid., p. 312.

79 See Roger Fisher, "Bringing Law to Bear on Governments"; Wolfgang Friedmann, *The Changing Structure of International Law*, pp. 89–95; Michael Barkun, *Law Without Sanctions*, esp. ch. 2.

80 See Lynn H. Miller, *Organizing Mankind: An Analysis of Contemporary International Organization*, esp. chs 3–5.

81 A convenient discussion of these matters is J. L. Brierly, *The Law of Nations*, esp. chs 2–3.

82 H. L. A. Hart, *The Concept of Law*, p. 214.

83 For a further discussion, see Richard A. Falk, "International Jurisdiction: Horizontal and Vertical Conceptions of Legal Order"; and Gidon Gottlieb, "The Nature of International Law: Toward a Second Concept of Law," esp. pp. 331–9.

84 One appropriate framework for such an analysis is provided by collective-goods theory. This project is begun in Ruggie, "Collective Goods and Future International Collaboration."

85 Hobbes, *Leviathan*, ch. 14, p. 117.

86 Ibid.

86 Ibid., pp. 116–17.

88 To say that the (prescriptive) international state of nature is made up of persons rather than states (or their representatives) is not to eliminate states from the purview of international theory. My claim here is that principles must be *justified* by considerations of individual rather than "national" rights. But there is no theoretical difficulty in holding that such principles still *apply* primarily to states.

89 Morgenthau, *Politics Among Nations*, p. 10.

90 The most elegant and subtle recent discussion of the issues raised here is Nagel, *The Possibility of Altruism*; on Hobbes, see Thomas Nagel, "Hobbes's Concept of Obligation."

91 A view of this kind is expressed in Philippa Foot, "Moral Beliefs," pp. 99–104.

92 H. L. A. Hart, "Are there Any Natural Rights?," p. 185.

93 See the illuminating discussion of the relation of rational self-interest and ethics in David P. Gauthier, "Morality and Advantage," esp. pp. 468–75.

94 John Locke, *Two Treatises of Government* [1689], II, sec. 9, pp. 290–1, sec. 14, pp. 294–5, and sec. 145, p. 383.

95 Ibid., II, sec. 6, p. 289. Compare Gierke, *Natural Law and the Theory of Society*, vol. 1, p. 97.

96 Only one chapter – chapter 16, "Of Conquest" – of the Second Treatise is devoted specifically to this subject. However, it has been argued that a concern for international problems animates much of the remainder of Locke's theory as well. See Richard Cox, *Locke on War and Peace*. This interpretation is highly speculative, and there is little direct textual evidence in its support.

97 Anglo-American scholars have paid too little attention to Pufendorf as a political and especially as an international theorist. There is a useful, largely historical, discussion of his views in Leonard Krieger, *The Politics of Discretion*. A brief, and I think accurate, account of his view of the law of nations can be found in Walter Schiffer, *The Legal Community of Mankind*, pp. 49–63. The best work is in German. See the bibliography in Horst Denzer, *Moralphilosophie und Naturrecht bei Samuel Pufendorf*, pp. 375–85.

98 Samuel Pufendorf, *De jure naturae et gentium, libri octo* [1688], VIII, i, p. 1138 (the order of the phrases has been reversed). See also II, ii, pp. 158–9.

99 Ibid., II, iii, p. 219. Pufendorf is responding to Hobbes's claim in *De Cive* (III, sec. 33, pp. 49–50) that "laws of nature . . . are not in propriety of speech laws" outside of civil society.

100 Pufendorf, *De jure naturae*, II, iii, p. 226; VII, ii, p. 983.

101 Ibid., VIII, ix, p. 1338; VIII, x, pp. 1342–3.

102 Ibid., II, iii, p. 163; VII, i, p. 949–63.

103 Ibid., VIII, vi, p. 1292.

104 Ibid., II, ii, p. 163; III, ii, p. 330; VIII, iv, p. 1253.

105 Ibid., II, ii, p. 176; VII, i, p. 962. Pufendorf gives no account of why this is the case. Rousseau held a similar view. See above, note 46.

106 Pufendorf, *De jure naturae*, VII, i, p. 949.

107 Ibid., II, ii, p. 163. Compare Hobbes, *Leviathan*, ch. 13, p. 115.

Bibliography

Acheson, Dean, "Ethics in International Relations Today," address given at Amherst College, December 9, 1964; *The New York Times*, December 10, 1964, p. 16.

Aron, Raymond, *Peace and War: A Theory of International Relations*, trans. Richard Howard and Annette Baker Fox. Garden City, NY: Doubleday, 1966.

Austin, John, *The Province of Jurisprudence Determined*. London: Weidenfeld and Nicolson, 1954.

Baier, Kurt, *The Moral Point of View: A Rational Basis for Ethics*. Ithaca, NY: Cornell University Press, 1958.

Barkun, Michael, *Law without Sanctions*. New Haven, CT: Yale University Press, 1968.

Barry, Brian, "Warrender and His Critics," *Philosophy* 42 (1968): 117–37.

Bodin, Jean, *Six Books of the Commonwealth*, trans. M. J. Tooley. Oxford: Basil Blackwell, 1955.

Bozeman, Adda B., *The Future of Law in a Multicultural World*. Princeton, NJ: Princeton University Press, 1971.

Brandt, Richard B., *Ethical Theory: The Problems of Normative and Critical Ethics*. Englewood Cliffs, NJ: Prentice-Hall, 1959.

Brierly, J. L., *The Law of Nations*, 6th edn., ed. Humphrey Waldock. Oxford: Clarendon Press, 1963.

Brown, Seyom, *New Forces in World Politics*. Washington, DC: The Brookings Institution, 1974.

Bull, Hedley, "Society and Anarchy in International Relations," in Herbert Butterfield and Martin Wright (eds.), *Diplomatic Investigations*. London: George Allen and Unwin, 1966, pp. 35–50.

Carr, Edward Hallett, *The Twenty Years' Crisis, 1919–1939*, 2nd edn. New York: Harper and Row, 1964.

Cooper, Richard N., "Economic Interdependence and Foreign Policy in the Seventies," *World Politics* 24 (1972): 159–81.

——, "Prolegomena to the Choice of an International Monetary System," *International Organization* 29 (1975): 63–97.

Cox, Richard, *Locke on War and Peace*. Oxford: Clarendon Press, 1960.

Denzer, Horst, *Moralphilosophie und Naturrecht bei Samuel Pufendorf*. Munich: C. H. Beck, 1972.

Falk, Richard A., "International Jurisdiction: Horizontal and Vertical Conceptions of Legal Order," *Temple Law Quarterly* 32 (1959): 295–320.

Fisher, Roger, "Bringing Law to Bear on Governments," *Harvard Law Review* 74 (1961): 1130–40.

Foot, Philippa, "Moral Beliefs," *Proceedings of the Aristotelian Society* 59 (1958–9): 83–104.

Frankel, Charles, *Morality and US Foreign Policy*. New York: Foreign Policy Association, 1975.

Frankena, W. K., *Ethics*, 2nd edn. Englewood Cliffs, NJ: Prentice-Hall, 1973.

Friedmann, Wolfgang, *The Changing Structure of International Law*. New York: Columbia University Press, 1964.

Gauthier, David P., "Morality and Advantage," *Philosophical Review* 76 (1967): 460–75.

——, *The Logic of Leviathan: The Moral and Political Theory of Thomas Hobbes*. Oxford: Clarendon Press, 1969.

Gottlieb, Gidon, "The Nature of International Law: Toward a Second Concept of Law," in Cyril E. Black and Richard A. Falk (eds.), *The Future of the International Legal Order*, vol. 4: *The Structure of the International Environment*. Princeton, NJ: Princeton University Press, 1972, pp. 331–83.

Haas, Ernest B., *Beyond the Nation-State*. Stanford, CA: Stanford University Press, 1964.

——, "The Study of Regional Integration," in Leon N. Lindberg and Stuart A. Scheingold (eds.), *Regional Integration*. Cambridge, MA: Harvard University Press, 1971, pp. 3–42.

——, Robert L. Butterworth, and Joseph S. Nye, *Conflict Management by International Organizations*. Morristown: General Learning Press, 1972.

Haas, Michael, "International Integration," in Michael Haas (ed.), *International Systems: A Behavioral Approach*. New York: Chandler, 1974, pp. 203–28.

Hart, H. L. A., "Are there Any Natural Rights?" *Philosophical Review* 64 (1955): 175–91.

——, *The Concept of Law*. Oxford: Clarendon Press, 1961.

Hobbes, Thomas, *Philosophical Rudiments concerning Government and Society* [*De Cive*], in Sir William Molesworth (ed.), *The English Works of Thomas Hobbes*, vol. 2. London: John Bohn, 1841.

——, *Leviathan*, in Sir William Molesworth (ed.), *The English Works of Thomas Hobbes*, vol. 3. London: John Bohn, 1841.

——, *De Corpore Politico*, in Sir William Molesworth (ed.), *The English Works of Thomas Hobbes*, vol. 4. London: John Bohn, 1845.

Hoffman, Stanley, "Notes on the Elusiveness of Modern Power," *International Journal* 30 (1975): 183–206.

Inkeles, Alex, "The Emerging Social Structure of the World," *World Politics* 27 (1975): 467–95.

Kant, Immanuel, *Perpetual Peace*, in Hans Reiss (ed.), *Kant's Political Writings*, trans. H. B. Nisbet. Cambridge: Cambridge University Press, 1971.

Kennan, George F., *Realities of American Foreign Policy*. Princeton, NJ: Princeton University Press, 1954.

Keohane, Robert O. and Joseph S. Nye, Jr. (eds.), *Transnational Relations and World Politics*. Cambridge, MA: Harvard University Press, 1972.

——, "Transgovernmental Relations and International Organizations," *World Politics* 21 (1974): 39–62.

——, *Power and Interdependence: World Politics in Transition*. Boston, MA: Little, Brown, 1977.

Krieger, Leonard, *The Politics of Discretion: Pufendorf and the Acceptance of National Law*. Chicago: University of Chicago Press, 1965.

Legault, Albert and George Lindsey, *The Dynamics of the Nuclear Balance*. Ithaca, NY: Cornell University Press, 1974.

Locke, John, *Two Treatises of Government*, 2nd edn., ed. Peter Laslett. Cambridge: Cambridge University Press, 1967.

Machiavelli, Niccolò, *The Prince*, trans. Luigi Ricci in Max Lerner (ed.), *The Prince and the Discourses*. New York: Random House, 1950, pp. 3–98.

——, *Discourses on the First Ten Books of Titus Livius*, trans. Christian E. Detmold, in Max Lerner (ed.), *The Prince and the Discourses*. New York: Random House, 1950, pp. 101–540.

Miller, Lynn H., *Organizing Mankind: An Analysis of Contemporary International Organization*. Boston, MA: Holbrook Press, 1972.

Mitrany, David, *A Working Peace System*, 4th edn. London: National Peace Council, 1946.

Morgenthau, Hans J., "The Twilight of International Morality," *Ethics* 58(2) (1948): 79–99.

——, *In Defense of the National Interest*. New York: Alfred A. Knopf, 1952.

——, *Politics among Nations*, 5th edn. New York: Alfred A. Knopf, 1973.

Morse, Edward L., "The Transformation of Foreign Policies: Modernization, Interdependence, and Externalization," *World Politics* 22 (1970): 371–92.

——, "Transnational Economic Processes," in Robert O. Keohane and Joseph S. Nye, Jr. (eds.), *Transnational Relations and World Politics*. Cambridge, MA: Harvard University Press, 1972, pp. 23–47.

Nagel, Thomas, *The Possibility of Altruism*. Oxford: Clarendon Press, 1970.

Northrup, F. S. C., *The Meeting of East and West*. New York: Macmillan, 1946.

Nye, Jr., Joseph S., *Peace in Parts: Integration and Conflict in Regional Organization*. Boston, MA: Little, Brown, 1971.

——, "Multinational Corporations in World Politics," *Foreign Affairs* 53 (1974): 153–75.

Pufendorf, Samuel, *De jure naturae et gentium, libri octo*, trans. C. H. and W. A. Oldfather. Oxford: Clarendon Press, 1934.

Rapoport, Anatol, *Strategy and Conscience*. New York: Schocken Books, 1964.

Raser, John R., "International Deterrence," in Michael Haas (ed.), *International Systems: A Behavioral Approach*. New York: Chandler, 1974, pp. 301–24.

Rosecrance, Richard, "Interdependence: Myth or Reality," *World Politics* 26 (1973): 1–27.

Rousseau, Jean-Jacques, *Discours sur l'inégalité*, in C. E. Vaughan (ed.), *The Political Writings of Jean-Jacques Rousseau*, vol. 1. New York: John Wiley, 1962, pp. 124–220.

——, "L'état de guerre," in C. E. Vaughan (ed.), *The Political Writings of Jean-Jacques Rousseau*, vol. 1. New York: John Wiley, 1962, pp. 293–307.

——, *Du contrat social*, in C. E. Vaughan (ed.), *The Political Writings of Jean-Jacques Rousseau*, vol. 2. New York: John Wiley, 1962, pp. 21–134.

Ruggie, John Gerard, "Collective Goods and Future International Collaboration," *American Political Science Review* 66 (1972): 874–93.

Schiffer, Walter, *The Legal Community of Mankind*. New York: Columbia University Press, 1954.

Schlesinger, Jr., Arthur, "The Necessary Amorality of Foreign Affairs," *Harper's Magazine* 243(1455) (1971): 72–3.

Sewell, James Patrick, *Functionalism and World Politics*. Princeton, NJ: Princeton University Press, 1966.

Sidgwick, Henry, *The Elements of Politics*, 4th edn. London: Macmillan, 1919.

Singer, J. David and Small, Melvin, "Alliance Aggregation and the Onset of War, 1815–1914," in J. David Singer (ed.), *Quantitative International Politics*. New York: Free Press, 1968, pp. 247–86.

Thompson, Kenneth W., *Political Realism and the Crisis of World Politics*. Princeton, NJ: Princeton University Press, 1960.

von Gierke, Otto, *Natural Law and the Theory of Society*, 2 vols., ed. and trans. Ernest Baker. Cambridge: Cambridge University Press, 1934.

Waltz, Kenneth N., *Man, the State, and War*. New York: Columbia University Press, 1959.

Warrender, Howard, *The Political Philosophy of Hobbes: His Theory of Obligation*. Oxford: Clarendon Press, 1957.

Warwick, Donald P., "Transnational Participation and International Peace," in Robert O. Keohane and Joseph S. Nye, Jr. (eds.), *Transnational Relations and World Politics*. Cambridge: Harvard University Press, 1972, pp. 305–24.

Watkins, J. W. N., *Hobbes's System of Ideas*, 2d edn. London: Hutchinson University Library, 1973.

Wolin, Sheldon S., *Politics and Vision*. Boston, MA: Little, Brown, 1960.

Young, Oran, "The Actors in World Politics," in James N. Rosenau et al. (ed.), *The Analysis of International Politics*. New York: Free Press, 1972, pp. 125–44.

Chapter 3

Cosmopolitanism and Sovereignty*
Thomas W. Pogge

The human future suddenly seems open. This is an inspiration; we can step back and think more freely. Instead of containment or détente, political scientists are discussing grand pictures: the end of history, or the inevitable proliferation and mutual pacifism of capitalist democracies. And politicians are speaking of a new world order. My inspiration is a little more concrete. After developing a rough, cosmopolitan specification of our task to promote moral progress, I offer an idea for gradual global institutional reform. Dispersing political authority over nested territorial units would decrease the intensity of the struggle for power and wealth within and among states, thereby reducing the incidence of war, poverty, and oppression. In such a multilayered scheme, borders could be redrawn more easily to accord with the aspirations of peoples and communities.

Institutional Cosmopolitanism Based on Human Rights

Three elements are shared by all cosmopolitan positions. First, *individualism*: the ultimate units of concern are human beings, or

persons[1] – rather than, say, family lines, tribes, ethnic, cultural, or religious communities, nations, or states. The latter may be units of concern only indirectly, in virtue of their individual members or citizens. Second, *universality*: the status of ultimate unit of concern attaches to every living human being equally[2] – not merely to some subset, such as men, aristocrats, Aryans, whites, or Muslims. Third, *generality*: this special status has global force. Persons are ultimate units of concern for everyone – not only for their compatriots, fellow religions, or such like.

Let me separate three cosmopolitan approaches by introducing two distinctions. The first is that between legal and moral cosmopolitanism. *Legal* cosmopolitanism is committed to a concrete political ideal of a global order under which all persons have equivalent legal rights and duties, that is, are fellow citizens of a universal republic.[3] *Moral* cosmopolitanism holds that all persons stand in certain moral relations to one another: we are required to respect one another's status as ultimate units of moral concern – a requirement that imposes limits upon our conduct and, in particular, upon our efforts to construct institutional schemes. This view is more abstract, and in this sense weaker, than legal cosmopolitanism: though

---

* From *Ethics* 103 (1992), pp. 48–75.

compatible with the latter, it is also compatible with other patterns of human interaction, for example, with a system of autonomous states and even with a plurality of self-contained communities. Here I present a variant of moral cosmopolitanism, though below I also discuss whether this position mandates efforts to move from our global status quo in the direction of a more cosmopolitan world order (in the sense of legal cosmopolitanism).

The central idea of moral cosmopolitanism is that every human being has a global stature as an ultimate unit of moral concern. Such moral concern can be fleshed out in countless ways. One may focus on subjective goods and ills (human happiness, desire fulfillment, preference satisfaction, or pain avoidance) or on more objective ones (such as human need fulfillment, capabilities, opportunities, or resources). Also, one might relativize these measures, for example, by defining the key ill as being worse off than anyone need be, or as falling below the mean – which is equivalent to replacing straightforward aggregation (sum ranking or averaging) by a version of maximin or equalitarianism, respectively. In order to get to my topic quickly, I do not discuss these matters but simply opt for a variant of moral cosmopolitanism that is formulated in terms of human rights (with straightforward aggregation).[4] In doing so, I capture what most other variants likewise consider essential. And my further reflections can, in any case, easily be generalized to other variants of moral cosmopolitanism.

My second distinction lies within the domain of the moral. It concerns the nature of the moral constraints to be imposed. An *institutional* conception postulates certain fundamental principles of justice. These apply to institutional schemes and are thus second-order principles: standards for assessing the ground rules and practices that regulate human interactions. An *interactional*

conception, by contrast, postulates certain fundamental principles of ethics. These principles, like institutional ground rules, are first order in that they apply directly to the conduct of persons and groups.[5]

Interactional cosmopolitanism assigns direct responsibility for the fulfillment of human rights to other (individual and collective) agents, whereas institutional cosmopolitanism assigns such responsibility to institutional schemes. On the latter view, the responsibility of persons is then indirect – a shared responsibility for the justice of any practices one supports: one ought not to participate in an unjust institutional scheme (one that violates human rights) without making reasonable efforts to aid its victims and to promote institutional reform.

Institutional and interactional conceptions are again compatible and thus may be combined.[6] Here I focus, however, on a variant of institutional cosmopolitanism while leaving open the question of its supplementation by a variant of interactional cosmopolitanism. I hope to show that making the institutional view primary leads to a much stronger and more plausible overall morality. Let us begin by examining how our two approaches would yield different accounts of human rights and human rights violations.

On the interactional view, human rights impose constraints on conduct, while on the institutional view they impose constraints upon shared practices. The latter approach has two straightforward limitations. First, its applicability is contingent, in that human rights are activated only through the emergence of social institutions. Where such institutions are lacking, human rights are merely latent and human rights violations cannot exist at all. Thus, if we accept a purely institutional conception of human rights, then we need some additional moral conception if we wish to deny that all is permitted in a very disorganized state of nature.

Second, the cosmopolitanism of the institutional approach is contingent as well, in that the global moral force of human rights is activated only through the emergence of a global scheme of social institutions, which triggers obligations to promote any feasible reforms of this scheme that would enhance the fulfillment of human rights. So long as there is a plurality of self-contained cultures, the responsibility for such violations does not extend beyond their boundaries.[7] It is only because all human beings are now participants in a single, global institutional scheme – involving such institutions as the territorial state and a system of international law and diplomacy as well as a world market for capital, goods, and services – that all human rights violations have come to be, at least potentially, everyone's concern.[8]

These two limitations do not violate generality. I have a duty toward every other person not to cooperate in imposing an unjust institutional scheme upon her, even while this duty triggers human-rights-based obligations only to fellow participants in the same institution scheme. This is analogous to how the duty to keep one's promises is general even while it triggers obligations only vis-à-vis persons to whom one has actually made a promise.

We see here how the institutional approach makes available an appealing intermediate position between two interactional extremes: it goes beyond simple libertarianism, according to which we may ignore harms that we do not directly bring about, without falling into a utilitarianism of rights à la Shue, which commands us to take account of all relevant harms whatsoever, regardless of our causal relation to these harms.[9]

Consider a human right not to be enslaved. On an international view, this right would constrain persons, who must not enslave one another. On an institutional view, the right would constrain legal and economic institutions: slavery must not be permitted or enforced. This leads to an important difference regarding the moral role of those who are neither slaves nor slaveholders. On the international view, such third parties have no responsibility vis-à-vis existing slaves, unless the human right in question involved, besides the negative duty not to enslave, also a positive duty to protect or rescue others from enslavement. Such positive duties have been notoriously controversial. On the institutional view, by contrast, some third parties may be implicated far more directly in the human rights violation. If they are not making reasonable efforts toward institutional reform, the more privileged participants in an institutional scheme in which slavery is permitted or even enforced – even those who own no slaves themselves – are here seen as cooperating in the enslavement, in violation of a negative duty. The institutional view thus broadens the circle of those who share responsibility for certain deprivations and abuses beyond what a simple libertarianism would justify, and it does so without having to affirm positive duties.

To be sure, working for institutional reform is doing something (positive). But, in the context of practices, this – as even libertarians recognize – does not entail that the duty in question is therefore a positive one: the negative duty not to abuse just practices may also generate positive obligations, as when one must act to keep a promise or contract one has made. Once one is a participant in social practices, it may no longer be true that one's negative duties require merely forbearance.

The move from an international to an institutional approach thus blocks one way in which the rich and mighty in today's developed countries like to see themselves as morally disconnected from the fate of the less fortunate denizens of the Third World. It overcomes the claim that one need only refrain from violating human rights directly, that one cannot reasonably be required to become a soldier in the global struggle against human rights violators and a comforter of their victims worldwide. This claim is not refuted but shown to be irrelevant. We are asked to be concerned about human rights violations not simply insofar as they exist at all, but only insofar as they are produced by social institutions in which we are significant participants. Our negative duty not to cooperate in the imposition of unjust practices, together with our continuing participation in an unjust institutional scheme, triggers obligations to promote feasible reforms of this scheme that would enhance the fulfillment of human rights.

One may think that a shared responsibility for the justice of the social institutions in which we participate cannot plausibly extend beyond our national institutional scheme, in which we participate as citizens, and which we can most immediately affect. But such a limitation is untenable because it treats as natural or God-given the existing global institutional framework, which is in fact imposed by human beings who are collectively quite capable of changing it. Therefore at least we – privileged citizens of powerful and approximately democratic countries – share a collective responsibility for the justice of the existing global order and hence also for any contribution it may make to the incidence of human rights violations.[10]

The practical importance of this conclusion evidently hinges on the extent to which our global institutional scheme is causally responsible for current deprivations. Consider this challenge: "Humans rights violations and their distribution have local explanations. In some countries torture is rampant, while it is virtually nonexistent in others. Some regions are embroiled in frequent wars, while others are not. In some countries democratic institutions thrive, while others bring forth a succession of autocrats. And again, some poor countries have

developed rapidly, while others are getting poorer year by year. Therefore our global institutional scheme has very little to do with the deplorable state of human rights fulfillment on earth."

This challenge appeals to true premises but draws an invalid inference. Our global institutional scheme can obviously not figure in the explanation of local humans rights violations, but only in the macroexplanation of their global incidence. This parallels how Japanese culture may figure in the explanation of the Japanese suicide rate or how the laxity of US handgun legislation may figure in the explanation of the North American homicide rate, without thereby explaining particular suicides/homicides or even intercity differentials in rates. In these parallel cases the need for a macroexplanation is obvious from the fact that there are other societies whose suicide/homicide rates are significantly lower. In the case of global institutions, the need for a macroexplanation of the overall incidence of human rights violations is less obvious because – apart from some rather inconclusive historical comparisons – the contrast to observable alternative global institutional schemes is lacking. Still, it is highly likely that there are feasible (i.e., practicable and accessible) alternative global regimes that would tend to engender lower rates of deprivation. This is clear, for example, in regard to economic institutions, where the centrifugal tendencies of certain free-market schemes are well understood from our experience with various national and regional schemes. This supports a generalization to the global plane, to the conjecture that the current constitution of the world market must figure prominently in the explanation of fact that our world is one of vast and increasing international inequalities in income and wealth (with consequent huge differentials in national rates of infant mortality, life expectancy, disease, and malnutrition). Such a macroexplanation does not preempt micro-explanations of why one poor country is developing rapidly and why another is not. It would explain why so few are while so many are not.

Consider this further challenge to the practical moral importance of our shared responsibility for the justice of our global institutional scheme: "An institutional scheme can be held responsible for only those deprivations it establishes, that is (at least implicitly), calls for. Thus, we cannot count against the current global regime the fact that it tends to engender a high incidence of war, torture, and starvation because nothing in the existing (written or unwritten) international ground rules calls for such deprivations – they actually forbid both torture and the waging of aggressive war. The prevalence of such deprivations therefore indicates no flaw in our global order and, a fortiori, no global duties on our part (though we do of course have some local duties to see to it that our government does not bring about torture, starvation, or an unjust war)."

This position is implausible. First, it would be irrational to assess social institutions without regard to the effects they predictably engender. For an institutional change (e.g., in economic ground rules) might benefit everyone (e.g., by increasing compliance, or through incentive effects). Second, social institutions are human artifacts (produced and abolished, perpetuated and revised by human beings), and it would be unprecedented not to take account of the predictable effects of human artifacts. (We choose between two engineering designs by considering not merely their suitability for their particular purpose but also their incidental effects, e.g., on pollution and the like, insofar as these are predictable.) Third, we consistently take incidental effects into account in debates about the design of domestic institutions (incentive effects of penal and tax codes, etc.).[11]

These arguments reaffirm my broadly consequentialist assessment of social institutions, which leads us to aim for the feasible global institutional scheme that produces the best pattern of human rights fulfillment, irrespective of the extent to which this pattern is established or engendered. We thus consider the existing global institutional scheme unjust insofar as the pattern of human rights fulfillment it tends to produce is inferior to the pattern that its best feasible alternatives would tend to produce. This broadly consequentialist variant of institutional cosmopolitanism accords with how the concern for human rights is understood within the *Universal Declaration of Human Rights*. Section 28 reads: "Everyone is entitled to a social *and International* order in which the rights and freedoms set forth in this Declaration can be fully realised" (my emphasis).[12]

This result suggests a further difference between the interactional and institutional approaches, concerning the way each counts violations of certain human rights. It cannot reasonably be required of an institutional scheme, for example, that it reduce the incidence of physical assaults to zero. This would be impossible, and approximating such an ideal as closely as possible would require a police state. The institutional approach thus counts a person's human right to physical integrity as fully satisfied if her physical integrity is reasonably secure.[13] This entails that – even in the presence of a shared institutional scheme – some of what count as human rights violations on the interactional view (e.g., certain assaults) do not count as human rights violations on the institutional view (because the persons whose physical integrity was violated were reasonably well protected). Conversely, some of what count as human rights violations on the institutional view (e.g., inadequate protection against assaults) may not register on the interactional view (as when insufficiently protected persons are not actually assaulted).

Let me close this more abstract part of my discussion with a sketch of how my institutional view relates to social and economic human rights and the notion of distributive justice. A man sympathetic to the moral claims of the poor, Michael Walzer, has written: "The idea of distributive justice presupposes a bounded world, a community, within which distributions take place, a group of people committed to dividing, exchanging, and sharing, first of all among themselves."[14] This is precisely the picture of distributive justice that Robert Nozick (among others) has so vigorously attacked. To the notion of dividing he objects that "there is no *central* distribution, no person or group entitled to control all the resources, jointly deciding how they are to be doled out."[15] And as for the rest, he would allow persons to do all the exchanging and sharing they like, but strongly reject any enforced sharing implemented by some redistribution bureaucracy.

The institutional approach involves a conception of distributive justice that differs sharply from the one Walzer supports and Nozick attacks. Here the issue of distributive justice is not how to distribute a given pool of resources or how to improve upon a given distribution but, rather, how to choose or design the economic ground rules, which regulate property, cooperation, and exchange and thereby condition production and distribution. (On the particular view I have defended, e.g., we should aim for a set of economic ground rules under which each participant would be able to meet her basic social and economic needs.) These economic ground rules – the object of distributive justice on the institutional approach – are prior to both production and distribution and therefore involve neither the idea of an already existing pool of stuff to be doled out nor the idea of already owned resources to be redistributed.

The institutional conception of distributive justice also does not presuppose the existence of a community of persons committed first of all to share with one another. Rather, it has a far more minimal rationale: we face a choice of economic ground rules that is partly open – not determined by causal necessity, nor preempted by some God-given or natural or neutral scheme that we must choose irrespective of its effects. This choice has a tremendous impact on human lives, an impact from which persons cannot be insulated and cannot insulate themselves. Our present global economic regime produces a stable pattern of widespread malnutrition and starvation among the poor (with some 20 million persons dying every year from hunger and trivial diseases), and there are likely to be feasible alternative regimes that would not produce similarly severe deprivations. In such a case of avoidable deprivations, we are confronted not by persons who are merely poor and starving but also by victims of an institutional scheme – impoverished and starved. There is an injustice in this economic scheme, which it would be wrong for its more affluent participants to perpetuate. And that is so quite independently of whether we and the starving are united by a communal bond or committed to sharing resources with one another, just as murdering a person is wrong irrespective of such considerations. This is what the assertion of social and economic human rights comes to within my institutional cosmopolitanism.

This institutional cosmopolitanism does not, as such, entail crisp practical conclusions. One reason for this is that I have not – apart from allusions to Rawls and the *Universal Declaration* – given a full list of precisely defined human rights together with relative weights or priority rules. Another reason is that this institutional cosmopolitanism bears upon the burning issues of the day only in an indirect way, mediated by empirical regularities and correlations. This is so chiefly because of its broadly consequentialist character, that is, its commitment to take the engendered consequences of an institutional scheme as seriously, morally, as its established consequences. Whether an institutional scheme establishes avoidable deprivations or inequalities (such as slavery or male suffrage) can be read off from the (written or unwritten) ground rules characterizing this scheme. With regard to engendered deprivations and inequalities, however, we face far more complex empirical questions about how the existing institutional scheme, compared to feasible modifications thereof, tends to affect the incidence of human rights violations, such as rates of infant mortality, child abuse, crime, war, malnutrition, poverty, personal dependence, and exclusion from education or health care.

The intervention of such empirical matters, and the openness of the notion of human rights, do not mean that no conclusions can be drawn about the burning issues, only that what we can conclude is less precise and less definite than one might have hoped.

The Idea of State Sovereignty

Before discussing how we should think about sovereignty in light of my institutional cosmopolitanism, let me define this term, in a somewhat unusual way, as a two-place relation: A is *sovereign* over B if and only if

1   A is a governmental body or officer ("agency"), and
2   B are persons, and
3   A has unsupervised and irrevocable authority over B
    (a)   to lay down rules constraining their conduct, or
    (b)   to judge their compliance with rules, or
    (c)   to enforce rules against them through preemption, prevention, or punishments, or
    (d)   to act in their behalf vis-à-vis other agencies (ones that do or do not have authority over them) or persons (ones whom A is sovereign over, or not).

A has *absolute sovereignty* over B if and only if

1   A is sovereign over B, and
2   no other agency has any authority over A or over B which is not supervised and revocable by A.

Any A having (absolute) sovereignty over some B can then be said to be an (absolute) sovereign (the one-place predicate).[16]

Central to contemporary political thought and reality is the idea of the autonomous territorial state as the preeminent mode of political organization. In the vertical dimension, sovereignty is very heavily concentrated at a single level; it is states and only states that merit separate colors on a political map of our world. For nearly every human being, and for almost every piece of territory, there is exactly one government with preeminent authority over, and primary responsibility for, this person or territory. And each person is thought to owe primary political allegiance and loyalty to this government with preeminent authority over him or her. National governments dominate and control the decision making of smaller political units as well as supranational decisions, which tend to be made through intergovernmental bargaining.[17]

From the standpoint of a cosmopolitan morality – which centers around the fundamental needs and interests of individual human beings, and of all human beings – this concentration of sovereignty at one level is no longer defensible. What I am proposing instead is not the idea of a world state, which is really a variant of the preeminent-state idea. Rather, the proposal is that governmental authority – or sovereignty – be widely dispersed in the vertical dimension. What we need is both centralization and decentralization, a kind of second-order decentralization away from the now dominant level of the state. Thus, persons should be citizens of, and govern themselves through, a number of political units of various sizes, without any one political unit being dominant and thus occupying the traditional role of state. And their political allegiance and loyalties[18] should be widely dispersed over these units: neighborhood, town, county, province, state, region, and world at large. People should be politically at home in all of them, without converging upon any one of them as the lodestar of their political identity.[19]

Before defending and developing this proposal by reference to my institutional cosmopolitanism, let me address two types of objection to any vertical division of sovereignty.

Objections of type 1 dispute that sovereignty can be divided at all. The traditional form of this objection rests on the belief that a juridical state (as distinct from a lawless state of nature) presupposes an absolute sovereign. This dogma of absolute sovereignty arises (e.g., in Hobbes and Kant) roughly as follows. A juridical state, by definition, involves a recognized decision mechanism that uniquely resolves any dispute. This mechanism requires some agency because a mere written or unwritten code (constitution, holy scripture) cannot settle disputes about its own interpretation. But so long as this agency is limited or divided – whether horizontally (i.e., by territory or by governmental function) or vertically (as in my proposal) – a juridical state has not been achieved because there is no recognized way in which conflicts over the precise location of the limit or division can be authoritatively resolved. A genuine state of peace requires then an agency of last resort – ultimate, supreme, and unconstrained. Such an agency may still be limited by (codified or uncodified) obligations. But these can obligate merely *in foro interno* because to authorize subjects, or some second agency, to determine whether the first agency is overstepping its bounds would enable conflicts about this question for which there would be no legal path of resolution.[20]

This argument, which – strictly construed – would require an absolute world sovereign, has been overtaken by the historical facts of the last two hundred years or so, which show conclusively that what cannot work in theory works quite well in practice. Law-governed coexistence is possible without a supreme and unconstrained agency. There is, it is true, the possibility of ultimate conflicts: of disputes in regard to which even the legally correct method of resolution is contested. To see this, one need only imagine how a constitutional democracy's three branches of government might engage in an all-out power struggle, each going to the very brink of what, on its understanding, it is constitutionally authorized to do. From a theoretical point of view, this possibility shows that we are not insured against, and thus live in permanent danger of, constitutional crises. But this no longer undermines our confidence in a genuine division of powers: we have learned that such crises need not be frequent or irresolvable. From a practical point of view, we know that constitutional democracies can endure and can ensure a robust juridical state.

This same point applies in the vertical dimension as well: just as it is nonsense to suppose that (in a juridical state) sovereignty must rest with one of the branches of government, it is similarly nonsensical to think that in a multilayered scheme sovereignty must be concentrated on one level exclusively. As the history of federalist regimes clearly shows, a vertical division of sovereignty can work quite well in practice, even while it leaves some conflicts over the constitutional allocation of powers without a legal path of authoritative resolution.

Objections of type 2 oppose, more specifically, a vertical dispersal of sovereignty: there are certain vertically indivisible governmental functions that form the core of sovereignty. Any political unit exercising these core functions must be dominant – free to determine the extent to which smaller units within it may engage in their own local political decision making, even while its own political process is immune to regulation and review by more inclusive units. Vertical distributions of sovereignty, if they are to exist at all, must therefore be lopsided (as in current federal regimes).

To be assessable, such a claim stands in need of two clarifications, which are rarely supplied. First, when one thinks about it more carefully, it turns out to be surprisingly difficult to come up with examples of indivisible governmental functions. Eminent domain, economic policy, foreign policy, judicial review; the control of raw materials, security forces, education, health care, and income support; the regulation and taxation of resource extraction and pollution, of work and consumption can all be handled at various levels and indeed are so handled in existing federal regimes and confederations. So what are the governmental functions that supposedly are vertically indivisible? Second, is their indivisibility supposed to be derived from a conceptual insight, from empirical exigencies, or from moral desiderata? And which ones?

Since I cannot here discuss all possible type 2 objections, let me concentrate on one paradigm case: Walzer's claim that the authority to fix membership, to admit and exclude, is at least part of an indivisible core of sovereignty: "At some level of political organization something like the sovereign state must take shape and claim the authority to make its own admissions policy, to control and sometimes to restrain the flow of immigrants."[21] Walzer's "must" does not reflect a conceptual or empirical necessity,

for in those senses the authority in question quite obviously can be divided – for example, by allowing political units on all levels to veto immigration. It is on moral grounds that Walzer rejects such an authority for provinces, towns, and neighborhoods: it would "create a thousand petty fortresses."[22] But if smaller units are to be precluded from controlling the influx of new members, then immigration must be controlled at the state level: "Only if the state makes a selection among would-be members and guarantees the loyalty, security, and welfare of the individuals it selects, can local communities take shape as 'indifferent' associations, determined only by personal preference and market capacity."[23] The asserted connection is again a moral one: it is certainly factually possible for local communities to exist as indifferent associations even while no control is exercised over migration at all; as Walzer says, "The fortresses too could be torn down, of course."[24] Walzer's point is, then, that the insistence on openness (to avoid a thousand petty fortresses) is asking too much of neighborhoods, unless the state has control over immigration: "The distinctiveness of cultures and groups depends upon closure. . . . If this distinctiveness is a value, . . . then closure must be permitted somewhere."[25]

But is the conventional model, with this rationale, really morally necessary? To be sure, Walzer is right to claim that the value of protecting cohesive neighborhood cultures is better served by national immigration control than by no control at all.[26] But it would be much better served still if the state were constrained to admit only immigrants who are planning to move into a neighborhood that is willing to accept them. Moreover, since a neighborhood culture can be as effectively destroyed by the influx of fellow nationals as by that of immigrants, neighborhoods would do even better, if they had some authority to select from among prospective domestic newcomers or to limit their number. Finally, neighborhoods may often want to bring in new members from abroad – persons to whom they have special ethnic, religious, or cultural ties – and they would therefore benefit from a role in the national immigration control process that would allow them to facilitate the admission of such persons. Thus there are at least three reasons for believing that Walzer's rationale – cohesive neighborhood cultures ought to be protected without becoming petty fortresses – is actually better served by a division of the authority to admit and exclude than by the conventional concentration of this authority at the level of the state.

Some Main Reasons for a Vertical Dispersal of Sovereignty

Having dealt with some preliminary obstacles, let me now sketch four main reasons favoring, over the status quo, a world in which sovereignty is widely distributed vertically.

1. *Peace/security* – Under the current regime, interstate rivalries are settled ultimately through military competition, including the threat and use of military force. Moreover, within their own territories, national governments are free to do virtually anything they like. Such governments therefore have very powerful incentives and very broad opportunities to develop their military might. This is bound to lead to the further proliferation of nuclear, biological, chemical, and conventional weapons of mass destruction. And in a world in which dozens of competing national governments control such weapons, the outbreak of devastating wars is only a matter of time. It is not feasible to reduce and eliminate national control over weapons of mass destruction through a program that depends upon the voluntary cooperation of each and every national government. What is needed, therefore, is the centrally enforced reduction and elimination of such weapons – in violation of the prevalent idea of state sovereignty. Such a program, if implemented soon, is much less dangerous than continuing the status quo. It could gain the support of most peoples and governments, if it increases the security of all on fair terms that are effectively adjudicated and enforced.

2. *Reducing oppression* – Under the current global regime, national governments are effectively free to control "their" populations in whatever way they see fit. Many make extensive use of this freedom by torturing and murdering their domestic opponents, censoring information, suppressing and subverting democratic procedures, prohibiting emigration, and so forth. This problem could be reduced through a vertical dispersal of sovereignty over various layers of political units that would check and balance one another as well as publicize one another's abuses.

3. *Global economic justice* – The magnitude and extent of current economic deprivations – over 20 million persons die every year from poverty-related causes – calls for some modification in the prevailing scheme of economic cooperation. One plausible reform would involve a global levy on the use of natural resources to support the economic development in the poorest areas.[27] Such a levy would tend to equalize per capita endowments and also encourage conservation. Reforms for the sake of economic justice would again involve some centralization – though without requiring anything like a global welfare bureaucracy.

Global economic justice is an end in its own right, which requires and therefore supports a reallocation of political authority. But it is also important as a means toward the first two purposes. War and oppression result from the contest for power within and among political units, which tends to be the more intense the higher the stakes. In fights to govern states, or to redraw their borders, far too much is now at stake by way of control of people and resources. We can best lower the stakes by dispersing political authority over several levels and institutionally securing economic justice at the global level.

This important point suggests why my first three considerations – though each supports some centralization – do not on balance support a world state. While a world state could lead to significant progress in terms of peace and economic justice, it also poses significant risks of oppression. Here the kind of multilayered scheme I propose has the great advantages of affording plenty of checks and balances and of assuring that, even when some political units turn tyrannical and oppressive, there will always be other, already fully organized political units (above, below, or on the same level) which can render aid and protection to the oppressed, publicize the abuses, and, if necessary, fight the oppressors.

There are two further important reasons against a world state. Cultural and social diversity are likely to be much better protected when the interests of cultural communities at all levels are represented (externally) and supported (internally) by coordinate political units. And the scheme I propose could be gradually reached from where we are now (through what I have called second-order decentralization), while a world state – involving, as it does, the annihilation of existing states – would seem reachable only through revolution or in the wake of some global catastrophe.

4. *Ecology* – Modern processes of production and consumption are liable to generate significant negative externalities that, to a large and increasing extent, transcend national borders. In a world of competing autonomous states, the internalization of such externalities is generally quite imperfect because of familiar isolation, assurance, and coordination problems. Treaties among a large number of very differently situated actors require difficult and time-consuming bargaining and negotiations, which often lead to only very slight progress, if any. And even when treaties are achieved, doubts about the full compliance of other parties tend to erode each party's own commitment to make good-faith efforts toward compliance.

Now one might think that this fourth reason goes beyond my institutional cosmopolitanism because there is no recognized human right to a clean environment. Why should people not be free to live in a degraded natural environment if they so choose? In response, perhaps they should be, but for now they won't have had a choice. The degradation of our natural environment ineluctably affects us all. And yet, most people are effectively excluded from any say about this issue which, in the current state-centric model, is regulated by national governments unilaterally or through intergovernmental bargaining heavily influenced by huge differentials in economic and military might.

This response suggests replacing *ecology* with a deeper and more general fourth reason, which might be labeled *democracy*: persons have a right to an institutional order under which those significantly and legitimately[28] affected by a political decision have a roughly equal opportunity to influence the making of this decision – directly or through elected delegates or representatives.[29] Such a human right to political participation also supports greater local autonomy in matters of purely local concern than exists in most current states or would exist in a world state, however democratic. In fact, it supports just the kind of multilayered institutional scheme I have proposed.

Before developing this idea further, let me consider an objection. One might say, against a human right to political participation, that what matters about political decisions is that they be correct, not that they be made democratically by those concerned. But this objection applies, first of all, only to political choices that are morally closed and thus can be decided correctly or incorrectly. I believe that we should reject a view on which almost all political choices are viewed as morally closed (with the correct decision determined, perhaps, through utility differentials), but I have no space here to defend this belief. Second, even when political choices are morally closed, the primary and ultimate responsibility for their being made correctly should lie with the persons concerned. Of course, some other decision procedure – such as a group of experts – may be more reliable for this or that kind of decision, and such procedures (judges, parliaments, cabinets, etc.) should then be put in place. This should be done, however, by the people delegating, or abstaining from, such decisions. It is ultimately up to them, and not to self-appointed experts, to recognize the greater reliability of, and to institutionalize, alternative decision-making procedures.

Given the postulated human right to political participation, the proper vertical distribution of sovereignty is determined by three sets of considerations. The first favor decentralization, the second centralization, while the third may correct the resulting balance in either direction.

First, decision making should be decentralized as far as possible. This is desirable in part, of course, in order to minimize the decision-making burdens upon individuals. But there are more important reasons as well. Insofar as decisions are morally closed, outsiders are more likely to lack the knowledge and sensitivities to make responsible judgments – and the only practicable and morally acceptable way of delimiting those who are capable of such judgments is by rough geographical criteria. Insofar as decisions are morally open, the end must be to maximize each person's opportunity to influence the social conditions that shape her life – which should not be diluted for the sake of enhancing persons' opportunities to influence decisions of merely local significance elsewhere. At least persons should be left free to decide for themselves to what extent to engage in such exchanges. The first consideration does not then rule out voluntary creation of central decision-making mechanisms (even though their structure – dependent upon unanimous consent – would tend to reflect the participants' bargaining power). Such centralization may be rational, for example, in cases of conflict between local and global rationality (tragedy-of-the-commons cases: fishing, grazing, pollution) and also in regard to desired projects that require many contributors because they involve coordination problems or economies of scale, for example, or because they are simply too expensive (construction and maintenance of transportation and communication systems, research and technology, space programs, and so forth).

The second consideration favors centralization insofar as this is necessary to avoid excluding persons from the making of decisions that significantly (and legitimately) affect them. Such decisions are of two – possibly three – kinds. Inhabiting the same natural environment and being significantly affected by what others do to it, we have a right to participate in regulating how it may be used. And since the lives each of us can lead are very significantly shaped by prevailing institutions – such as marriage, reproduction and birth control, property, money, markets, and forms of political organization – we have a right to participate in their choice and design. These two kinds of decision arise directly from Kant's point that human beings cannot avoid influencing one another: through direct contact and through their impact upon the natural world in which they coexist. A right to participate in decisions of the third kind is more controversial. There are contexts, one might say, in which we act as a species and thus should decide together how to act. Examples might be our conduct toward other biological species (extinction, genetic engineering, cruelty), ventures into outer space, and the preservation of our human heritage (ancient skeletons and artifacts, great works of art and architecture, places of exceptional natural beauty). In all these cases it would seem wrong for one person or group to take irremediable steps unilaterally.

The significance of the second consideration depends heavily upon empirical matters, though it does so in a rather straightforward and accessible way. It is obvious upon minimal reflection that the developments of the past few centuries have greatly increased the significance of this consideration in favor of centralization. This is so partly because of rising population density, but much more importantly because of our vastly more powerful technologies and the tremendously increased level of global interdependence. Concerning technologies, the fact that what a population does within its own national borders – stockpiling weapons of mass destruction, depleting nonrenewable resources, cutting down vegetation essential for the reproduction of oxygen, emitting pollutants that are destroying the ozone layer and cause global warming – now often imposes very significant harms and risks upon outsiders brings into play the political human rights of these outsiders, thereby morally undermining the conventional insistence on absolute state autonomy. Global interdependence is best illustrated by the emergence of truly global capital and commodity markets (as dramatically illustrated by the stock market crash of October 1987): a change in Japanese interest rates, or a speculative frenzy of short-selling on the Chicago Futures Exchange, can literally make the difference between life and death

for large numbers of people half a world away – in Africa, for example, where many countries depend upon foreign borrowing and cash crop exports. Such interdependence is not bad as such (it can hardly be scaled back in any case), but it does require democratic centralization of decision making: as more and more persons are significantly affected by certain institutions, more and more persons have a right to a political role in shaping them. The possibility of free bargaining over the design of such institutions does not satisfy the equal-opportunity principle, as is illustrated in the case of commodity markets by the fact that African populations simply lack the bargaining power that would allow them significantly to affect how such markets are organized. (This argument withstands the communitarian claim that we must reject supranational democratic processes for the sake of the value of national autonomy. Such rejection does indeed enhance the national autonomy of the advantaged First World populations. But their gain is purchased at the expense of poorer populations who, despite fictional or de jure state sovereignty, have virtually no control over the most basic parameters that shape their lives – a problem heightened by the fact that even their own, rather impotent governments face strong incentives to cater to foreign interests rather than to those of their constituents.)

The first two considerations by themselves yield the result that the authority to make decisions of some particular kind should rest with the democratic political process of a unit that (i) is as small as possible but still (ii) includes as equals all persons significantly and legitimately affected by decisions of this kind. In practice, some trading-off is required between these two considerations because there cannot always be an established political process that includes as equals all and only those significantly affected. A matter affecting the populations of two provinces, for example, might be referred to the national parliament or might be left to bargaining between the two provincial governments. The former solution caters to (ii) at the expense of (i): involving many persons who are not legitimately affected. The latter solution caters to (i) at the expense of (ii): giving the persons legitimately affected not an equal opportunity to influence the matter but one that depends on the relative bargaining power of the two provincial governments.

The first two considerations would suffice on the ideal-theory assumption that any decisions made satisfy all moral constraints with regard to both procedure (the equal-opportunity requirement) and output (this and other human rights). This assumption, however, could hardly be strictly true in practice. And so a third consideration must come into play: what would emerge as the proper vertical distribution of sovereignty from a balancing of the first two considerations alone should be modified – in either direction – if such modification significantly increases the democratic nature of decision making or its reliability (as measured in terms of human rights fulfillment). Let me briefly discuss how this third consideration might make a difference.

On the one hand, one must ask whether it would be a gain for human rights fulfillment on balance to transfer decision-making authority "upward" to larger units – or (perhaps more plausibly) to make the political process of smaller units subject to regulation and/or review by the political process of more inclusive units. Such authority would allow the larger unit, on human rights grounds,[30] to require revisions in the structure of the political process of the smaller one and/or to nullify its political decisions and perhaps also to enforce such revisions and nullifications.

Even when such interventions really do protect human rights, this regulation and review authority has some costs in terms of the political human rights of the members of the smaller unit. But then, of course, the larger unit's regulation and review process may itself be unreliable and thus may produce human rights violations either by overturning unobjectionable structures or decisions (at even greater cost to the political human right of members of the smaller unit) or by forcing the smaller unit to adopt structures and decisions that directly violate human rights.

On the other hand, there is also the inverse question: whether the third consideration might support a move in the direction of decentralization. Thus one must ask to what extent the political process of a larger unit is undemocratic or unreliable, and whether it might be a gain for human rights fulfillment on balance to transfer decision-making authority "downward" to smaller units – or to invest the political process of such sub-units with review authority. Such an authority might, for example, allow provincial governments, on human rights grounds, to block the application of national laws in their province. This authority is justified if and only if its benefits (laws passed in an undemocratic manner or violating human rights are not applied) outweigh its costs (unobjectionable laws are blocked in violation of the political rights of members of the larger unit).

How such matters should be weighed is a highly complex question, which I cannot here address with any precision. Let me make two points nevertheless. First, a good deal of weight should be given to the actual views of those who suffer abridgments of their human rights and for whose benefit a regulation and/or review authority might thus be called for. If most blacks in some state would rather suffer discrimination than see their state government constrained by the federal government, then the presumption against such an authority should be much weightier than if the opposition came only from the whites. This is not to deny that victims of injustice may be brainwashed or may suffer from false consciousness of various sorts. It may still be possible to make the case for a regulation and/or review authority. But it should be significantly more difficult to do so.

Second, commonalities of language, religion, ethnicity, or history are strictly irrelevant. Such commonalities do not give people a claim to be part of one another's political lives, nor does the lack of such commonalities argue against restraints. The presence or absence of such commonalities may still be empirically significant, however. Thus suppose that the members of some smaller unit share religious or ethnic characteristics that in the larger unit are in the minority (e.g., a Muslim province within a predominantly Hindu state). Our historical experience with such cases may well support the view that a regulation and review authority by the larger unit would probably be frequently abused or that a review authority by the smaller unit would tend to enhance human rights fulfillment overall. The relevance of such information brings out that the required weighings do not depend on value judgments alone. They also depend on reasonable expectations about how alternative arrangements would actually work in one or another concrete context.

The third consideration must also play a central role in a special case: the question of where decisions about the proper allocation of decision making should be made. For example, should a dispute between a provincial parliament and a national legislature over which of them is properly in charge of a particular decision be referred to the provincial or the national supreme court? Here again one must present arguments to the effect that the preferred locus of decision making is likely to be more reliable than its alternative.

Nothing definite can be said about the ideal number of levels or the exact distribution of legislative, executive, and judicial functions over them. These matters might vary in space and time, depending on the prevailing empirical facts to be accommodated by my second and third considerations (externalities, interdependence; unreliabilities) and on persons' preferences as shaped by the historical, cultural, linguistic, or religious ties among them. The human right to political participation also leaves room for a wide variety, hence regional diversity, of decision-making procedures – direct or representative, with or without political parties, and so on. Democracy may take many forms.

The Shaping and Reshaping of Political Units

One great advantage of the proposed multi-layered scheme is, I have said, that it can be reached gradually from where we are now. This requires moderate centralizing and decentralizing moves involving the strengthening of political units above and below the level of the state. In some cases, such units will have to be created, and so we need some ideas about how the geographical shape of new political units is to be determined. Or, seeing that there is considerable dissatisfaction about even the geographical shape of existing political units, we should ask more broadly: What principles ought to govern the geographical separation of political units on any level?

Guided again by the cosmopolitan ideal of democracy, I suggest these two procedural principles as a first approximation:

1   The inhabitants of any contiguous territory of reasonable shape may decide – through some majoritarian or supermajoritarian procedure – to join an existing political unit whose territory is

contiguous with theirs and whose population is willing – as assessed through some majoritarian or supermajoritarian procedure – to accept them as members.[31] This liberty is conditional upon the political unit or units that are truncated through such a move either remaining viable (with a contiguous territory of reasonable shape and sufficient population) or being willingly incorporated, pursuant to the first clause, into another political unit or other political units.

2   The inhabitants of any contiguous territory of reasonable shape, if sufficiently numerous, may decide – through some majoritarian or supermajoritarian procedure – to form themselves into a political unit of a level commensurate with their number. This liberty is subject to three constraints: there may be subgroups whose members, pursuant to their liberty under 1, are free to reject membership in the unit to be formed in favor of membership in another political unit. There may be subgroups whose members, pursuant to their liberty under 2, are free to reject membership in the unit to be formed in favor of forming their own political unit on the same level.[32] And the political unit or units truncated through the requested move must either remain viable (with a contiguous territory of reasonable shape and sufficient population) or be willingly incorporated, pursuant to the first clause of 1, into another political unit or other political units.

It will be said that acceptance of such principles would trigger an avalanche of applications. It is surely true that a large number of existing groups are unhappy with their current membership status; there is a significant backlog, so to speak, that might pose a serious short-term problem. Once this backlog will have been worked down, however, there may not be much redrawing activity as people will then be content with their political memberships, and most borders will be supported by stable majorities.

Moreover, as the advocated vertical dispersal of sovereignty is implemented, conflicts over borders will lose much of their intensity. In our world, many such conflicts are motivated by morally inappropriate considerations – especially the following two. There is competition over valuable or strategically important territories and groups because their possession importantly affects the distribution of international bargaining power (economic and military potential) for the indefinite future. And there are attempts by the more affluent to interpose borders between themselves and the poor in order to circumvent widely recognized duties of distributive justice among compatriots.[33] Under the proposed multilayered scheme – in which the political authority currently exercised by national governments is both constrained and dispersed over several layers, and in which economic justice is institutionalized at the global level and thus inescapable – territorial disputes on any level would be only slightly more intense than disputes about provincial or county lines are now. It is quite possible that my two principles are not suitable for defining a right to secession in our present world of excessively sovereign states.[34] But their plausibility will increase as the proposed second-order decentralization progresses.[35]

Finally, the incidence of applications can be reduced through two reasonable amendments. First, the burden of proof, in appealing to either of the two principles, should rest with the advocates of change, who must map out an appropriate territory, organize its population, and so forth. This burden would tend to discourage frivolous claims. Second, it may be best to require some supermajoritarian process (e.g., proponents must outnumber opponents plus nonvoters in three consecutive referenda over a two-year period). Some such provision would especially help prevent areas changing back and forth repeatedly (with outside supporters moving in, perhaps, in order to tip the scales).

Let me briefly illustrate how the two principles would work in the case of nested political units. Suppose the Kashmiris agree that they want to belong together as one province but are divided on whether this should be a province of India or of Pakistan. The majority West Kashmiris favor affiliation with Pakistan, the East Kashmiris favor affiliation with India. There are four plausible outcomes: a united Kashmiri province of Pakistan (P), a united Kashmiri province of India (I), a separate state of Kashmiri (S), and a divided Kashmir belonging partly to Pakistan and partly to India (D). Since the East Kashmiris can, by principle 2, unilaterally insist on D over P, they enjoy some protection against the West Kashmiri majority. They can use this protection for bargaining, which may result in outcome S (if this is the second preference on both sides) or even in outcome I (if that is the second preference of the West Kashmiris while the East Kashmiris prefer D or S over P).[36]

The conventional alternatives to my cosmopolitan view on settling the borders of political units reserve a special role either for historical states and their members (compatriots) or for nations and their members (fellow nationals). The former version is inherently conservative, the latter potentially revisionist (by including, e.g., the Arab, Kurdish, and Armenian nations and by excluding multinational states like the Soviet Union or the Sudan). The two key claims of such a position are: (*a*) Only (encompassing) groups of compatriots/fellow nationals have a right to self-government. (*b*) Such government may be exercised even over unwilling geographical subgroups of compatriots/fellow nationals (who at most have a

liberty of individual emigration).[37] Those who hold such a conventional position are liable to reject my cosmopolitan view as excessively individualist, contractarian, or voluntaristic. Examples of this sentiment are easy to find: "The more important human groupings need to be based on shared history, and on criteria of nonvoluntaristic (or at least not wholly contractarian) membership to have the value that they have."[38] Insofar as this is an empirical claim – about the preconditions of authentic solidarity and mutual trust, perhaps – I need not disagree with it.[39] If indeed a political unit is far more valuable for its members when they share a common descent and upbringing (language, culture, religion), then people will recognize this fact and will themselves seek to form political units along these lines. I don't doubt that groups seeking to change their political status under the two principles would for the most part be groups characterized by such unchosen commonalities.

But would I not give any other group, too, the right to change its political status, even if this means exchanging a more valuable for a less valuable membership? Margalit and Raz ridicule this idea through their examples of "the Tottenham Football Club supporters," "the fiction-reading public," and "the group of all the people whose surnames begin with a 'g' and end with an 'e.'"[40] Yet these examples – apart from being extremely farfetched – are ruled out by the contiguity requirement, which a "voluntarist" can and, I believe, should accept in light of the key function of government: to support shared rules among persons who cannot avoid influencing one another through direct interaction and through their impact upon their common environment. A more plausible example would then be that of the inhabitants of a culturally and linguistically Italian border village who prefer an (*ex hypothesi*) less valuable membership in France over a more valuable membership in Italy.

Here I ask, Do they not, France willing, have a right to err? Or should they be forced to remain in, or be turned over to, a superordinate political unit against their will?

This example brings out the underlying philosophical value conflict. My cosmopolitanism is committed to the freedom of individual persons and therefore envisions a pluralist global institutional scheme. Such a scheme is compatible with political units whose membership is homogeneous with respect to some partly unchosen criteria (nationality, ethnicity, native language, history, religion, etc.), and it would certainly engender such units. But it would do so only because persons choose to share their political life with others who are like themselves in such respects – not because persons are entitled to be part of one another's political lives if and only if they share certain unchosen features.

One way of supporting the conventional alternative involves rejecting the individualist premise that only human beings are ultimate units of moral concern.[41] One could then say that, once the moral claims of states/ nations are taken into account alongside those of persons, one may well find that, all things considered, justice requires institutional arrangements that are inferior, in human rights terms, to feasible alternatives – institutional arrangements, for example, under which the interest of Italy in its border village would prevail over the expressed interest of the villagers.

This justificatory strategy faces two main problems. It is unclear how states/nations can have interests or moral claims that are not reducible to interests and moral claims of their members (which can be accommodated within a conception of human rights). This idea smacks of bad metaphysics[42] and also is dangerously subject to political/ideological manipulation (as exemplified by Charles de Gaulle who was fond of adducing the interests of *la nation* against those of his French compatriots). Moreover, it is unclear why this idea should work here, but not in the case of other kinds of (sub- and supranational) political units, nor in that of religious, cultural, and athletic entities. Why need we not also take into account the moral claims of Catholicism, art, or baseball?

These problems suggest the other justificatory strategy, which accepts the individualist premise but then formulates the political rights of persons with essential reference to the state/nation whose members they are. This strategy has been defended, most prominently, by Michael Walzer, albeit in a treatise that focuses on international ethics (interactions) rather than international justice (institutions). Walzer approvingly quotes Westlake: "The duties and rights of states are nothing more than the duties and rights of the men who compose them," adding "the rights . . . [to] territorial integrity and political sovereignty . . . belong to states, but they derive ultimately from the rights of individuals, and from them they take their force. . . . States are neither organic wholes nor mystical unions."[43]

The key question is, of course, how such a derivation is supposed to work. There are two possibilities. The direct route would be to postulate either a human right to be governed by one's compatriots/fellow nationals[44] or a human right to participate in the exercise of sovereignty over one's compatriots/fellow nationals. The former of these rights is implausibly demanding upon others (the Bavarians could insist on being part of Germany, even if all the other Germans wanted nothing to do with them) and would still fail to establish *b*, unless it were also unwaivable – a duty, really. The latter right is implausibly demanding upon those obligated to continue to abide by the common will merely because they have once (however violently) been incorporated into a state or merely because they have once shared solidarity and sacrifices.

The indirect, instrumental route would involve the empirical claim that human rights (on a noneccentric definition) are more likely to be satisfied, or are satisfied to a greater extent, if there is, for each person, one political unit that decisively shapes her life and is dominated by her compatriots/fellow nationals. This route remains open on my cosmopolitan conception (via the third consideration), though the relevant empirical claim would not seem to be sustainable on the historical record.

Supposing that this sort of argument fails on empirical grounds, my institutional cosmopolitanism would favor a global order in which sovereignty is widely distributed vertically, while the geographical shape of political units is determined by the autonomous preferences of situated individuals in accordance with principles 1 and 2.

Notes

1   The differences between the notions of a person and a human being are not essential to the present discussion.

2   There is some debate about the extent to which we should give weight to the interests of future persons and also to those of past ones (whose deaths are still recent). I leave this issue aside because it is at right angles to the debate between cosmopolitanism and its alternatives.

3   One recent argument for a world state is advanced in Kai Nielsen, "World Government, Security, and Global Justice," in *Problems of International Justice*, ed. Steven Luper-Foy (Boulder, Colo.: Westview, 1988).

4   I have in mind here a rather minimal conception of human rights, one that rules out truly severe abuses, deprivations, and inequalities while still being compatible with a wide range of political, moral, and religious cultures. The recent development of, and progress within, both governmental and nongovernmental international organizations supports the hope, I believe, that such a conception might, in our world, become the object of a worldwide overlapping consensus. Compare Thomas W. Pogge, *Realizing Rawls* (Ithaca, N.Y.: Cornell University Press, 1989), chap. 5.

5   Interaction cosmopolitanism has been defended in numerous works. A paradigm example is Henry Shue, *Basic Rights* (Princeton, N.J.: Princeton University Press, 1980). Luban, another advocate of this position, puts the point as follows: "A human right, then, will be a right whose beneficiaries are all humans and whose obligors are all humans in a position to effect the right" (David Luban, "Just War and Human Rights," in *International Ethics*, ed. Charles Beitz et al. [Princeton, N.J.: Princeton University Press, 1985], p. 209). Robert Nozick's *Anarchy, State, and Utopia* (New York: Basic, 1974) – however surprising the rights he singles out as fundamental – is also an instance of interactional cosmopolitanism. For institutional cosmopolitanism, see Charles Beitz, *Political Theory and International Relations* (Princeton, N.J.: Princeton University Press, 1979), pt 3, and "Cosmopolitan Ideals and National Sentiment," *Journal of Philosophy* 80 (1983): 591–600; and Pogge, *Realizing Rawls*, chap. 6.

6   This is done, e.g., by John Rawls, who asserts (i) a natural duty to uphold and promote just institutions and also (ii) various other natural duties that do not presuppose shared institutions, such as duties to avoid injury and cruelty, duties to render mutual aid, and a duty to bring about just institutions where none presently exist. See John Rawls, *A Theory of Justice* (Cambridge, Mass.: Harvard University Press, 1971), pp. 114–15, 334.

7   On the interactional approach, by contrast, any positive human rights would impose duties on persons anywhere to give possible aid and protection in specified cases of need.

8   These two limitations are compatible with the belief that we have a duty to create a comprehensive institutional scheme. Thus, Kant believed that any persons and groups who cannot avoid influencing one another ought to enter into a juridical state. See Hans Reiss (ed.), *Kant's Political Writings* (Cambridge: Cambridge University Press, 1970), p. 73.

9   The second extreme I am here alluding to is consequentialism in ethics, i.e., any consequentialist view that applies directly to agents – be it of the ideal or real, of the act, rule, or motive variety. There are also noninteractional variants of consequentialism, such as Bentham's utilitarianism which applies to institutions.

10 Talk of such a contribution makes implicit reference to alternative feasible global regimes.

11 The supposed moral significance of the distinction between the established and the engendered effects of social institutions is extensively discussed in Pogge, *Realizing Rawls*, secs. 2–4.

12 Similarly also Rawls's first principle of justice: "Every person has the same indefeasible claim to a fully adequate scheme of equal basic liberties, which scheme is compatible with the same scheme of liberties for all" (latest version, unpublished). In both cases the postulated entitlement or claim is clearly second order.

13 This notion is defined in probabilistic terms, perhaps by taking account of various personal characteristics. Thus it is quite possible that the human right to physical integrity is today fulfilled in the United States for middle-aged whites or suburbanites but not for black youths or inner-city residents.

14 Michael Walzer, "The Distribution of Membership," in *Boundaries*, ed. Peter Brown and Henry Shue (Totowa, N.J.: Rowman & Littlefield, 1981), p. 1. Compare the largely identical chap. 2 of Michael Walzer, *Spheres of Justice* (New York: Basic, 1983), p. 31.

15 Nozick, p. 149.

16 It is quite possible, and not without historical justification, to define sovereignty the way I have defined absolute sovereignty. In that case the expression "distribution of sovereignty" would be an oxymoron.

17 One promising exception to this is the European Parliament.

18 This includes the sentiments of patriotism, if such there must be. Beitz points out two respects in which patriotic allegiance to political units may be desirable: it supports a sense of shared loyalty ("Cosmopolitan Ideals," p. 599); and it allows one to see oneself as a significant contributor to a common cultural project: "Just as we can see ourselves as striving to realize in our own lives various forms of individual perfection, so we can see our countries as striving for various forms of social and communal perfection" ("Cosmopolitan Ideals," p. 600). Neither of these considerations entail that, say, Britain must be the sole object of your patriotic allegiance rather than some combination of Glasgow, Scotland, Britain, Europe, humankind, and perhaps even such geographically dispersed units as the Anglican church, the World Trade Union Movement, PEN, or Amnesty International.

19 Many individuals might, of course, identify more with one of their citizenships than with the others. But in a multilayered scheme such prominent identifications would be less frequent and, most important, would not converge; even if some residents of Glasgow would see themselves as primarily British, others would identify more with Europe, with Scotland, with Glasgow, or with humankind at large.

20 This dogma – prefigured in Aquinas, Dante, Marsilius, and Bodin – is most fully stated in chaps 14, 26, and 29 of Thomas Hobbes, *Leviathan* (Harmondsworth: Penguin, 1981), who also introduces the idea of obligations *in foro interno*. For Kant's statements of it, see Reiss (ed.), pp. 75, 81, 144–5. The dogma maintained its hold well into the twentieth century, when it declined together with the Austinian conception of jurisprudence. See Geoffrey Marshall, *Parliamentary Sovereignty and the Commonwealth* (Oxford: Oxford University Press, 1957), pt 1; S. I. Benn and R. S. Peters, *Social Principles and the Democratic State* (London: Allen & Unwin, 1959), chaps 3, 12; and Herbert L. A. Hart, *The Concept of Law* (Oxford: Oxford University Press, 1961).

21 Walzer, "Distribution," p. 10.

22 Ibid., p. 9.

23 Ibid.

24 Ibid.

25 Ibid., pp. 9–10.

26 Ibid., p. 9.

27 For further discussion of such a reform –
backed perhaps by the idea that the world's
resources should be owned or controlled by
all its inhabitants as equals – see Beitz, *Political Theory*, pp. 136–43; and Pogge, *Realizing Rawls*, pp. 250–2, 263–5.

28 The qualification "legitimately" is necessary
to rule out claims such as this: "I should be
allowed a vote on the permissibility of homosexuality, in all parts of the world, because the
knowledge that homosexual acts are performed anywhere causes me great distress." I
cannot enter a discussion of this proviso here,
except to say that the arguments relevant to
its specification are by and large analogous to
the standard arguments relevant to the specification of Mill's no-harm principle.

29 I understand opportunity as being impaired
only by (social) disadvantages – not by
(natural) handicaps. This is plausible only on
a narrow construal of "handicap." Although
being black and being female are natural features, they reduce a person's chances to affect
political decisions only in certain social settings (in a racist/sexist culture). Such reductions should therefore count as disadvantages.
By contrast, those whose lesser ability to participate in public debate is due to their low
intelligence are not disadvantaged but handicapped. They do not count as having a less-than-equal opportunity. The postulated
human right is not a group right. Of course,
the inhabitants of a town may appeal to this
right to show that it was wrong for the
national government say, to impose some
political decision that affects only them. In
such a case, the townspeople form a group of
those having a grievance. But they do taut
have a grievance as a group. Rather, each of
them has such a grievance of not having been
given her due political weight – just the grievance she would have had, had the decision
been made by other townspeople with her
excluded.

30 Though not in defense of other procedural or
substantive constraints to which the smaller
unit may have chosen to commit itself.
Compare here the situation in the United
States, where federal courts may review
whether laws and decisions at the state level
accord with superordinate federal requirements, but not whether they accord with
superordinate requirements of that state
itself.

31 I won't try to be precise about "reasonable
shape." The idea is to rule out areas with
extremely long borders, or borders that divide
towns, integrated networks of economic
activity, or the like. Perhaps the inhabitants
in question should have to be minimally
numerous; but I think the threshold could be
quite low. If a tiny border village wants to
belong to the neighboring province, why
should it not be allowed to switch? The contiguity condition needs some relaxing to
allow territories consisting of a small number
of internally contiguous areas whose access to
one another is not controlled by other political units. The United States of America would
satisfy this relaxed condition through secure
access among Puerto Rico, Alaska, Hawaii,
and the remaining forty-eight contiguous
states.

32 What if minority subgroups are geographically dispersed (like the Serbs in Croatia)? In
such cases, there is no attractive way of
accommodating those opposed to the formation of the new political unit. My second
principle would let the preference of the
majority within the relevant territory prevail
nevertheless. This is defensible, I think, so
long as we can bracket any concern for human
rights violations. Where justice is not at stake,
it seems reasonable, if legitimate preferences
are opposed and some must be frustrated, to
let the majority prevail.

33 See Alan Buchanan, *Secession* (Boulder, Colo.:
Westview, 1991), pp. 114–25; and Thomas
W. Pogge, "Loopholes in Moralities," *Journal of Philosophy* 89 (1992): 79–98, pp. 88–90.

34 That topic is extensively discussed by
Buchanan. While he takes the current states
system for granted and adjusts his theory of
secession accordingly, I am arguing that a

more appealing theory of secession would be plausible in the context of a somewhat different global order. I thereby offer one more reason in favor of the latter.

35 For example, as European states will increasingly become subject to global regional constraints – regarding military might, pollution, exploitation of resources, treatment of its citizens etc. – the importance of whether there is one state (Czechoslovakia) or two states (one Czech, one Slovak) would tend to decline: for the Slovaks, for the Czechs, and for any third parties in the vicinity.

36 Obviously, this story is not meant to reflect the actual situation on the Indian subcontinent.

37 While the precise definition of 'nation' and 'nationality' is not essential to my discussion, I do assume that nationality is not defined entirely in voluntaristic terms (e.g., "a nation is a group of persons all of whom desire to constitute one political unit of which they are the only members"), in which case the two claims would become trivial. The definition may still contain significant voluntaristic elements, as in Renan's proposal: "A nation is a grand solidarity constituted by the sentiment of sacrifices which one has made and those one is disposed to make again. It supposes a past" (quote in Brian Barry, "Self-Government Revisited," in *The Nature of Political Theory*, ed. David Miller and Larry Siedentop [Oxford: Clarendon, 1983], p. 136). So long as some non-voluntaristic element is present, at least one of the two claims can get off the ground; those who want to belong together as one political unit may be prevented from doing so when they lack an appropriate history of solidarity and sacrifices.

38 Avishai Margalit and Joseph Raz, "National Self-Determination," *Journal of Philosophy* 57 (1990): 439–61, p. 456.

39 Though one should ask how this claim squares with the history of the United States, in the nineteenth century, say. Those who enjoyed the rights of citizenship were highly heterogeneous in descent and upbringing, and they came as immigrants, through sheer choice. I do not believe these facts significantly reduced the level of solidarity and mutual trust they enjoyed, compared to the levels enjoyed in the major European states of that period. A careful study of this case might well show that people can be bound together by a common decision to follow the call of a certain constitution and ideology as well as the promise of opportunities and adventure. If so, this would suggest that what matters for solidarity and mutual trust is the will to make a political life together and that such will is possible without unchosen commonalities. This result would hardly be surprising, seeing how easily the closest friendships we form transcend such commonalities of facial features, native language, cultural background, and religious convictions.

40 Margalit and Raz, pp. 443, 456.

41 For an example, see Brian Barry, "Do Countries have Moral Obligations?" in *The Tanner Lectures on Human Value*, vol. 2, ed. S. M. McMurrin (Salt Lake City: University of Utah Press, 1981), pp. 27–44.

42 Rawls makes this point: "We want to account for the social values, for the intrinsic good of institutional, community, and associative activities, by a conception of justice that in its theoretical basis is individualistic. For reasons of clarity among others we do not want to . . . suppose that society is an organic whole with a life of its own distinct from and superior to that of all its members in their relations with one another" (p. 264).

43 Michael Walzer, *Just and Unjust Wars* (New York: Basic, 1977), p. 53; cf. Walzer, "The Moral Standing of States," in Beitz et al. (eds), p. 219.

44 Walter suggests this tack: "Citizens of a sovereign state have a right, insofar as they are to be ravaged and coerced at all, to suffer only at one another's hand" (*Wars*, p. 86).

Part II

Rights to Self-Determination

Introduction

Do a people have a right to create their own political community? A people's right to self-determination is a right to self-government, entailing either the creation of a sphere of autonomy within an existing polity or secession from it. This is not merely a philosophical question but an important issue in current affairs. Nor are these debates new, as the anti-colonial movements in India, the United States of America, and elsewhere clearly demonstrate.

In chapter 4, Avishai Margalit and Joseph Raz focus their attention on whether a *moral* justification of self-determination is possible. They argue that the right to self-determination is composed of many distinct, but related, parts. These include the following:

1 A group must share a unitary character and culture.
2 The tastes of group members are shaped by their unified culture.
3 Group members recognize each other.
4 Group membership is earned through one's relationship to the group's culture, not personal achievement.

These (and other) factors create a group identity, an identity that is shared amongst its constituent members. Group interests are, thus, not personal interests.

Given this understanding of a group, Margalit and Raz argue that such groups may have a moral claim to self-government. Group membership is an important aspect of individual personality and well-being depending upon public expression, sometimes taking the form of political activities. Self-government is, thus, valuable to groups and can be justified. This claim, however, does not entail that a group has a right to self-determination. Groups may enjoy public expression in political matters and enjoy relative autonomy without having to secede. The crucial question is whether or not inclusion within a larger political community damages the collective value that group members have in their group. Thus, Margalit and Raz's argument for self-determination is instrumental in claiming "that members of a group are best placed to judge whether their group's prosperity will be jeopardized if it does not enjoy political independence."

Allen Buchanan challenges this picture in chapter 5. Unlike Margalit and Raz, Buchanan is uninterested in defending a *moral* justification of self-determination and secession. His reasons are simple. Any theory of secession should satisfy the condition of "minimal realism." That is, it must have a reasonably satisfactory likelihood of adoption by existing states in international law. Without any genuine degree of success, our theory is stillborn. In addition, any theory of secession should avoid creating "perverse incentives," such as encouraging discrimination or ethnic cleansing and discouraging more efficient government or further protections of human liberties.

Buchanan defends "remedial right only theorists" who argue that groups have a right to secede only if they have suffered tangible harm versus "primary rights theorists" who claim groups have rights to secede whether or not they have suffered harm. His argument is that secession is an issue to be decided by more than two parties: there are more legitimate interests beyond a state and a group wishing to secede from it. These legitimate interests are those of the global order, encoded in international laws and their guiding normative structure. Instead, we should adopt the view that harm to groups is the only legitimate justification for secession. This view is more consistent with international law and more likely to gain universal acceptance than primary rights theories, satisfying the condition of minimal realism. Moreover, perverse incentives are avoided as groups and states are under an obligation to avoid causing harm, whether to prevent groups seceding or assist the cause of secession or repression of minorities post-secession to further political consolidation.

The arguments in defense of a right to self-determination may take many forms. Margalit and Raz opt for a moral justification, whilst Buchanan defends a political, institutional justification. Which defense we choose has consequences for the world we live in as each defense may justify drawing new political boundaries in some parts of the world and not others. Nevertheless, these chapters help clarify our thinking about this issue whichever defense we might prefer.

Chapter 4

National Self-Determination*
Avishai Margalit and Joseph Raz

In the controversy-ridden fields of international law and international relations, the widespread recognition of the existence of national rights to self-determination provides a welcome point of agreement. Needless to say, the core consensus is but the eye of a raging storm concerning the precise definition of the right, its content, its bearers, and the proper means for its implementation. This paper will not address such questions, though indirectly it may help with their investigation. Its concern is with the moral justification of the case for national self-determination. Its purpose is critical and evaluative, its subject lies within the morality of international relations rather than within international law and international relations proper.

It is assumed throughout that states and international law should recognize such a right only if there is a sound moral case for it. This does not mean that international law should mirror morality. Its concern is with setting standards that enjoy the sort of clarity required to make them the foundations of international relations between states and fit for recognition and enforcement through international organs. These concerns give rise to special considerations that should be fully recognized in the subtle process of applying moral principles to the law. The derivation of legal principles from moral premises is never a matter of copying morality into law. Still, the justification of the law rests ultimately on moral considerations, and therefore those considerations should also help shape the contours of legal principles. That is why the conclusions of this paper bear on controversies concerning the proper way in which the law on this subject should develop, even though such issues are not here discussed directly.

Moral inquiry is sometimes understood in a utopian manner, i.e., as an inquiry into the principles that should prevail in an ideal world. It is doubtful whether this is a meaningful enterprise, but it is certainly not the one we are engaged in here. We assume that things are roughly as they are, especially that our world is a world of states and of a variety of ethnic, national, tribal, and other groups.[1] We do not question the justification for this state of affairs. Rather, we ask whether, given that this is how things are and for as long as they remain the same, a moral case can be made in support of national self-determination.

* From *The Journal of Philosophy* 87:9 (1990), pp. 439–61.

I Isolating the Issue

The core content of the claim to be examined is that there is a right to determine whether a certain territory shall become, or remain, a separate state (and possibly also whether it should enjoy autonomy within a larger state). The idea of national self-determination or (as we shall refer to it in order to avoid confusion) the idea of self-government encompasses much more. The value of national self-government is the value of entrusting the general political power over a group and its members to the group. If self-government is valuable then it is valuable that whatever is a proper matter for political decision should be subject to the political decision of the group in all matters concerning the group and its members. The idea of national self-government, in other words, speaks of groups determining the character of their social and economic environment, their fortunes, the course of their development, and the fortunes of their members by their own actions, i.e., by the action of those groups, in as much as these are matters which are properly within the realm of political action.[2] Given the current international state system, in which political power rests, in the main, with sovereign states,[3] the right to determine whether a territory should be an independent state is quite naturally regarded as the main instrument for realizing the ideal of self-determination. Consideration of this right usually dominates all discussions of national self-determination. To examine the justification of the right is the ultimate purpose of this article. But we shall continuously draw attention to the fact that, as we shall try to show, the right of self-determination so understood is not ultimate, but is grounded in the wider value of national self-government, which is itself to be only instrumentally justified.

The next section deals with the nature of the groups that might be the subject of such a right. Section III considers what value, if any, is served by the enjoyment of political independence by such groups. Section IV examines the case for conceding that there is a moral right to self-determination. This examination may lead to revising our understanding of the content of the right. It may reveal that moral considerations justify only a narrower right, or that the argument that justifies the right warrants giving it a wider scope. But the core as identified here will provide the working base from which to launch the inquiry.

Before we start, a few words about this way of identifying the problem may be in place. In two ways the chosen focus of our examination is narrower than many discussions of self-determination in international relations. First, we disregard the claims made, typically by third-world countries, in the name of self-determination, against the economic domination of multinational companies, the World Bank, or against powerful regional or world powers. The considerations canvassed in this paper are relevant to such issues, but fall short of directly tackling them. To be complete, a discussion of a right must examine both its grounds and its consequences. This paper is concerned mostly with the grounds for the right of self-determination. It asks the question: Who has the right and under what conditions is it to be exercised? It does not go into the question of the consequences of the right beyond the assumption, already stated, that it is a right that a territory be a self-governing state. A good deal of the current turmoil in international law, and international relations, has to do with the exploration of that last notion. What is entailed by the fact that a state is a sovereign, self-governing, entity? The claims that economic domination violate the right to self-determination belong to that discussion. The conclusions of this paper provide part of the grounds by which such claims are to be settled. But we do not propose to pursue this question here.

Second, claims of self-determination are invariably raised whenever one state invades and occupies another, or a territory belonging to another. Yet it is important to distinguish between the wrongness of military invasion or occupation, and the rights available against it, and the right (whatever it may turn out to be) to self-determination. In a word, the latter is a source of title, whereas the former is a possessory right based largely on public-order considerations. Any legal system, international law not excluded, recognizes certain ways as legitimate ways of solving disputes, and outlaws others. Subject to the exceptions of legitimate self-defense and self-help, the use of violence is forbidden. Violation of that prohibition gives rise to a right to have the *status quo ante* restored, before the deeper sources of the dispute between the parties are examined; that is, regardless of the soundness of one's title to a territory, one may not use force to occupy it. This is why the right to recover a territory lost by force is a possessory right. It does not depend on the ultimate soundness of one's title, and that is why it was said to be based on public-order considerations. A large part of its justification is in the need to establish that the proper means of dispute resolution be the only ones resorted to.

Not surprisingly, invocation of this possessory right is, however, accompanied by a claim of good title (the merits of which are not immediately relevant). The underlying title is often the right to self-determination. Hence the temptation to confuse the two. But notice that, apart from the different justificatory foundations, the two are far from identical in consequence. They merely overlap. The claims of a people who have been for many years ruled by another cannot be based on the possessory right that applies only against a recent occupier. On the other hand, the occupation of portions of Antarc-

tica, or of some uninhabited island, do violate the possessory right, but not the right of self-determination. The latter is that of the inhabitants, and does not apply when there are no inhabitants.[4]

II Groups

Assuming that self-determination is enjoyed by groups, what groups qualify? Given that the right is normally attributed to peoples or nations, it is tempting to give that as the answer and concentrate on characterizing "peoples" or "nations." The drawbacks of this approach are two: it assumes too much and it poses problems that may not require a solution.

It is far from clear that peoples or nations rather than tribes, ethnic groups, linguistic, religious, or geographical groups are the relevant reference group. What is it that makes peoples particularly suited to self-determination? The right concerns determination whether a certain territory shall be self-governing or not. It appears to affect most directly the residents of a territory, and their neighbors. If anyone, then residents of geographical regions seem intuitively to be the proper bearers of the right. Saying this does not get us very far. It does not help in identifying the residents of which regions should qualify. To be sure, this is the crucial question. But even posing it in this way shows that the answer, "the largest regions inhabited by one people or nation," is far from being the obvious answer.

We have some understanding of the benefits self-government might bring. We need to rely on this in looking for the characteristics that make groups suitable recipients of those benefits. We want, in other words, to identify groups by those characteristics which are relevant to the justification of the right. If it turns out that those do not apply to peoples or nations, we shall have shown that the right to self-determination is misconceived and, as recognized in international law, unjustified. Alternatively, the groups identified may encompass peoples (or some peoples) as well as other groups. This will provide a powerful case for redrawing the boundaries of the right. Either way we shall be saved much argument concerning the characterization of nations which, interesting as it is in itself, is irrelevant to our purpose.

Having said that, it may be useful to take nations and peoples as the obvious candidates for the right. We need not worry about their defining characteristics. But we may gain insight by comparing them with groups, e.g., the fiction-reading public, or Tottenham Football Club supporters, which obviously do not enjoy such a right. Reflection on such examples suggests six characteristics that in combination are relevant to a case for self-determination.

1.   The group has a common character and a common culture that encompass many, varied and important aspects of life, a culture that defines or marks a variety of forms or styles of life, types of activities, occupations, pursuits, and relationships. With national groups we expect to find national cuisines, distinctive architectural styles, a common language, distinctive literary and artistic traditions, national music, customs, dress, ceremonies and holidays, etc. None of these is necessary. They are but typical examples of the features that characterize peoples and other groups that are serious candidates for the right to self-determination. They have pervasive cultures, and their identity is determined at least in part by their culture. They possess cultural traditions that penetrate beyond a single or a few areas of human life, and display themselves in a whole range of areas, including many which are of great importance for the well-being of individuals.

2.   The correlative of the first feature is that people growing up among members of

the group will acquire the group culture, will be marked by its character. Their tastes and their options will be affected by that culture to a significant degree. The types of careers open to one, the leisure activities one learned to appreciate and is therefore able to choose from, the customs and habits that define and color relations with strangers and with friends, patterns of expectations and attitudes between spouses and among other members of the family, features of lifestyles with which one is capable of empathizing and for which one may therefore develop a taste – all these will be marked by the group culture.

They need not be indelibly marked. People may migrate to other environments, shed their previous culture, and acquire a new one. It is a painful and slow process, success in which is rarely complete. But it is possible, just as it is possible that socialization will fail and one will fail to be marked by the culture of one's environment, except negatively, to reject it. The point made is merely the modest one that, given the pervasive nature of the culture of the groups we are seeking to identify, their influence on individuals who grow up in their midst is profound and far-reaching. The point needs to be made in order to connect concern with the prosperity of the group with concern for the well-being of individuals. This tie between the individual and the collective is at the heart of the case for self-determination.

As one would expect, the tie does not necessarily extend to all members of the group, and failure of socialization is not the only reason. The group culture affects those who grow up among its members, be they members or not. But to say this is no more than to point to various anomalies and dilemmas that may arise. Most people live in groups of these kinds, so that those who belong to none are denied full access to the opportunities that are shaped in part by the group's culture. They are made to feel estranged and their chances to have a rewarding life are seriously damaged. The same is true of people who grow up among members of a group so that they absorb its culture, but are then denied access to it because they are denied full membership of the group.

Nothing in the above presupposes that groups of the kind we are exploring are geographically concentrated, let alone that their members are the only inhabitants of any region. Rather, by drawing on the transmission of the group culture through the socialization of the young, these comments emphasize the historical nature of the groups with which we are concerned. Given that they are identified by a common culture, at least in part, they also share a history, for it is through a shared history that cultures develop and are transmitted.

3. Membership in the group is, in part, a matter of mutual recognition. Typically, one belongs to such groups if, among other conditions, one is recognized by other members of the group as belonging to it. The other conditions (which maybe the accident of birth or the sharing of the group culture, etc.) are normally the grounds cited as reasons for such recognition. But those who meet those other conditions and are yet rejected by the group are at best marginal or problematic members of it. The groups concerned are not formal institutionalized groups, with formal procedures of admission. Membership in them is a matter of informal acknowledgment of belonging by others generally, and by other members specifically. The fiction-reading public fails our previous tests. It is not identified by its sharing a wide-ranging pervasive culture. It also fails the third test. To belong to the fiction-reading public all we have to do is to read fiction. It does not matter whether others recognize us as fiction-reading.[5]

4. The third feature prepares the way for, and usually goes hand in hand with, the importance of membership for one's self-identification. Consider the fiction-reading public again. It is a historically significant group. Historians may study the evolution of the fiction-reading public, how it spread from women to men, from one class to others, from reading aloud in small groups to silent reading, from reliance on libraries to book buying, etc.; how it is regarded as important to one's qualification as a cultured person in one country, but not in another; how it furnishes a common topic of conversation in some classes but not in others; how belonging to the group is a mark of political awareness in some countries, while being a sign of escapist retreat from social concerns in another.

Such studies will show, however, that it is only in some societies that the existence of these features of the fiction-reading public is widely known. For the most part, one can belong to the group without being aware that one is a typical reader, that one's profile is that of most readers. Sometimes this is a result of a mistaken group image's being current in that society. Our concern is rather with those cases where the society lacks any very distinct image of that group. This indicates that, in such societies, membership of that group does not have a highly visible social profile. It is not one of the facts by which people pigeonhole each other. One need not be aware who, among people one knows, friends, acquaintances, shopkeepers one patronizes, one's doctor, etc., shares the habit. In such societies, membership of the fiction-reading public is not highly visible, that is, it is not one of the things one will normally know about people one has contact with, one of the things that identify "who they are." But it happens in some countries that membership of the reading public becomes a highly visible mark of belonging to a social group, to the intelligentsia, etc. In such countries, talk of the recently published novel becomes a means of mutual recognition.

One of the most significant facts differentiating various football cultures is whether they are cultures of self-recognition: whether identification as a fan or supporter of this club or that is one of the features that are among the main markers of people in the society. The same is true of occupational groups. In some countries, membership is highly visible and is among the primary means of pigeonholing people, of establishing "who they are"; in others, it is not.

Our concern is with groups, membership of which has a high social profile, that is, groups, membership of which is one of the primary facts by which people are identified, and which form expectations as to what they are like, groups membership of which is one of the primary clues for people generally in interpreting the conduct of others. Since our perceptions of ourselves are in large measure determined by how we expect others to perceive us, it follows that membership of such groups is an important identifying feature for each about himself. These are groups, members of which are aware of their membership and typically regard it as an important clue in understanding who they are, in interpreting their actions and reactions, in understanding their tastes and their manner.

5.   Membership is a matter of belonging, not of achievement. One does not have to prove oneself, or to excel in anything, in order to belong and to be accepted as a full member. To the extent that membership normally involves recognition by others as a member, that recognition is not conditional on meeting qualifications that indicate any accomplishment. To be a good Irishman, it is true, is an achievement. But to be an Irishman is not. Qualification for membership is usually determined by nonvoluntary criteria. One cannot choose to belong. One belongs because of who one is. One can come to belong to such groups, but only by changing, e.g., by adopting their culture, changing one's tastes and habits accordingly

– a very slow process indeed. The fact that these are groups, membership of which is a matter of belonging and not of accomplishment, makes them suitable for their role as primary foci of identification. Identification is more secure, less liable to be threatened, if it does not depend on accomplishment. Although accomplishments play their role in people's sense of their own identity, it would seem that at the most fundamental level our sense of our own identity depends on criteria of belonging rather than on those of accomplishment. Secure identification at that level is particularly important to one's well-being.

6.   The groups concerned are not small face-to-face groups, members of which are generally known to all other members. They are anonymous groups where mutual recognition is secured by the possession of general characteristics. The exclusion of small groups from consideration is not merely ad hoc. Small groups that are based on personal familiarity of all with all are markedly different in the character of their relationships and interactions from anonymous groups. For example, given the importance of mutual recognition to members of these groups, they tend to develop conventional means of identification, such as the use of symbolic objects, participation in group ceremonies, special group manners, or special vocabulary, which help quickly to identify who is "one of us" and who is not.

The various features we listed do not entail each other but they tend to go together. It is not surprising that groups with pervasive cultures will be important in determining the main options and opportunities of their members, or that they will become focal points of identification, etc. The way things are in our world, just about everyone belongs to such a group, and not necessarily to one only. Membership is not exclusive and many people belong to several groups that answer to our description. Some of them are rather like national groups, e.g., tribes or ethnic groups. Others are very different. Some religious groups meet our conditions, as do social classes, and some racial groups. Not all religions or racial groups did develop rich and pervasive cultures. But some did and those qualify.

III   The Value of Self-government

(A)   The Value of Encompassing Groups

The description of the relevant groups in the preceding section may well disappoint the reader. Some will be disappointed by the imprecise nature of the criteria provided. This would be unjustified. The criteria are not meant to provide operational legal definitions. As such they clearly would not do. Their purpose is to pick on the features of groups which may explain the value of self-determination. As already mentioned, the key to the explanation is in the importance of these groups to the well-being of their members. This thought guided the selection of the features. They are meant to assist in identifying that link. It is not really surprising that they are all vague matters of degree, admitting of many variants and many nuances. One is tempted to say "that's life." It does not come in neatly parceled parts. While striving to identify the features that matter, we have to recognize that they come in many shapes, in many shades, and in many degrees rife with impurities in their concrete mixing.

A more justified source of disappointment is the suspicion that we have cast the net too wide. Social classes clearly do not have a right to self-determination. If they meet the above conditions then those conditions are at best incomplete. Here we can only crave the reader's patience. We tried to identify the features of groups which help explain the value of self-determination. These may apply not only beyond the sphere in which the right is commonly recognized. They may apply to groups that really should not possess it for other reasons yet to be explored.

The defining properties of the groups we identified are of two kinds. On the one hand, they pick out groups with pervasive cultures; on the other, they focus on groups, membership of which is important to one's self-identity. This combination makes such groups suitable candidates for self-rule. Let us call groups manifesting the six features *encompassing groups*. Individuals find in them a culture which shapes to a large degree their tastes and opportunities, and which provides an anchor for their self-identification and the safety of effortless secure belonging.

Individual well-being depends on the successful pursuit of worthwhile goals and relationships. Goals and relationships are culturally determined. Being social animals means not merely that the means for the satisfaction of people's goals are more readily available within society. More crucially it means that those goals themselves are (when one reaches beyond what is strictly necessary for biological survival) the creatures of society, the products of culture. Family relations, all other social relations between people, careers, leisure activities, the arts, sciences, and other obvious products of "high culture" are the fruits of society. They all depend for their existence on the sharing of patterns of expectations, on traditions preserving implicit knowledge of how to do what, of tacit conventions regarding what is part of this or that enterprise and what is not, what is appropriate and what is not, what is valuable and what is not. Familiarity with a culture determines the boundaries of the imaginable. Sharing in a culture, being part of it, determines the limits of the feasible.

It may be no more than a brute fact that our world is organized in a large measure around groups with pervasive cultures. But it is a fact with far-reaching consequences. It means, in the first place, that membership of such groups is of great importance to individual well-being, for it greatly affects one's opportunities, one's ability to engage in the relationships and pursuits marked by the culture. Secondly, it means that the prosperity of the culture is important to the well-being of its members. If the culture is decaying, or if it is persecuted or discriminated against, the options and opportunities open to its members will shrink, become less attractive, and their pursuit less likely to be successful.

It may be no more than a brute fact that people's sense of their own identity is bound up with their sense of belonging to encompassing groups and that their self-respect is affected by the esteem in which these groups are held. But these facts, too, have important consequences. They mean that individual dignity and self-respect require that the groups, membership of which contributes to one's sense of identity, be generally respected and not be made a subject of ridicule, hatred, discrimination, or persecution.

All this is mere common sense, and is meant to be hedged and qualified in the way our common understanding of these matters is. Of course, strangers can participate in activities marked by a culture. They are handicapped, but not always very seriously. Of course, there are other determinants of one's opportunities, and of one's sense of self-respect. Membership of an encompassing group is but one factor. Finally, one should mention that groups and their culture may be pernicious, based on exploitation of people, be they their members or not, or on the denigration and persecution of other groups. If so, then the case for their protection and flourishing is weakened, and may disappear altogether.

Having regard for this reservation, the case for holding the prosperity of encompassing groups as vital for the prosperity of their members is a powerful one. Group interests cannot be reduced to individual interests. It makes sense to talk of a group's prospering or declining, of actions and policies as serving the group's interest or of harming it, without having to cash this in terms of individual interests. The group may flourish if its culture prospers, but this need not mean that the lot of its members or of anyone else has improved. It is in the interest of the group to be held in high regard by others, but it does not follow that, if an American moon landing increases the world's admiration for the United States, Americans necessarily benefit from this. Group interests are conceptually connected to the interests of their members but such connections are nonreductive and generally indirect. For example, it is possible that what enhances the interest of the group provides opportunities for improvement for its members, or that it increases the chance that they will benefit.

This relative independence of group interest is compatible with the view that informs this article: that the moral importance of the group's interest depends on its value to individuals. A large decline in the fortunes of the group may, e.g., be of little consequence to its members. There is no a priori way of correlating group interest with that of its members or of other individuals. It depends on the circumstances of different groups at different times. One clear consequence of the fact that the moral significance of a group's interest is in its service to individuals is the fact that it will depend, in part, on the size of the group. The fortunes of a larger group may be material to the well-being of a larger number of people. Other things being equal, numbers matter.

(B)   The Instrumental Case

Does the interest of members in the prosperity of the group establish a right to self-determination? Certainly not, at least not yet, not without further argument. For one thing we have yet to see any connection between the prosperity of encompassing groups and their political independence. The easiest connection to establish under certain conditions is an instrumental one. Sometimes the prosperity of the group and its self-respect are aided by, sometimes they may be impossible to secure without, the group's enjoying political sovereignty over its own affairs. Sovereignty enables the group to conduct its own affairs in a way conducive to its prosperity.[6] There is no need to elaborate the point. It depends on historical conditions. Hence the prominence of a history of persecution in most debates concerning self-determination. But a history of persecution is neither a necessary nor a sufficient condition for the instrumental case for self-government. It is not a necessary condition, because persecution is not the only reason why the groups may suffer without independence. Suffering can be the result of neglect or ignorance of or indifference to the prosperity of a minority group by the majority. Such attitudes may be so well entrenched that there is no realistic prospect of changing them.

Persecution is not a sufficient condition, for there may be other ways to fight and overcome persecution and because whatever the advantages of independence it may, in the circumstances, lead to economic decline, cultural decay, or social disorder, which only make their members worse off. Besides, as mentioned above, pernicious groups may not deserve protection, especially if it will help them to pursue repressive practices with impunity. Finally, there are the interests of nonmembers to be considered. In short, the instrumental argument (as well as others) for self-government is sensitive to counterarguments pointing to its drawbacks, its cost in terms of human well-being, possible violations of human rights, etc.

We shall return to these issues below. First, let us consider the claim that the instrumental argument trivializes the case for self-government by overlooking its intrinsic value. Of the various arguments for the intrinsic value of self-government which have been and can be advanced, we examine one which seems the most promising.

(C) An Argument for the Intrinsic Value of Self-government

The argument is based on an extension of individual autonomy or of self-expression (if that is regarded as independently valuable). The argument unravels in stages: (1) people's membership of encompassing groups is an important aspect of their personality, and their well-being depends on giving it full expression; (2) expression of membership essentially includes manifestation of membership in the open, public life of the community; (3) this requires expressing one's membership in political activities within the community. The political is an essential arena of community life, and consequently of individual well-being; (4) therefore, self-government is inherently valuable, it is required to provide the group with a political dimension.

The first premise is unexceptionable. So is the second, though an ambiguity might be detected in the way it is often understood. Two elements need separating. First, given the importance of membership to one's well-being, it is vital that the dignity of the group be preserved. This depends, in part, on public manifestations of respect for the group and its culture, and on the absence of ridicule of the group, etc., from the public life of the society of which one is a member. One should not have to identify with or feel loyalty to a group that denigrates an encompassing group to which one belongs. Indeed, one should not have to live in an environment in which such attitudes are part of the common culture. Second, an aspect of well-being is an ability to express publicly one's identification with the group and to participate openly in its public culture. An encompassing group is centered on mutual recognition and is inevitably a group with a public culture. One cannot enjoy the benefits of membership without participation in its public culture, without public participation in its culture.

Both elements are of great importance. Both indicate the vital role played by public manifestations of group culture and group membership among the conditions of individual well-being. To the extent that a person's well-being is bound up with his identity as a member of an encompassing group it has an important public dimension. But that dimension is not necessarily political in the conventional narrow sense of the term. Even where it is, its political expression does not require a political organization whose boundaries coincide with those of the group. One may be politically active in a multinational, multicultural polity.

Here supporters of the argument for the intrinsic value of self-government may protest. The expression of membership in the political life of the community, they will say, involves more than its public expression. It involves the possibility of members of an encompassing group participating in the political life of their state, and fighting in the name of group interests in the political arena. Such actions, they will insist, may be not only instrumentally valuable to the group, but intrinsically important to its politically active members. They are valuable avenues of self-fullfilment. These points, too, have to be readily admitted. There is no reason to think that everyone must take part in politics, or else his or her development is stunted and personality or life are deficient. In normal times, politics is but an option that people may choose to take or to leave alone. Although its availability is important,

for its absence deprives people of valuable opportunities, its use is strictly optional. Even if it is possible to argue that one's personal well-being requires some involvement with larger groups, and the avoidance of exclusive preoccupation with one's own affairs and those of one's close relations or friends, that involvement can take nonpolitical forms, such as activity in a social club, interest in the fortunes of the arts in one's region, etc.

Politics is no more than an option, though this is true in normal times only. In times of political crises that have moral dimensions, it may well be the duty of everyone to stand up and be counted. In Weimar, Germans had a moral duty to become politically involved to oppose Nazism. There are many other situations where an apolitical attitude is not morally acceptable. But all of them are marked by moral crises. In the absence of crisis there is nothing wrong in being nonpolitical.

Having said this, we must repeat that the option of politics must remain open, and with it the option of fighting politically for causes to do with the interests of one's encompassing groups. But there is nothing here to suggest that this should be done in a political framework exclusive to one's group or dominated by it. There is nothing wrong with multinational states, in which members of the different communities compete in the political arena for public resources for their communities. Admittedly, prejudice, national fanaticism, etc., sometimes make such peaceful and equitable sharing of the political arena impossible. They may lead to friction and persecution. This may constitute a good argument for the value of self-government, but it is an instrumental argument of the kind canvassed above. There is nothing in the need for a public or even a political expression of one's membership of an encompassing group which points to an intrinsic value of self-government.

(D) The Subjective Element

In an indirect way, the attempt to argue for the intrinsic value of self-government does point to the danger of misinterpreting the instrumental approach to the question. First, the argument does not deny the intrinsic value of the existence of the political option as a venue for activity and self-expression to all (adult) members of society. We are not advocating a purely instrumentalist view of politics generally. The intrinsic value to individuals of the political option does not require expression in polities whose boundaries coincide with those of encompassing groups. That is the only point argued for above.

Second, the pragmatic, instrumentalist character of the approach advocated here should not be identified with an aggregating impersonal consequentialism. Some people tend to associate any instrumentalist approach with images of a bureaucracy trading off the interest of one person against that of another on the basis of some cost–benefit analysis designed to maximize overall satisfaction; a bureaucracy, moreover, in charge of determining for people what is really good for them, regardless of their own views of the matter. Nothing of the kind should be countenanced. Of course, conflicts among people's interests do arise, and call for rational resolution that is likely to involve sacrificing some interests of some people for the sake of others. Such conflicts, however, admit of a large degree of indeterminacy, and many alternative resolutions may be plausible or rational. In such contexts, talking of maximization, with its connotations of comparability of all options, is entirely out of place.

Furthermore, nothing in the instrumentalist and pragmatic nature of our approach should be allowed to disguise its sensitivity to subjective elements, its responsiveness to the perceptions and sensibilities of the people concerned. To a considerable extent, what matters is how well people feel in their environment: Do they feel at home in it or are they alienated from it? Do they feel respected or humiliated? etc. This leads to a delicate balance between "objective" factors and subjective perceptions. On the one hand, when prospects for the future are concerned, subjective perceptions of danger and likely persecution, etc., are not necessarily to be trusted. These are objective issues on which the opinion of independent spectators may be more reliable than that of those directly involved. On the other hand, the factual issue facing the independent spectators is how people will respond to their conditions, what will be their perceptions, their attitudes to their environment, to their neighbors, etc. Even a group that is not persecuted may suffer many of the ills of real persecution if it feels persecuted. That its perceptions are mistaken or exaggerated is important in pointing to the possibility of a different cure: removing the mistaken perception. But that is not always possible, and up to a point in matters of respect, identification, and dignity, subjective responses, justified or not, are the ultimate reality so far as the well-being of those who have them is concerned.

IV   A Right to Self-determination

It may seem that the case for self-government establishes a right to self-determination. That is, it establishes the reasons for the right sort of group, an encompassing group, to determine that a territory shall be self-governing. But things are not that simple. The case for self-government shows that sometimes, under certain conditions, it is best that the political unit be roughly an encompassing group. A group's right to self-determination is its right to determine that a territory be self-governing, regardless of whether the case for self-government, based on its benefits, is established or not. In other words, the right to self-determination answers the question "who is to decide?", not "what is the best decision?". In exercising the right, the group should act responsibly in light of all the considerations we mentioned so far. It should, in particular, consider not only the interests of its members but those of others who may be affected by its decision, But if it has the right to decide, its decision is binding even if it is wrong, even if the case for self-government is not made.[7]

The problem in conceding the existence of such a right is, of course, not the possibility that a group that would best be self-governing does not wish to be so. Given the strong subjectivist element in the instrumentalist argument, such reluctance to assume independence would suggest that the case for its being self-governing is much weakened. The problem is that the case for self-government is hedged by considerations of the interest of people other than members of the groups, and by the other interests of members of the groups, i.e., other than their interests as members of the groups. These include their fundamental individual interests which should be respected, e.g., by a group whose culture oppresses women or racial minorities. These considerations raise the question whether encompassing groups are the most suitable bodies to decide about the case for self-government. Can they be entrusted with the decision in a matter in which their group interests are in conflict with other interests of members of the group as well as with the interests of other people? At the very least this suggests that the right must be qualified and hedged to protect other interests.

More fundamental still is the question of how the right of self-determination fits within our general conception of democratic decision making. We are used to a two-level structure of argument concerning social issues, such as just taxation, the provision of public education, etc. First, we explore the principles that should govern the matter at issue. Second, we devise a form of democratic procedure for determining what shall be done. The first level answers the question "what should be done?". The second responds to the question "who should decide?".

On a simple majoritarian view, the issue of self-government seems to defy a democratic decision procedure. The question is "what is the relevant democratic unit?" and that question cannot be democratically decided, at least not entirely so. In fact, of course, we are not simple majoritarians. We adopt a whole range of democratic procedures such as constitution-making privileged majorities, ordinary legislative processes, plebiscites, administrative processes, and decisions by special agencies under conditions of public accountability and indirect democratic control. We match various democratic processes with various social and political problems. This means that there is no universal democratic formula serving as the universal answer to "who decides?" questions. Rather, we operate a mixed principled-democratic system in which principles, whose credentials do not derive entirely from their democratic backing, determine what form of a democratic procedure is suited for what problem. Within this mixed principled-democratic framework, the right to self-determination fits as just another qualified democratic process suited to its object.

What are the principles involved? It is tempting to see here a principle giving the part veto over the issue of membership in a larger whole. To form a new political unit, or to remain part of an existing one, all component parts should agree. To break up a political unit, or to foil the creation of a new one, all that is required is the will of the group that wants to secede or to stay out.

This principle derives its appeal from its voluntaristic aura. It seems to regard the justification of all political units as based on consent. But this is an undesirable illusion. It is undesirable since, as was explained above regarding encompassing groups, the more important human groupings need to be based on shared history, and on criteria of nonvoluntaristic (or at least not wholly contractarian) membership to have the value that they have. The principle presents no more than an illusion of a contractarian principle since it refers to groups, not to individuals. But the whole contractarian ethos derives its appeal from the claim that each individual's consent is a condition of the legitimacy of political units. Beyond all that, the principle simply begs the question that it is meant to answer, namely, what are the parts? Which groupings have the veto and which do not? Can the group of all the people whose surnames begin with a "*g*" and end with an "*e*" count for these purposes? Do they have the veto on membership in a larger political unit?

The right to self-determination derives from the value of membership in encompassing groups. It is a group right, deriving from the value of a collective good, and as such opposed in spirit to contractarian-individualistic[8] approaches to politics or to individual well-being. It rests on an appreciation of the great importance that membership in and identification with encompassing groups has in the life of individuals, and the importance of the prosperity and self-respect of such groups to the well-being of their members. That importance makes it reasonable to let the encompassing group that forms a substantial majority in a territory have the right to determine whether that territory shall form an independent state in order to protect the culture and self-respect of the group, provided that the new state is likely to respect the fundamental interests of its inhabitants, and provided that measures are adopted to prevent its creation from gravely damaging the just interests of other countries. This statement of the argument for the right requires elaboration.

(1) The argument is an instrumental one. It says, essentially, that members of a group are best placed to judge whether their group's prosperity will be jeopardized if it does not enjoy political independence. It is in keeping with the view that, even though participation in politics may have intrinsic value to individuals, the shape and boundaries of political units are to be determined by their service to individual well-being, i.e., by their instrumental value. In our world, encompassing groups that do not enjoy self-government are not infrequently persecuted, despised, or neglected. Given the importance of their prosperity and self-respect to the well-being of their members, it seems reasonable to entrust their members with the right to determine whether the groups should be self-governing. They may sacrifice their economic or other interests for the sake of group self-respect and prosperity. But such a sacrifice is, given the circumstances of this world, often not unreasonable.

One may ask why should such matters not be entrusted to international adjudication by an international court, or some other international agency. Instead of groups' having a right to self-determination which makes them judges in their own cause, the case for a group's becoming self-governing should be entrusted to the judgment of an impartial tribunal. This would have been a far superior solution to the question "who is to decide?". Unfortunately, there simply does not exist any international machinery of enforcement that can be relied upon in preference to a right of self-determination as the right of self-help, nor is there any prospect of one coming into existence in the near future. In the present structure of international relations, the most promising arrangement is one that recognizes group rights to self-determination and entrusts international bodies with the duty to help bring about its realization, and to see to it that the limits and preconditions of the right are observed (these are enumerated in the points two to five below),

(2) The right belongs to the group. But how should it be exercised? Not necessarily by a simple majority vote. Given the long-term and irreversible nature of the decision (remember that while independence is up to the group, merger or union is not), the wish for a state must be shared by an overwhelming majority, reflecting deep-seated beliefs and feelings of an enduring nature, and not mere temporary popularity. The precise institutional requirements for the exercise of the right are issues that transcend the topic of this paper. They are liable to vary with the circumstances of different national and ethnic groups. Whatever they are they should reflect the above principle.

(3) The right is over a territory. This simply reflects the territorial organization of our political world. The requirement that the group be a substantial majority of the territory stems from further considerations aimed at balancing the interest in self-government against the interests of nonmembers. First, it is designed to ensure that self-government for a territory does not generate a problem as great as it is meant to solve, by ensuring that the independence will not generate a large-scale new minority problem. That risk cannot be altogether avoided. As was remarked before, numbers count in the end.

A further factual assumption underlying this condition is that people are, even today, most directly affected by the goings-on in their region. It is true that one's economic conditions are affected by the economic activities in far away places. This, however, is more and more true of the international system generally. The ideal of economic autarchy died a natural death. (Correspond-

ingly, the condition of economic viability which used to figure in theories of the states in international relations has little role in the modern world.) What can be secured and protected, and what vitally matters to the quality of life, is its texture as determined by the local culture and custom, the nature of the physical environment, etc. Hence the right is given only to a group that is the majority in a territory. The case for self-government applies to groups that are not in the majority anywhere, but they do not have the right to self-determination anywhere. Their members, like other people, may have a right to immigration on an individual basis to a territory of their choice. But their case is governed by general principles of freedom of movement and the sovereign rights of existing states. This means that their communal interests remain an important consideration to be borne in mind by the decision makers, but they have no right, i.e., the decision is not up to them.

Do historical ties make a difference? Not to the right if voluntarily abandoned. Suppose that the group was unjustly removed from the country. In that case, the general principle of restitution applies, and the group has a right to self-determination and control over the territory it was expelled from, subject to the general principle of prescription. Prescription protects the interests of the current inhabitants. It is based on several deep-seated concerns. It is meant to prevent the revival of abandoned claims, and to protect those who are not personally to blame from having their life unsettled by claims of ancient wrongs, on the ground that their case now is as good as that of the wronged people or their descendants. Prescription, therefore, may lose the expelled group the right even though its members continue to suffer the effects of the past wrong. Their interest is a consideration to be borne in mind in decisions concerning immigration policies, and the like, but because of prescription they lost the right to self-determination. The outcome is not up to them to decide.

(4) The right is conditional on its being exercised for the right reasons, i.e., to secure conditions necessary for the prosperity and self-respect of the group. This is a major protection against abuse. Katanga cannot claim a right to self-determination as a way of securing its exclusive control over uranium mines within its territory. This condition does not negate the nature of a right. The group is still entrusted with the right to decide, and its decision is binding even if wrong, even if the case for self-government does not obtain, provided the reasons that motivate the group's decision are of the right kind.

(5) Finally, there are the two broad safeguards on which the exercise of the right is conditional. First, that the group is likely to respect the basic rights of its inhabitants, so that its establishment will do good rather than add to the ills of this world. Secondly, since the establishment of the new state may fundamentally endanger the interests of inhabitants of other countries, its exercise is conditional on measures being taken to prevent or minimize the occurrence of substantial damage of this kind. Such measures, which will vary greatly from case to case, include free-trade agreements, port facilities, granting of air routes, demilitarization of certain regions, etc.

Two kinds of interests do not call for special protection. One is the interest of a people to regard themselves as part of a larger rather than a smaller grouping or country. The English may have an interest in being part of Great Britain, rather than mere Englanders. But that interest can be justly satisfied only with the willing co-operation of, e.g., the Scots. If the other conditions for Scottish independence are met, this interest of the English should not stand in its way. Secondly, unjust economic gains, the product of colonial or other form of exploitation of one group by another, may be denied to the exploiting group without hesitation or compensation (barring arrangements for a transitory period). But where secession and independence will gravely affect other and legitimate interests of other countries, such interests should be protected by creating free-trade zones, demilitarized areas, etc.

(6) A right in one person is sufficient ground to hold some other person(s) to be under a duty.[9] What duties arise out of the right to self-determination? How is this matter to be settled? As the previous discussion makes clear, the right of self-determination is instrumentally justified, as the method of implementing the case for self-government, which itself is based on the fact that in many circumstances self-government is necessary for the prosperity and dignity of encompassing groups. Hence, in fixing the limits of the right, one has to bear in mind the existing system of international politics, and show that, given other elements in that system, certain duties can be derived from the right to self-determination, whereas others cannot. The first and most important duty arising out of the right is the duty not to impede the exercise of the right, i.e., not to impede groups in their attempts to decide whether appropriate territories should be independent, so long as they do so within the limits of the right. This duty affects in practice first and foremost the state that governs the territory concerned and its inhabitants.

There may be other duties following from the right of self-determination. In particular, there may be a duty on the state governing the territory to provide aid in exercising the right, and a duty on other states to aid the relevant group in realizing its right, and thus to oppose the state governing the territory if it impedes its implementation. But the extent of these duties must be subject to the general principles of international morality, which indicate what methods may and may not be used in pursuit of worthwhile goals and in preventing the violation of rights. As indicated at the outset, examination of the details of such implications of the right is beyond the scope of this article.

This brings to an end our consideration of the outlines of the case for a right to self-determination and its limits. It is an argument that proceeds in several stages from fundamental moral concerns to the ways in which they can be best implemented, given the way our world is organized. The argument is meant to present the normal justification for the right. It does not claim that there could not be alternative justifications. But it does claim to be the central case, which alternatives presuppose or of which they are variations.[10]

Two conclusions emerge from this discussion. On the one hand, the right to self-determination is neither absolute nor unconditional. It affects important and diverse interests of many people, from those who will be citizens of the new state, if it comes into being, to others far away from it. Those who may benefit from self-government cannot insist on it at all costs. Their interests have to be considered alongside those of others. On the other hand, the interests of members of an encompassing group in the self-respect and prosperity of the group are among the most vital human interests. Given their importance, their satisfaction is justified even at a considerable cost to other interests. Furthermore, given the absence of effective enforcement machinery in the international arena, the interest in group prosperity justifies entrusting the decision concerning self-government to the hands of an encompassing group that constitutes the vast majority of the population in the relevant territory, provided other vital interests are protected.

Notes

[1] This fact is doubly relevant. It is a natural fact about our world that it is a populated world with no unappropriated lands. It is a social and a moral fact that it is a world of nations, tribes, peoples, etc., that is, that people's perception of themselves and of others and their judgments of the opportunities and the responsibilities of life are shaped, to an extent, by the existence of such groups and their membership of them. It may be meaningful to claim that our views regarding national self-determination apply only to a populated world like ours. One may point to different principles that would prevail in a world with vast unoccupied fertile lands. Such speculation is utopian but it may serve to highlight some of the reasons for the principles that apply in our condition. To speculate concerning a reality different from ours in its basic social and moral constitution is pointless in a deeper way. Such social facts are constitutive of morality. Their absence undercuts morality's very foundations. We could say that under such changed conditions people will have normative beliefs and will be guided by some values. But they are not ones for which we can claim any validity.

[2] This qualification is to take account of the fact that, according to doctrines of limited government, certain matters are outside the realm of politics, and no political action regarding them may be undertaken.

[3] Among the exceptions to this rule are the slowly growing importance of supernational, especially regional, associations, such as the European Community, the growth of a doctrine of sovereignty limited by respect for fundamental human rights, and the continuing (usually thinly veiled) claims of some states that they are not bound by the international law regarding the sovereignty of states.

[4] The substantive right protected indirectly by the possessory right in cases of this kind is one of the other rights providing a title in a territory. The right to self-determination is only one of the possible sources of title.

5 The fiction-reading public can take the character of a literary elite with mutual recognition as part of its identity. The importance of "acceptability" in such groups has often been noted and analyzed.

6 This is not meant to suggest that there are not often drawbacks to self-rule. They will be considered below.

7 It should be made clear that these observations relate to the right to self-determination as it is commonly understood in the discourse of international relations and international morality. In principle, there could be a different right of self-determination, i.e., a right that, when the case for self-government is established, self-government should be granted, i.e., that all the international agents have a duty to take what action is necessary to grant self-government to the encompassing group regarding which the case for self-government has been established, That is, there could in principle have been a substantive right to have self-government when it is right that one should have it, rather than a "who is to decide" right, that an encompassing group should be entitled to decide whether it should be self-governing. Below we touch briefly on the reasons that explain why the right of self-determination as we know it today is not of this kind.

8 The reference is to moral individualism, or value individualism, not to methodological individualism. It is impossible here to deal with the matter adequately. Let us simply indicate our position briefly. There is no accepted characterization of the term. In *The Morality of Freedom* [(New York: Oxford, 1986), p. 198], Raz identified moral individualism with the view that only individual goods, and no collective goods, have intrinsic values. According to individualism so understood, membership of encompassing groups, and the prosperity of such groups, cannot be of intrinsic value. But we believe that it is intrinsically valuable. Hence, on this definition our approach is not individualistic. In "Three Grades of Social Involvement" [*Philosophy and Public Affairs*, XVIII (1989), p. 133], George Sher characterizes moral individualism as the belief that moral justification proceeds through premises relating to individuals and their preferences. His characterization is too vague to be conclusively disputed (e.g., all holistic justifications will include premises relating to preferences as well as to everything else – does that make them individualistic?). But if Sher has in mind the standard type of (actual or hypothetical) contractarian justifications, then our approach is not individualistic. Because actual individual preferences heavily depend on social practices, there is no reason to give them justificatory primacy. The content of hypothetical preferences is either too indefinite to yield any results or is made definite by assuming a certain social context to give them meaning. Either way it cannot be endowed with justificatory primacy, though of course people's capacity to respond to various conditions, and to form various goals and attachments, is central to any moral justification.

9 See Raz, *The Morality of Freedom*, ch. 7: The Nature of Rights. On the relations of moral and legal rights, see also Raz, "Legal Rights," *Oxford Journal of Legal Studies*, IV (1984), p. 1. Raz has applied this analysis to the case of constitutional rights in general in ch. 10 of *The Morality of Freedom*.

10 On the notion of a "normal justification," and the reasons why it cannot be analyzed as either a necessary or a sufficient condition, see Raz, *The Morality of Freedom*, ch. 3.

Chapter 5

Theories of Secession*
Allen Buchanan

After a long period of neglect, political philosophers have turned their attention to secession. A growing number of positions on the justification for, and scope of, the right to secede are being staked out. Yet, so far there has been no systematic account of the *types* of normative theories of secession. Nor has there been a systematic assessment of the comparative strengths and weaknesses of the theoretical options.

Indeed, as I shall argue, there is even considerable confusion about what sorts of considerations ought to count for or against a theory of the right to secede. Although some writers pay lip-service to the distinction between arguments to justify a moral right to secede and arguments to justify prescriptions for how international law should deal with secession, they have not appreciated how great the gulf is between their moral justifications and any useful guidance for international law. This article begins the task of remedying these deficiencies.

I The Institutional Question

Most existing theories either fail to distinguish between two quite different normative questions about secession, or fail to appreci-

* From *Philosophy & Public Affairs* 26:1 (1997), pp. 31–61.

ate that the two questions require quite different answers.

1. Under what conditions does a group have a moral right to secede, independently of any questions of *institutional* morality, and in particular apart from any consideration of international legal institutions and their relationship to moral principles?

2. Under what conditions should a group be recognized as having a right to secede as a matter of international *institutional* morality, including a morally defensible system of international law?

Both are *ethical* questions. The first is posed in an institutional vacuum and, even if answerable, may tell us little about what institutional responses are (ethically) appropriate. The second is a question about how international institutions, and especially international legal institutions, ought (ethically) to respond to secession.

Those who offer answers to the first question assume that answering it will provide valuable guidance for reforming international institutions. Whether this is the case, however, will depend upon whether the attractive features of noninstitutional theories remain attractive when attempts are made to institutionalize them. I shall argue that they do not: Otherwise appealing accounts of the right to secede are seen to be poor guides to institutional reform once it is appreciated that attempts to incorporate them into international institutions would create perverse incentives. In addition, I shall argue that moral theorizing about secession can provide significant guidance for international legal reform only if it coheres with and builds upon the most morally defensible elements of existing law, but that noninstitutional moral theories fail to satisfy this condition. I contend that unless institutional considerations are taken into account from the beginning in developing a normative theory of secession, the result is unlikely to be of much value for the task of providing moral guidance for institutional reform.

Which question one is trying to answer makes a difference, because different considerations can count for or against a theory of the right to secede. Because I believe that the more urgent and significant task for political philosophy at this time is to answer the second question, I will concentrate on theories of the right to secede understood as answers to it.[1]

The chief reason for believing that the institutional question is the more urgent one is that secession crises tend to have international consequences that call for international responses. If these international responses are to be consistent and morally progressive, they must build upon and contribute to the development of more effective and morally defensible international institutions, including the most formal of these, the international legal system.

Because secessionist attempts are usually resisted with deadly force by the state, human rights violations are common in secession. Often, the conflicts, as well as the refugees fleeing from them, spill across international borders. Recent events in the former Yugoslavia demonstrate both the deficiencies of international legal responses and the lack of consensus on sound ethical principles to undergird them.[2]

Some, perhaps most, recent writers offering accounts of the right to secede do not even state whether, or if so how, their proposals are intended to be incorporated into international legal regimes.[3] They refer only to "the right" to secede, without making it clear whether this means a noninstitutional ("natural") moral right or a proposed international legal right. Others signal that they are proposing changes in the way in which the international community responds to secession crises, and this presumably includes international legal responses, but they appear unaware of the gap between their arguments concerning the justification and scope of a moral right to secede and the requirements of a sound proposal for reforming international law.[4] Finally, some analysts acknowledge this gap and cautiously note that their theories are only intended to provide general guidance for the latter enterprise, but provide no clues as to how the gap might be bridged.[5] None of these three groups has articulated or even implicitly recognized the constraints that are imposed on accounts of the right to secede, once it is clearly understood that what is being proposed is an international legal right.

Keeping the institutional question in the foreground, I will first distinguish between two basic types of theories of the right to secede: *Remedial Right Only Theories* and *Primary Right Theories*. All normative theories of secession can be classified under these two headings. In addition, I will distinguish between two types of Primary Right Theories, according to what sorts of characteristics a group must possess to have a Primary Right to secede: *Ascriptive Group Theories* and *Associative Group Theories*.

Then I will articulate a set of criteria that ought to be satisfied by any moral theory of the right to secede capable of providing valuable guidance for determining what the international legal response to secession should be, and explain the rationale for each criterion.

Finally, after articulating the main features of what I take to be the most plausible instances of Remedial Right Only Theories and Primary Right Theories of secession, I will employ the aforementioned criteria in their comparative evaluation. The chief conclusion of this comparison will be that Remedial Right Theories are superior. Whatever cogency Primary Right Theories have they possess only when viewed in an institutional vacuum. They are of little use for developing an international institutional response to problems of secession.

II   Two Types of Normative Theories of Secession

All theories of the right to secede either understand the right as a *remedial* right only or also recognize a *primary* right to secede. By a right in this context is meant a *general*, not a *special*, right (one generated through promising, contract, or some special relationship). Remedial Right Only Theories assert that a group has a general right to secede if and only if it has suffered certain injustices, for which secession is the appropriate remedy of last resort.[6] Different Remedial Right Only Theories identify different injustices as warranting the remedy of secession,

Primary Right Theories, in contrast, assert that certain groups can have a (general) right to secede in the absence of any injustice. They do not limit legitimate secession to being a means of remedying an injustice. Different Primary Right Theories pick out different conditions that groups must satisfy to have a right to secede in the absence of injustices.

Remedial Right Only Theories. According to this first type of theory, the (general) right to secede is in important respects similar to

the right to revolution, as the latter is understood in what may be called the mainstream of normative theories of revolution. The latter are typified by John Locke's theory, according to which the people have the right to overthrow the government if and only if their fundamental rights are violated, and more peaceful means have been to no avail.[7]

The chief difference between the right to secede and the right to revolution, according to Remedial Right Only Theories, is that the right to secede accrues to a portion of the citizenry, concentrated in a part of the territory of the state. The object of the exercise of the right to secede is not to overthrow the government, but only to sever the government's control over that portion of the territory.

The recognition of a remedial right to secede can be seen as supplementing Locke's theory of revolution and theories like it. Locke tends to focus on cases where the government perpetrates injustices against "the people," not a particular group within the state, and seems to assume that the issue of revolution arises usually only when there has been a persistent pattern of abuses affecting large numbers of people throughout the state. This picture of legitimate revolution is conveniently simple: When the people suffer prolonged and serious injustices, the people will rise.

In some cases however, the grosser injustices are perpetrated, not against the citizenry at large, but against a particular group, concentrated in a region of the state. (Consider, for example, Iraq's genocidal policies against Kurds in northern Iraq.) Secession may be justified, and may be feasible, as a response to selective tyranny, when revolution is not a practical prospect.

If the only effective remedy against selective tyranny is to oppose the government, then a strategy of opposition that stops short of attempting to overthrow the government (revolution), but merely seeks to remove one's group and the territory it occupies from the control of the state (secession), seems both morally unexceptionable and, relatively speaking, moderate. For this reason, a Remedial Right Only approach to the right to secede can be seen as a valuable complement to the Lockean approach to the right to revolution understood as a remedial right. In both the case of revolution and that of secession, the right is understood as the right of persons subject to a political authority to defend themselves from serious injustices, as a remedy of last resort.

It was noted earlier that Remedial Right Only Theories hold that the *general* right to secession exists only where the group in question has suffered injustices. This qualification is critical. Remedial Right Only Theories allow that there can be *special* rights to secede if (1) the state grants a right to secede (as with the secession of Norway from Sweden in 1905), or if (2) the constitution of the state includes a right to secede (as does the 1993 Ethiopian Constitution), or perhaps if (3) the agreement by which the state was initially created out of previously independent political units included the implicit or explicit assumption that secession at a later point was permissible (as some American Southerners argued was true of the states of the Union). If any of these three conditions obtain, we can speak of a *special* right to secede. The point of Remedial Right Only Theories is not to deny that there can be special rights to secede in the absence of injustices. Rather, it is to deny that there is a *general* right to secede that is not a remedial right.

Because they allow for special rights to secede, Remedial Right Only Theories are not as restrictive as they might first appear. They do *not* limit permissible secession to cases where the seceding group has suffered injustices. They *do* restrict the general (as opposed to special) right to secede to such cases.

Depending upon which injustices they recognize as grievances sufficient to justify secession, Remedial Right Theories may be more liberal or more restrictive. What all Remedial Right Only Theories have in common is the thesis that there is no (general) right to secede from a just state.

A Remedial Right Only Theory. For purposes of comparison with the other basic type of theory, Primary Right Theories, I will take as a representative of Remedial Right Only Theories the particular version of this latter type of theory that I have argued for at length elsewhere.[8] According to this version, a group has a right to secede only if:

1 The physical survival of its members is threatened by actions of the state (as with the policy of the Iraqi government toward Kurds in Iraq) or it suffers violations of other basic human rights (as with the East Pakistanis who seceded to create Bangladesh in 1970), *or*
2 Its previously sovereign territory was unjustly taken by the state (as with the Baltic Republics).

I have also argued that other conditions ought to be satisfied if a group that suffers any of these injustices is to be recognized through international law or international political practice as having the right to secede.[9] Chief among these is that there be credible guarantees that the new state will respect the human rights of all of its citizens and that it will cooperate in the project of securing other *just terms* of secession.[10] (In addition to the protection of minority and human rights, the just terms of secession include a fair division of the national debt; a negotiated determination of new boundaries; arrangements for continuing, renegotiating, or terminating treaty obligations; and provisions for defense and security.) This bare sketch of the theory will suffice for the comparisons that follow.

Primary Right Theories. Primary Right Theories fall into two main classes: *Ascriptive Group Theories* and *Associative Group Theories.* Theories that include the Nationalist Principle (according to which every nation or people is entitled to its own state) fall under the first heading. Those that confer the right to secede on groups that can muster a majority in favor of independence in a plebiscite fall under the second.

Ascriptive Group Theories. According to Ascriptive Group versions of Primary Right Theories, it is groups whose memberships are defined by what are sometimes called ascriptive characteristics that have the right to secede (even in the absence of injustices). Ascriptive characteristics exist independently of any actual political association that the members of the group may have forged. In other words, according to Ascriptive Group Theories of secession, it is first and foremost certain *nonpolitical* characteristics of groups that ground the group's right to an independent political association.

Being a nation or people is an ascriptive characteristic. What makes a group a nation or people is the fact that it has a common culture, history, language, a sense of its own distinctiveness, and perhaps a shared aspiration for constituting its own political unit. No actual political organization of the group, nor any actual collective choice to form a political association, is necessary for the group to be a nation or people.

Thus Margalit and Raz appear to embrace the Nationalist Principle when they ascribe the right to secede to what they call "encompassing cultures," defined as large-scale, anonymous (rather than small-scale, face-to-face) groups that have a common culture and character that encompasses many important aspects of life and which marks the character of the life of its members, where membership in the group is in part a matter of mutual recognition and is important for one's self-identification and is a matter of belonging, not of achievement.[11]

Associative Group Theories. In contrast, Associative Group versions of Primary Right Theories do not require that a group have any ascriptive characteristic in common such as ethnicity or an encompassing culture, even as a necessary condition for having a right to secede. The members of the group need not even believe that they share any characteristics other than the desire to have their own state. Instead, Associative Group Theorists focus on the *voluntary political choice* of the members of a group (or the majority of them), their decision to form their own independent political unit. Any group, no matter how heterogeneous, can qualify for the right to secede. Nor need the secessionists have any common connection, historical or imagined, to the territory they wish to make into their own state. All that matters is that the members of the group voluntarily choose to associate together in an independent political unit of their own. Associative Group Theories, then, assert that there is a right to secede that is, or is an instance of, *the right of political association.*

The simplest version of Associative Group Primary Right Theory is what I have referred to elsewhere as the *pure plebiscite theory* of the right to secede.[12] According to this theory, any group that can constitute a majority (or, on some accounts, a "substantial" majority) in favor of secession within a portion of the state has the right to secede. It is difficult to find unambiguous instances of the pure plebiscite theory, but there are several accounts which begin with the plebiscite condition and then add weaker or stronger *provisos.*

One such variant is offered by Harry Beran.[13] On his account, any group is justified in seceding if (1) it constitutes a substantial majority in its portion of the state, wishes to secede, and (2) will be able to marshal the resources necessary for a viable independent state.[14] Beran grounds his theory of the right to secede in a *consent theory of political obligation.* According to Beran, actual (not "hypothetical" or "ideal contractarian") consent of the governed is a necessary condition for political obligation, and consent cannot be assured unless those who wish to secede are allowed to do so.

Christopher Wellman has more recently advanced another variant of plebiscite theory.[15] According to his theory, there is a primary right of political association, or, as he also calls it, of political self-determination. Like Beran's right, it is primary in the sense that it is not a remedial right, derived from the violation of other, independently characterizable rights. Wellman's right of political association is the right of any group that resides in a territory to form its own state if (1) that group constitutes a majority in that territory; if (2) the state it forms will be able to carry out effectively what was referred to earlier as the legitimating functions of a state (preeminently the provision of justice and security); and if (3) its severing the territory from the existing state will not impair the latter's ability to carry out effectively those same legitimating functions.

Like Beran's theory, Wellman's is an Associative Group, rather than an Ascriptive Group variant of Primary Right Theory, because any group that satisfies these three criteria, not just those with ascriptive properties (such as nations, peoples, ethnic groups, cultural groups, or encompassing groups) is said to have the right to secede. Both Beran and Wellman acknowledge that there can also be a right to secede grounded in the need to remedy injustices, but both are chiefly concerned to argue for a Primary Right, and thus to argue *against* all Remedial Right Only Theories.

According to Primary Right Theories, a group can have a (general) right to secede even if it suffers no injustices, and hence it may have a (general) right to secede from a perfectly just state. Ascriptive characteristics, such as being a people or nation, do not imply that the groups in question have suffered injustices. Similarly, according to Associative Group Theories, what confers the right to secede on a group is the voluntary choice of members of the group to form an independent state; no grievances are necessary.

Indeed, as we shall see, existing Primary Right Theories go so far as to recognize a right to secede even under conditions in which the state is effectively, indeed flawlessly, performing all of what are usually taken to be the *legitimating functions* of the state. As noted above in the description of Wellman's view, these functions consist chiefly, if not exclusively, in the provision of justice (the establishment and protection of rights) and of security.

Notice that in the statement that Primary Right Theories recognize a right to secede from perfectly just states the term "just" must be understood in what might be called the uncontroversial or standard or theory-neutral sense. In other words, a perfectly just state here is one that does not violate relatively uncontroversial individual moral rights, including above all human rights, and which does not engage in uncontroversially discriminatory policies toward minorities. This conception of justice is a neutral or relatively uncontroversial one in this sense: We may assume that it is acknowledged both by Remedial Right Only Theorists and Primary Right Only Theorists – that both types of theorists recognize these sorts of actions as injustices, though they may disagree in other ways as to the scope of justice. In contrast, to understand the term "just" here in such a fashion that a state is assumed to be *unjust* simply because it contains a minority people or nation (which lacks its own state) or simply because it includes a majority that seeks to secede but has not been permitted to do so, would be to employ a conception of the justice that begs the question in this context, because it includes elements that are denied by one of the parties to the debate, namely Remedial Right Only Theorists. To repeat: the point is that Primary Right Theories are committed to the view that there is a right to secede even from a state that is perfectly just in the standard and uncontroversial, and hence theory-neutral sense.[16]

III   Criteria for Evaluating Proposals for an International Legal Right to Secede

With this classification of types of theories of the right to secede in mind, we can now proceed to their comparative evaluation. Special attention will be given to considerations that loom large, once we look to these theories for guidance in formulating proposals for a practical and morally progressive international legal approach to dealing with secession crises. The following criteria for the comparative assessment of competing proposals for how international law ought to understand the right to secede are not offered as exhaustive. They will suffice, however, to establish two significant conclusions. First, theories of the moral right to secede that might initially appear reasonable are seen to be seriously deficient when viewed as elements of an institutional morality articulated in a system of international law. Second, some current theories of the right to secede are much more promising candidates for providing guidance for international law than others. Others fail to take into account some of the most critical considerations relevant to the project of providing a moral foundation for an international institutional response to secession crises.

1.   *Minimal Realism.* A proposal for an international legal right to secede ought to be morally progressive, yet at the same time at least minimally realistic. A *morally progressive* proposal is one which, if imple-

mented with a reasonable degree of success, would better serve basic values than the status quo. Preeminent among these values is the protection of human rights.

A proposal satisfies the requirement of *minimal realism* if it has a significant prospect of eventually being adopted in the foreseeable future, through the processes by which international law is actually made. As we shall see, it is important to keep in mind one crucial feature of this process: International law is made by existing states (that are recognized to be legitimate by the international community).[17]

Minimal realism is not slavish deference to current political feasibility. The task of the political philosopher concerned to provide principles for an international legal response to secession crises is in part to set moral targets – to make a persuasive case for trying to transcend the current limits of political feasibility in pursuit of moral progress. Nevertheless, moral targets should not be so distant that efforts to reach them are not only doomed to failure, but unlikely to produce any valuable results at all.

To summarize: A theory is morally progressive and minimally realistic if and only if its implementation would better serve basic values than the status quo and if it has some significant prospect of eventually being implemented through the actual processes by which international law is made and applied.

2.   *Consistency with Well-Entrenched, Morally Progressive Principles of International Law.* A proposal should build upon, or at least not squarely contradict, the more morally acceptable principles of existing international law, when these principles are interpreted in a morally progressive way. If at all possible, acceptance and implementation of a new principle should not come at the price of calling into question the validity of a well-entrenched, morally progressive principle.

3.   *Absence of Perverse Incentives.* At least when generally accepted and effectively implemented under reasonably favorable circumstances, a proposal should not create perverse incentives. In other words, acceptance of the proposal, and recognition that it is an element of the system of international institutional conflict resolution, should not encourage behavior that undermines morally sound principles of international law or of morality, nor should it hinder the pursuit of morally progressive strategies for conflict resolution, or the attainment of desirable outcomes such as greater efficiency in government or greater protection for individual liberty. (For example, an international legal principle concerning secession whose acceptance encouraged groups to engage in ethnic cleansing, or that encouraged states to pursue repressive immigration policies, or discriminatory development policies, would fail to meet this criterion.)

The chief way in which acceptance as a principle of international law creates incentives is by conferring *legitimacy* on certain types of actions. By doing so, international law reduces the costs of performing them and increases the cost of resisting them. (These costs consist not only of the risk of tangible economic or military sanctions, but also the stigma of condemnation and adverse public opinion, both domestic and international.) Hence, by conferring legitimacy on a certain type of action, international law gives those who have an interest in preventing those actions from occurring an incentive to act strategically to prevent the conditions for performing the actions from coming into existence.

To illustrate this crucial legitimating function of international law and the incentives to which it can give rise, suppose that a principle of international law were to emerge that recognized the legitimacy of secession by any federal unit following a majority plebiscite in that unit in favor of indepen-

dence. Such a principle, or rather *its acceptance* as a valid principle of international law, would create an incentive for a state that wishes to avoid fragmentation to resist efforts at federalization. For if the state remains centralized, then it will not face the possibility of a secessionist plebiscite, nor have to contend with international support for secession if the plebiscite is successful. As we shall see, some theories of secession create just such an incentive. The incentive is perverse, insofar as it disposes states to act in ways that preclude potentially beneficial decentralization.

Among the various benefits of decentralization (which include greater efficiency in administration and a check on concentrations of power that can endanger liberty) is the fact that it can provide meaningful autonomy for territorially concentrated minorities without dismembering the state. In some cases, federalization, rather than secession, may be the best response to legitimate demands for autonomy by groups within the state. Thus a theory of secession whose general acceptance would create incentives to block this alternative is defective, other things being equal.

4.   *Moral Accessibility.* A proposal for reforming international law should be morally accessible to a broad international audience. It should not require acceptance of a particular religious ethic or of ethical principles that are not shared by a wide range of secular and religious viewpoints. The *justifications* offered in support of the proposal should incorporate ethical principles and styles of argument that have broad, cross-cultural appeal and motivational power, and whose cogency is already acknowledged in the justifications given for well-established, morally sound principles of international law. This fourth criterion derives its force from the fact that international law, more so than domestic law, depends for its efficacy upon voluntary compliance.

Although these four criteria are relatively commonsensical and unexceptionable, together they impose significant constraints on what counts as an acceptable proposal for an international legal right to secede. They will enable us to gauge the comparative strengths of various accounts of the moral right to secede, at least so far as these are supposed to provide guidance for international institutional responses to secessionist crises.

IV   Comparing the Two Types of Theories

Remedial Right Only Theories have several substantial attractions. First, a Remedial Right Only Theory places significant constraints on the right to secede, while not ruling out secession entirely. No group has a (general) right to secede unless that group suffers what are uncontroversially regarded as injustices and has no reasonable prospect of relief short of secession. Given that the majority of secessions have resulted in considerable violence, with attendant large-scale violations of human rights and massive destruction of resources, common sense urges that secession should not be taken lightly.

Furthermore, there is good reason to believe that secession may in fact exacerbate the ethnic conflicts which often give rise to secessionist movements, for two reasons. First, in the real world, though not perhaps in the world of some normative theorists, many, perhaps most, secessions are by ethnic minorities. But when an ethnic minority secedes, the result is often that another ethnic group becomes a minority within the new state. All too often, the formerly persecuted become the persecutors. Second, in most cases, not all members of the seceding group lie within the seceding area, and the result is that those who do not become an even smaller minority and hence even more vulnerable to the discrimination and persecution that fueled the drive for secession in the first place.[18] Requiring serious grievances as a condition for legitimate secession creates a significant hurdle that reflects the gravity of state-breaking in our world and the fact that secession often does perpetuate and sometimes exacerbate the ethnic conflicts that give rise to it.

Minimal Realism. Remedial Right Only Theories score much better on the condition of minimal realism than Primary Right Theories. Other things being equal, proposals for international institutional responses to secessionist claims that do not pose pervasive threats to the territorial integrity of existing states are more likely to be adopted by the primary makers of international law – that is, states – than those which do.

Primary Right Theories are not likely to be adopted by the makers of international law because they authorize the dismemberment of states even when those states are perfectly performing what are generally recognized as the legitimating functions of states. Thus Primary Right Theories represent a direct and profound threat to the territorial integrity of states – even just states. Because Remedial Right Only Theories advance a much more restricted right to secede, they are less of a threat to the territorial integrity of existing states; hence, other things being equal, they are more likely to be incorporated into international law.

At this point it might be objected that the fact that states would be unlikely to incorporate Primary Right Theories into international law is of little significance, because their interest in resisting such a change is itself not morally legitimate. Of course, states will not be eager to endanger their own existence. Similarly, the fact that a ruling class of slaveholders would be unlikely to enact a law abolishing slavery would not be a very telling objection to a moral theory that says people have the right not to be enslaved.[19]

This objection would sap some of the force of the charge that Primary Right Theories score badly on the minimal realism requirement *if* states had no morally legitimate interest in resisting dismemberment. However, it is not just the self-interest of states that encourages them to reject theories of the right to secede that makes their control over territory much more fragile. States have a *morally legitimate interest* in maintaining their territorial integrity. The qualifier "morally legitimate" is crucial here. The nature of this morally legitimate interest will become clearer as we apply the next criterion to our comparative evaluation of the two types of theories.

Consistency with Well-Entrenched, Morally Progressive Principles of International Law. Unlike Primary Right Theories, Remedial Right Only Theories are consistent with, rather than in direct opposition to, a morally progressive interpretation of what is generally regarded as the single most fundamental principle of international law: the principle of the territorial integrity of existing states.

It is a mistake to view this principle simply as a monument to the self-interest of states in their own survival. Instead, I shall argue, it is a principle that serves some of the most basic morally legitimate interests of *individuals*.

The interest that existing states have in continuing to support the principle of territorial integrity is a morally legitimate interest because the recognition of that principle in international law and political practice promotes two morally important goals: (1) the protection of individuals' physical security, the preservation of their rights, and the stability of their expectations; and (2) an incentive structure in which it is reasonable for individuals and groups to invest themselves in participating in the fundamental processes of government in a conscientious and cooperative fashion over time. Each of these benefits of the maintenance of the principle of territorial integrity warrants explanation in detail.

Individuals' rights, the stability of individuals' expectations, and ultimately their physical security, depend upon the effective enforcement of a legal order. Effective enforcement requires effective *jurisdiction*, and this in turn requires a clearly bounded territory that is recognized to be the domain of an identified political authority. Even if political authority strictly speaking is exercised only over persons, not land, the effective exercise of political authority over persons depends, ultimately upon the establishment and maintenance of jurisdiction in the territorial sense. This fact rests upon an obvious but deep truth about human beings: They have bodies that occupy space, and the materials for living upon which they depend do so as well. Furthermore, if an effective legal order is to be possible, both the boundaries that define the jurisdiction and the identified political authority whose jurisdiction it is must persist over time.

So by making effective jurisdiction possible, observance of the principle of territorial integrity facilitates the functioning of a legal order and the creation of the benefits that only a legal order can bring. Compliance with the principle of territorial integrity, then, does not merely serve the self-interest of states in ensuring their own survival; it furthers the most basic morally legitimate interests of the individuals and groups that states are empowered to serve, their interest in the preservation of their rights, the security of their persons, and the stability of their expectations.

For this reason, states have a morally legitimate interest in maintaining the principle of territorial integrity. Indeed, that is to indulge in understatement: states, so far as their authority rests on their ability to serve the basic interests of individuals, have an *obligatory* interest in maintaining territorial integrity.

The principle of territorial integrity not only contributes to the possibility of maintaining an enforceable legal order and all the benefits that depend on it; it also gives citizens an incentive to invest themselves sincerely and cooperatively in the existing political processes. Where the principle of territorial integrity is supported, citizens can generally proceed on the assumption that they and their children and perhaps their children's children will be subject to laws that are made through the same processes to which they are now subject – and whose quality they can influence by the character of their participation.

For it to be reasonable for individuals and groups to so invest themselves in participating in political processes there must be considerable stability both in the effective jurisdiction of the laws that the processes create and in the membership of the state. Recognition of the principle of the territorial integrity of existing states contributes to both.

In Albert Hirschman's celebrated terminology, where exit is too easy, there is little incentive for voice – for sincere and constructive criticism and, more generally, for committed and conscientious political participation.[20] Citizens can exit the domain of the existing political authority in different ways. To take an example pertinent to our investigation of secession, if a minority could escape the authority of laws whose enactment it did not support by unilaterally redrawing political boundaries, it would have little incentive to submit to the majority's will, or to reason with the majority to change its mind.[21]

Of course, there are other ways to escape the reach of a political authority, emigration being the most obvious. But emigration is usually not a feasible option for minority groups and even where feasible is not likely to be attractive, since it will only involve trading minority status in one state for minority status in another. Staying where one is and attempting to transfer control over where one is to another, more congenial political authority is a much more attractive alternative, if one can manage it.

Moreover, in order to subvert democratic processes it is not even necessary that a group actually exit when the majority decision goes against it. All that may be needed is to issue a credible threat of exit, which can serve as a *de facto* minority veto.[22] However, in a system of states in which the principle of territorial integrity is given significant weight, the costs of exit are thereby increased, and the ability to use the threat of exit as a strategic bargaining tool is correspondingly decreased.

In addition, the ability of representative institutions to approximate the ideal of deliberative democracy, in which citizens strive together in the ongoing articulation of a conception of the public interest, also depends, in part, upon stable control over a definite territory, and thereby the effective exercise of political authority over those within it. This stability is essential if it is to be reasonable for citizens to invest themselves in cultivating and practicing the demanding virtues of deliberative democracy.

All citizens have a morally legitimate interest in the integrity of political participation. To the extent that the principle of territorial integrity helps to support the integrity of political participation, the legitimacy of this second interest adds moral weight to the principle.

To summarize: Adherence to the principle of territorial integrity serves two fundamental morally legitimate interests: the interest in the protection of individual security, rights, and expectations, and the interest in the integrity of political participation.

We can now see that this point is extremely significant for our earlier application of the criterion of minimal realism to the comparison of the two types of theories of secession. If the sole source of support for the principle of territorial integrity – and hence the sole source of states' resistance to implementing Primary Right Theories in international law – were the selfish or evil motives of states, then the fact that such theories have scant prospect of being incorporated into international law would be of little significance. For in that case the Primary Right Theorist could simply reply that the criterion of minimal realism gives undue weight to the interests of states in their own preservation.

That reply, however, rests on a misunderstanding of my argument. My point is that it is a strike against Primary Right Theories that they have little prospect of implementation even when states are motivated solely or primarily by interests that are among the most morally legitimate interests that states can have. Thus my application of the minimal realism requirement cannot be countered by objecting that it gives undue weight to the interests of states in their own preservation.

Before turning to the application of the third criterion, my argument that the principle of the territorial integrity of existing states serves morally legitimate interests requires an important qualification. That principle can be abused; it has often been invoked to shore up a morally defective status quo. However, some interpretations of the principle of territorial integrity are less likely to be misused to perpetuate injustices and more likely to promote moral progress, however.

The Morally Progressive Interpretation of the Principle of Territorial Integrity. What might be called the *absolutist* interpretation of the principle of the territorial integrity of existing states makes no distinction between legitimate and illegitimate states, extending protection to all existing states. *Any* theory that recognizes a (general) right to secede, whether remedial only, or primary as well as remedial, is inconsistent with the absolutist interpretation, since any such theory permits the nonconsensual breakup of existing states

under certain conditions. This first, absolutist interpretation has little to recommend it, however. For it is inconsistent with there being *any* circumstances in which other states, whether acting alone or collectively, may rightly intervene in the affairs of an existing state, even for the purpose of preventing the most serious human-rights abuses, including genocide.

According to the *progressive* interpretation, the principle that the territorial integrity of existing states is not to be violated applies only to *legitimate* states – and not all existing states are legitimate. There is, of course, room for disagreement about how stringent the relevant notion of legitimacy is. However, recent international law provides some guidance: States are *not* legitimate if they (1) threaten the lives of significant portions of their populations by a policy of ethnic or religious persecution, or if they (2) exhibit institutional racism that deprives a substantial proportion of the population of basic economic and political rights.

The most obvious case in which the organs of international law have treated an existing state as illegitimate was that of Apartheid South Africa (which satisfied condition [2]). The United Nations as well as various member states signaled this lack of legitimacy not only by various economic sanctions, but by refusing even to use the phrase "The Republic of South Africa" in public documents and pronouncements. More recently, the Iraqi government's genocidal actions toward Kurds within its borders (condition [1]) was accepted as a justification for infringing Iraq's territorial sovereignty in order to establish a "safe zone" in the North for the Kurds. To the extent that the injustices cited by a Remedial Right Only Theory are of the sort that international law regards as depriving a state of legitimacy, the right to secede is consistent with the principle of the territorial integrity of existing (legitimate) states.

Here, too, it is important to emphasize that the relevance of actual international law is conditional upon the moral legitimacy of the interests that the law, or in this case, changes in the law, serves. The key point is that the shift in international law away from the absolutist interpretation of the principle of territorial integrity toward the progressive interpretation serves morally legitimate interests and reflects a superior normative stance. So it is no mere conformity to existing law, but consonance with morally progressive developments in law, which speaks here in favor of Remedial Right Only Theories. Moreover, as I argued earlier, the principle that is undergoing a progressive interpretation, the principle of territorial integrity, is one that serves basic moral interests of individuals and groups, not just the interests of states.

In contrast, any theory of secession that recognizes a primary right to secede for any group within a state, in the absence of injustices that serve to delegitimize the state, directly contradicts the principle of the territorial integrity of existing states, *on its progressive interpretation.*[23] Accordingly, Remedial Right Only Theories have a singular advantage: Unlike Primary Right Theories, they are consistent with, rather than in direct opposition to, one of the most deeply entrenched principles of international law on its morally progressive interpretation. This point strengthens our contention that according to our second criterion Remedial Right Only Theories are superior to Primary Right Theories.

So far, the comparisons drawn have not relied upon the particulars of the various versions of the two types of theories. This has been intentional, since my main project is to compare the two basic *types* of theories. Further assessments become possible, as we examine the details of various Primary Right Theories.

V   Primary Right Theories

Avoiding Perverse Incentives. Remedial Right Only Theories also enjoy a third advantage: If incorporated into international law, they would create laudable incentives, while Primary Right Theories would engender very destructive ones (criterion 3).

A regime of international law that limits the right to secede to groups that suffer serious and persistent injustices at the hands of the state, when no other recourse is available to them, would provide protection and support to just states, by unambiguously sheltering them under the umbrella of the principle of the territorial integrity of existing (legitimate) states. States, therefore, would have an incentive to improve their records concerning the relevant injustices in order to reap the protection from dismemberment that they would enjoy as legitimate, rights-respecting states. States that persisted in treating groups of their citizens unjustly would suffer the consequences of international disapprobation and possibly more tangible sanctions as well. Furthermore, such states would be unable to appeal to international law to support them in attempts to preserve their territories intact.

In contrast, a regime of international law that recognized a right to secede in the absence of any injustices would encourage even just states to act in ways that would prevent groups from becoming claimants to the right to secede, and this might lead to the perpetration of injustices. For example, according to Wellman's version of Primary Right Theory, any group that becomes capable of having a functioning state of its own in the territory it occupies is a potential subject of the right to secede. Clearly, any state that seeks to avoid its own dissolution would have an incentive to implement policies designed to prevent groups from becoming prosperous enough and politically well-organized enough to satisfy this condition.

In other words, states would have an incentive to prevent regions within their borders from developing economic and political institutions that might eventually become capable of performing the legitimating functions of a state. In short, Wellman's version of Primary Right Theory gives the state incentives for fostering economic and political dependency. Notice that here, too, one need not attribute evil motives to states to generate the problem of perverse incentives. That problem arises even if states act only from the morally legitimate interest in preserving their territories.

In addition, a theory such as Wellman's, if used as a guide for international legal reform, would run directly contrary to what many view as the most promising response to the problems that can result in secessionist conflicts. I refer here to the proposal, allude to earlier and increasingly endorsed by international legal experts, that every effort be made to accommodate aspirations for autonomy of groups *within* the state, by exploring the possibilities for various forms of decentralization, including federalism.

Wellman might reply that the fact that the implementation of his theory would hinder efforts at decentralization is no objection, since on his account there is no reason to believe that decentralization is superior to secession. There are two reasons, however, why this reply is inadequate.

First, as we saw earlier, decentralization can be the best way to promote morally legitimate interests (in more efficient administration, and in avoiding excessive concentrations of power) in many contexts in which secession is not even an issue. Hence, any theory of secession whose general acceptance and institutionalization would inhibit decentralization is deficient, other things being equal. Second, and more importantly,

according to our second criterion for evaluating proposals for international legal reform, other things being equal, a theory is superior if it is consonant with the most well-entrenched, fundamental principles of international law on their morally progressive interpretations. The principle of territorial integrity, understood as conferring protection on legitimate states (roughly, those that respect basic rights) fits that description, and that principle favors first attempting to address groups' demands for autonomy by decentralization, since this is compatible with maintaining the territorial integrity of existing states. It follows that the Primary Right Theorists cannot reply that the presumption in favor of decentralization as opposed to secession gives too much moral weight to the interests *of states* and that there is no reason to prefer decentralization to secession. The point, rather, is that decentralization has its own moral attractions and in addition is favored by a well-entrenched, fundamental principle of international law that serves basic, morally legitimate interests of individuals (and groups).

Even if Wellman's view were never formally incorporated into international law, but merely endorsed and supported by major powers such as the United States, the predictable result would be to make centralized states even less responsive to demands for autonomy within them than they are now. Allowing groups within the state to develop their own local institutions of government and to achieve a degree of control over regional economic resources would run the risk of transforming them into successful claimants for the right to secede. Beran's version of Primary Right Theory suffers the same flaw, because it too gives states incentives to avoid decentralization in order to prevent secessionist majorities from forming in viable regions.

If either Wellman's or Beran's theories were implemented, the incentives regarding *immigration* would be equally perverse. States wishing to preserve their territory would have incentives to prevent potential secessionist majorities from concentrating in economically viable regions. The predictable result would be restrictions designed to prevent ethnic, cultural, or political groups who might become local majorities from moving into such regions, whether from other parts of the state or from other states. Similarly, groups that wished to create their own states would have an incentive to try to concentrate in economically viable regions in which they can *become* majorities – and to displace members of other groups from those regions.

There is a general lesson here. Theories according to which majorities in regions of the state are automatically legitimate candidates for a right to secede (in the absence of having suffered injustices) look more plausible if one assumes that populations are fixed. Once it is seen that acceptance of these theories would create incentives for population shifts and for the state to attempt to prevent them, they look much less plausible.

The same objections just noted in regard to the Primary Right Theories of Wellman and Beran also afflict that of Margalit and Raz, although it is an Ascriptive Group, rather than an Associative Group, variant. On Margalit and Raz's view, it is "encompassing groups" that have the right to secede.

Like the other Primary Right Theories already discussed, this one scores badly on the criteria of minimal realism and consistency with deeply entrenched, morally progressive principles of international law. Also, if incorporated in international law, it would create perverse incentives.

First, it is clear that no principle which identifies all "encompassing groups" as

bearers of the right of self-determination, where this is understood to include the right to secede from any existing state, would have much of a chance of being accepted in international law, even when states' actions were determined primarily by the pursuit of morally legitimate interest. The reason is straightforward: most, if not all, existing states include two or more encompassing groups; hence acceptance of Margalit and Raz's principle would authorize their own dismemberment. Second, the right to independent statehood, as Margalit and Raz understand it, is possessed by every encompassing group even in the absence of any injustices. Consequently, it too runs directly contrary to the principle of the territorial integrity of existing states on its most progressive interpretation (according to which just states are entitled to the protection the principle provides).

Third, if accepted as a matter of international law, the right endorsed by Margalit and Raz would give states incentives to embark on (or continue) all-too-familiar "nation-building" programs designed to obliterate minority group identities – to eliminate all "encompassing groups" within their borders save the one they favor for constituting "the nation" and to prevent new "encompassing groups" from emerging. Instead of encouraging states to support ethnic and cultural pluralism within their borders, Margalit and Raz's proposal would feed the reaction against pluralism.

Moral Accessibility. The last of the four criteria for assessment, moral accessibility, is perhaps the most difficult to apply. None of the accounts of the right to secede under consideration (with the possible exception of the Nationalist Principle in its cruder formulations) clearly fails the test of moral accessibility. Therefore, it may be that the comparative assessment of the rival theories must focus mainly on the other criteria, as I have done.

Nevertheless, it can be argued that Remedial Right Only Theories have a significant advantage, so far as moral accessibility is concerned. They restrict the right to secede to cases in which the most serious and widely recognized sorts of moral wrongs have been perpetrated against a group, namely violations of human rights and the unjust conquest of a sovereign state. That these are injustices is widely recognized. Hence if anything can justify secession, surely these injustices can. Whether *other* conditions also justify secession is more controversial, across the wide spectrum of moral and political views.

Recall that according to all Primary Right Theories, a group has the right to form its own state from a part of an existing state, even if the state is flawlessly performing what are generally taken to be the legitimating functions of states – even if perfect justice to all citizens and perfect security for all prevail. Presumably the intuitive moral appeal of this proposition is somewhat less than that of the thesis that the most serious injustices can justify secession.

VI   Political Liberty, the Harm Principle, and the Constraints of Institutional Morality

The Primary Right Theories advanced by Beran, Wellman, and Margalit and Raz share a fundamental feature. Each of these analysts begins with what might be called the *liberal presumption in favor of political liberty* (or freedom of political association). In other words, each develops a position on the right to secede that takes as its point of departure something very like the familiar liberal principle for *individuals*, which is so prominent in Mill's *On Liberty* and which Joel Feinberg has labeled "The Harm Principle."

According to the Harm Principle in its simplest formulation, individuals (at least those possessed of normal decision-making capacity) ought to enjoy liberty of action so long as their actions do not harm the legitimate interests of others. Wellman is most explicit in his application of the Harm Principle to the justification of secession:

> We begin with liberalism's presumption upon individual liberty, which provides a *prima facie* case *against* the government's coercion and for the permissibility of secession.... [T]his presumption in favor of secession ... is outweighed by the negative consequences of the exercise of such liberty. But if this is so, then the case for liberty is defeated only in those circumstances in which its exercise would lead to harmful conditions. And because harmful conditions would occur in only those cases in which either the seceding region or the remainder state is unable to perform its political function of protecting rights, secession is permissible in any case in which this peril would be avoided.[24]

Margalit and Raz similarly note that harmful consequences of the exercise of the right to secede can override the right, when they caution that the right must be exercised in such a way as to avoid actions that fundamentally endanger the interests either of the people of other countries or the inhabitants of the seceding region.[25] And Beran at one point complicates his theory by acknowledging that the right to secede by plebiscite is limited by the obligation to prevent harm to the state from which the group is seceding, as when the seceding region "occupies an area which is culturally, economically, or militarily essential to the existing state."[26]

What these theorists have failed to appreciate is that even if the Harm Principle is a valuable principle to *guide* the design of institutions (if they are to be liberal institutions), it cannot itself serve as an overriding principle *of* institutional ethics. An example unrelated to the controversy over the right to secede will illustrate this basic point.

Suppose that one is a physician contemplating whether to administer a lethal injection to end the life of a permanently unconscious patient whose autonomic functions are intact and who will continue to breathe unassisted for an indefinite period of time. Suppose that after careful consideration one correctly concludes that giving the injection will produce no harm to the patient (since the patient has no interests that would suffer a "setback" as a result of ending his permanent vegetative existence) or to the family or anyone else. As a matter of the morality of this individual decision – apart from any consideration of what might be an appropriate set of principles of institutional ethics, it may be permissible to administer the injection.

However, it is a quite different question as to whether the principles of the institution within which the action is to occur, whether as a matter of law or in some less formal way, ought to permit physicians to exercise their judgment as to whether to administer lethal injections to permanently unconscious patients. For one thing, a consideration of what would be the appropriate institutional principles requires that we look, not just at the harmful consequences *of this particular action*, but at the harmful consequences *of legitimizing actions of this sort*. The first, most obvious worry is that by legitimizing acts of active nonvoluntary euthanasia when no harm is expected to result we may encourage killings in situations that are in fact relevantly unlike the ideal case described above. For example, there may be factors (such as pressures of cost-containment or bias against certain ethnic groups or against the aged) that will lead some physicians to engage in active nonvoluntary euthanasia under circumstances in which a net harm to the patient or to others will result. Second, legitimizing the practice of physician-administered nonvoluntary euthanasia may encourage some individuals to engage in

other acts that have bad consequences. For example, if it became expected that physicians would administer lethal injections to elderly patients when their quality of life was very poor, a significant number of physicians might shun the practice of geriatric medicine, either because they have moral scruples against killing or because geriatric practice would come to be regarded as having a lower professional status. The result might be that geriatric medicine would either not attract a sufficient number of physicians or would attract the wrong type of individuals. Whether or not such consequences would occur and, if they would occur, how much moral weight they should be accorded is controversial. The point, however, is that they are relevant considerations for determining whether, as a matter of institutional morality, physicians ought to be empowered to engage in nonvoluntary active euthanasia.

Similarly, one cannot argue straightaway from hypothetical or actual cases in which secession harms no one's legitimate interests to the conclusion that, as a matter of international law, or even of informal political practice, we should recognize a right to secede whenever no harm to legitimate interests can be expected to result from the exercise of the putative right in the particular case. And we certainly cannot argue, as Beran and Wellman do, that the only legitimate interests to be considered are those of the two parties directly involved. (Margalit and Raz, at least, recognize that the legitimate interests of the inhabitants of all countries are relevant to determining the scope and limits of the right to secede, whereas Beran considers only the legitimate interests of the remainder state and Wellman only the legitimate interests of the people of the remainder state and those of the members of the seceding group.)

The most fundamental problem, however, is not that these theorists have failed to consider all the harmful effects of the particular exercise of the putative right to secede. Rather, it is that they have failed to understand that the institutionalization of an otherwise unexceptionable ethical principle that recognizes a right can create a situation in which uncacceptable harms will result, even if these harms do not result from any particular exercise of the putative right. Unacceptable harms may result, not from exercises of the putative right, but rather from strategic reactions on the part of states that have an interest in preventing the condition for exercising the putative right from coming about.

The chief mechanism by which this occurs, in the case of legal institutions, is by the encouragement to harmful behavior that can result from *legitimizing* certain actions. As I emphasized above, when a type of action is legitimized by international law, the costs of performing it are, other things being equal, lowered. But, for this very reason, those whose interests will be threatened by the performance of these actions have an incentive to prevent others from being in a position to satisfy the conditions that make performance of the actions legitimate.

For example, as was shown earlier, serious harms may occur as states apprehensive of their own dissolution take measures to prevent regions within them from developing the economic and political resources for independent statehood, or to prevent minorities from developing "encompassing cultures," or to bar groups from immigrating into an area where they might become a secessionist majority. In each case, the harms that would result from the incorporation of the putative right to secede into international law would *not* be caused by a particular group of secessionists who exercised the right so described. Instead, the harms would result from the actions of states reacting to incentives that would be created by the acceptance of this conception of the right as a principle for the international institutional order.

VII Ideal Versus Nonideal Theory

I have argued that Primary Right Theorists have not appreciated some of the most significant sorts of considerations that are relevant to making a case that a proposed principle of rightful secession ought to be recognized as such in the international system. Because of a lack of *institutional* focus, Primary Right Theories fail to appreciate the importance of states, both practically and morally. Once we focus squarely on institutions, and hence on the importance of states, we see that Primary Right Theories (1) are deficient according to the criterion of minimal realism (because they neglect the role of states as the makers of international law), (2) are not consistent with morally progressive principles of international law (because they contradict the principle of the territorial integrity even when it is restricted to the protection of morally legitimate states), and (3) create perverse incentives (because their proposed international principles would encourage morally regressive behavior by states in their domestic affairs). My contention has been that by failing to take institutional considerations seriously in attempting to formulate a right to secede these analysts have produced normative theories that have little value as guides to developing more humane and effective international responses to secessionist conflicts.

Before concluding, I will consider one final reply which those whose views I have criticized might make. The Primary Right Theorists might maintain that they and I are simply engaged in two different enterprises: I am offering a *nonideal* institutional theory of the right to secede; they are offering an *ideal*, but nonetheless, institutional theory. They are thinking institutionally, they would protest, but they are thinking about what international law concerning secession would look like under ideal conditions, where there is perfect compliance with all relevant principles of justice.[27] Thus, from the fact that in *our* imperfect world attempts to implement their principles would create perverse incentives or would be rejected by states genuinely concerned to prevent violations of human rights that might arise from making state borders much less resistant to change is quite irrelevant. None of these adverse consequences would occur under conditions of perfect compliance with (all) valid principles of justice.

This criticism raises complex issues about the distinction between ideal and nonideal political theory that I cannot hope to tackle here. However, I will conclude by noting that this strategy for rebutting the objections I have raised to Primary Right Theories comes at an exorbitant price: If such theories are only defensible under the assumption of perfect compliance with all relevant principles of justice, then they are even less useful for our world than my criticisms heretofore suggest – especially in the absence of a complete set of principles of justice for domestic and international relations.

International legal institutions are designed to deal with the problems of our world. A moral theory of international legal institutions for dealing with secessionist

conflicts in our world must respond to the problems that make secessionist conflicts a matter of moral concern for us, the residents of *this* world. A moral theory of institutions for a world that is so radically different from our world, not only as it is, but as it is likely ever to be, cannot provide valuable guidance for improving *our* institutions. The gap between that kind of "ideal" institutional theory and our non-ideal situation is simply too great.[28] Moreover, unless the full ideal theory of justice is produced or at least sketched, it is unilluminating to deflect objections by declaring that they would not arise if there were complete compliance with all principles of justice.

This is not to say, however, that there is no room for ideal theory of any sort. The Remedial Right Only Theory that I endorse is in a straightforward sense an ideal theory: It sets a moral target that can only be achieved through quite fundamental changes in international legal institutions and doctrine. (If I am right, this target is morally progressive, but not disastrously utopian.) My skepticism, rather, is directed only to theories that are so "ideal" that they fail to engage the very problems that lead us to seek institutional reform in the first place.

Notes

1   There is another question that a comprehensive normative theory of secession ought to answer: Under what conditions, if any, ought a constitution include a right to secede, and what form should such a right take? See Allen Buchanan, *Secession: The Morality of Political Divorce from Fort Sumter to Lithuania and Quebec* (Boulder, Col.: Westview Press, 1991), pp. 127–49.
2   International law recognizes a "right of all peoples to self-determination," which includes the right to choose independent

statehood. However, international legal practice has interpreted the right narrowly, restricting it to the most unambiguous cases of de-colonization. The consensus among legal scholars at this time is that international law does not recognize a right to secede in other circumstances, but that it does not unequivocally prohibit it either. Hurst Hannum, *Autonomy, Sovereignty and Self-Determination: The Accommodation of Conflicting Rights* (Philadelphia: University of Pennsylvania Press, 1990), pp. 27–39; W.

Ofuatey-Kodjoe, *The Principle of Self-Determination in International Law* (New York: Nellen, 1977); Christian Tomuschat (ed.), *Modern Law of Self-Determination* (Dordrecht: Martinus Nijhoff, 1993).

3 Harry Beran, *The Consent Theory of Political Obligation* (London: Croom Helm, 1987); David Copp, "Do Nations Have a Right of Self-Determination?" in Stanley G. French (ed.), *Philosophers Look at Canadian Confederation* (Montreal: Canadian Philosophical Association, 1979), pp. 71–95; David Gauthier, "Breaking Up: An Essay on Secession," *Canadian Journal of Philosophy* 24: 3 (1994), pp. 357–72.

4 Daniel Philpott, "In Defense of Self-Determination," *Ethics* 105 (January 1995): 352–85; David Gauthier, "Breaking Up: An Essay on Secession," pp. 357–72; Michael Walzer, "The New Tribalism," *Dissent* 39: 2 (Spring 1992), pp. 165–9.

5 Avishai Margalit and Joseph Raz, "National Self-Determination," *Journal of Philosophy* 86: 9 (1990), pp. 439–61. Christopher Wellman, "A Defense of Secession and Political Self-Determination," *Philosophy & Public Affairs* 24: 2 (Spring 1995), pp. 357–72.

6 Some versions of Remedial Right Only Theory, including the one considered below, add another necessary condition: the *proviso* that the new state makes credible guarantees that it will respect the human rights of all those who reside in it.

7 John Locke, *Second Treatise of Civil Government* (New York: Hackett, 1980), pp. 100–24. Strictly speaking, it may be incorrect to say that Locke affirms a right to revolution if by revolution is meant an attempt to overthrow the existing political authority. Locke's point is that if the government acts in ways that are not within the scope of the authority granted to it by the people's consent, then governmental authority ceases to exist. In that sense, instead of a Lockean right to revolution it would be more accurate to speak of the right of the people to constitute a new governmental authority.

8 Allen Buchanan, *Secession*, pp. 27–80.

9 Allen Buchanan, "Self-Determination, Secession, and the Rule of International Law," in Robert McKim and Jeffrey McMahan (eds.), *The Morality of Nationalism* (Oxford: Oxford University Press).

10 This proviso warrants elaboration. For one thing, virtually no existing state is without some infringements of human rights. Therefore, requiring credible guarantees that a new state will avoid *all* infringements of human rights seems excessive. Some might argue, instead, that the new state must simply do a better job of respecting human rights than the state from which it secedes. It can be argued, however, that the international community has a legitimate interest in requiring somewhat higher standards for recognizing new states as legitimate members of the system of states.

11 Avishai Margalit and Joseph Raz, "National Self-Determination," pp. 445–7.

12 Allen Buchanan, "Self-Determination, Secession, and the Rule of International Law."

13 Harry Beran, *The Consent Theory of Political Obligation*, p. 42.

14 Beran, *ibid.*, p. 42, adds another condition: that the secession not harm the remainder state's essential military, economic, or cultural interests.

15 Christopher Wellman, "A Defense of Secession and Self-Determination," p. 161.

16 It is advisable at this point to forestall a misunderstanding about the contrast between the two types of theories. Remedial Right Only Theories, as the name implies, recognize a (general) right to secede only as a remedy for injustice, but Primary Right Theories need not, and usually do not, deny that there is a remedial right to secede. They only deny that the right to secede is only a remedial right. Thus a Primary Right Theory is not necessarily a Primary Right Only Theory.

17 The statement that it is states that make international law requires a qualification: nongovernmental organizations (NGOs) are coming to exert more influence in the international legal arena. However, their impact is limited compared to that of states.

18 Donald Horowitz, "Self-Determination: Politics, Philosophy and Law" (1998) in *NOMOS XXXIX*.

19 This example is drawn from Christopher Wellman, "Political Self-Determination," unpublished manuscript.

20 Albert O. Hirschman, *Exit, Voice, and Loyalty* (Cambridge, Mass.: Harvard University Press, 1970).

21 Cass R. Sunstein, "Constitutionalism and Secession," *University of Chicago Law Review* 58 (1991), pp. 633–70.

22 Allen Buchanan, *Secession*, pp. 98–100.

23 Here it is important to repeat a qualification noted earlier: the progressive interpretation of the principle of territorial integrity operates within the limits of what I have called the relatively uncontroversial, standard, or theory-neutral conception of justice, as applied to the threshold condition that states must be minimally just in order to be legitimate and so to fall within the scope of the principle of territorial integrity. Therefore, it will not do for the Primary Right Theorist to reply that his theory is compatible with the progressive interpretation of the principle of territorial integrity because on his view a state that does not allow peoples or nations to secede or does not allow the secession of majorities that desire independent statehood *is* unjust. The problem with this reply is that it operates with a conception of justice that goes far beyond the normative basis of the progressive interpretation and in such a way as to beg the question by employing an understanding of the rights of groups that is not acknowledged by both parties to the theoretical debate.

24 Christopher Wellman, "A Defense of Secession and Self-Determination," p. 163.

25 Avishai Margalit and Joseph Raz, "National Self-Determination," pp. 459–60.

26 Harry Beran, *The Consent Theory of Political Obligation*, p. 42.

27 For a valuable discussion of the distinction between ideal and nonideal theory and for the beginning of a normative account of secession from the standpoint of domestic institutions (including constitutional provisions for secession), see Wayne Norman, "Domesticating Secession," unpublished paper. For a discussion of the idea of a constitutional right to secede, see Allen Buchanan, *Secession*, pp. 127–49.

28 I am indebted to Harry Brighouse for his suggestion that the sort of ideal theory which would have to be assumed by Primary Right Theorists in order to escape my objections is so extreme as to be practically irrelevant.

Part III

Human Rights

Introduction

Several centuries ago, philosophers such as Thomas Hobbes and John Locke argued for a conception of "natural rights." Whilst there are important differences between these accounts, all natural rights theorists broadly agree that all human beings possess rights "naturally." That is, you and I possess certain rights solely on account of our being human beings. Natural rights often include rights to own property, pursue a livelihood, create a family, and to one's own life (i.e., a right against being murdered). These rights are pre-legal: we have them independently of political institutions. Often natural rights proponents argue that these rights serve as legitimate moral constraints on the conduct of political leadership.

Human rights have much in common with natural rights, although there are important differences, too. Both are rights that people possess in virtue of their humanity. However, human rights are not merely moral, but political and enshrined in our institutions. Perhaps the most well-known document that sets out the human rights for all is contained in the United Nations' "Universal Declaration of Human Rights" (UDHR), reproduced in chapter 6 of this volume. The UDHR effectively enshrines a number of traditional natural rights (such as rights to life, liberty, and possessions). These rights are wide-ranging and controversial, including rights to a public trial for all, rights to travel to and from one's own country, and rights to choose one's marriage partner.

Despite its great promise, the UDHR is not enforced by a world-state or global police. We may well praise or condemn our fellow states for how well they abide by or deny human rights as set out in the UDHR. However, the violation of the UDHR does not itself trigger any coercive measures as such. The fact that a country has participated in gross human rights abuses may well motivate the United Nations' Security Council to pass punitive measures, whether they be economic sanctions or military action. However, the Security Council can pass such measures without the UDHR having been breached. Thus, the status of the UDHR limits it to a moral standard by which we might evaluate the activities of states.

In chapter 7, Leif Wenar examines the nature of rights, drawing on the influential work of Wesley Hohfeld. Hohfeld distinguishes between various rights claims, or "incidents," which include the privilege, the claim, the power, and the immunity. These incidents support one or more particular functions, such as exemption, discretion, authorization, protection, provision, and performance. Although Wenar argues that not all rights are claims, he does accept that all rights are incidents while rejecting the view that all incidents are rights. Thus, Wenar offers us a "several-functions theory of rights." The benefit of this view is that it can overcome "single-function" theories, such as the will theory (e.g., rights are incidents that offer the rights holder specific varieties of choices) and the interest theory (e.g., rights are incidents that further the well-being of the rights holder). Only the several functions theory can acknowledge that all rights must serve at least one function despite the fact there is not one function that all rights need share: "Rights have all of the functions that they do."

Chapter 8 examines the contemporary international practices concerning human rights. Charles R. Beitz argues that the protection and safeguarding of human rights is a necessary condition for the minimal legitimacy of any state. This view borrows from John Rawls's views presented in *The Law of Peoples* (see chapter 11). Rawls argues that any "decent" society must respect human rights. Such a society need not be liberal and it may adopt competing ways of life: a decent society need not be an advanced Western state and, thus, not parochial. Beitz adopts this perspective as a proper standard for measuring the legitimacy of any state. First, he argues that human rights have a political character tied to the international arena. Second, the existence of human rights must fulfill a standard of reasonableness, rather than complete agreement. If we uphold this understanding of human rights, according to Beitz, they will act as a proper constraint on states by providing a universal and legitimate basis with which to criticize the activities of states.

Thus far, our analysis of human rights has largely concentrated upon the rights of individual persons. In Chapter 9, Peter Jones makes an argument for group rights. He argues that rights are fundamentally about what is of significance to individuals. Part of what is significant to individuals is their identity in groups. Thus, rights can pertain to individuals and the groups they belong to. Jones sheds invaluable light on helping us distinguish between individual rights and group rights. He discusses both collective and corporate conceptions of group rights, arguing that these views are not mutually exclusive and that legitimate group rights can take both collective and corporatist forms.

Part III concludes with a timely look at torture by David Sussman. With the current "War on Terror," the possible justifications for the use of torture have been re-examined. Sussman argues that torture is morally repugnant not merely because it is violent, cruel, and degrading, but because it is more than this: it is "the pre-eminent instance of a kind of forced self-betrayal." The torture victim is both helpless at the hands of his interrogators and an active participate in his suffering, coerced to take part in the cruel ritual. Thus, the victim's autonomy is not merely violated, but perverted in the act of his being tortured. Torture is never justifiable.

Whilst the concept of human rights has been with us only a relatively short time, its importance in our normative and political assessment of domestic and international institutions has become widespread. Much hinges on what might serve as a human right and its violation. The following chapters in this Part aim to help us understand fully this crucial area of concern.

Chapter 6

Universal Declaration of Human Rights*
United Nations

On December 10, 1948 the General Assembly of the United Nations adopted and proclaimed the Universal Declaration of Human Rights the full text of which appears in the following pages. Following this historic act the Assembly called upon all Member countries to publicize the text of the Declaration and "to cause it to be disseminated, displayed, read and expounded principally in schools and other educational institutions, without distinction based on the political status of countries or territories."

Preamble

Whereas recognition of the inherent dignity and of the equal and inalienable rights of all members of the human family is the foundation of freedom, justice and peace in the world,

Whereas disregard and contempt for human rights have resulted in barbarous acts which have outraged the conscience of mankind, and the advent of a world in which human beings shall enjoy freedom of speech and belief and freedom from fear and want has been proclaimed as the highest aspiration of the common people,

Whereas it is essential, if man is not to be compelled to have recourse, as a last resort, to rebellion against tyranny and oppression, that human rights should be protected by the rule of law,

Whereas it is essential to promote the development of friendly relations between nations,

Whereas the peoples of the United Nations have in the Charter reaffirmed their faith in fundamental human rights, in the dignity and worth of the human person and in the equal rights of men and women and have determined to promote social progress and better standards of life in larger freedom,

Whereas Member States have pledged themselves to achieve, in co-operation with the United Nations, the promotion of universal respect for and observance of human rights and fundamental freedoms,

Whereas a common understanding of these rights and freedoms is of the greatest importance for the full realization of this pledge,

* From *Universal Declaration of Human Rights* (1948).

**Now, therefore THE GENERAL ASSEM-
BLY proclaims THIS UNIVERSAL
DECLARATION OF HUMAN RIGHTS**
as a common standard of achievement for
all peoples and all nations, to the end
that every individual and every organ of
society, keeping this Declaration constantly
in mind, shall strive by teaching and education to promote respect for these rights and
freedoms and by progressive measures,
national and international, to secure their
universal and effective recognition and
observance, both among the peoples of
Member States themselves and among
the peoples of territories under their
jurisdiction.

Article 1

All human beings are born free and equal
in dignity and rights. They are endowed
with reason and conscience and should
act towards one another in a spirit of
brotherhood.

Article 2

Everyone is entitled to all the rights and
freedoms set forth in this Declaration,
without distinction of any kind, such as
race, colour, sex, language, religion, political or other opinion, national or social
origin, property, birth or other status.
Furthermore, no distinction shall be made
on the basis of the political, jurisdictional
or international status of the country or
territory to which a person belongs,
whether it be independent, trust, non-
self-governing or under any other limitation of sovereignty.

Article 3

Everyone has the right to life, liberty and
security of person.

Article 4

No one shall be held in slavery or servitude; slavery and the slave trade shall be
prohibited in all their forms.

Article 5

No one shall be subjected to torture or to
cruel, inhuman or degrading treatment or
punishment.

Article 6

Everyone has the right to recognition
everywhere as a person before the law.

Article 7

All are equal before the law and are entitled without any discrimination to equal
protection of the law. All are entitled
to equal protection against any discrimination in violation of this Declaration
and against any incitement to such
discrimination.

Article 8

Everyone has the right to an effective
remedy by the competent national tribunals for acts violating the fundamental
rights granted him by the constitution or
by law.

Article 9

No one shall be subjected to arbitrary
arrest, detention or exile.

Article 10

Everyone is entitled in full equality to a
fair and public hearing by an independent
and impartial tribunal, in the determination of his rights and obligations and of
any criminal charge against him.

Article 11

(1) Everyone charged with a penal
offence has the right to be presumed
innocent until proved guilty according to
law in a public trial at which he has had
all the guarantees necessary for his
defence.

(2) No one shall be held guilty of any
penal offence on account of any act or
omission which did not constitute a penal
offence, under national or international

law, at the time when it was committed. Nor shall a heavier penalty be imposed than the one that was applicable at the time the penal offence was committed.

Article 12

No one shall be subjected to arbitrary interference with his privacy, family, home or correspondence, nor to attacks upon his honour and reputation. Everyone has the right to the protection of the law against such interference or attacks.

Article 13

(1) Everyone has the right to freedom of movement and residence within the borders of each state.

(2) Everyone has the right to leave any country, including his own, and to return to his country.

Article 14

(1) Everyone has the right to seek and to enjoy in other countries asylum from persecution.

(2) This right may not be invoked in the case of prosecutions genuinely arising from non-political crimes or from acts contrary to the purposes and principles of the United Nations.

Article 15

(1) Everyone has the right to a nationality.

(2) No one shall be arbitrarily deprived of his nationality nor denied the right to change his nationality.

Article 16

(1) Men and women of full age, without any limitation due to race, nationality or religion, have the right to marry and to found a family. They are entitled to equal rights as to marriage, during marriage and at its dissolution.

(2) Marriage shall be entered into only with the free and full consent of the intending spouses.

(3) The family is the natural and fundamental group unit of society and is entitled to protection by society and the State.

Article 17

(1) Everyone has the right to own property alone as well as in association with others.

(2) No one shall be arbitrarily deprived of his property.

Article 18

Everyone has the right to freedom of thought, conscience and religion; this right includes freedom to change his religion or belief, and freedom, either alone or in community with others and in public or private, to manifest his religion or belief in teaching, practice, worship and observance.

Article 19

Everyone has the right to freedom of opinion and expression; this right includes freedom to hold opinions without interference and to seek, receive and impart information and ideas through any media and regardless of frontiers.

Article 20

(1) Everyone has the right to freedom of peaceful assembly and association.

(2) No one may be compelled to belong to an association.

Article 21

(1) Everyone has the right to take part in the government of his country, directly or through freely chosen representatives.

(2) Everyone has the right of equal access to public service in his country.

(3) The will of the people shall be the basis of the authority of government; this will shall be expressed in periodic and genuine elections which shall be by universal and equal suffrage and shall be held by secret vote or by equivalent free voting procedures.

Article 22

Everyone, as a member of society, has the right to social security and is entitled to realization, through national effort and international co-operation and in accordance with the organization and resources of each State, of the economic, social and cultural rights indispensable for his dignity and the free development of his personality.

Article 23

(1) Everyone has the right to work, to free choice of employment, to just and favourable conditions of work and to protection against unemployment.

(2) Everyone, without any discrimination, has the right to equal pay for equal work.

(3) Everyone who works has the right to just and favourable remuneration ensuring for himself and his family an existence worthy of human dignity, and supplemented, if necessary, by other means of social protection.

(4) Everyone has the right to form and to join trade unions for the protection of his interests.

Article 24

Everyone has the right to rest and leisure, including reasonable limitation of working hours and periodic holidays with pay.

Article 25

(1) Everyone has the right to a standard of living adequate for the health and well-being of himself and of his family, including food, clothing, housing and medical care and necessary social services, and the right to security in the event of unemployment, sickness, disability, widowhood, old age or other lack of livelihood in circumstances beyond his control.

(2) Motherhood and childhood are entitled to special care and assistance. All children, whether born in or out of wedlock, shall enjoy the same social protection.

Article 26

(1) Everyone has the right to education. Education shall be free, at least in the elementary and fundamental stages. Elementary education shall be compulsory. Technical and professional education shall be made generally available and higher education shall be equally accessible to all on the basis of merit.

(2) Education shall be directed to the full development of the human personality and to the strengthening of respect for human rights and fundamental freedoms. It shall promote understanding, tolerance and friendship among all nations, racial or religious groups, and shall further the activities of the United Nations for the maintenance of peace.

(3) Parents have a prior right to choose the kind of education that shall be given to their children.

Article 27

(1) Everyone has the right freely to participate in the cultural life of the community, to enjoy the arts and to share in scientific advancement and its benefits.

(2) Everyone has the right to the protection of the moral and material interests resulting from any scientific, literary or artistic production of which he is the author.

Article 28

Everyone is entitled to a social and international order in which the rights and freedoms set forth in this Declaration can be fully realized.

Article 29

(1) Everyone has duties to the community in which alone the free and full development of his personality is possible.

(2) In the exercise of his rights and freedoms, everyone shall be subject only to such limitations as are determined by law solely for the purpose of securing due recognition and respect for the rights and freedoms of others and of meeting the just requirements of morality, public order and the general welfare in a democratic society.

(3) These rights and freedoms may in no case be exercised contrary to the purposes and principles of the United Nations.

Article 30

Nothing in this Declaration may be interpreted as implying for any State, group or person any right to engage in any activity or to perform any act aimed at the destruction of any of the rights and freedoms set forth herein.

Chapter 7

The Nature of Rights*
Leif Wenar

The twentieth century saw a vigorous debate over the nature of rights. Will theorists argued that the function of rights is to allocate domains of freedom. Interest theorists portrayed rights as defenders of well-being. Each side declared its conceptual analysis to be closer to an ordinary understanding of what rights there are, and to an ordinary understanding of what rights do for rightholders. Neither side could win a decisive victory, and the debate ended in a standoff.[1]

This article offers a new analysis of rights. The first half of the article sets out an analytical framework adequate for explicating all assertions of rights. This framework is an elaboration of Hohfeld's, designed around a template for displaying the often complex internal structures of rights. Those unfamiliar with Hohfeld's work should find that the exposition here presumes no prior knowledge of it. Those who know Hohfeld will find innovations in how the system is defined and presented. Any theorist wishing to specify precisely what is at stake within a controversy over some particular right may find this framework useful.

The analytical framework is then deployed in the second half of the article to resolve the dispute between the will and interest theories. Despite the appeal of freedom and well-being as organizing ideas, each of these theories is clearly too narrow. We accept rights, which do not (as the will theory holds) define domains of freedom; and we affirm rights whose aim is not (as the interest theory claims) to further the interests of the rightholder. A third theory, introduced here, is superior in describing the functions of rights as they are commonly understood.

Will theorists and interest theorists have erred in adopting analyses framed to favor their commitments in normative theory. This has turned the debate between them into a proxy for the debate between Kantianism and welfarism. Yet that normative dispute cannot be resolved through a conceptual analysis of rights. The third theory presented here is not fashioned to fortify any normative position. Rather, it is offered as a vernacular standard against which to measure the interpretations of rights that various normative theories press us to accept.

The ambitions of the article are thus principally descriptive. The first half of the article shows what kinds of things rights are (i.e., all

* From *Philosophy & Public Affairs* 33:3 (2005), pp. 223–52.

rights are Hohfeldian incidents). The second half shows what rights do for rightholders (i.e., which Hohfeldian incidents are rights). The two halves together complete an analysis of the concept of a right. The analysis here is general. It holds for all rights of conduct: moral rights, legal rights, customary rights, and so on.[2] The analysis aims to reveal the logical structure underlying our assertions of rights, while remaining faithful to an ordinary understanding of what rights there are, and of the significance rights have for those who hold them.

I   A Modified Hohfeldian Framework

The first half of the article sets out a modified Hohfeldian framework for explicating the meanings of rights assertions. The thesis of this section is that all assertions of rights can be understood in terms of four basic elements, known as the Hohfeldian incidents.[3]

There are two fundamental forms of rights assertions: "A has a right to phi" and "A has a right that B phi," where "phi" is an active verb. We begin by connecting these two fundamental forms of assertion to the four Hohfeldian incidents: the privilege, the claim, the power, and the immunity. In the process it will emerge that each of the two fundamental forms of assertion can also indicate complex "molecular" rights, whose structure will be resolvable into combinations of the four "atomic" incidents. Finally, at the end of this section we show how rights assertions that lack active verbs can be translated into active-verb form. We will then have covered all forms of rights assertions, and will have shown that all rights assertions can be understood in terms of the Hohfeldian incidents.

We begin with those rights assertions of the form "A has a right to phi" that indicate the privilege, the first of the four Hohfeldian incidents.

A   Privileges

A sheriff in hot pursuit of a suspect has the legal right to break down the door that the suspect has locked behind him. The sheriff's having a legal right to break down the door implies that he has no legal duty not to break down the door.

For rights like the sheriff's:

"A has a Y right to phi" implies "A has no Y duty not to phi."

(where "Y" is "legal," "moral," or "customary," and "phi" is an active verb)[4]

The type of right here is what Hohfeld called a "privilege," which is also called a "liberty" or a "license."[5] The sheriff's right is a single privilege. A right that is a single privilege confers an *exemption* from a general duty. While ordinary citizens have a duty not to break down doors, police officers have a privilege-right [no duty not] to break down doors. When President Nixon asserted that he had a legal right not to turn over the Watergate tapes, he was asserting "executive privilege." Ordinary citizens have a legal duty to turn over evidence when subpoenaed. Yet Nixon alleged that because he was President he had a legal right [no duty not] not to turn over his evidence. James Bond's license to kill is also an exemption from a general duty. Bond's (alleged) right exempts him from a duty not to do what civilians emphatically have a duty not to do, viz., to kill. Similarly, your driver's license gives you the right to drive. This right exempts you from a duty not to do what you would otherwise have a strong duty not to do – to operate dangerous machinery at high speeds.

We can represent a right that is a single privilege, such as your right to drive, in graphic terms as seen in Figure 7.1.

In Figure 7.1 your right to drive a car is displayed as a single privilege. This single

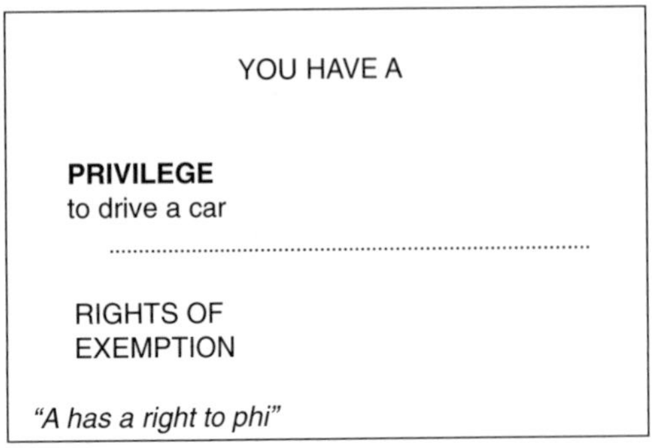

```
┌─────────────────────────────────────────────┐
│                                               │
│              YOU HAVE A                        │
│                                               │
│                                               │
│   PRIVILEGE                                    │
│   to drive a car                               │
│   ........................................     │
│                                               │
│   RIGHTS OF                                    │
│   EXEMPTION                                    │
│                                               │
│   "A has a right to phi"                       │
│                                               │
└─────────────────────────────────────────────┘
```

Figure 7.1 The right to drive as a single privilege

privilege is classified according to its function (a single privilege is a right of exemption), and according to the form of its assertion (a single privilege is asserted by expressions of the form "A has a right to phi").

Some assertions of the form "A has a right to phi" indicate not a single privilege, but a paired privilege. A paired privilege is composed of two privileges. The holder of a paired privilege has a privilege [no duty not] to phi, and also has a privilege [no duty not] *not* to phi. That is, for a right that is a paired privilege:

> "A has a Y right to phi" implies both "A has no Y duty not to phi" and "A has no Y duty to phi."

> (where "Y" is "legal," "moral," or "customary," and "phi" is an active verb)

A person vested with a paired privilege is entitled to perform some action, or not to perform that action, as he pleases. For instance, a chess player has the right to capture his opponent's pawn en passant. This right is a paired privilege: the player has a right [no duty not] to take en passant, and a right [no duty not] not to take en passant. The player may take his opponent's pawn, or not, as he thinks best. The function of a right

that is a paired privilege is to endow its bearer with *discretion*, or choice, concerning some action. The chess player's right gives the player discretion over whether to take his opponent's pawn, or to leave that pawn on the board.

Paired privileges can be enormously important. For instance, each person has extensive (if not unlimited) paired privilege-rights to move her body, and to use her property. In a liberal society each citizen also has extensive (if not unlimited) paired privilege-rights regarding her speech, association, and religious practice. These paired privilege-rights all entitle the rightholder to choose how to act within some domain: that is, they all specify what the rightholder has no duty (not) to do.

It may be noticed that while a paired privilege is composed of two privileges, the function of a right that is a paired privilege is not related to the function of a right that is a single privilege. The function of a single privilege-right is to confer an exemption from a general duty. Yet neither of the privileges that make up a paired privilege need confer an exemption from a general duty. Rather, the function of the two privileges in a paired privilege-right is together to endow the rightholder with discretion concerning some action. The function of the single privilege-right (exemption) and the function of the paired privilege-right (discretion) are entirely independent.[6]

We can represent the chess player's right in the same space as we represented your right to drive, so long as we indicate that the rights which occupy this space may have either of two distinct functions (Fig. 7.2).

In Figure 7.2, "Privileges (not) to capture a pawn en passant," indicates the paired privilege to capture and not to capture a pawn. This paired privilege-right is classified according to its function (a paired privilege-right is, unlike a single privilege-right, a right of discretion), and according to the form of

```
┌─────────────────────────────────────────┐
│                                         │
│          CHESS PLAYER HAS               │
│                                         │
│                                         │
│   PRIVILEGES                            │
│   (not) to capture                      │
│   a pawn en passant                     │
│                                         │
│   ......................................│
│                                         │
│   RIGHTS OF                             │
│   EXEMPTION                             │
│   OR DISCRETION                         │
│                                         │
│   "A has a right to phi"                │
│                                         │
└─────────────────────────────────────────┘
```

Figure 7.2 A chess player's right as a paired privilege

its assertion (a paired privilege-right is, like a single privilege-right, asserted by expressions of the form "A has a right to phi").

B Claims

We assert not only that "A has a right to phi," but that "A has a right that B phi." This second fundamental form of rights-assertion often implies not a lack of a duty in the right-holder A, but the presence of a duty in a second party B. In such cases:

> "A has a Y right that B phi" implies "B has a Y duty to A to phi."

> (where "Y" is "legal," "moral," or "customary," and "phi" is an active verb)

Ignoring the domain restriction "Y," let us examine the simple assertion "A has a right that B phi" when this implies "B has a duty to A to phi." The Hohfeldian incident here indicated is the claim. For every claim in A there is some B who has a duty to A. Your right that I not strike you correlates to my duty not to strike you. Your right that I help you correlates to my duty to help you. Your right that I do what I promised correlates to my duty to do what I promised.[7]

As these examples suggest, rights that are claims can have three different functions. A claim-right can entitle its bearer to *protection* against harm or paternalism, or to *provision* in case of need, or to specific *performance* of some agreed-upon, compensatory, or legally or conventionally specified action. Claims, like privileges, can be of signal importance. Your right against assault, and a child's right to a decent education, and an employee's right to his pay are all examples of rights that are claims.

Some rights are privileges, and some rights are claims. Many familiar rights are combinations of both of these Hohfeldian incidents. For example, in the United States arrestees have the right to remain silent. This is a "molecular" right made up of a privilege and a claim. The arrestee's privilege is a single privilege [no duty not] not to speak, which exempts the arrestee from the general duty to obey police instructions. The arrestee's claim correlates to the police officers' duties not to force him to speak, which protects the arrestee from the police (Fig. 7.3).

Figure 7.3 displays an arrestee's molecular right to remain silent. On the left is the single privilege: a right of exemption of the form "A has a right to phi." On the right is the claim: a right of protection of the form "A has a right that B phi." The privilege and the claim together make up the arrestee's right to remain silent.

C Powers and Immunities

"A has a right to phi" often implies a privilege, and "A has a right that B phi" often implies a claim. These implications hold often – not always – because each of these forms of rights-assertion can also indicate a different, "higher-order" Hohfeldian incident. We have not only privileges and claims, but rights to alter our privileges and claims, and rights that our privileges and claims not be altered.[8]

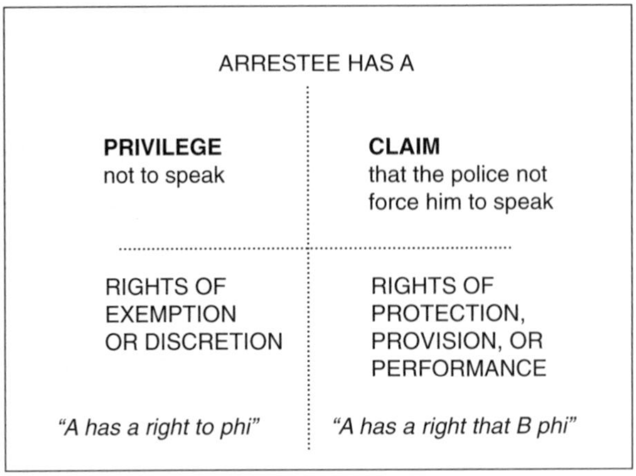

Figure 7.3   The right to remain silent as a privilege and a claim

The higher-order incident indicated by "A has a right to phi" is the power. To have a power is to have the ability within a set of rules to alter the normative situation of oneself or another. Specifically, to have a power is to have the ability within a set of rules to create, waive, or annul some lower-order incident(s). I have a right to promise to give you my fortune. Before I exercise this right I have no duty to give you my fortune, and you have no claim that I do. In exercising my power by making the promise, I create in you a claim to my fortune and thereby create in myself the duty to give it to you. Similarly, a judge has the legal right (power) to sentence a criminal to prison, meaning that a judge has the ability to annul the criminal's privileges of free movement. Or again: in a restaurant you have the customary right (power) to waive your claim to be served a sample of the wine before the bottle is poured, thereby annulling the waiter's customary duty to serve you this sample.

The power, like the privilege, is indicated by propositions of the form "A has a right to phi." All rights that are powers confer *authority*. Rights that are single powers confer nondiscretionary authority. For example, a judge's right to sentence a convicted criminal

under mandatory sentencing laws is a single power. The judge's right authorizes her to annul the criminal's right to free movement. Yet this is a single power because the judge has no discretion under the sentencing laws: she must use her authority to sentence the criminal to a specified term of years. A right that is a paired power confers discretionary authority. For example, you have the power to waive, and the power not to waive, the waiter's duty to serve you a sample of wine. Rights that are paired powers, like rights that are paired privileges, endow their bearers with discretion concerning some action. Rights that are paired powers are thus both authorizing and discretionary.[9]

The rights that are indicated by the form "A has a right to phi" have, in sum, three possible functions: single privileges mark an *exemption* from a general duty; both paired privileges and paired powers mark *discretion* within a certain domain; and both single powers and paired powers mark *authority* to alter the normative situation in some way.

Powers can range over the rights of others. Clearly such powers must not be unlimited. The fourth and final Hohfeldian incident is the immunity. One person has an immunity whenever another person lacks the ability

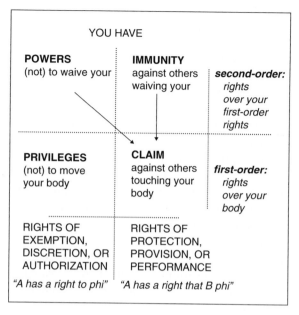

Figure 7.4 A complex molecular right

within a set of rules to change her normative situation in a particular respect. The immunity, like the claim, is signaled by the form "A has a right that B phi" (or, more commonly, "... that B not phi"). Rights that are immunities, like many rights that are claims, entitle their holders to *protection* against harm or paternalism.

A professor has the right to teach and research at her university. A tenured professor has the right that her university not annul her rights to teach and research. The right of tenure is an immunity. The tenured professor's right corresponds to the university's lack of a right (power) to fire her. Similarly, an American's right that Congress not restrict her privilege of free speech protects her against the general power of Congress to impose duties upon her. A witness granted a right against prosecution gains an immunity against being indicted for certain crimes. A defendant who desires to be punished may invoke a right against being required to present evidence that might lead to his acquittal. All of these rights are immunities,

and all protect the rightholder from harm or paternalism.[10]

Figure 7.4 displays all four Hohfeldian incidents working together within a complex right that you have over your body. This complex right comprises both first-order incidents (a paired privilege and a claim) and second-order incidents (a paired power and an immunity). On the first order, the paired privilege endows you with the discretion to move your body, or not to move your body, as you see fit. The claim on the first order affords you protection; it correlates to a duty in each other person not to touch your body. On the second order are your rights regarding the alteration of these first-order rights. Here we see the paired power that gives you the discretionary authority to waive your claim against others touching your body: your right, that is, to authorize others to touch your body. Also on the second order is your protective immunity against other people waiving your claim not to be touched: your right, that is, against anyone else authorizing others to touch your body.

As Figure 7.4 shows, the four incidents are positioned in the diagram according to their attributes. Rights over objects such as one's body are first-order privileges and claims. Rights over rights are second-order powers and immunities. As for the two columns, A's "active" rights on the left are privileges and powers, while A's "passive" rights on the right are claims and immunities. Privileges and powers are exercised, while claims and immunities are not exercised; they are merely enjoyed.[11] Moreover, there is an overlap in function between privileges (exemption, discretion) and powers (discretion, authorization) on the left; and an overlap in function between claims (protection, provision, performance) and immunities (protection) on the right.

Most rights are complex molecular rights like the one in Figure 7.4: rights made up of multiple Hohfeldian incidents.[12] Molecular rights indicated by the form "A has a right to phi" (where phi is an active verb) will always contain an incident from the left side of the diagram – a privilege or power – although they may contain incidents from the right side as well. Thus the right to move freely is a molecular right that contains privileges (not) to travel about the country; and the right to lead a meeting is a molecular right that contains the power to close a debate.[13] Molecular rights indicated by the form "A has the right that B phi" will always contain an incident from the right side of the diagram – a claim or immunity – although they may contain incidents from the left side as well. Thus the right that others respect one's privacy is a molecular right containing a claim against unwanted surveillance; and the right that the government not take one's property without due process is a molecular right containing an immunity against sudden expropriation.[14]

We have shown how the two fundamental forms of rights assertions can be understood in terms of the Hohfeldian incidents. In both of these fundamental forms of rights-assertion "phi" is an active verb. Assertions of rights in which "phi" is not an active verb but a noun ("Workers have the right to a decent wage") or in which "phi" is a passive verb ("Children have a right to be educated at state expense") are easily transposed into active verb forms. Workers have a right that their employers pay them a decent wage, and children have a right that the state pay for their education.[15] Explications of assertions of rights containing nouns and passive verbs merge in this way into the explication of the two fundamental forms of rights-assertion.

Finally, assertions of broad or indeterminate rights – such as the "right to free expression" – can be specified in several different ways into complexes of Hohfeldian incidents. The different specifications will correspond to different understandings of the right at stake. Indeed one of the virtues of the Hohfeldian framework is its capacity to display in exact terms various interpretations of what people might mean when they assert a broad or indeterminate right like the right to free expression. For example, should a controversial author assert that his right to free expression has been violated by a bookstore refusing to carry his book, a Hohfeldian explication will show that the author is not asserting the (usual) privilege-rights to expression insulated by protective claims and immunities. He is rather asserting a (tendentious) claim-right that others abet the spread of his expression. This Hohfeldian explication will be useful in evaluating the truth of the author's assertion that his right to free expression has been violated.

The framework for explicating rights assertions into assertions about Hohfeldian incidents is now complete. Any assertion of a right can be translated into an assertion about a single Hohfeldian incident, or into an assertion about a complex of incidents, or into a set of alternative assertions about such incidents. All rights are Hohfeldian incidents.

The proof of this thesis is inductive. In examining sample rights, we have found that:

(1) Each right can be identified with one or more of the Hohfeldian incidents; and

(2) Each right has one or more of the six specific functions (exemption, discretion, authorization, protection, provision, performance).

The inductive step is to say: All rights are like this. All rights can be analyzed into Hohfeldian diagrams. Our confidence in this inductive step will increase as we successfully explicate more and more rights with the Hohfeldian diagrams, and as we fail to find counterexamples. The reader may want to satisfy himself or herself that confidence in this inductive step is justified, and may wish to test the framework with more sample rights. The note below reproduces a list of rights from a recent text, which may be useful for evaluating the induction.[16]

Philosophers of law sometimes complain that the ordinary language of rights is loose, or confused. Yet there is nothing wrong with ordinary language. The word "right" in ordinary language is merely systematically ambiguous, like many other words, such as "free."[17] Assertions of rights can refer to various (combinations of) Hohfeldian incidents. Since these incidents have quite different logical forms, speakers may fall into contradiction if they do not understand the implications of their own assertions. For example, it is not uncommon for a speaker to assert a right that can only be a privilege, and then go on to infer from this assertion that someone owes him a duty. Yet this kind of error is not the result of a defect in ordinary language. It is rather a defect in the speaker's understanding of the various meanings of the word "right." Ordinary rights-talk can be entirely rigorous and error-free, provided that speakers understand how assertions of rights map onto the Hohfeldian incidents.

The Hohfeldian framework shows that the unity of rights is not a simple Thalesian monism; it is the unity of molecules composed of the atoms of the periodic table. Privilege-rights and claim-rights share the concept of duty, and range over physical objects. Power-rights and immunity-rights share the concept of authority, and range over lower-order incidents. Privilege-rights and power-rights are actively exercised, and overlap in their functions. Claim-rights and immunity-rights are passively enjoyed, and their functions also mesh. All of the rights that we know are built from these common elements, in ways determined by the natures of the elements themselves.

II The Functions of Rights

A Theories of the Functions of Rights

All rights are Hohfeldian incidents. Are all Hohfeldian incidents rights? That is, would any of the four Hohfeldian incidents, or any combination of incidents, count as A's right were it ascribed to A? We might label the theory that answers this question affirmatively the *any-incident* theory of rights. Both of the long-dominant theories of the functions of rights – the will theory and the interest theory – oppose this any-incident theory. According to the will theory and the interest theory, some (combinations of) Hohfeldian incidents do not qualify as rights because they do not perform the function that all rights perform. The will theory says that only those combinations of incidents that give their holders certain kinds of choices are properly regarded as rights. The interest theory limits the term "rights" to those incidents that further their holders' well-being. The will and interest theories are each "single-function" theories of rights.

According to these theories all rights have some single function, although the two theories differ as to what that function is. Both single-function theories would therefore reject the explication of rights assertions in the first part of this article, in which rights have six distinct functions.[18]

The long and unresolved historical contest between these two single-function theories stretches back through Bentham (an interest theorist) and Kant (a will theorist) into the Dark Ages.[19] In the twentieth century the scholarly contest between advocates of the two theories ended in stalemate. I believe that, as is often the case with unresolved historical debates, this situation is explained by each side giving a partial account of a larger terrain. Here I will briefly review the standing objections to each single-function theory in order to show how each is too restrictive as an account of the functions of rights, and to indicate how the weakness of each theory is the strength of the other.

A better alternative, I believe, is what might be called the *several functions* theory of rights. The several functions theory captures what is plausible in the will and interest theories; yet because it does not require that all rights have some single overall function it avoids the procrustean strictures of each. The test of a theory of the functions of rights is how well it captures our ordinary understanding of what rights there are and what significance rights have for rightholders. The several functions theory is, I will argue, preferable to both the will theory and the interest theory on these grounds.

B The Will Theory

The will theory of rights asserts that the single function of a right is to give the rightholder discretion over the duty of another. A land owner has a right, for instance, because he has the power to waive or not to waive the duties that others have not to enter

his land. A promisee has a right because she has the power to demand performance of the promisor's duty, or to waive performance, as she likes. As Hart describes the central thesis of the will theory, "The individual who has the right is a small scale sovereign to whom the duty is owed."[20]

The attraction of the will theory is that it reserves for rights the special role of securing dominion over significant spheres of action. Many important rights do endow rightholders with this kind of discretion, and so serve the freedom of those who hold them. The connection between rights and freedom, so powerful in modern politics, is for will theorists a matter of definition.

However, the will theorist's sole focus on a certain sort of freedom constrains what he recognizes as a right. The will theorist recognizes as a right only those Hohfeldian incidents that confer on their bearers the discretion to alter the duties of others. Thus the will theorist recognizes as rights only those molecular structures that include a paired power (not) to create, waive or annul a claim that one person has against another.[21] This view of the function of rights also entails a restriction on the class of potential rightholders. The will theorist recognizes as potential rightholders only those beings that have certain capacities: the capacities to exercise powers to alter the duties of others.

These constraints render the will theory implausibly narrow. This narrowness is evident, first, in the range of rights that the theory recognizes. Many important rights, such as the complex bodily right in Figure 7.4, do include a paired power to alter a claim. But many do not. For example, you have no legal power to waive or annul your claim against being enslaved, or your claim against being tortured to death. The will theory therefore does not recognize that you have a legal right against being enslaved, or against being tortured to death. Yet most would regard these unwaivable claims as rights, indeed as among the more important rights that individuals have.[22]

Will theorists have responded to this charge of narrowness in two ways. The first is to restrict the relevance of the theory to a limited context. Hart himself takes this strategy. He admits that the will theory is satisfactory "only at the level of the lawyer concerned with the working of the 'ordinary' law," and is not adequate to handle individual rights at the level of constitutional law.[23] The second strategy is to try to redeem the incidents in question as rights by finding someone who does have discretion with regards to them, such as a government official who has discretion over whether to prosecute a torturer.[24] Yet even were this search for "choosers" always successful, the result would fit poorly with an ordinary understanding of rights. For here the will theory is still committed to saying that you have no right against being tortured. Rather, the right that you not be tortured would be the district attorney's right, since the district attorney is the person with the discretion.

The limitations of the will theory are also evident in its inability to account for the rights of incompetent (e.g., comatose) adults, and of children.[25] The will theory can acknowledge rights only in those beings competent to exercise powers, which incompetent adults and children are not. Incompetent adults and children therefore cannot on this view have rights.[26] This is certainly a result at variance with ordinary understanding. Few would insist that it is conceptually impossible, for example, for children to have a right against severe abuse.

C   The Interest Theory

The will theory faces serious problems in explaining many rights that most believe there are. Yet where the will theory falters, the interest theory flourishes.[27] The interest theory holds that the single function of rights is to further their holders' interests. More specifically, rights are those incidents whose purpose is to promote the well-being of the rightholder.[28] As MacCormick puts it, "The essential feature of rules which confer rights is that they have as a specific aim the protection or advancement of individual interests or goods."[29]

The interest theory is not committed to the implausible thesis that each right is always in the interest of the rightholder. Some inheritances, for example, are more trouble than they are worth. Rather, the interest theory holds that the function of rights is to promote rightholders' interests in the general case: "To ascribe to all members of a class C a right to treatment T is to presuppose that T is, in all normal circumstances, a good for every member of C."[30]

Since the interest theory turns on the rightholder's interests instead of her choices, it can recognize as rights unwaivable claims such as the claims against enslavement and torture. The interest theory also has no trouble viewing children and incompetent adults as rightholders, since children and incompetent adults have interests that rights can protect. Moreover, the interest theory can accept a wide range of Hohfeldian incidents – such as a claim to another's assistance and the immunity that protects free speech – as promoting the well-being of their holders and so as rights. Finally, the interest theory can acknowledge that individuals may be better off having the power to make choices, and so can embrace many of the rights central to the will theory. The appeal of the interest theory emanates from the wide range of rights that it can endorse, and from the evident fact that having rights can make a life go better.

Yet the interest theory is also inadequate to our ordinary understanding of rights. There are many rights the purpose of which is not to further the well-being of the rightholder, even in the general case. This is clearest with rights that define occupational roles. A judge has a (power) right to sentence criminals, but this right is not designed to benefit the judge. Rather, judges are ascribed this right as part of a system of justice that protects the members of the community. A traffic warden has a (power) right to issue parking tickets; but the point of this right is to improve the lives of motorists, not the life of the warden. Similarly, an army captain may have the (power) right to order units, including his own, into battle; yet the specific aim of the rule that confers this right is not to further the captain's well-being. In each of these cases the right is ascribed in order to benefit parties beside the rightholder. The existence of such role-defining rights establishes that the interest theory is implausibly narrow.[31]

Interest theorists have taken two different paths in response to these kinds of cases. Raz tries to rescue the conceptual connection between rights and interests by reinforcing the interests of rightholders with the interests of others. On Raz's variant of the interest theory the existence of a right turns not on the purpose of the right's ascription, but on the sufficiency of the rightholder's interests in justifying the right's normative impact.[32] Raz's variant faces the same difficulty as faced by the original interest theory. Whatever interest a judge has in exercising her right to impose criminal punishments, for example, it cannot be sufficient to justify the dramatic normative effects of her exercise of this right. Raz's response to this difficulty attempts to boost the strength of the judge's interest in exercising her power by drawing attention to the fact that protecting the judge's interest also protects the interests of the public.[33] Yet this attempt to add the interests of the public to the interest of the judge merely highlights the fact that the judge's interest is in itself insufficient to ground this right. Role-bearers often do not

have interests in their rights sufficient to justify their having those rights. When they do not, they cannot within Raz's own analysis have rights.[34]

Kramer takes the other path of response to these role-defining rights, which is to deny that they are rights at all. A judge has no right to sentence criminals, a traffic warden has no right to issue tickets, an army captain has no right to give orders, and so on. This response reanimates a definitional stipulation found in Hohfeld's original 1913 article that "in the strictest sense" all rights are claims.[35] On this view a judge's power to sentence – because it is a power and not a claim – cannot be a right. This redefinition of "rights" does save the statement that "All rights further the interests of the rightholder," but only by withdrawing this statement from ordinary language. The interest theory so construed becomes valid for "rights" understood as a term within a specially constructed dialect of "strictly speaking." Yet the theory remains incorrect for "rights" as commonly understood.[36]

D   The Any-Incident Theory

The will theory and the interest theory are both inadequate to our understanding of rights, the weakness of each being the strength of the other. The will theory captures rights that give discretion to the rightholder without conferring benefits, but fails to capture rights that confer benefits without giving discretion. The interest theory accepts rights that confer benefits, but rejects rights whose holders do not benefit from holding them. In the most general terms, the will theory accounts better for the incidents on the left side of Figure 7.4, while the interest theory accounts better for the incidents on the right side. Each theory includes rights that the other cannot.

This is all to the advantage of the any-incident theory.[37] The any-incident theory holds that each Hohfeldian incident, and each combination of incidents, is rightly called a right. This theory counts as rights all of the rights identified by both the will and the interest theories. It counts as rights those incidents that confer choices, as well as those incidents that promote interests. The any-incident theory thus acknowledges as rights the judge's power to sentence as well as the child's claim against abuse. Yet the any-incident theory is not the concatenation of the other two theories. It does not say that Hohfeldian incidents are rights just in case they confer choices or just in case they benefit their bearers. The any-incident theory simply says that any Hohfeldian incident or complex of incidents is a right.

The inclusiveness of the any-incident theory brings it closer than the will or the interest theory to an ordinary understanding of rights. However, the any-incident theory is in fact too inclusive. It counts as rights some Hohfeldian incidents that we ordinarily would not.

In order to locate the over-inclusiveness of the any-incident theory, let us review Section I of this article. There we were concerned to show that all assertions of rights could be explicated in terms of the Hohfeldian diagrams. As we investigated different rights, we found that each right could be cashed out in terms of (combinations of) Hohfeldian incidents, and that each had a certain function or set of functions. For example, we found that rights that mark exemptions from duties are single privileges, that rights that entitle the rightholder to protection are claims or immunities, and so on. In all, we found six specific functions that rights can have (exemption, discretion, authorization, protection, provision, and performance) and we mapped these functions onto the different incidents.

The induction was that each right can be identified with one or more of the Hohfeldian incidents, and that each right has one or

more of the six specific functions. Yet we have not asserted, nor is it true, that all Hohfeldian incidents have one of the six specific functions. For example, although all rights that confer an exemption are single privileges, there are single privileges that do not confer an exemption or perform any of the other specific functions. Similarly, although many rights that protect are immunities, there are immunities that do not protect or perform any of the other specific functions. All rights are incidents and have one or more of the six functions, but some incidents have none of the six functions.

The space of incidents that do not perform any of the six functions is where the any-incident theory fails. The any-incident theory says that each incident or combination of incidents is a right, regardless of whether that incident or combination of incidents performs any function at all. The any-incident theory becomes overly inclusive when it counts as rights those Hohfeldian incidents that do not perform any of the six functions we found in Section I. Two examples illustrate this over-inclusiveness.

As Hart noted, not all immunities are regarded as rights.[38] One person has an immunity whenever another person lacks a power to alter his normative situation in some respect. Yet by this definition there exist many immunities that provide no protection. To take one of Hart's examples: your city council lacks the power to award you a pension. By the definition of the immunity, you therefore have an immunity against your city council's awarding you a pension. But it would be odd, Hart said, to hear you say that you have a *right* that your city council not award you a pension. Here we have an incident – an immunity – that does not perform any of the six functions. In particular, this immunity does not provide protection. What is more, this incident does not appear to be a right. Yet the any-incident theory says that all incidents are rights, and so the any-incident theory fails by including this immunity within the class of rights.[39]

We can see the same type of over-inclusiveness in another of Hart's examples, this time concerning the privilege. Each of us has no legal duty to assault other people on the street. We each therefore have a single legal privilege not to assault others on the street. But we would balk at saying that each of us has a legal right not to assault others on the street. The reason we balk is because this single privilege does not exempt us from a general duty. This single privilege does not perform the function that all single privilege-rights perform. The any-incident theory, by allowing incidents like this into the class of rights, allows too much.[40]

E   The Several Functions Theory

The several functions theory subtracts these counterintuitive cases from the any-incident theory. The several functions theory holds that any incident or combination of incidents is a right, but only if it performs one or more of the six functions shown in Figure 7.4. In other words, all (combinations of) incidents are rights so long as they mark exemption, discretion, or authorization, or entitle their holders to protection, provision, or performance. Only those (combinations of) incidents that perform at least one of the six specific functions are rights.

The several functions theory is superior to the any-incident theory in rejecting those incidents that are clearly not rights. Your immunity against your city council granting you a pension does not protect you against harm or paternalism, since being granted a pension would neither harm you nor interfere with your autonomy for your benefit.[41] Your single privilege not to assault others is not an exemption from a general duty to assault others, since there is no such general duty. Therefore according to the several functions theory, neither of these incidents is a right.[42]

The several functions theory is also superior to both the will theory and the interest theory without being simply their concatenation. Like the any-incident theory, the several functions theory counts as rights everything counted as a right by both of the single-function theories. It counts the judge's (discretionary) power to sentence, as well as the child's (protective) claim against abuse. The several functions theory thus resolves the standoff between the will theory and the interest theory by accepting all of the rights that are recognized by each of the procrustean single-function theories.

Moreover, the several functions theory also recognizes rights beyond those recognized by either the will theory or the interest theory. These are rights that neither give the rightholder discretionary power over the duty of another, nor promote the well-being of the rightholder. The discretionary right (paired privilege) of a citizen to restrain an attacker of a third party, and the discretionary right (paired privilege) of a parent to chastise a naughty child are one type of example. A judge's right (single power) to sentence a criminal to a specific term of years under mandatory sentencing laws, and a police officer's exemptive right (single privilege) to detain a suspect that he has been ordered to detain are another sort of example.[43] Since we would without hesitation call the incidents in these examples rights, this is further confirmation that the several functions theory captures our ordinary understanding of rights better than the will theory or the interest theory do.

Figure 7.5 displays the extensional relationships among the four theories of the functions of rights, within the realm of commonly accepted rights.

The several functions theory accepts that there is no one thing that rights do for rightholders. Rights have no fundamental normative purpose in this sense. Rather, rights play a number of different roles in our lives. Some rights give the rightholder discretion

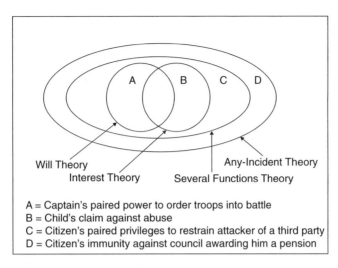

A = Captain's paired power to order troops into battle
B = Child's claim against abuse
C = Citizen's paired privileges to restrain attacker of a third party
D = Citizen's immunity against council awarding him a pension

Figure 7.5 The incidents that are rights according to the four theories of the functions of rights

over others' duties, some rights protect the rightholder from harm, some rights do neither of these things but something else altogether. All rights perform some function, but there is no one function that all rights have. There is no one function that all rights have, as there is no one function that all furniture has, and no one feature that all games have. Rights have all of the functions that they do.[44]

The great advantage of the several functions theory is its fit with our ordinary understanding of rights. It must be emphasized that will and interest theorists cannot evade this point by gesturing to the looseness or non-univocality of rights-talk in ordinary language. Will theorists, interest theorists, and several function theorists can agree that ordinary language will be perfectly tight and univocal so long as speakers understand how assertions of rights map onto the Hohfeldian incidents. This is not the issue. The debate among theorists of the functions of rights would persist even in the Hohfeldian utopia where ordinary language users make no inconsistent assertions about rights.

The issue is the functions of rights. All sides of the debate maintain that the primary standard for settling this dispute is an ordi-

nary understanding of what rights there are and what roles they play in our lives. The final accusation of will and interest theorists against each other has always been that the other side's theory yields counterintuitive results.[45] Or, rather, each side has accused the other of being *more* counterintuitive. Yet each single-function theory yields many more counterintuitive results than the several functions theory yields. Thus the several functions theory is superior when judged against the standard by which the single-function theories judge each other.[46]

The long debate between will and interest theorists has outlasted the plausibility of either of their theories as a conceptual analysis of rights. The explanation for this, I believe, is that the contest between them has become a proxy for a debate between strongly opposed normative commitments. Those theorists whose normative commitments entail that rights should be distributed so as to create equal domains of freedom – mostly Kantians like Steiner – champion the will theory as an analysis of the nature of rights. Their welfarist opponents like Raz, who hold that the point of morality or the law is to further individual well-being, fight for the interest theory. Each side attempts to portray that part of the ordinary concept that is most congruent with their normative theory as the whole concept. Each side is invested in securing victory for its own analysis, because each side is attempting to use its analysis to preempt objections to its preferred normative theory. A reader convinced that the best conceptual analysis of rights does not allow rights for children will be less concerned with a normative theory that offers none. A reader who believes that rights are conceptually tied to the rightholder's interests will be less likely to protest the manhandling of cases where the rightholder's interests do not ground the right.[47]

Any moral or legal theorist is of course free to stipulate what the word "right" means within his theory. Yet stipulation is effortless; it requires no argument, and it is not analysis. As a subject of scholarly inquiry, conceptual analysis has its own integrity. An analysis that is faithful to an ordinary understanding of rights will not reduce the justificatory burden on any normative theory of rights. Instead, such an analysis will partly determine the justificatory burden that a normative theory must discharge. A faithful analysis will enable us to gauge how much of our ordinary understanding of rights is captured by a normative theory's portrayal of rights, and to judge for ourselves whether that normative theory is compelling enough to convince us to give up the rest.[48] A strong normative argument will be able to withstand scrutiny as a normative argument, from the perspective of an unblinkered view of the conceptual terrain.

III   Conclusion

The congruence of the several functions theory with our ordinary understanding of rights makes it preferable to competing theories. Still, one might hope for a fuller account of the several functions of rights. Why, one might ask, are these particular six functions associated with our concept of a right? Why should rights be characterized by all of these six functions, and by only these six? If rights do not all have some single function, why do rights have the functions that they do?

For answers to these questions we would need to turn to history. The concept of a right has been reshaped, fitfully, and by strong social forces, for nearly two thousand years. Rights were extant in ancient law, and contested by Christian scholars of the Middle Ages. Rights were later stretched to define the offices of the burgeoning bureaucratic state. Throughout the modern period rights have been grasped by popular movements attempting to protect or empower the excluded, the exploited and the injured. We in the twenty-first century are the inheritors of a concept that has been pulled and cut by many hands, over many years. This is why, when we use the tools of philosophical analysis to detect the deep structure of our concept of rights, we find an irreducible complexity.[49]

One could hardly count oneself as a theorist if one did not seek a simpler unity – if one did not search for the single logical form, for the single function, that all rights share. The desire for unitary analyses is strong, and for any given concept it cannot be judged a priori whether this desire will be satisfiable. For rights, the desire cannot be satisfied. The standoff between rights theorists in the twentieth century showed that attempts to present some part of the concept of rights as though it were the whole concept will not succeed. Any analysis that cannot imagine the rights of judges and traffic wardens, of the comatose and of children, will not survive outside of the study. Any theory that must retreat to a technical language of "strictly speaking" is not, strictly speaking, a theory of rights. Theorists who try to tie reasoning about rights to a single pillar will bind their readers with ropes of sand.

All rights are Hohfeldian incidents. All Hohfeldian incidents are rights so long as they mark exemption, or discretion, or authorization, or entitle their holders to protection, provision, or performance. Therefore, rights are all those Hohfeldian incidents that perform these several functions.

Notes

1 For the history and current state of the debate between the will and interest theories, see Matthew Kramer, Nigel Simmonds, and Hillel Steiner, *A Debate over Rights* (Oxford: Oxford University Press, 1998), hereafter *DOR*. The description of the debate as a "standoff" is from L. W. Sumner, *The Moral Foundations of Rights* (Oxford: Oxford University Press, 1987), p. 51.

2 The analysis here is not meant to apply directly to epistemic rights (rights to believe, infer, doubt), to affective rights (rights to feel), or to conative rights (rights to want). I proposed some initial contrasts between rights of conduct and these attitudinal rights in Leif Wenar, "Legal Rights and Epistemic Rights," *Analysis* 63 (2003), pp. 142–6. An expanded version of that paper is available on request.

3 Wesley Hohfeld, *Fundamental Legal Conceptions as Applied in Judicial Reasoning* (New Haven: Yale University Press, 1919). Explorations of the Hohfeldian system include Stig Kanger, *New Foundations for Ethical Theory* (Stockholm: Stockholm University Press, 1957); Lars Lindahl, *Position and Change* (Dordrecht: D. Reidel, 1977); and Judith Jarvis Thomson, *The Realm of Rights* (Cambridge, Mass.: Harvard University Press, 1990). The framework presented here is obviously heavily indebted to Hohfeld and his many commentators, yet certain aspects of it are controversial or new. Some examples: (1) It is not assumed that all rights are claims; (2) The incidents are matched with specific functions; (3) For the purposes of this article the tables of jural correlatives and opposites are unnecessary, and the incidents are not here characterized in terms of the tables. Because the current framework contains differences at this level, the Hohfeldian cognoscenti may find it useful to approach the text de novo.

4 Similarly, "A has no Y right to phi" implies "A has a Y duty not to phi." See Wenar, "Legal Rights and Epistemic Rights."

5 "Privilege" is in some ways an unfortunate name for this incident, as it may have distracting connotations of hierarchy (compare "feudal privilege"). It is best regarded as a wholly technical term.

6 It may also be noticed that in asserting a single privilege-right one need neither affirm nor deny that the single privilege involved is also half of a paired privilege. The sheriff's right to break down the door is an exemptive single privilege. In asserting this right, one need take no position on whether the sheriff also has a single privilege not to break down the door. He may, or he may not (e.g., he may have been ordered to break it down). If the sheriff does also have the single privilege not to break down the door, then his two privileges together form a paired privilege-right: he has the right to break down the door at his discretion. But this discretionary right is distinct from the exemptive right originally asserted, and in asserting the exemptive right one need take no stand on whether he also has or lacks the discretionary right.

7 Notice here that B's duty is not simply to perform the action phi. It is a duty that is owed to or directed toward A. Explaining the "direction" of duties is not simple, and I put this issue to one side here. See Gopal Sreenivasan, "A Hybrid Theory of Claim Rights," *Oxford Journal of Legal Studies* 25 (2005).

8 See Sumner, *Moral Foundations*, pp. 27–31; Kramer in *DOR*, p. 20. There are not only "second-order" powers and immunities that range over claims and privileges, but "third-order" powers and immunities that range over second-order incidents, and so on. A complex structure of authority such as a

political constitution can be seen as a structure of incidents layered in this way.

9   The "paired power" described here is in fact a simple representation of a more complex structure of incidents. A paired power represents a paired privilege (not) to exercise a single power. This detail would be important in a full treatment of the incidents; here we simply "push" the paired privilege into the power, making the power into a paired power. Wayne Sumner emphasized the importance of retaining privileges here.

10   Several of these examples are taken from Michael Bayles, *Hart's Legal Philosophy* (Dordrecht: Kluwer, 1992), p. 164.

11   Carl Wellman, *A Theory of Rights* (Totowa, NJ: Rowman and Allanheld, 1985), pp. 70–1.

12   Carl Wellman posited in 1985 that every right consists of a "core" incident with "associated elements" surrounding it. This approach to understanding rights has proved fruitful (see his *Real Rights* [Oxford: Oxford University Press, 1995] and *An Approach to Rights* [Dodrecht: Kluwer, 1997]), and I believe its usefulness could be amplified by the method for representing rights in this article. I do not, however, here commit to Wellman's hypothesis. It should also be noted that the diagrams are not intended to capture all of the complexities of the rights that are displayed, for many of the rights have qualifications not here shown. For example, the legal privilege to move one's body does not contain the privilege to make "fighting words" gestures to others.

13   There are apparent exceptions to this rule because a few English verbs falsely take the active voice. For example, the verb "to inherit" appears active; yet one can inherit without performing any action. Sentences with falsely active verbs should be rephrased to bring out the true agent. Thus "The infant has a right to inherit the estate" should be read "The infant has a right that the executor pass the estate to him." The incident marked by falsely active verbs is ordinarily a claim, not a privilege or power.

14   Wellman argues (*A Theory of Rights*, pp. 75–9) that there are rights whose "core" is not one of the four incidents above, but is rather

a "liability" (A has a liability when A is on the "receiving end" of B's power). His examples are the right to be given an inheritance, and the right to be married. Yet these rights are better explained in terms of the four incidents. The right to be given an inheritance is a claim against the executor of the will to transfer the relevant funds. The right to be married is similar: a power jointly held by two people to create in themselves a claim against the relevant authority that this authority exercise its power to join the couple in marriage.

15   Some complex rights assertions combine simpler rights assertions of both of these forms. For example, "I have a right to walk on the bike path without being run over" resolves into "I have a right to walk on the bike path" and "I have a right that others not run me over while I am walking on the bike path." Jennifer Saul suggested this example.

16   "Under what basic headings should we classify the right to change one's name, the right of private security guards to make arrests, the exclusive right to decide who publishes (copyright), stock-purchase rights, the right to recover money damages for defamation, tenants' and landlords' rights, the right to smoke the dried leaves of some (but not all) plants, and the right to judicial review of the rulings of some administrative agencies? Are there purposes for which it is helpful to sort into two basic groupings – say, the positive and the negative – the right of legislative initiative, the right not to be denied a job because of sexual preference, the right to return to a job after taking unpaid maternity leave, the right to interstate travel, freedom of testation, and the right to inform authorities of a violation of the law? And what about hunting and fishing rights, the right to keep and bear arms, a landowner's right to abate nuisances upon his land, mineral rights, the right to present testimony about the victim of a crime in order to influence the sentencing of a perpetrator, pension rights, the right to give to charity tax-free, the right to recover a debt, the right to run for office, the right to view obscene materials at home?" Stephen Holmes

and Cass Sunstein, *The Costs of Rights* (New York: W.W. Norton, 1999), pp. 38–9.

We can take three of these rights as samples for analysis. The "core" of the right to give to charity tax-free is a paired power to transfer funds to a charity, the positive power of which is unqualified by the requirement that some percentage of all funds transferred pass to the government. The right not to be denied a job because of sexual preference is a claim that employers not take sexual preference into account when making employment decisions. The right to view obscene materials at home is a paired privilege to view obscene materials at home, plus a claim against the police interfering with one's doing so.

17 Leif Wenar, "The Meanings of Freedom," in *Contemporary Debates in Social Philosophy*, ed. Laurence Thomas (Oxford: Blackwell, 2005).

18 Jonathan Riley suggested the label "single-function theory."

19 See the historical sources cited in n. 49, especially the works by Tuck, Tierney, Brett, and Simmonds.

20 H. L. A. Hart, *Essays on Bentham* (Oxford: Oxford University Press, 1982), p. 183. Besides Hart, influential advocates of a choice-based approach to rights include Savigny, Kelsen, Wellman, and Steiner.

21 Hart, *Essays* pp., 183–4; cf. Wellman, *A Theory of Rights*, p. 199.

22 It is a peculiarity of the will theory that it regards one's trivial claims (such as your waivable claim not to have your left foot touched with a feather) as one's rights, while not being able to acknowledge one's weighty claims (such as your unwaivable claim against being tortured) as one's rights. See Neil MacCormick, "Rights in Legislation," in *Law, Morality and Society: Essays in Honour of H. L. A. Hart*, ed. P. M. S. Hacker and Joseph Raz (Oxford: Oxford University Press, 1977), pp. 189–209, 197.

23 Hart, *Essays*, pp. 185–6, 192–3.

24 Steiner in *DOR*, pp. 248–56.

25 Neil MacCormick, *Legal Right and Social Democracy* (Oxford: Oxford University Press, 1982), pp. 154–66.

26 Nor can animals. Hart saw it as a "substantial merit" of the will theory that it cannot assign rights to animals, because animals "are not spoken or thought of as having rights" (Hart, *Essays*, p. 185). Since animals are now often spoken and thought of as having rights, this feature of the will theory may now appear less meritorious. Hart did in a footnote allow that children can have rights, which rights are exercised by their representatives, e.g., parents (Hart, p. 184). Yet he was only able to reach this position by suppressing the central will theory thesis that a rightholder is sovereign over the duty of another.

27 Bentham gave the first modern statement of the interest theory; other champions include Ihering, Austin, Lyons, Raz, MacCormick and Kramer. For an exceptionally clear exposition of the interest theory, see Kramer's essay in *DOR*. I will here use both "interest" and "well-being" to indicate the interest theorist's central concept of what is good for a being. This concept can be construed broadly enough to include a person's agency interests in having and making choices over a range of options.

28 A more exact statement of the interest theory would be necessary to overcome the long-standing objection of third-party beneficiaries. Simmonds gives a good summary of the problem in *DOR*, pp. 197–8; for the classic objection and reply see Hart, *Essays*, pp. 180–1; David Lyons, *Rights, Welfare and Mill's Moral Theory* (Oxford: Oxford University Press, 1994), pp. 36–46. For an adaptation of Bentham's response to the objection see Kramer, *DOR*, pp. 81ff. Kramer's endorsement of "Bentham's test" produces an overly expansive version of the interest theory which I do not discuss here.

29 MacCormick, "Rights in Legislation," p. 192.

30 Neil MacCormick, "Children's Rights: A Test-Case for Theories of Rights," *Archiv für Rechts und Sozialphilosophie* 62 (1976): 311; see Joseph Raz, *The Morality of Freedom* (Oxford: Oxford University Press, 1986), p. 180.

31 See Wellman, *A Theory of Rights*, pp. 25–6; Peter Jones, *Rights* (New York: St. Martin's, 1994), pp. 31–2.

32 Raz, *Morality of Freedom*. ch. 7.

33 Joseph Raz, *Ethics in the Public Domain* (Oxford: Oxford University Press, 1994), pp. 149–51, 274–5.

34 To take another case, Raz describes a journalist's right to free speech as a function of the interests of the journalist's audience. Yet as Kamm observes, "If the satisfaction of the interests of others is the reason why the journalist gets a right to have his interest protected, his interest is *not sufficient* to give rise to the duty of non-interference with his speech" (Frances Kamm, "Rights," *Oxford handbook of Jurisprudence and Philosophy of Law* [Oxford: Oxford University Press, 2002], pp. 476–513, 485).

35 Hohfeld, *Fundamental Legal Conceptions*, p. 36. Raz does not use the Hohfeldian terminology, yet his characterization of rights implies that he also holds that, in effect, all rights are claims. So Raz is subject to both criticisms here. The criticism of his view in the previous paragraph would go through even were he to broaden his characterization to include other incidents as well.

36 Kramer, *DOR*, pp. 9–14, 93. It is important to note that when interest theorists and will theorists attempt to validate their theses by resorting to a technical discourse, they do not draw a line between legal discourse and lay discourse. Rather, they put lawyers and judges on the side of laypeople in using the "loose" ordinary language of rights. It is only philosophers of law who speak a "strict" dialect of rights. Of course the two types of theorists disagree on which "strict" dialect philosophers of law should speak. So on Kramer's strict philosophical usage judges would not have the right to sentence criminals, while on Wellman's strict philosophical usage infants would not have a right against abuse (Wellman, *A Theory of Rights*, p. 136). Yet, as emphasized above, ordinary language is not in fact loose in this way (although some people's understanding of it may be). The only reason to resort to a "strict" dialect is to rescue one of the single-function theories from counterexamples. I discuss this point at greater length in Leif Wenar, "The Functions of Rights," in *Law: Metaphysics, Meaning, and*

Objectivity, ed. Enrique Villanueva [New York: Rodopi].

37 To my knowledge the any-incident theory has not been proposed as an alternative to the will and interest theories, although something like it is suggested in Thomson, *The Realm of Rights.*

38 Hart, *Essays*, pp. 191–2; see also Lyons, *Rights, Welfare*, p. 11; Simmonds in *DOR*, pp. 153–4.

39 See also Kramer, "Getting Rights Right," in *Rights, Wrongs, and Responsibilities,* ed. Matthew Kramer (London: Macmillan, 2001), pp. 28–95, pp. 78–89. A will theorist might object to the definition of the immunity used in this article, and so to the construction of this example. In this article B has an immunity whenever A lacks a power to alter B's incidents. However, a will theorist might prefer to locate the immunity in the agency who has the power to nullify a putative alteration of B's incidents by A. Such a theorist might say in the pension example that it is not you but rather the Home Secretary who has the immunity against your being awarded a pension, since it is the Home Secretary who could nullify such an award. Yet even with the immunity so recharacterized Hart's point is valid. Even if the Home Secretary is said to have an immunity against your council awarding you a pension, it would be odd to say that he has a right that your council not do so. Hillel Steiner (in *DOR*) offered the proposed redefinition of the immunity.

40 Showing that incidents that lack the several functions are not rights also solves a riddle about powers that has vexed a number of authors. The law states that you have the ability – and so, by definition, that you have the power – to make yourself liable to prosecution by breaking the law. Yet of course the law does not give you the right to do anything by breaking the law. (See Kramer in *DOR*, p. 104 and the citations there.) The solution lies in seeing that the incident in question is again an incident lacking any of the functions of rights. The law does not give you the *authority* to do anything by breaking the law. So

although the law acknowledges that you have a legal power, it does not vest you with any law-breaking rights.

41 This is true whether we construe being harmed as being made worse off than one was, than one otherwise would be, or than one should (morally, legally, customarily) be; or whether "harm" is tied to violation of an agent's sovereignty. The several functions theory does not itself commit to any particular interpretation of "harm." Rather, the rights that the theory will count as protective will vary along with the variations in the definition of this term. As for paternalism, it might be thought that there are possible circumstances in which being granted a pension by one's city council would constitute a paternalistic interference with one's autonomy. For example, Simmonds imagines a case in which receiving a pension would threaten one's reputation for having a devil-may-care attitude (*DOR*, p. 154). Reflection on such possibilities lends further support to the several functions theory, since as Simmonds acknowledges, in such circumstances it becomes plausible to describe the immunity in question as a right. Gerald Gaus pointed out the importance of paternalism in the function of the claim.

42 It might be argued that an interest theory could explain why rights have the several function that they do, by showing how all of the functions serve interests in some way. Thus it might be argued that the immunity against being awarded a pension is not a right because it does not protect the rightholder's interests; and the privilege not to assault others is not a right because it does not exempt its bearer from a duty in a way that furthers the rightholder's interests. This proposal faces the threshold objection that a will theorist can make exactly parallel arguments (e.g., file immunity is not a right because it does not protect the agent's sovereignty). The more serious difficulty for the proposal, however, is that it does not overcome the counterexamples to the interest theory arising from role-related rights (as above, the judge's power to sentence is not grounded in the interests of the judge). A supplementary proposal could be advanced to attempt to overcome those counterexamples, this time expanding the interest theory to include as rights all those incidents that serve not just the rightholder's interests but anyone's interests. On this expanded interest theory, the judge would have a right because his power to sentence authorizes him in a way that serves the interests of the community. However, this proposed expansion would inflate the interest theory past the bursting point. For almost every incident, including the immunity against being awarded a pension and the privilege not to assault passersby, serves some interest or other. The interest theory retains it shape only when defined by the interests of the rightholder; removing this definitional element makes it swell toward the any-incident theory. The Editors of *Philosophy & Public Affairs* helped to clarify these points.

43 These sorts of examples are discussed in Hart, *Essays*, pp. 182–3; Wellman, *A Theory of Rights*, pp. 64–8.

44 To affirm that rights have only six basic functions is not to assert that rights can further only six values. The six functions are basic because they obtain whenever an incident is a right; but rights may, in performing their basic functions, further any number of values. For instance, a right that authorizes farmers to sell their land may increase productive efficiency; and a right that authorizes a minority group to vote may promote social equality. Indeed the six basic functions can themselves be seen as values, and these values may occasionally be furthered cross-categorically when rights perform their basic functions. The legal right against self-incrimination illustrates this possibility. The single privilege-right against self-incrimination exempts its bearer from the general duty to testify, and in so doing it protects its bearer from a requirement of self-harm. All single privilege-rights exempt; this privilege-right in exempting its bearer also protects its bearer.

45 A representative sample of passages: Steiner charges that the interest theory "places con-

siderable strain on our ordinary understanding of rights" (*DOR*, p. 287). MacCormick, by contrast, wonders who could accept the will theory, given that it "does such violence to common understanding" ("Rights in Legislation," p. 197). Kramer is even more severe with the will theory, "Many people would shrink from a theory which defines 'right' in a way that commits the proponents of the theory to the view that children and mentally infirm people have no rights at all. Even when stripped of its ghastliness by being carefully explained, such a view tends to sound outlandish when stated" (*DOR*, p. 69).

46   "Theories of rights don't come cheap. Buying either of them (the will theory or the interest theory) involves paying some price in the currency of counterintuitiveness. Nor, I should add, has this centuries-long debate about the nature of rights ever revealed any distinct third theory that even approaches their levels of generality, let alone promises to undercut their prices" (Steiner, *DOR*, p. 298). The several functions theory is this third theory.

47   As Raz himself puts it (*Morality of Freedom*, p. 16), "Moral and political philosophy has for long embraced the literary device (not always clearly recognized as such) of presenting substantive arguments in the guise of conceptual explorations," I discuss this theme at greater length in "The Functions of Rights."

48   Following are two examples – one classic, one contemporary – of how rights have been portrayed by normative theorists: "A right is a power of which the exercise by the individual or by some body of men is recognized by society either as itself directly essential to a common good or as conferred by an authority of which the maintenance is recognized as so essential" (Thomas Hill Green, *Lectures on the Principles* of *Political Obligation* [Cambridge: Cambridge University Press, 1986], p. 103); "In my view, rights are constraints on discretion to act that we believe to be important means for avoiding morally unacceptable consequences" (T. M. Scanlon, *The Difficulty of Tolerance* [Cambridge: Cambridge University Press, 2003], p. 151).

49   For perspectives on this history up to Hobbes, see Richard Sorabji, *Animal Minds and Human Morals* (London: Duckworth, 1993), pp. 50–57; Fred Miller, *Nature, Justice, and Rights in Aristotle's Politics* (Oxford: Oxford University Press, 1995), pp. 87–193; Barry Nicholas, *An Introduction to Roman Law* (Oxford: Oxford University Press, 1962), pp. 19–25, 98–405; Anthony Honoré, *Ulpian*, 2nd edn. (Oxford: Oxford University Press, 2002), pp. 84–93; Richard Tuck, *Natural Rights Theories* (Cambridge: Cambridge University Press, 1976); Brian Tierney, *The Idea of Natural Rights* (Atlanta: Scholars Press, 1997); Annabel Brett, *Liberty, Right, and Nature* (Cambridge: Cambridge University Press, 1997). See also Simmonds's reflections on the historical development of the modern jurisprudence of rights in *DOR*, pp. 113–232.

Chapter 8

Human Rights as a
Common Concern*
Charles R. Beitz

More than fifty years have passed since the UN General Assembly adopted the Universal Declaration of Human Rights, and in that time the doctrine of human rights has come to play a distinctive and in some respects an unexpected role in international life. This is primarily the role of a moral touchstone – a standard of assessment and criticism for domestic institutions, a standard of aspiration for their reform, and increasingly a standard of evaluation for the policies and practices of international economic and political organizations. This role is carried out in a variety of ways. Perhaps the most visible is the increasing willingness to regard concern about human rights violations as an acceptable justification for various kinds of international intervention, ranging from diplomatic and economic sanctions to military action, in the domestic affairs of states.

But coercive intervention in any form is exceptional, and the political functions of human rights usually are considerably less dramatic. For example, a government's human rights record may determine eligibility for development assistance programs, or human rights conditions may be attached to

internationally sponsored financial adjustment measures. The likely effect on satisfaction of human rights may function as a standard of evaluation for the policies of international financial and trade institutions. In the United States, legislation requires periodic reporting by the government regarding human rights practices in other countries and makes eligibility for certain forms of preferential treatment in US foreign policy dependent on satisfaction of minimum human rights standards. In various parts of the world, most notably in Europe, regional codes have been adopted, and there is a developing capacity for adjudication and something like enforcement (even the European Court of Human Rights' capacity to hold governments accountable lacks the machinery of coercion typically associated with adjudication within the state).[1]

The public role of human rights also has been important – more so perhaps than generally recognized in the United States – beyond the sphere of intergovernmental relations. Human rights have served as bases for standard setting, monitoring, reporting, and advocacy by nongovernmental organizations at both the domestic and the international levels of world politics (Best 1995; Korey 1998). To whatever extent

* From *American Political Science Review* 95:2 (2001), pp. 269–82.

contemporary international political life can be said to have a "sense of justice," its language is the language of human rights.

I do not mean to overstate the case. Notwithstanding the hopes of its authors, the Universal Declaration does not function today as an "international bill of rights." The international capacity to enforce the requirements of human rights law on states is at best embryonic. Outside Europe, most individual victims of human rights abuses have no effective appeal beyond their domestic courts, if there. And even in countries within the global "human rights culture" there is great variation in the degree to which internationally recognized human rights are embedded in domestic legal systems.[2] The juridical role of human rights is both limited and uneven. But none of this shows that the national foreign policy measures, international institutions, and nongovernmental organizations dedicated to the advancement of human rights are politically inconsequential. In fact, the global human rights regime is almost certainly more influential today than at any time since World War II.[3]

This fact recalls a longstanding worry about the doctrine of international human rights, expressed variously in terms of its alleged partiality or parochialism. In practice, the worry arises as an objection to external measures that are intended to induce a government to comply with the doctrine's requirements. Such measures by another government or an external organization are sometimes said to constitute the imposition of foreign values upon a culture whose history and conventional moral beliefs do not support them – in the extreme case, a kind of postcolonial imperialism.

There is a reflection of this worry at the theoretical level in a tension between two conceptions of human rights that can be found in philosophical thought. According to one conception, human rights represent the common element in a range of views about social justice or political legitimacy found among the world's cultures. A variant of this position, which is more permissive as to what might be counted as a human right but is motivated by a similar idea, regards human rights as political standards that would be reasonable to accept regardless of one's (culturally influenced) views about social justice or political legitimacy. This notion might be expressed by saying that human rights strive to be nonpartisan, nonparochial, or neutral among conflicting political cultures and ideologies.[4] I shall call this the nonpartisan or restricted conception of human rights.

The other conception regards human rights as distinctive of a particular view or family of views about social justice or political legitimacy. Although a list of human rights might not be a complete description of the requirements of social justice for a society, on this conception it would be more than the common element found among, or acceptable to, otherwise divergent views of social justice. That is, human rights identify conditions that society's institutions should meet if we are to consider them legitimate. But because there is no general reason to believe that these conditions are included in all the views about social justice or political legitimacy that exist in the world – or even among those that have achieved widespread acceptance in individual societies – there is no claim that human rights are nonpartisan. On this view, in contrast to the first, the advocate of human rights takes a stand on controverted questions of political theory. I call this the liberal or full conception of human rights.[5]

Many people will think that the restricted conception is the more plausible because it seems to embody a tolerance of culturally embedded moral differences that is missing from the liberal view. But there is something paradoxical about this thought. Once we begin to describe evaluative standards for social and political institutions, it is hard to explain why we should stop short of a full description of these requirements as we see them. Of course, any such standards should be appropriate for the empirical circumstances in which they are supposed to apply, and it is important to add that this will leave some room for variation. But the intent would still be to state conditions for the legitimacy of institutions. If this is the intent, then why should we stop short of a full, liberal conception of human rights? And what would be the principle of distinction between the full and the restricted conceptions?

My purpose here is to explore the thinking that might lead someone to advocate a nonpartisan or restricted view of human rights. More precisely, I shall take up one aspect of this subject: Does the nonpartisanship, nonparochialism, or neutrality of a set of rights, in itself, provide a reason to treat these rights, as opposed to a more extensive set like that found in international doctrine, as having a special status in international affairs? In putting the question this way, I mean to distinguish considerations of ideological and cultural pluralism from various other kinds of reasons for giving some political aims priority over others – for example, reasons of urgency, efficiency, and institutional competence. These other reasons are obviously important and may often prove decisive in establishing priorities for political action, but they are also more easily understood, so for now I lay them aside. I will conclude – tentatively, because I cannot give the view an affirmative defense here – that considerations of ideological and cultural pluralism need not, in themselves, limit the scope of a plausible doctrine of international human rights, although they may have important bearing on reasoning about the connection between human rights and political action.

International Human Rights as Partisan Standards

To place the theoretical question in its political context, I begin with some summary remarks about the history and content of the doctrine of human rights as we find it in international law and practice.

Although the contemporary international doctrine of human rights has many antecedents, both philosophical and political, it is principally a legacy of World War II. It arose, on the one hand, from the statement of allied war aims in the Atlantic Charter (1941) and, on the other, from persistent pressure brought by individuals and groups outside government for a declaration of political principles for the postwar world. The Preamble to the United Nations Charter (adopted in 1946) affirms "faith in fundamental human rights," and Article 1 commits the organization to encourage respect for "human rights and for fundamental freedoms for all." (By contrast, there was no mention of human rights or any analogous idea in the Covenant of the League of Nations [Lauren 1998, chaps. 5–6].) The charter does not give content to the idea of human rights and fundamental freedoms, however. For that one must refer to the Universal Declaration (1948) and two international covenants, one on civil and political rights and the other on economic, social, and cultural rights (both 1966). It bears remembering that the declaration is just that, a declaration of the General Assembly without the force of law, whereas the covenants are treaties to which national governments have acceded. Together these documents, which often are referred to collectively (and, as I suggested earlier, misleadingly) as the International Bill of Rights, constitute an authoritative catalog of internationally recognized human rights.

There are various ways to classify the rights enumerated in these documents. For our purposes it is useful to think of internationally recognized human rights as falling roughly into five categories, although it is less important to agree about categories than to appreciate the scope and detail of the enumerated rights.

1 Rights of the person refer to life, liberty, and security of the person; privacy and freedom of movement; ownership of property; freedom of thought, conscience, and religion, including freedom of religious teaching and practice "in public and private"; and prohibition of slavery, torture, and cruel or degrading punishment.
2 Rights associated with the rule of law include equal recognition before the law and equal protection of the law; effective legal remedy for violation of legal rights; impartial hearing and trial; presumption of innocence; and prohibition of arbitrary arrest.
3 Political rights encompass freedom of expression, assembly, and association; the right to take part in government; and periodic and genuine elections by universal and equal suffrage.
4 Economic and social rights refer to an adequate standard of living; free choice of employment; protection against unemployment; "just and favorable remuneration"; the right to join trade unions; "reasonable limitation of working hours"; free elementary education; social security; and the "highest attainable standard of physical and mental health."
5 Rights of communities include self-determination and protection of minority cultures.

I note, but shall not discuss, that other international agreements have elaborated and enlarged the scope of human rights in the areas of genocide, slavery and forced labor, racial discrimination, apartheid, discrimination against women, and the rights of children.[6]

There has been a longstanding dispute in official international discourse about human rights doctrine on two major points: whether the international community should recognize any priorities, either moral or pragmatic, among categories of rights (particularly between civil and political as against economic and social rights) and whether human rights doctrine should take note of cultural differences in a way that would make the content of a person's human rights depend upon features of that person's culture. The last major international conference on human rights, conducted in Vienna in 1993, considered these issues at length. The final act of the conference declined to set priorities among categories, holding that "all human rights are universal, indivisible and interdependent and interrelated." Although it recognized that "the significance of national and regional particularities . . . must be borne in mind," it declared that "it is the duty of States, regardless of their political, economic and cultural systems, to promote and protect all human rights and fundamental freedoms" (United Nations 1993, sec. I.5).

Human rights are sometimes thought to set a minimal standard, but it is not obvious what this can mean. The rights of the declaration and the two covenants, taken in their entirety, include requirements that bear on nearly every significant dimension of a society's basic institutional structure, ranging from protections against the misuse of state power to requirements concerning the political process, welfare policy, and the organization of the economy. In scope and detail, international human rights are not more minimal than, say, the requirements of Rawls's principles of social justice. And those principles are not minimal in any very interesting sense.

Still, one can acknowledge the scope and detail of internationally recognized human rights without giving up the idea that they are or should aspire to be neutral or nonparochial standards. So it may be useful to recall, briefly and without critical comment, some recent instances in which it has been said that human rights are not neutral because they conflict with practices endorsed by one or another of the world's major conventional moralities. All of these are familiar in the human rights literature.

One example is the dispute about "Asian values." In the last decade some East Asian political leaders (e.g., Lee Kwan Yew of Singapore and Mahathir Mohamad of Malaysia) argued that some of the political and civil rights found in the international doctrine – mainly freedom of expression and political participation – are incompatible with traditional Asian political beliefs, which value social harmony over public dispute and the collective pursuit of shared interests over the individual pursuit of private interest. The civil and political rights of the declaration were distinctively "Western" values. For this reason, it was said, international pressure for domestic political reform (exerted, e.g., by means of the attachment of political conditions to international financial arrangements) was inappropriate (Kausikan 1993).

Or consider the question of the subordination of women in traditional Islamic doctrine, elements of which are carried over into some authoritative modern interpretations. There is, for example, no presumption of equal treatment or equal protection of law, no protection against forced marriage, and either required or permitted forms of gender discrimination (e.g., mandatory veiling and sexual seclusion and segregation). To the extent that these elements are embodied in the public law and legally sanctioned practices of Islamic states, such as Iran and Pakistan (or for that matter Saudi Arabia), there is a clear conflict with the requirements of international human rights doctrine, and

pressure to conform to these requirements will be regarded as partisan.[7]

Finally, there is the much discussed matter of female genital mutilation (FGM), still practiced ritualistically in Sahelian Africa on as many as two million girls, at or before puberty, each year. FGM, which can take several forms, is sustained by cultural acceptance rather than the force of law, so it does not obviously represent a case of a human rights violation by the state. Yet, where it occurs, FGM is not an aberration; it is entrenched in local cultures and permitted or required by local moral codes. And it is subject to intervention, if not by the state, then by nongovernmental agencies that claim to be acting to defend the human rights of the women affected. There is controversy about the seriousness of the harms brought about by FGM in comparison with various practices found in Western cultures, but whatever one's view about that, it would be hard to argue that interference to curtail FGM constitutes the application of a culturally neutral standard.[8]

In each of these cases it has been said that the local moralities that permit or require practices inconsistent with international human rights are sufficiently complex to allow for an internal critique of the offending practices.[9] This is true and important, but it does not diminish the impression that human rights operate in all three settings in a nonneutral way. Indeed, the existence of disagreements internal to a culture, combined with the fact that the weight of human rights seems usually to favor the modernizing, cosmopolitan side of the disagreement, only strengthens the view of international human rights as a partisan rather than a neutral concern. Jack Donnelly (1999: 84) has written that internationally recognized human rights "set out as a hegemonic political model something very much like the liberal democratic welfare state of western Europe." No doubt this overstates the case, at least insofar as it suggests there is an unambiguous "liberal" position about the full range of the subject matter of international human rights (there is, e.g., no single liberal view about self-determination or the rights of minority cultures). But Donnelly is correct that the declaration and covenants cannot really be regarded as setting forth a culturally or politically ecumenical or syncretistic doctrine.

Neutrality and Paternalism

The evident partisanship of international human rights doctrine has led some philosophers to suggest that we should distinguish between the full set of values recognized as human rights in international law and a restricted subset variously referred to as "basic rights" (Shue 1996)[10] or "human rights proper" (Rawls 1999a: 80, n. 23). For expository purposes I shall call the restricted subset – whatever its contents turn out to be – "genuine" human rights. The fact that the rights in the subset could be regarded as nonpartisan, or ideologically or culturally neutral, might be seen as qualifying them to play a special role in foreign policy for which international human rights generally are not suited.

Among those who believe there are grounds for restricting genuine human rights to some sort of nonparochial or neutral core, it is not always clear what these grounds are or why we should care about them. In this section and the next, I discuss these questions in connection with each of two distinct interpretations of neutrality or nonparochialism.

Consider first an approach suggested by some remarks of Michael Walzer (although he does not make the connection with human rights explicit), who distinguishes between "thin" and "thick" moralities. Walzer (1994: 9–10) speculates that a comparison of the moral codes found in various societies might produce "a set of standards to which all societies can be held – negative injunctions, most likely, rules against murder, deceit, torture, oppression, and tyranny." These standards would constitute "the moral minimum," not a complete moral code but, rather, "reiterated features of particular thick or maximal moralities." Someone influenced by such a distinction might regard human rights as part of the "minimum" or "thin" morality, nonparochial in that they are part of a core of requirements shared by all conventional or "thick" moralities – the common elements in a global moral pluralism. Thus, for example, R. J. Vincent (1986: 48–9) writes of a "core of basic rights that is common to all cultures despite their apparently divergent theories," which he describes as a "lowest common denominator."[11]

As Walzer's speculation suggests, this conception of nonparochialism, if treated as a constraint on what we should count as genuine human rights, would yield a relatively short list. Among others, rights requiring democratic political forms, religious toleration, legal equality for women, and free choice of a marriage partner would certainly be excluded. Other rights might be excluded if they were understood to generate certain kinds of duties; if, for example, the right to a high standard of physical and mental health were thought to imply that society has an obligation to ensure the accessibility of health care for all, then the existence of disagreement about distributive responsibilities outside of families or local communities would presumably exclude this right as well.[12]

The narrowness of the resulting conception might encourage us to think that this interpretation of neutrality relies excessively on the metaphor of a "core" of rights common to the world's main conventional moralities. Perhaps this is too restrictive; after all, the idea of a right is itself culturally specific. So one might shift to a more elaborate conception that sees human rights as falling within an "overlapping consensus" of political moralities.[13] On such a view, nonparochial human rights would not necessarily be part of a common core in the sense of being recognized by all conventional moralities; instead, they would be rights that could be accepted by a reasonable person consistently with acceptance of any of the main conceptions of political and economic justice in the world. The idea here is that human rights should be the objects of a possible agreement among the world's political cultures; they are norms for the conduct of governments and international organizations that anyone who belongs to one of these cultures can accept without renouncing other important political principles.[14] Such a view would be narrow in comparison with the present international doctrine, but presumably it would be broader than the "common core": A value could count as a genuine human right even if it were not explicitly present in every culture, just in case members of each culture could reasonably accept it as consistent with their culture's moral conventions.

There are other forms of this basic idea, but rather than proliferate interpretations I shall turn instead to the question why we should care about a doctrine of human rights limited to either a common core or an overlapping consensus. In answering this question, we should remember that one function of human rights in international politics is to justify external interference in a society aimed at changing some aspect of the society's internal life. Such interference might aim, for example, to stop genocide or forceful political repression, to protect the innocent against civil violence when local authorities are unwilling or unable to do so, to restore a democratic government removed by force of arms, or to deliver humanitarian assistance to those imperiled by natural disaster or political collapse.

I believe the reason many people aspire to a nonparochial or culturally neutral doctrine of human rights is connected to this interference-justifying role. Those who object to interference to protect human rights may claim that the interference is unjustifiably paternalistic. It would be paternalistic in that it limits liberty on the grounds that those whose liberty is limited (the "subjects") will be better off as a result of the interference, and it would be unjustified either because the subjects are capable of making choices for themselves or because the intervenor judges "better off" by standards the subjects have no reason to accept. A doctrine of human rights that satisfies a neutrality constraint might seem to offer the best prospect of meeting the antipaternalism objection because, if the human rights at stake are neutral in an appropriate way, then it can be replied that the aims of interference are ones that its subjects themselves would accept if they were in a position to bring their own moral beliefs to bear on the matter at hand.

The antipaternalism objection, as interpreted above, faces the following problem. When we are concerned about a violation of human rights in another society, we are usually not confronted with a situation in which people are unanimous in endorsing standards of conduct that justify the behavior of concern to us.[15] The picture of a "we" who believe in human rights and a "they" who do not is badly misleading. Among the "they" are oppressors and victims, and usually there is little reason to believe that the victims all share the values that the oppressors think justify their conduct. What this shows is that the perception of interference to defend human rights as a form of paternalism can be a misapprehension. Paternalism is an intervention in a person's self-regarding choices on the grounds that the intervention is good for that person. The individual whose liberty is interfered with is the same person as the one whose good the interference is intended to advance. In typical cases of interference based on human rights, however, some people's liberties are infringed in order to protect the human rights of others. The justification appropriately appeals not to paternalistic considerations but to the desirability of preventing a harm or securing a benefit for someone threatened by another agent's wrongful actions or omissions. (Although not always: Interference to persuade a young girl not to undergo an FGM procedure is genuinely paternalistic, but noncoercive interference – such as providing information and so respecting the girl's capacity for choice – affords a different defense.) That this should not be immediately obvious is evidence of the continuing grip of the analogy of person and state, which tempts us to treat the state as if it had the moral attributes of an individual rather than as an aggregate of separate persons with wills and interests of their own.

In most cases, then, what I have called the antipaternalism objection, if it pertains at all, must be interpreted elliptically. It must hold that, for purposes of justifying external interference in a society, we should base our judgment of what constitutes harm or benefit to a member of that society on standards of value that belong to the conventional morality of the society, even if we have reason to believe that those on whose behalf the interference occurs would reject these values in their own cases. We might call this the principle of cultural deference.

In itself this is not necessarily a form of moral relativism, since it does not deny that sound cross-cultural moral judgments are possible. Nevertheless, taken as a general principle of practical reasoning, it is a strange, even a bizarre, view, for it allows the content of the doctrine of genuine human rights to be determined by the array of political moralities or conceptions of justice to be found in the world. Suppose a society with a racist political culture approves of the forced sterilization of a despised minority race as a means of population control. If we accept the principle of deference, we are forced to delete the right against genocide from the catalog of genuine human rights, because it is neither part of nor consistent with the racist conception. But surely we would resist doing so.

Someone might think that cases like that of a genocidal society are only theoretical possibilities, that no society would for long support such a horrible morality. Perhaps, over time, one expects a "normal distribution" of conventional moralities, each with a distinctive structure and content, but all converging on a substantial common core. This seems to me demonstrably too optimistic, but even if one regards the genocide case simply as a thought experiment, reflection about it suggests that the ground of our belief that, for example, genocide is a great wrong has to do not with the fact that other people agree it is so, but with the nature and consequences of genocide itself (compare Scanlon 1998: 337–8).[16]

Whether a standard should be accepted as a ground of action, and a fortiori as a ground of international action, does not turn on whether the standard is a part of, or implied by, existing conventional moralities. Actual agreement is too strong a condition to impose on any critical standard, and I believe it misrepresents the motivating idea of human rights. To say that human rights are "universal" is not to claim that they are necessarily either accepted by or acceptable to everyone, given their other political and ethical beliefs. Human rights are supposed to be universal in the sense that they apply to or may be claimed by everyone. To hold, also, that a substantive doctrine of human rights should be consistent with the moral beliefs and values found among the world's conventional moralities is to say something both more and different, and potentially subversive, of the doctrine's critical aims.

Decency and Minimal Legitimacy

I shall turn now to a different reason for limiting genuine human rights to a nonparochial core (and therefore a different idea of the way the core can be nonparochial). The basic idea is that we can distinguish between minimal and full legitimacy, with human rights serving as necessary conditions of minimal legitimacy. A minimally legitimate regime is one that merits respect as a cooperating member of international society, even if it falls short of being (what we would recognize as) fully legitimate or reasonably just.

Something like this distinction lies behind the conception of human rights found in Rawls's *The Law of Peoples* (1999a). It can be seen as an attempt to describe a view that is significantly nonparochial without being neutral in either of the senses I distinguished in the last section. As Rawls conceives of human rights, they are normative standards that would be satisfied by any "decent" regime, whether a liberal democracy or a (nonliberal, nondemocratic) "decent hierarchical society." For Rawls, "decency" is a term of art that serves to demarcate the boundaries of acceptable pluralism in international relations. Decent societies are those that liberal societies have reason to recognize as "equal participating members in good standing" of international society (the "Society of Peoples") (p. 59). Being so recognized, decent societies are entitled to a presumption against interference in their internal affairs; it would be wrong for foreign governments to intervene militarily, to attach political conditions to bilateral relationships and transactions, or to criticize. Rawls distinguishes decency from liberal justice: All liberal societies are decent, but not all decent societies are liberal. Human rights are common to all decent societies, whether they satisfy the requirements of liberal justice or

not. So conceived, human rights "cannot be rejected as peculiarly liberal or special to the Western tradition. They are not parochial" (p. 65).

What should count as genuine human rights? Rawls believes that all decent societies would respect the rights of the person, the rights associated with the rule of law, freedom of religious belief and thought, freedom of expression (although perhaps not as extensive as justice requires in liberal societies), and certain economic (mainly subsistence) rights. Decent societies might, however, diverge beyond this area of overlap; specifically, they are not required to provide for equal freedom of public religious practice (but there must be sufficient liberty to allow the practice of minority religions "in peace and without fear" [Rawls 1999a, 74]), equal access to public office, or a right to democratic political participation. Therefore, the corresponding rights of the declaration – equal freedom of public religious practice as opposed to freedom of conscience and private religious practice, the right to vote in free and fair elections – do not count as "human rights proper"; they "seem more aptly described as stating liberal aspirations" or "appear to presuppose specific kinds of institutions" (p. 80, n. 23).[17]

Rawls's view has been criticized for being too tolerant of illiberal regimes (e.g., Buchanan 2000; Téson 1994). This may turn out to be correct, but there is a danger of overstatement: The scope of international toleration in Rawls's theory depends on the idea of "decency," which as he understands it is more restrictive than it may seem. A decent regime renounces aggressive war as an instrument of policy; follows a "common good conception of justice," in which everyone's interests are taken into account (although perhaps not on an equal basis); and respects certain basic rights, including subsistence rights, for all (so that, among other things, official discrimination against women is not permitted) (Rawls 1999a: 64–7). It is true that decency is compatible with a state religion and with undemocratic, but not nonparticipatory, political institutions: decency is, and is intended to be, a weaker requirement than liberal justice.[18] Even so, the constraints of decency are hardly undemanding and, taken seriously, probably would exclude many of the nondemocratic regimes in the world today and possibly some ostensibly democratic ones as well. In the end this may not be enough to meet the criticism, but it helps avoid a distorted picture of the theory.

It is important to see that, unlike the common core or overlapping consensus views, Rawls's view does not require the content of the human rights doctrine to be restricted by the array of political-moral conceptions in the world. The content is determined from the beginning by the normative idea of decency; human rights are said to be nonparochial in relation to all decent societies, not all societies simpliciter. This is why Rawls's view is not open to the objection that it deprives the human rights doctrine of its capacity to serve as a basis of social criticism. But there is a price to be paid. As Rawls (1999a: 80–1) observes, human rights must be considered as "binding on all peoples and societies, including outlaw states" that violate these rights. But because human rights are conceived so that they are necessarily common only to decent societies, it cannot be argued that interference to protect human rights in other societies would always be consistent with the conventional moralities of those societies.

Of course, much depends on the facts of the case, particularly on the relationship between the nature of a government and the content of its society's conventional morality. The case of a rogue tyranny oppressing a population that shares a decent political morality is different from the earlier example of a genocidal government in a racist society.

But the possibility of variation does not affect the basic point that a doctrine such as Rawls's might justify interference in non-decent societies that could not easily be defended against complaints that it imposes alien values. Something more needs to be said to respond to such a complaint.

The response might have to do with the normative idea of decency itself, which serves to characterize the minimum requirements of legitimacy. Where does the force of this idea come from? The answer is not clear to me. The underlying thought is that a society should not have to satisfy liberal principles of justice in order to be regarded by other societies as legitimate; a society may be deficient by liberal standards yet still embody elements that distinguish it from a band of thieves who have achieved a modus vivendi. These elements include the rule of law, an acceptance that all persons have legal personality and the capacity to participate in public life, and a "common good idea of justice" that is shared, at least, by judges and other public officials. Such a society might be said to embody a form of reciprocity even if, from a liberal perspective, it is not the preferred form.[19] Unlike liberal societies, such a society might embody and promote a single, comprehensive view of the good life; but it would do so under conditions (including respect for "human rights proper") that render the society tolerable as a cooperating partner for liberal societies in the international order.

The question, however, is not whether a society that satisfies these criteria of decency is to be preferred to one that does not; so much is clear. At issue is whether, and if so why, decent but not just societies should be regarded as legitimate and, therefore, as qualified for treatment as "members in good standing" of the international order. Why – for the (limited) purposes of international political life – should decency be regarded as on a par with liberal justice?[20]

At one point Rawls (1999a: 67) writes that the definition of decency is simply stipulated for the purposes of the theory, and the reader must judge "whether a decent people . . . is to be tolerated and accepted." But it is a serious question whether we have enough to go on intuitively to make such a judgment. Do we have a clear enough common-sense idea of decency, as a standard for institutions distinct from that of social justice, to judge other than arbitrarily? At another point he suggests that the content of the idea of decency is related to the function this idea plays in the conduct of liberal foreign policy. Liberal states should tolerate decent nonliberal states (which respect "human rights proper") because they are so structured and governed as to be peaceful, cooperating members of international society and therefore do not threaten international stability, whereas interference is permissible in "outlaw" states (which do not respect these rights) because their internal features cause them to threaten international order (p. 81). As a practical matter this may be true, but it cannot give a plausible account of the basis of human rights, because it would locate the justification in the wrong place, not in the significance of human rights for the rights holders but in the beneficial consequences for international order of reducing the number of regimes that do not respect them.[21]

Rawls's most perspicuous argument for tolerating decent but illiberal regimes appeals to the consequences of toleration for these societies themselves. Decent societies, by definition, are open to internal, nonviolent change, and Rawls (1999a: 61–2) believes that the evolution of their institutions in a liberal direction is more likely if they are treated "with due respect" as equal members of international society. This is an empirical hypothesis about political development, and I suspect that some version of it is true in a significant range of cases (although I am not

sure what would count as evidence for it). Yet, although the political development hypothesis bears clearly on the question of how we should act toward a society, it does not bear so obviously on the question of the ethical significance of a society's political decency or, derivatively, of the proper scope of a doctrine of human rights. Perhaps the connection, in Rawls's view, is that human rights should be understood as a class of moral consideration whose *only* role in political discourse is to justify coercive intervention in a society's affairs. If that is correct, then the fact that a value is not sufficient to justify coercive intervention counts against identifying the value as a human right.

But whether Rawls holds this view or not, there are two reasons not to accept it. First, it is not true that the only role of human rights in international discourse is to justify coercive intervention. As I observed at the beginning, human rights are also, for example, invoked to justify noncoercive interference by outsiders (governments, international agencies, nongovernmental organizations) and to justify programs of reform by compatriots. We should conceptualize human rights in a way that is adequate to this larger role. Second, as before, the argument against interference does not easily extend to an argument for limiting the scope of human rights. Granting the political development hypothesis grants nothing about the moral standing of the values expressed as human rights; the hypothesis is about the best means of realizing these values, not about their standing as values. Indeed, the best argument against reform intervention in a decent society, assuming that the hypothesis is correct, is that intervention is more likely to retard than encourage the society's movement from decency to (liberal) justice. But such an argument depends on rather than repudiates the claim that the liberal conception is an appropriate standard for the society in question.

What is the upshot for human rights? I believe it is this. If it were possible to regard a decent society as minimally legitimate, in the sense of being, for purposes of its international relations, morally on a par with a liberally just society, then it would be possible to understand "human rights proper" as necessary conditions of minimal legitimacy. There would be a clear sense in which these human rights, as against the full catalog of internationally recognized human rights, could be defended as nonparochial. If the ethical significance of decency derives from that of liberal justice, however – for example, if its normative force depends on the hypothesis that decent societies, left to their own devices, are likely to develop into liberal ones – then the hypothesis might yield a reason not to interfere in decent societies, but there would be no deep distinction between "human rights proper" and other human rights that are part of liberal justice but not of decency. Indeed, it is hard to see any distinction of principle at all.

Purposes and Limits of International Human Rights

Notwithstanding these doubts about Rawls's interpretation of human rights, reflection about his view suggests two related precepts for any plausible conception. I shall try to formulate these precepts in a general way and then explain why they seem plausible.[22]

First, a satisfactory philosophical conception of human rights should be suited to the public role that we need human rights to play in international affairs. The doctrine of human rights is a political construction intended for certain political purposes and is to be understood against the background of a range of general assumptions about the character of the contemporary international environment.[23]

Second, the conception should interpret human rights as "common" in a special sense, not as the area of agreement among all existing political doctrines or comprehensive views, but as principles for international affairs that could be accepted by reasonable persons who hold conflicting reasonable conceptions of the good life.

Here are some points of clarification. First, to say that international human rights compose a doctrine adopted for certain political purposes is to reject some traditional views about the character of human rights, such as those that interpret human rights as a contemporary restatement of the (or a) theory of natural law or natural rights, or as a statement of a single comprehensive view about political justice or the political good that is supposed to apply to all human societies at all times and places.[24] Human rights are standards intended to play a regulative role for a range of actors in the political circumstances of the contemporary world. Yet, to describe human rights doctrine as a "political construction" is not to say that human rights are unrelated to these other kinds of views: In adhering to the doctrine or in criticizing it, one might be moved by beliefs about natural law or natural rights or by a comprehensive conception of the good. But it would be an error to identify these more fundamental moral beliefs with a political doctrine of human rights.

Second, according to these precepts, the particulars of the public political role expected of human rights are essential to a comprehension and defense of the doctrine. I shall say more about this role below. For now the essential point is that human rights are meant for certain political purposes, and we cannot think intelligently about their content and reach without taking account of these purposes. I do not mean to say that one should accept uncritically the conception of the political role of human rights prevailing in international affairs any more than one should accept the details of prevailing views of their content. But criticism must begin with some conception of the practice being examined, and the contours of this practice are to be found in the doctrine of human rights as we have it in contemporary international life.

Third, the second precept states that human rights should be acceptable to reasonable persons, not peoples. This is possibly in contrast to Rawls, who writes of peoples as corporate wholes with more or less widely shared conventional moralities. I have discussed my doubts about this elsewhere (Beitz 2000) and here simply call attention to the possible contrast and note its importance in thinking about the content of the human rights doctrine. In my view, human rights are ultimately justified by considerations about the reasonable interests of individuals, not those of whole societies conceived as corporate entities.

A view of this kind is at odds with some traditional conceptions in distinguishing between human rights as a political doctrine and various underlying views about social justice. Why should we accept the revisionist view? Part of the answer is that, as a historical matter, international human rights doctrine is not accurately interpreted as an effort to fill the same conceptual space as was filled by natural law or natural rights in the Western political tradition. Those ideas aimed to supply something different – a comprehensive conception of the good or just society, perhaps, or an account of the constraints a government should observe in the use of its monopoly of political power. By contrast, the international doctrine is a negotiated agreement (or set of agreements) that describes "a common standard of achievement for all peoples and all nations" (Universal Declaration, Preamble), and it is meant to provide guidance in the conduct of international political life by actors such as international organizations and their member states, nongovernmental organizations, and individuals.

But the argument need not rest on a historical observation. Contemporary international society needs a doctrine of the kind imagined by the framers of the Universal Declaration. One reason, which Rawls notices, arises from the developing international capacity and disposition to intervene coercively in the affairs of states to protect the interests of their own people. Standards are needed to guide the use of this coercive power. As I have been urging, however, human rights doctrine serves other purposes as well. The most general, albeit awkward, statement of these purposes might be this. The global political structure contains an array of institutions and practices, including the foreign policies of states, with the capacity to influence the conditions of life for individuals in their domestic societies. In some cases this influence comes about through intentional action, such as military intervention or the attachment of political conditions to development aid. In other cases it occurs through the normal operation of an institution, such as structural assistance provided by international financial bodies. Moreover, as I have been emphasizing, transnational action that affects human rights is not limited to the operations of governments and international organizations; it may also be carried out by nongovernmental organizations, acting in international fora or within the internal political processes of individual societies. The doctrine of human rights is a statement of standards to guide the structures and conduct of global political life insofar as these bear on the conditions of life for individuals in their societies.

To be more specific, a doctrine of human rights suited for contemporary international practice should be capable of playing at least three kinds of roles. First, it constrains the domestic constitutions of states and the fundamental rules of international organizations and regimes. (Whether this constraint should operate by means of the embodiment of these norms in constitutions, organizational charters, and so forth, I take to be another question, one not settled by theoretical considerations.) Second, it describes goals for social development applicable to all contemporary societies, to the extent that they are or can be influenced by such external forces as the foreign policies of other states and the practices of international institutions. (The degree and kinds of influence appropriate in particular cases is again another question, involving both normative and pragmatic considerations.) Third (and derivatively), the doctrine furnishes grounds of political criticism to which it would be appropriate to appeal in the setting of global politics by a range of international and transnational actors – not only governments but also officials of international institutions and nongovernmental organizations acting in their capacity as citizens of global society.

On this view the doctrine of human rights is significantly teleological. It is a statement of aspiration applicable to all contemporary societies, but all of its requirements may not be capable of being satisfied simultaneously or in the short run. Human rights may not bear on political choice as straightforwardly as they would if conceived in more traditional terms as side constraints or prohibitions. The actions required to satisfy a human right will depend on the case. This is not only because achieving a given end may require different strategies in different settings, but also because priorities will have to be set and compromises reached when, in the short term, the effort to secure one right threatens to block efforts to secure another. Joel Feinberg (1973: 95) observed long ago that some rights of the declarations seem to be more accurately conceived as rights "in an unusual new 'manifesto sense'" than on the model of legal claim-rights.[25] The view I sketch here is compatible with this observation.

A Case Study: Political Rights

According to the formula I suggest, the doctrine of human rights is "common" in the sense that, considered in light of the political purposes it is expected to serve, reasonable persons could accept it despite differences in their reasonable conceptions of the good. Because this formulation depends from the outset on judgments about which conceptions to count as reasonable, its effect is to frame the question of the justification of human rights as a substantive problem of political theory, comparable to problems such as the justification of principles of social justice for domestic society. What distinguishes the problem about human rights from the others is the special character of the international political environment in which these standards must operate. Concerns regarding cultural parochialism or political bias would arise, if at all, within the substantive argument for each of its elements.

To illustrate, let me consider whether the doctrine of human rights should recognize a right to democratic institutions. The Covenant on Civil and Political Rights is unequivocal. It holds that there are human rights to political institutions that afford every citizen an opportunity to participate in public affairs either directly or through "freely chosen representatives"; to compete for public office and to vote in "genuine periodic elections"; and to assemble peaceably without restrictions "other than those . . . which are necessary in a democratic society in the interests of national security or public safety" (Articles 21, 25). As a purely descriptive matter, there is no question that these requirements are nonneutral in the sense that they are not endorsed by all the major political moralities in the world. What is the ethical significance of this fact? Does it mean that we should not regard democratic rights as genuine human rights, or that we should not accept the defense or promotion of democratic rights as a justification for interference in a non-democratic society's domestic life?

These questions are worth special attention because the element of international human rights doctrine most often said to be objectionably parochial is that concerned with democratic rights. At the same time, there is a discernible trend in international law toward recognition of a universal right to democratic institutions (Franck 1995, chap. 4). So these questions mark a specific point of tension between the restricted conception of human rights prevalent in philosophical thought and the development of international law and practice.

Consider a hypothetical case. Imagine an authoritarian regime in a society in which historically the predominant political beliefs are not democratic. Citing the Covenant on Civil and Political Rights, a modernizing insurgency fighting for democratic reforms calls upon the international community for military and financial help. Given the society's cultural history, international interference, if successful, would produce a result that would be regarded as a change for the worse by a significant portion, perhaps even a majority, of the society. The question is whether this fact argues against interference to help the reformers and, if so, for what reason.

One possible reply returns to the issue of paternalism. Interference in this kind of case, perhaps in contrast to most interferences to defend human rights, would be genuinely paternalistic: It involves coercive interference in some people's liberty on the grounds that the results would be in their own interests. But it would not be justified paternalism. Normally, the justification of a paternalistic choice has at least three elements: (1) a claim that the subject is unable to choose rationally for himself owing to a failure of reason or will; (2) evidence that the choice is guided by

knowledge of the subject's own interests, to the extent they can be known, or by a reasonable conception of the interests it would be rational for the subject to have; and (3) a reasonable expectation that the subject will come to agree that the agent's choices on his behalf are the best that could be made under the circumstances.[26] In my example, because a significant portion or even a majority of the population does not share democratic political values, for this portion of the population the second element (and possibly the third) of the justification would fail. The interference does not appear to take seriously the moral beliefs of those whom it coerces.

This reply seems to me to yield the most plausible account of the ethical significance of the fact that many in our hypothetical society hold moral beliefs inconsistent with democracy. Yet, it is open to certain doubts. First, it may be questioned whether what I describe as people's "moral beliefs" accurately identify their political interests. This is primarily an empirical issue, and I have not worked out the case in enough detail to resolve it one way or the other. One would want to know, for example, about the nature of the evidence that many people reject democratic values, whether the society has any past experience with democratic forms, and whether there have been occasions for public political deliberation about forms of government.

On one set of assumptions, the very fact that political institutions lack the features characteristic of democracy – such as free expression, political competition, voting – would suggest that preferences about political forms are not either fully informed or freely arrived at. In that case the justification of paternalistic interference must fall back on a judgment about what it would be rational for people to want if they were in possession of full information and able to reason freely, and here we have no choice but to engage the substantive question of the value of democracy. Telescoping a long argument, suppose there is reason to believe that democratic institutions are instrumental to the enjoyment of certain (nonpolitical) human rights, including the rights of the person and subsistence rights. Then, assuming these other rights are not themselves culturally controversial, there is an argument that it would be rational to want democratic rights as means of ensuring the satisfaction of urgent human interests, whatever the present political values in a culture.[27] (There is also the counterargument that some other configurations of political institutions, like Rawls's "decent consultation hierarchy," would be equally effective in securing human rights. Which is correct depends on a historical and political judgment, not an ethical one.)

Second, the reply considers only the perspective of the nondemocratic portion of the population. What about the democratic insurgents who asked for outside help? Again, one needs more information, but presumably the insurgency has local causes and responds to local grievances and aspirations. From the perspective of this group, interference is not a matter of paternalism at all but of avoiding or reducing harm or protecting against injustice. It is hard to see how this issue can be addressed other than by examining the urgency of the interests at stake in relation to the costs of interference and its probability of success. Once again, it seems that the justifiability of interference to support the democratic reformers should be faced as a free-standing issue in political ethics in which the values that interference may achieve are compared with the costs and risks of making the attempt. There is no categorical conclusion possible about the sufficiency of democratic reform as a justification of intervention in a case like this.

These reflections suggest an alternative explanation of the ethical significance of local disagreement over political values. It may be that this bears on the feasibility of constructive interference, or on its prospects of success in the long run, rather than on the nature or scope of human rights themselves. If a significant portion of the population lacks democratic sympathies, then it is not likely that democratic institutions will be sustained even if a democratic insurgency attains its immediate objectives. In that case it could be true both that there is a human right to democratic institutions and that interference in support of a prodemocratic insurgency would be wrong.

Why, then, should we say there is a right at all? If the acceptability of interference to promote democratic institutions effectively depends on the extent of democratic commitment within a culture, have we not conceded that there is no universal (and hence no human) right to democracy? The answer is that we have not. The question trades on the idea that there can be no right without a remedy, or no right without some feasible strategy for its realization. But the fact that intervention is unlikely to succeed in establishing democratic institutions in a divided political culture does not imply that nothing ever will; institutional change is a complex historical process, usually accompanied by changes in political belief as well. Moreover, a human right to democracy may have practical force otherwise than by licensing coercive intervention. For example, it might call for efforts at persuasion and education or support for the development of elements of a democratic social infrastructure (associations, labor unions, and so on). Of course, to accept this as a reply to the objection, one must accept a conception of a human right as something different from a legal right or certain moral rights; for example, although it may generate duties for various agents, a human right cannot always be a ground for insisting on immediate compliance. But if human rights are regarded as political constructions in the way I have described, this is unremarkable.

Conclusion

The discourse on international human rights suffers from a strange juxtaposition. In major arenas of international politics concerns about human rights are more prominently expressed than ever before, and there is some reason to believe that these concerns increasingly motivate action. Yet, within contemporary political thought human rights are often regarded with suspicion. These suspicions are diverse. Some people think there is no such thing as *universal* human rights (i.e., rights that may be claimed by anyone). Some think there is no such thing as universal *human* rights (possessed by human beings independently of their relationships with others and their institutional memberships). Some think that "internationally recognized human rights" are not *rights* (at least not in any sense that would be familiar to someone influenced by Hohfeld). Some think the international doctrine of human rights is a good idea corrupted by overextension: Although there may be such a thing as a universal human right, some (perhaps many) of the rights specifically enumerated in the international instruments fail to qualify. And some believe the doctrine of human rights is a cloak for liberal political values, an instance of partisanship rather than a neutral basis for global agreement.

I have only addressed the last of these suspicions directly, although I have adverted to some of the others. I have observed that the doctrine of human rights, regarded for the moment as part of the positive law of international society, cannot plausibly be considered culturally or politically nonpartisan. And I have argued that this fact, in itself, does not count against the doctrine. What is distinctive about human rights as a category of normative standard is not their suppos-

edly symmetrical relationship to the conceptions of political justice or legitimacy to be found in the world's cultures but, rather, the role they play in international relations. Human rights state conditions for political and social institutions, the systematic violation of which may justify efforts to bring about reform by agents external to the society in which the violation occurs. This interference-justifying role may limit the content of the doctrine, but there is no reason to suppose the limitations will yield a neutral or nonpartisan view. Indeed, it is hard to see how things could be otherwise. In the words of the Vienna Declaration, human rights specify conditions that institutions should satisfy in order to respect "the dignity and worth inherent in the human person" (Preamble); but the concept of a person with inherent dignity and worth is a substantive moral idea and will almost certainly be more congenial to some than to other conceptions of justice or political good.

Is this kind of partisanship problematic for the doctrine? I believe not, provided that each of its elements can be defended by an appropriately general argument, as I suggest is possible for the right to democratic institutions. Such a defense would hold that human rights are "common" in a morally significant way without being, so to speak, empirically nonparochial. This, of course, is not to say that cultural and political differences do not come into deliberation about how to act. These differences may enter in a variety of ways – for example, as factors determining the feasibility and cost of a contemplated interference or the risks of collateral harm. They may also enter at a more basic level, as factors influencing a judgment about the rightness of using coercive means of interference, particularly when the purpose of the interference is genuinely paternalistic.

This conception of human rights faces a variety of objections. Here I note three of the most prominent and simply gesture at the kind of reply that might be offered to each. First, it may seem excessively pragmatic to regard human rights as a "political conception." Whatever else they are, human rights are surely moral standards, standards whose authority rests on recognizably moral considerations. To suggest otherwise, the objection holds, fails to take seriously both the character and the history of the idea of human rights. I believe, however, that the objection starts from a faulty premise. To say that the doctrine of human rights is a political conception is not to deny that its authority rests on moral considerations; human rights are political, not in the source of their authority, but in their role in public ethical life. As I have described them, human rights are standards to which it is reasonable to hold political institutions accountable in the processes of contemporary world politics. They operate as prima facie justifications of transnational (although not only transnational) political action aimed at bringing about change in the structure and operation of domestic (and international) institutions. Any account of the authority of human rights must take note of the political contexts in which they operate, but this hardly means that the account would exclude moral considerations; in fact, it would depend upon them.

Second, in some ways a contrasting objection is that a partisan conception of human rights is insufficiently realistic. According to this objection, unless a doctrine of human rights is culturally neutral it cannot possibly play the role that we need a doctrine of human rights to play in international affairs. The reason is that if a violation of human rights is not regarded as a shared basis for political action, then the capacity to enlist international support when it is most needed will deteriorate, and the doctrine of human rights will become little more than a sectarian hope. The latter proposition seems true

enough, but the point about neutrality does not obviously follow from it. It is an empirical question whether a political doctrine must be neutral in order to enlist enough international support to be influential, a claim that not only has not been proved but also is most likely false. The growth of the global human rights regime itself may be evidence to the contrary.

Third, there is a residual worry that an expansive doctrine of human rights can too easily be used as an instrument of neocolonial domination, as a way to rationalize the use of coercion by a hegemonic power to advance its own interests. Of course, there is one sense in which this is a legitimate worry if not almost a necessary truth. If an expansive doctrine of human rights embraces liberal political values, and if the hegemonic power identifies its interests with the advance of these values, then coercion that is soundly justified by human rights considerations also will advance the interests of the hegemonic power. What troubles people, however, seems to be not this kind of case but one in which human rights considerations are abused or distorted in order to make self-interested political action seem to be justified by other-regarding considerations. The fear is that an expansive doctrine will be more open to this sort of abuse than a minimalist one.

This is not an abstract fear. The history of intervention (e.g., by the United States in Central America) includes many instances of what plausibly can be seen as analogous abuses of the values of self-government and individual liberty as rationales for self-interested interference. Let us therefore concede the hypothesis that an expansive doctrine is more open to abuse by a hegemonic power than a more narrowly drawn conception. What follows? Since we are conceiving of human rights as a public, political doctrine, it cannot be replied that the possibility of abuse is irrelevant to the content of the doctrine. If this possibility were significant, and if unilateral intervention were the only mechanism realistically available to promote human rights, then a narrowing of the doctrine's content might be appropriate. But there is an alternative: It is to establish multilateral institutions to protect human rights doctrine from unilateral abuse. This is one source of the argument for a world human rights court, and it may also argue for something like the complex voting system found in the Security Council, which otherwise might be seen as objectionably constrained by its supermajority requirements and the great-power veto. If such mechanisms can be made to work, the potential for neocolonial abuse of human rights doctrine will not by itself argue for a limitation of the doctrine's substantive scope.

All of this only gestures at how one might defend a more robust theory of human rights than that presumed by those who regard neutrality as a virtue, and one more in keeping with the doctrine of human rights found in contemporary international practice. Plainly, more needs to be said to develop such a defense and to explore the objections that could be brought against it. And plainly, that would be beyond the scope of a single article.

So I will conclude with an observation on a different although related point. The question of whether an expansive conception of international human rights can be defended is different from the question of whether we ought to accord human rights a fundamental place in international political theory. As a central element in international practice, human rights are well established, and political theorists should strive for a critical understanding that takes seriously their practical role. But there are good reasons to resist thinking of human rights as the fundamental terms of international political theory. For example, rights are rarely self-evident and usually stand in need of justification, and the justification seldom terminates in another assertion of right. And because the satisfaction of a right typically imposes costs on others, we need a mechanism for assigning responsibility for bearing those costs. In itself, however, the concept of a human right is not much help in designing such a mechanism because it is concerned with the interests of the beneficiary of the right rather than with the relationship in which the right is satisfied. For both reasons it seems likely that a satisfactory theory of human rights is better conceived as an aspect of a more general theory of global justice.

Notes

1 Notwithstanding, governments seem to acknowledge the court's authority, as the decision by the British government regarding the treatment of homosexuals in the military illustrates (*Financial Times* 1999). On the variety of roles played by human rights in intergovernmental relations, see, e.g., Forsythe 2000, pt II; Vincent 1986, esp. chaps 4–6; and the case studies in Risse, Ropp, and Sikkink 1999.

2 The idea of a human rights culture derives from the Argentinean jurist Eduardo Rabossi (Rorty 1993: 115).

3 Precisely why this should be true is an interesting question. There is a provocative discussion that focuses on the growth of the European human rights regime in Moravcsik 2000.

4 In an article whose title ("Human Rights as a Neutral Concern") inspired the title of this paper, Scanlon (1979: 83) describes human rights as "a ground for action that is neutral with respect to the main political and economic divisions in the world" and as standards that "are not controversial in the way that other political and economic issues are."

He does not suggest, as do some of the writers considered below, that human rights aspire to be neutral among all conceptions of justice or legitimacy. Rawls (1999a: 65, n. 4 and accompanying text) cites the Scanlon article as a source for the conception of human rights in *The Law of Peoples*.

[5] Donnelly (1999: 81) characterizes human rights as "a distinctive, historically unusual set of social values and practices." Others who have espoused a liberal view of human rights include Waldron (1993: 10–24), Nino (1991, passim), and Rorty (1993). Needless to say, agreement about the scope of human rights can coexist with disagreement in other dimensions.

[6] These agreements, as well as the Universal Declaration and the two covenants, are conveniently collected in Brownlie 1992.

[7] See the analysis of contemporary sources of Islamic human rights law, including the 1981 Universal Islamic Declaration of Human Rights, in Mayer 1995: 95–6 and 117–18. On the extent of officially sanctioned human rights violations in the countries mentioned, see US Department of State 1999.

[8] Welch 1995: 87–97. For the criticism that concern about FGM is ethnocentric, see the discussion by Tamir (1996) and the response by Kamm (1996).

[9] See Sen 1999: 231–46, on Asian values, and An-Na'im 1990, chap. 7, esp. pp. 175–7, on gender in Islamic law. In general, compare Perry 1998: 76–8.

[10] Compare Miller 1995: 74–5. There is an interestingly different view in Buchanan 1999: 52–6 and 59–60.

[11] Similarly, Martin (1993: 75) believes human rights are principles that "would be regarded as reasonable by persons at different times or in different cultures. And such principles, again cross-culturally, would be thought to have connection . . . with a fairly wide range of differing conventional moralities."

[12] In Walzer's (1994: 28–31) view, distributive justice generally is part of thick but not thin morality; see his suggestive and interesting remarks on "the cure of souls and the cure of bodies in the medieval and modern West."

[13] The idea of an overlapping consensus is due to Rawls, but he does not use it in the analysis of human rights. See Nussbaum 1997: 286, and 1999: 37–9 and passim, for the application of this idea to human rights.

[14] I think this is consistent with Scanlon 1979, but it does not seem to be consistent with his view in *What We Owe to Each Other* (1998: 348). The position taken there allows judgments about the (un)reasonableness of culturally influenced beliefs about value to enter into bottom-line judgments about right and wrong; there is no guarantee that these judgments would satisfy the condition in the text. The latter seems to me to be closer to the truth.

[15] The point has often been noted. See, e.g., Nussbaum 1999: 10–12; Scanlon 1979: 88.

[16] Brown (1999: 119) claims to the contrary that "there are no general moral standards that apply" to "Bosnian Serbs who kill Bosnian Muslims" or "Muslim extremists who think that the death penalty is an appropriate response to apostasy" because in each case the agents do not believe the conduct in question is wrong. This cannot be right. The Bosnian Serbs who killed innocent civilians were wrong to do so, whether they accept this or not.

[17] Freedom of religion can be considered a human right "proper," in Rawls's sense, only if its scope is interpreted more narrowly than what some believe to be the intent of Article 18 of the Universal Declaration. The human right to freedom of religion, as Rawls understands it, forbids the persecution of minority religions, but it allows for a state religion that enjoys various political privileges, such as public offices open only to its members (1999a: 65, n. 2), and the state religion may, "on some questions, be the ultimate authority within society and may control government policy on certain important matters" (p. 74).

[18] In the political sphere, for example, a decent regime need not be democratic, but it must provide regular opportunities for all citizens to communicate their views and preferences to those authorized to make political decisions. Rawls (1999a: 64) calls such an arrange-

ment a "decent consultation hierarchy." The details are complex, and I pass over them here.

[19] I am grateful to Amy Gutmann for help in clarifying this thought.

[20] The restriction to international political life is important. Rawls need not (and does not) claim that decency and justice are "on a par" for any other purpose.

[21] I do not mean to say that Rawls himself gives such an account of human rights.

[22] Thomas Pogge's comments on an earlier draft helped me formulate these precepts.

[23] Jones (1996: 183–204) emphasizes the political character of Rawls's interpretation of human rights. Note, however, that Rawls (1999a: 81, n. 25) has reservations about this interpretation.

[24] For example, Finnis (1980: 198) believes human rights are "a contemporary idiom"

for natural rights (see pp. 210–30 for his view of the content and limits of the doctrine of international human rights).

[25] Feinberg's use of "manifesto sense" is not, as some writers have thought, derisory; he endorses and expresses sympathy for this usage. It is also worth noting that one can accept the idea that some human rights are "manifesto rights" without also accepting Feinberg's view that it is not possible to assign corresponding duties to them. That, I believe, is a mistake.

[26] I rely here on the discussion in *A Theory of Justice* (Rawls 1999b: 218–20).

[27] The argument is made in Shue 1996, 74–8, and Sen 1999, 178–86. I made a similar argument about the value of democracy, concentrating on the circumstances of developing societies, in Beitz 1981, 177–208.

References

An-Na'im, Abdullahi. 1990. *Toward an Islamic Reformation: Civil Liberties, Human Rights, and International Law* (Syracuse, NY: Syracuse University Press).

Beitz, Charles R. 1981. "Democracy in Developing Societies." In *Boundaries: National Autonomy and its Limits*, ed. Peter G. Brown and Henry Shue (Totowa, NJ: Rowman & Littlefield), pp. 177–208.

—— 2000. "Rawls's Law of Peoples." *Ethics* 110 (July): 669–96.

Best, Geoffrey. 1995. "Justice, International Relations, and Human Rights." *International Affairs* 71 (October): 775–800.

Brown, Chris. 1999. "Universal Human Rights: A Critique." In *Human Rights in Global Politics*, ed. Tim Dunne and Nicholas J. Wheeler (Cambridge: Cambridge University Press), pp. 103–27.

Brownlie, Ian, ed. 1992. *Basic Documents on Human Rights*, 3rd edn (Oxford: Clarendon Press).

Buchanan, Allen. 1999. "Recognitional Legitimacy." *Philosophy & Public Affairs* 28 (Winter): 52–6.

—— 2000. "Rawls's Law of Peoples." *Ethics* 110 (July): 697–721.

Donnelly, Jack. 1999. "The Social Construction of International Human Rights." In *Human Rights in Global Politics*, ed. Tim Dunne and Nicholas J. Wheeler (Cambridge: Cambridge University Press), pp. 71–102.

Feinberg, Joel. 1973. *Social Philosophy* (Englewood Cliffs, NJ: Prentice-Hall).

Financial Times. 1999. "Gays Win Case against Armed Services Ban." September 28, London edition, p. 16.

Finnis, John. 1980. *Natural Law and Natural Rights* (Oxford: Clarendon Press).

Forsythe, David P. 2000. *Human Rights in International Relations* (Cambridge: Cambridge University Press).

Franck, Thomas M. 1995. *Fairness in International Law and Institutions* (Oxford: Clarendon Press).

Jones, Peter. 1996. "International Human Rights: Philosophical or Political?" In *National Rights, International Obligations*, ed. Simon Caney, David George, and Peter Jones (Boulder, CO: Westview), pp. 183–204.

Kamm, F. M. 1996. "Is Body Intrusion Special?" *Boston Review* 21 (October/November). http://bostonreview.mit.edu/BR21.5/Kamm.html (accessed January 30, 2001).

Kausikan, Bilahari. 1993. "Asia's Different Standard." *Foreign Policy* 92 (Fall): 24–51.

Korey, William. 1998. *NGOs and the Universal Declaration of Human Rights: "A Curious Grapevine"* (New York: St Martin's Press).

Lauren, Paul Gordon. 1998. *The Evolution of International Human Rights: Visions Seen* (Philadelphia: University of Pennsylvania Press).

Martin, Rex. 1993. *A System of Rights* (Oxford: Clarendon Press).

Mayer, Ann Elizabeth. 1995. *Islam and Human Rights: Tradition and Politics*, 2nd edn. (Boulder, CO: Westview).

Miller, David. 1995. *On Nationality* (Oxford: Oxford University Press).

Moravcsik, Andrew. 2000. "The Origins of International Human Rights Regimes: Democratic Delegation in Postwar Europe." *International Organization* 54 (Spring): 217–52.

Nino, Carlos Santiago. 1991. *The Ethics of Human Rights* (Oxford: Clarendon Press).

Nussbaum, Martha. 1997. "Human Rights Theory: Capability and Human Rights." *Fordham Law Review* 66 (November): 273–300.

—— 1999. "In Defense of Universal Values." *The Fifth Annual Hesburgh Lectures on Ethics and Public Policy* (Notre Dame, IN: Joan B. Kroc Institute for International Peace Studies at the University of Notre Dame).

Perry, Michael J. 1998. *The Idea of Human Rights* (New York: Oxford University Press).

Rawls, John. 1999a. *The Law of Peoples* (Cambridge, MA: Harvard University Press).

—— 1999b. *A Theory of Justice*, rev. edn. (Cambridge, MA: Harvard University Press).

Risse, Thomas, Stephen C. Ropp, and Kathryn Sikkink (eds.) 1999. *The Power of Human Rights* (Cambridge: Cambridge University Press).

Rorty, Richard. 1993. "Human Rights, Rationality, and Sentimentality." In *On Human Rights: The Oxford Amnesty Lectures 1993*, ed. Stephen Shute and Susan Hurley (New York: Basic Books), pp. 111–34.

Scanlon, T. M. 1979. "Human Rights as a Neutral Concern." In *Human Rights and US Foreign Policy*, ed. Peter G. Brown and Douglas MacLean (Lexington, MA: Lexington Books), pp. 83–92.

—— 1998. *What We Owe to Each Other* (Cambridge, MA: Harvard University Press).

Sen, Amartya. 1999. *Development as Freedom* (New York: Alfred A. Knopf).

Shue, Henry. 1996. *Basic Rights: Subsistence, Affluence, and US Foreign Policy*, 2nd edn. (Princeton, NJ: Princeton University Press).

Tamir, Yael. 1996. "Hands Off Clitoridectomy: What Our Revulsion Reveals about Ourselves." *Boston Review* 21 (Summer). http://bostonreview.mit.edu/BR21.3/Tamir.html (accessed January 30, 2001).

Téson, Fernando. 1994. "Some Observations on John Rawls's 'The Law of Peoples.'" *American Society of International Law Proceedings* 88: 18–22.

United Nations. 1993. "Vienna Declaration and Programme of Action." World Conference on Human Rights. UN Doc. A/CONF.157/23 (July 12).

US Department of State. 1999. *Country Reports on Human Rights Practices for 1998: Near East and North Africa*. February 29. http://www.state.gov/www/global/human_rights/1998_hrp_report/98htp_report_nea.html (accessed January 30, 2001).

Vincent, R. J. 1986. *Human Rights and International Relations* (Cambridge: Cambridge University Press).

Waldron, Jeremy. 1993. *Liberal Rights: Collected Papers 1981–1991* (Cambridge: Cambridge University Press).

Walzer, Michael. 1994. *Thick and Thin: Moral Argument at Home and Abroad* (Notre Dame, IN: University of Notre Dame Press).

Welch, Claude E. 1995. *Protecting Human Rights in Africa: Roles and Strategies of Nongovernmental Organizations* (Philadelphia: University of Pennsylvania Press).

Chapter 9

Group Rights and Group Oppression*
Peter Jones

For much of the twentieth century, political philosophy has regarded the proposition that groups can hold rights with a mixture of scepticism and suspicion. In recent years, however, that proposition has been received more favourably. In part this revival in the fortunes of group rights has stemmed from a resigned acceptance that some longstanding and widely espoused rights, such as rights of national self-determination or rights to other forms of collective autonomy, cannot be convincingly disaggregated into the rights of individuals. It has also stemmed from new worries about the fate of ethnic and cultural minorities and from doubts about whether the concern and respect due to those minorities can be adequately secured merely by ascribing rights to their members individually. If a group enjoys a distinct mode of life and if that mode of life takes a collective form, perhaps our moral recognition of that mode of life has to be directed towards the group collectively rather than to its members severally. If we choose to express our concern for the group and its form of life in the language of rights, perhaps those have to be rights that we ascribe to the group qua group rather than to its members as separate individuals.

More generally, in moral philosophy and political life we commonly assert rights in relation to matters that we reckon to be of fundamental significance. Yet some of what is fundamentally important for people relates to identities that they can possess and to practices in which they can engage only in association with others. Consequently, it can seem merely arbitrary to insist that people can have rights only to goods that they can enjoy individually and never to goods that they can enjoy only collectively.

Yet, despite this shift in opinion, there is still considerable uncertainty over just what we should understand a group right to be, and also a degree of unease about the moral implications of ascribing rights to groups. In this article I hope to remove some of this uncertainty by distinguishing two conceptions of group rights. Both inhabit the current literature on group rights, but their difference has generally passed unnoticed and part of my concern is simply to articulate the separateness of these two conceptions. I also argue that each conception has different implications for, and raises different questions relating to, the status of individuals and their freedom. Group rights are

* From *The Journal of Political Philosophy* 7:4 (1999), pp. 353–77.

often articulated as demands for group freedom, but they are also feared as vehicles for group oppression. I aim to show that each conception provides us with different reasons for worrying about group rights.

My emphasis throughout will be on moral rather than legal rights, since my primary concern is with rights to which people appeal in arguing about the form that social and political arrangements should take. Indeed, much of my interest in this subject stems from the question of who we should regard as the relevant moral claimants in a plural society and a plural world – groups or individuals? – and, if we answer groups, how different conceptions of group rights can make for different responses to plurality. Some of what I say, however, also has a bearing upon institutional and legal rights.

Group Rights and Individual Rights

There is little about group rights that is uncontroversial but there is at least this much agreement upon the basic concept: a right is a group right only if it is a right held by a group rather than by its members severally. If rights are held by individuals separately, their shared rights do not add up to a group right even though their rights relate to a characteristic which marks them off, sociologically, as a group. A right is a group right only if it is a right held by a group qua group.

Rights are most conspicuously not group rights when they are ascribed to human individuals without reference to any further characteristic as, for example, in the case of human rights to freedom of expression and freedom of association. The possibility of confusion begins to arise when rights relate to identities that people share with others. For example, we might assert the right of Protestants to practise their religion or the

right of homosexuals not to suffer discrimination. However, relating a right to a characteristic that individuals share with others does not transform it into a group right. Individuals may share their Protestantism or their homosexuality with others but still hold their rights as individual Protestants or individual homosexuals. Indeed, we are likely to regard both of these rights as merely special instances of rights that are general to individuals – the rights of all individuals to enjoy freedom of religion and not to suffer discrimination because of their sexual orientation.

Rights can also be associated with group membership and group activity without being group rights. I can have a right to join a group, such as a tennis club or a ramblers' association, only if there is a group for me to join. Having joined the group, I may enjoy rights unique to members of the group. But normally these will be individual rights: if you prevent my joining the group or infringe my rights as a member of the group, it is my rights that you violate rather than rights that belong to the group. Of course, we might hold that if you prevent my joining a group, you violate not merely a right possessed by myself as would-be joiner but also a right possessed by the group; in that case a genuine group right will be at stake. My point is only that rights that relate to group membership and group activity need not, for that reason, be group rights. A group right is defined by its subject rather than its object: by who it is that holds the right rather than by what the right is a right to.

Two considerations further complicate the disentanglement of group rights from individual rights. First, if a legal or institutional group right is justified by a moral right, that moral right could be a right held by individuals rather than by the group as a collective entity; conversely, an individual legal right may be underwritten by a moral group right. Consider the use of group representation in legislatures. Clearly if groups are accorded constitutional rights to representation qua groups, these constitutional rights must be group rights. But those constitutional rights may be grounded in the moral rights of individual citizens. For instance, the defence could be that certain group identities are so fundamental to the life of a society that the only way to ensure that its individual citizens are adequately and equally represented is by making express provision for the representation of their group identities. Group representation will then be justified as a device that more effectively secures the equal rights of political participation possessed by individual citizens. Of course, the defence does not have to be of that sort: group representation may also be justified as a way of protecting goods to which groups are entitled only as groups. But group rights need not 'go all the way down': institutional group rights may sometimes be the instruments of more fundamental individual rights.

Similarly, moral group rights may sometimes secure institutional expression as individual rights. For instance, the collective and exclusive right of a tribe to fish certain waters may be institutionalized by according legal fishing rights to its individual members, so that those rights are exercizable separately by the tribe's members rather than only by the tribe collectively. We cannot simply take for granted therefore either that legal group rights are symptomatic of moral group rights or that moral group rights will find institutional expression only as legal group rights.

A second complication is that sorting rights into individual and group rights is not always a matter of mere analysis. Suppose, for example, that a society contains a linguistic minority and the government of that society prohibits or otherwise impedes the minority's use of its language. If that government violates a right, whose right does it violate? A possible answer is a right held by the linguistic minority as a group; but an equally possible answer is a right possessed individually by each member of the minority to be unprevented from speaking his or her native tongue. In other words, claims of right do not always divide themselves analytically into group rights or individual rights. Determining whether the relevant right should be ascribed to a group collectively or to its members severally will often be a matter of moral substance.

Thus, discriminating group rights from individual rights can require some care but that discrimination still remains to be made.

Group Rights: The Collective Conception

How then can a group have a right that is genuinely a group right? I begin by considering the answer offered by Joseph Raz, whose understanding of group rights I shall describe as the 'collective' conception.[1] Raz subscribes to the interest theory of rights and his version of that theory has been widely adopted by others, including by several exponents of group rights.[2]

Raz's general definition of a right runs as follows:

> 'X has a right' if and only if X can have rights, and, other things being equal, an aspect of X's well-being (his interest) is a sufficient reason for holding some other person(s) to be under a duty.[3]

He adds that an individual can have rights 'if and only if either his wellbeing is of ultimate value or he is an "artificial person" (for example, a corporation)'.[4]

Raz's definition refines earlier statements of the interest theory of rights and two of its features are worth emphasizing. First, like other interest theorists, Raz does not say that having an interest, of itself, yields a right; my interest yields a right only if it is an interest sufficiently significant to create a *duty* for another or others. Secondly, for Raz, rights and duties do not stand in a merely correlative relation; rather, normatively, the logic runs from rights to duties in that it is an aspect of my wellbeing that provides the reason for another's having a duty. In that way, rights *ground* duties.[5]

How does the idea of group rights fare on Raz's conception? Like most people, Raz is ready to accept the idea of a legal group right; legal systems typically accord rights to groups that they constitute or recognize as corporate entities. But Raz also holds that a group can have moral rights. It has those rights if those who make up the group possess a joint interest in a good that justifies the imposition of duties upon others. Raz specifies the following as the conditions that have to be met for there to be a group or 'collective' right.

> First, it exists because an aspect of the interest of human beings justifies holding some person(s) to be subject to a duty. Second, the interests in question are the interests of individuals as members of a group in a public good and the right is a right to that public good because it serves their interest as members of the group. Thirdly, the interest of no single member of that group in that public good is sufficient by itself to justify holding another person to be subject to a duty.[6]

Thus, suppose a society contains a cultural minority. Each individual member of that minority may have an interest in the maintenance of the culture in which he has developed, secured an identity and developed a way of life. The interest of any one individual may not suffice to justify imposing duties on the larger society to institute measures to protect and sustain that culture. But the joint interest of all members of the minority may well suffice, in which case we can ascribe the appropriate group right to the minority.

A cultural minority is likely to be a group with a distinct identity and a substantial common life. But the conditions Raz lays down for a group right imply that an identity of that sort is not essential.[7] Any set of individuals who possess a joint interest in a good can have group rights relating to that good provided that their joint interest is sufficiently significant to create duties for others. What unites and identifies a set of individuals as a group for right-holding purposes is simply their possessing a shared interest of sufficient moment.

Consider the case of cyclists and cycleways. Each cyclist may have an interest in there being a safe and convenient cycleway running through a city. The interest of any single cyclist will not be enough to create a duty for the city authority to construct the cycleway. But the shared interests of all cyclists might well suffice, in which case we could say that the cyclists collectively possess a right – a group right – that the cycleway be built.

Now interests in cycleways may not be the sort of interests that we normally associate with rights. I cite this example only to indicate that a group as thinly identified as cyclists could, in principle, meet Raz's criteria: it is the interests of cyclists that create the duty to build the cycleway; the cycleway is a good that is public to cyclists; and the interest of any single cyclist alone is insufficient to generate a duty to construct the cycleway. If cyclists do not have this group right, it would seem that the explanation, for Raz, must be found in the relative costs and benefits at stake rather than in any shortcomings of cyclists as a 'group'.

Here is another example. An entrepreneur builds a factory in the country of Boria at a site which borders on two other countries, Coria and Doria. The factory gives off polluting fumes and those fumes adversely affect sections of the population in Coria and Doria as well as people in Boria. Suppose that the fumes are insufficiently harmful to give any single individual a right that the factory shall stop its polluting activity. But suppose that the joint interest of all the affected individuals does provide sufficient reason for imposing on the factory-owner a duty to desist with his polluting activity. In that case, the collective conception allows us to say that the individuals living in the vicinity of the factory have a right, as a group, that the factory shall not pollute their environment. The individuals who make up the group can be drawn from Boria, Coria and Doria and those three sets of nationals may lead entirely separate lives and, sociologically, share nothing in common. Nevertheless, for the collective conception of group rights, their shared interest in the factory's ceasing its polluting activity can be enough to make them a group for right-holding purposes.

On this understanding of group rights, then, groups that possess rights can be sets of individuals who share nothing but an interest on a specific matter. I may belong to a whole variety of such 'interest groups' and the membership of each of these groups may be quite different, since I may have a whole variety of different and unrelated interests each of which I share with different sets of people.

We must, of course, avoid caricaturing Raz's position. Just how readily group interests translate into group rights depends upon how high we set the standard for that translation. It also depends upon all-things-considered judgements about how a group's interest interplays with other interests. A collective interest that, taken in isolation, may provide a prima facie case for a right may fail to provide a conclusive case once it is placed in a context of other, competing interests. My concern is to point out only that, on the collective conception of rights: (i) any set of individuals that has a common interest may possess a right qua group; (ii)

that the relevant common interest can be a shared interest on one matter only; and (iii) that no more is required for them to bear a group right than that their interests, taken collectively, are sufficiently weighty to do the job.[8]

That feature of the collective conception of group rights should, however, be set against another. In my cycling and pollution examples, the interests at stake are interests that individuals might have as independent individuals. Even if I were the only cyclist in a city, I would still have an interest in there being a cycleway and, even if I were the only person affected by factory pollution, I would still have an interest in a clean environment. But the collective conception need not suppose that the interests that combine to make the case for a group right must be interests that individuals could have as independent individuals. Consider, again, the case of a group distinguished by a common culture and a shared mode of life. The interest of the members of that group in their shared mode of life is not an interest they could have as isolated and independent individuals. The collective conception can happily recognize that the interests that make the case for a group right may be of this necessarily social and interdependent kind. But that recognition is consistent with its insistence that, ultimately, interrelated and interdependent interests have moral significance only as the interests of individuals.[9]

Raz's generous understanding of group rights has struck some as too generous. Denise Réaume is one theorist who finds it unsatisfactory for that reason.[10] She suggests we should adopt a more discriminating conception of group rights by being more selective about the kind of good to which a group can have a right. In other words, she seeks to narrow the compass of group rights by narrowing their possible objects rather than their possible subjects.

Réaume notices that a good can be a public good and yet be enjoyed privately rather than publicly. For example, clean air is a good public to a community of breathers, but it is a good consumed by members of that community privately rather than publicly: each inhales and enjoys the benefits of clean air as an individual. Indeed, the case of clean air indicates that some public goods might reasonably be the objects of individual rights. Suppose that the only duty entailed by the right to clean air is the duty to refrain from pollution. In that case, it does not seem unreasonable to hold that each individual, as an individual, has a right to clean air. Someone who pollutes the air violates the rights of each individual who is affected by that pollution, just as someone who poisons a water supply violates the rights of each separate consumer of that supply rather than a single collective right possessed by the entire body of consumers.[11] Hence, although a group can have a right only to a public good (a good public to the group), not all rights to public goods need be group rights.

However, Réaume points out, there is a sub-set of public goods that are 'public' in a special sense. These are 'participatory goods' – goods which, by their very nature, must be enjoyed publicly if they are to be enjoyed at all. They 'involve activities that not only require many in order to produce the good but are valuable only because of the joint involvement of many. The publicity of production itself is part of what is valued – the good *is* the participation'.[12] Friendship, a team game and a convivial party are each goods that are public to their participants in this way. Réaume cites living in a cultured society, sharing a common language and being a member of a religious community as other examples, although she accepts that these goods need not be participatory or even public in all of their aspects.

Thus, while there are some public goods to which individuals could conceivably hold

rights, only groups can have rights to participatory public goods. Individuals can hold rights only to what they can enjoy individually; participatory goods can be enjoyed only collectively, so only collectivities can hold rights to them. Réaume proposes that we understand group rights as rights to participatory goods.

Should we narrow our understanding of group rights in the way that Réaume suggests? While she defines her position in opposition to Raz's, her understanding of group rights shares at least one central feature with his. For Réaume as for Raz, what distinguishes a set of individuals as a right-holding group is their common interest in the good to which they have a right rather than anything that distinguishes them as a group independently of that good.[13] The implication of Réaume's analysis seems to be that any set of individuals who share in a participatory good possess a group right to that good provided only that their interest in that good is sufficiently weighty to be a source of duties for others. Given the nature of participatory goods, it may be that groups having rights to those goods will generally have stronger sociological identities as groups than groups who share only in non-participatory goods. Yet that remains a contingent feature of Réaume's analysis. As the examples of a game and a convivial party indicate, a set of individuals might share in a participatory good while sharing nothing else that identifies them as a group.

In addition, it is difficult to see how Réaume can combine the idea of participatory goods with Raz's general interest theory of rights in a way that removes altogether the possibility that groups may have rights to non-participatory goods. While Réaume quarrels with Raz's conception of group rights, she accepts his general claim that a person has a right if he or she has an interest that provides sufficient reason for holding another or others to be under a duty.[14] But, if one adopts that general conception of rights, it is hard to see how one can resist the logic that goes on to claim that a group of individuals may have shared interests in a good that ground a joint right to that good. Those interests may be interests in a participatory good; but they may also be interests in a non-participatory good. It may be that rights to participatory goods can only be group rights; it does not follow that group rights can only be rights to participatory goods. It is not clear, therefore, that Réaume's insights into the different natures of public goods provide us with reason for adopting a conception of group rights more narrowly focused than Raz's.

Group Rights:
The Corporate Conception

Whatever reservations we may have about Réaume's analysis of group rights, many of us are likely to share her sense that Raz's conception does not conform with what we often understand by group rights.[15] It seems unusually generous. It extends rights to collections of individuals some of whom might be better described as 'sets' than 'groups'. That sense points to a different conception of group rights – what I shall call the 'corporate' conception.[16]

Perhaps the best avenue into this alternative conception of group rights is to consider what people usually intend to ask when they ask whether a group *can* bear rights. Often that question is asked of groups in the way it is asked of infants or foetuses or animals or species or the dead or future generations. Questions of who or what can have rights are typically raised against a background assumption that rights can be possessed, uncontroversially, by 'persons' – that is, by adult human beings in full command of their faculties. The issue is whether beings or entities other than persons can possess rights.

What does that question turn upon? It turns upon the attribution of moral standing. To violate a right is to *wrong* the holder of the right. It is to fail to do what is *owed* to the right holder. That indicates that someone or something can hold rights only if it is the sort of thing to which duties can be owed and which is capable of being wronged. In other words, moral standing is a precondition of right-holding.

We may think that we have duties *in respect of* something, but we think of those duties as grounded in the rights of that something only if it is the sort of thing to which we can *owe* duties and that we *wrong* if we fail to perform those duties. Thus, for example, we may think that we have duties not to destroy beautiful paintings or buildings, but most of us would not conceive those as duties owed to paintings and buildings such that the wrong of their destruction can be explicated as wronging the paintings and buildings themselves. In other words, generally, we do not ascribe moral standing to paintings and buildings (as opposed to their owners or others who have an interest in their continued existence) and that is why we do not ascribe rights to paintings and buildings even though we ascribe value to them. A moral right is a moral title and only beings possessed of moral standing can possess entitlements which, in turn, are sources of moral obligation for others.[17]

Thus, to ask whether infants or animals or the dead can possess rights is to ask whether we should ascribe moral standing to infants or animals or the dead. Similarly, to ask whether groups can have rights is typically to ask whether we should ascribe moral standing to a group qua group rather than only to its individual members. If we should, we can think of a group's bearing rights in the same immediate and nonreducible way in which an individual person can bear rights.

That, in turn, implies a conception of group rights quite different from the collective conception. The collective conception does not require us to ascribe moral standing to a group separately from the moral standing we ascribe to its members severally. The right is possessed by the members of the group only as a group, but the interests that ground their jointly held right are the several, if shared and interrelated, interests of the group's members and, more particularly, the requisite moral standing is provided by the several individuals who make up the group rather than by the group as a collective entity.[18] There need be no suggestion that a group has, or can have, moral standing that is somehow separate from and not wholly reducible to the moral standing of the several individuals who constitute the group. But, on the corporate conception, a group does have moral standing qua group and it bears its rights as a single integral entity rather than as so many individuals who possess a joint claim.

Hence, what distinguishes a group as a group for right-holding purposes is quite different for the corporate than for the collective conception. Just as an individual has an identity and a standing as a person independently and in advance of the interests and rights that he or she possesses, so a group that bears a corporate right must have an identity and a standing independently and in advance of the interests it has and the rights it bears. Its being a group with moral standing as a group is a logical prerequisite of its being an entity that can bear corporate rights. So the 'groupness' of groups, for right-holding purposes, is understood quite differently by these two conceptions.[19]

Consider, for example, how each might interpret the moral significance of nationhood and the right of national self-determination. On the corporate conception, a nation will be conceived as an entity with a distinct life and identity of its own which others must recognize and respect. Accord-

ingly, it should receive political recognition and, more particularly, its right of self-determination must be acknowledged. To deny a nation that right is to affront its status as a nation, just as to deny someone the right to shape their own life is to affront their status as a person.

Contrast that view with the defence of national self-determination mounted by Margalit and Raz.[20] They catalogue a number of sociological and cultural features commonly possessed by groups that we describe as nations, and they go on to argue that the wellbeing of individuals who share in those features is, generally, best served by their having a collective right of self-determination. Thus, for Margalit and Raz, the case for national self-determination is made by way of the interests of those who make up a nation rather than by reference to the status of nationhood itself. A nation, in so far as it bears rights, is an 'interest group'. The interests at stake here are, of course, of a very special kind but, in the end, nations have rights of self-determination only because those rights serve the wellbeing of individuals. If, for some reason, people's interests would be better served by taking a section of the population of Nation A and a section of the population of Nation B and putting them together in a self-determining unit, neither Nation could claim that its rights had been violated. That is because implication of Margalit's and Raz's view is that nations, merely as such, do not have rights.

The contrast I have drawn here is not meant to imply that the corporate conception is incompatible with an interest theory of rights. A proponent of the corporate conception may hold that a group's interests must play a defining role in identifying its rights. But a right-identifying interest will be interpreted differently by the corporate than by the collective conception: it will be conceived as an interest of the group as a single entity rather than as an amalgam of the separate if identical interests of the group's constituent members. Moreover, unlike the collective conception, the corporate conception need not be wedded to an interest theory of rights. Interests seem pivotal for the collective conception for, without interests, it is hard to see what it could be that accumulates across individuals to make the case for a collective right.[21] But no such cumulative factor is necessary for the corporate conception, since, on that conception, a group has a pre-existing moral identity as a group. Consequently, the corporate conception can be used alongside other theories of rights – for example, a choice theory of rights which would identify a group's rights not by way of its interests but by reference to the duties the group is owed and over whose performance it can exercise control.[22]

In a moment, I shall argue that these two conceptions of group rights present us with different reasons for worrying about the way in which the claims of groups might imperil those of individuals. But first I want to say a little about three other matters that serve to emphasize the separateness of the two conceptions.

(1) The Significance of Group Identity

I shall not attempt a thorough investigation of the criteria that a group must satisfy if it is to possess corporate rights.[23] Clearly, those who agree in conceiving group right on the corporate model may disagree over the precise conditions a group must satisfy if it is to be a right-holding group. However, there is one condition upon which any proponent of a corporate conception must insist: that a right-holding group has a clear identity as a group.[24]

It would, perhaps, be unreasonable to inquire that a group be as sharply individu-ated as a human person before it can be recognized as a distinct entity. But rights must have possessor and, if we are using the corporate conception, a group must be sufficiently well-defined to enable the identification of the social entity that possesses the right. Recall that, for the corporate conception, a right-holding group must be identifiable as a morally significant entity independently of, and in advance of, the interests and rights it possesses. Consequently, it cannot rely upon its possession of interests and rights for its moral identity.[25]

A group's identity must also be sufficiently strong to withstand claims that it is subsumed by a larger identity or that it is a mere amalgam of smaller groups, each of whose separate identities discredits the larger group's claim to be a morally significant entity. One of the most common and effective ways of debunking a group's claim to rights is to challenge its integrity as a group. Claims that a particular set of people constitute a nation are often challenged in that way, as, indeed, is the very idea of 'nationhood'.[26]

This is not a matter that need trouble us if we adopt the collective conception – or, at least, not in the same way. For the collective conception, the only relevant consideration is whether a set of individuals shares an interest which adequately grounds a right. Sociologically, groups may be ragged at the edges, they may overlap, some may be contained within others, some may have less than uniform memberships. None of that complexity and untidiness is fundamentally problematic for the collective conception. All we need ask is whether, somewhere in all this sociological confusion, there is a set of individuals with a common interest of a sort that grounds a right. The complex and untidy nature of individuals' involvement with one another makes that judgement more complicated but, for the collective conception, that complication is a technical rather than a moral difficulty.

(2)   Scepticism about Group Rights

A second matter to which the two conceptions relate differently is scepticism about group rights. Some people take exception to the very idea that groups can hold rights. Their scepticism, I suggest, presupposes the corporate rather than the collective conception. If we accept that individuals can have rights that derive from their individual interests, it is hard to see how we can resist the logic of the collective conception that claims that groups of individuals can hold rights jointly that derive from their shared interests. Of course, whether any particular shared interest suffices to ground a joint right will always have to be argued, but it is hard to see how someone who accepts an interest theory of rights could find unacceptable the very idea that rights might be held by groups in the way that Raz suggests.

By contrast, it is entirely intelligible that someone faced with the corporate conception might reject the very notion of group rights. Their claim might be that individual persons are the only beings that have moral standing and that groups qua groups should be accorded no analogous moral status no matter how culturally and sociologically distinct they are. Indeed, the objection that is most commonly advanced against group rights is that groups have no moral standing that is not wholly reducible to the moral status of the individual persons who make them up.[27] But, as I have just indicated, that objection is of no force if it is directed against the collective rather than the corporate conception of group rights.

(3)   Which Rights?

The distinction I have drawn between the collective and the corporate conceptions turns upon different understandings of the subject of group rights. Does that distinction imply a difference in the possible objects of group rights – in what it is that groups might have rights to?

Many of the rights that might be ascribed to groups are capable of being group rights on either conception. I have explained how both conceptions can make sense of a group right of national self-determination. It is also easy to contemplate how both conceptions might ascribe rights to cultural and ethnic groups concerning recognition and respect for their identities and modes of life. However, while the domains of the two sorts of group right may overlap, they are unlikely to be entirely the same. Because the collective conception is more generous than the corporate conception about the kinds of group that can possess rights, it can also be more generous about the possible objects of group rights. For example, on the collective conception specific groups might have rights to clean air, coastal defences and community health safeguards; these are unlikely to be group rights on the corporate conception simply because the groups to which they relate are unlikely to be groups distinguished by the special sort of moral identity that is essential for that conception.

What about the converse? Are there any rights that might qualify as group rights for the corporate but not for the collective conception? That is more difficult to answer, but one possibility is rights that imply a possessor that is not wholly identifiable with a current set of individuals. Consider the right of a cultural group that its identity shall survive into the indefinite future. If there is such a right, it is hard to see how it could be explained solely by reference to the interests of current members of the cultural group. We might try to square it with the collective conception by invoking the interests of future generations but, since those future individuals have yet to acquire a cultural identity, we cannot convincingly impute to them membership of, and an interest in, a particular group's identity. If a long-term right of cultural survival is claimed for a group, it is more intelligibly claimed on the corporate than on the collective model.[28]

The same is true of some assertions of property rights. Nations are sometimes said to have rights over particular pieces of territory and tribes over particular tracts of land. Where those ownership rights are conceived as stretching back into the indefinite past and forward into the indefinite future, the 'owner' is more intelligibly conceived corporately than collectively. Similarly, rights bestowed on tribes or peoples by treaty, or reparating them for historical wrongs, are more readily intelligible as corporate than as collective rights. There are, then, some group rights which, if they are rights, make more sense as corporate than as collective rights.

Group Rights and the Status of Individuals

What is the significance of group rights for the status of individuals and, more particularly, for the freedom of individuals to shape their lives as they choose? Groups and individuals can be juxtaposed in too simple a fashion. Groups are made up of individuals and the fate of individuals is tied up with the fate of the groups to which they belong. Nor need we think of groups as monsters that tower threateningly over outsiders. Politically, one of the principal drives behind the assertion of rights has been a desire to protect the vulnerable. In recent years, group rights have received more sympathetic attention partly because they have been claimed by, or for, minorities who stand in a disadvantaged or vulnerable relationship with a larger society. Nor, again, need group rights be inimical to freedom. The right of a nation or a cultural group to be self-determining, for example, has often been asserted as a demand that the individuals who form that group should be able to shape their destiny free from interference by censorious outsiders.

Yet many people still look upon group rights with distrust. They fear that, when we ascribe rights to groups, we hand them a licence to oppress individuals. Is that fear justified? It may seem that we can make no progress in answering that question until we have decided upon the rights that groups have. Clearly, much will turn on the content that we give group rights. Yet there is a widely shared belief that there is something about group rights merely as such that is threatening to individuals. I shall examine whether there is indeed something in the very nature of group rights that justifies that anxiety.

Fear of group rights has two dimensions. One is the danger they pose for individuals *outside* the group. Rights are often ascribed to individuals as protections against the power of institutionalized groupings such as firms or trade unions and uninstitutionalized groupings such as opinionated majorities. If we ascribe rights to groups, we may seem to remove that protection. Rights will not safeguard individuals against groups if groups also have rights that they can use to match or trump the rights of individuals.

The other threat posed by group rights is to individuals *inside* the group. A group might claim rights against its own members so that the group can impose restrictions upon its members severally. Consequently, in embracing group rights we may be placing individuals at the mercy of collectivities. In addition, the effect of ascribing rights to groups may be to diminish the moral standing of their individual members: the independent moral identity of each individual will be 'lost' in the identity of the group and the group will replace the individual as the object of moral concern.

I have formulated these worries as worries about groups and individuals, and I shall go on to examine them in that simple form. However, similar worries may be expressed entirely in terms of groups. What, for example, will be the fate of small groups when they find themselves confronted by the rights of large groups? Groups that claim rights often contain within their ranks smaller groups with distinct identities and interests. How will the standing of those internal groups be affected if we ascribe rights to the larger group within which they fall? It would be a mistake, therefore, to see these worries about group oppression as no more than manifestations of an old rivalry between individualism and collectivism or a new rivalry between liberalism and communitarianism.

Groups versus Individuals: The Collective Conception

The collective theory of group rights seems potentially more threatening to individuals outside than to individuals inside the group.[29] That is because, on the collective theory, at least as it is articulated by Raz, numbers count. As Raz remarks, 'collective or group rights represent the cumulative interests of many individuals who are members of the relevant groups. It follows that there is nothing essentially non-aggregative about rights.'[30] Other things being equal, numbers would seem to bear upon collective rights in two ways. First, the greater the number of people who share an interest, the stronger the case for that interest's grounding a right. Secondly, the greater the number of people who enjoy a collective right in virtue of their shared interest, the weightier that collective right. Thus size matters. Numbers affect both which groups have rights and how weighty their rights are. Notice that as well as trading off one interest against another,

interest theorists are usually happy to trade off one right against another.[31] An interest theory of rights of the sort espoused by Raz mimics some of the aggregative and discounting features of utilitarianism and it can therefore arouse some of the same anxieties as utilitarianism about the fate of individuals and their rights. There is, then, something in the logic of the collective conception which provides reason for worrying that, when individuals and their rights come up against groups and their rights, it is individuals who will frequently be the losers.

Denise Réaume suggests that her version of group rights, in which groups have rights only to participatory goods, does not share the aggregative features of Raz's theory.[32] She accepts that numbers are relevant to whether groups have rights, but in a way quite different from that proposed by Raz. Participatory goods, such as the communal aspects of language use or religious practice, require a critical mass of participants to be viable. If they do not attract the required minimum of participants, those goods will not exist and there can be no rights to them. But if the critical mass of participants is achieved, numbers are of no further relevance. In particular, they do not affect the weight of a group's right to a participatory good. Yet it is not clear that Réaume can dismiss the relevance of numbers quite so easily given that, whatever her departures from Raz, she still works with his interest theory of rights. If we operate with that theory, the number of people who share an interest in a participatory good would still seem inescapably relevant to whether a group has a right and, if it does, to how weighty that right is.

In all of this, of course, much depends upon: (i) how we conceive the interests of individuals singly and in groups; (ii) how far the rights of groups actually rub up against those of individuals; and (iii) how the social costs of putative individual rights compare with those of putative group rights. The impact of numbers will be modified to the extent that it takes more to justify the duties consequent upon group rights than those entailed by individual rights. Even so, the aggregative nature of the collective conception provides some ground for fearing that group interests and group rights will overwhelm individual interests and individual rights.

The fate of individuals internal to the group seems much less troubling for the collective conception. Since, on that conception, an individual will be a member of a right-holding group only if he or she shares in the interest that grounds the right, it is hard to see how an individual could be disadvantaged by the group's right. The interest of the group must be identical with that of each of its members, so that anything that promotes the good of the group must promote the good of its members. However, there are two considerations that might disrupt a simple symmetry of interests amongst the holders of a collective right.

First, while a set of individuals may all have an interest in x, the extent of their interest in x may differ. For example, if I am almost bilingual I shall be less crucially interested in measures designed to protect my first language than if it is my only language. There seems nothing in the collective conception that requires that the interests that sum together to provide the case for a group right must be interests of equal moment for each member of the group.

Secondly, people may share an interest on one matter but have different and conflicting interests on another. Suppose that, like others, I have an interest in x but that, unlike others, I have a conflicting and greater interest in y. If people's shared interests in x justify a collective right to x, should I be included amongst the joint holders of that right because I have *some* interest in x, even though I have a conflicting and greater interest in y? The answer depends upon how we are to interpret the interest that makes the case for a right. If that should be an individual's all-things-considered interest, I shall fall outside the right-holding group. But if it can be an individual's partial interest, the logic of the collective conception seems to be that my interest in x can add to the case for a group right to x and I can figure as a joint holder of that right even though the right runs counter to my interest all things considered. Even in this latter case, however, the y that conflicts with x could not be the duty generated by the right to x. I cannot simultaneously share in a joint right to x and incur, singly or jointly, the duty consequent upon that right. A collective right, unlike a corporate right, cannot be held against those who make up the right-holding group. I postpone explaining this point until the next section.

Each of these complications is of limited significance and it remains true for the collective conception that if an individual is to figure as a member of a group that wields a right, she must retain an interest in that group's right. Her interests cannot be simply ignored, nor can she be made to 'disappear' into some larger entity within which she has no independent moral significance.

Groups versus Individuals: The Corporate Conception

The collective conception, then, may give us more reason to worry about how a group's rights bear upon individuals external to the group than upon those within the group. With the corporate theory the balance of concern tips in the other direction. A group might wield its corporate rights at the expense of individuals or smaller groups that fall outside its boundaries, but there are two considerations that modify that threat.

The first is that a corporate conception of group rights is likely to figure in a moral world in which groups confront other groups and, in some measure, hold their rights against one another as groups rather than against individuals. In other words, many of the duties entailed by corporate rights are likely to be corporate duties. For example, when a nation, in virtue of its separate identity, is accorded a right of self-determination, that is typically conceived as a right that it holds with respect to other nations. It is not usually conceived as a right whose corresponding duties are targeted at particular individuals within other nations. The same will often hold true, on the corporate conception, of rights that are assigned to groups in virtue of their ethnic or cultural identities. I do not pretend that this must be generally true; corporate rights can impose duties or costs upon individuals as well as upon groups.[33] But, in so far as corporate rights are targeted at other corporate entities, they will not set up a moral contest between a group Goliath and an individual David.

There is less reason to expect the collective theory to generate a separate domain of group-to-group interaction for, on that theory, the rights of groups derive from aggregations of interests and those interests vie with other interests whomsoever's interests they are – those of large groups or of small groups or of individuals taken singly.

A second feature of the corporate theory is that it can more readily accommodate a conception of group rights as equal rights. Each group, a corporate theorist might argue, presents us with an identity, each identity should command respect, and each should command equal respect. Taking any single dimension of identity, no group's identity matters more than any other's and, accordingly, no group's rights should count for more or less than another's. Thus, if we ascribe rights to nations or to cultural groups, we can ascribe rights to each of them equally. Size does not matter. Small nations, for example, will have the same rights, and rights

of the same weight, as large nations. A corporate conception of group rights can therefore happily accompany a commitment to group rights as equal rights.[34]

Again, that does not hold for the collective theory. On that theory, as we have seen, a large group of individuals is more likely to have a right, and a right of greater weight, than a small group. Of course, in some cases, it may turn out that the rights of a large group need be no greater than those of a small group to provide adequately for the larger group's interests. A large nation's rights of self-determination, for example, may need to be no different from a small nation's to provide adequately for its interest in self-determination. But, for the collective theory, that remains a contingent matter.

These two considerations, then, modify, without entirely removing, the threat posed by corporate group rights to outsiders. But the corporate conception gives us reason, that the collective conception does not, to worry about how a group right will bear upon the group's own members.

Perhaps the most obvious reason for that worry is that, on the corporate conception, a group can have rights against or over its own members. Let me explain why the corporate conception makes that possible, while the collective conception rules it out. By common consent people cannot hold rights against themselves. Consequently, there can be a right/duty or a right/liability relation only if we can separate the party that holds the right from the party that incurs the corresponding duty or liability. The corporate conception makes possible the separation of a group from its individual members because, morally, it attributes standing to a group separately from its members severally. Existentially, there may be no way in which we can or would wish to separate a group from its members; a corporate conception of group rights need not be wedded to a non-ethical ontological claim that a group as a whole has a being that is somehow separate from its parts. But, *morally*, by giving standing to a group qua group, the corporate conception does enable a group to be identified separately from its members. That separation, in turn, opens up the possibility that a group corporately may hold rights against, or over, its members severally.

By contrast, if we confine ourselves to an unadulterated collective conception, we cannot accept that group rights can be inwardly directed. Group rights cannot take that form because, morally, the group has no identity or standing that is separate from the individuals who make it up and who jointly hold its rights. If A and B and C hold a right jointly rather than separately, they still hold that right as so many independently identifiable individuals. To suppose that they might hold that joint right against A or B or C singly or against A and B and C collectively would be no less odd than to suppose that an individual might hold an individual right against himself. Individuals who incur the duty entailed by a collective right cannot figure amongst the holders of that right.[35] On the collective conception, then, a group's rights can only be externally directed.

There is one way in which a collective right might be linked to a corporate right that requires further comment. A set of individuals who, in conformity with the collective conception, make up a right-holding group might decide to constitute themselves – or might be constituted by an outside agency – as a group with a common decision procedure so that they can more effectively pursue their shared interests. The group could then use that procedure to make decisions binding upon each of its members and those decisions could, in turn, be said to create rights held by the group against its members severally. But that will have become possible only because the group has now acquired, institutionally, a corporate identity that it previously lacked: it has been formally constituted

as a body with a corporate identity and a status that distinguishes it from its individual members. It is that formal separation of the group (now institutionalized as a decision-making body) from its several members (now institutionally subject to its authority) that has created the possibility of the group's having rights over its own members.

Morally, the group's institutional corporate right might be grounded in its collective right but, *conceptually*, the two rights remain quite distinct. Nor need one right entail the other. A group with a collective right against the outside world need not institutionalize itself as a group that wields a corporate right over its own members. And a group that constitutes itself as a formal association with rights over its own members need not be a group that possesses a collective moral right against the outside world: *any* set of individuals can turn themselves into a formal association and empower themselves to make decisions as a group that bind each of them severally.

Moreover, if the case for a group's corporate right of self-government is grounded in its members' collective right, that case will stand only so long as the corporate right retain its symmetry with the group's collective right. Recall that, on the collective conception, I belong to a right-holding group only if I share in the interest that grounds the right of the group. If a group wields its corporate right to my disadvantage, the group cannot pretend that this use of its corporate right is merely an extension of a collective right in which I share. That is not to say that every corporate decision that affects me adversely must be at odds with the collective right: a decision which disbenefits me immediately may be part of an overall arrangement that works to my general advantage and my general gain may be greater than my particular loss. But if a group has the corporate authority to sacrifice my overall good for the sake of other members of the group, that authority cannot be excused as merely the instrument of a collective right of which I am myself a joint holder.

So one way in which the corporate, but not the collective, conception threatens individuals is by making it possible for a group to hold rights against its own members. Is it really appropriate to describe that as a 'threat'? After all, we are thoroughly familiar with associations that exercise authority over their members: such associations are ubiquitous and commonplace rather than exceptional and sinister. But my principal concern is with groups that are alleged to possess fundamental *moral* rights – groups that possess identities that demand moral recognition rather than groups that are created by acts of association. The most favoured candidates for these groups are nations, ethnic groups and cultural groups – groups whose membership is not chosen but naturally or socially given and whose members, on the strictest interpretation, cannot escape membership.[36] It is the association of corporate moral rights with this sort of involuntary group that makes the possibility of a group's having rights over its own members seem potentially oppressive.

Beyond that, very much depends, of course, on what specific rights we allow that a group might hold against its own members. At one extreme, a proponent of the corporate conception might ascribe unlimited internal rights to a group so that the individuals encompassed by the group are entirely at its corporate mercy. At the other extreme, that proponent might deny that a group has any inwardly directed rights: logically it seems possible to ascribe rights to a group on the corporate model but to limit those to externally directed rights.[37] However, as I shall now go on to show, even corporate rights directed at parties outside the group can have adverse implications for those inside the group.

Underlying worries about internally direct group rights are a more general concern.

Corporate rights are rights possessed only by groups that have moral standing qua groups. That moral standing can compete with the moral standing of the separate individuals who constitute the group's members. At the limit, a group as a corporate entity may possess a moral standing so inclusive and complete that it deprives the group's individual members of any independent moral standing: the group becomes everything, the individual nothing. But let us put aside that extreme possibility. Even if we attribute moral standing to individuals as well as to groups, we have still to wrestle with the issue of who has standing on what. Who, for any particular matter, has standing on that matter? Who is entitled to determine what is to be done – the group or its members separately?

That issue is perhaps most clearly apparent when it arises in relation to the demands a group makes upon outsiders. As long as a group of individuals is of one mind, it may make little practical difference whether the group presents its claims upon the outside world as corporate rights or as collective rights. But suppose that a group is not of one mind and that those who claim to speak for the group find themselves opposed by a body of internal dissenters. Suppose, for example, that a community decides to require its members to conform to its traditional religion and so institutes and enforces measures designed to ensure that everyone encompassed by the community complies with that religion. A dissenting minority objects and appeals to the outside world to intervene on its behalf. What should the outside world do? Assume that we leave practical complications to one side and focus only on the issue of principle. If religious belief and practice are matters on which individuals have standing, that opens the door to justified intervention. If, on the other hand, a community's internal affairs, including the place that religion has in its life, are matters on which only the community qua group has standing, external intervention designed to alter the character of the community's internal arrangements will be illicit. The outside world must recognize that its conduct should be governed by the voice of the group rather than by the voice of the internal malcontents.

An obvious objection to this conclusion is that a divided community cannot pretend to be a single group with a single set of interests and rights. But the corporate conception, in ascribing to a group irreducible identity and standing, enables us to contemplate the group separately from its members severally and to acknowledge that it has rights against us in spite of dissenting voices that reach us from within the group. In such cases, of course, some voice has to serve as the voice of the group other than the unanimous voice of all of the individuals encompassed by the group. That adds another layer of complication to the corporate conception. But the fundamental point about 'standing', in this context, is that it determines whose voice is to count and whose is not. If the group only has standing, the group's 'authoritative' or 'authentic' voice is the voice to which we, as outsiders, should attend; the voice of the individual or the sub-group has no status.[38]

Contrast that moral picture with the way the world appears if, instead, we adopt the collective conception of group rights and the moral assumptions upon which it is built. On that conception, individuals fall within a group that possesses a right only if they share in the interest that grounds the right. Suppose, again, that the members of a community have conflicting interests on a matter and that those interests divide them into a majority and a minority. If we follow the collective conception, the community will confront the outside world not with the single right of a single moral entity but with two conflicting claims, both of which demand the attention of outsiders. The outside world may ultimately conclude that it should accede to the wishes of the majority rather

than to those of the minority but, if it has reached that conclusion in a manner consonant with the moral assumptions that underpin the collective conception, it will have taken full account of the interests of the minority. It will have accorded 'standing' to members of the minority even though it has decided it should subordinate their wishes to those of the majority. It will not have merely ignored the minority on the grounds that the voice of the majority constitutes the single authentic voice of the community.

Thus, the internal threat posed by the corporate conception consists not only in its enabling a group to claim rights against its own members. It lies also in its propensity to allow the moral standing of the group to displace that of individuals and sub-groups who fall within the group's compass.

Conclusion

Throughout this article, I have counterposed the collective to the corporate conception and presented these as rival understandings of group rights. Interpreting a group right, such as a right of national or cultural self-determination, according to one conception rather than the other makes a fundamental difference to the sort of right it is. Yet these two conceptions need not be mutually exclusive. By that I mean not that a group's right might simultaneously assume both forms. Rather, I mean that there is no formal inconsistency in holding that some group rights take a collective form while others take a corporate form. We might, for example, hold both that urban populations have collective rights to clean air that they hold against potential polluters and that nations have corporate rights of self-determination that they hold against one another. It seems unlikely that those who embrace the idea of corporate rights would have any principled objection to the idea of collective rights. On the other hand, many who are willing to embrace the idea of collective rights may take exception to the idea of corporate rights simply because they are unwilling to ascribe moral standing to a group as such.

Of the various contrasting features of the two conceptions, the most fundamental concerns the locus of moral standing. The collective conception locates moral standing in the several individuals who jointly hold a right, while the corporate conception locates it in the group conceived as a single unitary entity. That difference in the moral structure of the two conceptions bears crucially on the debate over whether we should allow that groups can hold rights. It also bears crucially on the sorts of group that might hold rights and on the sorts of right a group might have.[39] Finally, it bears fundamentally on the implications of ascribing rights to groups for individuals (and other groups) that fall outside or inside the ranks of the right-holding group. Before we worry about the implications of according rights to groups, we need to know which of these two sorts of group right is at stake; only then can we know what it is that we should worry about.

Notes

[1] J. Raz, *The Morality of Freedom* (Oxford: Clarendon Press, 1986). For Raz's general analysis of rights, see pp. 165–216, 245–63; for his understanding of group rights, see pp. 207–8.

[2] See, for example, Nathan Brett, 'Language Laws and Collective Rights', *Canadian Journal of Law and Jurisprudence*, 4 (1991), 347–60; Michael Freeman, 'Are there Collective Human Rights?', *Political Studies*, 43 (special issue, 1995), 25–40; Leslie Green, 'Two Views of Collective Rights', *Canadian Journal of Law and Jurisprudence*, 4 (1991), 315–27, and 'Internal Minorities and their Rights', in *Group Rights*, ed. J. Baker (Toronto: University of Toronto Press, 1994), pp. 101–17; Avishai Margalit and Moshe Halbertal, 'Liberalism and the Right to Culture', *Social Research*, 61 (1994), 491–510; Denise G. Réaume, 'Individuals, Groups, and Rights to Public Goods', *University of Toronto Law Journal*, 38 (1988), 1–27, and 'The Group Right to Linguistic Security: Whose Right, What Duties?', in *Group Rights*, ed. Baker, pp. 118–41. I should add that, while these authors work with Raz's interest conception of rights, they do not always accept everything he says about rights in general or group rights in particular.

[3] Raz, *Morality of Freedom*, p. 166. Earlier influential statements of the interest theory were given by David Lyons in 'Rights, Claimants and Beneficiaries', *American Philosophical Quarterly*, 6 (1969), 173–85, and by Neil MacCormick in 'Rights in Legislation', in *Law, Morality and Society*, ed. P. M. S. Hacker and J. Raz (Oxford: Clarendon Press, 1977), pp. 189–209.

[4] Raz, *Morality of Freedom*, p. 166.

[5] Raz, *Morality of Freedom*, pp. 166–8, 170–2, 183–6. Not all duties need be grounded by rights since duties can exist for other reasons.

[6] Raz, *Morality of Freedom*, p. 208.

[7] Raz uses the phrase 'members of a group' in his definition of a collective right but I take that to refer to membership of the group identified by its shared interest in the relevant public good. I cannot see how, given his general conception of rights, Raz could justifiably restrict collective rights to groups that are distinguished as groups by some feature that is independent of the interest that grounds their right.

[8] The way in which Raz formally defines a right – X has a right if 'an aspect of X's well-being (his interest) is a *sufficient* reason for holding some other person(s) to be under a duty' – may suggest that X's right must be justified solely by X's interests. However, Raz indicates that the interests that provide the ground for a right can include interests that

will be promoted through the right-holder's having that right other than interests of the right-holder himself. That, in turn, implies that the interests that make the case for a group right, and that contribute to the weight of the right, might include interests other than those of the right-holding group. I ignore here any additional complications to which that might give rise. See Raz, *Morality of Freedom*, pp. 247–55, and 'Rights and Individual Well-being', in his *Ethics in the Public Domain* (Oxford: Clarendon, 1994, revised edn), pp. 44–59.

9   'Cultural, and other, groups have a life of their own. But their moral claim to respect and to prosperity rests entirely on their vital importance to the prosperity of individual human beings.' Raz, *Ethics in the Public Domain*, p. 178.

10   Réaume, 'Individuals, Groups, and Rights to Public Goods', and 'The Group Right to Linguistic Security'.

11   It would be odd, however, to ascribe to an individual a right to a public good *as a public* good. If we take the case of clean air, that would imply that *I* have a right that *everyone* should enjoy clean air, so that you ought to have clean air not because you are entitled to it but because I am entitled that you should have it. For an attempt to present even the rights to culture and to national self-determination as individual rather than collective rights, see Yael Tamir, *Liberal Nationalism* (Princeton, NJ: Princeton University Press, 1993), esp. chs 2 & 3.

12   Réaume, 'Individuals, Groups, and Rights to Public Goods', p. 10. For other accounts of participatory goods, see Jeremy Waldron, 'Can Communal Goods be Human Rights?', in his *Liberal Rights* (Cambridge: Cambridge University Press, 1993), pp. 354–9; and Leslie Green, *The Authority of the State* (Oxford: Clarendon Press, 1988), pp. 207–9. Waldron calls participatory goods 'communal goods' and Green calls them 'shared goods'.

13   Comparison between Réaume and Raz is complicated by Réaume's apparent misreading of Raz's understanding of group rights. She remarks that Raz 'characterises collective rights as individual rights arising out of the interest in collective goods' ('The Group Right to Linguistic Security', p. 123). But, while Raz conceives the interests that ground a collective right as the interests of the several individuals who make up the group, he insists that the right is held only by the group: members of the group hold a right jointly that none of them holds individually. Marlies Galenkamp misreads Raz in a similar fashion: *Individualism versus Collectivism: the Concept of Collective Rights* (Rotterdam: Rotterdamse Filosofische Studies, 1993), pp. 16, 19. Réaume is sometimes agnostic and sometimes ambivalent about whether her conception of group rights requires the attribution of moral standing to groups as such (what I go on to describe as a 'corporate' conception of group rights): 'Individuals, Groups, and Rights to Public Goods', pp. 11, 24, 27, 'The Group Right to Linguistic Security', pp. 124–5, 138. But a group's having a right to a participatory good is entirely consistent with Raz's conception of collective rights properly understood. For example, Réaume's statement that 'there be no individual right to a collective good but only a collective right, held jointly by all who share in the collective good' ('The Group Right to Linguistic Security', p. 121) might have been made by Raz himself.

14   Réaume, 'Individuals, Groups, and Rights to Public Goods', pp. 7, 14; and 'The Group Right to Linguistic Security', p. 119.

15   But note that Raz understands himself to be providing a 'philosophical definition' of a right rather than an explanation of 'the ordinary meaning of the term', and also a theory of rights that is adjusted to the current climate of thinking; *Morality of Freedom*, pp. 165, 249.

16   I use the label 'corporate' with some reluctance and for want of a better alternative. 'Corporate' might suggest 'characteristic of a legal corporation' but that is a fuller meaning than I intend. In this article, I use 'corporate' to denote nothing more than I expressly describe.

17   See further, my *Rights* (Basingstoke: Macmillan, 1994), pp. 36–9, 67–71.

18 Raz does not say this of his conception of collective rights but I take that to be an implicit feature of his conception. Cf. his discussion of ultimate value and the capacity to hold rights, *Morality of Freedom*, pp. 176–80. Whatever Raz's view, the location of moral standing in the several individuals who jointly hold a collective right is crucial to my own understanding of that right.

19 Because those laying claim to, or writing about, group rights have generally not worked consciously with the distinction I make between the collective and corporate conceptions, it is not always easy to assign authors to one or other school of thought. However, I believe the corporate conception captures what most people have understood by group rights until quite recently. In so far as the English pluralists embraced the idea of group rights, they conceived them in this way. See, in particular, John Neville Figgis, *Churches in the Modern State* (London: Longmans, Green, 1913). For examples of recent studies of group rights which are guided, more or less explicitly, by what I describe as the corporate conception (even though the authors may use the term 'collective' right) see: Marlies Galenkamp, *Individualism versus Collectivism: the Concept of Group Rights*, especially ch. 5; Larry May, *The Morality of Groups* (Notre Dame: University of Notre Dame Press, 1987), ch. 5; Michael McDonald, 'Should Communities have Rights? Reflections on Liberal Individualism', *Canadian Journal of Law and Jurisprudence*, 4 (1991), 217–37; Vernon Van Dyke, 'The Individual, the State, and Ethnic Communities in Political Theory', *World Politics*, 29 (1977), 343–69, and *Human Rights, Ethnicity, and Discrimination* (Westport: Greenwood Press, 1985); Adeno Addis, 'Individualism, Communitarianism, and the Rights of Ethnic Minorities', *Notre Dame Law Review*, 67 (1992), 615–76. See also, Roger Scruton, 'Corporate Persons', *Proceedings of the Aristotelian Society*, supplementary vol. 63 (1989), 239–66. Leslie Green has come closest to distinguishing two sorts of group right in the way that I do; see his 'Two Views of Collective Rights'.

20 Avishai Margalit and Joseph Raz, 'National Self-determination', *Journal of Philosophy*, 87 (1990), 439–61. See also Raz, *Morality of Freedom*, pp. 207–9.

21 The idea that is fundamental to the collective conception of group rights is not that of rights conceived according to the interest theory but of rights held jointly by a number of individuals. But, if we were to formulate the collective conception without reference to the interest theory, we should need something other than the shared interests of individuals that could explain why we should suppose that people might hold (moral) rights jointly rather than separately or corporately.

22 Cf. L. W. Sumner, *The Moral Foundation of Rights* (Oxford: Clarendon Press, 1987), pp. 209–11.

23 For studies of this issue and some possible answers, see Peter A. French, *Collective and Corporate Responsibility* (New York: Columbia University Press, 1984); Galenkamp, *Individualism versus Collectivism*; and May, *The Morality of Groups*. Since, on my view, right-holding depends crucially upon moral standing, the conditions of moral standing will provide the conditions a group has to satisfy if it is to be a corporate right-holder. But since the prerequisites of moral standing are controversial (as is evident from disputes over whether any entity other than human persons can possess rights), that controversy must infect the question of which groups, if any, can possess corporate rights.

24 This is, of course, a necessary not a sufficient condition for a corporate group right: even if we concede that a group has a clear identity, we need not concede that it has rights qua group.

25 What I say here does not exclude the possibility that the requisite identity may be imputed to, rather than experienced by, a group. One, perhaps surprising, exponent of corporate group rights is John Rawls. He ascribes various rights to 'peoples' and his insistence that the liberal conception of the person must not be transposed from liberal to nonliberal societies seems to rule out a 'collective' understanding of those group rights.

Moreover, the rights of peoples appears to have a fundamental rather than a derivative status for Rawls or, at least, as fundamental a status as his approach allows. See Rawls, 'The Law of Peoples', in On *Human Rights: the Oxford Amnesty Lectures 1993*, ed. S. Shute and S. Hurley (New York: Basic Books, 1993), pp. 41–82, and my 'International Human Rights: Philosophical or Political?', in *National Rights, International Obligations*, ed. S. Caney, D. George and P. Jones (Boulder, CO: Westview, 1996), pp. 183–204.

26 See, for example, Elie Kedourie, *Nationalism*, 4th edn (Oxford: Blackwell, 1993); and David George, 'National Identity and National Self-determination', and John Charvet, 'What is Nationality, and is there a Right to National Self-determination?', both in *National Rights, International Obligations*, ed. Caney, George and Jones, pp. 13–33, 53–68. For a similarly sceptical appraisal of the identity of cultural groups, see Chandran Kukathas, 'Are there any Cultural Rights?', *Political Theory*, 20 (1992), 105–39.

27 Here is a recent example of that scepticism: 'Individuals are natural units: organized collectivities are constructed "units". Ethnoculturally defined peoples are, I believe, groupings whose "unity" can be made to appear or disappear depending on which "ties that bind" one may wish to emphasize for political, anthropological, sociological, or historical purposes. The conception of a given ethnoculturally defined people replete with its rights and obligations is a politically and emotionally powerful fiction – but it is a fiction and nothing more. Fictitious entities have no rights . . .' (James A. Graff, 'Human Rights, Peoples and the Right to Self-determination', in *Group Rights*, ed. Baker, p. 194). For similarly sceptical dismissals of group rights, see Michael Hartney, 'Some Confusions concerning Collective Rights', and Jan Narveson, 'Collective Rights?', *Canadian Journal of Law and Jurisprudence*, 4 (1991), 293–314 and 329–45.

28 Cf. Leslie Green, 'Are Language Rights Fundamental?', *Osgoode Hall Law Journal*, 25 (1987), 639–69; and Denise Réaume, 'The Constitutional Protection of Language:

Survival or Security?', in *Language and the State: the Law and Politics of Identity*, ed. David Schneiderman (Cowansville, Quebec: Les Editions Yvon Blais, 1991), pp. 37–57.

29 'Inside/outside' here need not take a territorial form. For example, if the language rights of French speakers in Quebec or of Welsh speakers in Wales are interpreted as group rights, the 'outsiders' that are most likely to be affected by those rights are speakers of other languages resident in Quebec or Wales.

30 Raz, *Morality of Freedom*, p. 187; see also p. 209.

31 For an article that illustrates well the propensity of the interest theory to generate conflicts of rights and to deal with those conflicts by trading off rights against rights, see Jeremy Waldron, 'Rights in Conflict', in his *Liberal Rights*, pp. 203–24.

32 Réaume, 'Individuals, Groups, and Rights to Public Goods', pp. 25–6; 'The Group Right to Linguistic Security', pp. 126–7.

33 For example, corporate rights designed to protect a group's culture might restrict the conduct not only of other groups but also of individuals external to the protected group since their individual conduct might adversely affect the group's culture.

34 Minority groups are sometimes accorded rights that are not enjoyed by other groups. But those special rights are usually justified as devices that aim to correct for the unequal circumstances of groups. They need not be at odds therefore with a commitment to group rights as *fundamentally* equal.

35 Suppose, for example, that a factory owner lives in the vicinity of his own polluting factory. Suppose too that the environmental interests of those living near the factory make the case for their having a collective right that the owner shall stop his factory's polluting activity. Should we regard the factory owner as himself a joint holder of that collective right because he too has an interest in living in a clean environment and in spite of his incurring the duty consequent upon the right? The reason why we should not is that, if someone is to have a right, they must have not merely an interest but an interest that

grounds a duty. While the factory owner might have an interest in a clean environment (an interest in the state of affairs that will be brought about by the performance of his own duty), his own interest will not figure in the interests that generate his duty. His duty not to pollute is owed to others but not to himself and that is why he does not share in the joint right that they enjoy in respect of his duty. So he does not form part of the right-holding group even though he shares (partially if not all things considered) an interest with the group. Of course, none of this would hold if we were to allow that individuals might owe duties to, and so hold rights against, themselves.

[36] In stating the point in this way, I do not mean myself to assert that such groups are indeed devoid of any element of volition. On this issue, see the interesting remarks of Russell Hardin on group identification in his *One for All: the Logic of Group Conflict* (Princeton, NJ: Princeton University Press, 1995), pp. 45–71.

[37] This seems to be the option favoured by Will Kymlicka. Since his name has become closely associated with group rights, I should indicate where he stands in my own analysis of these. Kymlicka does not recognize group rights of any sort as fundamental moral rights. The fundamental units of his morality are individual persons. His principal concern is to argue that vulnerable cultural minorities require 'group-differentiated' or 'community-specific' rights if their fundamental interests are to be provided for on terms equal with other cultural groups. These group-differentiated rights can be invested either in individual members of the group or in the group as a collectivity. Kymlicka treats that as a largely technical choice – the form of right, individual or group, should be dictated by whichever will be the more appropriate instrument for the job. Thus, in so far as Kymlicka argues for group rights, he conceives these as institutionally created rights that are justified only by their efficacy in pro-

tecting or promoting the wellbeing of individuals. He is clearly wary of group rights and unhappy that they should enable a group to regiment the lives of its own members; rather, he argues, group-differentiated rights should be externally directed and should aim to protect or promote individuals' cultural interests against the outside world. That is more consonant with the collective conception of group rights than with the corporate conception, though, to my knowledge, Kymlicka nowhere allies himself with that conception. Perhaps the difficulty for Kymlicka is that institutionalized group rights, particularly rights of self-determination, typically take a corporate form. See Kymlicka, *Liberalism, Community and Culture* (Oxford: Clarendon Press, 1989), especially chs 2, 7–9, and *Multicultural Citizenship* (Oxford: Oxford University Press, 1995), especially chs 1, 3 and 8. Allen Buchanan makes a liberal case for group rights that has a structure similar to Kymlicka's and that is similarly qualified. See his 'The Role of Collective Rights in the Theory of Indigenous Peoples Rights', *Transnational Law and Contemporary Problems*, 3 (1993), 89–108; and 'Liberalism and Group Rights', in *In Harm's Way: Essays in Honor of Joel Feinberg*, ed. Jules L. Coleman and Allen Buchanan (Cambridge: Cambridge University Press, 1994), pp. 1–15.

[38] External intervention designed only to help dissenting individuals to leave the group might be consistent with a group's exclusive corporate right to order its internal affairs. On the other hand, the right of exit might be precisely what is at issue. See, for example, Thomas Isaac, 'Individual versus Collective Rights: Aboriginal People and the Significance of *Thomas* v. *Norris*', *Manitoba Law Journal*, 21 (1992), 618–30.

[39] I examine the significance of the distinction between collective and corporate rights for the debate over whether group rights can be human rights in Peter Jones, 'Human Rights, Group Rights and Peoples' Rights', *Human Rights Quarterly* (1999).

Chapter 10

What's Wrong with Torture?*
David Sussman

Why is torture morally wrong? This question has been neglected or avoided by recent moral philosophy, in part because torture is by its nature especially difficult to discuss. Torture involves degrees of pain and fear that are often said to be utterly indescribable; indeed, these experiences are sometimes said to destroy in their victims the very hope of any sort of communication or shared experience whatsoever.[1] Torture has proved surprisingly difficult to define.[2] There is no clear agreement on the distinction between torture, coercion, and manipulation, or whether such techniques as sleep and sensory deprivation, isolation, or prolonged questioning should count as forms of torture.[3] In addition, we may be fearful of deriving some sort of perverse titillation from the subject, or of being able to dispassionately contemplate the agonies of real victims of torture. Those who have not suffered torture may well feel it is not their place to offer any very substantive reflections on the practice, leaving the issue to those who unfortunately know what they are talking about. We might also worry that in just raising the question, we inadvertently give aid and comfort to

torturers, if only by supplying materials for disingenuous self-justification.

On the other hand, if we approach the question of torture's justifiability in good faith, it may seem so easy to answer as to be hardly worth asking. Torture involves the intentional infliction of extreme physical pain or psychological distress on a person, for such ends as inducing the betrayal of some cause or intimate, intimidating actual or potential opponents, or as an exercise of dominance or sadism simply for its own sake. Since at least Beccaria there has been a broad and confident consensus that torture is uniquely "barbaric" and "inhuman": the most profound violation possible of the dignity of a human being. In philosophical and political discussions, torture is commonly offered as one of the few unproblematic examples of a type of act that is morally impermissible without exception or qualification.[4]

Yet in the current "war on terrorism," the thought that torture may be an appropriate means of combating terrorists has emerged in respectable political and legal discussions in the United States and elsewhere.[5] We would not hope to justify torture that was meant to terrorize innocent civilians or dehumanize a population pursuant

* From *Philosophy & Public Affairs* 33:1 (2005), pp. 1–33.

to expulsion or genocide.[6] But could we justify the torture of a terrorist in order to find out the location of a bomb he has planted, or of a kidnapper to make him reveal the location of his captive while she might still be alive?[7] Here, torture might be understood as the sort of violence that can be permissible as part of the prosecution of a just war or legitimate police action, especially against people who have shown nothing but contempt for the laws of war and the rights of their victims. Nor is it entirely obvious why we should refuse to consider torture as a possible form of punishment, especially when we are willing to allow punishments of lengthy incarceration and perhaps even death. Yet while a convict might reasonably prefer torture to these other punishments, punitive torture remains officially beyond the pale even in an America that countenances the executions of juvenile and mentally retarded offenders. What is it about torture that sets it apart even from killing, maiming, or imprisoning someone, such that the circumstances that might justify inflicting such harms would not even begin to justify torture?[8]

In this article, I defend the intuition that there is something morally special about torture that distinguishes it from most other kinds of violence, cruelty, or degrading treatment. Torture is all these things, of course, and is morally objectionable simply as such. What I deny, however, is that the wrongness of torture can be fully grasped by understanding it as just an extreme instance of these more general moral categories. I argue that there is a core concept of what constitutes torture that corresponds to a distinctive kind of wrong that is not characteristically found in other forms of extreme violence or coercion, a special type of wrong that may explain why we find torture to be more morally offensive than other ways of inflicting great physical or psychological harm.[9]

My account is not meant to provide any very immediate way of resolving the "ticking bomb" or "Dirty Harry" dilemmas mentioned above. Instead, I am trying to articulate more clearly the moral structure of these dilemmas and the special reluctance we have to consider torture even in the face of such pressing claims. I do not here contend that torture is categorically wrong, but only that it bears an especially high burden of justification, greater in degree and different in kind from even that of killing.[10] Establishing such a special burden of justification may be a necessary step in defending a categorical proscription of torture, but it is not by itself sufficient for such a defense.

While not providing any immediate answers, this account will at least give us reason to resist assimilating these dilemmas to the problems posed by other uses of force in war and police action. My approach is broadly Kantian, but I do not construe the wrong of torture as just that of disregarding, thwarting, or undermining the victim's capacities for rational self-governance. Instead, I argue that torture forces its victim into the position of colluding against himself through his own affects and emotions, so that he experiences himself as simultaneously powerless and yet actively complicit in his own violation. So construed, torture turns out to be not just an extreme form of cruelty, but the pre-eminent instance of a kind of forced self-betrayal, more akin to rape than other kinds of violence characteristic of warfare or police action.

My discussion focuses on interrogational torture, i.e., torture that involves a protracted process of inflicting or threatening pain in a context of helplessness and dependence, so as to make its victim provide information, confessions, denunciations, and the like. Such torture is prevalent in the world today, and it is the sort of torture that seems most likely to be justifiable in sufficiently dire circumstances and against sufficiently ruthless and culpable foes. I foreground such torture because in it the central idea of a relationship that is not only morally wrong but also morally perverted finds its clearest illustration. Once this idea of a moral perversion is on the table, I turn to the other context where there may sometimes seem to be prima facie grounds for torture: legal punishment. Such torture is also objectionable as a travesty of the most basic practical relations between embodied agents, but the character of this distorted relation will differ in some important respects from that found in other forms of torture. Again, this examination is not intended to provide any immediate answers about whether torture might ultimately be justified in any particular case. Instead, it is meant only to expand our theoretical vocabulary, so that we can start to say what is morally special about torture without making torture so unique as to be beyond profitable philosophical discussion.

I

The United Nations Convention against Torture and Other Cruel, Inhuman, or Degrading Treatment or Punishment defines torture as

> [a]ny act by which severe pain or suffering, whether physical or mental, is intentionally inflicted on a person for such purposes as obtaining from him or a third person information or a confession, punishing him for an act he or a third person has committed or is suspected of having committed, or intimidating or coercing him or a third person, or for any reason based on discrimination of any kind, when such pain or suffering is inflicted by or at the instigation of or with the consent or acquiescence of a public official or other person acting in an official capacity. It does not include pain or suffering arising only from, inherent in or incidental to lawful sanctions.[11]

At a minimum, torture involves the deliberate infliction of great pain or some other intensely distressing affective state (fear, shame, disgust, and so forth) on an unwilling person for purposes that person does not and could not reasonably be expected to share. While one might accidentally kill or inadvertently maim, one cannot accidentally or inadvertently torture. But there are many ways of deliberately inflicting pain that we would hesitate to call torture. I might punch a stranger in the face, breaking his nose, and then run away. The victim here may experience great pain, but we would not normally say he had been subjected to torture. Two people might simultaneously inflict great pain on each other (e.g., wrestlers each applying submission holds to each other), but we would not normally describe this as torture either.

In addition to the intentional infliction of great pain, torture seems to require that its perpetrators and victims be placed in a distinctive kind of social setting and relationship to one another. Victims of torture must be, and must realize themselves to be, completely at the mercy of their tormentors. This condition involves two distinct elements. First, being at another's mercy requires that there be a profoundly asymmetric relation of dependence and vulnerability between the parties. The victim of torture must be unable to shield herself in any significant way, and she must be unable to effectively evade or retaliate against her tormenter. I may intentionally inflict great pain in a fight in order to make my foe do something; I may gouge his eyes in order to get him to stop choking me. Nevertheless, insofar as my opponent is not helpless before me, my eye-gouging is not an instance of torture, even though I am trying to force him to comply with my desires by inflicting pain on him. Police who use tear gas to disperse a crowd are not engaging in torture, regardless of how painful the gas may be.

In neither case are the victims forced to be passive before the infliction of suffering, their avenues of response limited to those narrowly defined by their tormentors. Instead, these victims still have it within their power to resist or mitigate the violence done to them: by retreating, devising ways of protecting themselves, or countering their assailants with new threats of their own. In such cases, the attackers are in the position of having to anticipate how their opponents, as free agents, might try to alter or upset the conditions that frame their conflict. In combat, each party recognizes the other to be capable of reshaping the practical task before them in an indefinitely wide variety of ways. In contrast, the torture victim real-izes that he has no room to maneuver against his antagonist, no way to fight back or protect himself, and he must realize that his antago-nist is aware of this as well. The victim may ultimately comply or not, but he has no prospect of surprising his tormentor in a way that might change the basic shape of the antagonism between them.

Second, the torture victim must see herself as being unable to put up any real moral or legal resistance to her tormentor. The victim takes her tormentor to be someone who can do anything he wants to her, who does not have to worry about answering any chal-lenges that the victim (or her representa-tives) might put to him. The torturer confronts no moral or legal impediments stemming from his victim's will, but evi-dently takes himself to be limited only by his own desires and interests, or the desires and interests of those he serves as an agent. Yet the torturer is in a position to demand any-thing from his victim as if by an enforceable right. The most intimate and private parts of a victim's life and body become publicly available tools for the torturer to exploit as he will. The victim is completely exposed, while the torturer is free to conceal anything he likes, even those things to which a victim clearly has a right and a profound interest. Typically, victims are kept in the dark about where they are, why they are being tortured, who might be making the ultimate decisions about their fates, how long they have been confined, or even whether it is day or night. The asymmetry of power, knowledge, and prerogative is absolute: the victim is in a position of complete vulnerability and expo-sure, the torturer in one of perfect control and inscrutability.

Characteristically, the torture victim finds herself to be not only physically and morally defenseless, but exposed to a will that appears largely if not completely arbitrary.[12] The victim's greatest interests are completely subject to the caprice of her torturers, who normally conceal just what it is they want or what their ultimate plans are, or represent their goals in inconsistent and ever-shifting ways. Of course, a victim might know that she is being tortured for a specific purpose (to obtain some particular piece of informa-tion, perhaps, or to incriminate someone) or that her torturers operate under some significant restrictions (perhaps they have orders not to kill or leave any permanent marks on the victim). Yet even in these cases, the victim's only grounds for such beliefs about her tormentors' ends and intentions come from how these tormentors choose to present themselves to her. Typically, a torture victim has no independent way of corrobo-rating any admissions or assurances of her torturers. Insofar as she is able to form any estimate of their motives and intentions, the victim must trust in the sincerity of people who have already shown that they have no scruples about how they treat her. A torturer may seem to want a particular piece of infor-mation, or recognize certain kinds of treat-ment to be off-limits, but such self-imposed restrictions might be abandoned or revised without warning at any moment.

The victim knows nothing of her torturer other than what he wants her to know, save that he is at best indifferent to her rights and interests. Even if the victim is willing to supply the information or confession that seems to be wanted, she has no reason to believe that her tormentor will accept it as accurate and complete. Perhaps she will continue to be tortured "just to make sure," or for some other reason entirely, or for no reason at all. She can neither verify any claims her tormentor makes, nor rely on any promises or assurances he offers. Instead, the victim can only guess at the real motives and intentions of her torturer, being forced into the position of trusting someone in a context that makes the very idea of trust seem insane.[13]

II

Torture should be distinguished from both coercion and brainwashing, even though all three may often overlap in particular cases. What is distinctive about torture is that it aims to manipulate its victims through their own responses, as agents, to the felt experience of their affects and emotions in a context of dependence, vulnerability, and disorientation. Coercion, in contrast, need only exploit the agent's rational responses to the cognitive content of these feelings. The coercer tries to influence his victims through their own appreciation of their reasons for action. Coercion presupposes that its victim thinks that his coercers intend to act against his interests should he act or fail to act in a particular way, and that the reason they have adopted such conditional intentions is to give him a stronger reason to do something than he had before. Coercion requires only that its victim have the capacities needed for practical reasoning and intentional action, and that he be able to recognize the expression of these powers in those who are trying to pressure him. Affect and emotion are not required, even though agents will normally take themselves to have very strong interests in avoiding certain kinds of affective experiences. In principle, we could coerce a being that has no emotional life at all (e.g., a corporate agent such as a state or a university), so long as this being had determinate interests that it rationally pursued in part by anticipating the intentions and actions of other rational agents. But we could not in principle torture this sort of artificial person who lacks any distinct sort of emotional or affective life.

Coercion, as a kind of hard bargaining by means of threats, involves too direct an appeal to its victim's rationality to count as torture. Brainwashing, in contrast, diverges from torture in failing to appeal to its victim's rational judgment at all. Like the use of drugs or sleep deprivation to put a victim into a hyper-suggestible state, brainwashing exploits the victim's affects and bodily responses so as to directly subvert or restructure his rational capacities and commitments. It is essential to this process that the victim cannot be fully aware of what is going on. The victim's beliefs, desires, and perceptions are supposed to be reshaped in a way that reflects the brainwasher's designs, while still appearing to the victim as being properly responsive to the world and his own authentic concerns. To recognize that one has been brainwashed is to begin to undo the process. In contrast, not only is it possible for someone to realize that she is being coerced, but such a realization is a constitutive feature of coercion as such. To be coerced, I need to do more than realize that someone else will do something I find undesirable should I fail to do what he wants. I must also realize that my coercer has adopted this intention in order to get me to do what he wants, and that I can expect him to anticipate and block my attempts to escape or modify this situation. To be coerced I must see myself as threatened in this way, as confronting another will that intends to consistently frustrate my actions for the sake of its interests. I experience the will of my coercer not just as distinct from my own, as an obstacle or impediment, but as my will's opponent, as a counter-will that is the systematic negation of my own in some area of activity. In contrast, successful brainwashing requires that its victim ultimately take up and identify with the will of another person, thereby losing any sense that this will is different from or opposed to her own.

Torture exists somewhere between coercion and brainwashing. Like coercion, torture requires its victim to have some minimal understanding of what is being done to him. The victim must realize himself to be at the mercy of someone else who is deliberately trying to get him to act against his own choices and commitments. Yet the torturer is not merely constructing a harsh set of options for the victim to rationally navigate as best he can. The felt experience of pain, fear, and uncertainty are essential elements of torture. Yet the torturer does not set out to exploit the immediate causal consequences of these feelings, as if pain were just a particularly cheap or effective form of truth serum. Rather, in torture the victim must confront his own feelings as a problem, as something he must respond to, where this response is something for which he may see himself to be in some way accountable. Torture is normally accompanied not just by pain and the constant threat of pain and death, but also by relentless (if evidently pointless) questioning. The victim is presented with a dilemma about submission or resistance (which can also be a dilemma about how or when to properly or effectively submit). And he must confront this dilemma not merely with respect to the disvalue of pain and fear, but while caught up in the experience of these very feelings themselves.

There need not always be a determinate answer as to whether some piece of manipu-

lation is really one of coercion, torture, or brainwashing. A particular act might simultaneously be an instance of more than one type of abuse. The torture victim subjected to repeated electrical shock is also being coerced. Even if he were completely dispassionate, he would realize that he was being given some very compelling reasons to submit to his tormentor. Torture will also sometimes approach brainwashing, insofar as the protracted experience of pain and terror seldom leaves an individual's rational capacities intact. The experience of torture may simply shatter a mind, making it immediately responsive to the suggestions of an interrogator, just as one may be brought to babble without inhibition or control by the influence of drugs. Any particular act of torture will tend to shade off in one direction or another: the more effectively the torture undermines the victim's rational capacities, the less effectively it can also be coercing him by appeal to his incentive structure (and vice versa). Yet while there can be such irreducibly overlapping cases, this does not entail that coercion, torture, and brainwashing all exhibit the same basic kind of wrong that varies only in terms of quantitative dimension.[14] As the roles of reason and sensibility shift along this spectrum, the relation of the victim to her tormentor and to herself can assume new shapes that take on different kinds of moral significance.

III

The question now emerges whether torture, so understood, represents a morally distinct and interesting category of action. This question has two aspects. The first is whether torture represents any sort of morally unified category at all, or whether it only refers to a heterogeneous collection of acts that bear various resemblances to one another. The worry here is that even if such acts are individually objectionable in some way or other, there may be no interesting type of wrong that they all involve.[15] The second aspect of the question concerns whether torture, if indeed a morally unified category, is sufficiently basic to be of analytical interest. Is there a special type of moral wrong characteristic of torture as such, or can this wrong (or wrongs) be fully captured by a broader description that might just as readily apply to different kinds of action? If there is such a basic wrong, does appeal to it illuminate what is fundamentally objectionable about torture, or does this appeal turn out to be only a way of repeating our basic conviction that torture is especially or uniquely bad?

The naive utilitarian objection to torture is that it produces tremendous suffering that typically fails to be sufficiently offset by any resulting benefits. A sufficiently nuanced utilitarianism may appeal not just to the intensity and quantity of pain that torture involves but also to the special disutilities associated with the "higher pains" only available to creatures that can experience dread, anguish, and self-disgust.[16] This utilitarian can also point to the lasting psychological and political effects of torture on human beings and institutions. The agony of torture typically continues to reproduce itself in the lives of victims and those close to them long after the physical torments stop.[17] Politically, torture tends to become an entrenched, ever-widening practice, progressively divorced from whatever legitimate aims it might have originally served. Torture that is resorted to as an emergency measure frequently becomes a permanent feature of a regime of terrorization for its actual and potential victims, an education in brutality for its perpetrators, and a corrosive that progressively dissolves the rule of law.[18] The sophisticated utilitarian will also point to the typical inefficiencies and self-defeating effects of torture. Torture is a notoriously unreliable way of gathering intelligence (although perhaps not all that more unreli-

able than the alternatives usually available). Torture is usually a counterproductive strategy of political control, undermining respect for legal authority and in the long run leaving a subject population more alienated and radicalized than cowed.

The utilitarian focuses on the actual harms involved in torture, and in so doing clearly captures an essential element of what is morally objectionable about such practices. However, utilitarianism will have trouble explaining the moral significance of the social and intentional structure of the "drama" that torture enacts. For it seems that all the harms that typically result from torture might just as readily result from what can sometimes be morally legitimate forms of warfare. It is doubtful that there is any form of pain or injury that can be delivered by a torturer that is categorically worse than the harms that can result from bullets and bombs. The torture victim may experience such terror and helplessness as to leave him permanently shattered psychologically, but so too may besieged soldiers subjected to artillery or aerial bombardments intended to destroy their morale.[19] Yet such tactics are not normally met with the sort of categorical condemnation that the torture of enemy soldiers receives.

If the special wrongness of torture reflected only the special badness of harms it inflicts, then a soldier who could rescue either a number of troops from a firefight or the same number of POWs from torture would be strictly obligated to do the latter, other concerns being equal. I take it that this conclusion does not correspond to how we intuitively understand the special moral status of torture. While we have strong moral reasons to prevent torture, they do not seem to be different in kind from the reasons we have to prevent the traumas of war. But we do seem to have a moral reason not to serve as someone's torturer that is qualitatively different, and more stringent, than the reasons we have not to make war on him. There seems to be something about the distinctive structure of the relationship of torturer to victim that is intrinsically objectionable and that goes beyond the badness of its usual effects.

Kantian moral theory may seem better suited to capture the distinct moral considerations posed by the structure of the relationship between torturer and victim. The Kantian argues that what is essentially wrong with torture is the profound disrespect it shows the humanity or autonomy of its victim. Here, torture is wrong as the most extreme instance of using someone as a mere means to purposes she does not or could not reasonably share. Although this explanation clearly captures part of what is morally significant about torture, the account is importantly incomplete. The Kantian's problem complements that of the utilitarian. The utilitarian focuses on the badness of the victim's agony but cannot readily grasp the significance of the characteristic interpersonal structure of torture. The Kantian can begin to make sense of that structure, but in turn has difficulty explaining why torture seems morally special because it specifically involves pain and other unpleasant feelings, rather than some other way that our ends might be frustrated or our agency disrupted.

For the orthodox Kantian, what is fundamentally objectionable about torture is that the victim, and the victim's agency, is put to use in ways to which she does not or could not reasonably consent. The fact that it is pain that is characteristically involved is of only indirect importance. What immediately matters to the Kantian is that the victim may reasonably and strongly object to such treatment. The use of pain is significant only insofar as pain is something someone may reasonably and strongly refuse to undergo. But just as the social setting of torture adds a special dimension to its wrongness, so too must the fact that torture involves pain and

action directly upon the victim's body rather than some other intensely unwanted imposition. I may deeply desire that some compromising photographs that have been stolen from me never be made public, and I might even be willing to endure great physical pain in order to prevent this. Yet my blackmailer is not doing anything of a piece with torturing me, even though she is thwarting my will through a means to which she has no right.

The orthodox Kantian can go a little farther toward accommodating the special significance of pain. Unlike other kinds of unwanted imposition, pain characteristically compromises or undermines the very capacities constitutive of autonomous agency itself. It is almost impossible to reflect, deliberate, or even think straight when one is in agony. When sufficiently intense, pain becomes a person's entire universe and his entire self, crowding out every other aspect of his mental life. Unlike other harms, pain takes its victim's agency apart "from the inside," such that the agent may never be able to reconstitute himself fully. The Kantian can thus recognize that torture is not only a violation of the value of rational agency, but a violation that is accomplished through the very annihilation of such agency itself, if only temporarily or incompletely.

This account faces the challenge of showing how disrupting rational self-governance through pain is interestingly different from disrupting self-governance through intense physical pleasure (or any other kind of affect that is not painful). Of course, intense pleasure is usually welcomed by its recipients, and as such may be fully consistent with their own autonomy. Moreover, it is normally quite difficult to "inflict" pleasure on someone against his will. Pain is certainly a simpler and more effective tool for such manipulation, particularly in the absence of sophisticated medical technology. Yet there seems to be no barrier in principle to undermining someone's agency through ecstasy rather than through suffering. Certain drugs might induce intense euphoria in someone regardless of what he wants and in a way that, like pain, makes it impossible to think or care about anything else. Perhaps such pleasure would make its victim liable to suggestion, such that he would reveal anything under questioning. If of a sufficiently ascetic or puritanical bent, this victim might well object as strongly to such techniques as other people would to electric shock. While such manipulation would clearly be a profound violation of agency, the orthodox Kantian seems compelled to say that it is wrong in precisely the same way as the normal agonistic forms of torture. The Kantian seems unable to do justice to what we would normally take to be a clearly non-accidental truth: the fact that torture *hurts*.

Even if the Kantian can account for this asymmetry between pleasure and pain, her view faces yet another hurdle. Any approach that condemns torture as a disruption of agency will have difficulty distinguishing torture from killing. After all, nothing could compromise or undermine rational self-governance more completely than the very death of the agent. Yet while there is a very strong moral presumption against both killing and torturing a human being, it seems that we take the presumption against torture to be even greater than that against homicide. This intuition seems to be just the opposite of what the Kantian account would lead us to expect. We normally think that we may kill in self-defense or as part of the prosecution of a just war. But we are much more reluctant to accept that we may torture in self-defense or as part of proper combat. Although the Kantian might be able to show that torturing a person is not much better than killing him, she seems unable to explain how inflicting torture might actually be *more* objectionable (or objectionable in a fundamentally different way) than ending his life.

IV

In "Torture," Henry Shue allows that the circumstances that justify killing could in principle justify torture.[20] However, Shue argues that whenever torture is a real option for an agent, that agent cannot be in any such circumstances. We may be justified in using deadly force only against someone who is actively posing some kind of substantial threat to someone or something. Yet if we are in a position to torture someone, Shue observes, we must be in a position of complete power over him, thus able to counter any danger he might pose. We might sometimes have to kill in self-defense, but we could not find ourselves in a situation where we would have to torture in self-defense. For Shue, torture, unlike killing, necessarily violates a basic principle of just combat: the prohibition against attacking the defenseless.

Must potential victims of torture be defenseless in this way? Consider again the captured terrorist who we know to have planted a powerful bomb in some crowded civilian area. Although the terrorist is in our power, he refuses to reveal the bomb's location, hoping to strike one last blow against us by allowing a train of events that he has set in motion to come to its intended conclusion. In one sense, the terrorist is indeed defenseless. We can do anything we like to him, and there is nothing he can do to resist or shield himself against us. But such helplessness means neither that the terrorist has ceased to engage in hostilities against us, nor that he is no longer an active military threat. His placing of the bomb was the beginning of an attack on us; his silence, although not any kind of further overt act, is nevertheless voluntary behavior undertaken for the sake of bringing that act to completion. His continued silence thus might well be considered a part of his attack, understood as a temporally extended action.

Consider a case where the police confront a very obese man who is trying to suffocate another by sitting on his chest. Like the terrorist, the fat man is defenseless before the police, who can wound or even kill him easily. Yet if the fat man dies or loses consciousness, the police lack the strength to shift him off his victim. Only the fat man can end his attack, even though he does not now need to do anything further in order for it to succeed. Here it seems that the police might well be justified in macing the fat man or twisting his arm (or threatening to kill him) in order to get him to derail a train of events that he has intentionally set in motion, even though he no longer has to actively contribute anything to it. The terrorist relies on a bomb's mechanism to accomplish his goal, the fat man on his weight, and it is hard to see how this difference of method could be of any great moral significance.

In response to such worries Shue argues that what is important is not only whether a potential target is defenseless, but also whether he has a real opportunity to surrender. In order for an enemy to be a legitimate target, there must be some way he can renounce hostilities, some form of exit from relations of conflict that he knows about and that can be legitimately demanded of him. Yet in the case of interrogational torture, it seems possible to satisfy this condition. After all, the bomb-planting terrorist knows very well what we want (the information), has the power to provide it, and knows that it is only for the sake of such information that we are moved to torture him. Telling us what we want to know might then appear to be something like the laying down of arms that must accompany any real surrender.

Shue replies that an interrogator cannot know for sure in any given case whether his prisoner actually possesses the information wanted. The ignorant terrorist (or unfortunate bystander) would have no way to effectively surrender, and thus no way to exit the

relationship of active hostility in which he finds himself. Shue may be right about such cases. However, this objection would establish the general impermissibility of interrogational torture only insofar as our belief that we had the right person needed to meet some standard of proof that we could never reasonably hope to attain. If we had to be absolutely certain that our prisoner has the information we want (and thus the capacity to surrender) then we might indeed never be in a proper position to torture. Yet this would be to hold torture to an epistemic test that we would never use in other areas of just combat or criminal punishment. Soldiers may continue to attack even when they cannot know with absolute certainty whether their enemy is still physically and psychologically capable of surrendering (especially true when warfare is conducted at great speed and distance, as with aerial or artillery bombardment). Yet if we scale back the demand for certainty to keep it in line with other forms of just combat, then torture may turn out to be justified in those cases where we have sufficiently strong evidence that our suspect possesses the information we want. By itself, the mere possibility of torturing the ignorant is no more of an objection to the permissibility of torture than the mere possibility of killing a noncombatant is to just warfare or the bare chance of punishing the innocent is to legal sanctions.

Shue contends we must not only afford our foes the opportunity of surrender, but that opportunity must also be such they can exercise it without having to make any unreasonable sacrifice. We hardly offer our foes any real opportunity for surrender if to do so they would have to allow their families to be killed, or humiliate themselves for a minor military purpose. In a similar vein, Shue argues that we could not require of a prisoner that he betray a cause to which he is committed in order to escape torture. Such a betrayal would so violate the prisoner's integrity that it would give him no more of a real opportunity for surrender than would the option of suicide. What remains unclear, however, is why we should be so solicitous of the terrorist's sense of his own integrity. The terrorist disregards the principles of just combat, striking at his enemies' loved ones simply because they are dear to him. The terrorist makes no effort to distinguish himself from civilians and other noncombatants, forcing his foe into the terrible choice of either waging war against innocents or failing to protect himself and those near to him. Given that the terrorist attacks his enemy's own integrity this way, it is hard to see how he is entitled to terms of surrender that do not require him to in any way compromise his cause. Plausibly, such terms should be reserved for combatants who accept certain risks (by wearing uniforms, living apart from civilian populations, and so on) and do so in order to allow fighting to proceed without forcing combatants to make such self-disfiguring choices. At least, Shue has given us no reason why the principles that govern the surrender of legitimate combatants should also be applied without modification to those who make no pretense of being bound by anything like the rules of war. Shue's argument also has the paradoxical consequence that it would be less objectionable to torture a morally sensitive collaborator who is ambivalent about waging war against us (and hence has no very firm or deep commitment to betray) than to torture the hate-filled fanatic who is wholeheartedly bent on our destruction.

V

Our problem his been to understand how torture is essentially different from other kinds of intentional injury, coercion, or killing, and why torture seems harder to justify than even such acts. Whatever solutions we are to offer, they must do justice to the different features of torture that the orthodox Kantian and utilitarian separately call to our attention. Whatever makes torture distinctively bad must have something to do with the sort of interpersonal relationship it enacts, a relationship that realizes a profound violation of the victim's humanity and autonomy. Yet the special iniquity of torture must also have something to do with the fact that torture characteristically involves the infliction of pain and the use of force directed immediately against the body and the emotions. If torture is morally distinctive in the ways that our intuitions suggest, there must be something about what pain is, and about its special relation to our own agency, that makes some important moral difference. We can preserve torture's special moral status only if we can find there to be some significant moral difference between being used as a mere means in general, and being used as such a means through one's own distressing affects and bodily responses.

Let me now sketch the beginnings of an account that might satisfy this burden. My suggestion is essentially an extension of the Kantian thought that torture fails to respect the dignity of its victim as a rationally self-governing agent. What is distinct about torture, however, is that it does not just traduce the value such dignity represents by treating its subject as a mere means. Rather torture, even in the "best" case, involves a deliberate perversion of that very value, turning our dignity against itself in a way that must be especially offensive to any morality that fundamentally honors it. To see this, we should consider what sort of experience of her own agency the victim must suffer in order for the torturer to succeed. The torturer wants something from his victim, something that the victim would not normally provide (information, confession, pleading, and so on). In response, her captors begin a protracted process of threatening and inflicting pain. Physical pain has a peculiar quality. On the one hand, we experience it as not a part of ourselves: it is something unbidden whose very nature is such that we want to expel it from ourselves, to abolish it or drive it away. In an obvious way, we are passive before physical pain; it is something that just happens to us, neither immediately evoked nor eliminated by any decisions or judgments we may make.

On the other hand, pain is also a primitive, unmediated aspect of our own agency. Pain is not something wholly alien to our wills, but something in which we find ourselves actively, if reluctantly, participating. My pain is, after all, *my* pain, an experience that in its very nature seems to demand, wheedle, or plead with me. Insofar as the experience of pain has any content, it seems to be that of a pure imperative. To feel pain is to confront something like a bodily demand to change something about one's condition, to do something to silence this very demand. Often a pain makes clear just what needs to be done or avoided, but such specificity is nor essential to its character as a pain. We can have acute nonspecific pains that we have no idea how to deal with, such as the visceral pains we might feel deep within our bodies after surgery. Yet even here we feel a need to do something in response: we writhe, grimace, or groan. Here pain still seems to be experienced as a kind of imperative, but one that refers only to itself, like someone incessantly screaming "Shut me up!" In this respect, pain seems to be importantly different in form from even physical pleasure. Such pleasure, while an important aspect of the will's embodiment, does not have the same kind of imperatival quality as pain, the same self-referential demandingness. To feel physical pleasure is to enjoy or luxuriate in one's state, to be content, satisfied, at rest. To be in pain is to confront some sort of insistent plea to do something; unlike pleasure, its very nature calls for a response from us.

Following Elaine Scarry, we might construe pain as something like the "voice" of the body.[21] The comparison to language is illuminating. In many respects, pain is like a sensation, but a sensation that seems to have a kind of immediate significance in which the agent already finds his attention and will to be invested. Normally, one cannot adopt a purely contemplative attitude toward one's own pain. In these respects, feeling pain resembles hearing the utterance of a meaningful sentence. I cannot hear a minimally grammatical English sentence as just noise; I cannot just choose whether or not to grasp its meaning (although I may try with some effort to divert my attention to other things). In hearing the sentence as meaningful, I find myself to be passively receiving an experience in which my active powers of understanding are already in play. If someone tells me to "Go away!" I cannot first contemplate the utterance and then consider how I might respond to it. Rather, in hearing the command, the possibility of going away has already become real for me, as something I must make some effort to disobey or disregard. I may challenge or ignore the order, but this is always a "second move" in response to an initial proposal in which I find myself to have already begun to participate. Similarly, I might ignore or disregard my pain, but to do so I must counter some motivational and evaluative "protocommitments" that have already begun to engage my will by the time I can actively confront the question of how to respond.[22]

Pain resembles a kind of primitive language of bodily commands and pleas that makes the same kind of insistent demands on our attention and response as our children's shrieking and whining. Understood as a kind of expressive voice, my pain is not unproblematically an exercise of my own agency (the way my reflectively adopted commitments might be), but neither is it something fully distinct from such agency. It is this peculiar duality that the torturer sets out to exploit. What the torturer does is to take his victim's pain, and through it his victim's body, and make it begin to express the torturer's will. The resisting victim is committed to remaining silent, but he now experiences within himself something quite intimate and familiar that speaks for the torturer, something that pleads a case or provides an excuse for giving in.[23] My suffering is experienced as not just something the torturer inflicts on me, but as something I do to myself, as a kind of self-betrayal worked through my body and its feelings. As Scarry observes,

> The ceaseless, self-announcing signal of the body in pain, at once so empty and undifferentiated and so full of blaring adversity, contains not only the feeling "my body hurts" but the feeling "my body hurts me"....[24]

In a similar vein, Susan Brison remarks that after being beaten, raped, and repeatedly strangled into unconsciousness, "My body was now perceived as an enemy, having betrayed my newfound trust and interest in it."[25]

It is perhaps not accidental that many of the most common forms of torture involve somehow pitting the victim against himself, making him an active participant in his own abuse. In Abu Ghraib, captives were made to masturbate in front of jeering captors. Here the captive was forced into the position of having to put his most intimate desires, memories, and fantasies into the service of his torturers, in a desperate attempt to arouse himself for their amusement. The US soldiers could beat and kill their prisoners, but only the prisoner himself could offer up his own erotic life to be used against himself in this way. A ubiquitous form of torture is the denial of regular access to toilet facilities. The torture here is not just the infantilizing and dehumanizing disgrace of soiling oneself,

but the futile struggle against one's own body not to do so. The victim confronts the question of whether she was simply forced to soil herself, or whether she allowed herself to do so, discovering herself to be willing to purchase some comfort at the price of public or personal humiliation.[26]

Torturers often force their victims to stand or maintain contorted postures ("stress positions") for prolonged periods of time. In these cases, the victim's own efforts to remain in a particular position serve as the immediate source of his suffering.[27] One of the most common forms of contemporary torture is "the submarine," a technique that involves repeated partial drownings.[28] I take it that the torture here is not just the agony of inhaling water, but the hopeless struggle against one's own desperate urge to breathe that precedes it. Not only does the victim find himself hurt by his body, but he also finds himself to be the one hurting his body as well, in some way pushing it against itself. The relationship of torturer to victim is thus replicated in the victim's own consciousness of himself as an embodied agent. In the most intimate aspects of his agency, the sufferer is made to experience himself not just as a passive victim, but as an active accomplice in his own debasement.[29]

When inflicted as part of torture, physical pain is importantly different from other kinds of agony that might result from disease or injury. In the case of natural pain, my body may seem to rebel against me, but it does not seem to rebel out of some other allegiance. The pain of disease may transfix me, but it does not seem to do so for any point of its own. Naturally caused pain is relatively inarticulate, manifesting itself as only the blank negation of my will by something that is nevertheless an intimate part of it. Torture is different, in that the sufferer experiences his pain as having a point. There is a will lurking behind his suffering, a will with a project that is somehow meant to be served by all the various torments. Part of the characteristic dynamic of torture is that the victim is led to hope (however falsely or unreasonably) that there might be something he could do to appease or mollify his tormentor. The victim almost invariably finds himself trying to anticipate his torturer's will, to figure out what it wants.[30] If the victim is in a position to provide what is wanted (say, some specific information), then he will find himself considering (despite himself), whether it might not be so bad to reveal the information, whether the betrayal would be so great, whether he has already endured more than could be asked of him. To head off this sort of dynamic, Jacobo Timerman recommends complete mental passivity, since any sort of active thought served only to aid his torturers:

> [I]t's best to allow yourself to be led meekly toward pain and through pain, rather than to struggle resolutely as if you were a normal human being. The vegetable attitude can save a life. . . . More than once I was brusquely awakened by someone shouting: "Think. Don't sleep, think." But I refused to think. . . . To think meant becoming conscious of what was happening to me, imagining what might be happening to my wife and children; to think meant trying to work out how to relieve this situation, how to wedge an opening in my relationship with the jailers. In that solitary universe of the tortured, any attempt to relate to reality was an immense painful effort leading to nothing.[31]

Despite his conscious commitments, the victim experiences within himself a dialectic where some part of him serves as the eager agent of his tormentor. Even if the victim is not in a position to provide the information or denunciations wanted, he still finds a part of himself taking his torturer's side. The ignorant victim must ask himself how he can best display his ignorance, or offer up some lie or substitute information that might

appease his tormentor, often in a feat of great inventiveness.[32] In either case, the victim finds in his pain, and his own immediate responses to that pain, a surrogate for the torturer. The victim's own voice, the voice of his body, has come in part to speak the torturer's mind. This is why torture requires there to be some protracted process in which pain is both inflicted and withheld (perhaps even assuaged) in a capricious and unpredictable way. This continuous dynamic of inflicting and withholding pain, seemingly at the whim of an omnipotent tormenter, puts the victim in the unavoidable position of betraying or colluding against himself, an experience the victim undergoes whether or not he actually informs or confesses.[33]

The situation is even worse in the case of terroristic torture. In the case of terroristic torture, there is nothing in particular that the torturer consistently demands in order to stop the torment. Yet such torture invariably involves relentless questioning, even if it is directed toward information that is obviously valueless or already known to the torturer. These demands are without any evident point, but they also suggest to the victim that something is wanted from him, but something of which he cannot make sense. Irena Martinez, another victim of the Argentine *junta,* recalls:

> Basically, they want you to feel that your life depends on them, that they are omnipotent, and that every nice thing that you do for them will have some influence on their decision about your life or death.[34]

The victim is forced into a position where she must try to anticipate and understand every little mood and quirk of her torturers. Despite herself, she finds herself trying to grasp her torturer's interests, anticipate his demands, and present herself in a way that might evoke pity or satisfaction from him.

Consider the climax of Winston Smith's torments in *1984*. When Smith is confronted with the rat-mask, there is nothing that he is called on to say or do to avoid this horror. Rather, it is Smith himself who, in an exercise of considerable ingenuity, has to come up with a self-violation extreme enough to satisfy O'Brien. Smith is undone not merely because his cry of "Do it to Julia!" is sincere; both Smith and Julia fully expected, and accepted, that they would betray each other again and again. Smith is undone because he takes the desperate initiative of putting his intimate knowledge of his own deepest loves and commitments into the service of O'Brien's torments. Despite himself, Smith ends up doing for O'Brien the one thing that O'Brien could not himself do, and so becomes an active part of the very apparatus of torture that is being applied to him.

The victim of torture finds within herself a surrogate of the torturer, a surrogate who does not merely advance a particular demand for information, denunciation, or confession. Rather, the victim's whole perspective is given over to that surrogate, to the extent that the only thing that matters to her is pleasing this other person, who appears infinitely distant, important, inscrutable, powerful, and free.[35] The will of the torturer is thus cast as something like the source of all value in his victim's world, a unique object of fascination from which the victim cannot hope to free herself. The torturer thereby makes himself into a kind of perverted God and forces his victim into a grotesque parody of love and adoration. Améry writes, "I also have not forgotten that there were moments when I felt a kind of wretched admiration for the agonizing sovereignty they exercised over me. For is not the one who can reduce a person so entirely to a body and a whimpering prey of death God or, at least, a demigod?"[36] Like love or religious devotion, such an attitude can develop an emotional hold that persists beyond the circumstances that initially created it, as the phenomenon of "traumatic bonding" or "Stockholm syndrome" attests. Judith Herman writes, "The sense that the perpetrator is still present, even after liberation, signifies a major alternation in the victim's relational world. The enforced relationship during captivity, which of necessity monopolizes the victim's attention, becomes part of the victim's inner life and continues to engross her attention after release."[37] Such attention is dominated by fear, but other forms of fascination and concern may be engendered as well. Conroy recounts several disturbing incidents in which victims, at their own initiative, have become the friends, comrades, and in one case even the lover of their former torturers.[38]

Torture thus turns out to be something like sexual seduction, accomplished through fear and pain rather than through erotic desire. After all, such desire can be almost as insistent and arresting as physical pain, and as able to "saturate" our bodies as thoroughly as fear or disgust. We can find ourselves to be simultaneously passive before and profoundly engaged by our sexual desires, which we experience as something like both an effect we suffer and an attitude we adopt. In seduction, we find ourselves becoming fixated on the wants, intentions, and body of another (and the physical possibilities of that body), through the non-voluntary arousal and frustration of our own desires. Successful seduction leads not just to appetite, but to a kind of fascination with another as an embodied agent that makes one acutely aware of one's own physical exposure before that other. In torture, as in sex, the body is touched in ways that make the most personal and intense feelings manifest themselves publicly and involuntarily (e.g., in erection, lubrication, sweat, shivering, urination, defecation, and centrally, spontaneous cries).[39] Of course, even an unwelcome attempt at seduction is not wrong in anything like the way torture is. Normally, the person seduced voluntarily enters into the interaction in question, and is able to voluntarily withdraw from or otherwise reshape the dynamics of the encounter. Just as the seducer works on the desire of his target, she may work on his, or end the interaction at her discretion. We talk about "playing games" in such erotic contexts, a description that never suggests itself in the case of real torture.

Where such possibilities of exit, resistance, and reply are absent, however, torture may well be realized through sexual desire rather than through physical pain. In fact, on the analysis I have offered it should be possible to torture someone through many different sorts of desires whether or not they are sexual in nature. Any suitably intense and relentless craving, whether for food, drugs, sleep, or just quiet, could be the medium through which a suitably constrained and dependent person might be tortured (such torture need not involve touching the victim's body, so long as his physical environment is appropriately controlled). Our sexual desires and responses are just particularly apt avenues of torture. This aptitude derives not just from the strength and attention-fixing powers of these responses, or the degree to which such feelings are potential sources of shame. In addition, the sexual is an area in which we have one of our basic experiences of ourselves and others as simultaneously free and embodied beings. Sexual interest provides the materials for profound forms of intimacy, self-revelation, and trust: as such, it is readily perverted into a mode of self-estrangement and self-betrayal.[40] Rape and the threat of rape are common means of torture,[41] as are prolonged nakedness, forcing couples to engage in sex in view of their tormentors, forcing a victim to watch a family member being raped, or forced sexual contact with animals (the forced masturbation of Abu Ghraib seems to be a recent innovation of the US military). In such cases, I suggest, victims are forced to experience the question of whether they are in some way aroused by or welcoming of these violations of themselves and their loved ones,[42] of whether despite their most sincere commitments they are ultimately in league with their torturer. Victims of both rape and torture often obsess over the question of whether they resisted enough or whether they let themselves "give in" too readily. In both cases, the victim must confront the question of whether her will really manifests her sincerest convictions, or whether it more readily expresses the will of another even as that other displays nothing but hatred or contempt for her.

VI

In "The Genesis of Shame," J. David Velleman argues that shame is primarily a response to an injury to one's public standing as a "self-presenting creature."[43] To be able to effectively communicate and cooperate, a rational agent must have the ability, and must be recognized by others as having the ability, to choose which of his feelings, desires, and emotions to present to others. Velleman observes that these abilities are called into question by such "bodily insubordination" as erection or blushing that reveals our feelings despite our best attempts to keep them to ourselves. We feel shame when we seem unable to keep from publicizing what we wish to keep private and hence seem unable to control the persona we present to others. For Velleman, shame is only properly occasioned by one's own inability to properly maintain one's privacy, not by the invasion of it, for "[W]hen people forcibly violate your privacy, no doubt is cast on your capacity for self-presentation."[44]

In torture, the victim suffers a violation that does cast doubt on something similar to his capacity for self-presentation, but deeper and more fundamental. This experience resembles but is worse than the sorts of shaming that Velleman discusses. Insofar as the victim experiences some part of himself to be in collusion with his tormentor, he confronts not just a loss of control over the way he presents himself to others. Rather, doubt is cast on his ability to have cares and commitments that are more immediately and authentically his own than those of another agent. Whatever its ultimate goal, torture aims to make its victim make himself into something that moral philosophy tells us should be impossible: a natural slave, a truly heteronomous will. The victim retains enough freedom and rationality to think of himself as accountable, while he nevertheless finds himself, despite all he can do, to be expressing the will of another, the will of a hated and feared enemy.[45]

Even if the victim does not break, he will still characteristically discover within himself a host of traitorous temptations. His problem is not just that his body is insubordinate, as when an erection reveals his desire in a way completely independent of his will, but that it is treacherous. This treachery is to be found not in the wayward physiological responses of his body, but in those feelings and desires in which he finds his will to be already incipiently invested. Even if the torturers seek only information, they nevertheless try to make their victim experience himself as a moral abomination, as a free and accountable agent whose freedom nevertheless truly belongs to the will of somebody else. The victim finds himself to be not only losing control of his persona. Rather, he also finds himself to be actively giving up control of his person, insofar as his personality is bound up with his ability to immediately define and know his concerns and commitments through his own sincere avowal of them.

Torture does not merely insult or damage its victim's agency, but rather turns such agency against itself, forcing the victim to experience herself as helpless yet complicit in her own violation. This is not just an assault on or violation of the victim's autonomy, but also a perversion of it, a kind of systematic mockery of the basic moral relations that an individual bears both to others and to herself. Perhaps this is why torture seems qualitatively worse than other forms of brutality or cruelty. The violence of war or police action may injure or insult an agent's capacities for rational and moral self-governance, but such violence need not make the victim an accomplice in his own violation. Torture, in contrast, involves not just the insults and injuries to be found in other kinds of violence, but a wrong that, by exploiting the victim's own participation, might best be called a humiliation.

VII

So far I have considered torture in contexts in which the victim is completely at the mercy of another person, a person who operates (or at least appears to operate) with no independent constraints on how he may treat his victim. I have argued that in such cases, what morally distinguishes torture from other forms of great violence is in part how the victim is put into a position where she is psychologically and rationally compelled to anticipate and identify with her tormentor's attitude toward her, thereby being forced to experience her affects, emotions, and imaginings as colluding against her. On this account, torture requires not just the complete helplessness and vulnerability of the victim, but a kind of open-ended freedom (real or perceived) on the part of the torturer.

Much actual torture has this character, especially the kinds that we are most tempted to think might sometimes be morally justified in combating terrorism. But torture need not have precisely this structure, especially when it is used not as a means of extracting information or confessions, but as a form of criminal punishment. A legal system might well exist in which after receiving due process of law, an individual is to be punished by a specific number of lashes or electric shocks of a particular intensity, where the infliction of such punishment is properly monitored by reliable third-party authorities (and perhaps legal and medical representatives of the victim as well). Normally we would call such sort of treatment torture, even though the victim, while helpless, is not (and does not take himself to be) exposed to the caprice of any other agent. Here, the victim is not called upon to answer any questions, or to present himself in some way that might satisfy his torturers. He knows instead that regardless of whatever he says or does, and regardless of what any of his tormentors think or want, he will receive the same punishment, without any possibility of its being eased or aggravated. In medieval legal parlance, such forms of torture were known as ordeals, where there was nothing for the victim to do but suffer in some very fixed and determinate way.

On the analysis I have offered, it may appear that such ordeals do not really qualify as torture; or more precisely, that they are not morally objectionable in the distinctive way other kinds of torture are (although they may be still be highly objectionable in the broader ways that any kind of violence may be). Yet while such ordeals do differ significantly from the central cases of torture I have so far discussed, there is a special objection to such treatment that is similar to the objections to torture "proper." Even in the case of ordeals, there is a way in which the basic structure of embodied agency is perverted or turned against itself.

What is important here is again not just the experience of pain and fear, but the fact that the pain is administered by another person, that it serves some purpose or point of another, and that the victim cannot effectively evade, retaliate, or shield himself against these assaults. Unlike other kinds of attack, here the victim must simply take it: there is no reply or counter open to him, nothing for him to do in response. In normal action, a person's movements and feelings are expressive of his prior attitudes, desires, or intentions, which then have their significance recognized by others. But in ordeals, this expressive relation between the public and the private is reversed. Another person or institution has some interest, project, or attitude toward the victim, realized immediately in the body and bodily affects of the victim, who experiences himself as merely the ultimate passive recipient of these acts. His thoughts, his attention, his interest assume whatever form his body demands. In a sense, his body ceases to be *his*, to be the substance in which he expresses his own attitudes, intentions, and feelings in a way that can be meaningful for others as a form of self-expression. Since the victim cannot effectively reassert himself physically against the assault (by fighting, fleeing, or shielding himself), his body becomes the medium in which someone else realizes or expresses his agency. The victim here becomes little more than a point of pure receptivity, having the most basic forms of agency effectively at the command of another.[46] Améry observes:

> The other person, *opposite* whom I exist physically in the world and *with* whom I can exist only as long as he does not touch my skin surface as border, forces his own corporeality on me with the first blow. . . . Certainly, if there is even a minimal prospect of successful resistance, a mechanism is set in motion that enables me to rectify the border violation by the other person. For my part, I can expand in urgent self-defense, objectify my own corporeality, restore the trust in my continued existence. . . .[47]

In such torture by ordeal, the victim is not actively colluding against himself: rather, it is as if basic conditions of his agency have been completely assimilated by another, having become so thoroughly his enemy's that even the idea of betrayal is out of place. Here the victim experiences his body in all its intimacy as the expressive medium of another will,[48] a will to which what is left of his personality finds itself immediately conforming. In the ordeal the victim's will is not annihilated, as in death, but turned into just a locus of suffering, as something that is aware of itself as a body available to and saturated by the active will of another.[49] The experience has been likened to a kind of paradoxical consciousness of oneself as dead.[50] Améry writes that

> [a]mazed, the tortured person experienced that in this world there can be the other as absolute sovereign. . . . Astonishment at the existence of the other, as he boundlessly asserts himself through torture, and astonishment at what one can become oneself: flesh and death. The tortured person never ceases to be amazed that all those things one may, according to inclination, call his soul, or his mind, or his

consciousness, or his identity, are destroyed when there is that cracking and splintering in the shoulder joints. That life is fragile is a truism he has always known. . . . But only through torture did he learn that a living person can be transformed so thoroughly into flesh and by that, *while still alive,* be partly made into a prey of death.[51]

Like interrogational torture, ordeals involve not just an insult or injury to the victim's agency. Through the combination of captivity, restraint, and pain, the physical and social bases of rational agency are actively turned against such agency itself. In torture, Améry writes, "one's fellow man was experienced as the antiman."[52] If so, then torture by ordeal should be objectionable in ways akin to torture that seeks some sort of response from its victim, insofar as both involve some sort of perversion of the most basic human relations. Whether such objections could ever be overcome by legitimate military or punitive interests is a question that waits upon more comprehensive understandings of the morality of punishment, warfare, and self-defense.

Notes

1. See, e.g., Jean Améry, "Torture" in *Art From the Ashes*, ed. Lawrence L. Langer (New York: Oxford University Press, 1995), pp. 130–1; Diana Kordon et al., "Torture in Argentina" in *Torture and its Consequences*, ed. Metin Basoglu (Cambridge: Cambridge University Press, 1992), pp. 443–4; Elaine Scarry, *The Body in Pain* (New York: Oxford University Press, 1985), pp. 34–8.

2. See Edward Peters, *Torture* (New York: Basil Blackwell, 1985), p. 154.

3. Donald Rumsfeld insists that what the prisoners at Abu Ghraib suffered was not "technically" torture but only "abuse," and the European Court of Human Rights has con-

cluded that while Great Britain had subjected suspected IRA sympathizers to "inhuman and degrading treatment," what they suffered was nevertheless "not quite torture." In neither case, however, was it made clear just what the relevant distinction was supposed to be (see n. 15 below).

4. "There can never be any justification for torture. It creates an escalation of violence in the internal affairs of states. It spreads like a contagious disease from country to country. It has lasting effects on the mental and physical health of the victim, and brutalizes the torturer" (*Declaration of the First Amnesty International Conference for the Abolition of*

Torture, as quoted in *A Glimpse of Hell*, ed. Duncan Forrest [London: Amnesty International UK, 1996], p. viii). Of course, all the same objections might be pressed against warfare in almost any form, without making war categorically unjustifiable.

5 See, e.g., Alan Dershowitz, "Torture of Terrorists" in *Shouting Fire* (Boston: Little Brown, 2002), pp. 470–7; Bruce Hoffman, "A Nasty Business," *Atlantic Monthly* (January 2002); and Anthony Lewis, "Making Torture Legal," *New York Review of Books* (June 15, 2004): 4–8.

6 Although many in the United States do seem open to torture as a form of entertainment, as attested by the popularity of "reality television" devoted to little more than the infliction of various humiliations and cruelties upon its (sometimes unwitting) participants. To cite one notable example: an episode of "Culture Shock" offered a prize to whichever of two contestants could endure being suspended in the back-bending "harness of pain" longer. At least in one case, it was a contestant's husband who was called upon to hold the rope that contorted her body. The contestant claims to have been permanently injured by the experience and has brought suit against the producers of "Culture Shock." See Adam Liptak, "Growing Rowdier, TV Reality Shows are Attracting Suits," *The New York Times* (January 7, 2003), Sec. A, p. 1.

7 See Richard Bernstein, "Kidnapping Has Germans Debating Police Torture," *The New York Times* (April 10, 2003), Sec. A, p. 3.

8 Even those who morally condemn capital punishment often consider it to be distinct from and less objectionable than punitive torture, as Amnesty International discovered when it decided to group capital punishment with torture and mutilation as the sort of human rights violation that Amnesty International would protest.

9 That is, than other forms of great violence that we sometimes countenance in war and police action. I do not mean to say that torture is absolutely unique morally: its distinctive wrongs may well also be found in rape and many kinds of spousal and child abuse. I suspect that in a comprehensive analysis, these latter would best be understood as special types of torture.

10 Which is not to say that when torture is wrong, it is worse than wrongful acts of maiming and killing. This I leave as an open question, to which there may not be any very general answer. My interest here is only with the prima facie objections to these acts, and what kinds of concerns may or may not properly counter such objections. Nothing I argue here entails that it is more important for us to prevent torture than it is to prevent murder, or that torturers should be condemned or punished more severely than murderers. The moral differences between torture, killing, and maiming may not always make a difference in such third-personal contexts.

11 Office of the High Commissioner for Human Rights, http://www.unhchr.ch/html/menu3/b/h_cat39.htm. The Convention entered into force in 1987.

12 See Metin Basoglu and Susan Mineka, "The Role of Uncontrollable and Unpredictable Stress in Post-Traumatic Stress Responses in Torture Survivors," in Basoglu, *Torture and its Consequences*, pp. 182–217.

13 In some consensual sado-masochistic acts, the "victim" may similarly occupy a position of complete vulnerability before another. Yet here the victim need not be entirely helpless before his tormentor, should there be agreed upon signals or "stop words" that he can use to call the session to a halt. Such acts may differ from real torture in that they are (at least sometimes) conducted with a shared understanding that the victim retains an effective power to withdraw consent, and hence that his subjection is merely a kind of pantomime (however real the pain). Of course, in such cases the victim must trust that his tormentor will respect that authority, but unlike real cases of torture, that trust need not be unreasonable. However, such pretend-torture may turn into real torture when the tormentor makes it clear that he does not recognize the victim's right to opt out, taking himself to be as unconstrained morally as he is physically.

14 In Northern Ireland, Great Britain employed what it called "interrogation in depth" against

suspected IRA sympathizers. Such interrogation consisted in hooding the prisoners,
keeping them in a room pervaded by the din
of a large engine or fan, depriving them of
food, water and sleep, and forcing them to
stand for long periods pressing themselves
against a wall. (Such techniques are also part
of current US interrogation procedures; see
Mark Danner, "The Logic of Torture" in *The
New York Review of Books* [June 24, 2004],
pp. 71–2). In the British case, the European
Court of Human Rights concluded that these
five techniques, while constituting "inhuman
and degrading treatment," were still "not
quite torture." See John Conroy, *Unspeakable
Acts, Ordinary People: The Dynamics of
Torture* (Berkeley: University of California
Press, 2000), p. 187. From what I have argued,
this judgment might be defended by appeal
to the fact that the isolation and sensory
disorientation were only (very successful)
attempts to undermine the victim's psychological integrity. However, hunger, thirst,
and the prolonged standing were intensely
painful, and conducted in an atmosphere in
which the prisoners continually feared for
their lives and health. Such techniques are
clearly forms of torture as I understand it.

15 For an interpretation along these lines, see
William Twining, "Torture and Philosophy,"
The Proceedings of the Aristotelian Society
(1978, supp. vol. 52): 147.

16 See, e.g., Barrie Paskins, "Torture and Philosophy," *The Proceedings of the Aristotelian
Society* (1978, supp. vol. 52): 165–94.

17 See Glenn R. Randall and Ellen L. Lutz,
Serving Survivors of Torture (Waldorf,
Maryland: AAAS Books, 1991), pp. 28–30.

18 Insofar as torture involves an arbitrary or
capricious use of power (or the appearance of
such a use), it tends to erode any legal strictures imposed upon it. The Romans initially
limited interrogational torture to slaves, and
when Europe reintroduced torture in the
thirteenth century it took care to exempt
"children, the elderly, pregnant women,
knights, barons, aristocrats, kings, professors,
and, usually, the clergy." In both cases,
however, these restrictions were gradually
relaxed until almost anyone could be tor-

tured pursuant to a judicial proceeding. See
Conroy, *Unspeakable Acts*, p. 30. Modern
attempts to introduce torture as a limited and
temporary emergency measure have generally met the same fate.

19 Randall and Lutz deny that there is any
unique "torture syndrome." Instead, they
argue, the psychological consequences of
torture are similar to those suffered by other
survivors of great stress and trauma, including combat and imprisonment. Randall and
Lutz, *Serving Survivors*, pp. 4–5.

20 Henry Shue, "Torture," *Philosophy & Public
Affairs* 7 (1978): 124–43.

21 Scarry, *Body in Pain*, pp. 45–51.

22 For a related discussion to which I am considerably indebted, see Christine Korsgaard,
The Sources of Normativity (Cambridge:
Cambridge University Press, 1996), pp. 138–
40, 145–60.

23 "There were times when he feebly tried to
compromise, when he said to himself: I will
confess, but not yet. I must hold out till the
pain becomes unbearable. Three more kicks,
two more kicks, and then I will tell them what
they want." George Orwell, *1984* (New York:
Plume Books, 1983), p. 215.

24 Scarry, *Body in Pain*, p. 47.

25 Susan J. Brison, *Aftermath: Violence and the
Remaking of a Self* (Princeton, N.J.: Princeton
University Press, 2002), p. 44.

26 Torturers also frequently heighten this experience of collusion and betrayal by making
victims witness or otherwise come to believe
that their loved ones are being tortured, with
the suggestion that this torture will cease if
the victim complies. See Randall and Lutz,
Serving Survivors, pp. 109–10; Basoglu and
Mineka, "The Role", pp. 205–6. Here, the
victim is forced into a kind of complicity with
his torturer on two levels. Overtly, his actions
determine whether his family or his comrades (or whoever else he might incriminate)
are tortured, or the degree or manner in
which they suffer. More deeply, the victim's
feelings of love for his family have been
mobilized by the torturer, and he has been
made to regret the fact that he cares for them.
The victim's love has been made to condemn
itself (a result that is also to be found in

hostage-taking and many kinds of terrorism).
My thanks to Christine Korsgaard for pressing me on this point.

27   Such as the hooded prisoner in the notorious
Abu Ghraib photograph, balancing on a box
and holding his wired arms apart in fear of
being electrocuted if he fell.

28   The US government admits to subjecting
Khalid Sheik Mohammed to this technique,
in a variation given the more sporting name
of "water-boarding."

29   Conroy, *Unspeakable Acts*, p. 169. Of course,
another reason why such techniques are so
common is that they are cheap and easy to
perform and tend to leave no incriminating
marks on their victims.

30   Brison tells of "the heightened lucidity that
had led me to memorize my assailant's face
during the attack, when my life had depended
on reading every gesture, hearing every noise,
taking everything down, storing it all away"
(Brison, *Aftermath*, p. 109). See also Jacobo
Timerman, *Prisoner without a Name, Cell
without a Number* (New York: Alfred A.
Knopf, 1981), p. 35.

31   Timerman, *Prisoner*, p. 35.

32   "I talked. I accused myself of invented absurd
political crimes, and even now I don't know
at all how they could have occurred to me,
dangling bundle that I was" (Améry,
"Torture," p. 133).

33   It is not surprising that victims of torture
typically suffer a kind of profound alienation
from their own affective and emotional lives.
Torture typically produces alexithymia, "the
inability to be aware of and to tolerate basic
feeling states" (Henry Krystal, "The Paradigm of Adult Catastrophic Trauma and
Infantile Trauma," as quoted in Randall and
Lutz, *Serving Survivors*, p. 42). Someone suffering alexithymia "cannot use [his] emotions as guidelines for action, is unable to
tolerate feelings that do occur and cannot
recognize these feelings, has a decreased
ability to conceive abstract thoughts, and has
a decreased ability to feel pleasure" (Randall
and Lutz, *Serving Survivors*, p. 42).

34   Conroy, *Unspeakable Acts*, p. 171.

35   Cf. Elie Wiesel's account of witnessing his
father being beaten by a concentration camp

guard: "I had watched the whole scene
without moving. I kept quiet. In fact I was
thinking of how to get farther away so that I
would not be hit myself. What is more, any
anger I felt at that moment was directed, not
at the [guard], but against my father. I was
angry with him, for not knowing how to avoid
Idek's outbreak. That is what concentration
camp life had made of me" (*Night*, as quoted
in Judith Herman, *Trauma and Recovery*
[New York: Basic Books, 1991], p. 84).

36   Améry, "Torture," p. 133. Timerman quotes
one of his tormentors remarking, "Only God
gives and takes life. But God is busy elsewhere, and we're the ones who must undertake this task in Argentina" (Timerman,
Prisoner, p. 31).

37   Herman, *Trauma*, p. 91.

38   Conroy, *Unspeakable Acts*, p. 175.

39   "De Sade claimed that the object of sexual
desire was to evoke involuntary responses
from one's partner, especially audible ones.
The infliction of pain is no doubt the most
efficient way to accomplish this, but it requires
a certain abrogation of one's own exposed
spontaneity" (Thomas Nagel, "Sexual Perversion" in *Mortal Questions* [Cambridge: Cambridge University Press, 1979], p. 50).

40   Scarry similarly considers torture and sex
both to involve some profound experience of
self-revelation, although in torture such self-
revelation serves only to destroy the possibilities of human intimacy. Here pain and fear
are used to bring "all the solitude of absolute
privacy with none of its safety, all the self-
exposure of the utterly public with none of
its possibility for camaraderie or shared experience" (Scarry, *Body in Pain*, p. 53).

41   See Inge Lunde and Jorgen Ortmann, "Sexual
Torture and the Treatment of its Consequences" in Basoglu, *Torture and its Consequences*, pp. 310–11.

42   See Lunde and Ortmann, "Sexual Torture,"
p. 314.

43   J. David Velleman, "The Genesis of Shame,"
Philosophy & Public Affairs 30 (2001): 37.

44   Velleman, "Genesis of Shame," p. 38.

45   Améry writes of the torturer "expand[ing]
into the body of his fellow man" ("Torture,"
p. 132). Cf. Brison, "This working through,

or remastering of, the traumatic memory involves going from being the medium of someone else's (the torturer's) speech to being the subject of one's own" (Brison. *Aftermath*, p. 56).

46 Améry, "Torture," p. 126: "The boundaries of my body are also the boundaries of my self. My skin surface shields me against the external world. If I am to have trust, I must feel on it only what I *want* to feel."

47 Améry, "Torture," p. 126.

48 This aspect of punitive torture may be shared to varying degrees with other problematic forms of corporal punishment such as mutilation, castration, and death (even when such punishments can be inflicted without causing physical pain). Cf. Jeffrey H. Reiman, "Justice, Civilization, and the Death Penalty: Answering van den Haag," *Philosophy & Public Affairs* 14 (1985): 115–48. Reiman argues that one of the principal objections to all forms of corporal punishment is the "urgency" and all-absorbing nature of physical pain or, in the case of execution, of the fear of death. However, it is unclear why the fear of a (painless) death is different in kind than the fear of a lengthy prison sentence, or the "reflective pain" of serving one out. Nor does Reiman consider potentially painless forms of corporal punishment, such as mutilation or branding, that seem objectionable just as immediate assaults on the body.

49 Cf. Herman, *Trauma*, p. 93: "Whatever new identity she develops in freedom must include the memory of her enslaved self. Her image of her body must include a body that can be controlled and violated. Her image of herself in relation to others must include a person who can lose and be lost to others."

50 See Brison, *Aftermath*, pp. 38–66.

51 Améry, "Torture," p. 136, my emphasis.

52 Améry, "Torture," p. 136.

Part IV

Rawl's *The Law of Peoples*

Introduction

The work of John Rawls has changed the way we think about political philosophy. No political philosopher rivals his influence on contemporary work and its continued direction, even after his recent death in 2002. In 1971, his *A Theory of Justice* revolutionized the way we consider justice in the state. Rawls's *The Law of Peoples* revolutionized the way we consider justice between states in the international sphere. This work began life as part of the 1993 Oxford Amnesty Lectures and developed over the following years, published in its more complete form in 1999.

This work proved highly controversial amongst Rawlsian scholars. Just as it was the case that many philosophers claimed Rawls had betrayed the project of *A Theory of Justice* in his following book, *Political Liberalism*, critics claimed *The Law of Peoples* was a double-betrayal of his previous work. Rather than discuss the controversies surrounding the reception of the development of Rawls's work, I will instead focus our attention on the main ideas of *The Law of Peoples*.[1]

In this work, Rawls defends a system of international justice he calls a "Law of Peoples" that governs the relations between members in "a Society of Peoples." A Society of Peoples is composed of reasonably just "liberal peoples" and "decent peoples." This fact is meant to represent the view that societies need not be liberal in order to possess complete legitimate status within international society. Decent peoples may be illiberal, yet respect the rule of law and permit dissent. The Law of Peoples is a realistic utopia that is practical and based upon the idea of public reason. If put into practice, peoples will lack any reason to engage in war with one another and a Kantian perpetual peace becomes a possibility (see chapter 16). From these basic building blocks, Rawls paints a revealing picture of how we might reconsider justice in the international sphere, not least the rights of peoples that we should uphold and defend.

The second chapter in this Part is an essay by Thomas W. Pogge. He argues that Rawls defends (in an earlier version of *The Law of Peoples* from 1993) a global order that lacks an egalitarian distributive principle that might help rectify global inequalities, a fact true of

---

[1] On these controversies, see Leif Wenar, "The Unity of Rawls's Work," *Journal of Moral Philosophy* 1 (2004): 265–75.

Rawls's final views on the subject as well. Pogge claims that a global order that adhered to Rawls's own principles of justice would become a more egalitarian order, adopting new features, such as a global resources tax. As wealthy states use more of the world's resources, they are required to contribute – through this tax – proceeds which are used, in turn, to improve the lot of the present and future global poor. Moreover, this tax would not only help alleviate global poverty, but it is realistically practical: Pogge notes that a $2 global resources tax on each barrel of crude oil would generate one-sixth of the resources necessary to help bring to an end the existence of severe poverty, raising the price of petroleum by only a mere 5¢ per gallon. Pogge argues that world citizens behind a global original position – persons placed behind "a veil of ignorance" and unaware of their social position, gender, occupation, and other characteristics – would support Pogge's picture over what Rawls himself presents. Thus, in a sense, Pogge uses Rawls against himself to shed light on what an egalitarian, Rawlsian world order might look like.

The work of John Rawls has been monumental in helping shape the direction of how we think about not only domestic justice but also international justice. The following selections from his *The Law of Peoples* gives us an important look at the power of his ideas and Pogge's essay is an example of one of the many ways Rawls helps us think more clearly about matters of global justice.

Chapter 11

*The Law of Peoples**
John Rawls

Introduction

1. By the "Law of Peoples" I mean a particular political conception of right and justice that applies to the principles and norms of international law and practice. I shall use the term "Society of Peoples" to mean all those peoples who follow the ideals and principles of the Law of Peoples in their mutual relations. These peoples have their own internal governments, which may be constitutional liberal democratic or non-liberal but decent[1] governments. In this book I consider how the content of the Law of Peoples might be developed out of a liberal idea of justice similar to, but more general than, the idea I called *justice as fairness* in *A Theory of Justice* (1971). This idea of justice is based on the familiar idea of the social contract, and the procedure followed before the principles of right and justice are selected and agreed upon is in some ways the same in both the domestic and the international case I shall discuss how such a Law of Peoples[2] fulfills certain conditions, which justify calling the

Society of Peoples a *realistic utopia* (see §1), and I shall also return to and explain why I have used the term "peoples" and not "states."

In §58 of *A Theory of Justice* I indicated how justice as fairness can be extended to international law (as I called it there) for the limited purpose of judging the aims and limits of just war. Here my discussion covers more ground. I propose considering five types of domestic societies. The first is *reasonable liberal peoples*; the second, *decent peoples* (see note 1 above). The basic structure of one kind of decent people has what I call a "decent consultation hierarchy," and these peoples I call "decent hierarchical peoples." Other possible kinds of decent peoples I do not try to describe, but simply leave in reserve, allowing that there may be other decent peoples whose basic structure does not fit my description of a consultation hierarchy, but who are worthy of membership in a Society of Peoples. (Liberal peoples and decent peoples I refer to together as "well-ordered peoples.") There are, third, *outlaw states* and, fourth, *societies burdened by unfavorable conditions*. Finally, fifth, we have societies that are *benevolent absolutisms*: they honor human rights; but, because their

* From John Rawls, *The Law of Peoples* (Cambridge, MA: Harvard University Press, 1999), pp. 3–4, 11–19, 23–43.

members are denied a meaningful role in making political decisions, they are not well-ordered.

. . .

I   The First Part of Ideal Theory

§1   The Law of Peoples as Realistic Utopia

1.1   Meaning of Realistic Utopia. . . . Political philosophy is realistically utopian when it extends what are ordinarily thought to be the limits of practicable political possibility and, in so doing, reconciles us to our political and social condition. Our hope for the future of our society rests on the belief that the social world allows a reasonably just constitutional democracy existing as a member of a reasonably just Society of Peoples. What would a reasonably just constitutional democracy be like under reasonably favorable historical conditions that are possible given the laws and tendencies of society? And how do these conditions relate to laws and tendencies bearing on the relations between peoples?

These historical conditions include, in a reasonably just domestic society, the fact of reasonable pluralism.[3] In the Society of Peoples, the parallel to reasonable pluralism is the diversity among reasonable peoples with their different cultures and traditions of thought, both religious and nonreligious. Even when two or more peoples have liberal constitutional regimes, their conceptions of constitutionalism may diverge and express different variations of liberalism. A (reasonable) Law of Peoples must be acceptable to reasonable peoples who are thus diverse; and it must be fair between them and effective in shaping the larger schemes of their cooperation.

This fact of reasonable pluralism limits what is practicably possible here and now, whatever may have been the case in other historical ages when, it is often said, people within a domestic society were united (though perhaps they never really have been) in affirming one comprehensive doctrine. I recognize that there are questions about how the limits of the practicably possible are discerned and what the conditions of our social world in fact are. The problem here is that the limits of the possible are not given by the actual, for we can to a greater or lesser extent change political and social institutions and much else. Hence we have to rely on conjecture and speculation, arguing as best we can that the social world we envision is feasible and might actually exist, if not now then at some future time under happier circumstances.

Eventually we want to ask whether reasonable pluralism within or between peoples is a historical condition to which we should be reconciled. Though we can imagine what we sometimes think would be a happier world – one in which everyone, or all peoples, have the same faith that we do – that is not the question, excluded as it is by the nature and culture of free institutions. To show that reasonable pluralism is not to be regretted, we must show that, given the socially feasible alternatives, the existence of reasonable pluralism allows a society of greater political justice and liberty. To argue this cogently would be to reconcile us to our contemporary political and social condition.

1.2   Conditions of the Domestic Case. I begin with a sketch of a reasonably just constitutional democratic society (hereafter sometimes referred to simply as a liberal society) as a realistic utopia and review seven conditions that are necessary for such a realistic utopia to obtain. Then I check whether parallel conditions would hold for a society of reasonably just and decent peoples who honor a Law of Peoples. Should those conditions also hold, the Society of Peoples is also a case of realistic utopia.

(i)   There are two necessary conditions for a liberal conception of justice to be *realistic*. The first is that it must rely on the actual laws of nature and achieve the kind of stability those laws allow, that is, stability for the right reasons.[4] It takes people as they are (by the laws of nature), and constitutional and civil laws as they might be, that is, as they would be in a reasonably just and well-ordered democratic society. Here I follow Rousseau's opening thought in *The Social Contract*:

> My purpose is to consider if, in political society, there can be any legitimate and sure principle of government, taking men as they are and laws as they might be. In this inquiry I shall try always to bring together what right permits with what interest requires so that justice and utility are in no way divided.

The second condition for a liberal political conception of justice to be realistic is that its first principles and precepts be workable and applicable to ongoing political and social arrangements. Here an example may be helpful: consider primary goods (basic rights and liberties, opportunities, income and wealth, and the social bases of self-respect) as used in justice as fairness. One of their main features is that they are workable. A citizen's share of these goods is openly observable and makes possible the required comparisons between citizens (so-called interpersonal comparisons). This can be done without appealing to such unworkable ideas as a people's overall utility, or to Sen's basic capabilities for various functionings (as he calls them).[5]

(ii)   A necessary condition for a political conception of justice to be *utopian* is that it use political (moral) ideals, principles, and concepts to specify a reasonable and just society. There is a family of reasonable liberal conceptions of justice, each of which has the following three characteristic principles:

the first enumerates basic rights and liberties of the kind familiar from a constitutional regime;

the second assigns these rights, liberties, and opportunities a special priority, especially with respect to the claims of the general good and perfectionism values; and

the third assures for all citizens the requisite primary goods to enable them to make intelligent and effective use of their freedoms.

The principles of these conceptions of justice must also satisfy the criterion of reciprocity. This criterion requires that, when terms are proposed as the most reasonable terms of fair cooperation, those proposing them must think it at least reasonable for others to accept them, as free and equal citizens, and not as dominated or manipulated or under pressure caused by an inferior political or social position.[6] Citizens will differ as to which of these conceptions they think the most reasonable, but they should be able to agree that all are reasonable, even if barely so. Each of these liberalisms endorses the underlying ideas of citizens as free and equal persons and of society as a fair system of cooperation over time. Yet since these ideas can be interpreted in various ways, we get different formulations of the principles of justice and different contents of public reason.[7] Political conceptions differ also in how they order, or balance, political principles and values even when they specify the same principles and values as significant. These liberalisms contain substantive principles of justice, and hence cover more than procedural justice. The principles are required to specify the religious liberties and freedoms of artistic expression of free and equal citizens, as well as substantive ideas of fairness assuring fair opportunity and adequate all-purpose means, and much else.[8]

(iii)   A third condition for a realistic utopia requires that the category of the political must contain within itself all the essential elements for a political conception of justice. For example, in political liberalism persons are viewed as citizens, and a political conception of justice is built up from political (moral) ideas available in the public political culture of a liberal constitutional regime. The idea of a free citizen is determined by a liberal political conception and not by any comprehensive doctrine, which always extends beyond the category of the political.

(iv) Because of the fact of reasonable pluralism, constitutional democracy must have political and social institutions that effectively lead its citizens to acquire the appropriate sense of justice as they grow up and take part in society. They will then be able to understand the principles and ideals of the political conception, to interpret and apply them to cases at hand, and they will normally be moved to act from them as circumstances require. This leads to stability for the right reasons.

Insofar as liberal conceptions require virtuous conduct of citizens, the necessary (political) virtues are those of political cooperation, such as a sense of fairness and tolerance and a willingness to meet others halfway. Moreover, liberal political principles and ideals can be satisfied by the basic structure of society even if numerous citizens lapse on occasion, provided that their conduct is outweighed by the appropriate conduct of a sufficient number of others.[9] The structure of political institutions remains just and stable (for the right reasons) over time.

This idea of realistic utopia is importantly institutional. In the domestic case it connects with the way citizens conduct themselves under the institutions and practices within which they have grown up; in the international case with the way a people's character has historically developed. We depend on the facts of social conduct as his-

torical knowledge and reflection establish them: for example, the facts that, historically, political and social unity do not depend on religious unity, and that well-ordered democratic peoples do not engage in war with one another. These observations and others will be essential as we proceed.

(v) Because religious, philosophical, or moral unity is neither possible nor necessary for social unity, if social stability is not merely a *modus vivendi*, it must be rooted in a reasonable political conception of right and justice affirmed by an overlapping consensus of comprehensive doctrines.

(vi) The political conception should have a reasonable idea of toleration derived entirely from ideas drawn from the category of the political.[10] This condition might not always be necessary, however, as we can think of cases when all the comprehensive doctrines held in society themselves provide for such a view. Nevertheless, the political conception will be strengthened if it contains a reasonable idea of toleration within itself, for that will show the reasonableness of toleration by public reason.

1.3 Parallel Conditions of Society of Peoples. Assuming that §1.2 above adequately indicates the conditions required for a reasonably just constitutional democracy, which I have called "a realistic utopia," what are the parallel conditions for a reasonably just Society of Peoples? This is too big a matter to discuss at this point in any detail. Yet it might be fruitful to note some of the parallels before we proceed, since doing so will foreshadow the argument to follow.

The first three conditions, I believe, are as strong in one case as in the other:

(i*) The reasonably just Society of well-ordered Peoples is *realistic* in the same ways as a liberal or decent domestic society. Here again we view peoples as they are (as organized within a reasonably just domestic society) and the Law of Peoples as it might be, that is, how it would be in a reasonably just Society of just and decent Peoples. The content of a reasonable Law of Peoples is ascertained by using the idea of the original position a second time with the parties now understood to be the representatives of peoples (§3). The idea of peoples rather than states is crucial at this point: it enables us to attribute moral motives – an allegiance to the principles of the Law of Peoples, which, for instance, permits wars only of self-defense – to peoples (as actors), which we cannot do for states (§2).[11]

The Law of Peoples is also realistic in a second way: it is workable and may be applied to ongoing cooperative political arrangements and relations between peoples. That this is the case cannot be shown until the content of the Law of Peoples is sketched (§4). For now, suffice it to say that the Law is expressed in the familiar terms of the freedom and equality of peoples, and it involves numerous jurisprudential and political (moral) ideas.

(ii*)   A reasonably just Law of Peoples is *utopian* in that it uses political (moral) ideals, principles, and concepts to specify the reasonably right and just political and social arrangements for the Society of Peoples. In the domestic case, liberal conceptions of justice distinguish between the reasonable and the rational, and lie between altruism on one side and egoism on the other. The Law of Peoples duplicates these features. For example, we say (§2) that a people's interests are specified by their land and territory, their reasonably just political and social institutions, and their free civic culture with its many associations. These various interests ground the distinctions between the reasonable and the rational and show us how the relations among peoples may remain just and stable (for the right reasons) over time.

(iii*)   A third condition requires that all the essential elements for a political conception of justice be contained within the category of the political. This condition will be satisfied for the Law of Peoples once we extend a liberal political conception for a constitutional democracy to the relations among peoples. Whether this extension can be carried out successfully has yet to be shown. But in any event, the extensions of the political always remain political, and comprehensive doctrines, religious, philosophical, and moral, always extend beyond it.

(iv*)   The degree to which a reasonably just, effective institutional process enables members of different well-ordered societies to develop a sense of justice and support their government in honoring the Law of Peoples may differ from one society to another in the wider Society of Peoples. The fact of reasonable pluralism is more evident within a society of well-ordered peoples than it is within one society alone. An allegiance to the Law of Peoples need not be equally strong in all peoples, but it must be, ideally speaking, sufficient. . . .

This brings us to the remaining two conditions.

(v*)   The unity of a reasonable Society of Peoples does not require religious unity. The Law of Peoples provides a content of public reason for the Society of Peoples parallel to the principles of justice in a democratic society.

(vi*)   The argument for toleration derived from the idea of the reasonable holds equally in the wider Society of Peoples; the same reasoning applies in one case as in the other. The effect of extending a liberal conception of justice to the Society of Peoples, which encompasses many more religious and other comprehensive doctrines than any single people, makes it inevitable that, if member peoples employ public reason in their dealings with one another, toleration must follow.

These conditions are discussed in more detail as we proceed. How likely it is that such a Society of Peoples can exist is an important question, yet political liberalism asserts that the possibility is consistent with the natural order and with constitutions and laws as they might be. The idea of public reason for the Society of Peoples is analogous to the idea of public reason in the domestic case when a shared basis of justification exists and can be uncovered by due reflection. Political liberalism, with its ideas of realistic utopia and public reason, denies what so much of political life suggests – that stability among peoples can never be more than a *modus vivendi*.

The idea of a reasonably just society of well-ordered peoples will not have an important place in a theory of international politics until such peoples exist and have learned to coordinate the actions of their governments in wider forms of political, economic, and social cooperation. When that happens, as I believe, following Kant, it will, the society of these peoples will form a group of satisfied peoples. As I shall maintain (§2), in view of their fundamental interests being satisfied, they will have no reason to go to war with one another. The familiar motives for war would be absent: such peoples do not seek to convert others to their religions, nor to conquer greater territory, nor to wield political power over another people. Through negotiation and trade they can fulfill their needs and economic interests. A detailed account of how and why all this takes shape over time will be an essential part of the theory of international politics.

. . .

§2   Why Peoples and Not States?

2.1 Basic Features of Peoples. This account of the Law of Peoples conceives of liberal democratic peoples (and decent peoples) as the actors in the Society of Peoples, just as citizens are the actors in domestic society.

Starting from a political conception of society, political liberalism describes both citizens and peoples by political conceptions that specify their nature, a conception of citizens in one case, of peoples acting through their governments in the other. Liberal peoples have three basic features: a reasonably just constitutional democratic government that serves their fundamental interests; citizens united by what Mill called "common sympathies"; and finally, a moral nature. The first is institutional, the second is cultural, and the third requires a firm attachment to a political (moral) conception of right and justice.[12]

By saying that a people have a reasonably just (though not necessarily a fully just) constitutional democratic government I mean that the government is effectively under their political and electoral control, and that it answers to and protects their fundamental interests as specified in a written or unwritten constitution and in its interpretation. The regime is not an autonomous agency pursuing its own bureaucratic ambitions. Moreover, it is not directed by the interests of large concentrations of private economic and corporate power veiled from public knowledge and almost entirely free from accountability. What institutions and practices might be necessary to keep a constitutional democratic government reasonably just, and to prevent it from being corrupted, is a large topic I cannot pursue here, beyond noting the truism that it is necessary to frame institutions in such a way as to motivate people sufficiently, both citizens and government officers, to honor them, and to remove the obvious temptations to corruption.[13]

As for a liberal people being united by common sympathies and a desire to be under the same democratic government, if those sympathies were entirely dependent upon a common language, history, and political culture, with a shared historical consciousness, this feature would rarely, if ever, be fully satisfied. Historical conquests and immigration have caused the intermingling of groups with different cultures and historical memories who now reside within the territory of most contemporary democratic governments. Notwithstanding, the Law of Peoples starts with the need for common sympathies, no matter what their source may be. My hope is that, if we begin in this simplified way, we can work out political principles that will, in due course, enable us to deal with more difficult cases where all the citizens are not united by a common language and shared historical memories. One thought that encourages this way of proceeding is that within a reasonably just liberal (or decent) polity it is possible, I believe, to satisfy the reasonable cultural interests and needs of groups with diverse ethnic and national backgrounds. We proceed on the assumption that the political principles for a reasonably just constitutional regime allow us to deal with a great variety of cases, if not all.[14]

Finally, liberal peoples have a certain moral characters. Like citizens in domestic society, liberal peoples are both reasonable and rational, and their rational conduct, as organized and expressed in their elections and votes, and the laws and policies of their government, is similarly constrained by their sense of what is reasonable. As reasonable citizens in domestic society offer to cooperate on fair terms with other citizens, so (reasonable) liberal (or decent) peoples offer fair terms of cooperation to other peoples. A people will honor these terms when assured that other peoples will do so as well. This leads us to the principles of political justice in the first case and the Law of Peoples in the other. It will be crucial to describe how this moral nature comes about and how it can be sustained from one generation to the next.

2.2 Peoples Lack Traditional Sovereignty. Another reason I use the term "peoples" is

to distinguish my thinking from that about political states as traditionally conceived, with their powers of sovereignty included in the (positive) international law for the three centuries after the Thirty Years' War (1618–48). These powers include the right to go to war in pursuit of state policies – Clausewitz's pursuit of politics by other means – with the ends of politics given by a state's rational prudential interests.[15] The powers of sovereignty also grant a state a certain autonomy (discussed below) in dealing with its own people. From my perspective this autonomy is wrong.

In developing the Law of Peoples the first step is to work out the principles of justice for domestic society. Here the original position takes into account only persons contained within such a society, since we are not considering relations with other societies. That position views society as closed: persons enter only by birth, and exit only by death. There is no need for armed forces, and the question of the government's right to be prepared militarily does not arise and would be denied if it did. An army is not to be used against its own people. The principles of domestic justice allow a police force to keep domestic order and a judiciary and other institutions to maintain an orderly rule of law.[16] All this is very different from an army that is needed to defend against outlaw states. Although domestic principles of justice are consistent with a qualified right to war, they do not of themselves establish that right. The basis of that right depends on the Law of Peoples, still to be worked out. This law, as we shall see, will restrict a state's internal sovereignty or (political) autonomy, its alleged right to do as it wills with people within its own borders.

Thus, in working out the Law of Peoples, a government as the political organization of its people is not, as it were, the author of all of its own powers. The war powers of governments, whatever they might be, are only those acceptable within a reasonable Law of Peoples. Presuming the existence of a government whereby a people is domestically organized with institutions of background justice does not prejudge these questions. We must reformulate the powers of sovereignty in light of a reasonable Law of Peoples and deny to states the traditional rights to war and to unrestricted internal autonomy.

Moreover, this reformulation accords with a recent dramatic shift in how many would like international law to be understood. Since World War II international law has become stricter. It tends to limit a state's right to wage war to instances of self-defense (also in the interests of collective security), and it also tends to restrict a state's right to internal sovereignty. The role of human rights connects most obviously with the latter change as part of the effort to provide a suitable definition of, and limits on, a government's internal sovereignty. At this point I leave aside the many difficulties of interpreting these rights and limits, and take their general meaning and tendency as clear enough. What is essential is that our elaboration of the Law of Peoples should fit these two basic changes, and give them a suitable rationale.[17]

The term "peoples," then, is meant to emphasize these singular features of peoples as distinct from states, as traditionally conceived, and to highlight their moral character and the reasonably just, or decent, nature of their regimes. It is significant that peoples rights and duties in regard to their so-called sovereignty derive from the Law of Peoples itself, to which they would agree along with other peoples in suitable circumstances. As just or decent peoples, the reasons for their conduct accord with the corresponding principles. They are not moved solely by their prudent or rational pursuit interests, the so-called reasons of state.

2.3   Basic Features of States.   The following remarks show that the character of a

people in the Law of Peoples is different from the character of what I refer to as states. States are the actors in many theories of international politics about the causes of war and the preservation of peace.[18] They are often seen as rational, anxiously concerned with their power – their capacity (military, economic, diplomatic) to influence other states – and always guided by their basic interests.[19] The typical view of international relations is fundamentally the same as it was in Thucydides' day and has not been transcended in modern times, when world politics' is still marked by the struggles of states for power, prestige, and wealth in a condition of global anarchy.[20] How far states differ from peoples rests on how rationality, the concern with power, and a state's basic interests are filled in. If *rationality* excludes the *reasonable* (that is, if a state is moved by the aims it has and ignores the criterion of reciprocity in dealing with other societies); if a state's concern with power is predominant; and if its interests include such things as converting other societies to the state's religion, enlarging its empire and winning territory, gaining dynastic or imperial or national prestige and glory, and increasing its relative economic strength – then the difference between states and peoples is enormous.[21] Such interests as these tend to put a state at odds with other states and peoples, and to threaten their safety and security, whether they are expansionist or not. The background conditions also threaten hegemonic war.[22]

A difference between liberal peoples and states is that just liberal peoples limit their basic interests as required by the reasonable. In contrast, the content of the interests of states does not allow them to be stable for the right reasons: that is, from firmly accepting and acting upon a just Law of Peoples. Liberal peoples do, however, have their fundamental interests as permitted by their conceptions of right and justice. They seek to protect their territory to ensure the security and safety of their citizens, and to preserve their free political institutions and the liberties and free culture of their civil society. Beyond these interests, a liberal people tries to assure reasonable justice for all its citizens and for all peoples; a liberal people can live with other peoples of like character in upholding justice and preserving peace. Any hope we have of reaching a realistic utopia rests on there being reasonable liberal constitutional (and decent) regimes sufficiently established and effective to yield a viable Society of Peoples.

§3   Two Original Positions

3.1   Original Position as Model of Representation.   This part describes the first step of ideal theory. Before beginning the extension of the liberal idea of the social contract to the Law of Peoples, let us note that the original position with a veil of ignorance is a model of representation for liberal societies.[23] In what I am now calling the first use of the original position, it models what we regard – you and I, here and now[24] – as fair and reasonable conditions for the parties, who are rational representatives of free and equal, reasonable and rational citizens, to specify fair terms of cooperation for regulating the basic structure of this society. Since the original position includes the veil of ignorance, it also models what we regard as appropriate restrictions on reasons for adopting a political conception of justice for that structure. Given these features, we conjecture that the conception of political justice the parties would select is the conception that you and I, here and now, would regard as reasonable and rational and supported by the best reasons. Whether our conjecture is borne out will depend on whether you and I, here and now, can, on due reflection, endorse the principles adopted. Even if the conjecture is intuitively plausible, there are different ways of interpreting the reasonable and the rational, and of specifying restric-

tions on reasons and explaining the primary goods. There is no *a priori* guarantee that we have matters right.

Here five features are essential: (1) the original position models[25] the parties as representing citizens fairly; (2) it models them as rational; and (3) it models them as selecting from among available principles of justice those to apply to the appropriate subject, in this case the basic structure, In addition, (4) the parties are modeled as making these selections for appropriate reasons, and (5) as selecting for reasons related to the fundamental interests of citizens as reasonable and rational. We check that these five conditions are satisfied by noting that citizens are indeed represented fairly (reasonably), in view of the symmetry (or the equality) of their representatives' situation in the original position.[26] Next, the parties are modeled as rational, in that their aim is to do the best they can for citizens whose basic interests they represent, as specified by the primary goods, which cover their basic needs as citizens. Finally, the parties decide for appropriate reasons, because the veil of ignorance prevents the parties from invoking inappropriate reasons, given the aim of representing citizens as free and equal persons.

I repeat here what I have said in *Political Liberalism*, since it is relevant below.[27] Not allowing the parties to know people's comprehensive doctrines is one way in which the veil of ignorance is thick as opposed to thin. Many have thought a thick veil of ignorance to be without justification and have queried its grounds, especially given the great significance of comprehensive doctrines, religious and nonreligious. Since we should justify features of the original position when we can, consider the following. Recall that we seek a political conception of justice for a democratic society, viewed as a system of fair cooperation among free and equal citizens who willingly accept, as politically autonomous, the publicly recognized principles of justice determining the fair terms of that cooperation. The society in question, however, is one in which there is a diversity of comprehensive doctrines, all perfectly reasonable. This is the fact of reasonable pluralism, as opposed to the fact of pluralism as such. Now if all citizens are freely to endorse the political conception of justice, that conception must be able to gain the support of citizens who affirm different and opposing, though reasonable, comprehensive doctrines, in which case we have an overlapping consensus of reasonable doctrines. I suggest that we leave aside how people's comprehensive doctrines connect with the content of the political conception of justice and, instead, regard that content as arising from the various fundamental ideas drawn from the public political culture of a democratic society. Putting people's comprehensive doctrines behind the veil of ignorance enables us to find a political conception of justice that can be the focus of an overlapping consensus and thereby serve as a public basis of justification in a society marked by the fact of reasonable pluralism. None of what I am arguing here puts in question the description of a political conception of justice as a freestanding view, but it does mean that to explain the rationale of the thick veil of ignorance we must look to the fact of reasonable pluralism and the idea of an overlapping consensus of reasonable comprehensive doctrines.

3.2 *Second Original Position as Model.* At
the next level, the idea of the original position is used again, but this time to extend a liberal conception to the Law of Peoples. As in the first instance, it is a model of representation, since it models what we would regard – you and I, here and now[28] – as fair conditions under which the parties, this time the rational representatives of liberal peoples, are to specify the Law of Peoples, guided by appropriate reasons. Both the parties as rep-

resentatives and the peoples they represent are situated symmetrically and therefore fairly. In addition, peoples are modeled as rational, since the parties select from among available principles for the Law of Peoples guided by the fundamental interests of democratic societies, where these interests are expressed by the liberal principles of justice for a democratic society. Finally, the parties are subject to a veil of ignorance properly adjusted for the case at hand: they do not know, for example, the size of the territory, or the population, or the relative strength of the people whose fundamental interests they represent. Though they do know that reasonably favorable conditions obtain that make constitutional democracy possible – since they know they represent liberal societies – they do not know the extent of their natural resources, or the level of their economic development, or other such information.

As members of societies well-ordered by liberal conceptions of justice, we conjecture that these features model what we would accept as fair – you and I, here and now – in specifying the basic terms of cooperation among peoples who, as liberal peoples, see themselves as free and equal. This makes the use of the original position at the second level a model of representation in exactly the same way it is at the first. Any differences are not in how the model of representation is used but in how it needs to be tailored given the agents modeled and the subject at hand.

Having said this, let us check that all five features are covered for the second original position. Thus, people's representatives are (1) reasonably and fairly situated as free and equal, and peoples are (2) modeled as rational. Also their representatives are (3) deliberating about the correct subject, in this case the content of the Law of Peoples. (Here we may view that law as governing the basic structure of the relations between peoples.)

Moreover, (4) their deliberations proceed in terms of the right reasons (as restricted by a veil of ignorance). Finally, the selection of principles for the Law of Peoples is based (5) on a people's fundamental interests, given in this case by a liberal conception of justice (already selected in the first original position). Thus, the conjecture would appear to be sound in this case as in the first. But again there can be no guarantee.

Two questions, though, may arise. One is that in describing peoples as free and equal, and so as fairly and reasonably represented, it may appear that we have proceeded differently than in the domestic case. There we counted citizens as free and equal because that is how they conceive of themselves as citizens in a democratic society. Thus, they think of themselves as having the moral power to have a conception of the good, and to affirm or revise that conception if they so decide. They also see themselves as self-authenticating sources of claims, and capable of taking responsibility for their ends.[29] In the Law of Peoples we do somewhat the same: we view *peoples* as conceiving of themselves as free and equal *peoples* in the Society of Peoples (according to the political conception of that society). This is parallel to, but not the same as, how in the domestic case the political conception determines the way citizens are to see themselves according to their moral powers and higher-order interests.

The second question involves another parallel to the domestic case. The original position denied to the representatives of citizens any knowledge of citizens' comprehensive conceptions of the good. That restriction called for a careful justification.[30] There is also a serious question in the present case. Why do we suppose that the representatives of liberal peoples ignore any knowledge of the people's comprehensive conception of the good? The answer is that a liberal society with a constitutional regime does not, *as a liberal society*, have a *comprehensive* conception of the good. Only the citizens and associations within the civic society in the domestic case have such conceptions.

3.3 Fundamental Interests of Peoples. In thinking of themselves as free and equal, how do peoples (in contrast to states) see themselves and their fundamental interests? These interests of liberal peoples are specified, I said (§2.3), by their reasonable conception of political justice. Thus, they strive to protect their political independence and their free culture with its civil liberties, to guarantee their security, territory, and the well-being of their citizens. Yet a further interest is also significant: applied to peoples, it falls under what Rousseau calls *amour-propre*.[31] This interest is a people's proper self-respect of themselves as a people, resting on their common awareness of their trials during their history and of their culture with its accomplishments. Altogether distinct from their self-concern for their security and the safety of their territory, this interest shows itself in a people's insisting on receiving from other peoples a proper respect and recognition of their equality. What distinguishes peoples from states – and this is crucial – is that just peoples are fully prepared to grant the very same proper respect and recognition to other peoples as equals. Their equality doesn't mean, however, that inequalities of certain kinds are not agreed to in various cooperative institutions among peoples, such as the United Nations, ideally conceived. This recognition of inequalities, rather, parallels citizens' accepting functional social and economic inequalities in their liberal society.

It is, therefore, part of a people's being reasonable and rational that they are ready to offer to other peoples fair terms of political and social cooperation. These fair terms are those that a people sincerely believes other equal peoples might accept also; and should they do so, a people will honor the terms it has proposed even in those cases where that people might profit by violating them.[32] Thus, the criterion of reciprocity applies to the Law of Peoples in the same way it does to the principles of justice for a constitutional regime. This reasonable sense of due respect, willingly accorded to other reasonable peoples, is an essential element of the idea of people who are satisfied with the status quo for the right reasons. It is compatible with ongoing cooperation among them over time and the mutual acceptance and adherence to the Law of Peoples. Part of the answer to political realism is that this reasonable sense of proper respect is not unrealistic, but is itself the outcome of democratic domestic institutions. I will come back to this argument later.

§4   The Principles of the Law of Peoples

4.1   Statement of the Principles.   Initially, we may assume that the outcome of working out the Law of Peoples only for liberal democratic societies will be the adoption of certain familiar principles of equality among peoples. These principles will also, I assume, make room for various forms of cooperative associations and federations among peoples, but will not affirm a world-state. Here I follow Kant's lead in *Perpetual Peace* (1795) in thinking that a world government – by which I mean a unified political regime with the legal powers normally exercised by central governments – would either be a global despotism or else would rule over a fragile empire torn by frequent civil strife as various regions and peoples tried to gain their political freedom and autonomy.[33] As I discuss below, it may turn out that there will be many different kinds of organizations subject to the judgment of the Law of Peoples and charged with regulating cooperation among them and meeting certain recognized duties.

Some of these organizations (such as the United Nations ideally conceived) may have the authority to express for the society of well-ordered peoples their condemnation of unjust domestic institutions in other countries and clear cases of the violation of human rights. In grave cases they may try to correct them by economic sanctions, or even by military intervention. The scope of these powers covers all peoples and reaches their domestic affairs.

These large conclusions call for some discussion. Proceeding in a way analogous to the procedure in *A Theory of Justice*,[34] let's look first at familiar and traditional principles of justice among free and democratic peoples:[35]

1   Peoples are free and independent, and their freedom and independence are to be respected by other peoples.
2   Peoples are to observe treaties and undertakings.
3   Peoples are equal and are parties to the agreements that bind them.
4   Peoples are to observe a duty of non-intervention.
5   Peoples have the right of self-defense but no right to instigate war for reasons other than self-defense.
6   Peoples are to honor human rights.
7   Peoples are to observe certain specified restrictions in the conduct of war.
8   Peoples have a duty to assist other peoples living under unfavorable conditions that prevent their having a just or decent political and social regime.

4.2   Comments and Qualifications.   This statement of principles is, admittedly, incomplete. Other principles need to be added, and the principles listed require much explanation and interpretation. Some are superfluous in a society of well-ordered peoples, for example, the seventh regarding the conduct of war and the sixth regarding human rights. Yet the main point is that free and independent well-ordered peoples are ready to recognize certain basic principles of political justice as governing their conduct. These principles constitute the basic charter of the Law of Peoples. A principle such as the fourth – that of non-intervention – will obviously have to be qualified in the general case of outlaw states and grave violations of human rights. Although suitable for a society of well-ordered peoples, it fails in the case of a society of disordered peoples in which wars and serious violations of human rights are endemic.

The right to independence, and equally the right to self-determination, hold only within certain limits, yet to be specified by the Law of Peoples for the general case.[36] Thus, no people has the right to self-determination, or a right to secession, at the expense of subjugating another people.[37] Nor may a people protest their condemnation by the world society when their domestic institutions violate human rights, or limit the rights of minorities living among them. A people's right to independence and self-determination is no shield from that condemnation, nor even from coercive intervention by other peoples in grave cases.

There will also be principles for forming and regulating federations (associations) of peoples, and standards of fairness for trade and other cooperative institutions.[38] Certain provisions will be included for mutual assistance among peoples in times of famine and drought and, insofar as it is possible, provisions for ensuring that in all reasonable liberal (and decent) societies people's basic needs are met.[39] These provisions will specify duties of assistance in certain situations, and they will vary in stringency with the severity of the case.

4.3 Role of Boundaries. An important role of a people's government, however arbitrary a society's boundaries may appear from a historical point of view, is to be the representative and effective agent of a people as they take responsibility for their territory and its environmental integrity, as well as for the size of their population. As I see it the point of the institution of property is that, unless a definite agent is given responsibility for maintaining an asset and bears the loss for not doing so, that asset tends to deteriorate. In this case the asset is the people's territory and its capacity to support them *in perpetuity*; and the agent is the people themselves as politically organized. As I noted in the Introduction, they are to recognize that they cannot make up for their irresponsibility in caring for their land and its natural resources by conquest in war or by migrating into other people's territory without their consent.[40]

It does not follow from the fact that boundaries are historically arbitrary that their role in the Law of Peoples cannot be justified. On the contrary, to fix on their arbitrariness is to fix on the wrong thing. In the absence of a world-state, there *must* be boundaries of some kind, which when viewed in isolation will seem arbitrary, and depend to some degree on historical circumstances. In a reasonably just (or at least decent) Society of Peoples, the inequalities of power and wealth are to be decided by all peoples for themselves. . . .

4.4 Argument in Second Original Position. A large part of the argument in the original position in the domestic case concerns selecting among the various formulations of the two principles of justice (when the view adopted is liberal), and between liberal principles and such alternatives as the classical, or the average, principle of utilitarianism, and various forms of rational intuitionism and moral perfectionism.[41] By contrast, the only alternatives for the parties to pick from in the second-level original positions are formulations of the Law of Peoples. Three main ways in which the first and the second use of original position are not analogous are these:

(1)   A people of a constitutional democracy has, as a *liberal* people, no *comprehensive* doctrine of the good (§3.2 above), whereas individual citizens within a liberal domestic society do have such conceptions, and to deal with their needs as citizens, the idea of primary goods is used.

(2)   A people's fundamental interests as a people are specified by its political conception of justice and the principles in the light of which they agree to the Law of Peoples, whereas citizens' fundamental interests are given by their conception of the good and their realizing to an adequate degree their two moral powers.

(3)   The parties in the second original position select among different formulations or interpretations of the eight principles of the Law of Peoples, as illustrated by the reasons mentioned for the restrictions of the two powers of sovereignty (§2.2).

Part of the versatility of the original position is displayed in how it is used in the two cases. These differences between the two cases depend importantly on how, in each instance, the parties are understood.

The parties' first task in the second original position is to specify the Law of Peoples – its ideals, principles, and standards – and how those norms apply to political relations among peoples. If a reasonable pluralism of comprehensive doctrines is a basic feature of a constitutional democracy with its free institutions, we may assume that there is an even greater diversity in the comprehensive doctrines affirmed among the members of the Society of Peoples with its many different cultures and traditions. Hence a classical, or average, utilitarian principle would not be accepted by peoples, since no people organized by its government is prepared to count, *as a first principle*, the benefits for another people as outweighing the hardships imposed on itself. Well-ordered peoples insist on an *equality* among themselves as peoples, and this insistence rules out any form of the principle of utility.

I contend that the eight principles of the Law of Peoples (see §4.1) are superior to any others. Much as in examining the distributive principles in justice as fairness, we begin with the baseline of equality – in the case of justice as fairness the equality of social and economic primary goods, in this case the equality of and the equal rights of all peoples. In the first case we asked whether any departure from the baseline of equality would be agreed to provided that it is to the benefit of all citizens of society and, in particular, the least advantaged. (I only hint here at the reasoning.) With the Law of Peoples, however, persons are not under one but many governments, and the representatives of peoples will want to preserve the equality and independence of their own society. In the working of organizations and loose[42] confederations of peoples, inequalities are designed to serve the many ends that peoples share. In this case the larger and smaller peoples will be ready to make larger and smaller contributions and to accept proportionately larger and smaller returns.

Thus, in the argument in the original position at the second level I consider the merits of only the eight principles of the Law of Peoples listed in §4.1. These familiar and largely traditional principles I take from the history and usages of international law and practice. The parties are not given a menu of alternative principles and ideals from which to select, as they are in *Political Liberalism*, or in *A Theory of Justice*. Rather, the representatives of well-ordered peoples simply reflect on the advantages of these principles of equality among peoples and see no reason to depart from them or to propose alternatives. These principles must, of course, satisfy the criterion of reciprocity, since this criterion holds at both levels –

both between citizens as citizens and peoples as peoples.

Certainly we could imagine alternatives. For example: principle (5) has the obvious alternative, long supported by the practice of European states in modern history, that a state may go to war in the rational pursuit of its own interests. These may be religious, dynastic, territorial, or the glory of conquest and empire. In view of [my] account of democratic peace, however, that alternative would be rejected by liberal peoples. As shown later [in my account], it would also be rejected by decent peoples.

The discussion in §2 of the two traditional powers of sovereignty brings out that the eight principles are open to different interpretations. It is these *interpretations*, of which there are many, that are to be debated in the second-level original position. Regarding the two powers of sovereignty, we ask: What kind of political norms do liberal peoples, given their fundamental interests, hope to establish to govern mutual relations both among themselves and with nonliberal peoples? Or what moral climate and political atmosphere do they wish to see in a reasonably just Society of well-ordered Peoples? In view of those fundamental interests, liberal peoples limit a state's right to engage in war to wars of self-defense (thus allowing collective security), and their concern for human rights leads them to limit a state's right of internal sovereignty. In the Law of Peoples the many difficulties of interpreting the eight principles I have listed take the place of the arguments for first principles in the domestic case. The problem of how to interpret these principles can always be raised and is to be debated from the point of view of the second-level original position.

4.5 Cooperative Organizations. In addition to agreeing to the principles that define the basic equality of all peoples, the parties will formulate guidelines for setting up coop-erative organizations and agree to standards of fairness for trade as well as certain provisions for mutual assistance. Suppose there are three such organizations: one framed to ensure fair trade among peoples; another to allow a people to borrow from a cooperative banking system; and the third an organization with a role similar to that of the United Nations, which I will now refer to as a Confederation of Peoples (not states).[43]

Consider fair trade: suppose that liberal peoples assume that, when suitably regulated by a fair background framework,[44] a free competitive-market trading scheme is to everyone's mutual advantage, at least in the longer run. A further assumption here is that the larger nations with the wealthier economies will not attempt to monopolize the market, or to conspire to form a cartel, or to act as an oligopoly. With these assumptions, and supposing as before that the veil of ignorance holds, so that no people knows whether its economy is large or small, all would agree to fair standards of trade to keep the market free and competitive (when such standards can be specified, followed, and enforced). Should these cooperative organizations have unjustified distributive effects between peoples, these would have to be corrected, and taken into account by the duty of assistance.

The two further cases of agreeing to a central bank and to a Confederation of Peoples can be treated in the same way. Always the veil of ignorance holds, and the organizations are mutually beneficial and are open to liberal democratic peoples free to make use of them on their own initiative. As in the domestic case, peoples think it reasonable to accept various functional inequalities once the baseline of equality is firmly established. Thus, depending on their size, some will make larger contributions to the cooperative bank than others (suitable interest being due on loans) and will pay larger dues in the organization of the Confederation of Peoples.[45]

Notes

[1] I use the term "decent" to describe nonliberal societies whose basic institutions meet certain specified conditions of political right and justice (including the right of citizens to play a substantial role, say through associations and groups, in making political decisions) and lead their citizens to honor a reasonably just law for the Society of Peoples.

[2] Throughout this book I will sometimes refer to *a* Law of Peoples, and sometimes to *the* Law of Peoples. As will become clear, there is no single possible Law of Peoples, but rather a family of reasonable such laws meeting all the conditions and criteria I will discuss, and satisfying the representatives of peoples who will be determining the specifics of the law.

[3] See the definition on p. 36 of *Political Liberalism*.

[4] Stability for the right reasons means stability brought about by citizens acting correctly according to the appropriate principles of their sense of justice, which they have acquired by growing up under and participating in just institutions.

[5] It doesn't follow, however, that Sen's idea of basic capabilities is not important here; and indeed, the contrary is the case. His thought is that society must look to the distribution of citizens' effective basic freedoms, as these are more fundamental for their lives than what they possess in primary goods, since citizens have different capabilities and skills in using those goods to achieve desirable ways of living their lives. The reply from the side of primary goods is to grant this claim – indeed, any use of primary goods must make certain simplifying assumptions about citizens' capabilities – but also to answer that to apply the idea of effective basic capabilities without those or similar assumptions calls for more information than political society can conceivably acquire and sensibly apply. Instead, by embedding primary goods into the specification of the principles of justice and ordering the basic structure of society accordingly, we may come as close as we can in practice to a just distribution of Sen's effective freedoms. His idea is essential because it is needed to explain the propriety of the use of primary goods. For Amartya Sen's view see his *Inequality Reexamined* (Cambridge, Mass.: Harvard University Press, 1992), esp. chapters 1–5.

[6] See *Political Liberalism*, II: §1, pp. 48–54, and "The Idea of Public Reason Revisited," pp. 136ff.

[7] Of these liberalisms, justice as fairness is the most egalitarian. See *Political Liberalism*, pp. 6ff.

[8] Some may think that the fact of reasonable pluralism means that the forms of fair adjudication among comprehensive doctrines must be only procedural and not substantive. This view is forcefully argued by Stuart Hampshire in *Innocence and Experience* (Cambridge, Mass.: Harvard University Press, 1989). In the text above, however, I assume that the several forms of liberalism are each substantive conceptions. For a thorough treatment of the issues, see the discussion by Joshua Cohen, "Pluralism and Proceduralism," *Chicago-Kent Law Review*, vol. 69, no. 3 (1994).

[9] Liberal conceptions are also what we may call "liberalisms of freedom." Their three principles guarantee the basic rights and liberties, assign them a special priority, and assure to all citizens sufficient all-purpose means so that their freedoms are not purely formal. In this they stand with Kant, Hegel, and less obviously J. S. Mill.

[10] See *Political Liberalism*, pp. 60ff. The main points of this conception of toleration can be set out in summary fashion as follows: (1) Reasonable persons do not all affirm the same comprehensive doctrine. This is said to be a consequence of the "burdens of judgment." (2) Many reasonable doctrines are affirmed, nor all of which can be true or right as judged from within any one comprehensive doctrine. (3) It is not unreasonable to affirm any one of the reasonable comprehensive doctrines. (4) Others who affirm reasonable doctrines different from ours are reasonable also. (5) In affirming our belief in a doctrine we recognize as reasonable, we

are not being unreasonable. (6) Reasonable persons think it unreasonable to use political power, should they possess it, to repress other doctrines that are reasonable yet different from their own. These points may seem too narrow; for I recognize that every society also contains numerous unreasonable doctrines. In regard to this point, however, what is important to see is that how far unreasonable doctrines can be active and tolerated is not decided by what is said above, but by the principles of justice and the kinds of actions they permit. I am indebted to Erin Kelly for discussion of this point.

11 A question sure to be asked is: Why does the Law of Peoples use an original position at the second level that is fair to peoples and not to individual persons? What is it about peoples that gives them the status of the (moral) actors in the Law of Peoples? Part of the answer is given in §2, in which the idea of peoples is specified. . . . Those who are troubled by this question should turn to it now.

12 I am much indebted to John Cooper for instructive discussion about these features.

13 An example worth mentioning is public financing of both elections and forums for public political discussion, without which sensible public politics is unlikely to flourish. When politicians are beholden to their constituents for essential campaign funds, and a very unequal distribution of income and wealth obtains in the background culture, with the great wealth being in the control of corporate economic power, is it any wonder that congressional legislation is, in effect, written by lobbyists, and Congress becomes a bargaining chamber in which laws are bought and sold?

14 Here I think of the idea of nation as distinct from the idea of government or state, and I interpret it as referring to a pattern of cultural values of the kind described by Mill. In thinking of the idea of nation in this way I follow Yael Tamir's highly instructive *Liberal Nationalism* (Princeton: Princeton University Press, 1993).

15 It would be unfair to Clausewitz not to add that for him the state's interests can include regulative moral aims of whatever kind, and thus the aims of war may be to defend democratic societies against tyrannical regimes, somewhat as in World War II. For him the aims of politics are not part of the theory of war, although they are ever-present and may properly affect the conduct of war. On this, see the instructive remarks of Peter Paret, "Clausewitz," in *The Makers of Modern Strategy*, ed. Peter Paret (Princeton: Princeton University Press, 1986), pp. 209–13. The view I have expressed in the text above characterizes the *raison d'état* as pursued by Frederick the Great. See Gerhard Ritter, *Frederick the Great*, trans. Peter Paret (Berkeley: University of California Press, 1968), chap. 10 and the statement on p. 197.

16 I stress here that the Law of Peoples does not question the legitimacy of government's authority to enforce the rule of democratic law. The supposed alternative to the government's so-called monopoly of power allows private violence for those with the will and the means to exercise it.

17 Daniel Philpott in his "Revolutions in Sovereignty," PhD dissertation (Harvard University, 1995), argues that the changes in the powers of sovereignty from one period to another arise from the changes that occur in peoples' ideas of right and just domestic government. Accepting this view as roughly correct, the explanation for the shift would seem to lie in the rise and acceptance of constitutional democratic regimes, their success in World Wars I and II, and the gradual loss of faith in Soviet communism.

18 See Robert Gilpin's *War and Change in World Politics* (Cambridge: Cambridge University Press, 1981), chap. 1, pp. 9–25. See also Robert Axelrod's *The Complexity of Cooperation* (Princeton: Princeton University Press, 1997), chap. 4, "Choosing Sides," with its account of the alignments of countries in World War II.

19 Lord Palmerston said: "England has no eternal friends, and no eternal enemies; only eternal interests." See Donald Kagan, *Origins of War and the Preservation of Peace* (New York: Doubleday, 1995), p. 144.

20 Gilpin's main thesis is that "the fundamental nature of international relations has not changed over the millennia. International relations continue to be a recurring struggle

for wealth and power among independent
actors in a state of anarchy. The history of
Thucydides is as meaningful a guide to the
behavior of states today as when it was written
in the fifth century B.C." See Gilpin, *War and
Change in World Politics*, p. 7. He presents his
reasons for this thesis in chapter 6.

21 In his great *History of the Peloponnesian War*,
trans. Rex Warner (London: Penguin Books,
1954), Thucydides tells the story of the fated
self-destruction of the Greek city-states in the
long war between Athens and Sparta. The
history ends in midstream, as if it is broken
off. Did Thucydides stop, or was he unable to
finish? It is as if he said: "and so on. . . ." The
tale of folly has gone on long enough. What
moves the city-states is what makes the
increasing self-destruction inevitable. Listen
to the Athenians' first speech to the Spartans:
"We have done nothing extraordinary, contrary to human nature in accepting empire
when it was offered to us, then refusing to
give it up. Very powerful motives prevent us
from doing so – security, honor and self-
interest. And we were not the first to act this
way, far from it. It was always the rule that
the weaker should be subject to the stronger,
and, besides, we consider that we are worthy
of our power. Up to the present moment you
too used to think that we were; but now, after
calculating your interests, you are beginning
to talk in terms of right and wrong. Considerations of this kind have never turned people
aside from opportunities of aggrandizement
offered by superior strength. Those who
really deserve praise are those who, while
human enough to enjoy power, nevertheless
pay more attention to justice than compelled
to by their situation. Certainly we think that
if anyone were in our position, it would be
evident whether we act in moderation or not"
(Book I: 76).

It is clear enough how the cycle of self-
destruction goes. Thucydides thinks that, if
the Athenians had followed Pericles' advice
not to expand their empire as long as the war
with Sparta and its allies lasted, they might
well have won. But with the invasion of Melos
and the folly of the Sicilian adventure urged
on by Alcibiades' advice and persuasion, they

were doomed to self-destruction. Napoleon
is reputed to have said, commenting on his
invasion of Russia: "Empires die of indiges-
tion." But he wasn't candid with himself.
Empires die of gluttony, of the ever-expand-
ing craving for power. What makes peace
among liberal democratic peoples possible is
the internal nature of peoples as constitutional democracies and the resulting change
of the motives of citizens. For the purposes
of our story of the possibility of realistic
utopia it is important to recognize that Athens
was not a liberal democracy, though it may
have thought of itself as such. It was an autocracy of the 35,000 male members of the
assembly over the total population of about
300,000.

22 Gilpin, *War and Change in World Politics*,
esp. chap. 5, discusses the features of hegemonic war.

23 See the discussion of the original position
and the veil of ignorance in *Political Liberalism*, I: §4.

24 Note: "you and I" are "here and now" citizens
of the same liberal democratic society working out the liberal conception of justice in
question.

25 What is modeled is a *relation*, in this case, the
relation of the parties representing citizens.
In the second original position at the second
level, what is modeled is the relation of the
parties representing peoples.

26 The idea here follows the precept of similar
cases: persons equal in all relevant respects
are to be represented equally.

27 This paragraph restates a long footnote on
pp. 24–5 of the 1996 paperback edition of
Political Liberalism. This footnote draws on
an essay by Wilfried Hinsch, to whom I am
much indebted, presented by him at Bad
Homburg, in July 1992.

28 In this case "you and I" are citizens of some
liberal democratic society, but not of the
same one.

29 See *Political Liberalism*, pp. 29–35.

30 See the long footnote on pp. 24–5 of the 1996
paperback edition of *Political Liberalism*,
restated above.

31 My account here follows N. J. H. Dent in his
Rousseau (Oxford: Basil Blackwell, 1988) and

Frederick Neuhouser's essay "Freedom and the General Will," *Philosophical Review*, July 1993. Donald Kagan in his *Origins of War and the Preservation of Peace* notes two meanings of honor. As I describe them in the text (above and in the next section), one is compatible with satisfied peoples and their stable peace, whereas the other is not, setting the stage for conflict. I believe Kagan underestimates the great difference between the two meanings of honor.

32 This account parallels the idea of the reasonable used in a liberal society. See *Political Liberalism*, II: §1.

33 See Chapter 16 in this Reader [ed.].

34 See *A Theory of Justice*, where chapter 2 discusses the principles of justice and chapter 3 gives the reasoning from the original position concerning the selection of principles. All references to *A Theory of Justice* are to the original edition (Harvard University Press, 1971).

35 See J. L. Brierly, *The Law of Nations: An Introduction to the Law of Peace*, 6th edn (Oxford: Clarendon Press, 1963); and Terry Nardin, *Law, Morality, and the Relations of States* (Princeton: Princeton University Press, 1983). Both Brierly and Nardin give similar lists as principles of international law.

36 Charles Beitz, *Political Theory and International Relations* (Princeton: Princeton University Press, 1979), chap. 2, has a valuable discussion of the question of the autonomy of states, with a summary of the main points on pp. 121–3. I owe much to his account.

37 A clear example regarding secession is whether the South had a right to secede in 1860–61. On my account it had no such right, since it seceded to perpetuate its domestic institution of slavery. This was as severe a violation of human rights as any, and it extended to nearly half the population.

38 On these principles, see Robert Keohane, *After Hegemony* (Princeton: Princeton University Press, 1984).

39 By basic needs I mean roughly those that must be met if citizens are to be in a position to take advantage of the rights, liberties, and opportunities of their society. These needs include economic means as well as institutional rights and freedoms.

40 This remark implies that a people has at least a qualified right to limit immigration. I leave aside here what these qualifications might be. . . . Another reason for limiting immigration is to protect a people's political culture and its constitutional principles. See Michael Walzer, *Spheres of Justice* (New York: Basic Books, 1983), pp. 38ff. for a good statement. He says on page 39: "To tear down the walls of the state is not, as Sidgwick worriedly suggested, to create a world without walls, but rather to create a thousand petty fortresses. The fortresses, too, can be torn down: all that is necessary is a global state sufficiently powerful to overwhelm the local communities. Then the result would be the world of the political economist, as Sidgwick described it [or of global capitalism, I might add] – a world of deracinated men and women."

41 See *A Theory of Justice*, chapters 2 and 3.

42 I use this adjective to emphasize that confederations are much less tight than federations and do not involve the powers of federal governments.

43 Think of the first two organizations as in some ways analogous to GATT and the World Bank.

44 Here I assume, as in the domestic case, that, unless fair background conditions exist and are maintained over time from one generation to the next, market transactions will not remain fair, and unjustified inequalities among peoples will gradually develop. These background conditions and all that they involve have a role analogous to that of the basic structure in domestic society.

45 What does the Law of Peoples say about the following situation? Suppose that two or more of the liberal democratic societies of Europe, say Belgium and the Netherlands, or these two together with France and Germany, decide they want to join and form a single society, or a single federal union. Assuming they are all liberal societies, any such union must be agreed to by an election in which in each society the decision whether to unite is thoroughly discussed. Moreover, since these societies are liberal, they adopt a liberal

political conception of justice, which has the three characteristic kinds of principles, as well as satisfying the criterion of reciprocity, as all liberal conceptions of justice must do (§1.2). Beyond this condition, the electorate of these societies must vote on which political conception they believe to be the *most* reasonable, although all such conceptions are at least reasonable. A voter in such an election might vote for the difference principle (the most egalitarian liberal conception), should he or she think it is the most reasonable. Yet so long as the criterion of reciprocity is satisfied, other variants of the three characteristic principles are consistent with political liberalism. To avoid confusion, I add that what I later call the "duty of assistance" applies only to the duty that liberal and decent peoples have to assist *burdened* societies. As I explain there, such societies are neither liberal nor decent.

Chapter 12

An Egalitarian Law of Peoples*
Thomas W. Pogge

Expanding on a brief sketch of over twenty years ago, Rawls has recently offered a more detailed extension of his theory of justice to the international domain.[1] Like that first sketch, the "law of peoples" he now proposes has no egalitarian distributive component. In my own extension of Rawls's framework, I had argued that a criterion of global justice must be sensitive to international social and economic inequalities.[2] Here I take another look at this issue in light of Rawls's new and more elaborate deliberations about it.

There are three components of Rawls's conception of domestic justice that, in his view (LP, p. 51), qualify it for the predicate "egalitarian":

(1)   His first principle of justice requires that institutions maintain the fair value of the political liberties, so that persons similarly motivated and endowed have, irrespective of their economic and social class, roughly equal chances to gain political office and to influence the political decisions that shape their lives (cf. TJ, p. 225).

(2)   His second principle of justice requires that institutions maintain fair equality of opportunity, so that equally talented and motivated persons have roughly equal chances to obtain a good education and professional position irrespective of their initial social class (cf. TJ, pp. 73, 301).

(3)   His second principle also requires that, insofar as they generate social or economic inequalities, social institutions must be designed to the maximum benefit of those at the bottom of these inequalities (the difference principle – cf. TJ, pp. 76f).

Each of these egalitarian components furnishes separate grounds on which the current basic structure of the United States can be criticized for producing excessive inequalities.

Analogous points can be made about our current world order:

(1)   It fails to give members of different peoples roughly equal chances to influence the transnational political decisions that shape their lives.

(2)   It fails to give equally talented and motivated persons roughly equal chances to obtain a good education and professional position irrespective of the society into which they were born.

(3)   It also generates international social and economic inequalities that are not

* From *Philosophy & Public Affairs*, 23 (1994), pp. 195–224.

to the maximum benefit of the world's worst-off persons.

These observations are certainly true. The question is: Do they show faults in the existing global order?

Rawls's law of peoples contains no egalitarian distributive principle of any sort; and he seems then to be committed to the view that none of the three analogous criticisms is valid, even though he explicitly attacks only the analogue to his third egalitarian concern: the proposal of a global difference principle. My own view still is that all three of the analogous egalitarian concerns are valid in a world characterized by the significant political and economic interdependencies that exist today and will in all likelihood persist into the indefinite future. Here I will, however, defend against Rawls a much weaker claim: A plausible conception of global justice must be sensitive to international social and economic inequalities.

My focus on this one disagreement should not obscure the fact that I agree with much in this Amnesty Lecture – both substantively and methodologically. Substantively, I agree with his view that a just world order can contain societies governed by a conception of justice that differs from his own political liberalism by being nonpolitical, nonliberal, or both (LP, pp. 42f, 46); and that a main demand to make upon how their institutions work domestically is that they secure human rights (LP, pp. 61–3, 68–71). Methodologically, I agree that it is too early to tell how his idea of the original position – initially devised to deal with a closed, self-contained society (*TJ*, pp. 4, 8, 457) – should best be adapted to the complexities of our interdependent world (LP, pp. 50, 65f). Various possibilities should be worked out in some detail. One main strategy is Rawls's: Apply the two principles to the basic structure of a national society, and then reconvene the parties for a second session to deal with the relations among such societies.

Another main strategy is to start with a global original position that deals with the world at large, even asking, as Rawls puts it (somewhat incredulously?), "whether, and in what form, there should be states, or peoples, at all" (LP, p. 50). Variants of this second strategy have been entertained by David Richards, Thomas Scanlon, Brian Barry, Charles Beitz, and myself. I can leave aside this second strategy here, because international egalitarian concerns can easily be accommodated within the first strategy; as we shall see, Rawls simply decides against doing so.

My focus on one disagreement should also not obscure the fact that there are others. Two of these are relevant here. First, I do not believe that the notion of "a people" is clear enough and significant enough in the human world to play the conceptual role and to have the moral significance that Rawls assigns to it. In many parts of the globe, official borders do not correlate with the main characteristics that are normally held to identify a people or a nation – such as a common ethnicity, language, culture, history, tradition. Moreover, whether some group does or does not constitute a people would seem, in important ways, to be a matter of more-or-less rather than either-or. I have suggested that these complexities might be better accommodated by a multilayered institutional scheme in which the powers of sovereignty are vertically dispersed rather than heavily concentrated on the single level of states.[3] But I will set aside this topic as well. Let us assume that there really is a clear-cut distinction between peoples and other kinds of groupings, that every person belongs to exactly one people, and that each national territory really does, nearly enough, contain all and only the members of a single people. In this highly idealized case, egalitarian concerns would seem to be least pressing. Hence, if I can make them plausible for this case, they should be plausible for more realistic scenarios as well.

Second, I do not believe that Rawls has an adequate response to the historical arbitrariness of national borders – to the fact that most borders have come about through violence and coercion. He writes:

> From the fact that boundaries are historically arbitrary it does not follow that their role in the law of peoples cannot be justified. To wit: that the boundaries between the several states of the United States are historically arbitrary does not argue to the elimination of our federal system, one way or the other. To fix on their arbitrariness is to fix on the wrong thing. The right question concerns the political values served by the several states in a federal system as compared with the values served by a central system. The answer is given by states' function and role: by the political values they serve as subunits, and whether their boundaries can be, or need to be, redrawn, and much else.   (LP, p. 223, n16)

Let us suppose that the mere fact of historical arbitrariness is indeed no argument against the status quo, that a forward-looking justification suffices. What such a justification should be able to justify is threefold: that there should be boundaries at all, that they should be where they are now, and that they should have the institutional significance they currently have. I am not interested in the first two issues: Let there be national borders and let them be just where they are today. The issue I am raising is the third: How can Rawls justify the enormous distributional significance national borders now have, and in a Rawlsian ideal world would continue to have, for determining the life prospects of persons born into different states? How can he justify that boundaries are, and would continue to be, associated with ownership of, full control over, and exclusive entitlement to all benefits from, land, natural resources, and capital stock? It is revealing that, in the midst of discussing national borders, Rawls switches to considering state borders within the US, which

have virtually no distributional significance. It does not really matter whether one is born in Kansas or in Iowa, and so there is not much to justify, as it were. On the other hand, it matters a great deal whether one is born a Mexican or a US citizen, and so we do need to justify to a Mexican why we should be entitled to life prospects that are so much superior to hers merely because we were born on the other side of some line – a difference that, on the face of it, is no less morally arbitrary than differences in sex, in skin color, or in the affluence of one's parents. Justifying this is more difficult when national borders are historically arbitrary or, to put it more descriptively, when the present distribution of national territories is indelibly tainted with past unjust conquest, genocide, colonialism, and enslavement. But let me set aside this difficulty as well and focus on moral rather than historical arbitrariness. Let us assume that peoples have come to be matched up with territories in the morally most benign way one can conceive.

My defense, against Rawls, of an egalitarian law of peoples labors then under a self-imposed triple handicap: I accept Rawls's stipulation that global justice is addressed in a second session of the original position, featuring representatives of peoples who take the nation state system as a given; I accept Rawls's fantasy that the world's population neatly divides into peoples cleanly separated by national borders; and I waive any support my egalitarian view could draw from the role that massive past crimes have played in the emergence of current national borders. I make these concessions strictly for the sake of the argument of Sections I–V and otherwise stand by my earlier contrary positions.

I   A Global Resources Tax

Some of the arguments Rawls advances against incorporating an egalitarian component into the law of peoples are pragmatic, mainly having to do with inadequate administrative capabilities and the dangers of a world government. To make it easier for you to assess these worries, I want to put before you a reasonably clear and specific institutional proposal and thereby give our central disagreement a concrete institutional form. I lack the space, however, to develop and defend a complete criterion of global justice and to show what specific institutional arrangements would be favored by this criterion. I will therefore employ a little shortcut. I will make an institutional proposal that virtually any plausible egalitarian conception of global justice would judge to be at least a step in the right direction. Rawls's law of peoples, by contrast, would not call for such a step. It would permit the step among consenting peoples, but would not view it as required or suggested by justice.

When sketching how a property-owning democracy might satisfy the difference principle, Rawls entertains a proportional income or consumption tax with a fixed exemption. The tax rate and exempt amount are to be set so as maximally to benefit the lowest economic position in the present and future generations. Focusing on one such (as he says) instrument "frees us from having to consider the difference principle on every question of policy."[4]

I have proposed a similar instrument to control international inequality: a global resources tax, or GRT.[5] The basic idea is that, while each people owns and fully controls all resources within its national territory,[6] it must pay a tax on any resources it chooses to extract. The Saudi people, for example, would not be required to extract crude oil or to allow others to do so. But if they chose to do so nonetheless, they would be required to pay a proportional tax on any crude extracted, whether it be for their own use or for sale abroad. This tax could be extended, along the same lines, to reusable resources: to land used in agriculture and ranching, for example, and, especially, to air and water used for the discharging of pollutants.

The burdens of the GRT would not be borne by the owners of resources alone. The tax would lead to higher prices for crude oil, minerals, and so forth. Therefore, some of the GRT on oil would ultimately fall upon the Japanese (who have no oil of their own, but import a good bit), even while the tax would be actually paid by the peoples who own oil reserves and choose to extract them. This point significantly mitigates the concern that the GRT proposal might be arbitrarily biased against some rich peoples, the resource-rich, and in favor of others. This concern is further mitigated by the GRT's pollution component.

The GRT is then a tax on consumption. But it taxes different kinds of consumption differentially. The cost of gasoline will contain a much higher portion of GRT than the cost of a ticket to an art museum. The tax falls on goods and services roughly in proportion to their resource content: in proportion to how much value each takes from our planet. The GRT can therefore be motivated not only forward-lookingly, in consequentialist and contractualist terms, but also backward-lookingly: as a proviso on unilateral appropriation, which requires compensation to those excluded thereby. Nations (or persons) may appropriate and use resources, but humankind at large still retains a kind of minority stake, which, somewhat like preferred stock, confers no control but a share of the material benefits. In this picture, my proposal can be presented as a global resources dividend, which operates as a modern Lockean proviso. It differs from Locke's own proviso by giving up the vague and unwieldy[7] condition of "leaving enough and as good for others": One may use unlimited amounts, but one must share some of the economic benefit. It is nevertheless similar enough to the original so that even such notoriously antiegalitarian thinkers as Locke and Nozick might find it plausible.[8]

National governments would be responsible for paying the GRT, and, with each society free to raise the requisite funds in any way it likes, no new administrative capabilities would need to be developed. Since extraction and pollution activities are relatively easy to quantify, the assurance problem would be manageable and total collection costs could be negligible.

Proceeds from the GRT are to be used toward the emancipation of the present and future global poor: toward assuring that all have access to education, health care, means of production (land) and/or jobs to a sufficient extent to be able to meet their own basic needs with dignity and to represent their rights and interests effectively against the rest of humankind: compatriots and foreigners. In an ideal world of reasonably just and well-ordered societies, GRT payments could be made directly to the governments of the poorest societies, based on their per capita income (converted through purchasing power parities) and population size. These data are readily available and easy to monitor – reliable and comprehensive data are currently being collected by the United Nations, the World Bank, the IMF, and various other organizations.[9]

GRT payments would enable the governments of the poorer peoples to maintain lower tax rates, higher tax exemptions and/or higher domestic spending for education, health care, microloans, infrastructure, etc. than would otherwise be possible. Insofar as they would actually do this, the whole GRT scheme would require no central bureaucracy and certainly nothing like a world government, as governments would simply transfer the GRT amounts to one another through some facilitating organization, such as the World Bank, perhaps, or the UN. The differences to traditional development aid are: Payments would be a matter of entitle-

ment rather than charity and – there being no matching of "donors" and recipients – would not be conditional upon rendering political or economic favors to a donor or upon adopting a donor's favored political or economic institutions.[10] Acceptance of GRT payments would of course be voluntary: A just society may certainly shun greater affluence if it, democratically, chooses to do so.

In a nonideal world like ours, corrupt governments in the poorer states pose a significant problem. Such governments may be inclined, for example, to use GRT funds to underwrite indispensable services while diverting any domestic tax revenue saved to the rulers' personal use. A government that behaves in this way may be cut off from GRT funds.[11] In such cases it may still be possible to administer meaningful development programs through existing UN agencies (World Food Program, WHO, UNICEF, etc.) or through suitable nongovernmental organizations (Oxfam). If GRT funds cannot be used effectively to improve the position of the poor in a particular country, then there is no reason to spend them there. They should rather be spent where they can make more of a difference in reducing poverty and disadvantage.

There are then three possibilities with regard to any country that is poor enough in aggregate to be eligible for GRT funds: Its poorer citizens may benefit through their government, they may benefit from development programs run by some other agency, or they may not benefit at all. Mixtures are, of course, also possible. (A country might receive 60 percent of the GRT funds it is eligible for, one third of this through the government and two thirds of it through other channels.) How are these matters to be decided? And by whom? The decisions are to be made by the facilitating organization, but pursuant to clear and straightforward general rules. These rules are to be designed, and possibly revised, by an international group of economists and international lawyers. Its task is to devise the rules so that the entire GRT scheme has the maximum possible positive impact on the world's poorest persons – the poorest quintile, say – in the long run. The qualification "in the long run" indicates that incentive effects must be taken into account. Governments and also the wealthier strata of a people stand to gain from GRT spending in various ways ("trickle-up") and therefore have an incentive to ensure that GRT funds are not cut off. The rules should be designed to take advantage of this incentive. They must make it clear to members of the political and economic elite of GRT-eligible countries that, if they want their society to receive GRT funds, they must cooperate in making these funds effective toward enhancing the opportunities and the standard of living of the domestic poor.[12]

Specifying how GRT funds should best be raised poses some complex problems, among them the following four: First, setting tax rates too high may significantly dampen economic activity – in extreme cases so much that revenues overall would decline. It must be noted, however, that the funds raised through the GRT scheme do not disappear: They are spent by, and for the benefit of, the global poor and thereby generate effective market demand that spurs economic activity. Second, imposing any GRT on land use for cultivation of basic commodities (grains, beans, cotton, etc.) might increase their prices and thereby have a deleterious effect on the position of the globally worst-off. Hence it may make sense to confine any GRT on land to land used in other ways (e.g. to raise cattle or to grow tobacco, coffee, cocoa, or flowers). Third, the setting of tax rates should also take into account the interests of the future globally worst-off. The GRT should target the extraction of nonrenewable resources liable to run out within a few decades in preference to that of resources of which we have an abundant supply; it

should target the discharging of pollutants that will persist for centuries in preference to the discharging of pollutants that decay more quickly. Finally, while designing the GRT is inevitably difficult and complicated, the tax itself should be easy to understand and to apply. It should, for example, be based on resources and pollutants whose extraction or discharge is reasonably easy to monitor or estimate, in order to ensure that every people is paying its fair share and also to assure every people that this is so.

The general point behind these brief remarks is that GRT liabilities should be targeted so as to optimize their collateral effects. What is perhaps surprising is that these effects may on the whole be positive, on account of the GRT's considerable benefits for environmental protection and conservation. These benefits are hard to secure in a less concerted way because of familiar collective-action problems ("tragedy of the commons").

What about the overall magnitude of the GRT? In light of today's vast global social and economic inequalities, one may think that a massive GRT scheme would be necessary to support global background justice. But I do not think this is so. Current inequalities are the cumulative result of decades and centuries in which the more-developed peoples used their advantages in capital and knowledge to expand these advantages ever further. They show the power of long-term compounding rather than overwhelmingly powerful centrifugal tendencies of our global market system. Even a rather small GRT may then be sufficient continuously to balance these ordinary centrifugal tendencies of market systems enough to prevent the development of excessive inequalities and to maintain in equilibrium a rough global distributional profile that preserves global background justice.

I cannot here work through all the complexities involved in determining the appropriate magnitude of the GRT scheme. To achieve some concreteness nevertheless, let us, somewhat arbitrarily, settle for a GRT of up to 1 percent of world product – less than 1 percent if a smaller amount would better advance the interests of the globally worst-off in the long run. Almost any egalitarian conception of global justice would probably recognize this proposal as an improvement over the status quo. A 1 percent GRT would currently raise revenues of roughly $270 billion per annum. This amount is quite large relative to the total income of the world's poorest one billion persons and, if well targeted and effectively spent, would make a phenomenal difference to them even within a few years. On the other hand, the amount is rather small for the rest of us: not only less than the annual defense budget of the US alone, but also a good bit less than the market price of the current annual crude oil production, which is in the neighborhood of $400 billion (c. 60 million barrels per day at about $18 per barrel). Thus the entire revenue target could be raised by taxing a small number of resource uses – ones whose discouragement seems especially desirable for the sake of future generations. A $2-per-barrel GRT on crude oil extraction, for example, would raise about one sixth of the overall revenue target – while increasing the price of petroleum products by about 5¢ a gallon. It would have some substitution effects, welcome in terms of conservation and environmental protection; and, if it had any dampening effect on overall economic activity at all, this effect would be quite slight.

Having tried to show that introducing a 1 percent GRT would be an instantly feasible and morally attractive institutional reform of the existing global order,[13] let me now focus on its plausibility as a piece of ideal theory. To do this, we append my GRT proposal to Rawls's law of peoples.[14] The resulting alternative to Rawls is not my considered position on global justice. Its point is rather to allow us to focus sharply on the topic of international inequality. Egalitarian concerns will be vindicated, if it can be shown that the amended law of peoples is morally more plausible than Rawls's original – and especially so, if this can be shown on Rawlsian grounds.

II   Rawls's Position on International Distributive Justice

In his initial sketch, Rawls's brief discussion of international justice was characterized by a tension between three views:

(1)   He speaks of the second session of the original position as featuring *persons* from the various societies who make a rational choice of principles so as best to protect their interests while "they know nothing about the particular circumstances of their own society, its power and strength in comparison with other nations, *nor do they know their place in their own society*" (*TJ*, p. 378, my emphasis). I called this reading R_1 (*RR*, pp. 242ff).

(2)   On the same page, Rawls also speaks of this second session as featuring "representatives of *states* [who are] to make a rational choice to protect their interests" (*TJ*, p. 378, my emphasis). Here, "the national interest of a just state is defined by the principles of justice that have already been acknowledged. Therefore such a nation will aim above all to maintain and to preserve its just institutions and the conditions that make them possible" (*TJ*, p. 379). I called this reading R_2 (*RR*, pp. 243ff).

(3)   Rawls also wanted to endorse the traditional (pre-World War II) principles of international law as outlined by James Brierly.

I have tried to show (*RR*, §21) that no two of these views are compatible.

Rawls has now fully resolved the tension by clearly and consistently endorsing the second view, R_2 – without, however, offering any reasons for favoring it over R_1. He stipulates that the parties "are representatives of peoples" (LP, p. 48) and "subject to a veil of ignorance: They do not know, for example, the size of the territory, or the population, or the relative strength of the people whose fundamental interests they represent. Although they know that reasonably favorable conditions obtain that make democracy possible, they do not know the extent of their natural resources, or level of their economic development, or other such related information" (LP, p. 54).

And what are those fundamental interests of a people? As in his initial account of R_2, Rawls takes each people to have only one such fundamental interest: that its domestic institutions satisfy its conception of justice (LP, pp. 54, 64). And while the parties to the first session of the original position do not know the particular conceptions of the good of the persons they represent, Rawls assumes, without justifying the disanalogy, that each party to the second session does know what conception of domestic justice "her" people subscribes to. It would seem that the various delegates would then favor different versions of the law of peoples, each one especially hospitable to a particular conception of domestic justice.[15] Rawls claims, however, that within a certain range of conceptions of domestic justice the interests of peoples regarding the law of peoples coincide: delegates of peoples whose conception of domestic justice is either *liberal* or *hierarchical* would all favor exactly the same law of peoples (LP, p. 60). This is then the law of peoples that we, as members of a society with a liberal conception of justice, should endorse: It is hospitable to liberal regimes and to the more palatable nonliberal regimes as well. The regimes it does not accommodate are "outlaw regimes" of various sorts or else committed to an expansionist foreign policy (LP, pp. 72f). Rawls's law of peoples cannot be justified to them as being (behind the veil of ignorance) in their interest as well. But this fact cannot count against it from our point of view – which, after all, is the one to which we seek to give systematic expression.

Given this structure of his account, Rawls decides to run the second session twice: Once to show that delegates of peoples with any liberal conception of domestic justice would favor his law of peoples and then to show that delegates of peoples with any hierarchical conception of domestic justice would do so as well.[16] He does not actually perform either of these two runs in any detail, and I am quite unclear as to how the second is supposed to go.

In the next two sections, I shall focus exclusively on the liberal run, in which "the parties deliberate among available principles for the law of peoples by reference to the fundamental interests of democratic societies in accordance with, or as presupposed by, the liberal principles of domestic justice" (LP, p. 54). A *liberal* conception of justice is defined (LP, p. 51) as one that

– demands that certain rights, liberties, and opportunities be secure for all citizens

– gives this demand a high priority vis-à-vis other values and interests, and

– demands that all citizens should have adequate means to take advantage of their rights, freedoms, and opportunities.

Liberal conceptions of justice may differ from Rawls's by being comprehensive rather than political, for example, or by lacking some or all of the three egalitarian components he incorporates.

Rawls makes each delegate assume that her people is interested exclusively in being constituted as a just liberal society and he asserts that delegates with this sole interest would adopt his law of peoples, which lacks any egalitarian component. I will now argue against his stipulation that the delegates have only this one interest (Section III) and then against his claim that delegates with this sole interest would adopt his law of peoples (Section IV). If only one of my two arguments succeeds, Rawls's account is in trouble.

III   Against Rawls's Stipulation

An obvious alternative to the stipulation is this: Each delegate assumes that her people has an ultimate interest not only in the justice of its domestic institutions, but also in the well-being of its members (beyond the minimum necessary for just domestic institutions). Each delegate assumes, that is, that her people would, other things equal, prefer to have a higher rather than a lower average standard of living.[17]

Delegates so described would favor the GRT amendment. This is clearly true if, like the parties to the domestic session, they deliberate according to the maximin rule. But it is also true if they focus on average expectations: The GRT amendment would benefit all peoples by reducing pollution and environmental degradation. It is unclear whether it would have a positive or negative effect on per capita income for the world at large. But it would keep national per capita incomes closer together and thereby, given the decreasing marginal significance of income for well-being, raise the average standard of living as anticipated in the original position. An increase in national per capita income at the bottom matters more than an equal decrease in national per capita income at the top – in terms of a people's ability to structure its social world and national territory in accordance with its collective values and preferences, for example,

and also in terms of its members' quality of life.

We need not stipulate that a people's interest in well-being is strong relative to its interest in domestic justice. For suppose we have each delegate assume that her people's interest in well-being is very slight and subordinate to the interest in domestic justice. Then the delegate will care relatively little about what her people would gain through the amendment in case it would otherwise be poorer. But then she will also care little about what it would lose through the amendment in case it would otherwise be more affluent. She would care little both ways, and therefore would still have reason to adopt the amendment if, as I have argued, the gains outweigh the losses.

I conclude that, if a delegate assumes her people to have an interest in well-being, and be it ever so slight, then she will favor my amendment – regardless of whether she seeks to maximize her people's average or worst-case expectations. Rawls must therefore posit the opposite: Each delegate assumes that her people has no interest at all in its standard of living (beyond its interest in the minimum necessary for just domestic institutions). This is, of course, precisely what his stipulation entails. But why should we find this stipulation plausible once we see what it excludes?

There are several reasons to find it *implausible*. There are, for one thing, variants of liberalism that – unlike Rawls's own – are committed to continued economic growth and progress; and a people committed to one of them should be presumed to want to avoid economic stagnation and decline. There are also cosmopolitan variants of liberalism which extend the egalitarian concerns that Rawls confines to the domestic case to all human beings worldwide; and a people committed to one of them should be presumed to want to avoid relative deprivation for itself as well as for others.

The stipulation also has implausible side effects. In explicating the outcome of the liberal run of his second session, Rawls writes: "There should be certain provisions for mutual assistance between peoples in times of famine and drought and, were it feasible, as it should be, provisions for ensuring that in all reasonably developed liberal societies people's basic needs are met" (LP, p. 56). Does he really mean what this sentence suggests: that provisions are called for to meet basic needs only in reasonably developed societies? His account may well leave him no other choice. In his second session, each delegate cares solely about her people's achieving domestic justice. However, helping a people meet their basic needs may not enable them to achieve domestic justice, if their society is still quite undeveloped. Hence aid to members of such societies is not a requirement of global justice on Rawls's stipulation. His law of peoples requires basic food aid, say, only to peoples who but for their poverty would be able to maintain just domestic institutions.

Now it would be outrageous to suggest that Rawls deems it a matter of moral indifference whether members of undeveloped societies are starving or not. But, given his stipulation, he would have to say that such aid is an ethical duty, which we might discharge individually, or collectively through our government. International *justice* requires institutions designed to meet basic needs in societies where this contributes to domestic justice, but not in societies where it does not. Yet this looks counterintuitive: Why, after all, do liberals want the law of peoples to be supportive of the internal justice of all societies, if not for the sake of the persons living in them? And if our concern for the domestic justice of societies is ultimately a concern for their individual members, then why should we focus so narrowly on how well a law of peoples accom-

modates their interest in living under just domestic institutions and not also, more broadly, on how well it accommodates their underlying and indisputable interest in secure access to food, clothing, shelter, education, and health care, even where a reasonably developed liberal society is still out of the question?

The danger here is not merely moral implausibility, but also philosophical incoherence between Rawls's conceptions of domestic and of global justice. According to the latter, a just domestic regime is an end in itself. According to the former, however, it is not an end in itself, but rather something we ought to realize for the sake of individual human persons, who are the ultimate units of moral concern. Our natural duty to create and uphold just domestic institutions is a duty owed to them (TJ, p. 115). Their well-being is the *point* of social institutions and therefore, through the first session of the original position, gives content to Rawls's conception of domestic justice.

The incoherence might be displayed as follows. Suppose the parties to the first, domestic session knew that the persons they represent are the members of one society among a plurality of interdependent societies; and suppose they also knew that a delegate will represent this society in a subsequent international session, in which a law of peoples is to be adopted. How would they describe to this delegate the fundamental interests of their society? Of course they would want her to push for a law of peoples that is supportive of the kind of national institutions favored by the two principles of justice which, according to Rawls, they have adopted for the domestic case. But their concern for such domestic institutions is derivative on their concern for the higher-order interests of the individual human persons they themselves represent in the domestic original position. Therefore, they would want the delegate to push for the law of peoples that best accommodates, on the whole, those higher-order interests of individuals.[18] They would want her to consider not only how alternative proposals for a law of peoples would affect their clients' prospects to live under just domestic institutions, but also how these proposals would affect their clients' life prospects in other ways – for example through the affluence of their society. This point, by the way, strongly suggests that those committed to a Rawlsian (or, indeed, any other liberal) conception of domestic justice should want the delegates to any global original position to be conceived as representatives of persons rather than peoples.

I suspect that Rawls wants his second session of the original position to be informed by the interests of peoples, conceived as irreducible to the interests of persons, because the latter would inject an individualistic element that he deems unacceptable to hierarchical societies. The problem he sees is real enough, but his solution accommodates the hierarchicals at the expense of not being able to accommodate the liberals. I will return to this point in Section V.

IV Against Rawls's Reasoning

The foregoing arguments notwithstanding, let us now allow the stipulation. Let us assume that each people really does have only the one interest in the justice of its own domestic institutions, and that its delegate to the second session of the original position is instructed accordingly. Would such delegates prefer Rawls's law of peoples over my more egalitarian alternative? The answer, clearly, is NO: They would at most be indifferent between the two proposals. I don't know why Rawls thinks otherwise. But he may have been misled by an unrecognized presumption that a laissez-faire global eco-

nomic order is the natural or neutral benchmark which the delegates would endorse unless they have definite reasons to depart from it.

This presumption would explain his discussion of a global difference principle, which is peculiar in two respects. First, Rawls considers such a principle only in regard to one part of nonideal theory: coping with unfavorable conditions (LP, p. 75), although it has generally, if not always, been proposed as an analogue to the domestic difference principle, which is used primarily to design the ideal basic structure.[19] Second, the tenor of his remarks throughout is that a global difference principle is too strong for the international case, that it demands too much from hierarchical societies (e.g., LP, p. 75). This suggests a view of the difference principle as a principle of *re*distribution, which takes from some to give to others: The more it redistributes, the more demanding is the principle. But this view of the difference principle loses an insight that is crucial to understanding Rawls's own, domestic difference principle: There is no prior distribution, no natural baseline or neutral way of arranging the economy, relative to which the difference principle could be seen to make *re*distributive modifications. Rather, there are countless ways of designing economic institutions, none initially privileged, of which one and only one will be implemented. The difference principle selects the scheme that ought to be chosen. The selected economic ground rules, whatever their content, do not *re*distribute, but rather govern how economic benefits and burdens get distributed in the first place.

This point is crucial for Rawls's reply to Nozick's critique. Nozick wants to make it appear that laissez-faire institutions are natural and define the baseline distribution which Rawls then seeks to revise *ex post* through redistributive transfers. Nozick views the first option as natural and the second as making great demands upon the diligent and the gifted. He allows that, with unanimous consent, people can make the switch to the second scheme; but, if some object, we must stick to the first.[20] Rawls can respond that a libertarian basic structure and his own more egalitarian liberal-democratic alternative are options on the same footing: the second is, in a sense, demanding on the gifted, if they would do better under the first – but then the first is, in the same sense and symmetrically, demanding on the less gifted, who would do much better under the second scheme.

In his discussion of the global difference principle, Rawls's presentation of the issue is the analogue to Nozick's in the domestic case. It is somehow natural or neutral to arrange the world economy so that each society has absolute control over, and unlimited ownership of, all natural resources within its territory. Any departures from this baseline, such as my GRT proposal, are demanding and, it turns out, too demanding on some societies. I want to give the analogue to the Rawlsian domestic response: Yes, egalitarian institutions are demanding upon naturally and historically favored societies, as they would do better in a scheme with unlimited ownership rights. But then, symmetrically, a scheme with unlimited ownership rights is at least equally demanding upon naturally and historically disfavored societies, since they and their members would do much better under a more egalitarian global basic structure.

I have argued that Rawls has given no reason why the delegates – even if each of them cares solely about her people's prospects to live under just domestic institutions – should prefer his inegalitarian law of peoples over more egalitarian alternatives. Might they have a reason for the opposite preference? I believe that they do. In a world with large international inequalities, the domestic institutions of the poorer societies are vulnerable to being corrupted by powerful political and economic interests abroad. This is something we see all around us: politicians and business people from the rich nations self-servingly manipulating and interfering with the internal political, judicial, and economic processes of third-world societies.

Rawls is presumably aware of this phenomenon, but he fails to see its roots in gross international inequality: In poorer societies, he writes, "the problem is commonly the nature of the public political culture and the religious and philosophical traditions that underlie its institutions. The great social evils in poorer societies are likely to be oppressive government and corrupt elites" (LP, p. 77). Now Rawls is surely right that many poor countries have corrupt institutions and ruling elites, which do not serve the interests of the people and contribute to their poverty. But the inverse is certainly true as well: Relative poverty breeds corruptibility and corruption. Powerful foreign governments support their favorite faction of the local elite and often manage to keep or install it in power – through financial and organizational help for winning elections, if possible, or through support for security forces, coups d'état, or "revolutions" otherwise. Third-world politicians are bribed or pressured by firms from the rich societies to cater to their sex tourism business, to accept their hazardous wastes and industrial facilities, and to buy useless products at government expense. Agribusinesses, promising foreign exchange earnings that can be used for luxury imports, manage to get land use converted from staple foods to export crops: Wealthy foreigners get coffee and flowers year-round, while many locals cannot afford the higher prices for basic foodstuffs. Examples could be multiplied; but I think it is indisputable that the oppression and corruption in the poorer countries, which Rawls rightly deplores, is by no means entirely homegrown. So it is true, but not the whole truth, that governments and institutions of poor countries are often corrupt: They are actively being corrupted, continually and very significantly, by private and official agents from vastly more wealthy societies. It is entirely unrealistic to expect that such foreign-sponsored corruption can be eradicated without reducing the enormous differentials in per capita GNP.

So long as the delegates to Rawls's second session are merely presumed to know that large international inequalities *may* have a negative impact upon the domestic justice of the poorer societies, they have a tie-breaking reason to favor a more egalitarian law of peoples over Rawls's.[21]

V Another Way of Understanding Rawls's Liberal Delegates

If only one of my two arguments is sound, then delegates of liberal societies would prefer a more egalitarian law of peoples over Rawls's inegalitarian alternative. I suppose Rawls would regret this fact, if it destroys the desired coincidence between the law of peoples adopted by delegates of liberal societies (at step 1 of his second session) and the law of peoples adopted by delegates of hierarchical societies (at step 2). But this coincidence fails, in any case, on account of human rights.

Rawls claims that both sets of delegates would adopt precisely the same law of peoples (LP, p. 60), which includes a list of human rights (LP, pp. 62f, 68, 70) featuring minimum rights to life (means of subsistence and security), to liberty (freedom from slavery, serfdom, and forced occupations), to personal property, to "a measure" (LP, p. 63) of liberty of conscience and freedom of thought and "a certain" (LP, p. 68)

freedom of association (compatible with an established religion), to emigration, and to the rule of law and formal equality as expressed by the rules of natural justice (for example that similar cases be treated similarly). He gives no reason, and I can see none, historical or philosophical, for believing that hierarchical societies, as such, would incorporate these human rights into their favored law of peoples. Perhaps many such societies can honor these rights while retaining their hierarchical, nonliberal character, as Rawls suggests (LP, p. 70); but this hardly shows that they would choose to be bound by them. Human rights are not essential to hierarchical societies, as they are essential to liberal ones.

Not only is it highly doubtful that delegates of hierarchical societies would choose to commit themselves to so much; it is also quite unclear why delegates of liberal societies would not want to incorporate more than Rawls's list, which specifically excludes freedom of speech (LP, p. 62), democratic political rights (LP, pp. 62, 69f), and equal liberty of conscience and freedom of thought (LP, pp. 63, 65).

Rawls's quest for a "politically neutral" (LP, p. 69) law of peoples – one that liberals and hierarchicals would independently favor on the basis of their respective values and interests – thus holds little promise: Those who are really committed to a liberal conception of justice will envision a law of peoples which demands that persons everywhere enjoy the protection of the full list of human rights as well as adequate opportunities and material means that are not radically unequal. The friends of hierarchical societies will prefer a world order that is much less protective of the basic interests of persons as individuals. The former will want the interests of persons to be represented in the second session of the original position. The latter will care only about the interests of peoples.

Occasionally, Rawls suggests a different picture, which jettisons the claim to political neutrality. On this picture, the law of peoples he proposes is not what liberals would ideally want, but rather is affected by the existence of hierarchical societies. The alleged coincidence of the results of the two runs of the second session is then not luck, but design. It comes about because good liberals seek to accommodate hierarchical societies by adjusting their ideal of global justice so as to "express liberalism's own principle of toleration for other reasonable ways of ordering society" (LP, p. 43).[22] Just as Rawls himself may be expressing this desire by conceiving the second session of the original position in nonindividualistic terms, he may conceive of his liberal delegates as having a similar desire to adopt a law of peoples acceptable to hierarchical societies. This could explain their – otherwise incredible – decisions against certain human rights (precisely those most offensive to the hierarchicals) and against any egalitarian principle.

This picture is not at all that of a negotiated compromise in which the liberal delegates agree to surrender their egalitarian concerns and some human rights in exchange for the hierarchical delegates accepting the remainder. Such a bargaining model is quite un-Rawlsian and also does not fit with his account, on which the two groups of delegates deliberate in mutual isolation. The toleration model is more noble than this: The liberal delegates, informed that their societies share a world with many hierarchical societies, seek to design a law of peoples that hierarchical societies, on the basis of their values and interests as such, can reasonably accept. Yet, for all its nobility, the toleration model has a drawback that the bargaining model avoids: It is rather one-sided. The hierarchicals, unencumbered by any principle of toleration, get their favorite law of peoples, while the liberals, "to express liberalism's own principle of toleration," surrender their egalitarian concerns and some important human rights.[23] This fits the witty definition of a liberal as someone who will not take her own side in any disagreement.

What goes wrong here is that Rawls, insofar as he is committed to this picture, does not clearly distinguish two views, and hence is prone to accept the second with the first:

(1) Liberalism involves a commitment to tolerance and diversity that extends beyond the family of liberal conceptions: A liberal world order will therefore leave room for certain kinds of nonliberal national regimes.

(2) Liberalism involves a commitment to tolerance and diversity that extends beyond the family of liberal conceptions: It would thus be illiberal to impose a liberal global order on a world that contains many peoples who do not share our liberal values.

By acknowledging (1), we are not compromising our liberal convictions. To the contrary: We would be compromising our liberal convictions if we did not envision a liberal world order in this way. A world order would not be genuinely liberal if it did not leave room for certain nonliberal national regimes. Those who acknowledge (2), by contrast, *are* compromising their liberal convictions for the sake of accommodating those who do not share them. Liberals should then accept (1) and reject (2).

This reasoning is the analogue to what Rawls himself would say about the domestic case. Consider:

(1′) A liberal society must leave room for certain nonliberal communities and lifestyles.

(2′) It would be illiberal to impose liberal institutions on a society that contains many persons who do not share our liberal values.

Rawls would clearly accept (1′) and reject (2′). He could give the following rationale for this: While our society can contain many different kinds of communities, associations, and conceptions of the good, some liberal in character and others not, it can be structured or organized in only one way. If my neighbor wants to be a Catholic and I an atheist, we can *not* both have our way, can both lead the life each deems best. But if my neighbor wants the US to be organized like the Catholic Church and I want it to be a liberal state, we can *not* both have our way. There is no room for accommodation here, and, if I really believe in egalitarian liberal principles, I should politically support them and the institutions they favor against their opponents. These institutions will not vary with the shifting political strength of groups advocating various religious, moral, or philosophical doctrines.[24]

My rationale is the analogue to this: While the world can contain societies that are structured in a variety of ways, some liberal and some not, it cannot itself be structured in a variety of ways. If the Algerians want their society to be organized as a religious state consistent with a just global order and we want ours to be a liberal democracy, we can both have our way. But if the Algerians want the world to be organized according to the Koran, and we want it to accord with liberal principles, then we can *not* both have our way. There is no room for accommodation here, and, if we really believe in egalitarian liberal principles – in every person's equal claim to freedom and dignity – then we should politically support these principles, and the global institutions they favor, against their opponents. These institutions will not vary with the shifting political strength of states committed to various conceptions of domestic justice.

I conclude that Rawls has failed to show that the law of peoples liberals would favor and the law of peoples favored by hierarchicals either coincide by sheer luck or can be made to coincide by morally plausible design. We should then work toward a global order that – though tolerant of certain nonliberal regimes, just as a liberal society is tolerant of certain nonliberal sects and movements – is itself decidedly liberal in character, for example by conceiving of individual persons and of them alone as ultimate units of equal moral concern. This quest will put us at odds with many hierarchical societies whose ideal of a fully just world order will be different from ours.

It may seem then that my more assertive liberalism will lead to greater international conflict. And this may well be so in the area of human rights. But it may not be so in the area here at issue: international inequality. Rawls rejects all egalitarian distributive principles of international justice on the ground (among others) that they are inseparable from liberal values and therefore unacceptable to hierarchical societies (LP, p. 75).[25] But in the real world, the chief opponents of proposals along the lines of my GRT are the affluent liberal societies. We are, after all, also the wealthy ones and account for a vastly disproportionate share of global resource depletion and pollution. If we submitted the GRT proposal to the rest of the world, I believe it would be accepted by most societies with some enthusiasm.[26]

Given that institutional progress is politically possible, it would be perverse to oppose it by saying to the rest of the world: "We care deeply about equality, and we would very much like it to be the case that you are not so much worse off than we are. But, unfortunately, we do not believe that you ultimately care about equality the way we do. Therefore we feel entitled to refuse any global institutional reforms that would lead to greater international equality." One reason this would be perverse is that those touting hierarchical values and those suffering most from global inequality are rarely the same. Those whose lot a GRT would do most to improve – poor women and rural laborers in the third world, for example – rarely give the hierarchical values of their rulers and oppressors their considered and reflective endorsement.[27]

VI   The Problem of Stability

Delegates of liberal societies might *prefer* an egalitarian law of peoples and yet *adopt* Rawls's inegalitarian alternative.[28] For they might believe that a scheme like the GRT would simply not work: The moral motives ("sense of justice") that a just world order would engender in peoples and their governments would not be strong enough to ensure compliance. There would always be some wealthy peoples refusing to pay their fair share, and this in turn would undermine others' willingness to participate. In short: The GRT scheme is practicable only if backed by sanctions.[29] And sanctions presuppose a world government, which the delegates have abundant reasons to reject.

In response, I accept the claim that the GRT scheme would have to be backed by sanctions. But sanctions do not require a world government. They could work as follows: Once the agency facilitating the flow of GRT payments reports that a country has not met its obligations under the scheme, all other countries are required to impose duties on imports from, and perhaps also similar levies on exports to, this country to raise funds equivalent to its GRT obligations plus the cost of these enforcement measures. Such decentralized sanctions stand a very good chance of discouraging *small*-scale defections. Our world is now, and is likely to remain, highly interdependent economically; most countries export and import between 10 percent and 50 percent of their

gross domestic product. None of them would benefit from shutting down foreign trade for the sake of avoiding a GRT obligation of around 1 percent of GDP. And each would have reasons to meet its GRT obligation voluntarily: to retain full control over how the funds are raised, to avoid paying for enforcement measures in addition, and to avoid the negative publicity associated with noncompliance.

This leaves the problem of *large*-scale defections, and the related problem of getting most of the more affluent societies to agree to something like the GRT scheme in the first place. This scheme could not work in our world without the willing cooperation of most of the wealthier countries. You may be tempted to look at the world as it is and conclude that the hope for such willing cooperation is not realistic. So you would have the delegates to any global original position choose Rawls's law of peoples after all. And you might then give the following speech to the global poor: "We care deeply about equality, and we would very much like it to be the case that you are not so much worse off than we are. But, unfortunately, it is not realistic to expect that we would actually comply with more egalitarian global institutions. Since no one would benefit from a futile attempt to maintain impracticable institutions, we should all just rest content with the global inequalities of the status quo."

This little speech is not quite as nefarious as I have made it sound, because the "we" in the first sentence denotes a significantly smaller group than the "we" in the second, which refers to the entire population of the first world. Still, if it is true that reflection on our (wide sense) liberal values would support a preference for more egalitarian global economic institutions, then we (narrow sense) should at least try to stimulate such reflection in our compatriots before declaring such institutions to be impracticable. We should seek to make it become widely recognized among citizens of the developed West that such institutions are required by justice. I have already suggested one reason for believing that this may be a feasible undertaking – a scheme like the GRT can be justified by appeal to different (and perhaps incompatible) values prominent in Western moral thought:

(a) It can be supported by libertarian arguments as a global resources dividend that satisfies a modern Lockean proviso on unilateral appropriation.[30]
(b) It can be supported as a general way of mitigating the effects of grievous historical wrongs that cannot be mitigated in any more specific fashion.[31]
(c) It is also supported by forward-looking considerations as exemplified in the hypothetical-contract (Rawls) and consequentialist traditions.

These rationales are not unassailable. For one thing, they all hinge upon empirical facts of interdependence:

(a) Peoples must share the same planet with its limited resources.
(b) The common history that has produced peoples and national territories as they now exist and will continue to exist in the forseeable future is replete with massive wrongs and injustices.
(c) Existing peoples interact within a single global framework of political and economic institutions which tends to produce and reproduce rather stable patterns of inequalities and deprivations.

To undermine those rationales and the moral conclusion they support, first-worlders often downplay these interdependencies and think of real societies as "self-sufficient" (*TJ*, p. 4), "closed," "isolated" (*TJ*, p. 8), and "self-contained" (*TJ*, p. 457).[32] Like the closely related notion that the causes of third-world poverty are indigenous, this fiction is a severe distortion of the truth – most clearly in the especially relevant case of today's most unfortunate societies, which are still reeling from the effects of slavery and colonial oppression and exploitation and are also highly vulnerable to global market forces and destabilization from abroad.

The three rationales are also frequently confronted with notions of national partiality: It is perfectly permissible for us and our government, in a spirit of patriotic fellow-feeling, to concentrate on promoting the interests of our own society and compatriots, even if foreigners are much worse off. I need not deny this claim, only qualify it: Partiality is legitimate only in the context of a *fair* competition. This idea is familiar and widely accepted in the domestic case: It is perfectly all right for persons to concentrate on promoting the interests of themselves and their relatives, provided they do so on a "level playing field" whose substantive fairness is continually preserved. Partiality toward one's family is decidedly not acceptable when we, *qua* citizens, face political decisions in which that level playing field itself is at stake. It would be morally wrong, for example, even (or perhaps especially) if one's children are white boys, to use one's political influence to oppose equal access to higher education for women or blacks. Most citizens in the developed West understand and accept this point without question. It should not be all that hard to make them understand that for closely analogous reasons national partiality is morally acceptable only on condition that the fairness of international competition is continually preserved, and that it is morally wrong in just the same way for the rich Western states to use their vastly superior bargaining power to impose upon the poor societies a global economic order that tends to perpetuate and perhaps aggravate their inferiority.[33]

If the three rationales can be properly developed and defended against these and other challenges, a moral commitment to something like the GRT scheme may gradually emerge and become widespread in the developed West. Even if this were to occur, however, there would still be the further question whether our governments could be moved to introduce and comply with such institutions. I think that an affirmative answer to this question can be supported by some historical evidence. Perhaps the most dramatic such evidence is provided by the suppression of the slave trade in the nineteenth century. Great Britain was in the forefront of these efforts, actively enforcing a ban on the entire maritime slave trade irrespective of a vessel's ownership, registration, port of origin, or destination. Britain bore the entire cost of its enforcement efforts and could not hope to gain significant benefits from it – in fact, Britain bore additional opportunity costs in the form of lost trade, especially with Latin America. States do sometimes act for moral reasons.[34]

It should also be said that institutional reforms establishing a GRT need not go against the national interest of the developed states. I have already said that the GRT would slow pollution and resource depletion and thereby benefit all peoples in the long run. Let me now add that the fiction of mutual independence, and the cult of state sovereignty associated with it, have become highly dangerous in the modern world. Technological progress offers rapidly expanding possibilities of major devastations, of which those associated with nuclear, chemical, or biological weapons and accidents are only the most dramatic and the most obvious. If responsibility for guarding against such possibilities remains territorially divided over some two hundred national governments, the chances of avoiding them in the long run are slim. No state or group of states can protect itself against all externally induced gradual or catastrophic deteriorations of its environment. The present geopolitical constellation offers a unique opportunity for bringing the more dangerous technologies under central international control. If the most powerful states were to try to mandate such control unilaterally, they would likely encounter determined resistance and would have to resort to force. It would seem more promising to pursue the same goal in a multilateral fashion, by relaxing the idea of state sovereignty in a more balanced way: We, the first world, give up the notion that all our great affluence is ours alone, fit to be brought to bear in our bargaining with the rest of the world so as to entrench and expand our advantage. They, the rest, give up the notion that each society has a sovereign right to develop and control by itself all the technological capacities we already possess.

This scenario shows another reason for believing that it may be possible for a commitment to the GRT scheme to become and remain widespread among our compatriots in the first world: We, too, like the global poor, have a strong interest in a gradual erosion of the doctrine of absolute state sovereignty through a strengthening concern for the welfare of humankind at large,[35] though our interest is a more long-term one than theirs. It may seem that a commitment motivated along these lines would be excessively prudential. But then our concern to protect our environment is not merely prudential, but also moral: We do care about the victims of Bhopal and Chernobyl, as well as about future generations. And once the new institutions begin to take hold and to draw the members of different societies closer together, the commitment would in any case tend gradually to assume a more moral character.

I conclude that there is no convincing reason to believe that a widespread moral commitment on the part of the more affluent peoples and governments to a scheme like the GRT could not be sustained in the world as we know it. Delegates of liberal societies as Rawls conceives them would therefore not merely *prefer*, but would *choose*, my more egalitarian law of peoples over his inegalitarian alternative. In doing so, they would also envision a more democratic world order, a greater role for central organizations, and, in this sense, more world government than we have at present – though nothing like *a* world government on the model of current national governments.

"The politician," Rawls writes, "looks to the next election, the statesman to the next generation, and philosophy to the indefinite future."[36] Our task as philosophers requires that we try to imagine new, better political structures and different, better moral sentiments. Yes, we must be realistic, but not to the point of presenting to the parties in the original position the essentials of the status quo as unalterable facts.

Notes

[1] John Rawls, "The Law of Peoples," in *On Human Rights*, ed. Stephen Shute and Susan Hurley (New York: Basic Books, 1993), pp. 41–82, 220–30. Page numbers preceded by "LP" refer to this lecture. The earlier sketch is on pp. 378f of *A Theory of Justice* (Cambridge, MA: Harvard University Press, 1971); henceforth *TJ*.

[2] See Chapter 6 of *Realizing Rawls* (Ithaca, NY: Cornell University Press 1989); henceforth *RR*.

[3] "Cosmopolitanism and Sovereignty," *Ethics* 103 (1992), pp. 48–75.

[4] John Rawls, "Justice as Fairness: Revisited, Revised, Recast," 1992, typescript, p. 136.

[5] *RR*, pp. 256n18, 264f. See also "An Institutional Approach to Humanitarian Intervention," *Public Affairs Quarterly* 6 (1992), pp. 89–103, p. 96.

[6] This accommodates Rawls's remark that "unless a definite agent is given responsibility for maintaining an asset and bears the loss of not doing so, that asset tends to deteriorate" (LP, p. 57).

[7] Consider: Must we leave enough and as good for future generations? For how many? Are air and water pollution ruled out entirely because the air and water left behind is not as good?

[8] Cf. John Locke, *Second Treatise*, §§27, 33; Robert Nozick, *Anarchy, State, and Utopia* (New York: Basic Books 1974), pp. 175–7 and chapter 4.

[9] One may think that domestic income distribution should be taken into account as well. Even if two states have the same per capita income, the poor in the one may still be much worse off than the poor in the other. The problem with taking account of this fact is that it may provide a perverse incentive to governments to neglect their domestic poor in order to receive larger GRT payments. This incentive is bad, because governments might act on it, and also because governments might, wrongly, be thought to act or be accused of acting on it (appearance and assurance problems).

[10] For a detailed account of how the latter feature renders current aid highly inefficient, if not useless, see the cover story "Why Aid is an Empty Promise," *The Economist* 331/7862: (May 7, 1994), pp. 13–14, 21–4.

[11] For a contrary conception, see Brian Barry, "Humanity and Justice in Global Perspective," in *NOMOS XXIV, Ethics, Economics, and the Law*, ed. J. R. Pennock and J. W. Chapman (New York: New York University Press, 1982), pp. 219–52. Barry holds that the governments of poor societies should receive funds regardless of their domestic policies.

[12] In some GRT-eligible countries there may well be factions of the ruling elite for whom

these incentives would be outweighed by their interest in keeping the poor uneducated, impotent, and dependent. Still, the incentives will shift the balance of forces in the direction of reform.

13 This is a bit of an exaggeration: I have not yet given you any reason not to dismiss my GRT proposal as unfeasible in the political sense. This I hope to do in the final section.

14 Rawls characterizes this law of peoples by the following list of principles (LP, p. 55): "(1) Peoples (as organized by their government) are free and independent and their freedom and independence is to be respected by other peoples. (2) Peoples are equal and parties to their own agreements. (3) Peoples have the right of self-defense but no right to war. (4) Peoples are to observe a duty of nonintervention. (5) Peoples are to observe treaties and undertakings. (6) Peoples are to observe certain specified restrictions on the conduct of war (assumed to be in self-defense). (7) Peoples are to honor human rights." Though this list is not meant to be complete (ibid.), the complete list would not contain an egalitarian distributive principle (LP, pp. 75f). Throughout Rawls makes no attempt to show that representatives of peoples would, in his second session of the original position, adopt these principles. The presentation is far less rigorous than the one he had offered in support of his two principles of domestic justice. My response in this essay is then not so much a critique of Rawls as a detailed and, I hope, constructive invitation to defend his conclusions.

15 I say that any global (session of the) original position features *delegates* rather than parties or representatives. This is my expression, not Rawls's. Its sole purpose is to make more perspicuous that the reference is to deliberators about global rather than domestic institutions.

16 See LP, pp. 52 and 60 for Rawls's distinction of these two steps, as he calls them, of his account of international ideal theory.

17 Rawls makes the analogous stipulation for the domestic session of the original position, remarking that it cannot hurt a person to have greater means at her disposal: one can always give them away or forego their use (*TJ*, pp. 142f).

18 For Rawls's account of the three higher-order interests of the persons whom the parties to the first, domestic session represent, see his *Political Liberalism* (New York: Columbia University Press 1993), pp. 74f, 106.

19 In the penultimate draft of "The Law of Peoples," Rawls did argue also against the global difference principle as a proposal for ideal theory, but he has deleted those arguments.

20 See *Anarchy, State, and Utopia*, pp. 167–74, 198–204, 280–92.

21 While the delegates to an R_2-type second session would view my modification as an improvement, they would presumably like even better the addition of a more statist egalitarian component, such as Brian Barry's proposal cited in note 11. This does not worry me, because it was only for the sake of the argument that I have here accepted Rawls's R_2 set-up, which treats peoples, not persons, as ultimate units of moral concern. I am confident that a more plausible construal of a global original position – G, for example, as defended in *RR* §§22–3 – would support something very much like the GRT as an essential part of a fully just law of peoples.

22 Another, related reason might be, as Rawls remarks in another context, that "all principles and standards proposed for the law of peoples must, to be feasible, prove acceptable to the considered and reflective public opinion of peoples and their governments" (LP, p. 50).

23 And probably some additional human rights as well, if I was right to argue that the hierarchical delegates would not adopt even the truncated list that Rawls incorporates into his law of peoples.

24 In supporting his view that our conception of justice should not, in the manner of (2'), be sensitive to what competing views happen to be prevalent among our compatriots, Rawls also stresses that such sensitivity would render this conception "political in the wrong way," thus leading to some of the problems associated with institutions that reflect a *modus*

vivendi. (See *Political Liberalism*, Lecture IV, esp. pp. 141–8.) This concern, too, has an analogue on the global plane (see *RR*, Chapter 5).

25 I believe, to the contrary, that rather a lot could be said to support the GRT scheme in terms of nonliberal values prevalent in many hierarchical societies today, though I cannot undertake this task here.

26 Witness the debates during the 1970s, in UNCTAD and the General Assembly of the United Nations, about a new international economic order.

27 Should I apologize for my liberal bias here, for being concerned with endorsement by individual persons rather than by whole peoples (as expressed, presumably, by their governments and "elites")?

28 The problem I try to deal with in this final section is not one raised by Rawls, who holds that the delegates would even *prefer* his law of peoples. So nothing I say in response to the problem is meant to be critical of him.

29 One might justify including this claim among the general knowledge available to the delegates by pointing to how lax many states have been about paying their much smaller membership dues to the UN.

30 Cf. the far more radical idea that on a Lockean account "each individual has a right to an equal share of the basic nonhuman means of production" (i.e., means of production other than labor which are not themselves produced: resources in the sense of my GRT), as presented in Hillel Steiner, "The Natural Right to the Means of Production," *Philosophical Quarterly* 27 (1977), pp. 41–9, p. 49; and further developed in G. A. Cohen, "Self-Ownership, World Ownership, and Equality: Part II," *Social Philosophy and Policy* 3 (1986), 77–96, pp. 87–95.

31 Nozick entertains this backward-looking rationale for the difference principle: If we cannot disentangle and surgically neutralize the effects of past wrongs, then implementing Rawls's difference principle may be the best way of satisfying Nozick's principle of rectification at least approximately. See *Anarchy, State, and Utopia*, p. 231.

32 Rawls describes societies in this way only for purposes of a "first approximation." See *Political Liberalism*, p. 272.

33 For a different argument, to the effect that unqualified partiality constitutes a loophole, see my "Loopholes in Moralities," *Journal of Philosophy* 89 (1992), pp. 79–98, pp. 84–98.

34 I owe this example to W. Ben Hunt. Obviously, much more could and should be said about the various similarities and dissimilarities between this nineteenth-century case and our current global situation. I mention the case here mainly as a preliminary, but I think powerful, empirical obstacle to the claim that governments never act contrary to what they take to be in their own, or their society's, best interest. There are, I believe, many other less dramatic, but also more recent, counter-examples to this claim.

35 Note the success of recent programs under which third-world governments are forgiven some of their foreign debts in exchange for their undertaking certain environmental initiatives in their territory.

36 "The Idea of an Overlapping Consensus," *Oxford Journal of Legal Studies* 7 (1987): p. 24.

Part V

Nationalism and Patriotism

Introduction

In Parts V and VI we will examine essays on nationalism and cosmopolitanism. There are many forms and supporting arguments for both these concepts. One common difference is that nationalists are more favorable to recognizing special obligations to compatriots whereas cosmopolitans more often argue for obligations to distant others beyond our state. Robert E. Goodin begins this Part (chapter 13) with an analysis of the moral significance of our relationships with others. He argues that, *contra* nationalists, there is nothing fundamentally special morally about persons residing within national boundaries. What is special about boundaries more generally is that they provide an invaluable method for fixing our duties with a particular agent (e.g., the state). In other words, it is far easier to consider the rights and responsibilities of individuals within a state given the important role of the state in our lives. We might then think we have a special relationship to compatriots given our sharing this important political community. However, there is nothing morally significant about duties to compatriots that is greater in weight than to non-compatriots given the contingent fact of our communal membership.

In contrast, David Miller's essay "The Ethics of Nationality" (chapter 14) argues that we have special obligations to fellow citizens, even if we also possess certain moral obligations to all. He claims that our social attachments have moral significance. Our membership in groups gives a special weight to fellow group members. This weight is shared mutually: all group members give a special weight to fellow members on account of their connection. Nationality is an important source of our identity. We feel a loyalty to each other. These obligations are public, not private, and expressed in the political life of our state.

This Part closes with a reading by Martha C. Nussbaum (chapter 15), who argues that our highest obligations are to our fellow human beings, whether or not we are fellow citizens. She draws on the cosmopolitan tradition represented by Diogenes the Cynic and Kant to make a case for a cosmopolitan patriotism. This view does not deny that we have special connections with those in close relationship with us, whether family, friends or neighbors. Instead, this view holds that these are some of many overlapping forms of relationships we have with members of humanity *including humanity as a whole*. Our task should be to bring them all closer together. The rest of her essay is dedicated to considerations in education reform that might give best effect to cosmopolitanism, providing a very powerful critique of nationalism.

Nationalism and patriotism are more than just waving flags and singing traditional songs. Too often extremist elements in contemporary society use the idea of the nation and the patriotic ties that bind the community together, twisting them in their favor, damaging the view of nationalism and patriotism in the eyes of many. However, these readings demonstrate that there is nothing unsavory in the view that we have obligations to members of our nation and that our national membership has significance for us. It is then left for us to consider the meaning of nationalism and patriotic duties for our lives in light of what we learn here.

Chapter 13

What is so Special about our Fellow Countrymen?*
Robert E. Goodin

There are some "general duties" that we have toward other people, merely because they are people. Over and above those, there are also some "special duties" that we have toward particular individuals because they stand in some special relation to us. Among those are standardly supposed to be special duties toward our families, our friends, our pupils, our patients. Also among them are standardly supposed to be special duties toward our fellow countrymen.

Where those special duties come from and how they fit with the rest of morality is a moot point. I shall say little about such foundational issues, at least at the outset. In my view, the best way of exploring foundations is by examining carefully the edifice built upon them.

The bit of the edifice that I find particularly revealing is this: When reflecting upon what "special treatment" is due to those who stand in any of these special relations to us, ordinarily we imagine that to be especially *good* treatment. Close inspection of the case of compatriots reveals that that is not completely true, however. At least in some respects, we are obliged to be more scrupulous – not less – in our treatment of nonnationals

than we are in our treatment of our own compatriots.[1]

This in itself is a politically important result. It shows that at least some of our general duties to those beyond our borders are at least sometimes more compelling, morally speaking, than at least some of our special duties to our fellow citizens.

This finding has the further effect of forcing us to reconsider the bases of our special duties to compatriots, with yet further political consequences. Morally, what ultimately matters is not nationality per se. It is instead some further feature that is only contingently and imperfectly associated with shared nationality. This further feature may sometimes be found among foreigners as well. When it is, we would have duties toward those foreigners that are similar in their form, their basis, and perhaps even their strength to the duties that we ordinarily acknowledge toward our fellow countrymen.

I The Particularist's Challenge

A

Modern moral philosophy has long been insistently universalistic. That is not to say that it enjoins identical performances,

* From *Ethics* 98 (July 1988), pp. 663–86.

regardless of divergent circumstances. Of course universal laws play themselves out in different ways in different venues and demand different things from differently placed agents. But while their particular applications might vary, the ultimate moral principles, their form and content, has long been regarded as essentially invariant across people. The same basic precepts apply to everyone, everywhere, the same.

A corollary of this universality is impartiality.[2] It has long been supposed that moral principles – and therefore moral agents – must, at root, treat everyone the same. Of course, here again, basic principles that are perfectly impartial can (indeed, usually will) play themselves out in particular applications in such a way as to allow (or even to require) us to treat different people differently. But the ultimate principles of morality must not themselves play favorites.

On this much, at least utilitarians and Kantians – the great contending tribes of modern moral philosophy – can agree. Everyone counts for one, no one for more than one, in the Benthamite calculus. While as an upshot of those calculations some people might gain and others lose, the calculations themselves are perfectly impartial. So too with Kant's Categorical Imperative. Treating people as ends in themselves, and respecting the rationality embodied in others, may require us to do different things to, for, or with different people. But that is not a manifestation of any partiality between different people or their various projects. It is, instead, a manifestation of our impartial respect for each and every one of them.

Furthermore, this respect for universality and impartiality is no mere quirk of currently fashionable moral doctrines. Arguably, at least, those are defining features of morality itself. That is to say, they arguably must be embodied in any moral code in order for it to count as a moral code at all.

B

Despite this strong attachment to canons of universality and impartiality, we all nonetheless ordinarily acknowledge various special duties. These are different in content and form from the general duties that universalistic, impartial moralities would most obviously generate for us. Whereas our general duties tell us how we should treat anyone, and are hence the same toward everyone, special duties vary from person to person. In contrast to the universality of the general moral law, some people have special duties that other people do not. In contrast to the impartiality of the general moral law, we all have special duties to some people that we do not have to others.[3]

Special duties, in short, bind particular people to particular other people. How this particularism of special duties fits with the universality and impartiality of the general moral law is problematical. Some say that it points to a whole other branch of the moral law, not captured by any of the standard canons. Others, Kantians and utilitarians among them, say that it is derivative in some way or another from more general moral laws. Yet others say that this particularism marks the limits of our psychological capacities for living up to the harsh standards that the general moral law sets for us.[4]

Be all these foundational questions as they may, it is not hard to find intuitively compelling examples of special duties that we would all acknowledge. At the level of preposterous examples so favored among philosophers, consider this case. Suppose your house is on fire. Suppose two people are trapped in the fire, and you will clearly have time to rescue only one before the roof collapses killing the other. One of those trapped is a great public benefactor who was visiting you. The other is your own mother. Which should you rescue?

This is a story told originally by an impartialist, William Godwin. Being a particularly blunt proto-utilitarian, he had no trouble plunking for the impartialist position: "What magic is there in the pronoun 'my' that should justify us in overturning the decisions of impartial truth?"[5] Nowadays, however, it is a story told more often against impartialists. Few, then or now, have found themselves able to accept the impartialist conclusion with quite such equanimity as Godwin. Many regard the example as a reductio ad absurdum of the impartialist position. And even those who want to stick up for the impartialist side are obliged to concede that impartialists have a case to answer here.[6]

But the debate is not confined to crazy cases like that one. In real life, just as surely as in moral fantasies, we find ourselves involved in special relations of all sorts with other people. And just as we intuitively feel that we should save our own mothers rather than Archbishop Fenelon in Godwin's example, so too do we intuitively feel we should show favoritism of some sort to all those other people likewise. The "mere enumeration" of people linked to us in this way is relatively uncontentious and has changed little from Sidgwick's day to Parfit's. Included in both their lists are family, friends, benefactors, clients, and co-workers, and – especially important, in the present context – compatriots.[7]

Intuitively, we suppose that, on account of those special relations between us, we owe all of those people special treatment of some sort or another: special "kindnesses," "services," or "sacrifices"; "we believe that we ought to try to give them certain kinds of benefit."[8] According to Parfit, "Common-Sense Morality largely consists in such obligations"; and, within commonsense morality, those obligations are particularly strong ones, capable of overriding (at least

at the margins) our general duties to aid strangers.[9]

C

Here, I do not propose to focus (initially, at least) upon the precise strength of those duties. Rather, I want to direct attention to their general tendency. Notice that there is a presumption, running through all those standard discussions of special duties, that the special treatment due to those who are linked to us by some special relation is especially *good* treatment. We are said to be obliged to do more for those people than for unrelated others in an effort to spare them harm or to bring them benefits. To those who stand in some special relation to us, we are said to owe special "kindnesses," "services," or "sacrifices."

That assumption seems to me unwarranted. Agreed, special relations do sometimes permit (and sometimes even require) us to treat those specially related to us better than we need to, absent such a link. Other times, however, special relations permit (and perhaps even sometimes require) us to treat those thus linked to us worse than we would be obliged to treat them, absent such a link.[10] Exploring how that is so, and why, sheds light upon the true nature and strength of special duties. It also, not incidentally, limits the claims for exclusive special treatment that can be entertained under that heading.

II   The Case of Compatriots

When discussing what special claims compatriots, in particular, have against us, it is ordinarily assumed that we owe more to our fellow countrymen and less to foreigners. The standard presumption is that "compatriots take priority" over foreigners, "at least in the case of duties to aid"; "the state in determining what use shall be made of its own moneys, may legitimately consult the welfare of its own citizens rather than that of aliens."[11] Thus, it makes a salutary start to my analysis to recall that, at least with respect to certain sorts of duties, we must be more scrupulous – not less – in our treatment of foreigners.

In the discussion that follows, "we" will be understood to mean "our community, through its sovereign representatives." In discussing what "we" may and may not do to people, I shall require some rough-and-ready guide to what our settled moral principles actually are. For these purposes, I shall have recourse to established principles of our legal codes: though the correspondence is obviously less than perfect, presumably the latter at least constitute a rough approximation to the former. Public international law will be taken as indicative of what we may do to foreigners, domestic public law as indicative of what we may do to our compatriots. In both cases, the emphasis will be upon customary higher law rather than upon merely stipulative codes (treaties, statutes, etc.).[12]

Consider, then, all these ways in which we must treat foreigners in general better than we need to treat our compatriots:[13]

Example a. – We, through our public officials, may quite properly take the property of our fellow citizens for public purposes, provided they are duly compensated for their losses; this is especially true if the property is within our national boundaries but is even true if it is outside them. We cannot, however, thus commandeer an identical piece of property from a foreigner for an identical purpose in return for identical compensation. This is especially true if the property is beyond our borders;[14] but it is even true if the property is actually in our country, in transit.[15]

Example b. – We can conscript fellow citizens for service in our armed forces, even if they are resident abroad.[16] We cannot so con-

script foreign nationals, even if they are resident within our own country.[17]

Example c. – We can tax fellow citizens, even if they are resident abroad.[18] We cannot so tax foreigners residing abroad on income earned abroad.[19]

Example d. – We can dam or divert the flow of a river lying wholly within our national territory to the disadvantage of fellow citizens living downstream. We may not so dam or divert rivers flowing across international boundaries to the disadvantage of foreigners downstream.[20]

Example e. – We can allow the emission of noxious factory fumes that damage the persons or property of fellow citizens. We may not do so if those fumes cross international frontiers, causing similar damage to the persons or property of foreigners there.[21]

Example f. – We may set arbitrarily low limits on the legal liability of manufacturers for damages done by their production processes or products domestically to our fellow citizens. We may not so limit the damage recoverable from them for harm done across international boundaries to foreigners.[22]

Example g. – According to international law, we may treat our fellow citizens "arbitrarily according to [our own] discretion." To aliens within our national territory, however, we must afford their persons and property protection "in accordance with certain rules and principles of international law," that is, "in accordance with ordinary standards of civilization."[23] Commentators on international law pointedly add, "It is no excuse that [a] State does not provide any protection whatever for its own subjects" in those respects.[24]

These are all examples of ways in which we must treat foreigners better than compatriots. In a great many other respects, of course, the conventional wisdom is perfectly right that we owe better treatment to our compatriots than we do to foreigners. For example, we have a duty to protect the persons and property of compatriots against attack, even when they are abroad.[25] Absent treaty obligations, we have no such duty to protect noncitizens beyond our borders. We have a duty – morally, and perhaps even legally – to provide a minimum level of basic necessities for compatriots. Absent treaty obligations, we have no such duty – legally, anyway – to assist needy noncitizens beyond our borders.

Even within our borders, we may treat citizens better in all sorts of ways than we treat noncitizens, just so long as some "reasonable" grounds for those discriminations can be produced and just so long as the protection we provide aliens' persons and property comes up to minimal internationally acceptable standards.[26] Not only are aliens standardly denied political rights, like voting and office-holding, but they are also standardly excluded from "public service." This has, in the past, been interpreted very broadly indeed: in the United States, an alien could have been debarred from being an "optometrist, dentist, doctor, nurse, architect, teacher, lawyer, policeman, engineer, corporate officer, real estate broker, public accountant, mortician, physiotherapist, pharmacist, pedlar, pool or gambling-hall operator";[27] in the United Kingdom the range of prohibited occupations has included harbor pilots, masters of merchant ships, and skippers of fishing vessels.[28] Besides all those quasi-public functions from which aliens are excluded, they also suffer other disadvantages of a purely material sort. Perhaps the most significant among them are the rules, found in some states denying aliens the right to own land.[29] All of this can be perfectly permissible, both under international law and under higher domestic law.

Thus, the situation is very much a mixed one. Sometimes we are indeed permitted (sometimes even required) to treat our fellow citizens better than we treat those who do not share that status with us. Other times, however, we are required to treat nonciti-

zens better than we need to treat our own fellow citizens.

I pass no judgment on which pattern, on balance, predominates. The point I want to make here is merely that the situation is much more mixed than ordinary philosophical thinking on special duties leads us to expect. That in itself is significant, as I shall now proceed to show.

III   Special Duties as Magnifiers and Multipliers

In attempting to construe the effect that special relationships have on our moral duties, commonsense morality tends to employ either of two basic models (or both of them: they are nowise incompatible). On the face of things, these two models can only offer reinforcing interpretations for the same one half of the phenomenon observed in Section II above. Digging deeper to see how such models might account for that other half of the phenomenon drives us toward a model that is even more deeply and familiarly flawed.

A

One standard way of construing the effect of special relationships on our moral duties is to say that special relationships "merely magnify" preexisting moral duties. That is to say, they merely make more stringent duties which we have, in weaker form, vis-à-vis everyone at large; or, "imperfect duties" are transformed by special relationships into "perfect" ones. Thus, perhaps it is wrong to let anyone starve, but it is especially wrong to let kin or compatriots starve. And so on.

That kind of account fits only half the facts, as sketched in Section II above, though. If special relationships were merely magnifiers of preexisting duties, then the magnification should be symmetrical in both positive and negative directions. Positive duties (i.e., duties to provide positive assistance to others) should become more strongly positive vis-à-vis those linked to us by some special relationship. Negative duties (i.e., duties not to harm others) should become more strongly negative vis-à-vis those linked to us by some special relationship. When it comes to our duties in relation to compatriots, however, the former is broadly speaking true, while the latter is not.

It is perfectly true that there is a variety of goods that we may or must provide to compatriots that we may at the same time legitimately deny to nonnationals (especially nonresident nonnationals). Rights to vote, to hold property, and to the protection of their persons and property abroad are among them. In the positive dimension, then, the "magnifier" model is broadly appropriate.[30]

In the negative dimension, it is not. All the examples *a* through *f* in Section II above point to ways in which we may legitimately impose burdens upon compatriots that may not properly be imposed upon non-nationals (especially nonresident nonnationals). We may poison our compatriots' air, stop their flow of water, deprive them of liberty by conscription, deny them legal remedies for damage to their persons and their property – all in a way that we cannot do to nonresident nonnationals. If anything, it is our negative duties toward nonnationals, not our negative duties toward compatriots, that are here magnified.

B

A second way of construing the effect of special relationships on our moral duties is to say that special relationships "multiply" as well as magnify preexisting duties. That is to say, special relationships do not just make

our ordinary general duties particularly stringent in relation to those bound to us by some special relationship; they also create new special duties, over and above the more general ones that we ordinarily owe to anyone and everyone in the world at large. Thus, contracts, for example, create duties de novo. I am under no general duty, strong or weak, to let Dick Merelman inhabit a room in my house; that duty arises only when, and only because, we sign a lease. The special (here, contractual) relationship has created a new duty from scratch.

The "multiplier" model bolsters the "mere magnifier" model's already broadly adequate account of why we have especially strong positive duties toward those linked to us by some special relationship. Sometimes those special relationships strengthen positive duties we owe, less strongly, to everyone at large. Other times, special relationships create new positive duties that we owe peculiarly to those thus linked to us. Either way, we have more and stronger positive duties toward those who stand in special relationships to us than we do the world at large. And that broadly fits the pattern of our special duties vis-à-vis compatriots, as revealed in Section II above.

On the face of it, though, it is hard to see how this multiplier model can account for the weakening of negative duties toward compatriots observed there. If special relationships multiply duties, then we would ordinarily expect that that multiplication would produce more new duties in each direction. Consider the paradigm case of contracts. Sometimes contracts create new special duties enjoining us to help others in ways that we would not otherwise be bound to do. Other times, contracts create new special duties enjoining us not to harm others (e.g., by withdrawing trade, labor, or raw materials) in ways that we would otherwise be at liberty to do. It is hard, on the face of it, at least, to see what the attraction of special duties would be – either for agents who are anxious to incur them or for philosophers who are anxious to impose them – if they make people worse off, opening them up to new harms from which they would otherwise be protected.

Yet, judging from examples *a* through *f* in Section II above, that is precisely what happens in the special relationship between compatriots. Far from simply creating new negative duties among compatriots, that special relationship seems sometimes to have the effect of canceling (or at least weakening or mitigating) some of the negative duties that people owe to others in general. That hardly looks like the result of an act of multiplication. Ordinarily, we would expect that multiplication should produce more – not fewer – duties.

C

Digging deeper, we find that there may be a way to explain why special relationships have this curious tendency to strengthen positive duties while weakening negative ones. This model quickly collapses into another, more familiar one – and ultimately falls prey to the same objections standardly lodged against it, as Section IV will show. Still, it is worth noting how quickly all the standard theories about special duties, when confronted with certain elementary facts about the case of compatriots, collapse into that familiar and flawed model that ordinarily we might have regarded as only one among many possible ways of filling out those theories.

The crucial move in reconciling standard theories about special duties with the elementary facts about compatriots laid out in Section II is just this: whether special relationships multiply duties or merely magnify them, the point remains that a relationship is inherently a two-way affair. The same

special relation that binds me to you also binds you to me. Special duties for each of us will usually follow from that fact.[31]

Each of us will ordinarily benefit from others' being bound by those extra (or extra strong) duties to do for us things that they are not obliged (or not so powerfully obliged) to do for the world at large. Hence the apparent "strengthening" of positive duties in consequence of special relationships.

Each of us will also ordinarily suffer from those extra (or extra strong) duties imposing an extra burden on us. Hence the apparent "weakening" of negative duties in consequence of the special relationship. We may legitimately impose burdens upon those standing in special relationships to us that we may not impose upon those in no special relation to us, merely because we have special rights against them, and they have special duties toward us. Those extra burdens upon them are no more, and no less, than the fair price of our being under special duties to provide them with valued assistance.

Many of the findings of Section II above lend themselves quite naturally to some such interpretation. When we say that compatriots may have their incomes taxed, their trucks commandeered, or other liberties curtailed by conscription, that is surely to say little more than that people may be required to do what is required in order to meet their special duties toward their fellow citizens – duties born of their fellow citizens' similar sacrifices to benefit them.[32] When we say that nonnationals (especially nonresident nonnationals) may not be treated in such ways, that is merely to say that we have no such special claims against them nor they any such special duties toward us.

Others of the examples in Section II above (especially examples *d* through *g*) do not lend themselves quite so obviously to this sort of analysis. But perhaps, with a sufficiently long story that is sufficiently rich in lurid details, we might be persuaded that polluting the air, damming rivers, limiting liability for damages, and denying people due process of law really is to the good of all; and suffering occasional misfortunes of those sorts really is just the fair price that compatriots should be required to pay for the benefits that they derive from those broader practices.

Notice that, given this account, the motivational quandary in Section III*B* disappears. People welcome special relationships – along with the attendant special rights and special duties (i.e., along with the strengthening of positive duties and the weakening of negative ones) – because the two come as part of an inseparable package, and people are on net better off as a result of it. That is just to say, their gains from having others' positive duties toward them strengthened exceeds their costs from having others' negative duties toward them weakened, and it is impossible for them to realize the gains without incurring the costs.

Notice, however, how quickly these standard theories of how special relationships work on our moral duties – the magnifier and the multiplier models – have been reduced to a very particular theory about "mutual-benefit societies." Initially, the magnifier and multiplier theories seemed to be much broader than that, open to a much wider variety of interpretations and not committing us to any particular theory about why or how the "magnification" or "multiplication" of duties occurred. Yet if those models are to fit the elementary facts about duties toward compatriots in Section II at all, they must fall back on a sort of mutual-benefit logic that provides a very particular answer to the question of how and why the magnification or multiplication of duties occurred. As Section IV will show, that is not an altogether happy result.

IV   The Mutual-Benefit-Society Model

According to the conventional wisdom about international relations, we have a peculiarly strong obligation to leave foreigners as we found them. "Nonintervention" has long bid fair to constitute the master norm of international law.[33] That is not to say that it is actually wrong to help foreigners, of course. It is, however, to say that it is much, much more important not to harm them than it is to help them. Where compatriots are concerned, almost the opposite is true. According to the flip side of that conventional wisdom, it is deeply wrong to be utterly indifferent toward your fellow countrymen; yet it is perfectly permissible for fellow countrymen to impose hardships on themselves and on one another to promote the well-being of their shared community.

Perhaps the best way to make sense of all this is to say that, within the conventional wisdom about international relations, nation-states are conceptualized as ongoing mutual-benefit societies. Within mutual-benefit-society logic, it would be perfectly permissible to impose sacrifices on some people now so that they themselves might benefit in the future; it may even be permissible to impose sacrifices on some now so that others will benefit, either now or in the future.

Precisely what sorts of contractarian or utilitarian theories are required to underpin this logic can be safely left to one side here. It is the broad outline, rather than the finer detail, that matters for present purposes. The bottom line is always that, in a mutual-benefit society, imposing harms is always permissible – but only on condition that some positive good comes of it, and only on condition that those suffering the harm are in some sense party to the society in question.

Suppose, now, that national boundaries are thought to circumscribe mutual-benefit societies of this sort.[34] Then the broad pattern of duties toward compatriots and foreigners, respectively, as described in Section II above, becomes perfectly comprehensible. In dealing with other people in general (i.e., those who are not party to the society), the prime directive is "avoid harm": those outside our mutual-benefit society ought not be made to bear any of our burdens; but neither, of course, have they any claim on any of the benefits which we have produced for ourselves, through our own sacrifices. In dealing with others in the club (i.e., compatriots), positive duties wax while negative ones wane: it is perfectly permissible to impose hardships, so long as some positive good somehow comes of doing so; but the point of a mutual-benefit society, in the final analysis, must always be to produce positive benefits for those who are party to it.

There are many familiar problems involved in modeling political communities as mutual-benefit societies.[35] The one to which I wish to draw particular attention here is the problem of determining who is inside the club and who is outside it. Analysis of this problem, in turn, forces us back to the foundational questions skirted at the outset of the article. These will be readdressed in Section V below, where I construct an alternative model of special duties as not very special, after all.

From the legalist perspective that dominates discussion of such duties, formal status is what matters. Who is a citizen? Who is not? That, almost exclusively, determines what we may or must do to people, qua members of the club.

Yet formal status is only imperfectly and contingently related to who is actually generating and receiving the benefits of the mutual-benefit society. The mismatch is most glaring as regards resident aliens: they are often net contributors to the society, yet they are equally often denied its full benefits.[36] The mismatch also appears only slightly less glaringly, as regards natural-born citizens who retain that status although they are and will inevitably (because, e.g., severely handicapped) continue to be net drains on the mutual-benefit society.[37]

In its starkest form, mutual-benefit-society logic should require that people's benefits from the society be strictly proportional to the contributions they have made toward the production of those benefits. Or, minimally, it should require that no one draw out more than he has paid in: the allocation of any surplus created by people's joint efforts may be left open. On that logic, we have special duties toward those whose cooperation benefits us, and to them alone. That they share the same color passport – or, indeed, the same parentage – is related only contingently, at best, to that crucial consideration.

It may well be that mutual-benefit logic, in so stark a form, is utterly inoperable. Constantly changing circumstances mean that everything from social insurance to speculative business ventures might benefit us all in the long run, even if at any given moment some of them constitute net drains on the system. And lines on the map, though inherently arbitrary at the margins, may be as good a way as any of identifying cheaply the members of a beneficially interacting community. So we may end up embracing the formalistic devices for identifying members of the mutual-benefit society, knowing that they are imperfect second-bests but also knowing that doing better is impossible or prohibitively expensive.

The point remains, however, that there are some clear, straightforward adjustments that ought to be made to such "first stab" definitions of membership, if mutual-benefit logic underlay membership. That they are not made – and that we think at least one of them ought not be made – clearly indicates that it is not mutual-benefit logic that underlies membership, after all.

Reflect, again, upon the case of resident aliens who are performing socially useful functions over a long period of time. Many societies egregiously exploit "guest workers," denying them many of the rights and privileges accorded to citizens despite the fact that they make major and continuing contributions to the society. Politically and economically, it is no mystery why they are deprived of the full fruits of their labors in this way.[38] But if the moral justification of society is to be traced to mutual-benefit logic, that is transparently wrong. The entry ticket to a mutual-benefit society should, logically, just be conferring net benefits on the society.[39] That membership is nonetheless denied to those who confer benefits on the society demonstrates that the society is not acting consistently on that moral premise. Either it is acting on some other moral premise or else it is acting on none at all (or none consistently, which morally amounts to the same).

Or consider, again, the case of the congenitally handicapped. Though born of native parents in the homeland, and by formalistic criteria therefore clearly qualified for citizenship, such persons will never be net contributors to the mutual-benefit society. If it were merely the logic of mutual benefit that determined membership such persons would clearly be excluded from the benefits of society.[40] (If their parents cared about them, they could give them some of *their* well-earned benefits.) Yet that does not happen, no matter how sure we are that handicapped persons will be net drains on the society for the duration of their lives. And most of us intuitively imagine that it is a good thing, morally, that it does not happen. Thus, society here again seems to be operating on something other than mutual-

benefit logic; and here, at least, we are glad that it is.

V The Assigned Responsibility Model

The magnifier, multiplier, and mutual-benefit-society models all take the special-ness of special duties particularly seriously. They treat such duties as if they were, at least in (large) part, possessed of an independent existence or of an independent moral force. I want to deny both of those propositions.

My preferred approach to special duties is to regard them as being merely "distributed general duties." That is to say, special duties are in my view merely devices whereby the moral community's general duties get assigned to particular agents. For this reason, I call mine an "assigned responsibility" model.[41]

This approach treats special duties as much more nearly derivative from general duties than any of the other approaches so far considered. Certainly it is true that, on this account, special duties derive the whole of their moral force from the moral force of those general duties. It may not quite be the case that, existentially, they are wholly derivative from general duties: we cannot always deduce from considerations of general duties alone who in particular should take it upon themselves to discharge them; where the general principle leaves that question open, some further (independent, often largely arbitrary) "responsibility principle" is required to specify it. Still, on this account, special duties are *largely* if not wholly derivative from considerations of general duty.

The practical consequences of this finding are substantial. If special duties can be shown to derive the whole of their moral force from their connections to general duties, then they are susceptible to being overridden (at least at the margins, or in exceptional circumstances) by those more general considerations. In this way, it turns out that "our fellow countrymen" are not so very special after all. The same thing that makes us worry mainly about them should also make us worry, at least a little, about the rest of the world, too.

These arguments draw upon larger themes developed elsewhere.[42] Here I shall concentrate narrowly upon their specific application to the problem of our special duties toward compatriots. The strategy I shall pursue here is to start from the presumption that there are, at root, no distinct special duties but only general ones. I then proceed to show how implementing those general duties gives rise to special duties much like those we observe in the practice of international relations. And finally I shall show how those special duties arising from general duties are much more tightly circumscribed in their extended implications than are the special duties deriving from any of the other models.[43]

A

Let us start, then, from the assumption that we all have certain general duties, of both a positive and negative sort, toward one another. Those general injunctions get applied to specific people in a variety of ways. Some are quasi-naturalistic. Others are frankly social in character.

For an example of the former, suppose we operate under some general injunction to save someone who is drowning, if you and you alone can do so. Suppose, further, that you happen to find yourself in such a position one day. Then that general injunction becomes a compelling commandment addressed specifically to you.

The same example is easily adapted to provide an instance of the second mode as well. Suppose, now, that there are hundreds of people on the beach watching the drowning swimmer flounder. None is conspicuously closer or conspicuously the stronger swimmer; none is related to the swimmer. In short, none is in any way "naturalistically" picked out as the appropriate person to help. If all of them tried to help simultaneously, however they would merely get in each other's way; the probable result of such a melee would be multiple drownings rather than the single one now in prospect. Let us suppose, finally, that there is one person who is not naturalistically but, rather, "socially" picked out as the person who should effect the rescue: the duly-appointed lifeguard.[44] In such a case, it is clearly that person upon whom the general duty of rescue devolves as a special duty.

Notice that it is not a matter of indifference whom we choose to vest with special responsibility for discharging our general moral duties. Obviously, some people would, for purely naturalistic reasons, make better lifeguards than others. It is for these naturalistic reasons that we appoint them to the position rather than appointing someone else. But their special responsibility in the matter derives wholly from the fact that they *were* appointed, and not at all from any facts about why they were appointed.

Should the appointed individuals prove incompetent, then of course it is perfectly proper for us to retract their commissions and appoint others in their places. If responsibility is allocated merely upon the bases here suggested, then its reallocation is always a live issue. But it is an issue to be taken up at another level, and in another forum.[45] Absent such a thoroughgoing reconsideration of the allocation of responsibilities, it will almost always be better to let those who have been assigned responsibility get on with the job. In all but the most exceptional cases of clear and gross incompetence on the part of the appointed individual, it will clearly be better to get out of the way and let the duly appointed lifeguard have an unimpeded chance at pulling the drowning swimmer out of the water.

That seems to provide a good model for many of our so-called special duties. A great many general duties point to tasks that, for one reason or another, are pursued more effectively if they are subdivided and particular people are assigned special responsibility for particular portions of the task. Sometimes the reason this is so has to do with the advantage of specialization and division of labor. Other times, it has to do with lumpiness in the information required to do a good job, and the limits on people's capacity for processing requisite quantities of information about a great many cases at once. And still other times it is because there is some process at work (the adversarial system in law, or the psychological processes at work in child development, e.g.) that presuppose that each person will have some particular advocate and champion.[46] Whatever the reason, however, it is simply the case that our general duties toward people are sometimes more effectively discharged by assigning special responsibility for that matter to some particular agents. When that is the case, then that clearly is what should be done.[47]

Thus, hospital patients are better cared for by being assigned to particular doctors rather than having all the hospital's doctors devote one *n*th of their time to each of the hospital's *n* patients. Someone accused of a crime is better served, legally, by being assigned some particular advocate, rather than having a different attorney appear from the common pool of attorneys to represent him at each different court date.[48] Of course, some doctors are better than others, and some lawyers are better than others; so it is not a matter of indifference which one is handling your case. But any one is better than all at once.

B

National boundaries, I suggest, perform much the same function. The duties that states (or, more precisely, their officials) have vis-à-vis their own citizens are not in any deep sense special. At root, they are merely the general duties that everyone has toward everyone else worldwide. National boundaries simply visit upon those particular state agents special responsibility for discharging those general obligations vis-à-vis those individuals who happen to be their own citizens.[49]

Nothing in this argument claims that one's nationality is a matter of indifference. There are all sorts of reasons for wishing national boundaries to be drawn in such a way that you are lumped together with others "of your own kind"; these range from mundane considerations of the ease and efficiency of administration to deep psychological attachments and a sense of self that may thereby be promoted.[50] My only point is that those are all considerations that bear on the drawing and redrawing of boundaries; they are not, in and of themselves, the source of special responsibilities toward people with those shared characteristics.[51]

The elementary facts about international responsibilities set out in Section II above can all be regarded as fair "first approximations" to the implications of this assigned responsibility model. States are assigned special responsibility for protecting and promoting the interests of those who are their citizens. Other states do them a prima facie wrong when they inflict injuries on their citizens; it is the prima facie duty of a state, acting on behalf of injured citizens, to demand redress. But ordinarily no state has any claim against other states for positive assistance in promoting its own citizens' interests: that is its own responsibility. Among its own citizens, however, it is perfectly proper that in discharging that responsibility the state should compel its citizens to comply with various schemes that require occasional sacrifices so that all may prosper.[52]

C

So far, the story is strictly analogous in its practical implications to that told about mutual-benefit societies in Section IV above. Here, as there, we have special duties for promoting the well-being of compatriots. Here, as there, we are basically obliged to leave foreigners as we found them. The rationale is different: here, it is that we have been assigned responsibility for compatriots, in a way that we have not been assigned any responsibility for foreigners. But the end result is much the same – so far, at least.

There are, however, two important points of distinction between these stories. The first concerns the proper treatment of the useless and the helpless. So far as a mutual-benefit society is concerned, useless members would be superfluous members. Not only may they be cast out, they ought to be cast out. If the raison d'être of the society is mutual benefit, and those people are not benefiting anyone, then it is actually wrong, on mutual-benefit logic, for them to be included. (That is true, at least insofar as their inclusion is in any way costly to the rest of the society – ergo, it is clearly wrong, in those terms, for the severely handicapped to draw any benefits from a mutual-benefit society.) The same is true with the helpless, that is, refugees and stateless persons. If they are going to benefit society, then a mutual-benefit society ought to take them in. But if they are only going to be a net drain on society (as most of the "boat people" presumably appeared to be, e.g.), then a mutual-benefit society not only may but *must*, on its own principles, deny them entry. The fact that they are without any other protector in the international

system is, for mutual-benefit logic, neither here nor there.

My model, wherein states' special responsibilities are derived from general ones of everyone to everyone, cancels both those implications. States are stuck with the charges assigned to them, whether those people are a net benefit to the rest of society or not. Casting off useless members of society would simply amount to shirking their assigned responsibility.

The "helpless" constitute the converse case. They have been (or, anyway, they are now) assigned to no one particular state for protection. That does not mean that all states may therefore ignore or abuse them, however. Quite the contrary. What justifies states in pressing the particular claims of their own citizens is, on my account, the presumption that everyone has been assigned an advocate/protector.[53] Then, and only then, will a system of universal special pleading lead to maximal fulfillment of everyone's general duties toward everyone else worldwide.

Suppose, however, that someone has been left without a protector. Either he has never been assigned one, or else the one he was assigned has proven unwilling or unable to provide the sort of protection it was his job to provide. Then, far from being at the mercy of everyone, the person becomes the "residual responsibility" of all.[54] The situation here is akin to that of a hospital patient who, through some clerical error, was admitted with some acute illness without being assigned to any particular physician's list: he then becomes the residual responsibility of all staff physicians of that hospital.

To be sure, that responsibility is an "imperfect" one as against any particular state. It is the responsibility of the set of states, taken as a whole, to give the refugee a home; but it is not the duty of any one of them in particular.[55] At the very least, though, we can say this much: it would be wrong for any state to press the claims of its own citizens strongly, to the disadvantage of those who have no advocate in the system;[56] and it would not be wrong (as, perversely, it would be on the mutual-benefit-society model) for any state to agree to give refugees a home. Both these things follow from the fact that the state's special responsibility to its own citizens is, at root, derived from the same considerations that underlie its general duty to the refugee.

The second important difference between my model and mutual-benefit logic concerns the critique of international boundaries and the obligation to share resources between nations. On mutual-benefit logic, boundaries should circumscribe groups of people who produce benefits for one another. Expanding those boundaries is permissible only if by so doing we can incorporate yet more mutually beneficial collaborators into our society; contracting those boundaries is proper if by so doing we can expel some people who are nothing but liabilities to our cooperative unit. On mutual-benefit logic, furthermore, transfers across international boundaries are permissible only if they constitute mutually beneficial exchanges. The practical consequence of all this is, characteristically, that the rich get richer and the poor get poorer.[57]

On the model I have proposed, none of this would follow. Special responsibilities are, on my account, assigned merely as an administrative device for discharging our general duties more efficiently. If that is the aim, then they should be assigned to agents capable of discharging them effectively; and that, in turn, means that sufficient resources ought to have been given to every such state agent to allow for the effective discharge of those responsibilities. If there has been a misallocation of some sort, so that some states have been assigned care of many more people than they have been assigned resources to care for them, then a reallocation is called

for.[58] This follows not from any special theory of justice but, rather, merely from the basis of special duties in general ones.[59]

If some states prove incapable of discharging their responsibilities effectively, then they should either be reconstituted or assisted.[60] Whereas on mutual-benefit logic it would actually be wrong for nations to take on burdens that would in no way benefit their citizens, on my model it would certainly not be wrong for them to do so; and it would in some diffuse way be right for them to do so, in discharge of the general duties that all of them share and that underwrite their own grant of special responsibility for their own citizens in the first place.[61]

VI Conclusion

Boundaries matter, I conclude. But it is the boundaries around people, not the boundaries around territories, that really matter morally. Territorial boundaries are merely useful devices for "matching" one person to one protector. Citizenship is merely a device for fixing special responsibility in some agent for discharging our general duties vis-à-vis each particular person. At root, however, it is the person and the general duty that we all have toward him that matters morally.

If all has gone well with the assignment of responsibilities, then respecting special responsibilities and the priority of compatriots to which they give rise would be the best way of discharging those general duties. But the assignment of responsibility will never work perfectly, and there is much to make us suppose that the assignment embodied in the present world system is very imperfect indeed. In such cases, the derivative special responsibilities cannot bar the way to our discharging the more general duties from which they are derived. In the present world system, it is often – perhaps ordinarily – wrong to give priority to the claims of our compatriots.

Notes

1 Unlike David Miller, "The Moral Significance of Nationality" (*Ethics*, 1988), I shall here make no distinction between "state" and "nation," or between "citizenship" and "nationality." They will be used interchangeably here.

2 Or so it is standardly supposed. Actually, there could be a "rule of universal partiality" (e.g. "everyone ought to pursue his own interests," or "everyone ought to take care of his own children"). A variant of this figures largely in my argument in Section V below.

3 The terms "special" and "general" duties – and to a large extent the analysis of them as well – are borrowed from H. L. A. Hart, "Are there any Natural Rights?," *Philosophical Review* 64 (1955), pp. 175–91.

4 See Robert E. Goodin, *Protecting the Vulnerable* (Chicago: University of Chicago Press, 1985), ch. 1 and the references therein. The strongest arguments for such partiality have to do with the need to center one's sense of self, through personal attachments to particular people and projects; see, e.g., Bernard Williams, *Moral Luck* (Cambridge: Cambridge University Press, 1981), ch. I. But surely those arguments apply most strongly to more personal links, and only very weakly, if at all, to impersonal links through shared race or nationality. John Cottingham pursues such points in "Partiality, Favouritism and Morality," *Philosophical Quarterly* 36 (1986), pp. 357–73, pp. 370–1.

5 William Godwin, *Enquiry Concerning Political Justice* (1793; reprint, Oxford: Clarendon, 1971), bk. 2, ch. 2.

6 See, e.g., Williams, *Moral Luck*, pp. 17–18, for the former position; and R. M. Hare, *Moral Thinking* (Oxford: Clarendon Press, 1981), p. 138, for the latter.

7 Henry Sidgwick, *The Methods of Ethics*, 7th edn. (London: Macmillan, 1907), bk. 3, ch. 4, sec. 3; Derek Parfit, *Reasons and Persons* (Oxford: Clarendon Press, 1984), pp. 95, 485.

8 Sidgwick, *The Methods of Ethics*, bk. 3, ch. 4, sec. 3; Parfit, *Reasons and Persons*, pp. 95, 485.

9 Parfit, *Reasons and Persons*, p. 95.

10 Sometimes special duties specifically require the opposite. Parents, teachers, and prison wardens are all, from time to time, required by special duties to inflict punishment upon those under their care. But at least some – and arguably all – of these are pains inflicted for the recipient's own greater, long-term good. See Herbert Morris, "A Paternalistic Theory of Punishment," *American Philosophical Quarterly* 18 (1981), pp. 263–71; cf. John Deigh, "On the Right to Be Punished: Some Doubts," *Ethics* 94 (1984), pp. 191–211.

11 Henry Shue, *Basic Rights* (Princeton, NJ: Princeton University Press, 1980), p. 132; Benjamin Cardozo, *People v. Crane*, 214 NY 154, 164,108 NE 427, 437. This report of what constitutes the conventional wisdom is echoed by: Thomas Nagel, "Ruthlessness in Public Life," in *Public and Private Morality*, ed. Stuart Hampshire (Cambridge: Cambridge University Press, 1978), pp. 75–93, p. 81; Charles R. Beitz, *Political Theory and International Relations* (Princeton, NJ: Princeton University Press, 1979), p. 163; and Goodin, *Protecting the Vulnerable*, chs. 1 and 2. Among them, only Cardozo could be said to accept that conventional wisdom uncritically.

12 Unlike stipulative law, which might be made by a small body of people on the spur of the moment, customary law represents the settled judgments of a great many people over some long period. Thus, it is better qualified for use in a quasi-Rawlsian "reflective equilibrium." For other uses of legal principles in such a role, see Robert E. Goodin, *The Politics of Rational Man* (London: John Wiley, 1976), ch. 7, and *Protecting the Vulnerable*, ch. 5.

13 These all refer to ways that we must treat foreigners in general, absent specific contractual or treaty commitments. The latter may require better treatment, or permit worse, or both in different respects. The principles set out in the text, however, constitute the normative background against which such contracts or treaties are negotiated.

14 This is true even if it is a piece of movable property, so there is no question of expropriating a piece of another nation's territory. Suppose, e.g., that the British government needs to requisition a privately owned ship to provision troops in the South Atlantic: it may so requisition a ship of British registry, even if it is lying in Dutch waters; it may not so requisition a ship of Dutch registry, even if lying in British waters (except in a case of extreme emergency).

15 Adrian S. Fisher, chief reporter, *Restatement (Second) of the Foreign Relations Law of the United States* (St. Paul, MN: American Law Institute, 1965), sec. 185c. The "right of safe passage" for people and goods in transit, for purposes of commerce or study, was firmly established even in early modern international law; see Hugo Grotius, *On the Law of War and Peace*, trans. F. W. Kelsey (1625; reprint, Oxford: Clarendon Press, 1925), bk. 2, ch. 2, secs. 13–15; Christian Wolff, *The Law of Nations Treated according to a Scientific Method*, trans. Joseph H. Drake (1749; reprint, Oxford: Clarendon, 1934), sec. 346; and Emerich de Vattel, *The Law of Nations, or the Principles of Natural Law*, trans. Joseph Chitty (1758; reprint, Philadelphia: T. and J. W. Johnson, 1863), bk. 2, ch. 10, sec. 132. This rule, too, is subject to an "extreme emergency" exception.

16 L. Oppenheim, *International Law: A Treatise*, ed. H. Lauterpact (London: Longman, 1955), 1:288. This, and the similar result in example *c* below, follows from the fact that a state enjoys continuing "personal" sovereignty over its own citizens but possesses merely those powers derived from its "territorial" sovereignty over aliens within its borders. This distinction, emphasized in modern international law (e.g., throughout the first volume of Oppenheim's treatise, *International Law*), appears in a particularly clear early formulation in Francisco Suárez's 1612 *Treatise on Laws and God the Lawgiver*, in *Selections from Three Works*, trans. and ed. Gwladys L. Williams, Ammi Brown, John Waldron, and Henry Davis (Oxford: Clarendon Press, 1944), ch. 30, sec. 12.

17 Oppenheim, 1:288. The practice in the United States, of course, is to conscript alien nationals who are permanently resident in the country into its armed forces; see Alexander M. Bickel, *The Morality of Consent* (New Haven, CT: Yale University Press, 1975), p. 49. But the long-standing rule in international law is that, while we may require resident aliens to help with police, fire, and flood protection, foreigners are exempt from serving in the militia; see Vattel, bk. 2, ch. 8, secs. 105–6 for one early statement of the rule.

18 Oppenheim, 1:288. Bickel, p. 48. Again, this is a long-standing rule of international law; see Wolff, sec. 324; and Vattel, bk. 2, ch. 8, sec. 106. Of course, having the right to tax nationals abroad, states may waive that right (as, e.g., through double-taxation agreements).

19 A partial exception to this rule might be that an alien with permanent residency in one state but temporarily resident in another might be taxable in the first country for earnings in the second; the United States, at least, would try to collect. Some authors maintain that even resident aliens should be exempt from certain sorts of taxes. One example Wolff offers (sec. 324) is a poll tax: since aliens are precluded by reason of noncitizenship from voting, they ought for that reason to be exempt from a poll tax, too. Another example, offered by Battel (bk. 2, ch. 8, sec. 106), is that foreigners should be "exempt from taxes . . . destined for the support of the rights of the nation"; since resident aliens are under no obligation to fight in defense of the nation, they should be under no obligation to pay taxes earmarked for the defense of the nation either.

20 Oppenheim, 1:290–1, 348, 475.

21 Ibid., 1:291.

22 Thus, e.g., the Price-Anderson Act sets the limit for liability of operators of civilian nuclear reactors within the United States at $560 million. But had the Fermi reactor in Detroit experienced a partial meltdown similar to that at Chernobyl, spreading pollution to Canada, international law would

not have recognized the legitimacy of that limit in fixing damages due to Canadians. "It is," according to Oppenheim's *International Law*, 1:350, "a well-established principle that a State cannot invoke its municipal legislation as a reason for avoiding its international obligations."

23 Oppenheim, 1:686–7. Indeed, "black letter" international law – as codified in the American Law Institute's *Restatement (Second) of the Foreign Relations Law of the United States*, sec. 165(1)(a) – holds that "conduct attributable to a state and causing injury to an alien is wrongful under international law . . . if it departs from the international standard of justice." For elaboration, see Oppenheim, 1:290, 350, 641; and J. L. Brierly, *The Law of Nations*, 2nd edn. (Oxford: Clarendon, 1936), pp. 172 ff.

24 Oppenheim, 1:687–8. Elsewhere Oppenheim explicitly draws attention to the "paradoxical result" that "individuals, when residing as aliens in a foreign state, enjoy a measure of protection . . . denied to nationals of a State within its own territory" (1:641, n. 1). In the past, this has been the subject of some controversy. Premodern international lawyers tended to hold that there was some external (god-given) standard of "just suitable" laws that must be adhered to in prescribing differential treatment for aliens; see Suárez, ch. 33, sec. 7. But early modern writers like Wolff (sec. 302) and Vattel (bk. 2, ch. 8, sec. 100) – right down to Henry Sidgwick, *The Elements of Politics* (London: Macmillan, 1891), pp. 235–6 – seemed to suppose that, since the state could refuse admission to aliens altogether, it could impose any conditions it liked upon their remaining in the country, however discriminatory and however short that treatment may fall from any international standards of civilized conduct. At the very least, aliens are not wronged if they are treated no worse than nationals – or so it was thought by many (predominantly European and Latin American) international lawyers prior to 1940 (Ian Brownlie, *Principles of Public International Law* [Oxford: Clarendon Press, 1966], p. 425). By now, it is decidedly the

"prevailing rule" of international law that "there is an international standard of justice that a state must observe in the treatment of aliens, even if the state does not observe it in the treatment of its own nationals, and even if the standard is inconsistent with its own law" (*Restatement [Second] of the Foreign Relations of the United States*, sec. 165, comment *a*; and Louis B. Sohn and R. R. Baxter, "Responsibility of States for Injuries to the Economic Interests of Aliens (Harvard Law School Draft Convention)," *American Journal of International Law* 55 [1961], 545–84, pp. 547–8. There is no longer any doubt that "national treatment" is not enough; the only persisting question is whether the international standard demanded should vary with, e.g., the wealth or educational attainments of the people to whom it is being applied – as, e.g., standards of "due diligence" and "reasonable care" perhaps should (Brownlie, p. 427).

25 States are under obligations arising from customary and higher domestic law to do so, even if those obligations are unenforceable under international law, as they seem to be (see Oppenheim, 1:686–7).

26 Suárez, ch. 33, sec. 7; Wolff, sec. 303; Sidgwick, *Elements of Politics*, p. 235; Brierly, pp. 172–3; Oppenheim, 1:689–91; Brownlie, pp. 424–48; Gerald M. Rosberg, "The Protection of Aliens from Discriminatory Treatment by the National Government," *Supreme Court Review* (1977), pp. 275–339; Edward S. Corwin, *The Constitution, and What it Means Today*, ed. H. W. Chase and C. R. Ducat (Princeton, NJ: Princeton University Press, 1978), pp. 90–2, and *1980 Supplement*, pp. 159–61; "Developments in the Law: Immigration Policy and the Rights of Aliens," *Harvard Law Review* 96 (1983): 1286–1465.

27 Bickel, pp. 45–6. Also, see Corwin, pp. 90–2, and *1980 Supplement*, pp. 159–61; and "Developments in the Law."

28 Brierly, p. 173; Oppenheim, 1:690.

29 Brierly, p. 173; Bickel, p. 46; "Developments in the Law," pp. 1300–1.

30 "Broadly," because example *g* above arguably does not fit this pattern. It all depends upon

whether we construe this as a positive duty to provide aliens with something good ("due process of law") or as a negative duty not to do something bad to them ("deny them due process of law"). This, in turn, depends upon where we set the baseline of how well off they would have been absent our intervention in the first place.

31   I say "usually" because there are some unilateral power relations (like that of doctor and patient or parent and child) that might imply special duties for one but not the other party to the relationship; see Goodin, *Protecting the Vulnerable.*

32   The sacrifices might be actual or merely hypothetical (i.e., should the occasion arise, they would make the sacrifice).

33   Standard prescriptions along these lines of medieval churchmen were strengthened by each of the early modern international lawyers in turn – Grotius, Wolff, and Vattel – so that by the time of Sidgwick's *Elements of Politics,* the "principle of mutual non-interference" (p. 231) could be said to be "the fundamental principle" of international morality with no equivocation. It remains so to this day, in the view of most lawyers and of many philosophers; see, e.g., Michael Walzer, *Just and Unjust Wars* (New York: Basic Books, 1977), and "The Moral Standing of States," *Philosophy and Public Affairs* 9 (1980), pp. 209–30.

34   This thought finds its fullest contemporary expression in the notion of the "circumstances of justice" that John Rawls, *A Theory of Justice* (Cambridge, MA: Harvard University Press, 1971), pp. 126–30, borrows from David Hume, *A Treatise of Human Nature* (London: John Noon, 1739), bk. 3, pt. 2, sec. 2, and *An Enquiry Concerning the Principles of Morals* (London: Cadell, 1777), sec. 3, pt. 1. Some international relations theorists defend this analysis at length; see e.g., Wolff's *Law of Nations,* and Beitz's *Political Theory and International Relations,* pp. 143–53 (cf. his "Cosmopolitan Ideals and National Sentiment," *Journal of Philosophy* 80 [1983]: 591–600, p. 595). Other commentators seem almost to fall into this way of talking without thinking (see Nagel, p. 81; and Tony Honoré, "The Human Community and the Principle

of Majority Rule," in *Community as a Social Ideal,* ed. Eugene Kamenka [London: Edward Arnold, 1982], pp. 147–60, p. 154).

35   These are addressed, in their particular applications to the mutual-benefit model of international obligations, in Brian Barry, "Humanity and Justice in Global Perspective," in *NOMOS XXIV: Ethics, Economics and the Law,* ed. J. R. Pennock and J. W. Chapman (New York: New York University Press, 1982), pp. 219–52, pp. 225–43; and in Goodin, *Protecting the Vulnerable,* pp. 154–60.

36   Both domestic and international law go some way toward recognizing that in many respects resident aliens are much more like citizens than they are like nonresident aliens. But by and large those acknowledgments come *not* in the form of awarding them the same benefits as are enjoyed by citizens but, rather, in the form of imposing many of the same burdens on resident aliens as on citizens. A state may, e.g., compel resident aliens to pay taxes and rates and to serve in local police forces and fire brigades "for the purpose of maintaining public order and safety" in a way it may not require of nonresident aliens; Oppenheim, 1:680–1.

37   Brian Barry, "Justice as Reciprocity," in *Justice,* ed. Eugene Kamenka and Alice E.-S. Tay (London: Edward Arnold, 1979), pp. 50–78, pp. 68–9; Robert E. Goodin, *Political Theory and Public Policy* (Chicago: University of Chicago Press, 1982), pp. 77–9.

38   The argument here would perfectly parallel that for supposing that, if a workers' cooperative needed more labor, it would hire workers rather than selling more people shares in the cooperative. Demonstrations of this have been developed independently by J. E. Meade, "The Theory of Labour-Managed Firms and of Profit Sharing," *Economic Journal* 82 (1972), 402–28; and David Miller, "Market Neutrality and the Failure of Cooperatives," *British Journal of Political Science* 11 (1981): 309–21.

39   The "participation" model of citizenship is a close cousin to this mutual-benefit-society model. Participating in a society is usually (if not quite always) a precondition for produc-

ing benefits for others in that society; and usually (if not quite always) the reason we think participants in society deserve to enjoy the fruits of formal membership is that that is seen as fair return for the benefits they have produced for the society. See "Developments in the Law," pp. 1303–11; and Peter H. Schuck, "The Transformation of Immigration Law," *Columbia Law Review* 84 (1984): 1–90.

40 Since they are, ex hypothesi, congenital handicaps, there is no motive for those who have safely been born without suffering the handicap to set up a mutual insurance scheme to protect themselves against those risks.

41 "Nationality" and the duties to compatriots to which such notions give rise are just the sorts of "institutions" that Henry Shue ("Mediating Duties," in *Ethics*, 1988) shows to be so crucial in implementing any duties of a positive sort. How, precisely, the "assignment" of responsibility is accomplished can safely be left open: sometimes, people and peoples get assigned to some national community by some specific agency (e.g., the UN Trusteeship Council); more often, assignments are the products of historical accidents and conventions. However they are accomplished, these "assignments" must specify both who is responsible for you and what they are responsible for doing for you. Even so-called perfect duties, which specify the former precisely, are characteristically vague on the latter matter (specifying, e.g., a duty to provide a "healthful diet" for your children), and require further inputs of a vaguely "institutional" sort to flesh out their content.

42 Goodin, *Protecting the Vulnerable*; Philip Pettit and Robert E. Goodin, "The Possibility of Special Duties," *Canadian Journal of Philosophy* 16 (1986): 651–76.

43 Broadly the same strategy is pursued by Shue in "Mediating Duties."

44 This, incidentally, provides an alternative explanation for why we should appoint lifeguards for crowded but not uncrowded beaches. The standard logic – true, too, in its way – is that it is a more efficient allocation of scarce resources since it is more likely that

more people will need rescuing on crowded beaches. Over and above all that, however, it is also true that an "obvious" lifesaver will be needed more on crowded than uncrowded beaches to keep uncoordinated helpers from doing each other harm.

45 That is to say that the ascription of "role responsibilities" takes on the same two-tier structure familiar to us from discussions of "indirect consequentialism"; see Hare, pp. 135–40, 201–5; and Bernard Williams, "Professional Morality and Its Dispositions," in *The Good Lawyer*, ed. David Luban (Totowa, NJ: Rowman & Allanheld, 1983), pp. 259–69.

46 Nagel, p. 81; Williams, *Moral Luck*, ch. 1.

47 Assigning responsibility to some might have the effect of letting others off the hook too easily. It is the job of the police to stop murders, so none of the onlookers watching Kitty Genovese's murder thought it their place to get involved; it is the lifeguard's job to rescue drowning swimmers, so onlookers might stand idly by watching her botch the job rather than stepping in to help themselves; and so on. This emphasizes the importance of back-up responsibilities, to be discussed below, specifying whose responsibility it is when the first person assigned the responsibility fails to discharge it.

48 This is the "division of labor model" of the adversary system discussed by Richard Wasserstrom, "Lawyers as Professionals: Some Moral Issues," *Human Rights* 5 (1975), pp. 1–24, p. 9, and "Roles and Morality," in Luban, ed., pp. 25–37, p. 30.

49 This is, I believe, broadly in line with Christian Wolff's early analysis. Certainly he believes that we have special duties toward our own nations: "Every nation ought to care for its own self, and every person in a nation ought to care for his nation" (sec. 135). But it is clear from Wolff's preface (secs. 9–15) that those special rights and duties are set in the context of, and derived from, a scheme to promote the greater common good of all nations as a whole. Among contemporary writers, this argument is canvassed, not altogether approvingly, by Shue, *Basic Rights*, pp. 139–44; and William K. Frankena, "Moral

Philosophy and World Hunger," in *World Hunger and Moral Obligation*, ed. William Aiken and Hugh La Follette (Englewood Cliffs, NJ: Prentice-Hall, 1977), pp. 66–84, p. 81. Hare, pp. 201–2, is more bullish on the proposal.

50   Sidgwick, *Elements of Politics*, ch. 14; Brian Barry, "Self-government Revisited," in *The Nature of Political Theory*, ed. David Miller and Larry Siedentop (Oxford: Clarendon, 1983), pp. 121–54; Alasdair MacIntyre, "Is Patriotism a Virtue?" (Lawrence: University of Kansas, Lindley Lecture, March 26, 1984). Compare Cottingham, pp. 370–4. Notice that the principle urged by David Miller in arguing for "The Moral Significance of Nationality" is very much in line with my own in its practical implications: *if* people have national sentiments, then social institutions should be arranged so as to respect them; but Miller gives no reason for believing that people should or must have such sentiments, nor does he pose any objection to people's extending such sentiments to embrace the world at large if they so choose.

51   That is to say, if general duties would be better discharged by assigning special responsibilities to a group of people who enjoy helping one another, then we should so assign responsibilities – not because there is anything intrinsically good about enjoying helping one another, but merely because that is the best means to the intrinsically good discharging of general duties.

52   If example *g* in Section II is construed as a special positive duty toward aliens, as n. 30 above suggests it might be, then it poses something of a problem for all three other models of special responsibilities. All three, for diverse reasons, would expect *positive* duties to be stronger vis-à-vis compatriots, not toward aliens. The assigned responsibility model alone is capable of explaining the phenomenon, as a manifestation of our general duty toward everyone at large which persists even after special responsibilities have been allocated. More will be said of that residual general duty below.

53   Thus, in international law aliens typically have no right themselves to protest directly

to host states if they have been mistreated by it; instead, they are expected to petition their home governments, who make representations to the host state in turn (Oppenheim, vol. 1, chap. 3). Similarly, the reason aliens may be denied political rights in their host states is presumably that they have access to the political process in their home states. It is an implication of my argument here that, if states want to press the special claims of their own citizens to the exclusion of all others, then they have a duty to make sure that everyone has a competent protector – just as if everyone at the seashore wants to bathe undisturbed by any duty to rescue drowning swimmers, then they have a duty to appoint a lifeguard.

54   See Goodin, *Protecting the Vulnerable*, ch. 5; and Pettit and Goodin, "The Possibility of Special Duties," pp. 673–6.

55   Vattel, bk. 1, ch. 19, sec. 230; see, similarly, Wolff, secs. 147–9; and Grotius, bk. 2, ch. 2, sec. 16. Vattel and Wolff specifically assert the right of the exile to dwell anywhere in the world, subject to the permission of the host state – permission which the host may properly refuse only for "good" and "special reasons" (having to do, in Vattel's formulation at least, with the strict scarcity of resources in the nation for satisfying the needs of its preexisting members). The duty of the international community (i.e., the "set of states, as a whole") to care for refugees derives from the fact that refugees "have no remaining recourse other than to seek international restitution of their need," as the point has been put by Andrew E. Shacknove, "Who is a Refugee?" *Ethics* 95 (1985): 274–84.

56   Similarly, in the "advocacy model" in the law, it is morally proper for attorneys to press their clients' cases as hard as they can if and only if everyone has legal representation; if institutions fail to guarantee that, it is wrong for attorneys to do so. See Wasserstrom, "Lawyers as Professionals," pp. 12–13, and "Roles and Morality," pp. 36–7.

57   Ideally, of course, this model would have both the rich getting richer and the poor getting richer. Even in this ideal world,

however, it is almost inevitable that the rich would get richer at a faster rate than the poor. Assuming that the needs of the poor grow more quickly than those of the rich, then in some real sense it may well be inevitable, even in this ideal world, that the poor will actually get (relatively) poorer.

58 Or, as Miller puts it, it is wrong to put the poorly-off in charge of the poorly-off and the well-off in charge of the well-off ("The Moral Significance of Nationality"). That is not a critique of my model but, instead, a critique of existing international boundaries from within my model.

59 Compare Barry, "Self-government Revisited," pp. 234–9.

60 Some have offered, as a reductio of my argument, the observation that one way of "reconstituting" state boundaries as I suggest might be for a particularly poor state to volunteer to become a colony of another richer country. But that would be a true implication of my argument only if (a) citizens of the would-be colony have no very strong interests in their national autonomy and (b) the colonial power truly discharges its duties to protect and promote the interests of the colony, rather than exploiting it. The sense that this example constitutes a reductio of my argument derives, I submit, from a sense that one or the other of those propositions is false. But in that case, it would not be an implication of my argument, either.

61 This duty to render assistance across poorly constituted boundaries might be regarded as a "secondary, back-up responsibility" that comes into play when those assigned primary responsibility prove unwilling or unable to discharge it. In *Protecting the Vulnerable*, ch. 5, I argue that such responsibilities come into play whatever the reason for the default on the part of the agent with primary responsibility. There, I also argue that one of our more important duties is to organize political action to press for our community as a whole to discharge these duties, rather than necessarily trying to do it all by ourselves. That saves my model from the counterintuitive consequence that well-off Swedes, knowing that the welfare state will feed their own children if they do not, should send all their own food to starving Africans who would not otherwise be fed rather than giving any of it to their own children.

Chapter 14

The Ethics of Nationality*
David Miller

I

The second proposition contained in the idea of nationality is that nations are ethical communities. In acknowledging a national identity, I am also acknowledging that I owe special obligations to fellow members of my nation which I do not owe to other human beings. This proposition is a contentious one, for it seems to cut against a powerful humanitarian sentiment which can be expressed by saying that every human being should matter equally to us. Each person can feel happiness and pain, each person can feel respected when his or her claims are recognized and demeaned when they are not, so how can it be right to give priority or special treatment to some human beings just because they are tied to us by the kind of bonds identified in the last chapter? From an ethical point of view, nationality may seem to give our feelings for our compatriots a role in our practical reasoning that is rationally indefensible.

To get a grip on the issues here, I am going to begin by distinguishing between ethical universalism and ethical particular-

ism. These are two competing accounts of the structure of ethical thought, and I shall argue that it makes a big difference to our understanding of nationality which account we accept. The division between them is not, however, rigid: it is possible to start from a universalist position and then to move some considerable distance to accommodate particularist concerns, and vice versa. It is also important not to confuse this question of the structure of an ethical theory with the question of its content. Someone who subscribes to ethical universalism might, for instance, be a utilitarian or on the other hand a defender of natural rights. How far the division between universalism and particularism coincides with substantive differences over the content of ethics is not an issue I can address here.

So where does the distinction lie? Ethical universalism gives us a certain picture of what ethics is about, the elements of which are individuals with their generic human capacities, considered for these purposes as standing apart from and prior to their relationships to other individuals. Each person is an agent capable of making choices surrounded by a universe of other such agents, and the principles of ethics specify what he must do towards them, and what he may

* From David Miller, *On Nationality* (Oxford: Oxford University Press, 1995), pp. 49–80.

claim in return from them. Because the principles are to be universal in form, only general facts about other individuals can serve to determine my duties towards them. Thus, a principle that might figure in a universalist ethics might be 'Relieve the needy', and then it would be relevant fact, in working out what I owe to Tom, that he is in need and that I have resources which could be used to allay his need. On the other hand, what we might call relational facts about Tom, facts about some relationship in which he already stands to me, cannot enter the picture at this fundamental level. So the fact that Tom is my brother or my neighbour cannot, on a universalist view of ethics, count in determining my duty towards him *at the basic level.* Now as we shall see shortly, an ethical universalist may well want to argue that at a less fundamental level facts such as these should count in determining my duty towards Tom. But these have to be brought in by means of an argument showing why, in the light of the fundamental principles, it may be justifiable to act on the basis of such relational facts. No ethical universalist can allow 'because he is my brother' to stand as a basic reason for action.

Ethical particularism is simply the opposite of this. It holds that relations between persons are part of the basic subject-matter of ethics, so that fundamental principles may be attached directly to these relations. It invokes a different picture of the ethical universe, in which agents are already encumbered with a variety of ties and commitments to particular other agents, or to groups or collectivities, and they begin their ethical reasoning from those commitments. Different forms of ethical particularism will portray these ties in different ways, and attach significance to different relational facts. Moreover, to say that we must begin our ethical reasoning by taking account of the various relationships in which we stand to others is not to say that we must conclude by endorsing the moral demands that conventionally attach to those relationships. 'Because he is my brother' can count as a basic reason for the particularist, but this does not mean that I am bound to behave towards him as convention dictates that brothers should behave towards one another.

Now it seems that both ethical universalism and ethical particularism have strong arguments in their favour. On the one hand, there is little doubt that we do feel a sense of responsibility to other human beings considered merely as such. On the other hand, in our everyday life we decide what to do primarily by considering what our relationships to others, and our memberships of various groups, demand of us. So it seems natural to look for some compromise view that would do justice to both of these powerful intuitions.[1] How, starting from a universalist perspective, might we try to explain and justify particular ethical commitments?

There are two broad avenues that we might follow. (Which we choose will depend in part on the *content* of our universalist ethics.) First, we might argue that, in order to realize the values that lie at the base of our ethical theory most effectively, it makes sense for each agent to pursue those values in relation to particular other agents rather than the whole universe of agents. There is, so to speak, a parcelling out of the basic duties so that I am given a relatively concrete set of duties to carry out in my day-to-day existence.[2] Thus, to take the example given earlier, suppose that one of our basic principles is 'relieve the needy'. It may be that this principle is discharged most effectively if each of us takes care of the needy in our immediate environment. Why is this? Well, first of all, there are many possible relievers and many people in need, so there is a problem of coordination. We want to ensure that everyone in need gets taken care of, and that as far as possible there is no duplication of the relief. If we say that each person should look after their own family first, next their immediate neighbours, then after that other members of their local community, and so forth, we may hope to achieve these two desiderata. Second, I am likely to be far better placed to relieve the needs of some people than others, partly because it is simply more feasible for me to transfer the necessary resources, and partly because I will know more about what is actually needed by the particular people in question.[3] I am likely to know *in detail* what members of my family need, and I can get resources to them easily. So, we require conventions to decide who is to discharge duties such as this in particular cases, and it is easy to see that the most effective conventions will be ones that take account of relationships like those we find in families. Let us call this the 'useful convention' method of getting from universal duties to particular ones. The idea is that, if everyone acts on the convention in question ('Help members of your family first', etc.), all of us together will end up better discharging a duty that is universal in form.

The second avenue involves arguing that, from the universal perspective, each of us is empowered to create special relationships of various kinds, establishing particular sets of rights and obligations.[4] The simplest case would be a promise or contract: by making a promise or entering a contract, we confer special rights on our partners in agreement, and undertake special duties towards them. This is justified from a universalist perspective because it is seen as valuable for people to have the moral power to enter such agreements. (It promotes their well-being, it is an essential part of their freedom, etc.) The argument can be extended to relationships within the family and to membership of other groups by portraying these groups as voluntary associations: I am entitled freely to enter such associations, and once I have become a member I am subject to the rules and obligations of membership. (It is implicit in the story that I cannot enter *any* such association, but at the very least only those associations whose purpose does not contravene the basic principles of universal ethics.) Let us call this the 'voluntary creation' route from universal duties to particular ones. The general idea, to summarize, is that it is valuable from a universal point of view for people to have the moral power to bind themselves into special relationships with ethical content.

If these are the ways in which universalists typically try to accommodate our sense that special relationships and special loyalties matter to us ethically, how do particularists try to account for universal duties? The picture of ethical life favoured by particularists tends to be pluralistic. That is, we are tied in to many different relationships – families, work groups, voluntary associations, religious and other such communities, nations – each of which makes demands on us, and there is no single overarching perspective from which we can order or rank these demands. In case of conflict – say, where I have to decide whether to use my resources to help my brother or my colleague at work – I simply have to weigh their respective claims, reflecting both on the nature of my relationship to the two individuals and on the benefits that each would get from the help I can give. Given a picture of this kind, it is relatively straightforward to include the claim that I owe something to my fellow human beings considered merely as such. The relationships in which I stand vary considerably in their complexity and closeness. There is nothing in particularism which prevents me from recognizing that I stand in *some* relationship to all other human beings by virtue of our common humanity and our sharing of a single world. The problem is rather to decide on what ethical demands stem from this relationship, and to weigh it against other more specific loyalties.

Despite these conciliatory manœuvres made to incorporate the moral intuitions appealed to by the other side, there still remains a fundamental gulf between ethical universalism and particularism. One way of expressing this, which I shall try to show is misleading, is that universalists believe in ethical *impartiality*, whereas particularists believe in ethical *partiality*. This may seem to be an accurate way of describing the contrast because, from a universalist point of view, what the particularist is advocating is naturally referred to as 'favouring your own family' or 'showing preference for your own community', and this appears to be a case of 'showing partiality', whereas 'favouring everyone equally' looks like 'being impartial'. But in fact this is wrong. 'Impartiality' always gains its meaning from a specific context, and it means something like 'applying the rules and the criteria appropriate to that context in a uniform way, and in particular without allowing personal prejudice or interest to interfere'.[5] So a judge is being impartial when she applies the rule of law even-handedly to the cases that come before her, not taking bribes or allowing racial prejudice, say, to influence her verdicts. But she need be impartial only towards the cases that come before her, and she is not being partial because the rules she applies require her to punish crimes more leniently than the equivalent crimes are punished in some other jurisdiction. Equally, a father may deal impartially with his children, but this doesn't require him to dole out the same treatment to his neighbour's children as he gives to his own.[6]

The ethical particularist is not an advocate of partiality. He will agree that ethical conduct must be impartial, but he will simply deny that impartiality consists in taking up a universalist perspective. Thus, if I am a member of group G, then I must act towards all the other members of group G in certain ways, and that will require me to be impartial even if I happen to like Elizabeth more than John; and so forth. But I am not required to act in the same way towards people who are not members of G, and in refusing them what I would be obliged to give to people who are members, I am not displaying partiality.[7] Partiality (in the morally relevant sense) means treating someone (possibly yourself) favourably in defiance of ethically sanctioned rules and procedures, so we don't know what it consists in until we know what those rules and procedures are in a given case.

Describing the contrast between universalism and particularism in terms of a contrast between impartiality and partiality muddles up a question about the structure of ethics with a different question. This second question has to do with how far ethical demands, *however construed*, may justifiably constrain individuals' pursuit of their own projects and goals. Several recent authors, most notably perhaps Bernard Williams and Thomas Nagel, have explored the conflicts that arise between impersonal morality and what Nagel calls 'the personal standpoint' – the agent's view of himself as someone with particular concerns and interests whose satisfaction is vitally important to him.[8] This may indeed legitimately be presented as a conflict between impartiality and partiality, since what goes into the scales against impersonal morality is the agent's concern that his own life should go well. It is important to see that the conflict between personal and impersonal standpoints can be just as severe when 'impartial morality' is construed in particularist terms – for instance, when a person has to choose between pursuing his own ambitions and doing what his profession or his country requires of him. Both Williams and Nagel veil this point to some extent, by thinking of impartiality in universalist terms. So the picture they present is of an agent with his own projects confronted with the demands of some global principle such as utility or equality.[9] But the position is really much more complex than that. What constrains the pursuit of individual projects is typically a whole raft of demands and obligations, stemming from someone's commitments, memberships, and allegiances, as well as from the rights or needs of humanity as such. All of these, I have argued, can best be seen as (possibly conflicting) requirements of impartiality.

How, then, *should* we understand what is at stake in the contest between universalism and particularism in ethics? We can get a better grasp of it by seeing what the universalist will identify as the main weakness in particularism, and conversely what the particularist will regard as the main weakness in universalism. To begin with the first of these, to the universalist, particularism appears as the capitulation of reason before sentiment, prejudice, convention, and other such rationally dubious factors. By allowing existing commitments, relationships, and loyalties to enter our ethical thinking at a basic level, the particularist signally fails to subject these bonds to rational scrutiny. And this exposes him immediately to two dangers. One is moral conservatism, the sanctification of merely traditional ethical relations, based perhaps on the interests of dominant social groups, on outmoded philosophies, or perhaps on sheer ignorance. The other is incoherence, where the ethical demands that stem from relationships of different kinds are not brought into any rational relation with one another, so that a person who follows a particularistic ethics would receive no guidance in cases where he was pulled in one direction by one set of obligations and in the opposite direction by a second set – the position, for instance, of Sartre's young Frenchman [. . .]. Indeed, because different aspects of the situation might appear salient on different occasions, such a person might

act inconsistently – and inconsistent behaviour would seem to be the epitome of irrationality.

The ethical universalist aspires instead to a model of the following sort; rational reflection on the foundations of ethics will lead us to a single basic principle, or else to an ordered set of principles, with universal scope – for instance to the principle of utility, or a principle of basic human rights, or some version of the principle of equality. In the light of this basic principle, we will then be able to scrutinize our more specific ethical intuitions (say, about our familial obligations), accepting some, rejecting others, modifying yet others, and assigning them consistent weights to be used in cases of conflict. We would then have something that deserved the name of an ethical *system*, a set of principles and rules of varying scope that together would guide our conduct consistently, and that could resolve moral dilemmas such as the one described above. Of course, adopting a universalist perspective does not entail discovering such a system – it may turn out that there is simply an irreducible plurality of basic ethical principles – but the idea that we should at least *try* to devise such a system seems to me to provide a good deal of the motive force behind universalism.

Let me now turn the question around and ask what particularists are likely to see as the main defect of ethical universalism. The answer, I think, is that in two respects at least universalism relies upon an implausible picture of moral agency, of the person who is to be the bearer of responsibilities and duties. It draws a sharp line between moral agency and personal identity on the one hand, and between moral agency and personal motivation on the other. According to the universalist, we discover what our duties are by abstract reflection on the human condition and on what others can legitimately ask of us. When we act morally, we act out of a regard for these purely rational considerations; for instance, having decided that the basis of ethics is the general happiness, we resolve to act according to those rules of conduct that are best calculated to promote that objective. But, the particularist will argue, this involves driving a wedge between ethical duty and personal identity. No considerations about who I am, where I have come from, or which communities I see myself as attached to are to be allowed to influence my ethical reasoning. As Alasdair MacIntyre has put the point, a position of this kind:

> requires of me to assume an abstract and artificial – perhaps even an impossible – stance, that of a rational being as such, responding to the requirements of morality not *qua* parent or farmer or quarterback, but *qua* rational agent who has abstracted him or herself from all social particularity, who has become not merely Adam Smith's impartial spectator, but a correspondingly impartial actor, and one who in his impartiality is doomed to rootlessness, to be a citizen of nowhere. How can I justify to myself performing this act of abstraction and detachment?[10]

Equally, the particularist will claim, universalism rests upon an implausible account of ethical motivation. When I act on moral principle, I am supposed to act simply out of a rational conviction that I am doing what morality requires of me. I am not to be influenced by my sentiments towards the objects of my duty, nor am I to allow the reactions of those around me in my community to guide my behaviour. So, for instance, thoughts such as 'I'd be letting down my family if I did that' or 'This is not how a good Christian should behave' have to be seen as extraneous to ethics proper. But it seems unlikely that rational conviction can carry the weight required of it, except perhaps in the case of a small number of heroic individuals who are genuinely able to govern

their lives by considerations of pure principle. For the mass of mankind, ethical life must be a social institution whose principles must accommodate natural sentiments towards relatives, colleagues, and so forth, and which must rely on a complex set of motives to get people to comply with its requirements – motives such as love, pride, and shame as well as purely rational conviction.[11]

II

These arguments and counter-arguments could be spelt out at much greater length than is possible here, but my aim has simply been to identify what is at stake in the contest between universalism and particularism in ethics. The universalist sees in particularism a failure of rationality; the particularist sees in universalism a commitment to abstract rationality that exceeds the capacities of ordinary human beings. These are the main charges that each side has to rebut if it is to provide a convincing account of ethical life. So let us now turn our attention back to nationality and ask about its ethical significance. It should be clear from what has been said that national allegiances could have intrinsic significance only if we adopt some form of ethical particularism. If we begin from a universalist position, then the fact that Elizabeth is my compatriot cannot justify my having special obligations towards her at the basic level. On the other hand, it is not so clear that nationality must be devoid of ethical significance at a less basic level. Perhaps special obligations to compatriots can be derived by universalists in one of the ways in which they seek to derive limited obligations generally. So let us see how an ethical universalist might try to do this.

In this investigation we must guard against one possible source of confusion. We have on the one hand groups of people who share a national identity ... On the other hand we have people who are involved in common schemes of political co-opera-tion, in the sense that they are subject to the same set of laws, contribute to one another's welfare through schemes of taxation, and so forth; the most familiar case is those who are citizens of the same state. Now of course relationships of these two kinds may coin-cide, as they do when we have genuine nation-states in which all citizens share a common nationality. But equally, as we have already seen, there can be groups of compa-triots who are not (now) involved in common schemes of political co-operation (e.g. are citizens of different states), and people may share a common citizenship even though they are the bearers of separate national identities. So we need to be clear whether we are trying to assess the ethical significance of nationality as such, or instead the ethical sig-nificance of membership in a scheme of political co-operation. The importance of this will shortly be apparent.

How, then, might an ethical universalist try to justify special obligations among com-patriots? We have seen that there are two broad strategies that he might follow. Con-sider first the 'voluntary creation' strategy. This would seek to portray a nation as a voluntary association which someone might choose to join, and would argue that the special rights and obligations attached to nationality are justified in roughly the same way as the rights and obligations of more immediate associations such as families and sports clubs. Such an argument runs into difficulties immediately. We have seen already how misleading it is to suppose that nationality could be interpreted on the model of a voluntary association. Bearing a national identity means seeing oneself as part of a historic community which in part makes one the person that one is: to regard membership as something one has chosen is to give way to an untenable form of social atomism which first abstracts the individual

from his or her social relationships and then supposes that those relationships can be explained as the voluntary choices of the individual thus abstracted. Now admittedly, it is possible to renounce one's nationality, in the sense of removing oneself from the society in question, making no further claims against it, and acknowledging no further obligations. But for this renuncia-tion to be genuine, one or other identity – the person's or the nation's – must have changed in such a radical way that the person in question could no longer see herself as a member of that nation – the position, for instance, of a Jew in Hitler's Germany. The fact that in certain circum-stances membership must be renounced does not make continuing acknowledge-ment of one's nationality a matter of volun-tary choice.

Even if this difficulty could be surmounted, there would be the further question whether nations *qua* voluntary associations are the kind of things one could *legitimately* join according to universalist principles. What, positively, are the moral gains, or the gains in personal welfare, that flow from member-ship of large agglomerations of people such as nations usually are? It is very difficult to see how the arguments deployed by universalists to justify obligation-creating practices such as promises and contracts which involve small numbers of individuals could be extended to these more extensive communities. And indeed, if we look at the arguments actually used by universalists in this area, we find that they are targeted not on nations as such but on schemes of politi-cal co-operation, or, more specifically, states, What the arguments actually try to justify are the special rights and obligations one has as citizen of this or that state.

To take a familiar instance of this argu-ment, assume that our universal obligation is to secure the basic rights of everyone else – rights to life, liberty, and so forth. Suppose that we are the subjects of a state which fulfils this duty reasonably effectively in the case of its own members, and does not actively violate the rights of outsiders. Then it may be claimed that we may discharge our individual obligations by supporting the state to which we belong. We have contracted into a scheme of co-operation which can be justified in terms that the universalist accepts, and so we ought properly to acknowledge the special responsibilities that we incur under the scheme.

This approach still has to face the problem involved in viewing the state as a voluntary association. States demand the allegiance of their subjects: the long history of attempts to show that, appearances notwithstanding, each of these subjects has actually *consented* to membership of the state reveals the nature of the problem. It may be circumvented, however, by regarding political co-operation not as a voluntary matter in the strict sense but as *quasi-contractual* in nature. Here the emphasis is placed not on consent but on the mutual exchange of benefits. My obligations to the state and to my fellow-citizens derive from our common participation in a practice from which all may expect to benefit. The appeal here is to a principle of fair play which does not require that I should have made a voluntary decision to join the practice.[12] Now this principle has an important role to play in our understanding of the obligations of nationality, as I shall show in due course. But it cannot bear all the weight that it is being asked to bear here.

Observe that the quasi-contractual approach to limited obligations proceeds entirely by appeal to existing practices. Because, as a matter of fact, I am part of an on-going scheme of co-operation from which I derive benefits, I have an obligation to contribute to the scheme as its rules require. The fair play principle lays down some conditions on the kind of scheme that will generate obligations in this way – for

instance, it cannot operate in such a way that one group of participants exploits another group by receiving a disproportionate share of the benefits – but it does not provide positive reasons for having such a scheme, or for preferring one such scheme to an alternative with a wider or a narrower membership. So, although it may show why individuals derive obligations from their participation in the state, it cannot show why *this* kind of practice is preferable to one that has a universal, or for that matter a much narrower, scope.

Putting this another way, the quasi-contractual approach only generates conditional obligations. It says that, *if* you are the beneficiary of a scheme of political co-operation, you should do your fair share to sustain the scheme. But it does nothing to show why such schemes should exist. It does not show that it is desirable for there to be such things as states; it only shows that, where they do exist, people may have special obligations as a result. And equally, of course, it has nothing to say about the ethical significance of nationality. It attaches no weight to the fact that we feel a sense of common identity with this group of people rather than that. It is interested only in the fact of co-operation, regardless of whether this is based on a shared national identity or upon the mere contingency of being thrown together (metaphorically or actually) in a lifeboat.

However one tries to spell it out, the 'voluntary creation' approach to special obligations is not going to endow nationality with ethical significance (nor, indeed, will it even strongly justify the existence of states). What about the second strategy available to universalists, the 'useful convention' approach? This side-steps all the problems of consent and voluntariness, for there is no implication that useful conventions must be ones that have emerged by free agreement. But it faces the same difficulty in explaining why any significance should attach to national boundaries as such.

Consider one example of this approach. Goodin writes: 'Special responsibilities are, on my account, assigned merely as an administrative device for discharging our general duties more efficiently.'[13] To illustrate this account, he takes the case of a swimmer drowning off a beach that has an official lifeguard. To avoid chaos in the water, we need to be able to assign to someone the responsibility of rescuing the swimmer, and since the lifeguard is the designated person, the duty falls in the first place on him. This is a convincing example of the way in which a duty borne by everyone – the duty to save life – can be assigned in a particular case to a specific person. But notice how the example works. First, there is a social convention – the appointing of an official lifeguard – which means that we can all recognize who bears the duty in this case. But the assignment is not purely arbitrary. The lifeguard will have been selected because he is a strong swimmer, and will have been trained in life-saving techniques. So we all have good reason to think that the object of our duty – saving the swimmer – will be served best by our getting out of the lifeguard's way and letting him perform the rescue.

Now compare the case of obligations to compatriots as a way of discharging our general duties to humanity. Here again we find a convention whereby each state is held responsible for protecting the rights and serving the welfare of its own citizens. Although there is no act of assignment, as there has been in the case of the lifeguard, the convention in question seems to be universally recognized. But does this convention ensure that those who are assigned responsibility for each portion of humanity are the most competent to undertake that task? Why does it make sense to assign responsibility for the rights and welfare of Swedes to other Swedes and the rights and welfare of Somalians to other Somalians, if we are looking at the question from a global

perspective? What is the equivalent here to the selection and training of the lifeguard?

Two bad answers to this question are physical proximity and administrative ease. Neither of these has any intrinsic connection with nationality. Physical proximity suggests taking responsibility for those in your locality regardless of their nationality. Administrative ease brings us back once again to states, as the institutions that are currently most effective in protecting rights and delivering welfare; but it provides no answer to such questions as 'Why should the boundaries of states be located here rather than there?' 'Why not have sub-national or supra-national units performing these tasks?' A better answer is that cultural similarities mean that co-nationals are better informed about one another than they are about outsiders, and therefore better placed to say, for example, when their fellows are in need, or are deprived of their rights. This, I think, is the strongest argument that can be given, from a universalist point of view, for acknowledging special obligations to compatriots. But it confronts an argument in the opposite direction which is at least as powerful. Nations are hugely unequal in their capacity to provide for their own members. In so far as the obligations we are considering include the obligation to provide for human needs up to a certain point, it would seem odd to put the well off in charge of the well off and the badly off in charge of the badly off. Simple co-ordination rules like 'Help the person standing next to you' make sense when, as far as we know, each is equally in need of help, and each equally able to provide it. But the international picture is very different from this. To put Swedes, with a per capita annual income of \$24,000, in charge of their own needy, and Somalians, with a per capita annual income of \$120, in charge of *their* needy would seem grossly irrational from a universal standpoint.[14] As Shue has argued, if we want to devise a reasonable institutional scheme to link together right-holders and duty-bearers, ability to pay would seem the natural way of assigning the duties.[15]

I conclude, therefore, that attempts to justify the principle of nationality from the perspective of ethical universalism are doomed to failure. The consistent universalist should regard nationality not as a justifiable source of ethical identity but as a limitation to be overcome. Nationality should be looked upon as a *sentiment* that may have certain uses in the short term – given the weakness of people's attachment to universal principles – but which, in the long term, should be transcended in the name of humanity. Thus, Sidgwick, representing the utilitarian brand of universalism, contrasted the national ideal with the cosmopolitan ideal. The latter was 'the ideal of the future', but to apply it now 'allows too little for the national and patriotic sentiments which have in any case to be reckoned with as an actually powerful political force, and which appear to be at present indispensable to social well-being. We cannot yet hope to substitute for these sentiments, in sufficient diffusion and intensity, the wider sentiment connected with the conception of our common humanity.'[16] Here is a consistent universalist, not trying *per impossibile* to demonstrate the moral worth of nationality, but arguing that practical ethics must, for the foreseeable future, bow to the force of national sentiments.

Nothing I have said so far is intended as a critique of universalism in itself. A universalist approach to ethics might still be the correct one. What I have been trying to dispel is the comforting thought that one can embrace universalism in ethics while continuing to give priority to one's compatriots in one's practical reasoning. The choice, as I see it, is either to adopt a more heroic version of universalism, which attaches no intrinsic significance to national boundaries, or else

to embrace ethical particularism and see whether one can defend oneself against the charge that one is succumbing to irrational sentiment in giving weight to national allegiances.

III

The particularist defence of nationality begins with the assumption that memberships and attachments in general have ethical significance. Because I identify with my family, my college, or my local community, I properly acknowledge obligations to members of these groups that are distinct from the obligations I owe to people generally. Seeing myself as a member, I feel a loyalty to the group, and this expresses itself, among other things, in my giving special weight to the interests of fellow-members. So, if my time is restricted and two students each ask if they can consult me, I give priority to the one who belongs to my college.[17]

These loyalties, and the obligations that go with them, are seen as mutual. I expect other members to give special weight to my interests in the same way as I give special weight to theirs. This doesn't mean that the relationship is one of strict reciprocity. For various reasons it may not be possible for the person whose interests I promote to return the favour in kind: the student I advise is not likely to be in a position to reciprocate with advice of the same sort. But perhaps she has computing skills which I lack, in which case she may be in a position to offer help of a different sort, and then I expect her to weight my interests in the same way as I weight hers. If this mutuality fails – not in a particular case, but in general – the character of the group or community to which I think I belong is put in question. Perhaps I have the romantic belief that my college is an academic community, whereas in fact it is simply an agglomeration of self-interested individuals using the institution to advance their careers. It is important that the obligations I acknowledge may be either appropriate or inappropriate as the case may be, depending on the relationships that really obtain within the group in question.

The obligations that I should acknowledge in a case like this are likely to be coloured by the general ethos of the group or community. This will determine, to some degree at least, the interests that I can be called on to promote. The college example that I used above traded to some extent on the fact that a college is an academic institution, so that giving academic advice is a paradigm of the sort of act that I can be called on to perform. But if this point is pushed too far, we are in danger of reducing communities of all kinds to instrumental associations. My collegial obligations extend to general human interests, so that if there are two students who need to be driven urgently to hospital, and I can take only one, then again, I ought to give priority to the one who belongs to my college, taking the other only if his need is considerably more urgent. But the interests are interpreted in the light of the community's values. A good example is provided by the medieval Jewish communities described by Michael Walzer.[18] Members of these communities recognized an obligation to provide for one another's needs, but needs in turn were understood in relation to religious ideals; this meant, for instance, that education was seen as a need for boys but not for girls; that food was distributed to the poorest members of the communities on the eve of the religious festivals; and so forth.

Before going on to see whether this picture of the ethics of community can plausibly be extended to nations, it is worth dwelling for a moment on the motivational strengths of ethical ties of this kind. First, to the extent that I really do identify with the group or community in question, there need be no sharp conflict between fulfilling my obligations and pursuing my own goals and purposes. The group's interests are among the goals that I set myself to advance; they may of course conflict with other goals that are equally important to me, but we are far away from the position where an individual with essentially private aims and purposes has to balance these against the obligations of a universalist morality such as utilitarianism. In that position there would almost always be a simple trade-off: the more a person does what morality requires of him, the less scope he has to pursue his personal goals. If this were indeed a correct picture of ethical life, one might be forgiven for thinking that morality would have rather little motivational power. But when I see my own welfare as bound up with the community to which I belong, contributing towards it is also a form of goal-fulfilment.

Second, because of the loose reciprocity that characterizes the ethics of community, a person who acts to aid some other member of his group can be sustained by the thought that in different circumstances he might expect to be the beneficiary of the relationship. I do not mean to suggest that such a person will act *in order* to receive some future benefit. From a self-interested point of view, it may be irrational to assume such an obligation, because it may be clear enough that the expected benefits are smaller than the expected costs. The point is a weaker one: the act of making a contribution is not a pure loss, from the point of view of the private interests of the person making it, because he is helping to sustain a set of relationships from which he stands to benefit to some degree. The point again is not that particularistic relationships serve to eradicate conflict between an individual's interests and the interests of others in the group or community, but that they soften the conflict so that ethical behaviour becomes easier for imperfectly altruistic agents.

Finally, we should observe that groups and communities form natural sites on which more formal systems of reciprocity can establish themselves. They mark out sets of people who are already well disposed to one another in certain respects, and this makes it easier to create formal practices for mutual benefit.[19] Thus, a group of neighbours may decide to form a shopping collective or share a school run. These practices are likely to be governed by tighter norms of reciprocity, in the sense that each person will have equal responsibilities and these will be more formally defined – it will be my job to visit the warehouse on the third Saturday of every month, say. When practices of this kind emerge, their effect will be to reinforce the less formal bonds that constituted the community in the first place, and to blur still further the contrast between a person's interests and her communal obligations.

How far, then, can these arguments be applied to nations? Does it make sense to regard nations as communities which generate rights and obligations in the same way as communities of a more immediate sort? Can the particularistic arguments I have been deploying serve to defend obligations to compatriots? In the last chapter I tried to bring out the various features that distinguish nations *qua* communities from communities of a more direct and immediate kind, and I want now to explore the ethical implications of this in somewhat greater depth.

Nationality is, as I have argued already, a powerful source of personal identity; but paradoxically, it is strangely amorphous when we come to ask about the rights and obligations that flow from it. It is capable of evoking fierce, and indeed often supreme, loyalty, manifested in people's willingness to give up their lives for their country; but if we were to ask those who share this loyalty what precisely their obligations consist in, we would I think receive answers that were very vague. People would no doubt say, first of all, that they had a duty to defend their

nation and its ancestral territory, in other words to preserve the community's culture and its physical integrity. They would also say that they bore a special responsibility towards their fellow-nationals, that they were justified in giving them priority both when acting as individuals and when deciding upon public policy. But if asked to be more specific about the *content* of those special responsibilities, it would be hard to elicit any determinate general answer.

This reminds us of the abstract character of nationality, its quality of 'imagined community'. Whereas in face-to-face communities, especially perhaps those with defined objectives, there is a clear understanding of what each is expected to contribute towards the welfare of other members, in the case of nationality we are in no position to grasp the demands and expectation of other members directly, nor they ours. Into this vacuum there flows what I have called a public culture, a set of ideas about the character of the community which also helps to fix responsibilities. This public culture is to some extent a product of political debate, and depends for its dissemination upon mass media. (This will be particularly true, of course, where the nation in question has its own state, or equivalent system of political authority.) It will therefore have an ideological coloration. Some national cultures may attach value to individual self-sufficiency, for example, and will therefore construe their members' obligations to one another mainly in terms of providing the conditions under which individuals can fashion their own lives; others will lay greater stress on collective goods, and regard compatriots as having duties to involve themselves in various forms of national service, to enhance the literary and artistic heritage of the nation, and so forth. So, although at any time it may be possible to say roughly what the obligations of the members of nation A are, these obligations in their particular content are an artefact of the public culture of that nation.

Now this may at first sight appear a very unsatisfactory conclusion to reach. We set out to show that particular ethical obligations could legitimately be derived from membership in a national community. Normally we would expect such obligations to be independently derived, and to serve as reasons in the process of political decision-making. For instance, we might appeal to obligations to provide welfare in the course of advocating policies or institutions that would serve to meet the needs, for instance the medical needs, of fellow-nationals. But it turns out that the obligations themselves stem from a public culture that has been shaped by political debate in the past.

But although this shows that we cannot derive the obligations of nationality simply from reflection on what it means for a group of people to constitute a nation in the first place, we should not exaggerate the significance of this point. It certainly does not imply that my obligations *qua* member of nation A are merely whatever I take them to be. The culture in question *is* a public phenomenon: any one individual may interpret it rightly or wrongly, and draw correct or incorrect conclusions about his obligations to compatriots as a result. Moreover, although the public culture is shaped by political debate, this does not mean that it is easily manipulable by political actors in the short term. It is often quite resilient: a relevant example is the failure of the British Conservative Party under Mrs Thatcher to bring about any across-the-board changes in national culture, despite holding the reins of government for eleven years.[20] Because of this relative stability, the idea that the public culture can serve as a source of ideas that may then be used to justify or criticize the policies of a particular government remains valid.

The fact that the public culture, and the obligations of nationality that derive from

it, can be reshaped over time has a welcome consequence. I said that one main charge levelled against all forms of ethical particularism is that they amount to the sanctification of merely traditional ethical relations. To the extent that national identities, and the public cultures that help to compose them, are shaped by processes of rational reflection to which members of the community can contribute on an equal footing, this charge no longer applies. The obligations that we now acknowledge are not merely traditional, but will bear the imprint of the various reasons that have been offered over time in the course of these debates. Thus, if, in a democratic community I have an obligation to support a national health service, that obligation is grounded in the reasons given for having the health service when it was first introduced, and reaffirmed from time to time when the health service is debated. (I may not know these reasons myself, and may simply take it for granted that supporting a national health service is part of what we believe in round here; none the less, the point remains that the obligations have a grounding in something more than mere tradition.) How far this ideal condition is met will depend on the political institutions we have, the quality of political debate both within the formal institutions and outside them, the general level of education, and so forth. These are matters that I shall return to later, when I discuss the ideal of national self-determination.

I have so far claimed that the ethical implications of nationality differ from those of lesser communities in two main respects. The potency of nationality as a source of personal identity means that its obligations are strongly felt and may extend very far – people are willing to sacrifice themselves for their country in a way that they are not for other groups and associations. But at the same time, these obligations are somewhat indeterminate and likely to be the subject of political debate; in the best case, they will flow from a shared public culture which results from rational deliberation over time about what it means to belong to the nation in question. However, to grasp the full force of the obligations of nationality, we need to consider what happens when national boundaries coincide with state boundaries, so that a formal scheme of political co-operation is superimposed on the national community.

In this case people will have rights and obligations of citizenship as well as rights and obligations of nationality. Rights and obligations of the first kind stem simply from their participation in a practice from which they stand to benefit, via the principle of reciprocity. As citizens they enjoy rights of personal protection, welfare rights, and so forth, and in return they have an obligation to keep the law, to pay taxes, and generally to uphold the co-operative scheme.[21] To a very large extent, their obligations of nationality are discharged through the state, provided that the latter pursues the right kind of policies. And this has the immediate advantage that people can play their part in the scheme in the knowledge that most others will (if necessary) be compelled to play theirs. Whereas in small communities each member can see for himself whether others are carrying out their obligations or not, in a nation-state we have to rely on the presence of enforcement mechanisms to get that assurance.

It would, however, be a great mistake to suppose that, once a practice of political co-operation is in place, nationality drops out of the picture as an irrelevance – that we simply have the rights and obligations of citizens interacting with other citizens. The bonds of nationality give the practice a different shape from the one that it would have without them. Let us try to imagine how the rights and obligations of citizenship might look if the citizens were tied to one another

by nothing beyond the practice of citizenship itself, and were motivated by the principle of fairness.[22] They would insist on strict reciprocity. In other words, each would expect to benefit from their association in proportion to his or her contribution, taking as a baseline the hypothetical state of affairs in which there was no political co-operation between them. So, for instance, redistributive taxation would be agreed to only in circumstances in which each person thought it was rational to insure him- or herself through the state against the possibility of falling below a certain level of resources.[23] Given the possibility of private insurance, we would expect states that lacked a communitarian background such as nationality provides to be little more than minimal states, providing only basic security to their members.[24] In particular, it is difficult to explain why states should provide opportunities and resources to people with permanent handicaps if one is simply following the logic of reciprocity. It is because we have prior obligations of nationality that include obligations to provide for needs that arise in this way that the practice of citizenship properly includes redistributive elements of the kind that we commonly find in contemporary states.

It may be asked how this analysis squares with the fact that citizenship is frequently extended to residents of the state who acknowledge a different nationality from the majority. Although it is possible to devise two categories of citizenship in these circumstances – e.g. by classifying non-nationals as 'guest workers' – there are strong reasons for extending a single common citizenship to everyone who is subject to the authority of the same state. When this happens, most citizens will find that their obligations of citizenship based on reciprocity are backed up by obligations stemming from common nationality; but some will not. Such a state of affairs may well be tolerated, particularly if the number of nonnationals is fairly small, but it is potentially unstable. The instability might be resolved either by slimming down the obligations of citizenship – turning the state into something closer to a minimal state – or by making state and nation coincide more closely. If the latter option is pursued, there are again two alternatives: to try to assimilate the nonnationals so that they come to share in a common national identity, or to partition the state in such a way that the new political units are more exactly isomorphic with national divisions [. . .] The point that I want to underline here is that there are strong ethical reasons for making the bounds of nationality and the bounds of the state coincide. Where this obtains, obligations of nationality are strengthened by being given expression in a formal scheme of political co-operation;[25] and the scheme of co-operation can be based on loose rather than strict reciprocity, meaning that redistributive elements can be built in which go beyond what the rational self-interest of each participant would dictate.

IV

The particularistic defence of nationality that I have been building up might seem convincing in its own terms; but the universalist will want to ask whether there are not also obligations to human beings as such, and if so how they can be reconciled with the picture so far presented. Does the ethics of nationality not entail moral indifference to outsiders? Here it is important to begin by recognizing that, when we talk about outsiders, we are not talking about isolated individuals, but about people who are themselves members of national communities. Of course there are exceptions to this – stateless persons, or refugees who for good reasons can no longer embrace their past national identity. But in general, in considering relationships to outsiders, we should not fall into the trap of thinking that our only relationship to them is of one human being to another. We are certainly related in that way; but, in considering my ethical relationship to, say, a Tanzanian, I should not forget that we are also related as Briton to Tanzanian. Each of us is linked internally to our own national community, and this creates a second dimension to our relationship alongside the first, which complicates the ethical picture.

If we consider just the first dimension, then the obligations that it imposes are probably best captured by a theory of basic rights. There are generic conditions for living a decent life which can be expressed in terms of rights to bodily integrity, personal freedom, a minimum level of resources, and so forth.[26] We have obligations to respect these rights in others that derive simply from our common humanity; mostly these are rights to forbearance of various kinds – rights to be left alone, not to be injured in various ways, etc. – but they may also include rights to provision, for example in cases where a natural shortage of resources means that people will starve or suffer bodily injury if others do not provide for them.

So much is relatively commonplace: nearly all ethical universalists would wish to endorse such a list of rights and their corresponding obligations, though many would argue that our responsibilities to other human beings go somewhat further than this. And I can see no reason why those who hold particularist views should not also endorse such a list of basic rights. The divergence occurs when we juxtapose relationships between persons abstractly conceived with relationships between persons as members of communities, including national communities.

For now the basic rights and the obligations that correspond to them are overlain by the special responsibilities that we have as members of these communities. Moreover, in each community there will be a specific understanding of the needs and interests of members which generate obligations on the part of other members. I argued above that a community will embody a common ethos which enters into the definition of the needs and interests that count for these purposes; in the case of nations, this common ethos takes the form of a public culture. Thus, in one national community (the Republic of Ireland, for example) religious education may be regarded as a shared need which should properly be funded by the community as a whole, whereas in another (the United States for example) it may be seen as a private matter which should be left to each person to consider, and to provide for their children as they saw fit. Given that there is a limit to the resources available in any given community to meet these commonly recognized needs, conflicts may then arise in any of the following three ways.

First, there may be a simple conflict between providing for the needs people have as members of a national community and respecting the basic rights of outsiders, to the extent that the latter involves some form of positive provision. For example, given that there is no obvious limit to the quantity of resources that might be expended in providing for health needs, how should we weigh the demands of the domestic national health service against the costs of immunization programmes in other countries? Considerations of urgency point in one direction; the relative strength of our obligations to different groups of people points in the other. No simple doctrine of 'basic rights first' seems acceptable in such cases.

Second, it may turn out that our own understanding of basic rights, coloured as it will undoubtedly be by the ethos of our own community, conflicts in certain respects with the priorities attached to various needs in

other communities. We might see formal education as a basic right; but there may be communities in which this is regarded as disruptive of cultural bonds and therefore as not, ultimately, in the best interests of the individuals concerned. In these circumstances, do we have obligations to promote basic rights as we see them, or should we rather give priority to community-based conceptions of need which we do not ourselves share?

Although these first two points seem to me quite powerful, they do not by themselves challenge a universal obligation to protect basic rights at a sufficiently fundamental level – say, to protect people from death by starvation. At this level we should expect conceptions of need to converge, and, provided the cost of protecting these rights is relatively small, it would be difficult to argue that the obligation must always yield to the demands of justice within the national community. But the third point cuts deeper still. *Who* has the obligation to protect these basic rights? Given what has been said so far about the role of shared identities in generating obligations, we must suppose that it falls in the first place on the national and smaller local communities to which the rights-bearer belongs. So why should we, as outsiders, have obligations to provide resources which ought to be provided in each case by fellow-nationals and/or local communities and other such groups?

The only answer that can be given here is that the rights will not be effectively protected unless there is provision across national boundaries. But again, we must ask why this should be the case. The most compelling argument for international provision is that it is simply impossible for the national community in question to protect the basic rights of its members – say, because of resource shortages caused by drought or flooding. In these circumstances we can say that there is a general obligation, falling equally on all those in a position to provide aid, to step in and safeguard the basic rights of those threatened by famine.[27] But if we take 'impossible' literally, this case is probably quite rare. Much more often, nations cannot protect the basic rights of their members because of other decisions they have taken: famines may result from misguided economic decisions made in the past, and they may be perpetuated by the institutional rules that continue to be applied.[28] Or again, the cause may simply be the unwillingness of better off people in the society in question to make the changes that would secure the rights of the worst off, for instance to introduce publicly funded welfare schemes.[29] What then follows for the obligations of outsiders?

Consider the general case in which B has a general right, primary responsibility for respecting which falls upon A (through some process of assignment), who fails to discharge his obligation. What responsibility does some third party, C, then have? We do not automatically conclude that C should herself provide what is needed to satisfy B's right. Her first obligation is surely to try to get A to acknowledge his responsibility, by persuasion if possible, but failing this by such force as is commensurate with the right in question. If these approaches fail, then at some point we will probably say that C should take care of B herself, though the obligation to do so would be weaker than A's original obligation. If we translate this pattern of reasoning to the international arena, then, if nation A fails to protect the rights of a set of its members B, the obligation of nation C is first of all to use all reasonable means to induce A to protect the rights of B. This might involve, for instance, trying by public condemnation to shame policy-makers in A to respect these rights, threatening to sever trade links or withdraw military co-operation unless the policy is changed, and in the last resort attempting directly to remove from power those responsible for the policies leading to the rights violations.

Measures such as this would be widely regarded as compromising the self-determination of the nation in question, and for that reason as unacceptable. This demonstrates the incongruity in holding together two principles which are indeed often held together by liberals: one attaches value to national self-determination and argues that nations have no right to interfere in one another's domestic affairs (except perhaps in very extreme cases); the other holds that we have a positive obligation to protect the basic rights of our fellow human beings. My point is that acceptance of the first principle places severe limits on the scope of the second. For if the obligation in question falls first of all on fellow-nationals, and if outsiders are prohibited by the first principle from intervening in a heavy-handed way when this obligation fails to be discharged, then it seems that they can at most have a weak obligation to provide the necessary resources themselves. If C is prohibited from compelling A to discharge his obligation to B when A defaults, C cannot then be placed under an equally strong obligation to fulfil B's rights.[30]

To put this point another way, I believe that ethical universalists who believe in a duty to protect basic rights of the kind I have been discussing – and, even more so, those who believe in a general utilitarian duty to promote the welfare of fellow human beings – ought to take seriously the case for benevolent imperialism. Given that many existing states signally fail to protect the basic rights of their members, and given also that on universalist grounds we can attach no intrinsic value to the obligations of community or to national self-determination, why not subject the members of these states to benign outside rule? Of course in most cases this proposal would not be practicable because of local resistance, but (again in universalist terms) such resistance must be seen as misguided if we allow that the imperialism is benevolent.[31] Why make a fetish of self-government if your basic rights will be better protected by outsiders? That few of those who now write as universalists are prepared to draw such conclusions shows, I think, that, while they are often ready to condemn their own countrymen as blinkered for their attachment to the idea of nationality, they are not prepared to pass the same judgement on outsiders.[32]

There is an appealing compromise between ethical universalism and ethical particularism which holds that it is justifiable to act on special loyalties and recognize special obligations to compatriots *provided* that this does not involve violating the basic rights of outsiders.[33] Basic rights come first; so long as they are respected, it is ethically acceptable to give preference to the needs and interests of fellow-countrymen (and to members of other such communities). Unfortunately, this position turns out to be too simple. At the very least, we need to draw a distinction between violating basic rights by one's own actions, and allowing them to be violated by others. It is probably true that the ethical claims of nationality could not justify anyone in violating the rights of an outsider by, say, killing or injuring him.[34] But if we take nationality seriously, then we must also accept that positive obligations to protect basic rights (e.g. to relieve hunger) fall in the first place on co-nationals, so that outsiders would have strong obligations in this respect only where it was strictly impossible for the rights to be protected within the national community. If bad policies or vested interests in nation A mean that some of its citizens go needy, then, if nation C decides that its own welfare requirements mean that it cannot afford to give much (or anything) to the needy in A, it has not directly violated

their rights; at most, it has permitted them to be violated, and in the circumstances this may be justifiable.

[...] So my account of the ethics of nationality is not yet fully executed. But since the argumentative strategy of this chapter has been a little oblique, let me conclude here by retracing its main steps. I began by distinguishing between ethical universalism and ethical particularism. I then argued that neither of the two approaches commonly used by universalists to justify special loyalties and duties – I call them the "useful convention" and "voluntary creation" approaches – stood much chance of accounting for commonly recognized obligations to fellow-nationals. The consistent ethical universalist ought to be a cosmopolitan. I then presented a justifying account of particularism, pointing out that, where obligations spring from communal relations, the opposition between self-interest and ethical obligation is diminished. I drew particular attention to the way in which communities can support formal practices of reciprocity in such a way that each reinforces the obligations deriving from the other. A nation-state in which a formal scheme of political co-operation is superimposed on a national community is a paradigmatic example of this. Finally, I asked whether ethical particularism of the kind defended here is compatible with the recognition of universal human rights. The answer is affirmative, but the obligations corresponding to these rights turn out to fall primarily on co-nationals. One corollary of this is that we are not in most cases required by justice to intervene to safeguard the human rights of foreigners, though humanitarian considerations may lead us to do so.

This argument is something less than a frontal assault on ethical universalism, which would carry us far away from the main focus of my book. My aim has been the more modest one of showing that the ethics of nationality is plausible, resting as it does on well established facts about human identity and human motivation. The onus is on the universalist to show that, in widening the scope of ethical ties to encompass equally the whole of the human species, he does not also drain them of their binding force.

Notes

1   Alternatively, members of either camp may try to tough it out, holding on to simple and rigorous forms of universalism and particularism respectively. The best example of a tough-minded universalist is perhaps William Godwin, well known for his rejection of special relationships of all kinds, including family relationships, as carrying any ethical weight. On the other side, one could cite extreme forms of nationalism such as that advocated by Fichte, in which the nation is presented as the supreme object of loyalty and duty.

2   This avenue is followed in R. Goodin, *Protecting the Vulnerable* (Chicago: University of Chicago Press, 1985), especially chs. 4–5. Goodin assigns duties to B according to how far the interests of others are vulnerable to his choices. 'If A's interests are vulnerable to B's actions and choices, B has a special responsibility to protect A's interests; the strength of the responsibility depends strictly upon the degree to which B can affect A's interests' (p. 118).

3   This is the line of argument used by Peter Singer to explain special responsibilities in 'Reconsidering the Famine Relief Argument', in P. G. Brown and H. Shue (eds.), *Food Policy* (New York: Free Press, 1977), p. 44.

4   For an example of this approach, see A. Gewirth, 'Ethical Universalism and Particularism', *Journal of Philosophy* 85 (1988), pp. 283–302.

5   At least, this is the meaning of impartiality in its morally relevant sense. There may perhaps also be a morally neutral sense in which any discrimination in the way that I treat people can be called partiality.

6   Cf. here the analysis of impartiality in J. Cottingham, 'Ethics and Impartiality', *Philosophical Studies* 43 (1983), pp. 83–99.

7   The argument here runs parallel to that made in A. Oldenquist, 'Loyalties', *Journal of Philosophy* 79 (1982), pp. 173–93. Oldenquist argues that the demand for 'impartiality' always in reality amounts to the demand that we should consider equally the interests of a wider 'tribe' of people than the present objects of our concern.

8   See B. Williams, 'Persons, Character and Morality', in *Moral Luck* (Cambridge: Cambridge University Press, 1981); T. Nagel, *Equality and Partiality* (New York: Oxford University Press, 1991).

9   This point is made in criticism of Williams in A. MacIntyre, 'The Magic in the Pronoun "My"', *Ethics* 94 (1983–4), pp. 113–25. It bears especially upon Williams's discussion in 'Persons, Character and Morality', and it may be worth adding that, in providing a general characterization of ethics in *Ethics and the Limits of Philosophy* (London: Fontana, 1985), Williams makes it very clear that he does not identify the ethical standpoint with universalism. Nagel is also somewhat inconsistent on this question: when explaining the general distinction between impartiality and partiality, he treats national solidarity as a form of partiality, but in other places he focuses on the tension between the pursuit of private interests and the responsibilities people have to other members of their political community as an instance of the conflict between personal and impersonal standpoints.

10 A. MacIntyre, *Is Patriotism a Virtue?*, Lindley Lecture (Lawrence, KS: University of Kansas, 1984), p. 12.

11 One way of putting this is to say that the view of ethics invoked by particularists is Humean rather than Kantian. Hume saw that morality had to be understood in relation to natural sentiments, so that the judgements we make

about others must reflect their (and our) natural preferences for kinsmen and associates. 'When experience has once given us a competent knowledge of human affairs, and has taught us the proportion they bear to human passion, we perceive, that the generosity of men is very limited, and that it seldom extends beyond their friends and family, or, at most, beyond their native country. Being thus acquainted with the nature of man, we expect not any impossibilities from him; but confine our view to that narrow circle, in which any person moves, in order to form a judgement of his moral character. When the natural tendency of his passions leads him to be serviceable and useful within his sphere, we approve of his character, and love his person, by a sympathy with the sentiments of those, who have a more particular connexion with him' (D. Hume, *A Treatise of Human Nature*, ed. L. A. Selby-Bigge, rev. P. H. Nidditch (Oxford: Clarendon Press, 1978), p. 602. I have discussed Hume's account of morality more extensively in D. Miller, *Philosophy and Ideology in Hume's Political Thought* (Oxford: Clarendon Press, 1981), especially chs. 2 and 5.

12 For formulations of the principle, see H. L. A. Hart, 'Are There any Natural Rights?' in A. Quinton. (ed.), *Political Philosophy* (Oxford: Oxford University Press, 1967); J. Rawls, 'Legal Obligation and the Duty of Fair Play', in S. Hook (ed.), *Law and Philosophy* (New York: New York University Press, 1964). A full discussion can be found in G. Klosko, *The Principle of Fairness and Political Obligation* (Lanham, MD: Rowman & Littlefield, 1992).

13 R. E. Goodin, 'What is so Special about Our Fellow Countrymen?', *Ethics* 98 (1987–8), p. 685.

14 Figures for 1990 are from *World Tables 1993* (Baltimore, MD: Johns Hopkins University Press, 1993).

15 H. Shue, 'Mediating Duties', *Ethics* 98 (1987–8), p. 703.

16 H. Sidgwick, *The Elements of Politics*, 2nd edn. (London: Macmillan, 1897), p. 308. Sidgwick's position has more recently been reaffirmed in C. Beitz, 'Cosmopolitan Ideals and National Sentiment', *Journal of Philosophy* 80 (1983), pp. 591–600. But compare the tougher-minded utilitarian universalism of Peter Singer: 'Sentiments like love, affection and community feeling are a large part of what makes life worthwhile. But sentiments are likely to lead us astray in moral reasoning, seducing us into accepting positions that are based, not on an impartial consideration of the interests of all involved, but rather on our own likes and dislikes' ('Reconsidering the Famine Relief Argument', p. 43).

17 I am supposing that I have no formal responsibilities to either student; they just happen to be working on a subject where I am able to give them some guidance. I am not suggesting that obligations of membership should always take precedence over formally assigned or contractual obligations to outsiders.

18 M. Walzer, *Spheres of Justice* (Oxford: Martin Robertson, 1983), pp. 71–8.

19 I don't mean to suggest that communities are a necessary condition for mutual benefit practices to appear. If any set of individuals is so placed that there is mutual advantage to be gained by establishing a co-operative practice, there is some chance that the practice will emerge. But often there is a problem in deciding who should be included in the scope of the practice, and there may be set-up costs that no individual is willing to incur alone. (I have looked at this issue in some depth in D. Miller, 'Public Goods without the State', *Critical Review 7* (1993), pp. 505–23.) In any case, the present point is not so much that communities facilitate mutual benefit practices as that, where they have this effect, the members' motivational ties to the group are reinforced.

20 For evidence, see I. Crewe, 'Has the Electorate Become Thatcherite?' in R. Skidelsky (ed), *Thatcherism* (Oxford: Blackwell Publishers, 1989).

21 As will be apparent, I am here describing citizenship in a well functioning liberal democracy. For discussion of the circumstances under which the fair-play principle can generate obligations to the state, see Klosko, *Principle of Fairness*, especially chs. 2–4.

22 Why not assume a higher degree of altruism? If we do this, we face the problem of explaining why altruistic concern should be directed towards one's fellow-citizens, rather than towards those who are neediest regardless of their citizenship. As I noted above, the only plausible argument here is one that appeals to our superior knowledge of the needs of our fellow citizens. So to show why citizens who were not linked by bonds of nationality should agree to compulsory redistribution among themselves, we would need to show (*a*) that they had sufficient general altruism, but also (*b*) that they had good reason to think that their altruism was best directed towards their fellow-citizens to whom, to repeat, they had no special ties beyond the institutions of common citizenship.

23 This point emerges clearly in Brian Barry's analysis of the idea of reciprocity in 'Justice as Reciprocity' in his *Democracy, Power and Justice* (Oxford: Clarendon Press, 1989), although it is somewhat overlooked in his later paper in the same volume, "The Continuing Relevance of Socialism".

24 A comparison between Canada and the USA might seem to rebut this claim: the USA has the stronger sense of national identity, yet redistributes less in favour of its worse-off members than does Canada with its welfare state.

25 Strengthened in the sense that, besides the obligations that I have that stem directly from a shared national identity, I have largely overlapping obligations of citizenship based on reciprocity. If I ask myself: 'Why pay my taxes?' two answers can be given: I have duty *qua* member of this nation to support common projects and to fulfil the needs of fellow members; and I have a duty *qua* citizen to sustain institutions from which I can expect in turn to benefit. Either of these reasons taken separately is vulnerable; together they make a powerful case for contribution.

26 There are many accounts of basic rights. Among the best, not least because it resists the temptation to expand the list of basic rights to include things that are socially desirable but not really basic, is H. Shue, *Basic Rights: Subsistence, Affluence and American*

Foreign Policy (Princeton, NJ: Princeton University Press, 1980).

27 I am considering here the international obligations that would arise in the absence of any ongoing scheme of co-operation between the national communities in question. Later I discuss the obligations of reciprocity that occur when there exists a practice of mutual aid between states to cope with natural disasters of various kinds.

28 The second alternative corresponds to Amartya Sen's thesis that starvation typically occurs because of failures of entitlement rather than unavailability of food in general; see A. Sen, *Poverty and Famines: An Essay on Entitlement and Deprivation* (Oxford: Clarendon Press, 1981).

29 In saying this I do not mean to deny that the economic policies pursued by one nation-state may make it more difficult for another to protect the basic rights of its citizens.

30 I do not mean that C should not act to fulfil B's rights; this may still be the right thing to do. But it would be hard to blame C if she decided not to do this. This suggests that there could only be a humanitarian obligation to, for example, send relief to famine victims in circumstances where relief was being withheld by their own government (whereas if the government *cannot* send relief, then there is a good case for saying that outside agencies have a duty of justice to supply it).

31 Several readers have said that the objection to benevolent imperialism is simply that we have no reason to think that imperialism can be benevolent. I think this is merely a way of avoiding a difficult question. Consider a proposal to put most of sub-Saharan Africa under the administrative control of members of the EU, acting perhaps on behalf of the United Nations. What reason is there to think that the Dutch, the Austrians, or the Swedes – even perhaps the French or the British – could not govern Tanzania, Angola, or Rwanda in a more efficient and humane way than their present rulers? That proposals such as this are today ruled out on principle testifies to the force that the idea of national self-determination has for us.

32 At one point Peter Singer makes the far weaker proposal that "we might make offers of aid to countries with rapidly increasing populations conditional on effective steps being taken to halt population growth". But, he goes on, "I imagine that many people who have agreed with me up to this point will be reluctant to accept this conclusion. It will be said that it would be an attempt to impose our own ideas on other, independent, sovereign nations" ("Reconsidering the Famine Relief Argument", p. 47). Singer goes on to defend his proposal, but he is fully aware of how controversial it is to suggest even this.

33 For examples of this position, see S. Gorovitz, "Bigotry, Loyalty, and Malnutrition", in P. G. Brown and H. Shue (eds.), *Food Policy* (New York: Free Press, 1977); S. Nathanson, *Patriotism, Morality and Peace* (Lanham, MD: Rowman & Littlefield, 1993), especially chs. 4 and 13.

34 Unless this was necessary in order to protect the basic rights of a compatriot, as for instance in case of war.

Chapter 15

Patriotism and Cosmopolitanism*
Martha C. Nussbaum

When anyone asked him where he came from, he said, "I am a citizen of the world."
    Diogenes Laertius, *Life of Diogenes the Cynic*

I

In Rabindranath Tagore's novel *The Home and the World*, the young wife Bimala, entranced by the patriotic rhetoric of her husband's friend Sandip, becomes an eager devotee of the *Swadeshi* movement, which has organized a boycott of foreign goods. The slogan of the movement is *Bande Mataram* (Hail Motherland). Bimala complains that her husband, the cosmopolitan Hindu landlord Nikhil, is cool in his devotion to the cause:

> And yet it was not that my husband refused to support *Swadeshi*, or was in any way against the Cause. Only he had not been able whole-heartedly to accept the spirit of *Bande Mataram*.
>
> "I am willing," he said, "to serve my country; but my worship I reserve for Right which is far greater than my country. To worship my country as a god is to bring a curse upon it."

* From Joshua Cohen (ed.), *For Love of Country? Debating the Limits of Patriotism* (Boston, MA: Beacon Press, 2002), pp. 2–17, 145 (notes).

Americans have frequently supported the principle of *Bande Mataram*, giving the fact of being American a special salience in moral and political deliberation, and pride in a specifically American identity and a specifically American citizenship a special power among the motivations to political action. I believe, as do Tagore and his character Nikhil, that this emphasis on patriotic pride is both morally dangerous and, ultimately, subversive of some of the worthy goals patriotism sets out to serve – for example, the goal of national unity in devotion to worthy moral ideals of justice and equality. These goals, I shall argue, would be better served by an ideal that is in any case more adequate to our situation in the contemporary world, namely the very old ideal of the cosmopolitan, the person whose allegiance is to the worldwide community of human beings.

My articulation of these issues is motivated, in part, by my experience working on international quality-of-life issues in an institute for development economics connected with the United Nations. It is also motivated by the renewal of appeals to the nation, and national pride, in some recent discussions of American character and American education. In a well-known op-ed piece in the *New York Times* (13 February

1994), philosopher Richard Rorty urges Americans, especially the American left, not to disdain patriotism as a value, and indeed to give central importance to "the emotion of national pride" and "a sense of shared national identity." Rorty argues that we cannot even criticize ourselves well unless we also "rejoice" in our American identity and define ourselves fundamentally in terms of that identity. Rorty seems to hold that the primary alternative to a politics based on patriotism and national identity is what he calls a "politics of difference," one based on internal divisions among America's ethnic, racial, religious, and other subgroups. He nowhere considers the possibility of a more international basis for political emotion and concern.

This is no isolated case. Rorty's piece responds to and defends Sheldon Hackney's recent call for a "national conversation" to discuss American identity.[1] As a participant in its early phase, I was made vividly aware that the project, as initially conceived,[2] proposed an inward-looking task, bounded by the borders of the nation, rather than considering ties of obligation and commitment that join America to the rest of the world. As with Rorty's piece, the primary contrast drawn in the project was between a politics based on ethnic and racial and religious difference and a politics based on a shared national identity. What we share as both rational and mutually dependent human beings was simply not on the agenda.

One might wonder, however, how far the politics of nationalism really is from the politics of difference. *The Home and the World* (better known, perhaps, in Satyajit Ray's haunting film of the same title) is a tragic story of the defeat of a reasonable and principled cosmopolitanism by the forces of nationalism and ethnocentrism. I believe that Tagore sees deeply when he observes that, at bottom, nationalism and ethnocentric particularism are not alien to one

another, but akin – that to give support to nationalist sentiments subverts, ultimately, even the values that hold a nation together, because it substitutes a colorful idol for the substantive universal values of justice and right. Once someone has said, I am an Indian first, a citizen of the world second, once he or she has made that morally questionable move of self-definition by a morally irrelevant characteristic, then what, indeed, will stop that person from saying, as Tagore's characters so quickly learn to say, I am a Hindu first, and an Indian second, or I am an upper-caste landlord first, and a Hindu second? Only the cosmopolitan stance of the landlord Nikhil – so boringly flat in the eyes of his young wife Bimala and his passionate nationalist friend Sandip – has the promise of transcending these divisions, because only this stance asks us to give our first allegiance to what is morally good – and that which, being good, I can commend as such to all human beings.

Proponents of nationalism in politics and in education frequently make a weak concession to cosmopolitanism. They may argue, for example, that although nations should in general base education and political deliberation on shared national values, a commitment to basic human rights should be part of any national education system, and that this commitment will in a sense hold many nations together.[3] This seems to be a fair comment on practical reality; and the emphasis on human rights is certainly necessary for a world in which nations interact all the time on terms (let us hope) of justice and mutual respect.

But is it sufficient? As students here grow up, is it sufficient for them to learn that they are above all citizens of the United States but that they ought to respect the basic human rights of citizens of India, Bolivia, Nigeria, and Norway? Or should they – as I think – in addition to giving special attention to the history and current situation of their own nation, learn a good deal more than they frequently do about the rest of the world in which they live, about India and Bolivia and Nigeria and Norway and their histories, problems, and comparative successes? Should they learn only that citizens of India have equal basic human rights, or should they also learn about the problems of hunger and pollution in India, and the implications of these problems for the larger issues of global hunger and global ecology? Most important, should they be taught that they are, above all, citizens of the United States, or should they instead be taught that they are, above all, citizens of a world of human beings, and that, while they happen to be situated in the United States, they have to share this world with the citizens of other countries? I suggest four arguments for the second concept of education, which I call *cosmopolitan education*. But first I introduce a historical digression, which traces cosmopolitanism to its origins, and in the process recover some excellent arguments that have traditionally supported it.

II

When Diogenes the Cynic replied, "I am a citizen of the world," he meant, apparently, that he refused to be defined by his local origins and group memberships, so central to the self-image of the conventional Greek male; instead, he defined himself in terms of more universal aspirations and concerns. The Stoics, who followed his lead, further developed his image of the *kosmou politês* (world citizen) arguing that each of us dwells, in effect, in two communities – the local community of our birth, and the community of human argument and aspiration that "is truly great and truly common, in which we look neither to this corner nor to that, but measure the boundaries of our nation by the sun" (Seneca, *De Otio*). It is this community that is, fundamentally, the source of

our moral obligations. With respect to the most basic moral values, such as justice, "We should regard all human beings as our fellow citizens and neighbors" (Plutarch, *On the Fortunes of Alexander*). We should regard our deliberations as, first and foremost, deliberations about human problems of people in particular concrete situations, not problems growing out of a national identity that is altogether unlike that of others. Diogenes knew that the invitation to think as a world citizen was, in a sense, an invitation to be an exile from the comfort of patriotism and its easy sentiments, to see our own ways of life from the point of view of justice and the good. The accident of where one is born is just that, an accident; any human being might have been born in any nation. Recognizing this, his Stoic successors held, we should not allow differences of nationality or class or ethnic membership or even gender to erect barriers between us and our fellow human beings. We should recognize humanity wherever it occurs, and give its fundamental ingredients, reason and moral capacity, our first allegiance and respect.

This clearly did not mean that the Stoics were proposing the abolition of local and national forms of political organization and the creation of a world state. Their point was even more radical: that we should give our first allegiance to no mere form of government, no temporal power, but to the moral community made up by the humanity of all human beings. The idea of the world citizen is in this way the ancestor and the source of Kant's idea of the "kingdom of ends," and has a similar function in inspiring and regulating moral and political conduct. One should always behave so as to treat with equal respect the dignity of reason and moral choice in every human being. It is this concept that also inspires Tagore's novel, as the cosmopolitan landlord struggles to stem the tide of nationalism and factionalism by appeals to universal moral norms. Many of the speeches of the character Nikhil were drawn from Tagore's own cosmopolitan political writings.

Stoics who hold that good civic education is education for world citizenship recommend this attitude on three grounds. First, they hold that the study of humanity as it is realized in the whole world is valuable for self-knowledge: we see ourselves more clearly when we see our ways in relation to those of other reasonable people.

Second, they argue, as does Tagore, that we will be better able to solve our problems if we face them in this way. No theme is deeper in Stoicism than the damage done by faction and local allegiances to the political life of a group. Political deliberation, they argue, is sabotaged again and again by partisan loyalties, whether to one's team at the Circus or to one's nation. Only by making our fundamental allegiance to the world community of justice and reason do we avoid these dangers.

Finally, they insist that the stance of the *kosmou politês* is intrinsically valuable, for it recognizes in people what is especially fundamental about them, most worthy of respect and acknowledgment: their aspirations to justice and goodness and their capacities for reasoning in this connection. These qualities may be less colorful than local or national traditions and identities – it is on this basis that the young wife in Tagore's novel spurns them in favor of qualities in the nationalist orator Sandip that she later comes to see as superficial – but they are, the Stoics argue, both lasting and deep.

The Stoics stress that to be a citizen of the world one does not need to give up local identifications, which can be a source of great richness in life. They suggest that we think of ourselves not as devoid of local affiliations, but as surrounded by a series of concentric circles. The first one encircles the self, the next takes in the immediate family, then follows the extended family, then, in order, neighbors or local groups, fellow city-dwellers, and fellow countrymen – and we can easily add to this list groupings based on ethnic, linguistic, historical, professional, gender, or sexual identities. Outside all these circles is the largest one, humanity as a whole. Our task as citizens of the world will be to "draw the circles somehow toward the center" (Stoic philosopher Hierocles, 1st–2nd CE), making all human beings more like our fellow city-dwellers, and so on. We need not give up our special affections and identifications, whether ethnic or gender-based or religious. We need not think of them as superficial, and we may think of our identity as constituted partly by them. We may and should devote special attention to them in education. But we should also work to make all human beings part of our community of dialogue and concern, base our political deliberations on that interlocking commonality, and give the circle that defines our humanity special attention and respect.

In educational terms, this means that students in the United States, for example, may continue to regard themselves as defined partly by their particular loves – their families, their religious, ethnic, or racial communities, or even their country. But they must also, and centrally, learn to recognize humanity wherever they encounter it, undeterred by traits that are strange to them, and be eager to understand humanity in all its strange guises. They must learn enough about the different to recognize common aims, aspirations, and values, and enough about these common ends to see how variously they are instantiated in the many cultures and their histories. Stoic writers insist that the vivid imagining of the different is an essential task of education, and that it requires, in turn, a mastery of many facts about the different. Marcus Aurelius gives himself the following advice, which might be called the basis for cosmopolitan education: "Accustom yourself not to be inattentive to what another person says, and as far as possible enter into that person's mind" (VI. 53). "Generally," he adds, "one must first learn many things before one can judge another's action with understanding."

A favored exercise in this process of world thinking is to conceive of the entire world of human beings as a single body, its many people as so many limbs. Referring to the fact that it takes only changing a single letter in Greek to convert the word "limb" (*melos*) into the word "part" (*meros*), Marcus says: "If, changing the word, you call yourself merely a [detached] part rather than a limb, you do not yet love your fellow men from the heart, nor derive complete joy from doing good; you will do it merely as a duty, not as doing good to yourself" (VII. 13). It is important to recall that, as emperor, he gave himself that advice in connection with daily duties that required coming to grips with the cultures of remote and, initially, strange civilizations, such as Parthia and Sarmatia.

I would like to see education adopt this cosmopolitan Stoic stance. The organic model could, of course, be abused – if, for example, it was taken to deny the fundamental importance of the separateness of people and of fundamental personal liberties. Stoics were not always sufficiently attentive to these values and to their political salience; in that sense, their thought is not always a good basis for a scheme of democratic deliberation and education. But as the image is primarily intended – as a reminder of the interdependence of all human beings and communities – it has fundamental significance. There is clearly a huge amount to be said about how such ideas might be realized in curricula at many levels. Instead of beginning that more concrete task, however, I focus on the present day and offer four arguments for making world citizenship, rather than democratic or national citizenship, the focus for civic education.

III

Through Cosmopolitan Education, We Learn More about Ourselves

One of the greatest barriers to rational deliberation in politics is the unexamined feeling that one's own preferences and ways are neutral and natural. An education that takes national boundaries as morally salient too often reinforces this kind of irrationality, by lending to what is an accident of history a false aim of moral weight and glory. By looking at ourselves through the lens of the other, we come to see what in our practices is local and nonessential, what is more broadly or deeply shared. Our nation is appallingly ignorant of most of the rest of the world. I think this means that it is also, in many crucial ways, ignorant of itself.

To give just one example of this: If we want to understand our own history and our choices about child-rearing and the structure of the family, we are helped immeasurably by looking around the world to see in what configurations families exist, and through what strategies children are in fact being cared for. (This would include a study of the history of the family, both in our own and other traditions.) Such a study can show us, for example, that the two-parent nuclear family, in which the mother is the primary homemaker and the father the primary breadwinner, is by no means a pervasive style of child-rearing in today's world. The extended family, clusters of families, the village, women's associations – all these groups, and others, in various places in the world have major child-rearing responsibilities. Seeing this, we can begin to ask questions – for example, about how much child abuse there is in a family that involves grandparents and other relatives in child-rearing, as compared with the relatively isolated Western-style nuclear family; or about how the different structures of child care support women's work.[4] If we do not undertake this kind of educational project, we risk assuming that the options familiar to us are the only ones there are, and that they are somehow "normal" and "natural" for all humans. Much the same can be said about conceptions of gender and sexuality, about conceptions of work and its division, about schemes of property holding, or about the treatment of children and the aged.

We Make Headway Solving Problems that Require International Cooperation

The air does not obey national boundaries. This simple fact can be, for children, the beginning of the recognition that, like it or not, we live in a world in which the destinies of nations are closely intertwined with respect to basic goods and survival itself. The pollution of third-world nations that are attempting to attain our high standard of living will, in some cases, end up in our air. No matter what account of these matters we will finally adopt, any intelligent deliberation about ecology – as, also, about the food supply and population – requires global planning, global knowledge, and the recognition of a shared future.

To conduct this sort of global dialogue, we need knowledge not only of the geography and ecology of other nations – something that would already entail much revision in our curricula – but also a great deal about their people, so that in talking with them we may be capable of respecting their traditions and commitments. Cosmopolitan education would supply the background necessary for this type of deliberation.

We Recognize Moral Obligations to the Rest of the World that are Real and that Otherwise would go Unrecognized

What are Americans to make of the fact that the high living standard we enjoy is one that

very likely cannot be universalized, at least given the present costs of pollution controls and the present economic situation of developing nations, without ecological disaster? If we take Kantian morality at all seriously, as we should, we need to educate our children to be troubled by this fact. Otherwise we are educating a nation of moral hypocrites who talk the language of universalizability but whose universe has a self-serving, narrow scope.

This point may appear to presuppose universalism, rather than being an argument in its favor. But here one may note that the values on which Americans may most justly pride themselves are, in a deep sense, Stoic values: respect for human dignity and the opportunity for each person to pursue happiness. If we really do believe that all human beings are created equal and endowed with certain inalienable rights, we are morally required to think about what that conception requires us to do with and for the rest of the world.

Once again, that does not mean that one may not permissibly give one's own sphere a special degree of concern. Politics, like child care, will be poorly done if each thinks herself equally responsible for all, rather than giving the immediate surroundings special attention and care. To give one's own sphere special care is justifiable in universalist terms, and I think this is its most compelling justification. To take one example, we do not really think our own children are morally more important than other people's children, even though almost all of us who have children would give our own children far more love and care than we give others'. It is good for children, on the whole, that things work this way, and that is why our special care is good, rather than selfish. Education may and should reflect those special concerns – for example, in a given nation, spending more time on that nation's history and politics. But my argument does entail the idea that we should not confine our thinking to our own sphere, that in making choices in both political and economic matters we should most seriously consider the right of other human beings to life, liberty, and the pursuit of happiness, and that we should work to acquire the knowledge that will enable us to deliberate well about those rights. I believe this sort of thinking will have large-scale economic and political consequences.

We Make a Consistent and Coherent Argument Based on Distinctions We are Prepared to Defend

In Richard Rorty's and Sheldon Hackney's eloquent appeals to shared values, there is something that makes me very uneasy. They seem to argue effectively when they insist on the centrality to democratic deliberation of certain values that bind all citizens together. But why should these values, which instruct us to join hands across boundaries of ethnicity, class, gender, and race, lose steam when they get to the borders of the nation? By conceding that a morally arbitrary boundary such as the boundary of the nation has a deep and formative role in our deliberations, we seems to deprive ourselves of any principled way of persuading citizens they should in fact join hands across these other barriers.

For one thing, the very same groups exist both outside and inside. Why should we think of people from China as our fellows the minute they dwell in a certain place, namely the United States, but not when they dwell in a certain other place, namely China? What is it about the national boundary that magically converts people toward whom we are both incurious and indifferent into people to whom we have duties of mutual respect? I think, in short, that we undercut the very case for multicultural respect within a nation by failing to make central to education a broader world respect. Richard Rorty's

patriotism may be a way of bringing all Americans together; but patriotism is very close to jingoism, and I'm afraid I don't see in Rorty's argument any proposal for coping with this very obvious danger.

Furthermore, the defense of shared national values in both Rorty and Hackney, as I understand it, requires appealing to certain basic features of human personhood that obviously also transcend national boundaries. So if we fail to educate children to cross those boundaries in their minds and imaginations, we are tacitly giving them the message that we don't really mean what we say. We say that respect should be accorded to humanity as such, but we really mean that Americans as such are worthy of special respect. And that, I think, is a story that Americans have told for far too long.

IV

Becoming a citizen of the world is often a lonely business. It is, as Diogenes said, a kind of exile – from the comfort of local truths, from this warm, nestling feeling of patriotism, from the absorbing drama of pride in oneself and one's own. In the writings of Marcus Aurelius (as in those of his American followers Emerson and Thoreau), a reader can sometimes sense a boundless loneliness, as if the removal of the props of habit and local boundaries had left life bereft of any warmth or security. If one begins life as a child who loves and trusts his or her parents, it is tempting to want to reconstruct citizenship along the same lines, finding in an idealized image of a nation a surrogate parent who will do one's thinking for one. Cosmopolitanism offers no such refuge; it offers only reason and the love of humanity, which may seem at times less colorful than other sources of belonging.

In Tagore's novel, the appeal to world citizenship fails. It fails because patriotism is full of color and intensity and passion, whereas cosmopolitanism seems to have a hard time gripping the imagination. And yet in its very failure, Tagore shows, it succeeds. For the novel is a story of education for world citizenship, since the entire tragic story is told by the widowed Bimala, who understands, if too late, that Nikhil's morality was vastly superior to Sandip's empty symbol-mongering, that what looked like passion in Sandip was egocentric self-exaltation, and that what looked like lack of passion in Nikhil contained a truly loving perception of her as a person. If one goes today to Santiniketan, a town several hours by train from Calcutta where Tagore founded his cosmopolitan university, Vishvabharati (which means "all the world") – one feels the tragedy once more. For all-the-world university has not achieved the anticipated influence or distinction within India, and the ideals of the cosmopolitan community of Santiniketan are increasingly under siege from militant forces of ethnocentric particularism and Hindu-fundamentalist nationalism. And yet, in the very decline of Tagore's ideal, which now threatens the very existence of the secular and tolerant Indian state, the observer sees its worth. To worship one's country as if it were a god is indeed to bring a curse upon it. Recent electoral reactions against Hindu nationalism give some grounds for optimism that this recognition of worth is widespread and may prove efficacious, averting a tragic ending of the sort that Tagore describes.

And since I am in fact optimistic that Tagore's ideal can be successfully realized in schools and universities in democracies around the world, and in the formation of public policy, let me conclude with a story of cosmopolitanism that has a happy ending. It is told by Diogenes Laertius about the courtship and marriage of the Cynic cosmopolitan philosophers Crates and Hipparchia (one of the most eminent female philosophers of antiquity), in order, presumably, to show that casting off the symbols of status and nation can sometimes be a way to succeed in love. The background is that Hipparchia is from a good family, attached, as most Greek families were, to social status and pedigree. They resent the cosmopolitan philosopher Crates, with his strange ideas of world citizenship and his strange disdain for rank and boundaries.

[Hipparchia] fell in love with Crates' arguments and his way of life and paid no attention to any of her suitors nor to wealth or high birth or good looks. Crates, though, was everything to her. Moreover, she told her parents that she would kill herself if she were not married off to him. So Crates was called on by her parents to talk their daughter out of it; he did all he could, but in the end he didn't persuade her. So he stood up and threw off his clothes in front of her and said, "Here is your bridegroom; these are his possessions; make your decision accordingly – for you cannot be my companion unless you undertake the same way of life." The girl chose him. Adopting the same clothing and style of life she went around with her husband and they copulated in public and they went off together to dinner parties. And once she went to a dinner party at the house of Lysimachus and there refuted Theodorus the Atheist, with a sophism like this: "If it wouldn't be judged wrong for Theodorus to do something, then it wouldn't be judged wrong for Hipparchia to do it either; but Theodorus does no wrong if he beats himself; so Hipparchia too does no wrong if she beats Theodorus." And when Theodorus could not reply to her argument, he ripped off her cloak. But Hipparchia was not upset or distraught as a woman would normally be. (DL 6.96–8)[5]

I am not exactly recommending Crates and Hipparchia as the marital ideal for students in my hypothetical cosmopolitan schools (or Theodorus the Atheist as their logic teacher).[6] But the story does reveal this: that the life of the cosmopolitan, who puts right before country and universal reason before the symbols of national belonging, need not be boring, flat, or lacking in love.

Notes

1   See Hackney's speech to the National Press Club, which was circulated to all participants in the planning meeting.

2   This is an important qualification. A short essay of mine on international issues was eventually included in the Scholar's Pamphlet issued by the project: "A National Conversation on American Pluralism and Identity: Scholar's Essays," MacArthur Foundation.

3   A recent example of this argument is in Amy Gutmann's "Multiculturalism and Democratic Education," presented at a conference on "Equality and Its Critics" held at Brown University in March 1994. My article originated as a comment on Gutmann's paper.

4   For some related questions about women and work, see the articles in Martha C. Nussbaum and Jonathan Glover (eds.), *Women, Culture, and Development* (Oxford: Clarendon Press, 1995).

5   I am grateful to Brad Inwood for permission to use his unpublished translation of this section.

6   I exempt Hipparchia from criticism, since she was clearly trying to show him up and she did not endorse the fallacious inference seriously.

Part VI

Cosmopolitanism

Introduction

Cosmopolitanism differs from nationalism in that while nationalists hold that we have special obligations to compatriots, cosmopolitans see our obligations to all persons as sharing in equality in the light of our common humanity. Perhaps the most influential modern work defending the cosmopolitan position is Immanuel Kant's famous *Perpetual Peace*, first published in 1795. In this essay, Kant argues that perpetual peace amongst states is possible (chapter 16). Of course, it cannot be said that we naturally live in a state of peace: peaceful relations must be established amongst us. Kant starts by arguing that if people needed to offer their consent in order for their state to go to war that the community would rarely, if ever, choose war over peace. A representative state would not only choose peace, but would help establish "a league of nations" so that they might use diplomacy with other states to avoid conflict and maintain peaceful relations. Kant denies that this situation would give rise to a world-state: instead, he sees the league of nations as "a federation" of similar, representative states. Such a view has become known by international relations scholars as the "democratic peace thesis": democracies do not wage war with other democracies. Kant's position is *cosmopolitan* because he argues that there is a universal standard, "the law of world citizenship," that helps govern the relations between nations. In other words, what is just for one state is just for all: the condition of perpetual peace is a possibility for all states. Without a league of nations, each state would be the ultimate arbiter of right and wrong – a view taken by classical realists, such as Hegel.[1] Instead, reason is our ultimate guide to discerning the demands of justice. Kant argues that through a league of nations each polity will gradually harmonize their views of justice leading to a shared understanding of justice and peaceful co-existence.

In chapter 17, Jürgen Habermas begins with a fascinating introduction to Kant's main arguments in *Perpetual Peace*, which is as illuminating as it is critical. This is followed by an examination of how this theory has fared historically. Habermas argues that Kant's "league of nations" is a community of nations. These nations are interrelated through international

---

[1] See G. W. F. Hegel, *Elements of the Philosophy of Right*, ed. Allen W. Wood, trans. H. B. Nisbet (Cambridge: Cambridge University Press, 1991), §§330–40 and my *Hegel's Political Philosophy* (Edinburgh: Edinburgh University Press, 2007), chapter 8.

trade and share a common political structure in the form of the United Nations. This situation creates the possibility of a form of "cosmopolitan democracy" of cosmopolitan citizens, rather than a world-state. Yet, Habermas remains skeptical of this political structure's ability to safeguard global human rights, given its lack of sufficient authority. He recommends a number of measures, including reform of the UN's Security Council and expansion of the World Court's powers. These reforms are necessary for a cosmopolitan world order: human rights violations should be seen as international criminal activities as judged by the international community, not by the whim of individual states. We possess these rights in virtue of our common humanity, not different nationalities.

The final reading is by Thomas W. Pogge. He defends moral universalism: the view that certain fundamental moral principles should be held equally by all persons. This position has major implications for global economic justice. Pogge spares no detail in painting a harrowing picture of the size and extent of severe global poverty. He nowhere denies that corrupt leaders have played a part in the continuation of severe poverty, taking advantage of an "international resource privilege" (related to "the resource curse") and repression. Nevertheless, Pogge argues that the global poor suffer from a global order, supported and maintained by wealthy states, that is coercively imposed upon them. We in the affluent West are responsible for severe poverty because the coercive global order we uphold generates deprivations amongst the global poor. These deprivations harm the most fundamental of moral principles, such as rights to life and liberty. Global economic justice is not only cosmopolitan in upholding a minimal standard of justice universally, but it demands structural changes in the global order in order to alleviate the continuation of severe poverty. Thus, we in the affluent West possess both a causal *and* moral responsibility to eradicate poverty amongst the global poor. We possess a negative duty of assistance in helping to fight global poverty because our activities contribute to its existence and scale, rather than a positive duty to assist the poor grounded in charity.

Cosmopolitanism has tremendous appeal to both the best in political philosophy's past and present. Whether or not it is worthy of defense instead of nationalism will be left for the reader to decide.

Chapter 16

*Perpetual Peace**
Immanuel Kant

Section I
Containing the Preliminary Articles for Perpetual Peace among States

"1.   No Treaty of Peace Shall Be Held Valid in Which There is Tacitly Reserved Matter for a Future War"

Otherwise a treaty would be only a truce, a suspension of hostilities but not peace, which means the end of all hostilities – so much so that even to attach the word "perpetual" to it is a dubious pleonasm. The causes for making future wars (which are perhaps unknown to the contracting parties) are without exception annihilated by the treaty of peace, even if they should be dug out of dusty documents by acute sleuthing. When one or both parties to a treaty of peace, being too exhausted to continue warring with each other, make a tacit reservation (*reservatio mentalis)* in regard to old claims to be elaborated only at some more favorable opportunity in the future, the treaty is made in bad

* From Immanuel Kant, *Perpetual Peace*, ed. Lewis White Beck (Indianapolis, IN: Bobbs–Merrill, 1957), Sections I and II, pp. 3–21, 23–34.

faith, and we have an artifice worthy of the casuistry of a Jesuit. Considered by itself, it is beneath the dignity of a sovereign, just as the readiness to indulge in this kind of reasoning is unworthy of the dignity of his minister.

But if, in consequence of enlightened concepts of statecraft, the glory of the state is placed in its continual aggrandizement by whatever means, my conclusion will appear merely academic and pedantic.

"2.   No Independent States, Large or Small, Shall Come under the Dominion of Another State by Inheritance, Exchange, Purchase, or Donation"

A state is not, like the ground which it occupies, a piece of property (*patrimonium*). It is a society of men whom no one else has any right to command or to dispose except the state itself. It is a trunk with its own roots. But to incorporate it into another state, like a graft, is to destroy its existence as a moral person, reducing it to a thing; such incorporation thus contradicts the idea of the original contract without which no right over a people can be conceived. Everyone knows to what dangers Europe, the only part of the world where this manner of acquisition is known, has been brought, even down to the most recent times, by the presumption that states could espouse one another; it is in part a new kind of industry for gaining ascendancy by means of family alliances and without expenditure of forces, and in part a way of extending one's domain. Also the hiring-out of troops by one state to another, so that they can be used against an enemy not common to both, is to be counted under this principle; for in this manner the subjects, as though they were things to be manipulated at pleasure, are used and also used up.

"3.   Standing Armies (miles perpetuus) Shall in Time Be Totally Abolished"

For they incessantly menace other states by their readiness to appear at all times prepared for war; they incite them to compete with each other in the number of armed men, and there is no limit to this. For this reason, the cost of peace finally becomes more oppressive than that of a short war, and consequently a standing army is itself a cause of offensive war waged in order to relieve the state of this burden. Add to this that to pay men to kill or to be killed seems to entail using them as mere machines and tools in the hand of another (the state), and this is hardly compatible with the rights of mankind in our own person. But the periodic and voluntary military exercises of citizens who thereby secure themselves and their country against foreign aggression are entirely different.

The accumulation of treasure would have the same effect, for, of the three powers – the power of armies, of alliances, and of money – the third is perhaps the most dependable weapon. Such accumulation of treasure is regarded by other states as a threat of war, and if it were not for the difficulties in learning the amount, it would force the other state to make an early attack.

"4.   National Debts Shall Not Be Contracted with a View to the External Friction of States"

This expedient of seeking aid within or without the state is above suspicion when the purpose is domestic economy (e.g., the improvement of roads, new settlements, establishment of stores against unfruitful years, etc.). But as an opposing machine in the antagonism of powers, a credit system which grows beyond sight and which is yet a safe debt for the present requirements – because all the creditors do not require payment at one time – constitutes a dangerous money power. This ingenious invention of a commercial people [England] in this century is dangerous because it is a war treasure which exceeds the treasures of all other states; it cannot be exhausted except by default of taxes (which is inevitable), though it can be long delayed by the stimulus to trade which occurs through the reaction of credit on industry and commerce. This facility in making war, together with the inclination to do so on the part of rulers – an inclination which seems inborn in human nature – is thus a great hindrance to perpetual peace. Therefore, to forbid this credit system must be a preliminary article of perpetual peace all the more because it must eventually entangle many innocent states in the inevitable bankruptcy and openly harm them. They are therefore justified in allying themselves against such a state and its measures.

"5.   No State Shall by Force Interfere with the Constitution or Government of Another State"

For what is there to authorize it to do so? The offense, perhaps, which a state gives to the subjects of another state? Rather the example of the evil into which a state has fallen because of its lawlessness should serve as a warning. Moreover, the bad example which one free person affords another as a *scandalum acceptum* is not an infringement of his rights. But it would be quite different if a state, by internal rebellion, should fall into two parts, each of which pretended to be a separate state making claim to the whole. To lend assistance to one of these cannot to be considered an interference in the constitution of the other state (for it is then in a state of anarchy). But so long as the internal dissension has not come to this critical point, such interference by foreign powers would infringe on the rights of an independent people struggling with its internal disease; hence it would itself be an offense and would render the autonomy of all states insecure.

"6. No State Shall, during War, Permit Such Acts of Hostility Which Would Make Mutual Confidence in the Subsequent Peace Impossible: Such Are the Employment of Assassins (percussores), Poisoners (venefici), Breach of Capitulation and Incitement to Treason (perduellio) in the Opposing State"

These are dishonorable stratagems. For some confidence in the character of the enemy must remain even in the midst of war, as otherwise no peace could be concluded and the hostilities would degenerate into a war of extermination (*bellum internecinum*). War, however, is only the sad recourse in the state of nature (where there is no tribunal which could judge with the force of law) by which each state asserts its right by violence and in which neither party can be adjudged unjust (for that would presuppose a juridical decision); in lieu of such a decision, the issue of the conflict (as if given by a so-called "judgment of God") decides on which side justice lies. But between states no punitive war

(*bellum punitivum*) is conceivable, because there is no relation between them of master and servant.

It follows that a war of extermination, in which the destruction of both parties and of all justice can result, would permit perpetual peace only in the vast burial ground of the human race. Therefore, such a war and the use of all means leading to it must be absolutely forbidden. But that the means cited do inevitably lead to it is clear from the fact that these infernal arts, vile in themselves, when once used would not long be confined to the sphere of war. Take, for instance, the use of spies (*uti exploratoribus*). In this, one employs the infamy of others (which can never be entirely eradicated) only to encourage its persistence even into the state of peace, to the undoing of the very spirit of peace.

Although the laws stated are objectively, i.e., in so far as they express the intention of rulers, mere prohibitions (*leges prohibitivae*), some of them are of that strict kind which hold regardless of circumstances (*leges strictae*) and which demand prompt execution. Such are Nos. 1, 5, and 6. Others, like Nos. 2, 3, and 4, while not exceptions from the rule of law, nevertheless are subjectively broader (*leges latae*) in respect to their observation, containing permission to delay their execution without, however, losing sight of the end. This permission does not authorize, under No. 2, for example, delaying until doomsday [. . .] the re-establishment of the freedom of states which have been deprived of it – i.e., it does not permit us to fail to do it, but it allows a delay to prevent precipitation which might injure the goal striven for. For the prohibition concerns only the manner of acquisition which is no longer permitted, but not the possession, which, though not bearing a requisite title of right, has nevertheless been held lawful in all states by the public opinion of the time (the time of the putative acquisition).

Section II
Containing the Definitive Articles for Perpetual Peace among States

The state of peace among men living side by side is not the natural state (*status naturalis*); the natural state is one of war. This does not always mean open hostilities, but at least an unceasing threat of war. A state of peace, therefore, must be *established*, for in order to be secured against hostility it is not sufficient that hostilities simply be not committed; and, unless this security is pledged to each by his neighbor (a thing that can occur only in a civil state), each may treat his neighbor, from whom he demands this security, as an enemy.[1]

First Definitive Article for Perpetual Peace

"The Civil Constitution of Every State Should Be Republican"

The only constitution which derives from the idea of the original compact, and on which all juridical legislation of a people must be based, is the republican.[2] This constitution is established, firstly, by principle of the freedom of the members of a society (as men); secondly, by principles of dependence of all upon a single common legislation (as subjects); and, thirdly, by the law of their equality (as citizens). The republican constitution, therefore, is, with respect to law, the one which is the original basis of every form of civil constitution. The only question now is: Is it also the one which can lead to perpetual peace?

The republican constitution, besides the purity of its origin (having sprung from the pure source of the concept of law), also gives a favorable prospect for the desired consequence, i.e., perpetual peace. The reason is this: if the consent of the citizens required in order to decide that war should be declared (and in this constitution it cannot but be the case), nothing is more natural than that they would be very cautious in commencing such a poor game, decreeing for themselves all the calamities of war. Among the latter would be: having to fight, having to pay the costs of war from their own resources, having painfully to repair the devastation war leaves behind, and, to fill up the measure of evils, load themselves with a heavy national debt that would embitter peace itself and that can never be liquidated on account of constant wars in the future. But, on the other hand, in a constitution which is not republican, and under which the subjects are not citizens, a declaration of war is the easiest thing in the world to decide upon, because war does not require of the ruler, who is the proprietor and not a member of the state, the least sacrifice of the pleasures of his table, the chase, his country houses, his court functions, and the like. He may, therefore, resolve on war as on a pleasure party for the most trivial reasons, and with perfect indifference leave the justification which decency requires to the diplomatic corps who are ever ready to provide it.

In order not to confuse the republican constitution with the democratic (as is commonly done), the following should be noted. The forms of a state (*civitas*) can be divided either according to the persons who possess the sovereign power or according to the mode of administration exercised over the people by the chief, whoever he may be. The first is properly called the form of sovereignty (*forma imperii*), and there are only three possible forms of it: autocracy, in which one, aristocracy, in which some associated together, or democracy, in which all those who constitute society, possess sovereign power. They may be characterized, respectively, as the power of a monarch, of the nobility, or of the people. The second division is that by the form of government (*forma regiminis*) and is based on the way in which the state makes use of its power; this way is based on the constitution, which is the act of the general will through which the many persons become one nation. In this respect government is either republican or despotic. Republicanism is the political principle of the separation of the executive power (the administration) from the legislative; despotism is that of the autonomous execution by the state of laws which it has itself decreed. Thus in a despotism the public will is administered by the ruler as his own will. Of the three forms of the state, that of democracy is, properly speaking, necessarily a despotism, because it establishes an executive power in which "all" decide for or even against one who does not agree; that is, "all," who are not quite all, decide, and this is a contradiction of the general will with itself and with freedom.

Every form of government which is not representative is, properly speaking, without form. The legislator can unite in one and the same person his function as legislative and as executor of his will just as little as the universal of the major premise in a syllogism can also be the subsumption of the particular under the universal in the minor. And even though the other two constitutions are always defective to the extent that they do leave room for this mode of administration, it is at least possible for them to assume a mode of government conforming to the spirit of a representative system (as when Frederick II at least *said* he was merely the first servant of the state). On the other hand, the democratic mode of government makes this impossible, since everyone wishes to be master. Therefore, we can say: the smaller the personnel of the government (the smaller the number of rulers), the greater is their representation and the more nearly the constitution approaches to the possibility of republicanism; thus the constitution may be expected by gradual reform finally to raise itself to republicanism. For these reasons it is more difficult for an aristocracy than for a monarchy to achieve the one completely juridical constitution, and it is impossible for a democracy to do so except by violent revolution.

The mode of government, however, is incomparably more important to the people than the form of sovereignty, although much depends on the greater or lesser suitability of the latter to the end of [good] government. To conform to the concept of law, however, government must have a representative form, and in this system only a republican mode of government is possible; without it, government is despotic and arbitrary, whatever the constitution may be. None of the ancient so-called "republics" knew this system, and they all finally and inevitably degenerated into despotism under the sovereignty of one, which is the most bearable of all forms of despotism.

Second Definitive Article for a Perpetual Peace

"The Law of Nations Shall be Founded on a Federation of Free States"

Peoples, as states, like individuals, may be judged to injure one another merely by their coexistence in the state of nature (i.e., while independent of external laws). Each of them may and should for the sake of its own security demand that the others enter with it into a constitution similar to the civil constitution, for under such a constitution each can be secure in his right. This would be a league of nations, but it would not have to be a state consisting of nations. That would be contradictory, since a state implies the relation of a superior (legislating) to an inferior (obeying), i.e., the people, and many nations in one state would then constitute only one nation. This contradicts the presupposition, for here we have to weigh the rights of nations against each other so far as they are distinct states and not amalgamated into one.

When we see the attachment of savages to their lawless freedom, preferring ceaseless combat to subjection to a lawful constraint which they might establish, and thus preferring senseless freedom to rational freedom, we regard it with deep contempt as barbarity, rudeness, and a brutish degradation of humanity. Accordingly, one would think that civilized people (each united in a state) would hasten all the more to escape, the sooner the better, from such a depraved condition. But, instead, each state places its majesty (for it is absurd to speak of the majesty of the people) in being subject to no external juridical restraint, and the splendor of its sovereign consists in the fact that many thousands stand at his command to sacrifice themselves for something that does not concern them and without his needing to place himself in the least danger. The chief difference between European and American savages lies in the fact that many tribes of the latter have been eaten by their enemies, while the former know how to make better use of their conquered enemies than to dine off them; they know better how to use them to increase the number of their subjects and thus the quantity of instruments for even more extensive wars.

When we consider the perverseness of human nature which is nakedly revealed in the uncontrolled relations between nations (this perverseness being veiled in the state of civil law by the constraint exercised by government), we may well be astonished that the word "law" has not yet been banished from war politics as pedantic, and that no state has yet been bold enough to advocate this point of view. Up to the present, Hugo Grotius, Pufendorf, Vattel, and many other irritating comforters have been cited in justification of war, though their code, phil-osophically or diplomatically formulated, has not and cannot have the least legal force, because states as such do not stand under a common external power. There is no instance on record that a state has ever been moved to desist from its purpose because of arguments backed up by the testimony of such great men. But the homage which each state pays (at least in words) to the concept of law proves that there is slumbering in man an even greater moral disposition to become master of the evil principle in himself (which he cannot disclaim) and to hope for the same from others. Otherwise the word "law" would never be pronounced by states which wish to war upon one another; it would be used only ironically, as a Gallic prince interpreted it when he said, "It is the prerogative which nature has given the stronger that the weaker should obey him."

States do not plead their cause before a tribunal; war alone is their way of bringing suit. But by war and its favorable issue in victory, right is not decided, and though by a treaty of peace this particular war is brought to an end, the state of war, of always finding a new pretext to hostilities, is not terminated. Nor can this be declared wrong, considering the fact that in this state each is the judge of his own case. Notwithstanding, the obligation which men in a lawless condition have under the natural law, and which requires them to abandon the state of nature, does not quite apply to states under the law of nations, for as states they already have an internal juridical constitution and have thus outgrown compulsion from others to submit to a more extended lawful constitution according to their ideas of right. This is true in spite of the fact that reason, from its throne of supreme moral legislating authority, absolutely condemns war as a legal recourse and makes a state of peace a direct duty, even though peace cannot be established or secured except by a compact among nations.

For these reasons there must be a league of a particular kind, which can be called a league of peace (*foedus pacificum*), and which would be distinguished from a treaty of peace (*pactum pacis*) by the fact that the latter terminates only one war, while the former seeks to make an end of all wars forever. This league does not tend to any dominion over the power of the state but only to the maintenance and security of the freedom of the state itself and of other states in league with it, without there being any need for them to submit to civil laws and their compulsion, as men in a state of nature must submit.

The practicability (objective reality) of this idea of federation, which should gradually spread to all states and thus lead to perpetual peace, can be proved. For if fortune directs that a powerful and enlightened people can make itself a republic, which by its nature must be included to perpetual peace, this gives a fulcrum to the federation with other states so that they may adhere to it and thus secure freedom under the idea of the law of nations. By more and more such associations, the federation may be gradually extended.

We may readily conceive that a people should say, "There ought to be no war among us, for we want to make ourselves into a state; that is, we want to establish a supreme legislative, executive, and judiciary power which will reconcile our differences peaceably." But when this state says, "There ought to be no war between myself and other states, even though I acknowledge no supreme legislative power by which our rights are mutually guaranteed," it is not at all clear on what I can base my confidence in my own rights unless it is the free federation, the surrogate of the civil social order, which reason necessarily associates with the concept of the law of nations – assuming that something is really meant by the latter.

The concept of a law of nations as a right to make war does not really mean anything, because it is then a law of deciding what is right by unilateral maxims through force and not by universally valid public laws which restrict the freedom of each one. The only conceivable meaning of such a law of nations might be that it serves men right who are so inclined that they should destroy each other and thus find perpetual peace in the vast grate that swallows both the atrocities and their perpetrators. For states in their relation to each other, there cannot be any reasonable way out of the lawless condition which entails only war except that they, like individual men, should give up their savage (lawless) freedom, adjust themselves to the constraints of public law, and thus establish a continuously growing state consisting of various nations (*civitas gentium*), which will ultimately include all the nations of the world. But under the idea of the law of nations they do not wish this, and reject in practice what is correct in theory. If all is not to be lost, there can be, then, in place of the positive idea of a world republic, only the negative surrogate of an alliance which averts war, endures, spreads, and holds hack the stream of those hostile passions which fear the law, though such an alliance is in constant peril of their breaking loose again. [. . .]

Third Definitive Article for a Perpetual Peace

"The Law of World Citizenship Shall Be Limited to Conditions of Universal Hospitality"

Here, as in the preceding articles, it is not a question of philanthropy but of right. Hospitality means the right of a stranger not to be treated as an enemy when he arrives in the land of another. One may refuse to receive him when this can be done without causing his destruction; but, so long as he peacefully occupies his place, one may not treat him with hostility. It is not the right to be a permanent visitor that one may demand. A special beneficent agreement would be needed in order to give an outsider a right to become a fellow inhabitant for a certain length of time. It is only a right of temporary sojourn, a right to associate, which all men have. They have it by virtue of their common possession of the surface of the earth, where, as a globe, they cannot infinitely disperse and hence must finally tolerate the presence of each other. Originally, no one had more right than another to a particular part of the earth.

Uninhabitable parts of the earth – the sea and the deserts – divide this community of all men, but the ship and the camel (the desert ship) enable them to approach each other across these unruled regions and to establish communication by using the common right to the face of the earth, which belongs to human beings generally. The inhospitality of the inhabitants of coasts (for instance, of the Barbary Coast) in robbing ships in neighboring seas or enslaving stranded travelers, or the inhospitality of the inhabitants of the deserts (for instance, the Bedouin Arabs) who view contact with nomadic tribes as conferring the right to plunder them, is thus opposed to natural law, even though it extends the right of hospitality, i.e., the privilege of foreign arrivals, no further than to conditions of the possibility of seeking to communicate with the prior inhabitants. In this way distant parts of the world can come into peaceable relations with each other, and these are finally publicly established by law. Thus the human race can gradually be brought closer and closer to a constitution establishing world citizenship.

But to this perfection compare the inhospitable actions of the civilized and especially of the commercial states of our part of the world. The injustice which they show to lands and peoples they visit (which is equivalent to conquering them) is carried by them to terrifying lengths. [. . .]

Since the narrower or wider community of the peoples of the earth has developed so far that a violation of rights in one place is felt throughout the world, the idea of a law of world citizenship is no high-flown or exaggerated notion. It is a supplement to the unwritten code of the civil and international law, indispensable for the maintenance of the public human rights and hence also of perpetual peace. One cannot flatter oneself into believing one can approach this peace except under the condition outlined here.

First Supplement
Of the Guarantee for
Perpetual Peace

The guarantee of perpetual peace is nothing less than that great artist, nature (*nature daedala rerum*). In her mechanical course we see that her aim is to produce a harmony among men, against their will and indeed through their discord. As a necessity working according to laws we do not know, we call it destiny. But, considering its design in world history, we call it "providence," inasmuch as we discern in it the profound wisdom of a higher cause which predetermines the course of nature and directs it to the objective final end of the human race. We do not observe or infer this providence in the cunning contrivances of nature, but, as in questions of the relation of the form of things to ends in general, we can and must supply it from our own minds in order to conceive of its possibility by analogy to actions of human art. The idea of the relationship and harmony between these actions and the end which reason directly assigns to us is transcendent from a theoretical point of view; from a practical standpoint, with respect, for example, to the ideal of perpetual peace, the concept is dogmatic and its reality is well established, and thus the mechanism of nature may be employed to that end. The use of the word "nature" is more fitting to the limits of human reason and more modest than an expression indicating a providence unknown to us. This is especially true when we are dealing with questions of theory and not of religion, as at present, for human reason in questions of the relation of effects to their causes must remain within the limits of possible experience. On the other hand, the use of the word "providence" here intimates the possession of wings like those of Icarus, conducting us toward the secret of its unfathomable purpose.

Before we more narrowly define the guarantee which nature gives, it is necessary to examine the situation in which she has placed her actors on her vast stage, a situation which finally assures peace among them. Then we shall see how she accomplishes the latter. Her preparatory arrangements are:

1 In every region of the world she has made it possible for men to live.
2 By war she has driven them even into the most inhospitable regions in order to populate them.
3 By the same means, she has forced them into more or less lawful relations with each other.

That in the cold wastes by the Arctic Ocean the moss grows which the reindeer digs from the snow in order to make itself the prey or the conveyance of the Ostyak or Samoyed; or that the saline sandy deserts are inhabited by the camel which appears created as it were in order that they might not go unused – that is already wonderful. Still clearer is the end when we see how besides the furry animals of the Arctic there are also the seal, the walrus, and the whale which afford the inhabitants food from their flesh and warmth from their blubber. But the care of nature excites the greatest wonder when

we see how she brings wood (though the inhabitants do not know whence it comes) to these barren climates, without which they would have neither canoes, weapons, nor huts, and when we see how these natives are so occupied with their war against the animals that they live in peace with each other – but what drove them there was presumably nothing else than war.

The first instrument of war among the animals which man learned to tame and to domesticate was the horse (for the elephant belongs to later times, to the luxury of already established states). The art of cultivating certain types of plants (grain) whose original characteristics we do not know, and the increase and improvement of fruits by transplantation and grafting (in Europe perhaps only the crab apple and the wild pear), could arise only under conditions prevailing in already established states where property was secure. Before this could take place, it was necessary that men who had first subsisted in anarchic freedom by hunting, fishing, and sheepherding should have been forced into an agricultural life. Then salt and iron were discovered. These were perhaps the first articles of commerce for the various peoples and were sought far and wide; in this way a peaceful traffic among nations was established, and thus understanding, conventions, and peaceable relations were established among the most distant peoples.

As nature saw to it that men *could* live everywhere in the world, she also despotically willed that they *should* do so, even against their inclination and without this *ought* being based on a concept of duty to which they were bound by a moral law. She chose war as the means to this end [. . .].

War itself requires no special motive but appears to be engrafted on human nature; it passes even for something noble, to which the love of glory impels men quite apart from any selfish urges. Thus among the American savages, just as much as among those of Europe during the age of chivalry, military valor is held to be of great worth in itself, not only during war (which is natural) but in order that there should be war. Often war is waged only in order to show valor; thus an inner dignity is ascribed to war itself, and even some philosophers have praised it as an ennoblement of humanity, forgetting the pronouncement of the Greek who said, "War is an evil inasmuch as it produces more wicked men than it takes away." So much for the measures nature takes to lead the human race, considered as a class of animals, to her own end.

Now we come to the question concerning that which is most essential in the design of perpetual peace: What has nature done with regard to this end which man's own reason makes his duty? That is, what has nature done to favor man's moral purpose, and how has she guaranteed (by compulsion but without prejudice to his freedom) that he shall do that which he ought to but does not do under the laws of freedom? This question refers to all three phases of public law, namely, civil law, the law of nations, and the law of world citizenship. If I say of nature that she wills that this or that occur, I do not mean that she imposes a duty on us to do it, for this can be done only by free practical reason; rather I mean that she herself does it, whether we will or not [. . .].

1.   Even if a people were not forced by internal discord to submit to public laws, war would compel them to do so, for we have already seen that nature has placed each people near another which presses upon it, and against this it must form itself into a state in order to defend itself. Now the republican constitution is the only one entirely fitting to the rights of man. But it is the most difficult to establish and even harder to preserve, so that many say a republic would have to be a nation of angels, because men with their selfish inclinations are not capable of a constitution of such

sublime form. But precisely with these inclinations nature comes to the aid of the general will established on reason, which is revered even though impotent in practice. Thus it is only a question of a good organization of the state (which does lie in man's power), whereby the powers of each selfish inclination are so arranged in opposition that one moderates or destroys the ruinous effect of the other. The consequence for reason is the same as if none of them existed, and man is forced to be a good citizen even if not a morally good person.

The problem of organizing a state, however hard it may seem, can be solved even for a race of devils, if only they are intelligent. The problem is: "Given a multitude of rational beings requiring universal laws for their preservation, but each of whom is secretly inclined to exempt himself from them, to establish a constitution in such a way that, although their private intentions conflict, they check each other, with the result that their public conduct is the same as if they had no such intentions."

A problem like this must be capable of solution; it does not require that we know how to attain the moral improvement of men but only that we should know the mechanism of nature in order to use it on men, organizing the conflict of the hostile intentions present in a people in such a way that they must compel themselves to submit to coercive laws. Thus a state of peace is established in which laws have force. We can see, even in actual states, which are far from perfectly organized, that in their foreign relations they approach that which the idea of right prescribes. This is so in spite of the fact that the intrinsic element of morality is certainly not the cause of it. (A good constitution is not to be expected from morality, but, conversely, a good moral condition of a people is to be expected only under a good constitution.) Instead of genuine morality, the mechanism of nature brings it to pass through selfish inclinations, which naturally conflict outwardly but which can be used by reason as a means for its own end, the sovereignty of law, and, as concerns the state, for promoting and securing internal and external peace.

This, then, is the truth of the matter: Nature inexorably wills that the right should finally triumph. What we neglect to do comes about by itself, though with great inconveniences to us. "If you bend the reed too much, you break it; and he who attempts too much attempts nothing" (Bouterwek).

2.   The idea of international law presupposes the separate existence of many independent but neighboring states. Although this condition is itself a state of war (unless a federative union prevents the outbreak of hostilities), this is rationally preferable to the amalgamation of states under one superior power, as this would end in one universal monarchy, and laws always lose in vigor what government gains in extent; hence a soulless despotism falls into anarchy after stifling the seeds of the good. Nevertheless, every state, or its ruler, desires to establish lasting peace in this way, aspiring if possible to rule the whole world. But nature wills otherwise. She employs two means to separate peoples and to prevent them from mixing: differences of language and of religion. These differences involve a tendency to mutual hatred and pretexts for war, but the progress of civilization and men's gradual approach to greater harmony in their principles finally leads to peaceful agreement, This is not like that peace which despotism (in the burial ground of freedom) produces through a weakening of all powers; it is, on the contrary, produced and maintained by their equilibrium in liveliest competition.

3.   Just as nature wisely separates nations, which the will of every state, sanctioned by the principles of international law, would gladly unite by artifice or force, nations which could not have secured themselves against violence and war by means of the law of world citizenship unite because of mutual interest. The spirit of commerce, which is incompatible with war, sooner or later gains the upper hand in every state. As the power of money is perhaps the most dependable of all the powers (means) included under the state power, states see themselves forced, without any moral urge, to promote honorable peace and by mediation to prevent war wherever it threatens to break out. They do so exactly as if they stood in perpetual alliances, for great offensive alliances are in the nature of the case rare and even less often successful.

In this manner nature guarantees perpetual peace by the mechanism of human passions. Certainly she does not do so with sufficient certainty for us to predict the future in any theoretical sense, but adequately from a practical point of view, making it our duty to work toward this end, which is not just a chimerical one.

Second Supplement
Secret Article for Perpetual Peace

A secret article in contracts under public law is objectively, i.e., from the standpoint of its content, a contradiction. Subjectively, however, a secret clause can be present in them, because the persons who dictate it might find it compromising to their dignity to declare openly that they are its authors.

The only article of this kind is contained in the statement: "The opinions of philosophers on the conditions of the possibility of public peace shall be consulted by those states armed for war."

But it appears humiliating to the legislative authority of a state, to whom we must naturally attribute the utmost wisdom, to seek instruction from subjects (the philosophers) on principles of conduct toward other states. It is nevertheless very advisable to do so. Therefore, the state tacitly and secretly invites them to give their opinions, that is, the state will let them publicly and freely talk about the general maxims of warfare and of the establishment of peace (for they will do that of themselves, provided they are not forbidden to do so). It does not require a particular convention among states to see that this is done, since their agreement on this point lies in an obligation already established by universal human reason which is morally legislative.

I do not mean that the state should give the principles of philosophers any preference over the decisions of lawyers (the representatives of the state power); I only ask that they be given a hearing. The lawyer, who has made not only the scales of right but also the sword of justice his symbol, generally uses the latter not merely to keep back all foreign influences from the former, but, if the scale does not sink the way he wishes, he also throws the sword into it (*vae victis*), a practice to which he often has the greatest temptation because he is not also a philosopher, even in morality. His office is only to apply positive laws, not to inquire whether they might not need improvement. The administrative function, which is the lower one in his faculty, he counts as the higher because it is invested with power (as is the case also with the other faculties [of medicine and theology]). The philosophical faculty occupies a very low rank against this allied power. Thus it is said of philosophy, for example, that she is the handmaiden to theology, and the other faculties claim as much. But one does not see distinctly whether she precedes her mistress with a flambeau or follows bearing her train.

That kings should philosophize or philosophers become kings is not to be expected. Nor is it to be wished, since the possession of power inevitably corrupts the untrammeled judgment of reason. But kings or kinglike peoples which rule themselves under laws of equality should not suffer the class of philosophers to disappear or to be silent, but should let them speak openly. This is indispensable to the enlightenment of the business of government, and, since the class of philosophers is by nature incapable of plotting and lobbying, it is above suspicion of being made up of propagandists.

Notes

[1] We ordinarily assume that no one may act inimically toward another except when he has been actively injured by the other. This is quite correct if both are under civil law, for, by entering into such a state, they afford each other the requisite security through the sovereign which has power over both. Man (or the people) in the state of nature deprives me of this security and injures me, if he is near me, by this mere status of his, even though he does not injure me actively (*facto*); he does so by the lawlessness of his condition (*statu iniusto*) which constantly threatens me. Therefore, I can compel him either to enter with me into a state of civil law or to remove himself from my neighborhood. The postulate which is basic to all the following articles is: All men who can reciprocally influence each other must stand under some civil constitution.

Every juridical constitution which concerns the person who stands under it is one of the following:

(1) The constitution conforming to the civil law of men in a nation (*ius civitatis*).
(2) The constitution conforming to the law of nations in their relation to one another (*ius gentium*).
(3) The constitution conforming to the law of world citizenship, so far as men and states are considered as citizens of a universal state of men, in their external mutual relationships (*ius cosmopoliticum*).

This division is not arbitrary, being necessary in relation to the idea of perpetual peace. For if only one state were related to another by physical influence and were yet in a state of nature, war would necessarily follow, and our purpose here is precisely to free ourselves of war.

2   Juridical (and hence) external freedom cannot be defined, as is usual, by the privilege of doing anything one wills so long as he does not injure another. For what is a privilege? It is the possibility of an action so far as one does not injure anyone by it. Then the definition would read: Freedom is the possibility of those actions by which one does no one an injury. One does another no injury (he may do as he pleases) only if he does another no injury – an empty tautology. Rather, my external (juridical) freedom is to be defined as follows: It is the privilege to lend obedience to no external laws except those to which I could have given consent. Similarly, external (juridical) equality in a state is that relationship among the citizens in which no one can lawfully bind another without at the same time subjecting himself to the law by which he also can be bound. No definition of juridical dependence is needed, as this already lies in the concept of a state's constitution as such.

The validity of these inborn rights, which are inalienable and belong necessarily to humanity, is raised to an even higher level by the principle of the juridical relation of man to higher beings, for, if he believes in them, he regards himself by the same principles as a citizen of a supersensuous world. For in what concerns my freedom, I have no obligation with respect to divine law, which can be acknowledged by my reason alone, except in so far as I could have give my consent to it. Indeed, it is only through the law of freedom of my own reason that I frame a concept of the divine will. With regard to the most sublime reason in the world that I can think of, with the exception of God – say, the great Aeon – when I do my duty in my post as he does in his, there is no reason under the law of equality why obedience to duty should fall only to me and the right to command only to him. The reason why this principle of equality does not pertain to our relation to God (as the principle of freedom does) is that this Being is the only one to which the concept of duty does not apply. [. . .]

Chapter 17

Kant's Idea of Perpetual Peace, with the Benefit of Two Hundred Years' Hindsight*
Jürgen Habermas

First espoused by the Abbé St. Pierre, "perpetual peace" is for Kant an ideal that lends intuitive force to the idea of a cosmopolitan order. In this way, Kant introduces a third dimension into his "Doctrine of Right." Along with the civil law of states and in place of international law, he now introduces an innovation with broad implications: the idea of a cosmopolitan law based on the rights of the world citizen. The republican order of a democratic constitutional state, founded on human rights, demanded more than a weak binding of states in their foreign affairs through international law. Rather, the legal order within each state was supposed to lead ultimately to a global legal order that unites all peoples and abolishes war. "All forms of the state are based in the idea of a constitution which is compatible with the natural rights of man, so that those who obey the law should act as a unified body of legislators. And if we accordingly think of the commonwealth in terms of the concepts of pure reason, it may be called a Platonic ideal [*respublica noumenon*], which is not an empty figment of the imagination, but the eternal norm of all civil constitutions whatsoever, and a means to abolish all wars."[1] It is the concluding phrase, "and a means to abolish all wars," that surprises us. It points toward the norms of international law which regulate war and peace, if only peremptorily; they are valid only until pacification through law shows the way to a cosmopolitan order that abolishes war, the possibility of which Kant develops in "Toward Perpetual Peace."

Of course, Kant developed this idea using the concepts drawn from the debates concerning modern natural law and the specific historical experiences of his times. Differences in conceptual framework and temporal distance now separate us from Kant. With the superior and undeserved knowledge of later generations, we see today that his proposals suffer from conceptual difficulties and that they are no longer appropriate to our historical experiences. In the following, I will therefore first sketch out the premises that constitute Kant's starting point. These premises affect all three steps of his argument: the definition of the goal, namely, perpetual peace; the description of the actual project, which takes the legal form of a federation of nations; and, finally, the solution to this problem posed by this project

* From James Bohman and Matthias Lutz-Bachmann (eds.), *Perpetual Peace: Essays on Kant's Cosmopolitan Ideal* (Cambridge, MA: MIT Press, 1997), pp. 113–53.

in the philosophy of history, the gradual realization of the idea of a cosmopolitan order. Following upon this analysis, in the second section I examine how Kant's idea of peace fares in light of the historical experience of the last 200 years. In the third section, I turn to the question of how it must he reformulated with a view to the contemporary global situation. The alternatives to the return to the state of nature proposed by legal scholars, political scientists, and philosophers have evoked strong objections to the universalism of the proposed cosmopolitan law and its politics of human rights, objections which lose their force once we draw the appropriate distinction between law and morality within the concept of human rights. Such a distinction also offers the key to a metacriticism of Carl Schmitt's influential arguments against the humanistic foundation of legal pacifism.

1

Kant defines the *goal* of the achievement of a "legal order" among peoples negatively, as the abolition of war: "There shall be no war," proclaiming that the "disastrous practice of war" must be brought to an end.[2] Kant justifies the desirability of such a peace through the evils of those forms of warfare which the princes of Europe were waging at that time with their mercenary armies. In discussing its evils, Kant mentions first and foremost not the victims of war but rather the "horrors of violence," the "devastation," and, above all, the plundering and impoverishment of a country resulting from the considerable burdens of debt that arise from war, as well as other possible consequences of war, including subjugation, the loss of liberty, and foreign domination. Added to them is moral decline brought about when subjects are induced to such criminal acts as spying and spreading of false information or reduced to the maliciousness of snipers or

assassins. Here Kant has in mind the panorama of limited war as it had been institutionalized in the system of the balance of power as a legitimate means to solve conflicts by international law ever since the Peace of Westphalia. The end of such a war defines the conditions of peace. And, as a specific peace treaty ends the evil of an individual war between nations, so the peace compact among all peoples "puts an end to war forever" and does away with the evils of war as such. This is the meaning of Kant's phrase "perpetual peace." But it is a peace as limited as the model of war upon which it is based.

Kant is thinking here of spatially limited wars between individual states or alliances, not of world wars. He is thinking of wars conducted between ministers and states, but not yet of anything like civil wars. He is thinking of technically limited wars that still permit the distinction between fighting troops and the civilian population, and not yet of anything like guerrilla warfare and the terror of bombardment. He is thinking of wars with politically defined aims, and not yet of anything like ideologically motivated wars of destruction and expulsion.[3] Given the premises of limited warfare, the normative regulation of international law extends only to rules for the conduct of war and for the settlement of peace. The "right to go to war" [*ius ad bellum*] is the basis for legal regulation both "during" and "after" war; it is, strictly speaking, no right at all, for it merely expresses the arbitrary freedom accorded the subjects of international law in the state of nature, that is, in the lawless condition that characterizes their external relations to each other.[4] The only criminal law backed by sanctions that can intervene into this lawless state relates to the conduct of war itself, and even then it is only carried out by the courts of those states that are currently waging war. War crimes are merely those crimes committed *during* war. Now that wars are unlimited, the concept of peace has also been correspondingly expanded to include the claim that war itself, in the form of a war of aggression, is a crime that deserves to be despised and punished. For Kant, however, there is not yet a crime *of* war.

While a perpetual peace provides one of its more important characteristics, it is only a symptom of a cosmopolitan order. Kant must still solve the *conceptual problem* of how this order could be thought of from the viewpoint of law. He must find the proper difference between cosmopolitan law and classical international law, and thus what is specific to *ius cosmopoliticum*.

Like all rights in the state of nature, international law is only provisionally valid; by contrast, cosmopolitan law resembles state sanctioned civil law in that both definitively end the state of nature. When describing the transition to the cosmopolitan order, Kant therefore repeatedly draws on the analogy to the first act of leaving the state of nature, through which the establishment of a particular state makes it possible for citizens of a particular area to live in legally guaranteed freedom. Just as the social contract ended the state of nature between individuals who are otherwise left to their own devices, so too, Kant suggests, the state of nature between warring states now comes to an end. In "Theory and Practice," published two years before "Toward Perpetual Peace," Kant draws strict parallels between these two processes. There he still speaks of a "universal state of all peoples, to whose powers all states shall freely submit themselves."[5] Here, too, he mentions the destruction of human well-being and the loss of freedom as the greatest evils of war, and then continues: "There is no possible way of counteracting this except a state based on the law of peoples, upon enforceable public laws to which each state must submit (by analogy to the civil state among individual human beings). For a lasting universal peace by means of the so-

called European balance of power is nothing but an illusion."[6] Kant speaks here of a "universal state of all peoples, under whose authority all states should freely submit themselves." But only two years later, in "Toward Perpetual Peace," Kant carefully distinguishes between "a federation of nations" and "a state of all peoples."

From now on a distinctly "cosmopolitan" order was to be distinguished from the legal order within states by virtue of the fact that, unlike individual citizens, states do not subject themselves to the public coercive laws of some supreme power; instead, they retain their existence as individual states. In the federation of free states that forgo war in their external relations, the sovereignty of each member remains inviolable. The states associated with one another in this way preserve their sovereign powers and jurisdiction and do not dissolve into a world republic modeled after a state writ large. In place of the "positive idea of a world republic" is put the "negative substitute of an enduring and gradually expanding federation likely to prevent war."[7] Such a federation emerges through sovereign acts of will exercised in many different contracts under international law, which are now no longer to be thought of on the model of the social contract. For these contracts do not establish any claims to enforceable rights by the parties over and against each other, but rather bind members to an alliance whose continued existence depends on an "enduring and voluntary association." But this act of association goes beyond the binding power of the international law of peoples only in virtue of its feature of "permanence." Hence, Kant compares the federation of nations to a "permanent congress of states."[8]

The contradictory character of this construction is quite apparent. In other passages, Kant asserts that a congress "merely signifies a voluntary gathering of various states that can be dissolved at any time, not an association which, like the American states, is based on a political constitution."[9] Kant never explains just how this union is to be permanent, the feature on which a civilized resolution of international conflict depends, without the binding character of law based on the establishment of something analogous to a constitution. On the one hand, Kant wants to preserve the sovereignty of its members by the proviso that they may dissolve their compact; this is what makes possible the comparison of the federation with congresses and voluntary associations. On the other hand, a federation that creates the conditions of peace in the long run must differ from merely provisional alliances to the extent that its members must feel *obligated* to subordinate their own *raison d'etat* to the jointly declared goal of "not deciding their differences by war, but by a process analogous to a court of law." Without this element of obligation, the peaceable congress of nations cannot become "permanent," nor can its voluntary association become "enduring"; instead, it would remain hostage to an unstable constellation of interests that is likely to degenerate and fall apart, much as the League of Nations did years later. Kant cannot have any *legal* obligation in mind here, since his federation of nations is not organized around the organs of a common government that could acquire coercive authority. Rather, he is forced to rely exclusively on each government's own *moral* self-binding. But such trust is hardly compatible with Kant's own soberly realistic descriptions of the politics of his times.

Kant is thoroughly aware of this problem, but he covers it over with a simple appeal to reason: "If a state says: 'There shall be no war between myself and other states even though I do not recognize any supreme legislative power which could secure my rights and whose rights I should in turn secure,' it is impossible to understand what justification I can have for placing any trust in my rights,

unless I can rely on some substitute for the union of civil society, namely, on the free federation. If the concept of a law of peoples is to have any significance, reason must connect it with a federation of this kind."[10] This assurance leaves open the decisive question: How is a permanent self-binding of states which continue as sovereign to be ensured? This is not even the empirical issue of how to approximate the idea; it is a conceptual problem with the idea itself. If the union of peoples is not a moral but a legal arrangement, then all the qualities of a "good constitutional state" that Kant enumerates some pages later would be present and would make it possible for such an organization to do more than rely on the "good moral culture" of its members; it now could, when appropriate, make its own binding demands.

Viewed historically, Kant's reticence concerning the project of a *constitutionally* organized community of peoples is certainly realistic. The democratic constitutional state, which had just emerged from the American and French Revolutions, was still the exception rather than the rule. The existing system of the balance of power functioned on the assumption that only sovereign states could be the subjects of the law of peoples. Under these conditions, external sovereignty designates the capacity of states, each acting independently in the international arena to defend the integrity of its borders by military means when needed. Internal sovereignty refers to the capacity, based on the state's monopoly over the means of violence, for maintaining peace and order by means of administrative power and positive law. *Raison d'etat* is thus defined according to the principles of a prudential power politics that includes the possibility of limited wars, whereby domestic policy is always subordinated to the primacy of foreign policy. The clear separation of foreign and domestic policy stems from a narrow and politically well-defined concept of power according to which, in the final analysis, power is measured in terms of the degree to which those in power have command over the means of violence stored in the barracks of the military and the police.

As long as this classical-modern world of nation states remains an unsurpassable conceptual limit, any attempt at a cosmopolitan constitution that does not respect the sovereignty of states necessarily appears unrealistic. This explains why Kant never considers the possibility of a community of peoples under the hegemony of a powerful state as a viable alternative; indeed, he always presents it with the image of a "universal monarchy."[11] Under such premises, such supreme political power would result in "the most terrible despotism."[12] Because Kant does not escape the limited horizon of his historical experience, it becomes equally difficult to establish any moral motivation for creating and maintaining a federation among free states that are all still dedicated to power politics. In order to provide a solution to this problem, Kant proposes a philosophy of history with a cosmopolitan intent, which is supposed to make plausible the improbable "agreement between politics and morality" through a hidden "intention of nature."

2

Kant identifies three naturally occurring tendencies which meet reason halfway and which explain why a federation of nations could be in the enlightened self-interest of states: the peaceful nature of republics, the power of world trade to create communal ties, and the function of the political public sphere. It is informative to cast a historical glance back at these arguments in two respects. On the one hand, they have been falsified by developments in the nineteenth and twentieth centuries. On the other, they refer to historical trends that betray a

peculiar dialectical quality. These very same trends reveal that the premises on which Kant based his theory reflect the conditions he perceived at the close of the eighteenth century that no longer hold. Yet these trends would seem to support the claim that a conception of cosmopolitan law that was properly reformulated in contemporary terms might well find support in a constellation of forces that meets it halfway.

(1)   Kant's first argument claims that international relations lose their bellicose character to the extent that the republican form of government is achieved within states; this is because the population of democratic constitutional states demand that their governments pursue peaceful policies out of their own self-interest. "If, as is the case under such a constitution, the consent of the citizens is required to decide whether or not war is declared, it is very natural that they will have great hesitation in embarking on so dangerous and costly a game."[13] This optimistic assumption has been disproved by the mobilizing power of an idea, the ambivalence of which Kant was in no position to perceive in 1795. Nationalism was certainly a vehicle for the desired transformation of subordinated subjects into active citizens who identify with their state. However, its existence makes the nation state no more peaceful than its predecessor, the dynastic absolutist state.[14] From the viewpoint of nationalist movements, the classical self-assertion of sovereign states gains the connotations of freedom and national independence. Therefore, the republican convictions of citizens create the willingness to fight and die for nation and fatherland. With some justification, Kant considered the mercenary armies of his day to be instruments for "the use of human beings as mere machines . . . in the hands of someone else" and called for the establishment of the citizen militia. But he was not able to foresee that

the mass mobilization of young men obligated to military service would stir nationalist passions and produce an age of devastating, ideologically unlimited wars of liberation.

At the same time, the idea that a democratic state domestically encourages a pacifistic stance toward the outside world is not completely false. Historical and statistical research shows that states with democratic constitutions do not necessarily conduct fewer wars than authoritarian regimes (of whatever kind), but that they are less likely to be warlike in their relations toward one another. This finding can be given an interesting interpretation.[15] To the extent that the universalist value orientations of a population accustomed to free institutions also influence foreign policy, the republican polity does not behave more peaceably as a whole; however, this orientation does change the character of the wars which it conducts. The foreign policy of the state changes according to the motivations of its citizenry. The use of military force is no longer exclusively determined not only by an essentially particularist vision of *raison d'etat* but also by the desire to promote the international proliferation of non-authoritarian forms of state and government. More important, if value preferences transcend preserving national interests and extend rather to the implementation of democracy and human rights, then the very conditions under which the balance of power operates have changed irrevocably.

(2)   The history we now survey also permits us to understand Kant's second argument in a similarly dialectical manner. Kant's direct assertions were certainly wrong, but in a more indirect way he also turns out to have been correct in a crucial respect. Indeed, Kant considered the growing interdependence of societies produced through the exchange of information, persons, and commodities, and especially through the expansion of trade, to be favorable to the peaceful association of peoples.[16] Trade relations expanded in early modernity into the dense network of a world market, which according to Kant "provides the basis for an interest in the security of peaceful relations through mutual gain." As Kant puts it: "The spirit of commerce cannot coexist with war."[17] However, Kant had not yet learned, as Hegel would from the English economists,[18] that capitalist development would lead to an opposition among classes that would in turn threaten both peace itself and the presumed readiness to live in peace in politically liberal societies. He could not foresee that the social tensions that only increased with accelerating process of capitalistic industrialization would both strain domestic politics with civil wars and lead foreign policy down the path toward imperialist wars. Throughout the nineteenth century and the first half of the twentieth, European governments repeatedly drew on the force of nationalism in order to divert social conflicts outward and to neutralize them with foreign-policy successes.

It was only after the catastrophes of World War II led to the depletion of integrating nationalist energies that the successful pacification of class antagonisms by means of the welfare state was possible. Only then did the internal situation of the industrialized nations change to such an extent that, at least within the OECD countries, economic interdependence led to the very "economization of international politics"[19] that Kant had rightly hoped would have a pacifying effect. Today globally dispersed media, networks, and systems necessitate a density of symbolic and social relationships, which bring about the constant reciprocal influence between local and quite distant events.[20] These processes of globalization rendered complex societies, with their delicate technological infrastructures, ever more vulnerable. As military confrontations between the nuclear-armed great powers became more and more improbable because of the huge risks, local conflicts piled up comparably numerous and terrible sacrifices. At the same time, globalization put into question the presuppositions of classical international law, namely, the sovereignty of states and the sharp distinction between domestic and foreign policies.

Non-governmental actors such as multi-national corporations and internationally influential private banks render the formal sovereignty of nation states increasingly hollow. Even the governments of the eco-nomically most powerful countries today are keenly aware that they are caught on the horns of a dilemma: on the one hand, their scope for action is limited by the structures of the nation state; on the other hand, they must respond to imperatives based not entirely on world trade but also on increasingly global networks of productive relations. Sovereign states could profit from their economies so long as they were "national economies" that could be influenced by political means. With the denationalization of the economy, in particular with the interdependencies in the world financial markets and in industrial production itself, national politics loses its control over the general conditions of production[21] – and with it any leverage for maintaining its standard of living.

At the same time, there is a blurring of the boundaries between domestic and foreign policy that are constitutive of state sover-eignty. The classical image of power politics is being changed not only by additional normative features such as a politics of democratization or of human rights, but also through a peculiar diffusion of power itself. With the growing pressure for cooperation, more or less indirect influence is becoming more important than direct implementation of one's own goals through the exercise of administrative power or threats of violence. Instead, power is now exerted indirectly in the structuring of perceived situations, in the creation of contacts, in the interruption of flows of communication, or in the definition of agendas and problems; in short, it is exercised on the boundary conditions within which actors make their decisions.[22] "Soft power" forces "hard power" aside and robs the subjects Kant had counted on in his asso-ciation of free states of the very basis for their independence.

(3)   Similar tendencies emerge once again in considering Kant's third argument, which he puts forward in order to blunt the suspi-cions that the projected federation of nations is a "mere chimera." In a republican polity, constitutional principles become the stan-dards by which policies must be publicly measured. Such governments do not dare try to "justify their policies publicly through clever slights of hand alone,"[23] even though they may need principles only to pay lip service to them. To this extent, criticism in the civic public sphere can prevent the execution of intentions that neither can withstand the light of day nor are consistent with publicly defensible maxims. On Kant's view, public criticism also has a program-matic function to the extent that philoso-phers, in their capacity as public teachers of the law or as public intellectuals, are permit-ted to "talk freely and publicly about the maxims of waging war and creating peace" and to convince the public of all citizens of the validity of their basic principles. Kant probably had the example of Voltaire and Frederick II in mind when he wrote the fol-lowing moving sentence: "It is not to be expected that kings will philosophize or that philosophers will become kings; nor is it to be desired, however, since the possession of power inevitably corrupts the free judgment of reason. Kings and sovereign peoples who governed themselves by egalitarian laws should not, however, force the class of phi-losophers to disappear or to remain silent,

but should allow them to speak publicly. This is essential in both cases in order that light may be thrown on their affairs and . . . beyond suspicion."[24]

As the atheism controversy involving Fichte would show only a few years later, Kant had every reason to fear censorship. We may also forgive his trust in the power of philosophy to convince others and in the sincerity of philosophers; historical skepticism about reason belongs more to the nineteenth century, and it was not until the twentieth century that intellectuals engaged in the gravest betrayals. What is more important is that Kant obviously counted on the existence of a transparent and surveyable public sphere formed by literary means and open to arguments, the membership of which would be borne by a small class of educated citizens. He could not foresee the structural transformation of the bourgeois public sphere in the future: a public sphere dominated by the electronic mass media, semantically degenerated, and taken over by images and virtual realities. He could hardly even imagine that the milieu of an Enlightenment of "speech and discussion" could be so utterly transformed into forms of indoctrination without language and linguistic deception.

This veil of ignorance probably explains why Kant dared to anticipate something so far in the future that it is only now actually coming about: namely, his brilliant anticipation of a global public sphere. The existence of the world public sphere emerges in the wake of global communication: "The process by which all the peoples of the earth have entered into a universal community has come to the point where a violation of rights in one part of the world is felt everywhere; this means that the idea of cosmopolitan law is no longer a fantastical or overly exaggerated idea. It is a necessary complement to civil and international law, transforming it into public law of humanity (or human rights [*Menschenrechte*]); only under this condition (namely, the existence of a functioning global public sphere) can we flatter ourselves that we are continually advancing toward perpetual peace."[25]

The first events that actually drew the attention of the world public sphere, and polarized its opinion on a global scale, were the wars in Vietnam and the Persian Gulf. It was only very recently that the United Nations organized in rapid succession a series of conferences on global issues, including ecology (in Rio de Janeiro), population growth (in Cairo), poverty (in Copenhagen), and global warming (in Berlin). These "world summits" can be interpreted as so many attempts to bring some political pressure to bear on governments simply by making the problems of human survival themes for the global public – that is, by appealing to the force of world opinion. One should not overlook the fact that this temporary public attention is still issue-specific and channeled through the established structures of national public spheres. Supporting structures are needed to stabilize communication between spatially distant participants, who exchange contributions at the same time on the same themes with equal relevance. In this sense there is not yet a global public sphere, let alone a European one, as urgently needed as it is. However, the central role played by a new type of organization, namely non-governmental organizations such as Greenpeace or Amnesty International, is not confined to conferences, but more generally concerns creating and mobilizing transnational public spheres. Their role is at the least an indication of the growing impact on the press and the other media of actors who confront the states from within the network of international civil society.[26]

The important role that Kant gives to publicity and to the public sphere raises the question of the relationship between the legal constitution and the political culture of a polity.[27] A liberal political culture forms the ground in which the institutions of freedom put down their roots; at the same time, it is also the medium through which progress in the political process of civilizing a population takes place.[28] Certainly, Kant speaks of the "growth of culture" that leads toward greater agreement over principles[29]; he also expected that the public use of communicative freedom would be transformed into processes of enlightenment that would affect the attitudes and ways of thinking of the populace in political socialization. In this context, Kant speaks of "the heartfelt sympathy which any enlightened person inevitably feels for anything good as he comes to understand it fully."[30] However, such remarks lack any systematic importance, because the dichotomous conceptual frame of transcendental philosophy separates internal from external conditions, morality from legality. In particular, Kant does not recognize the relationship in a liberal political culture between prudential pursuit of one's interests and moral insights and habits, between tradition and critique. The practices of such a culture mediate between morality, law, and politics and at the same time form the suitable context for a public sphere that encourages political learning processes.[31] Kant did not really need to retreat to some metaphysical "intention of nature" in order to explain how a "pathologically enforced social union can be transformed into a moral whole."[32]

As these critical reflections show, Kant's idea of a cosmopolitan order must be reformulated if it is not to lose touch with a world situation that has fundamentally changed. The long-overdue revision of Kant's basic conceptual framework is made easier by the fact that the cosmopolitan idea itself has not remained fixed. Ever since Woodrow Wilson's initiative and the founding of the League of Nations in Geneva, the idea of a cosmopolitan order has been repeatedly taken up and implemented in politics. After

the end of World War II, the idea of perpetual peace was given more tangible form in the institutions, declarations, and policies of the United Nations (as well as in other transnational organizations). The challenge of the incomparable catastrophes of the twentieth century has also given new impetus to Kant's idea. Against this somber background, the World Spirit, as Hegel would have put it, has jerked unsteadily forward.

European societies confronted the horror of a spatially and technologically unlimited war during World War I. World War II brought home the mass crimes of an ideologically unlimited war. Behind the veil of the total war contrived by Hitler, the breakdown of civilization was so complete that a shaken world accelerated the transition from international law to cosmopolitan law based on the rights of the world citizen. First, the outlawing of war initially mentioned in the 1928 Kellogg-Briand Pact was transferred into the war-crimes tribunals of Nuremberg and Tokyo. These tribunals did not limit themselves to crimes committed during war, but rather incriminated war itself as a crime. From this point onward, the "crime *of* war" could be prosecuted. Second, criminal law is now expanded to include "crimes against humanity" – that is, crimes carried out by legally empowered organs of the state with the assistance of countless members of organizations, functionaries, civil servants, businessmen, and private individuals. With these two innovations, governmental subjects of international law lost their general presumption of innocence in a supposed state of nature.

3

Any fundamental conceptual revision of Kant's proposal ought to focus on three aspects: (1) the external sovereignty of states and the changed nature of relations among them, (2) the internal sovereignty of states and the normal limitations of classical power politics, and (3) the stratification of world society and a globalizations of dangers which make it necessary for us to rethink what we mean by "peace."

(1) Kant's concept of a permanent federations of nations that respects the sovereignty of each is, as I have shown, inconsistent. The rights of the world citizen must be institutionalized in such a way that it actually binds individual governments. The community of peoples must at least be able to hold its members to legally appropriate behavior through the threat of sanctions. Only then will the unstable system of states asserting their sovereignty through mutual threat be transformed into a federation whose common institutions take over state functions: it will legally regulate the relations among its members and monitor their compliance with its rules. The external relationship of contractually regulated international relations among states, where each forms the environment for the others, then becomes the internally structured relationship among the members of a common organization based on a charter or a constitution. The Charter of the United Nations has precisely this significance in that it prohibits offensive wars (with the prohibition of violence in article 2.4) and empowers the Security Council to use appropriate means, including military action, "whenever a threat or violation of peace or an attack is present." At the same time, the UN Charter expressly forbids the intervention in the internal affairs of a state (in article 2.7). Each state retains the right to military self-defense. In December of 1991, the General Assembly reaffirmed this principle: "The sovereignty, territorial integrity, and national unity of a state must be fully respected in accordance with the Charter of the United Nations."[33]

With these ambiguous regulations, which both limit and guarantee the sovereignty of individual states, the Charter makes allowances for its own transitional status. The UN does not have its own military forces, or even any which it could deploy under its own command, much less any by means of which it might enjoy a monopoly over the means of violence. It is dependent on the voluntary cooperation of its members. The missing power base is supposed to be compensated for by the Security Council, in which the superpowers are bound to the world organization in return for veto rights and permanent membership. As everyone knows, this structure led to the consequence that the superpowers blocked each other's moves for decades. And when the Security Council does take the initiative, it makes highly selective use of its capacities for judgment through a disregard for the principle of treating similar cases similarly.[34] This problem once again become relevant through the events of the Gulf War.[35] Although not unimportant in this regard, the World Court in The Hague possesses only a symbolic significance. It is not always in session, nor can it as yet obligate governments to abide by its judgments (as was shown once again in the case of Nicaragua versus the United States).

(2) Because Kant believed that the barriers of national sovereignty were insurmountable, he conceived of the cosmopolitan community as a federation of states, not of world citizens. This assumption proved inconsistent, insofar as Kant derived every legal order, including that within the state, from a more original law, which gives rights to every person "qua human being." Every individual has the right to equal freedom under universal laws (since "everyone decides for everyone, and each decides for himself"[36]). This founding of law in human rights designates individuals as the bearers of rights and gives to all modern legal orders an inviolable individualistic character.[37] If Kant holds that this guarantee of freedom – "that

which human beings ought to do in accordance with the laws of freedom" – is precisely the essential purpose of perpetual peace, "indeed for all three variants of public law, civil, international and cosmopolitan law,"[38] then he ought not allow the autonomy of citizens to be mediated through the sovereignty of their states.

The point of cosmopolitan law is, rather, that it goes over the heads of the collective subjects of international law to give legal status to the individual subjects and justifies their unmediated membership in the association of free and equal world citizens. Carl Schmitt grasped this point and saw that this conception implies that "each individual is at the same time a world citizen (in the full juridical sense of the word) and a citizen of a state."[39] The higher-level legal power to define authority itself [*Kompetenz-Kompetenz*] now falls to the unified world state, giving individuals a legally unmediated relation to this international community; this transforms the individual state into "a mere agency [*Kompetenz*] for specific human beings who take on double roles in their international and national functions."[40] The most important consequence of a form of law that is able to puncture the sovereignty of states is the arrest of individual persons for crimes committed in the service of a state and its military.

Even in this respect, current developments have outstripped Kant. Based on the 1941 North Atlantic Charter, the UN Charter imposes the general obligation on its member states to observe and attempt to realize human rights. The General Assembly made these rights precise in an exemplary fashion in the General Declaration of Human Rights, which has been further developed by means of numerous resolutions.[41] The United Nations does not simply leave the protection of human rights to the nation states; it also possesses its own instruments for *establishing* that human-rights violations have

occurred. The Human Rights Commission possesses various observer functions and reporting procedures that concern themselves with basic social, economic, and cultural rights (although under the "proviso of what is possible"); further, there are procedures for bringing complaints about violations of civil and political rights. In theoretical terms (although not in terms recognized by all signatory states), the rights of individuals to bring formal complaints, which give all citizens the legal means to challenge their own governments, are more significant than the complaints brought by states. But there has been no criminal court that can test and decide upon well-established cases of human-rights violations. Even the proposal to institute a United Nations High Commissioner for Human Rights could not be implemented in the recent Vienna conference on human rights. Ad hoc war-crimes tribunals on the model of the Nuremberg and Tokyo international military tribunals are still the exception.[42] Certainly the General Assembly of the United Nations has recognized the guiding principles on which the judgments of these tribunals were based as the "principles of international law." Nonetheless, this assertion is false to the extent that these trials against leading Nazi military figures, diplomats, ministers, doctors, bankers, and industrial leaders have been treated as "unique" events without the force of legal precedent.[43]

The weak link in the global protection of human rights remains the lack of any executive power that could secure, when necessary, the General Declarations of Human Rights through interventions into nation states, despite their "supreme power" over their territory. Since human rights must in many cases be implemented against the will of the governments of nation states, the prohibition against intervention in international law must be revised. In cases where functioning state power has not disappeared entirely (as it did in Somalia), the world organization undertakes intervention only with the agreement of the affected governments (as in Liberia or in Croatia and Bosnia). Without a doubt, the United Nations took the first steps down a new path during the Gulf War with Resolution 688 in April of 1991, de facto if not de jure. The United Nations based its right of intervention in cases of "threats to international security" on chapter VII of its charter. To this extent, the UN did not, from a juridical point of view, intervene in "the internal affairs" of a sovereign state. But the US-led coalition did precisely this, as the allies certainly knew, when it instituted no-fly zones in Iraqi airspace and deployed ground troops in northern Iraq in order to secure safe areas for Kurd refugees, thus protecting the members of a national minority against their own state.[44] The British Foreign Minister spoke on this occasion of an "expansion of the limits of international action."[45]

(3)   The revisions necessary in light of the changed character of international relations and the need to limit the actions of sovereign states relate most directly to the conception of the federation of peoples and cosmopolitan order. Both are the locations in which very demanding norms are put in practice, norms which to some degree already exist. However, there is still, as much as ever, a discrepancy between the letter and the execution of these norms. The contemporary world situation can be understood in the best-case scenario as a period of transition from international to cosmopolitan law, but many other indications seem to support a regression to nationalism. How one assesses the situation depends in the first instance on how one estimates the effects of the dynamic processes at work in history that meet cosmopolitanism halfway. We have followed out the dialectic of these tendencies, which Kant had in mind under the headings of the

peaceful character of republics, the unifying power of global markets, and the normative pressure of liberal public spheres. Today such tendencies join together in an unprecedented and unforeseeable constellation.

Kant imagined the expansion of the association of free states in such a way that more and more democratic states would crystallize around the core of an avant-garde of peaceful republics: ". . . if by good fortune one powerful and enlightened nation can form a republic, this will provide a focal point for a federal association among other states . . . and gradually spread through associations of this kind."[46] As a matter of fact, a world organization has today united *all* states under one roof and indeed independent of whether they have already established republics or whether they respect human rights. The political unity of the world finds its expression in the General Assembly of the United Nations, in which all governments are represented with equal rights. In this way, the world organization abstracts not only from the differences in legitimation among its member states but also from their status differences within a stratified world society. I speak of a world society because communication systems and markets have created a global context; at the same time, it is also important to speak of a stratified world society, because the mechanism of the world market couples increasing productivity with increasing impoverishment, development with underdevelopment processes. Globalization both divides the world and forces it to cooperative action as a community of shared risks.

From the perspective of political science, the world has since 1917 disintegrated into three worlds. The terms "First World," "Second World," and "Third World" have different meanings since 1989.[47] The "Third World" today consists of those territories where the state infrastructure and monopoly of the means of violence are so weakly developed (Somalia) or so decayed (Yugoslavia) and where the social tensions are so high and the tolerance levels of political culture so low that indirect violence of a Mafia or fundamentalist variety disrupts internal order. These societies are also threatened by processes of nationalist, ethnic, and religious fragmentation. Indeed, the wars that have occurred here in the last few decades are mostly civil wars, which have often gone unnoticed in the world public sphere. The "Second World" is shaped by the heritage of power politics that individual nation states that have emerged from decolonization have taken over from Europe. Internally these states balance their unstable relations through authoritarian constitutions and obstinately insist on sovereignty and nonintervention from the outside (as in the Persian Gulf region). They emphasize military violence and exclusively obey the logic of the balance of power. Only the states of the "First World" can to a certain degree succeed in bringing their national interests into harmony with the normative claims established by the United Nations, an organization that has come at least part of the way toward achieving the cosmopolitan level.

As indicators of belonging to the First World, Richard Cooper lists the decreasing relevance of external boundaries and the toleration of a legally flourishing internal pluralism; the influence of states on one another's traditionally domestic concerns, with an increasing fusion between domestic and foreign policy; the sensitivity to the pressures of a liberal public sphere; the rejection of military force as a means of solving conflicts; the juridification of international relations; and the favoring of partnerships that base security on transparency and trust in expectations. The First World thus constitutes the temporal meridian of the present, as it were, by which the political simultaneity

of economic and cultural nonsimultaneity is measured. As a child of the eighteenth century, Kant thought unhistorically, ignored these facts, and thereby overlooked the *real abstraction* that must be accomplished by the organization of the community of nations and which it must also take into account in its policies.

The politics of the United Nations can take this real abstraction seriously only if it works to overcome social divisions and economic imbalances. This aim could, in turn, succeed in the face of the stratification of world society only on the condition that a consensus forms in three areas: a historical consciousness shared by all members concerning the nonsimultaneity of the societies simultaneously related by peaceful coexistence; a normative agreement concerning human rights, the interpretation of which remains disputed between the Europeans and the Asians and Africans; and a shared understanding concerning the meaning of the goal of peace.[48] Kant was satisfied with a purely negative conception of peace. This is unsatisfactory not only because all limits on the conduct of war have now been surpassed but also because of the new global circumstances that link the emergence of wars to specifically societal causes.

According to a proposal made by Dieter and Eva Senghaas,[49] the complexity of the causes of war requires a conception that understands peace as a *process* accomplished by nonviolent means. However, its aim is not merely to prevent violence per se but also to satisfy the real necessary conditions for a common life without tensions among groups and peoples. Such a strategy of nonviolent intervention works in favor of processes of democratization[50] that take into account the fact that global interconnections have now made *all* states dependent on their environment and sensitive to the "soft" power of indirect influence, up to the point of explicitly threatened economic sanctions.

With the increasing complexity of these goals and the burdensome character of these strategies, it must also be admitted that increasing difficulties are holding the leading powers back from taking the initiative and bearing its costs. I want to conclude this section by mentioning the four most important variables in this regard: the composition of the Security Council, which has to always act in concert; the political culture of the leading powers, the governments of which can adopt a "selfless" policy only for the short term, and only then if they are forced to react to the normative pressures of a mobilized public sphere; the formation of regional regimes, which would for the first time provide the world organization with an effective substructure; and the gentle compulsion to globally coordinated action that starts with an undistorted perception of current global dangers. The threats are obvious: ecological imbalance; asymmetries of standards of living and economic power; powerful technologies of an unprecedented scale; the arms trade, especially the spread of atomic, biological, and chemical weapons; terrorism and the rise of drug-related criminality; and so on. In light of this growing list, those of us who do not doubt the capacity of the international system to learn have to place our hopes in the fact that the very globalization of these dangers has already objectively brought the world together into an involuntary community of shared risks.

4

On the one hand, the contemporary reformulation of the Kantian idea of a cosmopolitan pacification of the state of nature between states has inspired energetic efforts to reform the United Nations and, more generally, to create effective supranational organizations in various regions of the world. Such efforts aim at the improvement of the institutional framework necessary for a feasible politics based on human rights, which has suffered serious setbacks since it was first attempted during the presidency of Jimmy Carter (1). On the other hand, this form of politics has evoked a strong opposition that sees any institutional implementation of human rights as a self-defeating moralization of politics. Such policies are, however, based on an unclear conception of human rights that does not sufficiently distinguish between politics and morality (2).

(1)   The "rhetoric of universalism" against which this critique is directed finds its most intelligent formulation in proposals to reconstruct the United Nations in the form of a "cosmopolitan democracy." These proposal for reform concentrate on three points: establishing of a world parliament, developing a more complete world court system, and beginning the long overdue reorganization of the Security Council.[51]

The United Nations still clings to features of a "permanent congress of states." If it is no longer to be a mere assembly of government delegations, the General Assembly must be transformed into a kind of parliament that shares its powers with a second chamber. In such a parliament, peoples will be represented not by their governments but by the elected representatives of the totality of world citizens. Countries that refuse to allow representatives to be elected by democratic procedures (procedures that also give special consideration to their national minorities) could be represented in the meantime by non-governmental organizations that the World Parliament itself selects as the representatives of oppressed populations.

The World Court in The Hague currently lacks the power to press charges and make claims; it cannot make binding decisions, and thus it is limited to the function of an umpire. Its jurisdiction is now restricted to the relations among states; it does not extend to conflicts between individual persons or between individual citizens and their governments. In all these respects, the powers of the World Court must be expanded along the lines of proposals made by Hans Kelsen in 1944.[52] International criminal prosecution, which has up to now only been established on an ad hoc basis for specific war-crimes trials, must be permanently institutionalized.

The Security Council was conceived to be a counterweight to the egalitarian General Assembly. It is supposed to reflect the de facto relations of power in the world. Some five decades later, this reasonable principle must be altered to fit the changed world situation; such an adaptation should not be limited to simply expanding the representation of the most influential states (for example, by accepting Germany or Japan as a permanent member). Instead, it has been proposed that, along with the world powers (such as the United States), regional regimes (such as the European Union) should also be given a privileged vote. It is also necessary that the requirement of unanimity among the permanent members be abolished in favor of an appropriate form of majority rule. Following the model of Brussels' ministry of the European Union, the Security Council as a whole could be reformed into an executive power capable of carrying out policies. States will adjust their traditional foreign policies according to the imperatives of world domestic policy only if the world organization possesses a military force under its own command and exercises its own policing functions.

These reflections are conventional, in the sense that they are oriented to the organizational components of national constitutions. The implementation of a properly clarified conception of cosmopolitan law demands somewhat more institutional imagination. In any case, the moral universalism that guided Kant's proposals remains the structuring normative intuition. Beginning with

Hegel's criticisms of Kant's morality of humanity, an argument directed against this moral-practical self-understanding of modernity has been especially influential in Germany and has left deep traces.[53] Carl Schmitt has given this argument its sharpest formulation, based on reasoning that is incisive and confused at the same time.

Schmitt turns the slogan. "he who says humanity wants to deceive" into the powerful formula "Humanity, Bestiality." According to Schmitt, "the deception of humanism" has its roots in the hypocrisy of a legal pacifism that wants to conduct "just wars" in the name of peace and cosmopolitan rights. "When a state fights its political enemy in the name of humanity, it is not a war for the sake of humanity, but rather a war in which a particular state tries to usurp a universal concept in its struggle against its enemy, in the same way that one can misuse peace, justice, progress and civilization in order to vindicate oneself and to discredit the foe. The concept of 'Humanity' is an especially useful ideological instrument. . . ."[54]

Schmitt later extended this argument (directed in 1932 against the United States and the other victors of Versailles) to the actions of the League of Nations and the United Nations. The politics of a world organization inspired by Kant's idea of perpetual peace and oriented to the creation of a cosmopolitan order obeys the same logic: its pan-interventionism necessarily leads to a pan-criminalization and with it to the perversion of the goal it is supposed to serve.[55]

(2)   Before I consider the specific context of these reflections, I would like to deal with the argument at a general level and uncover its problematic core. Its two basic propositions are that the politics of human rights leads to wars that are disguised as police actions to lend them a moral quality and that this moralization stamps the enemy as an inhuman criminal and thus opens the floodgates. "We

are acquainted with the secret law behind this vocabulary and know today that the most terrible wars are conducted in the name of peace and that the worst inhumanity is committed in the name of humanity."[56] These two statements are justified with the aid of two further premises: (a) that the politics of human rights serves to implement norms that are a part of universalistic morality and (b) that, in accordance with the moral code of "good" and "evil," these negative moral evaluations of an enemy (or a political opponent in war) destroy the legally institutionalized limitation of military conflict (or of political struggle more generally). Whereas the first premise is false, the second premise suggests a false presupposition with regard to the politics of human rights.

On premise (a): Human rights in the modern sense can be traced back to the Virginia Bill of Rights and to the 1776 American Declaration of Independence, as well as to the 1789 Declaration des droits de l'homme et du citoyen. These declarations are inspired by the political philosophy of modern natural law, especially that of Locke and Rousseau. It is no accident that human rights first take on concrete form in the context of these first constitutions precisely as basic rights guaranteed in the context of the legal order of the nation state. However, they have a double character: as constitutional norms they enjoy a positive validity (of instituted law), but as rights that are attributed to each person as a human being they acquire a suprapositive validity.

In the philosophical discussion of human rights, this ambiguity has provoked much irritation.[57] According to one interpretation, human rights are supposed to have a status between moral and positive law; according to the other interpretation, they appear with identical content in the form of both moral and juridical rights [*Rechte*]; that is, "as a law [*Recht*] valid [*gültig*] prior to any state, but not for that reason already in force [*geltend*]."

Human rights are then "not actually preserved or rejected, but nonetheless guaranteed or disrespected."[58] These formulas reflect philosophical embarrassment and suggest that the constitutional legislator only disguises already given moral norms in the form of positive law. This recourse to the classical distinction between natural and instituted law sets up the lines of debate in the wrong way. The conception of human rights does not have its origins in morality; rather, it bears the imprint of the modern concept of individual liberties and is therefore distinctly juridical in character. What gives human rights the appearance of being moral rights is neither their content nor even their structure but rather their form of validity, which points beyond the legal order of the nation state.

The historical texts of various constitutions appeal to "innate" rights and have the form of "declarations": both are supposed to militate against what we now call a positivist misunderstanding and express the fact that human rights are "not under the control of any legislator."[59] But this rhetorical proviso cannot save human rights from the fate of all positive law; they, too, can be changed or even abolished with the change of regimes. As a component of a democratic legal order, they share with all other legal norms a dual sense of "validity": not only are they valid de facto and implemented by the sanctioning power of state violence; they can also claim normative legitimacy (that is, they are capable of being rationally justified). It is in their justification that basic rights do indeed have a remarkable status.

As constitutional norms, human rights have a certain primacy, shown by the fact that they are constitutive for legal order as such and by the extent to which they determine a framework within which normal legislative activity is possible. But even among constitutional norms as a whole, basic rights stand out. On the one hand, liberal and social basic rights have the form of general norms addressed to citizens in their properties as "human beings" and not merely as members of a polity. Even if human rights can be realized only within the framework of the legal order of a nation state, they are justified in this sphere of validity as rights for all persons and not merely for citizens. The more one explores the content of the German Basic Law [Germany's constitution] from the viewpoint of human rights, the more the legal status of resident noncitizens living in Germany resembles that of citizens. It is this universal validity, applied to every human being as such, that basic rights share with moral norms. As can be shown in the recent controversy in Germany over the right of resident aliens to vote, this same point applies to basic political rights too. This points to a second and even more important aspect: Basic rights are equipped with such universal validity claims precisely because they can be justified *exclusively* from the moral point of view. Other legal norms can certainly *also* be justified with the help of moral arguments, but in general further ethical-political and pragmatic considerations play a role in their justification – considerations that have to do with the particular concrete form of life of a historical legal community or with the concrete goals of particular policies. Basic rights, on the contrary, regulate matters of such generality that moral arguments are *sufficient for their justification*. These arguments show why the guarantee of such rules is in the equal interest of all persons qua persons, and thus why they are equally good for *everyone*.

This mode of justification in no way undermines the juridical quality of basic rights, nor does it turn them into moral norms. Legal norms – in the modern sense of positive law – retain their legal form even if their claim to legitimacy can be justified with the help of this further sort of reason. This character is due to their structure, not to their content. According to this structure, basic rights are enforceable individual rights, the meaning of which is to unbind legal persons in very specific ways from moral commands by creating a sphere of action in which each person can act according to his or her own preferences. Whereas moral rights can only be justified as duties that bind the free will of autonomous persons, legal duties are primarily entitlements to voluntary action; indeed, they derive precisely through the legal limitation of these very same individual liberties that they permit.[60]

The conceptual privileging of rights over duties results from the structure of modern coercive law first elaborated by Hobbes. Hobbes introduced a shift in perspective away from pre-modern law, which was still justified from a religious or metaphysical perspective. In a manner quite different from the grounding of duties in deontological morality, law here serves the purpose of protecting the freedom of the individual according to the principle that everything is permitted that is not explicitly forbidden according to those general laws that limit freedom. Certainly, the generality of such laws satisfies the moral point of view of justice, especially if the individual rights derived from them are supposed to be legitimate. The individual rights that protect a sphere of liberty give modern legal order its basic structure. Hence, Kant conceives of law as "the sum of the conditions under which the choices of each can be united with the freedom of others according to general laws of freedom."[61] According to Kant, all special human rights have their justification in the single original right of each individual to equal freedom: "To the extent that it can coexist with the freedom of all in accordance with a universal law, freedom (as independence from being constrained by the arbitrary will of others) is the only original right, belonging to each human being simply by virtue of his or her humanity."[62]

For this reason, Kant has no other place to put human rights than in his "Doctrine of Right." Like other individual rights, as rights they have a moral content. But this content is in no way altered by the fact that human rights structurally belong within an order of positive and coercive law in which claims to individual rights are enforceable. To this extent, it is constitutive of the meaning of human rights that, according to their status as basic rights, they belong within a framework of some existing legal order, whether it be national, international, or global, in which they can be protected. The mistake of conflating them with moral rights results from their peculiar nature: apart from their universal validity *claims*, these rights have had an unambiguously positive form only within the national legal order of the democratic state. Moreover, they possess only weak validity in international law, and they await institutionalization within the framework of a cosmopolitan order which is only now emerging.

On premise (b): If the first premise of the counterargument (that human rights are by nature moral rights) is false, then the first of the two auxiliary propositions (the statement that the global implementation of human rights necessarily follows a moral logic that would lead to interventions disguised as police actions) is also undercut. At the same time, the second statement (that an interventionist politics of human rights would have to disguise itself as a "struggle against evil") is also refuted. In any case this statement suggests the false presupposition that a classical international law oriented to limited wars would be sufficient to steer military conflicts down a "civilized" path. Even if this presupposition still held, the police actions of a democratically legitimate world organization capable of taking action would better earn the title of the means for "civilizing" international conflicts than would limited war. Establishing a cosmopolitan order

means that violations of human rights are no longer condemned and fought from the moral point of view in an unmediated way, but are rather prosecuted as criminal actions within the framework of a state-organized legal order according to institutionalized legal procedures. Precisely such a justification of the state of nature among states would protect us from a moral de-differentiation of law and would guarantee to the accused full legal protection, even in cases of war crimes and crimes of humanity. Even such cases are protected from unmediated moral discrimination.[63]

5

I would like to develop this metacritical argument further by dealing specifically with Carl Schmitt's objections. I return to these objections because Schmitt did not always link the various levels of his argument in an especially transparent way. Schmitt's criticism of a form of cosmopolitan law that does not stop at the sovereignty of individual states was especially preoccupied with a morally discriminating conception of war. In this way, his argument seems to have a clear legal focus. It is directed against the prohibition of offensive war codified in the United Nations Charter and against the arrest of individual persons for war crimes, both of which were unknown in classical international law before World War I. But this juridical discussion, harmless in itself, is laden with both political considerations and metaphysical justifications. We must unfold the existing theory that lies in the background (1) in order to uncover the critique of morality at the core of the argument (2).

(1) Taken at face value, this juridical argument has the goal of civilizing war through international law (a); and it is connected with a political argument that only appears

to be consistent with preserving the existing international order (b).

(a)   Schmitt does not reject the distinction between offensive and defensive wars simply because it is difficult pragmatically to operationalize it. Rather, the juridical reason is that only a morally neutral conception of war, which excludes the possibility of personal arrest of war criminals, is consistent with the sovereignty of the subjects of international law. If that is true, then *ius ad bellum*, the right to begin a war for any reason whatsoever, constitutes the sovereignty of states. At this level of the argument, Schmitt is not yet concerned with the supposedly disastrous consequences of moral universalism (as he is in other writings[64]); rather, he is concerned with any limitation on how wars are conducted. Only the practice of not discriminating among types of wars is supposed to succeed in limiting military actions in war and thus to protect us from the evil of a total war, which Schmitt analyzed before World War II with admirable clarity.[65]

Schmitt tries to present the return to the status quo ante of limited war as a realistic alternative to the cosmopolitan pacification of the state of nature among states. In comparison with civilizing it, abolishing war altogether is a much more extensive and apparently utopian goal. Admittedly, the "realism" of this proposal can be doubted for good empirical reasons. The simple appeal to an international law, as it emerged out of the wars of religion as one of the great achievements of Western rationalism, does not point the way toward reestablishing the classical-modern world of the balance of power. The classical form of such international law had already failed in the face of the total wars unleashed in the twentieth century. Powerful forces have already brought about a territorial, technical, and ideological delimitation of war. These forces could more likely be tamed through the sanctions and interventions of an organized community of peoples than through the juridically ineffective appeal to the insight of sovereign governments. Precisely at a time when they ought to change their uncivilized behavior, a return to the classical international legal order would hand back to collective actors an unfettered freedom of action. This argumentative weakness is a first indication that the juridical argument only forms a facade, behind which misgivings of a different sort are hidden.

After World War II, Schmitt could save the consistency of his purely juridical argument only by bracketing the mass crimes of the Nazi period as a sui generis category, in order to preserve at least the appearance of moral neutrality for war. In a brief prepared in 1945 for the Nuremberg defendant Friedrich Flick, Schmitt rigorously distinguished between war crimes and "atrocities," stating that the latter transcend human understanding "as the characteristic expression of an inhuman mentality." He admits that "the commands of a superior cannot justify or pardon such outrages committed by those under him."[66] That Schmitt the lawyer was motivated by purely tactical considerations in making this distinction in the context of the Nuremberg trials became brutally clear in the texts written in his diary a few years later. From his "Glossorarium" it is clear that Schmitt not only wanted to see offensive wars decriminalized but also saw the absolute breakdown of civilization in the extermination of the Jews on the same level. He asks: "Was it a 'crime against humanity'? Is there such a thing as a crime against love?" Furthermore, he doubts whether the Holocaust is to be considered a juridical state of affairs at all, because the "object of protection and attack" of such a crime cannot be sufficiently precisely delimited: "Genocide, the murder of peoples, moving concept. I have experienced an example of it in my own body: the destruction of the German-Prussian civil service in 1945." This rather ticklish understanding of genocide leads Schmitt to an even farther-reaching conclusion: "The concept of 'crimes against humanity' is only the most general of all general clauses for use in exterminating an enemy." In another passage, Schmitt puts it this way: "There are crimes against humanity and crimes for humanity. Crimes against humanity were committed by the Germans. Crimes for humanity were perpetrated on the Germans."[67]

Here yet another argument apparently emerges. The implementation of cosmopolitan law with the consequence of the use of a discriminating conception of war is not only considered a false reaction to the development of total war, but is now its cause. Total war is the contemporary form of "just war" and necessarily encourages an interventionist politics of human rights: "What is decisive is that the total character of the war belongs to its claim of being just."[68] In this way, moral universalism takes on the role of an explanandum, and the argument shifts from the juridical to the moral level. Schmitt seems at first to have recommended the return to classical international law as a way to avoid total war. But it is not at all certain that he truly saw the total delimiting of war and hence the inhuman character of the conduct of war as the real evil, or whether it is much more the case that he mostly feared the discrediting of war as such. In any case, in an addition to *The Concept of the Political* written in 1938 Schmitt describes the totalitarian expansion of war to nonmilitary areas in such a way that he sees total war as a hygienic service for peoples: "The step beyond the purely military view of war not only brings with it a quantitative expansion, it also produces a qualitative jump. For this reason total war does not signify a lessening, but rather an intensification of hatred of the enemy. With the mere possibility of such an increase in intensity, the concepts of friend and foe become political once again and are freed from the sphere of private and psychological forms of speech in which they had become completely drained of their political character."[69]

(b)   Although it should come as no surprise that an inveterate foe of pacificism should not be so concerned with the problem of the taming of wars unleashed by totalitarianism, Schmitt could also have something else in mind: the preservation of an international order in which wars can still be waged and used to solve conflicts. The practice suggested by a nondiscriminating conception of war keeps intact the mechanism of unlimited national self-assertion as the basis of order. The evil to be avoided is therefore not total war, but rather the decline of the sphere of the political that rests upon the classical distinction of domestic and foreign politics. This distinction is justified by Schmitt through his own peculiar theory of the political. According to this theory, legally pacified domestic politics must be supplemented by a bellicose foreign policy licensed by international law; with its monopoly over the means of violence, the state can maintain law and order against the virulent subversive power of domestic enemies only if it preserves and regenerates its political substance in struggle against its foreign foes. This substance is renewed in the willingness of members of a nation to kill and be killed, since it is of the essence of the political to be related to "the real possibility of physical death." What is "political" is the capacity and will of a people to recognize its foes and to assert itself against "the negation of its existence" though the "otherness of the foreign."[70]

These scurrilous reflections on "the essence of the political" interest us here only for their usefulness in Schmitt's argument. The vitalistic content loaded into the concept of the political is the background for the assertion that its creative power has to be transformed into a destructive power as soon as it is shut off from the "conquering violence" of the predatory international arena. Supposedly for the sake of world peace, the global implementation of human rights and democracy would have the unintended effect of allowing war to step beyond the limits within which it is held by "formally just" international law. Without being permitted to run free in its hunting ground, war will become autonomous, overwhelm the spheres of civil life in modern society, and thus eliminate the complexity of differentiated societies. This warning against the catastrophic consequences of abolishing war through the pacification of law is explicable only through a metaphysics that is at best a relic of its time and which in the meantime also invokes the somewhat naked aesthetics of war as "the storm of steel."[71]

(2)   One can certainly distill and specify a particular viewpoint out of this bellicose *Lebensphilosophie*. According to Schmitt, behind the ideological justification of the call for a "war against war" is the universalism of the Kantian morality of humanity, which transforms the temporally, socially, and technologically limited military struggle between organized "units of peoples" into an unlimited paramilitary civil war.

All indications are that Schmitt would react to the United Nations' peacekeeping and peacemaking efforts in precisely the same way as Hans Magnus Enzensberger: "The rhetoric of universalism is specific to the West. The postulates advanced in this way are supposed to be valid without exception or differences for all. Universalism thus knows no distinctions between near and far; it is unconditional and abstract. . . . But since all our possibilities of action are finite,

the gap between claim and reality opens up wider and wider. Soon the limit of objective hypocrisy is also transgressed; it is then that universalism proves itself to be a moral trap."[72] It is therefore the false abstractions of the morality of humanity, an abstract morality that produces self-deception and a hypocritical overburdening of our moral capacities. The limits which such a morality transgresses are seen by Enzensberger and Gehlen as anthropologically deep-seated conceptions of space and time: a being such as a human, made out of such flimsy materials, functions morally only in the proximate perceptual environment.[73]

Schmitt comes closer to Hegel's criticism of Kant when he speaks of hypocrisy. He furnishes the contemptuous formula "humanity, bestiality" with an ambiguous commentary, which at first glance might have come from Horkheimer: "We speak of the main city cemetery and tactfully keep quiet about the slaughter house. But slaughtering is self-evident, and it would be inhumane, even bestial, to say the word 'to slaughter' out loud."[74] This aphorism is ambiguous to the extent that it seems at first to signify an ideology critique directed against the false and transfiguring abstraction of a Platonic general concept with which we often only cover up the dark side of the civilization of the victors, namely the suffering of marginalized victims. But this reading would nonetheless require a kind of egalitarian respect and universal compassion validated by the very moral universalism Schmitt so vehemently rejects. What Schmitt's antihumanism seeks to affirm (along with Mussolini's and Lenin's interpretations of Hegel[75]) is not the slaughtered calf, but rather the battle [*Schlacht*], Hegel's slaughter bench [*Schlachtbank*] of peoples, the "honor of war." For this reason his commentary states further on that "humanity does not wage war . . . the concept of humanity excludes the possibility of the concept of a foe."[76] According to Schmitt, the morality of humanity falsely abstracts from the natural order of the political, namely the supposedly unavoidable distinction between friend and foe. Because it subsumes political relationships under the categories of "good" and "evil," it turns the enemy in war into "an inhuman monster who can not only be defended against but also must be definitively annihilated."[77] And because the discriminating concept of war derives from the universalism of human rights, it is ultimately the infection of international law with morality that explains why the inhumanity of modern war and civil war occurs "in the name of humanity."

Independent of the context in which Schmitt employs it, this critique of morality has had baneful effects through the history of its reception. It fuses a correct insight with a fatal mistake fed by the friend–foe conception of the political. The true thesis at the core of the argument consists in the fact that an *unmediated* moralization of law and politics would in fact serve to break down those protected spheres that we as legal persons have good moral reasons to want to secure. But it is mistaken in its assumption that such a moralization is hindered only by keeping international law free of law and the law free of morality. Both are false under the premises of the constitutional state and democracy: the idea of a constitutional state demands that the coercive violence of the state be channeled both externally and internally through legitimate law; and the democratic legitimation of law is supposed to guarantee that law remain in harmony with recognized moral principles. Cosmopolitan law is thus a consequence of the idea of the constitutional state. In it, symmetry is finally established between the juridification of social and political relations both inside and outside the state's boundaries.

Schmitt's most informative inconsistency is his insistence upon an asymmetry between a pacified legal order within the state and a bellicose one outside it. Since he also imagines legal peace within the state to consist only in the latent conflict between the organs of the state and the enemies whom the state represses by means of struggle, he hands law over completely to the occupiers of state power and declares representatives of the opposition within the state to be domestic enemies – a practice that has left traces in the Federal Republic of Germany.[78] Quite distinct from the democratic constitutional state in which independent courts and the whole body of citizens (sometimes, in extreme cases, activated through civil disobedience) decide about sensible questions concerning unconstitutional behavior, Schmitt weighs the interests of the current holders of power and criminalizes political opponents into enemies in civil war. This loosening of constitutional controls in the border zones of domestic affairs has precisely the effects that Schmitt fears in the pacification of foreign affairs between states: the thorough penetration of moral categories into the legally protected zone of political action and the stylization of opponents into agents of evil. But it would be entirely inconsistent then to demand that international relations remain immune from regulations analogous to those in the constitutional state.

As a matter of fact, an *unmediated* moralization of politics in the international arena would be just as damaging as the struggle of governments with their domestic enemies – something Schmitt permits because he localizes the damage in the wrong place. In both cases, the damage only occurs in light of the false coding of legally protected political and state actions: such actions are falsely moralized, judged according to criteria of "good" and "evil"; they are then criminalized and thus judged according to criteria of "legal" and "illegal." All the while, Schmitt ignores the decisive moment – the legal presupposition of an authority that judges impartially and fulfills the conditions of neutral criminal punishment.

The politics of human rights undertaken by a world organization turns into a fundamentalism of human rights only when it undertakes an intervention that is really nothing more than the struggle of one party against the other and thus uses a moral legitimation as a cover for a false juridical justification. In such cases, the world organization (or the alliance acting in its name) does engage in "deception," because it portrays what is actually a military confrontation between two warring parties as a neutral police action justified by actual law and by the judgments of a criminal court. "Morally justified appeals threaten to take on fundamentalist features when they do not aim at the implementation of a legal procedure [for the positivization and] for the application and achievement of human rights, but rather seize directly upon the interpretive scheme by which violations of human rights are attributed, or when such moral appeals are the sole source of the demanded sanctions."[79]

Schmitt also defends the assertion that the juridification of power politics outside the boundaries of states (and thus the implementation of human rights in an arena previously dominated by military force) _always and necessarily_ leads to such a human-rights fundamentalism. This assertion is false, since it is based on the false premise that human rights have a moral nature and thus that their implementation signifies a form of moralization. The problematic side of the juridification of international affairs already mentioned does not consist in the placing of actions previously understood as "political" under legal categories. Quite different from morality, the legal code in no way requires

unmediated moral evaluation according to the criteria of "good" and "evil." Klaus Günther clarifies the central point: "That a purely political interpretation of human rights (in the sense of Carl Schmitt) is excluded does not mean that an unmediated moralistic interpretation should be put in its place."[80] Human rights should not be confused with moral rights.

The difference between law and morality that Günther insists upon does not in any way signify that positive law has no moral content. Through the democratic procedure of the political process of legislation, moral arguments (along with other types of reasons) flow into the justification of relevant norm-making activities and in this way into law itself. As Kant already saw, law is distinguished from morality through the formal properties of legality. This means that some aspects of morally evaluated action (for example, intentions and motives) ought not be the proper subjects of legal regulation. Above all, the legal code makes binding the judgments and sanctions of the agencies authorized to protect those affected through narrowly interpreted, intersubjectively testable conditions of the procedures of the constitutional state. Whereas the moral person stands naked before the inner court of his or her conscience, the moral person remains clothed with the cloak of the rights to freedom that are justified by good moral reasons. The correct solution to the problem of the moralization of power politics is therefore "not the demoralization of politics, but rather the democratic transformation of morality into a positive system of law with legal procedures of application and implementation."[81] Fundamentalism about human rights is to be avoided not by giving up on the politics of human rights, but rather only through the cosmopolitan transformation of the state of nature among states into a legal order.

Notes

1 Immanuel Kant, "The Contest of Faculties," in *Kant's Political Writings* (Cambridge, 1970), p. 187; *Werke* XI (Suhrkamp, 1977), p. 364.

2 In the conclusion to "Rechtslehre" in *Metaphysics of Morals* (*Kant's Political Writings*, pp. 173–4); *Werke* VIII, p. 478.

3 Indeed, Kant does mention in his "Doctrine of Right" the "unjust enemy," whose "publicly expressed will, whether in word or deed, displays a maxim that would make peace among nations impossible" (*Metaphysics of Morals*, section 60; *Political Writings*, p. 170). However, the examples he gives, such as breaking an international treaty or the division of a conquered country (e.g., Poland in his own time) illuminate the accidental character of this conception. A "punitive war" against unjust enemies is an idea with no real practical consequences, so long as states are considered entities with unlimited sovereignty. Such a punishment could only be given by a juridical authority which judges impartially in terms of violations of the rules of international conduct; but no state could recognize such an authority without limiting its own sovereignty. Only the outcome of the conflict can decide "who is in the right" (*Political Writings*, p. 96; *Werke* XI, p. 200).

4 Kant, *Political Writings*, p. 113; *Werke* XI, p. 212.

5 Kant, "Theory and Practice," in *Political Writings*, p. 92; *Werke* XI, p. 172.

6 Kant, "Theory and Practice," p. 92; *Werke* XI, p. 172.

7 Kant, "Toward Perpetual Peace," in *Political Writings*, p. 105; *Werke* XI, p. 213.

8 In "The Doctrine of Right," *Metaphysics of Morals*, section 61; *Kant's Political Writings*, p. 171.

9 Kant, *Metaphysics of Morals* in *Political Writings*, p. 171; *Werke* VIII, p. 475.

10 "Toward Perpetual Peace," pp. 104–5; *Werke* XI, p. 212.

11 "Toward Perpetual Peace," p. 127; *Werke* XI, p. 225.

12 "Theory and Practice," p. 90; *Werke* XI, p. 169.

13 "Toward Perpetual Peace," p. 100; *Werke* XI, pp. 205–6.

14 H. Schulze, *Staat und Nation in der Europäischen Geschichte* (Munich, 1994).

15 See D. Archibugi and D. Held's "Introduction" to their collection *Cosmopolitan Democracy* (Cambridge, 1995), p. 10ff.

16 See "The Doctrine of Right," *Metaphysics of Morals*, section 62; *Political Writings*, p. 172.

17 "Toward Perpetual Peace," 114, *Werke* XI, p. 226.

18 See Georg Lukacs, *Der junge Hegel* (Zurich, 1948).

19 Dieter Senghaas, "Internationale Politik im Lichte ihrer strukturellen Dilemmata," in *Wohin driftet die Welt?* (Frankfurt, 1994), p. 121ff; here p. 132.

20 This is Anthony Giddens's definition of globalization in *The Consequences of Modernity* (Cambridge, 1990), p. 64.

21 R. Knieper, *Nationale Souveränität* (Frankfurt, 1991).

22 J. S. Nye, "Soft Power," *Foreign* Policy 80 (1990), pp. 152–71.

23 "Toward Perpetual Peace," p. 121; *Werke* XI, p. 238.

24 Kant, "Toward Perpetual Peace," p. 115; *Werke* XI, p. 228.

25 "Toward Perpetual Peace," p. 108; *Werke* XI, p. 216f. (bracketed words inserted by Habermas – translator).

26 On the theme of a farewell to the world of nation states see E. O. Czempiel, *Weltpolitik im Umbruch* (Munich, 1993), p. 105ff.

27 See the essays by Albrecht Wellmer and Axel Honneth in *Gemeinschaft und Gerechtigkeit*, ed. M. Brumlik and H. Brunkhorst (Frankfurt, 1993), p. 173ff and p. 260ff.

28 See the title essay in my book *Die Normalität einer Berliner Republik* (Munich, 1995), p. 165ff.

29 "Toward Perpetual Peace," p. 114; *Werke* XI, p. 226.

30 *Kant's Political Writings*, p. 51; "Idee zu einer Allgemeinen Geschichte," in *Werke* XI, p. 46ff.

31   On the idea of "a people as a learning sover-
      eign," see H. Brunkhorst, *Demokratie und
      Differenz* (Frankfurt, 1994), p. 199ff.

32   "Idea of a Universal History," in *Kant's Politi-
      cal Writings.* p. 45; "Idee zu einer Allgemei-
      nen Geschichte," in *Werke* XI, p. 38.

33   J. Isensee defends a qualified prohibition of
      intervention against the increasing tendency
      to deviate from the norm with the surprising
      construction of "basic rights for states" in
      "Weltpolizei für Menschenrechten," *Jurist-
      ische Zeitung* 9 (1995), pp. 421–30. "What is
      valid for the basic rights of individuals is also
      valid mutatis mutandis for the 'basic rights'
      of states, including their sovereign equality,
      their self-determination as the power over
      persons and territory." Constructing an
      analogy between the sovereignty of states re-
      cognized by international law and the basic
      guaranteed right to freedom granted to indi-
      vidual persons misses not only the funda-
      mental importance of individual rights and
      the individualist orientation of modern legal
      order; it also misses the specifically juridical
      meaning of human rights as the individual
      rights of citizens in a cosmopolitan order.

34   See the examples in Charles Greenwood,
      "Gibt es ein Recht auf humanitäre Interven-
      tion?" *Europa-Archiv* 4 (1993), p. 94.

35   For my account of these events, see *Ver-
      gangenheit als Zukunft* (Munich, 1993),
      pp. 10–44.

36   Kant, "Theory and Practice," p. 77; *Werke* XI,
      p. 144.

37   See J. Habermas, "Struggles for Recognition
      in the Democratic Constitutional State," in
      Multiculturalism, ed. A. Guttman (Princeton,
      NJ, 1994).

38   "Toward Perpetual Peace," p. 111; *Werke* XI,
      p. 223.

39   As shown in a treatment of this work by
      Georges Scelle, *Precis de droit de gens* (two
      volumes; Paris, 1932 and 1934). See Carl
      Schmitt, *Die Wendung zum diskriminierenden
      Kriegsbegriff* (Berlin, 1988), p. 16.

40   Schmitt, *Kriegsbegriff*, p. 19.

41   On the Vienna conference on human rights
      see R. Wolfrum, "Die Entwicklung des
      internationalen Menschenrechtsschutzes,"
      Europa-Archiv 23 (1993): 681–90. On the

status of disputed rights to solidarity see W.
Huber, "Menschenrechte/Menschenwürde,"
in *Theologische Realenzyklopädie* (Berlin and
New York, 1992), volume XXII, pp. 577–602;
see also E. Riedel, "Menschenrechte der
dritten Dimension," *Europäische Grundre-
chte-Zeitschrift* 16 (1989): pp. 9–21.

42   In 1993 the Security Council established such
      a tribunal for the prosecution of war crimes
      and crimes against humanity in the former
      Yugoslavia.

43   As argued by H. Quaritsch in his "Postscript"
      to C. Schmitt, *Das internationalrechtliche
      Verbrechen des Angriffskrieges* (1945) (Berlin,
      1994), pp. 125–247, here from p. 236ff.

44   Greenwood (1993, p. 104) comes to the fol-
      lowing conclusion: "The idea that the United
      Nations can use the powers granted in its
      Charter to intervene in a state for humanitar-
      ian reasons appears now to be much more
      strongly established."

45   As cited by Greenwood, p. 96.

46   "Toward Perpetual Peace," p. 104; *Werke* XI,
      p. 211ff.

47   See R. Cooper. "Gibt es eine neue Weltord-
      nung?" *Europa-Archiv* 18 (1993), pp.
      509–16.

48   T. Lindholm offers a reasonable proposal for
      the framework of such a discussion of human
      rights in *The Cross-Cultural Legitimacy of
      Human Rights* (report no. 3, Norwegian
      Institute of Human Rights, 1990).

49   D. and E. Senghaas, "Si vis pacem, par
      posem," *Leviathan* (1990), pp. 230–47.

50   E. O. Czempiel has investigated these strate-
      gies in light of many different examples in
      Sonderheft der Zeitschrift für Politik, ed. G.
      Schwarz (Zurich, 1989); see pp. 55–75.

51   Here I am following D. Archibugi, "From the
      United Nations to Cosmopolitan Democ-
      racy," in *Cosmopolitan Democracy*.

52   See Hans Kelsen, *Peace through Law* (Chapel
      Hill, NC, 1944).

53   Habermas, *The Philosophical Discourse of
      Modernity* (Cambridge, MA, 1987), p. 336ff.

54   Carl Schmitt, *The Concept of the Political*
      (New Brunswick, 1976), p. 52. Isensee ("Welt-
      polizei für Menschenrechten," p. 429) makes
      the same argument: "Ever since there have
      been interventions, they have served ideolo-

gies: confessional ones in the sixteenth and seventeenth centuries; monarchical, Jacobin, and humanitarian principles; the socialist world revolution. Now human rights and democracy join the series. In the long history of intervention, ideology has served to disguise the interest in power of those intervening and to impart their effectiveness with the aura of legitimacy."

55 Schmitt, *Glossarium, 1947–1951* (Berlin, 1991), p. 76.

56 Schmitt, *Concept of the Political*, p. 36.

57 See the essays in *On Human Rights*, ed. S. Schute and S. Hurley (New York, 1993).

58 O. Höffe, "Die Menschenrechte als Legitimation und kritischer Massstab der Demokratie," in *Menschenrechte und Demokratie*, ed. J Schwardtländer (Stuttgart, 1981), p. 250. See also Höffe, *Politische Gerechtigkeit* (Frankfurt, 1987).

59 S. König, *Zur Begründung der Menschenrechte: Hobbes-Locke-Kant* (Freiburg, 1994), p. 26ff.

60 See Hugo Bedau's analysis of the structure of human rights (developed in dialogue with Henry Shue's position), "International Human Rights," in *And Justice for All*, ed. T. Regan and D. van de Weer (Totowa, 1983): "The emphasis on duties is meant to avoid leaving the defense of human rights in a vacuum, bereft of any moral significance for the specific conduct of others. But the duties are not intended to explain or generate rights: if anything, the rights are supposed to explain and generate the duties." (p. 297)

61 Kant, *Metaphysics of Morals* (Cambridge, 1991), p. 56 [translation modified]; *Werke* VIII, p. 345.

62 *Metaphysics of Morals*, p. 63; *Werke* VIII, p. 345.

63 On distinguishing the spheres of ethics, law, and morality, see R. Forst, *Kontexte der Gerechtigkeit* (Frankfurt, 1994).

64 Specifically, in his *Das internationalrechtliche Verbrechen des Angriffskrieges.*

65 In both *The Concept of the Political* (1963) and *Die Wendung zur diskriminerenden Kriegsbegriff* (1988).

66 Schmitt, *Das Verbrechen*, p. 19,

67 Schmitt, *Glossarium*, pp. 113, 265, 146, 282.

68 Schmitt, *Die Wendung*, p. 1.

69 Schmitt, *Der Begriff des Politischen* (Berlin, 1963). (This section is not included in the English translations – translator.)

70 Schmitt, *Concept of the Political*, p. 33.

71 This is a reference to Ernst Junger's novel, *Stahlgewetter*, a model of the aesthetization of war for Heidegger as well. – translator.

72 Hans Magnus Enzensberger, *Aussichten auf den Bürgerkrieg* (Frankfurt, 1993), p. 73ff. Enzensberger rests his case on an extremely selective description of the current international situation, in which the extraordinary expansion of democratic forms of the state in Latin America, Africa, and Eastern Europe is not considered. On this development see Czempiel, *Welt im Umbruch*, p. 107ff. He quickly converts the complex relationships between fundamentalist opportunism with regard to conflicts within states on the one hand and social deprivations and the lack of liberal traditions on the other into anthropological constants. But it is precisely an expanded conception of peace that has affinities with preventive and nonviolent strategies and makes us aware of the pragmatic limitations which undermine humanitarian interventions, as the examples of Somalia and the former Yugoslavia show. For a casuistry of various types of intervention see Senghaas, p. 185ff.

73 Arnold Gehlen, *Moral und Hypermoral* (Frankfurt, 1969).

74 Schmitt, *Glossarium*, p. 259.

75 Ibid., p. 229; see also *Concept of the Political*, p. 63.

76 *Concept of the Political*, p. 54ff.

77 *Concept of the Political*, p. 36.

78 See Habermas, *Kleine Politische Schriften I–IV* (Frankfurt, 1981), pp. 328–39.

79 Klaus Günther, "Kampf gegen das Böse? Wider die ethische Aufrüstung der Kriminalpolitik," *Kritische Justiz* 17 (1994), p. 144. (Bracketed phrase inserted by Habermas – translator.)

80 Ibid.

81 Ibid.

Chapter 18

Moral Universalism and Global Economic Justice*
Thomas W. Pogge

Introduction

Socioeconomic rights, such as that "to a standard of living adequate for the health and well-being of oneself and one's family, including food, clothing, housing, and medical care" (*UDHR*, Article 25), are currently, and by far, the most frequently unfulfilled human rights. Their widespread underfulfillment also plays a major role in explaining global deficits in civil and political human rights demanding democracy, due process, and the rule of law. Extremely poor people – often physically and mentally stunted owing to malnutrition in infancy, illiterate owing to lack of schooling, and much preoccupied with their family's survival – can cause little harm or benefit to the politicians and bureaucrats who rule them. Such officials therefore pay much less attention to the interests of the poor than to the interests of agents more capable of reciprocation, including foreign governments, companies, and tourists.

It is not surprising, perhaps, that those who live in protected affluence manage to reconcile themselves, morally, to such severe poverty and oppression. Still, it is interesting to examine how, and how convincingly, they do so. In this regard, earlier generations of European civilization had two noteworthy advantages over ours. First, the advanced industrial societies were then much less affluent in absolute and relative terms.[1] Fifty years ago, the eradication of severe poverty worldwide would have required a major shift in the global income distribution, imposing substantial opportunity costs upon the advanced industrialized societies. Today, the required shift would be small and the opportunity cost for the developed countries barely noticeable.[2] Second, earlier generations of European civilization were not committed to moral universalism. Their rejection of this idea was forcefully expressed, for instance, when the Anglo-Saxon powers blocked Japan's proposal to include language endorsing racial equality in the Covenant of the League of Nations.[3] Today, by contrast, the equal moral status of all human beings is widely accepted in the developed West. These two historical changes make our acquiescence in severe poverty abroad harder to justify than it would have been in the past. Still, we are quite tolerant of the persistence of extensive and severe poverty abroad even though it would not cost us much to reduce

* From Thomas W. Pogge, *World Poverty and Human Rights* (Cambridge: Polity, 2002), pp. 91–117, 230–6.

it dramatically. How well does this tolerance really fit with our commitment to moral universalism?

Moral Universalism

A moral conception, such as a conception of social justice, can be said to be universalistic if and only if

(A)   it subjects all persons to the same system of fundamental moral principles;

(B)   these principles assign the same fundamental moral benefits (e.g. claims, liberties, powers, and immunities) and burdens (e.g. duties and liabilities) to all; and

(C)   these fundamental moral benefits and burdens are formulated in general terms so as not to privilege or disadvantage certain persons or groups arbitrarily.

I cannot fully explicate these three conditions here, but some brief comments are essential.

Condition A allows a universalistic moral conception to be compatible with moral rules that hold for some people and not for others. But such differences must be generated pursuant to fundamental principles that hold for all. Generated *special* moral benefits and burden can arise in many ways: from contracts or promises, through election or appointment to an office, from country-specific legislation, from conventions prevalent in a certain culture or region, from committing or suffering a crime, from being especially rich or needy, from producing offspring, from practicing a certain occupation, from having an ill parent, from encountering a drowning child, and so on. Only *fundamental* moral principles, including those pursuant to which special moral benefits and burdens are generated, must be

the same for all persons. This condition raises the difficult question of who is to count as a person in the relevant sense: what about the severely mentally disabled, infants, higher animals, artificial or extraterrestrial intelligences?

Condition B raises various problems about how a universalistic moral conception can respond to pragmatic pressures toward allowing the assignment of lesser fundamental moral benefits and burdens to children and to the mentally disabled and perhaps greater fundamental moral burdens to the specially gifted. It is possible that the development of a plausible universalistic moral conception requires that this condition be relaxed somewhat to allow certain departures from equality. Still, equality remains the default – the burden of proof weighs on those favoring specific departures. This suffices to disqualify traditional assignments of unequal fundamental moral benefits and burdens to persons of different sex, skin color, or ancestry.

Moral universalism is clearly incompatible with fundamental principles containing proper names or rigid descriptions of persons or groups. But fundamental principles may legitimately involve other discriminations, as when they enjoin us to respect our parents or to give support to the needy. This distinction between acceptable and unacceptable discriminations cannot be drawn on the basis of formal, grammatical criteria, because it is possible to design gimmicky general descriptions that favor particular persons or groups arbitrarily. Thus, principles meant to discriminate against the Dutch need not refer to them by name, but can refer instead to persons born at especially low elevations or something of this kind – and similarly in other cases. If moral universalism is not to be robbed of all content, we must understand condition C as including the demand that a moral conception must justify the discriminations enshrined in its fundamental principles. An injunction to show special concern for the well-being of the needy can be given a plausible rationale – for instance by reference to the fact that they need help more than others do or that such aid yields larger marginal benefits to its recipients. An injunction to be especially concerned with the well-being of lawyers, by contrast, lacks such a rationale. Why should lawyer, of all people, enjoy special care? Why not also public prosecutors, brokers, dentists?

From this reflection we can see that moral universalism cannot be defined formally. (This is why it makes sense to explicate it through an exemplary application: to the topic of economic justice.) All three conditions raise substantive questions. Who is to count as a person? Can persons differ from one another so much that somewhat different fundamental principles may hold for them? And when is a distinction made by a fundamental principle arbitrary? These are difficult questions that have more than one plausible answer. And even if we could agree on how to answer them, we still would not have achieved moral agreement. From the fact that the rule of helping the needy, for instance, cannot be disqualified as arbitrary, nothing follows about whether this rule is morally valid and, if so, what moral weight it has. Universalism is thus not a moral position with a clearly defined content, but merely an approach – a general schema that can be filled in to yield a variety of substantive moral positions. Universalism can at best provide necessary, not sufficient, conditions for the acceptability of a moral conception. These conditions amount to a call for systematic coherence in morality: the moral assessment of persons and their conduct, of social rules and states of affairs, must be based on fundamental principles that hold for all persons equally; and any discriminations built into such funda-

mental principles must be given a plausible rationale.

Our Moral Assessments of National and Global Economic Orders

Consider two important questions about economic justice:

1   What fundamental moral claims do persons have on the global economic order and what fundamental responsibilities do these claims entail for those who impose it?
2   What fundamental moral claims do persons have on their national economic order and what fundamental responsibilities do these claims entail for those who impose it?

The prevailing opinion is that the correct answers to these questions are very different, that moral claims and burdens are far less substantial in the first case than in the second. But this discrepancy in moral assessment, much like preferential concern for the well-being of lawyers, looks arbitrary. Why should our moral duties, constraining what economic order we may impose upon one another, be so different in the two cases? Let us consider whether this discrepancy stands in need of justification as moral universalism affirms, and whether such a justification is available.

In discussions of national economic justice it is commonly mentioned that national populations, like families, may understand themselves as solidaristic or fraternal communities bound together by specialties of fellow feeling. Such ties generate special moral claims and burdens, and our responsibilities toward fellow citizens and family members may then greatly exceed, and weaken, our responsibilities toward outsiders.[4] Conceding all this does not, however, invalidate the universalist challenge, but merely gives it a different form, involving more specific versions of our two questions:

1′ What moral constraints are there on the kinds of global economic order persons may impose on others even when they have no bond of solidarity with them and a strong bond of solidarity with a smaller group such as their own nation?

2′ What moral constraints are there on the kinds of national economic order persons may impose on others even when they have no bond of solidarity with them and a strong bond of solidarity with a smaller group such as their own family?

The latter question is not concerned with the more ambitious criteria to which specific societies might choose to subject their national economic order, but with the weaker criterion of justice to which we would subject *any* national economic order, regardless of how the society in question understands itself. This weaker criterion is still much stronger than the criterion we apply to the global economic order. There is, then, a discrepancy between the *minimal* criteria of economic justice we apply on the global and national levels. Moral universalism demands that this discrepancy be given a plausible rationale.

Let us first examine, however, whether such a discrepancy is really widely presumed, as I claim. My impression is that most people in the rich countries think of our global economic order as basically just – although this order does not meet two important minimal requirements we place on any national economic order.

The first minimal requirement is that, at least within the limits of what justice allows, social rules should be liable to peaceful change by any large majority of those on whom they are imposed. The global economic order, though it does stabilize a largely violence-free coordination of actors, nonetheless relies on latent violence in two ways. On the one hand, its stability – like that of any other realistically conceivable economic order – depends on the presence of substantial police forces that prevent and deter rule violations. On the other hand, the design of the global economic order – in contrast to that of a democratically governed state – is determined by a tiny minority of its participants whose oligarchic control of the rules ultimately also rests on a huge preponderance of military power. The crucial asymmetry concerns the latter point: we deem it unjust when a national economic order is coercively imposed by a powerful minority and demand that any large majority of its participants should be able to change its rules without the use of force. But few in the wealthy countries place the same moral requirement on the global economic order – most would dismiss it as ridiculous or absurd.

The second minimal requirement is that avoidable life-threatening poverty must be avoided. Insofar as is reasonably possible, an economic order must be shaped to produce an economic distribution such that its participants can meet their most basic standard needs. In regard to the global economic order, most citizens of the rich countries would reject this requirement as well. We know that billions abroad are exposed to life-threatening poverty. We think that we should perhaps help these people with sporadic donations, just as we should occasionally support the worse-off in our own country. But few of us believe that this extensive and severe poverty, even if avoidable, shows our global economic order to be unjust.

Some Factual Background about the Global Economic Order

The moral assessment of an economic order must be responsive to information about three factors: the extent of absolute poverty, how severe and widespread it is; the extent of inequality, which is a rough measure of the avoidability of poverty and of the opportunity cost to the privileged of its avoidance; and the trend of the first two factors, that is, how poverty and inequality tend to develop over time. Let me summarize the state of our world in regard to these three factors.

The Extent of World Poverty

The World Bank estimates that 1,214 out of 5,820 million human beings were in 1998 living below the international poverty line, which it currently defines in terms of $32.74 PPP 1993 per month or $1.08 PPP 1993 per day.[5] "PPP" stands for "purchasing power parity." So the income per person per year of people at the international poverty line has as much purchasing power as $393 had in the US in 1993. According to the US consumer price index, $393 had as much purchasing power in 1993 as $483 has in 2001 (www.bls.gov/cpi/home.htm). The World Bank's $1/day poverty line corresponds, then, roughly to an income of $483 per person per year.[6] Those living below this poverty line fall, on average, 30 percent below it.[7] So they live on roughly $338 PPP 2001 per person per year on average. Now the $PPP incomes the World Bank ascribes to people in poor countries are on average at least four times higher than their actual incomes at market exchange rates.[8] Since virtually all the global poor live in such poor countries, we can then estimate that

their annual *per capita* income of $338 PPP 2001 corresponds to at most $85 at market exchange rates. On average, the global poor can buy about as much per person per year as can be bought with $338 in a typical rich country or with $85 in a typical poor one.

These are the poorest of the poor. The World Bank provides data also for a less scanty poverty line that is twice as high: $786 PPP 1993 ($965 PPP or roughly $241 in the year 2001) per person per year. It counts 2,801 million people as living below this higher poverty line,[9] falling 44.4 percent below it on average.[10] This much larger group of people – nearly half of humankind – can, then, on average buy as much per person per year as can be bought with $537 in a typical rich country or with $134 in a typical poor one.

The consequences of such extreme poverty are foreseeable and extensively documented: 14 percent of the world's population (826 million) are undernourished, 16 percent (968 million) lack access to safe drinking water, 40 percent (2,400 million) lack access to basic sanitation, and 854 million adults are illiterate.[11] Of all human beings 15 percent (more than 880 million) lack access to health services,[12] 17 percent (approximately 1,000 million) have no adequate shelter, and 33 percent (2,000 million) no electricity.[13] "Two out of five children in the developing world are stunted, one in three is underweight and one in ten is wasted."[14] One-quarter of all 5- to 14-year-olds work outside their family for wages, often under harsh conditions, in mining, textile and carpet production, prostitution, factories, and agriculture.[15]

These statistics are depressing enough. Yet, they can plausibly be accused of making things look better than they are. By focusing on human beings *alive at any given time*, all these statistics give less weight to persons whose lives are short. Thus, if the poorest third of humankind live, on average, half as long as the rest (which is approximately true), then they account for fully half of all human lives. To give the same weight to each human life irrespective of its duration, all the above statistics would have to be similarly adjusted for differences in life expectancy. No such adjustment is needed for statistics about births and deaths, as they already give equal weight to every human life. One-third of all human deaths are due to poverty-related causes, such as starvation, diarrhea, pneumonia, tuberculosis, malaria, measles, and perinatal conditions, all of which could be prevented or cured cheaply through food, safe drinking water, vaccinations, rehydration packs, or medicines.[16] If the developed Western countries had their proportional shares of these deaths, severe poverty would kill some 3,500 Britons and 16,500 Americans per week. Each year, 15 times as many US citizens would die of poverty-related causes as were lost in the entire Vietnam War.

The extent of human suffering and premature deaths due to poverty-related causes is not well known in the West. As the media presented retrospectives on the twentieth century, they gave ample space to some of its human-made horrors: 11 million murdered in the German holocaust, 30 million starved to death in Mao's Great Leap Forward, 11 million wiped out by Stalin, 2 million killed by the Khmer Rouge, 800,000 hacked to death in Rwanda. The media also give considerable attention to natural disasters. When there are earthquakes, storms, and floods, we have them on the evening news, with footage of desperate parents grieving for their dead children. Not mentioned in the retrospectives and not shown on the evening news are the ordinary deaths from starvation and preventable diseases – some 250 million people, mostly children, in the 14 years since the end of the Cold War. The names of these people, if listed in the style of the Vietnam War Memorial, would cover a wall 350 miles long.[17]

The Extent of Global Inequality

Severe poverty is nothing new. What is new is the extent of global inequality. Real wealth is no longer limited to a small elite. Hundreds of millions enjoy a high standard of living with plenty of spare time, travel, education, cars, domestic appliances, mobile phones, computers, stereos, and so on. The "high-income economies" (comprising 32 countries plus Hong Kong), with 14.9 percent of world population and 79.7 percent of aggregate global income, have annual *per capita* income of $27.510.[18] For the world as a whole, annual *per capita* income is $5,150.[19] With annual *per capita* income of about $85, the collective income of the bottom quintile is about $103 billion annually, or one-third of 1 percent of aggregate global income. This contrast gives us a sense of how cheaply severe poverty could be avoided: one-eightieth of our share is triple theirs[20] – which should give pause to those who conclude from the very large number of extremely poor people that eradicating world poverty would dramatically impoverish the developed countries.

Global inequality is even greater in regard to property and wealth. Affluent people typically have more wealth than annual income, while the poor normally own significantly less than one annual income. The enormous fortunes of the super-rich in developed societies were given special emphasis in recent *Human Development Reports:* "The world's 200 richest people more than doubled their net worth in the four years to 1998, to more than $1 trillion. The assets of the top three billionaires are more than the combined GNP of all least developed countries and their 600 million people."[21]

Trends in World
Poverty and Inequality

The last 50 years give the impression of rapid progress, punctuated by a long series of human-rights declarations and treaties, new initiatives, summits, as well as detailed research into the quantification, causes, and effects of poverty. Such things are not unimportant. But they disguise the fact that real progress for the poor themselves is less impressive. Yes, life expectancy has risen markedly in many countries and infant mortality has fallen substantially owing to better disease control. But the number of people in poverty has not declined since 1987[22] – despite the fact that this period has seen exceptional technological and economic progress as well as a dramatic decline in defense expenditures.[23] Since 1996, when 186 governments made the very modest commitment to halve the number of undernourished people within 19 years, this number has barely changed – despite a 22 percent drop in the real wholesale prices of basic foodstuffs.[24] These trends are all the more disturbing as the ranks of the poor and undernourished are continuously thinned by some 50,000 premature deaths daily from poverty-related causes.

While poverty and malnutrition are stagnant, global inequality, and hence the avoidability of poverty, is escalating dramatically: "The income gap between the fifth of the world's people living in the richest countries and the fifth in the poorest was 74 to 1 in 1997, up from 60 to 1 in 1990 and 30 to 1 in 1960. [Earlier] the income gap between the top and bottom countries increased from 3 to 1 in 1820 to 7 to 1 in 1870 to 11 to 1 in 1913."[25] There is a long-established trend toward ever greater international income inequality – a trend that has certainly not decelerated since the end of the colonial era 40 years ago.[26]

So much by way of data about the world economy which is deemed tolerably just here in the developed countries.

Conceptions of National and Global Economic Justice Contrasted

Let us compare this case to that of a national society in which the various economic parameters we have considered resemble those of the world at large. No national society displays anything like the current degree of global income inequality, but because Brazil has one of the highest quintile income inequality ratios (24.4),[27] and because its PPP gross national income *per capita* is close to that of the world at large,[28] we might call our fictional country Subbrazil. The point of the contrast is to pose this challenge: if we consider Subbrazil's economic order unjust, how can we find the global economic order morally acceptable?

One may object here that the economic order of Subbrazil is not really unjust. It appears unjust to us because we imagine that most of its citizens, like most citizens of European countries, conceive of their society as being, at least in some weak sense, a solidaristic community. Subbrazil's failure to meet even weak solidaristic standards constitutes no injustice, however, because most Subbrazilians do not want their national economic order to meet such a standard. If they desired otherwise, a majority of Subbrazilians could reform their economic order through the ballot box.

This objection could be contested by asserting that we do not accept as just a national economic order that avoidably produces life-threatening poverty for a sizable minority merely because this economic order is approved by the majority. But even if we accept the objection despite this worry, the challenge is not yet dissolved. The objection assumes that the Subbrazilian economy meets at least the first minimal requirement. It assumes that, if some large majority of Subbrazilians wanted to reform their national economic order so as to reduce life-threatening poverty, they could bring about such reforms. I can thus circumvent the objection by weakening my claim. Instead of claiming that we would condemn as unjust any national economic order that does not meet *both* minimal requirements, I claim instead that we would condemn as unjust any national economic order that does not meet at least *one* of them.

Let us imagine, then, a fictive Sub-Subbrazil: a society whose economic order avoidably produces life-threatening poverty for a sizable minority and is also not subject to peaceful change from below, even by a large majority.[29] Such an economic order would be condemned as unjust by most people in the developed countries. (What is to count as an unjust national economic order, if not this?) And we arrive then at this reformulated challenge: if we condemn as unjust the imposition of the national economic order of Sub-Subbrazil, how can we condone the imposition, by governments acting in our name, of the existing global economic order? The latter order is, after all, like the former in the extent of poverty and inequality it produces and also in that even a large majority of those on whom it is imposed – the poorest four-fifths of humankind, for instance – cannot reform it by peaceful means. How can the flagrant discrepancy between our minimal criteria of national and global economic justice be justified?

As here explicated, moral universalism demands such a justification. In the face of this demand, we have three options. First, we can evade the demand by surrendering the discrepancy: by strengthening the minimal criterion we apply to the global economic order and/or by weakening the minimal criterion we apply to any national economic order (perhaps even reversing our opinion that Sub-Subbrazil's economic order is unjust). Second, we can try to meet the demand by defending a discrepancy of minimal criteria – by justifying the view that our global economic order may not be unjust even if it fails to meet the minimal criterion of justice we apply to any national economic order. Third, we can insist on a discrepancy of minimal criteria while rejecting the universalist demand to justify this discrepancy.

Responses of the first two kinds accept the universalist challenge and are willing to engage in the debate about minimal criteria of national and global economic justice. The third response declines to join this debate with the tripartite claim that national economic regimes are subject to some minimal criterion of justice, that the global economic order is not subject to this criterion, and that no justification can or need be given for this discrepancy. [The next section] focuses on this third, most antagonistic response.

Moral Universalism and David Miller's Contextualism

The third response can point to existing moral intuitions or convictions. Our discrepant criteria of national and global economic justice are fixed points that any philosophical account of our morality must reaffirm. An account that does not vindicate our deepest convictions must be ejected for this reason alone. We are deeply convinced that we do not share responsibility for starvation abroad. This conviction, which we are more sure of than we could ever be of the merits of any complex philosophical argument, refutes any moral conception that concludes otherwise. To be sure, our discrepant standards of economic justice may seem incoherent. But the moral data (our intuitions or deepest convictions) are what they are, and coherence, in any case, is in the eye of the beholder.

In this simple version, the third response is hard to swallow. The view that moral reflection exhausts itself in compiling our favorite convictions, that what we firmly enough believe to be right is right, trivializes the ambition of leading a moral life. But perhaps the third response can be made more palatable by presenting it as including a justification for its rejection of the universalist demand for justification. David Miller may appear to develop such a more sophisticated position, arguing for the anti-universalist claim that we should allow diverse moral principles to hold in different contexts without demanding any justification for such diversity.[30] I try to show that this appearance is misleading, that Miller's contextualism overlaps with moral universalism, and that moral conceptions within this overlap seem more promising than moral conceptions exemplifying more extreme variants of either universalism or contextualism. Let me add that I am here setting aside Miller's interesting and important work on national and international justice,[31] attending solely to his more general account of contextualism.

Miller may appear to embrace the general statement of the anti-universalist response when he associates the contextualism he favors – "a species of intuitionism in Rawls's sense"[32] – with bald, conversation-stopping pronouncements of the form "equality is simply the appropriate principle to use in circumstances C."[33] He also argues against the demand for justification: attempts to construct a unified account of all of morality cannot achieve "a reasonably close fit between the theory and our pre-theoretical considered judgements."[34] Such attempts, he believes, lead to the proliferation of neat but implausible moral theories whose disagreements raise questions we cannot convinc-

ingly resolve and therefore foster a skeptical attitude toward morality which sets back efforts toward achieving moral progress on concrete and urgent practical problems.

I respect and share these concerns. But it is not clear that anti-universalism can do any better. Those who walk out of specific moral discussions with an emphatic declaration that C_1 and C_2 simply *are* different contexts to which different principles P_1 and P_2 are appropriate will fail to convince, and quite possibly seem offensive to, those who believe otherwise – even if they also argue in general terms that morality is too heterogeneous to yield to the universalist demand for justifications. (Think of those who, in accord with the convictions of their time, emphatically declared that moral principles appropriate to one social class simply *are* inappropriate to another.) By declining to give any specific reasons for delimiting the various contexts, and for assigning the various moral principles to them, in the way they do, such people will moreover foster a cynical attitude toward moral theorizing as the bare assertion of favorite convictions, invariably distorted by the asserter's interests, social position, and prejudices.

Miller is sensitive to these countervailing concerns when – setting his contextualism apart from conventionalism – he writes: "Contextualism . . . recognizes that we are likely to find different principles of justice being used at different times and in different places, but it argues that this variation itself has an underlying logic that we can both grasp and use as a critical tool when assessing the prevailing conceptions of justice at any particular moment."[35] This remark shows, I believe, that Miller rejects the third response by recognizing that morality is subject to an underlying transcontextual logic which may, on the one hand, provide a rationale for applying different moral principles in different contexts (e.g. under different natural, historical, cultural, technological, economic, or demographic conditions) and may also, on the other hand, serve as a basis for criticizing prevailing moral conceptions. Once we can, by appeal to such an underlying logic, formulate justifying reasons for or against the application of different moral standards to persons from different social classes, and for or against the differential assessment of national and global economic regimes, we have moved beyond *dogmatic* contextualism and the unsupported endorsements or rejections it takes to be appropriate responses to moral disagreement.

Insofar as contextualism endorses a justificatory discourse about the delimitation of contexts and the variation of principles across them – and other work by Miller (see n. 31) contains plenty of argument in this vein – it overlaps with moral universalism. As explicated here, universalism does not require that, if moral principles P_1, P_2, P_3 are to apply in contexts C_1, C_2, C_3, respectively, then there must be one supreme "transcendent" principle or set of principles of which P_1, P_2, P_3 are contextual applications (as "drive no faster than 30 miles per hour" is a contextual application of "move no faster than is both safe and legal"). To be sure, moral universalism *permits* such highly unified anti-contextualist moral conceptions, as exemplified by utilitarianism. But it *also* permits the *critical* contextualist alternative suggested in the last-quoted sentence from Miller: a moral conception holding that fundamental principles P_1, P_2, P_3 apply in contexts C_1, C_2, C_3, respectively, and offering a justification for delimiting the various contexts, and for assigning the various moral principles to them, in these ways.

I find this contextualist moral universalism far more plausible than its anti-contextualist (monistic) alternative. Regarding our general view of moral theorizing, Miller and I may converge then upon an intermediate view – critical contextualism – defined by the rejection of monistic univer-

salism on the one hand and dogmatic contextualism on the other. We both envision different fundamental moral principles applying in different contexts, and we both seek justifications for the delimitation of contexts and the formulation of fundamental principles appropriate to them. We differ in regard to what delimitations, context-specific principles, and justifications we find acceptable.

Because the proposed intermediate view of moral theorizing is unfamiliar, I develop it somewhat further through a discussion of Rawls's work, which provides both an illustration and a violation of the contextualist moral universalism I favor.

Contextualist Moral Universalism and John Rawls's Moral Conception

Rawls wants to confine his theory of justice to a specific context: to the basic structure of a self-contained society existing under the circumstances of justice. His theory commits him to certain moral demands on the political conduct of citizens – they must support and promote a just basic structure. But Rawls wants to leave open what moral principles may apply to their personal conduct. He has been attacked for this aloofness by monistic universalists, such as Gerald Cohen and Liam Murphy.[36] According to them, any fundamental moral principle that applies to social institutions must also apply to personal conduct. Thus, if the difference principle requires that a society's economic order should erase any socioeconomic inequality that does not optimize the lowest socioeconomic position, then individuals must also be required, in their personal conduct, to erase any socioeconomic inequality that does not optimize the lowest socioeconomic position.[37]

Rawls's contextualism can be defended against this critique. Rawls has important reasons for limiting the range of his principles of justice to the basic structure. These reasons – invoking *inter alia* the fact of pluralism as well as the need to avoid overdemandingness and to achieve stability (compliance) – show that basic social institutions should be treated as a separate context to which distinct moral principles apply.[38] These reasons illustrate how limiting the range of moral principles can be justified without the invocation of any deeper, trans-contextual principles from which context-specific principles are then derived. The case at hand thus shows how it is possible to justify moral principles as range-limited or context-specific even while also maintaining that they are fundamental. Insofar as the justification for the Rawlsian range limit satisfies the three conditions of moral universalism, his account of the justice of basic social institutions is an instance not merely of critical contextualism, but also, and more specifically, of contextualist moral universalism.

Whereas this Rawlsian separation of contexts instantiates contextualist moral universalism, another separation of contexts, central to his latest work, instantiates its violation. Rawls insists there on applying quite different fundamental principles to national and international institutional schemes, but fails to give an adequate justification for the separation of contexts. This failure occurs on three distinct levels.

First, Rawls strongly rejects the difference principle as a requirement of global justice on the ground that it is unacceptable for one people to bear certain costs of decisions made by another – decisions affecting industrialization or the birth rate, for example.[39] But he fails to explain why this ground should not analogously disqualify the difference principle for national societies as well. Why is it not likewise unacceptable for one province, township, or family to bear such costs of decisions made by another?[40] And if, despite such sharing of costs, the difference

principle is the most reasonable one for us to advocate in regard to the domestic economic order, then why is it not also the most reasonable one for us to advocate in regard to the global economic order? Rawls provides no answer.

Rawls also fails to explain how his rejection of the difference principle for the global order accords with his argument in *A Theory of Justice*, which he continues to endorse. There Rawls discusses how a human population of indeterminate size and explicitly conceived as "self-contained" and "a closed system"[41] should institutionally organize itself. His inquiry leads to the difference principle as a requirement of economic justice. He takes this principle to be acceptable – indeed ideal – for the US, even though this society diverges from the task description by not being a self-contained closed system. So why should the difference principle be unacceptable for the world at large, which fits the task description precisely? There is, again, no answer in Rawls.

It might be objected that this unjustified discrepancy is not important. Perhaps Rawls should concede that a global economic order designed to satisfy the difference principle is not, as such, unacceptable. But the goal of such an order is nonetheless morally inappropriate to our world, because many people oppose the difference principle and not unreasonably so.

Against this objection, one needs to point out that such opposition exists at home as well as abroad. Increasingly sensitive to this fact, Rawls continues to propose the difference principle, which he had associated with the ideal of fraternity,[42] as the most reasonable one for the domestic economic order of modern liberal societies including, first and foremost, the US. But he allows that other societies may reasonably subject their national economic regimes to other criteria. And he is even willing to concede that his difference principle is not uniquely reasonable even for the US: his fellow citizens would not be unreasonable if they gave their political support to some other liberal criterion of economic justice.[43] At least according to Rawls's later work, then, a society that deliberately fails to satisfy the difference principle may nonetheless not be unjust. Rather, to count as just (or not-unjust), a national society need merely endorse and (approximately) satisfy *some* not-unreasonable liberal standard of economic justice.

Now if this, rather than the difference principle, is Rawls's minimal criterion of national economic justice, it defines a second level on which the challenge from moral universalism arises: Rawls should either hold that a global order, too, can count as just only if it satisfies this minimal criterion of economic justice or else justify his failure to do so.

Rawls does neither; but he suggests that one reason against applying liberal standards globally is the need to accommodate certain – "decent" – nonliberal societies. (Decent societies are ones to which, Rawls believes, liberal societies should offer reciprocal recognition as full and equal members in good standing within a well-ordered system of states.) This is a strange suggestion because, in our world, nonliberal societies and their populations tend to be poor and quite willing to cooperate in reforms that would bring the global economic order closer to meeting a liberal standard of economic justice. The much more affluent liberal societies are the ones blocking such reforms, and it is not clear how their obstruction can be justified by the concern to accommodate decent societies. Granted, these reforms are not required by decency, decent societies thus could oppose them, and liberal societies might then have reason to accommodate such opposition. But when there exists no decent society actually opposing the reforms, then the concern to accommodate decent societies cannot be a reason for liberal societies to block them contrary to the minimal criterion, and hence to every more specific criterion, of liberal economic justice.

Suppose that the foregoing argument fails or that there are some decent societies opposed to economic reform. If so, the challenge of moral universalism arises one last time on a yet lower level: Rawls should either disqualify as less-than-decent any global economic order that does not meet whatever requirements any national economic order must meet to count as decent or else justify his refusal to do so.

But again, it seems that Rawls wants to insist on an unjustified double standard. He writes that a decent society's "system of law must follow a common good idea of justice that takes into account what it sees as the fundamental interests of everyone in society."[44] Rawls is quite vague on what constraints he takes this condition to place on the national economic order of a decent society. But he does not require the global economic order to meet even these weaker constraints of decency. All he asks is that no peoples should have to live "under unfavorable conditions that prevent their having a just or decent political and social regime."[45] And even this demand does not constrain global economic institutions, but only the conduct of other peoples. We may impose a global economic order that generates strong centrifugal tendencies and ever increasing international inequality, provided we "assist" the societies impoverished by this order just enough to keep them above some basic threshold.[46]

Despite considerable vagueness in his treatment of economic institutions, it seems clear, then, that Rawls endorses double standards on three different levels: in regard to national economic regimes, the difference principle is part of Rawls's highest aspiration for justice; in regard to the global economic order, however, Rawls disavows this aspiration and even rejects the difference principle as unacceptable. Rawls suggests a weaker minimal criterion of liberal economic justice on the national level; but he holds that the global order can fully accord with liberal conceptions of justice without satisfying this criterion. And Rawls suggests an even weaker criterion of economic decency on the national level; but he holds that the global order can be not merely decent, but even just, without satisfying this criterion. Insofar as he offers no plausible rationales for these three double standards, Rawls runs afoul of moral universalism. He fails to meet the burden of showing that his applying different moral principles to national and global institutional schemes does not amount to arbitrary discrimination in favor of affluent societies and against the global poor.

Rationalizing Divergent Moral Assessments through a Double Standard

Most citizens of the developed countries reconcile themselves to massive and avoidable poverty abroad by not holding such poverty against the global economic order as they would hold similar poverty within a national society against its domestic economic order. The common and obvious way of rationalizing such a divergence is through a double standard: by subjecting the global economic order to weaker moral demands than any national economic order. Such double standards are widely employed in ordinary and academic discourse. They are often dogmatically taken for granted, perhaps with a general appeal to "our moral convictions" or a general argument for dogmatic contextualism. This is the "third response" to moral universalism. [. . .]

Rawls seems willing to defend a double standard in regard to national and global economic justice and thus exemplifies the second response to the universalist challenge. But the defenses he actually provides are incomplete, because he does not face up to the comparative nature of the task. It is not enough, for instance, to provide arguments against a global application of the difference principle. One must also show that these arguments create the desired asymmetry, that they have more weight than analogous arguments against a national application of the difference principle. Rawls does not even begin to do this.

His failure is typical of academic and popular rationalizations of double standards of economic justice. There are reasons for, and reasons against, a strong criterion of economic justice. Discussions of the national economic order tend to highlight the reasons for, discussions of the global order tend to highlight the reasons against. But to justify the desired asymmetry, one must discuss the relevant reasons of both kinds in respect to both contexts. In particular, one must show that some reasons for a strong criterion have more weight in the balance of reasons concerning national than they have in the balance of reasons concerning global economic justice – and/or, conversely, that some reasons for a weak criterion have less weight in the balance of reasons concerning national than they have in the balance of reasons concerning global economic justice.

Arguments for a weak criterion of economic justice typically appeal to cultural diversity or to the autonomy of, or special ties within, smaller groups. Such arguments are often used to justify acquiescence in a global economic order that engenders great poverty and inequality. But all three factors exist within nations as well. And they can then be useful in the defense of a double standard only if one can show them to be significantly less relevant domestically. As we have seen, showing this is not so easy.[47]

In a sense this is a modest result. Many different double standards could be formulated with regard to our topic, and various rationales might be offered for each such formulation. No one can anticipate and refute all conceivable such accounts. But this very impossibility of showing conclusively that no sufficiently large discrepancy of standards can be justified provides a subsidiary reason for what I have presented as an essential element of moral universalism: the assignment of the burden of proof to those who *favor* a double standard. They can bear this burden, as they need only make good on an existential quantifier by formulating *one* version of the desired double standard and then giving a plausible rationale for it. And yet, the *moral* reason remains primary: we owe the global poor an account of why we take ourselves to be entitled to impose on them a global economic order in violation of the minimal moral constraints we ourselves place on the imposition of any national economic order.

If the burden of proof indeed weighs on those favoring a double standard, then the result of my discussion is not so modest after all. We, the affluent countries and their citizens, continue to impose a global economic order under which millions avoidably die each year from poverty-related causes. We would regard it as a grave injustice if such an economic order were imposed within a national society. We must regard our imposition of the present global order as a grave injustice unless we have a plausible rationale for a suitable double standard. We do not have such a plausible rationale.

Rationalizing Divergent Moral Assessments without a Double Standard

There is another way of rationalizing the failure of the affluent to hold massive and avoidable poverty abroad against the global economic order as they would hold similar poverty within a national society against its domestic economic order. The next four paragraphs give a summary statement of this rationalization, which invokes the idea of institutional responsibility.

We tend to recoil from an institutional order described as one that is imposed upon people of whom many avoidably are very poor. But let us not be fooled by mere rhetoric. An economic order under which there is a lot of avoidable love sickness is not, for this reason, morally flawed. This example drives home that the moral quality of an institutional order under which avoidable starvation occurs depends on whether and how that order is causally related to this starvation. It depends, that is, on the extent to which starvation could be avoided through institutional modification. And it also depends on the manner in which the institutional order in question engenders more starvation than its best feasible alternative would. Does it, for example, require serfs to do unremunerated work for aristocrats or does it merely fail to tax the more productive participants enough to underwrite an adequate welfare system?

This insight is relevant to our topic. We have been discussing the moral assessment of two kinds of economic order (national and global) that, in the real world, differ greatly in their causal impact. The global economic order plays a marginal role in the perpetuation of extensive and severe poverty worldwide. This poverty is substantially caused not by global, systemic factors, but – in the countries where it occurs – by their flawed national economic regimes and by their corrupt and incompetent elites, both of which impede national economic growth and a fairer distribution of the national product. Such domestic defects are the main reason why these countries become ever poorer in relative and often even in absolute terms and why the burdens of this impoverishment fall upon their poorest citizens most heavily.[48] Excessive poverty and inequality within countries, by contrast, are to a considerable extent traceable to systemic factors and are then, causally and morally, the responsibility of the politically and economically influential elites who uphold the relevant national economic regimes.

We do indeed judge our global economic order, under which a great deal of poverty and inequality persists, less harshly than we would a national economic order associated with similar poverty and inequality data. But these discrepant assessments do not reflect a double standard concerning the significance of extreme poverty and inequality in the moral assessment of global and national regimes. Rather, they reflect a single standard uniformly applied to both kinds of regime, yet a standard that is sensitive not merely to the incidence of avoidable poverty but also to the regime's causal role in its occurrence.

The reconciling force of this empirical rationalization depends on complex economic causalities, on the correct explanation of persisting severe poverty worldwide and of the expansion of global inequality. We must convince ourselves that the global economic order is not a significant causal contributor to these phenomena. Many citizens of the affluent countries are convinced of this, and convinced even that the global economic order could not be modified into a significant causal contributor to the eradication of extreme poverty and inequality. These people believe that, for such progress to occur, the poor countries themselves must get their house in order, must give themselves governments and political institutions that are more responsive to the needs of their populations. With respect to this task, outsiders can help only to a very limited extent. This is so because it would be morally unacceptable to impose what we think of as reasonable leaders or social institutions upon such countries and also because any resolute interference in the internal affairs of poor

countries could easily turn out to be counterproductive as corrupt rulers manage further to entrench their rule by denouncing our supposed imperialism or neocolonialism. Sad as it is, our hands are tied. We can try to alleviate world poverty through development assistance, given *ad hoc* by affluent societies and individuals or built into the global order as in the Tobin Tax proposal. But such attempts will not succeed well because we cannot prevent the corrupt elites from siphoning off much of our aid into their own pockets. Perhaps 1.21 percent of our incomes would indeed suffice to raise all the incomes of all human beings to the World Bank's higher poverty line (see n. 2). But, as things stand, there is unfortunately no way of getting such a donation to the world's poorest people in a concentrated way.

Responding to this empirical rationalization, I do not deny the analysis sketched in the preceding paragraph. The eradication of poverty in the poor countries indeed depends strongly on their governments and social institutions: on how their economies are structured and on whether there exists genuine democratic competition for political office which gives politicians an incentive to be responsive to the interests of the poor majority. But this analysis is nevertheless ultimately unsatisfactory, because it portrays the corrupt social institutions and corrupt elites prevalent in the poor countries as an exogenous fact: as a fact that explains, but does not itself stand in need of explanation. "Some poor countries manage to give themselves reasonable political institutions, but many others fail or do not even try. This is just the way things are." An explanation that runs out at this point does not explain very much. An adequate explanation of persistent global poverty must not merely adduce the prevalence of flawed social institutions and of corrupt, oppressive, incompetent elites in the poor countries but must also provide an explanation for this prevalence.

Social scientists do indeed provide deeper explanations responsive to this need. These are, for the most part, "nationalist" explanations which trace flaws in a country's political and economic institutions and the corruption and incompetence of its ruling elite back to this country's history, culture, or natural environment.[49] Because there are substantial differences in how countries, and the incidence of poverty within them, develop over time, it is clear that such nationalist explanations must play a role in explaining national trajectories and international differentials. From this it does not follow, however, that the global economic order does not also play a substantial causal role by shaping how the culture of each poor country evolves and by influencing how a poor country's history, culture, and natural environment affect the development of its domestic institutional order, ruling elite, economic growth, and income distribution. In these ways global institutional factors might contribute substantially to the persistence of severe poverty in particular countries and in the world at large. The next section shows that this is indeed the case, contrary to the central claim of the empirical rationalization.

The Causal Role of Global Institutions in the Persistence of Severe Poverty

My case can be made by example, and I focus on two highly significant aspects of the existing global order.[50] Any group controlling a preponderance of the means of coercion within a country is internationally recognized as the legitimate government of this country's territory and people – regardless of how this group came to power, of how it exercises power, and of the extent to which it may be supported or opposed by the population it rules.[51] That such a group exercising effective power receives international recognition means not merely that we engage it in negotiations. It means also that we accept this group's right to act for the people it rules and, in particular, confer upon it the privileges freely to borrow in the country's name (international borrowing privilege) and freely to dispose of the country's natural resources (international resource privilege).

The resource privilege we confer upon a group in power is much more than our acquiescence in its effective control over the natural resources of the country in question. This privilege includes the power[52] to effect legally valid transfers of ownership rights in such resources. Thus a corporation that has purchased resources from the Saudis or Suharto, or from Mobuto or Abacha, has thereby become entitled to be – and actually *is* – recognized anywhere in the world as the legitimate owner of these resources. This is a remarkable feature of our global institutional order. A group that overpowers the guards and takes control of a warehouse may be able to give some of the merchandise to others, accepting money in exchange. But the fence who pays them becomes merely the possessor, not the owner, of the loot. Contrast this with a group that overpowers an elected government and takes control of a country. Such a group, too, can give away some of the country's natural resources, accepting money in exchange. In this case, however, the purchaser acquires not merely possession, but all the rights and liberties of ownership, which are supposed to be – and actually *are* – protected and enforced by all other states' courts and police forces. The international resource privilege, then, is the legal power to confer globally valid ownership rights in the country's resources.

Indifferent to how governmental power is acquired, the international resource privilege provides powerful incentives toward coup attempts and civil wars in the resource-rich countries. Consider Nigeria, for instance, where oil exports of $6–10 billion annually constitute roughly a quarter of GDP. Whoever takes power there, by whatever means, can count on this revenue stream to enrich himself and to cement his rule. This is quite a temptation for military officers, and during 28 of the past 32 years Nigeria has indeed been ruled by military strongmen who took power and ruled by force. Able to buy means of repression abroad and support from other officers at home, such rulers were not dependent on popular support and thus made few productive investments toward stimulating poverty eradication or even economic growth.[53]

After the sudden death of Sani Abacha, Nigeria is now ruled by a civilian ex-general, Olusegun Obasanjo, who – a prominent member of the Advisory Council of Transparency International (TI) – raised great expectations for reform. These expectations have been disappointed: Nigeria continues to be listed near the bottom of TI's own international corruption chart.[54] This failure has evoked surprise. But it makes sense against the background of the international resource privilege: Nigeria's military officers know well that they can capture the oil revenues by overthrowing Obasanjo. To survive in power, he must therefore keep them content enough with the status quo so that the potential gains from a coup attempt do not seem worth the risk of failure. Corruption in Nigeria is not just a local phenomenon rooted in tribal culture and traditions, but encouraged and sustained by the international resource privilege.

Nigeria is just one instance of a broader pattern also exemplified by the Congo/Zaire, Kenya, Angola, Mozambique, Brazil, Venezuela, the Philippines, Burma/Myanmar, the oil states of the Middle East, and many smaller resource-rich but poverty-stricken countries.[55] In fact, there is a significant negative correlation, known as the Dutch Disease, between the size of countries' resource sectors and their rates of economic growth. This correlation has a "nationalist" explanation: national resource abundance causes bad government and flawed institutions by encouraging coups and civil wars and by facilitating authoritarian entrenchment and corruption. But this nationalist explanation crucially depends on a global background factor, the international resource privilege, without which a poor country's generous resource endowment would not handicap its progress toward democratic government, economic growth, and the eradication of poverty – certainly not to the same extent.[56]

Similar points can be made about the international borrowing privilege, according to which any group holding governmental power in a national territory – no matter how it acquired or exercises this power – is entitled to borrow funds in the name of the whole society, thereby imposing internationally valid legal obligations upon the country at large. Any successor government that refuses to honor debts incurred by an ever so corrupt, brutal, undemocratic, unconstitutional, repressive, unpopular predecessor will be severely punished by the banks and governments of other countries; at minimum it will lose its own borrowing privilege by being excluded from the international financial markets. Such refusals are therefore quite rare, as governments, even when newly elected after a dramatic break with the past, are compelled to pay the debts of their ever so awful predecessors.

The international borrowing privilege has three important negative effects on the corruption and poverty problems in the poor countries. First, it puts a country's full credit at the disposal of even the most loathsome rulers who took power in a coup and maintain it through violence and repression. Such rulers can then borrow more money and can do so more cheaply than they could do if they alone, rather than the entire country, were obliged to repay. In this way, the international borrowing privilege helps such rulers to maintain themselves in power even against near-universal popular opposition. Second, indifferent to how governmental power is acquired, the international borrowing privilege strengthens incentives toward coup attempts and civil war: whoever succeeds in bringing a preponderance of the means of coercion under his control gets the borrowing privilege as an additional reward. Third, when the yoke of dictatorship can be thrown off, the international borrowing privilege saddles the country with the often huge debts of the former oppressors. It thereby saps the capacity of its fledgling democratic government to implement structural reforms and other political programs, thus rendering it less successful and less stable than it would otherwise be.[57] (It is small consolation that putschists are sometimes weakened by being held liable for the debts of their elected predecessors.)

I have shown how two aspects of the global economic order, imposed by the wealthy societies and cherished also by authoritarian rulers and corrupt elites in the poorer countries, contribute substantially to the persistence of severe poverty. The two privileges crucially affect what sorts of persons jostle for political power and then shape national policy in the poor countries, what incentives these persons face, what options they have, and what impact these options would have on the lives of their compatriots. These global factors thereby strongly affect the overall incidence of oppression and poverty and also, through their greater impact on resource-rich countries, international differentials in oppression and poverty.

This result is not altered by the fact that reforms of the two privileges are not easy to devise and might well, by raising the prices of natural resources, prove quite costly for the affluent consumer societies and for other states dependent on resource imports. I am arguing that the citizens and governments of the wealthy societies, by imposing the present global economic order, significantly contribute to the persistence of severe poverty and thus share institutional moral responsibility for it. I am not yet discussing what we should do about persistent global poverty in light of our moral responsibility for it.

It is easier to disconnect oneself from extensive and severe poverty suffered by wholly innocent people abroad when there are others who clearly are to blame for it. My argument in this section was therefore focused specifically on how the national causal factors we most like to highlight – tyranny, corruption, coups d'état, civil wars – are encouraged and sustained by central aspects of the present global economic order. The argument shows that, those national causal factors notwithstanding, we share causal and moral responsibility. This insight should not lessen the moral responsibility we assign to dictators, warlords, corrupt officials, and cruel employers in the poor countries any more than our initial insight into their moral responsibility should lessen the moral responsibility we assign to ourselves.

The focus of my argument should also not obscure the other ways in which the present global economic order contributes to the persistence of poverty. By greatly increasing international interdependence, this order exacerbates the vulnerability of the weaker national economies to exogenous shocks through decisions and policies made – without input from or concern for the poorer societies – in the US or EU (e.g. interest rates set by the US and EU central banks, speculation-induced moves on commodity and currency markets). Moreover, the components of this global economic order emerge through highly complex intergovernmental negotiations in which the governments and negotiators of the developed countries enjoy a crushing advantage in bargaining power and expertise. Agreements resulting from such negotiations therefore reflect the interests of these rich countries' governments, corporations, and populations – regardless of whether the relevant representatives of the developing countries are corrupt or are selflessly devoted to poverty eradication. And agreements that are good for the rich countries may not be good for the global poor, as is amply demonstrated in the report on the Uruguay Round discussed in section IV of the General Introduction.

Conclusion

The previous section showed what is obvious to people in the poor, marginal countries: that the rules structuring the world economy have a profound impact on the global economic distribution just as the economic order of a national society has a profound impact on its domestic economic distribution. The empirical rationalization is not empirically sustainable.

Spreading awareness of its unsustainability could turn out to be of great practical importance in reshaping both the explanatory and the moral debates about world poverty. As it is, the explanatory debate is largely focused on nationalist explanations: on the question of what national economic institutions and policies in poor countries hamper or promote the eradication of domestic poverty. Some argue for free markets with a minimum in taxes and governmental regulations (the Asian tigers model), others for increased governmental investment in education, medical care, and infrastructure (the Kerala model). This debate is certainly important. But it would also be quite important to examine what *global* economic institutions hamper or promote the eradication of poverty world-

wide. Modest such inquiries are familiar: economists and politicians debate alternative structures and missions for the IMF and the World Bank and the international impact of the 1995 Trade-Related Aspects of Intellectual Property Rights (TRIPS) agreement reached within the WTO. But with respect to larger issues, such as the international resource and borrowing privileges and the political mechanisms through which the rules of the world economy are created and revised, the status quo is largely taken for granted as a given background much like the basic natural features of our planet.

As it is, the moral debate is largely focused on the extent to which affluent societies and persons have obligations to help others worse off than themselves. Some deny all such obligations, others claim them to be quite demanding. Both sides easily take for granted that it is as potential helpers that we are morally related to the starving abroad.[58] This is true, of course. But the debate ignores that we are also and more significantly related to them as supporters of, and beneficiaries from, a global institutional order that substantially contributes to their destitution.

If the empirical rationalization fails, if national and global economic regimes are comparable in their workings and impact, then we are after all employing a double standard when we count avoidable extremes of poverty and inequality against national economic regimes only. And we do then face moral universalism's challenge to our easy acceptance of extensive, severe poverty abroad. Without a plausible rationale, our discrepant assessments constitute covert arbitrary discrimination in favor of the wealthy societies and against the global poor.

Notes

[1] See text at n. 25.

[2] See nn. 5–10 and accompanying text. The global poverty gap is about $44 billion annu-

ally for the World Bank's official international poverty line and $300 billion annually for its doubled poverty line. These figures correspond to 0.14 and 0.96 percent, respectively, of aggregate global income ($31,171 billion annually) and to 0.18 and 1.21 percent, respectively, of the combined gross national incomes of the high-income economies ($24,829 billion annually). See World Bank, *Report 2002*, p. 233, reporting data for the year 2000.

3 April 11, 1919. The proposal received a majority in the committee (11 of the 17 members present), but Woodrow Wilson, as chair, ruled that this particular amendment needed unanimous support to pass. See Naoko Shimazu, *Japan, Race and Equality*, p. 30.

4 The appeal is usually made in behalf of societies that could easily build just and thriving national communities even in a more egalitarian global economic order. The difference would be that the remaining majority of humankind might then enjoy the same luxury.

5 See www.worldbank.org/research/povmonitor/, which is periodically updated. The poverty line is explained in World Bank, *Report 2000/2001*, pp. 17 and 23.

6 I say "roughly" because the two equivalences cannot be combined by transitivity. The reason is that they are based on different goods-baskets. One goods-basket was used to determine what amount of a foreign currency had, in 1993, the same purchasing power as $393 then had in the US. Another goods-basket (defining the US consumer price index) was used to determine what amount of $s have, in 2001, the same purchasing power as $393 had in the US in 1993.

7 Chen and Ravallion, "How Did the World's Poorest Fare in the 1990s?," tables 2 and 4, dividing the poverty gap index by the head-count index.

8 Thus the World Bank equates India's *per capita* gross national income of $460 to $2,390 PPP, China's $840 to $3,940 PPP, Nigeria's $260 to $790 PPP, Pakistan's $470 to $1,960 PPP, Bangladesh's $380 to $1,650 PPP, Ethiopia's $100 to $660 PPP, Vietnam's $390 to $2,030 PPP, and so on (World Bank, *Report 2002*, pp. 232–3).

9 Chen and Ravallion, "How Did the World's Poorest Fare in the 1990s?," table 3. The figure given is 2,801.03 million for 1998.

10 Ibid., tables 3 and 4, again dividing the poverty gap index by the head-count index.

11 These four figures are from UNDP, *Report 2001*, pp. 22 and 9.

12 UNDP, *Report 1999*, p. 22.

13 UNDP, *Report 1998*, p. 49.

14 FAO, *The State of Food Insecurity in the World 1999*, p. 11.

15 World Bank, *Report 1999/2000*, p. 62. According to the International Labor Organization "some 250 million children between the ages of 5 and 14 are working in developing countries – 120 million full time, 130 million part time" (www.ilo.org/public/english/standards/ipec/simpoc/stats/4stt.htm).

16 In 2000, there were 55.694 million human deaths. The main causes highly correlated with poverty were (with death tolls in thousands): diarrhea (2,124) and malnutrition (445), perinatal (2,439) and maternal conditions (495), childhood diseases (1,385), tuberculosis (1,660), malaria (1,080), meningitis (156), hepatitis (128), tropical diseases (124), respiratory infections (3,941 – mainly pneumonia), HIV/AIDS (2,943) and sexually transmitted diseases (217) (WHO, *The World Health Report 2001*, annex table 2). Cf. also FAO, *The State of Food Insecurity in the World 1999*, UNICEF, *The State of the World's Children 2002*, and USDA, *U.S. Action Plan on Food Security*, p. III: "Worldwide 34,000 children under age five die daily from hunger and preventable diseases."

17 The Vietnam War Memorial in Washington, designed by Maya Ying Lin, is a black granite wall, 439½ feet long, on which the names of 58,226 fallen US soldiers are engraved.

18 World Bank, *Report 2002*, p. 233.

19 Ibid., reflecting aggregate global income (sum of all gross national incomes) of $31,171 billion annually and a world population of 6,054 million (year 2000). Each quintile thus contains 1,211 million human beings.

20 Cf. also the figures provided in n. 2. Curiously, the World Bank does not publish data about the *per capita* or the collective income of the global poor, about their share of aggregate global income, or about the amount of extra income needed for all of them to reach the relevant poverty line.

[21] UNDP, *Report 1999*, p. 3. "The additional cost of achieving and maintaining universal access to basic education for all, basic health care for all, reproductive health care for all women, adequate food for all and safe water and sanitation for all is . . . less than 4% of the combined wealth of the 225 richest people in the world" (UNDP, *Report 1998*, p. 30).

[22] The number of people below the doubled international poverty line (cf. n. 9) has increased by 9.9 percent – or 20.7 percent if the special case of China is excluded (World Bank, *Report 2000/2001*, p. 23). Global population growth during the same period (1987–98) was about 18 percent (www.census.gov/ipc/www/worldpop.html).

[23] Thanks to the end of the Cold War, the high-income economies were able to reduce their military expenditures from 4.1 percent of their combined GDPs in 1985 to 2.2 percent in 1998 (UNDP, *Report 1998*, p. 197; UNDP, *Report 2000*, p. 217). Their annual "peace dividend" currently amounts to over $450 billion (1.9 percent of their combined GDPs of currently $23,982 billion – UNDP, *Report 2001*, p. 181). In the same period, the same countries chose to reduce their combined net official development assistance from 0.34 percent of their combined GNPs to 0.24 percent (ibid., p. 190, giving details for each affluent country). Preliminary figures for the year 2000 indicate that the rich countries have further reduced their ODA to 0.22 percent of their combined GNPs (www.oecd.org/media/release/ODA_april01.pdf).

[24] The 1996 *Rome Declaration on World Food Security* described "more than 800 million people" as undernourished. This number has officially developed as follows: "nearly 800 million" (UNDP, *Report 1995*, p. 16, and UNDP, *Report 1996*, p. 20), "some 840 million" (UNDP, *Report 1997*, p. 5), "841 million" (UNDP, *Report 1998*, p. 49), "about 840 million" (UNDP, *Report 1999*, p. 22), "about 790 million" (UNDP, *Report 2000*, p. 8), "826 million" (UNDP, *Report 2001*, p. 22). The World Bank's Food Price Index fell from 124 in 1985 to 108 in 1996 to 84.5 in 2000 (statistics from "Global Commodity Markets" published by the World Bank's Development Prospects Group).

[25] UNDP, *Report 1999*, p. 3. These ratios are based on market exchange rates, not purchasing power parities. This is appropriate when one is focusing, as I am throughout, not on income inequality as such, but on the avoidability of poverty. The global quintile income inequality ratio is much greater, if one compares individuals (or household averages) rather than country averages. One would then, in the top quintile, replace the poorest citizens of rich countries with richer persons in poorer countries and analogously, in the bottom quintile, replace the wealthiest citizens of poor countries with poorer citizens in less-poor countries. So calculated, the global quintile income inequality ratio rose from 78 in 1988 to 113 in 1993, indicating an average annual growth gap of 7.7 percent (personal communication from Branko Milanovic, World Bank). This trend has continued. Today, the top quintile of human beings have around 90 percent of global income and the bottom quintile about one-third of 1 percent (see text following n. 19), which puts the global quintile income inequality ratio at about 270.

[26] The figures just cited indicate an average annual growth gap of 1.66 percent for the colonial era (1820–1960), 2.34 percent for the period 1960–90, and 3.04 percent for the period 1990–97.

[27] UNDP, *Report 2001*, p. 183. Outside Latin America, most national quintile income inequality ratios are between 4 and 10, e.g. Austria 3.2; Japan 3.4; Germany 4.7; Bangladesh 4.9; Spain 5.4; France 5.6; India 5.7; Switzerland 5.8; United Kingdom 6.5; Australia 7.0; China 8.0; USA 9.0; Malaysia 12.4; Nigeria 12.8; South Africa 22.6 (ibid., pp. 182–4).

[28] $7,320 versus $7,350 (World Bank, *Report 2002*, pp. 232–3).

[29] North Korea comes to mind, China around 1960, and the Soviet Union around 1930. But none of these cases displays the extreme income inequality of Sub-Subbrazil.

[30] In this general statement, anti-universalism is entirely consistent with the thesis that the two

minimal requirements (conjunctively or disjunctively) apply to the present global economic order. I address such anti-universalism, then, not because it threatens this thesis, but because it threatens the way I support this thesis here.

31 See esp. Miller, "Justice and Global Inequality," "National Self-Determination and Global Justice," and his forthcoming "The Ethics of Assistance: Morality, Affluence and the Distant Needy," which he has kindly allowed me to read.

32 Miller, "Two Ways to Think about Justice," p. 20.

33 Ibid., p. 16.

34 Ibid., p. 6.

35 Ibid., pp. 12–13.

36 The word "monism" is introduced in Murphy, "Institutions and the Demands of Justice." According to his usage, monism denies that there is a plurality of different contexts, or domains of value, each with its own fundamental moral principle(s). The fundamental principles of monistic moral conceptions thus are not contextually limited in range. Such a conception could nonetheless feature a plurality of fundamental moral principles and thus need not be monistic in the more usual sense.

37 Ibid., p. 280; Cohen, "Where the Action Is," pp. 22–3.

38 For an elaboration of these reasons, see Pogge, "On the Site of Distributive Justice." In accordance with his method of avoidance, Rawls would probably prefer to make the weaker claim: to have shown that the moral principles appropriate to the basic structure *may* not be appropriate to other contexts or, generally, that different moral principles *may* be appropriate to different "domains of value." See the cautious formulations he employs in his discussion of a "model case of an overlapping consensus" in Rawls, *Political Liberalism*, pp. 169–71.

39 Rawls, *The Law of Peoples*, pp. 116–18. This argument exemplifies the strategy of justifying inequality by appeal to group autonomy.

40 See Pogge, *Realizing Rawls*, pp. 252–3, cf. "An Egalitarian Law of Peoples," pp. 211–13.

41 Rawls, *A Theory of Justice*, pp. 401, 7.

42 Ibid., pp. 90–1.

43 With regard to his own fellow citizens, Rawls writes: "It is inevitable and often desirable that citizens have different views as to the most appropriate political conception; for the public political culture is bound to contain different fundamental ideas that can be developed in different ways. An orderly contest between them over time is a reliable way to find which one, if any, is most reasonable." Rawls, *Political Liberalism*, p. 227, see also pp. 164 and 241.

44 Rawls, *The Law of Peoples*, pp. 67–8.

45 Ibid., p. 37.

46 This objection to Rawls's account is presented more fully in Pogge, "Rawls on International Justice."

47 See text at n. 4 for the appeal to special ties, text at n. 39 for the appeal to group autonomy, and the discussion of "decent peoples" in Rawls for the appeal to cultural diversity. This last appeal comes in two variants. Cultural diversity is adduced to justify that we may suspend our moral standards in dealing with foreigners who do not share our commitment to these standards (see Pogge, *Realizing Rawls*, pp. 269–70). But why may we then not likewise suspend these standards in dealing with compatriots who do not share this commitment? Cultural diversity is also adduced to argue that, given non-liberal cultures abroad, we may not reform the global economic order in light of liberal notions of fairness and equality of opportunity. But why may we then, despite the presence of US non-liberal cultures, realize such liberal notions in the national economic order?

48 Rawls offers a version of this view, suggesting that the causes of international inequality are purely domestic: "the causes of the wealth of a people and the forms it takes lie in their political culture and in the religious, philosophical, and moral traditions that support the basic structure of their political and social institutions, as well as in the industriousness and cooperative talents of its members, all supported by their political virtues.... Crucial also is the country's population policy" (Rawls, *The Law of Peoples*, p. 108). If a

society does not want to be poor, it can curb its population growth or industrialize (ibid., pp. 117–18) and, in any case, "if it is not satisfied, it can continue to increase savings, or, if this is not feasible, borrow from other members of the Society of Peoples" (ibid., p. 114). With the right culture and policies, even resource-poor countries like Japan can do very well. With the wrong culture and policies, resource-rich countries like Argentina may do very poorly (ibid., p. 108). Every people is master of its own fate – except perhaps the Arctic Eskimos (ibid., p. 108 n. 34).

49 The spirit of many nationalist explanations reverting to history and culture is captured in Walzer's remark that "it is not the sign for some collective derangement or radical incapacity for a political community to produce an authoritarian regime. Indeed, the history, culture, and religion of the community may be such that authoritarian regimes come, as it were, naturally, reflecting a widely shared world view or way of life" (Walzer, "The Moral Standing of States," pp. 224–5). Detailed accounts are provided in Landes, *The Wealth and Poverty of Nations*, and in the essays collected in Harrison and Huntington: *Culture Matters*. Nationalist explanations reverting to societies' natural environments are exemplified in Diamond, *Guns, Germs, and Steel*.

50 Other aspects, though less significant, are considerably more obvious and, perhaps for this reason, currently under attack. One such obvious aspect is diplomatic immunity – recently invoked by General Augusto Pinochet – which shields crimes committed by high officials from prosecution in other countries. Another such obvious aspect is corporate bribery of foreign officials, which most developed countries have permitted and encouraged until recently. The nongovernmental organization Transparency International (TI) has worked hard to publicize this problem, and its work has contributed to the 1997 *Convention on Combating Bribery of Foreign Officials in International Business Transactions*. Even if this *Convention* were to stamp out international bribery completely, the deep entrenchment of corruption

in many ex-colonies would still be traceable (by way of a historical explanation) to the extensive bribery they were subjected to, with official encouragement from the affluent states, during their formative years.

51 See § 5, second paragraph.

52 As explicated in Hohfeld, *Fundamental Legal Conceptions*, a power involves the legally recognized authority to alter the distribution of first-order liberties, claims, and duties. Having *a* power or powers in this sense is distinct from having power (i.e. control over physical force and/or means of coercion).

53 For some background, see "Going on down," *The Economist*, June 8, 1996, pp. 46–8. A later update reports: "Oil revenues [are] paid directly to the government at the highest level. . . . The head of state has supreme power and control of all the cash. He depends on nobody and nothing but oil. Patronage and corruption spread downwards from the top" (*The Economist*, December 12, 1998, p. 19). Despite its huge oil revenues, Nigeria's real *per capita* GDP has declined by 22 percent between 1977 and 1998 (UNDP, *Report 2000*, p. 185).

54 In October 2003, Nigeria received a score of 1.4 out of 10 on the Corruption Perception Index, second from the bottom (www.transparency.org/cpi/2003/cpi2003.en.html).

55 For the 1975–99 period, these countries had long-term average annual rates of change in real GDP *per capita* as follows: Nigeria −0.8 percent, Congo/Zaire −4.7* percent, Kenya 0.4 percent, Angola −2.1* percent, Mozambique 1.3* percent, Brazil 0.8 percent, Venezuela −1.0 percent, Saudi Arabia −2.2 percent, United Arab Emirates −3.7* percent, Oman 2.8* percent, Kuwait −1.5* percent, Bahrain −0.5* percent, Brunei −2.1* percent. Indonesia 4.6 percent, the Philippines 0.1 percent (UNDP, *Report 2001*, pp. 178–81; stars indicate that a somewhat different period was used due to insufficient data). As a group, the resource-rich developing countries thus fell far below the 2.2 percent annual rate in real *per capita* growth of the high-income economies – even while the developing countries on the whole kept pace (with 2.3 percent) thanks to rapid growth in China

and the rest of East and Southeast Asia (ibid., p. 181).

56 I add this caution because coups, civil wars, and oppression may be encouraged by the prospect of mere possession of resources, even without the power to confer internationally valid ownership rights. As I have learned from Josiah Ober, this is elegantly observed already in Thucydides, *The History of the Peloponnesian War*, book 1, ch. 2.

57 Many poor countries are weighed down by large debt service obligations that their unelected rulers incurred for unproductive purposes (including, most typically, purchases of weapons needed for internal repression). In Nigeria, for instance, the military rulers did not only steal and waste the oil revenues of several decades, but also left behind a national debt of $30 billion or 78.8 percent of GNP. Debt/GNP ratios for some other countries are as follows: Congo/Zaire 232 percent, Kenya 61.5 percent, Angola 297.1 percent, Mozambique 223.0 percent, Brazil 30.6 percent, Venezuela 39.6 percent, Indonesia 176.5 percent, the Philippines 70.1 percent (UNDP, *Report 2000*, pp. 219–21; for Congo/Zaire, the figure is from UNDP, *Report 1999*, p. 195). When the burden of debt service becomes too oppressive, the high-income countries occasionally grant some debt relief, thereby protecting their own banks from losses and, as a side effect, encouraging further lending to corrupt authoritarian rulers.

58 Singer ("Famine, Affluence and Morality" – see Chapter 19 of this volume) has famously built his case for demanding obligations on an analogy with the situation of a healthy adult chancing upon a drowning infant whom he alone can rescue from a shallow pond. Many others have followed his lead, discussing the question on the basis of the tacit assumption that we are not contributing to the distress we are able to alleviate.

Bibliography

Chen, Shaohua and Martin Ravallion, "How Did the World's Poorest Fare in the 1990s?" Working paper, August 2000. www.worldbank.org/research/povmonitor/pdfs/methodology.pdf

Cohen, G.A., "Where the Action Is: On the Site of Distributive Justice," *Philosophy & Public Affairs* 26 (1997): 3–30.

Diamond, Jared, *Guns, Germs, and Steel: the Fates of Human Societies*. New York: W. W. Norton, 1999.

FAO, *The State of Food Insecurity in the World 1999*. www.fao.org/news/1999/img/sofi99-e.pdf

Harrison, Lawrence E. and Samuel P. Huntington (eds.), *Culture Matters: How Values Shape Human Progress*. New York: Basic Books, 2001.

Hohfeld, W. A., *Fundamental Legal Conceptions*. New Haven, CT: Yale University Press, 1919.

Landes, David, *The Wealth and Poverty of Nations: Why Some are so Rich and Some so Poor*. New York: W. W. Norton, 1998.

Miller, David, "Justice and Global Inequality," in Andrew Hurrell and Ngaire Woods (eds.), *Inequality, Globalization and World Politics*. Oxford: Oxford University Press, 1999, pp. 187–210.

Miller, David, "Two Ways to Think about Justice," *Politics, Philosophy, and Economics* 1 (2002): 5–28.

Pogge, Thomas W., *Realizing Rawls*. Ithaca, NY: Cornell University Press, 1989.

Pogge, Thomas W., "An Egalitarian Law of Peoples," *Philosophy & Public Affairs* 23 (1994): 195–224.

Pogge, Thomas W., "On the Site of Distributive Justice: Reflections on Cohen and Murphy," *Philosophy & Public Affairs* 29 (2000): 137–69.

Pogge, Thomas W., "Rawls on International Justice," *Philosophical Quarterly* 51 (2001): 246–53.

Rawls, John, *Political Liberalism*. New York: Columbia University Press, 1993.

Rawls, John, *The Law of Peoples*. Cambridge, MA: Harvard University Press, 1999.

Shimazu, Naoko, *Japan, Race and Equality: The Racial Equality Proposal of 1919.* London: Routledge, 1998.

Singer, Peter, "Famine, Affluence, and Morality," *Philosophy & Public Affairs* 1 (1972): 229–43.

UNDP, *Human Development Report 1995.* New York: Oxford University Press, 1995.

UNDP, *Human Development Report 1996.* New York: Oxford University Press, 1996.

UNDP, *Human Development Report 1997.* New York: Oxford University Press, 1997.

UNDP, *Human Development Report 1998.* New York: Oxford University Press, 1998.

UNDP, *Human Development Report 1999.* New York: Oxford University Press, 1999.

UNDP, *Human Development Report 2000.* New York: Oxford University Press, 2000.

UNDP, *Human Development Report 2001.* New York: Oxford University Press, 2001.

UNICEF, *The State of the World's Children 2002.* New York: UNICEF, 2002. www.unicef.org/sow02/pdf/sowc2002-eng-full.pdf

USDA, *US Action Plan on Food Security.* 1999. www.fas.usda.gov/icd/summit/pressdoc.html

Walzer, Michael, "The Moral Standing of States," *Philosophy & Public Affairs* 9 (1980): 209–29.

World Bank, *World Development Report 1999/2000.* New York: Oxford University Press, 2000. www.worldbank.org.wdr/2000/fullreport.html

World Bank, *World Development Report 2000/2001.* New York: Oxford University Press, 2001. www.worldbank.org/poverty/wdrpoverty/report/index.htm

World Bank, *World Development Report 2002.* New York: Oxford University Press, 2001. http://econ.worldbank.org/wdr/structured_doc.php?sp=2391&st=&sd=2394

WHO, *The World Health Report 2001.* Geneva: WHO Publications, 2001.

Part VII

Global Poverty and International Distributive Justice

Introduction

Perhaps the single most popular concern that we find in the global justice literature is an interest in the problems of global poverty and inequality, as well as solutions to how best to address these problems. This Part begins with a reading that many credit with first raising greater interest in global justice amongst political philosophers: Peter Singer's essay "Famine, Affluence, and Morality," first published in 1972 (chapter 19). Singer famously endorses the position that "if it is in our power to prevent something bad from happening, without thereby sacrificing anything of comparable moral importance, we ought, morally, to do it." As an example, Singer tells us that we should enter a pond to rescue a drowning child even if it made our clothes muddy: we sacrifice nothing of comparable moral importance (such as the state of our clothes) in preventing something bad from happening (such as the death of a child). Importantly, the distance between the suffering and those who can offer help is immaterial to satisfy the moral argument. Singer will argue that because there is suffering in the world and the moral costs to wealthy nations pale in comparison then wealthy nations have a duty to help those in need. This help is a moral duty rather than an act of charity.

In the next reading, Leif Wenar considers "What We Owe to Distant Others." He argues that there are two questions we must answer. First, we must offer an account of what are our duties to those in need. Second, we must offer an account of what we might do to fulfill our duties. After considering the role that contractualism may play in helping us provide an answer to the first "normative" question, Wenar turns his attention to a consideration of the second "empirical" question. He challenges the conventional view (argued for by Singer in chapter 19) that there is a strong relationship between the resources a wealthy person contributes to those in need and the resources those in need actually receive. Instead of arguing we should simply offer aid to the poor, Wenar argues convincingly that more work must be done on issues of aid effectiveness, including greater transparency from our national governments regarding international poverty alleviation initiatives.

In chapter 21, Thomas Nagel investigates the possibility of global socio-economic justice. He argues that sovereignty must be established prior to legitimacy. Political institutions need to be first established and then we should shape these institutions in a way that would best facilitate global distributive justice. Part of the justification for this view rests on a realist assumption. That is, Nagel argues that global justice will only become a reality after there are first global institutions. It is likely that these institutions will be unjust and serve the interests of affluent states. Nevertheless, it is necessary for these institutions to first take a grip before they can be used for good: "the path from anarchy to justice must go through injustice" or "the cunning of history."

In Part VI, Thomas Pogge provides a powerful argument for the alleviation of severe poverty. He argues that we in the affluent West uphold a coercive global order that perpetuates severe poverty amongst the global poor. We are both causally and morally responsible to alleviate their suffering. In this Part, Pogge puts forward a solution: the global resources dividend (chapter 22). He argues that everyone, including the global poor, own a stake in the earth's limited resources and they suffer burdens when the environment is degraded by affluent states perpetuating their lifestyles. Affluent states therefore should pay a global resources dividend: a small tax on the natural resources they use, resources that are shared by all. The proceeds will go to alleviating global poverty, providing a major improvement in conditions amongst the global poor without requiring great sacrifice amongst affluent states. Thus, the dividend is both morally required and practically feasible.

In the final reading, Lisa L. Fuller discusses not simply whether or not affluent states should redistribute at least part of their wealth to help alleviate global poverty, but how this redistribution might take place (chapter 23). Fuller identifies a central problem with all accounts of international distributive justice: if affluent states are obliged to redistribute wealth, then how can we ensure they will comply? In particular, she pays close attention to Pogge's global resources dividend argued for in chapter 22. Fuller's claim is not that Pogge fails to provide an adequate moral defense of his proposal, but that he fails to offer an adequate defense of the proposal's realistic implementation, challenging Pogge's contention that the dividend is practically feasible. Instead, Fuller argues for reform of NGO-delivered aid to the global poor, fostering a transparent and accountable system that is more likely to succeed and alleviate severe poverty than more ambitious proposals, such as the global resources dividend put forward by Pogge.

Global poverty has long existed as a major worry. As inequalities across the globe increase and the size of suffering continues to grow, there is an ever more urgent need to rethink our strategies for dealing with such a large and seemingly intractable problem on a horrific scale. The following chapters help shed light on what may well be the single most important moral issue of the day.

Chapter 19

Famine, Affluence, and Morality*

Peter Singer

As I write this, in November 1971, people are dying in East Bengal from lack of food, shelter, and medical care. The suffering and death that are occurring there now are not inevitable, not unavoidable in any fatalistic sense of the term. Constant poverty, a cyclone, and a civil war have turned at least nine million people into destitute refugees; nevertheless, it is not beyond the capacity of the richer nations to give enough assistance to reduce any further suffering to very small proportions. The decisions and actions of human beings can prevent this kind of suffering. Unfortunately, human beings have not made the necessary decisions. At the individual level, people have, with very few exceptions, not responded to the situation in any significant way. Generally speaking, people have not given large sums to relief funds; they have not written to their parliamentary representatives demanding increased government assistance; they have not demonstrated in the streets, held symbolic fasts, or done anything else directed toward providing the refugees with the means to satisfy their essential needs. At the government level, no government has given the sort of massive aid that would enable the refugees to survive for more than a few days. Britain, for instance, has given rather more than most countries. It has, to date, given £14,750,000. For comparative purposes, Britain's share of the nonrecoverable development costs of the Anglo-French Concorde project is already in excess of £275,000,000, and on present estimates will reach £440,000,000. The implication is that the British government values a supersonic transport more than thirty times as highly as it values the lives of the nine million refugees. Australia is another country which, on a per capita basis, is well up in the "aid to Bengal" table. Australia's aid, however, amounts to less than one-twelfth of the cost of Sydney's new opera house. The total amount given, from all sources, now stands at about £65,000,000. The estimated cost of keeping the refugees alive for one year is £464,000,000. Most of the refugees have now been in the camps for more than six months. The World Bank has said that India needs a minimum of £300,000,000 in assistance from other countries before the end of the year. It seems obvious that assistance on this scale will not be forthcoming. India will be forced to choose between letting the refugees starve or diverting funds from her own development program, which will mean that

* From *Philosophy & Public Affairs* 1:3 (1972), pp. 229–43.

more of her own people will starve in the future.[1]

These are the essential facts about the present situation in Bengal. So far as it concerns us here, there is nothing unique about this situation except its magnitude. The Bengal emergency is just the latest and most acute of a series of major emergencies in various parts of the world, arising both from natural and from man-made causes. There are also many parts of the world in which people die from malnutrition and lack of food independent of any special emergency. I take Bengal as my example only because it is the present concern, and because the size of the problem has ensured that it has been given adequate publicity. Neither individuals nor governments can claim to be unaware of what is happening there.

What are the moral implications of a situation like this? In what follows, I shall argue that the way people in relatively affluent countries react to a situation like that in Bengal cannot be justified; indeed, the whole way we look at moral issues – our moral conceptual scheme – needs to be altered, and with it, the way of life that has come to be taken for granted in our society.

In arguing for this conclusion I will not, of course, claim to be morally neutral. I shall, however, try to argue for the moral position that I take, so that anyone who accepts certain assumptions, to be made explicit, will, I hope, accept my conclusion.

I begin with the assumption that suffering and death from lack of food, shelter, and medical care are bad. I think most people will agree about this, although one may reach the same view by different routes. I shall not argue for this view. People can hold all sorts of eccentric positions, and perhaps from some of them it would not follow that death by starvation is in itself bad. It is difficult, perhaps impossible, to refute such positions, and so for brevity I will henceforth take this assumption as accepted. Those who disagree need read no further.

My next point is this: if it is in our power to prevent something bad from happening, without thereby sacrificing anything of comparable moral importance, we ought, morally, to do it. By "without sacrificing anything of comparable moral importance" I mean without causing anything else comparably bad to happen, or doing something that is wrong in itself, or failing to promote some moral good, comparable in significance to the bad thing that we can prevent. This principle seems almost as uncontroversial as the last one. It requires us only to prevent what is bad, and not to promote what is good, and it requires this of us only when we can do it without sacrificing anything that is, from the moral point of view, comparably important. I could even, as far as the application of my argument to the Bengal emergency is concerned, qualify the point so as to make it: if it is in our power to prevent something very bad from happening, without thereby sacrificing anything morally significant, we ought, morally, to do it. An application of this principle would be as follows: if I am walking past a shallow pond and see a child drowning in it, I ought to wade in and pull the child out. This will mean getting my clothes muddy, but this is insignificant, while the death of the child would presumably be a very bad thing.

The uncontroversial appearance of the principle just stated is deceptive. If it were acted upon, even in its qualified form, our lives, our society, and our world would be fundamentally changed. For the principle takes, firstly, no account of proximity or distance. It makes no moral difference whether the person I can help is a neighbor's child ten yards from me or a Bengali whose name I shall never know, ten thousand miles away. Secondly the principle makes no distinction between cases in which I am the only person who could possibly do anything and cases in which I am just one among millions in the same position.

I do not think I need to say much in defense of the refusal to take proximity and distance into account. The fact that a person is physically near to us, so that we have personal contact with him, may make it more likely that we *shall* assist him, but this does not show that we *ought* to help him rather than another who happens to be further away. If we accept any principle of impartiality, universalizability, equality, or whatever, we cannot discriminate against someone merely because he is far away from us (or we are far away from him). Admittedly, it is possible that we are in a better position to judge what needs to be done to help a person near to us than one far away, and perhaps also to provide the assistance we judge to be necessary. If this were the case, it would be a reason for helping those near to us first. This may once have been a justification for being more concerned with the poor in one's own town than with famine victims in India. Unfortunately for those who like to keep their moral responsibilities limited, instant communication and swift transportation have changed the situation. From the moral point of view, the development of the world into a "global village" has made an important, though still unrecognized, difference to our moral situation. Expert observers and supervisors, sent out by famine relief organizations or permanently stationed in famine-prone areas, can direct our aid to a refugee in Bengal almost as effectively as we could get it to someone in our own block. There would seem, therefore, to be no possible justification for discriminating on geographical grounds.

There may be a greater need to defend the second implication of my principle – that the fact that there are millions of other people in the same position, in respect to the Bengali refugees, as I am, does not make the situation significantly different from a situation in which I am the only person who can prevent something very bad from occurring. Again, of course, I admit that there is a psychological difference between the cases; one feels less guilty about doing nothing if one can point to others, similarly placed, who have also done nothing. Yet this can make no real difference to our moral obligations.[2] Should I consider that I am less obliged to pull the drowning child out of the pond if on looking around I see other people, no further away than I am, who have also noticed the child but are doing nothing? One has only to ask this question to see the absurdity of the view that numbers lessen obligation. It is a view that is an ideal excuse for inactivity; unfortunately most of the major evils – poverty, overpopulation, pollution – are problems in which everyone is almost equally involved.

The view that numbers do make a difference can be made plausible if stated in this way: if everyone in circumstances like mine gave £5 to the Bengal Relief Fund, there would be enough to provide food, shelter, and medical care for the refugees; there is no reason why I should give more than anyone else in the same circumstances as I am; therefore I have no obligation to give more than £5. Each premise in this argument is true, and the argument looks sound. It may convince us, unless we notice that it is based on a hypothetical premise, although the conclusion is not stated hypothetically. The argument would be sound if the conclusion were: if everyone in circumstances like mine were to give £5, I would have no obligation to give more than £5. If the conclusion were so stated, however, it would be obvious that the argument has no bearing on a situation in which it is not the case that everyone else gives £5. This, of course, is the actual situation. It is more or less certain that not everyone in circumstances like mine will give £5. So there will not be enough to provide the needed food, shelter, and medical care. Therefore by giving more than £5 I will prevent more suffering than I would if I gave just £5.

It might be thought that this argument has an absurd consequence. Since the situation appears to be that very few people are likely to give substantial amounts, it follows that I and everyone else in similar circumstances ought to give as much as possible, that is, at least up to the point at which by giving more one would begin to cause serious suffering for oneself and one's dependents – perhaps even beyond this point to the point of marginal utility, at which by giving more one would cause oneself and one's dependents as much suffering as one would prevent in Bengal. If everyone does this, however, there will be more than can be used for the benefit of the refugees, and some of the sacrifice will have been unnecessary. Thus, if everyone does what he ought to do, the result will not be as good as it would be if everyone did a little less than he ought to do, or if only some do all that they ought to do.

The paradox here arises only if we assume that the actions in question – sending money to the relief funds – are performed more or less simultaneously, and are also unexpected. For if it is to be expected that everyone is going to contribute something, then clearly each is not obliged to give as much as he would have been obliged to had others not been giving too. And if everyone is not acting more or less simultaneously, then those giving later will know how much more is needed, and will have no obligation to give more than is necessary to reach this amount. To say this is not to deny the principle that people in the same circumstances have the same obligations, but to point out that the fact that others have given, or may be expected to give, is a relevant circumstance: those giving after it has become known that many others are giving and those giving before are not in the same circumstances. So the seemingly absurd consequence of the principle I have put forward can occur only

if people are in error about the actual circumstances – that is, if they think they are giving when others are not, but in fact they are giving when others are. The result of everyone doing what he really ought to do cannot be worse than the result of everyone doing less than he ought to do, although the result of everyone doing what he reasonably believes he ought to do could be.

If my argument so far has been sound, neither our distance from a preventable evil nor the number of other people who, in respect to that evil, are in the same situation as we are, lessens our obligation to mitigate or prevent that evil. I shall therefore take as established the principle I asserted earlier. As I have already said, I need to assert it only in its qualified form: if it is in our power to prevent something very bad from happening, without thereby sacrificing anything else morally significant, we ought, morally, to do it.

The outcome of this argument is that our traditional moral categories are upset. The traditional distinction between duty and charity cannot be drawn, or at least, not in the place we normally draw it. Giving money to the Bengal Relief Fund is regarded as an act of charity in our society. The bodies which collect money are known as "charities." These organizations see themselves in this way – if you send them a check, you will be thanked for your "generosity." Because giving money is regarded as an act of charity, it is not thought that there is anything wrong with not giving. The charitable man may be praised, but the man who is not charitable is not condemned. People do not feel in any way ashamed or guilty about spending money on new clothes or a new car instead of giving it to famine relief. (Indeed, the alternative does not occur to them.) This way of looking at the matter cannot be justified. When we buy new clothes not to keep ourselves warm but to look "well-dressed" we are not providing for any important need.

We would not be sacrificing anything significant if we were to continue to wear our old clothes, and give the money to famine relief. By doing so, we would be preventing another person from starving. It follows from what I have said earlier that we ought to give money away, rather than spend it on clothes which we do not need to keep us warm. To do so is not charitable, or generous. Nor is it the kind of act which philosophers and theologians have called "supererogatory" – an act which it would be good to do, but not wrong not to do. On the contrary, we ought to give the money away, and it is wrong not to do so.

I am not maintaining that there are no acts which are charitable, or that there are no acts which it would be good to do but not wrong not to do. It may be possible to redraw the distinction between duty and charity in some other place. All I am arguing here is that the present way of drawing the distinction, which makes it an act of charity for a man living at the level of affluence which most people in the "developed nations" enjoy to give money to save someone else from starvation, cannot be supported. It is beyond the scope of my argument to consider whether the distinction should be redrawn or abolished altogether. There would be many other possible ways of drawing the distinction – for instance, one might decide that it is good to make other people as happy as possible, but not wrong not to do so.

Despite the limited nature of the revision in our moral conceptual scheme which I am proposing, the revision would, given the extent of both affluence and famine in the world today, have radical implications. These implications may lead to further objections, distinct from those I have already considered. I shall discuss two of these.

One objection to the position I have taken might be simply that it is too drastic a revision of our moral scheme. People do not ordinarily judge in the way I have suggested they should. Most people reserve their moral condemnation for those who violate some moral norm, such as the norm against taking another person's property. They do not condemn those who indulge in luxury instead of giving to famine relief. But given that I did not set out to present a morally neutral description of the way people make moral judgments, the way people do in fact judge has nothing to do with the validity of my conclusion. My conclusion follows from the principle which I advanced earlier, and unless that principle is rejected, or the arguments shown to be unsound, I think the conclusion must stand, however strange it appears.

It might, nevertheless, be interesting to consider why our society, and most other societies, do judge differently from the way I have suggested they should. In a well-known article, J. O. Urmson suggests that the imperatives of duty, which tell us what we must do, as distinct from what it would be good to do but not wrong not to do, function so as to prohibit behavior that is intolerable if men are to live together in society.[3] This may explain the origin and continued existence of the present division between acts of duty and acts of charity. Moral attitudes are shaped by the needs of society, and no doubt society needs people who will observe the rules that make social existence tolerable. From the point of view of a particular society, it is essential to prevent violations of norms against killing, stealing, and so on. It is quite inessential, however, to help people outside one's own society.

If this is an explanation of our common distinction between duty and supererogation, however, it is not a justification of it. The moral point of view requires us to look beyond the interests of our own society. Previously, as I have already mentioned, this may hardly have been feasible, but it is quite feasible now. From the moral point of view, the prevention of the starvation of millions of people outside our society must be considered at least as pressing as the upholding of property norms within our society.

It has been argued by some writers, among them Sidgwick and Urmson, that we need to have a basic moral code which is not too far beyond the capacities of the ordinary man, for otherwise there will be a general break-down of compliance with the moral code. Crudely stated, this argument suggests that if we tell people that they ought to refrain from murder and give everything they do not really need to famine relief, they will do neither, whereas if we tell them that they ought to refrain from murder and that it is good to give to famine relief but not wrong not to do so, they will at least refrain from murder. The issue here is: Where should we drawn the line between conduct that is required and conduct that is good although not required, so as to get the best possible result? This would seem to be an empirical question, although a very difficult one. One objection to the Sidgwick–Urmson line of argument is that it takes insufficient account of the effect that moral standards can have on the decisions we make. Given a society in which a wealthy man who gives five percent of his income to famine relief is regarded as most generous, it is not surprising that a proposal that we all ought to give away half our incomes will be thought to be absurdly unrealistic. In a society which held that no man should have more than enough while others have less than they need, such a pro-posal might seem narrow-minded. What it is possible for a man to do and what he is likely to do are both, I think, very greatly influenced by what people around him are doing and expecting him to do. In any case, the possibility that by spreading the idea that we ought to be doing very much more than we are to relieve famine we shall bring about a general breakdown of moral behavior

seems remote. If the stakes are an end to widespread starvation, it is worth the risk. Finally, it should be emphasized that these considerations are relevant only to the issue of what we should require from others, and not to what we ourselves ought to do.

The second objection to my attack on the present distinction between duty and charity is one which has from time to time been made against utilitarianism. It follows from some forms of utilitarian theory that we all ought, morally, to be working full time to increase the balance of happiness over misery. The position I have taken here would not lead to this conclusion in all circum-stances, for if there were no bad occurrences that we could prevent without sacrificing something of comparable moral importance, my argument would have no application. Given the present conditions in many parts of the world, however, it does follow from my argument that we ought, morally, to be working full time to relieve great suffering of the sort that occurs as a result of famine or other disasters. Of course, mitigating cir-cumstances can be adduced – for instance, that if we wear ourselves out through over-work, we shall be less effective than we would otherwise have been. Nevertheless, when all considerations of this sort have been taken into account, the conclusion remains: we ought to be preventing as much suffering as we can without sacrificing something else of comparable moral importance. This conclu-sion is one which we may be reluctant to face. I cannot see, though, why it should be regarded as a criticism of the position for which I have argued, rather than a criticism of our ordinary standards of behavior. Since most people are self-interested to some degree, very few of us are likely to do every-thing that we ought to do. It would, however, hardly be honest to take this as evidence that it is not the case that we ought to do it.

It may still be thought that my conclu-sions are so wildly out of line with what everyone else thinks and has always thought that there must be something wrong with the argument somewhere. In order to show that my conclusions, while certainly contrary to contemporary Western moral standards, would not have seemed so extraordinary at other times and in other places, I would like to quote a passage from a writer not normally thought of as a way-out radical, Thomas Aquinas.

> Now, according to the natural order instituted by divine providence, material goods are provided for the satisfaction of human needs. Therefore the division and appropriation of property, which proceeds from human law, must not hinder the satisfaction of man's necessity from such goods. Equally, whatever a man has in superabundance is owed, of natural right, to the poor for their sustenance. So Ambrosius says, and it is also to be found in the *Decretum Gratiani*: "The bread which you withhold belongs to the hungry; the clothing you shut away, to the naked; and the money you bury in the earth is the redemption and freedom of the penniless."[4]

I now want to consider a number of points, more practical than philosophical, which are relevant to the application of the moral conclusion we have reached. These points challenge not the idea that we ought to be doing all we can to prevent starvation, but the idea that giving away a great deal of money is the best means to this end.

It is sometimes said that overseas aid should be a government responsibility, and that therefore one ought not to give to privately run charities. Giving privately, it is said, allows the government and the non-contributing members of society to escape their responsibilities.

This argument seems to assume that the more people there are who give to privately organized famine relief funds, the less likely it is that the government will take over full responsibility for such aid. This assumption is unsupported, and does not strike me as at all plausible. The opposite view – that if no one gives voluntarily, a government will assume that its citizens are uninterested in famine relief and would not wish to be forced into giving aid – seems more plausible. In any case, unless there were a definite probability that by refusing to give one would be helping to bring about massive government assistance, people who do refuse to make voluntary contributions are refusing to prevent a certain amount of suffering without being able to point to any tangible beneficial consequence of their refusal. So the onus of showing how their refusal will bring about government action is on those who refuse to give.

I do not, of course, want to dispute the contention that governments of affluent nations should be giving many times the amount of genuine, no-strings-attached aid that they are giving now. I agree, too, that giving privately is not enough, and that we ought to be campaigning actively for entirely new standards for both public and private contributions to famine relief. Indeed, I would sympathize with someone who thought that campaigning was more important than giving oneself, although I doubt whether preaching what one does not practice would be very effective. Unfortunately, for many people the idea that "it's the government's responsibility" is a reason for not giving which does not appear to entail any political action either.

Another, more serious reason for not giving to famine relief funds is that until there is effective population control, relieving famine merely postpones starvation. If we save the Bengal refugees now, others, perhaps the children of these refugees, will face starvation in a few years' time. In support of this, one may cite the now well-known facts about the population explosion and the relatively limited scope for expanded production.

This point, like the previous one, is an argument against relieving suffering that is happening now, because of a belief about what might happen in the future; it is unlike the previous point in that very good evidence can be adduced in support of this belief about the future. I will not go into the evidence here. I accept that the earth cannot support indefinitely a population rising at the present rate. This certainly poses a problem for anyone who thinks it important to prevent famine. Again, however, one could accept the argument without drawing the conclusion that it absolves one from any obligation to do anything to prevent famine. The conclusion that should be drawn is that the best means of preventing famine, in the long run, is population control. It would then follow from the position reached earlier that one ought to be doing all one can to promote population control (unless one held that all forms of population control were wrong in themselves, or would have significantly bad consequences). Since there are organizations working specifically for population control, one would then support them rather than more orthodox methods of preventing famine.

A third point raised by the conclusion reached earlier relates to the question of just how much we all ought to be giving away. One possibility, which has already been mentioned, is that we ought to give until we reach the level of marginal utility – that is, the level at which, by giving more, I would cause as much suffering to myself or my dependents as I would relieve by my gift. This would mean, of course, that one would reduce oneself to very near the material circumstances of a Bengali refugee. It will be recalled that earlier I put forward both a strong and a moderate version of the principle of preventing bad occurrences. The strong version, which required us to prevent bad things from happening unless in doing so we would be sacrificing something of comparable moral significance, does seem to require reducing ourselves to the level of marginal utility. I should also say that the strong version seems to me to be the correct one. I proposed the more moderate version – that we should prevent bad occurrences unless, to do so, we had to sacrifice something morally significant – only in order to show that even on this surely undeniable principle a great change in our way of life is required. On the more moderate principle, it may not follow that we ought to reduce ourselves to the level of marginal utility, for one might hold that to reduce oneself and one's family to this level is to cause something significantly bad to happen. Whether this is so I shall not discuss, since, as I have said, I can see no good reason for holding the moderate version of the principle rather than the strong version. Even if we accepted the principle only in its moderate form, however, it should be clear that we would have to give away enough to ensure that the consumer society, dependent as it is on people spending on trivia rather than giving to famine relief, would slow down and perhaps disappear entirely. There are several reasons why this would be desirable in itself. The value and necessity of economic growth are now being questioned not only by conservationists, but by economists as well.[5] There is no doubt, too, that the consumer society has had a distorting effect on the goals and purposes of its members. Yet looking at the matter purely from the point of view of overseas aid, there must be a limit to the extent to which we should deliberately slow down our economy; for it might be the case that if we gave away, say, forty percent of our Gross National Product, we would slow down the economy so much that in absolute terms we would be giving less than if we gave twenty-five percent of the much larger GNP that we would have if we limited our contribution to this smaller percentage.

I mention this only as an indication of the sort of factor that one would have to take into account in working out an ideal. Since Western societies generally consider one percent of the GNP an acceptable level for overseas aid, the matter is entirely academic. Nor does it affect the question of how much an individual should give in a society in which very few are giving substantial amounts.

It is sometimes said, though less often now than it used to be, that philosophers have no special role to play in public affairs, since most public issues depend primarily on an assessment of facts. On questions of fact, it is said, philosophers as such have no special expertise, and so it has been possible to engage in philosophy without committing oneself to any position on major public issues. No doubt there are some issues of social policy and foreign policy about which it can truly be said that a really expert assessment of the facts is required before taking sides or acting, but the issue of famine is surely not one of these. The facts about the existence of suffering are beyond dispute. Nor, I think, is it disputed that we can do something about it, either through orthodox methods of famine relief or through popula-

tion control or both. This is therefore an issue on which philosophers are competent to take a position. The issue is one which faces everyone who has more money than he needs to support himself and his dependents, or who is in a position to take some sort of political action. These categories must include practically every teacher and student of philosophy in the universities of the Western world. If philosophy is to deal with matters that are relevant to both teachers and students, this is an issue that philosophers should discuss.

Discussion, though, is not enough. What is the point of relating philosophy to public (and personal) affairs if we do not take our conclusions seriously? In this instance, taking our conclusion seriously means acting upon it. The philosopher will not find it any easier than anyone else to alter his attitudes and way of life to the extent that, if I am right, is involved in doing everything that we ought to be doing. At the very least, though, one can make a start. The philosopher who does so will have to sacrifice some of the benefits of the consumer society, but he can find compensation in the satisfaction of a way of life in which theory and practice, if not yet in harmony, are at least coming together.

Notes

[1] There was also a third possibility: that India would go to war to enable the refugees to return to their lands. Since I wrote this paper [in 1971], India has taken this way out. The situation is no longer that described above, but this does not affect my argument, as the next paragraph indicates.

[2] In view of the special sense philosophers often give to the term, I should say that I use "obligation" simply as the abstract noun derived from "ought," so that "I have an obligation to" means no more, and no less, than

"I ought to." This usage is in accordance with the definition of "ought" given by the *Shorter Oxford English Dictionary*: "the general verb to express duty or obligation." I do not think any issue of substance hangs on the way the term is used; sentences in which I use "obligation" could all be rewritten, although somewhat clumsily, as sentences in which a clause containing "ought" replaces the term "obligation."

[3] J. O. Urmson, "Saints and Heroes," in *Essays in Moral Philosophy*, ed. Abraham I. Melden (Seattle and London, 1958), p. 214. For a

related but significantly different view see also Henry Sidgwick, *The Methods of Ethics*, 7th edn. (London, 1907), pp. 220–1, 492–3.

4   *Summa Theologica*, II–II, Question 66, Article 7, in *Aquinas, Selected Political Writings*, ed. A. P. d'Entreves, trans. J. G. Dawson (Oxford, 1948), p. 171.

5   See, for instance, John Kenneth Galbraith, *The New Industrial State* (Boston, MA: 1967), and E. J. Mishan, *The Costs of Economic Growth* (London, 1967).

Chapter 20

What We Owe to Distant Others*
Leif Wenar

What morality requires of us in a world of poverty and inequality depends both on what our duties are in the abstract, and on what we can do to help.

T. M. Scanlon addresses the first question.[1] Scanlon's contractualism, like Rawls's justice as fairness, is intended as a theoretical alternative to utilitarianism. Yet Scanlon's is a theory not of institutional design, but of individual duty – of what you and I owe to each other, and to each other person in the world. In this article I first evaluate how well Scanlon's theory explains the patterns and content of our reasoning about our duties to distant others. I will suggest that contractualism does isolate the moral factors that frame our deliberations about the extent of our obligations in situations of need. To this extent, contractualism matches and clarifies our common-sense understanding of our duties to distant others.

The second, empirical question then becomes vital. What we as individuals need to know is *how* to fulfil our duties to the distant poor. We need to know what we must actually do. Moral theorists tend to base their prescriptions on simple assump-

tions about how the rich can help the poor. Yet a survey of the empirical literature shows how urgently we need more information on this topic before we can know what contractualist morality – or any plausible morality – requires of us.

1   Justifying One's Actions to Others

Like Immanuel Kant, Scanlon begins with the question of moral motivation in order to reach the question of moral requirement. Scanlon holds that the fundamental moral motivation is the desire to justify one's actions to others on grounds that those others could reasonably accept.[2] This desire to justify oneself to others is a direct response to the value that one perceives in them. Others are (as we are) capable of assessing the reasons they have to live their lives in different ways, and are capable of guiding their actions by their assessments of these reasons. When we act in ways that are justifiable to others, we acknowledge the capacities that others have to govern their lives in accordance with their judgements of what is worthwhile.[3]

Of course in some sense utilitarianism can also be said to respond to the value of

* From *Politics, Philosophy & Economics* 2 (2003), pp. 283–304.

others, but contractualism is distinguished from utilitarianism both by the characteristics it deems valuable and by the response to value that it deems appropriate. Contractualism attends in the first instance to the capacity rationally to direct one's own life, rather than to feelings of pleasure and pain or well-being more generally. In this sense the contractualist motivation tracks the value *of* people, instead of the value *in* people. Moreover, the contractualist attitude toward value is not, as a utilitarian account would suggest, that it is always simply 'to be promoted'. Rather, the correct response to perceiving the rational natures of other individuals is to be motivated to justify one's actions to them.

The fundamental contractualist duty is then to act in accordance with principles that everyone could reasonably accept. This formula focuses on individuals, and not (as in utilitarianism) on collectivities. For each action we are to ask whether a rule permitting the action would be reasonably acceptable to each other individual, instead of asking whether the rule would promote the well-being of all people taken together. The rules that would be acceptable to all define the content of our duties from a contractualist perspective.

How well do these contractualist accounts of moral motivation and moral reasoning mesh with the structure of our moral sensitivities? The fit often appears to be good. For instance, contractualism can explain why we are attentive to the effects of our actions both on those who are better off and on those who are worse off, since our actions will have to be justified to both. Contractualism can in addition explain why our moral concern is usually first directed to the plight of the worst off, since the complaints of the worst off are often the strongest grounds for rejecting a potential principle.[4]

Contractualism can also explain why our moral concern tends to be activated by one-to-one comparisons of well-being, rather than by aggregative considerations. As charitable organizations have long known, those of us who live in the rich world tend to respond strongly to images of *individuals* in dire straits whose plights seem unjustifiable given our own surplus of resources. The contractualist interpretation of this reaction is that our moral concern is roused by the necessity of justifying our actions (or inaction) to such individuals, independently of the numbers of individuals in like circumstances.

An aggregative theory like utilitarianism might attempt to explain this focus on individuals by saying that our concern is raised by the possibility of increasing total happiness by transferring our surplus resources to individuals like the ones we see in the commercials. But a utilitarian theory will find it more difficult to explain, as contractualism easily can, why our moral concern would be triggered much more intensely by seeing a single person in great need than it would by seeing thousands slightly worse off than ourselves.

Scanlon sometimes expresses the contractualist moral motivation as reflecting 'The reason we have to *live with others* on terms that they could not reasonably reject'.[5] This way of putting it highlights the question of the relative priority of the contractualist desire with respect to other motivations that might compete for our attention. After all, the sense in which we 'live with' most of those whose value we must recognize is quite attenuated. We 'live with' the poorest in the world, for instance, in the sense that each group's actions indirectly affect the political and physical environments of the other group – and in the sense that we in the rich countries have the potential to affect the poor by devoting our resources to charitable causes and political activism. This is a much lesser way to live with others than, for example, the ways in which we live with our friends, our colleagues, and our fellow citizens. What does contractualism have to say about the relative priority of the reasons we have to live with these different sets of people on particular terms, and how well does this correspond to our sense of what priorities these types of relations should have?

On the purely theoretical level contractualism says, as I believe it must, that the reasons we have to justify our actions to other human beings, regardless of our relation to them, take precedence over the more particular reasons we have to engage with those closer to us.[6] In other words, our closer relations of friendship, family, and fellow citizenship have a 'built-in sensitivity to the demands of right and wrong'.[7] If they did not, we would not find them acceptable: we do not see these closer relations as licences for immorality. The universal morality sets the structure in which our closer relations must fit, and this is so even though any plausible universal morality will acknowledge the value of closer relations by making room for them in its requirements and permissions. The universal relation has priority over the particular, and its demands shape the acceptable forms of these special relations even as it takes the possible value of these special relations (so shaped) into account.

This priority of the universal is, I believe, the only intellectually satisfying construal of the priority relation. Moreover, contractualism plausibly locates the source of this priority in the great value that we recognize in each other person regardless of our relation to them. Yet although we acknowledge the priority of the universal, in everyday life this is typically a source of unease. We may register the moral importance of helping distant others in need, even as we turn to devote our time and resources to the routine expectations of those near and dear. This kind of 'bad conscience' in favouring the local over the urgent is a familiar feature of modern moral consciousness. It is a phenomenon that a contractualist moral psychology can go some way to explain.

A contractualist moral psychology says that our desires to act are responses to reasons and values. Specifically, our motivations to act flow from judgements about reasons to act that spring from our perceptions of value 'in the world'. When we perceive something valuable, we judge that there is a reason to engage in a course of action that protects it, or pursues it, or promotes it, or honours it, and so on. When we judge that there is a reason to engage in some course of action, we thereby (insofar as we are rational) come to have a motivation to engage in that course. In this way, our motivations are responses to our perceptions of the values that there are 'out there'.[8] This holds for all of our motivations – your desire to contribute to the wildlife sanctuary is a response to the value you perceive in nature, just as my desire to eat the chocolate right now is a response to the value I perceive in the chocolate.

However, the strengths of our actual motivations do not always correspond to the relative importance of the values in the world, because our attention is constantly being drawn toward rather small portions of all the values that there are. Our biology and our social conditioning determine our psychology to keep drawing our attention back to more 'local' values and reasons – to the value of eating good food, to the value of attending to the needs of those we love, and to the value of engaging in the pleasures of discussions with colleagues. Our characters are set with a particular constellation of what Scanlon calls 'desires in the directed attention sense', so that certain kinds of considerations persistently present themselves to our consciousness in a favourable light.[9] The contractualist ideal of virtue would be a person whose attention was always directed toward those values that were the most important for her to respond to at the time.

None of us lives up to this ideal of character, and because we do not our attentions are constantly being pulled toward the charms of things that, objectively, matter less.

This habitual drawing of attention to nearer horizons can account for the fact that our recognition of the needs of distant others often has quite temporary motivational power. We will acknowledge the strong reasons we have to help distant others when we are presented with these reasons. But we are not so constituted that we can easily focus on these reasons over time. Our attention keeps getting dragged bock to the reasons we have to engage with people and events close at hand.

Of course this motivational story has nothing to say about what we should actually *do* for distant others. That will be the subject of the rest of the article. But this contractualist account of motivation can explain why, when we are asked how much we should *attend* to the topic of our duties to distant others, we will invariably say: 'More'.

Contractualism can explain both why we judge that we should attend more to the needs of distant others, and why this judgement is correct. What then does contractualism require us to do in response to the needs of the world's poor? I believe that contractualism isolates and clarifies, but does not resolve, the two most difficult problems that the rich face in thinking about their duties to the distant poor. One problem is empirical, and we need to make progress on it through empirical research. The other problem is normative, and the contractualist approach shows how difficult it is to make progress on it at all.

2   The Normative Question

In sections 18 and 19 of *A Theory of Justice*, John Rawls conjectured that there should be an extension of the approach of justice as fairness to the question of what actions are morally right for individuals to perform. He called this conjectural theory 'rightness as fairness', and said that it would provide 'a way for eliminating customary phrases in terms of other expressions' so as to give 'a definition or explication of the concept [of] . . . right'.[10]

I believe that Scanlon's contractualism is a theory of 'rightness as fairness' – or more precisely, a theory of 'wrongness as unfairness'. The contractualist characterization of wrongness focuses on principles that all could reasonably accept, or, equivalently, on principles that none could reasonably reject. It asks us to evaluate potential principles of conduct by examining the strength of the complaints that those affected by a principle could lodge against it. If a complaint to a principle is strong enough, that principle can reasonably be rejected. The grounds for reasonable rejection of a proposed principle typically resolve, I believe, into complaints that the principle is unfair.[11]

Below I summarize three types of complaint against a proposed principle of conduct, all of which are complaints of unfairness. The first two will concern us especially in what follows.

1   *Disadvantage.* The proposed principle would leave some people badly off, and there are other principles available under which no one would be as badly off as those people would be under the proposed principle.
2   *Sacrifice.* The proposed principle requires a sacrifice from some that is too great, given the size of the benefit that others would gain from this sacrifice.
3   *Distribution by irrelevant criterion.* The proposed principle allows advantages to some people, but for no reason related to the justification of the overall distribution.

The complaint of *disadvantage* is the basis for the contractualist interpretation of some of the deepest rules of right and wrong.[12] For example, consider the grounds for rejecting a principle that allows wanton killing. A principle allowing wanton killing can be reasonably rejected by those who would be killed. This is because this principle would leave these victims badly off, and there are other principles available (forbidding wanton killing) under which no one would be as badly off as the victims would be under the proposed principle. In essence, a principle allowing wanton killing is unfair because it is worse to be killed than it is to be a frustrated killer. Since any principle allowing wanton killing could be reasonably rejected, wanton killing is morally wrong.

The complaint of *sacrifice* can be illustrated by an objection that is sometimes heard during debates over the priorities for a national health service. It would be unfair, it is said, to transfer the entire budget for 'optional' procedures like fertility enhancement into the budget for expensive treatments that prolong the lives of the terminally ill. The sacrifice for the groups needing the 'optional' procedures would be too great, it is said, given the small gains in longevity for the terminally ill that these sacrifices would buy. This is so even though the terminally ill are of course much worse off than those who would be asked to sacrifice the fertility-enhancement procedures.

The complaint of *distribution by irrelevant criterion* grounds Scanlon's discussion of free riding.[13] It is unfair for some arbitrarily to gain extra advantages within a cooperative scheme in which all bear burdens, even if their gaining this extra advantage would not make anyone else worse off. So, for example, it would be wrong for some to be allowed secretly to exempt themselves from a scheme that reduces emissions from automobiles, even though the pollution that they would thereby cause is in fact too slight to endanger anyone.

The idea of fairness lies behind both the complaint of disadvantage and the complaint of sacrifice. Yet these two fairness-based complaints push contractualist morality in opposite directions. Consider for example the principles appropriate for two groups, the Rich and the Poor. The complaint of disadvantage puts pressure on contractualism to require redistribution of resources from the Rich toward the Poor – and at the limit, toward equalizing resources between Rich and Poor. This is because for any proposed principle that allows the Rich to control more resources than the Poor, there is a more egalitarian principle under which the Poor do better. So the Poor have grounds for rejecting principles that keep them poor, given the availability of principles that would redistribute resources to make them richer. On the other hand, the complaint of sacrifice puts pressure on contractualism to resist redistribution. The Rich cannot in fairness be required to give up huge amounts of resources just to provide the smallest gains to the Poor. The Poor, in other words, cannot reasonably reject a proposed principle *simply* because there is an alternative under which they would be better off, without consideration to the amount of sacrifice that the proposed principle would impose upon the Rich.[14]

In the context of our duties to distant people in need, the complaint of sacrifice may seem to be irrelevant. It may appear to be obvious that we in rich countries could easily sacrifice what is of little importance to us in order to bring about large welfare gains to those in poor countries. Yet right now I just want to emphasize the more abstract point that considerations of sacrifice are part of our thinking about our moral duties, and so that the complaint of sacrifice will have a place in any plausible moral theory. The complaints of the poor cannot have absolute priority.[15]

Indeed I believe that it is a virtue of contractualism that it isolates so clearly two of the factors that guide our reasoning about redistribution: the complaint of disadvantage and the complaint of sacrifice. The rich man should give some money to the destitute family at his door. Yet the rich man need not give up his entire fortune if somehow this would provide the destitute family with only a single extra penny. Our judgements in these extreme cases are certain, and they are explained by one and then the other complaint dominating our reasoning. It is the cases between these extremes, where both complaints have weight, that make us uncertain. How much sacrifice is enough?

Scanlon's own proposed principle of duties to distant others is a compromise between the complaints of disadvantage and sacrifice. His 'Rescue Principle' requires the rich to aid those in desperate straits (for example, those starving), but only if the rich can do so at 'slight or moderate' cost to themselves. Here the sacrifice required of the better off is clearly being weighed against the benefit to the badly off, the result being a principle that is only mildly burdensome to the better off.[16]

One might be tempted to express disappointment that Scanlon's principle requiring aid to distant others is relatively undemanding. Yet there is a deeper indeterminacy within contractualism that is more significant. Contractualism locates the two most important factors in our reasoning about our duties to aid distant others: the benefit to the poor, and the amount of sacrifice from the rich. But it gives us no tools for understanding how to resolve the tension between these two factors. It would be churlish to require a moral theory to give us an exact schedule of trade-offs between benefits and sacrifices. Contractualism, as far as I can see,

provides no guidance whatsoever. It leaves the large area between the extreme cases (about which we were already certain) to be decided entirely by individual judgement. The fact that Scanlon's judgement about trade-offs (as expressed in his Rescue Principle) may be different from your own judgement highlights how little assistance contractualism gives in specifying our duties in the crucial 'intermediate' cases.

Here, for example, is Thomas Nagel's judgement on what principles of aid could be reasonably rejected:

> While no one could reasonably reject some requirement of aid from the affluent to the destitute, the cumulative effect on an individual life of an essentially unlimited requirement to give to those who are very much worse off than yourself, whatever other affluent people are doing, would simply rule out the pursuit of a wide range of individualistic values – aesthetic, hedonistic, intellectual, cultural, romantic, athletic and so forth. Would the certain abandonment of all these things provide reasonable ground for rejection of a principle that required it – even in the face of the starving millions? The question for Scanlon's model would be whether it could be offered as a justification to *each one* of those millions, and my sense is that perhaps it could, that one could say: "I cannot be condemned as unreasonable if I reject a principle that would require me to abandon most of the substance of my life to save yours."[17]

Nagel here reaffirms our intuitions about time 'extreme' cases. The rich cannot reasonably reject 'some requirement of aid'; yet 'an unlimited requirement to give' would be unreasonable. What is distinctive in the passage is Nagel's judgement that it would be unreasonable to require the rich to give up 'most of the substance of [their lives]' in order to keep the poor from starving. The rich cannot, Nagel says, reasonably be expected to give up their aesthetic, hedonistic, intellectual, cultural, romantic, and athletic pursuits for the sake of improving the lives of the destitute.

How can contractualism help us in evaluating Nagel's judgements here? There are at least two kinds of objections that could be levelled at Nagel's proposal. First, someone might object that certain interests of the rich (for example, their hedonistic or athletic interests) have almost no moral significance when compared to the interests of the poor in avoiding the grotesque sufferings of deprivation. Nagel has, it might be said, taken these complaints from the rich too seriously. Second, someone might object that Nagel's proposal, even if accepted, leaves a great deal of uncertainty about what is actually required of the rich. Would affluent Americans be excessively burdened if they were required to sacrifice until they reached the average level of affluent Europeans? Until they reached the average level reached by their grandparents' generation? Would it be too much to require rich Americans to sacrifice 50 percent of their wealth and income for the sake of relieving the destitution of the poorest?

Each of us can come to a view with respect to the questions raised by these two objections. As we do so, however, we will be relying entirely on our own judgement, and not at all on resources that contractualism provides for us. Contractualism is useful in clarifying the structure of our reasoning about our abstract moral duties to aid distant others. But it does not help us further by showing us how to determine more exactly what the extent of our duties is, even in the abstract. So far as the extent of these duties is concerned, contractualism leaves us clearer about why we are where we already were.[18]

On the one hand, this will not encourage those who have worried about the seemingly *ad hoc* nature of contractualist reasoning.[19] On the other hand, contractualism seems to have captured a central tension in our ordinary moral reasoning, and given the nature of this reasoning it is difficult to see how the theory could go on to say anything more definite than it does. Whether one thinks that contractualism should be criticized for leaving a large role to individual judgement will depend on what one expects from moral theory. What is certain, however, is that contractualism in itself leaves unanswered important questions about what we owe to distant others.

3   The Empirical Question

I mentioned above that worries about how the sacrifice of the rich relates to the benefit to the poor might seem irrelevant to our current situation, since clearly what the rich could sacrifice would be of little importance to them compared to the tremendous benefits that their sacrifices could bring to the world's impoverished people. The situation of the rich is obviously at the 'extreme' where small or moderate sacrifice could bring great benefit – and contractualism echoes ordinary moral judgement in saying that in such cases some amount sacrifice is morally required. This empirical thesis that small sacrifice from the rich can bring great benefit to the poor is implicit in many public appeals for charitable contributions. This empirical thesis that small sacrifice can bring great benefit is also explicit in almost all analytical moral theorizing about our duties to distant others, as it has been since Peter Singer's classic 1972 article on famine relief.[20]

I believe that the confidence expressed in this familiar empirical thesis is seriously misplaced. It is in fact quite difficult to determine how much the sacrifices of a rich individual will contribute to the long-term well-being of distant people in need. There is nothing clear or obvious about the relation between what a rich individual sacrifices and what the distant poor gain. If progress is to be made in contractualist theory or elsewhere about our duties to distant others, the empirical questions in this area require our attention.

We tend to pass quickly over the empirical questions about our duties to distant others. In everyday life, the thought that short-circuits the empirical questions says 'We must be able to do *something*'. For philosophers, it is the high professional standards of abstract clarity that tend to screen off the relevance of the empirical issues. We are doing moral philosophy, after all, not political theory or economics, and this can appear to license the assumption that individuals in the rich world can assist the distant poor almost instantly and without mediation.

Yet this natural assumption in moral theory ignores the extraordinarily complex causal nexus that lies between the rich and those distant from them who live in poverty. These causal connections between the rich and poor are relevant to the conclusions that moral theory can reach. Individuals must after all carry out their moral duties in this world, in all its reality and detail. If moral theorists demand action to this world, they should be able to give firm empirical support for their claims that the actions they require will have the effects that they predict.

The empirical question that rich individuals must be able to answer in order to understand their moral duties to aid distant others is this: *How will each dollar, given by me or my government, affect the long-term well-being of the poor?*

One cannot expect a precise answer to such a question. As with many complex issues we must be satisfied with informed, reasonable guesses. Nor of course will the answer to such a question be simple. There are many ways of giving, and many dimensions of well-being.[21] Yet when one approaches the empirical (as opposed to the moral) literature that bears on this topic, four things are particularly striking. The first is that the question above is nowhere discussed. What

rich individuals need to know is how each dollar they can give, or each hour they can devote to campaigning for more foreign aid, will affect the long-term welfare of distant people who need help the most. Perhaps understandably, the specialized social scientists who produce the empirical literature have not seen answering such questions as an important goal of their inquiries.

The second thing that strikes one in the empirical literature is what most researchers agree on. Certain gross facts in the history of poverty and aid are fairly widely accepted. Over the past 50 years the percentage of people living in dire poverty has declined, while the absolute number has increased. Aid flows during this period have been greater than the period before, yet in absolute terms have been fairly small. Many aid initiatives appear to have averted crises and reduced poverty. But the money spent on other initiatives has been worse than wasted – it has, for example, disrupted local systems of production, intensified corruption, or simply delayed democratic reforms. The direction of aid has often been guided by strategic and institutional rather than by humanitarian imperatives.[22] Yet even the best-intentioned efforts have had unintended side-effects that have overwhelmed their benefits, and the projects that have seemed the most likely to have salutary effects sometimes have not.

Indeed the third thing that strikes one in the empirical literature is how much of this material is pessimistic about the effectiveness of aid. Here I will just report some of the main strands of pessimism that run through the literature on aid.

There are two main categories of aid: humanitarian assistance and development assistance. Humanitarian assistance is directed toward those in immediate peril. It includes provision of food and shelter, dehydration relief, and medical attention for those injured by armed conflict. This assistance aims at short or medium-term benefits for those that receive it. Yet the wider effects of humanitarian assistance are often less certain.[23] The most pressing concern is that the efforts of relief organizations unavoidably affect the political situation of the area. This is especially clear in armed conflicts. Relief organizations may for example have to turn food aid over to a local army in order to gain access to the needy. The very presence of 'free' food or medical care may encourage combatants to continue fighting, or it may encourage them to drive 'unwanted' minorities out of the country into refugee camps. The camps themselves may also become havens for soldiers as they regroup to launch further attacks.[24]

In non-combat situations, the availability of humanitarian assistance may encourage governments to shirk responsibility for the fates of their most impoverished citizens – that is, it may encourage them to divert funds to other programmes or, worse, to 'disown' the poorest completely. Similarly, the availability of humanitarian assistance may undermine systems of local self-help (for example, the training of native doctors) and it may thwart efforts (even by foreign aid groups) to promote long-term self-reliance. In both combat and non-combat contexts, aid agencies must often hand over a significant percentage of their 'project' budgets to authoritarian governments, to corrupt officials, and to criminals in order to maintain their headquarters in the national capital, and in order to 'get things done' in the field. Dependence, moral hazard, fuelling conflict and oppression and corruption and crime: these are the major risks of inserting resources into the complex political disequilibria that define wars and other humanitarian crises.[25] They are the major risks of humanitarian assistance.

Development assistance attempts to promote long-term, self-sustaining political and economic improvements in poor areas.

Development aid includes intergovernmental grants and loans (sometimes administered by the World Bank or the International Monetary Fund) that are intended to spur economic growth or to stimulate specific reforms in public policy in the recipient country. Development aid also includes direct initiatives by multilaterals and non-governmental organization (NGOs) to improve education, sanitation, contraception awareness, and so on. The complexities here are enormous, and some of the data available on bilateral and multilateral aid are particularly discouraging.[26] The influential World Bank special report *Assessing Aid*, for instance, is about as sceptical about the past 50 years of bilateral and multilateral aid as such a report can be, given that it is issued by an organization whose future existence depends on providing aid.[27] Some studies have found that, overall, bilateral and multilateral aid to governments has had little or no impact on economic growth, and has not benefited the poor.[28] Efforts by donors to 'target' intergovernmental aid at specific public policy areas like health or education are usually unsuccessful, since recipient governments simply spend elsewhere the money they would have spent in the targeted area.[29] Moreover, some studies indicate that development aid has not overall been an incentive for recipient governments to change their policies in the 'right' directions, and indeed has often delayed reform.[30] Worse still, aid has made some government elites more concerned with appearing to respond to foreign donors than to their own citizens, especially in Africa.[31] One set of cross-country regressions from more than 100 developing countries indicates that higher bilateral or multilateral aid has had no correlation with decreased infant mortality, and has had a slightly negative correlation with life expectancy and primary schooling.[32]

Non-governmental organizations do have advantages over governments in administering development assistance. The greatest potential advantage of NGOs is political independence.[33] Yet NGOs have had real difficulties coordinating their efforts with local governments and with each other, and have had some tendency simply to 'plant a flag' on particular projects regardless of the effectiveness of those projects.[34] The locally directed development efforts that NGOs specialize in also face the general dilemma that these programmes must be extremely sensitive to local circumstances to ensure recipient participation (and so success), yet aim to impose large-scale changes on the political, productive, or reproductive practices of those who are meant to participate. (The dilemmas here can be appreciated by imagining oneself to be part of a 'recipient population' of development assistance.)

The strong sceptical currents in the empirical literature on aid effectiveness bring us to the fourth and most striking fact, which is the overall uncertainty in the empirical literature about what aid really works.[35] Several of the pessimistic studies of development aid effectiveness cited above have spawned fierce debates in the literature.[36] This is perhaps not surprising given how highly charged the topics are ideologically. Yet what is remarkable in these debates is how deep the disagreements run about what economic methods are appropriate for assessing the data, and about what data are relevant for evaluating particular development strategies. Indeed, even the most widely used World Bank statistics addressing elementary questions like how many poor people there are in the world, and whether that number is increasing or decreasing, have been strongly criticized by responsible academics as 'neither reliable nor meaningful'.[37] In fact it is sometimes remarkable how little of what appear to be relevant data about development aid are even recorded at all.[38]

At the micro level, the obstacles for collecting and interpreting the data on aid effectiveness are even greater. Evaluations of the effectiveness of the particular projects carried out by aid agencies lack a standardization that would make meta-analyses of their impact on welfare possible. These evaluations are also often surprisingly limited in scope, tending to focus on short-term, 'concrete' criteria of success instead of long-term welfare benefits.[39] This is especially true of NGO self-evaluations,[40] and the relatively few independent evaluations of NGO projects have not borne out the NGOs' claims of success. The largest study to date of NGO effectiveness asserts that:

A repeated and consistent conclusion drawn across countries and in relation to all clusters of studies is that the data are exceptionally poor. There is a paucity of data and information from which to draw firm conclusions about the impact of projects, about efficiency and effectiveness, about sustainability, the gender and environmental impact of projects and their contribution to strengthening democratic forces, institutions and organizations and building civil society. There is even less firm data with which to assess the impact of NGO development interventions beyond discrete projects, not least those involved in building and strengthening institutional capacity.[41]

Having reviewed this study and the other major study of NGO project effectiveness, one scholar concludes: 'These two multi-country studies raise serious doubts as to whether many NGOs *know* what they are doing, in the sense of their overall impact on people's lives.'[42]

It may appear unseemly to question the efforts of the most active donors and aid organizations. For example, the Scandinavian governments have been relatively generous in their bilateral grants, and Oxfam, Unicef, and Medicins Sans Frontieres have made heroic efforts in tending wounds, distributing food, limiting epidemics, and teaching reproductive health. Indeed, the most common reply to worries about the effectiveness of aid is to call attention to the experience and conscientiousness of the people who staff government agencies and aid organizations. Why should we not expect that the efforts of good people familiar with the problems of administering aid will end up providing significant benefits?[43]

There is no doubt that many people who work in aid agencies are knowledgeable and conscientious. Yet one might think that it takes more than this reliably to effect long-term increases in human well-being within recipient communities. When one looks at the institutional incentives – what individuals need to do to succeed within their organizations, and what organizations need to do to succeed in competition with other organizations – one finds that there are relatively few incentives for attending to the long-term well-being of the neediest, and unfortunately many incentives for ignoring or even counteracting this long-term well-being.

For instance, it will not surprise many to find that the main institutional incentive of the US government to provide food aid has been to respond to the powerful US industries who are the producers and shippers of excess American-grown food. Nor is it a surprise that it is often in the interest of officials in recipient governments to maximize aid flows into their countries, as this gives them more resources to exchange for patronage, and more independence from electoral polities. Both of these tendencies have had long-term negative impacts on the politics and economic self-sufficiency of countries which have received inter-governmental aid.

It is less well known that NGOs and those who work within them often face some of the same diversionary incentives. NGOs have incentives to propose projects that will meet the goals of those who will approve the projects (for example, the local government or the United States Agency for International Development). There is often little incentive for NGOs to study the long-term impact of the projects they propose, since projects are frequently accepted for reasons besides their anticipated effectiveness. Nor is there a strong institutional imperative to follow up projects with careful studies of their long-term effects, since future funding is often not dependent on past long-term project success. NGOs also have incentives to exaggerate humanitarian crises in order to increase their funding, and to exaggerate their own efficiency and effectiveness since this helps with fund-raising. Moreover, there is very little independent oversight of claims in these areas. This does not mean, of course, that there are no effective projects addressing real crises, but it does mean that it can be quite difficult for outsiders to know which projects these are.

We can express concern about these institutional incentives without impugning the motives of individuals working within aid agencies. Many politicians, bureaucrats, and NGO staff want to increase the power of their organizations, and their own power within their organizations, so that they can try to do more good. The difficulty comes when what people need to do to attain this success fails to track the long-term well-being of those who are badly off.

The institutional incentives of aid organizations are as they are because of a historical deficiency in external accountability. Aid organizations have evolved to a great extent unchecked by the four major checking mechanisms on bureaucratic organizations. These four mechanisms are democratic politics, regulatory oversight, press scrutiny, and academic review. Because of this historical deficiency in accountability, it is not surprising that many aid organizations have become places where it is difficult for the good people within them to do good.

It is no part of my intention to argue that aid cannot be effective. I have reported on the scepticism about aid that appears in the empirical literature, but none of the studies I have cited are definitive and several have been vigorously criticized. I have described the structure of diversionary incentives faced by the individuals and organizations involved in aid, but people can overcome such incentives. I have not sought in any way to show that we know that aid cannot work.

Rather, I have hoped to bring out how difficult it is for us to determine the effects of individual contributions to aid efforts, and how urgent it is to gain better empirical information about what aid is effective. The simple empirical assumption that small sacrifice brings great benefit has been nearly universal in theorizing about our moral duties in the face of poverty. Yet we can only be as confident about such theorizing as we are about this assumption. Given the difficult history of aid, it is no longer sufficient for moral philosophers simply to inform their readers of the cost of an oral rehydration kit.[44] We need more information on the efficacy of aid. Moreover, the information we need is comprehensive and systematic information, instead of anecdotal reports of aid efforts that have succeeded or failed.

I have throughout emphasized the long-term effects of aid on human welfare because of the importance of the long term to moral theory. Recall that the contractualist motivation turns on 'The reason we have to *live with others* on terms that they could not reasonably reject'.[45] We 'live with' the poorest in the third world in the sense that our everyday actions indirectly affect their political and physical environments, and in the sense that we in the rich world have the potential to affect the poor by devoting our resources to aid. Yet this is the same way that we 'live with' the descendants of today's poor, and indeed with the descendants of today's potential donors. We must therefore justify our actions to future generations as much as to those now living. We must consider the possibility that current aid projects will hurt in the long run, even if (as not all do) they help in the short term. We must work to determine when our situation is like being able to pull a drowning child out of a shallow pond, and when it is more like trying to push through a crowd at the edge of a dock to save the child who has already fallen in.[46]

4   Conclusion

I have suggested that contractualism isolates, but does not answer, the two most important questions regarding our moral duties to distant others. The abstract normative question is how much sacrifice from rich individuals is required for the sake of how much benefit to the poor. The empirical question is how rich individuals can effectively promote the long-term welfare of the poor. Without progress in answering these questions, the nature and extent of our duties will remain indeterminate.

The danger of this indeterminacy is that it will lead to what might be called 'the selfishness of uncertainty'. Even those who wish to justify their actions to others must at some point decide to give a particular percentage of their income, or to devote a particular number of hours per week to advocacy. Yet settling on any particular level of contribution implies that one has arrived at defensible answers to our two questions: how much sacrifice is morally required, given how much one can reasonably expect others to benefit from this sacrifice. Defending answers to such questions is exactly what seems so difficult. The frustration associated with answering these questions then spurs avoidance of the entire topic.

The devastating magnitude of global poverty makes this response inadequate.[47] We live in a world where poverty causes massive human suffering. Ignoring this fact can hardly be justified. The familiar response of moral theorists *simply* to send more aid is, I believe, no longer appropriate. A more reasonable plan of action has, I believe, several elements.

First, we should support in any way we can independent research into aid effectiveness. This research can be carried out in universities, by the media, by governmental regulatory organizations, or by 'aid-watch' NGOs. Second, we should put pressure on aid agencies to become more accountable. Agencies must provide thorough assessments of the effectiveness of their projects – even though this will mean spending less on the projects themselves. These assessments should include detailed descriptions of all agency expenditures (costs of maintaining in-country headquarters, bribes paid, and so on). The assessments should also include evaluations of the impact of projects on the long-term well-being of recipient communities, carried out or certified by groups which have no incentive to provide positive reports.

Third, insofar as we do support aid projects, we should try to understand the political and economic contexts into which our resources will flow, and to seek out those projects which appear to combine the greatest potential for positive long-term impact with the fewest risks of counterproductive intervention (immunizing children against infectious diseases and iodizing salt supplies might be examples). Fourth, we should require high standards of transparency and effectiveness from our own governments' foreign aid programmes, and insist that foreign aid not be regarded as just another mechanism for promoting domestic political and economic interests. In practical terms, following these four proposals could mean doing our own research on aid effectiveness; offering conditional financial support to aid organizations; writing letters to politicians, aid organizations, and newspapers; and being careful when casting our votes.

We must also ask whether 'aid' is the only category that captures the content of our duties to the global poor. This article has been concerned specifically with questions about the rich aiding the poor, and so with questions about the *redistribution* of resources from the rich to the poor. Our discussion has presupposed, as Scanlon says, 'a framework of entitlements'.[48] Yet we can also question the fairness of the system of rules that has contributed to the rich being as rich as they are, and the poor being as poor. There is an elaborate set of rules that shape the outcomes of the global economic and political system – rules concerning trade barriers and domestic subsidies, intellectual property rights, the incurring and relief of national debts, and much else. It is plausible that the rich countries have used their overwhelming political power to skew these rules in their own favour, and that these rules could be reformed in ways that are beneficial to the poor without being tremendously burdensome to the rich. If this is correct, our practical duties with respect to the poor might direct us toward demanding, for example, that our own governments reduce domestic agricultural subsidies and tariff levels.[49] When we do moral theory we focus on individual duty, not on institutional design. Yet global poverty may present us with a situation in which we can best discharge some of our moral duties by working to improve the structure of global institutions.

Much more work is required for us to understand our specific duties with respect to the world's poor. Making this effort is part of what we owe to distant others. The desperate situation of billions of human beings who live far from us is the contemporary moral problem with the greatest claim on our attention. We owe it to these people to keep our attention focused upon it.

Notes

1   T. M. Scanlon, *What We Owe to Each Other* (Cambridge, MA: Harvard University Press, 1998).

2   In this article I will not distinguish between 'what all could reasonably accept' and 'what no one could reasonably reject'. I will also use the word 'desire' to refer generically to our motivations.

3   Scanlon, *What We Owe to Each Other*, pp. 103–6. In this way Scanlon's contractualism is like that part of Kant's moral theory that results in the Formula of Humanity: act so as to treat humanity whether in oneself or others always as an end in itself and never merely as a means. On Kant's view it is 'humanity' (the ability rationally to set and pursue ends) that is of unconditional worth. This is quite close to Scanlon's location of value in the ability to recognize and respond to reasons. In both Scanlon's and Kant's theories, moral motivation is a reaction to the reasons generated by the practical rationality of others. Indeed, echoes of Kant's imperative against instrumentalizing humanity can be heard in Scanlon's contractualist formula. The Kantian requirement that one accommodate others' capacities to set ends when pursuing one's own ends is analogous to the requirement of living by rules that others can reasonably accept. Moreover, Kant's demand that one heed the ends that others have actually set is parallel to the injunction to imagine the complaints that others might have to what one proposes to do.

4   T. M. Scanlon, 'Contractualism and Utilitarianism', in *Utilitarianism and Beyond*, ed. A. Sen and B. Williams (Cambridge: Cambridge University Press, 1982), p. 123.

5   Scanlon, *What We Owe to Each Other*, p. 154 (emphasis added); compare also p. 162.

6   I am using 'other human beings' as a convenient marker to indicate the largest class to which justification is due, without meaning to prejudge the question as to whether the scope of morality might be wider.

7   Scanlon, *What We Owe to Each Other*, p. 166.

8   Ibid., pp. 7–64.

9   Ibid., p. 39. In this paragraph and the next the description of a contractualist moral psychology is an extrapolation from what Scanlon has written. The sketch of the contractualist ideal of virtue, for instance, is mine not Scanlon's.

10 J. Rawls, *A Theory of Justice*, revised edn (Cambridge, MA: Harvard University Press, 1999). pp. 95–6.

11 This interpretation of contractualism as a theory of 'rightness as fairness', as well as the formulation of the complaints of unfairness that follow, are my own. Scanlon has not characterized contractualism in these ways.

12 See Scanlon, 'Contractualism and Utilitarianism', p. 123.

13 Scanlon, *What We Owe to Each Other*, pp. 211–13.

14 I discuss this tension at greater length in 'Contractualism and Global Economic Justice', *Metaphilosophy* 32 (2001), pp. 79–94 (reprinted in *Global Justice*, edited by T. Pogge (Oxford: Blackwell Publishing, 2002), pp. 79–82). It might be noticed that the complaint of disadvantage involves the claim that some are 'badly off', and so complaints of disadvantage will become weaker the better off the poor are in absolute terms. Since our concern here is with the global poor, and many of the global poor are about as badly off as humans can be while still being alive, we can put this complexity to one side. We can assume, that is, that absolute deprivation of many of the world's poor makes their current disadvantage-based complaint about as strong as such a complaint could be.

15 As Scanlon observes in *What We Owe to Each Other*, pp. 228–9, Rawls's argument for the difference principle (which does give absolute priority to the worst off) is something of a special case. First, the reasoning is confined to one particular arena: the justice of the basic structure of a society. Second, the argument proceeds from a baseline of equality – the assumption that equal citizens are all prima facie entitled to equal shares of the benefits of social cooperation. This baseline assumption gives a great deal of weight to the

complaints of those who would be worse off under any proposed inegalitarian principles. Yet even so, one might note that Rawls himself ends up defending the difference principle from objections of sacrifice – saying that it is empirically unlikely that the rich will have to make great sacrifices to provide tiny benefit to the poorest. See Rawls, *A Theory of Justice*, pp. 135–7.

16 Scanlon, *What We Owe to Each Other*, pp. 224–5. It is important to note that we are here discussing principles of *aid* and *redistribution*. In such a discussion we are assuming that the rich have the right to control certain resources and that the poor do not. As Scanlon says in *What We Owe to Each Other*, p. 214, in discussing aid 'we need to presuppose a framework of entitlements.' This article is primarily concerned with duties to aid, but our duties to distant others may also require us to work to revise the frameworks of global economic and political rules that work to produce these entitlements. I return to this point in the paper's conclusion.

17 T. Nagel, *Concealment and Exposure* (Oxford: Oxford University Press, 2002), p. 154.

18 Rahul Kumar's sensitive discussion of the contractualist duty of mutual aid is not intended to address this kind of indeterminacy in contractualism. Kumar, like Nagel, lists a variety of considerations that might allow an agent to resist certain principles of mutual aid. For instance, Kumar mentions having control enough over one's life to be able to make and execute plans, the costs of keeping oneself alert for occasions when aid may be required, and the ability to control with whom one forms significant relationships. Kumar does not discuss global poverty, and only a few of the considerations he mentions are relevant to this context. More importantly for our discussion, Kumar does not mean to comment in this article on how we might go about weighting the kinds of considerations he mentions against the countervailing considerations that favour requiring aid. See R. Kumar, 'Defending the Moral Moderate: Contractualism and Common Sense', *Philosophy and Public Affairs* 28 (1999): 275–309. For a subtle discussion of

contractualism with contrasting emphases to Kumar's, see E. Ashford, 'The Demandingness of Scanlon's Contractualism', *Ethics* 113 (2003), pp. 273–302.

19 T. Pogge, 'What We Can Reasonably Reject', *NOÛS* 11 (2001), p. 138 writes: 'When Scanlon actually tries to settle substantive moral questions by reference to [the contractualist formula], he must invoke extraneous intuitions and considerations that (though he repeatedly assures the reader that they are not *ad hoc*) have no discernible basis in his formulas. Yes, Scanlon is right to caution us against the quest for a fully determinate algorithm. But one may surely expect something advertised as a "general criterion of wrongness" to contribute more content than Scanlon manages to milk out of his formula'.

20 P. Singer, 'Famine, Affluence, and Morality', *Philosophy and Public Affairs* 1 (1972), pp. 229–43.

21 On well-being see, for example, A. Sen, *Development as Freedom* (Oxford: Oxford University Press, 1999), pp. 14–110.

22 See A. Alesina and D. Dollar, 'Who Gives Foreign Aid to Whom and Why?' *NBER Working Paper 6612* (1998), p. i, who write regarding bilateral aid: 'We find considerable evidence that the direction of foreign aid is dictated by political and strategic considerations, much more than by the economic needs and policy performance of the recipients.' See also R. J. Barro and J. W. Lee, 'IMF Programs: Who is Chosen and What are the Effects?' *IMF Working Paper* (2001), http://www.imf.org/external/pubs/ft/staffp/2001/00-00/pdf/rbjl.pdf.

23 A good summary of critiques of 'classic humanitarian' assistance is in C. Collins, 'Critiques of Humanitarianism and Humanitarian Action', *Humanitarian Coordination: Lessons Learned* (New York: Office for the Coordination of Humanitarian Affairs, 1998), pp. 12–26. An extensive survey of the humanitarian assistance literature is J. Gundel, 'Humanitarian Assistance: Breaking the Waves of Complex Political Emergencies', *Report for the Center for Development Research*, Copenhagen (1999),

http://www.cdr.dk/working_papers/wp-99-5.htm. For strong first-hand anecdotal criticisms of aid efforts in Africa, see M. Maren, *The Road to Hell: The Ravaging Effects of Foreign Aid and International Charity* (New York: Free Press, 1997). Alex de Waal, *Famines Crimes: Politics and the Disaster Relief Industry in Africa* (Oxford: James Currey, 1997) presents a more systematic exposition of the thesis that most current humanitarian efforts in Africa are useless or damaging because they disrupt local practices and political institutions.

[24] The refugee camps set up by international charity groups in Rwanda were used by government soldiers and Hutu extremists as staging points for further genocidal assaults. See J. Burton et al., 'The International Response to Conflict and Genocide: Lessons from the Rwanda Experience', *Journal of Humanitarian Assistance* (1996), http://www.reliefweb.int/library/nordic/book3/pb022.html. NGO activities during the Rwandan disaster spurred serious debates and new declarations of policy among aid agencies that work in conflict zones, although it remains uncertain how these agencies would do differently were a Rwanda-type situation to recur. See, for example, the charters set out in the SPHERE project, http://www.sphereproject.org/, consulted July 1, 2003: 'Rwanda Scenario', *Humanitarian Assistance Ombudsman*, http://www.oneworld.org/ombudsman/scen2.html. For a frank appraisal of the difficulties of this sort of aid see F. Terry, *Condemned to Repeat? The Paradox of Humanitarian Action* (Ithaca, NY: Cornell University Press, 2002).

[25] Thomas G. Weiss, 'Principles, Politics and Humanitarian Action', *Humanitarianism and War Project* (1998), http://hwproject.tufts.edu/publications/electronic/e_ppaha.html, writes: 'The "dark side" of humanitarian action would include: food and other aid usurped by belligerents to sustain a war economy (for example, in Liberia); assistance that has given legitimacy to illegitimate political authorities, particularly those with a guns economy (for example, in Somalia); aid distribution patterns that have influ-

enced the movement of refugees (for example, in eastern Zaire); resource allocations that have promoted the proliferation of aid agencies and created a wasteful aid market that encourages parties to play organizations against one another (for example, in Afghanistan); elites that have benefited from the relief economy (for example, it Bosnia); and resources that have affected strategic equilibriums (for example, in Sierra Leone) . . . Although humanitarian agencies go to great lengths to present themselves as nonpartisan and their motives as pure, they are deeply enmeshed in politics. Budget allocations and turf protection require vigilance. Humanitarians also negotiate with local authorities for visas, transport, and access, which all require compromises. They feel the pain of helping ethnic cleansers, feeding war criminals, and rewarding military strategies that herd civilians into camps. They decide whether or not to publicize human rights abuses. They look aside when bribes occur and food aid is diverted for military purposes. They provide foreign exchange and contribute to the growth of war economies that redistribute assets from the weak to the strong.'

[26] See for example S. Davarajan, D. Dollar, and T. Holmgren, *Aid and Reform in Africa* (Washington, DC: World Bank Publishing, 2001) on the detrimental effects of aid grants to African countries such as Zaire (now the Democratic Republic of Congo) and Nigeria. W. Easterly, *The Elusive Quest for Growth* (Cambridge, MA: MIT Press, 2001) is an accessible account, written by a former World Bank economist, of why the successive paradigms for international development since World War II have resulted in ineffective or counterproductive aid strategies.

[27] World Bank, *Assessing Aid* (Oxford: Oxford University Press, 1998), http://www.worldbank.org/research/aid/aidpub.htm.

[28] P. Boone, 'Politics and the Effectiveness of Foreign Aid', *European Economic Review* 40 (1996), pp. 289–329; P. Boone and J. P. Faguet, 'Multilateral Aid, Politics, and Poverty', in *The Global Crisis in Foreign Aid*, ed. Grant and Nijman (Syracuse, NY: Syracuse

University Press, 1998); W. Easterly, 'The Effects of IMF and World Bank Programs on Poverty', *IMF Working Paper* (2000), http://www.imf.org/external/pubs/ft/staffp/2000/00-00/e.pdf; R. J. Barro and J. W. Lee, 'IMF Programs: Who is Chosen and What are the Effects?'; and see the citations in World Bank *Global Development Finance 1999*, http://www.worldbank.org/prospects/gdf99, p. 74. A. Przeworski and J. R. Vreeland, 'The Effect of IMF Programs on Economic Growth', *Journal of Development Economics* 62 (2000): 385, conclude: 'We find evidence that governments enter into agreements with the IMF under the pressures of a foreign reserves crisis but they also bring in the Fund to shield themselves from the political costs of adjustment policies. Program participation lowers growth rates for as long as countries remain under a program. Once countries leave the program, they grow faster than if they had remained, but not faster than they would have without participation.'

David Dollar, in reports that have been influential for current World Bank policy, argues that aid has had a positive effect on growth in countries with a 'good policy environment'. See C. Burnside and D. Dollar, 'Aid, Policies, and Growth' (1997) and 'Aid, the Incentive Regime, and Poverty Reduction' (1998); and P. Collier and D. Dollar, 'Aid Allocation and Poverty Reduction' (1998) *World Bank Research Papers*, http://www.worldbank.org/research/aid/background/toc.htm. Yet see also the arguments that Dollar's thesis is too pessimistic in the works cited in footnote 36 below.

29 World Bank, *Global Development Finance 1999*, p. 75; World Bank *Assessing Aid*, pp. 5, 19–20, 60–79. World Bank *Assessing Aid*, p. 74 states: 'Donors are, more or less, financing whatever the government decides to do.'

30 J. W. Gunning, 'Rethinking Aid' (2000) *World Bank Research Papers* http://www.worldbank.org/research/abcde/washington_12/pdf_files/gunning.pdf; Burnside and Dollar. 'Aid, Policies and Growth'; World Bank, *Global Development Finance 1999*, p. 74.

31 T. Dietz and J. Houtcamp, 'Foreign Aid to Africa', in *The Global Crisis in Foreign Aid*, ed. Grant and Nijman, pp. 89–102.

32 Boone and Faguet, 'Multilateral Aid, Politics, and Poverty', pp. 15–19.

33 P. Burnell, *Foreign Aid in a Changing World* (Buckingham: Open University Press, 1997), pp. 184–6; R. Cassen et al., *Does Aid Work?* 2nd edn. (Oxford: Oxford University Press, 1994), pp. 51–2.

34 N. van de Walle and T. Johnston, *Improving Aid to Africa* (Washington, DC: Johns Hopkins University Press, 1996); Cassen et al., *Does Aid Work?*, pp. 174–5, 229; Iain Guest, 'Misplaced Charity Undermines Kosovo's Self-Reliance', http://www.bard.edu/hrp/hhrs/guest.htm.

35 In a large evaluation of Swedish aid effectiveness, H. White, *Dollars, Dialogue and Development: An Evaluation of Swedish Program Aid* (Stockholm: SIDA, 1999): 89, http://www.sida.se/Sida/articles/4700-4799/4782/pdf/utv99-17.pdf, sums up this phenomenon as 'The difficulty with saying anything'.

36 See, for example, the debate around the influential 'Dollar hypotheses' on aid. H. Hansen and F. Tarp, 'Aid Effectiveness Disputed', *Journal of International Development* 12 (2001): 375–98; R. Lensink and H. White, 'Aid Allocation, Poverty Reduction, and the *Assessing Aid* Report', *Journal of International Development* 12 (2001): 399–412; J. Beynon, 'Policy Implications for Aid Allocations of Recent Research on Aid Effectiveness and Selectivity: A Summary' (2001), http://193.51.65.78/dac/pdf/aid_effecti/beynon_1.pdf; the essays in *Changing the Conditions for Development Aid: A New Paradigm?*, edited by N. Hermes and R. Lensink (London: Frank Cass, 2001); and P. Collier and D. Dollar, 'World Bank Development Effectiveness: What Have We Learnt?' (2001), http://193.51.65.78/dac/htm/pubs/aid_effectiv.htm.

37 S. Reddy and T. Pogge, 'How Not to Count the Poor', (2001), p. 1: http://www.columbia.edu/~sr793/, write: 'The estimates of the extent, distribution and trend of global income poverty provided in the World Bank's World Development Reports for 1990 and

2000/01 are neither meaningful nor reliable. The Bank uses an arbitrary international poverty line unrelated to any clear conception of what poverty is. It employs a misleading and inaccurate measure of purchasing power "equivalence" that creates serious and irreparable difficulties for international and inter-temporal comparisons of income poverty. It extrapolates incorrectly from limited data and thereby creates an appearance of precision that masks the high probable error of its estimates. The systematic distortion introduced by these three flaws likely leads to a large understatement of the extent of global income poverty and to an incorrect inference that it has declined. A new methodology of global poverty assessment is feasible and necessary'.

38   For example, there has only recently begun an initiative in the Development Assistance Committee of the Organization for Economic Cooperation and Development to record what proportion of overseas development assistance is spent on basic social services in the recipient countries. See J. Harrington, C. Porter, and S. Reddy, 'Financing Basic Social Services', in *Choices for the Poor* (2001): 173–202, http://www.undp.org/dpa/publications/choicesforpoor/ENGLISH.

39   For example, an aid project might be evaluated as 'successful' were it to meet its objective of installing a fresh water conduit system into a village, without being sensitive to the fact that after the aid agency leaves the system breaks down, or is captured by local powers as a source of revenue, thus forcing the poorest villagers to travel even farther than before to find a source of fresh water.

40   The qualified positive answer that Cassen et al. give to the question of their book, *Does Aid Work?*, is actually relative to a slightly different question: Do aid efforts work in meeting their own objectives? The authors are candid about the methodological limitations of aid evaluation, and give several suggestions for improvements. They are also explicit that their conclusions do not take into account a variety of political and social 'systematic' effects of the type mentioned above. Cassen et al., *Does Aid Work?* pp. 86–

142, 174–5, 225. See also Burnell, *Foreign Aid in a Changing World*, pp. 176–7.

41   R. C. Riddell, et al., 'Searching for Impact and Methods: NGO Evaluation Synthesis Study', p. 99: http://www.valt.helsinki.fi/ids/ngo. Similar conclusions are reached in P. Oakley, *Overview Report. The Danish NGO Impact Study. A Review of Danish NGO Activities in Developing Countries* (Oxford: INTRAC, 1999).

42   R. Davies, 'Monitoring and Evaluating NGO Achievements' (2001): http://www.mande.co.uk/docs/arnold.htm.

43   Peter Singer has emphasized in conversation the importance of meeting this objection. See also his response in *One World* (New Haven, CT: Yale University Press, 2002), pp. 189–91, to a conference draft of the current article.

44   See, for example, Peter Unger's brief discussion of the empirical factors affecting the costs of improving one child's life-chances in *Living High and Letting Die* (Oxford: Oxford University Press), pp. 146–9. The empirical research cited in Unger's book concerning the efficacy of aid consists of a newspaper editorial on polio (p. 6 note 5), a book review by Amartya Sen (p. 37 note 6), two articles about cyclone shelters from an Oxfam newsletter and a newspaper (pp. 43–4, notes 11–13), and a telephone call to an official at the World Bank to get some summary figures (p. 147, note 3).

45   Scanlon, *What We Owe to Each Other*, p. 154 (emphasis added).

46   The first metaphor is from Singer, 'Famine, Affluence, and Morality', p. 231.

47   Pogge's overview of some World Bank statistics gives a sense of the magnitude of the current situation. 'Out of a global population of six billion, some 2.8 billion have less than $2 per day to live on, and nearly 1.2 billion of these have less than $1 per duty. [These are purchasing power figures, so this means that 1.2 billion people can at most purchase daily the equivalent of *what $1 can buy in the USA.*] 815 million people are undernourished, 1.1 billion lack access to safe water, 2.4 billion lack access to basic sanitation, and more than 880 million lack access to basic health

services. Approximately 1 billion have no adequate shelter and 2 billion no electricity.' T. Pogge, '"Assisting" the Global Poor', in *The Ethics of Assistance: Morality and the Distant Needy*, ed. D. K. Chatterjee (Cambridge University Press).

48 Scanlon, *What We Owe to Each Other*, p. 214.

49 On this theme see the work of Thomas Pogge, especially his recent book *World Poverty and Human Rights* (Cambridge: Polity Press, 2002). Pogge argues that the imposition by the rich countries of the current global economic and political institutional order implies that citizens of rich countries are violating a negative duty not to harm the world's poor. He offers specific proposals for reforming the global order so as to make it more just structurally.

Chapter 21

The Problem of Global Justice*
Thomas Nagel

I

We do not live in a just world. This may be the least controversial claim one could make in political theory. But it is much less clear what, if anything, justice on a world scale might mean, or what the hope for justice should lead us to want in the domain of international or global institutions, and in the policies of states that are in a position to affect the world order.

By comparison with the perplexing and undeveloped state of this subject, domestic political theory is very well understood, with multiple highly developed theories offering alternative solutions to well-defined problems. By contrast, concepts and theories of global justice are in the early stages of formation, and it is not clear what the main questions are, let alone the main possible answers. I believe that the need for workable ideas about the global or international case presents political theory with its most important current task, and even perhaps with the opportunity to make a practical contribution in the long run, though perhaps only the very long run.

The theoretical and normative questions I want to discuss are closely related to pressing practical questions that we now face about the legitimate path forward in the governance of the world. These are, inevitably, questions about institutions, many of which do not yet exist. However imperfectly, the nation-state is the primary locus of political legitimacy and the pursuit of justice, and it is one of the advantages of domestic political theory that nation-states actually exist. But when we are presented with the need for collective action on a global scale, it is very unclear what, if anything, could play a comparable role.

The concept of justice can be used in evaluating many different things, from the criminal law to the market economy. In a broad sense of the term, the international requirements of justice include standards governing the justification and conduct of war and standards that define the most basic human rights. Some standards of these two kinds have achieved a measure of international recognition over the past half-century. They define certain types of criminal conduct, usually by states, against other states or against individuals or ethnic groups. But this is not the aspect of global justice that I will concentrate on. My concern here is not with

* From *Philosophy & Public Affairs* 33:2 (2005), pp. 113–47.

war crimes or crimes against humanity but with socio-economic justice, and whether anything can be made of it on a world scale.

I will approach the question by focusing on the application to the world as a whole of two central issues of traditional political theory: the relation between justice and sovereignty, and the scope and limits of equality as a demand of justice. The two issues are related, and both are of crucial importance in determining whether we can even form an intelligible ideal of global justice.

The issue of justice and sovereignty was memorably formulated by Hobbes. He argued that although we can discover true principles of justice by moral reasoning alone, actual justice cannot be achieved except within a sovereign state. Justice as a property of the relations among human beings (and also injustice, for the most part) requires government as an enabling condition. Hobbes drew the obvious consequence for the international arena, where he saw separate sovereigns inevitably facing each other in a state of war, from which both justice and injustice are absent.

The issue of justice and equality is posed with particular clarity by one of the controversies between Rawls and his critics. Rawls argued that the liberal requirements of justice include a strong component of equality among citizens, but that this is a specifically political demand, which applies to the basic structure of a unified nation-state. It does not apply to the personal (nonpolitical) choices of individuals living in such a society, nor does it apply to the relations between one society and another, or between the members of different societies. Egalitarian justice is a requirement on the internal political, economic, and social structure of nation-states and cannot be extrapolated to different contexts, which require different standards. This issue is independent of the specific standards of egalitarian justice

found in Rawls's theory. Whatever standards of equal rights or equal opportunity apply domestically, the question is whether consistency requires that they also apply globally.

If Hobbes is right, the idea of global justice without a world government is a chimera. If Rawls is right, perhaps there can be something that might be called justice or injustice in the relations between states, but it bears only a distant relation to the evaluation of societies themselves as just or unjust: for the most part, the ideal of a just world for Rawls would have to be the ideal of a world of internally just states.

II

It seems to me very difficult to resist Hobbes's claim about the relation between justice and sovereignty. There is much more to his political theory than this, of course. Among other things, he based political legitimacy and the principles of justice on collective self-interest, rather than on any irreducibly moral premises. And he defended absolute monarchy as the best form of sovereignty. But the relation between justice and sovereignty is a separable question, and Hobbes's position can be defended in connection with theories of justice and moral evaluation very different from his.

What creates the link between justice and sovereignty is something common to a wide range of conceptions of justice: they all depend on the coordinated conduct of large numbers of people, which cannot be achieved without law backed up by a monopoly of force. Hobbes construed the principles of justice, and more broadly the moral law, as a set of rules and practices that would serve everyone's interest if everyone conformed to them. This collective self-interest cannot be realized by the independent motivation of self-interested individuals unless each of them has the assurance that others will conform if he does. That assurance requires the external incentive provided by the sovereign, who sees to it that individual and collective self-interest coincide. At least among sizable populations, it cannot be provided by voluntary conventions supported solely by the mutual recognition of a common interest.

But the same need for assurance is present if one construes the principles of justice differently, and attributes to individuals a non-self-interested motive that leads them to want to live on fair terms of some kind with other people. Even if justice is taken to include not only collective self-interest but also the elimination of morally arbitrary inequalities, or the protection of rights to liberty, the existence of a just order still depends on consistent patterns of conduct and persisting institutions that have a pervasive effect on the shape of people's lives. Separate individuals, however attached to such an ideal, have no motive, or even opportunity, to conform to such patterns or institutions on their own, without the assurance that their conduct will in fact be part of a reliable and effective system.

The only way to provide that assurance is through some form of law, with centralized authority to determine the rules and a centralized monopoly of the power of enforcement. This is needed even in a community most of whose members are attached to a common ideal of justice, both in order to provide terms of coordination and because it doesn't take many defectors to make such a system unravel. The kind of all-encompassing collective practice or institution that is capable of being just in the primary sense can exist only under sovereign government. It is only the operation of such a system that one can judge to be just or unjust.

According to Hobbes, in the absence of the enabling condition of sovereign power, individuals are famously thrown back on their own resources and led by the legitimate motive of self-preservation to a defensive, distrustful posture of war. They hope for the conditions of peace and justice and support their creation whenever it seems safe to do so, but they cannot pursue justice by themselves.

I believe that the situation is structurally not very different for conceptions of justice that are based on much more other-regarding motives. Without the enabling condition of sovereignty to confer stability on just institutions, individuals however morally motivated can only fall back on a pure aspiration for justice that has no practical expression, apart from the willingness to support just institutions should they become possible.

The other-regarding motives that support adherence to just institutions when they exist do not provide clear guidance where the enabling conditions for such institutions do not exist, as seems to be true for the world as a whole. Those motives, even if they make us dissatisfied with our relations to other human beings, are baffled and left without an avenue of expression, except for the expression of moral frustration.

III

Hobbes himself was not disturbed by the appearance of this problem in the international case, since he believed that the essential aim of justice, collective security and self-interest, could be effectively provided for individuals through the sovereignty of separate states. In a famous passage, he says:

> [I]n all times, kings, and persons of sovereign authority, because of their independency, are in continual jealousies, and in the state and posture of gladiators; having their weapons pointing, and their eyes fixed on one another; that is, their forts, garrisons, and guns upon the frontiers of their kingdoms; and continual spies upon their neighbours; which is a posture

of war. But because they uphold thereby, the industry of their subjects; there does not follow from it, that misery, which accompanies the liberty of particular men.[1]

The absence of sovereignty over the globe, in other words, is not a serious obstacle to justice in the relations among the citizens of each sovereign state, and that is what matters.

This position is more problematic for those who do not share Hobbes's belief that the foundation of justice is collective self-interest and that the attachment of any individual to just institutions is based solely on his own good. If Hobbes were right, a person's interest in justice would be served provided he himself lived in a stable society governed in accordance with the rules of peace, security, and economic order. But for most of us, the ideal of justice stems from moral motives that cannot be entirely reduced to self-interest.

It includes much more than a condition of legally enforced peace and security among interacting individuals, together with stable property rights and the reliability of contracts. Most modern conceptions of justice impose some limits on the powers of sovereignty – in the name of non-Hobbesian individual rights to liberty – and some condition of fairness or equality in the way the institutions of a just society treat its citizens, not only politically but economically and socially. It is this last element that creates unease over the complete absence of any comparable standards of fairness or equality of opportunity from the practices that govern our relations with individuals in other societies.

The gruesome facts of inequality in the world economy are familiar. Roughly 20 percent of the world's population live on less than a dollar a day, and more than 45 percent live on less than two dollars a day, whereas the 15 percent who live in the high-income economies have an average per capita income

of seventy-five dollars a day.[2] How are we to respond to such facts?

There is a peculiar problem here for our discussion: The facts are so grim that justice may be a side issue. Whatever view one takes of the applicability or inapplicability of standards of justice to such a situation, it is clearly a disaster from a more broadly humanitarian point of view. I assume there is some minimal concern we owe to fellow human beings threatened with starvation or severe malnutrition and early death from easily preventable diseases, as all these people in dire poverty are. Although there is plenty of room for disagreement about the most effective methods, some form of humane assistance from the well-off to those in extremis is clearly called for quite apart from any demand of justice, if we are not simply ethical egoists. The urgent current issue is what can be done in the world economy to reduce extreme global poverty.

These more basic duties of humanity also present serious problems of what we should do individually and collectively to fulfill them in the absence of global sovereignty, and in spite of the obstacles often presented by malfunctioning state sovereignty. But now I am posing a different question, one that is morally less urgent but philosophically harder. Justice as ordinarily understood requires more than mere humanitarian assistance to those in desperate need, and injustice can exist without anyone being on the verge of starvation.

Humanitarian duties hold in virtue of the absolute rather than the relative level of need of the people we are in a position to help. Justice, by contrast, is concerned with the relations between the conditions of different classes of people, and the causes of inequality between them. My question is about how to respond to world inequality in general from the point of view of justice and injustice rather than humanity alone. The answer to that question will depend crucially on one's moral conception of the relation between the value of justice and the existence of the institutions that sovereign authority makes possible. There are two principal conceptions that I want to consider.

According to the first conception, which is usually called *cosmopolitanism,* the demands of justice derive from an equal concern or a duty of fairness that we owe in principle to all our fellow human beings, and the institutions to which standards of justice can be applied are instruments for the fulfillment of that duty. Such instruments are in fact only selectively available: We may be able to live on just terms only with those others who are fellow members of sufficiently robust and well-ordered sovereign states. But the moral basis for the requirements of justice that should govern those states is universal in scope: it is a concern for the fairness of the terms on which we share the world with anyone.[3]

If one takes the cosmopolitan view, the existence of separate sovereign states is an unfortunate obstacle, though perhaps for the foreseeable future an insurmountable one, to the establishment or even the pursuit of global justice. But it would be morally inconsistent not to wish, for the world as a whole, a common system of institutions that could attempt to realize the same standards of fairness or equal opportunity that one wants for one's own society. The accident of being born in a poor rather than a rich country is as arbitrary a determinant of one's fate as the accident of being born into a poor rather than a rich family in the same country. In the absence of global sovereignty we may not be able to describe the world order as *un*just, but the absence of justice is a defect all the same.

Cosmopolitan justice could be realized in a federal system, in which the members of individual nation-states had special responsibilities toward one another that they did not have for everyone in the world. But that would be legitimate only against the background of a global system that prevented such special responsibilities from generating injustice on a larger scale. This would be analogous to the requirement that within a state, the institutions of private property, which allow people to pursue their private ends without constantly taking into account the aims of justice, should nevertheless be arranged so that societal injustice is not their indirect consequence.[4]

Unlike cosmopolitanism, the second conception of justice does not have a standard name, but let me call it the *political* conception, since it is exemplified by Rawls's view that justice should be understood as a specifically political value, rather than being derived from a comprehensive moral system, so that it is essentially a virtue – the first virtue – of social institutions.

On the political conception, sovereign states are not merely instruments for realizing the preinstitutional value of justice among human beings. Instead, their existence is precisely what gives the value of justice its application, by putting the fellow citizens of a sovereign state into a relation that they do not have with the rest of humanity, an institutional relation which must then be evaluated by the special standards of fairness and equality that fill out the content of justice.

Another representative of the political conception is Ronald Dworkin, who expresses it this way:

A political community that exercises dominion over its own citizens, and demands from them allegiance and obedience to its laws, must take up an impartial, objective attitude toward them all, and each of its citizens must vote, and its officials must enact laws and form governmental policies, with that responsibility in mind. Equal concern . . . is the special and indispensable virtue of sovereigns.[5]

Every state has the boundaries and population it has for all sorts of accidental and historical reasons; but given that it exercises sovereign power over its citizens and in their name, those citizens have a duty of justice toward one another through the legal, social, and economic institutions that sovereign power makes possible. This duty is *sui generis,* and is not owed to everyone in the world, nor is it an indirect consequence of any other duty that may be owed to everyone in the world, such as a duty of humanity. Justice is something we owe through our shared institutions only to those with whom we stand in a strong political relation. It is, in the standard terminology, an *associative* obligation.

Furthermore, though the obligations of justice arise as a result of a special relation, there is no obligation to enter into that relation with those to whom we do not yet have it, thereby acquiring those obligations toward them. If we find ourselves in such a relation, then we must accept the obligations, but we do not have to seek them out, and may even try to avoid incurring them, as with other contingent obligations of a more personal kind: one does not have to marry and have children, for example.

If one takes this political view, one will not find the absence of global justice a cause for distress. There is a lot else to be distressed about: world misery, for example, and also the egregious internal injustice of so many of the world's sovereign states. Someone who accepts the political conception of justice may even hold that there is a secondary duty to promote just institutions for societies that do not have them. But the requirements of justice themselves do not, on this view, apply to the world as a whole, unless and until, as a result of historical developments not required by justice, the world comes to be governed by a unified sovereign power.

The political conception of justice therefore arrives, by a different route, at the same conclusion as Hobbes: The full standards of justice, though they can be known by moral reasoning, apply only within the boundaries of a sovereign state, however arbitrary those boundaries may be. Internationally, there may well be standards, but they do not merit the full name of justice.

IV

On either the cosmopolitan or the political view, global justice would require global sovereignty. But there is still a huge difference between the two views in the attitude they take toward this conclusion. On the political view, the absence of global justice need not be a matter of regret; on the cosmopolitan view, it is, and the obstacles to global sovereignty pose a serious moral problem. Let me consider the issue of principle between the two conceptions. While we should keep in mind that different views about the content of justice can be combined with either of these two conceptions of its scope, I will continue to use Rawls to exemplify the political view. But most of what I will say is independent of the main disagreements over the content of domestic justice – political, economic, or social.

Rawls's political conception of justice is an example of a more general feature of his approach to moral theory, his rejection of what Liam Murphy calls *monism.* Murphy has introduced this term to designate the idea that "any plausible overall political/ moral view must, at the fundamental level, evaluate the justice of institutions with normative principles that apply also to people's choices." The opposite view, which Murphy calls dualism, is that "the two practical problems of institutional design and personal conduct require, at the fundamental level, two different kinds of practical principle."[6] (The term "dualism" is not ideal for the contrast, since, as we shall see, there are more than two levels at which independent moral principles may apply.)

Rawls is famous for insisting that different principles apply to different types of entities: that "the correct regulative principle for a thing depends on the nature of that thing."[7] The most noted instance of this is his argument against utilitarianism, which he criticizes for applying to a society of individuals the principles of aggregating and maximizing net benefits minus costs that are appropriate within the life of a single individual, but inappropriate for groups of individuals. "Utilitarianism," he says, "does not take seriously the distinction between persons."[8]

But the point applies more widely. Rawls's anti-monism is essential to understanding both his domestic theory of a just society and his view of the relation between domestic and international principles, as expressed in *The Law of Peoples*. His two principles of justice are designed to regulate neither the personal conduct of individuals living in a just society, nor the governance of private associations, nor the international relations of societies to one another, but only the basic structure of separate nation-states. It is the nature of sovereign states, he believes, and in particular their comprehensive control over the framework of their citizens' lives, that creates the special demands for justification and the special constraints on ends and means that constitute the requirements of justice.

In Rawls's domestic theory this expresses itself in two ways: first, in the priority of individual liberty, which leaves people free to pursue their own personal ends rather than requiring them to pursue just outcomes privately; and, second, in the application of the difference principle not to the distribution of advantages and disadvantages to individuals, but rather to the probabilistic distribution of ex ante life prospects (which always include a range) to those born into

different socio-economic classes. Even if the basic structure supported by law satisfies the difference principle by arranging inequalities to maximize the expectations of the lowest class in this sense, individual choices are not expected to be governed by that principle. Those choices will result in substantial inequalities in actual outcomes among individuals within each socio-economic class, in addition to the inequalities in ex ante life prospects between classes permitted by the difference principle itself.

So Rawls's egalitarianism does not apply either to individual morality or to individual outcomes within the bounds of an egalitarian state. But neither does it apply to the relations between states, nor between the individual members of different states. These are all different cases or types of relation, and the principles that govern them have to be arrived at separately. They cannot be reached by extending to the international case the principles of domestic justice.

Internationally, Rawls finds the main expression of moral constraints not in a relation among individuals but in a limited requirement of mutual respect and equality of status among peoples. This is more constraining than the traditional Hobbesian privileges of sovereignty on the world stage; it is a substantial moral order, far from the state of nature. But the moral units of the order are peoples, not individuals, and the values have to do with the relations among these collective units rather than the relations of individuals across the world.

Just as, within a state, what we owe one another as fellow citizens through our common institutions is very different from what we owe one another as private individuals, so internationally, what we owe to other inhabitants of the globe through our society's respect for the societies of which they are citizens is different both from what we owe to our fellow citizens and from what we as individuals owe to all our fellow human beings. The duties governing the relations among peoples include, according to Rawls, not only nonaggression and fidelity to treaties, but also some developmental assistance to "peoples living under unfavorable conditions that prevent their having a just or decent political and social regime."[9] But they do not include any analogue of liberal socioeconomic justice.

This limitation is rejected by cosmopolitan critics of Rawls. The issue is the choice of moral units. The monist idea is that the basic constituency for all morality must be individuals, not societies or peoples, and that whatever moral requirements apply either to social institutions or to international relations must ultimately be justified by their effects on individuals – and by a morality that governs the treatment of all individuals by all other individuals.

From this point of view it seems natural to conclude that any such morality must count all individual lives as equally valuable or important, and that in particular it must not allow international boundaries to count at the most basic level in determining how one individual should take into consideration the interests of another. The consequence seems to be that if one wants to avoid moral inconsistency, and is sympathetic to Rawls's theory of justice, one should favor a global difference principle, perhaps backed up by a global original position in which all individuals are represented behind the veil of ignorance.[10]

But whatever we think about the original position, Rawls must resist the charge that moral consistency requires him to take individuals as the moral units in a conception of global justice. To do so would make a huge difference, for it would mean that applying the principles of justice within the bounds of the nation-state was at best a practical stop-gap.

Rawls's anti-monism is in essence a theoretical rejection of such standards for moral consistency. Just as there is no inconsistency in governing interpersonal relations by principles very different from those that govern legal institutions, so there need be no inconsistency in governing the world differently from its political subdivisions. But if what we are looking for is moral, and not just logical, consistency, the differences between the cases must in some way explain why different principles are appropriate.

The way to resist cosmopolitanism fundamentally would be to deny that there is a universal pressure toward equal concern, equal status, and equal opportunity. One could admit a universal humanitarian requirement of minimal concern (which, even in the world as it is, would not be terribly onerous, provided all the prosperous countries did their share). But the defense of the political conception of justice would have to hold that beyond the basic humanitarian duties, further requirements of equal treatment depend on a strong condition of associative responsibility, that such responsibility is created by specific and contingent relations such as fellow citizenship, and that there is no general moral requirement to take responsibility for others by getting into those sorts of relations with as many of them as possible.

This would still count as a universal principle, but it would imply a strongly differentiated system of moral obligations. If the conditions of even the poorest societies should come to meet a livable minimum, the political conception might not even see a general humanitarian claim for redistribution. This makes it a very convenient view for those living in rich societies to hold. But that alone doesn't make it false.

V

I find the choice between these two incompatible moral conceptions difficult. The cosmopolitan conception has considerable moral appeal, because it seems highly arbitrary that the average individual born into a poor society should have radically lower life prospects than the average individual born into a rich one, just as arbitrary as the corresponding difference between rich and poor in a rich but unjust society. The cosmopolitan conception points us toward the utopian goal of trying to extend legitimate democratic governance to ever-larger domains in pursuit of more global justice.

But I will not explore that possibility further. Without trying to refute cosmopolitanism I will instead pursue a fuller account of the grounds and content of the political conception. I am going to follow this fork in the path partly because I believe the political conception is accepted by most people in the privileged nations of the world, so that, true or false, it will have a significant role in determining what happens. I also think it is probably correct.

Let me try to spell out the kind of political conception that seems to me plausible. Even though I am skeptical about grounding it in a hypothetical contract of the type Rawls proposes, its debt to the social contract tradition will be obvious.[11]

We can begin by noting that even on the political conception, some conditions of justice do not depend on associative obligations. The protection, under sovereign power, of negative rights like bodily inviolability, freedom of expression, and freedom of religion is morally unmysterious. Those rights, if they exist, set universal and prepolitical limits to the legitimate use of power, independent of special forms of association. It is wrong for any individual or group to deny such rights to any other individual or group, and we do not give them up as a condition of membership in a political society, even though their precise boundaries and methods of protection through law will have to be determined politically in light of each society's particular circumstances.

Socioeconomic justice is different. On the political conception it is fully associative. It depends on positive rights that we do not have against all other persons or groups, rights that arise only because we are joined together with certain others in a political society under strong centralized control. It is only from such a system, and from our fellow members through its institutions, that we can claim a right to democracy, equal citizenship, nondiscrimination, equality of opportunity, and the amelioration through public policy of unfairness in the distribution of social and economic goods.

In presenting the intuitive moral case for the particular principles of justice he favors as the embodiment of these ideals, Rawls appeals repeatedly to the importance of eliminating or reducing morally arbitrary sources of inequality in people's life prospects.[12] He means inequalities flowing from characteristics of people that they have done nothing to deserve, like their race, their sex, the wealth or poverty of their parents, and their inborn natural endowments. To the extent that such factors, through the operation of a particular social system, generate differences in people's expectations, at birth, of better or worse lives, they present a problem for the justification of that system. In some respects these arbitrary sources of inequality can be eliminated, but Rawls holds that where they remain, some other justification needs to be found for permitting them.

The important point for our purposes is that Rawls believes that this moral presumption against arbitrary inequalities is not a principle of universal application. It might have considerable appeal if recast as a universal principle, to the effect that there is something prima facie objectionable to anyone's having lower life prospects at birth than anyone else just because of a difference between the two of them, such as the wealth of their parents or their nationality, over which neither of them had any control. But this is not the principle Rawls is appealing to. Rather, in his theory the objection to arbitrary inequalities gets a foothold only because of the societal context. What is objectionable is that we should be fellow participants in a collective enterprise of coercively imposed legal and political institutions that generates such arbitrary inequalities.

What is interesting and somewhat surprising about this condition is that such co-membership is itself arbitrary, so an arbitrary distinction is responsible for the scope of the presumption against arbitrariness. We do not deserve to have been born into a particular society any more than we deserve to have been born into a particular family. Those who are not immigrants have done nothing to become members of their society. The egalitarian requirement is based not on actual choice, consent, or contract, but on involuntary membership. It is only the internal character of the system in which we arbitrarily find ourselves that gives rise to the special presumption against further arbitrary distinctions within it.

Since there are equally arbitrary extrasocietal distinctions that do not carry the same moral weight, the ground for the presumption cannot be merely that these intrasocietal inequalities have a profound effect on people's lives. The fact that they shape people's life prospects from birth is necessary but not sufficient to explain the presumption against them. So what is the additional necessary condition?

I believe it comes from a special involvement of agency or the will that is inseparable from membership in a political society. Not the will to become or remain a member, for most people have no choice in that regard, but the engagement of the will that is essential to life inside a society, in the dual role each member plays both as one of the society's subjects and as one of those in whose name its authority is exercised. One might even say that we are all participants in the general will.

A sovereign state is not just a cooperative enterprise for mutual advantage. The societal rules determining its basic structure are coercively imposed: it is not a voluntary association. I submit that it is this complex fact – that we are both putative joint authors of the coercively imposed system, and subject to its norms, i.e., expected to accept their authority even when the collective decision diverges from our personal preferences – that creates the special presumption against arbitrary inequalities in our treatment by the system.

Without being given a choice, we are assigned a role in the collective life of a particular society. The society makes us responsible for its acts, which are taken in our name and on which, in a democracy, we may even have some influence; and it holds us responsible for obeying its laws and conforming to its norms, thereby supporting the institutions through which advantages and disadvantages are created and distributed.[13] Insofar as those institutions admit arbitrary inequalities, we are, even though the responsibility has been simply handed to us, responsible for them, and we therefore have standing to ask why we should accept them. This request for justification has moral weight even if we have in practice no choice but to live under the existing regime. The reason is that its requirements claim our active cooperation, and this cannot be legitimately done without justification – otherwise it is pure coercion.[14]

The required active engagement of the will of each member of the society in its operation is crucial. It is not enough to appeal to the large material effects that the system imposes on its members. The immigration policies of one country may impose large effects on the lives of those living in other countries, but under the political conception that by itself does not imply that such policies should be determined in a way that gives the interests and opportunities of those others equal consideration. Immigration policies are simply enforced against the nationals of other states; the laws are not imposed in their name, nor are they asked to accept and uphold those laws. Since no acceptance is demanded of them, no justification is required that explains why they should accept such discriminatory policies, or why their interests have been given equal consideration. It is sufficient justification to claim that the policies do not violate their prepolitical human rights.

That does not mean that on the political conception one state may do anything whatever to the citizens of another. States are entitled to be left to their own devices, but only on the condition that they not harm others. Even a nation's immunity from the need to justify to outsiders the limits on access to its territory is not absolute. In extreme circumstances, denial of the right of immigration may constitute a failure to respect human rights or the universal duty of rescue. This is recognized in special provisions for political asylum, for example. The most basic rights and duties are universal, and not contingent on specific institutional relations between people. Only the heightened requirements of equal treatment embodied in principles of justice, including political equality, equality of opportunity, and distributive justice, are contingent in this way.

To be sure, even within a state, through economic competition for example, some members or associations of members may impose serious consequences on others without any implication that the others are asked to accept or authorize the actions that have those consequences. Citizens are not expected to treat each other equally in private transactions. But the broader legal framework that makes those actions possible and that legally sustains their results is subject to collective authority and justification and therefore to principles of social justice: not act by act, but for the system as a whole.

In short, the state makes unique demands on the will of its members – or the members make unique demands on one another through the institutions of the state – and those exceptional demands bring with them exceptional obligations, the positive obligations of justice. Those obligations reach no farther than the demands do and that explains the special character of the political conception.

VI

What is the overall moral outlook that best fits the political conception of justice? Although it is based on a rejection of monism and does not derive its content from a universal moral relation in which we stand to all persons, the political conception does not deny that there is such a relation. Political institutions create contingent, selective moral relations, but there are also noncontingent, universal relations in which we stand to everyone, and political justice is surrounded by this larger moral context.

The normative force of the most basic human rights against violence, enslavement, and coercion, and of the most basic humanitarian duties of rescue from immediate danger, depends only on our capacity to put ourselves in other people's shoes. The interests protected by such moral requirements are so fundamental, and the burdens they impose, considered statistically, so much slighter, that a criterion of universalizability of the Kantian type clearly supports them. I say "statistically" because the restrictions implied by individual rights can in particular cases be very demanding: you may not kill an innocent person to save your life, for example. But the importance to all of us of blanket immunity from such violation dominates the slight danger that we will be called on to lose our lives rather than violate the constraint. This is based not on a utilitarian calculation but on the great importance to each person of the kind of inviolability conferred by rights. Rights are a guarantee to each of us of a certain protected status, rather than a net benefit to the aggregate.

This minimal humanitarian morality governs our relation to all other persons. It does not require us to make their ends our own, but it does require us to pursue our ends within boundaries that leave them free to pursue theirs, and to relieve them from extreme threats and obstacles to such freedom if we can do so without serious sacrifice of our own ends. I take this to be the consequence of the type of contractualist standard expressed by Kant's categorical imperative and developed in one version by Scanlon. To specify it any less vaguely would require a full moral theory, which I will not attempt even to sketch here.

This moral minimum does not depend on the existence of any institutional connection between ourselves and other persons: It governs our relations with everyone in the world. However, it may be impossible to fulfill even our minimal moral duties to others without the help of institutions of some kind short of sovereignty. We do not need institutions to enable us to refrain from violating other people's rights, but institutions are indispensable to enable us to fulfill the duty of rescue toward people in dire straits all over the world. Further, it seems clear that human rights generate a secondary obligation to do something, if we can, to protect people outside of our society against their most egregious violation, and this is practically impossible, on a world scale, without some institutionalized methods of verification and enforcement.

The first of these roles, that of rescue, can be filled to some extent by NGOs that operate internationally but privately, providing individuals with the opportunity to contribute to relief of famine and disease. Even the second role, protection of rights, has its private institutional actors in the form of organizations like Amnesty International and Human Rights Watch. But successful action on a much larger scale would be possible through international institutions supported by governments, both with funds and with enforcement. The World Bank is in some respects such an institution, and the International Criminal Court aspires to be. The question is whether international developments will countenance the bending of national sovereignty needed to extend the authority of such institutions, both to command funds and to curb domestic rights violations with force, if necessary.

But even if this is the direction of global governance for the future, there remains a clear line, according to the political conception of justice, between the call for such institutions and a call for the institution of global socio-economic justice. Everyone may have the right to live in a just society, but we do not have an obligation to live in a just society with everyone. The right to justice is the right that the society one lives in be justly governed. Any claims this creates against other societies and their members are distinctly secondary to those it creates against one's fellow citizens.

Is this stark division of levels of responsibility morally acceptable, or is it too radical an exclusion of humanity at large from full moral concern? The answer from the point of view of the political conception must be that there is no single level of full moral concern, because morality is essentially multilayered.

Even within the framework of a just society special obligations arise from contingent personal relations and voluntary associations or undertakings by individuals. The whole point of the political conception is that social justice itself is a rise in exclusive obligation, but with a broader associative range and from a lower moral baseline than the personal obligations. And it depends on the contingency of involuntary rather than voluntary association.

Perhaps this move to a new moral level can be best understood as a consequence of the more basic obligation, emphasized by both Hobbes and Kant, that all humans have to create and support a state of some kind – to leave and stay out of the state of nature. It is not an obligation to all other persons, in fact it has no clear boundaries; it is merely an obligation to create the conditions of peace and a legal order, with whatever community offers itself.

This requirement is based not on a comprehensive value of equality, but on the imperative of securing basic rights, which can be done more or less locally. But once the state exists, we are in a new moral situation, where the value of equality has purchase. The difference between the political and the cosmopolitan conceptions is that the latter sees the formation of the state as answering also a universal demand for equality, even if as a practical matter it can be realized only locally. On the political conception, by contrast, the only universal requirement of equality is conditional in form: We are required to accord equal status to anyone with whom we are joined in a strong and coercively imposed political community.

Some standard of universalizability underlies even this conditional requirement. It is part of a multilayered conception of morality, shaped by the Kantian ideal of a kingdom of ends whose members do not share a common set of ends. The heightened obligations that arise from contingent particular associations do not subtract from a prior condition of universal concern, but rather move our moral relations selectively to a new level, at which more ends and responsibilities are shared. The universality

of this morality consists in its applying to anyone who happens to be or to become a member of our society: no one is excluded in advance, and in that sense all persons are regarded as morally equal.

Such a morality also leaves space for voluntary combinations in the pursuit of common ends, which are not in general governed by standards of equality. But political institutions are different, because adherence to them is not voluntary: Emigration aside, one is not permitted to declare oneself not a member of one's society and hence not subject to its rules, and other members may coerce one's compliance if one tries to refuse. An institution that one has no choice about joining must offer terms of membership that meet a higher standard.

VII

My thoughts about this subject were kindled by Rawls's treatment of the ethics of international relations in *The Law of Peoples*, but his approach is different, so let me say something about it. First of all, he poses the question not as a general one about international obligations or global justice, but as a question about what principles should govern the foreign policy of a liberal society. So it is an elaboration of his account of a just society, rather than an independent account of a just world. And he sees the answer to this question as having to do primarily with how such a society should deal with the other societies with which it shares the world, whether these be liberal, or nonliberal but still "decent," in his term, or whether they be outlaw societies that fail to respect human rights and the restraints of international law.

As already noted, the moral units of this international morality are not individual human beings but separate societies, or "peoples," and it is equality among these collective units that is the basis of Rawls's conception. For that reason Charles Beitz has given it the name *social liberalism,* to contrast it with his own view, which he calls *cosmopolitan liberalism.*[15] Our obligations as members of a liberal society toward the members of other societies are not direct, but are filtered through the relations between our societies. That is because, as Rawls puts it, societies have a "moral nature," which deserves equal respect, provided they meet the basic conditions of decency. But individuals per se are not entitled to equal treatment internationally.

Rawls holds that the requirement of equal respect for other peoples is strong enough to impose on liberal societies a tolerance for nonliberal states that meet a minimal condition of decency, so that the foreign policy of a liberal state should not have the aim of moving all other societies toward liberalism, if possible. This is analogous to the restraint liberalism imposes internally against the use of state power to promote a particular comprehensive moral or religious view. It is surprising that internationally, equal respect should result precisely in toleration for the absence of such restraint in nonliberal societies. But Rawls believes that this consequence follows if we accord a moral nature and a moral right of equality to peoples, which are not themselves derived from the equality of individuals, and which take precedence over domestic liberal values in the international case.

The claims of individuals take over only at a much lower threshold, that of basic human rights. A society that does not respect the human rights of its subjects forfeits, in Rawls's view, the moral status that demands respect, equality, and noninterference. But that is not necessarily true of a theocratic society with no elections, for example, provided it does not persecute minorities and observes due process of law.[16]

This seems to me a mistake. The political conception of justice need not be based on the strong personification of peoples and need not imply the principled toleration of nonliberal societies. I would take a more individualistic position than Rawls does. The question of international toleration is difficult, but I believe that although there are obvious practical reasons for liberal societies not to try to impose liberal domestic justice universally, there are no moral reasons for restraint of the kind Rawls offers. It is more plausible to say that liberal states are not obliged either to tolerate nonliberal states or to try to transform them, because the duties of justice are essentially duties to our fellow citizens. But there seems nothing wrong with being particularly supportive of transformations in a liberal direction.

Whether other basic international obligations, such as those embodied in just war theory, can be accounted for without the moral personification of peoples is another question, but I would give a similar answer. People engaged in a legitimate collective enterprise deserve respect and noninterference, especially if it is an obligatory enterprise like the provision of security, law, and social peace. We owe it to other people – considered as individuals – to allow them, and to some degree enable them, to collectively help themselves. So respect for the autonomy of other societies can be thought of as respect for the human rights of their members, rather than as respect for the equality of peoples, taken as moral units in their own right.

Rawls's conception is that sovereignty is constrained internally by the moral equality of individuals who are subjects of the state, but that the same force does not operate externally: From outside, sovereignty is constrained by the moral equality of other peoples, which imposes requirements even on a state that does not owe its members what it owes its own. I am prepared to accept the first part of this claim, about the source of internal constraints, but would offer universal human rights rather than the equality of peoples or societies as the source of the constraints on the external exercise of sovereign power.[17]

VIII

The implications of the political conception for world politics tend to be conservative, but that is not the end of the story; the conservatism comes under pressure from powerful forces in the other direction. The source of that pressure lies both in existing global or international institutions and in the increasingly felt need to strengthen such institutions and to create new ones, for three types of purpose: the protection of human rights; the provision of humanitarian aid; and the provision of global public goods that benefit everyone, such as free trade, collective security, and environmental protection. Institutions that serve these purposes are not designed to extend democratic legitimacy and socio-economic justice, but they naturally give rise to claims for both, in respect to their design and functioning. And they put pressure on national sovereignty by their need for power to be effective. They thus present a clearly perceived threat to the limits on claims of justice imposed by the political conception.

This poses a familiar dilemma: Prosperous nations have reasons to want more governance on a world scale, but they do not want the increased obligations and demands for legitimacy that may follow in its wake. They do not want to increase the range of those to whom they are obliged as they are toward their own citizens; and this reflects the convictions of their citizens, not just of their governments.

Resistance to the erosion of sovereignty has resulted in the US refusal to join the Kyoto Treaty on atmospheric emissions and the International Criminal Court, decisions that have been widely criticized. Similar questions arise over who is to determine the policies of the International Monetary Fund and the World Bank, and over the authority of the United Nations in matters of international peace and security. But by far the most important institutions from this point of view are those of the international economy itself.

The global economy, within which the familiar inequalities are now generated, requires a stable international system of property rights and contractual obligations that provide the conditions for international commerce. These include: the rights of sovereign states to sell or confer legal title to the exploitation of their natural resources internationally; their right to borrow internationally and to create obligations of repayment on successor governments; the rights of commercial enterprises in one country to establish or acquire subsidiaries in other countries, and to profit from such investments; international extensions of antitrust law; regulation of financial markets to permit the orderly international flow of capital; the laws of patent and copyright; the rules of international trade, including penalties for violations of agreed restrictions on protective tariffs, dumping, preferential subsidies, and so forth.[18] Many of the goods that contemporary persons consume, or their components, are produced in other countries. We are clearly in some kind of institutional relation – legal and economic – with people the world over.

This brings us to an issue that is internal to the political conception, rather than being about the choice between the political and the cosmopolitan conceptions. Some would argue that the present level of world economic interdependence already brings into force a version of the political conception of justice, so that Rawls's principles, or some alternative principles of distributive justice, are applicable over the domain covered by the existing cooperative institutions.[19] This would be a very strong result, but I believe that it is not the case, precisely because such institutions do not rise to the level of statehood.

The absence of sovereign authority over participant states and their members not only makes it practically infeasible for such institutions to pursue justice but also makes them, under the political conception, an inappropriate site for claims of justice. For such claims to become applicable it is not enough that a number of individuals or groups be engaged in a collective activity that serves their mutual advantage. Mere economic interaction does not trigger the heightened standards of socio-economic justice.

Current international rules and institutions may be the thin end of a wedge that will eventually expand to seriously dislodge the dominant sovereignty of separate nation-states, both morally and politically, but for the moment they lack something that according to the political conception is crucial for the application and implementation of standards of justice: They are not collectively enacted and coercively imposed in the name of all the individuals whose lives they affect; and they do not ask for the kind of authorization by individuals that carries with it a responsibility to treat all those individuals in some sense equally. Instead, they are set up by bargaining among mutually self-interested sovereign parties. International institutions act not in the name of individuals, but in the name of the states or state instruments and agencies that have created them. Hence the responsibility of those institutions toward individuals is filtered through the states that represent and bear primary responsibility for those individuals.

But while international governance falls far short of global sovereignty, and is ultimately dependent on the sovereignty of separate states, international institutions are not all alike. Some involve delegation of

authority, by states, to a supranational institution, generally by treaty, where this amounts to a partial limitation of sovereignty. Under NAFTA, for example, the domestic courts of the United States, Canada, and Mexico are expected to enforce the judgments of its tribunals. And judgments of the European Court of Justice are enforced by the national courts of member states of the European Union.

Then there are the traditional international organizations, such as the UN, the WHO, the IMF, and the World Bank, which are controlled and financed by their member states and are empowered to act in various ways to pursue agreed-upon goals, but are not, with the exception of the Security Council, empowered to exercise coercive enforcement against states or individuals. Even the coercive authority of the Security Council is primarily a form of collective self-defense exercised by traditional sovereign powers, although there is some erosion of sovereignty in the move toward intervention to prevent domestic genocide.

Finally, there are a number of less formal structures that are responsible for a great deal of international governance – structures that have been enlighteningly described by Anne-Marie Slaughter in her recent book on government networks.[20] Such networks typically bring together officials of different countries with a common area of expertise and responsibility, who meet or communicate regularly, harmonize their practices and policies, and operate by consensus, without having been granted decision-making authority by any treaty. Examples are networks of environmental regulators, antitrust regulators, central bankers, finance ministers, securities commissioners, insurance supervisors, or police officials. The Basel Committee on Banking Supervision, for example, "is now composed of the representatives of thirteen central banks that regulate the world's largest banking markets."[21] It has developed standards for the division of tasks between home-country and host-country regulators, and has set uniform capital adequacy standards. Agreements are reached by consensus and implemented by the central banks themselves, acting under the sovereign authority of their several states. Slaughter argues that networks of this kind, which link the disaggregated subparts of sovereign states sharing common competences and responsibilities rather than the (notionally) unitary states themselves, will become increasingly important in global governance, and should be recognized as the wave of the future.

It is a convincing case. It is important to recognize that the traditional model of international organizations based on treaties between sovereign states has been transcended. Nevertheless, I believe that the newer forms of international governance share with the old a markedly indirect relation to individual citizens and that this is morally significant. All these networks bring together representatives not of individuals, but of state functions and institutions. Those institutions are responsible to their own citizens and may have a significant role to play in the support of social justice for those citizens. But a global or regional network does not have a similar responsibility of social justice for the combined citizenry of all the states involved, a responsibility that if it existed would have to be exercised collectively by the representatives of the member states. Rather, the aim of such institutions is to find ways in which the member states, or state-parts, can cooperate to better advance their separate aims, which will presumably include the pursuit of domestic social justice in some form. Very importantly, they rely for enforcement on the power of the separate sovereign states, not of a supranational force responsible to all.

Individuals are not the constituents of such institutions. Even if the more powerful states are motivated to some extent by humanitarian concerns to shape the rules in consideration of the weakest and poorest members of the international community, that does not change the situation fundamentally. Justice is not merely the pursuit of common aims by unequal parties whose self-interest is softened by charity. Justice, on the political conception, requires a collectively imposed social framework, enacted in the name of all those governed by it, and aspiring to command their acceptance of its authority even when they disagree with the substance of its decisions.

Justice applies, in other words, only to a form of organization that claims political legitimacy and the right to impose decisions by force, and not to a voluntary association or contract among independent parties concerned to advance their common interests. I believe this holds even if the natural incentives to join such an association, and the costs of exit, are substantial, as is true of some international organizations and agreements. There is a difference between voluntary association, however strongly motivated, and coercively imposed collective authority.

IX

A second, somewhat different objection to this limitation of justice to the nation-state is that it assumes an unrealistically sharp dichotomy between sovereign states and existing global institutions with respect to agency, authorization, and authority. So even if economic globalization does not trigger the full standards of social justice, it entails them in a modified form.

In fact, according to this objection, there is a sliding scale of degrees of co-membership in a nested or sometimes overlapping set of governing institutions, of which the state is only the most salient. If we accept the moral framework of the political conception, we should conclude that there is a corresponding spectrum of degrees of egalitarian justice that we owe to our fellow participants in these collective structures in proportion to our degrees of joint responsibility for and subjection to their authority. My relation of co-membership in the system of international trade with the Brazilian who grows my coffee or the Philippine worker who assembles my computer is weaker than my relation of co-membership in US society with the Californian who picks my lettuce or the New Yorker who irons my shirts. But doesn't the first pair of relations as well as the second justify concern about the moral arbitrariness of the inequalities that arise through our joint participation in this system? One may even see an appeal to such a value in the call for standards of minimum compensation, fair labor practices, and protection of worker health and safety as conditions on international trade agreements – even if the real motivation behind it is protectionism against cheap third world labor.

Perhaps such a theory of justice as a "continuous" function of degrees of collective responsibility could be worked out. It is in fact a natural suggestion, in light of the general theory that morality is multilayered. But I doubt that the rules of international trade rise to the level of collective action needed to trigger demands for justice, even in diluted form. The relation remains essentially one of bargaining, until a leap has been made to the creation of collectively authorized sovereign authority.

On the "discontinuous" political conception I am defending, international treaties or conventions, such as those that set up the rules of trade, have a quite different moral character from contracts between self-interested parties within a sovereign state. The latter may be part of a just socio-economic system because of the background of collectively imposed property and tax law

in which they are embedded. But contracts between sovereign states have no such background: They are "pure" contracts, and nothing guarantees the justice of their results. They are like the contracts favored by libertarians, but unless one accepts the libertarian conception of legitimacy, the obligations they create are not and need not be underwritten by any kind of socio-economic justice. They are more primitive than that.

On the political conception, the same is true of the economic relation in which I stand to Brazilian or Philippine workers. Within our respective societies the contracts and laws on which this relation depends are subject to standards of social justice. Insofar as they transcend societal boundaries, however, the requirements of background justice are filtered out and commercial relations become instead something much thinner: instruments for the common pursuit of self-interest. The representatives of distinct societies that establish the framework within which such transactions can be undertaken will be guided by the interests of their own members, including their interest in domestic social justice. But a more comprehensive criterion of global socioeconomic justice is not part of the picture.

By contrast a "continuous" or sliding scale of requirements of justice would have to depend on a scale of degrees of collective engagement. I am related to the person who assembled my computer in the Philippines through the combination of US and Philippine property, commercial and labor law, the international currency markets, the international application of patent law, and the agreements on trade overseen by the World Trade Organization. The claim would have to be that since we are both participating members of this network of institutions, this puts us in the same boat for purposes of raising issues of justice, but somehow a different and perhaps leakier boat than that created by a common nation-state.

Leaving aside the practical problems of implementing even a weaker standard of economic justice through such institutions, does the idea make moral sense? Is there a plausible position covering this case that is intermediate between the political and the cosmopolitan conceptions? (The cosmopolitan conception would say that, ideally, the full standards of justice should apply, but that practically, they cannot be implemented given the limited power of international institutions.) Although it is far from clear what the answer is, it seems to me that such a sliding standard of obligation is considerably less plausible than either the cosmopolitan (one-place) or political (two-place) standard. It is supposed to be a variation on the political conception, according to which one can be moved above the default position defined by human rights and collective self-interest through participation in the institutional structures that make complex economic interaction possible. But if those institutions do not act in the name of all the individuals concerned, and are sustained by those individuals only through the agency of their respective governments or branches of those governments, what is the characteristic in virtue of which they create obligations of justice and presumptions in favor of equal consideration for all those individuals? If the default really is a basic humanitarianism, permitting voluntary interaction for the pursuit of common interests, then something more is needed to move us up toward the higher standard of equal consideration. It will not emerge merely from cooperation and the conventions that make cooperation possible.

I would add two qualifications to this rather uncompromising claim. First, there are good reasons, not deriving from global socio-economic justice, to be concerned about the consequences of economic relations with states that are *internally* egregiously unjust. Even if internal justice is the primary responsibility of each state, the complicity of other states in the active support or perpetuation of an unjust regime is a secondary offense against justice.

Secondly, even self-interested bargaining between states should be tempered by considerations of humanity, and the best way of doing this in the present world is to allow poor societies to benefit from their comparative advantage in labor costs to become competitors in world markets. WTO negotiations have finally begun to show some sense that it is indecent, for example, when subsidies by wealthy nations to their own farmers cripple the market for agricultural products from developing countries, both for export and domestically.

X

That is more or less where we are now. But I said there was a dilemma, stemming from the need for more effective global institutions to deal with our collective problems, from global warming to free trade. It is not only the fear of tyranny but also the resistance to expanded democracy, expanded demands for legitimacy, and expanded scope for the claims of justice that inhibits the development of powerful supranational institutions. Fortunate nations, at any rate, fear such developments. They therefore face the problem of how to create a global order that will have its own legitimacy, but not the kind of legitimacy that undermines the strict limits on their responsibilities.[22]

The resistance to expanded democracy is sometimes explained on the ground that the right kind of *demos* does not exist internationally to permit democratic government beyond the nation-state. Even in the subglobal and much less unequal space of Europe this is a serious problem, which has given rise to significant debate. If there is not now a European civil society, is there nevertheless the hope of one? Is the possibility compatible with the linguistic diversity of Europe? Could it perhaps be brought into existence as the *result* of democratic European political institutions, rather than serving as a precondition of their creation?

But this, I believe, is not the main issue. Multilingual and multinational states have their problems, and they may have functioned most successfully before the era of democracy. But if there came into being a genuine European federation with some form of democratically elected representative government, politics would eventually develop on a European scale to compete for control of this centralized power. The real problem is that any such government would be subject to claims of legitimacy and justice that are more than the several European populations are willing to submit themselves to. That reflects in part a conviction that they are not morally obliged to expand their moral vulnerabilities in this way. (The recent expansion of the European Union, by increasing its economic inequality, will almost certainly inhibit the growth of its federal power for just this reason.)

Globally there are a number of ways in which greater international authority would be desirable. Resources for development aid and emergency relief could be more effectively obtained by a systematic assessment or tax than by the present system of voluntary contributions. Global public goods like atmospheric protection and free trade could obviously benefit from increased international authority. Both the protection of human rights and the provision of basic humanitarian aid would be easier if regimes found to be responsible for the oppression or destitution of their own subjects in these respects were regarded as having forfeited their sovereign rights against outside interference. Not only the prevention of genocide but the relief of famine may sometimes require a change of government, and the intervention of collective outside forces and agencies. This would mean establishing a link between internal and external legitimacy

as a qualification of the general right of noninterference.[23]

But all these types of increased international authority would bring with them increased responsibilities. An authority capable of carrying out these functions and imposing its decisions would naturally be subject to claims of legitimacy, pressures toward democracy, and pressures to apply standards of justice in the distribution of burdens and benefits through its policies. There is a big difference between agreements or consensus among separate states committed to the advancement of their own interests and a binding procedure, based on some kind of collective authority, charged with securing the common good. The potential costs are much more serious than the risks that led to the US refusal to join the International Criminal Court.

This leaves us with the question whether some form of legitimacy is possible for the global or international case that does not depend on supranational sovereignty or democracy – let alone distributive justice – and yet can be embodied in institutions that are less cumbersome and feeble than those that depend for their creation and functioning on unanimous voluntary acceptance by sovereign states. For the moment, I do not see such a possibility though perhaps it can be invented. The alternative to global sovereignty may not be global anarchy, but a clear and limited form of such governance remains elusive.

XI

Yet in thinking about the future, we should keep in mind that political power is rarely created as a result of demands for legitimacy, and that there is little reason to think that things will be different in this case.

If we look at the historical development of conceptions of justice and legitimacy for the nation-state, it appears that sovereignty usually precedes legitimacy. First there is the concentration of power; then, gradually, there grows a demand for consideration of the interests of the governed, and for giving them a greater voice in the exercise of power. The demand may be reformist, or it may be revolutionary, or it may be a demand for reform made credible by the threat of revolution, but it is the existence of concentrated sovereign power that prompts the demand, and makes legitimacy an issue. War may result in the destruction of a sovereign power, leading to reconfigurations of sovereignty in response to claims of legitimacy; but even in that case the conquerors who exercise power become the targets of those claims.

Even in the most famous case of the creation of a democratic federation, illegitimacy preceded legitimacy. The foundation of the United States depended on the protection of slavery, without which unanimity among the thirteen ex-colonies could not have been achieved. In fighting the civil war to preserve the Union, Lincoln knew that the preservation of sovereign power over the entire territory was the essential condition for progress in the pursuit of democratic legitimacy and justice. The battle for more political and social equality has continued ever since, but it has been possible only because centralized power was kept in existence, so that people could contest the legitimacy of the way it was being used.

So I close with a speculation. While it is conceivable in theory that political authority should be created in response to an antecedent demand for legitimacy, I believe this is unlikely to happen in practice. What is more likely is the increase and deployment of power in the interests of those who hold it, followed by a gradual growth of pressure to make its exercise more just, and to free its organization from the historical legacy of the balance of forces that went into its creation. Unjust and illegitimate regimes are the necessary precursors of the progress toward

legitimacy and democracy, because they create the centralized power that can then be contested, and perhaps turned in other directions without being destroyed. For this reason, I believe the most likely path toward some version of global justice is through the creation of patently unjust and illegitimate global structures of power that are tolerable to the interests of the most powerful current nation-states. Only in that way will institutions come into being that are worth taking over in the service of more democratic purposes, and only in that way will there be something concrete for the demand for legitimacy to go to work on.

This point is independent of the dispute between the political and cosmopolitan conceptions. We are unlikely to see the spread of global justice in the long run unless we first create strong supranational institutions that do not aim at justice but that pursue common interests and reflect the inequalities of bargaining power among existing states. The question is whether these conditions can be realized by units established through voluntary agreement rather than by involuntary imposition. The path of conquest, responsible for so much of the scope of sovereign authority in the past, is no longer an option on a large scale. Other historical developments would have to create the illegitimate concentrations of power that can nurture demands for legitimacy, and provide them with something that is both worth taking over and not too easy to break up.

My conclusion, though it presupposes a conception of justice that Hobbes did not accept, is Hobbesian in spirit: the path from anarchy to justice must go through injustice. It is often unclear whether, for a given problem, international anarchy is preferable to international injustice. But if we accept the political conception, the global scope of justice will expand only through developments that first increase the injustice of the world by introducing effective but illegitimate institutions to which the standards of justice apply, standards by which we may hope they will eventually be transformed. An example, perhaps, of the cunning of history.

Notes

1 Thomas Hobbes, *Leviathan*, ch. 13.

2 These figures, from a few years ago, come from Thomas Pogge, *World Poverty and Human Rights* (Cambridge: Polity Press, 2002), pp. 97–9. See also Joseph Stiglitz, *Globalization and Its Discontents* (London: Penguin, 2002), p. 25. The situation seems to be improving, as population growth slows down and productivity growth speeds up in some of the biggest poor countries, China, India, and Bangladesh. See Martin Wolf, *Why Globalization Works* (New Haven, CT: Yale University Press, 2004), pp. 157–63.

3 See Peter Singer, *One World* (New Haven, CT: Yale University Press, 2002); Thomas Pogge, *Realizing Rawls* (Ithaca, NY: Cornell University Press, 1989), pp. 240–80; Pogge, *World Poverty and Human Rights*; Charles Beitz, *Political Theory and International Relations* (Princeton, NJ: Princeton University Press, 1979). I am leaving aside here the very important differences over what the universal foundation of cosmopolitan justice is. Cosmopolitans can be utilitarians, or liberal egalitarians, or even libertarian defenders of laissez faire, provided they think these moral standards of equal treatment apply in principle to our relations to all other persons, not just to our fellow citizens.

4 A subtle version of such a system has been outlined by Janos Kis in "The Unity of Mankind and the Plurality of States" (unpublished manuscript). He calls it a *supranation-state regime*: separate states would retain primary responsibility for just governance, but share sovereign power with international institutions with special authority defined functionally and not territorially, with respect to trade, the environment, human rights, and so forth. See Section VIII below for some questions about applying cosmopolitan norms at this level.

5 Ronald Dworkin, *Sovereign Virtue* (Cambridge, MA: Harvard University Press, 2000), p. 6.

6 Liam Murphy, "Institutions and the Demands of Justice," *Philosophy & Public Affairs* 27 (1998), pp. 251–91, at pp. 253–4.

7 John Rawls, *A Theory of Justice*, rev. edn (Cambridge, MA: Harvard University Press, 1999), p. 25.

8 Ibid., p. 24.

9 John Rawls, *The Law of Peoples* (Cambridge, MA: Harvard University Press, 1999), p. 37.

10 Rawls himself proposes a "second original position," with representatives of peoples as the parties behind the veil of ignorance, but he does not really try to arrive at principles on this basis (*The Law of Peoples*, pp. 32–42). I should mention that Rawls's *original* original position, the attempt to model a moral choice for handling conflicts of interest among distinct parties by the device of an individual choice under radical uncertainty about which of the parties one is, seems to me to violate Rawls's own insistence that different principles are appropriate for answering different kinds of questions. The original position might even be charged with failing to take seriously the distinction between persons, since no individual choice, even a choice under uncertainty, is equivalent to a choice for a group. This is confirmed by the difficulty Rawls has in showing that his principles of justice would be chosen by individuals in the original position. For example, he has to exclude any assignment of probabilities to their belonging to one social class rather than another, an exclusion that seems arbitrary when we think of the original position purely as a self-regarding choice under uncertainty.

11 In "Distributive Justice, State Coercion, and Autonomy," *Philosophy & Public Affairs* 30 (2001), pp. 257–96, Michael Blake defends

very similar moral conclusions – specifically that although absolute deprivation is an international concern, relative deprivation is not. But he bases his argument on the rather different ground of autonomy and what is needed to justify coercion.

12 See *A Theory of Justice,* chapter II, and John Rawls, *Justice as Fairness: A Restatement* (Cambridge, MA: Harvard University Press, 2001), part II.

13 Janos Kis has pointed out to me that there is also a significant negative aspect to our collective responsibility for one another. If our society has inflicted wrongs that demand compensation, we are obliged to contribute to those reparations whether we individually played a part in the wrongs or not. So there is more than one way in which, to use a phrase of Rawls, the members of a society "share one another's fate."

14 I have stated these conditions of justice in a way that applies to self-governing societies. Robert Post has put to me the excellent question whether on the political conception justice is owed to the subjects of regimes that are imposed from outside, such as colonial regimes or regimes of military occupation (such as those imposed on Germany and Japan after World War II). Even if we set aside the issue of whether colonial rule is ipso facto unjust, I believe the answer to Post's question is yes. Does this require a modification of my conditions? I believe it requires a broad interpretation of what it is for a society to be governed in the name of its members. But I think it can be said that if a colonial or occupying power claims political authority over a population, it purports not to rule by force alone. It is providing and enforcing a system of law that those subject to it are expected to uphold as participants, and which is intended to serve their interests even if they are not its legislators. Since their normative engagement is required, there is a sense in which it is being imposed in their name.

15 See the Afterword to the second edition of Charles Beitz, *Political Theory and International Relations* (Princeton, NJ: Princeton University Press, 1999), pp. 214–16; and "Rawls's Law of Peoples," Beitz's discussion in *Ethics* 110 (2000), pp. 669–96.

16 See his discussion of a decent hierarchical society in *The Law of Peoples*, pp. 75–8.

17 For a more broadly sympathetic discussion of Rawls's approach, see Stephen Macedo, "What Self-governing Peoples Owe to One Another: Universalism, Diversity, and *The Law of Peoples*," *Fordham Law Review* 72 (2004), pp. 1721–38. Macedo defends Rawls both on the refusal to extend distributive justice internationally and on the toleration of nonliberal peoples.

18 Thomas Pogge places particular emphasis on the first two of these factors as sources of global responsibility, since they are so important in propping up authoritarian states that treat their own citizens unjustly.

19 See Brian Barry, *The Liberal Theory of Justice* (Oxford: Oxford University Press, 1973), pp. 128–33; Beitsz, *Political Theory and International Relations,* pp. 150–3.

20 Anne-Marie Slaughter, *A New World Order* (Princeton, NJ: Princeton University Press, 2004).

21 Ibid., p. 43.

22 The undemocratic rulers of many poor nations have strong reasons of a different kind to protect their sovereign authority against international encroachment, but that is another topic.

23 For a forceful statement of this view, see Brian Barry, "Statism and Nationalism: A Cosmopolitan Critique" in *Global Justice*, Nomos 41, ed. Ian Shapiro and Lea Brilmayer (New York: New York University Press, 1999), pp. 12–65.

Chapter 22

Eradicating Systemic Poverty: Brief for a Global Resources Dividend*
Thomas W. Pogge

Introduction

In three previous essays I have sketched and defended the proposal of a Global Resources Dividend or GRD.[1] This proposal envisions that states and their governments shall not have full libertarian property rights with respect to the natural resources in their territory, but can be required to share a small part of the value of any resources they decide to use or sell. This payment they must make is called a dividend because it is based on the idea that the global poor own an inalienable stake in all limited natural resources. As in the case of preferred stock, this stake confers no right to participate in decisions about whether or how natural resources are to be used and so does not interfere with national control over resources, or eminent domain. But it does entitle its holders to a share of the economic value of the resource in question, if indeed the decision is to use it. This idea could be extended to limited resources that are not destroyed through use but merely eroded, worn down, or occupied, such as air and water used for discharging

pollutants or land used for farming, ranching, or buildings.

Proceeds from the GRD are to be used toward ensuring that all human beings can meet their own basic needs with dignity. The goal is not merely to improve the nutrition, medical care, and sanitary conditions of the poor, but also to make it possible that they can themselves effectively defend and realize their basic interests. This capacity presupposes that they are freed from bondage and other relations of personal dependence, that they are able to read and write and to learn a profession, that they can participate as equals in politics and in the labor market, and that their status is protected by appropriate legal rights which they can understand and effectively enforce through an open and fair legal system.

The GRD proposal is meant to show that there are feasible alternative ways of organizing our global economic order, that the choice among these alternatives makes a substantial difference to how much severe poverty there is worldwide, and that there are weighty moral reasons to make this choice so as to minimize such poverty. With the benefit of some critical responses[2] and spirited defenses,[3] I include here a more

* From *The Journal of Human Development* 2:1 (2001), pp. 59–77.

concise statement of the proposal and its justification.

1 Radical Inequality and Our Responsibility

One great challenge to any morally sensitive person today is the extent and severity of global poverty. There are two ways of conceiving such poverty as a moral challenge to us: we may be failing to fulfill our *positive* duty to help persons in acute distress; and we may be failing to fulfill our more stringent *negative* duty not to uphold injustice, not to contribute to or profit from the unjust impoverishment of others.

These two views differ in important ways. The positive formulation is easier to substantiate. It need be shown only that they are very badly off, that we are very much better off, and that we could relieve some of their suffering without becoming badly off ourselves. But this ease comes at a price. Some who accept the positive formulation think of the moral reasons it provides as weak and discretionary and thus do not feel obligated to promote worthy causes, especially costly ones. Many feel entitled, at least, to support good causes of their choice – their church or alma mater, cancer research or the environment – rather than putting themselves out for total strangers half a world away, with whom they share no bond of community or culture. It is of some importance, therefore, to investigate whether existing global poverty involves our violating a *negative* duty. This is important for us, if we want to lead a moral life and important also for the poor, because it makes a great difference to them whether we affluent do or do not see global poverty as an injustice we help maintain.

Some believe that the mere fact of *radical inequality* shows a violation of negative duty. Radical inequality may be defined by reference to five conditions:[4]

1 The worse-off are very badly off in absolute terms.
2 They are also very badly off in relative terms – very much worse off than many others.
3 The inequality is impervious: it is difficult or impossible for the worse-off substantially to improve their lot; and most of the better-off never experience life at the bottom for even a few months and have no vivid idea of what it is like to live in that way.
4 The inequality is pervasive: it concerns not merely some aspects of life, such as the climate or access to natural beauty or high culture, but most aspects or all.
5 The inequality is avoidable: the better-off can improve the circumstances of the worse-off without becoming badly off themselves.

World poverty clearly exemplifies radical inequality as defined. But I doubt that these five conditions suffice to invoke more than a merely positive duty. And I suspect most citizens of the developed West would also find them insufficient. They might appeal to the following parallel. Suppose we discovered people on Venus who are very badly off, and suppose we could help them at little cost to ourselves. If we did nothing, we would surely violate a positive duty of beneficence. But we would not be violating a negative duty of justice, because we would not be *contributing* to the perpetuation of their misery.

This point could be further disputed. But let me here accept the Venus argument and examine what *further* conditions must be satisfied for radical inequality to manifest an injustice that involves violation of a negative duty by the better-off. I see three plausible approaches to this question, invoking three different grounds of injustice: the *effects of shared social institutions*, the *uncompensated exclusion from the use of natural resources*, and *the effects of a common and violent history.* These approaches exemplify distinct and competing political philosophies. We need nevertheless not decide among them here if, as I argue, the following two theses are true. First, *all three approaches classify the existing radical inequality as unjust and its coercive maintenance as a violation of negative duty.* Second, *all three approaches can agree on the same feasible reform of the status quo as a major step toward justice.* If these two theses can be supported, then it may be possible to gather adherents of the dominant strands of Western normative political thought into a coalition focused on eradicating world poverty through the introduction of a Global Resources Dividend or GRD.

2 Three Grounds of Injustice

The Effects of Shared Social Institutions

The first approach[5] puts forward three additional conditions:

6 There is a shared institutional order that is shaped by the better-off and imposed on the worse-off.

7 This institutional order is implicated in the reproduction of radical inequality in that there is a feasible institutional alternative under which such severe and extensive poverty would not persist.

8 The radical inequality cannot be traced to extra-social factors (such as genetic handicaps or natural disasters) which, as such, affect different human beings differentially.

Present radical global inequality meets condition **6** in that the global poor live within a worldwide states system based on internationally recognized territorial domains, interconnected through a global network of market trade and diplomacy. The presence and relevance of shared institutions is shown

by how dramatically we affect the circumstances of the global poor through investments, loans, trade, bribes, military aid, sex tourism, culture exports, and much else. Their very survival often crucially depends on our consumption choices, which may determine the price of their foodstuffs and their opportunities to find work. In sharp contrast to the Venus case, we are causally deeply involved in their misery. This does not mean that we should hold ourselves responsible for the remoter effects of our economic decisions. These effects reverberate around the world and interact with the effects of countless other such decisions and thus cannot be traced, let alone predicted. Nor need we draw the dubious and utopian conclusion that global interdependence must be undone by isolating states or groups of states from one another. But we must be concerned with how the rules structuring international interactions foreseeably affect the incidence of extreme poverty. The developed countries, thanks to their vastly superior military and economic strength, control these rules and therefore share responsibility for their foreseeable effects.

Condition **7** involves tracing the poverty of individuals in an explanatory way to the structure of social institutions. This exercise is familiar in regard to national institutions, whose explanatory importance has been powerfully illustrated by domestic regime changes in China, eastern Europe, and elsewhere. In regard to the global economic order, the exercise is unfamiliar and shunned even by economists. This is due in part, no doubt, to powerful resistance against seeing oneself as connected to the unimaginable deprivations suffered by the global poor. This resistance biases us against data, arguments, and researchers liable to upset our preferred world view and thus biases the competition for professional success against anyone exploring the wider causal context of world poverty. This bias is reinforced by our cognitive tendency to overlook the causal significance of stable background factors (e.g. the role of atmospheric oxygen in the outbreak of a fire), as our attention is naturally drawn to geographically or temporally variable factors. Looking at the incidence of poverty worldwide, we are struck by dramatic local changes and international variations, which point to local explanatory factors. The heavy focus on such local factors then encourages the illusion that they completely explain global poverty.

This illusion conceals how profoundly local factors and their effects are influenced by the existing global order. Yes, a culture of corruption pervades the political system and the economy of many developing countries. But is this culture unrelated to the fact that most affluent countries have, until quite recently, allowed their firms to bribe foreign officials and even made such bribes tax-deductible? Yes, developing countries have shown themselves prone to oppressive government and to horrific wars and civil wars. But is the frequency of such brutality unrelated to the international arms trade,[6] and unrelated to international rules that entitle anyone holding effective power in such a country to borrow in its name and to sell ownership rights in its natural resources? Yes, the world is diverse, and poverty is declining in some countries and worsening in others. But the larger pattern of increasing global inequality is quite stable, reaching far back into the colonial era. The affluent countries have been using their power to shape the rules of the world economy according to their own interests and thereby have deprived the poorest populations of a fair share of global economic growth – quite avoidably so, as the GRD proposal shows.

Global poverty meets condition **8** insofar as the global poor, if only they had been born into different social circumstances, would be just as able and likely to lead healthy, happy, and productive lives as the rest of us. The root cause of their suffering is their abysmal social starting position which does not give them much of a chance to become anything but poor, vulnerable, and dependent – unable to give their children a better start than they had themselves.

It is because the three additional conditions are met that existing global poverty has, according to the first approach, the special moral urgency we associate with negative duties, so that we should take it much more seriously than otherwise similar suffering on Venus. The reason is that the citizens and governments of the affluent countries – whether intentionally or not – are imposing a global institutional order that foreseeably and avoidably reproduces severe and widespread poverty. The worse-off are not merely poor and often starving, but are *being* impoverished and starved under our shared institutional arrangements, which inescapably shape their lives.

The first approach can be presented in a consequentialist guise, as in Bentham, or in a contractualist guise, as in Rawls or Habermas. In both cases, the central thought is that social institutions are to be assessed in a forward-looking way, by reference to their effects. In the present international order, billions are born into social starting positions that give them extremely low prospects for a fulfilling life. Their misery could be justified only if there were no institutional alternative under which such massive misery would be avoided. If, as the GRD proposal shows, there is such an alternative, then we must ascribe this misery to the existing global order and therefore ultimately to ourselves.

Uncompensated Exclusion from the Use of Natural Resources

The second approach adds (in place of conditions **6–8**) only one condition to the five of radical inequality:

9 The better-off enjoy significant advantages in the use of a single natural resource base from whose benefits the worse-off are largely, and without compensation, excluded.

Currently, appropriation of wealth from our planet is highly uneven. Affluent people use vastly more of the world's resources, and they do so unilaterally, without giving any compensation to the global poor for their disproportionate consumption. Yes, the affluent often pay for the resources they use, such as imported crude oil. But these payments go to other affluent people, such as the Saudi family or the Nigerian kleptocracy, with very little, if anything, trickling down to the global poor. So the question remains: what entitles a global elite to use up the world's natural resources on mutually agreeable terms while leaving the global poor empty-handed?

Defenders of capitalist institutions have developed conceptions of justice that support rights to unilateral appropriation of disproportionate shares of resources while accepting that all inhabitants of the earth ultimately have equal claims to its resources. These conceptions are based on the thought that such rights are justified if all are better off with them than anyone would be if appropriation were limited to proportional shares.

This pattern of justification is exemplified with particular clarity in John Locke.[7] Locke is assuming that, in a state of nature without money, persons are subject to the moral constraint that their unilateral appropriations must always leave "enough, and as good" for others, that is, must be confined to a proportional share.[8] This so-called Lockean Proviso may, however, be lifted with universal consent.[9] Locke subjects such a lifting to a second-order proviso, which requires that the rules of human coexistence may be changed only if all can *ratio-* *nally* consent to the alteration, that is, only if everyone will be better off under the new rules than anyone would be under the old. And he claims that the lifting of the enough-and-as-good constraint through the general acceptance of money does satisfy this second-order proviso. A day laborer in England feeds, lodges, and is clad better than a king of a large fruitful territory in the Americas.[10]

It is hard to believe that Locke's claim was true in his time. In any case, it is surely false on the global plane today. Billions are born into a world where all accessible resources are already owned by others. It is true that they can rent out their labor and then buy natural resources on the same terms as the affluent can. But their educational and employment opportunities are almost always so restricted that, no matter how hard they work, they can barely earn enough for their survival and certainly cannot secure anything like a proportionate share of the world's natural resources. The global poor get to share the burdens resulting from the degradation of our natural environment while having to watch helplessly as the affluent distribute the planet's abundant natural wealth amongst themselves. With average annual *per capita* income of about $85, corresponding to the purchasing power of $338 in the US, the poorest fifth of humankind are today just about as badly off, economically, as human beings could be while still alive. It is, then, not true, what according to Locke and Nozick would need to be true, that all are better off under the existing appropriation and pollution rules than anyone would be with the Lockean Proviso. According to the second approach, the citizens and governments of the affluent states are therefore violating a negative duty of justice when they, in collaboration with the ruling elites of the poor countries, coercively exclude the poor from a proportional resource share.

The Effects of a Common and Violent History

The third approach adds one condition to the five of radical inequality:

10 The social starting positions of the worse-off and the better-off have emerged from a single historical process that was pervaded by massive, grievous wrongs.

The present circumstances of the global poor are significantly shaped by a dramatic period of conquest and colonization, with severe oppression, enslavement, even genocide, through which the native institutions and cultures of four continents were destroyed or severely traumatized. This is not to say (or to deny) that affluent descendants of those who took part in these crimes bear some special restitutive responsibility toward impoverished descendants of those who were victims of these crimes. The thought is rather that we must not uphold extreme inequality in social starting positions when the allocation of these positions depends upon historical processes in which moral principles and legal rules were massively violated. A morally deeply tarnished history should not be allowed to result in *radical* inequality.

This third approach is independent of the others. For suppose we reject the other two approaches and affirm that radical inequality is morally acceptable when it comes about pursuant to rules of the game that are morally at least somewhat plausible and observed at least for the most part. The existing radical inequality is then still condemned by the third approach on the ground that the rules were in fact massively violated through countless horrible crimes whose momentous effects cannot be surgically neutralized decades and centuries later.[11]

Some friends of the present distribution claim that standards of living, in Africa and Europe for instance, would be approximately the same if Africa had never been colonized. Even if this claim were both clear and true, it would still be ineffective, because my argument applies to persons, not continents. If world history had transpired without colonization and enslavement, then there would perhaps now still be affluent people in Europe and poor ones in Africa, much as in the Venus scenario. But these would be persons and populations quite different from those now actually living there. So we cannot tell starving Africans that *they* would be starving and *we* would be affluent even if the crimes of colonialism had never occurred. Without these crimes there would not be the actually existing radical inequality which consists in *these* persons being affluent and *those* being extremely poor.

So the third approach, too, leads to the conclusion that the existing radical inequality is unjust, that coercively upholding it violates a negative duty, and that we have urgent moral reason to eradicate world poverty.

3   A Moderate Proposal

The reform proposal now to be sketched is meant to support my second thesis: that the status quo can be reformed in a way that all three approaches would recognize as a major step toward justice. But it is also needed to close gaps in my argument for the first thesis. The proposal should show that the existing radical inequality can be traced to the structure of our global economic order (condition **7**). And it should also show that condition **5** is met; for, according to all three approaches, the status quo is unjust only if we can improve the circumstances of the global poor without thereby becoming badly off ourselves.

I am formulating my reform proposal in line with the second approach, because the other two would support almost any reform that would improve the circumstances of the global poor. The second approach narrows the field by suggesting a more specific idea: those who make more extensive use of our planet's resources should compensate those who, involuntarily, use very little. This idea does not require that we conceive of global resources as the common property of humankind, to be shared equally. My proposal is far more modest by leaving each government in control of the natural resources in its territory. Modesty is important if the proposed institutional alternative is to gain the support necessary to implement it and is to be able to sustain itself in the world as we know it. I hope that the GRD satisfies these two desiderata by staying close to the global order now in place and by being evidently responsive to each of the three approaches.

In light of the vast extent of global poverty today, one may think that a massive GRD would be necessary to solve the problem. But I doubt this is so. Present radical inequality is the cumulative result of decades and centuries in which the more affluent societies and groups have used their advantages in capital and knowledge to expand these advantages ever further. This inequality demonstrates the power of long-term compounding more than powerful centrifugal tendencies of our global market system. It is, then, quite possible that, if radical inequality has once been eradicated, quite a small GRD may, in the context of a fair and open global market system, be sufficient continuously to balance those ordinary centrifugal tendencies of markets enough to forestall its reemergence. The great magnitude of the problem does suggest, however, that initially more may be needed so that it does not take too long before severe poverty is erased and an acceptable distributional profile is reached. To get a concrete sense of the magnitudes involved, let us consider an initial, maximal figure of 1 percent of aggregate global income, currently about $312 billion annually.[12] This corresponds to the income shortfall that separates the 2,801 million human beings living below the World Bank's $2/day (strictly: $2.15 PPP 1993) poverty line from this line.[13] Such an amount, if well targeted and effectively spent, would make a phenomenal difference to the poor even within a few years. On the other hand, the amount is rather small for the rest of us: close to the annual defense budget of just the US alone, two-thirds of the annual "peace dividend", and about half the market value of the current annual crude oil production.[14]

Let us stay with the case of crude oil for a moment and examine the likely effects of a $2 per barrel GRD on crude oil extraction. This dividend would be owed by the countries in which oil is extracted, though most of this cost would be passed along, through higher world market prices, to the end-users of petroleum products. At $2 per barrel, over 18 percent of the high initial revenue target could be raised from crude oil alone – and comfortably so: at the expense of raising the price of petroleum products by about a nickel per gallon. It is thus clearly possible – without major changes to our global economic order – to eradicate world hunger within a few years by raising a sufficient revenue stream from a limited number of resources and pollutants. These should be selected carefully, with an eye to all collateral effects. This suggests the following desiderata. The GRD should, first, be easy to understand and to apply. It should, for instance, be based on resources and pollutants whose extraction or discharge is easy to monitor or estimate, in order to ensure that every society is paying its fair share and to assure everyone that this is so. Such transparency also helps fulfill a second desideratum of keeping overall collection costs low. The GRD should, third, have only a small impact on the price of goods consumed to satisfy basic needs. And it should, fourth, be focused on resource uses whose discouragement is especially important for conservation and environmental protection. In this last respect, the GRD reform can produce great ecological benefits that are hard to secure in a less concerted way because of familiar collective-action problems: each society has little incentive to restrain its consumption and pollution, because the opportunity cost of such restraint falls on it alone while the costs of depletion and pollution are spread worldwide and into the future.

The scheme for disbursing GRD funds is to be designed so as to make these funds maximally effective toward ensuring that all human beings can meet their own basic needs with dignity. Such design must draw upon the expertise of economists and international lawyers. Let me nonetheless make some provisional suggestions to give more concreteness to the proposed reform. Disbursement should be made pursuant to clear and straightforward general rules whose administration is cheap and transparent. Transparency is important to exclude political favoritism and the appearance thereof. It is important also for giving the government of any developing country clear and strong incentives toward eradicating domestic poverty. To optimize such incentive effects, the disbursement rules should reward progress: by allocating more funds to this country and/or by assigning more of its allocation directly to its government.

This incentive may not always prevail. In some poor countries, the rulers care more about keeping their subjects destitute, uneducated, docile, dependent, and hence exploitable. In such cases, it may still be possible to find other ways of improving the circumstances and opportunities of the domestic poor: by making cash payments directly to them or to their organizations or by funding development programs administered through UN agencies or effective non-governmental organizations. When, in extreme cases, GRD funds cannot be used effectively in a particular country, then there is no reason to spend them there rather than in those many other places where these funds can make a real difference in reducing poverty and disadvantage.

Even if the incentives provided by the GRD disbursement rules do not always prevail, they shift the political balance of forces in the right direction. A good government brings enhanced prosperity through GRD support and thereby generates more popular support which in turn tends to make it safer from coup attempts. A bad government finds the poor harder to oppress when they receive GRD funds through other channels and when all strata of the population have an interest in realizing GRD-accelerated economic improvement under a different government more committed to poverty eradication. With the GRD in place, reforms will be pursued more vigorously and in more countries, and will succeed more often and sooner, than would otherwise be the case. Combined with suitable disbursement rules, the GRD can stimulate a peaceful international competition in effective poverty eradication.

This rough and revisable sketch has shown, I hope, that the GRD proposal deserves serious examination as an alternative to conventional development assistance. While the latter has an aura of handouts and dependence, the GRD avoids any appearance of arrogant generosity. It merely incorporates into our global institutional order the moral claim of the poor to partake in the benefits from the use of planetary resources. It implements a moral right – and one that can be justified in multiple ways: namely also forward-looking, by reference to its effects, and backward-looking, by reference to the evolution of the present economic distribution.

Moreover, the GRD would also be vastly more efficient. The disbursement of conventional development assistance is governed by political considerations:[15] only 19 percent of the $56 billion in official development assistance (year 1999) goes to the 43 least developed countries.[16] And only 8.3 percent is spent on meeting basic needs – much less than the 20 percent the high-income countries promised in the "20:20 compact" made within the OECD.[17] All high-income countries together thus spend about $4.65 billion annually on meeting basic needs abroad – 0.02 percent of their combined GNPs, about $5.15 annually from each citizen of the developed world and $3.83 annually for each person in the poorest quintile. The GRD, by contrast, would initially raise 67 times as much exclusively toward meeting the basic needs of the global poor.

Since the GRD would cost more and return less in direct political benefits, many of the wealthier and more powerful states might be tempted to refuse compliance. Wouldn't the GRD scheme then require a global enforcement agency, something like a world government? In response, I agree that the GRD would have to be backed by sanctions. But sanctions could be decentralized. Once the agency facilitating the flow of GRD payments reports that a country has not met its obligation under the scheme, all other countries are required to impose duties on imports from, and perhaps also similar levies on exports to, this country to raise funds equivalent to its GRD obligations plus the cost of these enforcement measures. Such decentralized sanctions stand a very good chance of discouraging small-scale defections. Our world is now, and is likely to remain, highly interdependent economically. Most countries export and import between 10 and 50 percent of their gross domestic product. No country would profit from shutting down foreign trade for the sake of avoiding its GRD obligation. And each would have reasons to fulfill its GRD

obligation voluntarily: to retain control over how the funds are raised, to avoid paying extra for enforcement measures, and to avoid the adverse publicity associated with non-compliance.

To be sure, such a scheme of decentralized sanctions could work only so long as both the US and the EU continue to comply and continue to participate in the sanction mechanism. I assume that both will do this, provided they can be brought to commit themselves to the GRD scheme in the first place. This prerequisite, which is decisive for the success of the proposal, is addressed later. It should be clear, however, that a refusal by the US or the EU to participate in the eradication of world poverty would not affect the implications of the present section 8. The feasibility of the GRD suffices to show that extensive and severe poverty is avoidable at moderate cost (condition **5**), that the existing global order plays an important role in its persistence (condition **7**) and that we can take what all three approaches would recognize as a major step toward justice (second thesis).

4 The Moral Argument for the Proposed Reform

By showing that conditions **1–10** are met, I hope to have demonstrated that present global poverty manifests a grievous injustice that can and should be abolished through institutional reform – involving the GRD scheme, perhaps, or some superior alternative. To make this train of thought as transparent and criticizable as possible, I restate it now as an argument in six steps. The first two steps involve new formulations, so I comment on them briefly at the end.

(1)   If a society or comparable social system, connected and regulated by a shared institutional order (condition **6**),

displays radical inequality (conditions **1–5**), then this institutional order is *prima facie* unjust and requires justification. Here the burden of proof is on those who wish to defend this order and its coercive imposition as compatible with justice.

(2) Such a justification of an institutional order under which radical inequality persists would need to show either

    (**2a**)   that condition **10** is not met, perhaps because the existing radical inequality came about fairly: through a historical process that transpired in accordance with morally plausible rules that were generally observed; or

    (**2b**)   that condition **9** is not met, because the worse-off can adequately benefit from the use of the common natural resource base through access to a proportional share or through some at least equivalent substitute; or

    (**2c**)   that condition **8** is not met, because the existing radical inequality can be traced to extra-social factors (such as genetic handicaps or natural disasters) which, as such, affect different persons differentially; or

    (**2d**)   that condition **7** is not met, because any proposed alternative to the existing institutional order either

- is impracticable, that is, cannot be stably maintained in the long run; or
- cannot be instituted in a morally acceptable way even with good will by all concerned; or
- would not substantially improve the circumstances of the worse-off; or
- would have other morally serious disadvantages that offset any improvement in the circumstances of the worse-off.

(3) Humankind is connected and regulated by a shared global institutional order under which radical inequality persists.

(4) This global institutional order therefore requires justification ⟨from (**1**) and (**3**)⟩.

(5) This global institutional order can be given no justification of forms (**2a**), (**2b**), or (**2c**). A justification of form (**2d**) fails as well, because a reform involving introduction of a GRD provides an alternative that is practicable, can (with some good will by all concerned) be instituted in a morally acceptable way, would substantially improve the circumstances of the worse-off, and would not have disadvantages of comparable moral significance.

(6) The existing global order cannot be justified ⟨from (**4**), (**2**), and (**5**)⟩ and hence is unjust ⟨from (**1**)⟩.

In presenting this argument, I have not attempted to satisfy the strictest demands of logical form, which would have required various qualifications and repetitions. I have merely tried to clarify the structure of the argument so as to make clear how it can be attacked.

One might attack the first step. But this moral premise is quite weak, applying only if the existing inequality occurs within a shared institutional order (condition **6**) *and* is radical, that is, involves truly extreme poverty and extreme differentials in standards of living (conditions **1–5**). Moreover, the first premise does not flatly exclude any institutional order under which radical inequality persists, but merely demands that it be justified. Since social institutions are created and upheld, perpetuated or reformed by human beings, this demand cannot plausibly be refused.

One might attack the second step. But this moral premise, too, is weak, in that it demands of the defender of the status quo only one of the four possible showings, (2a)–(2d), leaving him free to try each of the conceptions of economic justice outlined in section 2 even though he can hardly endorse all of them at once. Still, it remains open to argue that an institutional order reproducing radical inequality can be justified in a way that differs from the four, (2a)–(2d), I have described.

One might try to show that the existing global order does not meet one of the ten conditions. Depending on which condition is targeted, one would thereby deny the third premise or give a justification of forms (2a) or (2b), or (2c), or show that my reform proposal runs into one of the four problems listed under (2d).

The conclusion of the argument is reached only if all ten conditions are met. Existing global poverty then manifests a *core injustice*: a phenomenon that the dominant strands of Western normative political thought jointly – albeit for diverse reasons – classify as unjust and can jointly seek to eradicate. Insofar as advantaged and influential participants in the present international order grant the argument, we acknowledge our shared responsibility for its injustice. We are violating a negative duty of justice insofar as we contribute to (and fail to mitigate) the harms it reproduces and insofar as we resist suitable reforms.

5   Is the Reform Proposal Realistic?

Even if the GRD proposal is practicable, and even if it could be implemented with the good will of all concerned, there remains the problem of generating this good will, especially on the part of the rich and mighty. Without the support of the US and the EU, massive global poverty and starvation will certainly not be eradicated in our lifetimes. How realistic is the hope of mobilizing such support? I have two answers to this question.

First, even if this hope is not realistic, it is still important to insist that present global poverty manifests a grievous injustice according to Western normative political thought. We are not merely distant witnesses of a problem unrelated to ourselves, with a weak, positive duty to help. Rather we are, both causally and morally, intimately involved in the fate of the poor by imposing upon them a global institutional order that regularly produces severe poverty and/or by effectively excluding them from a fair share of the value of exploited natural resources and/or by upholding a radical inequality that evolved through a historical process pervaded by horrendous crimes. We can realistically end our involvement in their severe poverty not by extricating ourselves from this involvement, but only by ending such poverty through economic reform. If feasible reforms are blocked by others, then we may in the end be unable to do more than mitigate some of the harms we also help produce. But even then a difference would remain, because our effort would fulfill not a duty to help the needy, but a duty to protect victims of any injustice to which we contribute. The latter duty is, other things being equal, much more stringent than the former, especially when we can fulfill it out of the benefits we derive from this injustice.

My second answer is that the hope may not be so unrealistic after all. My provisional optimism is based on two considerations. The first is that moral convictions can have real effects even in international politics – as even some political realists admit, albeit with regret. Sometimes these are the moral convictions of politicians. But more commonly politics is influenced by the moral convictions of citizens. One dramatic example of this is the abolitionist movement which, in the nineteenth century, pressured the British government into suppressing the slave trade.[18] A similar moral mobilization may be possible also for the sake of eradicating world poverty – provided the citizens of the more powerful states can be convinced of a moral conclusion that really can be soundly supported and a path can be shown that makes only modest demands on each of us.

The GRD proposal is morally compelling. It can be broadly anchored in the dominant strands of Western normative political thought outlined in section 2. And it also has the morally significant advantage of shifting consumption in ways that restrain global pollution and resource depletion for the benefit of future generations in particular. Because it can be backed by these four important and mutually independent moral rationales, the GRD proposal is well positioned to benefit from the fact that moral reasons can have effects in the world. If some help can be secured from economists, political scientists, and lawyers, then moral acceptance of the GRD may gradually emerge and become widespread in the developed West.

Eradicating world poverty through a scheme like the GRD also involves more realistic demands than a solution through private initiatives and conventional development aid. Continual mitigation of poverty leads to fatigue, aversion, even contempt. It requires the more affluent citizens and governments to rally to the cause again and again while knowing full well that most others similarly situated contribute nothing or very little, that their own contributions are legally optional, and that, no matter how much they give, they could for just a little more always save yet further children from sickness or starvation.

The inefficiency of conventional development aid is also sustained by the competitive situation among the governments of the donor countries, who feel morally entitled to decline to do more by pointing to their even less generous competitors. This explanation supports the optimistic assumption that the affluent societies would be prepared, in joint reciprocity, to commit themselves to more than what they tend to do each on its own. Analogous considerations apply to environmental protection and conservation, with respect to which the GRD also contributes to a collective solution. When many parties decide separately in this matter, then the best solution for all is not achieved, because each gets almost the full benefit of its pollution and wastefulness while the resulting harms are shared by all ("tragedy of the commons"). An additional point is that national development-aid and environmental-protection measures must be politically fought for or defended year after year, while acceptance of the GRD scheme would require only one – albeit rather more far-reaching – political decision.

The other optimistic consideration has to do with prudence. The times when we could afford to ignore what goes on in the developing countries are over for good. Their economic growth will have a great impact on our environment and their military and technological gains are accompanied by serious dangers, among which those associated with nuclear, biological, and chemical weapons and technologies are only the most obvious. The transnational imposition of externalities and risks will ever more become a two-way street as no state or group of states, however rich and mighty, will be able effectively to insulate itself from external influences: from military and terrorist attacks, illegal immigrants, epidemics and the drug trade, pollution and climate change, price fluctuations and scientific-technological and cultural innovations. It is, then, increasingly in our interest, too, that stable democratic institutions should emerge in the developing countries – institutions under which governmental power is effectively constrained through procedural rules and basic rights. So long as large segments of these peoples lack elementary education and have no assurance that they will be able to meet even their most basic needs, such democratic institutions are much less likely than explosive mixtures of religious and ideological fanaticism, violent opposition movements, death squads, and corrupt and politicized militaries. To expose ourselves to the occasional explosions of these mixtures would be increasingly dangerous and also more costly in the long run than the proposed GRD.

This prudential consideration has a moral side as well. A future that is pervaded by radical inequality and hence is unstable would endanger not only the security of ourselves and our progeny, but also the long-term survival of our society, values, and culture. Not only that: such a future would, quite generally, endanger the security of all other human beings and their descendants as well as the survival of their societies, values, and cultures. And so the interest in peace – in a future world in which different societies, values, and cultures can coexist and interact peacefully – is obviously also, and importantly, a moral interest.

Realizing our prudential and moral interest in a peaceful and ecologically sound future will – and here I go beyond my earlier modesty – require supranational institutions and organizations that limit the sovereignty rights of states more severely than is the current practice. The most powerful states could try to impose such limitations upon all the rest while exempting themselves. It is doubtful, however, that today's great powers will summon the political will to make this attempt before it is too late. And it is doubtful also whether they could succeed. For such an attempt would provoke the bitter resistance of many other states, which would simultaneously try very hard, through military buildup, to gain access to the club of great powers. For such a project, the "elites" in many developing countries could probably mobilize their populations quite easily, as the recent examples of India and Pakistan illustrate.

It might, then, make more sense for all to work toward supranational institutions and organizations that limit the sovereignty rights of all states equally. But this solution can work only if at least a large majority of the states participating in these institutions and organizations are stable democracies, which presupposes, in turn, that their citizens are assured that they can meet their basic needs and can attain a decent level of education and social position.

The current geopolitical development drifts toward a world in which militarily and technologically highly advanced states and groups, growing in number, pose an ever greater danger for an ever larger subset of humankind. Deflecting this development in a more reasonable direction realistically requires considerable support from those other 85 percent of humankind who want to reduce our economic advantage and achieve our high standard of living. Through the introduction of the GRD or some similar reform we can gain such support by showing concretely that our relations to the rest of the world are not solely devoted to cementing our economic hegemony and that the global poor will be able peacefully to achieve a considerable improvement in their circumstances. In this way and only in this way can we refute the conviction, understandably widespread in the poor countries, that we will not give a damn about their misery until they have the economic and military power to do us serious harm. And only in this way can we undermine the popular support that aggressive political movements of all kinds can derive from this conviction.

6 Conclusion

We are familiar, through charity appeals, with the assertion that it lies in our hands to save the lives of many or, by doing nothing, to let these people die. We are less familiar with the assertion examined here of a weightier responsibility: that most of us do not merely let people starve but also participate in starving them. It is not surprising that our initial reaction to this more unpleasant assertion is indignation, even hostility – that, rather than think it through or discuss it, we want to forget it or put it aside as plainly absurd.

I have tried to respond constructively to the assertion and to show its plausibility. I don't pretend to have proved it conclusively, but my argument should at least raise grave doubts about our commonsense prejudices, which we must in any case treat with

suspicion on account of how strongly our self-interest is engaged in this matter. The great moral importance of reaching the correct judgment on this issue also counsels against lightly dismissing the assertion here defended. The essential data about the lives and deaths of the global poor are, after all, indisputable. In view of very considerable global interdependence, it is extremely unlikely that their poverty is due exclusively to local factors and that no feasible reform of the present global order could thus affect either that poverty or these local factors. No less incredible is the view that ours is the best of all possible global orders, that any modification of it could only aggravate poverty. So we should work together across disciplines to conceive a comprehensive solution to the problem of world poverty, and across borders for the political implementation of this solution.

Notes

1 Pogge, "An Egalitarian Law of Peoples," "Eine globale Rohstoffdividende," and "A Global Resources Dividend."

2 Reichel, "Internationaler Handel," Kesselring, "Weltarmut und Ressourcen-Zugang," Crisp and Jamieson, "Egalitarianism and a Global Resources Tax."

3 Kreide, "Armut, Gerechtigkeit und Demokratie," and Mandle, "Globalization and Justice."

4 Extending Nagel, "Poverty and Food."

5 Suggested in O'Neill, "Lifeboat Earth"; Nagel, "Poverty and Food"; and Pogge, *Realizing Rawls*, § 24.

6 Arms sold to the developing countries facilitate repression, fuel civil wars, and divert funds from meeting basic needs. In 2000, the rich countries spent about $4,650 million on development assistance for meeting basic needs abroad while also selling the developing countries an estimated $25,438 million in conventional weapons. This represents 69 percent of the entire international trade in conventional weapons (valued at $36,862

million). The main sellers of arms are the US, with over 50 percent of sales, then Russia, France, Germany, and the UK, with another 37 percent. See Congressional Research Service, *Conventional Arms Transfers to Developing Nations*.

7 See also Nozick, *Anarchy, State, and Utopia*, ch. 4.

8 Locke, "An Essay Concerning the True Original," § 27 and § 33.

9 Ibid., § 36.

10 Ibid., § 41 and § 37.

11 See Nozick, *Anarchy, State, and Utopia*, p. 231.

12 Aggregate global income was $31,171 billion in the year 2000.

13 The poverty gap relative to the World Bank's better-known $1/day (strictly: $1.08 PPP 1993) poverty line is only $44 billion annually. But this line is too low to define an acceptable goal in a world as affluent in aggregate as ours. Even the higher poverty line allows a family of four to buy only as much each month as can be bought with $322 in

the US. And bringing all human beings up to the higher poverty line would still leave the average person in the high-income economies with over 100 times more money and 28 times more purchasing power.

[14] Crude oil production is currently about 77 million barrels daily or about 28 billion barrels annually. At a typical price of $25 per barrel, this comes to $700 billion annually though prices are higher or lower at times.

[15] Alesina and Dollar, "Who Gives Foreign Aid to Whom and Why?"

[16] UNDP, *Report 2001*, p. 190.

[17] UNDP, *Report 2000*, p. 79.

[18] Drescher, *Capitalism and Antislavery.*

Bibliography

Alesina, Alberto and David Dollar, "Who Gives Foreign Aid to Whom and Why?" *Journal of Economic Growth* 5 (2000): 33–64.

Congressional Research Service, *Conventional Arms Transfers to Developing Nations, 1993–2000*. Washington, DC: Library of Congress, 2001. http://usinfo.state.gov/topical/pol/arms/stories/01082201.htm

Crisp, Roger and Dale Jamieson, "Egalitarianism and a Global Resources Tax: Pogge on Rawls," in Victoria Davion and Clark Wolf (eds.), *The Idea of a Political Liberalism: Essays on Rawls*. Lanham, MD: Rowman and Littlefield, 2000, pp. 90–101.

Drescher, Seymour, *Capitalism and Antislavery: British Mobilization in Comparative Perspective*. Oxford: Oxford University Press, 1986.

Kesselring, Thomas, "Weltarmut und Ressourcen-Zugang," *Analyse und Kritik* 19 (1997): 242–54.

Kreide, Regina, "Armut, Gerechtigkeit und Demokratie," *Analyse und Kritik* 20 (1998): 245–62.

Locke, John, "An Essay Concerning the True Original, Extent, and End of Civil Government," in his *Two Treatises of Government*, ed. Peter Laslett. Cambridge: Cambridge University Press, 1960.

Mandle, Jon, "Globalization and Justice," *Annals of the American Academy* 570 (2000): 126–39.

Nagel, Thomas, "Poverty and Food: Why Charity is not Enough," in Peter Brown and Henry Shue (eds.), *Food Policy: The Responsibility of the United States in the Life and Death Choices*. New York: The Free Press, 1977, pp. 54–62.

Nozick, Robert, *Anarchy, State, and Utopia*. New York: Basic Books, 1974.

O'Neill, Onora, "Lifeboat Earth," *Philosophy & Public Affairs* 4 (1974): 273–92.

Pogge, Thomas W., *Realizing Rawls*. Ithaca, NY: Cornell University Press, 1989.

Pogge, Thomas W., "An Egalitarian Law of Peoples," *Philosophy & Public Affairs* 23 (1994): 195–224.

Pogge, Thomas W., "A Global Resources Dividend," in David A. Crocker and Toby Linden (eds.), *Ethics of Consumption: The Good Life, Justice, and Global Stewardship*. Lanham, MD: Rowman and Littlefield, 1998, pp. 501–36.

Reichel, Richard, "Internationaler Handel, Tauschgerechtigkeit und die globale Rohstoffdividende," *Analyse und Kritik* 19 (1997): 229–41.

UNDP, *Human Development Report 2000*. New York: Oxford University Press, 2000.

UNDP, *Human Development Report 2001*. New York: Oxford University Press, 2001.

Chapter 23

Poverty Relief, Global Institutions, and the Problem of Compliance*
Lisa L. Fuller

Among the many challenges associated with globalization, eradicating poverty stands out as both extremely urgent and ethically complex. While it is clear that what we want is a significant lessening of death and disease due to poverty, how this can be achieved and who is responsible for carrying it out are far less clear. The enormous gap between the rich and poor indicates that a redistribution of wealth from the former to the latter would make the world more just, but this fact, taken on its own, is not very illuminating. It is only when we turn to the task of hammering out a concrete solution that we can begin to see, and to work through, those issues that stand in the way of instantiating global justice. Among them are fundamental questions about the obligations of nation-states and other international actors, the nature and purpose of their interactions, and the most desirable shape of international institutions. The resolution of these background issues is by no means a simple undertaking, but the urgency of the problem demands that we take them up as they arise – keeping in mind that, ultimately, we are after practical strategies for addressing the

* From The *Journal of Moral Philosophy* 2:3 (2005), pp. 285–97.

problem. In what follows, I will explain and criticize what I call 'the institutional view' of poverty relief, and sketch out an alternative that both avoids its main defect and relies on a less ideal conception of international relations. My own view focuses on the kind of improvements that would be required for conventional international aid to acquire the legitimacy and accountability that it now lacks.

The Individual View vs. the Institutional View

In the philosophical literature, there are two standard approaches to the problem of global poverty. The first is exemplified by the work of Peter Singer, who maintains that *as individuals* we have a moral obligation to give generously to organizations such as Oxfam in order to prevent harm caused by extreme poverty. We might call this 'the individual duty view'. By contrast, philosophers such as Thomas Pogge and Andrew Kuper suggest that we should support a systemic or 'institutional' solution to global poverty. The institutional view directs our attention away from the acts of individuals and toward the institutional rules to which all individuals and states are subject. On this view, global poverty is both caused and perpetuated by political and market institutions that are badly slanted in favour of powerful nation-states. The argument for this claim goes, roughly, as follows: Historically, powerful states have used their military and economic strength to shape the way interactions take place at the global level. They have 'made the rules', so to speak. Under the current rules, many poor countries fare quite badly. Only if there were no feasible alternatives that could avoid this outcome could these rules be justified. However, there *are* feasible institutional alternatives under which poor countries would fare much better. As such, the perpetuation of the status quo amounts to the coercive imposition of an unjust order on poor countries, by affluent ones. Pogge sums this up nicely when he says:

> Citizens and governments of the affluent countries – whether intentionally or not – are imposing a global institutional order that forseeably and avoidably reproduces severe and widespread poverty. The worse-off are not merely poor and often starving, but are being impoverished and starved under our shared institutional arrangements.[1]

According to this view, institutions are at the root of the problem and so institutional reform is clearly the solution. While there are potentially very many alternative arrangements that would improve the lot of poor countries, I will restrict my focus here to the one suggested by Pogge himself. He calls his alternative scheme the 'Global Resources Dividend' (or GRD). It would work like this: those people who make extensive use of the planet's resources would compensate those who, involuntarily, are able to use very little. For instance, a $2 per barrel GRD tax on crude oil could be instituted, which would be payable to a central fund. The countries from which the oil is extracted would pay the tax, but the extra cost would ultimately be passed on to end users in the marketplace. The funds collected by the central fund could then be redistributed such that they are 'maximally effective toward ensuring that all human beings can meet their basic needs with dignity'.[2]

Pogge suggests that the disbursement of these funds should be governed by clear, straightforward rules that are cheap to administer. The disbursing body should also be maximally transparent, in order to 'exclude political favoritism and the appearance thereof'.[3] Since the allocation of funds would be exclusively geared toward meeting the basic needs of the poor (rather than toward securing other political benefits for the donors), it would be much more efficient than conventional development assistance. Moreover, the disbursement scheme should create incentives for developing countries by rewarding significant gains in eradicating poverty – the more progress a country makes in this regard, the more funds should be allocated to it.

Having outlined the institutional view, we can now ask why Pogge and Kuper might prefer this type of solution to the individual duty view. The main reason seems to be that they regard traditional methods of development aid as seriously flawed. For instance, Kuper asserts that non-governmental organizations (NGOs) 'can never be the primary agents of justice and aid in the long run', for several reasons.[4] First, their funding is too capricious, depending as it does on the inclinations of donor countries and individuals. Second, their access to particular populations depends on the whims of others (usually rulers), whose interests often diverge significantly from the aims of NGOs. Third, they are not democratically elected or sufficiently accountable for their actions and aims, and finally, they cannot produce large-scale growth or redistribution.

Pogge suggests additional reasons why we ought to reject NGO aid. He notes that it engenders donor fatigue and even contempt for the poor by requiring 'affluent citizens and governments to rally to the cause again and again while knowing full well that most others similarly situated contribute nothing or very little'.[5] Further, he thinks that NGO aid 'has an aura of handouts and dependence' which would be avoided by an institutional solution.[6]

Thus, the argument for an institutional solution to global poverty actually proceeds on two fronts: by pointing out the merits of a scheme such as the GRD, and by criticizing the current system of NGO relief programmes. It is my intention here to challenge both of these lines of argument. However, far from simply suggesting that individual generosity rather than institutional reform is the answer, I would like to suggest that framing the problem in this dichotomous manner blinds us to a third possibility that does not suffer from the defects of either. So far, we have seen the defects of the NGO alternative. I'll now point out some drawbacks of the institutional approach.

Problems for the Institutional View

The central problem for institutional solutions such as Pogge's is how to generate enough goodwill among rich states that they would be willing to commit themselves to these types of reforms. Indeed, Pogge even admits that 'the GRD would cost more and return less in direct political benefits' than traditional development or humanitarian aid.[7] As a result, he recognizes that powerful states might be reluctant to comply. However, he gives two reasons for believing that the compliance of the world's two strongest powers – the United States and the European Union – could be secured. First, he notes that 'moral convictions can have real effects even in international

politics . . . provided the citizens of the more powerful states can be convinced of a moral conclusion that really can be soundly supported and a path can be shown that makes only modest demands on each of us'.[8] He cites the abolition of the slave trade in Britain as an example of how the moral convictions of citizens can impact international norms in a positive manner.

Secondly, Pogge argues that an enterprise such as the GRD has clear prudential value, even for powerful states, and so they might be persuaded to cooperate on this basis. He claims that we can no longer afford to ignore what is going on in the developing world. He suggests that creating greater equality between states and more prosperity in developing countries would help mitigate against the spread of terrorist attacks, epidemics, the drug trade, and pollution, all of which will threaten rich states more in the future. Contributing to the GRD would be cheaper overall for powerful states than exposing themselves to these other threats.[9]

In addition, Pogge argues that greater prosperity in developing countries will enable governments to protect the basic rights of their citizens and provide elementary education, which will, in turn, tend toward the creation of well-ordered, democratic regimes. The emergence of democratic institutions in developing countries is in the interest of powerful states, and this aim would be promoted by entering into a scheme such as the GRD.

While I admire Pogge's optimism in this regard, I still think there are several considerations that work against the possibility of obtaining compliance from *both* very powerful and less powerful states. My first worry is about his argument from the moral consensus of citizens. Indeed, it is sometimes the case that change can be heavily influenced by the attitudes of citizens in affluent countries, but Pogge has an overly idealistic view of the dynamics of international relations. Thomas

Weiss characterizes a Pogge-type view of the foundations of international politics as 'efforts to agree upon desirable international public policies within governmental, intergovernmental and nongovernmental arenas'.[10] This type of view focuses on the cooperation evident between states when they form treaties and cooperate in institutions such as the United Nations. On the other hand, it is possible to view international politics as, in Weiss's words, 'the competition among states for survival and supremacy and for maximizing national interests in an anarchical world'.[11] While I am no realist, and so would not wholly subscribe to the latter view, it does seem somewhat naïve to discount it altogether. Pogge knows this, since he admits that powerful governments and multinational corporations have historically 'negotiate[d] and re-negotiate[d] the rules of the game among themselves with each pressing vigorously for its own advantage, using war and threat of war when this seems opportune and showing no concern for the interests or even survival of the weakest "players"'.[12]

The point here is that the power of moral consensus is always going to be tempered by considerations of national interest – and it does not seem realistic to presume that the citizens of affluent countries will be able to sustain a preference for morality over economic interest, especially when economic times are bad. In the case of slavery, its abolition affected only some of the British population for the worse, namely, slave-traders. A measure such as the GRD affects virtually everyone in affluent states, including those with not much money relative to their fellow citizens. I am sceptical that they could be convinced to cooperate, and importantly, to *lend continued support* to cooperation.

Further, history has shown that global institutions such as the UN are typically susceptible to the interests of the most powerful states, and so any 'moral mission' they

adopt is going to be strongly influenced by these interests. This is the main reason such organizations have worked only imperfectly in the past, and I see no reason to suppose that this will change in the near future. While I recognize that this is exactly the type of power manoeuvering that Pogge is trying to circumvent with his proposal, the problem is how to get there from here. In any political struggle between the more powerful and the less so (or, if you prefer, the exploiters and the exploited), this is the major hurdle it must surmount. It seems to me that moral consensus is not likely to secure compliance on its own.

Likewise, Pogge's prudential argument rests on shaky foundations. It presupposes that powerful states will see the promotion of democracy as in their long-term interest. Even if we grant this assumption, there is one main problem with it – that a state's long-term interest may conflict with its short-term interest, particularly in economic matters. Given that presidents and prime ministers need to be re-elected, it is not likely that they will support reforms which leave their people as a whole economically worse-off, even in the name of democracy. In fact, the opposite has often been the case – affluent states have been known to prop up dictators for the sake of securing economic benefits.

But these concerns pale in comparison with the final difficulty facing Pogge's proposal – the cooperation problem. Again, he is aware of this particular difficulty and has even gone so far as to give it a name. He calls it 'appealing to the sucker exemption'.[13] Rich states can refuse to unilaterally institute reforms that favour the global poor on the grounds that this would put them at a competitive disadvantage relative to other states, who we can presume are looking out for their own interests and so would take advantage of this situation to the fullest extent. Pogge addresses this problem when he says, '[b]ut if each such society so defended itself by pointing to the others, the reasonable response would surely be to ask them all to work out a multilateral reform that affects all of them equally and thus does not alter their competitive positions, vis-à-vis one another'.[14]

In theory, this sounds good. However, in order for such a reform to work, all or most states would have to institute the GRD at roughly the same time. From a logistical point of view this seems obviously problematic, since democratic governments must be receptive to the changing attitudes of their citizens. Also, making reforms dependent upon cooperation on such a large scale sets up the real possibility of a drawn-out 'waiting game' in which each state waits for others to move towards compliance. This difficulty is made immeasurably worse by the fact that if states forgo regular aid until such time as all states can implement reform, many people will die in the meantime.[15]

Even if this logistical difficulty could be somehow worked out, continued compliance would need to be guaranteed. In order to ensure that no states renege on their obligations, there would have to be some type of global enforcement. Pogge suggests that the EU and/or the US could implement trade sanctions on those less powerful countries that fail to comply. While they may be perfectly *able* to do this, they may be reluctant to take on the role of enforcers, since sanctioned countries may then retaliate by setting up their own trade barriers which would negatively affect their 'sanctioners'. We should not discount the force of the profit motive which lies in the background here.

In addition, if the US and the EU were to be the *de facto* enforcement mechanism for the GRD, then their own compliance with the reform would always be voluntary. In international politics, there is no effective way to 'regulate the regulators', and so the US and the EU would be free to come in and out of compliance as they saw fit. *Knowing* that the US and EU need only comply when it is in their interest, it doesn't seem reasonable for any less powerful state to agree to this type of solution in the first place, because it puts them at risk of incurring sanctions for non-compliance without the assurance that the powerful states will also do their part. This is, of course, one version of a classic problem associated with international cooperation.

Ideal Theory and the Best Outcome

Since they are obviously aware of the many difficulties associated with the institutional view, why do Pogge and Kuper (among others) still cling to it? What makes them want to defend something with so many flaws that must be overcome? Kuper makes his reasons explicit, and I am willing to conjecture that Pogge is similarly motivated. The institutional view is attractive because *if* it could work (and that is a big 'if – '), it would most certainly be the best solution to the problem. Kuper argues against the individual duty view precisely because he thinks it is not the best solution overall. He wants to know what policies are '*the most* beneficial to global development and poverty relief', and claims that 'an articulated philosophy is not going to recommend *sub-optimal* . . . courses of action'.[16]

Kuper specifically likens his view to the structural analysis of Marxism, which, famously, outright rejects piecemeal solutions to impoverishment in favour of the wholesale reorganization of societies. He notes that

[a] theory that does not include a contextual and institutional analysis . . . is condemned to recommending brief symptomatic relief, or even damaging and counterproductive action. This is not a peculiarly Marxist point, and one

does not need to sympathize with Marxists to think that telling the bourgeoisie to be more charitable as individual actors is unlikely to produce deep changes.[17]

No doubt there are multiple alternative structures that would be an improvement on the current rules of international interaction. However, the main issue for me is which options have some practical plausibility – not which one would create the best outcome in theory. I would be willing to settle for a 'sub-optimal' solution if it would improve the current situation of the global poor and was a realistic practical alternative. As such, I prefer to work from the type of institutions we have and ask how they might be improved and made justifiable, rather than focusing on refining my conception of the optimal solution. This difference in approach ultimately comes down to conflicting background views about the relevance of ideal theory for applied ethics and political philosophy.

Kuper argues that an ideal conception of justice is a '*valuable orienteering mechanism for action*' because it allows us to see whether we are moving closer or further away from where we want to be.[18] Additionally, he notes that having such a standard in mind means that we can be pro-active in working towards it. Even when tough choices need to be made along the way, since we know where we are headed, then we will not "unwittingly make sub-optimal choices".[19]

While I agree that ideal theory has a role to play, it is important to see that it is limited in its practical applicability. This is because, as Kai Nielsen points out, ideal theory is interested in which principles or institutions rational people would agree to '*assuming everyone will fully comply*'.[20] Moreover, Nielsen notes that even in ideal theory we must take into account 'what is humanly possible', that is, we must have an adequate conception of human nature and how soci-

eties work, before we can paint even an ideal picture of international justice.[21] Mere logical possibilities cannot do the work here. My point in bringing in the ideal/non-ideal distinction is that non-ideal theory can admit that not everyone will comply with whatever scheme is put in place. It can also admit that even if it is possible for people to comply, they often will not. Taking this fact about human nature into account, non-ideal theory can still ask what we ought to do for the worse-off.

And this seems to me to be the right question to ask, because full compliance with any cooperation scheme in a political arena that lacks effective enforcement is not a genuine possibility. Further, poverty affects peoples' well-being right now, and we do not need a picture of the ideally just world in order to take small steps in the right direction.

To be fair, Pogge argues that it is the very feasibility of the GRD which demonstrates the injustice of the current world order. As such, he is trying to appeal to what is humanly possible. Still, he does not treat the compliance problem as central. Instead, he addresses it after he has worked out his solution, and so in my view, takes up the issues in exactly the wrong order. Another reason to think that Pogge is working from ideal theory is that he does not consider what the implementation of the GRD would look like in the real world. One of the main problems with creating supranational institutions and organizations is that they are too large, and so are susceptible to any number of abuses by people and states behaving 'non-ideally' – that is, acting according to a sense of their interests that does not correspond with the cooperative aims of the group. One problem of this sort might be that it is hard to know in advance if the end users would really pay the GRD tax. The way new taxes affect behaviour is notoriously hard to predict, and no doubt power relations would have an influence at this level as well.

In addition, the size of the central administration required for a scheme such as the GRD is another strike against it. Large bureaucracies invite tyranny and bureaucratic waste. Pogge cannot simply stipulate that its administration should be cheap, effective and transparent. Rather, he needs to tell us how these administrative features of the scheme could be maintained on such a grand scale.

In the spirit of non-ideal theory, Onora O'Neill suggests that we ought to examine the concrete capabilities of various international actors in order to determine 'which obligations of justice they can hold and discharge'.[22] She notes that, 'the value of focusing on capabilities is that this foregrounds an explicit concern with action and the results that agents or agencies can achieve in actual circumstances, and so provides a *seriously realistic starting point for normative reasoning*'.[23] In particular, she directs our attention to the capacities of non-state actors, which she defines as 'institutions that are neither states, nor international in the sense of being either interstatal or intergovernmental, nor directly subordinate to individual states or governments, but that interact across borders with states or state institutions'.[24] NGO aid agencies are among these actors.

According to the definition just presented, we should understand NGOs as part of international civil society, and not as privately run charities that exist outside the political realm. Kuper sees them as distinctly private entities since he says, 'we cooperate and succeed ... through social rules and institutions. Effective poverty relief will thus require above all else extensive cooperation with other agents – indeed, it will require the creation ... of agencies to reduce poverty'.[25] As Singer points out, NGOs such as Oxfam and Doctors Without Borders already do this.[26] What exactly is Kuper suggesting then? He must be suggesting the creation of supranational institutions (like Pogge) because

he thinks NGOs are not genuine political institutions. His problem with NGOs, then, is not that they cannot deliver the goods. Rather, it is that they are not a permanent, systematic, integrated set of agencies that are created by nation-states.

While it might be true that NGOs do not constitute a single coherent system, it is not true that they do not have either a political, or an institutional character. They are large, established, complex organizations that operate according to their own standards as well as the requirements of international law. They negotiate with both donor and recipient governments. They often represent the interests of their beneficiaries in intergovernmental forums. Some (though not all) are internally democratic. Most importantly, they *already have* the capabilities to relieve suffering due to poverty in even the most remote regions of the world. Perhaps many NGOs are not ideally structured, but it still seems gratuitous to create a whole new set of institutions to address poverty when we already have them. Moreover, it might turn out to be a good thing that NGOs are members of civil society, rather than answerable to governments.[27]

NGO Aid Reform: A Third Alternative

It should be apparent by now that I favour reform of NGO-delivered aid over the creation of new supranational institutions. However, I am not thus subscribing to the individual duty view as it is usually understood. This is because I reject the idea that the international aid community is a bunch of private organizations from which it is inappropriate to expect the type of accountability and legitimacy characteristic of political institutions. They are already an established part of the international political scene, and I will argue that certain reforms could address their weaknesses and increase their viability as a vital poverty-reduction mechanism.

My main reason for recommending NGO aid reform is that this type of solution does not suffer from the compliance problems which afflict the institutional view. However, in order for my view to be persuasive, I should also address those concerns that caused Pogge and Kuper to rule out this option in the first place. Let us recall what they were: (1) NGO funding is too capricious, (2) they are not democratically elected or accountable, (3) they are not effective on a large scale and, finally, (4) they create donor fatigue.

I will now sketch out a programme of reform intended to address these problems. My first recommendation is that donations to NGOs should be 'general' rather than directed at specific recipients. This would eliminate much of the control donor countries have over who receives aid. As a result, aid could be more efficiently directed at eradicating poverty than it is now. Indeed, Singer points out that 'three of the biggest donors – the United States, France, and Japan – direct their aid, not to those countries where it will be most effective in fostering growth and reducing poverty, but to countries where aid will further their own strategic or cultural interests'.[28] In fact, many donors already agree to make substantial general donations when they deal with certain NGOs.[29]

General donations would also eliminate the problem of competition among NGOs for funds that are too often directed exclusively at 'popular' recipients, that is, those that are currently in the news. If NGOs had greater leeway to decide where to allocate funds, they would also be better able to cooperate amongst themselves such that more populations in different areas could be helped. Also, if NGOs were to require all donations to be general in form, then they would not have to move money around

according to the whims of donors and so could do more long-range projects.

One might worry that such a requirement would discourage donations, but it does not seem to do so for individuals, most of whom make their donations to a particular agency and not to a particular recipient country. Further, it seems unlikely that governments would simply stop giving to NGOs altogether, if all or most of them were to institute this requirement. After all, NGOs are the organizations that most often implement aid programmes on the ground, and it would be very costly for governments to duplicate this type of expertise for their own purposes. Finally, at least some countries already prefer their money to go to those places where it will be most efficiently used.[30]

My second recommendation would be to require all practising international NGOs to be 'accountable for reasonableness' in the sense that Norman Daniels and James Sabin have outlined.[31] This entails engaging in a process of deliberation in which the reasons for decisions are both available to all stakeholders and rationally defended. A fair and accountable process of this sort must meet several conditions – it must be publicly accessible, allow the possibility of appeals, and be effectively regulated.[32]

The first condition requires that decisions and their rationales be made publicly available. Allocation decisions, and the rationales behind them, would then begin to resemble a kind of 'case law' to which people could turn for precedents and to make objections. Daniels and Sabin argue that this would increase the fairness of decisions both substantively and procedurally – substantively because it encourages people to give justifications that are well thought out, and procedurally because like cases would be treated alike.[33] Both the transparency of public deliberations and their increased fairness would strengthen the legitimacy of international NGOs.

The 'appeals' condition requires that '[t]here must be mechanisms for challenge and dispute resolution . . . and more broadly, opportunities for revision and improvement of policies in the light of new evidence or arguments'.[34] This condition would allow potential recipients of aid, current recipients of aid, governments, and the public to put forward arguments when they disagree with certain decisions. This opportunity would likely bring much needed additional information to the table and so increase aid effectiveness. More importantly, an appeals process would greatly increase NGO accountability, because they would be forced to either justify their practices in light of objections, or change them.

What I have in mind here is *not* that donor interests and concerns would be the focus of the justification and appeals processes. Rather, I am specifically thinking about how to generate greater accountability to recipients. More transparency and public accountability would shed light on a number of key concerns, such as the nature of negotiations or agreements with local authorities, the degree of risk to which recipients are exposed as the result of unintended consequences of aid, and the reasons for changing or discontinuing projects.

Finally, Daniels and Sabin's regulation condition requires that some type of official monitoring take place to ensure that the other conditions are met. Third-party monitoring bodies could be set up, in which democratically elected members would review the practices and decisions of NGOs based in their country at set intervals. The members of these bodies could be a combination of experienced aid practitioners, representatives from developing countries and donor representatives. Decentralized monitoring would allow NGOs to retain most of their flexibility with regard to project design and location, since it would not create too much additional bureaucracy. The purpose of the monitoring would not be to standardize the activities of NGOs everywhere, but rather to increase their transparency, produce greater accountability, and check their effectiveness – recognizing that organizations may have different mandates and methods.

Unlike powerful nation-states, it would be possible to effectively regulate NGOs with relatively small, impartial monitoring bodies. NGOs could be licensed to practise by such entities, and their continued good standing could depend on being successfully reviewed. Indeed, the introduction of a licence would improve aid quality in many respects, since it would weed out those organizations that do not demonstrate sufficient expertise.

These reforms would increase NGO accountability, improve their effectiveness and allow them to cooperate better in order to widen the scope of their action. As for their funding being capricious, most of the larger, more successful NGOs have solved that problem by restricting the amount any particular government can contribute in any given year, and by developing a strong base of private supporters. They also sign contracts with certain governments that extend over a period of several years to lock in their funds. By ensuring that their funding comes from many sources, they have greater control over the planning of their future projects. Moving from general to specific donations would only give them more independence in this regard, and so it seems to me that this objection is not particularly worrisome.

By contrast, the fact that NGOs create donor fatigue and exude 'an aura of dependence' may simply be something we have to live with.[35] Indeed, as we have seen, even a solution such as the GRD depends significantly on the continuing goodwill of powerful states. Certainly citizens might just as easily become 'fatigued' by a tax increase on natural resources as they are by their governments' contributions to foreign aid. Until developing countries are powerful enough to bargain on a more equal footing in the economic realm, they will always be dependent in some way on the goodwill of the stronger states. I cannot see how introducing the GRD would be more effective at rectifying this imbalance than conventional development assistance, since both depend on the goodwill of the stronger party.

These suggested reforms have one final feature to recommend them – they do not suffer from compliance problems. NGOs could institute the internal reforms and opt-in to the review process one at a time. Indeed, once the review systems were set up, the increased legitimacy and credibility participation would confer upon them would act as an incentive for NGOs to participate. Donors, too, could choose to contribute funds to those NGOs that comply with the reforms one at a time. They need not wait to see what other states will do because they would be using the same funds that they typically allocate to foreign aid in any given year.

Conclusion

The reforms just sketched out are not an ideal solution to poverty relief. In fact, they only apply to the roughly 36 per cent of aid that is distributed by NGOs.[36] This means that the remaining bilateral aid would still be plagued by the problems associated with the political interests and hard-bargaining of donor states. However, these reforms would have a considerable impact on the effectiveness and accountability of aid *as it is delivered right now*. Further, these recommendations focus on those international actors that are the least affected by considerations of national interest and profit. This makes them a more realistic alternative than sweeping suggestions of new, state-centred, global institutions. We *can* have a transparent, accountable, effective system of poverty relief, which seems to be the wish of philosophers such as Pogge and Kuper. It might just look different than they thought it would.

Notes

1 Thomas Pogge, *World Poverty and Human Rights* (Oxford: Blackwell Publishing, 2002), p. 201.
2 Pogge, *World Poverty and Human Rights*, p. 206.
3 Pogge, *World Poverty and Human Rights*, p. 206.
4 Andrew Kuper, 'More than Charity: Cosmopolitan Alternatives to the Singer Solution', *Ethics and International Affairs* 16 (2002), pp. 107–20 (p. 114).
5 Pogge. *World Poverty and Human Rights*, p. 212.
6 Pogge, *World Poverty and Human Rights*, p. 207.
7 Pogge, *World Poverty and Human Rights*, p. 207.
8 Pogge, *World Poverty and Human Rights*, p. 211.
9 Pogge, *World Poverty and Human Rights*, p. 213.
10 Thomas Weiss, 'Principles, Politics and Humanitarian Action', *Ethics & International Affairs* 13 (1999), pp. 1–22, p. 11.
11 Weiss, 'Principles, Politics and Humanitarian Action', p. 11.
12 Pogge, *World Poverty and Human Rights*, p. 128.
13 Pogge, *World Poverty and Human Rights*, p. 128.
14 Pogge. *World Poverty and Human Rights*, p. 128.
15 Kuper, 'More than Charity', p. 115.
16 Kuper, 'More than Charity', p. 118, my emphasis.
17 Kuper, 'More than Charity', p. 113.
18 Kuper, 'More than Charity', p. 115.
19 Kuper, 'More than Charity', p. 116.

[20] Kai Nielsen, 'Ideal and Non-Ideal Theory: How Should We Approach Questions of Global Justice?', *International Journal of Applied Philosophy* 2 (1985), pp. 33–41 (p. 35), emphasis added.

[21] Nielsen, 'Ideal and Non-Ideal Theory', p. 36.

[22] Onora O'Neill, 'Agents of Justice', *Metaphilosophy* 32 (2001), pp. 180–95 (pp. 189–90).

[23] O'Neill, 'Agents of Justice', p. 189, original italics.

[24] O'Neill, 'Agents of Justice', p. 191.

[25] Kuper, 'More than Charity', p. 115.

[26] Peter Singer, 'Poverty, Facts, and Political Philosophies', *Ethics and International Affairs* 16 (2002), pp. 121–4 (p. 123).

[27] To clarify, I am mainly thinking of large, international NGOs. I am not referring to agencies that are exclusively concerned with monitoring and reporting, such as Amnesty International, religious groups, or small-scale, local NGOs. So for the purpose of the recommendations I am about to make, I am using the term 'NGO' in this limited sense.

[28] Peter Singer, *One World* (New Haven, CT: Yale University Press, 2002), p. 191.

[29] For instance, Médecins sans Frontières (Doctors without Borders) does not accept 'targeted' donations, but they still receive significant government aid.

[30] Peter Singer notes that the Nordic countries in Europe already do this. See Singer, *One World*, p. 191.

[31] Norman Daniels and James Sabin, *Setting Limits Fairly* (Oxford: Oxford University Press, 2002), p. 44.

[32] Daniels and Sabin, *Setting Limits Fairly*, p. 45.

[33] Daniels and Sabin, *Setting Limits Fairly*, p. 48.

[34] Daniels and Sabin, *Setting Limits Fairly*, p. 45.

[35] Pogge, *World Poverty and Human Rights*, p. 207.

[36] Daniel Little, *The Paradox of Wealth and Poverty* (Cambridge, MA: Westview Press, 2003), p. 177. Here he is citing the World Bank.

Part VIII

Just War

Introduction

It may be paradoxical to consider the subject of a "just war" if we believe that no use of violence can be justified. However, there is a long and venerable tradition of conceiving moral limits to legitimate warfare that continues to develop to the present day. One early statement of just war theory can be found in St. Thomas Aquinas' magnificent work *Summa Theologiae* (see chapter 24). Aquinas presents us with a number of questions (denoted as "*articulus*") followed by several possible objections (or "*obietio*") where Aquinas gives us his own arguments (under "*responsio*") and occasionally supplemented with some additional arguments (or "*ad*"). Certainly the form that Aquinas adopts to make his arguments will be unfamiliar to most contemporary students of political philosophy. However, the arguments he offers us are perhaps the most influential on the topic and well worth careful study.

Aquinas tells us that three things are necessary for a just war: (a) a just government, (b) a just cause, and (c) a just intent. A government cannot wage a just war if it is illegitimate. Legitimate governments can only wage just war with a just cause and just intent. In other words, the offending state must have performed some act of wrongdoing. Moreover, a state must not only be legitimate and wage war for a just cause, but it must have a just intent. Our intent must only be to spread good or help avert evil. We cannot wage just war if we lack righteous intentions even if the state we want to attack deserves punishment for its actions. These ideas have remained highly influential, particularly Aquinas' distinction between *jus ad bellum* (the justifiability of the war) and *jus in bello* (the justifiability of the way war is waged). The remainder of this reading considers various questions regarding sedition and treason, as well as the right to execute persons innocent or deserving, with clear implications for questions of just war and the study of terrorism.

Chapter 25 contains an excerpt from John Stuart Mill's fine essay "A Few Words on Non-Intervention." Mill agrees in part with Aquinas: wars should only *normally* be defensive, not aggressive. A state can fight an aggressive, not defensive, war on occasion. While he seems favorable to the view that civilized states almost inevitably find themselves in the position of conquering "barbarian" states, it seems clear that freedom for the population of a state is something that they must struggle for, rather than something a just, but foreign, power offers them: "No people ever was and remained free, but because it was determined to be so . . . for, unless the spirit of liberty is strong in a people, those who have the executive in their hands easily work any institutions to the purposes of despotism." Thus, all states should adopt the policy of non-intervention.

In the next reading I have included Chapter VII ("Action with Respect to Threats to the Peace, Breaches of the Peace, and Acts of Aggression") of the United Nations' *Charter*. We find that power is placed entirely in the United Nation's Security Council. The Security Council is empowered to decide whether or not the United Nations should maintain peace and security in trouble spots or authorize the use of force. It is worth noting both the wide discretionary powers of the Security Council, as well as the fact that it is possible for a state to engage in legitimate war without gaining the prior acceptance of the Security Council without contravening the *Charter*. One example is the right of all states to defend themselves against foreign aggression. It is worth noting the explicit language: "the inherent right of individual or collective self-defence if an *armed attack occurs* against a Member of the United Nations" (emphasis added). Some argue this is just right, while others claim it is too limited.

Next, in his classic essay "War and Massacre," Thomas Nagel examines the means and ends of warfare. He argues that there should be clear "absolutist" (e.g., deontological) principles that guide the conduct of a war, such as a prohibition on killing innocent civilians (noncombatants). If we do not hold firm to this conviction, then we risk opening a Pandora's box to possible gross injustices, such as bombing civilian cities in order to gain an advantage in military strategy. Targeting civilians in combat is something that should never be done. For Nagel, this fact is intuitive because we do not believe that such an action is capable of justification. It is not a question of ends justifying the means, but rather that some means are wholly illegitimate and wrong no matter the ends.

In chapter 28, Michael Walzer examines an important issue in thinking about just war. One view of just war holds that states have a right to self-defense and engage in war against an aggressive enemy. A second view holds that states may have the right to enter preventative war: we can attack another country in order to prevent unlawful aggression between states. Walzer examines a position in between the two. Can we justify waging war if we anticipate an aggressive act which has not yet happened? Indeed, this is an issue that was discussed by the United States government over Iraq: if we can anticipate that Iraq would become an aggressive, terrorist country that might threaten the United States and its interests if left alone, then why should we wait for Iraq to fire first before taking action? An analogy is that we would be foolish to wait for a sniper to fire his rifle at us if we can already see him point his rifle at us and know he intends to cause us harm. Walzer considers a variety of different perspectives, introducing new concepts such as the necessity of "just fear" of attack rather than simply being fearful of an attack. We can have a "just fear" and be morally justified to wage a pre-emptive strike so long as the threat is sufficiently established: the state to be attacked must be like a sniper actively preparing to harm us and simply waiting for the most opportune moment to strike.

Part VIII concludes with a reading by Jeff McMahan, "Just Cause for War" (chapter 29). McMahan argues that a just war is only possible if the war has a just cause. In other words, we fail to fight a just war if our cause is unjust, even if the conduct of our military campaign is otherwise morally justified. Moreover, a just cause for war may take forms that differ from traditional war theories, such as the prevention of future aggression.

The justification of war carries with it tremendous importance. No matter how just our cause or noble our conduct, many innocent people will inevitably be killed. These high moral stakes reinforce the necessity of sharpening our thinking about just war. It is hoped that the following chapters will provide just this.

Chapter 24

War, Sedition and Killing
St. Thomas Aquinas

(a) Summa Theologiae
IIaIIae 40: On War

. . .

Articulus 1: Whether It Is Always a Sin to Wage War

It seems that it is always a sin to wage war.

obiectio 1: For punishment is not inflicted for anything except sin. But those who wage war are threatened by the Lord with punishment, according to Matthew 26:52: "All that take the sword shall perish by the sword." Therefore all war is unlawful.

obiectio 2: Moreover, whatever is contrary to a Divine precept is a sin. But to wage war is contrary to a Divine precept, for it is said at Matthew 5:39: "But I say unto you, That ye resist not evil", and at Romans 12:19: "Dearly beloved, avenge not yourselves, but rather give place unto wrath." Therefore to wage war is always a sin.

* From St. Thomas Aquinas, *Political Writings*, ed. R. W. Dyson (Cambridge: Cambridge University Press, 2002), pp. 239–42, 247–8, 251–6, 261–6.

obiectio 3: Moreover, nothing is contrary to an act of virtue except sin. But war is contrary to peace. Therefore war is always a sin.

obiectio 4: Moreover, every kind of legitimate contest is lawful, as is clear in the case of contests of reason. But the martial contests which take place in tournaments are prohibited by the Church, for those who die in such events are deprived of ecclesiastical burial. Therefore it seems that war is a sin absolutely.

[. . .]

responsio: If a war is to be just, three things are required. First, the authority of the prince by whose command war is to be waged. For it does not pertain to a private person to declare war, because he can prosecute his rights at the tribunal of his superior; similarly, it does not pertain to a private person to summon the people together, which must be done in time of war. Rather, since the care of the commonwealth is entrusted to princes, it pertains to them to protect the commonwealth of the city or kingdom or province subject to them. And just as it is lawful for them to use the material sword in defence of the commonwealth against those who trouble it from within, when they punish evildoers, according to the Apostle (Romans 13:4), "He beareth not the sword in vain: for he is the minister of God, a revenger to execute wrath upon him that doeth evil": so too, it pertains to them to use the sword of war to protect the commonwealth against enemies from without. Hence it is said to princes at Psalm 82:4: "Deliver the poor and needy: rid them out of the hand of the wicked." Hence also Augustine says: "The natural order accommodated to the peace of mortal men requires that the authority to declare and counsel war should be vested in princes."

Second, a just cause is required: that is, those against whom war is to be waged must deserve to have war waged against them because of some wrongdoing. Hence Augustine says in the book *Quaestiones in heptateuchum*: "A just war is customarily defined as one which avenges injuries, as when a nation or state deserves to be punished because it has neglected either to put right the wrongs done by its people or to restore what it has unjustly seized."

Third, it is required that those who wage war should have a righteous intent: that is, they should intend either to promote a good cause or avert an evil. Hence Augustine says: "Among true worshippers of God, those wars which are waged not out of greed or cruelty, but with the object of securing peace by coercing the wicked and helping the good, are regarded as peaceful." For it can happen that even if war is declared by a legitimate authority and for a just cause, that war may be rendered unlawful by a wicked intent. For Augustine says in the book *Contra Faustum*: "The desire to do harm, the cruelty of vengeance, an unpeaceable and implacable spirit, the fever of rebellion, the lust to dominate, and similar things: these are rightly condemned in war."

ad 1: As Augustine says: "He 'takes the sword' who arms himself to shed another's blood without the command or permission of a superior or lawful power." But one who, as a private person, makes use of the sword by the authority of the prince or judge, or, as a public person, through zeal for justice, as if by the authority of God, does not "take the sword", but uses it as one commissioned by another, and so does not deserve to suffer punishment. Even those who use the sword sinfully are not always slain by the sword; yet they always "perish" by their own sword nonetheless, for, unless they repent, they are punished eternally for their sinful use of the sword.

ad 2: As Augustine says, one should always be prepared in spirit to observe precepts of this kind: that is, a man should always be prepared not to resist or not to defend himself if need be. But it is sometimes necessary to act otherwise than this for the common good: even, indeed, for the good of those against whom one is fighting. Hence Augustine says:

> Many things must be done which are against the wishes of those whom we have to punish with, as it were, a kindly severity. When we take away from someone the freedom to do wrong, it is beneficial for him that he should be vanquished, for nothing is more unfortunate than the happiness of sinners, when impunity nourishes guilt and an evil will arises like an enemy within.

ad 3: Those who wage just wars intend to secure peace, and so they are not opposed to any peace except that evil peace which the Lord "came not to send" upon the earth (Matthew 10:34). Hence Augustine says: "We do not seek peace in order to wage war; rather, we wage war in order to achieve peace. Be peaceful, therefore, in making war, so that, in vanquishing those against whom you fight, you may lead them to the benefit of peace."

ad 4: Men are certainly not forbidden to engage in every kind of exercise involving feats of arms, but only in those exercises which are disorderly and perilous and which lead to slaying and looting. Among the people of antiquity warlike contests were held without such perils, and so were called "armed practice" or "wars without blood," as Jerome states in one of his letters.

[. . .]

(b) *Summa Theologiae* IIaIIae 42: On Sedition

We come next to sedition, and here there are two things to consider:

1 Whether it is a specific sin
2 Whether it is a mortal sin

Articulus 1: Whether Sedition is a specific sin Distinct from others

It seems that sedition is not a specific sin distinct from others.

obiectio 1: For, as Isidore says in the book *Etymologies,* "a seditious man is one who causes dissent among minds, and begets discord." But one who causes a sin to be committed does not himself sin by any other kind of sin than that which he caused to be committed. Therefore it seems that sedition is not a specific sin distinct from discord.

obiectio 2: Moreover, sedition implies a kind of division. But "schism" takes its name from *scissura* ["separation"], as stated above. Therefore it seems that the sin of sedition is not distinct from the sin of schism.

obiectio 3: Moreover, every specific sin which is distinct from others is either a capital vice or arises from some capital vice. But sedition is reckoned neither among the capital vices nor among those vices which arise from them, as appears from *Moralia* 31, where the vices of both kinds are enumerated. Therefore sedition is not a specific sin distinct from others.

responsio: Sedition is a specific kind of sin, resembling war and strife in certain ways but differing from them in others. It resembles them in so far as it implies a kind of opposition. But it differs from them in two respects. First, because war and strife signify actual fighting with one another, whereas sedition can be said to involve either actual fighting or preparation for such fighting. Hence the [interlinear] gloss on 2 Corinthians 12:20 says that seditions are "tumults leading to conflict": because, that is, certain persons are preparing and intending to fight. Second, they differ in that, properly speaking, war is carried on against external enemies, being as it were between one community and another, whereas strife occurs between one individual and another, or between a few people on one side and few on the other, while sedition, properly so called, arises as between parts of a single community who dissent from one another, as when one part of the city rises in tumult against another. And so, since sedition is opposed to a special kind of good, namely the unity and peace of a community, it is therefore a special kind of sin.

[. . .]

(c) *Summa Theologiae* IIaIIae 64: On Homicide

[. . .]

Articulus 1: Whether It Is Unlawful to Kill Any Living Thing

It seems that it is unlawful to kill any living thing.

obiectio 1: For the Apostle says (Romans 13:2) that those who resist the ordinance of God receive to themselves damnation. But, according to Psalm 147:8f, by the ordinance of Divine providence, "Who maketh grass to grow upon the mountains; Who giveth to beasts their food," all living things should be preserved. Therefore it seems unlawful to kill any living thing.

obiectio 2: Moreover, homicide is a sin because it deprives a man of life. But life is common to all animals and plants. Therefore for the same reason it seems to be a sin to slay brute beasts and plants.

obiectio 3: Moreover, a specific punishment is not appointed in the Divine law for anything except sin. But a punishment is appointed in the Divine law for one who kills another's ox or sheep, as is shown at Exodus 22:1. Therefore the killing of brute beasts is a sin.

sed contra: Augustine says at *De civitate Dei* 1: "When we hear it said, 'Thou shalt not kill', we do not take this as applying to trees, for they have no sensation, nor to non-rational animals, because they have no fellowship with us. The conclusion remains, therefore, that we are to take 'Thou shalt not kill' as applying to man."

responsio: There is no sin in using something for its proper purpose. Now in the natural order of things, imperfect things exist for the sake of perfect, just as, in the process of generation, nature proceeds from the imperfect to the perfect. Hence, just as in the generation of man there was first a living thing, then an animal, and finally a man, so too

such things as plants, which merely have life, all exist for the sake of animals, and all animals exist for the sake of man. And so it is not unlawful if man makes use of plants for the benefit of animals, and animals for the benefit of men, as the Philosopher shows at *Politics* 1. But among the possible uses, the most necessary seems to be that animals use plants, and men animals, as food; and this cannot be done without killing them. And so it is lawful both to kill plants for the use of animals, and animals for the use of men; and this, indeed, is by Divine ordinance, for it is said at Genesis 1:29f: "Behold I have given you every herb and all trees to be your meat, and to all beasts of the earth." Again, it is said at Genesis 9:3: "Everything that moveth and liveth shall be meat for you."

ad 1: The life of animals and plants is preserved by Divine ordinance not for their own sake, but for man's. Hence, as Augustine says at *De civitate Dei* 1, "by the most just ordinance of their Creator, both their life and death are subject to our needs."

ad 2: Brute beasts and plants do not have a life governed by reason so that they can set themselves to work. Rather, they are always set to work at the behest, as it were, of another, by a certain impulse of nature. And this is a sign that they are naturally enslaved and accommodated to the uses of others.

ad 3: He who kills another's ox sins not with regard to the killing of the ox, but because he has injured a man with respect to his property. Hence this is not contained under the sin of homicide but under the sin of theft or robbery.

Articulus 2: Whether It Is Lawful to Kill Sinners

It seems that it is not lawful to kill men who have sinned.

obiectio 1: For in a parable (Matthew 13:29f) the Lord forbade the uprooting of the tares which in the same place (vs. 38) are said to be "the children of the wicked one." But everything forbidden by God is a sin. Therefore it is a sin to kill a sinner.

obiectio 2: Moreover, human justice takes its form from Divine justice. But according to Divine justice sinners are reserved for repentance, according to Ezekiel 18:23 and 33:11, "I desire not the death of the sinner, but that the wicked turn from his way and live." Therefore it seems altogether unjust for sinners to be killed.

obiectio 3: Moreover, as Augustine shows in the book *Contra mendacium* and the Philosopher at *Ethics* II, that which is evil in itself should not be done even for the sake of a good end. But to kill a man is evil in itself, for we must have charity towards all men, and "we wish our friends to live and to exist," as is said at *Ethics* IX. Therefore it is in no way lawful to kill a man who has sinned.

sed contra: It is said at Exodus 22:18, "Thou shalt not suffer a witch to live," and at Psalm 101:8: "I will early destroy all the wicked of the land."

responsio: As stated above, it is lawful to kill brute beasts insofar as they are naturally ordained to man's use as imperfect is ordained to perfect. Now every part is directed to the whole as imperfect to perfect; and so every part naturally exists for the sake of the whole. For this reason we see that if the health of the whole body requires the removal of some member, perhaps because it is diseased or causing the corruption of other members, it will be both praiseworthy and wholesome for it to be cut away. Now every individual person stands in relation to the whole community as part to whole. And so if some man is dangerous to the community, causing its corruption because of some sin, it is praiseworthy and wholesome that he be slain in order to preserve the common good; for "a little leaven corrupteth the whole lump" (1 Corinthians 5:6).

ad 1: The Lord commanded them to abstain from uprooting the tares in order to spare the wheat, that is, the good. This commandment applies when the wicked cannot be slain without at the same time also slaying the good, either because the wicked lie hidden among the good, or because the wicked have so many followers that they cannot be killed without endangering the good, as Augustine says. Hence the Lord teaches that it is better that the wicked be suffered to live and vengeance reserved to the Final Judgment than that the good be slain together with the wicked. When, however, the good incur no peril, but rather are protected and saved by the slaying of the wicked, then the latter may lawfully be slain.

ad 2: According to the order of His wisdom, God sometimes slays sinners at once, in order to deliver the good, and sometimes grants them time for repentance, according as He knows what is expedient for His elect. And this also human justice imitates as far as it can; for it slays those who are dangerous to others, while it reserves for repentance those who sin without grievously harming others.

ad 3: By sinning, man withdraws himself from the order of reason, and in so doing falls away from the dignity of his humanity, by which he is naturally free and exists for himself, and descends instead towards the slavish condition of the beasts: becoming liable, that is, to be disposed of in whatever way is useful to others, according to Psalm 49:20: "Man, when he was in honour, did not understand; he hath been compared to senseless beasts, and made like to them"; and it is said at Proverbs 11:29: "The fool shall serve the wise." And so although it is evil in itself to slay a man while he remains in his dignity, it can nonetheless be good to slay a man who is a sinner, just as it can be to slay a beast. For a wicked man is worse than a beast, and does more harm, as the Philosopher says at *Politics* I and *Ethics* VII.

Articulus 3: Whether It Is Lawful for a Private Person to Kill a Man Who Has Sinned

It seems that it is lawful for a private person to kill a man who has sinned.

obiectio 1: For nothing unlawful is commanded in the Divine law. But at Exodus 32:27 Moses commanded: "Let every man kill his brother, and friend, and neighbour" because of the sin of the molten calf. Therefore it is lawful for even private persons to kill a sinner.

obiectio 2: Moreover, as stated above, man, on account of sin, "hath been compared" to the beasts. But it is lawful for any private person to kill a wild beast, especially a harmful one. Therefore he may for the same reason kill a man who has sinned.

obiectio 3: Moreover, a man, even if he is private person, is worthy of praise if he does something beneficial to the common good. But the slaying of malefactors is beneficial to the common good, as stated above. Therefore it is praiseworthy for even private persons to kill malefactors.

sed contra: Augustine says: "A man who, without exercising any public office, kills a malefactor, shall be lodged guilty of homicide, and all the more so since he has not feared to usurp a power which God has not granted him."

responsio: As stated above, it is lawful to kill a malefactor insofar as doing so is directed to the health of the whole community; but so to do pertains only to him to whom the task of preserving the community's health has been entrusted, just as it pertains to the physician to cut off a decayed member when he has been entrusted with the care of the health of the whole body. Now the care of the common good is entrusted to princes having public authority; and so they alone, and not private individuals, can lawfully kill malefactors.

ad 1: As Dionysius shows at *De caelesti hierarchia* XIII, responsibility for an act belongs to the person by whose authority the act is done. And so, as Augustine says at *De civitate Dei* 1, "He does not slay who is the servant of one who commands him, just as the sword is only the instrument of him who wields it." Hence those who slew their neighbours and friends at the Lord's command seem not to have done this themselves, but by His authority, just as the soldier slays the enemy by the authority of the prince and the executioner the robber by that of the judge.

ad 2: A beast is distinct by nature from man. Hence no one needs to be authorised to kill a wild beast, whereas such authorisation is necessary in the case of domestic animals: although not for their sake, but only by reason of the owner's loss. But a man who is a sinner is not distinct by nature from righteous men; and so public authorisation is needed if he is to be condemned to death for the common good.

ad 3: It is lawful for any private person to do something for the common benefit provided that no harm is thereby done to anyone; but if anyone is harmed, this cannot be done except by the judgment of him to whom it pertains to decide what is to be taken away from the parts in order to secure the welfare of the whole.

[. . .]

Articulus 6: Whether It Is Lawful to Kill the Innocent

It seems that it is in some cases lawful to kill the innocent.

obiectio 1: For the fear of God is never shown through a sinful act; rather, "The fear of the Lord driveth out sin," as is said at Ecclesiasticus 1:27. But Abraham was commended for his fear of the Lord because he was willing to slay his innocent son. Therefore one can without sin slay the innocent.

obiectio 2: Moreover, among those sins which are committed against one's neighbour, the greater sins seem to be those which do the greater harm to the one sinned against. Now to be slain does greater harm to a sinner than to one who is innocent, since by death the latter passes immediately from the misery of this life to the glory of heaven. Since, therefore, it is in certain cases lawful to slay a sinner, so much more is it lawful to slay one who is innocent or righteous.

obiectio 3: Moreover, that which is done according to the order of justice is not a sin. But sometimes one is compelled to slay an innocent man according to the order of justice: for example, when a judge, who has to judge according to the evidence, condemns to death someone whom he knows to be innocent but who has been traduced by false witnesses; and, similarly, the executioner who in obedience to the judge slays the man who has been unjustly sentenced.

sed contra: It is said at Exodus 23:7: "The innocent and righteous thou shalt not slay."

responsia: A man can be considered in two ways. In one way, in himself, in another way, in relation to something else. If a man be considered in himself, it is unlawful to kill anyone, since in everyone, even the sinner, we ought to love the nature which God has made, and which is destroyed by slaying him. On the other hand, as stated above, the slaying of a sinner becomes lawful in relation to the common good, which is corrupted by sin, whereas the common good is conserved and promoted by the life of righteous men, for they are the foremost part of the community. Therefore it is in no way lawful to slay the innocent.

ad 1: God has lordship over death and life, for it is by His ordinance that both the sinful and the righteous die. And so he who slays the innocent at God's command does not sin, any more than God does, at Whose behest he acts: indeed, his fear of God is shown by his willing obedience to His commands.

ad 2: In weighing the gravity of a sin, consideration must be given to what is essential rather than accidental. Hence one who slays a righteous man sins more grievously than one who slays a sinner: first, because he injures one whom he ought to love more, and so acts more against charity; second, because he inflicts an injury on someone who is less deserving of one, and so acts more against justice; third, because he deprives the community of a greater good; fourth, because he despises God more, according to Luke 10:16, "He that despiseth you despiseth Me." But it is accidental to the slaying that the righteous man who is slain is received by God into glory.

ad 3: If the judge knows that someone has been convicted by false witnesses and is innocent, he must examine the witnesses more carefully, so that he may find occasion for letting the blameless man go free, as Daniel did (Daniel 13:51). If he cannot do this, he should remit him for judgment to a higher court. If he cannot do this either, he does not sin if he pronounces sentence according to the evidence; for it is not he who kills the innocent man, but they who asserted his guilt. Again, if the sentence contains an intolerable error, the executioner who is to carry out the sentence of the judge who has condemned an innocent man should not obey him; otherwise the torturers who slew the martyrs would be excused. If, however, the sentence does not contain a manifest injustice, he does not sin if he carries out the judge's command, for has no right to scrutinise the judgment of his superior; nor is it he who slays the innocent man, but the judge at whose behest he acts.

Articulus 7: Whether It Is Lawful to Kill Someone in Self-Defence

It seems that it is not lawful to kill someone in self-defence.

obiectio 1: For Augustine says to Publicola: I do not like the advice that one may kill someone in order to avoid being killed by him: unless, however, one is a soldier carrying out a public function, in which case one acts not for oneself but for others, with power to do whatever is consistent with one's duty. But he who kills someone in self-defence kills him to avoid being killed by him. Therefore this would seem to be unlawful.

obiectio 2: Moreover, at *De libero arbitrio* 1 he says: "How are they free from sin in the sight of Divine providence, who are polluted by human slaughter for the sake of things which ought to be despised?" And, as is shown by what occurs earlier in the same passage, among the "things which ought to be despised" are "those things which men

may lose against their will," one of which is the life of the body. Therefore it is not lawful for anyone to take another's life in order to preserve the life of his own body.

obiectio 3: Further, Pope Nicholas says, and this is noted in the *Decretum*:

> Concerning the clerics about whom you have consulted us, namely, those who have killed a pagan in self-defence, as to whether they may after penance return to their former state or rise to a higher one: know that it is in no case lawful for them to kill any man in any circumstances whatsoever, nor can anyone give them licence to do so.

But clerics and laymen alike are bound to observe moral precepts. Therefore nor is it lawful for laymen to kill anyone in self-defence.

obiectio 4: Moreover, homicide is a more grievous sin than simple fornication or adultery. But no one may lawfully commit simple fornication or adultery or any other mortal sin whatsoever to save his own life; for the life of the spirit is to be preferred to that of the body. Therefore no one may lawfully take another's life in self-defence in order to preserve his own life.

obiectio 5: Moreover, if the tree is evil, so will the fruit be also, as is said at Matthew 7:17. But self-defence itself seems to be unlawful, according to Romans 12:19: "Dearly beloved, avenge not yourselves." Therefore the slaying of a man which proceeds from it is unlawful also.

sed contra: It is said at Exodus 22:2: "If a thief be found breaking into an house and be smitten that he die, he that struck him shall not be guilty of blood." But it is much more lawful to defend one's life than one's house. No one, therefore, is guilty if he slays a man in defence of his own life.

responsio: Nothing prevents a single act from having two effects, only one of which is intended while the other is beside the intention. Now moral acts take their species from what is intended, not from what is beside the intention, since this is accidental, as explained above. Accordingly, an act of self-defence may have two effects, one of which is the saving of one's own life while the other is the slaying of an attacker. If one's intention is to save one's own life, the act is not unlawful, because it is natural for everything to keep itself in being as far as possible. Yet an act may be rendered unlawful even though proceeding from a good intention if it is out of proportion to the end. Hence if a man uses more violence in self-defence than is necessary, this will be unlawful, whereas if he repels force with force in moderation, his defence will be lawful because, according to the laws, "it is lawful to repel force by force, provided that one does not exceed the limits of blameless defence." Nor is it necessary to salvation that a man refrain from an act of moderate self-defence in order to avoid killing another man, since one is bound to take more care of one's own life than of another's. But since it is unlawful for anyone to take a man's life except a public authority acting for the common good, as stated above, it is not lawful for one man to intend to kill another in self-defence, except in the case of those who have pubic authority, who, though intending to kill a man in self-defence, refer this to the public good: for instance, a soldier fighting against the enemy and a minister of the judge fighting with robbers; although even these sin if they are motivated by private animosity.

ad 1: The authority of Augustine is to be understood here as referring to a case where one man intends to kill another in order to save himself from death. The passage from *De libero arbitrio* [quoted in the second *obiectio*] is to be understood in the same sense.

It is precisely to indicate this kind of intention that he says, "for the sake of things [which ought to be despised]." By this the reply to the second *obiectio* is also shown.

ad 2: Irregularity is a consequence of the act, even though sinless, of taking a man's life, as appears in the case of a judge who justly condemns a man to death. For this reason a cleric, if he brings about the death of someone in self-defence, is irregular, even if he intended not to kill him, but only to defend himself.

ad 3: The act of fornication or adultery is not necessarily directed to the preservation of one's own life, as is the act which sometimes results in the taking of someone's life.

ad 4: The defence forbidden in this passage is that which is accompanied by vengeful spite. Hence a gloss says: "Avenge not yourselves – that is, do not strike your enemies back."

Articulus 8: Where One Incurs the Guilt of Homicide through Slaying a Man by Chance

It seems that one does incur the guilt of homicide through slaying a man by chance.

obiectio 1: For we read that Lamech slew a man believing himself to be slaying a wild beast, and that he was reputed guilty of homicide. One who slays man by chance therefore incurs the guilt of homicide.

obiectio 2: Moreover, it is said at Exodus 21:22f that: "If one strike a woman with child, and she miscarry indeed, if her death ensue thereupon, he shall render life for life." But this can be done without any intention of killing her. Therefore one is guilty of homicide through killing someone by chance.

obiectio 3: Moreover, in the *Decretum* there are several canons which prescribe punishments for unintentional homicide. But punishment is not due to anything except guilt. Therefore he who slays a man by chance incurs the guilt of homicide.

sed contra: Augustine says to Publicola: "God forbid that guilt should be imputed to us if, when we do something for a good and lawful purpose, we cause harm to anyone without intending to." But it sometimes happens that someone is killed by chance as a consequence of something done for a good purpose. Therefore guilt is not to be imputed to the person who did it.

responsio: According to the Philosopher at *Physics* ii, "chance is a cause which acts beyond anyone's intention." Strictly speaking, therefore, things which happen by chance are neither intended nor voluntary. And since every sin is voluntary, according to Augustine, it follows that chance occurrences, as such, are not sins. It does happen, however, that something which is not voluntary and intended actually and of itself is voluntary and intended accidentally, inasmuch as he who removes an obstacle to something happening is an accidental cause of it. Hence he who does not remove something from which homicide results will,

if he ought to have removed it, be in that sense guilty of voluntary homicide. This happens in two ways. In one way, when someone brings about another's death by occupying himself with unlawful things which he ought to avoid; in another way, when he does not take proper care. And so, according to the laws, if anyone does what he may lawfully do and takes due care, yet someone loses his life as a result, he does not incur the guilt of homicide; whereas if he is occupied with some unlawful pursuit, or even if he is occupied with something lawful but without due care, he does not escape the guilt of homicide if a man's death follows as a result of what he does.

ad 1: Lamech did not take sufficient care to avoid taking a man's life, and so he did not escape the guilt of homicide.

ad 2: One who strikes a woman with child does an unlawful act. And so if the death either of the woman or of her unborn child results, he will not avoid the crime of homicide, especially since death may so easily result from such a blow.

ad 3: According to the canons, a penalty is imposed upon those who cause death unintentionally through doing something unlawful or not taking due care.

Chapter 25

A Few Words on Non-Intervention*
John Stuart Mill

[. . .]

There seems to be no little need that the whole doctrine of non-interference with foreign nations should be reconsidered, if it can be said to have as yet been considered as a really moral question at all. We have heard something lately about being willing to go to war for an idea. To go to war for an idea, if the war is aggressive, not defensive, is as criminal as to go to war for territory or revenue; for it is as little justifiable to force our ideas on other people, as to compel them to submit to our will in any other respect. But there assuredly are cases in which it is allowable to go to war, without having been ourselves attacked, or threatened with attack; and it is very important that nations should make up their minds in time, as to what these cases are. There are few questions which more require to be taken in hand by ethical and political philosophers, with a view to establish some rule or criterion whereby the justifiableness of intervening in the affairs of other countries, and (what is sometimes fully as questionable) the justifi-

* From *The Collected Works of John Stuart Mill*, ed. John M. Robson (Toronto: University of Toronto Press, 1984), vol. XXI, pp. 118–24.

ableness of refraining from intervention, may be brought to a definite and rational test. Whoever attempts this, will be led to recognise more than one fundamental distinction, not yet by any means familiar to the public mind, and in general quite lost sight of by those who write in strains of indignant morality on the subject. There is a great difference (for example) between the case in which the nations concerned are of the same, or something like the same, degree of civilization, and that in which one of the parties to the situation is of a high, and the other of a very low, grade of social improvement. To suppose that the same international customs, and the same rules of international morality, can obtain between one civilized nation and another, and between civilized nations and barbarians, is a grave error, and one which no statesman can fall into, however it may be with those who, from a safe and unresponsible position, criticise statesmen. Among many reasons why the same rules cannot be applicable to situations so different, the two following are among the most important. In the first place, the rules of ordinary international morality imply reciprocity. But barbarians will not reciprocate. They cannot be depended on for observing any rules. Their minds are not capable of so great an effort, nor their will sufficiently under the influence of distant motives. In the next place, nations which are still barbarous have not got beyond the period during which it is likely to be for their benefit that they should be conquered and held in subjection by foreigners. Independence and nationality, so essential to the due growth and development of a people further advanced in improvement, are generally impediments to theirs. The sacred duties which civilized nations owe to the independence and nationality of each other, are not binding towards those to whom nationality and independence are either a certain evil, or at best a questionable good. The Romans were not the most clean-handed of conquerors, yet would it have been better for Gaul and Spain, Numidia and Dacia, never to have formed part of the Roman Empire? To characterize any conduct whatever towards a barbarous people as a violation of the law of nations, only shows that he who so speaks has never considered the subject. A violation of great principles of morality it may easily be; but barbarians have no rights as a *nation*, except a right to such treatment as may, at the earliest possible period, fit them for becoming one. The only moral laws for the relation between a civilized and a barbarous government are the universal rules of morality between man and man.

The criticisms, therefore, which are so often made upon the conduct of the French in Algeria, or of the English in India, proceed, it would seem, mostly on a wrong principle. The true standard by which to judge their proceedings never having been laid down, they escape such comment and censure as might really have an improving effect, while they are tried by a standard which can have no influence on those practically engaged in such transactions, knowing as they do that it cannot, and if it could, ought not to be observed, because no human being would be the better, and many much the worse, for its

observance. A civilized government cannot help having barbarous neighbours: when it has, it cannot always content itself with a defensive position, one of mere resistance to aggression. After a longer or shorter interval of forbearance, it either finds itself obliged to conquer them, or to assert so much authority over them, and so break their spirit, that they gradually sink into a state of dependence upon itself: and when that time arrives, they are indeed no longer formidable to it, but it has had so much to do with setting up and pulling down their governments, and they have grown so accustomed to lean on it, that it has become morally responsible for all evil it allows them to do. This is the history of the relations of the British Government with the native States of India. It never was secure in its own Indian possessions until it had reduced the military power of those States to a nullity. But a despotic government only exists by its military power. When we had taken away theirs, we were forced, by the necessity of the case, to offer them ours instead of it. To enable them to dispense with large armies of their own, we bound ourselves to place at their disposal, and they bound themselves to receive, such an amount of military force as made us in fact masters of the country. We engaged that this force should fulfil the purposes of a force, by defending the prince against all foreign and internal enemies. But being thus assured of the protection of a civilized power, and freed from the fear of internal rebellion or foreign conquest, the only checks which either restrain the passions or keep any vigour in the character of an Asiatic despot, the native Governments either became so oppressive and extortionate as to desolate the country, or fell into such a state of nerveless imbecility, that every one, subject to their will, who had not the means of defending himself by his own armed followers, was the prey of anybody who had a band of ruffians in his pay. The British Government felt this deplorable state of things to be its own work; being the direct consequence of the position in which, for its own security, it had placed itself towards the native governments. Had it permitted this to go on indefinitely, it would have deserved to be accounted among the worst political malefactors. In some cases (unhappily not in all) it had endeavoured to take precaution against these mischiefs by a special article in the treaty, binding the prince to reform his administration, and in future to govern in conformity to the advice of the British Government. Among the treaties in which a provision of this sort had been inserted, was that with Oude. For fifty years and more did the British Government allow this engagement to be treated with entire disregard; not without frequent remonstrances, and occasionally threats, but without ever carrying into effect what it threatened. During this period of half a century, England was morally accountable for a mixture of tyranny and anarchy, the picture of which, by men who knew it well, is appalling to all who read it. The act by which the Government of British India at last set aside treaties which had been so pertinaciously violated, and assumed the power of fulfilling the obligation it had so long before incurred, of giving to the people of Oude a tolerable government, far from being the political crime it is so often ignorantly called, was a criminally tardy discharge of an imperative duty. And the fact, that nothing which had been done in all this century by the East India Company's Government made it so unpopular in England, is one of the most striking instances of what was noticed in a former part of this article – the predisposition of English public opinion to look unfavourably upon every act by which territory or "revenue" are acquired from foreign States, and to take part with any government, however unworthy, which can make out the merest semblance of a case of injustice against our own country.

But among civilized peoples, members of an equal community of nations, like Christian Europe, the question assumes another aspect, and must be decided on totally different principles. It would be an affront to the reader to discuss the immorality of wars of conquest, or of conquest even as the consequence of lawful war; the annexation of any civilized people to the dominion of another, unless by their own spontaneous election. Up to this point, there is no difference of opinion among honest people; nor on the wickedness of commencing an aggressive war for any interest of our own, except when necessary to avert from ourselves an obviously impending wrong. The disputed question is that of interfering in the regulation of another country's internal concerns; the question whether a nation is justified in taking part, on either side, in the civil wars or party contests of another; and chiefly, whether it may justifiably aid the people of another country in struggling for liberty; or may impose on a country any particular government or institutions, either as being best for the country itself, or as necessary for the security of its neighbours.

Of these cases, that of a people in arms for liberty is the only one of any nicety, or which, theoretically at least, is likely to present conflicting moral considerations. The other cases which have been mentioned hardly admit of discussion. Assistance to the government of a country in keeping down the people, unhappily by far the most frequent case of foreign intervention, no one writing in a free country needs take the trouble of stigmatizing. A government which needs foreign support to enforce obedience from its own citizens, is one which ought not to exist; and the assistance given to it by foreigners is hardly ever anything but the sympathy of one despotism with another. A case requiring consideration is that of a protracted civil war, in which the contending parties are so equally balanced that there is no probability of a speedy issue; or if there is, the victorious side cannot hope to keep down the vanquished but by severities repugnant to humanity, and injurious to the permanent welfare of the country. In this exceptional case it seems now to be an admitted doctrine, that the neighbouring nations, or one powerful neighbour with the acquiescence of the rest, are warranted in demanding that the contest shall cease, and a reconciliation take place on equitable terms of compromise. Intervention of this description has been repeatedly practised during the present generation, with such general approval, that its legitimacy may be considered to have passed into a maxim of what is called international law. The interference of the European Powers between Greece and Turkey, and between Turkey and Egypt, were cases in point. That between Holland and Belgium was still more so. The intervention of England in Portugal, a few years ago, which is probably less remembered than the others, because it took effect without the employment of actual force, belongs to the same category. At the time, this interposition had the appearance of a bad and dishonest backing of the government against the people, being so timed as to hit the exact moment when the popular party had obtained a marked advantage, and seemed on the eve of overthrowing the government, or reducing it to terms. But if ever a political act which looked ill in the commencement could be justified by the event, this was: for, as the fact turned out, instead of giving ascendancy to a party, it proved a really healing measure; and the chiefs of the so-called rebellion were, within a few years, the honoured and successful ministers of the throne against which they had so lately fought.

With respect to the question, whether one country is justified in helping the people of another in a struggle against their government for free institutions, the answer will be different, according as the yoke which the people are attempting to throw off is that of a purely native government, or of foreigners; considering as one of foreigners, every government which maintains itself by foreign support. When the contest is only with native rulers, and with such native strength as those rulers can enlist in their defence, the answer I should give to the question of the legitimacy of intervention is, as a general rule, No. The reason is, that there can seldom be anything approaching to assurance that intervention, even if successful, would be for the good of the people themselves. The only test possessing any real value, of a people's having become fit for popular institutions, is that they, or a sufficient portion of them to prevail in the contest, are willing to brave labour and danger for their liberation. I know all that may be said. I know it may be urged that the virtues of freemen cannot be learnt in the school of slavery, and that if a people are not fit for freedom, to have any chance of becoming so they must first be free. And this would be conclusive, if the intervention recommended would really give them freedom. But the evil is, that if they have not sufficient love of liberty to be able to wrest it from merely domestic oppressors, the liberty which is bestowed on them by other hands than their own, will have nothing real, nothing permanent. No people ever was and remained free, but because it was determined to be so: because neither its rulers nor any other party in the nation could compel it to be otherwise. If a people – especially one whose freedom has not yet become prescriptive – does not value it sufficiently to fight for it, and maintain it against any force which can be mustered *within* the country, even by those who have the command of the public revenue, it is only a question in how few years or months that people will be enslaved. Either the government which it has given to itself, or some military leader or knot of conspirators who contrive to subvert the government, will speedily put an end to all popular institutions: unless indeed it suits their convenience better to leave them standing, and be content with reducing them to mere forms; for, unless the spirit of liberty is strong in a people, those who have the executive in their hands easily work any institutions to the purposes of despotism. There is no sure guarantee against this deplorable issue, even in a country which has achieved its own freedom; as may be seen in the present day by striking examples both in the Old and New Worlds: but when freedom has been achieved *for* them, they have little prospect indeed of escaping this fate. When a people has had the misfortune to be ruled by a government under which the feelings and the virtues needful for maintaining freedom could not develop themselves, it is during an arduous struggle to become free by their own efforts that these feelings and virtues have the best chance of springing up. Men become attached to that which they have long fought for and made sacrifices for; they learn to appreciate that on which their thoughts have been much engaged; and a contest in which many have been called on to devote themselves for their country, is a school in which they learn to value their country's interest above their own.

It can seldom, therefore – I will not go so far as to say never – be either judicious on right, in a country which has a free government, to assist, otherwise than by the moral support of its opinion, the endeavours of another to extort the same blessing from its native rulers. We must except, of course, any case in which such assistance is a measure of legitimate self-defence. If (a contingency by no means unlikely to occur) this country, on account of its freedom, which is a standing reproach to despotism everywhere, and an encouragement to throw it off, should find itself menaced with attack by a coalition of Continental despots, it ought to consider the popular party in every nation of the Continent as its natural ally: the Liberals should be to it, what the Protestants of Europe were to the Government of Queen Elizabeth. So, again, when a nation, in her own defence, has gone to war with a despot, and has had the rare good fortune not only to succeed in her resistance, but to hold the conditions of peace in her own hands, she is entitled to say that she will make no treaty, unless with some other ruler than the one whose existence as such may be a perpetual menace to her safety and freedom. These exceptions do but set in a clearer light the reasons of the rule; because they do not depend on any failure of those reasons, but on considerations paramount to them, and coming under a different principle.

But the case of a people struggling against a foreign yoke, or against a native tyranny upheld by foreign arms, illustrates the reasons for non-intervention in an opposite way; for in this case the reasons themselves do not exist. A people the most attached to freedom, the most capable of defending and of making a good use of free institutions, may be unable to contend successfully for them against the military strength of another nation much more powerful. To assist a people thus kept down, is not to disturb the balance of forces on which the permanent maintenance of freedom in a country depends, but to redress that balance when it is already unfairly and violently disturbed. The doctrine of non-intervention, to be a legitimate principle of morality, must be accepted by all governments. The despots must consent to be bound by it as well as the free States. Unless they do, the profession of it by free countries comes but to this miserable issue, that the wrong side may help the wrong, but the right must not help the right. Intervention to enforce non-intervention is always rightful, always moral, if not always prudent. Though it be a mistake to *give* freedom to a people who do not value the boon, it cannot but be right to insist that if they do value it, they shall not be hindered from the pursuit of it by foreign coercion. It might not have been right for England (even apart from the question of prudence) to have taken part with Hungary in its noble struggle against Austria; although the Austrian Government in Hungary was in some sense a foreign yoke. But when, the Hungarians having shown themselves likely to prevail in this struggle, the Russian despot interposed, and joining his force to that of Austria, delivered back the Hungarians, bound hand and foot, to their exasperated oppressors, it would have been an honourable and virtuous act on the part of England to have declared that this should not be, and that if Russia gave assistance to the wrong side, England would aid the right. It might not have been consistent with the regard which every nation is bound to pay to its own safety, for England to have taken up this position single-handed. But England and France together could have done it; and if they had, the Russian armed intervention would never have taken place, or would have been disastrous to Russia alone: while all that those Powers gained by not doing it, was that they had to fight Russia five years afterwards, under more difficult circumstances, and without Hungary for an ally. The first nation which, being powerful enough to make its voice effectual, has the spirit and courage to say that not a gun shall be fired in Europe by the soldiers of one Power against the revolted subjects of another, will be the idol of the friends of freedom throughout Europe. That declaration alone will ensure the almost immediate emancipation of every people which desires liberty sufficiently to be capable of maintaining it: and the nation which gives the word will soon find itself at the head of an alliance of free peoples, so strong as to defy the efforts of any number of confederated despots to bring it down. The prize is too glorious not to be snatched sooner or later by some free country; and the time may not be distant when England, if she does not take this heroic part because of its heroism, will be compelled to take it from consideration for her own safety.

Chapter 26

*Charter**
United Nations

Chapter VII

Action with Respect to Threats to the Peace, Breaches of the Peace, and Acts of Aggression

Article 39

The Security Council shall determine the existence of any threat to the peace, breach of the peace, or act of aggression and shall make recommendations, or decide what measures shall be taken in accordance with Articles 41 and 42, to maintain or restore international peace and security.

Article 40

In order to prevent an aggravation of the situation, the Security Council may, before making the recommendations or deciding upon the measures provided for in Article 39, call upon the parties concerned to comply with such provisional measures as it deems necessary or desirable. Such provisional measures shall be without prejudice to the rights, claims, or position of the parties concerned. The Security Council shall duly take account of failure to comply with such provisional measures.

Article 41

The Security Council may decide what measures not involving the use of armed force are to be employed to give effect to its decisions, and it may call upon the Members of the United Nations to apply such measures. These may include complete or partial interruption of economic relations and of rail, sea, air, postal, telegraphic, radio, and other means of communication, and the severance of diplomatic relations.

Article 42

Should the Security Council consider that measures provided for in Article 41 would be inadequate or have proved to be inadequate, it may take such action by air, sea, or land forces as may be necessary to maintain or restore international peace and security. Such action may include demonstrations, blockade, and other operations by air, sea, or land forces of Members of the United Nations.

* From United Nations, *Charter*, ch. VII (1946), http://www.un.org.

Article 43

1 All Members of the United Nations, in order to contribute to the maintenance of international peace and security, undertake to make available to the Security Council, on its call and in accordance with a special agreement or agreements, armed forces, assistance, and facilities, including rights of passage, necessary for the purpose of maintaining international peace and security.

2 Such agreement or agreements shall govern the numbers and types of forces, their degree of readiness and general location, and the nature of the facilities and assistance to be provided.

3 The agreement or agreements shall be negotiated as soon as possible on the initiative of the Security Council. They shall be concluded between the Security Council and Members or between the Security Council and groups of Members and shall be subject to ratification by the signatory states in accordance with their respective constitutional processes.

Article 44

When the Security Council has decided to use force it shall, before calling upon a Member not represented on it to provide armed forces in fulfilment of the obligations assumed under Article 43, invite that Member, if the Member so desires, to participate in the decisions of the Security Council concerning the employment of contingents of that Member's armed forces.

Article 45

In order to enable the United Nations to take urgent military measures, Members shall hold immediately available national air-force contingents for combined international enforcement action. The strength and degree of readiness of these contingents and plans for their combined action shall be determined within the limits laid down in the special agreement or agreements referred to in Article 43, by the Security Council with the assistance of the Military Staff Committee.

Article 46

Plans for the application of armed force shall be made by the Security Council with the assistance of the Military Staff Committee.

Article 47

1 There shall be established a Military Staff Committee to advise and assist the Security Council on all questions relating to the Security Council's military requirements for the maintenance of international peace and security, the employment and command of forces placed at its disposal, the regulation of armaments, and possible disarmament.

2 The Military Staff Committee shall consist of the Chiefs of Staff of the permanent members of the Security Council or their representatives. Any Member of the United Nations not permanently represented on the Committee shall be invited by the Committee to be associated with it when the efficient discharge of the Committee's responsibilities requires the participation of that Member in its work.

3 The Military Staff Committee shall be responsible under the Security Council for the strategic direction of any armed forces placed at the disposal of the Security Council. Questions relating to the command of such forces shall be worked out subsequently.

4   The Military Staff Committee, with the authorization of the Security Council and after consultation with appropriate regional agencies, may establish regional subcommittees.

Article 48

1   The action required to carry out the decisions of the Security Council for the maintenance of international peace and security shall be taken by all the Members of the United Nations or by some of them, as the Security Council may determine.
2   Such decisions shall be carried out by the Members of the United Nations directly and through their action in the appropriate international agencies of which they are members.

Article 49

The Members of the United Nations shall join in affording mutual assistance in carrying out the measures decided upon by the Security Council.

Article 50

If preventive or enforcement measures against any state are taken by the Security Council, any other state, whether a Member of the United Nations or not, which finds itself confronted with special economic problems arising from the carrying out of those measures shall have the right to consult the Security Council with regard to a solution of those problems.

Article 51

Nothing in the present Charter shall impair the inherent right of individual or collective self-defence if an armed attack occurs against a Member of the United Nations, until the Security Council has taken measures necessary to maintain international peace and security. Measures taken by Members in the exercise of this right of self-defence shall be immediately reported to the Security Council and shall not in any way affect the authority and responsibility of the Security Council under the present Charter to take at any time such action as it deems necessary in order to maintain or restore international peace and security.

Chapter 27

War and Massacre*
Thomas Nagel

From the apathetic reaction to atrocities committed in Vietnam by the United States and its allies, one may conclude that moral restrictions on the conduct of war command almost as little sympathy among the general public as they do among those charged with the formation of US military policy. Even when restrictions on the conduct of warfare are defended, it is usually on legal grounds alone: their moral basis is often poorly understood. I wish to argue that certain restrictions are neither arbitrary nor merely conventional, and that their validity does not depend simply on their usefulness. There is, in other words, a moral basis for the rules of war, even though the conventions now officially in force are far from giving it perfect expression.

I

No elaborate moral theory is required to account for what is wrong in cases like the Mylai massacre, since it did not serve, and was not intended to serve, any strategic

* From *Philosophy & Public Affairs* 1:2 (1972), pp. 123–44.

purpose. Moreover, if the participation of the United States in the Indo-Chinese war is entirely wrong to begin with, then that engagement is incapable of providing a justification for *any* measures taken in its pursuit – not only for the measures which are atrocities in every war, however just its aims.

But this war has revealed attitudes of a more general kind, that influenced the conduct of earlier wars as well. After it has ended, we shall still be faced with the problem of how warfare may be conducted, and the attitudes that have resulted in the specific conduct of this war will not have disappeared. Moreover, similar problems can arise in wars or rebellions fought for very different reasons, and against very different opponents. It is not easy to keep a firm grip on the idea of what is not permissible in warfare, because while some military actions are obvious atrocities, other cases are more difficult to assess and the general principles underlying these judgments remain obscure. Such obscurity can lead to the abandonment of sound intuitions in favor of criteria whose rationale may be more obvious. If such a tendency is to be resisted, it will require a better understanding of the restrictions than we now have.

I propose to discuss the most general moral problem raised by the conduct of warfare: the problem of means and ends. In one view, there are limits on what may be done even in the service of an end worth pursuing – and even when adherence to the restriction may be very costly. A person who acknowledges the force of such restrictions can find himself in acute moral dilemmas. He may believe, for example, that by torturing a prisoner he can obtain information necessary to prevent a disaster, or that by obliterating one village with bombs he can halt a campaign of terrorism. If he believes that the gains from a certain measure will clearly outweigh its costs, yet still suspects that he ought not to adopt it, then he is in a dilemma produced by the conflict between two disparate categories of moral reason: categories that may be called *utilitarian* and *absolutist*.

Utilitarianism gives primacy to a concern with what will *happen*. Absolutism gives primacy to a concern with what one is *doing*. The conflict between them arises because the alternatives we face are rarely just choices between *total outcomes*: they are also choices between alternative pathways or measures to be taken. When one of the choices is to do terrible things to another person, the problem is altered fundamentally; it is no longer merely a question of which outcome would be worse.

Few of us are completely immune to either of these types of moral intuition, though in some people, either naturally or for doctrinal reasons, one type will be dominant and the other suppressed or weak. But it is perfectly possible to feel the force of both types of reason very strongly; in that case the moral dilemma in certain situations of crisis will be acute, and it may appear that every possible course of action or inaction is unacceptable for one reason or another.

II

Although it is this dilemma that I propose to explore, most of the discussion will be devoted to its absolutist component. The utilitarian component is straightforward by comparison, and has a natural appeal to anyone who is not a complete skeptic about ethics. Utilitarianism says that one should try, either individually or through institutions, to maximize good and minimize evil (the definition of these categories need not enter into the schematic formulation of the view), and that if faced with the possibility of preventing a great evil by producing a lesser, one should choose the lesser evil. There are certainly problems about the formulation of utilitarianism, and much has been written about it, but its intent is morally transparent. Nevertheless, despite the addition of various refinements, it continues to leave large portions of ethics unaccounted for. I do not suggest that some form of absolutism can account for them all, only that an examination of absolutism will lead us to see the complexity, and perhaps the incoherence, of our moral ideas.

Utilitarianism certainly justifies *some* restrictions on the conduct of warfare. There are strong utilitarian reasons for adhering to any limitation which seems natural to most people – particularly if the limitation is widely accepted already. An exceptional measure which seems to be justified by its results in a particular conflict may create a precedent with disastrous long-term effects.[1] It may even be argued that war involves violence on such a scale that it is never justified on utilitarian grounds – the consequences of refusing to go to war will never be as bad as the war itself would be, even if atrocities were not committed. Or in a more sophisticated vein it might be claimed that a uniform policy of never resorting to military force would do less harm in the long run, if followed consistently, than a policy of deciding each case on utilitarian grounds (even though on occasion particular applications of the pacifist policy might have worse results than a specific utilitarian decision). But I shall not consider these arguments, for my concern is with reasons of a different kind, which may remain when reasons of utility and interest fail.[2]

In the final analysis, I believe that the dilemma cannot always be resolved. While not every conflict between absolutism and utilitarianism creates an insoluble dilemma, and while it is certainly right to adhere to absolutist restrictions unless the utilitarian considerations favoring violation are overpoweringly weighty and extremely certain – nevertheless, when that special condition is met, it may become impossible to adhere to an absolutist position. What I shall offer, therefore, is a somewhat qualified defense of absolutism. I believe it underlies a valid and fundamental type of moral judgment – which cannot be reduced to or overridden by other principles. And while there may be other principles just as fundamental, it is particularly important not to lose confidence in our absolutist intuitions, for they are often the only barrier before the abyss of utilitarian apologetics for large-scale murder.

III

One absolutist position that creates no problems of interpretation is pacifism: the view that one may not kill another person under any circumstances, no matter what good would be achieved or evil averted thereby. The type of absolutist position that I am going to discuss is different. Pacifism draws the conflict with utilitarian considerations very starkly. But there are other views according to which violence may be undertaken, even on a large scale, in a clearly just cause, so long as certain absolute restrictions on the character and direction of that violence are

observed. The line is drawn somewhat closer to the bone, but it exists.

The philosopher who has done most to advance contemporary philosophical discussion of such a view, and to explain it to those unfamiliar with its extensive treatment in Roman Catholic moral theology, is G. E. M. Anscombe. In 1958 Miss Anscombe published a pamphlet entitled *Mr. Truman's Degree*,[3] on the occasion of the award by Oxford University of an honorary doctorate to Harry Truman. The pamphlet explained why she had opposed the decision to award that degree, recounted the story of her unsuccessful opposition, and offered some reflections on the history of Truman's decision to drop atom bombs on Hiroshima and Nagasaki, and on the difference between murder and allowable killing in warfare. She pointed out that the policy of deliberately killing large numbers of civilians either as a means or as an end in itself did not originate with Truman, and was common practice among all parties during World War II for some time before Hiroshima. The Allied area bombings of German cities by conventional explosives included raids which killed more civilians than did the atomic attacks; the same is true of certain fire-bomb raids on Japan.

The policy of attacking the civilian population in order to induce an enemy to surrender, or to damage his morale, seems to have been widely accepted in the civilized world, and seems to be accepted still, at least if the stakes are high enough. It gives evidence of a moral conviction that the deliberate killing of noncombatants – women, children, old people – is permissible if enough can be gained by it. This follows from the more general position that any means can in principle be justified if it leads to a sufficiently worthy end. Such an attitude is evident not only in the more spectacular current weapons systems but also in the day-to-day conduct of the nonglobal war in Indochina: the indiscriminate destructiveness of antipersonnel weapons, napalm, and aerial bombardment; cruelty to prisoners; massive relocation of civilians; destruction of crops; and so forth. An absolutist position opposes to this the view that certain acts cannot be justified no matter what the consequences. Among those acts is murder – the deliberate killing of the harmless: civilians, prisoners of war, and medical personnel.

In the present war such measures are sometimes said to be regrettable, but they are generally defended by reference to military necessity and the importance of the long-term consequences of success or failure in the war. I shall pass over the inadequacy of this consequentialist defense in its own terms. (That is the dominant form of moral criticism of the war, for it is part of what people mean when they ask, "Is it worth it?") I am concerned rather to account for the inappropriateness of offering any defense of that kind for such actions.

Many people feel, without being able to say much more about it, that something has gone seriously wrong when certain measures are admitted into consideration in the first place. The fundamental mistake is made there, rather than at the point where the overall benefit of some monstrous measure is judged to outweigh its disadvantages, and it is adopted. An account of absolutism might help us to understand this. If it is not allowable to *do* certain things, such as killing unarmed prisoners or civilians, then no argument about what will happen if one doesn't do them can show that doing them would be all right.

Absolutism does not, of course, require one to ignore the consequences of one's acts. It operates as a limitation on utilitarian reasoning, not as a substitute for it. An absolutist can be expected to try to maximize good and minimize evil, so long as this does not require him to transgress an absolute prohibition like that against murder. But when such a conflict occurs, the prohibition takes complete precedence over any consideration of consequences. Some of the results of this view are clear enough. It requires us to forgo certain potentially useful military measures, such as the slaughter of hostages and prisoners or indiscriminate attempts to reduce the enemy civilian population by starvation, epidemic infectious diseases like anthrax and bubonic plague, or mass incineration. It means that we cannot deliberate on whether such measures are justified by the fact that they will avert still greater evils, for as intentional measures they cannot be justified in terms of any consequences whatever.

Someone unfamiliar with the events of this century might imagine that utilitarian arguments, or arguments of national interest, would suffice to deter measures of this sort. But it has become evident that such considerations are insufficient to prevent the adoption and employment of enormous antipopulation weapons once their use is considered a serious moral possibility. The same is true of the piecemeal wiping out of rural civilian populations in airborne antiguerrilla warfare. Once the door is opened to calculations of utility and national interest, the usual speculations about the future of freedom, peace, and economic prosperity can be brought to bear to ease the consciences of those responsible for a certain number of charred babies.

For this reason alone it is important to decide what is wrong with the frame of mind which allows such arguments to begin. But it is also important to understand absolutism in the cases where it genuinely conflicts with utility. Despite its appeal, it is a paradoxical position, for it can require that one refrain from choosing the lesser of two evils when that is the only choice one has. And it is additionally paradoxical because, unlike pacifism, it permits one to do horrible things to people in some circumstances but not in others.

IV

Before going on to say what, if anything, lies behind the position, there remain a few relatively technical matters which are best discussed at this point.

First, it is important to specify as clearly as possible the kind of thing to which absolutist prohibitions can apply. We must take seriously the proviso that they concern what we deliberately do to people. There could not, for example, without incoherence, be an absolute prohibition against *bringing about* the death of an innocent person. For one may find oneself in a situation in which, no matter what one does, some innocent people will die as a result. I do not mean just that there are cases in which someone will die no matter what one does, because one is not in a position to affect the outcome one way or the other. That, it is to be hoped, is one's relation to the deaths of most innocent people. I have in mind, rather, a case in which someone is bound to die, but who it is will depend on what one does. Sometimes these situations have natural causes, as when too few resources (medicine, lifeboats) are available to rescue everyone threatened with a certain catastrophe. Sometimes the situations are man-made, as when the only way to control a campaign of terrorism is to employ terrorist tactics against the community from which it has arisen. Whatever one does in cases such as these, some innocent people will die as a result. If the absolutist prohibition forbade doing what would result in the deaths of innocent people, it would have the consequence that in such cases nothing one could do would be morally permissible.

This problem is avoided, however, because what absolutism forbids is *doing* certain things to people, rather than bringing about certain *results*. Not everything that happens to others as a result of what one does is something that one has *done* to them. Catholic moral theology seeks to make this distinction precise in a doctrine known as the law of double effect, which asserts that there is a morally relevant distinction between bringing about the death of an innocent person deliberately, either as an end in itself or as a means, and bringing it about as a side effect of something else one does deliberately. In the latter case, even if the outcome is foreseen, it is not murder, and does not fall under the absolute prohibition, though of course it may still be wrong for other reasons (reasons of utility, for example). Briefly, the principle states that one is sometimes permitted knowingly to bring about as a side effect of one's actions something which it would be absolutely impermissible to bring about deliberately as an end or as a means. In application to war or revolution, the law of double effect permits a certain amount of civilian carnage as a side effect of bombing munitions plants or attacking enemy soldiers. And even this is permissible only if the cost is not too great to be justified by one's objectives.

However, despite its importance and its usefulness in accounting for certain plausible moral judgments, I do not believe that the law of double effect is a generally applicable test for the consequences of an absolutist position. Its own application is not always clear, so that it introduces uncertainty where there need not be uncertainty.

In Indochina, for example, there is a great deal of aerial bombardment, strafing, spraying of napalm, and employment of pellet- or needle-spraying antipersonnel weapons against rural villages in which guerrillas are suspected to be hiding, or from which small-arms fire has been received. The majority of those killed and wounded in these aerial attacks are reported to be women and children, even when some combatants are caught as well. However, the government regards these civilian casualties as a regrettable side effect of what is a legitimate attack against an armed enemy.

It might be thought easy to dismiss this as sophistry: if one bombs, burns, or strafes a village containing a hundred people, twenty of whom one believes to be guerrillas, so that by killing most of them one will be statistically likely to kill most of the guerrillas, then isn't one's attack on the group of one hundred a *means* of destroying the guerrillas, pure and simple? If one makes no attempt to discriminate between guerrillas and civilians, as is impossible in an aerial attack on a small village, then one cannot regard as a mere side effect the deaths of those in the group that one would not have bothered to kill if more selective means had been available.

The difficulty is that this argument depends on one particular description of the act, and the reply might be that the means used against the guerrillas is not: killing everybody in the village – but rather: obliteration bombing of the *area* in which the twenty guerrillas are known to be located. If there are civilians in the area as well, they will be killed as a side effect of such action.[4]

Because of casuistical problems like this, I prefer to stay with the original, unanalyzed distinction between what one does to people and what merely happens to them as a result of what one does. The law of double effect provides an approximation to that distinction in many cases, and perhaps it can be sharpened to the point where it does better than that. Certainly the original distinction itself needs clarification, particularly since some of the things we do to people involve things happening to them as a result of other things we do. In a case like the one discussed, however, it is clear that by bombing the village one slaughters and maims the civilians in it. Whereas by giving the only available medicine to one of two sufferers from a disease, one does not kill the other, even if he dies as a result.

The second technical point to take up concerns a possible misinterpretation of this feature of the position. The absolutist focus on actions rather than outcomes does not merely introduce a new, outstanding item into the catalogue of evils. That is, it does not say that the worst thing in the world is the deliberate murder of an innocent person. For if that were all, then one could presumably justify one such murder on the ground that it would prevent several others, or ten thousand on the ground that they would prevent a hundred thousand more. That is a familiar argument. But if this is allowable, then there is no absolute prohibition against murder after all. Absolutism requires that we *avoid* murder at all costs, not that we *prevent* it at all costs.[5]

Finally, let me remark on a frequent criticism of absolutism that depends on a misunderstanding. It is sometimes suggested that such prohibitions depend on a kind of moral self-interest, a primary obligation to preserve one's own moral purity, to keep one's hands clean no matter what happens to the rest of the world. If this were the position, it might be exposed to the charge of self-indulgence. After all, what gives one man a right to put the purity of his soul or the cleanness of his hands above the lives or welfare of large numbers of other people? It might be argued that a public servant like Truman has no right to put himself first in that way; therefore if he is convinced that the alternatives would be worse, he must give the order to drop the bombs, and take the burden of those deaths on himself, as he must do other distasteful things for the general good.

But there are two confusions behind the view that moral self-interest underlies moral absolutism. First, it is a confusion to suggest that the need to preserve one's moral purity might be the *source* of an obligation. For if by committing murder one sacrifices one's moral purity or integrity, that can only be because there is *already* something wrong with murder. The general reason against committing murder cannot therefore be merely that it makes one an immoral person. Secondly, the notion that one might sacrifice one's moral integrity justifiably, in the service of a sufficiently worthy end, is an incoherent notion. For if one were justified in making such a sacrifice (or even morally required to make it), then one would not be sacrificing one's moral integrity by adopting that course: one would be preserving it.

Moral absolutism is not unique among moral theories in requiring each person to do what will preserve his own moral purity in all circumstances. This is equally true of utilitarianism, or of any other theory which distinguishes between right and wrong. Any theory which defines the right course of action in various circumstances and asserts that one should adopt that course, ipso facto asserts that one should do what will preserve one's moral purity, simply because the right course of action *is* what will preserve one's moral purity in those circumstances. Of course utilitarianism does not assert that this is *why* one should adopt that course, but we have seen that the same is true of absolutism.

V

It is easier to dispose of false explanations of absolutism than to produce a true one. A positive account of the matter must begin with the observation that war, conflict, and aggression are relations between persons. The view that it can be wrong to consider merely the overall effect of one's actions on the general welfare comes into prominence when those actions involve relations with others. A man's acts usually affect more people than he deals with directly, and those effects must naturally be considered in his

decisions. But if there are special principles governing the manner in which he should *treat* people, that will require special attention to the particular persons toward whom the act is directed, rather than just to its total effect.

Absolutist restrictions in warfare appear to be of two types: restrictions on the class of persons at whom aggression or violence may be directed and restrictions on the manner of attack, given that the object falls within that class. These can be combined, however, under the principle that hostile treatment of any person must be justified in terms of something *about that person* which makes the treatment appropriate. Hostility is a personal relation, and it must be suited to its target. One consequence of this condition will be that certain persons may not be subjected to hostile treatment in war at all, since nothing about them justifies such treatment. Others will be proper objects of hostility only in certain circumstances, or when they are engaged in certain pursuits. And the appropriate manner and extent of hostile treatment will depend on what is justified by the particular case.

A coherent view of this type will hold that extremely hostile behavior toward another is compatible with treating him as a person – even perhaps as an end in himself. This is possible only if one has not automatically stopped treating him as a person as soon as one starts to fight with him. If hostile, aggressive, or combative treatment of others always violated the condition that they be treated as human beings, it would be difficult to make further distinctions on that score *within* the class of hostile actions. That point of view, on the level of international relations, leads to the position that if complete pacifism is not accepted, no holds need be barred at all, and we may slaughter and massacre to our hearts' content, if it seems advisable. Such a position is often expressed in discussions of war crimes.

But the fact is that ordinary people do not believe this about conflicts, physical or otherwise, between individuals, and there is no more reason why it should be true of conflicts between nations. There seems to be a perfectly natural conception of the distinction between fighting clean and fighting dirty. To fight dirty is to direct one's hostility or aggression not at its proper object, but at a peripheral target which may be more vulnerable, and through which the proper object can be attacked indirectly. This applies in a fist fight, an election campaign, a duel, or a philosophical argument. If the concept is general enough to apply to all these matters, it should apply to war – both to the conduct of individual soldiers and to the conduct of nations.

Suppose that you are a candidate for public office, convinced that the election of your opponent would be a disaster, that he is an unscrupulous demagogue who will serve a narrow range of interests and seriously infringe the rights of those who disagree with him; and suppose you are convinced that you cannot defeat him by conventional means. Now imagine that various unconventional means present themselves as possibilities: you possess information about his sex life which would scandalize the electorate if made public; or you learn that his wife is an alcoholic or that in his youth he was associated for a brief period with a proscribed political party, and you believe that this information could be used to blackmail him into withdrawing his candidacy; or you can have a team of your supporters flatten the tires of a crucial subset of his supporters on election day; or you are in a position to stuff the ballot boxes; or, more simply, you can have him assassinated. What is wrong with these methods, given that they will achieve an overwhelmingly desirable result?

There are, of course, many things wrong with them: some are against the law; some

infringe the procedures of an electoral process to which you are presumably committed by taking part in it; very importantly, some may backfire, and it is in the interest of all political candidates to adhere to an unspoken agreement not to allow certain personal matters to intrude into a campaign. But that is not all. We have in addition the feeling that these measures, these methods of attack are *irrelevant* to the issue between you and your opponent, that in taking them up you would not be directing yourself to that which makes him an object of your opposition. You would be directing your attack not at the true target of your hostility, but at peripheral targets that happen to be vulnerable.

The same is true of a fight or argument outside the framework of any system of regulations or law. In an altercation with a taxi driver over an excessive fare, it is inappropriate to taunt him about his accent, flatten one of his tires, or smear chewing gum on his windshield; and it remains inappropriate even if he casts aspersions on your race, politics, or religion, or dumps the contents of your suitcase into the street.[6]

The importance of such restrictions may vary with the seriousness of the case; and what is unjustifiable in one case may be justified in a more extreme one. But they all derive from a single principle: that hostility or aggression should be directed at its true object. This means both that it should be directed at the person or persons who provoke it and that it should aim more specifically at what is provocative about them. The second condition will determine what form the hostility may appropriately take.

It is evident that some idea of the relation in which one should stand to other people underlies this principle, but the idea is difficult to state. I believe it is roughly this: whatever one does to another person intentionally must be aimed at him as a subject, with the intention that he receive it as a subject. It should manifest an attitude to *him* rather than just to the situation, and he should be able to recognize it and identify himself as its object. The procedures by which such an attitude is manifested need not be addressed to the person directly. Surgery, for example, is not a form of personal confrontation but part of a medical treatment that can be offered to a patient face to face and received by him as a response to his needs and the natural outcome of an attitude toward *him*.

Hostile treatment, unlike surgery, is already addressed *to* a person, and does not take its interpersonal meaning from a wider context. But hostile acts can serve as the expression or implementation of only a limited range of attitudes to the person who is attacked. Those attitudes in turn have as objects certain real or presumed characteristics or activities of the person which are thought to justify them. When this background is absent, hostile or aggressive behavior can no longer be intended for the reception of the victim as a subject. Instead it takes on the character of a purely bureaucratic operation. This occurs when one attacks someone who is not the true object of one's hostility – the true object may be someone else, who can be attacked through the victim; or one may not be manifesting a hostile attitude toward anyone, but merely using the easiest available path to some desired goal. One finds oneself not facing or addressing the victim at all, but operating on him – without the larger context of personal interaction that surrounds a surgical operation.

If absolutism is to defend its claim to priority over considerations of utility, it must hold that the maintenance of a direct interpersonal response to the people one deals with is a requirement which no advantages can justify one in abandoning. The requirement is absolute only if it rules out any calculation of what would justify its violation. I have said earlier that there may be circum-

stances so extreme that they render an absolutist position untenable. One may find then that one has no choice but to do something terrible. Nevertheless, even in such cases absolutism retains its force in that one cannot claim *justification* for the violation. It does not become *all right*.

As a tentative effort to explain this, let me try to connect absolutist limitations with the possibility of justifying *to the victim* what is being done to him. If one abandons a person in the course of rescuing several others from a fire or a sinking ship, one *could* say to him, "You understand, I have to leave you to save the others." Similarly, if one subjects an unwilling child to a painful surgical procedure, one can say to him, "If you could understand, you would realize that I am doing this to help you." One could *even* say, as one bayonets an enemy soldier, "It's either you or me." But one cannot really say while torturing a prisoner, "You understand, I have to pull out your finger-nails because it is absolutely essential that we have the names of your confederates"; nor can one say to the victims of Hiroshima, "You understand, we have to incinerate you to provide the Japanese government with an incentive to surrender."

This does not take us very far, of course, since a utilitarian would presumably be willing to offer justifications of the latter sort to his victims, in cases where he thought they were sufficient. They are really justifications to the world at large, which the victim, as a reasonable man, would be expected to appreciate. However, there seems to me something wrong with this view, for it ignores the possibility that to treat someone else horribly puts you in a special relation to him, which may have to be defended in terms of other features of your relation to him. The suggestion needs much more development; but it may help us to understand how there may be requirements which are absolute in the sense that there can be no justification for violating them. If the justification for what one did to another person had to be such that it could be offered to him specifically, rather than just to the world at large, that would be a significant source of restraint.

If the account is to be deepened, I would hope for some results along the following lines. Absolutism is associated with a view of oneself as a small being interacting with others in a large world. The justifications it requires are primarily interpersonal. Utilitarianism is associated with a view of oneself as a benevolent bureaucrat distributing such benefits as one can control to countless other beings, with whom one may have various relations or none. The justifications it requires are primarily administrative. The argument between the two moral attitudes may depend on the relative priority of these two conceptions.[7]

VI

Some of the restrictions on methods of warfare which have been adhered to from time to time are to be explained by the mutual interests of the involved parties: restrictions on weaponry, treatment of prisoners, etc. But that is not all there is to it. The conditions of directness and relevance which I have argued apply to relations of conflict and aggression apply to war as well. I have said that there are two types of absolutist restrictions on the conduct of war: those that limit the legitimate targets of hostility and those that limit its character, even when the target is acceptable. I shall say something about each of these. As will become clear, the principle I have sketched does not yield an unambiguous answer in every case.

First let us see how it implies that attacks on some people are allowed, but not attacks on others. It may seem paradoxical to assert that to fire a machine gun at someone who is throwing hand grenades at your emplacement is to treat him as a human being. Yet the relation with him is direct and straightforward.[8] The attack is aimed specifically against the threat presented by a dangerous adversary, and not against a peripheral target through which he happens to be vulnerable but which has nothing to do with that threat. For example, you might stop him by machine-gunning his wife and children, who are standing nearby, thus distracting him from his aim of blowing you up and enabling you to capture him. But if his wife and children are not threatening your life, that would be to treat them as means with a vengeance.

This, however, is just Hiroshima on a smaller scale. One objection to weapons of mass annihilation – nuclear, thermonuclear, biological, or chemical – is that their indiscriminateness disqualifies them as direct instruments for the expression of hostile relations. In attacking the civilian population, one treats neither the military enemy nor the civilians with that minimal respect which is owed to them as human beings. This is clearly true of the direct attack on people who present no threat at all. But it is also true of the character of the attack on those who *are* threatening you, viz., the government and military forces of the enemy. Your aggression is directed against an area of vulnerability quite distinct from any threat presented by them which you may be justified in meeting. You are taking aim at them through the mundane life and survival of their countrymen, instead of aiming at the destruction of their military capacity. And of course it does not require hydrogen bombs to commit such crimes.

This way of looking at the matter also helps us to understand the importance of the distinction between combatants and noncombatants, and the irrelevance of much of the criticism offered against its intelligibility and moral significance. According to an absolutist position, deliberate killing of the innocent is murder, and in warfare the role of the innocent is filled by noncombatants. This has been thought to raise two sorts of problems: first, the widely imagined difficulty of making a division, in modern warfare, between combatants and noncombatants; second, problems deriving from the connotation of the word "innocence."

Let me take up the latter question first.[9] In the absolutist position, the operative notion of innocence is not moral innocence, and it is not opposed to moral guilt. If it were, then we would be justified in killing a wicked but noncombatant hairdresser in an enemy city who supported the evil policies of his government, and unjustified in killing a morally pure conscript who was driving a tank toward us with the profoundest regrets and nothing but love in his heart. But moral innocence has very little to do with it, for in the definition of murder "innocent" means "currently harmless," and it is opposed not to "guilty" but to "doing harm." It should be noted that such an analysis has the consequence that in war we may often be justified in killing people who do not deserve to die, and unjustified in killing people who do deserve to die, if anyone does.

So we must distinguish combatants from noncombatants on the basis of their immediate threat or harmfulness. I do not claim that the line is a sharp one, but it is not so difficult as is often supposed to place individuals on one side of it or the other. Children are not combatants even though they may join the armed forces if they are allowed to grow up. Women are not combatants just because they bear children or offer comfort to the soldiers. More problematic are the supporting personnel, whether in or out of uniform, from drivers of munitions trucks and army cooks to civilian munitions workers and farmers. I believe they can be plausibly classified by applying the condition that the prosecution of conflict must direct itself to the cause of danger, and not to what is peripheral. The threat presented by an army and its members does not consist merely in the fact that they are men, but in the fact that they are armed and are using their arms in the pursuit of certain objectives. Contributions to their arms and logistics are contributions to this threat; contributions to their mere existence as men are not. It is therefore wrong to direct an attack against those who merely serve the combatants' needs as human beings, such as farmers and food suppliers, even though survival as a human being is a necessary condition of efficient functioning as a soldier.

This brings us to the second group of restrictions: those that limit what may be done even to combatants. These limits are harder to explain clearly. Some of them may be arbitrary or conventional, and some may have to be derived from other sources; but I believe that the condition of directness and relevance in hostile relations accounts for them to a considerable extent.

Consider first a case which involves both a protected class of noncombatants and a restriction on the measures that may be used against combatants. One provision of the rules of war which is universally recognized, though it seems to be turning into a dead letter in Vietnam, is the special status of medical personnel and the wounded in warfare. It might be more efficient to shoot medical officers on sight and to let the enemy wounded die rather than be patched up to fight another day. But someone with medical insignia is supposed to be left alone and permitted to tend and retrieve the wounded. I believe this is because medical attention is a species of attention to completely general human needs, not specifically the needs of a combat soldier, and our conflict with the soldier is not with his existence as a human being.

By extending the application of this idea, one can justify prohibitions against certain particularly cruel weapons: starvation, poisoning, infectious diseases (supposing they could be inflicted on combatants only), weapons designed to maim or disfigure or torture the opponent rather than merely to stop him. It is not, I think, mere casuistry to claim that such weapons attack the men, not the soldiers. The effect of dum-dum bullets, for example, is much more extended than necessary to cope with the combat situation in which they are used. They abandon any attempt to discriminate in their effects between the combatant and the human being. For this reason the use of flamethrowers and napalm is an atrocity in all circumstances that I can imagine, whoever the target may be. Burns are both extremely painful and extremely disfiguring – far more than any other category of wound. That this well-known fact plays no (inhibiting) part in the determination of US weapons policy suggests that moral sensitivity among public officials has not increased markedly since the Spanish Inquisition.[10]

Finally, the same condition of appropriateness to the true object of hostility should limit the scope of attacks on an enemy country: its economy, agriculture, transportation system, and so forth. Even if the parties to a military conflict are considered to be not armies or governments but entire nations (which is usually a grave error), that does not justify one nation in warring against every aspect or element of another nation. That is not justified in a conflict between individuals, and nations are even more complex than individuals, so the same reasons apply. Like a human being, a nation is engaged in countless other pursuits while waging war, and it is not in those respects that it is an enemy.

The burden of the argument has been that absolutism about murder has a foundation in principles governing all one's relations to other persons, whether aggressive or amiable, and that these principles, and that absolutism, apply to warfare as well, with the result

that certain measures are impermissible no matter what the consequences.[11] I do not mean to romanticize war. It is sufficiently utopian to suggest that when nations conflict they might rise to the level of limited barbarity that typically characterizes violent conflict between individuals, rather than wallowing in the moral pit where they appear to have settled, surrounded by enormous arsenals.

VII

Having described the elements of the absolutist position, we must now return to the conflict between it and utilitarianism. Even if certain types of dirty tactics become acceptable when the stakes are high enough, the most serious of the prohibited acts, like murder and torture, are not just supposed to require unusually strong justification. They are supposed *never* to be done, because no quantity of resulting benefit is thought capable of *justifying* such treatment of a person.

The fact remains that when an absolutist knows or believes that the utilitarian cost of refusing to adopt a prohibited course will be very high, he may hold to his refusal to adopt it, but he will find it difficult to feel that a moral dilemma has been satisfactorily resolved. The same may be true of someone who rejects an absolutist requirement and adopts instead the course yielding the most acceptable consequences. In either case, it is possible to feel that one has acted for reasons insufficient to justify violation of the opposing principle. In situations of deadly conflict, particularly where a weaker party is threatened with annihilation or enslavement by a stronger one, the argument for resorting to atrocities can be powerful, and the dilemma acute.

There may exist principles, not yet codified, which would enable us to resolve such dilemmas. But then again there may not. We must face the pessimistic alternative that these two forms of moral intuition are not capable of being brought together into a single, coherent moral system, and that the world can present us with situations in which there is no honorable or moral course for a man to take, no course free of guilt and responsibility for evil.

The idea of a moral blind alley is a perfectly intelligible one. It is possible to get into such a situation by one's own fault, and people do it all the time. If, for example, one makes two incompatible promises or commitments – becomes engaged to two people, for example – then there is no course one can take which is not wrong, for one must break one's promise to at least one of them. Making a clean breast of the whole thing will not be enough to remove one's reprehensibility. The existence of such cases is not morally disturbing, however, because we feel that the situation was not unavoidable: one

had to do something wrong in the first place to get into it. But what if the world itself, or someone else's actions, could face a previously innocent person with a choice between morally abominable courses of action, and leave him no way to escape with his honor? Our intuitions rebel at the idea, for we feel that the constructibility of such a case must show a contradiction in our moral views. But it is not in itself a contradiction to say that someone can do X or not do X, and that for him to take either course would be wrong. It merely contradicts the supposition that *ought* implies *can* – since presumably one ought to refrain from what is wrong, and in such a case it is impossible to do so.[12] Given the limitations on human action, it is naïve to suppose that there is a solution to every moral problem with which the world can face us. We have always known that the world is a bad place. It appears that it may be an evil place as well.

Notes

[1] Straightforward considerations of national interest often tend in the same direction: the inadvisability of using nuclear weapons seems to be overdetermined in this way.

[2] These reasons, moreover, have special importance in that they are available even to one who denies the appropriateness of utilitarian considerations in international matters. He may acknowledge limitations on what may be done to the soldiers and civilians of other countries in pursuit of his nation's military objectives, while denying that one country should in general consider the interests of nationals of other countries in determining its policies.

[3] Privately printed. See also her essay "War and Murder," in *Nuclear Weapons and Christian Conscience*, ed. Walter Stein (London, 1963). The present paper is much indebted to these two essays throughout. These and related subjects are extensively treated by Paul Ramsey in *The Just War* (New York, 1968). Among recent writings that bear on the moral

problem are Jonathan Bennett, "Whatever the Consequences," *Analysis* 26:3 (1966), pp. 83–102; and Philippa Foot, "The Problem of Abortion and the Doctrine of the Double Effect," *The Oxford Review* 5 (1967), pp. 5–15. Miss Anscombe's replies are "A Note on Mr. Bennett," *Analysis* 26:3 (1966), p. 208, and "Who is Wronged?" *The Oxford Review* 5 (1967), pp. 16–17.

[4] This counter-argument was suggested by Rogers Albritton.

[5] Someone might of course acknowledge the *moral relevance* of the distinction between deliberate and nondeliberate killing, without being an absolutist. That is, he might believe simply that it was *worse* to bring about a death deliberately than as a secondary effect. But that would be merely a special assignment of value, and not an absolute prohibition.

[6] Why, on the other hand, does it seem appropriate, rather than irrelevant, to punch someone in the mouth if he insults you? The

answer is that in our culture it is an insult to punch someone in the mouth, and not just an injury. This reveals, by the way, a perfectly unobjectionable sense in which convention may play a part in determining exactly what falls under an absolutist restriction and what does not. I am indebted to Robert Fogelin for this point.

7 Finally, I should mention a different possibility, suggested by Robert Nozick: that there is a strong general presumption against benefiting from the calamity of another, whether or not it has been deliberately inflicted for that or any other reason. This broader principle may well lend its force to the absolutist position.

8 It has been remarked that according to my view, shooting at someone establishes an I–thou relationship.

9 What I say on this subject derives from Anscombe.

10 Beyond this I feel uncertain. Ordinary bullets, after all, can cause death, and nothing is more permanent than that. I am not at all sure why we are justified in trying to kill those who are trying to kill us (rather than merely in trying to stop them with force which may also result in their deaths). It is often argued that incapacitating gases are a relatively humane weapon (when not used, as in Vietnam, merely to make people easier to shoot). Perhaps the legitimacy of restrictions against them must depend on the dangers of escalation, and the great utility of maintaining *any* conventional category of restriction so long as nations are willing to adhere to it.

Let me make clear that I do not regard my argument as a defense of the moral immutability of the Hague and Geneva Conventions. Rather, I believe that they rest partly on a moral foundation, and that modifications of them should also be assessed on moral grounds.

But even this connection with the actual laws of war is not essential to my claims about what is permissible and what is not. Since completing this paper I have read an essay by Richard Wasserstrom entitled "The Laws of War" (which appeared in *The Monist*), which argues that the existing laws and conventions do not even attempt to embody a decent moral position: that their provisions have been determined by other interests, that they are in fact immoral in substance, and that it is a grave mistake to refer to them as standards in forming moral judgments about warfare. This possibility deserves serious consideration, and I am not sure what to say about it, but it does not affect my view of the moral issues.

11 It is possible to draw a more radical conclusion, which I shall not pursue here. Perhaps the technology and organization of modern war are such as to make it impossible to wage as an acceptable form of interpersonal or even international hostility. Perhaps it is too impersonal and large-scale for that. If so, then absolutism would in practice imply pacifism, given the present state of things. On the other hand, I am skeptical about the unstated assumption that a technology dictates its own use.

12 This was first pointed out to me by Christopher Boorse.

Chapter 28

Anticipations*
Michael Walzer

The first questions asked when states go to war are also the easiest to answer: who started the shooting? who sent troops across the border? These are questions of fact, not of judgment, and if the answers are disputed, it is only because of the lies that governments tell. The lies don't, in any case, detain us long; the truth comes out soon enough. Governments lie so as to absolve themselves from the charge of aggression. But it is not on the answers to questions such as these that our final judgments about aggression depend. There are further arguments to make, justifications to offer, lies to tell, before the moral issue is directly confronted. For aggression often begins without shots being fired or borders crossed.

Both individuals and states can rightfully defend themselves against violence that is imminent but not actual; they can fire the first shots if they know themselves about to be attacked. This is a right recognized in domestic law and also in the legalist paradigm for international society. In most legal accounts, however, it is severely restricted. Indeed, once one has stated the restrictions, it is no longer clear whether the right has any substance at all. Thus the argument of Secretary of State Daniel Webster in the *Caroline* case of 1842 (the details of which need not concern us here): in order to justify pre-emptive violence, Webster wrote, there must be shown "a necessity of self-defense . . . instant, overwhelming, leaving no choice of means, and no moment for deliberation."[1] That would permit us to do little more than respond to an attack *once we had seen it coming* but before we had felt its impact. Pre-emption on this view is like a reflex action, a throwing up of one's arms at the very last minute. But it hardly requires much of a "showing" to justify a movement of that sort. Even the most presumptuous aggressor is not likely to insist, as a matter of right, that his victims stand still until he lands the first blow. Webster's formula seems to be the favored one among students of international law, but I don't believe that it addresses itself usefully to the experience of imminent war. There is often plenty of time for deliberation, agonizing hours, days, even weeks of deliberation, when one doubts that war can be avoided and wonders whether or not to strike first. The debate is couched, I suppose, in strategic more than in moral terms. But the decision is judged morally, and the expectation of that judgment, of the effects it will have in allied and neutral states

* From Michael Walzer, *Just and Unjust War: A Moral Argument with Historical Illustrations*, 3rd edn. (New York: Basic Books, 2000), pp. 74–85, 340–1 (notes).

and among one's own people, is itself a strategic factor. So it is important to get the terms of the judgment right, and that requires some revision of the legalist paradigm. For the paradigm is more restrictive than the judgments we actually make. We are disposed to sympathize with potential victims even before they confront an instant and overwhelming necessity.

Imagine a spectrum of anticipation: at one end is Webster's reflex, necessary and determined; at the other end is preventive war, an attack that responds to a distant danger, a matter of foresight and free choice. I want to begin at the far end of the spectrum, where danger is a matter of judgment and political decision is unconstrained, and then edge my way along to the point where we currently draw the line between justified and unjustified attacks. What is involved at that point is something very different from Webster's reflex; it is still possible to make choices, to begin the fighting or to arm oneself and wait. Hence the decision to begin at least resembles the decision to fight a preventive war, and it is important to distinguish the criteria by which it is defended from those that were once thought to justify prevention. Why not draw the line at the far end of the spectrum? The reasons are central to an understanding of the position we now hold.

Preventive War and the Balance of Power

Preventive war presupposes some standard against which danger is to be measured. That standard does not exist, as it were, on the ground; it has nothing to do with the immediate security of boundaries. It exists in the mind's eye, in the idea of a balance of power, probably the dominant idea in international politics from the seventeenth century to the present day. A preventive war is a war fought to maintain the balance, to stop what is thought to be an even distribution of power from shifting into a relation of dominance and inferiority. The balance is often talked about as if it were the key to peace among states. But it cannot be that, else it would not need to be defended so often by force of arms. "The balance of power, the pride of modern policy . . . invented to preserve the general peace as well as the freedom of Europe," wrote Edmund Burke in 1760, "has only preserved its liberty. It has been the original of innumerable and fruitless wars."[2] In fact, of course, the wars to which Burke is referring are easily numbered. Whether or not they were fruitless depends upon how one views the connection between preventive war and the preservation of liberty. Eighteenth-century British statesmen and their intellectual supporters obviously thought the connection very close. A radically unbalanced system, they recognized, would more likely make for peace, but they were "alarmed by the danger of universal monarchy."* When they went to war on

---

* The line is from David Hume's essay "Of the Balance of Power," where Hume describes three British wars on behalf of the balance as having been "begun with justice, and even, perhaps, from necessity." I would have considered his argument at length had I found it possible to place it within his philosophy. But in his *Enquiry Concerning the Principles of Morals* (Section III, Part I), Hume writes: "The rage and violence of public war: what is it but a suspension of justice among the warring parties, who perceive that this virtue is now no longer of any *use* or advantage to them?" Nor is it possible, according to Hume, that this suspension itself be just or unjust; it is entirely a matter of necessity, as in the (Hobbist) state of nature where individuals "consult the dictates of self-preservation alone." That standards of justice exist alongside the pressures of necessity is a discovery of the *Essays*. This is another example, perhaps, of the impossibility of carrying over certain philosophical positions into ordinary moral discourse. In any case, the three wars Hume discusses were none of them necessary to the preservation of Britain. He may have thought them just because he thought the balance generally useful.

behalf of the balance, they thought they were defending, not national interest alone, but an international order that made liberty possible throughout Europe.

That is the classic argument for prevention. It requires of the rulers of states, as Francis Bacon had argued a century earlier, that they "keep due sentinel, that none of their neighbors do overgrow so (by increase of territory, by embracing of trade, by approaches, or the like) as they become more able to annoy them, than they were."[3] And if their neighbors do "overgrow," then they must be fought, sooner rather than later, and without waiting for the first blow. "Neither is the opinion of some of the Schoolmen to be received: that a war cannot justly be made, but upon a precedent injury or provocation. For there is no question, but a just fear of an imminent danger, though no blow be given, is a lawful cause of war." Imminence here is not a matter of hours or days. The sentinels stare into temporal as well as geographic distance as they watch the growth of their neighbor's power. They will fear that growth as soon as it tips or seems likely to tip the balance. War is justified (as in Hobbes' philosophy) by fear alone and not by anything other states actually do or any signs they give of their malign intentions. Prudent rulers assume malign intentions.

The argument is utilitarian in form; it can be summed up in two propositions: (1) that the balance of power actually does preserve the liberties of Europe (perhaps also the happiness of Europeans) and is therefore worth defending even at some cost, and (2) that to fight early, before the balance tips in any decisive way, greatly reduces the cost of the defense, while waiting doesn't mean avoiding war (unless one also gives up liberty) but only fighting on a larger scale and at worse odds. The argument is plausible enough, but it is possible to imagine a second-level utilitarian response: (3) that the acceptance of propositions (1) and (2) is dangerous (not useful) and certain to lead to "innumerable and fruitless wars" whenever shifts in power relations occur; but increments and losses of power are a constant feature of international politics, and perfect equilibrium, like perfect security, is a utopian dream; therefore it is best to fall back upon the legalist paradigm or some similar rule and wait until the overgrowth of power is put to some overbearing use. This is also plausible enough, but it is important to stress that the position to which we are asked to fall back is not a prepared position, that is, it does not itself rest on any utilitarian calculation. Given the radical uncertainties of power politics, there probably is no practical way of making out that position – deciding when to fight and when not – on utilitarian principles. Think of what one would have to know to perform the calculations, of the experiments one would have to conduct, the wars one would have to fight – and leave unfought! In any case, we mark off moral lines on the anticipation spectrum in an entirely different way.

It isn't really prudent to assume the malign intent of one's neighbors, it is merely cynical, an example of the worldly wisdom which no one lives by or could live by. We need to make judgments about our neighbor's intentions, and if such judgments are to be possible we must stipulate certain acts or sets of acts that will count as evidence of malignity. These stipulations are not arbitrary; they are generated, I think, when we reflect upon what it means *to be threatened*. Not merely *to be afraid*, though rational men and women may well respond fearfully to a genuine threat, and their subjective experience is not an unimportant part of the argument for anticipation. But we also need an objective standard, as Bacon's phrase "just fear" suggests. That standard must refer to the threatening acts of some neighboring state, for (leaving aside the dangers of natural disaster) I can only be threatened by someone who is threatening me, where "threaten" means what the dictionary says it means: "to hold out or offer (some injury) by way of a threat, to declare one's intention of inflicting injury."[4] It is with some such notion as this that we must judge the wars fought for the sake of the balance of power. Consider, then, the Spanish Succession, regarded in the eighteenth century as a paradigmatic case for preventive war, and yet, I think, a negative example of threatening behavior.

The War of the Spanish Succession

Writing in the 1750s, the Swiss jurist Vattel suggested the following criteria for legitimate prevention: "Whenever a state has given signs of injustice, rapacity, pride, ambition, or of an imperious thirst of rule, it becomes a suspicious neighbor to be guarded against: and at a juncture when it is on the point of receiving a formidable augmentation of power, securities may be asked, and on its making any difficulty to give them, its designs may be prevented by force of arms."[5] These criteria were formulated with explicit reference to the events of 1700 and 1701, when the King of Spain, last of his line, lay ill and dying. Long before those years, Louis XIV had given Europe evident signs of injustice, rapacity, pride, and so on. His foreign policy was openly expansionist and aggressive (which is not to say that justifications were not offered, ancient claims and titles uncovered, for every intended territorial acquisition). In 1700, he seemed about to receive a "formidable augmentation of power" – his grandson, the Duke of Anjou, was offered the Spanish throne. With his usual arrogance, Louis refused to provide any assurances or guarantees to his fellow monarchs. Most importantly, he refused to bar Anjou from the French succession, thus holding open the possibility of a unified and powerful Franco–Spanish state. And then, an alliance of European powers, led by Great Britain, went to war against what they assumed was Louis' "design" to dominate Europe. Having drawn his criteria so closely to his case, however, Vattel concludes on a sobering note: "it has since appeared that the policy [of the Allies] was too suspicious." That is wisdom after the fact, of course, but still wisdom, and one would expect some effort to restate the criteria in its light.

The mere augmentation of power, it seems to me, cannot be a warrant for war or even the beginning of warrant, and for much the same reason that Bacon's commercial expansion ("embracing of trade") is also and even more obviously insufficient. For both of these suggest developments that may not be politically designed at all and hence cannot be taken as evidence of intent. As Vattel says, Anjou had been invited to his throne "by the [Spanish] nation, conformably to the will of its last sovereign" – that is, though there can be no question here of democratic decision-making, he had been invited for Spanish and not for French reasons. "Have not these two Realms," asked Jonathan Swift in a pamphlet opposing the British war, "their separate maxims of Policy . . . ?"[6] Nor is Louis' refusal to make promises relating to some future time to be taken as evidence of design – only, perhaps, of hope. If Anjou's succession made immediately for a closer alliance between Spain and France, the appropriate answer would seem to have been a closer alliance between Britain and Austria. Then one could wait and judge anew the intentions of Louis.

But there is a deeper issue here. When we stipulate threatening acts, we are looking not only for indications of intent, but also for rights of response. To characterize certain acts as threats is to characterize them in a moral way, and in a way that makes a military response morally comprehensible. The utilitarian arguments for prevention don't do that, not because the wars they generate are too frequent, but because they are too common in another sense: *too ordinary*. Like Clausewitz's description of war as the continuation of policy by other means, they radically underestimate the importance of the shift from diplomacy to force. They don't recognize the problem that killing and being killed poses. Perhaps the recognition depends upon a certain way of valuing human life, which was not the way of eighteenth-century statesmen. (How many of the British soldiers who shipped to the continent with Marlborough ever returned? Did anyone bother to count?) But the point is an important one anyway, for it suggests why people have come to feel uneasy about preventive war. We don't want to fight until we are threatened, because only then can we rightly fight. It is a question of moral security. That is why Vattel's concluding remark about the War of the Spanish Succession, and Burke's general argument about the fruitlessness of such wars, is so worrying. It is inevitable, of course, that political calculations will sometimes go wrong; so will moral choices; there is no such thing as perfect security. But there is a great difference, nonetheless, between killing and being killed by soldiers who can plausibly be described as the present instruments of an aggressive intention, and killing and being killed by soldiers who may or may not represent a distant danger to our country. In the first case, we confront an army recognizably hostile, ready for war, fixed in a posture of attack. In the second, the hostility is prospective and imaginary, and it will always be a charge against us that we have made war upon soldiers who were themselves engaged in entirely legitimate (nonthreatening) activities. Hence the moral necessity of rejecting any attack that is merely preventive in character, that does not wait upon and respond to the willful acts of an adversary.

Pre-emptive Strikes

Now, what acts are to count, what acts do count as threats sufficiently serious to justify war? It is not possible to put together a list, because state action, like human action generally, takes on significance from its context. But there are some negative points worth making. The boastful ranting to which political leaders are often prone isn't in itself threatening; injury must be "offered" in some material sense as well. Nor does the kind of military preparation that is a feature of the classic arms race count as a threat, unless it violates some formally or tacitly agreed-upon limit. What the lawyers call "hostile acts short of war," even if these involve violence, are not too quickly to be taken as signs of an intent to make war; they may represent an essay in restraint, an offer to quarrel within limits. Finally, provocations are not the same as threats. "Injury and provocation" are commonly linked by Scholastic writers as the two causes of just war. But the Schoolmen were too accepting of contemporary notions about the honor of states and, more importantly, of sovereigns.[7] The moral significance of such ideas is dubious at best. Insults are not occasions for wars, any more than they are (these days) occasions for duels.

For the rest, military alliances, mobilizations, troop movements, border incursions, naval blockades – all these, with or without verbal menace, sometimes count and sometimes do not count as sufficient indications of hostile intent. But it is, at least, these sorts of actions with which we are concerned. We move along the anticipation spectrum in search, as it were, of enemies: not possible or potential enemies, not merely present illwishers, but states and nations that are already, to use a phrase I shall use again with reference to the distinction of combatants and noncombatants, *engaged in harming us* (and who have already harmed us, by their threats, even if they have not yet inflicted any physical injury). And this search, though it carries us beyond preventive war, clearly brings us up short of Webster's pre-emption. The line between legitimate and illegitimate first strikes is not going to be drawn at the point of imminent attack but at the point of sufficient threat. That phrase is necessarily vague. I mean it to cover three things: a manifest intent to injure, a degree of active preparation that makes that intent a positive danger, and a general situation in which waiting, or doing anything other than fighting, greatly magnifies the risk. The argument may be made more clear if I compare these criteria to Vattel's. Instead of previous signs of rapacity and ambition, current and particular signs are required; instead of an "augmentation of power," actual preparation for war; instead of the refusal of future securities, the intensification of present dangers. Preventive war looks to the past and future, Webster's reflex action to the immediate moment, while the idea of being under a threat focuses on what we had best call simply *the present*. I cannot specify a time span; it is a span within which one can still make choices, and within which it is possible to feel straitened.[8]

What such a time is like is best revealed concretely. We can study it in the three weeks that preceded the Six Day War of 1967. Here is a case as crucial for an understanding of anticipation in the twentieth century as the War of the Spanish Succession was for the eighteenth, and one suggesting that the shift from dynastic to national politics, the costs of which have so often been stressed, has also brought some moral gains. For nations, especially democratic nations, are less likely to fight preventive wars than dynasties are.

The Six Day War

Actual fighting between Israel and Egypt began on June 5, 1967, with an Israeli first strike. In the early hours of the war, the Israelis did not acknowledge that they had sought the advantages of surprise, but the deception was not maintained. In fact, they believed themselves justified in attacking first by the dramatic events of the previous weeks. So we must focus on those events and their moral significance. It would be possible, of course, to look further back still, to the whole course of the Arab–Jewish conflict in the Middle East. Wars undoubtedly have long political and moral pre-histories. But anticipation needs to be understood within a narrower frame. The Egyptians believed that the founding of Israel in 1948 had been unjust, that the state had no rightful existence, and hence that it could be attacked at any time. It follows from this that Israel had no right of anticipation since it had no right of self-defense. But self-defense seems the primary and indisputable right of any political community, merely because it is *there* and whatever the circumstances under which it achieved statehood.* Perhaps this is why the Egyptians fell back in their more formal arguments upon the claim that a state of war already existed between Egypt and Israel and that this condition justified the military moves they undertook in May 1967.[9] But the same condition would justify Israel's first strike. It is best to assume, I think, that the existing cease-fire between the two countries was at least a near-peace and that the outbreak of the war requires a moral explanation – the burden falling on the Israelis, who began the fighting.

The crisis apparently had its origins in reports, circulated by Soviet officials in mid-May, that Israel was massing its forces on the Syrian border. The falsity of these reports

---

* The only limitation on this right has to do with internal, not external legitimacy: a state (or government) established against the will of its own people, ruling violently, may well forfeit its right to defend itself even against a foreign invasion.

was almost immediately vouched for by United Nations observers on the scene. Nevertheless, on May 14, the Egyptian government put its armed forces on "maximum alert" and began a major buildup of its troops in the Sinai. Four days later, Egypt expelled the United Nations Emergency Force from the Sinai and the Gaza Strip; its withdrawal began immediately, though I do not think that its title had been intended to suggest that it would depart so quickly in event of emergency. The Egyptian military buildup continued, and on May 22, President Nasser announced that the Straits of Tiran would henceforth be closed to Israeli shipping.

In the aftermath of the Suez War of 1956, the Straits had been recognized by the world community as an international waterway. That meant that their closing would constitute a *casus belli*, and the Israelis had stated at that time, and on many occasions since, that they would so regard it. The war might then be dated from May 22, and the Israeli attack of June 5 described simply as its first military incident: wars often begin before the fighting of them does. But the fact is that after May 22, the Israeli cabinet was still debating whether or not to go to war. And, in any case, the actual initiation of violence is a crucial moral event. If it can sometimes be justified by reference to previous events, it nevertheless has to be justified. In a major speech on May 29, Nasser made that justification much easier by announcing that if war came the Egyptian goal would be nothing less than the destruction of Israel. On May 30, King Hussein of Jordan flew to Cairo to sign a treaty placing the Jordanian army under Egyptian command in event of war, thus associating himself with the Egyptian purpose. Syria already had agreed to such an arrangement, and several days later Iraq joined the alliance. The Israelis struck on the day after the Iraqi annoucement.

For all the excitement and fear that their actions generated, it is unlikely that the Egyptians intended to begin the war themselves. After the fighting was over, Israel published documents, captured in its course, that included plans for an invasion of the Negev; but these were probably plans for a counterattack, once an Israeli offensive had spent itself in the Sinai, or for a first strike at some later time. Nasser would almost certainly have regarded it as a great victory if he could have closed the Straits and maintained his army on Israel's borders without war. Indeed, it would have been a great victory, not only because of the economic blockade it would have established, but also because of the strain it would have placed on the Israeli defense system. "There was a basic assymetry in the structure of forces: the Egyptians could deploy . . . their large army of long-term regulars on the Israeli border and keep it there indefinitely; the Israelis could only counter their deployment by mobilizing reserve formations, and reservists could not be kept in uniform for very long . . . Egypt could therefore stay on the defensive while Israel would have to attack unless the crisis was defused diplomatically."[10] *Would have to attack:* the necessity cannot be called instant and overwhelming; nor, however, would an Israeli decision to allow Nasser his victory have meant nothing more than a shift in the balance of power posing possible dangers at some future time. It would have opened Israel to attack at any time. It would have represented a drastic erosion of Israeli security such as only a determined enemy would hope to bring about.

The initial Israeli response was not similiarly determined but, for domestic political reasons having to do in part with the democratic character of the state, hesitant and confused. Israel's leaders sought a political resolution of the crisis – the opening of the Straits and a demobilization of forces on both sides – which they did not have the political strength or support to effect. A flurry of diplomatic activity ensued, serving only to reveal what might have been predicted in advance: the unwillingness of the Western powers to pressure or coerce the Egyptians. One always wants to see diplomacy tried before the resort to war, so that we are sure that war is the last resort. But it would be difficult in this case to make an argument for its necessity. Day by day, diplomatic efforts seemed only to intensify Israel's isolation.

Meanwhile, "an intense fear spread in the country." The extraordinary Israeli triumph, once fighting began, makes it difficult to recall the preceding weeks of anxiety. Egypt was in the grip of a war fever, familiar enough from European history, a celebration in advance of expected victories. The Israeli mood was very different, suggesting what it means to live under threat: rumors of coming disasters were endlessly repeated; frightened men and women raided food shops, buying up their entire stock, despite government announcements that there were ample reserves; thousands of graves were dug in the military cemeteries; Israel's political and military leaders lived on the edge of nervous exhaustion.[11] I have already argued that fear by itself establishes no right of anticipation. But Israeli anxiety during those weeks seems an almost classical example of "just fear" – first, because Israel really was in danger (as foreign observers readily agreed), and second, because it was Nasser's intention to put it in danger. He said this often enough, but it is also and more importantly true that his military moves served no other, more limited goal.

The Israeli first strike is, I think, a clear case of legitimate anticipation. To say that, however, is to suggest a major revision of the legalist paradigm. For it means that aggression can be made out not only in the absence of a military attack or invasion but in the (probable) absence of any immediate intention to launch such an attack or invasion. The general formula must go something like this: states may use military force in the face of threats of war, whenever the failure to do so would seriously risk their territorial integrity or political independence. Under such circumstances it can fairly be said that they have been forced to fight and that they are the victims of aggression. Since there are no police upon whom they can call, the moment at which states are forced to fight probably comes sooner than it would for individuals in a settled domestic society. But if we imagine an unstable society, like the "wild west" of American fiction, the analogy can be restated: a state under threat is like an individual hunted by an enemy who has announced his intention of killing or injuring him. Surely such a person may surprise his hunter, if he is able to do so.

The formula is permissive, but it implies restrictions that can usefully be unpacked only with reference to particular cases. It is obvious, for example, that measures short of war are preferable to war itself whenever they hold out the hope of similar or nearly similar effectiveness. But what those measures might be, or how long they must be tried, cannot he a matter of *a priori* stipulation. In the case of the Six Day War, the "asymmetry in the structure of forces" set a time limit on diplomatic efforts that would have no relevance to conflicts involving other sorts of states and armies. A general rule containing words like "seriously" opens a broad path for human judgment – which it is, no doubt, the purpose of the legalist paradigm to narrow or block altogether. But it is a fact of our moral life that political leaders make such judgments, and that once they are made the rest of us do not uniformly condemn them. Rather, we weigh and evaluate their actions on the basis of criteria like those I have tried to describe. When we do that we are acknowledging that there are threats with which no nation can be expected to live. And that acknowledgment is an important part of our understanding of aggression.

Notes

1 D. W. Bowett, *Self-Defense in International Law* (New York, 1958), p. 59. My own position has been influenced by Julius Stone's critique of the legalist argument: *Aggression and World Order* (Berkeley, CA, 1968).

2 Quoted from the *Annual Register*, in H. Butterfield, "The Balance of Power," *Diplomatic Investigations*, pp. 144–5.

3 Francis Bacon, Essays ("Of Empire"); see also his treatise *Considerations Touching a War with Spain* (1624), in *The Works of Francis Bacon*, ed. James Spedding et al. (London, 1874), XIV, pp. 469–505.

4 *Oxford English Dictionary*, "threaten."

5 M. D. Vattel, *The Law of Nations* (Northampton, MA, 1805), bk. III, ch. III, paras. 42–4, pp. 357–78. Cf. John Westlake, *Chapters on the Principles of International Law* (Cambridge, England, 1894), p. 120.

6 Jonathan Swift, *The Conduct of the Allies and of the Late Ministry in Beginning and Carrying on the Present War* (1711), in *Prose Works*, ed. Temple Scott (London, 1901), V, 116.

7 As late as the eighteenth century, Vattel still argued that a prince "has a right to demand, even by force of arms, the reparation of an insult." *Law of Nations*, bk. II, ch. IV, para. 48, p. 216.

8 Compare the argument of Hugo Grotius: "The danger . . . must be immediate and imminent in point of time. I admit, to be sure, that if the assailant seizes weapons in such a way that his intent to kill is manifest, the crime can be forestalled; for in morals as in material things a point is not to be found which does not have a certain breadth." *The Law of War and Peace*, trans. Francis W. Kelsey (Indianapolis, n.d.), bk. II, ch. I, section V, p. 173.

9 Walter Laquer, *The Road to War: The Origin and Aftermath of the Arab–Israeli Conflict, 1967–8* (Baltimore 1969), p. 110.

10 Edward Luttwak and Dan Horowitz, *The Israeli Army* (New York, 1975), p. 212.

11 Luttwak and Horowitz, p. 224.

Chapter 29

Just Cause for War*
Jeff McMahan

Perhaps it should be rather heartening that democratic leaders who wish to take their countries to war are now obliged to advertise the war as having a "just cause." Politicians now routinely invoke this rather quaint phrase drawn from the traditional theory of the just war. Indeed, when the administration of George H. W. Bush decided to invade Panama, it christened its war "Operation Just Cause," thereby appropriating a label that George W. Bush might later have found serviceable had it still been available. But despite the increasing prominence of the notion of just cause in political discourse, there are few serious discussions of it, and those there are tend to be perfunctory. The usual practice is to offer a simple characterization of the requirement of just cause – for example, that it is the requirement that there be a good or compelling reason to go to war – and then to observe that, at least until quite recently, contemporary just war theory and international law have recognized only one just cause for war: self- or other-defense against aggression. It is then often noted that the consensus on this point is currently being challenged by those who claim that the pre-

vention of large-scale violations of people's human rights by their own government also provides just cause for war. Occasionally, skeptics of just war theory will also, for satirical effect, cite instances from the classical literature of causes for war that are now rejected but were once widely accepted as just, such as the punishment of wrongdoing and the spread of the Christian religion.

In this essay I advance a conception of the requirement of just cause that is revisionist in the context of contemporary just war theory, but that has roots in an older tradition of thought about the just war with which contemporary theorists have lost touch to a considerable extent. This revisionist conception has various heterodox – indeed, heretical – implications that I will highlight and defend: for example, that a just cause is necessary for the satisfaction of any of the other conditions of a just war, that there can be various just causes for war other than defense against aggression, that both sides in a war can have a just cause, and so on. The conception of just cause for which I will argue must ultimately be assessed by reference to the moral plausibility both of these implications and of the larger understanding of a just war in which the conception is embedded. As I will make clear below, I

* From *Ethics & International Affairs* 19:3 (2005). pp. 55–75.

mean by a just war something more than merely a morally justified war.

Resort to War, Continuation of War, and Termination of War

In the just war tradition, just cause is one of the requirements of *jus ad bellum* – that is, one of the conditions of justification for the resort to war. Contemporary just war theorists often assume, therefore, that the requirement of just cause applies only to the initial resort to war, and that after war has begun all that matters is how the war is conducted. But this cannot be right. It is possible that a war can begin without a just cause but become just when a just cause arises during the course of the fighting and takes over as the goal of the war. When this happens, it would be absurd to say that an unjust war has concluded and a new, just war has begun. Rather, one and the same war may cease to be unjust and become just – just as a war that begins with a just cause may continue after that cause has been achieved or has simply disappeared on its own.[1] But if a war in progress can either acquire or cease to have a just cause, then the requirement of just cause must apply not only to the resort to war but also to the continuation of war.[2] A just cause is, indeed, always required for engaging in war. Just cause specifies the ends for which it is permissible to engage in war, or that it is permissible to pursue by means of war.

One important implication of the idea that any engagement in war requires a just cause is that when the just cause of a war has been achieved, continuation of the war lacks justification and is therefore impermissible. Just cause thus determines the conditions for the termination of war.

There are, however, complexities here of which it is important to be aware. Although theorists in the just war tradition often write as if just cause were always a single, unitary goal, such as collective self-defense, there is

no reason to suppose that a war may have only one just cause. Even if the requirement of just cause applied only to the resort to war, there could in principle be two or more just causes. It is even possible that, if there were two or more just causes, no one on its own would be sufficiently important to make the resort to war proportionate, though all together would be. And assuming that the requirement of just cause applies not only to the initial resort to war but also to the continuation of war, it is also possible for there to be different just causes for the same war at different times. Consider, for example, a war that has self-defense against unjust aggression as its initial just cause. It might be justifiable to continue the war even after the initial aggression had been defeated in order to protect people in a justly occupied area or to ensure the effective disarmament of the aggressor. These would be just causes that, while not part of the justification for the recourse to war, may legitimately be pursued by the continuation of the war.

The idea that war may not be continued in the absence of a just cause explains why it cannot be permissible to demand that an adversary surrender unconditionally. For the idea that it could be permissible to demand unconditional surrender presupposes that the denial of *any* condition that the other side might set for surrender would itself be a just cause for the continuation of war. And that cannot be the case. Suppose the enemy insists on something perfectly reasonable as a condition of surrender – for example, that the victors pledge not to kill the prisoners of war they are holding. If it were permissible for the victors to insist on unconditional surrender and to continue the war until they secured it, that would presuppose that it is permissible for them to assert by means of war their alleged right to withhold a pledge not to kill prisoners.

This of course leaves open the question of what may be done when an adversary who has fought without justification demands as a condition of surrender something to which they are not entitled, yet the demand is also of a type that it would not be permissible to resist by means of war. Suppose, for example, that an adversary who has been largely defeated militarily demands as a condition of surrender that they be allowed to continue certain unjust domestic practices, such as certain forms of religious discrimination (for example, providing state funding for schools that promulgate the state religion, but not for others). Just as it may be necessary for an individual not to resist certain forms of wrongdoing when the only effective response would be inappropriate or excessive in relation to the offense, so it may be necessary in war to grant certain undeserved concessions when the only alternative is to continue to fight without sufficient justification.

The Moral Priority of Just Cause in *Jus ad Bellum*

It is not only unjust aims that cannot permissibly be pursued by means of war. There are also many good or legitimate aims that cannot permissibly be pursued by means of war. The requirement of just cause is not simply that war must have a just or worthy goal. Nor is it a requirement that there be a worthy goal, the achievement of which would outweigh the bad effects of war. In the just war tradition, the task of assessing the comparative importance of the goal or goals of war is assigned to the independent *jus ad bellum* requirement of proportionality. Proportionality requires, roughly, that the relevant bad effects attributable to the war must not be excessive in relation to the relevant good effects.[3] According to the view I accept, it might in principle be possible for considerations of proportionality to be fully subsumed within the requirement of just cause.

Many just war theorists would resist this suggestion, however, because they believe that the goods that count in the proportionality calculation are not restricted to those specified by the just cause. But unless just cause fully accounts for considerations of proportionality, it ought not to say anything about the scale, magnitude, or comparative importance of the goods to be achieved by war. For it would be uneconomical and indeed pointless to divide the work of weighing and measuring values between two requirements – for example, by having just cause stipulate that the goal of a war must be to achieve some very great good, while proportionality would require that the good be great enough to outweigh the relevant bad effects of the war.

I suggest, therefore, that just cause says *nothing* about considerations of scale or magnitude, but functions entirely as a restriction on the *type* of aim or end that may legitimately be pursued by means of war. It does not require that there be a great deal of good to be gained from war; nor does it imply that if there *is* a great deal of good to be gained, there is therefore a just cause.

This way of understanding the requirement of just cause parallels commonsense beliefs about the morality of individual action. Consider killing, for example, which occurs on a large scale in war. Suppose – to alter the details of Dostoyevsky's *Crime and Punishment* only slightly – that by killing the miserly and misanthropic old moneylender, Raskolnikov could have divided her wealth among a large number of poor people, bringing significant benefits to each that together would have greatly outweighed the harm to her. Most people think that this is not even the right *kind* of justification for killing. It is widely held that only certain *types* of aims – such as self-defense against an unjust attack – can provide a justification for killing. In the same way, there are numerous worthy and important goals that cannot justify the resort to war, or the practice of war. It cannot, for example, be a justification for going to war against a people that it would stimulate the world economy, no matter how great the economic benefits would be.[4]

I will soon turn to the question of how those types of goal that might provide a just cause for war may be distinguished from those that cannot. For the moment I will say more about the relation between just cause and proportionality.

Because just cause is only a restriction on the type of aim that can justify war, the proportionality requirement may have a larger role than many people suspect. Suppose, for example, that the defense of a state's territorial integrity against even partial annexation by another state is a just cause for war, as many people believe. If just cause is not a matter of scale, then there would be a just cause for war if a neighboring country were about to capture an acre of our territory on its border – an acre that it regards as a holy site, but that we are using only as a garbage dump. In this case, the reason why it would be wrong for us to go to war to retain our possession of that acre is not that our aim would be too trivial to constitute a just cause; it is, rather, that our just cause would be too trivial for war to be proportionate. (Something of this sort might have been argued with respect to Britain's resort to war when Argentina seized the Falkland Islands – though defenders of that war argued that the proportionality calculation had to take into account the importance of deterring even limited acts of aggression in order to uphold the principle of territorial integrity.)

If this is right, there is a sense in which just cause does less work than many have supposed, while proportionality does more. But there is also a sense in which just cause has a kind of priority over all the other requirements of *jus ad bellum*. In most statements of the traditional theory, the following requirements are included among the principles *of jus ad bellum*: just cause, competent authority, right intention, reasonable hope of success, necessity, and proportionality. The satisfaction of each is held to be necessary in order for the resort to war to be justified. And in that sense all the requirements are of equal importance. But I believe that just cause has priority over the other valid requirements in this sense: the others cannot be satisfied, even in principle, unless just cause is satisfied.

Admittedly, this is not true of the traditional requirement of competent authority, but I reject that component of the traditional theory for reasons I will not present here.[5] I also think that the plausible element in the requirement of "reasonable hope of success" is subsumed by the proportionality requirement.

That leaves right intention, necessity, and proportionality. Although it is not obvious to me that right intention is a valid requirement, suppose for the sake of argument that it is. It requires that war be pursued for the reasons that actually justify the war. It insists that those reasons not simply serve as a cover for the pursuit of other aims. What this means is that right intention is the requirement that war be pursued *in order* to achieve the just cause. Without a just cause, therefore, there are no reasons that can properly motivate the resort to war.

There is, it might be argued, one way in which right intention could be satisfied even in the absence of a just cause: if people falsely believed that there was a just cause and fought with the intention of achieving it. Yet it seems to me that this would clearly *not* be the *right* intention in the circumstances, though it might well be a *good* intention.

Consider next the requirement of necessity. This requirement demands that war be a necessary means of achieving the just cause. The claim that war is necessary for something other than the achievement of a just cause has no justificatory force.

In the case of proportionality, there is an equally simple argument. If just cause indicates the range of goods that may permissibly be pursued by war, then no goods that fail to come within the scope of the just cause, or are instrumental to achieving it, can count in the proportionality calculation. If they did, that would imply that a war is justified, at least in part, by the fact that it would achieve certain goods that cannot permissibly be achieved by means of war. (For those who are unconvinced by this simple argument, I will say more on this point in a later section on just cause and proportionality.)

Just Cause and *Jus in Bello*

I have argued that none of the valid requirements of *jus ad bellum* can be satisfied in the absence of a just cause. I also believe something even more controversial, which is that the requirements of *jus in bello* also cannot – except in rare instances – be satisfied in the absence of a just cause. This is a highly unorthodox claim. It is an axiom of contemporary just war theory that whether action in war is permissible or impermissible does not depend on whether there is a just cause. Just cause, on this view, governs only the resort to war. It is an *ad bellum* requirement, and as such has no role in the account of *jus in bello*. For the requirements of *jus in bello* and those of *jus ad bellum* are, as Michael Walzer puts it, "logically independent"; hence, just as a war that one is justified in fighting may be fought in an unjust manner, so a war that is itself unjustified may nevertheless be fought in a just manner or, as Walzer says, "in strict accordance with the rules."[6] The requirements of *jus ad bellum* are, moreover, thought to apply only to the political leaders, those with the authority to commit a people to war, and not to those who do the actual fighting. On this view, there is a moral division of labor that makes

soldiers responsible for adherence only to the principles of *jus in bello*, which must therefore be satisfiable whether or not their war meets the conditions of *jus ad bellum*. It would be intolerable to suppose that all soldiers who are commanded to fight in an unjust war, or who fight in such a war without knowing that it lacks a just cause, are for that reason criminals or even murderers.

It may seem obvious, in any case, that at least some of the requirements of *jus in bello* can be satisfied even by those who fight without just cause. The requirement of discrimination, for example, requires only that combatants restrict their attacks to military targets – that they target only other combatants and not noncombatants. This is implicit in the widely used alternative label for the requirement: the "requirement of noncombatant immunity."

But this is in fact just one interpretation of the requirement of discrimination, which in generic terms is simply the requirement to discriminate between legitimate and illegitimate targets and to make deliberate attacks only on the former. In my view, which I have defended elsewhere, the distinction between legitimate and illegitimate targets does not coincide with that between combatants and noncombatants. Rather, what discrimination requires is that soldiers target only those who are morally responsible for an unjust threat or for some other grievance that provides a just cause for war. If that is right, soldiers who lack a just cause also lack legitimate targets.[7]

Similarly, if soldiers lack a just cause, there are no goods that they are justified in pursuing by means of war. So even if there are goods for which belligerent action is necessary, they are not goods that can permissibly be achieved in that way. And when there are no goods that may be pursued by means of war, there are no goods that can properly be weighed against the bad effects that an act of war would cause; therefore, no act of war can be proportionate in the absence of a just cause.[8] In short, when there is no just cause, acts of war can be neither discriminate, necessary, nor proportionate.

There is, I concede, a small class of exceptions to this general claim. These are acts of war by those who lack a just cause that are necessary to prevent their adversaries from acting in ways that would be seriously wrong – for example, to prevent those fighting with a just cause from pursuing it by illegitimate means, such as by attacking people who are innocent in the relevant sense as a means of coercing those people's government to surrender.[9]

This concession necessitates that we distinguish between a *just cause for war*, which can contribute to the justification for going to war and may legitimately be pursued by means of war, and what I will call a *discrete just aim*, which cannot contribute to the justification for the resort to war or for its continuation, but may legitimately be pursued by means of war if war is in progress. Such aims are "discrete" because they occur in isolation and are unconnected with the larger aims of the unjust war of which they are a part. The permissibility of pursuing a discrete just aim by means of war is doubly conditional: it may be pursued *if* war is already in progress and *if* the wrong to be prevented cannot be avoided by surrendering on morally acceptable terms.

In general, however, a just cause is necessary for an act of war to be justified. It is for this reason that war must cease once the just cause has been achieved. Soldiers may not continue to fight once the aims that justified their fighting have been achieved. And if this is true, it should also be true that they may not fight at all if there are not and never were any aims that justify their being at war. Just cause is necessary not only for it to be permissible for political leaders to resort to war; it is also necessary for it to be permissible to *participate* in war.

This is not to say that those who participate in war without a just cause are necessarily culpable or deserving of punishment. Just as in the law a person may be fully exculpated for action that is objectively in breach of a statute, so most soldiers who fight without a just cause may have a variety of excuses that partially or even fully exculpate them. And even if the excuses that soldiers have for fighting in an unjust war never fully exculpate them, it is possible, and almost certainly highly desirable, not to treat mere participation in an unjust war as punishable under international law.

The Connection between Just Cause and Moral Liability to Attack

These claims about the dependence of *jus in bello* on just cause deviate substantially from the currently orthodox understanding of the just war. I will now advance a view about what types of aim can be just causes for war that is also heretical, given the consensus that has developed between international law and contemporary just war theory that defense against aggression is the sole just cause for war (with the possible exception of the prevention of large-scale violations of human rights, such as genocide). The view about what may be a just cause for war that I will defend does, however, have roots in the writings of earlier just war theorists and earlier theorists of international law.

Thomas Aquinas, for example, was close to the truth when he wrote that "a just cause is required, viz. that those who are to be warred upon should deserve to be warred upon because of some fault."[10] This claim is, however, in one respect too narrow and in another too broad. It is too narrow in its insistence that it is necessary for just cause that those attacked should *deserve* to be attacked. I take the claim that a person *deserves* to be harmed to imply that there is a moral reason to harm him even when harming him is unnecessary for the achievement of any other aim – for example, when harming him would not prevent, deter, or rectify any other harm or wrong. In this sense, people seldom if ever deserve to be warred upon.

The notion I would substitute for desert is *liability*. To say that a person is liable to be attacked is not to say that there is a reason to attack him no matter what; it is only to say that he would not be *wronged* by being attacked, given certain conditions, though perhaps only in a particular way or by a particular agent. This notion is broader than desert in that, while desert implies liability, liability does not imply desert.

Although liability to attack usually or perhaps always arises from action that is wrongful, there is no necessary connection between liability and punishment or retribution. To say that a person is liable to be harmed even though he does not deserve to be harmed is just to say that if it is unavoidable that someone must be harmed, there is reason that he should be the one who is harmed and that he will not be wronged by being harmed.

Substituting the notion of liability for that of desert, we can say that there is just cause for war only when those attacked have made themselves liable to be warred upon. But Aquinas's claim that the basis of their liability is fault, or culpability, may be both too broad and too strong. It is possible to read his claim as implying that *any* fault that might make a person deserving of harm could be a basis of liability to attack, in which case it would be too broad. For the relevant fault must be specifically for a wrong that war against the perpetrators would prevent or redress. And the insistence on fault, or culpability, may in principle be too strong in that it is possible – though not likely – that a people could make themselves liable to be warred upon by being morally responsible, though faultlessly, for a wrong that war against them would prevent or redress.[11]

Here, then, is a statement of the formal concept of just cause. There is just cause for war when one group of people – often a state, but possibly a nation or other organized collective – is morally responsible for action that threatens to wrong or has already wronged other people in certain ways, and that makes the perpetrators liable to military attack as a means of preventing the threatened wrong or redressing or correcting the wrong that has already been done.

The connection I am claiming between just cause and liability maybe found, though not altogether explicitly, in the work of some of the earlier jurists writing in the just war tradition. These writers typically insisted that just cause is founded in an injury, by which they meant a wrong or a violation of rights. Hugo Grotius, for example, noted with approval that "St. Augustine, in defining those to be just wars, which are made to avenge injuries, has taken the word avenge in a general sense of removing and preventing, as well as punishing aggressions."[12] Similarly, Emmerich de Vattel claimed that "the foundation, or cause of every just war is injury, either already done or threatened. . . . And, in order to determine what is to be considered as an injury, we must be acquainted with a nation's *rights*. . . . Whatever strikes at these rights is an injury, and a just cause of war."[13] But the most explicit of the classical writers is Francisco de Vitoria, who argued that a political leader "cannot have greater authority over foreigners than he has over his own subjects; but he may not draw the sword against his own subjects unless they have done some wrong; therefore he cannot do so against foreigners except in the same circumstances. . . . It follows from this that we may not use the sword [that is, resort to war] against those who have not harmed us; to kill the innocent is prohibited by natural law."[14] It is an implication of this view that those who fight by permissible means in a just cause are innocent and may not permissibly be attacked.

To kill the innocent, Vitoria says, is impermissible. And the innocent are those who have done no wrong; they are those who have done nothing to make themselves morally liable to be killed. This, as Vitoria recognizes, supports the view for which I argued above – that the requirement of discrimination cannot be satisfied in the absence of a just cause. For a war that lacks a just cause is a war fought against those who have not made themselves liable to attack. It is a war fought against the innocent. Vitoria therefore concludes that if a person is certain that a war is unjust, he must not fight in it, even if he is commanded to do so by a legitimate authority. For "one may not lawfully kill an innocent man on any authority, and in the case we are speaking of the enemy must be innocent. Therefore it is unlawful to kill them."[15] This view – that only those who fight in an unjust war are liable to attack – is shared by Francisco Suárez, who asserts that "no one may be deprived of his life save for reason of his own guilt"; thus, the innocent include all those who "have not shared in the crime nor in the unjust war."[16]

Contemporary just war theorists think that this is a crude mistake. "Innocent," they point out, contrasts in this case with "threatening," not with "guilty" or "culpable." Anyone who poses a threat is noninnocent, and therefore soldiers on both sides are noninnocent in the sense that is relevant for determining liability to attack.[17] This, after all, is what gives the distinction between combatants and noncombatants its moral significance: combatants pose a threat to others; noncombatants do not. Thus, because all soldiers are noninnocent, even those who have a just cause are not wronged when they are killed by those who lack a just cause.

Simply to be a soldier is to make oneself liable to be killed.

But this is an implausible understanding of the basis of liability. If simply posing a threat were a basis of liability to attack, those individuals who engage in justified self-defense would thereby make themselves liable to preemptive counterattack by those who have wrongfully attacked them. And police would not be wronged by being preemptively attacked by those whom they were about to attack in order to prevent them from committing crimes.

Why, then, do most contemporary just war theorists think that such an account of liability is appropriate in the case of war? I suspect that it has to do with their conviction that most ordinary soldiers are not criminals, even if they fight in a war that lacks a just cause. They believe that it is reasonable to absolve ordinary soldiers of responsibility for determining whether a war is just or unjust. That responsibility lies with others. Soldiers may thus see themselves *and their adversaries* as engaged in an activity dictated by goals for which they are not responsible and over which they have no control. They are bound by a code of honor that is suited to and distinctive of their role as warriors, but they are not holy warriors with a mandate to eradicate evil. They must not, for example, take vengeance on prisoners or seek to punish the vanquished. This is the only fair way for soldiers to view and treat other soldiers, given the various pressures and constraints under which they all must act. And, it is often argued, this way of understanding the morality of war also works out far better in practice than a view that treats those who fight with a just cause as innocent in the way their civilian population is innocent, but treats those who fight without a just cause as wrongdoers. To regard the liability of soldiers as a function merely of their role as combatants not only limits their liability to matters of *jus in bello*, and thus rules out the legitimacy of punishment merely for fighting on the wrong side, but also has as a corollary the prohibition of deliberate attacks on civilians. The separation of *jus in bello* from the question of just cause thus effectively limits or constrains the savagery of war.

What this view leaves out, however, is the insight of the classical jurists – that people are treated unjustly if they are deliberately killed without having done wrong. The currently orthodox view, which holds that the moral status of soldiers is unaffected by whether they have a just cause, implies that a person who takes up arms to defend himself and others from a threat of unjust aggression thereby makes himself morally liable to be killed by the aggressors, who then act permissibly, and do him no wrong, if they go on to kill him. It is very hard to believe that this could be right. Moreover, at least some of the practical benefits that are attributed to this orthodox view may be attained just as well by regarding some of those who fight without a just cause as excused for rather than as morally justified in fighting.

The contemporary theory of the just war seems, in short, to be less concerned than the tradition it claims to represent with what is just and unjust in war, and is instead more concerned with the consequences of war and the conventions that are useful in controlling those consequences.[18]

A Substantive Account of the Requirement of Just Cause

Thus far I have offered only a formal account of the requirement of just cause, claiming that there is a just cause for war only when those attacked are liable to be warred upon. A substantive account of just cause has to go further by providing a criterion for determining what sorts of action engender liability to military attack.

The classical jurists to whom I have referred typically offer a short list of just causes for war. The jurists tend to agree that the just causes for war are basically these: defense against unjust threats; recovery of or indemnity for what has been wrongfully taken, or compensation for the violation of rights; and punishment of wrongdoing, not solely for the purpose of retribution but to prevent or deter further wrongful action by the culprit or by others.[19] These suggested just causes for war are all consistent with the insistence that, for war to be just, those attacked must be morally liable to attack. But a unified account of the morality of war ought also to explain why certain forms of action give rise to liability to attack while others do not. In this section I will offer a preliminary sketch of a method for determining whether a certain goal can be a just cause for war.

War involves killing and maiming; or, rather, war that involves killing and maiming is what requires a just cause. In principle and even in law, there might be a wholly nonviolent war – for example, one declared by opposing belligerent powers but terminated by agreement before their forces engage. That is not my topic. War, as I understand it here, necessarily involves killing and maiming, typically on a large scale. A just cause, then, has to be a goal of a type that can justify killing and maiming.

Contrary to what I wrote earlier, this gives considerations of scale a role in the concept of just cause.[20] Only aims that are sufficiently serious and significant to justify killing can be just causes. Beyond this, however, considerations of scale are irrelevant to just cause.

Let us assume that people can make themselves liable to be killed (for example, in self-defense or as punishment) only by virtue of seriously wronging or threatening to wrong others. On this assumption, the just causes for war are limited to *the prevention or correction of wrongs that are serious enough to make the perpetrators liable to be killed or maimed.*

If this is right, it does not automatically generate a list of just causes, but it does provide some much-needed guidance in identifying what may be a just cause for war. We can, in particular, consult our beliefs – which are quite robust and stable – about which kinds of wrong are sufficiently serious that the killing or maiming of the perpetrator could be justified if it were necessary to prevent or correct the wrong. Most people agree, for example, that one person may permissibly kill another if that is necessary to prevent the other person from wrongfully killing, torturing, mutilating, raping, kidnapping, enslaving or, perhaps, imprisoning her. Many people would also accept that it can be permissible to kill in defense against unjust and permanent expulsion from one's home or homeland, and even, perhaps, in defense against theft – though here questions of scale are obviously relevant to proportionality. It is only when theft would threaten extreme and protracted deprivation that killing could be a proportionate means of defense. Perhaps what we should say is not that it can be permissible to kill to prevent theft, but that it can be permissible to kill to prevent any sort of act that would wrongfully reduce a person to utter destitution.

If each of these types of wrong is such that its prevention – or, when possible, its correction – can justify killing, then its prevention or correction can also be a just cause for war. There are, of course, complexities and complications involved in extrapolating from the individual to the collective level. Except for heuristic purposes, we cannot rely on what Walzer calls the "domestic analogy," applying the principles that govern relations between individuals to relations between collectives, as if collectives were individuals. For a collective is not an individual: it does not have a single will, a single set of desires, or a unitary good. Extrapolation has to proceed by composition rather than by analogy, but even the most reductive form of individualism must take account of distinctively collective goods, such as collective self-identification or collective self-determination, and thus recognize that there may be wrongs that are not entirely reducible to wrongs against individuals because they have a collective as their subject. I cannot pursue these complications here.

Instead, I will explore in the following section a few of the implications of the view I have sketched.

Just and Unjust Causes

Recovery of Goods Lost to Prior Aggression

In morality, if not in law, just cause is not limited to self-defense against armed aggression. It is, for example, possible for an offensive war to be just. This is clearest in cases in which defense against wrongful aggression fails and the aggressor achieves its aim – for example, by seizing and occupying territory, or by imposing an alien or collaborationist government that will do its bidding. In such cases it would be absurd to suppose that the victims lose their rights when they lose their war of defense. If it later becomes possible for them (or third parties acting on their behalf) to reassert through armed rebellion the rights that were violated by the earlier aggression, and thereby to recover the territory or political independence of which they were unjustly deprived, they will not wrong the aggressor if they do so. Successful aggressors remain liable to attack as long as they retain the spoils of their wrongful aggression. (Recall that just cause is not the sole condition of a just war. War must also be, among other things, necessary. Unjust occupation or political subordination may often be more effectively defeated, and with far fewer casualties, by means of nonviolent resistance, particularly when the occupier is a democratic society with a free press – as, for example, Israel is.)[21]

There is, however, a moral statute of limitations here, particularly with respect to territorial rights. If, following an unjust seizure of territory, enough time passes for a new society with its own infrastructure to arise within the territory, the members of that society may acquire an increasingly strong moral claim to stay, particularly as new generations who are entirely innocent of the initial aggression establish their own lives there. This is why Israeli settlements outside the borders Israel was assigned by the UN are properly regarded as instruments of insidious territorial aggression. The longer the settlers stay, the more they build, and the more children they have, the stronger their moral claim to the land becomes. Consequently, Israelis who move to the settlements voluntarily are morally responsible participants in unjust aggression, and as such are morally liable to defensive attack – though their young children are not. Even when they do not themselves bear arms, which they usually do, their presence in the occupied territories is possible only because of a background threat of military protection. There is, therefore, a case for regarding them as having combatant status and thus as being liable, even according to the orthodox theory of the just war. If there are those who refuse to bear arms, they are morally like civilians who make themselves liable by voluntarily acting as shields for combatants engaged in territorial aggression, and who thereby facilitate aggression by forcing the other side to have to kill civilians in order to resist.

Humanitarian Intervention

Governments sometimes gravely wrong their own citizens, particularly members of ethnic or other minorities or political dissidents. These wrongs may make their perpetrators liable to attack for purposes of defense or correction. Just as resistance to these wrongs may in rare instances lead to justified civil war by the victims against the perpetrators, so military intervention by third parties may also be justified on behalf of the victims. There are, of course, various conditions that must be met if humanitarian intervention is to be permissible. It must, for example, either be requested, or there must at least be compelling evidence that the intended beneficiaries would welcome rather than oppose intervention by the particular intervening agent or agents. (One reason why the American invasion of Iraq in 2003 was not a justifiable instance of humanitarian intervention is that there was no evidence that ordinary Iraqis wanted to be freed from the Ba'athist dictatorship *by the United States* – a country that a little more than a decade earlier, and under the leadership of the current president's father, had bombed their capital, decimated their civilian infrastructure, and successfully pressed for the institution and perpetuation of sanctions that subsequently resulted in many thousands of deaths among civilians.)

Many people have thought that considerations of national self-determination militate against humanitarian intervention. This objection is often specious, however, when the intervention is desired by the victims of governmental persecution. For in such cases the gulf between victims and perpetrators is typically so wide that there is no longer (if there ever was) a single collective "self" whose autonomy is threatened, but rather two or more distinct collective selves, one of which is engaged in wrongful action that is not protected by its right of self-determination.[22] There are various other objections to humanitarian intervention, but the most serious are of a pragmatic nature, having to do with such considerations as the likelihood of self-interested abuse of any norm recognizing the legitimacy of war for altruistic reasons. But no such objections show that certain aims of humanitarian intervention cannot be just causes for war.

The Prevention of Future Aggression

It is highly contentious whether the prevention of future aggression can be a just cause for war. By prevention of future aggression I mean action taken to address a threat of unjust attack that is neither in progress nor imminent, but temporally more remote. Whether this can be a just cause for war is obviously central to the issue of the legitimacy of preventive war.

Many theorists of the just war accept that the prevention of future aggression can be a legitimate aim of war once war is already in progress. Samuel Pufendorf, for example, writes: "It is permitted to apply force against an enemy not only to the point where I have repelled the danger which he threatens against me, or where I have recovered or wrested from him that which he has unjustly seized from or refused to furnish me; but I can also proceed against him in order to obtain a guarantee for the future. So long as the other allows this to be wrested from him through force, he gives sufficient indication that he still intends to injure me even thereafter."[23] Similarly, Vattel acknowledges that prevention through forcible disarmament can be permissible once aggression has occurred. But he insists on a prior injury as a condition of legitimacy. "For an injury gives us a right to provide for our future safety, by depriving the unjust aggressor of the means of injuring us."[24] Here Vattel echoes his predecessor, Vitoria, who, as I noted above in the discussion of moral liability to attack, asserted that violence may be done only to those who have "done some wrong." If, as these writers claim, the prevention of future aggression can be a legitimate aim of war once war is already in progress, that implies, on the understanding of just cause for which I have argued, that it can be a just cause for

war. For a just cause is any aim that may legitimately be pursued by means of war; it may justify only a phase of a war or even just a single act of war without justifying the resort to war or the war as a whole.

I once thought, as these classical writers imply, the prevention of future aggression could not *on its own* be a just cause for war. In a paper drafted during the Gulf War of 1990–91, Robert McKim and I drew a distinction between an *independent* just cause, which could justify war or the resort to war on its own, and a *conditional* just cause, which could contribute to the justification for war, but only when triggered or activated by the presence of an independent just cause.[25] I thought at the time that the prevention of future aggression could be only a conditional just cause – that is, that it could legitimately be pursued only when war was already justified by reference to an independent just cause arising from a wrong that had been done, was being done, or was on the verge of being done. I thought that only an act that made a country liable to attack for some reason other than prevention could also make it liable to preventive attack. I now think that this view is mistaken.

It is true that when the prevention of future aggression is a just cause for war, it is in most cases because a country is already committing a wrong – for example, is engaged in an act of unjust aggression – that makes it simultaneously liable to both defensive and preventive attack. In these cases, a single wrongful act makes the offending country liable to attack for more than one reason. But all that is necessary for prevention of future aggression to be a just cause is that a country should have done something to make itself liable to be attacked as a means of preventing it from committing a wrong in the future. And the kind of action that engenders this form of liability need not engender liability to attack for any other reason. In other words, the prevention of future aggression may, in some cases, be the *sole* just cause for war. In these cases, the country that is liable to preventive attack may be guilty of no wrong other than the kind recognized in the area of criminal law concerned with conspiracy: the kind of wrong that involves collaborators manifestly intending and actively preparing to commit a crime. In order for this kind of activity to constitute a just cause for war, the intended wrong must be grave enough that its prevention could justify killing and maiming.[26]

Just War as One Type of Morally Justified War

Consider now a different kind of case. Suppose that country A is about to be unjustly invaded by a ruthless and more powerful country, B. A's only hope of successful defense is to station forces in the territory of a smaller, weaker, neighboring country, C, in order to be able to attack B's forces from prepared positions as they approach A along the border between B and C. A's government requests permission from the government of C to deploy its forces on C's territory for this purpose, but C's government, foreseeing that allowing A to use its territory in this way would result in considerable destruction, denies the request. Suppose that C is within its rights to deny A the use of its territory but that, all things considered, it is nonetheless justifiable for A to avoid an otherwise inevitable defeat at the hands of B by going to war against C in order to be able to deploy troops there, provided that it will withdraw immediately after fighting off the invading forces from A. (One historical case that approximates this scenario is Russia's war against Finland in 1939–40. The Russian government believed that control of Finnish territory within artillery range of Leningrad was necessary to protect the city from Nazi bombardment. It offered the Finns an exchange of territory,

but the offer was refused, and the Russians then went to war to capture the territory they thought was necessary as a buffer against the Nazis. One reason this is only an approximation of my hypothetical example is that the Finns had good reason not to trust Stalin's assurances that Russia's aims were limited, since, among other things, Russia had only a short time earlier collaborated with the Germans in carving up Poland.)

Given that C is not morally required to sacrifice its territory for the sake of A, it seems that C does nothing to make itself liable to attack by A. On the account I have offered, therefore, A does not have a just cause for war against C. Yet if A is nevertheless morally justified in going to war against C, it must be possible for there to be wars that are morally justified yet unjust. A war is just when there is a just cause and all other relevant conditions of justification are also satisfied. But, while all just wars are morally justified, it seems that not all morally justified wars are just wars. As the example of A, B, and C suggests, there seem to be wars that are morally justified despite their requiring the targeting of those who are innocent in the relevant sense, so that at least some necessary phases of the war, and perhaps indeed all of its phases, lack a just cause. The form of justification in these latter cases is familiar: in rare circumstances, considerations of consequences override constraints on action that would otherwise be decisive. It is commonly recognized, for example, that it can in principle be permissible intentionally to harm or kill an innocent person if that is necessary to avert some great disaster. The necessity of preventing the disaster outweighs the grave injustice done to the individual victim.

If war may be justified in the absence of a just cause, one may wonder how significant the notion of just cause can be.[27] The answer is that the presence or absence of a just cause has a dramatic effect on the stringency of the proportionality requirement. When there is no just cause, all those who are targeted in war are innocent. And harms inflicted on the innocent weigh more heavily against the goals of a war than harms inflicted on those who are liable. The burden of justification is therefore very substantially greater in the absence of a just cause.

Deterrence

Deterrence is problematic as a just cause for the same reason it is problematic as the sole aim of punishment. In both cases it seems objectionable because it uses the harming of some as a means of influencing the action of others. So, for example, even if a government's systematic violations of the human rights of some of its citizens are sufficient to make it liable to attack for the purpose of stopping the violations, they do not obviously make that government liable to further or harsher attacks intended to warn other governments of the penalties for violating human rights. And certainly the violation of its citizens' human rights cannot make a government liable to attack as a show of force intended to deter other countries from engaging in the different crime of aggression.

Yet deterrence of others *can* be a just cause and thus contribute to the justification for war *if* the wrong committed by the country that is attacked would itself otherwise increase the probability that other countries would commit wrongs of a sort that would constitute a just cause for war. For in that case the country's wrongful action would make it to some degree responsible for the increased risk of further wrongful action by others. That responsibility makes it liable to belligerent action necessary to deter the wrongs that its own action had made more likely. Suppose, to take a historical example, that Argentina's seizure of the Falkland Islands, if unopposed, would have

emboldened other countries wrongfully to seize by force certain territories to which they believed they had a historical claim. In that case, the aim of restoring the deterrence of such ambitions to previous levels could have contributed to the justification for Britain's going to war and for its action during the war.

Although deterrence may thus be a just cause, it is, unlike the prevention of future aggression, unlikely ever to be the sole just cause for war. For any action that is sufficient to make a country liable to be used as a means of deterring others will almost necessarily be the sort of action that gives rise to another just cause as well. For example, it seems that a country can make itself liable to attack as a means of deterring others from engaging in aggression only by itself engaging in aggression, in which case defense against that aggression will also be a just cause. And the same seems true for other wrongs that may make a country liable to be attacked for the purpose of deterrence.

Democratization

The Bush administration has contended that war can be justified as a means of bringing democracy to people who lack it – that is, that democratization can be a just cause. But one does not even need a substantive account of just cause to rule this out; it is ruled out by the formal claim that just cause is always correlated with liability to attack on the part of those targeted for attack. For people cannot be liable to killing and maiming simply for failing to organize their internal affairs in a democratic manner, even if democracy would be better for them and for their relations with others.

There might be a just cause for war if a people were being forcibly *prevented* by a tyrannical government from organizing themselves democratically, for then the government itself might be liable to attack for wronging its citizens. A war to stop the suppression of a people's democratic aspirations would not be a war for the promotion of democracy, but would instead come within the category of humanitarian intervention, as its fundamental aim would be to stop a government from violating the rights of its citizens.

This admittedly presupposes a conception of humanitarian intervention that is rather more expansive than the prevailing conception. If the concept of humanitarian intervention is insufficiently elastic to include interventions that are necessary to defend the right of a people to democratic self-government from suppression by a tyrannical regime, this suggests the need for a further category of intervention – namely, intervention that is necessary for the defense of the rights of a people against violation by others within their own state, particularly by their own government. But note that what is really at issue here is not the concept of humanitarian intervention or the right to democracy, but the permissibility of military intervention to defend a people's right to collective self-determination. Such intervention might be justified even if what people want is not democracy but rule by what they perceive to be the law of god, while their government insists on subjecting them to some different form of rule instead. One important question here is whether interventionary war could be justified even when a people's aspirations for self-determination were being suppressed not by force but merely by a threat of force. If what I have claimed earlier is right, the way to think about this is to ask whether those who are responsible for the suppression thereby make themselves liable to be killed if that is necessary in order to end it. A useful test is to consider whether the people whose rights are being violated would be justified in resorting to armed rebellion in defense of those rights. If they would be, that suggests

that external military intervention on their behalf would be justified as well, other things being equal.

Just Cause and Proportionality

I claimed in the earlier section on the moral priority of just cause that only the achievement of aims that are specified by a just cause can contribute to the satisfaction of the *ad bellum* proportionality requirement. No other goods that might be realized by war may weigh against the bad effects that would be attributable to the war in determining whether war would be proportionate. In light of the formal and substantive elements of the account of just cause I have sketched, it may now be clearer why this is so. A just cause is necessarily connected with moral liability to attack on the part of those targeted for attack. The basis for liability is moral responsibility for a wrong that belligerent action would either prevent or somehow rectify. The substantive component of the account specifies the types of wrong that may permissibly be prevented or corrected by means of war – namely, wrongs that are sufficiently serious to make those responsible for them liable to be killed or maimed, if necessary, in order to prevent or correct them.

To see that only the prevention or correction of wrongs can weigh against the evils of war in the proportionality calculation, consider what would follow if other desirable goals were allowed to count as well. I am assuming that people can become morally *liable* to be killed or maimed only by virtue of action (which I take to include knowingly allowing things to happen) that wrongs or threatens to wrong others. If that is right and we assume that desirable goals unconnected with the prevention or correction of wrongs can count in the proportionality calculation, it follows that the achievement of these goals could justify (or contribute to the justification for) deliberately killing or maiming innocent (that is, nonliable) people. Although I have conceded that this may be true in extreme cases in which the alternative to killing the innocent would be a catastrophe involving substantially greater harm to the innocent, I have also claimed that a war fought in this way would not be a *just* war.

It seems, therefore, that the only goods that can count in the *ad bellum* proportionality calculation involve the prevention or correction of wrongs for which those warred against are responsible (for again it would be obviously unjust to prevent or correct a wrong by going to war against people not responsible for that wrong). If, moreover, war could be expected to prevent or correct wrongs that are insufficiently serious to make those responsible for them liable to killing or maiming, it seems that those good effects must also be excluded from the proportionality calculation. One argument for this claim invites us to suppose, to the contrary, that good effects of this sort – that is, the prevention or correction of wrongs that do not rise to the level of just cause for war – could figure in the proportionality calculation and thus contribute to the justification for the war. Suppose, for example, that the prevention or alleviation of certain forms of religious oppression, such as coercing women to wear veils, cannot be a just cause for war. Yet suppose there is a just cause for war against a certain country, and that going to war against that country could be expected also to mitigate the harshness of the religious oppression that many of its citizens suffer. It may seem that the expectation of alleviating religious oppression could contribute to the justification for war by weighing against the bad effects in the proportionality calculation, at least if those warred against were responsible for the oppression. But this seems to imply that the pursuit of an end that is insufficient to justify killing and maiming – namely, alleviating religious

oppression – can contribute to the justification for an activity – war – that necessarily involves killing and maiming. And that makes no sense. It seems, therefore, that the only ends that can weigh against the bad effects of war in the proportionality calculation are those specified by the just cause or causes for war.

There is, however, a forceful challenge to this argument. Not all of the bad effects of war involve killing or maiming. There are many lesser types of bad effect. Even if the relief or mitigation of minor religious oppression cannot justify killing or maiming, perhaps it can weigh against, and therefore justify, the infliction of some of the lesser bad effects of war. If that is so, perhaps certain expected good effects that do not rise to the level of just cause can count in the proportionality calculation, provided that they are weighed only against lesser expected harms and not against the inevitable killing and maiming. Only those goods specified by a just cause can be weighed against the killing and maiming.

If good effects beneath the threshold of just cause can weigh only against the lesser bad effects of war, it follows that in certain cases some such effects cannot count at all. If, for example, a war would have twice as many good effects beneath the level of just cause as it would have lesser bad effects, half the good effects would count in canceling out the bad, but the other half would have no justificatory role at all.

This understanding of the proportionality calculation may, however, require comparisons of expected effects that are too fine-grained to be possible. It seems unrealistic to suppose that we could separate both the good and bad expected effects of war into two categories and compare the expected effects in one category only with the expected effects in the corresponding category. So assuming that this challenge to the claim that only goods specified by a just cause can count in the proportionality calculation is correct, its practical significance may be negligible.

Can More Than One Belligerent have a Just Cause?

I noted in the introduction that the received view in international law and contemporary just war theory is that the only just cause for war is defense against aggression. This is pleasing to orthodox theorists because it coheres well with the traditional view that at most one side in a war can have a just cause.[28] But if, as I have argued, there are more just causes than defense against aggression, and if, as seems obvious, a country can pursue both just and unjust causes in the same war, then it is clearly possible for both sides in a war to have a just cause.

Here is what I take to be a clear case in which two opposing belligerents both have a just cause. A and B both plot to conquer territory belonging to the other. A seizes a piece of B's territory and B seizes a piece of A's territory – not as a reprisal but in accordance with plans formulated in advance. Both are pursuing unjust causes, but each side's unjust cause gives the other a just cause: namely, self-defense or the recovery of captured territory. But neither is simultaneously fighting two wars, one of aggression and another of defense; rather, each is fighting one war on two fronts. Each has the aim of defeating the other militarily, thereby enabling itself to reclaim its own territory, but also to annex the coveted part of the other's territory.

This kind of example forces us to reconsider what might be meant by the assertion that a war as a whole is either just or unjust. For what this case shows is that at least in some instances a war may have elements or phases that are just even though other elements or phases are unjust. It is not clear how these can be aggregated to yield an overall judgment of a war as a whole. One coherent questions, of course, whether the war is such that it is better that it be fought than not. But that question, even if we take account of considerations of justice in answering it, is not equivalent to the question of whether the war as a whole is just.

"Comparative Justice"

The idea that both sides in a war may simultaneously or sequentially pursue both just and unjust causes is different from the view of the US Catholic Bishops that both opponents in a war may have some degree of justice on their side, and that just cause is therefore a matter of "comparative" rather than absolute justice. On their view, just cause is a matter of "the comparative justice of the positions of the respective adversaries or enemies. In essence: Which side is sufficiently 'right' in a dispute. . . ?"[29] A similar though more carefully worked out view is advanced by A. J. Coates. He argues that both sides can have just cause (what he calls "bilateral justice"), though it may be that only one is justified in fighting. "Though never absolute or unilateral, there may be such a preponderance of justice on one side and injustice on the other as to constitute just cause, and even sufficient perhaps to justify recourse to war."[30]

But the plausible idea that neither side may be absolutely right and the other absolutely wrong – the idea that both sides may have legitimate claims and grievances – does not belong in our conception of just cause. Certainly both sides in a war may have legitimate complaints and grievances. But to suppose that just cause is compounded out of all these elements is to presuppose an overly broad conception of just cause.

Compare individual self-defense. Prior to a conflict, both parties may have legitimate grievances or claims and each may be guilty of wrongful provocations. But this is compatible with one having a right of self-defense and the other having no right at all in the conflict – for example, if one party unjustifiably succumbs to provocation and attacks the other as a means of resolving their disputes. It is the single act of aggression that makes the aggressor liable and gives the defender a right of self-defense. The same may be true in war.

The Plurality of Causes and the Moral Status of Combatants

There are many cases in which one side in a war has no just cause at all. All of its war aims are unjust. There are also cases in which one side in a war has one or more just causes but still ought not to be fighting at all – for example, because its war is disproportionate, or because it is simultaneously pursuing a larger unjust cause that all its acts of war tend to advance. It is also possible that a country may have a just cause or set of just causes sufficient to justify its being at war, but that this country also and simultaneously pursues other aims – either aims that are laudable but inappropriate for pursuit by means of war or aims that are positively unjust. These cases, which may even constitute the great majority of cases in which we have been inclined to judge that a war was just overall, pose a number of problems. I will close by mentioning just one of the problems that I think is particularly important. Recall that I argued earlier that a soldier's moral status and what he may permissibly do – his immunities and rights – both depend on whether he has a just cause. The problem is that one and the same soldier may at one time act to serve a just cause but at another act to serve an unjust cause, and

may not himself even know which is which. Or it may well be that a single act by this one soldier will serve both a just and an unjust cause.

In these cases, what is that soldier's status? Is he liable to attack when his action serves an unjust cause but not when it advances a just cause? And what presumptions are soldiers on the other side entitled to act on, given that in practice they cannot have knowledge about whether a particular adversary's action supports a just or unjust cause? Matters would be clearer if we could assume that all soldiers on one side have a just cause while all those on the other side do not.

One thing we *can* say is that those who fight in a war that is unjust overall might be morally liable to attack even at a time when they are pursuing a just cause, because they will soon revert to the pursuit of the larger unjust cause or causes that give the war its overall status as unjust. When they are pursuing a just cause they are nevertheless at the time engaged in fighting an unjust war – just as they are while they are asleep.

There is a great deal more to be said about this vexed set of issues, but here is not the place to try to say it. I hope, however, to have advanced and defended a conception of just cause for war that ties it closely to an adversary's liability to attack as a result of a wrong for which that adversary is or, in the absence of defensive action, would be responsible. I have tried to show that this conception, which has deep roots in the work of classical theorists in the just war tradition but is in many ways antithetical to contemporary just war theory, has radical implications for our thinking about the morality of war. I hope to explore these implications further in future work.[31]

Notes

[1] Grotius observed that "a war may be just in its origin, and yet the intentions of its authors may become unjust in the course of its prosecution." See Hugo Grotius, *The Rights of War and Peace* (1625), tr. A. C. Campbell (London: M. Walter Dunne, 1901), p. 273.

But a shift of intention does not entail the disappearance of the just cause. Thus, Grotius goes on to say that "such motives, though blamable, when even connected with a just war, do not render the war *ITSELF* unjust."

2 Here I am in agreement with David Mellow, "A Critique of Just War Theory" (PhD dissertation, University of Calgary, 2003), p. 201.

3 This is not, as some have supposed, a requirement that the bad effects, or expected bad effects, not exceed the good. A war might kill more people than it saves and still be proportionate if, for example, the majority of those killed are combatants who fight without a just cause, so that the war achieves a net saving of the lives of those who are fully innocent in the relevant sense. I will not pursue these complexities here. For discussion, see Thomas Hurka, "Proportionality in the Morality of War," *Philosophy & Public Affairs* 33 (2005), pp. 34–66; and Jeff McMahan and Robert McKim, "The Just War and the Gulf War," *Canadian Journal of Philosophy* 23:4 (1993), pp. 506–18.

4 See McMahan and McKim, "The Just War and the Gulf War," pp. 502, 512–13. There we acknowledge our debt on this point to Thomas Hurka, whose "Proportionality in the Morality of War" is one of the most probing and rigorous contributions to just war theory in recent decades.

5 Although I reject competent authority as a necessary condition of a just war, I concede that it is of practical importance to restrict the authority to take certain actions to certain individuals or bodies when we seek to give institutional expression or embodiment to the requirements of a just war. It may be that, once certain institutions are established, some just causes for war can permissibly be pursued only by those with proper authority.

6 Michael Walzer, *Just and Unjust Wars* (Harmondsworth, UK: Penguin, 1977), p. 21.

7 For elaboration, see Jeff McMahan, "The Ethics of Killing in War," *Ethics* 114:4 (2004), esp. pp. 718–29.

8 I have argued at length for the claim that those who fight without just cause cannot satisfy the *jus in bello* requirement of proportionality. See ibid., pp. 708–18.

9 Ibid., pp. 712–14.

10 Thomas Aquinas, *Summa Theologiae,* IIaIIae, q. 40, art. 1, resp., quoted in Jonathan Barnes, "The Just War," in Norman Kretzmann, Anthony Kenny, and Jan Pinborg (eds.), *The Cambridge History of Later Medieval Philosophy* (Cambridge: Cambridge University Press, 1982), p. 777. Since the only citation is to the Latin text, I assume that the translation is Barnes's own.

11 Some people accept that if you reasonably but mistakenly believe that I am culpably trying to kill you, you may be morally and legally justified in killing me. Even if this were so (I think it is not, but I cannot argue for that here), this would not imply that I would be liable to be killed. I cannot be made liable by your mistake, even if it is a reasonable one. The basis of moral liability must be some form of responsible action by the person who is liable. For discussion, see Jeff McMahan, "The Basis of Moral Liability to Defensive Killing," *Philosophical Issues* 15 (2005).

12 Grotius, *The Rights of War and Peace,* p. 76.

13 Emmerich de Vattel, *The Law of Nations* (1758), tr. Joseph Chitty (Philadelphia: Johnson, 1863), p. 302.

14 Francisco de Vitoria, "On the Law of War," in *Political Writings,* Anthony Pagden and Jeremy Lawrance (eds.) (Cambridge: Cambridge University Press, 1991), pp. 303–4.

15 Ibid., p. 307. Vitoria seems to accept a subjective account of justification, according to which it is wrong for a person to fight in a war that he believes to be unjust, even if his belief is mistaken (p. 308). This account of justification may not be *fully* subjective, however, because elsewhere Vitoria suggests that only *reasonable* belief is sufficient for justification (p. 306). But this means that he accepts that a person can be *justified* in fighting in an unjust war, provided that he reasonably believes that it is just; and Vitoria suggests that whenever there is uncertainty about whether a war is just, it is reasonable for a citizen to accept the assurance of his government that it *is* just (pp. 312–13).

16 Francisco Suárez, "On war" (Disputation XIII, *De Triplici Virtute Theologica: Charitate*) (c. 1610), in *Selections from Three Works,*

trans. Gladys L. Williams, Ammi Brown, and John Waldron (Oxford: Clarendon Press, 1944), pp. 845–6.

17 See, e.g., Thomas Nagel, "War and Massacre," in Charles R. Beitz, Marshall Cohen, Thomas Scanlon, and A. John Simmons, eds., *International Ethics* (Princeton: Princeton University Press, 1985), p. 69; Anthony Kenny, *The Logic of Deterrence* (London: Firethorn Press, 1985), p. 10; and Michael Walzer, *Just and Unjust Wars*, p. 145. Elizabeth Anscombe, another influential contributor to the literature on the just war, is inconsistent on this point. In her justly celebrated pamphlet opposing Oxford's award of an honorary degree to President Truman (on the ground, in effect, that mass murderers ought not to be awarded honorary degrees), she wrote that "'innocent' . . . is not a term referring to personal responsibility at all. It means rather 'not harming.' But the people fighting are 'harming,' so they can be attacked." (Anscombe, "Mr. Truman's Degree," in *Ethics, Religion, and Politics: Collected Philosophical Papers*, vol. 3 [Minneapolis: University of Minnesota Press, 1981], p. 67.) But in a later paper she wrote that "what is required, for the people attacked to be non-innocent in the relevant sense, is that they should themselves be engaged in an objectively unjust proceeding which the attacker has the right to make his concern; or – the commonest case – should be unjustly attacking him." ("War and Murder," in the same volume, p. 53.) In this quotation, "non-innocent" means neither "harming or threatening" nor "guilty," but "engaged in objectively wrongful action." So when she wrote the second essay, she had reverted to a position more in keeping with the older just war tradition but inconsistent with the contemporary orthodoxy.

18 For an argument that it is necessary for the law of war to diverge from the underlying, nonconventional morality of war, see Jeff McMahan, "The Laws of War and the Morality of War," in David Rodin and Henry Shue (eds.), *Just and Unjust Warriors*.

19 See e.g., Grotius, *The Rights of War and Peace*, pp.75–6; Vitoria, "On the Law of War," pp.

302–6; Vattel, *The Law of Nations*, pp. 301–14; and Samuel Pufendorf, *De Jure Naturae et Gentium, Libri Octo* (Oxford: Clarendon Press, 1934), p. 1294.

20 I am grateful to Rachel Cohon for calling this to my attention.

21 I believe, though this cannot be proven, that if the Palestinians had produced a leader like Gandhi rather than Arafat, they could have had their own state decades ago and could now be free and prosperous, and that this, by removing one potent source of grievance and humiliation among Arabs and Muslims, could in turn have helped forestall some of the worst instances of recent terrorism. Palestinian terrorism has, in short, been not only morally shameful but also self-defeating.

22 For detailed discussion, see Jeff McMahan, "Intervention and Collective Self-Determination," *Ethics & International Affairs* 10 (1996), pp. 1–24.

23 Craig L. Carr (ed.), *The Political Writings of Samuel Pufendorf*, trans. Michael Seidler (New York: Oxford University Press, 1994), p. 259.

24 Vattel, *The Law of Nations*, p. 310.

25 McMahan and McKim, "The Just War and the Gulf War," pp. 502–6. In this article we used the terms "sufficient just aim" and "contributing just aim," rather than the more perspicuous terms "independent just cause" and "conditional just cause."

26 For a more detailed discussion of these issues, see Jeff McMahan, "Preventive War and the Killing of the Innocent," in David Rodin and Richard Sorabji (eds.), *The Ethics of War Shared Problems in Different Traditions* (Aldershot, UK: Ashgate, 2005), pp. 169–90. See also Allen Buchanan and Robert O. Keohane, "Governing the Preventive Use of Force: A Cosmopolitan Institutional Proposal," *Ethics & International Affairs* 18: 1 (2004), pp. 1–22.

27 Thanks to Jon Mandle for pressing me on this point.

28 In answering the question "whether war can be just on both sides," Vitoria writes that "except in ignorance, it is clear *that this cannot happen*." The exception he makes for ignorance is a mistake. After correctly noting

that "invincible error is a valid excuse," he then concludes that those who fight in good faith, erroneously believing their cause to be just, are justified in fighting. But excuse excludes rather than entails justification. (Vitoria, "On the Law of War," pp. 312–13.) Vattel too asserts that "war cannot be just on both sides," but says, more plausibly, of a party fighting an unjust war, that "if he acts in consequence of invincible ignorance or error, the injustice of his arms is not imput-

able to him." (Vattel, *The Law of Nations*, p. 306.)

29 The Pastoral Letter of the US Catholic Bishops, *The Challenge of Peace* (London: CTS/SPCK, 1983), p. 27.

30 A. J. Coates, *The Ethics of War* (Manchester, UK: Manchester University Press, 1997), p. 151.

31 Most comprehensively in a book called *The Ethics of Killing: Self-Defense, War, and Punishment* (New York: Oxford University Press).

Part IX

Terrorism

Introduction

Perhaps the issue that looms largest with our politicians and much of the public is terrorism. The terrorist attacks on the United States of America on September 11, 2001 changed many things forever, not least the centrality of how best to respond to terrorism in the context of global justice. The readings in this section provide provocative views on the status of noncombatants, the definition of terrorism, and the reasons why we normally condemn terrorism universally.

In chapter 30, Michael Walzer considers the place of noncombatants in war. He begins with several fascinating accounts told by soldiers on the front line where they discuss cases where they refrained from killing a fellow soldier because he "looked funny" or was taking a bath. If correct, this demonstrates that soldiers clearly do not always view enemy soldiers as combatants that they may justifiably kill in battle. Many soldiers therefore only view enemy soldiers actively engaged in battle as combatants they might harm. The next question then regards the status of civilians. We might think that civilians that actively support their troops become legitimate targets in combat. However, Walzer distinguishes between different varieties of support. Those civilians involved in tasks that bring benefit to all – such as those who grow and sell food or those that provide utilities to all citizens – are noncombatants in a complete sense. The fact that soldiers might be supported by their efforts is not reason to harm them as their efforts are not specifically aimed at benefiting soldiers, but rather the whole community. However, civilians may make themselves legitimate targets if their activities are specifically aimed at benefiting soldiers. The line between civilian, soldier, and legitimate targets is imprecise and may be drawn in a variety of ways depending on particular circumstances.

Walzer's essay is followed by David Rodin's provocative "Terrorism without Intention" (chapter 31). Rodin argues that terrorism is wrong and commonly understood as wrong because it is violence against innocent persons. He claims that terrorist use of violence need not be used intentionally against noncombatants: violence may be used negligently and recklessly as well. By adopting a new view of terrorism (and its immorality), we may help prevent a war against terrorism from descending into "a terrorist war."

In chapter 32, Saul Smilansky claims that terrorism may be justified, but most of the terrorism that has taken place is not justified. After rejecting the view that the IRA,

Palestinians, or Al-Qaeda possess just grounds for terrorism, he then turns to other cases. Smilansky argues that terrorism may be justified if, and only if, there is a clear and present danger to the existence of a people and/or mass extermination of innocent noncombatants. By virtue of the fact that the vast majority of unjustified activities have been labeled "terrorism," this presents us with strong reasons to reject the possibility that any terrorism can be justified. In fact, the justification of terrorism is situated in a context of various illusions.

Can civilians ever be legitimate targets? Need we intentionally aim at causing fear for our actions to be considered terrorism? Is it possible to commit justified terrorism? These are just a few questions the following essays force us to consider. It is then up to the reader to decide what are the best answers to these questions.

Chapter 30

Noncombatant Immunity and Military Necessity*
Michael Walzer

The Status of Individuals

The first principle of the war convention is that, once war has begun, soldiers are subject to attack at any time (unless they are wounded or captured). And the first criticism of the convention is that this principle is unfair; it is an example of class legislation. It does not take into account that few soldiers are wholeheartedly committed to the business of fighting. Most of them do not identify themselves as warriors; at least, that is not their only or their chief identity; nor is fighting their chosen occupation. Nor, again, do they spend most of their time fighting; they neglect war whenever they can. I want to turn now to a recurrent incident in military history in which soldiers, simply by not fighting, appear to regain their right to life. In fact, they do not regain it, but the appearance will help us understand the grounds on which the right is held, and the facts of the case will clarify the meaning of its forfeiture.

* From Michael Walzer, *Just and Unjust Wars: A Moral Argument with Historical Illustration*, 3rd edn. (New York: Basic Books, 2000), pp. 138–59, 343–4 (notes).

Naked Soldiers

The same tale appears again and again in war memoirs and in letters from the front. It has this general form: a soldier on patrol or on sniper duty catches an enemy soldier unaware, holds him in his gunsight, easy to kill, and then must decide whether to shoot him or let the opportunity pass. There is at such moments a great reluctance to shoot – not always for moral reasons, but for reasons that are relevant nonetheless to the moral argument I want to make. No doubt, a deep psychological uneasiness about killing plays a part in these cases. This uneasiness, in fact, has been offered as a general explanation of the reluctance of soldiers to fight at all. In the course of a study of combat behavior in World War II, S. L. A. Marshall discovered that the great majority of men on the front line never fired their guns.[1] He thought this the result above all of their civilian upbringing, of the powerful inhibitions acquired in its course against deliberately injuring another human being. But in the cases I shall list, this inhibition does not seem a critical factor. None of the five soldiers who wrote the accounts was a "non-firer," nor, so far as I can tell, were the other men who figure importantly in their stories. Moreover, they give reasons for not killing or for hesitating to kill, and this the soldiers interviewed by Marshall were rarely able to do.

(1) I have taken the first case from a letter written by the poet Wilfred Owen to his brother in England on May 14, 1917.

> When we were marching along a sunken road, we got the wind up once. We knew we must have passed the German outposts somewhere on our left rear. All at once, the cry rang down, "Line the bank." There was a tremendous scurry of fixing bayonets, tugging of breech covers, and opening pouches, but when we peeped over, behold a solitary German, haring along toward us, with his head down and his arms stretched in front of him, as if he were going to take a high dive through the earth (which I have no doubt he would like to have done). Nobody offered to shoot him, he looked too funny . . .[2]

Perhaps everyone was waiting for an order to shoot, but Owen's meaning is undoubtedly that no one wanted to shoot. A soldier who looks funny is not at that moment a military threat; he is not a fighting man but simply a man, and one does not kill men. In this case, indeed, it would have been superfluous to do so: the comical German was soon taken prisoner. But that is not always possible, as the remaining cases suggest, and the reluctance or refusal to kill has nothing to do with the existence of a military alternative. There is always a nonmilitary alternative.

(2) In his autobiography *Good-bye to All That*, Robert Graves recalls the only time that he "refrained from shooting a German" who was neither wounded nor a prisoner.

> While sniping from a knoll in the support line, where we had a concealed loop-hole, I saw a German, about seven hundred yards away, through my telescopic sights. He was taking a bath in the German third line. I disliked the

idea of shooting a naked man, so I handed the rifle to the sergeant with me. "Here, take this. You're a better shot than I am." He got him; but I had not stayed to watch.[3]

I hesitate to say that what is involved here is a moral feeling, certainly not a moral feeling that is conceived to extend across class lines. But even if we describe it as the disdain of an officer and a gentleman for conduct that appears to be unmanly or unheroic, Graves's "dislike" still depends upon a morally important recognition. A naked man, like a funny man, is not a soldier. And what if the obedient and presumably unfeeling sergeant had not been with him?

(3) During the Spanish Civil War, George Orwell had a similar experience as a sniper working from a forward position in the republican lines. It would probably never have occurred to Orwell to hand his gun down the hierarchy of ranks; in any case, his was an anarchist battalion, and there was no hierarchy.

> At this moment a man, presumably carrying a message to an officer, jumped out of the trench and ran along the top of the parapet in full view. He was half-dressed and was holding up his trousers with both hands as he ran. I refrained from shooting at him. It is true that I am a poor shot and unlikely to hit a running man at a hundred yards . . . Still, I did not shoot partly because of that detail about the trousers. I had come here to shoot at "Fascists;" but a man who is holding up his trousers isn't a "Fascist," he is visibly a fellow-creature, similar to yourself, and you don't feel like shooting at him.[4]

Orwell says, "you don't feel like" rather than "you should not," and the difference between these two is important. But the fundamental recognition is the same as in the other cases and more fully articulated. Moreover, Orwell tells us that this "is the kind of thing that happens all the time in wars," though with what evidence he says that, and whether he means that one doesn't feel like shooting or that one doesn't shoot "all the time," I don't know.

(4) Raleigh Trevelyan, a British soldier in World War II, has published a "diary of Anzio" in which he recounts the following episode.

> There was a wonderfully vulgar sunrise. Everything was the color of pink geraniums, and birds were singing. We felt like Noah must have done when he saw his rainbow. Suddenly Viner pointed across the stretch of scrubby heath. An individual, dressed in German uniform, was wandering like a sleep-walker across our line of fire. It was clear that for the moment he had forgotten war and – as we had been doing – was reveling in the promise of warmth and spring. "Shall I bump him off?" asked Viner, without a note of expression in his voice. I had to decide quickly. "No," I replied, "just scare him away."[5]

Here, as in the Orwell passage, the crucial feature is the discovery of a man "similar to yourself," doing "as we had been doing." Of course, two soldiers shooting at one another are quite precisely similar; one is doing what the other is doing, and both are engaged in what can be called a peculiarly human activity. But the sense of being a "fellow-creature" depends for obvious reasons upon a different sort of identity, one that is entirely dissociated from anything threatening. The fellowship of spring (reveling in the sun) is a good example, though even that is not untouched by the pressures of "military necessity."

> Only Sergeant Chesteron didn't laugh. He said that we should have killed the fellow, since his friends would now be told precisely where our trenches were.

Sergeants seem to bear much of the burden of war.

(5) The most reflective of the accounts I have found is by an Italian soldier who fought the Austrians in World War I: Emilio Lussu, later a socialist leader and anti-fascist exile. Lussu, then a lieutenant, together with a corporal, had moved during the night into a position overlooking the Austrian trenches. He watched the Austrians having morning coffee and felt a kind of amazement, as if he had not expected to find anything human in the enemy lines.

> Those strongly defended trenches, which we had attacked so many times without success, had ended by seeming to us inanimate, like desolate buildings uninhabited by men, the refuge only of mysterious and terrible beings of whom we knew nothing. Now they were showing themselves to us as they really were, men and soldiers like us, in uniform like us, moving about, talking, and drinking coffee, just as our own comrades behind us were doing at that moment.[6]

A young officer appears and Lussu takes aim at him; then the Austrian lights a cigarette and Lussu pauses. "This cigarette formed an invisible link between us. No sooner did I see its smoke than I wanted a cigarette myself . . ." Behind perfect cover, he has time to think about his decision. He felt the war justified, "a hard necessity." He recognized that he had obligations to the men under his command. "I knew it was my duty to fire." And yet he did not. He hesitated, he writes, because the Austrian officer was so entirely oblivious to the danger that threatened him.

> I reasoned like this: To lead a hundred, even a thousand, men against another hundred, or thousand, was one thing; but to detach one man from the rest and say to him, as it were: "Don't move, I'm going to shoot you. I'm going to kill you" – that was different . . . To fight is one thing, but to kill a man is another. And to kill him like that is to murder him.

Lussu, like Graves, turned to his corporal but (perhaps because he was a socialist) with a question, not an order. "Look here – I'm not going to fire on a man alone, like that. Will you?" . . . "No, I won't either." Here the line has been clearly drawn between the member of an army who makes war together with his comrades and the individual who stands alone. Lussu objected to stalking a human prey. What else, however, does a sniper do?

It is not against the rules of war as we currently understand them to kill soldiers who look funny, who are taking a bath, holding up their pants, reveling in the sun, smoking a cigarette. The refusal of these five men, nevertheless, seems to go to the heart of the war convention. For what does it mean to say that someone has a right to life? To say that is to recognize a fellow creature, who is not threatening me, whose activities have the savor of peace and camaraderie, whose person is as valuable as my own. An enemy has to be described differently, and though the stereotypes through which he is seen are often grotesque, they have a certain truth. He alienates himself from me when he tries to kill me, and from our common humanity. But the alienation is temporary, the humanity imminent. It is restored, as it were, by the prosaic acts that break down the stereotypes in each of the five stories. Because he is funny, naked, and so on, my enemy is changed, as Lussu says, into a man. "A man!"

The case might be different if we imagine this man to be a wholehearted soldier. In his bath, smoking his morning cigarette, he is thinking only of the coming battle and of how many of his enemies he will kill. He is engaged in war-making just as I am engaged in writing this book; he thinks about it all the time or at the oddest moments. But this is an unlikely picture of an ordinary soldier. War is not in fact his enterprise, but rather surviving this battle, avoiding the next. Mostly, he hides, is frightened, doesn't fire,

prays for a minor wound, a voyage home, a long rest. And when we see him at rest, we assume that he is thinking of home and peace, as we would be. If that is so, how can it be justified to kill him? Yet it is justified, as most of the soldiers in the five stories understand. Their refusals seem, even to them, to fly in the face of military duty. Rooted in a moral recognition, they are nevertheless more passionate than principled decisions. They are acts of kindness, and insofar as they entail any danger at all or lower minutely the odds for victory later, they may be likened to superogatory acts. Not that they involve doing more than is morally required; they involve doing less than is permitted.

The standards of permissibility rest on the rights of individuals, but they are not precisely defined by those rights. For definition is a complex process, historical as well as theoretical in character, and conditioned in a significant way by the pressure of military necessity. It is time now to try to see what that pressure can and cannot do, and the "naked soldier" cases provide a useful instance. In the nineteenth century, an effort was made to protect one type of "naked soldier": the man on guard duty outside his post or at the edge of his lines. The reasons given for singling out this lone figure are similar to those expressed in the five stories. "No other term than murder," wrote an English student of war, "expresses the killing of a lone sentry by a pot shot at long range. It [is] like shooting a partridge sitting."[7] The same idea is obviously at work in the code of military conduct that Francis Lieber drafted for the Union Army in the American Civil War: "Outposts, sentinels, pickets are not to be fired upon, except to drive them in . . ."[8] Now, a war is easily imaginable in which this idea was extended, so that only soldiers actually fighting, hundreds against hundreds, thousands against thousands, as Lussu says, could be attacked. Such a war would be constituted as a series of set battles, formally or informally announced in advance, and broken off in some clear fashion. The pursuit of a defeated army could be allowed, so neither side need be denied the possibility of a decisive victory. But perpetual harassment, sniping, ambush, surprise attack – all these would be ruled out. Wars have indeed been fought in this way, but the arrangements have never been stable, because they give a systematic advantage to the army that is larger and better equipped. It is the weaker side that persistently refuses to fix any limits on the vulnerability of enemy soldiers (the extreme form of this refusal is guerrilla war), pleading military necessity. What does this mean?

The Nature of Necessity (1)

The plea takes a standard form. This or that course of action, it is said, "is necessary to compel the submission of the enemy with the least possible expenditure of time, life, and money."[9] That is the core of what the Germans call *kriegsraison*, reason of war. The doctrine justifies not only whatever is necessary to win the war, but also whatever is necessary to reduce the risks of losing, or simply to reduce losses or the likelihood of losses in the course of the war. In fact, it is not about necessity at all; it is a way of speaking in code, or a hyperbolical way of speaking, about probability and risk. Even if one grants the right of states and armies and individual soldiers to reduce their risks, a particular course of action would be *necessary* to that end only if no other course improved the odds of battle at all. But there will always be a range of tactical and strategic options that conceivably could improve the odds. There will be choices to make, and these are moral as well as military choices. Some of them are permitted and some ruled out by the war convention. If the convention did not discriminate in this way, it would

have little impact upon the actual fighting of wars and battles; it would simply be a code of expediency – which is what Sidgwick's twofold rule is likely to come to, under the pressure of actual warfare.

"Reason of war" can only justify the killing of people we already have reason to think are liable to be killed. What is involved here is not so much a calculation of probability and risk as a reflection on the status of the men and women whose lives are at stake. The case of the "naked soldier" is resolved in this way: soldiers as a class are set apart from the world of peaceful activity; they are trained to fight, provided with weapons, required to fight on command. No doubt, they do not always fight; nor is war their personal enterprise. But it is the enterprise of their class, and this fact radically distinguishes the individual soldier from the civilians he leaves behind.* If he is warned that he is always in danger, it is not so great a disruption of his life as it would be in the case of the civilian. Indeed, to warn the civilian is in effect to force him to fight, *but the soldier has already been forced to fight*. That is, he has joined the army because he thinks his country must be defended, or he has been conscripted. It is important to stress, however, that he has not

---

* In his moving account of the French defeat in 1940, Marc Bloch has criticized this distinction: "Confronted by the nation's peril and by the duties that it lays on every citizen, all adults are equal and only a curiously warped mind would claim for any of them the privilege of immunity. What, after all, is a 'civilian' in time of war? He is nothing more than a man whose weight of years, whose health, whose profession . . . prevents him from bearing arms effectively . . . Why should [these factors] confer on him the right to escape from the common danger?" (*Strange Defeat*, trans. Gerard Hopkins, New York, 1968, p. 130) But the theoretical problem is not to describe how immunity is gained, but how it is lost. We are all immune to start with; our right not to be attacked is a feature of normal human relationships. That right is lost by those who bear arms "effectively" because they pose a danger to other people. It is retained by those who don't bear arms at all.

been forced to fight by a direct attack upon his person; that would repeat the crime of aggression at the level of the individual. He can be personally attacked only because he already is a fighter. He has been made into a dangerous man, and though his options may have been few, it is nevertheless accurate to say that he has allowed himself to be made into a dangerous man. For that reason, he finds himself endangered. The actual risks he lives with may be reduced or heightened: here notions of military necessity, and also of kindness and magnanimity, have free play. But the risks can be raised to their highest pitch without violating his rights.

It is harder to understand the extension of combatant status beyond the class of soldiers, though in modern war this has been common enough. The development of military technology, it might be said, has dictated it, for war today is as much an economic as a military activity. Vast numbers of workers must be mobilized before an army can even appear in the field; and once they are engaged, soldiers are radically dependent on a continuing stream of equipment, fuel, ammunition, food, and so on. It is a great temptation, then, to attack the enemy army behind its own lines, especially if the battle itself is not going well. But to attack behind the lines is to make war against people who are at least nominally civilians. How can this be justified? Here again, the judgments we make depend upon our understanding of the men and women involved. We try to draw a line between those who have lost their rights because of their warlike activities and those who have not. On the one side are a class of people, loosely called "munitions workers," who make weapons for the army or whose work directly contributes to the business of war. On the other side are all those people who, in the words of the British philosopher G. E. M. Anscombe, "are not fighting and are not engaged in supplying those who are with the means of fighting."[10]

The relevant distinction is not between those who work for the war effort and those who do not, but between those who make what soldiers need to fight and those who make what they need to live, like all the rest of us. When it is militarily necessary, workers in a tank factory can be attacked and killed, but not workers in a food processing plant. The former are assimilated to the class of soldiers – partially assimilated, I should say, because these are not armed men, ready to fight, and so they can be attacked only in their factory (not in their homes), when they are actually engaged in activities threatening and harmful to their enemies. The latter, even if they process nothing but army rations, are not similarly engaged. They are like workers manufacturing medical supplies, or clothing, or anything else that would be needed, in one form or another, in peacetime as well as war. An army, to be sure, has an enormous belly, and it must he fed if it is to fight. But it is not its belly but its arms that make it an army. Those men and women who supply its belly are doing nothing peculiarly warlike. Hence their immunity from attack: they are assimilated to the rest of the civilian population. We call them *innocent* people, a term of art which means that they have done nothing, and are doing nothing, that entails the loss of their rights.

This is a plausible line, I think, though it may be too finely drawn. What is more important is that it is drawn under pressure. We begin with the distinction between soldiers engaged in combat and soldiers at rest; then we shift to the distinction between soldiers as a class and civilians; and then we concede this or that group of civilians as the processes of economic mobilization establish its direct contribution to the business of fighting. Once the contribution has been plainly established, only "military necessity" can determine whether the civilians involved are attacked or not. They ought not to be attacked if their activities can be stopped, or their products seized or destroyed, in some other way and without significant risk. The laws of war have regularly recognized this obligation. Under the naval code, for example, merchant seamen on ships carrying military supplies were once regarded as civilians who had, despite the work they were doing, a right not to be attacked, for it was possible (and it sometimes still is) to seize their ships without shooting at them. But whenever seizure without shooting ceases to be possible, the obligation ceases also and the right lapses. It is not a retained but a war right, and rests only on the agreement of states and on the doctrine of military necessity. The history of submarine warfare nicely illustrates this process, through which groups of civilians are, as it were, incorporated into hell. It will also enable me to suggest the point at which it becomes morally necessary to resist the incorporation.

Submarine Warfare: The Laconia Affair

Naval warfare has traditionally been the most gentlemanly form of fighting, possibly because so many gentlemen went into the navy, but also and more importantly because of the nature of the sea as a battlefield. The only comparable land environment is the desert; these two have in common the absence or relative absence of civilian inhabitants. Hence battle is especially pure, a combat between combatants, with no one else involved – just what we intuitively want war to be. The purity is marred, however, by the fact that the sea is extensively used for transport. Warships encounter merchant ships. The rules governing this encounter are, or were, fairly elaborate.[11] Worked out before the invention of the submarine, they bear the marks of their technological as well as their moral assumptions. A merchant ship carrying military supplies could lawfully be stopped on the high seas, boarded, seized,

and brought into port by a prize crew. If the merchant seamen resisted this process at any stage, whatever force was necessary to overcome the resistance was also lawful. If they submitted peacefully, no force could be used against them. If it was impossible to bring the ship into port, it could be sunk, "subject to the absolute duty of providing for the safety of the crew, passengers, and papers." Most often, this was done by taking all three on board the warship. The crew and passengers were then to be regarded not as prisoners of war, for their encounter with the warship was not a battle, but as civilian internees.

Now, in World War I, submarine commanders (and the state officials who commanded them) openly refused to act in accordance with this "absolute duty," pleading military necessity. They could not surface before firing their torpedoes, for their ships were lightly armed above decks and highly vulnerable to ramming; they could not provide prize crews from their own small number, unless they, too, were to return to port; nor could they take merchant seamen on board, for there was no room. Hence their policy was to "sink on sight," though they did accept some responsibility to assist survivors after the ship was down. "Sink on sight" was especially the policy of the German government. The only alternative, its defenders have argued, was not to use submarines at all, or to use them ineffectively, which would have conceded control of the sea to the British navy. After the war was over, perhaps because the Germans lost it, the traditional rules were reaffirmed. The London Naval Protocol of 1936, ratified by all the major participants in the last and the next great war (by the Germans in 1939), explicitly provided that "in their action with regard to merchant ships, submarines must conform to the rules of international law to which surface ships are subject." This is still the "binding rule," according to respected authorities on naval law, though anyone who defends the rule must do so "notwithstanding the experience of the Second World War."[12]

We can best gain access to this experience by turning immediately to the famous "*Laconia* order" issued by Admiral Doenitz of the German U-boat command in 1942. Doenitz required not only that submarines strike without warning, but also that they do nothing whatsoever to help the crew members of a sunken ship: "All attempts to rescue the crews of sunken ships should cease, including picking up men from the sea, righting capsized lifeboats, and supplying food and water."[13] This order provoked great indignation at the time, and after the war its promulgation was among the crimes with which Doenitz was charged at Nuremberg. But the judges refused to convict on this charge. I want to look closely at the reasons for their decision. Since their language is obscure, however, I shall also ask what their reasons might have been and what reasons we might have for requiring or not requiring rescue at sea.

The issue clearly was rescue and nothing else; despite the "binding rule" of international law, the policy of "sink on sight" was not challenged by the court. The judges apparently decided that the distinction between merchant ships and warships no longer made much sense.

> Shortly after the outbreak of the war, the British Admiralty . . . armed its merchant vessels, in many cases convoyed them with armed escort, gave orders to send position reports upon sighting submarines, thus integrating merchant vessels into the warning system of naval intelligence. On October 1, 1939, the Admiralty announced [that] British merchant ships had been ordered to ram U-boats if possible.

At this point, the court seemed to reason, merchant seamen had been conscripted for military service; hence it was permissible to attack them by surprise exactly as if they were soldiers. But this argument, by itself, is not a very good one. For if the conscription of merchant seamen was a response to illegitimate submarine attacks (or even to the strong probability of such attacks), it cannot be invoked to justify those same attacks. It must be the case that the "sink on sight" policy was justified in the first place. The inventions of the submarine had made it "necessary." The old rules were morally if not legally suspended because supply by sea – a military enterprise whose participants had always been liable to attack – had ceased now to be subject to nonviolent interdiction.

The "*Laconia* order" reached much further than this, however, for it suggested that seamen helpless in the sea, unlike wounded soldiers on hand, need not be helped once the battle was over. Doenitz's argument was that the battle, in fact, was never over until the submarine was safe in its home port. The sinking of a merchant vessel was only the first blow of a long and tense struggle. Radar and the airplane had turned the wide seas into a single battlefield, and unless the submarine immediately began evasive maneuvers, it was or might be in great trouble.[15] Seamen had once been better off than soldiers, a privileged class of near-combatants treated as if they were civilians; now, suddenly, they were worse off.

Here again is the argument from military necessity, and again we can see that it is above all an argument about risk. The lives of the submarine crew would be endangered, Doenitz claimed, and the probability of detection and attack increased by this or that extent, if they attempted to rescue their victims. Now, this is clearly not always the case: in his account of the destruction of an allied convoy in the Arctic Sea, David Irving describes a number of incidents in which German submarines surfaced and offered assistance to merchant seamen in lifeboats without increasing their own risks.

Lieutenant-Commander Teichert's U-456... had fired the striking torpedoes. Teichert took his submarine alongside the lifeboats and ordered the Master, Captain Strand, to come aboard; he was taken prisoner. The seamen were asked whether they had sufficient water and they were handed tinned meat and bread by the submarine officers. They were told that they would be picked up by destroyers a few days later.[16]

This occurred only a few months before Doenitz's order prohibited such assistance, and under conditions which made it perfectly safe. Convoy PQ 17 had dispersed, abandoned by its escorts; it was no longer in any sense a fighting force; the Germans controlled the air as well as the sea. The battle was clearly over, and military necessity could hardly have justified a refusal to help. I should think that if such a refusal, under similar circumstances, could be attributed to the "*Laconia* order," Doenitz would indeed be guilty of a war crime. But nothing like this was demonstrated at Nuremberg.

Nor, however, did the court openly adopt the argument from military necessity: that under different circumstances the refusal to help was justified by the risks it entailed. Instead, the judges reaffirmed the binding rule. "If the Commander cannot rescue," they argued, "then . . . he cannot sink a merchant vessel . . ." But they did not enforce the rule and punish Doenitz. Admiral Nimitz of the US Navy, called to testify by Doenitz's attorney, had told them that "US submarines [generally] did not rescue enemy survivors if by so doing the vessels were exposed to unnecessary or additional risk." British policy had been similar. In view of this, the judges declared that "the sentence of Doenitz is not assessed on the ground of his breaches of the international law of submarine warfare."[17] They did not accept the argument of the defense attorneys that the law had effectively been rewritten by informal collusion among the belligerents. But they apparently felt that this collusion did

make the law unenforceable (or at least unenforceable against only one of the parties to its violation) – a proper judicial decision, but one that leaves open the moral question.

In fact, Doenitz and his allied counterparts had reasons for the policy they adopted, and these reasons fit roughly into the framework of the war convention. Wounded or helpless combatants are no longer subject to attack; in that sense they have regained their right to life. But they are not entitled to assistance so long as the battle continues and the victory of their enemies is uncertain. What is decisive here is not military necessity but the assimilation of merchant seamen to the class of combatants. Soldiers need not risk their lives for the sake of their enemies, for both they and their enemies have exposed themselves to the coerciveness of war. There are some people, however, who are safe against that coerciveness, or who ought to be safeguarded against it, and these people also have a part in the *Laconia* affair.

The *Laconia* was a liner carrying 268 British servicemen and their families, returning home from pre-war stations in the Middle East, and 1800 Italian prisoners of war. It was torpedoed and sunk off the west coast of Africa by a U-boat whose commander did not know who its passengers were (liners were used extensively by the Allies as troopships). When Doenitz learned of the sinking, and of the identity of the people in the water, he ordered a massive rescue effort involving, initially, a number of other submarines.[18] Italian warships were also asked to hurry to the scene, and the U-boat commander responsible for the sinking radioed in English a general call for help. But the submarines were instead attacked by several Allied planes whose pilots presumably did not know what was going on in the seas below or did not believe what they were told. The confusion is typical enough in time of war: ignorance on all sides, compounded by mutual fear and suspicion.

In fact, the planes did little damage, but Doenitz's response was harsh. He directed he German commanders to confine their rescue efforts to the Italian prisoners; the British soldiers and their families were to be set adrift. It was this spectacle of women and children abandoned at sea, and the subsequent order that seemed to require its repetition, that was widely thought to be outrageous – and rightly so, it seems to me, even though "unrestricted" submarine warfare was by then commonly accepted. For we draw a circle of rights around civilians, and soldiers are supposed to accept (some) risks in order to save civilian lives. It is not a question of going out of their way or of being, or not being, good samaritans. They are the ones who endanger civilian lives in the first place, and even if they do this in the course of legitimate military operations, they must still make some positive effort to restrict the range of the damage they do. This indeed was Doenitz's own position before the Allied attack, a position he maintained despite criticism from other members of the German High Command: "I cannot put these people into the water. I shall carry on [the rescue effort]." It is not kindness that is involved here, but duty, and it is in terms of that duty that we judge the "*Laconia* order." A rescue effort undertaken for the sake of noncombatants can be broken off temporarily because of an attack, but it cannot be called off in advance of any attack merely because an attack may occur (or recur). For one attack at least has already occurred and put innocent people in danger of death. Now they must be helped.

Double Effect

The second principle of the war convention is that noncombatants cannot be attacked at any time. They can never be the objects or the targets of military activity. But as the *Laconia* affair suggests, noncombatants are often endangered not because anyone sets out to attack them, but only because of their proximity to a battle that is being fought against someone else. I have tried to argue that what is then required is not that the battle be stopped, but that some degree of care be taken not to harm civilians – which means, very simply, that we recognize their rights as best we can within the context of war. But what degree of care should be taken? And at what cost to the individual soldiers who are involved? The laws of war say nothing about such matters; they leave the cruelest decisions to be made by the men on the spot with reference only to their ordinary moral notions or the military traditions of the army in which they serve. Occasionally one of these soldiers will write about his own decisions, and that can be like a light going on in a dark place. Here is an incident from Frank Richards' memoir of the First World War, one of the few accounts by a man from the ranks.

> When bombing dug-outs or cellars, it was always wise to throw the bombs into them first and have a look around them after. But we had to be very careful in this village as there were civilians in some of the cellars. We shouted down to them to make sure. Another man and I shouted down one cellar twice and receiving no reply were just about to pull the pins out of our bombs when we heard a woman's voice and a young lady came up the cellar steps . . . She and the members of her family . . . had not left [the cellar] for some days. They guessed an attack was being made and when we first shouted down had been too frightened to answer. If the young lady had not cried out when she did, we would have innocently murdered them all.[19]

Innocently murdered, because they had shouted first; but if they had not shouted, and then killed the French family, it would have been, Richards believed, murder simply. And yet he was accepting a certain risk in shouting, for had there been German soldiers in the cellar, they might have scrambled out, firing as they came. It would have been more prudent to throw the bombs without warning, which means that military necessity would have justified him in doing so. Indeed, he would have been justified on other grounds, too, as we shall see. And yet he shouted.

The moral doctrine most often invoked in such cases is the principle of double effect. First worked out by Catholic casuists in the Middle Ages, double effect is a complex notion, but it is at the same time closely related to our ordinary ways of thinking about moral life. I have often found it being used in military and political debates. Officers will tend to speak in its terms, knowingly or unknowingly, whenever the activity they are planning is likely to injure noncombatants. Catholic writers themselves frequently use military examples; it is one of their purposes to suggest what we ought to think when "a soldier in firing at the enemy foresees that he will shoot some civilians who are nearby."[20] Such foresight is common enough in war; soldiers could probably not fight at all, except in the desert and at sea, without endangering nearby civilians. And yet it is not proximity but only some contribution to the fighting that makes a civilian liable to attack. Double effect is a way of reconciling the absolute prohibition against attacking noncombatants with the legitimate conduct of military activity. I shall want to argue, following the example of Frank Richards, that the reconciliation comes too easily, but first we must see exactly how it is worked out.

The argument goes this way: it is permitted to perform an act likely to have evil consequences (the killing of noncombatants) provided the following four conditions hold.

(1) The act is good in itself or at least indifferent, which means, for our purposes, that it is a legitimate act of war.

(2) The direct effect is morally acceptable – the destruction of military supplies, for example, or the killing of enemy soldiers.

(3) The intention of the actor is good, that is, he aims only at the acceptable effect: the evil effect is not one of his ends, nor is it a means to his ends.

(4) The good effect is sufficiently good to compensate for allowing the evil effect; it must be justifiable under Sidgwick's proportionality rule.[21]

The burden of the argument is carried by the third clause. The "good" and evil effects that come together, the killing of soldiers and nearby civilians, are to be defended only insofar as they are the product of a single intention, directed at the first and not the second. The argument suggests the great importance of taking aim in wartime, and it correctly restricts the targets at which one can aim. But we have to worry, I think, about all those unintended but foreseeable deaths, for their number can be large; and subject only to the proportionality rule – a weak constraint – double effect provides a blanket justification. The principle for that reason invites an angry or a cynical response: what difference does it make whether civilian deaths are a direct or an indirect effect of my actions? It can hardly matter to the dead civilians, and if I know in advance that I am likely to kill so many innocent people and go ahead anyway, how can I be blameless?[22]

We can ask the question in a more concrete way. Would Frank Richards have been blameless if he had thrown his bombs without warning? The principle of double effect would have permitted him to do so. He was engaged in a legitimate military activity, for many cellars were in fact being used by enemy soldiers. The effects of making "bomb without warning" his general policy would have been to reduce the risks of his being killed or disabled and to speed up the capture of the village, and these are "good" effects. Moreover, they were clearly the only ones he intended; civilian deaths would have served no purpose of his own. And finally, over an extended period of time, the proportions would probably have worked out favorably or at least not unfavorably; the mischief done would, let us assume, be balanced by the contribution to victory. And yet Richards was surely doing the right thing when he shouted his warning. He was acting as a moral man ought to act; his is not an example of fighting heroically, above and beyond the call of duty, but simply of fighting well. It is what we expect of soldiers. Before trying to state that expectation more precisely, however, I want to see how it works in more complex combat situations.

Bombardment in Korea

I am going to follow here a British journalist's account of the way the American army waged war in Korea. Whether it is an entirely just account I do not know, but I am more interested in the moral issues it raises than in its historical accuracy. This, then, was a "typical" encounter on the road to Pyongyang. A battalion of American troops advanced slowly, without opposition, under the shadow of low hills. "We were well into the valley now, halfway down the straight . . . strung out along the open road, when it came, the harsh stutter of automatic fire sputtering the dust around us."[23] The troops stopped and dove for cover. Three tanks moved up, "pounding their shells into the . . . hillside and shattering the air with their machine guns. It was impossible in this remarkable inferno of sound to detect the enemy, or to assess his fire." Within fifteen minutes, several fighter planes arrived, "diving down upon the hillside with their rockets." This is the new technique of warfare, writes the British journalist, "born

of immense productive and material might": "the cautious advance, the enemy small arms fire, the halt, the close support air strike, artillery, the cautious advance, and so on." It is designed to save the lives of soldiers, and it may or may not have that effect. "It is certain that it kills civilian men, women, and children, indiscriminately and in great numbers, and destroys all that they have."

Now there is another way to fight, though it is only open to soldiers who have had a "soldierly" training and who are not "roadbound" in their habits. A patrol can be sent forward to outflank the enemy position. In the end, it often comes to that anyway, as it did in this case, for the tanks and planes failed to hit the North Korean machine gunners. "At last, after more than an hour . . . a platoon from Baker Company began working their way through the scrub just under the ridge of the hill." But the first reliance was always on bombardment. "Every enemy shot released a deluge of destruction." And the bombardment had, or sometimes had, its characteristic double effect: enemy soldiers were killed, and so were any civilians who happened to be nearby. It was not the intention of the officers who called in the artillery and planes to kill civilians; they were acting out of a concern for their own men. And that is a legitimate concern. No one would want to be commanded in wartime by an officer who did not value the lives of his soldiers. But he must also value civilian lives, and so must his soldiers. He cannot save them, because they cannot save themselves, by killing innocent people. It is not just that they can't kill a lot of innocent people. Even if the proportions work out favorably, in particular cases or over a period of time, we would still want to say, I think, that the patrol must be sent out, the risk accepted, before the big guns are brought to bear. The soldiers sent on patrol can plausibly argue that they never chose to make war in Korea;

they are soldiers nevertheless; there are obligations that go with their war rights, and the first of these is the obligation to attend to the rights of civilians – more precisely, of those civilians whose lives they themselves endanger.

The principle of double effect, then, stands in need of correction. Double effect is defensible, I want to argue, only when the two outcomes are the product of a *double intention*: first, that the "good" be achieved; second, that the foreseeable evil be reduced as far as possible. So the third of the conditions listed above can be restated:

(3) The intention of the actor is good, that is, he aims narrowly at the acceptable effect; the evil effect is not one of his ends, nor is it a means to his ends, and, aware of the evil involved, he seeks to minimize it, accepting costs to himself.

Simply not to intend the death of civilians is too easy; most often, under battle conditions, the intentions of soldiers are focused narrowly on the enemy. What we look for in such cases is some sign of a positive commitment to save civilian lives. Not merely to apply the proportionality rule and kill no more civilians than is militarily necessary – that rule applies to soldiers as well; no one can be killed for trivial purposes. Civilians have a right to something more. And if saving civilian lives means risking soldier's lives, the risk must be accepted. But there is a limit to the risks that we require. These are, after all, unintended deaths and legitimate military operations, and the absolute rule against attacking civilians does not apply. War necessarily places civilians in danger; that is another aspect of its hellishness. We can only ask soldiers to minimize the dangers they impose.

Exactly how far they must go in doing that is hard to say, and for that reason it may seem odd to claim that civilians have rights in such matters. What can this mean? Do civilians have a right not only not to be attacked but also not to be put at risk to such and such a degree, so that imposing a one-in-ten chance of death on them is justified, while imposing a three-in-ten chance is unjustified? In fact, the degree of risk that is permissible is going to vary with the nature of the target, the urgency of the moment, the available technology, and so on. It is best, I think, to say simply that civilians have a right that "due care" be taken.[24]* The case is the same in domestic society: when the gas company works on the lines that run under my street, I have a right that its workmen observe very strict safety standards. But if the work is urgently required by the imminent danger of an explosion on a neighboring street, the standards may be relaxed and my rights not violated. Now, military necessity works exactly like civil emergency, except that in war the standards with which we are familiar in domestic society are always relaxed. That is not to say, however, that there are no standards at all, and no rights involved. Whenever there is likely to be a second effect, a second intention is morally required. We can move some way toward defining the limits of that second intention if we consider two more wartime examples.

---

* Since judgments of "due care" involve calculations of relative value, urgency, and so on, it has to be said that utilitarian arguments and rights arguments (relative at least to indirect effects) are not wholly distinct. Nevertheless, the calculations required by the proportionality principle and those required by "due care" are not the same. Even after the highest possible standards of care have been accepted, the probable civilian losses may still be disproportionate to the value of the target; then the attack must he called off. Or, more often, military planners may decide that the losses entailed by the attack, even if it is carried out at minimal risk to the attackers, are not disproportionate to the value of the target: then "due care" is an additional requirement.

The Bombing of Occupied France and the Vemork Raid

During World War II, the Free French air force carried out bombing raids against military targets in occupied France. Inevitably, their bombs killed Frenchmen working (under coercion) for the German war effort; inevitably too, they killed Frenchmen who simply happened to live in the vicinity of the factories under attack. This posed a cruel dilemma for the pilots, which they resolved not by giving up the raids or asking someone else to carry them out, but by accepting greater risks for themselves. "It was . . . this persistent question of bombing France itself," says Pierre Mendes-France, who served in the air force after his escape from a German prison, "which led us to specialize more and more in precision bombing – that is, flying at a very low altitude. It was more risky, but it also permitted greater precision . . ."[25] The same factories, of course, could have been (perhaps should have been) attacked by squads of partisans or commandos carrying explosives; their aim would have been perfect, not merely more precise, and no civilians except those working in the factories would have been endangered. But such raids would have been extremely dangerous and the chances of success, and especially of reiterated success, very slim. Risks of that sort were more than the French expected, even of their own soldiers. The limits of risk are fixed, then, roughly at that point where any further risk-taking would almost certainly doom the military venture or make it so costly that it could not be repeated.

There is obviously leeway for military judgment here: strategists and planners will for reasons of their own weigh the importance of their target against the importance of their soldiers' lives. But even if the target is very important, and the number of innocent people threatened relatively small, they must risk soldiers before they kill civilians. Consider, for example, the one case I have found from the Second World War where a commando raid was tried instead of an air attack. In 1943, the heavy water plant at Vemork in occupied Norway was destroyed by Norwegian commandos operating on behalf of the British SOE (Special Operations Executive). It was vitally important to stop the production of heavy water so as to delay the development of an atomic bomb by German scientists. British and Norwegian officials debated whether to make the attempt from the air or on the ground and chose the latter approach because it was less likely to injure civilians.[26] But it was very dangerous for the commandos. The first attempt failed, and thirty-four men were killed in its course; the second attempt, by a smaller number of men, succeeded without casualties – to the surprise of everyone involved, including the commandos. It was possible to accept such risks for a single operation that would not, it was thought, have to be repeated. For a "battle" that extended over time, consisting of many separate incidents, it would not have been possible.

Later in the war, after production was resumed at Vemork and security considerably tightened, the plant was bombed from the air by American planes. The bombing was successful, but it resulted in the deaths of twenty-two Norwegian civilians. At this point, double effect seems to work, justifying the air attack. Indeed, in its unrevised form it would have worked sooner. The importance of the military aim and the actual casualty figures (foreseeable in advance, let us assume) would have justified a bombing raid in the first place. But the special value we attach to civilian lives precluded it.

Now, the same value attaches to the lives of German as to those of French or Norwegian civilians. There are, of course, additional moral as well as emotional reasons for paying that respect and accepting its costs in the case of one's own people or one's allies (and it is no accident that my two examples involve attacks on occupied territory). Soldiers have direct obligations to the civilians they leave behind, which have to do with the very purpose of soldiering and with their own political allegiance. But the structure of rights stands independently of political allegiance; it establishes obligations that are owed, so to speak, to humanity itself and to particular human beings and not merely to one's fellow citizens. The rights of German civilians – who did no fighting and were not engaged in supplying the armed forces with the means of fighting – were no different from those of their French counterparts, just as the war rights of German soldiers were no different from those of French soldiers, whatever we think of their war.

The case of occupied France (or Norway) is, however, complex in another way. Even if the French pilots had reduced their risks and flown at high altitudes, we would not hold them solely responsible for the additional civilian deaths they caused. They would have shared that responsibility with the Germans – in part because the Germans had attacked and conquered France, but also (and more importantly for our immediate purposes) because they had mobilized the French economy for their own strategic ends, forcing French workers to serve the German war machine, turning French factories into legitimate military targets, and putting the adjacent residential areas in danger. The question of direct and indirect effect is complicated by the question of coercion. When we judge the unintended killing of civilians, we need to know how those civilians came to be in a battle zone in the first place. This is, perhaps, only another way of asking who put them at risk and what positive efforts were made to save them. But it raises issues that I have not yet addressed and that are most dramatically visible when we turn to another, and a much older, kind of warfare.

Notes

1. S. L. A. Marshall, *Men Against Fire* (New York, 1966), chs. 5 and 6.
2. Wilfred Owen, *Collected Letters*, ed. Harold Owen and John Bell (London, 1967), p. 458 (14 May 1917).
3. *Good-bye to All That* (rev. edn, New York, 1957), p. 132.
4. *The Collected Essays, Journalism and Letters of George Orwell*, ed. Sonia Orwell and Ian Angus (New York, 1968), vol. II, p. 254.
5. *The Fortress: A Diary of Anzio and After* (Harmondsworth, 1958), p. 21.
6. *Sardinian Brigade: A Memoir of World War I*, trans. Marion Rawson (New York, 1970), pp. 166–71.
7. Archibald Forbes, quoted in J. M. Spaight, *War Rights on Land* (London, 1911), p. 104.
8. *Instructions for the Government of Armies of the United States in the Field*, General Orders 100, April, 1863 (Washington, 1898), Article 69.
9. M. Greenspan, *The Modern Law of Land Warfare* (Berkeley, 1959), pp. 313–14.
10. G. E. M. Anscombe, *Mr. Truman's Degree* (privately printed, 1958), p. 7; see also "War and Murder" in *Nuclear Weapons and Christian Conscience*, ed. Walter Stein (London, 1963).
11. See Sir Frederick Smith, *The Destruction of Merchant Ships under International Law* (London, 1917) and Robert W. Tucker, *Law of War and Neutrality at Sea* (Washington, DC, 1957).
12. H. A. Smith, *Law and Custom of the Sea* (London, 1950), p. 123.
13. Turker, p. 72.
14. Tucker, p. 67.
15. Doenitz, *Memoirs: Ten Years and Twenty Days*, trans. K. H. Stevens (London, 1959), p. 261.

16 *The Destruction of Convoy PQ 17* (New York, n.d.), p. 157; for other examples, see pp. 145, 192–3.

17 *Nazi Conspiracy and Aggression: Opinion and Judgment* (Washington, DC, 1947), p. 140.

18 Doenitz, *Memoirs*, p. 259.

19 *Old Soldiers Never Die* (New York, 1966), p. 198.

20 Kenneth Dougherty, *General Ethics: An Introduction to the Basic Principles of the Moral Life According to St Thomas Aquinas* (Peekskill, NY, 1959), p. 64.

21 Dougherty, pp. 65–6; cf. John C. Ford, S. J. "The Morality of Obliteration Bombing," in *War and Morality*, ed. Richard Wasserstrom (Belmont, CA, 1970). I cannot make any effort here to review the philosophical controversies over double effect. Dougherty provides a (very simple) text book description, Ford a careful (and courageous) application.

22 For a philosophical version of the argument that it cannot make a difference whether the killing of innocent people is direct or indirect, see Jonathan Bennett, "Whatever the Consequences," *Ethics*, ed. Judith Jarvis Thomson and Gerald Dworkin (New York, 1968).

23 Reginald Thompson, *Cry Korea* (London, 1951), pp. 54, 142–3.

24 I have been helped in thinking about these questions by Charles Fried's discussion of "Imposing Risks on Others," *An Anatomy of Values: Problems of Personal and Social Choice* (Cambridge, MA, 1970), ch. XI.

25 Quoted from the published text of Marcel Ophuls' documentary film, *The Sorrow and the Pity* (New York, 1972), p. 131.

26 Thomas Gallagher, *Assault in Norway* (New York, 1975), pp. 19–20, 50.

Chapter 31

Terrorism without Intention*
David Rodin

If we are to be engaged in a "war on terrorism," then we had better get clear about what terrorism is. Until we achieve a clear and coherent understanding of what the morally relevant features of terrorism are, we cannot hope to develop an appropriate moral response to the "war on terrorism" now being prosecuted by the United States and its allies – its proper aims, scope, limitations, and potential exceptional permissions.

In this chapter, I present a unified way of understanding the moral significance of terrorism. I begin by briefly identifying four different strategies for defining terrorism. I then introduce a definition of terrorism which locates its moral significance in the object of attack – terrorism is given its distinctive moral character by the fact that it uses force against those who should not have force used against them. In the idiom of the just war theory, it uses force against noncombatants.

It has sometimes been claimed that certain military actions of key Western powers such as the United States, NATO, and Israel are properly described as acts of terrorism because they cause the death of a large number of noncombatants. This is a coun-terintuitive claim. But by examining the doctrine of double effect and contrasting it with the categories of reckless and negligent harming, I will argue that there are good reasons for thinking that these claims may sometimes be correct. Some harms inflicted unintentionally on noncombatants – so called collateral damage – may indeed be properly categorized as terrorist. I will conclude by briefly indicating some of the implications which this analysis has for our thinking about the ethics of war.

I Defining Terrorism

The concept of terrorism has been so deformed by rhetorical usage that it is probably not possible to provide a full analysis of its use in common language. At best what we can discern is a loose family resemblance. I shall suggest, however, that it is possible to provide a moral definition of the term. By this I mean an analysis of the features of acknowledged core instances of terrorism which merit and explain the moral reaction which most of us have toward them. These reactions are undeniably negative; most of us regard acts of terrorism with abhorrence. This in turn raises the question of whether the moral definition of a pejorative concept

* From *Ethics* 114 (July 2004), pp. 752–71.

makes the specified act wrong by definition. There is certainly truth in the thought that wrongness is part of the meaning of terrorism – in this respect the concept is more like that of murder than it is of killing. Yet it is not the case that establishing a moral definition trivializes the task of morally assessing terrorism by turning it into a matter of simple definition. This is because, first, it is part of the function of a moral definition to *explain why* the class of actions is wrong. The strategy I employ in this chapter is to explain an explicitly normative concept through definitional elements that are at least less normative. Second, once we have discovered the set of features that accounts for our negative moral reaction to a class of action, it is still an open question whether there exist cases in which the act so defined may be justified or excused (e.g., because of overwhelming consequentialist considerations). Understood in this way, a moral definition does not seek to encompass all potential usages of a term but rather to unearth and explain the distinctive features which enable the concept to play the role it does in our moral thinking.

Many philosophers and theorists of various kinds have attempted to define terrorism. These attempted definitions are too numerous to review here in detail, but they may be usefully classified as making appeal to four different sets of consideration. The taxonomy is not meant to be exclusive; theorists can and often do appeal to more than one. Nevertheless, the fourfold classification usefully identifies and orders the differing theoretical approaches to terrorism.

1.   *Tactical and Operational Definition*

This may be phrased in terms of the weapons deployed; for example, Carlos Marighela, the Brazilian revolutionary, defined terrorism simply as "the use of bomb attacks."[1] Clearly this is too narrow. Any such defini-

tion would have to be enlarged to include a range of further operational modalities, some of which are distinctive to terrorism (such as plane hijacking), but others may include more familiar military practices. Another form of operational definition focuses not on the weapon systems themselves but on the mode of their employment. Michael Walzer claims that "randomness is the crucial feature of terrorist activity."[2] The point here is not that terrorist attacks are unplanned or untargeted but rather that the violence appears random from the perspective of the victim. Violence comes unpredictably, often without warning, and people are killed or escape death by merest chance. Some authors have insisted that terrorism involves violence or its threat against persons.[3] Others allow violence against property to count.[4] Still others have denied a necessary connection with violence, claiming there can be nonviolent terrorism.[5]

2.   *Teleological Definition*

This focuses on the ends or goals of violence. Many writers claim that terrorism must be a political act.[6] The definition of the UK Terrorism Act 2000 is somewhat broader, specifying that it be "for the purpose of advancing a political, religious or ideological cause."[7] Beyond this, some authors have argued that a necessary feature of terrorism is that it is coercive, aiming to get people or groups to do things they would not otherwise do.[8] Finally, "terrorism" is etymologically connected to "terror", and some authors have argued that the creation of terror among a given community is definitional of terrorism.[9]

3.   *Agent-focused Definition*

In contrast to tactical and teleological definitions which focus on the nature of the act, this approach focuses on the nature of the actor. For example, Walter Laqueur defines terrorism as "the substate application of violence."[10] Unsurprisingly, such a definition which excludes state action from the definition of terrorism has been enthusiastically endorsed by states themselves: for example, the US State Department definition of "terrorism" restricts it to "violence perpetrated . . . by sub-national groups or clandestine agents."[11]

4. Object-focused Definition

Finally, terrorism has been defined as attacks against a particular class of target variously described as "innocent," "neutral," "civilian," or "noncombatant,"[12] Igor Primoratz goes further, arguing that "terrorism has a certain basic structure. It has not one, but two targets: the immediate, direct target, which is of secondary importance, and the indirect target which is really important."[13]

What are we to make of this multiplicity of definitional elements? The first thing to note is that it is plausible that each of these definitional features may have utility in different contexts. For example, for the purposes of a military-strategic, or sociological, or psychological investigation it may be highly relevant to distinguish between violence committed by state and nonstate actors, between different tactical modalities, and between violence directed to different teleological aims. However, it will be my argument that for the purposes of a moral definition of terrorism, the crucial factor is the fourth element – the object against which force is used. The key to a moral understanding of terrorism is that it consists in the use of force against those who should not have force used against them. A teleological definitional element is necessary to distinguish terrorism from common domestic forms of criminal activity, but it is the object-focused aspect that really directs and explains our typical moral judgments.

With this in mind, I propose to introduce the following moral definition: *terrorism is the deliberate, negligent, or reckless use of force against noncombatants, by state or nonstate actors for ideological ends and in the absence of a substantively just legal process.* Like all definitions, this one contains a number of suppressed arguments, and it is important that we make them explicit in order to see what is doing the moral and conceptual work. The aspect of my definition which is likely to be most controversial is the claim that terrorism may include negligent and reckless as well as deliberate uses of force, and this will be defended in a separate section below. Before doing this I propose to explain each clause of the definition in some detail.

Use of force. This is a deliberately broader notion than that of violence, with its connotations of wild and explosive physical harming. Clearly the kinds of force used and the methods of its deployment must be interpreted widely. Use of conventional weapons, weapons of mass destruction, hostage taking, poisoning, systematic incidences of rape, and destruction of property may all be terroristic.[14]

There will inevitably be a certain difficulty in determining what level of force is required to reach the threshold of terrorism, and there will certainly be many borderline cases. But equally clearly, for a use of force to count morally as terrorism it must cause very substantial harm to the lives and interests of its victims. The paradigm of terrorism is the employment of extreme and shocking force, for example, killing, maiming, and hostage taking. It is doubtful, indeed, whether lesser uses of force such as slapping or spanking could ever count morally as terrorism. It has often been claimed that the threat of force may count morally as terroristic.[15] This is plausible, but the threats must be credible, and usually this will be achieved by the prior use of actual force.

Ideological ends. The term 'ideological' is used here in its broadest sense to signify "a systematic scheme of ideas, usually relating to politics or society, or to the conduct of a class or group, and regarded as justifying actions."[16] It is meant only to signify a commitment to some systematic and socially directed end beyond the motives of fear, anger, lust, and personal enrichment, which are the typical motives of common violent crimes.

This teleological element is required in the definition to distinguish terrorism from common crime. Though terrorism is a species of crime, it is distinguished from common murder, rape, and destruction of property by the fact it is directed toward a broader agenda. Usually the ideological nature of terrorism will mean that it is committed by organized groups with an established infrastructure, but this is not an invariable feature, as cases of lone terrorist activity have been known to exist (e.g., the Unabomber, who conducted a prolonged series of bomb attacks in America).

Reference to "political ends", which is the preferred characterization of many authors, is not fully adequate because it fails to capture the numerous species of terrorist motivation beyond the purely political. Terrorism may, for example, be national separatist (IRA, ETA, PLO, Tamil Tigers), religious (Al-Qaida), racist (Ku Klux Klan), environmental (Animal Liberation Front, Earth Liberation Front), millennial fatalist (Aum Shinrikyo), antitechnologist (the Unabomber), or anti-federalist (Timothy McVeigh, who bombed the Oklahoma federal office building).

Noncombatants. Clearly this clause of the definition contains the crux of the moral argument. It is designed to capture the intuition that terrorism has the significance it does in our moral thinking because the targets it attacks are morally inappropriate. Put simply, terrorism involves the use of force against those who should not have force used against them, and to do so is a moral crime. Thus, terrorism is the political or ideological species of common violent crime. It is the criminality (and in its most serious form, the murderousness) of terrorism which explains its moral status and the reaction we rightly have to it.

Now to characterize terrorism in this way is implicitly to invoke some principled way of distinguishing those who are morally liable to the use of force and those who are not. In the Western tradition the most widely accepted way of doing this in the context of political conflict is by reference to the principle of discrimination within the just war theory. This stipulates that the only appropriate objects of force in a conflict are combatants – those who are engaged in fighting and are therefore either individually or collectively offering harm to the putative agent of force or to another.[17] All others are to be regarded as noncombatants and excluded from attack.

The just war principle of discrimination is not without its critics. It has been doubted, for example, whether the notion of a combatant really identifies sufficient conditions for being an appropriate object of force. For being a combatant or offering harm is a material fact about the agent; it need say nothing about his moral responsibility for the fact that he is offering harm (he might, e.g., be an unwilling and largely blameless conscript).[18] But for our present purposes we need make no judgment about the soundness of the permissive side of the principle of discrimination. As Michael Walzer says, "The theoretical problem is not to describe how immunity is gained, but how it is lost. We are all immune to start with; our right not to be attacked is a feature of normal human relationships."[19] This is surely right, the immunity of noncombatants from attack is the foundational element in our moral thinking, and whether or not the just war theory is ultimately able to sustain the permissibility of killing combatants is irrelevant to this fact. It is this basic moral judgment that ordinary people who are not engaged in any threatening combat operations should not be subject to attack that explains and underlies the moral repugnance we justifiably feel about acts of terrorism.

The term "noncombatant" is preferable to the related term "civilian" often employed in international law.[20] The reason for this can be seen from consideration of the bomb attack on the American destroyer USS *Cole* in the port of Aden in October 2000 (probably by members of Al-Qaida). The crew members killed were uniformed servicemen and therefore not civilians, but they were noncombatants in the morally relevant sense. They were in port on a routine friendly visit and were not involved in any combat operations at the time. Because of this, the attack on the *Cole* is rightly seen by most observers as terroristic. Similarly, soldiers who are wounded, sick, or have surrendered (*hors de combat*) are noncombatant in the relevant sense, and attacks against them may be morally terroristic.

State or nonstate actor.   Strictly this element is superfluous to the definition – it has been inserted only to make the universality of the definition explicit.

Universality is a basic principle of the interpretation of moral rules. There are, to be sure, exceptions to this principle, cases in which the identity of the agent is relevant to the permissibility of a given act. For example, though I am not permitted to cut people open and remove their kidneys, doctors often are. Cases like this, however, are exceptional, and all depend upon a rich moral context which explains the normative particularity (the doctor's special status and training, his duty of care, the presence of the patient's prior consent, and so on). Though there is no a priori way to rule out such

a contextual moral distinction between state and nonstate use of extralegal force against noncombatants, it is certainly far from obvious how such an account could proceed.

On the contrary, the proposition that acts of terrorism may be committed by state as well as nonstate actors should be obvious once one has accepted that the key to a moral understanding of terrorism is that it uses force against inappropriate objects. One may consider the 1985 bomb attack (with the loss of one life) on the Greenpeace vessel *Rainbow Warrior* in Auckland harbor by French secret agents. This was a paradigmatic terrorist attack; it involved the killing of noncombatants in the absence of substantively just legal process for ideological purposes. It is difficult to see how the fact that the perpetrator was a state government (and a liberal democratic one at that) could be relevant to our moral assessment of the attack as terroristic.

Substantively just legal process.   The purpose of this clause is to create a qualified exception to the definition. The exception is required because without it the use of force by agents of the state to enforce the law would be classed as terrorism. That cannot be right. Proper enforcement of the law by state agents is not an instance of terrorism; indeed it is a paradigm of morally justified use of force.

However, the wording of the clause is designed to capture the limits of this claim. For not all uses of force which are sanctioned by a legal process are morally justified. If the legal process itself is substantively unjust, then it cannot confer moral justification on the use of force. There are both historical and moral reasons for thinking that when this is the case the use of force may properly be regarded as terroristic.

When the term 'terrorism' was first coined in the late eighteenth century, it was employed to describe the use of terror as a tool of government by the Jacobin party after the French Revolution. Soon it came to signify the internal use of terror by states more widely, what today we would principally call totalitarian or repressive government. Thus, in contrast to many modern definitions which explicitly exclude state violence, in its original meaning terrorism was an act which could *only* be committed by states. Today the word is seldom used in this way, but it is apparent that from a moral perspective such use of force shares relevant features with more familiar acts of terrorism such as bombings and hijackings by nonstate actors: it too directs force against inappropriate targets, attacking those who should not be attacked for ideological ends. The wording of this clause, therefore, is designed to allow such uses of force to be included in the moral definition of terrorism. Thus regimes that systematically inflict unjust force on their own populations are rightly described as terrorist regimes.

Reference to a "substantively just" legal process is meant to signify a contrast with a more procedural interpretation of justice. Thus totalitarian and repressive states often use violence in a way that is procedurally legalistic but which fails to conform to a substantively just legal process. It is the procedurally legalistic but substantively unjust use of force by states which qualifies for inclusion under the moral definition of terrorism.

Just what makes a legal process substantively just is a central question of political philosophy and cannot be properly explored here. Indeed, it may seem a defect of my definition that it includes reference to such a contested and explicitly normative notion as substantive justice. But I take it that any adequate political philosophy must contain some way of distinguishing substantively just from unjust legal processes. The proper way of understanding this element of the definition is to view the term 'substantively just' as a marker or placeholder for the particular theory of justice one wishes to endorse. As such, the definition appropriately recognizes the way in which one's commitments in the theory of justice have implications for the moral scope of terrorism (as indeed they will have implications for many other normative concepts). The positive claim I want to make is that when a state uses force against noncombatants in accordance with a legal system which fails the substantive justice test (however one chooses to fully characterize that test), there is good reason to count this morally as terrorism.[21]

It is worth noting that it is the legal processes themselves which must be substantively unjust in order to satisfy the definition. Isolated miscarriages of justice within an otherwise just legal system do not constitute terrorism. However, the systematic application of unjust legal processes in ways that constitute a significant use of force against the lives and interests of noncombatants certainly may constitute terrorism.

One further element of my definition is operative by way of omission. I have made no mention of the further teleological and agent-focused features which some authors have thought definitional of terrorism: the claim that it is coercive, the claim that there is a necessary distinction between direct and indirect targets, and the link between terrorism and terror. Jenny Teichman says "we will look pretty silly if we do not mention terror in our account of terrorism."[22] Michael Walzer has said that what is distinctive about terrorism is that it "reaches beyond all limits; it is infinitely threatening to whole peoples, whose individual members are systematically exposed to violent death at any and every moment in the course of their (largely innocuous) lives."[23]

Well, is it silly to omit mention of terror in a moral definition of terrorism? The first thing to note is that Walzer's characterization is itself a considerable exaggeration. Anyone who has lived or worked in London or Jerusalem or New York knows that this is not (necessarily) what it is like to live under threat of terrorist attack. Only in the most extreme cases do terrorist attacks cause a genuine terror or panic in the population as a whole. Shocking as the attacks may be, ordinary people generally get on with their lives and think about the threat only when personally affected or when the violence is reported in the news. Such, apparently, is the grim resilience of the human spirit.

It does not seem to be the case that terrorism invariably has the effect of causing terror in a population. On the contrary, there have been instances in which communities have grown stronger and more resilient as a result of terrorist attacks. London during the blitz is the classic (though doubtless over-romanticized) example. If terrorism does not of necessity create terror in the population against which it is directed, then terror cannot be part of the moral definition of the crime.

But it may be that to focus on actual effects is misleading. It may be that the term "terrorism" is akin to "teaching"; one can be engaged in the activity of teaching even if there isn't much learning going on in the classroom. Perhaps the relevant fact is that the terrorist intends to cause terror in the population. But this too seems inadequate. Perhaps the terrorist is just confused about what the effects are likely to be, or perhaps his moral compass is so distorted that he believes himself to be benefiting his victims and their community, as is apparently the case with members of the Aum Shinrikyo cult.[24] Should these suppositions prove correct, I can see no reason to alter our moral appraisal that such acts constitute terrorism. A similar line of argument can be constructed to exclude from the definition the other putative features, namely, coerciveness and the "double targeting" of terrorist attacks.[25]

The key point to understand here is the distinction between definitional and aggravating features of an offense. A definitional feature of an offense identifies, as it were, a certain quantum of opprobrium – a step change in moral seriousness. We may be guided here by a domestic analogy. If a man in domestic society commits an act of murder and it is a feature of his crime that it causes (or was intended to cause) widespread terror, or if it was used to coerce a certain group of people or to attack an indirect target distinct from his direct target, then these are all aggravating features. They will cause us to view his crime with greater seriousness than otherwise, but they do not change the fact that what he is guilty of is an act of *murder* (albeit a particularly egregious one). In a similar way it would seem that the coercive and terrifying features of terrorism (when they are present) are aggravating but not definitional features of the offense.

II The Doctrine of Double Effect and the Distinction between Terror Bombing and Tactical Bombing

The final element of my definition is intended to be somewhat more revisionary than the preceding analysis. Because the definition includes "negligent and reckless" uses of force, it implicitly entails that some harms unintentionally inflicted on noncombatants in the course of war are a form of terrorism. The issue arises particularly in the case of aerial bombardment against targets within or adjacent to civilian populations which is almost certain to generate noncombatant casualties. Although new targeting technologies have significantly increased the bombing accuracy of Western air forces, the number of noncombatant casualties in modern air campaigns such as Kosovo, Afghanistan, and Iraq remains high in absolute terms. For example, though it is difficult to verify the reliability of figures, on some estimates the number of noncombatants killed by Operation Enduring Freedom in Afghanistan exceeded the number killed in the attacks on the Pentagon and World Trade Center.[26]

According to traditional moral theory, such "collateral casualties" are considered the regrettable but generally permissible side effect of legitimate military activity and are strongly distinguished from terrorism. In what follows I aim to cast doubt on this assessment. Doing so will entail examining a feature of moral theory which has long been thought to support it: the doctrine or principle of double effect. A standard formulation of the principle of double effect is as follows. One may never intentionally bring about an evil, either as an end in itself, or as a means to some greater good. Nonetheless, one may use neutral or good means to achieve a good end which one foresees will have evil consequences provided that (i) the evil consequences are not disproportionate to the intended good, (ii) the action is necessary in the sense that there is no less costly way of achieving the good.[27]

The double-effect principle has traditionally been taken to ground a moral distinction between the deliberate targeting of noncombatants, often called terror bombing, and tactical bombing, which aims at military targets but may cause collateral damage among noncombatants. In terror bombing, so the argument goes, the agent intends the death of noncombatants as a means to his ends. This is always wrong, though the goodness and viability of the ends may be very great indeed. In tactical bombing, on the other hand, the agent intends only to strike at legitimate military targets. The death of noncombatants, while it is a foreseen consequence of the action, is not intended either as a means or as an end (in Bentham's terms it is an oblique intention but not a direct intention). Provided the requirements of

necessity and proportionality are met, therefore, the action, together with its foreseen consequences, is not impermissible.

Now many philosophers have been deeply skeptical of the view that the intention of the agent in performing an action can be determinative of the permissibility of the act in this way. As several authors have pointed out, we have no satisfactory theoretical explanation of why intention in the sense here invoked should make a difference to the permissibility of actions.[28] Moreover, J. J. Thomson has spoken about the peculiarity of the principle when applied in action-guiding contexts. If a bomber pilot came to ask for your advice as to the permissibility of a raid which will destroy a military installation and also cause significant civilian casualties, it would seem absurd if you said to him that it all depends on your direct intention: if your intention is to destroy the installation, foreseeing but not intending the death of the civilians, this is permissible. But if your intention is to kill the civilians, merely foreseeing the destruction of the installation, this would be impermissible.[29] Even writers sympathetic to double effect such as Elizabeth Anscombe and John Ford have stressed the care with which it must be applied and the dangers – both intellectual and moral – of its abuse.[30]

Important as these criticisms are, I would like to raise a different set of questions about the principle of double effect by contrasting it with two considerations that explain how legal and moral culpability may exist in the absence of direct intention: these are the concepts of recklessness and negligence. Recklessness may be characterized as the culpable bringing about of unintentional evil consequences (or the risk thereof) that are in fact unreasonable and unjustified in the circumstances. Though recklessness is distinguished in law from intention proper, it is nonetheless a form of mens rea – a mental state sufficient for criminal liability. In law there are two forms of recklessness, subjective recklessness, which requires that the agent consciously foresaw the risk of evil consequences, and objective recklessness, in which the agent did not foresee the risk but where a reasonable person would have done so. Objective recklessness is very similar in content to negligence, which is the failure to take reasonable precautions in the face of a foreseeable risk. Negligence is primarily a civil law concept, but it may constitute a ground for criminal liability where the negligence is gross.

Judgments involving negligence and recklessness sit uncomfortably with the principle of double effect. Take the case of a motorist who drives across a crowded school yard to deliver a sick person to a hospital. The motorist certainly has no direct intention to harm the children – he aims at their death neither as a means nor as an end. His conduct may be necessary in the context, and if we imagine that the risk of death to his passenger and to the children are roughly balanced, then it will also be proportionate. Yet if he strikes and kills a child he will be held liable, in law and in morality, for manslaughter because of the recklessness of his actions. Similarly, a medical researcher who prematurely tests an unsafe new vaccine on humans out of a desire to speed the development of the product and thereby save lives is guilty of negligent action and may be liable for manslaughter. This is true even though his action may fulfill all the requirements of the double-effect principle.

One might object that there can be no tension between the concepts of recklessness and negligence on the one hand, and the doctrine of double effect on the other, because reckless and negligent risks must be such that they are in fact unreasonable in the circumstances. But we have already said that actions that pass the double-effect test must be necessary and proportionate, and surely action that is necessary and proportionate is ipso facto reasonable.[31] To construe the notion of reasonableness in this way, however, is to miss a crucial point. Persons have rights against being harmed or used for the benefit of others, rights which can only be alienated in very specific ways, usually having to do with actions and decisions they have freely and responsibly taken. Because of this there is an additional element to the reasonableness test which goes beyond the necessity and proportionality requirements, namely: is it justifiable to inflict such a risk upon this particular person? What motivates our intuition in the case of driving to the hospital through the school yard and the vaccine case is that those who are being forced to bear the risk have a right not to have such grave risks inflicted upon them. The fact that the risks are necessary (from the perspective of the beneficiaries of the risky activity) and proportionate (from the impersonal perspective of the world at large) is not sufficient to defeat the personal right not to be endangered or used in this way.

Now these observations about negligence and recklessness do not strictly contradict the doctrine of double effect because that doctrine, on its traditional interpretation, does not purport to identify sufficient conditions for innocence, only sufficient conditions for guilt. Nonetheless, there is clearly a tension here. The principle is supposed to show how the absence of a direct intention on the part of the agent can materially affect the permissibility of acts with harmful consequences. The concepts of negligence and recklessness, on the other hand, approach the idea of permissibility by drawing on the idea of a requirement to observe a reasonable standard of care in one's actions and not to undertake unreasonable risks. But one may fail to observe a reasonable standard of care either by possessing a direct intention to cause harm, by possessing an oblique intention to cause harm, or by possessing no intentional attitude toward the harm at all, as when one fails to foresee a harmful consequence of one's action that one could have been reasonably expected to foresee and avoid. Considerations of recklessness and negligence threaten not to disprove the principle of double effect but rather in certain contexts to render it irrelevant.

III   Standards of Care in Military Operations

What does all this imply for our discussion of aerial bombardment and the definition of terrorism? Clearly it shifts the focus of attention away from the direct intention of those engaged in the activity and onto the question of what constitutes an appropriate standard of care in military operations. In general, standards of care are contextual and depend on a large number of conditions specific to the agent, activity, and situation, but it is possible to identify some common elements. For instance, the more dangerous the activity one is engaged in, the higher the standard of care required. Thus a higher standard of care is required in the operation of a car than in riding a bicycle, and a higher standard still is required in the operation of a jumbo jet. Standards of care are also higher in activities that have a higher causal immediacy to harm. Thus, those who perform roadwork are subject to a higher standard of care than those who play football, even though footballs sometimes roll onto the road and cause accidents. Standards of care are often linked to professional relationships, and the standard of care expected of a professional is generally higher than that expected of a nonprofessional engaged in the same activity.

If we apply these observations to the activity of aerial bombardment, we will observe that bombardment is a highly dangerous activity, that there is a high causal immediacy between the dropping of bombs and resulting fatalities, and that the activity

is carried out by highly trained professionals. All of these observations will naturally lead us to the thought that the standard of care required of those engaged in military activities such as aerial bombardment is very high indeed, and that consequently when noncombatant fatalities are caused as the unintended but foreseen side effect of bombardment, this must raise serious questions of culpable negligence or recklessness.

Balanced against this is the fact that in certain circumstances, often in emergencies, it is justifiable to observe a lower standard of care and to incur a higher degree of risk than would otherwise be appropriate. So, for example, it may be justified for a surgeon to perform an operation in which there is an extremely high risk of death to the patient, if the alternative to surgery is an even higher risk of death or of great suffering. Moreover, police cars and ambulances are permitted to exceed the speed limit and pass red lights in emergencies (though of course strict requirements of care remain, e.g., the requirement to display warning lights, the requirement to slow down when entering intersections, and the requirement to generally minimize the risk to others). Finally, road engineers are permitted to make a reasonable trade-off between cost and safety when designing a road, though they know that this will lead to a certain number of otherwise avoidable fatalities.

Perhaps military operations which carry a high risk of noncombatant casualties are not reckless or negligent because the risks are justifiable in a similar way. But the analogy is not a good one. For in all the above examples a crucial part of what makes the risk justifiable is that the party assuming the risk is also the beneficiary of the risk-producing activity. This is obvious in the case of the patient undergoing risky surgery, but it is also true, in a statistical sense, of the risks of speeding police cars and less-than-perfectly safe roads. Because the risk of death to any particular person is spread more or less evenly throughout the community, one may rightly say that the community which enjoys the benefits of improved apprehension of criminals and an affordable road system also bears the risks incurred. Why should this idea be important to our sense that the risk in these cases is justifiable? The answer, I think, is that it links to the idea of autonomous agency and free acceptance of risk. A patient decides whether to assume the risk profile of a given operation, and every community makes its own collective decision about how to make the trade-offs involved in building roads and apprehending criminals. The risks are justifiable in these cases, at least in part, because they have been autonomously assumed either individually or collectively by those who bear them.

Contrast this with the case of aerial bombardment which imposes a substantial risk upon enemy noncombatants. In standard cases of military conflict there is no sense in which the party who bears the risk of harm benefits from the risky activity.[32] Neither have they autonomously chosen, either individually or collectively, to bear the risks of the bombardment. It is extremely doubtful, therefore, whether the risks imposed on enemy noncombatants can be justified in an analogous way to the risks imposed in domestic emergency situations.

If one is persuaded by these interlinked lines of argument then one will feel that the standard of care required of those engaged in military operations is high – higher than is currently reflected in the laws of war. One will be inclined to view many of the noncombatant casualties caused in the course of military operations (including those of Western nations) to be culpably reckless or negligent. One will feel this despite the considerations adduced by the principle of double effect.

IV Recklessness and Negligence as Mens Rea for Terrorism

Even if one is not persuaded that standards of care in the course of military operations are as high as I have suggested, one will have to accept that there is *some* standard of care incumbent on soldiers engaged in military operations and that when harm is caused as a consequence of their action falling below this standard, those harms will be culpable by reason of negligence or recklessness. The question then arises whether such reckless and negligent harming of noncombatants may properly be regarded as terrorist. Under the moral definition which I have been defending, there is strong reason to suppose that it may, for both share an underlying moral structure with more familiar forms of terrorism. Both constitute a culpable use of force for ideological ends, by a state or non-state actor, against noncombatants, and without substantively just legal process. Under the principle that like cases be treated alike, there is good reason to class both under the single moral heading of terrorism.

There is no denying, however, that such an analysis is at odds with the current common usage of the term, which generally restricts terrorism to acts of intentional harming. This may lead one to the following response: why should we meddle with the moral definition of terrorism, when we already possess an adequate set of conceptual tools for dealing with the issues raised in this article, in the form of the proportionality requirement within the laws of war?[33] Military action which causes unacceptable unintended harm to noncombatants can be condemned as disproportionate use of force. What is significant about the arguments I have presented here is that they show that the hurdle for proportionate use of force is much higher than has been commonly believed. But the appropriate way to deal with this is to strengthen the proportionality requirement, not to deform the ordinary meaning of terrorism.

There are two reasons why I think this response is not adequate. The first has to do with a general observation about the proportionality requirement in the laws of war. The notion of proportionality has its most natural application in the domestic sphere. If I kill an assailant who was about to kill me, it is easy to see that this is a proportionate use of force, just as it is easy to see that killing someone to defend my prize apple pie from premature and wrongful consumption is a disproportionate use of force. But in the context of war the proportionality requirement is much more difficult to interpret. The *jus in bello* proportionality requirement states that the harm done in the course of a military operation must not be disproportionate to the concrete military advantage likely to be gained. But it is not at all obvious that the two values of military advantage and harm against noncombatants are morally commensurable. Exactly what metric is one supposed to use to determine the level of military advantage required to offset the foreseeable deaths of a given number of non-combatants? Tweaking the proportionality requirement is unlikely to be an effective response to the concerns I have raised until we have a clearer conception of what proportionality in war is and how precisely it functions.

The second and deeper reason for the inadequacy of the proportionality response is that it rests on a misunderstanding of the reasons why the unintended infliction of harm or risk upon noncombatants is morally problematic. The proportionality requirement is most naturally interpreted as a quasi-consequentialist principle which states that there is a moral limit upon prima facie justified actions which is triggered when such

actions do more harm than good. The doubts about collateral damage which I have been raising in this article have an entirely different source. They derive rather from a conception of persons as beings with rights against being harmed, or exposed to risk of harm, in the absence of justifying conditions relating specifically to their autonomous actions and decisions.

Consider a domestic example. If the only way I can flee an assailant is to kill or impose a significant risk of death upon an innocent bystander, such action would certainly be proportionate on any reasonable interpretation of proportionality. But most people would view such action as wrong, and the reason for this is that there is no relevant moral fact about the bystander which could justify inflicting this (admittedly proportionate) harm upon him or her. In the same way, the conclusion that much collateral damage caused by military operations is negligent or reckless is not motivated only by the thought that the force is disproportionate (though it may well be that also). It is rather motivated by the thought that it is inflicted upon those who should not have force inflicted upon them – those who because they are noncombatants have no liability to have force (not even proportionate force) used against them.[34] Proportionality, therefore, is not the appropriate locus for the kind of moral issue I have been raising.

One may accept all of this, however, and still have reservations about extending the definition of the term 'terrorism' to include unintentional, albeit reckless and negligent, use of force against noncombatants. One might feel that to do so would be an act of disreputable persuasive redefinition akin to arguments that seek to define inequality and poverty as forms of violence. But in reality, very little turns on the purely terminological question of the usage of the word 'terrorism'. The important issue is whether one accepts the substantive argument put forward in this article: that the unintentional killing of some noncombatants in the course of military operations is morally culpable to the same degree and for the same reasons that typical acts of terrorism are culpable.

If one does accept this conclusion, then I think there are two entirely reasonable ways to settle the terminological question. The first is to restrict the definition of terrorism to the intentional (in the narrow sense of directly intended) use of force against noncombatants and to categorize the reckless and negligent use of force against noncombatants as a separate class of offense. This has the virtue of mirroring the distinction made in criminal law between murder, which requires the mens rea of intention, and the lesser offense of manslaughter, for which recklessness or negligence suffices (in the United States the distinction is between first- and second-degree murder). This is not an intrinsically objectionable way of settling the terminological question, however the manslaughter/murder distinction has been criticized by legal scholars as unhelpful and ad hoc. Indeed, murder is one of the few criminal offenses for which recklessness is not a sufficient mens rea. What is more, we have no term in our moral vocabulary for the reckless, as opposed to intentional, use of force against noncombatants for ideological reasons. An artificial term would need to be introduced (perhaps "reckless terrorism" or "terrorist manslaughter") which may have difficulty in gaining general currency.

The second response, reflected in my moral definition, is to hold that the crucial point about terrorism is not the direct intention of the agent but the wrongfulness of the act. Many acts which would generally be considered as sufficient for terrorism such as assault, battery, or the threat of the use of force, are lesser offenses than reckless manslaughter. It is difficult to see why such intentional acts should be included in the definition of terrorism, while the more serious offense of reckless manslaughter is excluded. Following this line of logic, my moral definition of terrorism makes reference to the "deliberate, reckless, or negligent" use of force against noncombatants. I believe that this definition best articulates what is morally most important about the phenomenon of terrorism.

V Conclusion

What conclusions for policy can be drawn from this moral analysis of terrorism? There are, I think, two broad and tentative lines of thought which emerge and which concern the *jus ad bellum* and the *jus in bello* of any engagement with terrorist adversaries. The first is that we should be extremely cautious about extending the rules of *jus ad bellum* so as to include terrorism as a just cause for war. What has come to be called "the Bush doctrine" asserts that countries have the right to use force (and indeed to engage in preemptive war) if they believe they may be subject to a tangible terrorist threat. But if my analysis is correct, it is apparent that terrorism in the morally relevant sense is a relatively broad military and political practice which is frequently utilized by states, including the United States and her allies. This has been obviously true in cases such as the terror bombing of Germany and Japan during the Second World War. But, as I have here suggested, terrorism in the sense of the reckless use of force against noncombatants has also been an issue in several recent conflicts including NATO's bombing campaign against the Federal Republic of Yugoslavia in 1999, Operation Enduring Freedom in Afghanistan, the war in Iraq, and, perhaps most clearly, Israel's military response to the Palestinian intifada. Viewing terrorism as itself a just cause for war would therefore result in a dangerous and unwelcome extension of the right to resort to force, one which would expose a number of

Western powers themselves to the use of military force.

Second, in terms of the *jus in bello*, it seems intuitively correct that any engagement which has as part of its goal the elimination of terrorist threats and which is called a "war on terror" should not, if it is to be legitimate, use terrorist tactics itself. At a minimum this will require much greater care to eliminate noncombatant casualties than has been demonstrated by Western powers in recent operations. So-called smart targetable munitions have the potential to revolutionize the humanitarian aspects of war. But aerial bombardments in Iraq, Afghanistan, and Kosovo have all resulted in very significant noncom-batant casualties, and Western powers continue to use substantially indiscriminate weapons such as cluster munitions and land mines. Moreover, the increased ability to target accurately means that we must pay greater attention to the nature of targets selected. The increasing tendency to target "dual use" facilities such as power stations, transport, and media infrastructure is particularly worrying in this context, for destroying such targets has the potential to cause very significant noncombatant deaths for months and even years after the conflict has ended.[35] If the war against terrorism is to avoid being a terrorist war, then such practices must be seriously reconsidered.

Notes

[1] Quoted in C. A. J. Coady, "The Morality of Terrorism," *Philosophy* 60 (1985), pp. 47–69, p. 47.

[2] Michael Walzer, *Just and Unjust Wars* (New York: Basic Books, 1977), p. 197. Walter Laqueur, on the other hand, explicitly denies that randomness is necessary to terrorism. See Walter Laqueur, *The Age of Terrorism* (Boston: Little, Brown, 1987), pp. 143–4.

[3] Igor Primoratz, "What is Terrorism?" *Journal of Applied Philosophy* 7 (1990), pp. 129–38, p. 135.

[4] Coady, "The Morality of Terrorism," p. 52.

[5] Carl Wellman, "On Terrorism Itself," *Journal of Value Enquiry* 13 (Winter 1979), pp. 250–8, p. 251.

[6] See Coady, "The Morality of Terrorism," p. 52; Jenny Teichman, "How to Define Terrorism," *Philosophy* 64 (1989): 512–13.

[7] UK Terrorism Act, 2000, pt. 1, sec. 1.

[8] Wellman, "On Terrorism Itself," p. 250.

[9] Ibid.

[10] Walter Laqueur, "Postmodern Terrorism," *Foreign Affairs* 75 (1996), pp. 24–36, p. 24.

[11] Quoted in George Lopez and Neve Gordon, "Terrorism in the Arab–Israeli Conflict," in *Ethics in International Affairs*, ed. Andrew Valls (Lanham, MD: Rowman & Littlefield, 2000), pp. 99–113, p. 103.

[12] For "innocent," see Primoratz, "What is Terrorism?" pp. 131, 133; for "neutral," see Teichman, "How to Define Terrorism," p. 513; and for "noncombatant," see Coady, "The Morality of Terrorism," p. 52.

[13] Primoratz, "What is Terrorism?" p. 131.

[14] There may be some doubt as to whether the disruption of information systems (cyberterrorism) can be properly described as a "use of force." Some incidences clearly are. For example, one of the most frightening possibilities envisioned by Pentagon scenario planners is the use of a high-altitude electromagnetic pulse (or HEMP) to attack the information infrastructure of the United States. A single nuclear device detonated at an altitude of 300 kilometers could devastate electrical systems across 90 percent of the continental United States, though the blast itself would cause no harm to persons on the ground. Such an attack is certainly a use of force and would count as an act of terrorism in the morally relevant sense. In contrast, the use of computer hacking to disrupt web sites and information systems does not employ physical force, though it is often included under the heading of cyberterrorism. Such acts are probably best seen as borderline cases of terrorism. Though they do not involve

physical force, they are still properly described as "attacks" upon property (albeit of an intangible kind) and may cause significant harm to the lives and interests of their victims.

15 For example, Walter Sinnott-Armstrong includes the threat of force in his definition of terrorism (Walter Sinnott-Armstrong, "On Primoratz's Definition of Terrorism," *Journal of Value Enquiry* 8 [1991]: 116), and it is explicitly included in the UK Terrorism Act, 2000, definition (pt. 1, sec. I).

16 *Oxford English Dictionary*, 2nd edn.

17 Thus the rather confusing equation within just war theory between noncombatants and "the innocent." "Innocent" is the negation of 'nocent', meaning harmful or injurious.

18 For a critique of the claim that it can be justifiable to use force against a morally innocent "material aggressor," see David Rodin, *War and Self-Defense* (Oxford: Oxford University Press, 2002), ch. 4, esp. pp. 83ff.

19 Walzer, *Just and Unjust Wars*, p. 145n.

20 See, e.g., *Protocol Additional to the Geneva Conventions of 12 August 1949, and Relating to the Protection of Victims of International Armed Conflicts (Protocol 1)* (1977), art. 51, sec. 2: "the civilian population as such, as well as individual civilians, shall not be the object of attack."

21 It would seem that as a minimum we may say that a substantively just legal system must involve the application of laws that do not violate basic human rights; impartial enforcement and judicial bodies; fair rules of evidence; and ideally effective procedures of appeal and review.

22 Teichman, "How to Define Terrorism," p. 511.

23 Walzer, *Just and Unjust Wars*, p. 200.

24 Laqueur, "Postmodern Terrorism," sec. 2.

25 None of this, of course, should obscure the significance of such features for the moral assessment of terrorism. It is a vitally important feature of the crime of terrorism that it will frequently cause severe and widespread fear and social dislocation. The claim is simply that these features ought not be made part of the definition of the crime. They are rather, as Tony Coady says, important empir-

ical insights into the sociology and motivational psychology of terrorism (Coady, "The Morality of Terrorism," p. 53).

26 Carl Conetta puts the figure at 1,000–1,300 civilian deaths directly from aerial bombardment and a minimum of 3,000 civilian deaths attributable to the impact of the bombing campaign and war on the nation's refugee and famine crises (*Strange Victory: A Critical Appraisal of Operation Enduring Freedom and the Afghanistan War*, Project on Defense Alternatives, Research Monograph no. 6 [Cambridge, MA: Commonwealth Foundation, January 2002]).

27 See Frances M. Kamm, "The Doctrine of Triple Effect and Why a Rational Agent Need Not Intend the Means to His End," *The Aristotelian Society Supplementary, Volume 74*, no. 1 (2000), pp. 21–39, p. 23.

28 T. M. Scanlon, "Intention and Permissibility," *The Aristotelian Society Supplementary Volume 74*, no. 1 (2000): 301–17, p. 303.

29 See Judith Jarvis Thomson, "Self-Defense," *Philosophy & Public Affairs* 20 (1991), pp. 283–311, p. 293.

30 G. E. M. Anscombe, "War and Murder," in *Moral Problems*, ed. James Rachels (New York: HarperCollins, 1979); J. C. Ford, "The Morality of Obliteration Bombing," in *War and Morality*, ed. Richard Wasserstrom (Belmont, CA: Wadsworth, 1970), pp. 15–41. Partly as a response to worries such as these, T. M. Scanlon has, in a recent paper, suggested a way of interpreting typical double-effect cases in a way that does not invoke the distinction between direct and oblique intention: T. M. Scanlon, "Intention and Permissibility," *The Aristotelian Society Supplementary Volume 74*, no. 1 (2000): 301–17.

31 I am indebted to Jeff McMahan for raising this point.

32 A possible exception to this observation may be in the case of humanitarian intervention.

33 For the legal definition of *jus in bello* proportionality see *Protocol Additional to the Geneva Conventions of 12 August 1949, and Relating to the Protection of Victims of International Armed Conflicts (Protocol 1)* (1977), art. 51 (5)(b) and art. 57 (2)(b).

[34] This analysis, of course, raises a difficult question about how it can ever be justifiable to impose risk upon those who have not through their actions made themselves specifically morally vulnerable to it. This question is beyond the scope of this article, but my sense is that the answer has to do with two kinds of consideration. The first is the kind of free collective consent to beneficial but risky activities assumed by communities, such as was discussed in Sec. III above. The second has to do with the much rarer set of cases in which there are such overwhelming consequentialist considerations that we are inclined to believe that it is justifiable to impose risks upon those who have done nothing to deserve their imposition. Such cases, of course, necessarily take us far beyond the bounds of any plausible conception of proportionality.

[35] See Henry Shue and David Wippman, "Limiting Attacks on Dual-Use Facilities Performing Indispensable Civilian Functions," *Cornell International Law Journal* 35 (2002), pp. 559–79.

Chapter 32

Terrorism, Justification, and Illusion*
Saul Smilansky

Bernard Williams once said that doing moral philosophy could be hazardous because there, presumably unlike in other areas of philosophy, we may run the risk of misleading people on important matters.[1] This risk seems to be particularly present when considering the topic of terrorism. I would like to discuss what seems to be a most striking feature of contemporary terrorism, a feature that, as far as I know, has not been noted. This has implications concerning the way that we should view terrorism (and counterterrorism) and shows the force of a number of neglected illusions surrounding the issue of terrorism, as well as its justification.

I Preliminaries

First I will quickly go over some definitions and clarify some of my assumptions. There is a broad sense in which terrorism can be understood as "intentionally targeting noncombatants with lethal or severe violence for political purposes."[2] In ethical terms, this formulation seems to capture the salient feature of the practice, the intentional targeting of noncombatants (and not in the context

of crime or the like). However, I wish to focus here on terrorism in a narrower sense, as practiced by members of small or weak groups that lack the capacity to field an army and engage in warfare. Henceforth when I speak of terrorism I shall refer to this narrower sense. The distinction between combatants and noncombatants and its relation to the notion of innocence are problematic, but to a lesser extent in the context of terrorism than in that of warfare. Terrorism has typically and specifically targeted civilians without concern for their innocence; this is a large part of the indiscriminate murderousness and randomness that terrorizes. Similarly, terrorists themselves are typically not coerced conscripts or people ignorant of the nature of their commitments, of whom one can wonder whether they might not be significantly morally innocent.

Two dominant claims on this issue that will concern us later on are

(a) The Principle of Noncombatant Immunity (PNI): it is never permissible to aim to kill (or severely harm) noncombatants; PNI forbids terrorist as well as counterterrorist activities aimed at killing (or severely harming) noncombatants.

* From *Ethics* 114 (July 2004), pp. 790–805.

(b) The Antioppression Exception to PNI: PNI is correct in general, but there are exceptions when weak forces are fighting unjust oppression. In our context, the Antioppression Exception permits terrorist targeting of noncombatants if it is necessary in combating oppressive regimes. Violating PNI in counterterrorist activity is still, however, forbidden.

Some general remarks about the normative views underlying this chapter. Some philosophers follow PNI and categorically reject terrorism as such. Coady, for example, writes, "I . . . object to the technique of terrorism as immoral wherever and whenever it is used or proposed."[3] I do not hold any such unambiguous position. Following in the footsteps of previous discussions, I think that matters are more complicated and that, as we shall see, the attempt to stick the square absolutist-deontological peg into the shapeless hole of terrorism cannot always be successful.[4] At the same time, I recognize the moral force of the deontological insistence on strict noncombatant immunity: according to this position the only permitted intentional targets are combatants, broadly understood, for it is only they who have in some sense forfeited the universal human right of security, by seeking to endanger others.[5] In my view unless there are overwhelming countervailing reasons, the strict constraint on the intentional targeting of noncombatants should be followed. But such reasons may occasionally exist, in extreme situations.[6]

Moreover, as has been often pointed out, the widespread acquiescence in the idea of nuclear deterrence makes it difficult to maintain the absolute deontological adherence to PNI. The relationship between *jus in bello* and *jus ad bellum* also seems to me to be closer than PNI requires, so that we would need to pay close attention to *jus ad bellum*.[7] And the distinction between what is philo-

sophically justified and what it would be pragmatically best to do also makes its presence felt in the issue of terrorism. These and other matters will concern us in detail ahead. For now all I wish to do is to note that all these complications suggest a multilevel pluralism (of various deontological and nondeontological ethical concerns and of principled versus pragmatic considerations) that defies easy codification.

II   Terrorism and Justification in Practice

It seems to me that the relationship between terrorism and moral justification in the world today is striking: the major instances of terrorism are not justified, while in cases where terrorism might be justified, there is no or relatively little terrorism. In other words, in the world today we have abundant terrorism without justification and possibly-justified terrorism that does not materialize! We shall take up the issue of what this means in Section III. Here I shall defend the claim just made. In all three of our test cases I shall only be able to outline the factors relevant for our issue, while the wealth of historical detail and complex nuances lie beyond our scope.

The following examples of terrorism are the most prominent ones of the post-Second World War era: (1) the Irish Republican Army (IRA) struggle against the British and Protestants in Northern Ireland, (2) the Palestinian struggle against Israel, and (3) the Al-Qaida struggle against the West in general and others who refuse to recognize the exclusive authority of fundamentalist Islam.

A   The IRA

In order to see the hopelessness of the case for IRA terrorism, it is enough to note the following facts:

(a) There is adjoining Northern Ireland an independent, flourishing, and democratic Irish state, namely, the Republic of Ireland. Established in 1921, it covers some 85 percent of the island. The Republic fully enables the right of the Irish nation to self-determination, to cultural and religious development, and to unencumbered formation of identities as Irishmen and Irishwomen. Any Catholic living in Northern Ireland need only move south or west the distance of an hour's drive, and all of the above rights and privileges will readily be available to him or her.

(b) If choosing to remain in Northern Ireland, any Catholic is a citizen of the United Kingdom, which is similarly a wealthy and democratic state and an open society. He or she will enjoy full political rights and religious freedom as a British subject and be represented in the British Parliament, as well as in democratic local government within Northern Ireland.

(c) Living conditions for most Catholics in Northern Ireland, while unequal to those of most Protestants, partly due to discrimination, have throughout the period not been terribly harsh. Discounting certain measures arising from the need to deal with terrorism, there has been little violence inflicted on the civilian population by the British authorities and hardly anything that can be described as tyranny or repression.

(d) There is complete freedom of movement and ample possibility for cultural interaction with the Republic of Ireland for any Catholic choosing to remain in Northern Ireland.

Irish Catholics have a strong historical case for resentment against the English. Under contemporary conditions, however, the Catholics of Northern Ireland are arguably among the few percentiles of the world's population who are the most fortunate,

in most respects that matter – political, cultural, economic, and religious. The case for armed struggle, let alone for continuous terrorism, is very weak. There is, in terms of just war theory, no just cause. Unless one implausibly makes almost every grievance or interest justification for terrorism, the IRA's terrorist campaigns have no ethical justification. (Unionist terrorism in Northern Ireland can similarly be shown to be unjustified. Even immediate unification of the whole of Ireland could not justify terrorism by Protestants, for reasons parallel to the above.)

B   The Palestinians

In the case of Palestinian terrorism the major factors that make for the absence of justification are the clear existence of alternatives to terrorism and the fact that the condition of the Palestinians has largely followed from their own choices. Consider the following:

(a) Israel was established in 1948 following a decision in 1947 by a large majority in the United Nations to partition what remained of the British mandate over Palestine (the part west of the River Jordan) into two independent states, a Jewish State and an Arab State (Resolution 181). The Jewish leadership accepted the decision. The official leadership of the Palestinian Arabs rejected the very idea of an independent state for the Jews as well as the compromise partition plan, and the Palestinians began fighting; this included a terrorist campaign, combined with the invasion of the military forces of five Arab armies. Hence, already in 1948 the Palestinians could have had an independent state alongside Israel.

(b) Between 1948 and 1967 the Palestinians could have called for and attempted to establish an independent Palestinian state in the West Bank and East Jerusalem (captured by Jordan in the 1948 war) and in the

Gaza Strip (captured by Egypt in the 1948 war), both areas intended to be within the Palestinian-Arab state according to the partition plan. The Palestinians made no such attempt, aiming their political efforts, coupled with continuous terrorist incursions, at Israel. Cross-border terrorism was led in the pre-1967 period by the mainstream Palestinian Fatah movement, headed (since 1964) with Yasser Arafat, with the avowed intention of provoking a war between Israel and the Arab states.

(c)   The uncompromising Palestinian denial of Israel's right to exist continued after the Six Day War in 1967, in which Israel captured the West Bank, East Jerusalem, and the Gaza Strip, until the late 1980s and the signing of the Oslo peace accords in 1993. Indiscriminate terrorism aimed at targets such as airplanes, synagogues, schools, and supermarkets was continuous.

(d)   It seems that once these territories were in Israeli hands, Israel became a classic target for nonviolent resistance, as practiced by Gandhi in India. The fact that Israel is a democracy, the moral traditions and sensibilities of Jews who were continuously persecuted when themselves nonviolent, and Israel's dependence on and support from similarly open and principled societies all could have made such a nonterrorist campaign (if aimed at the establishment of a Palestinian state alongside Israel and not instead of it) particularly successful.[8] But the opposite course has been repeatedly taken.

(e)   In 1978 Israel signed a peace treaty with Egypt. In that treaty Israel recognized the legitimate rights of the Palestinian people; one of the provisions of that treaty was the establishment of Palestinian "full autonomy" in the territories, followed by negotiations toward a permanent settlement. That plan could also have led to the establishment of a Palestinian state. The Palestinians refused to join the talks when invited by the Egyptian

President Anwar el-Sadat and rejected that plan.

(f)   In 1993 Israel, led by Yitzhak Rabin, and the Palestinians, led by Arafat, signed the Oslo agreement. This arranged for the gradual withdrawal of Israel from territories in the West Bank and Gaza Strip, in return for the commitment by the Palestinian authority (which was strengthened and well-armed following the agreement) to recognize Israel's right to exist, cease terrorism, and combat terrorism by other Palestinian groups that continued to call for its annihilation. This conditional "land for peace" agreement was soon broken: devastating terrorist attacks within Israeli cities occurred, often launched from Palestinian controlled territory, with the Palestinian Authority doing very little to stop them. This campaign resulted in the defeat of Rabin's successor, the Israeli Labor Premier Shimon Peres, in the 1996 elections, to the Likud candidate Benjamin Netanyahu, who, although continuing to give some further territory to the Palestinians, did not implement the Oslo accords in good faith. By then the Palestinians had some control of around 40 percent of the territories, including the major Palestinian population centers. The Palestinian state-on-the-way was once again derailed by Palestinian terrorism.

(g)   In 1999, a Labor candidate, Ehud Barak, was again elected prime minister. Barak, in the Camp David negotiations (summer 2000) and in the following months at the Egyptian city of Taba (partly even after violence had begun), made the Palestinians dramatic offers: accounts of the details vary somewhat, but in Camp David the offers included the Gaza Strip, 90 percent of the West Bank, and a capital in East Jerusalem, with most Israeli settlements to be dismantled. The Palestinians rejected the offers, made no counteroffer, and resorted to violence. In Taba, the offers included around 97 percent of the West Bank, and Barak offered even to hand over to the Palestinians some pre-1967 areas from within Israel itself (making it overall a roughly "100% deal"). Palestinian independence and the end to Israeli control seemed imminent. However, "like déjà vu all over again," the Palestinians rejected these offers as well as Clinton's bridging proposals, and they resorted to violence and armed struggle from the beginning, and shortly afterward – to systematic terrorism and suicide bombings. It is important to note the central role played in the terrorist campaign by the Palestinian mainstream led by Arafat's Fatah movement, and not only by radical Islamic groups like Hamas and Islamic Jihad. The view that the Palestinians only want a state of their own alongside Israel and, if that is granted, that they would truly recognize Israel and let it be (rather than use any territory that would be conceded as a springboard for seeking to destroy it) was perceived to have been discredited once again. The Israeli public in a political backlash elected Ariel Sharon. He has publicly supported the idea of a Palestinian state once terrorism ceases, although it is not clear what his intentions are.

None of this is to deny that certain Israeli actions have been morally unacceptable and that some Palestinian resentment has justification. No doubt, as in the case of Northern Ireland, the narrative is more complex and might be interpreted in somewhat different ways at various points. But our question is specific: whether terrorism has been justified. And in this case as well, the negative conclusion is clear: the Palestinians have repeatedly had peaceful opportunities for gaining a state of their own and, tragically, have opted instead for terrorism. For this there is no ethical justification. In terms of just war theory, the just Palestinian aim of establishing a state of their own alongside Israel did not require terrorism: the necessity condition was not met. Historical circumstances have changed over the years, but the

Palestinians have always seemed to prefer the hopes of annihilating Israel in concert with Arab states, or the romance of violent struggle, to constructive accommodation. Rather than terrorism being required in order to establish a Palestinian state, it is on the contrary the Palestinians that have repeatedly sabotaged the establishment of an independent Palestine alongside Israel, both directly, and indirectly through the influence of their choices and actions on the Israeli democratic process. (Instances of terrorism by Jews since the establishment of Israel also lack any credible moral justification.)

C   Al-Qaida

Al-Qaida seems to have developed after the success of the fight against the Soviet occupation of Afghanistan into a network seeking to establish fundamentalist Islamic hegemony, a self-declared "Universal Jihad." Al-Qaida has targeted Western states and westerners in general, Russians, Jews, nonsympathetic Islamic regimes and targets within Muslim countries, and other areas where Muslims may gain power (such as the Philippines). The ideology of this group is radical: it is antidemocratic and totalitarian, utopian, opposes universal human rights and the emancipation of women, anti-Western and anti-Semitic, and in favor of a continuous violent struggle toward the establishment of universal fundamentalist Muslim rule.

I trust that little needs to be said on why there is nothing here that can morally justify the most violent terrorist operations staged by Al-Qaida, which purposefully and typically discount noncombat immunity and moral innocence. Primarily, there is, in terms of just war theory, simply no just cause. There are twenty-two independent countries that are members in the Arab league and dozens of explicitly Islamic countries (the exact number depends on how those are defined). There is ample potential for Islamic self-expression, the development of Muslim culture, and the practice of Islam, the religion of over one billion people. There are many problems within Muslim societies, as well as vast wealth derived from oil that could help deal with them, but nothing here can justify a terror campaign.[9]

D   Where Might Terrorism Be Justifiable?

We have seen, then, that the most concerted terrorist efforts since the Second World War, those of the IRA, the Palestinians, and Al-Qaida, seem to lie very low in any plausible scheme of moral justification. This evaluation is not dependent on a subtle balancing of considerations but is apparent to any sensible informed analysis.

What about the other side of the equation? Here, since we are thinking hypothetically, it is much harder to judge, and, in any case, one must be very careful when suggesting that terrorist activity that might have been justified did not materialize. Making a convincing case here would also require a very detailed description of the situations. However, I do not think that as philosophers we can hide from ourselves that such cases can probably be made.

One situation where terrorism might be justified lies in situations where there is clear danger to a group's very existence or the mass extermination of noncombatants. There have been a number of almost genocidal situations in the post-World War II period we are considering – Biafra, Cambodia, Rwanda, Sudan, and East Timor. It is not clear whether terrorism would have been effective in stopping the horrors in those cases, or that there were not other untried means for doing so, but, if such a case for unique effectiveness could have been made, perhaps in those cases it might have been, overall, justified.

Another possible area we might examine is that of limited terrorist actions aimed at galvanizing public attention to the plight of poor people in the Third World. With millions in Africa starving, with further millions dying because they cannot afford to buy inexpensive and readily available medication, and so on, a consequentialist perspective, at least, certainly justifies great moral outrage. It might be argued that terrorism is unlikely to have a successful coercive effect here. However, if selective, limited, and symbolic, it could certainly raise the issues to the headlines. Whether there are other as yet untried alternatives, and whether terrorism can be a positive influence here overall, are questions that, again, would require detailed investigation. But for our purposes it suffices that we pay attention to the interesting fact that no serious attempts of this kind – whether justified or not – have occurred. Terrorism has continuously rocked the world, but such moral and idealistic aims have not been its targets.

Third, there is the issue of limited and narrowly focused terrorism aimed at toppling dictatorial regimes and establishing democracy. Many Third World regimes (or indeed Second World ones, until the fall of communism) are not only undemocratic but also severely oppressive. In many countries there is no likely possibility of improvement unless present rulers are toppled. It could be argued that such regimes would not care about even a great deal of harm inflicted on their civilian population; hence, terrorism would not be effective. However, the regime's control over power might weaken, and selective terrorism might at least be a means of "communication," rallying opposition forces in social orders where other forms of communications are tightly controlled. Other means of reform are perhaps not available, while limited terrorism focused on discrediting the regime or on influencing or harming the often-narrow elite might work. Again, great care must be taken here, and the possibility of making a proterrorism case should be viewed skeptically. The surprising fact, however, is, once again, how relatively uncommon terrorism has been in such contexts. The typical targets of terrorism in the narrow sense have been liberal democratic societies: consider which airlines have been hijacked, for instance. Terrorism has usually not targeted the worst but rather the best type of regimes in the world. These are doubtless easier targets, but not morally fitting ones.

III Illusions

I have argued, in a nutshell, that by and large where there has been terrorism it has not been justified, and where it perhaps could have been justified, it has not occurred. What follows from this?

A The Impotence of Justification

One would have thought that there would be some significant positive correlation between the practice of terrorism and moral justification. But not only is there no direct positive correlation, the two go in opposite directions. It might be argued that terrorists and those assisting them cannot be expected to follow intricate discussions of analytic philosophy. But that was not the expectation: there is, after all, political leadership, public discussion, media coverage, academic research, and individual moral reflection that might have been thought to have some positive effect, to help get things right. The continuous nature of terrorism as practiced in all these cases also precludes the thought that what we have here are some simple errors of calculation (e.g., the thought that limited acts of terrorism will ensure quick success) or some spontaneous reaction. Rather, long-term, well-developed, and seemingly self-sufficient bloody "cultures of terrorism" are involved.

Our result implies that the world is curiously disjointed. Perhaps there are situations where terrorism has been contemplated but not pursued as a result of good moral reasoning. Still, in a striking way the role of adequate moral reflection is shown in its emptiness – both when the efforts at justification ought to yield negative results and when they ought perhaps to yield positive ones. Within the societies and cultures that have generated terrorism, or support it, moral deliberation on our topic has failed to be effective. The thought that terrorism can be adequately guided by processes of justification is an illusion.

What, then, is going on? I think that an alternative "justification bypassing" explanation of the different situations can be provided, but doing this in detail is of course beyond our scope. Terrorism exists in our three major examples for historical, sociological, cultural, and psychological reasons. It is not by chance that, in all three cases, religion plays a large role. The nationalistic and religious hatred lying behind IRA, Palestinian, and Al-Qaida terrorism goes a long way toward explaining it. It is not so much substantive moral concerns – with massive danger to life, collective self-determination, personal freedom, basic cultural and religious rights, lack of alternatives, or the like – that lie behind these instances of terrorism, but the ghosts of history, the depths of ill will, and the temptations of power. Fanatical religious and nationalistic pride and intolerance, the psychological attractions of being a "victim" rather than assuming responsibility for one's difficulties, an uncritical culture of resentment and envy, romantic idealizations of struggle and violence, open hatred of the other for its otherness, irrational myths, the self-destructive desire for mastery, and other such beliefs and passions seem to lie behind contemporary terrorism.

B   Being Careful

The general project of moral justification makes certain demands: for instance, that the existence of real needs and just aims be established, that severe violence should be used only as a last resort, that reasonable proportionality be maintained, and that standards of universalization can be applied to the would-be justification.

What does the considerable impotence of this project in the present context imply about what we should do? At the very least, it seems to me to suggest that we take great care with this issue. For those deontologists who would condemn every instance of terrorism as such, matters are simpler. But even without dismissing the possibility that terrorism can be justified, we have nevertheless concluded that, in the major examples of its prevalence, terrorism has been unjustified. This conclusion should lead us to be very skeptical about the idea of permitting terrorism. It might be countered that the absence of actualization of those examples where terrorism might be justified should lead us, by the same token, to be more daring in allowing it. But I do not think that matters are symmetrical here. Our conclusion, in brief, is that the connection between justification and actualization is severed: under such conditions, engaging with the issues in the hope of "fine tuning" the permission of terrorist activity is far too risky. We should err on the side of not allowing terrorism.

In a still deeper way, we need to confront the fundamental power of illusory forces. In the past, illusory ideas of superiority and fanatical hunger for power coupled with fantasies of world mastery, such as those of the Nazis, overtook whole nations. The record of modern terrorism shows some of those elemental illusory forces at play and, in any case, exhibits a similar gross blindness to, or disdain of, acceptable standards of moral justification. There is a grand struggle between moral justification and the temptations of terrorism, and at least where terrorism has occurred, so far moral justification has seemed to have but little effectiveness. This applies both at the grassroots level and with the respective elites. All of this does not mean that we should give up the effort at clarifying standards of moral justification or give up the ideals of public enlightenment. We should, nevertheless, know where we are rather than fool ourselves.

C   Absolutist PNI as a "Positive Illusion"

Under such conditions, the Principle of Noncombatant Immunity, or PNI, has a lot to be said for it pragmatically; PNI might be socially useful even though philosophically it is unpersuasively strict. Perhaps, in its insistence on absolute constraints, in its taboo on intentionally targeting noncombatants, it is, by and large, a "positive illusion."[10]

A pertinent factor here follows from the general features of combat. Because of its lethal nature, the psychological tendency of situations of combat to lead to strong feelings of hatred and revenge seeking, and because of the temptations in situations where normal restraints against violence are left behind, absolute prohibitions are perhaps pragmatically necessary in order to achieve actual restraint. While with many matters ethical sensitivity can be problematic, in the case of warfare the dangers typically lie on the other side.[11] Concerning the intentional targeting of noncombatants, and perhaps a number of other "temptations" of combat, it is better that people believe in absolute constraints and not make exceptions. It is far from obvious, in other words, that the philosophical–ethical complexity should be applied in practice, say, in the minds of soldiers and their commanders. Such a widening gap between theory and practice is, however, problematic in itself.[12]

The absolutist line concerning noncombatant immunity has become dominant in Western public debate and in the laws concerning the conduct of warfare. This has had a large emotional influence, which goes much beyond any possible force that a merely conventional understanding of the constraints might elicit. Noncombatant immunity is enshrined in international law and, with the exception of nuclear deterrence, is widely respected, at least by First World countries. It has a civilizing influence that, other things staying constant, may be extended. Among the things that may not stay constant is terrorism, particularly as it receives support from established states and seeks to acquire nonconventional weaponry.

D The Dangerous Illusion of the Antioppression Exception

The Antioppression Exception to PNI, the modified version of PNI that allows the targeting of noncombatants by weak groups in the struggle against oppression, is a clear casualty of our discussion. All three of our major examples of terrorism are frequently assumed to be permitted by the Antioppression Exception. If there is no justification for terrorism in these cases, then our confidence in following this common lenient viewpoint should fade.

Moreover, if indeed the strict adherence to PNI is pragmatically so important, we see how dangerous the Antioppression Exception is to respect for PNI. The more "antioppression" by the weak is tolerated as a justification for terrorism, the more does the one-sided constraint put upon any counterterrorist transgressions of PNI seem unreasonable, adding pressure toward the abandonment of such counterterrorist constraint. Consider the following: "*Purity of Arms:* The IDF servicemen and women will use their weapons and force only for the purpose of their mission, only to the necessary extent and will maintain their humanity even during combat. IDF soldiers will not use their weapons and force *to harm human beings who are not combatants* or prisoners of war, and will do all in their power to avoid causing harm to their lives, bodies, dignity and property" (my emphasis).[13] Such limits follow from relevant parts of international law, which clearly incorporate deontological constraints upon combat: "The civilian population as such, as well as individual civilians, shall not be the object of attack. Acts or threats of violence the primary purpose of which is to spread terror among the civilian population are prohibited."[14] Potentially useful ideas such as the following are all forbidden by PNI:

(a)   threatening to kill noncombatants that terrorists care about in order to deter the terrorists;

(b)   intentionally killing noncombatants as a means to hinder terrorist activity;

(c)   indifference to noncombatant casualties during counterterrorist activity;

(d)   the idea that some terrorists or their leaders are beyond moral conversational reach, and hence everything may be done – including targeting noncombatants – in order to suppress them.

Now, recall the thoughts of David Hume: "And thus justice establishes itself by a kind of convention or agreement; that is, by a sense of interest, suppos'd to be common to all, and where every single act is perform'd in expectation that others are to perform the like. Without such a convention, no one wou'd ever have dream'd, that there was such a virtue as justice, or have been induc'd to conform his actions to it. . . . 'Tis only upon the supposition, that others are to imitate my example, that I can be induc'd to embrace that virtue."[15] This may well seem too extreme to many, and I would certainly put independent moral weight on PNI and think that views such as Hume's should be resisted. However, when for terrorists the indiscriminate murder of innocent civilians is the declared epitome of operational success, the idea that PNI is to be a strict constraint on self-defense from terrorism, with harmful operational repercussions, becomes psychologically problematic, more difficult to maintain in practice, and dubious at least in consequentialist and contractual ways. Even if PNI is maintained, and even if any accidental noncombatant enemy casualties are perceived as an operational failure by forces combating terrorism, concern for them, at least when they occur in the form of "collateral damage," would tend to diminish. And when terrorism becomes overwhelming, more direct "reciprocal" approaches that are ready to dismiss PNI in return for effectiveness can be expected. Moreover, as the experience in Northern Ireland attests, such anti-PNI escalation can itself take the form of terrorism, with both Catholic and Protestant sides engaging in it. By contrast, a firm insistence on PNI can limit divergence from PNI in counterterrorism and mutual terrorism.

Why can the Antioppression Exception be thought to be attractive as compared to strict PNI? The reason cannot simply lie with the moral weight of oppression, for oppression is not the only, nor is it the worse, form of badness that may need to be struggled against. So what line can the proponents of the Antioppression Exception take, given that they want to maintain the permission to transgress PNI as an exception available only for the weak? Perhaps the most plausible argument, from fairness or mutuality, might go like this: "You defenders of strict PNI are actually defending the strong against the weak, which is not fair. The forces of oppression, of course, wish to

limit struggle to armies or combatants, because that is where they are strong and we, the opponents of oppression, are weak. Well, we are ready – give us an equal share of your tanks, missiles, and warplanes, and we will fight only combatants and forgo terrorism. Until you do so, however, the only way we can defend ourselves and combat oppression is by attacking the oppressors at their weak point, namely, by targeting their noncombatants." Now, one may or may not find this persuasive as a basis for permissible terrorism, but, if one does find it persuasive, I do not think that the break with PNI can be contained. On the contrary, if we leave PNI behind, there is no reason why counterterrorist activities oblivious to PNI could not be defended. If the terrorists are killing noncombatants, counterterrorist activities can bring forth similar claims for "necessity," because they may argue that they are confronted by a mirror image of the limitations that the terrorists fighting oppression confront. Those fighting terrorism can just as well say that they would be happy not to have to fight terrorism by targeting noncombatants but cannot afford such luxury because terrorists are elusively blending into their noncombatant environment, and only by targeting noncombatants is the justified struggle against terrorism possible. They would be quite ready to forgo the unfortunate killing of noncombatants, if the terrorists would only stop hiding and come out in the open.

Of course this leaves open the substantive question whether the aim is justified, as well as whether other conditions such as proportionality are being met. But this equally can be asked of the proponents of the Antioppression Exception in specific cases. The general question is simply whether the pursuit of just aims may proceed at the expense of PNI. There is nothing unique in the struggle against oppression by terrorists representing weak groups that can justify the principled break with PNI through terrorism but can still stop in principle similar justifications for counterterrorism. Such a gross "Asymmetry Claim" needs firm justification, but one cannot imagine what that might be. My claim is not that a breach of PNI can be justified in the very same case both on the side of terrorism and of counterterrorism. Rather, it is that if it is just or otherwise morally justified to breach noncombatant immunity on the side of terrorism, it is likely to be sometimes so on the side of counterterrorism. It is an illusion that you can do morally nasty things in the name of, say, national liberation, but symmetrical justifications could not be found for counterterrorist breaches of PNI. Wherever we draw the line, it cannot reasonably apply only to one side.

It might be argued that the disappearance of the Antioppression Exception could have harmful consequences, emboldening the oppressors who would know that terrorist resistance would not be thought legitimate. This does not take into account the widespread use that oppressors currently make of the claim that repression is necessary because of the threat of terrorism, a claim which would also be set back. But, in any case, matters are symmetrical here as well: it might similarly be argued that ruthless non-PNI counterterrorism has a useful deterrent effect against terrorists, who would otherwise be able to count on the fact that, whatever they do, those fighting against them were limited by PNI!

In fact one of the particularly nasty features of terrorism is its "parasitic" nature: as in our three test cases, the terrorist infringement of PNI occurs just because the terrorists know that they can rely on their enemies not to react in a similar, ruthless manner. Sometimes terrorism aims to provoke reaction, but its perpetrators also know that such reaction is typically constrained by PNI and other limitations. This is one of the reasons why contemporary terrorism has typically targeted Western democracies, exploiting the principled respect for PNI.

As I have claimed, a number of different illusions (sometimes conflicting, and held by different groups) seem to be present in the context of terrorism and justification:

(a) the illusion of the efficacy of justification: that processes of credible ethical reflection and justification can be relied upon in generating what actually happens;

(b) the illusion that the major instances of modern terrorism have a significant justification;

(c) the overwhelming spread and force, in our context, of illusions – nationalistic, religious, ethnic, and cultural – irrational forces carrying great emotional weight with millions of people and leading to terrorism and the support of terrorism;

(d) the arguably positive illusory belief, encouraged by the international laws of warfare, that terrorism is never justified, as embedded in something such as the absolutist constraints of PNI;

(e) the illusion that we might and should permit this line to be crossed, but only in the fight by the weak against oppression (the Antioppression Exception).

The widespread impotence of the project of public moral justification and the prevalence of illusion, in the context of terrorism, merit further critical examination. What seems already clear is that these two factors should make us, as human beings, considerably more apprehensive, and as intellectuals, more humble.

Notes

1 Bernard Williams, *Morality* (Harmondsworth: Penguin, 1973), p. 9.

2 C. A. J. Coady, "Terrorism," in *Encyclopedia of Ethics*, ed. Lawrence C. Becker and Charlotte B. Becker, 2nd edn. (New York: Routledge, 2001), p. 1697.

3 C. A. J. Coady, "The Morality of Terrorism," *Philosophy* 60 (1985), p. 58; see also Jeffrie G. Murphy, "The Killing of the Innocent," *Monist* 57 (1973), pp. 547–8.

4 See, e.g., Michael Walzer, *Just and Unjust Wars* (Harmondsworth: Penguin, 1978); R. G. Frey and Christopher W. Morris, "Violence, Terrorism and Justice," in *Violence, Terrorism and Justice*, ed. R. G. Frey and Christopher W. Morris (Cambridge: Cambridge University Press, 1991), pp. 1–17; Virginia Held, "Terrorism, Rights and Political Goals," in Frey and Morris (eds.), pp. 59–85. To avoid misunderstanding, the type of deontological view I refer to is that which poses absolute constraints on intentionally harming noncombatants. Thomas Nagel, in his influential "War and Massacre," in *War and Moral Responsibility*, ed. Marshall Cohen, Thomas Nagel, and Thomas Scanlon (Princeton, NJ: Princeton University Press, 1974), calls deontology "absolutism," thereby capturing this feature.

5 See, e.g., Murphy, pp. 547–8. This is sometimes grounded in the principle of self-defense: see, e.g., Robert K. Fullinwider, "War and Innocence," in *International Ethics*, ed. Charles R. Beitz, Marshall Cohen, Thomas Scanlon, and A. John Simmons (Princeton, NJ: Princeton University Press, 1985), p. 94.

6 Such a view is sometimes called "moderate deontology" or "threshold deontology," but this seems to me misleading. On the need for conceptual clarity here, see my "Can Deontologists Be Moderate?" *Utilitas* 15 (2003), pp. 71–5.

7 For an extreme view on this, see Jeff McMahan, "Innocence, Self-Defense, and Killing in War," *Journal of Political Philosophy* 2 (1994), pp. 193–221, and his article, "The Ethics of Killing in War," *Ethics* 114 (July 2004).

8 This was suggested to me by Jeff McMahan.

9 It might be thought that by limiting my discussion to post–World War II events I have avoided the pertinent grievances that might justify terrorism. Since I think that the intentional targeting of noncombatants is morally so bad, very strong justification is required to overcome the constraint against it. It is hard to see why old historical grievances lying generations away, even if substantial, can justify killing noncombatants in the present. To do so would open the door to virtually unlimited worldwide violence, for historically nearly every national territorial holding has been acquired unjustly (and imagine, e.g., any effort to address slavery, colonialism, or the Holocaust through terrorism!). This has interesting implications that limit the role of considerations of justice within moral justification, but this matter cannot be pursued here. In any case, I do not see that in our three cases the grievances are now morally salient, although a footnote is not the place for a thorough defense of this claim. The Protestants have been in Northern Ireland for hundreds of years, and one cannot seriously think of current Protestants as invaders or upstarts. Jews have been in what the Romans (seeking to eliminate Jewish national identity) called Palestine for longer, of course, and even before the modern Zionist movement of the 1870s had a significant presence there (there was a Jewish majority in Jerusalem, e.g.). The return of Jews to their ancient homeland was a way of reestablishing political and cultural self-determination, as other peoples had, with the hopes for security in a dangerous world. Zionist immigration was nonviolent and made into a politically undefined place (at the beginning of the process the local Arabs saw themselves as part of the larger Arab entity, and Palestinian national identity itself developed as a response to the Jewish immigration, which of course does not imply that it is not now morally legitimate or important). I cannot begin to imagine how a serious argument for historical justification

of terrorism is supposed to work with Al-Qaida; judging from the rhetoric perhaps the Crusaders are the main culprits.

[10] On this notion, see Saul Smilansky, *Free Will and Illusion* (Oxford: Oxford University Press, 2000), ch. 7. The usefulness of a "positive illusion" typically depends on its not being recognized as such.

[11] See Saul Smilansky, "The Ethical Dangers of Ethical Sensitivity," *Journal of Applied Philosophy* 13 (1996), pp. 13–20.

[12] See Smilansky, *Free Will and Illusion*, ch. 11.

[13] This quotation is from "The Spirit of the IDF" (the revised ethical code of the Israeli army; Israeli Defense Force official publication, accepted September 2001), available

at the Israeli Defense Forces' official web site, "Doctrine of Ethics," http://www1.idf.il/DOVER/site/mainpage.asp?sl=en&id=23.

[14] The quotation is from the 1977 Protocol to the Geneva Convention, Article 13.2. See "Protocols additional to the Geneva Convention of 12 August 1949, and relating to the Protection of Victims of Non-international Armed Conflicts (Protocol II), 8 June 1977," available at the UN Office of the High Commissioner for Human Rights web site, http://www.unchr.ch/html/menu3/b/94.htm.

[15] David Hume, *A Treatise of Human Nature*, 2nd edn. (Oxford: Clarendon Press, 1987), p. 498.

Part X

Women and Global Justice

Introduction

The contributions by women to considerations of global justice have been remarkable and wide ranging. This work alerts us to new problems in how we consider questions of global justice, and it provides important and highly compelling new strategies for conceiving the future of global justice.

This Part begins with Susan Moller Okin's famous essay "Is Multiculturalism Bad for Women?" (chapter 33). She argues that we should respect group rights only insofar as they do not violate individual rights. We have a tendency to consider groups monolithically, failing to note the differences within groups. A variety of groups perpetuate violations of individual rights, namely, the rights of women. These violations take the form of female genital mutilation, polygamy, forced marriages, and worse, such as the discrimination of (and tolerated violence against) women who are not virgins and women who have been raped. These practices may all be part of contemporary cultures, but this does nothing to justify the practices. We harm the rights of women if we permit such group rights. Women must form part of any discussion on the permissibility of group rights as too often the rights of women are endangered by permitting many group rights.

The next two readings are by Martha C. Nussbaum. In the first, Nussbaum presents us with "the capabilities approach." Nussbaum reacts against critics who argue that universal norms do not exist. She presents us with a universal approach to thinking about political principles, as applicable in Calcutta as in either Chicago or Newcastle upon Tyne. Nussbaum then defends a particular set of capabilities to which all human beings are entitled, including: life; bodily health; bodily integrity; senses, imagination, and thought; emotions; practical reason; affiliation; other species; play; and control over one's environment. Governments have a moral duty to permit their citizens the opportunity to exercise their full range of capabilities, leaving the choice up to the individual whether or not she wants to fulfill any capability. Moreover, the capabilities approach is not only universalistic in its application to all cultures, but, importantly, universalistic in its applicability to both men and women.

Nussbaum's second reading considers "The Role of Religion" (chapter 35). Liberal communities often defend the right of citizens to exercise freedom of religious expression, while forms of religious expression may infringe the freedom of citizens. Here Nussbaum considers distinctly feminist responses to this challenge, arguing in favor of "the intrinsic value of religious capabilities." She claims that the ability to participate in religious activities is an important human good. Nussbaum defends broad freedoms of religious expression, while placing an important limit on their free exercise, namely, violation of other capabilities.

In the final reading, Carol C. Gould argues for "a more embodied politics" that is sensitive to group identities, and in particular focussing on women. She seeks to make human rights more responsive to what is of value to women. Gould argues for the centrality of the notion of care. Thus, it is precisely because we *care* about the well-being of others that we defend and recognize the human rights of others. Care is not simply something we find amongst family and friends, but something we can easily extend to all human beings internationally whether male or female. Thus, the feminist notion of care helps us understand the value we place on the rights of all.

Despite the volumes of work on global justice that have been written over the centuries, on the whole this work has failed (and quite miserably) to account satisfactorily for half the human race, namely women. What is more, the following chapters offer us various insights into not only what is in error about contemporary theorizing, but, most importantly, how we might improve our understanding of global justice. It will be left to the reader to consider whether or not the criticisms hit their target and whether their recommendations go far enough.

Chapter 33

Is Multiculturalism Bad for Women?*
Susan Moller Okin

Until the past few decades, minority groups – immigrants as well as indigenous peoples – were typically expected to assimilate into majority cultures. This assimilationist expectation is now often considered oppressive, and many Western countries are seeking to devise new policies that are more responsive to persistent cultural differences. The appropriate policies vary with context: countries such as England, with established churches or state-supported religious education, find it difficult to resist demands to extend state support to minority religious schools; countries such as France, with traditions of strictly secular public education, struggle over whether the clothing required by minority religions may be worn in the public schools. But one issue recurs across all contexts, though it has gone virtually unnoticed in current debate: what should be done when the claims of minority cultures or religions clash with the norm of gender equality that is at least formally endorsed by liberal states (however much they continue to violate it in their practices)?

In the late 1980s, for example, a sharp public controversy erupted in France about whether Magrébin girls could attend school wearing the traditional Muslim head scarves regarded as proper attire for postpubescent young women. Staunch defenders of secular education lined up with some feminists and far-right nationalists against the practice; much of the Old Left supported the multiculturalist demands for flexibility and respect for diversity, accusing opponents of racism or cultural imperialism. At the very same time, however, the public was virtually silent about a problem of vastly greater importance to many French Arab and African immigrant women: polygamy.

During the 1980s, the French government quietly permitted immigrant men to bring multiple wives into the country, to the point where an estimated 200,000 families in Paris are now polygamous. Any suspicion that official concern over head scarves was motivated by an impulse toward gender equality is belied by the easy adoption of a permissive policy on polygamy, despite the burdens this practice imposes on women and the warnings disseminated by women from the relevant cultures.[1] On this issue, no politically effective opposition galvanized. But once reporters finally got around to interviewing

* From Susan Moller Okin, *Is Multiculturalism Bad for Women?*, ed. Joshua Cohen, Matthew Howard, and Martha C. Nussbaum (Princeton, NJ: Princeton University Press, 1999), pp. 9–24, 133–5 (notes).

the wives, they discovered what the government could have learned years earlier: that the women affected by polygamy regarded it as an inescapable and barely tolerable institution in their African countries of origin, and an unbearable imposition in the French context. Overcrowded apartments and the lack of private space for each wife led to immense hostility, resentment, even violence both among the wives and against each other's children.

In part because of the strain on the welfare system caused by families with twenty to thirty members, the French government has recently decided to recognize only one wife and to consider all the other marriages annulled. But what will happen to all the other wives and children? Having ignored women's views on polygamy for so long, the government now seems to be abdicating its responsibility for the vulnerability that its rash policy has inflicted on women and children.

The French accommodation of polygamy illustrates a deep and growing tension between feminism and multiculturalist concern for protecting cultural diversity. I think we – especially those of us who consider ourselves politically progressive and opposed to all forms of oppression – have been too quick to assume that feminism and multiculturalism are both good things which are easily reconciled. I shall argue instead that there is considerable likelihood of tension between them – more precisely, between feminism and a multiculturalist commitment to group rights for minority cultures.

A few words to explain the terms and focus of my argument. By *feminism*, I mean the belief that women should not be disadvantaged by their sex, that they should be recognized as having human dignity equal to that of men, and that they should have the opportunity to live as fulfilling and as freely chosen lives as men can. *Multiculturalism* is harder to pin down, but the particular aspect that concerns me here is the claim, made in the context of basically liberal democracies, that minority cultures or ways of life are not sufficiently protected by the practice of ensuring the individual rights of their members, and as a consequence these should also be protected through special *group* rights or privileges. In the French case, for example, the right to contract polygamous marriages clearly constituted a group right not available to the rest of the population. In other cases, groups have claimed rights to govern themselves, to have guaranteed political representation, or to be exempt from certain generally applicable laws.

Demands for such group rights are growing – from indigenous native populations, minority ethnic or religious groups, and formerly colonized peoples (at least when the latter immigrate to the former colonial state). These groups, it is argued, have their own "societal cultures" which – as Will Kymlicka, the foremost contemporary defender of cultural group rights, says – provide "members with meaningful ways of life across the full range of human activities, including social, educational, religious, recreational, and economic life, encompassing both public and private spheres."[2] Because societal cultures play so pervasive and fundamental a role in the lives of their members, and because such cultures are threatened with extinction, minority cultures should be protected by special rights. That, in essence, is the case for group rights.

Some proponents of group rights argue that even cultures that "flout the rights of [their individual members] in a liberal society"[3] should be accorded group rights or privileges if their minority status endangers the culture's continued existence. Others do not claim that all minority cultural groups should have special rights, but rather that such groups – even illiberal ones that violate their individual members' rights, requiring them to conform to group beliefs or norms – have the right to be "left alone" in a liberal society.[4] Both claims seem clearly inconsistent with the basic liberal value of individual freedom, which entails that group rights should not trump the individual rights of its members; thus I will not address the additional problems they present for feminists here.[5] But some defenders of multiculturalism confine their defense of group rights largely to groups that are internally liberal.[6] Even with these restrictions, feminists – everyone, that is, who endorses the moral equality of men and women – should remain skeptical. So I will argue.

Gender and Culture

Most cultures are suffused with practices and ideologies concerning gender. Suppose, then, that a culture endorses and facilitates the control of men over women in various ways (even if informally, in the private sphere of domestic life). Suppose, too, that there are fairly clear disparities in power between the sexes, such that the more powerful, male members are those who are generally in a position to determine and articulate the group's beliefs, practices, and interests. Under such conditions, group rights are potentially, and in many cases actually, antifeminist. They substantially limit the capacities of women and girls of that culture to live with human dignity equal to that of men and boys, and to live as freely chosen lives as they can.

Advocates of group rights for minorities within liberal states have not adequately addressed this simple critique of group rights, for at least two reasons. First, they tend to treat cultural groups as monoliths – to pay more attention to differences between and among groups than to differences within them. Specifically, they accord little or no recognition to the fact that minority cultural groups, like the societies in which they exist

(though to a greater or lesser extent), are themselves *gendered*, with substantial differences in power and advantage between men and women. Second, advocates of group rights pay little or no attention to the private sphere. Some of the most persuasive liberal defenses of group rights urge that individuals need "a culture of their own," and that only within such a culture can people develop a sense of self-esteem or self-respect, as well as the capacity to decide what kind of life is good for them. But such arguments typically neglect both the different roles that cultural groups impose on their members and the context in which persons' senses of themselves and their capacities are first formed *and* in which culture is first transmitted – the realm of domestic or family life.

When we correct for these deficiencies by paying attention to internal differences and to the private arena, two particularly important connections between culture and gender come into sharp relief, both of which underscore the force of this simple critique of group rights. First, the sphere of personal, sexual, and reproductive life functions as a central focus of most cultures, a dominant theme in cultural practices and rules. Religious or cultural groups often are particularly concerned with "personal law" – the laws of marriage, divorce, child custody, division and control of family property, and inheritance.[7] As a rule, then, the defense of "cultural practices" is likely to have much greater impact on the lives of women and girls than on those of men and boys, since far more of women's time and energy goes into preserving and maintaining the personal, familial, and reproductive side of life. Obviously, culture is not only about domestic arrangements, but they do provide a major focus of most contemporary cultures. Home is, after all, where much of culture is practiced, preserved, and transmitted to the young. On the other hand, the distribution of responsibilities and power at home has a major impact on who can participate in and influence the more public parts of the cultural life, where rules and regulations about both public and private life are made. The more a culture requires or expects of women in the domestic sphere, the less opportunity they have of achieving equality with men in either sphere.

The second important connection between culture and gender is that most cultures have as one of their principal aims the control of women by men.[8] Consider, for example, the founding myths of Greek and Roman antiquity, and of Judaism, Christianity, and Islam: they are rife with attempts to justify the control and subordination of women. These myths consist of a combination of denials of women's role in reproduction; appropriations by men of the power to reproduce themselves; characterizations of women as overly emotional, untrustworthy, evil, or sexually dangerous; and refusals to acknowledge mothers' rights over the disposition of their children.[9] Think of Athena, sprung from the head of Zeus, and of Romulus and Remus, reared without a human mother. Or Adam, made by a male God, who then (at least according to one of the two biblical versions of the story) created Eve out of part of Adam. Consider Eve, whose weakness led Adam astray. Think of all those endless "begats" in Genesis, where women's primary role in reproduction is completely ignored, or of the textual justifications for polygamy, once practiced in Judaism, still practiced in many parts of the Islamic world and (though illegally) by Mormons in some parts of the United States. Consider, too, the story of Abraham, a pivotal turning point in the development of monotheism.[10] God commands Abraham to sacrifice "his" beloved son. Abraham prepares to do exactly what God asks of him, without even telling, much less asking, Isaac's mother, Sarah. Abraham's absolute obedience to God makes him the central,

fundamental model of faith for all three religions.

Although the powerful drive to control women – and to blame and punish them for men's difficulty in controlling their own sexual impulses – has been softened considerably in the more progressive, reformed versions of Judaism, Christianity, and Islam, it remains strong in their more orthodox or fundamentalist versions. Moreover, it is by no means confined to Western or monotheistic cultures. Many of the world's traditions and cultures, including those practiced within formerly conquered or colonized nation-states – which certainly encompasses most of the peoples of Africa, the Middle East, Latin America, and Asia – are quite distinctly patriarchal. They too have elaborate patterns of socialization, rituals, matrimonial customs, and other cultural practices (including systems of property ownership and control of resources) aimed at bringing women's sexuality and reproductive capabilities under men's control. Many such practices make it virtually impossible for women to choose to live independently of men, to be celibate or lesbian, or to decide not to have children.

Those who practice some of the most controversial of such customs – clitoridectomy, polygamy, the marriage of children or marriages that are otherwise coerced – sometimes explicitly defend them as necessary for controlling women and openly acknowledge that the customs persist at men's insistence. In an interview with *New York Times* reporter Celia Dugger, practitioners of clitoridectomy in Côte d'Ivoire and Togo explained that the practice "helps insure a girl's virginity before marriage and fidelity afterward by reducing sex to a marital obligation." As a female exciser said, "[a] woman's role in life is to care for her children, keep house and cook. If she has not been cut, [she] might think about her own sexual pleasure."[11] In Egypt, where a law banning female genital cutting was recently overturned by a court, supporters of the practice say it "curbs a girl's sexual appetite and makes her more marriageable."[12] Moreover, in such societies, many women have no economically viable alternative to marriage.

In polygamous cultures, too, men readily acknowledge that the practice accords with their self-interest and is a means of controlling women. As a French immigrant from Mali said in a recent interview: "When my wife is sick and I don't have another, who will care for me? . . . [O]ne wife on her own is trouble. When there are several, they are forced to be polite and well behaved. If they misbehave, you threaten that you'll take another wife." Women apparently see polygamy very differently. French African immigrant women deny that they like polygamy and say that not only are they given "no choice" in the matter, but their female forebears in Africa did not like it either.[13] As for child or otherwise coerced marriage: this practice is clearly a way not only of controlling who the girls or young women marry but also of ensuring that they are virgins at the time of marriage and, often, of enhancing the husband's power by creating a significant age difference between husbands and wives.

Consider too, the practice – common in much of Latin America, rural Southeast Asia and parts of West Africa – of pressuring or even requiring a rape victim to marry the rapist. In many such cultures – including fourteen countries in Central and South America – rapists are legally exonerated if they marry or (in some cases) simply offer to marry their victims. Clearly, rape is not seen in these cultures primarily as a violent assault on the girl or woman herself but rather as a serious injury to her family and its honor. By marrying his victim, the rapist can help restore the family's honor and relieve it of a daughter who, as "damaged goods," has become unmarriageable. In Peru, this barbaric law was amended for the worse in 1991: the codefendants in a gang rape now are all exonerated if just one of them offers to marry the victim (feminists are fighting to get the law repealed). As a Peruvian taxi driver explained: "Marriage is the right and proper thing to do after a rape. A raped woman is a used item. No one wants her. At least with this law the woman will get a husband."[14] It is difficult to imagine a worse fate for a woman than being pressured into marrying the man who has raped her. But worse fates do exist in some cultures – notably in Pakistan and parts of the Arab Middle East, where women who bring rape charges quite frequently are charged themselves with the serious Muslim offense of *zina*, or sex outside of marriage. Law allows for the whipping or imprisonment of such women, and culture condones the killing or pressuring into suicide of a raped woman by relatives intent on restoring the family's honor.[15]

Thus many culturally based customs aim to control women and render them, especially sexually and reproductively, servile to men's desires and interests. Sometimes, moreover, "culture" or "traditions" are so closely linked with the control of women that they are virtually equated. In a recent news report about a small community of Orthodox Jews living in the mountains of Yemen, the elderly leader of this small polygamous sect is quoted as saying: "We are Orthodox Jews, very keen on our traditions. If we go to Israel, we will lose hold over our daughters, our wives and our sisters." One of his sons added, "We are like Muslims, we do not allow our women to uncover their faces."[16] Thus the servitude of women is presented as virtually synonymous with "our traditions." (Ironically, from a feminist point of view, the story was entitled "Yemen's Small Jewish Community Thrives on Mixed Traditions." Only blindness to sexual servitude can explain the title; it is inconceivable that the article would have carried such a title if it were about a community that practiced any kind of slavery but sexual slavery.)

While virtually all of the world's cultures have distinctly patriarchal pasts, some – mostly, though by no means exclusively, Western liberal cultures – have departed far further from them than others. Western cultures, of course, still practice many forms of sex discrimination. They place far more importance on beauty, thinness, and youth in females and on intellectual accomplishment, skill, and strength in males. They expect women to perform for no economic reward far more than half of the unpaid work related to home and family, whether or not they also work for wages; partly as a consequence of this and partly because of workplace discrimination, women are far more likely than men to become poor. Girls and women are also subjected by men to a great deal of (illegal) violence, including sexual violence. But women in more liberal cultures are, at the same time, legally guaranteed many of the same freedoms and opportunities as men. In addition, most families in such cultures, with the exception of some religious fundamentalists, do not communicate to their daughters that they are of less value than boys, that their lives are to be confined to domesticity and service to men and children, and that their sexuality is of value only in marriage, in the service of men, and for reproductive ends. This situation, as we have seen, is quite different from that of women in many of the world's other cultures, including many of those from which immigrants to Europe and North America come.

Group Rights?

Most cultures are patriarchal, then, and many (though not all) of the cultural minorities that claim group rights are more patriarchal than the surrounding cultures. So it is no surprise that the cultural importance of maintaining control over women shouts out to us in the examples given in the literature on cultural diversity and group rights within liberal states. Yet, though it shouts out, it is seldom explicitly addressed.[17]

A paper by Sebastian Poulter about the legal rights and culture-based claims of various immigrant groups and Gypsies in contemporary Britain mentions the roles and status of women as "one very clear example" of the "clash of cultures."[18] In it, Poulter discusses claims put forward by members of such groups for special legal treatment on account of their cultural differences. A few are non-gender-related claims; for example, a Muslim schoolteacher's being allowed to be absent part of Friday afternoons in order to pray, and Gypsy children's being subject to less stringent schooling requirements than others on account of their itinerant lifestyle. But the vast majority of the examples concern gender inequalities: child marriages, forced marriages, divorce systems biased against women, polygamy, and clitoridectomy. Almost all of the legal cases discussed by Poulter stemmed from women's or girls' claims that their individual rights were being truncated or violated by the practices of their own cultural groups. In a recent article by political philosopher Amy Gutmann, fully half her examples have to do with gender issues – polygamy, abortion, sexual harassment, clitoridectomy, and purdah.[19] This is quite typical in the literature on subnational multicultural issues. Moreover, the same linkage between culture and gender occurs in practice in the international arena, where women's human rights are often rejected by the leaders of countries or groups of countries as incompatible with their various cultures.[20]

Similarly, the overwhelming majority of "cultural defenses" that are increasingly being invoked in US criminal cases involving members of cultural minorities are connected with gender – in particular with male control over women and children.[21]

Occasionally, cultural defenses are cited in explanation of expectable violence among men or the ritual sacrifice of animals. Much more common, however, is the argument that, in the defendant's cultural group, women are not human beings of equal worth but rather subordinates whose primary (if not only) function is to serve men sexually and domestically. Indeed, the four types of cases in which cultural defenses have been used most successfully are: (1) kidnap and rape by Hmong men who claim that their actions are part of their cultural practice of *zij poj niam*, or "marriage by capture"; (2) wife-murder by immigrants from Asian and Middle Eastern countries whose wives have either committed adultery or treated their husbands in a servile way; (3) murder of children by Japanese or Chinese mothers who have also tried but failed to kill themselves, and who claim that because of their cultural backgrounds the shame of their husbands' infidelity drove them to the culturally condoned practice of mother–child suicide; and (4) in France – though not yet in the United States, in part because the practice was criminalized only in 1996 – clitoridectomy. In a number of such cases, expert testimony about the accused's or defendant's cultural background has resulted in dropped or reduced charges, culturally based assessments of *mens rea*, or significantly reduced sentences. In a well-known recent case in the United States, an immigrant from rural Iraq married his two daughters, aged 13 and 14, to two of his friends, aged 28 and 34. Subsequently, when the older daughter ran away with her 20-year-old boyfriend, the father sought the help of the police in finding her. When they located her, they charged the father with child abuse and the two husbands and boyfriend with statutory rape. The Iraqis' defense is based in part on their cultural marriage practices.[22]

As the four examples show, the defendants are not always male, nor the victims always female. Both a Chinese immigrant man in New York who battered his wife to death for committing adultery and a Japanese immigrant woman in California who drowned her children and tried to drown herself because her husband's adultery had shamed the family relied on cultural defenses to win reduced charges (from first-degree murder to second-degree murder or involuntary manslaughter). It might seem, then, that the cultural defense was biased toward the male in the first case and the female in the second. But though defendants of different sexes were cited, in both cases, the cultural message is similarly gender-biased: women (and children, in the second case) are ancillary to men and should bear the blame and the shame for any departure from monogamy. Whoever is guilty of the infidelity, the wife suffers: in the first case, by being brutally killed on account of her husband's rage at her shameful infidelity; in the second, by being so shamed and branded such a failure by his infidelity that she is driven to kill herself and her children. Again, the idea that girls and women are first and foremost sexual servants of men – that their virginity before marriage and fidelity within it are their preeminent virtues – emerges in many of the statements made in defense of cultural practices.

Western majority cultures, largely at the urging of feminists, have recently made substantial efforts to preclude or limit excuses for brutalizing women. Well within living memory, American men were routinely held less accountable for killing their wives if they explained their conduct as a crime of passion, driven as they were by jealousy and rage over the wife's infidelity. Also not long ago, female rape victims who did not have completely celibate pasts or who did not struggle – even when to do so meant endangering themselves – were routinely blamed for the attack. Things have now changed to some extent, and doubts about the turn toward cultural defenses undoubtedly are prompted in part by a concern to preserve recent advances.

Another concern is that such defenses can distort perceptions of minority cultures by drawing excessive attention to negative aspects of them. But perhaps the primary concern is that, by failing to protect women and sometimes children of minority cultures from male and sometimes material violence, cultural defenses violate women's and children's rights to equal protection of the laws.[23] When a woman from a more patriarchal culture comes to the United States (or some other Western, basically liberal, state), why should she be less protected from male violence than other women are? Many women from minority cultures have protested the double standard that is being applied on behalf of their aggressors.[24]

Liberal Defense

Despite all this evidence of cultural practices that control and subordinate women, none of the prominent defenders of multicultural group rights has adequately or even directly addressed the troubling connections between gender and culture or the conflicts that arise so commonly between feminism and multiculturalism. Will Kymlicka's discussion is, in this respect, representative.

Kymlicka's arguments for group rights are based on the rights of individuals and confine such privileges and protection to cultural groups that are internally liberal. Following John Rawls, Kymlicka emphasizes the fundamental importance of self-respect in a person's life. He argues that membership in a "rich and secure cultural structure,"[25] with its own language and history, is essential both for the development of self-respect and for giving persons a context in which they can develop the capacity to make choices about how to lead their lives. Cultural minorities need special rights, then, because their cultures may otherwise be threatened with extinction, and cultural extinction would be likely to undermine the

self-respect and freedom of group members. Special rights, in short, put minorities on an equal footing with the majority

The value of freedom plays an important role in Kymlicka's argument. As a result, except in rare circumstances of cultural vulnerability, a group that claims special rights must govern itself by recognizably liberal principles, neither infringing on the basic liberties of its own members by placing internal restrictions on them nor discriminating among them on grounds of sex, race, or sexual preference.[26] This requirement is of great importance to a consistently liberal justification of group rights, because a "closed" or discriminatory culture cannot provide the context for individual development that liberalism requires, and because otherwise collective rights might result in subcultures of oppression within and facilitated by liberal societies. As Kymlicka says, "To inhibit people from questioning their inherited social roles can condemn them to unsatisfying, even oppressive lives."[27]

As Kymlicka acknowledges, this requirement of internal liberalism rules out the justification of group rights for the "many fundamentalists of all political and religious stripes who think that the best community is one in which all but their preferred religious, sexual, or aesthetic practices are outlawed." For the promotion and support of *these* cultures undermines "the very reason we had for being concerned with cultural membership – that it allows for meaningful individual choice."[28] But the examples I cited earlier suggest that far fewer minority cultures than Kymlicka seems to think will be able to claim group rights under his liberal justification. Though they may not impose their beliefs or practices on others, and though they may appear to respect the basic civil and political liberties of women and girls, many cultures do not, especially in the private sphere, treat them with anything like the same concern and respect with which men and boys are treated, or allow them to enjoy the same freedoms. Discrimination against and control of the freedom of females are practiced, to a greater or lesser extent, by virtually all cultures, past and present, but especially by religious ones and those that look to the past – to ancient texts or revered traditions – for guidelines or rules about how to live in the contemporary world. Sometimes more patriarchal minority cultures exist in the midst of less patriarchal majority cultures; sometimes the reverse is true. In either case, the degree to which each culture is patriarchal and its willingness to become less so should be crucial factors in judgment about the justifications of group rights – once women's equality is taken seriously.

Clearly, Kymlicka regards cultures that discriminate overtly and formally against women – by denying them education or the right to vote or hold office – as not deserving special rights.[29] But sex discrimination is often far less overt. In many cultures, strict control of women is enforced in the private sphere by the authority of either actual or symbolic fathers, often acting through, or with the complicity of, the older women of the culture. In many cultures in which women's basic civil rights and liberties are formally assured, discrimination practiced against women and girls within the household not only severely constrains their choices but also seriously threatens their well-being and even their lives.[30] And such sex discrimination – whether severe or more mild – often has very powerful *cultural* roots.

Although Kymlicka rightly objects, then, in the granting of group rights to minority cultures that practice overt sex discrimination, his arguments for multiculturalism fail to register what he acknowledges elsewhere: that the subordination of women is often informal and private, and that virtually no culture in the world today, minority or majority, could pass his "no sex discrimination" test if it were applied in the private

sphere.[31] Those who defend group rights on liberal grounds need to address these very private, culturally reinforced kinds of discrimination. For surely self-respect and self-esteem require more than simple membership in a viable culture. Surely it is *not* enough for one to be able to "question one's inherited social roles" and to have the capacity to make choices about the life one wants to lead, that one's culture be protected. At least as important to the development of self-respect and self-esteem is *our place within our culture*. And at least as pertinent to our capacity to question our social roles is *whether our culture instills in us and forces on us particular social roles*. To the extent that a girl's culture is patriarchal, in both these respects her healthy development is endangered.

Part of the Solution?

It is by no means clear, then, from a feminist point of view, that minority group rights are "part of the solution." They may well exacerbate the problem. In the case of a more patriarchal minority culture in the context of a less patriarchal majority culture, no argument can be made on the basis of self-respect or freedom that the female members of the culture have a clear interest in its preservation. Indeed, they *might* be much better off if the culture into which they were born were either to become extinct (so that its members would become integrated into the less sexist surrounding culture) or, preferably, to be encouraged to alter itself so as to reinforce the equality of women – at least to the degree to which this value is upheld in the majority culture. Other considerations would, of course, need to be taken into account, such as whether the minority group speaks a language that requires protection, and whether the group suffers from prejudices such as racial discrimination. But it would take significant factors weighing in the other direction to counterbalance evidence that a culture severely constrains women's choices or otherwise undermines their well-being.

What some of the examples discussed above illustrate is how culturally endorsed practices that are oppressive to women can often remain hidden in the private or domestic sphere. In the Iraqi child marriage case mentioned above, if the father himself had not called in agents of the state, his daughters' plight might well not have become public. And when Congress in 1996 passed a law criminalizing clitoridectomy, a number of US doctors objected to the law on the basis that it concerned a private matter which, as one said, "should be decided by a physician, the family, and the child."[32] It can take more or less extraordinary circumstances for such abuses of girls or women to become public or for the state to be able to intervene protectively.

Thus it is clear that many instances of private-sphere discrimination against women on cultural grounds are never likely to emerge in public, where courts can enforce the women's rights and political theorists can label such practices as illiberal and therefore unjustified violations of women's physical or mental integrity. Establishing group rights to enable some minority cultures to

preserve themselves may not be in the best interests of the girls and women of those cultures, even if it benefits the men.

Those who make liberal arguments for the rights of groups, then, must take special care to look at inequalities within those groups. It is especially important to consider inequalities between the sexes, since they are likely to be less public, and thus less easily discernible. Moreover, policies designed to respond to the needs and claims of cultural minority groups must take seriously the urgency of adequately representing less powerful members of such groups. Because attention to the rights of minority cultural groups, if it is to be consistent with the fundamentals of liberalism, must ultimately be aimed at furthering the well-being of the members of these groups, there can be no justification for assuming that the groups' self-proclaimed leaders – invariably composed mainly of their older and their male members represent the interests of all of the groups' members. Unless women – and, more specifically, young women (since older women often are co-opted into reinforcing gender inequality) – are fully represented in negotiations about group rights, their interests may be harmed rather than promoted by the granting of such rights.

Notes

1   *International Herald Tribune*, 2 February 1996, News section.

2   Will Kymlicka, *Multicultural Citizenship: A Liberal Theory of Minority Rights* (Oxford: Oxford University Press, 1995), pp. 89, 76. See also Kymlicka, *Liberalism, Community and Culture* (Oxford: Clarendon Press, 1989). It should be noted that Kymlicka himself does not argue for extensive or permanent group rights for those who have voluntarily immigrated.

3   Avishai Margalit and Moshe Halbertal, "Liberalism and the Right to Culture," *Social Research* 61: 3 (Fall 1994), p. 491.

4   For example, Chandran Kukathas, "Are there Any Cultural Rights?," *Political Theory* 20: 1 (1992), pp. 105–39.

5   Okin, "Feminism and Multiculturalism: Some Tensions," *Ethics* 108: 4 (July 1998), pp. 661–84.

6   For example, Kymlicka, *Liberalism, Community, and Culture* and *Multicultural Citizenship* (esp. ch. 8). Kymlicka does not apply his requirement that groups be internally liberal to those he terms "national minorities," but I will not address that aspect of his theory here.

7   See, for example, Kirti Singh, "Obstacles to Women's Rights in India," in *Human Rights*

of Women: National and International Perspectives, ed. Rebecca J. Cook (Philadephia: University of Pennsylvania Press, 1994), pp. 375–96, esp. pp. 378–89.

8   I cannot discuss here the roots of this male preoccupation, except to say (following feminist theorists Dorothy Dinnerstein, Nancy Chodorow, Jessica Benjamin, and, before them, Jesuit anthropologist Walter Ong) that it seems to have a lot to do with female primary parenting. It is also clearly related to the uncertainty of paternity, which technology has now counteracted. If these issues are at the root of it, then the cultural preoccupation with controlling women is not an inevitable fact of human life but a contingent factor that feminists have a considerable interest in changing.

9   See, for example, Arvind Sharma (ed.), *Women in World Religions* (Albany, NY: SUNY Press, 1987); John Stratton Hawley (ed.), *Fundamentalism and Gender* (Oxford: Oxford University Press, 1994).

10 See Carol Delaney, *Abraham on Trial: The Social Legacy of Biblical Myth* (Princeton: Princeton University Press, 1998). Note that in the Qur'anic version, it is not Isaac but Ishmael whom Abraham prepares to sacrifice.

11 *New York Times*, 5 October 1996, A4. The role that older women in such cultures play in perpetuating these practices is important but complex and cannot be addressed here.

12 *New York Times*, 26 June 1997, A9.

13 *International Herald Tribune*, 2 February 1996, News section.

14 *New York Times*, 12 March 1997, A8.

15 This practice is discussed in Henry S. Richardson, *Practical Reasoning about Final Ends* (Cambridge: Cambridge University Press, 1994), esp. pp. 240–3, 262–3, 282–4.

16 *Agence France Presse*, 18 May 1997, International News section.

17 See, however, Bhikhu Parekh's "Minority Practices and Principles of Toleration," *International Migration Review* (April 1996), pp. 251–84, in which he directly addresses and critiques a number of cultural practices that devalue the status of women.

18 Sebastian Poulter, "Ethnic Minority Customs, English Law, and Human Rights," *International and Comparative Law Quarterly* 36: 3 (1987), pp. 589–615.

19 Amy Gutmann, "The Challenge of Multiculturalism in Political Ethics," *Philosophy and Public Affairs* 22: 3 (Summer 1993), pp. 171–204.

20 Mahnaz Afkhami (ed.), *Faith and Freedom: Women's Human Rights in the Muslim World* (Syracuse: Syracuse University Press, 1995); Valentine M. Moghadam (ed.), *Identity Politics and Women: Cultural Reassertions and Feminisms in International Perspective* (Boulder, CO: Westview Press, 1994); Susan Moller Okin, "Culture, Religion, and Female Identity Formation" (unpublished manuscript, 1997).

21 For one of the best and most recent accounts of this, and for legal citations for the cases mentioned below, see Doriane Lambelet Coleman, "Individualizing Justice through Multiculturalism: The Liberals' Dilemma," *Columbia Law Review* 96: 5 (1996), pp. 1093–167.

22 *New York Times*, 2 December 1996, A6.

23 See Coleman, "Individualizing Justice through Multiculturalism."

24 See, for example, Nilda Rimonte, "A Question of Culture: Cultural Approval of Violence against Women in the Asian-Pacific Community and the Cultural Defense," *Stanford Law Review* 43 (1991), pp. 1311–26.

25 Kymlicka, *Liberalism, Community and Culture*, p. 165.

26 Ibid., pp. 168–72, 195–8.

27 Kymlicka, *Multicultural Citizenship*, p. 92.

28 Kymlicka, *Liberalism, Community and Culture*, pp. 171–2.

29 Kymlicka, *Multicultural Citizenship*, pp. 153, 165.

30 See, for example, Amartya Sen, "More Than One Hundred Million Women Are Missing," *New York Review of Books*, 20 December 1990.

31 Will Kymlicka, *Contemporary Political Philosophy: An Introduction* (Oxford: The Clarendon Press, 1990), pp. 239–62.

32 *New York Times*, 12 October 1996, A6. Similar views were expressed on national public radio.

Chapter 34

Capabilities as Fundamental Entitlements: Sen and Social Justice*
Martha C. Nussbaum

I The Capabilities Approach and Social Justice[1]

Throughout his career, Amartya Sen has been preoccupied with questions of social justice. Inequalities between women and men have been especially important in his thinking, and the achievement of gender justice in society has been among the most central goals of his theoretical enterprise. Against the dominant emphasis on economic growth as an indicator of a nation's quality of life, Sen has insisted on the importance of *capabilities*, what people are actually able to do and to be.[2] Frequently his arguments in favor of this shift in thinking deal with issues of gender.[3] Growth is a bad indicator of life quality because it fails to tell us how deprived people are doing; women figure in the argument as people who are often unable to enjoy the fruits of a nation's general prosperity. If we ask what people are actually able to do and to be, we come much closer to understanding the barriers societies have erected against full justice for women. Similarly, Sen criticizes approaches that measure well-being in terms of utility by

pointing to the fact that women frequently exhibit "adaptive preferences," preferences that have adjusted to their second-class status (Amartya Sen 1990, 1995). Thus the utilitarian framework, which asks people what they currently prefer and how satisfied they are, proves inadequate to confront the most pressing issues of gender justice. We can only have an adequate theory of gender justice, and of social justice more generally, if we are willing to make claims about fundamental entitlements that are to some extent independent of the preferences that people happen to have, preferences shaped, often, by unjust background conditions.

This critique of dominant paradigms in terms of ideas of gender justice is a pervasive feature in Sen's work, and it is obvious that one central motivation for his elaboration of the "capabilities approach" is its superior potential for developing a theory of gender justice. But the reader who looks for a fully formulated account of social justice generally, and gender justice in particular, in Sen's work will not find one; she will need to extrapolate one from the suggestive materials Sen provides. *Development as Freedom* develops one pertinent line of thought, arguing that capabilities provide the best basis for thinking about the goals of devel-

* From *Feminist Economics* 9:2–3 (2003), pp. 33–50, 56–9.

opment (Amartya Sen 1999). Both when nations are compared by international measures of welfare and when each nation strives internally to achieve a higher level of development for its people, capabilities provide us with an attractive way of understanding the normative content of the idea of development. Thinking of development's goal as increase in GNP per capita occluded distributional inequalities, which are particularly central when we are thinking about sex equality. It also failed to disaggregate and separately consider important aspects of development, such as health and education, that are demonstrably not very well correlated with GNP, even when we take distribution into account. Thinking of development's goal in terms of utility at least has the merit of looking at what processes do for people. But utility, Sen argues, is inadequate to capture the heterogeneity and noncommensurability of the diverse aspects of development. Because it fails to take account of the fact of adaptive preferences, it also biases the development process in favor of the status quo, when used as a normative benchmark. Finally, it suggests that the goal of development is a state or condition of persons (e.g., a state of satisfaction), and thus understates the importance of agency and freedom in the development process.

All these failings, he stresses, loom large when we confront the theory with inequalities based on sex: for women's lives reflect a striving after many different elements of well-being, including health, education, mobility, political participation, and others. Women's current preferences often show distortions that are the result of unjust background conditions. And agency and freedom are particularly important goals for women, who have so often been treated as passive dependants. This line of argument has close links with the feminist critique of Utilitarianism and dominant economic paradigms (e.g. Elizabeth Anderson 1993; Bina Agarwal

1997). It also connects fruitfully with writings by activist-scholars who stress the importance of women's agency and participation (e.g. Martha Chen 1983; Bina Agarwal 1994).

Not surprisingly, I endorse these arguments. But I think that they do not take us very far in thinking about social justice. They give us a general sense of what societies ought to be striving to achieve, but because of Sen's reluctance to make commitments about substance (which capabilities a society ought most centrally to pursue), even that guidance remains but an outline. And they give us no sense of what a minimum level of capability for a just society might be. The use of capabilities in development is typically comparative merely, as in the *Human Development Reports* of the UNDP. Thus, nations are compared in areas such as health and educational attainment. But concerning what level of health service, or what level of educational provision, a just society would deliver as a fundamental entitlement of all its citizens, the view is suggestive, but basically silent.

A different line of argument pursued by Sen in works from "Equality of What?" to *Inequality Reexamined* seems more closely related to concerns of social justice. This argument begins from the idea of equality as a central political value (Amartya Sen 1992). Most states consider equality important, Sen argues, and yet they often do not ask perspicuously enough what the right space is within which to make the relevant comparisons. With arguments closely related to his arguments about the goals of development, Sen argues that the space of capabilities provides the most fruitful and ethically satisfactory way of looking at equality as a political goal. Equality of utility or welfare falls short for the reasons I have already summarized. Equality of resources falls short because it fails to take account of the fact that individuals need differing levels of resources if they are to come up to the same level of capability to function. They also have differing abilities to convert resources into actual functioning.

Some of these differences are straightforwardly physical: a child needs more protein than an adult to achieve a similar level of healthy functioning, and a pregnant woman more nutrients than a nonpregnant woman. But the differences that most interest Sen are social, and connected with entrenched discrimination of various types. Thus, in a nation where women are traditionally discouraged from pursuing an education it will usually take more resources to produce female literacy than male literacy. Or, to cite Sen's famous example, a person in a wheelchair will require more resources connected with mobility than will the person with "nominal" mobility, if the two are to attain a similar level of ability to get around (Amartya Sen 1980).[4]

Sen's arguments about equality seem to have the following bearing on issues of social justice and public policy: to the extent that a society values the equality of persons and pursues that as among its social goals, equality of capabilities looks like the most relevant sort of equality to aim at. And it is clear that equality is a central goal for women who pursue social justice; once again, then, the arguments have particular force and relevance in the context of feminism. But Sen never says to what extent equality of capability *ought* to be a social goal,[5] or how it ought to be combined with other political values in the pursuit of social justice. Thus the connection of his equality arguments with a theory of justice remains as yet unclear.

In this chapter I shall suggest that the capabilities approach is indeed a valuable way to approach the question of fundamental entitlements, one that is especially pertinent to issues of sex equality.[6] I shall argue that it is superior to other approaches to

social justice in the Western tradition when we confront it with problems of sex equality. It is closely allied to, but in some ways superior to, the familiar human rights paradigm, in ways that emerge most vividly in the area of sex difference. And it is superior to approaches deriving from the Western notion of the social contract, because of the way in which it can handle issues of care, issues that are fundamental to achieving sex equality, as recent feminist work has demonstrated.[7]

I shall argue, however, that the capabilities approach will supply definite and useful guidance, and prove an ally in the pursuit of sex equality, only if we formulate a definite list of the most central capabilities, even one that is tentative and revisable, using capabilities so defined to elaborate a partial account of social justice, a set of basic entitlements without which no society can lay claim to justice.

II   Capabilities and Rights

The capabilities that Sen mentions in illustrating his approach, and those that are part of my more explicit list, include many of the entitlements that are also stressed in the human rights movement: political liberties, the freedom of association, the free choice of occupation, and a variety of economic and social rights. And capabilities, like human rights, supply a moral and humanly rich set of goals for development, in place of "the wealth and poverty of the economists," as Marx so nicely put it (Karl Marx 1844). Thus capabilities have a very close relationship to human rights, as understood in contemporary international discussions. In effect they cover the terrain covered by both the so-called "first-generation rights" (political and civil liberties) and the so-called second-generation rights (economic and social rights). And they play a similar role, providing both a basis for cross-cultural comparison and the philosophical underpinning for basic constitutional principles.

Both Sen and I connect the capabilities approach closely to the idea of human rights, and in Martha Nussbaum (2001a: Ch. 1) I have described the relationship between the two ideas at some length (see also Martha Nussbaum 1997). The human rights approach has frequently been criticized by feminists for being male-centered, and for not including as fundamental entitlements some abilities and opportunities that are fundamental to women in their struggle for sex equality. They have proposed adding to international rights documents such rights as the right to bodily integrity, the right to be free from violence in the home, and from sexual harassment in the workplace. My list of capabilities explicitly incorporates that proposal, and Sen's would appear to do so implicitly.[8] But the theoretical reasons for supplementing the language of rights with the language of capabilities still require comment.

Capabilities, I would argue, are very closely linked to rights, but the language of capabilities gives important precision and supplementation to the language of rights. The idea of human rights is by no means a crystal-clear idea. Rights have been understood in many different ways, and difficult theoretical questions are frequently obscured by the use of rights language, which can give the illusion of agreement where there is deep philosophical disagreement. People differ about what the *basis* of a rights claim is: rationality, sentience, and mere life have all had their defenders. They differ, too, about whether rights are prepolitical or artifacts of laws and institutions. They differ about whether rights belong only to individual persons, or also to groups. They differ about whether rights are to be regarded as side-constraints on goal-promoting action, or rather as one part of the social goal that is being promoted. They differ, again, about

the relationship between rights and duties: if A has a right to S, then does this mean that there is always someone who has a duty to provide S, and how shall we decide who that someone is? They differ, finally, about what rights are to be understood as rights *to*. Are human rights primarily rights to be treated in certain ways? Rights to a certain level of achieved well-being? Rights to resources with which one may pursue one's life plan? Rights to certain opportunities and capacities with which one may make choices about one's life plan?

The capabilities approach has the advantage of taking clear positions on these disputed issues, while stating clearly what the motivating concerns are and what the goal is. The relationship between the two notions, however, needs further scrutiny, given the dominance of rights language in international feminism.

Regarding fundamental rights, I would argue that the best way of thinking about what it is to secure them to people is to think in terms of capabilities. The right to political participation, the right to religious free exercise, the right of free speech – these and others are all best thought of as secured to people only when the relevant capabilities to function are present. In other words, to secure a right to citizens in these areas is to put them in a position of capability to function in that area. To the extent that rights are used in defining social justice, we should not grant that the society is just unless the capabilities have been effectively achieved. Of course people may have a prepolitical right to good treatment in this area that has not yet been recognized or implemented; or it may be recognized formally and yet not implemented. But by defining the securing of rights in terms of capabilities, we make it clear that a people in country C don't really have an effective right to political participation, for example, a right in the sense that matters for judging that the society is a just

one, simply because this language exists on
paper: they really have been given a right
only if there are effective measures to make
people truly capable of political exercise.
Women in many nations have a nominal
right of political participation without having this right in the sense of capability; for
example, they may be threatened with violence should they leave the home. In short,
thinking in terms of capability gives us a
benchmark as we think about what it is really
to secure a right to someone. It makes clear
that this involves affirmative material and
institutional support, not simply a failure
to impede.

We see here a major advantage of the
capabilities approach over understandings of
rights – very influential and widespread –
that derive from the tradition within liberalism that is now called "neoliberal," for which
the key idea is that of "negative liberty."
Often fundamental entitlements have been
understood as prohibitions against interfering state action, and if the state keeps its
hands off, those rights are taken to have been
secured; the state has no further affirmative
task. Indeed, the US Constitution suggests
this conception directly: for negative phras-
ing concerning state action predominates,
as in the First Amendment: "Congress shall
make no law respecting an establishment of
religion, or prohibiting the free exercise
thereof; or abridging the freedom of speech,
or of the press; or the right of the people
peaceably to assemble, and petition the
Government for a redress of grievances."
Similarly, the Fourteenth Amendment's all-
important guarantees are also stated in terms
of what the state may not do: "No State shall
make or enforce any law which shall abridge
the privileges or immunities of citizens of the
United States; nor shall any State deprive any
person of life, liberty, or property, without
due process of law; nor deny to any person
within its jurisdiction the equal protection of
the laws." This phraseology, deriving from

the Enlightenment tradition of negative
liberty, leaves things notoriously indeterminate as to whether impediments supplied by
the market, or private actors, are to be considered violations of fundamental rights of
citizens (Martha Nussbaum forthcoming).

The Indian Constitution, by contrast,
typically specifies rights affirmatively.[9] Thus
for example: "All citizens shall have the right
to freedom of speech and expression; to
assemble peaceably and without arms; to
form associations or unions; . . . [etc.]" (Art.
19). These locutions have usually been
understood to imply that impediments supplied by nonstate actors my also be deemed
to be violative of constitutional rights. Moreover, the Indian Constitution is quite explicit
that affirmative action programs to aid the
lower castes and women are not only not
incompatible with constitutional guarantees,
but are actually in their spirit. Such an
approach seems very important for gender
justice: the state needs to take action if traditionally marginalized groups are to achieve
full equality. Whether a nation has a written
constitution or not, it should understand
fundamental entitlements in this way.

The capabilities approach, we may now
say, sides with the Indian Constitution, and
against the neoliberal interpretation of the
US Constitution.[10] It makes it clear that
securing a right to someone requires more
than the absence of negative state action.
Measures such as the recent constitutional
amendments in India that guarantee women
one-third representation in the local *pan-
chayats*, or village councils, are strongly suggested by the capabilities approach, which
directs government to think from the start
about what obstacles there are to full and
effective empowerment for all citizens,
and to devise measures that address these
obstacles.

A further advantage of the capabilities
approach is that, by focusing from the start
on what people are actually able to do and

to be, it is well placed to foreground and address inequalities that women suffer inside the family: inequalities in resources and opportunities, educational deprivations, the failure of work to be recognized as work, insults to bodily integrity. Traditional rights talk has neglected these issues, and this is no accident, I would argue: for rights language is strongly linked with the traditional distinction between a public sphere, which the state regulates, and a private sphere, which it must leave alone.

The language of capabilities has one further advantage over the language of rights: it is not strongly linked to one particular cultural and historical tradition, as the language of rights is believed to be. This belief is not very accurate, as Sen has effectively argued: although the term "rights" is associated with the European Enlightenment, its component ideas have deep roots in many traditions (Amartya Sen 1997; Martha Nussbaum 2000a). Nonetheless, the language of capabilities enables us to bypass this troublesome debate. When we speak simply of what people are actually able to do and to be, we do not even give the appearance of privileging a Western idea. Ideas of activity and ability are everywhere, and there is no culture in which people do not ask themselves what they are able to do and what opportunities they have for functioning.

If we have the language of capabilities, do we also need the language of rights? The language of rights still plays, I believe, four important roles in public discourse, despite its unsatisfactory features. First, when used as in the sentence "A has a right to have the basic political liberties secured to her by her government," it reminds us that people have justified and urgent claims to certain types of urgent treatment, no matter what the world around them has done about that. It imports the idea of an urgent claim based upon justice. This is important particularly for women, who may lack political rights.

However, the capabilities approach can make this idea of a fundamental entitlement clear in other ways, particularly, as I shall be arguing, by operating with a list of capabilities which are held to be fundamental entitlements of all citizens based upon justice.

Rights language also has value because of the emphasis it places on people's choice and autonomy. The language of capabilities, as both Sen and I employ it, is designed to leave room for choice, and to communicate the idea that there is a big difference between pushing people into functioning in ways you consider valuable and leaving the choice up to them. Sen makes this point very effectively in *Development as Freedom* (Sen 1999). But we make this emphasis clear if we combine the capabilities analysis with the language of rights, as my list of capabilities does at several points, and as the Indian Constitution typically does.[11]

III Endorsing a List

One obvious difference between Sen's writings and my own is that for some time I have endorsed a specific list of the Central Human Capabilities as a focus both for comparative quality-of-life measurement and for the formulation of basic political principles of the sort that can play a role in fundamental constitutional guarantees.

The basic idea of my version of the capabilities approach, in *Women and Human Development* (2000a), is that we begin with a conception of the dignity of the human being, and of a life that is worthy of that dignity – a life that has available in it "truly human functioning," in the sense described by Marx in his 1844 *Economic and Philosophical Manuscripts*. With this basic idea as a starting point, I then attempt to justify a list of ten capabilities as central requirements of a life with dignity. These ten capabilities are supposed to be general goals that can be further specified by the society in question, as it works on the account of fundamental entitlements it wishes to endorse (Nussbaum 2000a; Ch. 1). But in some form all are part of a minimum account of social justice: a society that does not guarantee these to all its citizens, at some appropriate threshold level, falls short of being a fully just society, whatever its level of opulence. Moreover, the capabilities are held to be important for each and every person: each person is treated as an end, and none as a mere adjunct or means to the ends of others. And although in practical terms priorities may have to be set temporarily, the capabilities are understood as both mutually supportive and all of central relevance to social justice. Thus a society that neglects one of them to promote the others has shortchanged its citizens, and there is a failure of justice in the shortchanging (Martha Nussbaum 2001b). (Of course someone may feel that one or more of the capabilities on my list should not enjoy this central status, but then she will be differing with me about what ought to be on the list, not about the more general project of using a list to define a minimal conception of social justice.)

The list itself is open-ended and has undergone modification over time; no doubt it will undergo further modification in the light of criticism. But here is the current version.

The Central Human Capabilities

1 **Life.** Being able to live to the end of a human life of normal length; not dying prematurely, or before one's life is so reduced as to be not worth living.
2 **Bodily Health.** Being able to have good health, including reproductive health; to be adequately nourished; to have adequate shelter.
3 **Bodily Integrity.** Being able to move freely from place to place; to be secure against violent assault, including sexual

assault amid domestic violence; having opportunities for sexual satisfaction and for choice in matter of reproduction.
4 **Senses, Imagination, and Thought.** Being able to use the senses, to imagine, think, and reason – and to do these things in a "truly human" way, a way informed and cultivated by an adequate education, including, but by no means limited to, literacy and basic mathematical and scientific training. Being able to use imagination and thought in connection with experiencing and producing works and events of one's own choice, religious, literary, musical, and so forth. Being able to use one's mind in ways protected by guarantees of freedom of expression with respect to both political and artistic speech, and freedom of religious exercise. Being able to have pleasurable experiences and to avoid nonbeneficial pain.
5 **Emotions.** Being able to have attachments to things and people outside ourselves; to love those who love and care for us, to grieve at their absence; in general, to love, to grieve, to experience longing, gratitude, and justified anger. Not having one's emotional development blighted by fear and anxiety. (Supporting this capability means supporting forms of human association that can be shown to be crucial in their development.)
6 **Practical Reason.** Being able to form a conception of the good and to engage in critical reflection about the planning of one's life. (This entails protection for the liberty of conscience and religious observance.)
7 **Affiliation.**
   A. Being able to live with and toward others, to recognize and show concern for other human beings, to engage in various forms of social interaction; to be able to imagine

the situation of another. (Protecting this capability means protecting institutions that constitute and nourish such forms of affiliation, and also protecting the freedom of assembly and political speech.)

B. Having the social bases of self-respect and nonhumiliation; being able to be treated as a dignified being whose worth is equal to that of others. This entails provisions of nondiscrimination on the basis of race, sex, sexual orientation, ethnicity, caste, religion, national origin.

8 **Other Species.** Being able to live with concern for and in relation to animals, plants, and the world of nature.

9 **Play.** Being able to laugh, to play, to enjoy recreational activities.

10 **Control Over One's Environment.**

A. Political. Being able to participate effectively in political choices that govern one's life; having the right of political participation, protections of free speech and association.

B. Material. Being able to hold property (both land and movable goods), and having property rights on an equal basis with others; having the right to seek employment on an equal basis with others; having the freedom from unwarranted search and seizure. In work, being able to work as a human being, exercising practical reason, and entering into meaningful relationships of mutual recognition with other workers.

Because considerations of pluralism have been on my mind since the beginning, I have worked a sensitivity to cultural difference into my understanding of the list in several ways.

First, I consider the list as open-ended and subject to ongoing revision and rethinking, in the way that any society's account of its most fundamental entitlements is always subject to supplementation (or deletion).

I also insist, second, that the items on the list ought to be specified in a somewhat abstract and general way, precisely in order to leave room for the activities of specifying and deliberating by citizens and their legislatures and courts that all democratic nations contain. Within certain parameters it is perfectly appropriate that different nations should do this somewhat differently, taking their histories and special circumstances into account. Thus, for example, a free speech right that suits Germany well might be too restrictive in the different climate of the United States.

Third, I consider the list to be a free-standing "partial moral conception," to use John Rawls's phrase: that is, it is explicitly introduced for political purposes only, and without any grounding in metaphysical ideas of the sort that divide people along lines of culture and religion.[12] As Rawls says: we can view this list as a "module" that can be endorsed by people who otherwise have very different conceptions of the ultimate meaning and purpose of life; they will connect it to their religious or secular comprehensive doctrines in many ways.

Fourth, if we insist that the appropriate political target is capability and not functioning, we protect pluralism here again.[13] Many people who are willing to support a given capability as a fundamental entitlement would feel violated were the associated functioning made basic. Thus, the right to vote can be endorsed by believing citizens who would feel deeply violated by mandatory voting, because it goes against their religious conception. (The American Amish are in this category: they believe that it is wrong to participate in political life, but they endorse the right of citizens to vote.) The free expression of religion can be endorsed by people who would totally object to any establishment of religion that would involve dragooning all citizens into some type of religious functioning.

Fifth, the major liberties that protect pluralism are central items on the list: the freedom of speech, the freedom of association, the freedom of conscience.[14] By placing them on the list we give them a central and nonnegotiable place.

Sixth and finally, I insist on a rather strong separation between issues of justification and issues of implementation. I believe that we can justify this list as a good basis for political principles all round the world. But this does not mean that we thereby license intervention with the affairs of a state that does not recognize them. It is a basis for persuasion, but I hold that military and economic sanctions are justified only in certain very grave circumstances involving traditionally recognized crimes against humanity (Martha Nussbaum 2002). So it seems less objectionable to recommend something to everyone, once we point out that it is part of the view that state sovereignty, grounded in the consent of the people, is a very important part of the whole package.

Where does Sen stand on these questions? I find a puzzling tension in his writings at this point. On the one hand, he speaks as if certain specific capabilities are absolutely central and nonnegotiable. One cannot read his discussions of health, education, political and civil liberties, and the free choice of occupation without feeling that he agrees totally with my view that these human capabilities should enjoy a strong priority and should be made central by states the world over, as fundamental entitlements of each and every citizen (although he says little about how a threshold level of each capability would be constructed). In the case of liberty, he actually endorses giving liberty a

considerable priority, though without giving an exhaustive enumeration of the liberties that would fall under this principle. His role in the formulation of the measures that go into the *Human Development Reports*, moreover, clearly shows him endorsing a group of health- and education-related capabilities as the appropriate way to measure quality of life across nations.

On the other hand, Sen has conspicuously refused to endorse any account of the central capabilities. Thus the examples mentioned above remain in limbo: clearly they are examples of some things he thinks very important, but it is not clear to what extent he is prepared to recommend them as important goals for all the world's people, goals connected with the idea of social justice itself. And it is equally unclear whether there are other capabilities not mentioned so frequently that might be equally important, and, if so, what those capabilities might be. The reason for this appears to be his respect for democratic deliberation.[15] He feels that people should be allowed to settle these matters for themselves. Of course, as I have said above, I do too, in the sense of implementation. But Sen goes further, suggesting that democracy is inhibited by the endorsement of a set of central entitlements in international political debate, as when feminists insist on certain requirements of gender justice in international documents and deliberations.

In *Development as Freedom* things become, I believe, even more problematic. For Sen speaks throughout the work of "the perspective of freedom" and uses language, again and again, suggesting that freedom is a general all-purpose social good, and that capabilities are to be seen as instances of this more general good of human freedom. Such a view is not incompatible with ranking some freedoms ahead of others for political purposes, of course. But it does seem to go in a problematic direction.

First of all, it is unclear whether the idea of promoting freedom is even a coherent political project. Some freedoms limit others. The freedom of rich people to make large donations to political campaigns limits the equal worth of the right to vote. The freedom of businesses to pollute the environment limits the freedom of citizens to enjoy an unpolluted environment. The freedom of landowners to keep their land limits projects of land reform that might be argued to be central to many freedoms for the poor. And so on. Obviously these freedoms are not among those that Sen considers, but he says nothing to limit the account of freedom or to rule out conflicts of this type. Indeed, we can go further: any particular freedom involves the idea of constraint: for person P is only free to do action A if other people are constrained from interfering with A.[16]

Furthermore, even if there were a coherent project that viewed all freedoms as desirable social goals, it is not at all clear this is the sort of project someone with Sen's political and ethical views ought to endorse. The examples I have just given show us that any political project that is going to protect the equal worth of certain basic liberties for the poor, and to improve their living conditions, needs to say forthrightly that some freedoms are central for political purposes, and some are distinctly not. Some freedoms involve basic social entitlements, and others do not. Some lie at the heart of a view of political justice, and others do not. Among the ones that do not lie at the core, some are simply less important, but others may be positively bad.

For example, the freedom of rich people to make large campaign contributions, though defended by many Americans in the name of the general good of freedom, seems to me not among those freedoms that lie at the heart of a set of basic entitlements to which a just society should commit itself. In many circumstances, it is actually a bad

thing, and constraint on it a very good thing. Similarly, the freedom of industry to pollute the environment, though cherished by many Americans in the name of the general good of freedom, seems to me not among those freedoms that should enjoy protection; beyond a certain point, the freedom to pollute is bad, and should be constrained by law. And while property rights are certainly a good thing up to a point and in some ways, the freedom of large landowners in India to hold property under gender-discriminatory ceiling laws – laws that some early Supreme Court decisions have held to enjoy constitutional protection – is not part of the account of property rights as central human entitlements that a just society would want to endorse. To define property capabilities so broadly is actually a bad thing, because giving women equal access to land rights is essential to social justice (see generally Agarwal 1994).

To speak more generally, gender justice cannot be successfully pursued without limiting male freedom. For example, the "right" to have intercourse with one's wife whether she consents or not has been understood as a time-honored male prerogative in most societies, and men have greatly resented the curtailment of liberty that followed from laws against marital rape – one reason why about half of the states in the US still do not treat nonconsensual intercourse within marriage as genuine rape, and why many societies the world over still lack laws against it. The freedom to harass women in the workplace is a tenaciously guarded prerogative of males the world over: the minute sexual harassment regulations are introduced, one always hears protests invoking the idea of liberty. Terms like "femi-nazis" are used to suggests that feminists are against freedom for supporting these policies. And of course in one sense feminists are indeed insisting on a restriction of liberty, on the grounds that certain liberties are inimical both to equalities and to women's liberties and opportunities.

In short, no society that pursues equality or even an ample social minimum can avoid curtailing freedom in very many ways, and what it ought to say is: those freedoms are not good, they are not part of a core group of entitlements required by the notion of social justice, and in many ways, indeed, they subvert those core entitlements. Of other freedoms, for example the freedom of motorcyclists to drive without helmets, a society can say, these freedoms are not very important; they are neither very bad nor very good. They are not implicit in our conception of social justice, but they do not subvert it either.

In other words, all societies that pursue a reasonably just political conception have to evaluate human freedoms, saying that some are central and some trivial, some good and some actively bad. This evaluation also affects the way we will assess an abridgment of a freedom. Certain freedoms are taken to be entitlements of citizens based upon justice. When any one of these is abridged, that is an especially grave failure of the political system. In such cases, people feel that the abridgment is not just a cost to be borne; it is a cost of a distinctive kind, involving a violation of basic justice. When some freedom outside the core is abridged, that may be a small cost or a large cost to some actor or actors, but it is not a cost of exactly that same kind, one that in justice no citizen should be asked to bear. This qualitative difference is independent of the cost, at least in terms of standard subjective willingness-to-pay models. Thus, motorcyclists may mind greatly a law that tells them to wear a helmet. In terms of standard willingness-to-pay models, they might be willing to pay quite a lot for the right to drive without a helmet. On the other hand, many citizens probably would not think that not being able to vote was a big cost. In terms of standard willingness-to-pay models, at least, they would not pay much for the right to vote, and some might have to be paid for voting. And yet I would want to say that the right to vote is a fundamental entitlement based upon justice, whereas the right to drive without a helmet is not (Nussbaum 2001b).

Sen's response to these questions, in public discussion (Bielefeld, July 2001), has been to say that freedom per se is always good, although it can be badly used. Freedom, he said, is like male strength: male strength is per se a good thing, although it can be used to beat up women. I am not satisfied by this reply. For so much depends on how one specifies the freedoms in question. Some freedoms include injustice in their very definition. Thus, the freedom to rape one's wife without penalty, the freedom to hang out a sign saying "No Blacks here," the freedom of an employer to discriminate on grounds of race or sex or religion – those are freedoms all right, and some people zealously defend them. But it seems absurd to say that they are good per se, and bad only in use. Any society that allows people these freedoms has allowed a fundamental injustice, involving the subordination of a vulnerable group. Of other freedoms, for example, the freedom of the motorcycle rider to ride without a helmet, we should not say, "good in itself, bad only in use," we should say "neutral and trivial in itself, probably bad in use." Once again, attention to the all-important issue of content is vital.

Thus Sen cannot avoid committing himself to a core list of fundamental capabilities, once he faces such questions. If capabilities are to be used in advancing a conception of social justice, they will obviously have to be specified, if only in the open-ended and humble way I have outlined. Either a society has a conception of basic justice or it does not. If it has one, we have to know what its content is, and what opportunities and liberties it takes to be fundamental entitlements of all citizens. One cannot have a conception of social justice that says, simply, "All citizens are entitled to freedom understood as capability." Besides being wrong and misleading in the ways I have already argued, such a blanket endorsement of freedom/capability as goal would be hopelessly vague. It would be impossible to say whether the society in question was just or unjust.

Someone may now say, sure, there has to be a definite list in the case of each nation that is striving for justice, but why not leave the list-making to them, and to their processes of public discussion? Of course, as I have already said, in the sense of *implementation*, and also in the sense of *more precise* specification, I do so. So, to be a real objection to my proposal, the question must be, why should we hold out to all nations a set of norms that we believe justified by a good philosophical argument, as when feminists work out norms of sex equality in documents such as CEDAW, rather than letting each one justify its own set of norms? The answer to this question, however, is given in all of Sen's work: some human matters are too important to be left to whim and caprice, or even to the dictates of a cultural tradition. To say that education for women, or adequate healthcare, is not justified just in case some nation believes that it is not justified seems like a capitulation to subjective preferences, of the sort that Sen has opposed throughout his career. As he has repeatedly stated: capabilities have intrinsic importance. But if we believe that, we also believe that it is right to say to nations that don't sufficiently recognize one of them: you know, you too should endorse equal education for girls, and understand it as a fundamental constitutional entitlement. You too should provide a certain level of healthcare to all citizens, and view this as among their fundamental constitutional entitlements. Just because the US does not choose to rec-

ognize a fundamental right to healthcare, that doesn't make the US right, morally justified. A very important part of public discussion is radical moral statement and the arguments supporting those statements. Such statements may be justified long before they are widely accepted. Such was true of the statements of Gandhi, of Martin Luther King, Jr., of early feminists. Where feminist demands are not yet widely accepted, it is true of those demands today: although public debate has not yet accepted them, they are a part of that debate right now, and a part that has already presented adequate moral justification for basic human entitlements.

In short: it makes sense to take the issue of social justice seriously, and to use a norm of justice to assess the various nations of the world and their practices. But if the issue of social justice is important, then the content of a conception of justice is important. Social justice has always been a profoundly normative concept, and its role is typically critical: we work out an account of what is just, and we then use it to find reality deficient in various ways. Sen's whole career has been devoted to developing norms of justice in exactly this way, and holding them up against reality to produce valuable criticisms. It seems to me that his commitment to normative thinking about justice requires the endorsement of some definite content. One cannot say, "I'm for justice, but any conception of justice anyone comes up with is all right with me." Moreover, Sen, of course, does not say that. He is a radical thinker, who has taken a definite stand on many matters, including matters of sex equality. He has never been afraid to be definite when misogyny is afoot, or to supply a quite definite account of why many societies are defective. So it is somewhat mysterious to me why he has recently moved in the direction of endorsing freedom as a general good. Certainly there is no such retreat in his practical policies regarding women. In recent writing such as "The Many Faces of Misogyny" he is extremely definite about what is just and unjust in laws and institutions, and one can infer a rich account of fundamental human entitlements from his critique (Amartya Sen 2001). But then it would appear that he cannot actually believe that the content of an account of fundamental entitlements should be left up for grabs.

Such leaving-up-for-grabs is all the more dangerous when we are confronting women's issues. For obviously enough, many traditional conceptions of social justice and fundamental entitlements have made women second-class citizens, if citizens at all. Women's liberties, opportunities, property right, and political rights have been construed as unequal to men, and this has been taken to be a just state of affairs. Nor have traditional accounts of justice attended at all to issues that are particularly urgent for women, such as issues of bodily integrity, sexual harassment, and the issue of public support for care to children, the disabled, and the elderly.

Some supporters of a capabilities approach might be reluctant to endorse a list because of concerns about pluralism.[17] But here we may make two points that pertain specifically to the norm of respect for pluralism. First, the value of respect for pluralism itself requires a commitment to some cross-cultural principles as fundamental entitlements. Real respect for pluralism means strong and unwavering protection for religious freedom, for the freedom of association, for the freedom of speech. If we say that we are for pluralism, and yet refuse to commit ourselves to the nonnegotiability of these items as fundamental building blocks of a just political order, we show that we are really half-hearted about pluralism.

I am sure that Sen would agree with this. I am sure, too, that he would say the same about other items on my list, such as health and education: if a nation says that they are for human capabilities, but refuses to give these special protection for all citizens, citing reasons of cultural or religious pluralism, Sen will surely say that they are not making a good argument, or giving genuine protection to pluralism. Instead, they are, very often, denying people (often, women in particular) the chance to figure out what culture and form of life they actually want. So they are actually curtailing the most meaningful kind of pluralism, which requires having a life of one's own and some choices regarding it. And that goal surely requires a certain level of basic health and education.

But then we are both, in effect, making a list of such entitlements, and the only question then must be what shall go on the list, and, how long it will be.

The second argument is one that derives from the Rawlsian idea of political liberalism, and I am not certain that Sen would endorse it. The argument says that classical liberalism erred by endorsing freedom or autonomy as a general good in human life. Both earlier liberals such as John Stuart Mill and modern comprehensive liberals such as Joseph Raz hold that autonomy and freedom of choice are essential ingredients in valuable human lives, and society is entitled to promote across the board. Rawls, and I with him, hold that this general endorsement of freedom shows deficient respect for citizens whose comprehensive conceptions of the good human life do not make freedom and autonomy central human values. People who belong to an authoritarian religion cannot agree with Raz or Mill that autonomy is a generally good thing. Mill responds, in Chapter 3 of *On Liberty*, by denigrating such people (he understands Calvinists to be such people) (John Stuart Mill 1859). Presumably the Millean state would denigrate them too, and would design education and other institutions to disfavor them, although their civil liberties would not be restricted. Rawls and I agree that this strategy shows deficient respect for a reasonable pluralism of different comprehensive conceptions of the good life. We should respect people who prefer a life within an authoritarian religion (or personal relationship), so long as certain basic opportunities and exit options are firmly guaranteed.

I hold that this respect for pluralism is fostered both by making capability and not functioning the appropriate political goal and also by endorsing a relatively small list of core capabilities for political purposes. Thus we say two things to religious citizens. We say, first, that endorsing the capabilities list does not require them to endorse the associated functioning as a good in their own lives, a point I have stressed earlier in this section. And we say, second, that the very fact that it is a short list shows that we are leaving them lots of room to value other things in mapping out their plan of life. We do not ask them to endorse freedom as a general good – as we might seem to do if we talk a lot about freedom but fail to make a list. Instead, we just ask them to endorse this short list of freedoms (as capabilities) for political purposes and as applicable to all citizens. They may then get on with the lives they prefer.

The expectation is that a Roman Catholic citizen, say, can endorse this short list of fundamental liberties for political purposes, without feeling that her view of Church authority and its decisive role in her life is thereby being denigrated. Even an Amish citizen, who believes that all participation in public life is simply wrong, can still feel that it's all right to endorse the capabilities list for political purposes, because no general endorsement of autonomy as an end tells her that her life is less worthwhile than other lives. And, as I argued in Nussbaum (2000a: Chs. 1 and 3), even a woman who believes that the seclusion of women is right may

endorse this small menu of liberties and opportunities for all women, though she herself will use few of them – and she will feel that the conception is one that respects her, because it does not announce that only autonomous lives are worthwhile.

I am not certain whether Sen is in this sense a comprehensive liberal like Raz, or a political liberal like Rawls and me. But to the extent that he finds Rawls's arguments on this score persuasive, he has yet a further reason to endorse a definite and relatively circumscribed list of capabilities as political goals, rather than to praise freedom as a general social good.

The question of how to frame such a list, and what to put on it, is surely a difficult one, in many ways. But I have argued that there is no way to take the capabilities approach forward, making it really productive for political thought about basic social justice, without facing this question and giving it the best answer one can.

[. . .]

The capabilities approach is a powerful tool in crafting an adequate account of social justice. But the bare idea of capabilities as a space within which comparisons are made and inequalities assessed is insufficient. To get a vision of social justice that will have the requisite critical force and definiteness to direct social policy, we need to have an account, for political purposes, of what the central human capabilities are, even if we know that this account will always be contested and remade. Women all over the world are making critical proposals in public discussion, proposals that embody their radical demand for lives with full human dignity. While we await the day when the world as a whole accepts such ideas, the capabilities list is one way of giving theoretical shape to women's definite, and justified, demands.

Notes

1 I develop related arguments similar to those developed in this paper, but with a focus on constitutional and legal issues, in Martha Nussbaum (forthcoming).

2 See Amartya Sen (1980, 1982, 1985, 1992, 1999).

3 See for example Amartya Sen (1990, 1995, 1999).

4 Although Sen tends to treat this example as one of straightforward physical difference, it should not be so treated, since the reasons why wheelchair persons cannot get around are thoroughly social – the absence of ramps, etc. (for elaboration, see Nussbaum 2001a). See also Martha Nussbaum (2004), where I point out that all societies cater to the disabilities of the average person. Thus we do not have staircases with steps so high that only giants can climb them.

A further problem not mentioned by Sen, but relevant to his critique of Rawls: even if the person in the wheelchair were equally well off with regard to economic well-being, there is a separate issue of dignity and self-respect.

5 Obviously the case for this depends very much both on what capability we are considering and on how we describe it. Thus, equality of capability seems to be important when we consider the right to vote, the freedom of religion, and so on; but if we consider the capability to play basketball, it seems ludicrous to suppose that society should be very much concerned about even a minimum threshold level of it, much less complete equality. With something like health, much hangs on whether we define the relevant capability as "access to the social bases of health" or "the ability to be healthy." The former seems like something that a just society should distribute on a basis of equality; the latter contains an element of chance that no just society could, or should, altogether eliminate. So the question whether equality of capability is a good social goal cannot be well answered without specifying a list of the relevant capabilities.

6 One way of using it, discussed elsewhere, is as a basis for constitutional accounts of fundamental entitlements of all citizens (see Nussbaum 2000a; 2004).

7 See especially Eva Kittay (1999), Nancy Folbre (1999, 2001), Joan Williams (2000), Mona Harrington (1999). Earlier influential work in this area includes: Martha Fineman (1991, 1995), Sarah Ruddick (1989), Joan Tronto (1993), Virginia Held (1993), Robin West (1997). For an excellent collection of articles from diverse feminist perspectives, see Held (1995). See also Martha Nussbaum (2000b). And, finally, see United Nations Development Programme, *Human Development Report 1999*.

8 See his reply to letters concerning Amartya Sen (2001).

9 Not invariably: Art. 14, closely modeled on the equal protection clause of the US Fourteenth Amendment, reads: "The State shall not deny to any person equality before the law or the equal protection of the laws within the territory of India."

10 Of course this account of both is in many ways too simple; I refer primarily to the wording of the documents here, not to the complicated jurisprudential traditions stemming from them.

11 On a difference with Sen concerning the role of rights as "side-constraints," see Martha Nussbaum (1997).

12 For the relation of this idea to objectivity, see Martha Nussbaum (2001c).

13 See my discussion of this issue in Nussbaum (2000a: Ch. 1); and for a rejoinder to perfectionist critics, see Martha Nussbaum (2000c).

14 I am very skeptical of attempts to add group cultural right to the list, because every group contains hierarchy; see Martha Nussbaum (2004).

15 This is what Sen said in response to the present paper at the conference on his work at the Zentrum für interdisziplinäre Forschung in Bielefeld at which it was first presented, in July 2001.

[16] Thus, I do not see that we can coherently frame the notion of an increase or decrease in freedom, without specification of whose freedom, and freedom to do what. See John Rawls (1971: 202): "liberty can always be explained by a reference to three items: the agents who are free, the restrictions or limitations which they are free from, and what it is that they are free to do or not to do."

[17] Sen stated at the Bielefeld conference that this is not his concern.

References

Agarwal, Bina (1994) *A Field of One's Own: Gender and Land Rights in South Asia* (Cambridge: Cambridge University Press).

—— (1997) "'Bargaining' and Gender Relations: Within and Beyond the Household." *Feminist Economics* 3(1), pp. 1–15.

Anderson, Elizabeth (1993) *Value in Ethics and Economics* (Cambridge, MA: Harvard University Press).

Bérubé, Michael (1996) *Life As We Know It: A Father, A Family, and An Exceptional Child* (New York: Vintage).

Chen, Martha A. (1983) *A Quiet Revolution: Women in Transition in Rural Bangladesh* (Cambridge, MA: Schenkman).

Fineman, Martha (1991) *The Illusion of Equality* (Chicago: University of Chicago Press).

—— (1995) *The Neutered Mother, the Sexual Family and Other Twentieth Century Tragedies* (New York: Routledge).

Folbre, Nancy (1999) "Care and the Global Economy." Background paper prepared for *Human Development Report 1999*.

—— (2001) *The Invisible Heart: Economics and Family Values* (New York: New Press).

Gauthier, David (1986) *Morals by Agreement* (New York: Oxford University Press).

Harrington, Mona (1999) *Care and Equality* (New York: Alfred A. Knopf).

Held, Virginia (1993) *Feminist Morality: Transforming Culture, Society, and Politics* (Chicago: University of Chicago Press).

—— (ed.) (1995) *Justice and Care: Essential Readings in Feminist Ethics* (Boulder, CO: Westview Press).

Kittay, Eva (1999) *Love's Labor: Essays on Women, Equality, and Dependency* (New York: Routledge).

Locke, John (1698) *The Second Treatises of Government*. In Peter Laslett (ed.), *Two Treatise of Government* (Cambridge: Cambridge University Press, 1960).

Marx, Karl (1844) *Economic and Philosophical Manuscripts of 1844*. In Karl Marx, *Early Writings*, trans. and ed. T. Bottomore (New York: McGraw-Hill, 1964).

Nussbaum, Martha (1997) "Capabilities and Human Rights." *Fordham Law Review* 66, pp. 273–300.

—— (2000a) *Women and Human Development: The Capabilities Approach* (Cambridge: Cambridge University Press).

—— (2000b) "The Future of Feminist Liberalism." Presidential Address delivered to the Central Division of the American Philosophical Association. *Proceeding and Addresses of the American Philosophical Association* 74, pp. 47–79.

—— (2000c) "Aristotle, Politics, and Human Capabilities: A Response to Antony, Arneson, Charlesworth, and Mulgan." *Ethics* 111, pp. 102–40.

—— (2000d) "Animal Rights: The Need for a Theoretical Basis." *Harvard Law Review* 114(5), pp. 1506–49 (a review of Wise 2000).

—— (2001a) "Disabled Lives: Who Cares?" *The New York Review of Books* 48, pp. 34–7.

—— (2001b) "The Costs of Tragedy: Some Moral Limits of Cost–Benefit Analysis," in Matthew D. Adler and Eric A. Posner (eds.). *Cost–Benefit Analysis: Legal, Economic, and Philosophical Perspectives*, pp. 169–200 (Chicago: University of Chicago Press).

—— (2001c) "Political Objectivity." *New Literary History* 32, pp. 883–906.

—— (2002) "Women and the Law of Peoples." *Philosophy, Politics, and Economics* 1(3), pp. 283–306.

—— (2003) "The Complexity of Groups." *Philosophy and Social Criticism* 29, pp. 57–69.

——(2004) *Hiding from Humanity: Disgust, Shame, and the Law* (Princeton, NJ: Princeton University Press).

——Forthcoming. "Constitutions and Capabilities," In M. Krausz and D. Chatterjee (eds.) *Globalization, Development and Democracy: Philosophical Perspectives* (Oxford: Oxford University Press).

Rachels, James (1990) *Created from Animals: The Moral Implications of Darwinism* (New York: Oxford University Press).

Rawls, John (1971) *A Theory of Justice* (Cambridge, MA: Harvard University Press).

——(1980) *Kantian Constructivism in Moral Theory: The Dewey Lectures. The Journal of Philosophy* 77, pp. 515–71.

——(1996) *Political Liberalism.* Expanded Paperback Edition (New York: Columbia University Press).

Ruddick, Sarah (1989) *Maternal Thinking* (New York: Beacon Press).

Sen, Amartya (1980) "Equality of What?" in S. M. McMurrin (ed.), *Tanner Lectures on Human Values* (Salt Lake City: University of Utah Press). Reprinted in Sen 1982, pp. 353–69.

——(1982) *Choice, Welfare and Measurement* (Oxford, UK: Blackwell).

——(1985) *Commodities and Capabilities* (Amsterdam: North-Holland).

——(1990) "Gender and Cooperative Conflicts," in Irene Tinker (ed.), *Persistent Inequalities,* pp. 123–49 (New York: Oxford: Oxford University Press).

——(1992) *Inequality Reexamined* (New York and Cambridge, MA: Russell Sage and Harvard University Press).

——(1995) "Gender Inequality and Theories of Justice," in M. Nussbaum and J. Glover (eds.) *Women, Culture and Development,* pp. 259–73. (Oxford: Clarendon Press).

——(1997) "Human Rights and Asian values." *The New Republic* (July 14/21), pp. 33–40.

——(1999) *Development as Freedom* (New York: Knopf).

——(2001) "The Many Faces of Misogyny." *The New Republic* (September 17), pp. 35–40.

Tronto, Joan (1993) *Moral Boundaries: A Political Argument for an Ethic of Care* (New York: Routledge).

West, Robin (1997) *Caring for Justice* (New York: New York University Press).

Williams, Joan (2000) *Unbending Gender: Why Family and Work Conflict and What to Do About It* (New York: Oxford University Press).

Wise, Steven (2000) *Rattling the Cage: Toward Legal Rights for Animals* (Cambridge, MA: Perseus Books).

Chapter 35

The Role of Religion
Martha C. Nussbaum

I Religious Liberty and Sex Equality: A Dilemma

Modern liberal democracies typically hold that religious liberty is an extremely important value, and that its protection is among the most important functions of government. These democracies also typically defend as central a wide range of other human interests, liberties, and opportunities. Among these are the freedom of movement, the right to seek employment outside the home, the right to assemble, the right to bodily integrity, the right to education, and the right to hold and to inherit property. Sometimes, however, the religions do not support these other liberties. Sometimes, indeed, they deny such liberties to classes of people in accordance with a morally irrelevant characteristic, such as race or caste or sex. Such denials may not mean much in nations where the religions do not wield much legal power. But in nations such as India, where religions run large parts of the legal system, they are fundamental determinants of many lives.

In this way, a dilemma is created for the liberal state. On the one hand, to interfere with the freedom of religious expression is to strike a blow against citizens in an area of intimate self-definition and basic liberty. Not to interfere, however, permits other abridgments of self-definition and liberty. It is not surprising that modern democracies should find themselves torn in this area – particularly a democracy like India, which has committed itself to the equality of the sexes and nondiscrimination on the basis of sex in the list of Fundamental Rights enumerated in its Constitution – alongside commitments to religious liberty and nondiscrimination on the basis of religion.[1]

Consider these three cases, all involving conflicts between claims of religious free exercise and women's claims to other important rights under the Indian Constitution:

1. In 1983, Mary Roy, a Syrian Christian woman, daughter of wealthy parents, went to court to challenge the Travancore Christian Act, under which daughters inherit only one-fourth the share of sons, subject to a maximum of Rs. 5,000. The Indian Supreme Court declared that the relevant law superseding the Travancore Christian Act was the Indian Succession Act of 1925, which gives equal rights to daughters and sons.[2]

* From Martha C. Nussbaum, *Women and Human Development: The Capabilities Approach* (Cambridge: Cambridge University Press, 2000), pp. 167–212, 235–40.

(By ruling in this narrowly technical way, the Court avoided confronting the question whether the act violates constitutional guarantees of sex equality.) The Court also declared the change retroactive to 1951, thus bringing the property of many Christian males into dispute. Protest greeted the judgment. A Christian MP from Kerala (representing a district including many wealthy Christian landlords) introduced a Private Member's Bill in Congress seeking to block the retroactive effect of the law. Meanwhile, the Christian churches of Kerala vociferously protested the Court's interference with the free exercise of religion. It was argued that the judgment would "open up a floodgate of litigation and destroy the traditional harmony and goodwill that exists in Christian families."[3] The Synod of Christian Churches took an official position against the ruling and actively mobilized protests against it.[4] Priests belonging to the Roman Catholic, Jacobite, Church of South India, and Kananya Christian Churches all criticized the judgment from the pulpit. One reason for the strength of opposition may be that a portion of the traditional daughter's inheritance automatically went to the church; this would not be the case under the Indian Succession Act.[5]

2. In 1947, at the time of Independence, the Hindu Law Committee submitted a list of recommendations to reform the system of Hindu personal law. These were presented to Parliament in the form of the Hindu Code Bill. Backed by Nehru's law minister, B. R. Ambedkar, the bill proposed to grant women a right to divorce, remove the option of polygamous marriage for men, abolish child marriage for young women, and grant women more nearly equal property rights.[6] A storm of protest from Hindu MPs (led by conservative Pandits or Hindu religious authorities) greeted the proposed legislation. Debate focused on the new laws' alleged violations of the free exercise of religion, as

guaranteed in the new Constitution. Pandit Mukul Behrilal Bhargava held that equal property rights for women represented a forcible intrusion of Muslim ideas into the Hindu tradition. (Muslim women in India had had somewhat more equal inheritance rights since 1937, when the Shariat was substituted for customary law.)[7] Others objected to the fact that monogamy would be required for Hindus but not for Muslims. Still others objected to the whole idea of state-initiated reform of the Hindu code: "Hindu law is intimately connected with Hindu religion and no Hindu can tolerate a non-Hindu being an authority on Hindu law." Traditional Hindu MPs attacked female MPs for violating Hindu tradition, speaking of "the tyranny of modern women . . . [T]he days of their persecution are gone, it is nowadays men who are being persecuted."

Shortly after the new Constitution took effect, in the summer of 1951, a tumultuous session of Parliament formally debated the bill; conservative Pandit Govind Malviya spoke for two hours against the bill, which he called "wrong in principle, atrocious in detail and uncalled for in expediency." Despite Ambedkar's passionate support, the bill seemed bound for defeat, and even Nehru withdrew his support for the time being. In consequence, Dr Ambedkar resigned his ministerial position, saying: "To leave untouched the inequality between class and class, between sex and sex, and to go on passing legislation relating to economic problems is to make a farce of our Constitution and so build a palace on a dung-heap." The bill lapsed. Its provisions were eventually adopted in 1954, 1955, and 1956.

Fifty years after the initial proposal, these provisions continue to arouse controversy. The new laws are weakly enforced. Child marriage, for example, remains common in some regions, and is vigorously defended in both religious and cultural terms.[8] With the rise of Hindu fundamentalism, charges of violation of free exercise and discrimination in favor of Muslims are increasing, especially over the issue of polygamy. Substantial numbers of Hindu men continue to make bigamous marriages; others have converted to Islam in order to escape the polygamy prohibition.[9] To make things more complex still, Hindu courts have recently adopted an extremely stringent definition of a valid marriage, with the result that a large number of existing Hindu marriages, if challenged in court, would not withstand scrutiny, and the male would be acquitted of charges of bigamy attendant on a second marriage.[10]

3. In Madhya Pradesh in 1978, an elderly Muslim woman named Shah Bano was thrown out of her home by her husband, a prosperous lawyer, after forty-four years of marriage. (The occasion seems to have been a quarrel over inheritance between the children of Shah Bano and the children of the husband's other wife.) As required by Islamic personal law, he returned to her the *mehr*, or marriage settlement, that she had originally brought into the marriage – Rs. 3,000 (less than $100 by today's exchange rates). Like many Muslim women facing divorce without sufficient maintenance, she sued for regular maintenance payments under Section 125 of the uniform Criminal Procedure Code, which forbids a man "of adequate means" to permit various close relatives, including (by special amendment in 1973) an ex-wife,[11] to remain in a state of "destitution and vagrancy." This remedy had long been recognized as a solution to the inadequate maintenance granted by Islamic personal law, and many women had won similar cases. What was different about Shah Bano's case was that the Chief Justice of the Supreme Court of India, awarding her maintenance of Rs. 180 per month, remarked in his lengthy opinion that the Islamic system was very unfair to women, and that it was high time that the nation should indeed secure a Uniform Civil Code, as the Constitution had

long ago directed it to do. The Chief Justice wrote, "Undoubtedly, the Muslim husband enjoys the privilege of being able to discard his wife whenever he chooses to do so, for reason good, bad, or indifferent. Indeed, for no reason at all." Although of Hindu origin, the Chief Justice also undertook to interpret various Islamic sacred texts and to argue that there was no textual barrier in Islam to providing a much more adequate maintenance for women.

A storm of public protest greeted the opinion. Although some liberal Muslims backed Chief Justice Chandrachud, he had made their task difficult by his zealous incursion into the interpretation of sacred Islamic texts. The Islamic clergy and the Muslim Personal Law Board organized widespread protest against the ruling, claiming that it violated their free exercise of religion. In response to the widespread outcry, the government of Rajiv Gandhi introduced the Muslim Women's (Protection after Divorce) Act of 1986, which deprived all and only Muslim women of the right of maintenance guaranteed under the Criminal Procedure Code. Women's groups tried to get this law declared unconstitutional on grounds of both religious discrimination and sex equality, but the Supreme Court (in rapid retreat from charges of religious intolerance and excessive activism) refused to hear their claim. Hindu activists, meanwhile, complained that the 1986 law discriminates against Hindus, giving Muslim men "special privileges."[12]

Here are three examples of our dilemma, no different in kind from dilemmas that arise in the US and Europe, but different in degree, since the religions in India control so much of the legal system. On one side is the claim of religious free exercise; on the other, women's claims to various fundamental rights. In the first case, women won a clear victory – interestingly, in a case involving a small and politically powerless religion. In the second case, women made some strides, but the provisions are weakly enforced, and the current climate of Hindu fundamentalism and conservatism makes the future very unclear. In the third case, women suffered a particularly painful and prominent defeat. Free exercise and sex equality appear, at least sometimes, to be on a collision course.

II   Secular Humanists and Traditionalists

Feminists have taken a range of positions on this dilemma. Here are two extremes, both prominent in the international debate. The first position, which I shall call the position of *secular humanist feminism*, treats the dilemma as, basically, a non-dilemma.[13] The values of women's equality and dignity, and of the basic human rights and capabilities more generally, so outweigh any religious claim that any conflict between them should not be seen as a serious conflict, except in practical political terms. Indeed, the secular feminist tends to view religion itself as irredeemably patriarchal, and a powerful ally of women's oppression throughout the ages. She is not unhappy to muzzle it, and does not see it as doing a whole lot of good in anyone's life.[14]

Many secular humanist feminists are Marxists; if they follow Marx on religion, they are bound to take a negative view of religion's social role, and are unlikely even to give the free exercise of religion a high degree of respect. But some liberal feminists also take a secular humanist line. These feminists – usually comprehensive rather than political liberals – will be committed to preserving the liberty of conscience, but only within limits firmly set by a secular moral understanding of basic human rights and capabilities: religion, as Kant would have it, "within the limits of reason alone." This is in effect the position of J. S. Mill in *On Liberty*, where he excoriates Calvinism as an

"insidious . . . theory of life" that creates a "pinched and hidebound type of human character." Mill holds that it is perfectly proper for public policy to be based on the view that by teaching obedience as a good, Calvinism undermines "the desirable condition of human nature." He thus advocates liberalism as a comprehensive doctrine of life, rather than (in political-liberal fashion) as simply the basis for core political principles.[15] Some secular humanists in this comprehensive liberal tradition manifest, like Marxists, a general hostility to religion; Bertrand Russell is just one obvious example of a widely held view among liberal intellectuals. Others are not hostile to religion as such, but simply insist that it fall in line with a rational secular understanding of value; Joseph Raz and Susan Okin would seem to be in this group.

The second approach, which I shall call that of *traditionalist feminism*, also sees the dilemma as basically a non-dilemma. The understandings of each community, both religious and traditional, are our best, perhaps our only, guides in charting women's course for the future. All moral claims not rooted in a particular community's understanding of the good are suspect from the start; but those that challenge the roots of traditional religious practices are more than usually suspect, since they threaten sources of value that have over the ages been enormously important to women and men, forming the very core of their search for the meaning of existence.[16] Although such a position will frequently converge with mere traditionalism and antifeminism, I think it can be a genuine type of feminism, in the sense that its proponents are committed to defining feminism in terms of what has deep importance to real women, and in sheltering those deep values from the assault of other feminists.

Some traditionalist feminists are cultural relativists, who hold that as a matter of theory it is impossible to justify any cross-cultural moral norms. Some, on the other hand, are worried more about normative moral substance than about justification: they simply think local sources of value are more likely to be good for people than are international human rights norms, more in tune with and beneficial to the real lives people lead. In Indian terms, traditionalist feminists typically make common cause with other "nativist" defenders of tradition, opponents of secularization and modernization, who hold that the essence of Indian national identity resides in Hindu tradition,[17] and that traditional female roles lie at the core of a Hindu identity. (Analogous claims are made on the Muslim side.) Nativists often support their attack on human rights norms by holding that Indian values are radically different from Western values. I have extensively criticized this position. . .

Secular humanism is deeply appealing to feminists, since there is no doubt that the world's major religions, in their actual historical form, have been unjust to women both theoretically and practically. In contemporary politics, religious groups have frequently had a pernicious influence on women's lives, as our three cases from India suggest. It is indeed very tempting to say, fine, let religion exist, but let it clean up its act like anything else, bringing its own norms and conduct into line with a basic set of international moral standards, without receiving any special protections from the state.[18] When religion is clearly doing wrong, this position seems sensible. This was, it seems, the position of Chief Justice Chandrachud in the Shah Bano case, when he called for an end to state protection for religious courts.[19]

There are deep pragmatic difficulties with secular humanism, as the Shah Bano case shows us. It is rash and usually counterproductive to approach religious people with a set of apparently external moral demands, telling them that these norms are better than the norms of their religion. In the Indian situation it was bad enough when the demands were made by Hindus to Hindus; but when similar demands were made by Hindus to Muslims, they were read, to some extent correctly, as both insulting and threatening, showing a lack of respect for the autonomy of a minority cultural and religious tradition. Today, such demands are all the more clearly threatening, since the call for reform of Muslim personal law has been taken up as a rallying cry by Hindu nationalist forces, eager to portray Hinduism as enlightened toward women, and Islam as backward and oppressive. Although the goal of a uniform code continues to be backed by many feminist and otherwise progressive thinkers, in practice it is so prominent a part of the goals of Hindu fundamentalism that it is difficult to dissociate it from the idea of Hindu supremacy and a relegation of Muslim citizens to second-class status.

A related pragmatic error of the secular humanist is to fail to pursue alliances with feminist forces within each religious tradition. Religious traditions have indeed been powerful sources of oppression for women; but they have also been powerful sources of protection for human rights, of commitment to justice, and of energy for social change. For example, they have been primary sources of US abolitionism and of the more recent civil rights movement, and in India they have been primary sources of the Gandhian anticolonialism and of the contemporary Gandhian SEWA movement.[20] Muslim feminists like Heera Nawaz find ideas of justice in their religion important sources of empowerment. By announcing that she wants nothing to do with religion, or even (in the milder cases) by announcing that religion will be respected only insofar as it lives up to a comprehensive liberal view of life, the secular humanist dooms herself to a lonely and less-than-promising struggle, and insults many people who would otherwise be her allies. In the Indian context especially, secularist grassroots politics has had a hard time capturing people's imaginations. By ceding religion's moral authority and all its energy of symbol and metaphor to the side of patriarchy, or even (in the milder cases) by insisting that religions be feminist or liberal in all respects, the secularist further compromises her own political goals. Finally, she abandons the terrain of argument on which she is strongest, namely sex equality, and wades into contentious metaphysical issues. Why do this, when she doesn't need to?

But the difficulties with secular humanism are not merely pragmatic and political. Three arguments cast doubt upon it at a deeper level. First is an argument from the *intrinsic value of religious capabilities*. The liberty of religious belief, membership, and activity is among the central human capabilities. Because the religious capabilities have multiple aspects, I have included them among the capabilities of the senses, imagination, and thought, and also in the category of affiliation. This strategy reflects my view that religion is one extremely important way of pursuing these general capability goals, but not the only one that deserves protection.[21] I do insist, however, that it is among the specifications of these general capability goals that it is most important to protect for political purposes. To be able to search for an understanding of the ultimate meaning of life in one's own way is among the most important aspects of a life that is truly human. One of the ways in which this has most frequently been done historically is through religious belief and practice; to burden these practices is thus to inhibit many people's search for the ultimate good. Religion has also been intimately and fruitfully bound up with other human capabilities, such as the capabilities of artistic, ethical,

and intellectual expression. It has been a central locus of the moral education of the young, both in the family and in the larger community. Finally, it has typically been a central vehicle of cultural continuity, hence an invaluable support for other forms of human affiliation and interaction. To strike at religion is thus to risk eviscerating people's moral, cultural, and artistic, as well as spiritual, lives. Even if substitute forms of expression and activity are available in and through the secular state, a state that deprives citizens of the option to pursue religion has done them a grave wrong in these important areas.

For political purposes, the capabilities approach aims at religious capability or opportunity, rather than religious functioning, in order to leave to citizens the choice whether to pursue the pertinent human functions at all, and whether to pursue them through religion or through secular activity. For political purposes, then, the liberal state, as I envisage it, takes the position that citizens may reasonably pursue both religious and nonreligious conceptions of the good – or no definite conception. But the very fact that we insist that religious forms of these capabilities are among the specifications that must be defended for all citizens involves the recognition that religious functioning has had in many cases high intrinsic value: religious conceptions of value are among the reasonable ones that we are determined to make room for, as expressions of human powers.

Because religion is so important to people, such a major source of identity, there is also a strong argument from *respect for persons* that supplements these considerations of intrinsic value. When we tell people that they cannot define the ultimate meaning of life in their own way – even if we are sure we are right, and that their way is not a very good way – we do not show full respect for them as persons. In that sense, the secular humanist view is at bottom quite illiberal. It is precisely this consideration that led me to prefer *political liberalism* to *comprehensive liberalism*; the secular humanist view is a form of comprehensive liberalism. Obviously no state can allow its citizens to search for the ultimate meaning of life in any way they wish, especially when that way involves harm to others. But secular humanism frequently errs in the opposite direction, taking a dismissive and disrespectful stance toward religion even when no question of harm has arisen. Even if such a position were correct, even if a certain group of religious beliefs (or even all beliefs) were nothing more than retrograde superstition, we would not be respecting the autonomy of our fellow citizens if we did not allow them these avenues of inquiry and self-determination. As Roman Catholic thinker Jacques Maritain expressed the point:

> There is real and genuine tolerance only when a man is firmly and absolutely convinced of a truth, or of what he holds to be a truth, and when he at the same time recognizes the right of those who deny this truth to exist, and to contradict him, and to speak their own mind, not because they are free from truth but because they seek truth in their own way, and because he respects in them human nature and human dignity and those very resources and living springs of the intellect and of conscience which make them potentially capable of attaining the truth he loves, if someday they happen to see it.[22]

Frequently I sense that my fellow feminists do not sufficiently respect the "springs of conscience" in religious women (and men), when they treat religion dismissively, as a mere "opiate of the masses."

Finally, there is an argument from the *internal diversity of the religions.* Secular humanists who marginalize religion tend to treat religion as an enemy of women's progress. In so doing, they make a most unfortunate concession to their traditionalist opponents: they agree in defining religion as equivalent to certain reactionary, often highly patriarchal, voices.[23] This, as I have already said, is a pragmatic error: the humanist feminist thus alienates people who could become some of her most influential allies, by indicating that she considers their whole enterprise of effecting change (or a return to better earlier norms) within their religious traditions a silly waste of time. Sometimes she even reveals ignorance of the very existence of such contesting voices.[24] But her error is also a theoretical error about what a religious tradition is. I have criticized the error of treating cultures as homogeneous, neglecting internal diversity and conflict. The same point can be made at least as emphatically about religious traditions. No religious tradition consists simply of authority and sheeplike subservience. All contain argument, diversity of beliefs and practices, and a plurality of voices – including the voices of women, which have not always been clearly heard. All, further, are dynamic: because they involve a committed search for ultimate meaning, they shift in at least some ways in response to participants' changing views of meaning; and because they are forms of communal organization, they shift in response to their members' judgments about the sort of community in which they want to live.[25] What counts as Jewish, or Muslim, or Christian is not in any simple way read off from the past: although traditions vary in the degree and nature of their dynamism, they are defined at least in some ways by where their members want to go.

Thus any account of Judaism that fails to include the fact that Reform and Reconstructionist congregations address God as "you" rather than "he," and acknowledge the (four) mothers alongside the (three) fathers, is a false account of what the Jewish tradition is.[26] By this argument, secular-humanist feminists are giving a false account of Judaism when they call it inherently patriarchal; equally false is the account given by political forces in Israel that would refuse recognition to non-Orthodox branches of Judaism.[27] Any account of the Roman Catholic tradition that treats it as in principle anti-Semitic neglects a recent evolution in doctrine prompted by statements and actions of the current Pope. Jews may have good historical reasons for doubting whether the leopard can change its spots, but they also should not be deaf to what is going on. A similar evolution may eventually take place with regard to women's role in the priesthood; many Catholics support such a change. Such changes, of course, have already been made in most major Protestant denominations.[28] Any account of the Hindu tradition that holds that Rama is the one central divinity, or that Hinduism is in principle inseparable from the tradition of misogyny exemplified by the *Laws of Manu*, is again a false account, one that neglects the tremendous regional, temporal, and ideological diversity that has always obtained within Hinduism – including the deep religious commitments of campaigners for sex equality such as Rammohun Roy in the eighteenth century, Rabindranath Tagore in the early twentieth century, and Ela Bhatt of our own generation, all of whom have understood themselves to be representing an authentic Hinduism, freed from historical and cultural distortions.[29] Any account of Islam that holds it to be essentially and irredeemably misogynistic once again confuses fundamentalist voices (which frequently purvey their own highly synthetic accounts of tradition) with the whole of the tradition, and displays considerable ignorance about the texts (for example, about the fact that equal inheritance for women was secured by a return to the Quran from less authoritative interpretations, and that both Quran and Hadith regard men and women as sharing a single essential nature).[30]

Such ignorance is offensive to fellow citizens, and is objectionable for that reason alone – but it is also simply bad to be wrong!

If secular humanism has these practical and theoretical problems, how does traditionalist feminism fare? Interestingly enough, it suffers from very similar problems. In practical terms, as we shall soon see in more detail, it is highly divisive to neglect critical and dissenting voices within a religious tradition, equating it with its most patriarchal elements[31] and failing to acknowledge each tradition's dynamic character. Such ways of thinking about both Islam and Hinduism are implicated in the current bad state of group relations in India; narrow and static representations of tradition by the members of the traditions themselves are at least as much to blame for this as are ignorant representations by outsiders. Similarly, traditionalists about women's role have made the pragmatic political error of dividing where they could fruitfully pursue alliances, since feminists of all stripes share certain common goals in the area of material well-being.

In the theoretical domain too, similar problems can be identified. The traditionalist feminist seems to slight the intrinsic value of women's religious capabilities just as much as does the secular humanist, refusing to acknowledge the many ways people search for religious meanings outside the most patriarchal[32] element of a tradition. The ultraorthodox in Israel slight the intrinsic value of religious capabilities when they deny Conservative and Reform Jews the free exercise of their religion in areas such as marriage, divorce, and conversion; in similar ways, traditionalist Hindu, Islamic, and Christian authorities slight the value of dissident types of functioning in their own traditions, defining their way as the only legitimate way. This error is not only an assault on intrinsic value, it is also very much an assault on one's fellow citizens, who ought to be respected when they search for the good in their own ways, even when one holds, as fundamentalists typically do, that critical ways are erroneous departures from the correct way. Finally, it is evident that these traditionalists are frequently engaged in massive simplifications and rewritings of their own traditions, which distort and deform tradition and history by denying both diversity and dynamism, just as surely as do secularist feminists' misreadings.

The traditionalist view has one further difficulty that does not appear to be present in the secular humanist view. Namely, in at least some of its political forms, it rides roughshod over other human capabilities, giving religion (tendentiously interpreted) broad latitude to determine a woman's quality of life, even when that threatens not only dignity and equality, but also health, the wherewithal to live, and bodily integrity. The secular humanist is at least motivated by an admirable goal: to guarantee to women the full range of rights and capabilities, including both those already on the agenda for men and those that involve women's freedom from gender-specific abuses. I have argued that in the process, she slights a very important range of concerns related to religious capabilities and respect for persons; but she does so, often, without fully recognizing this fact, and with an eye to promoting women's equal citizenship. I don't think there is anything so positive to be said about the motives lying behind traditionalism, where women are concerned. It is rare to find a serious argument to the effect that a certain type of harm or inequality toward women is required, as such, by the spiritual or moral values inherent in a religious tradition. It was not argued that unequal inheritance rights for Mary Roy were a noble goal, essential to Christian worship; that polygamy and child marriage were of the essence of Hindu spiritual values; or that the failure to pay a monthly maintenance to Shah Bano was a

high moment in Islam. Usually, instead, even the overt arguments of traditionalists allude to the value of preserving the power of traditional religious courts of law and traditional religious authorities – a value far more dubious in moral terms than the value of the basic human capabilities. And frequently their arguments have the paradoxical result of allowing women to suffer discrimination in regard to property rights, or maintenance, or whatever, just because they happen to be members of that particular religion – surely a dubious way of showing respect for the moral values inherent in that tradition. At some point we must draw the line and deny that these approaches deserve the title "feminist" at all; that point is surely reached when not even a show is made of defending the traditional norms as supportive of women's interests. Insofar as serious moral argument is made, it is most commonly indirect, alleging that the power of traditional authorities or courts is necessary for the maintenance of other valuable aspects of tradition.[33] But such claims are empirical, and should be tested.

III Two Orienting Principles

Any adequate approach to the dilemma must, then, begin by treating it as a real dilemma, acknowledging the weight of the values on both sides. I have argued that it must respect the intrinsic value of religious capabilities and of religious women and men as choosers of a way of life (a basic commitment of political liberalism), while at the same time taking just as seriously the importance of the full range of the human capabilities that are sometimes at risk for women in traditional religious cultures. Finally, it must understand and respect the plurality and diversity of voices in each religious tradition, both traditional and critical, both female and male. This entails being skeptical from the start of any account that fails to recognize the complexity both of religion and of women's interests.

Two further principles now orient my approach. The first guiding principle has been with us from the start of this project: it is the *principle of each person as end*, reinterpreted as *a principle of each person's capability*. Like all the central capabilities, religious capabilities are capabilities of individual people, not, in the first instance, of groups. It is the person whose freedom of conscience and freedom of religious practice we should most fundamentally consider. Although religious functioning is usually relational and interactive (like political functioning and functioning in the family), and although it often involves shared goals and ends, the capabilities involved are important *for each*, and it is *each person* who should be allowed access to these capabilities. As with politics and the family, so here: an organic good for the group as group is unacceptable if it does not do good for the members taken one by one. Citizens of liberal democracies typically hold that not just some but *all* citizens should enjoy the political rights and liberties. The religious analogue is the idea that *all* (in the sense of *each and every one*)[34] should enjoy the liberty of conscience and religious exercise (and the other human capabilities). Thus, any solution that appears good for a religious group will have to be tested to see whether it does indeed promote the religious capabilities (and other capabilities) of the group's members, taken one by one. To subordinate the capabilities of some to the organic purposes of the whole is to violate people with respect to a capability that may lie at the heart of their lives.

I am emphatically not saying that all religious functioning, to be acceptable, must be individualistic, in the sense that the individual regards herself as an independent and self-willed member of the religious group. Such an account of religious functioning and capability would obviously leave out many of the ways in which people search for the good by subordinating themselves to authority or hierarchy, or by aligning themselves with the purposes of a corporate body. What is ruled out by the type of focus on the person for which I have argued is any approach that seeks a good for Hinduism or Judaism, let us say, by denying the liberty of conscience of individual Hindus or Jews. Israel's failure to give legal recognition to Reform and Conservative Judaism, for example, violates this principle: for it says, for the sake of a strong Judaism let us forbid individual Jews to worship in their own way, where marriage, conversion, and divorce are concerned. Whether this is indeed conducive to a strong Judaism may be doubted; but it certainly runs afoul of my principle.[35] So does the failure of the Indian system generally to allow individuals free egress from one religious tradition into another, given the impossibility of extricating ancestral property from the system of personal law into which one is born.

A good way of thinking of the type of focus on the individual person in religious matters that I am proposing is to think of the twin US constitutional principles of non-establishment and free exercise. The motivation behind the establishment clause is to prevent citizens from being violated in conscience and practice by the pressures of a dominant religious group backed by political and legal power; the motivation behind the free exercise clause is to prevent belief and worship from being impeded or burdened by public action. The history of these clauses is notoriously difficult and tortuous. At times they have appeared to be on a collision course with one another; at other times it is difficult to separate the strands of argument that the two clauses suggest. But in the most abstract terms we can say that together they aim at a regime in which each citizen's liberty of conscience is preserved inviolate, despite the pressures that corporate bodies of various types, whether religious or secular, may bring to bear. As we shall see, this tradition has been cognizant of the fact that one way of denying individuals the free exercise of their religion would be to destroy a group or tradition of which that person is a member; so group values do enter into the equation.[36] But they are not considered to be ends in their own right, and certainly they are not permitted to trump the value of the individual person's conscience.

My second orienting principle is one that I shall call *the principle of moral constraint*. Religion is given a high degree of deference and protection in many constitutional conceptions, as it will be in mine. One reason for this deference is surely that religion is extremely important to religious people, as a way of searching for the ultimate good. But another important part of this deference involves the role religions play in transmitting and fostering moral views of the conduct of life. As Heera Nawaz says: the major religions are all, at their heart, concerned with the conduct of life, and all the major traditions can plausibly be seen as attempts to reform or improve the conduct of life. Furthermore, it would not be too bold to add that all the major religions embody an idea of compassion for human suffering, and an idea that it is wrong for innocent people to suffer. All, finally, embody some kind of a notion of justice. This doesn't mean that religions do not concern many other things, such as faith and ritual practice and celebration and pleasure and contemplation; but at least a part of what they are about is moral.

When we give deference to religion in politics, we do not do so simply because of the moral role of the religion; nor need the political liberal assert that this moral role is the central object of the state's interest. To say such things would involve an unacceptably paternalistic stance toward religious traditions and what is central in them. We may and do, however, judge that any cult or so-called religion that diverges too far from the shared moral understanding that is embodied in the core of the political conception does not deserve the honorific name of religion. Thus US law has persistently refused to give religious status to satanist cults and other related groups. Controversies over Scientology have a similar character: insofar as states judge that this organization is really a shady con game, they refuse to give it the honorific status of religion. Comprehensive ethical or political views do not suffice to constitute a religion under US law; I shall express my own unease about this situation below. But systematic views of the conduct of life that are nontraditional, and in the end rather hard to distinguish from comprehensive ethical views, have been granted religious status in two draft board cases.[37] It has been explicitly stated that belief in a deity is not required: otherwise Buddhism and Taoism would not be protected, as they clearly are. A moral constraint is applied, then, to the definition of what counts as religion when we protect religion.

Furthermore – what interests me here – such a constraint is also applied to state protection of the recognized religions. Even when a group clearly counts as a religion, we sometimes judge that it forfeits its claim to state deference when it goes outside of certain moral understandings, especially those that are protected in the core of the basic constitutional conception. Thus US constitutional law has consistently denied that expressions of racial segregation or hierarchy are legitimate prerogatives of religion as such, when the state gives religion special tax benefits.[38] The Indian Constitution made a similar move when it offered religion protection similar to that given it under the US Constitution, and yet made untouchability illegal; Hinduism is protected only within moral constraints supplied by the core constitutional understanding of the equal worth of citizens. Laws against *sati* express a similar idea.

In keeping with the idea of political principles, we understand the moral constraints in terms of the list of central capabilities, in the following way. We should refuse to give deference to religion when its practices harm people in the areas covered by the major capabilities. Obviously problematic will be practices involving harm to nonmembers of the religion (e.g., a refusal by Hindus of a certain caste to allow any woman to go outside because their own caste norms forbid that); but practices involving harms to coreligionists will also be problematic, where they significantly infringe a central capability – particularly where there is reason to doubt the voluntariness of the practice.[39] (Such problems are especially grave when there are reasons to suppose that individual members do not have the opportunity to leave the religion should they disapprove of it.) Thus refusals by Hindus to allow Hindu women to go outside to work will also get critical scrutiny, especially when we feel that women are under duress and threat in this matter, and also when we have doubts about their opportunity to define themselves as non-Hindu should they wish to.

Formally and in the core of the political conception, the *principle of moral constraint* says nothing about matters internal to the religion itself. Political liberalism prevents this: the public political conception should take no stand on disputed issues of the good outside the core of the constitutional principles. But the principle of moral constraint has an informal social corollary, which members of the religion may use in discourse with one another, and which may also be used across religious lines in informal social deliberation. One of our greatest problems, in talking about the prerogatives of religious actors and groups, is to decide when there is a legitimate religious issue on the table, and when the issue is, instead, cultural or

political. Religions are intertwined in complex ways with politics and culture. Even when a religion is based on a set of authoritative texts, culture and politics enter into the interpretation of texts and the institutionalized form of traditional practice. Jews differ about where to draw the line between what is genuinely religious in the tradition and what is the work of specific contextual and historical shaping. Similar debates arise in Christianity and Islam. In all cases, many interpreters are inclined to regard at least a part of the tradition or even the text as a historical or cultural artifact, expressive of human ideas of the good at a particular time, but not binding without translation for our time.[40] Where Hinduism is concerned, the absence of scriptural authority makes it all the more difficult, if not virtually impossible, to identify a necessary religious core distinct from layers of history and culture, all powerfully infused with imperfect people's desire for political power.

When, then, we are thinking of curtailing some activity highly desired by some religious actor or actors speaking in the name of religion, it is useful to determine whether they are *really* speaking religiously, accurately understanding the core of that religion, or just going all out for political power. But it is more than just difficult to discover this; sometimes there may be no determinate answer to be discovered. Judges are not well qualified to judge in such matters, and in general they are rightly deferential to the claims of religious actors about what a legitimate claim of free exercise in their religion is.[41] They properly stick to a strictly limited *political use* of the *principle of moral constraint*. But in more informal social discourse it is sometimes important to take a stand. Do the Christians have a case that Mary Roy's inheritance claim jeopardizes Christian worship, or is this simply a ploy on the part of church leaders to keep tax revenue? Do Nehru's and Ambedkar's opponents have superior insight into the essence of Hinduism, or are they just trying to shore up power of religious courts?

The *social version* of the principle allows us to go further in commenting on these questions. It suggests that when we assess such debates we should be skeptical of any element that seems prima facie cruel or unjust – again, especially in the area of the central capabilities. But now, in addition to saying that we may not give such elements state deference, we press the question whether that element really is central to the religion. You say that your religion is dedicated to the good, we argue. But this is so patently bad that it seems dubious that it can really be a part of the religion, as we understand its central purpose.

This social principle would strike me as a valuable one even if major religions had not endorsed it. But it clearly has deep roots in Indian religious history, as well as in the West. When the emperor Ashoka (a convert to Buddhism who reigned during the third century BC) saw acts of religious intolerance being carried out in the name of religion, he invoked the principle of moral constraint in order to conclude that damage to other religions is simply not a way of expressing or exalting one's own:

> . . . the sects of other people all deserve reverence for one reason or another. By thus acting, a man exalts his own sect, and at the same time does service to the sects of other people. By acting contrariwise, a man hurts his own sect, and does disservice to the sects of other people. For he who does reverence to his own sect while disparaging the sects of others wholly from attachment to his own, with intent to enhance the splendour of his own sect, in reality by such conduct inflicts the severest injury on his own sect.[42]

In other words, no matter what religious actors say about their conduct, we may conclude that they are in error about what religion requires: acts of intolerant harm damage, and do not express or glorify, one's own religion, Hindu or Buddhist. Had he been a state actor in a political-liberal state, Ashoka would have been well advised to speak in a more restrained way, simply saying that when people behave this way they forfeit a claim to state protection. But his informal social use of the stronger social version of the principle is highly effective.

A similar appeal to the principle of moral constraint was made by US President Abraham Lincoln, in his second inaugural address, delivered at the end of the Civil War. Speaking of the fact that both (former) slaveholders and abolitionists think of themselves as Christian and their cause as a Christian cause, he commented:

> Both read the same Bible, and pray to the same God; and each invokes His aid against the other. It may seem strange that any men should dare to ask a just God's assistance in wringing their bread from the sweat of other men's faces; but let us judge not that we be not judged.[43]

Lincoln, like Ashoka, says in effect: whatever they think about the religious character of their acts, if the acts are unjust we must be highly skeptical. The idea that God is just lies behind and constrains more specific ideas of what God does and does not endorse. That God is really a backer of slavery is highly implausible.[44] Again, US courts speak more agnostically, simply saying that segregationists lose a claim to state protection in tax matters; but Lincoln's use of the stronger form of the principle is valuable, when religion is being invoked to back evil. For a Christian leader to say that slavery is anti-Christian does not seem to exceed the boundaries of public reason.

Moral constraint arguments naturally arise in the context of women's livelihood. A young wife in Bangladesh, told by local mullahs that religion forbade her to work in the fields alongside men, said that if Allah really was requiring them to stay hungry, then "Allah has sinned." She meant, of course, to express skepticism about the mullah's interpretation. Her view of her religion was that a just and good God would not permit women to starve simply on the ground that it seems to some men improper for a woman to go out of the house. A just God, presumably, would let her gain her livelihood and ask men to conduct themselves modestly toward her (as the Quran, in any case, explicitly requires).[45] Since Allah, by definition, does not sin, then any statement that implies that he does sin must be false. In general, this is the style of argument feminists in all religions have typically used to bring about change: if we're agreed that God is just and good, and if we can show you that a certain form of conduct is egregiously bad, then it follows that this conduct does not lie at the heart of religion, and must be a form of human error, which can be remedied while leaving religion itself intact. Again, it was a bad idea for the Chief Justice to say something like this; in his judicial role, especially as a Hindu, he should have confined himself to the more restricted political version of the principle. But these women, speaking socially and within their own religion, make a powerful use of its stronger social version.

Such arguments are common in both the Hindu and Muslim traditions in India, where women's issues are concerned. Nineteenth-century Bengali reformers Rammohun Roy and Iswarchandra Vidyasagar, campaigning against *sati*, child marriage, and polygamy, based their campaign on a recalling of Hindu tradition to its moral core. Similar moral arguments about Muslim conceptions of modesty are made by reformers, such as Rokeya Sakhawat Hossain, who challenge the seclusion of women from within religious orthodoxy, by pointing to its morally

objectionable consequences as well as its non-necessity for truly moral conduct.[46] The Indian Constitution uses the more restricted political version of the principle, as seems appropriate for basic constitutional matters in a pluralistic democracy. It makes no pronouncements about what Hinduism is or is not, it simply makes untouchability illegal. But moral constraint arguments do valuable work socially, in connection with such constitutional reforms.

To invoke the social version of the principle of moral constraint, we need not deny that a given form of immorality may at one time have been absolutely central to the beliefs and practices of the religion. It would be foolish, for example, to deny that the subordination of women was central in many religions at many times, that the caste system was a core feature of Hinduism, that racial hierarchy was a prominent feature of the Church of Jesus Christ of Latter-day Saints,[47] and so forth. What we are saying is that what makes religion worthy of a special place in human life (and of special political and legal treatment) is something having to do with ideals and aspirations, something that remains alive even when formerly core understandings shift in the light of moral debate, and indeed, something that guides that evolution. In the following section I shall focus on the narrower political use of the principle. But we shall later see that the informal social version of the principle does valuable work in guiding debate in a time of religious upheaval.

IV   Central Capabilities as Compelling State Interests

Let me recapitulate. We have two constraints that limit interference with religion: respect for the intrinsic value of religious capabilities, and respect for religious people as citizens. Next, we have a constraint that pushes the other way, toward at least some scrutiny of religion and religious actors: respect for the other central human capabilities. Next, we have two orienting principles: the principle of each person's capability, and the principle of moral constraint, interpreted in terms of the central capabilities. And finally, we have a fact that both secular humanists and traditionalists generally neglect, the internal diversity and plurality of the religions themselves. I shall now describe the approach that I would favor, arguing that it does not violate the constraints and is a good way to follow the guidance of the orienting principles. I shall then show how it would handle each of the three problem cases.

This proposal is conceived of as a good idea, not necessarily as the best reading of any particular constitutional tradition. It draws on ideas in US law, and it is very easy to adapt to the Indian constitutional tradition, which in most cases draws heavily on US constitutional jurisprudence for precedents involving the interpretation of fundamental rights. But obviously, interpreting a particular constitutional tradition involves asking question other than whether something is a good idea, questions about precedent, text, history, and institutional competence. I have not attempted that larger task here.

My approach is modeled on the United Stated Religious Freedom Restoration Act of 1993 (RFRA). This act prohibits any agency, department, or official of the United States, or of any state, from "substantially burden[ing] a person's exercise of religion even if the burden results from a rule of general applicability," unless the government can demonstrate that this burden "(1) is in furtherance of a compelling government interest; and (2) is the least restrictive means of furthering that compelling governmental interest."

We now need some background on the origin and current status of this law, in order to see how it grew out of a concern for the protection of minority religions, a central concern in my own argument. For some years there had been an issue, in First Amendment jurisprudence, about how far laws "of general applicability" might be upheld against a religious group or religious individuals, when those individuals claim that the law imposes a "substantial burden" on their exercise of their religion. For quite a few years, the legal situation was, theoretically at least, more or less as RFRA later reestablished it: the Supreme Court consistently held that laws of general applicability might impose a substantial burden on an individual's free exercise of religion only if the law furthered a compelling state interest, and in the least burdensome manner possible. The governing case was *Sherbert v. Verner* (1963).[48] A South Carolina woman refused to work on Saturday, because her Seventh-Day Adventist beliefs forbade it. After being fired, she was also refused state unemployment benefits on the grounds that she had refused suitable employment. She claimed that the state had violated her religious free exercise; the US Supreme Court agreed. The Court held that to attach to a benefit a condition that required violation of a religious duty did impose a substantial burden on her free exercise of her religion; the problem was compounded, the Court held, by the discriminatory impact of the benefits laws on workers who celebrate the Sabbath on Saturday. Under the regime established by *Sherbert*, other laws of general applicability were also found to violate religious free exercise; notable in this regard is the case of compulsory public education of Amish children in *Wisconsin v. Yoder*.[49]

In 1990, however, the Supreme Court changed course with its decision in *Employment Division v. Smith*.[50] Significantly, this case involved an unpopular minority religion and the threatening topic of legalized drug use.[51] The case concerned native American tribes in the state of Oregon, who claimed that it was essential to their religion to use peyote in a particular ceremony, and thus claimed exemption (not generally, but in this one ceremonial instance) from the drug laws of the state of Oregon.[52] The sincerity of their religious claim was not disputed, nor the centrality of the peyote ceremony to their religion.[53] In a lengthy opinion by Justice Scalia, the court held that the free exercise clause did not protect the plaintiffs, since "[w]e have never held that an individual's religious beliefs excuse him from compliance with an otherwise valid law prohibiting conduct that the State is free to regulate." The Court explicitly rejected the "compelling government interest" requirement, as making the lawmakers' job far too difficult.[54] The dissenters, however, emphasized the danger of disfavoring minority religions,[55] and invoked the Founders' interest in securing "the widest possible toleration of conflicting views." Justice O'Connor, who joined this part of the dissenting opinion, concluded: "The compelling interest test reflects the First Amendment's mandate of preserving religious liberty to the fullest extent possible in a pluralistic society. For the Court to deem this command a 'luxury,' is to denigrate "[t]he very purpose of a Bill of Rights." This is an important moment for my approach, because the need to protect minority religions is my central reason for favoring the ample protection of RFRA to the regime inaugurated by *Smith*.

The decision generated public outrage.[56] RFRA was passed in 1993 by an overwhelming bipartisan majority in both houses, and signed into law by President Clinton.[57] It was declared unconstitutional in June 1997, on grounds relating to the scope of Congress's powers under the Fourteenth Amendment.[58] The principle involved in RFRA continues to enjoy strong support, including, it would appear, the support of a vast majority of the American people. The unresolved issue is how to translate this support into law, and,

in particular, how to resolve the thorny issues of institutional competence raised by the clash between the legislative and judicial branches. Since I believe that each nation must resolve those particular issues on its own, in the light of its own traditions and constitution, I make no suggestion on that aspect of the issue here.

My own RFRA-based proposal has two parts: first, that the principle of RFRA be accepted as the guiding principle in dealing with the religious dilemma. The state and its agents may impose a substantial burden on religion only when it can show a compelling interest. *But*, second, protection of the central capabilities of citizens should always be understood to ground a compelling state interest: this is the way we interpret the principle of moral constraint and give content to the otherwise vague and amorphous notion of "compelling state interest."[59] In legal terms, I have suggested that the central capabilities are like a list of fundamental rights that might be embodied in constitutional guarantees. Many of them are already so embodied in the Indian Constitution, and in other constitutions around the world; others are embodied in human rights instruments that most of the nations under discussion have endorsed; still others are embodied in legal precedents through which Indian constitutional law has incorporated considerations of bodily integrity into its jurisprudence. So my proposal is meant as a set of moral guidelines that could in many respects be legally implemented under existing law.

On this principle, *Smith* ought to come out the other way. No compelling government interest was established in the case as argued, nor would thinking about the central capabilities help us to make a stronger argument than was in fact made. One might point to the parallel Indian case of the legalization of marijuana use during Holi, the Hindu spring festival: it seems just right to say that there is no compelling government interest in forbidding this festival use, and that forbidding it would impose a substantial burden on Hindu religion. (It is obvious, indeed, that Holi raises a far more serious issue for public order than the Native American ceremony, to put it mildly: for when a majority of the population is getting stoned, that can and has led to rioting and looting. Nonetheless, the Indian government is correct, in my view, to tolerate this exception and to focus on controlling disorder.) Other areas in which this principle would support an exemption would include the wearing of yarmulkes in the military,[60] the wearing of religious jewelry in prisons,[61] and reasonable accommodation of the religious dietary needs of prisoners.[62] On the other hand, a case like *Bob Jones*[63] would come out as it did: the government's interest in eradicating humiliating and stigmatizing racial discrimination would count as a compelling interest, in connection with the account of the central capabilities. Later, after I have discussed my Indian cases of sex discrimination, I shall say more about what latitude a religion might have for engaging in forms of sex discrimination internal to that religion; but *Bob Jones* already gives us one paradigm to employ: the government must not give favorable treatment to practices that humiliate and stigmatize individuals on account of their sex, especially where the voluntariness of the individuals' participation in those practices is far from certain.[64] I have already argued that such forms of discrimination are straightforward cases of capability failure, in that they compromise the social bases of dignity and non-humiliation.

I do not at all neglect the difficulty of appropriately specifying the level of each capability, but I think that this difficulty obtains in any constitutional tradition when we are trying to hammer out the best account of basic rights and liberties and say when a substantial burden has been applied to one of them. The best way to fix the boundaries

more precisely is an incremental way, relying on cases to enlarge our understanding of what we want to say. As I have already stated, I remain agnostic about the proper role of the legislature and the judiciary in this evolution; the resolution of such institutional questions depends on contextual features about the nature of democratic traditions in each nation.

This two-part approach seems to do well by the guidelines I have set out. It respects religious citizens and the intrinsic value of religious capabilities, by imposing a taxing standard on the state in any case of state action that would substantially burden religious free exercise. It also respects the claims of the other human capabilities, giving them a central place in the account of potential limits on religious freedom. It respects the principle of each person's capability by framing the question as that of when government may legitimately burden citizens' free exercise of their religion; it remains to be seen precisely how interference with religious leaders and the authority of religious courts may be related to such burdens. Finally, it obeys the principle of moral constraint, by saying that when a religion does violate a central human capability (whether religious or nonreligious) we will not give religion the deference that is usually due to it.

The most powerful objection to my approach will come from the side of Justice Scalia and the *Smith* opinion. Scalia's claim is that we give too much latitude to religion when we allow it to be a ground for the violation of otherwise valid laws of general applicability, even in the absence of a "compelling state interest." A public law that is neutral (that applies similarly to all the religions and to the nonreligious) and that has a rational basis, should be obeyed by all citizens, no matter what their religious convictions. Otherwise, Scalia argues, we will face a flood of claims for exemption to the law, and it will be beyond the capacity of judges to sort these out in a way compatible with public consistency and order. Insofar as Scalia's argument rests purely on an issue of institutional competence (he does not, for example, object to the granting of exemptions by individual state legislatures), I have no general disagreement with it; for I have said that questions of institutional division of labor must be settled by each separate constitutional tradition as it evolves. Insofar as the argument rests on more general concerns about arbitrariness of judgment, and on a general view that laws of general applicability should be exceptionless, I believe that it is insufficiently protective of religion, especially of minority religion. But his argument raises important concerns, which must be faced by any proposal in this area. By offering a clear account of "compelling government interest," my capability-based account of what constitutes a "compelling state interest" goes some way, I think, toward reducing the dangers about which he worries. If, however, we can show that even my very generous account of the role of religion still renders unacceptable many actions taken by the religions in the context of sex equality, we will also have shown, a fortiori, that such actions are unacceptable by the more stringent Scalia test.

We now face an important issue: does the approach require equality in basic capabilities, or only a basic minimum threshold? In other words, does sex discrimination with respect to the basic capabilities trigger a claim of compelling state interest, or only discrimination that pushes women into a situation of destitution or extreme capability failure? Let's try to get at this by looking at things in the other direction. Typically, the state has been held to impose a substantial burden on religion when it treats members of one religious group unequally. The plaintiff in *Sherbert v. Verner* was losing a benefit that the state might not have offered at all; but the holding was that, so long as it does offer such benefits, to condition them on a

practice that violates some people's religious freedom is to impose a substantial burden on the free exercise of religion. Forcing her to choose between the exercise of her religion and forfeiting benefits was said to be equivalent to fining someone for Saturday worship – a practice that would be unacceptable no matter how small the fine and no matter how great the individual's ability to pay. The inequality of treatment is itself a violation; to make X jump through hoops that Y is not forced to jump through, on account of X's religion, is ipso facto to burden the exercise of that religion. (It may also involve an establishment clause issue, although that was not the way *Sherbert* was argued.) So too, I think we should say, with the capabilities on the other side. The very singling out of women for differential treatment in a central area of human functioning is itself unacceptable, and gives rise to a compelling state interest in eradicating that discrimination, even if women are not by this means pushed into a basement level of functioning. Here we have the Indian Constitution on our side, since, unlike the US Constitution, it contains an explicit provision of nondiscrimination on the basis of sex, listing this among the fundamental rights of citizens. Moreover, as with race, any discrimination that stigmatizes and humiliates is ipso facto a case of capability failure: so even outside the domain of the other capabilities there will be little scope for permissible discrimination, although I shall argue below that some choices internal to the religion should still be protected.

V Nonreligion, Establishment, Balancing

Finally, my RFRA-based approach faces three very difficult questions. First, should religion be singled out for specially protective treatment, or should the same protections apply to all other expressive or ultimate-truth-pursuing activities? In framing and commenting on my list of the central capabilities, I have already suggested that religion is one of the ways in which people use thought and imagination in pursuit of an understanding of what is most important in life; it is also among the ways in which people pursue community and affiliation. But there are other ways, some involving comprehensive ethical views, some involving less systematic forms of personal search, some involving poetry, music, and the other arts. It seems difficult to distinguish religious belief-systems from the nonreligious beliefs and practices in any principled and systematic way. The features that make religion worthy of deference are frequently found in nonreligious belief-systems and practices. Moreover, even if one were to argue that religion is to be preferred not because of its role in people's search for meaning and community, but because it involves loyalty to a transcendent source of authority,[65] an argument I would not favor, this still would not yield a principled way of dividing what is conventionally called religion from what is conventionally called nonreligion: not all religions are theistic, Buddhism and Taoism being only two examples. One attractive feature of the *Smith* decision, for some of its supporters, is its fairness to nonreligious belief systems.[66] To accommodate religion and to reject a similar accommodation for Thoreau's philosophy[67] seems to many arbitrary and unfair.

US constitutional law has handled this question in a very complex and sometimes quite murky manner, through the twin principles of nonestablishment and free exercise. With respect to free exercise claims, religion is given special deference. But any privileging of religion over nonreligion can potentially trigger an establishment clause issue, and with respect to establishment issues, religion is in some respects more curtailed than nonreligion. Thus a public display honoring Thoreau would present no problem; such a display honoring Moses, or Jesus, would potentially raise an establishment issue. Government endorsement of environmentalism is appropriate; government endorsement of Christianity is not. The two clauses to some extent balance one another; thus, it has recently been argued that any free exercise exemption to laws of general applicability "offends Establishment Clause principles" and "connotes sponsorship and endorsement."[68] If we focus only on the free exercise side, however, we ought to feel uneasy when a religious capability is supported and another highly similar human capability is impeded. Since I shall recommend remaining neutral about establishment, this is an especially serious problem for my approach.

We have two distinct issues, a theoretical/moral issue and a practical issue. On the side of theory, there seems little to be said in favor of privileging religion over nonreligious beliefs and practices. A political-liberal political conception based on an idea of human capability should not play favorites among the comprehensive conceptions of the good citizens may reasonably hold; my approach reflects this by making religion one of the permissible ways of pursuing a wide variety of human capabilities, rather than a separate capability all its own, albeit one that is singled out on the list as deserving of protection for all citizens.

On the practical side, however, there are enormous difficulties involved in treating religious and nonreligious conceptions equally. Religion is usually organized and involves some publicly accepted body of doctrine or practice. It is not open to any and every believer to state ad hoc that a given law offends against his religion; however difficult such an inquiry may be, and however problematic an exercise of judicial faculties it may involve, such an inquiry must and frequently does take place. The Court in *Yoder* satisfied itself of the centrality of work in the Amish understanding of community; the Court in *Smith* granted the centrality of the peyote ceremony in Native American religious ceremonies. With nonreligion, such inquiries become absurdly taxing, and frequently they will yield no definite answer. If the belief system is comprehensive and textually based (as, for example, in the Thoreau case), things may not be too bad; but in many other perfectly legitimate cases the task of assessing the claim will be absurdly difficult, beyond the competence of any court or legislative body. If X says that his personal search for the meaning of life requires him to get stoned and listen to Mahler, he may be entirely sincere, and he may well have just as good a case morally as those who use drugs in a religious context; but ascertaining the centrality of this practice to his search for meaning will be virtually impossible, and granting exemptions in this way would quickly make a mockery of the drug laws, of mandatory military service, and many other laws of general applicability.

For some, these difficulties provide a strong reason to prefer *Smith*. Given that I continue to prefer to give religion a larger measure of deference, because of the pressing danger of disfavoring minority religions and their members, how do I propose to handle such problems? Tentatively, I believe that they can be handled in the following way. First, we confine the explicit area of potential exemptions to religion; but we allow religion to be somewhat broadly defined, including non-theistic belief systems such as the one that won Seeger his draft exemption.[69] It remains essential, however, to determine that the exercise of freedom of conscience is religion-like in having a systematic and non-arbitrary character; thus my Mahler fan, however sincere his practice, would still be excluded.

The disadvantage that would thereby be incurred by the nonreligious can at least to some extent be remedied by adopting strong protections for expressive speech and conduct. Thus, although the Mahler fan will not get an exemption from the drug laws, he can at least count on the protection of his right to listen to the music of his choice, to read the books of his choice, and so forth. By recognizing that the expressive interests involved in artistic and philosophical speech may be very religion-like, involving people's search for meaning and understanding, we give some account of why they should not be peripheral to the concerns of free speech jurisprudence.[70] But these subtleties take us rather far from our topic, since all of our Indian cases involve claims made by undisputed religions to exemptions from generally applicable laws involving sex equality.

Our second difficult question is, however, directly pertinent to the case of India. It is the question of religious establishment. I have presented my approach so far in terms of the concept of free exercise alone; I have argued that the central concern in the area of religion is that of religious capabilities, set over against the other capabilities of citizens. But I have also said that in the US case the *combination* of the free exercise clause and the establishment clause offered us a good way of thinking about what it would be to protect religious capabilities: the motivation behind the establishment clause is to prevent citizens from being violated in conscience and practice by the pressures of a dominant religious group with political and legal power behind it; the motivation behind the free exercise clause is to prevent belief and worship from being impeded or burdened by public action. Why, then, have I so far been silent about religious establishment? The answer emerges from the way I have interpreted the function of the establishment clause in the US setting: its function is to protect the capabilities of citizens. In other words, I understand nonestablishment as, at bottom, another way of shoring up free exercise, together with other capabilities of citizens. This approach suggests to me that it should be a contingent contextual question whether that protection is best accomplished through a regime of nonestablishment or through a regime of limited establishment with sufficient safeguards for citizen equality and free exercise. Given the specific history of intolerance toward minority religions, in the US it seems wise for the US to support a strong form of nonestablishment; only this regime, in the social context, guarantees all citizens a genuinely equal religious liberty. In the Scandinavian states, however, it seems plausible that the established Lutheran Churches actually protect religious pluralism more effectively than would a purely secular regime: they have been staunch defenders of religious pluralism in education, for example, and of other measures favorable to minorities. This is absolutely crucial to the case of India, because the existing regime of secularism in India involves a type of limited plural establishment: certain religions are entitled to maintain their own systems of civil law, and others (those too small or too new to have a codified system of personal law) use the secular system. In the next section I shall give this system a highly qualified type of support; given the history of Muslims in India, it seems apparent that any abolition of the system of Islamic law would be a grave threat to religious liberty and a statement that Muslims are not fully equal as citizens, and that even total nonestablishment would be de facto a type of Hindu establishment.

One might argue that any type of establishment puts minorities in a situation of indignity: in the public square a declaration is made that some believers are more privileged than others, even if the rights of others are duly protected. This is a grave point, which should not be dismissed. But I am inclined to think that this argument, too, must be assessed contextually. It is probably true of Britain, given Britain's history of anti-Semitism and xenophobia. But in India it would be disestablishment that would constitute a statement that Muslims were not fully equal citizens, absent a time of mutual respect and civic harmony, which may not come about in the foreseeable future. In the meantime, it seems to me that the totally nonestablished religions in India (Judaism, Buddhism) are not in grave difficulty because of their nonestablished status: in many ways they have an easier time than the others, since they simply go straight to the secular system, avoiding many difficult issues involving conflicts of laws.

In short: if the important issues underlying nonestablishment are really issues about both free exercise and full equality of citizens, it is plausible to suppose that, although nonestablishment is usually the best way of promoting those goals, this may not always be the case.

Finally, a deep methodological issue arises. I have said that the list of capabilities is a list of irreducibly distinct items, each of which is held by the public conception to be essential. We cannot make up for the removal of one by giving citizens more of another. When circumstances beyond the state's control force it to make such trade-offs, it should be acknowledged that a tragic event has occurred. Here, by contrast, I have favored a balancing test involving distinct capabilities, without suggesting that the choice need be tragic. Is this inconsistent with what I said about the list elsewhere?

I believe it is not. The cases I have mentioned all involve balancing above the threshold. So too, I believe, do the cases to be described later. Attention to the compelling interests represented by the other capabilities (for example, requiring equal property rights, or mobility, or even compulsory education) does not push the religious capabilities of citizens below the threshold. That is not to say that there could never be such a case – and yet even in *Wisconsin v. Yoder*, it was not maintained that survival of the religion required a totally unacceptable approach to education (for example, no secondary education), which would have triggered an overriding claim of compelling state interest. I recognize in section VIII below that there may be an element of tragedy in some cases using my approach; and yet, usually it is just not correct that protection of the other capabilities involves an unacceptable level of damage to a religious way of life. This is so, in part, because of the dynamic character of religious traditions, which have a way of evolving to meet the challenges of new situations.

Like any balancing test, mine requires a use of judgment in its application to the particular. Notions such as "compelling state interest" and "substantial burden" can certainly be given more definite content than they typically have been under US constitutional law – and I have attempted to make them more definite, through my use of the list of capabilities. Nonetheless, an irreducible element of judgment remains. To those who follow Rawls in wishing to have pure procedural solutions that involve no element of "intuitionism," the approach will therefore perhaps seem defective – even though balancing, here, occurs only at a later stage of political choice, after basic constitutional values are fixed. I can only say that this is indeed an issue worth pondering; but I can reply to the Rawlsian that it appears likely to be unavoidable in any plural list of the elements of the political good. Rawls's own list of primary goods is somewhat thinner than my list of capabilities, but it might still generate conflicts at the legislative stage, just as mine does – where, for example, the freedom of worship might seem to conflict with fully equal equality of opportunity. So I do not think that Rawls's theoretical assault on

intuitionism really succeeds in removing this problem; nor does my own approach appear to me to have an unacceptable amount of reliance on intuition – or, as I prefer to say, judgment.

[...]

VIII Capabilities and Loss

What is lost, if we follow my approach? Do these proposals involve a tragic aspect? The principle of moral constraint suggests to us that nothing of value is lost when we tell people that they cannot lord it over other people in immoral and harmful ways. By using the central capabilities as our guide, we allow considerable latitude for the preservation of tradition in cases that do not involve grave harms to others. And yet one should nonetheless acknowledge that there are some valuable ways of life that will become difficult to sustain in a climate of choice. Although an emphasis on the capabilities does not in any way preclude the choice to live a traditional hierarchical life, and indeed is intended to protect that opportunity; although we carefully create spaces within which such forms of life may continue and be supported; and although we stress that religion has always been a diverse and changing set of practices, and therefore won't be gravely damaged by being nudged in the direction of support for the capabilities – nonetheless, despite all this, we should acknowledge that at least some price will be paid for the sheer emphasis on choice and capability. There are some ways of life that people find deeply satisfying, and that probably do not involve unacceptable levels of indignity or capability inequality, which are likely to cease to exist in a regime of choice, simply because of social pressure and the availability of alternative choices. Veiling is available in a regime that does not make veiling mandatory, and it seems quite wrong of a regime to impose veiling by force on women who do not choose it. And yet the motivation for such a move can at least be comprehended, when we recognize that women who may wish to remain veiled have an extremely difficult time doing so in a fast-moving capitalist society in which their husbands are likely to be working for multinational corporations, many of whose members view veiling as primitive.

One such story was told to anthropologist Hannah Papanek by an elderly Indian Muslim woman, Hamida Khala.[71] It helps us see where the tragic potential lies in a regime of choice, and also helps us understand how human ingenuity and the dynamic nature of religious practices can surmount tragedy.

Brought up in an educated family in north India, Hamida Khala had a fine education under her father's supervision, and longed to wear the *burqua* as a sign of maturity. At the age of thirteen she was betrothed to a much older widower in the civil service, reputed to be of "modern" views. Hamida consented to the marriage on the condition that if her husband asked her to stop observing purdah she would return to her family. She began living with him at the age of fifteen, and he took her to Calcutta, far away from her family. As a civil servant, he worked with British, Hindu, and Muslim colleagues, and social life was organized around couples who typically attended dinners and tea parties together. Her husband began to resent her seclusion, which was cramping his own social life and his professional advancement. Although some colleagues arranged dinner parties at which women sat in a separate room, many refused to do so. And at last one host played a trick.

One night the women were seated at a table with empty seats at every other place. Suddenly a group of men came in and sat in the vacant seats. Hamida recalls this event with tremendous pain:

What I experienced, I just can't tell you. There was darkness all around me. I couldn't see anything. I had tears in my eyes . . . What I ate I don't remember . . . All my attempts, my endeavours to keep my purdah were over. I felt I was without faith, I had sinned. I had gone in front of so many men, all these friends of my husband. They've seen me. My purdah was broken, my purdah that was my faith.

Her husband insisted that he had not been aware of the plan, and apologized profoundly to her. Nonetheless, she recognized that her life would have to change if she were to stay with him. She wrote to her father, asking his advice. He told her that if her marriage might be endangered, she would have to leave purdah, adding that her extreme type of purdah does not represent an ancient Islamic tradition; she could behave with reticence and modesty even after leaving it. After reading sacred texts on her own, she came to the conclusion that there was a way of living as a devout Muslim outside of strict purdah. She worked out her own rules of modest dress and demeanor – long-sleeved blouses, downcast eyes, no makeup or jewelry – and followed them the rest of her life, while going outside and learning how to conduct daily business and social affairs. Her husband supported her and showed respect for her religion.

Hamida reports some good aspects of the change. She developed greater physical agility and strength by walking outside. She learned how to manage accounts, which came in handy when her husband died prematurely of a heart attack. Coming to the conclusion that "the real purdah is modesty," she refused to lend her support to a political campaign to bring back mandatory veiling in Pakistan, when a conservative leader asked her for help. She feels that she has been able to define successfully a Muslim identity that includes the central precepts of her religion – and yet, she acknowledges that there has been a real cost. "It was a big sacrifice for me to leave purdah." If that is so even in this very favorable case, where, because of Hamida's personal strength and her husband's respect, she was able to construct a viable religious alternative, we can easily imagine that other women might experience the sacrifice without discovering a viable alternative. Hard though it is for western feminists to imagine a life in which physical movement, practical command, and a variety of associative ties are not central, we can see that Hamida's old life contained genuine religious values and did not strike her, even in retrospect, as humiliating or as unacceptably subordinating. She does judge that women should focus more on exercise, and should learn to manage things in case they need to: in these respects she faults the earlier regime. Papanek adds evidence that women in purdah have been and are frequently cheated by middlemen, when they are unable to deal with managers and employers directly.[72] But she appears to think that the old regime was not, as such, unacceptable, and might have accommodated these changes.

This case shows, I believe, that a capability-based approach to religious liberty does involve the potential for tragedy. Nonetheless, it also shows how resourceful deeply religious women and men can be in adapting the religion's moral understanding to a changing reality. It is especially significant that Hamida Khala strongly opposed mandatory purdah. Her final judgment was that she and her husband "learned a lot from each other." Indeed, her response to the conservative leader – which she reported, Papanek says, with great delight – showed that she thinks the problem of modesty can be well solved by women without purdah, if only men will cooperate. "Let a thousand women come out at once, not just a few," she reported herself as saying. "Then you will see how quickly men get used to seeing women and think nothing of it." She had

kept her modesty while coming out of purdah, she added to the leader, and that is what really matters.

Through religion, people search for the transcendent. But religious groups and practices are human phenomena. The humanity of religion means that its practices are fallible, and need continual scrutiny in the light of the important human interests that it is the state's business to protect. On the other hand, religion is itself among the important human interests, both in itself and because it represents a central exercise of human choice. For these reasons, any solution to the dilemmas created when religion and sex equality clash must be complex, relying on the ability of judges and other political actors to balance multiple factors with discernment. One thing they should not do, however, is to abandon a commitment to equal justice, in the face of political intimidation.

On November 2, 1985, Shah Bano, in the presence of four male witnesses, signed with her thumbprint an open letter to all Muslims, stating that Islamic leaders had explained to her the commands concerning divorce and maintenance, in the light of Quran and Hadith. Using legal language that she is extremely unlikely to have chosen herself or perhaps even to have understood, she renounces her claim to maintenance and demands that the Indian government withdraw the Supreme Court decision. She further states that "Article 44 of the Indian Constitution, in which there is a directive for enacting a uniform civil code for all, is quite contrary to the Quran and the Hadith." She asks that the government renounce the goal of uniformity and resolve that "no interference would be ever attempted in future" with the operation of the Islamic courts. "In the end," she concludes, "I thank Manulana Habib Yar Khan and Haji Abdul Ghaffar Saheb of Indore who showed me the straight path and helped me follow the Truth and thus saved me in this world and in the hereafter."[73]

It is extremely difficult to avoid the conclusion that the faith of a devout and penniless women is being exploited for political purposes. And, to paraphrase Lincoln, it seems extremely strange that a just God would indeed require a destitute aged woman to renounce her claim to a minimal livelihood. Respecting the freedom of religion does not mean giving a small number of religious leaders limitless license to perpetuate human misery, to inhibit the religious freedom of individuals, and to push the law around. It is not an assault on religious freedom, but a deeper defense of its basic principle, to say that in such cases, the law indeed must "come to the rescue" in order that "society should move on."

Notes

[1] Article 14 guarantees the equal protection of the laws to all persons; Article 15 prohibits discrimination on the grounds of religion, race, caste, sex, or place of birth; Article 16 guarantees all citizens equality in matters relating to employment, and prohibits employment discrimination on the basis of religion, race, caste, sex, descent, place of birth, and residence; Article 17 abolishes untouchability: "its practice in any form is forbidden." Article 19 guarantees all citizens rights of free speech and expression, assembly, association, free movement, choice of residence, choice of occupation; Article 21 (the basis for privacy jurisprudence in cases involving marital rape and restitution of conjugal rights) says that "no citizen shall be deprived of his life or personal liberty" without due process of law; Article 25 states that all citizens are "equally entitled to freedom of conscience and the right freely to profess, practice and propagate religion," although there is an explicit qualification stating that this does not prevent government from abolishing the caste system and "throwing open . . . Hindu religious institutions of a public nature to all classes and sections of Hindus"; Article 26 gives religious denominations the right to manage their own affairs and to acquire property, "subject to public order, morality, and health"; Article 28 guarantees freedom to attend religious schools, states that no religious instruction shall be provided in institutions wholly funded by the state, and also states that where a school is aided by state funds students may not be compelled to perform religious observances. Finally, Article 13 renders invalid all "laws in force" that conflict with any of these Fundamental Rights and forbids the state to make any new laws that take away or abridge a Fundamental Right. (A subsequent judicial decision, however, declared that "laws in force does not include the religious systems of personal law": see *State of Bombay v. Narasu Appa Mali*, 1952.) For related constitutional discussion, see my "Religion and Women's Human Rights," in *Religion and Contemporary Liberalism*, ed. Paul Weithman (Notre Dame: University of Notre Dame Press, 1997), pp. 93–137, and, in a revised form, my *Sex and Social Justice* (New York: Oxford University Press, 1999).

[2] *Mrs. Mary Roy v. State of Kerala and Others*, AIR 1986 SC 1011. (Mary Roy is the mother of Booker Prize-winning novelist Arundhati Roy.) For discussion of this case, see Bina Agarwal, *A Field of One's Own: Gender and Land Rights in South Asia* (Cambridge: Cambridge University Press, 1994), 224–6, and Archana Parashar, *Women and Family Law Reform in India: Uniform Civil Code and Gender Equality* (Delhi: Sage, 1992), pp. 190–2. For a general description of the system of personal laws, see the following discussion.

[3] P. J. Kurien, author of the Private Member's Bill, in a public statement.

[4] See *Indian Express*, June 20, 1986.

[5] See E. D. Devadasan, *Christian Law in India* (Delhi: DSI Publications, 1974).

[6] For discussion of the debates, with many references, see Shahida Lateef, "Defining

Women through Legislation," in Zoya Hasan (ed.), *Forging Identities: Gender, Communities, and the State in India* (Boulder: Westview, 1994), pp. 38–58. This issue had already been dealt with in the Child Marriage Restraint Act of 1929, the first occasion on which the Indian women's movement achieved a big legislative success. It was now included in a more comprehensive package of reforms for the new republic.

7   The year 1937 saw passage of the Shariat Act, which stopped the custom of leaving all property to male heirs and returned the Muslim community from customary law to the prescriptions of the Shariat (where, however, women do not have fully equal shares). The bill was supported by Jinnah on grounds of sex equality: he stated that "the economic position of woman is the foundation of her being recognized as the equal of man and shar[ing] the life of man to the fullest extent." Nonetheless, the bill explicitly exempted agricultural land; thus many inequalities remained unaddressed. See Parashar, pp. 145–50; Agarwal, *A Field of One's Own*, pp. 98–9, 227–37; Agarwal, "Women and Legal Rights in Agricultural Land," *Economic and Political Weekly*, March 25, 1995.

8   See "Children Are Still Married off in Indian State," Agence-France Press, May 26, 1997, describing mass ceremonies in Rajasthan involving girls as young as seven, and supported by overwhelming community sentiment. Also John F. Burns, "Though Illegal, Child Marriage Is Popular in Part of India," *New York Times*, May 1998, pp. A1, 8. Police say that if nobody makes a complaint they cannot arrest anyone. Child marriage does not necessarily imply sexual consummation, which is usually delayed until after puberty. Nonetheless, the child bride leaves her natal home and is transferred to the power of the husband's home; usually her schooling ends at this point.

9   See Indira Jaising, "Towards an Egalitarian Civil Code," in Jaising (ed.), *Justice, for Women: Personal Laws, Women's Rights and Law Reform* (Mapusa, Goa: Other India Press, 1996), p. 24, describing a conversion and remarriage in Bombay high society; six

months later, however, the Supreme Court declared the new marriage invalid and stated that the husband was liable to be prosecuted for bigamy.

10   The requirement is now that all steps of the traditional Brahminic religious ceremony must have been performed. Many couples omit one or more steps – in some cases in some cases in order to indicate opposition to women's subordination. Others use distinct regional forms, or simply marry before a registrar; in all these cases marriages have been declared invalid. See descussion of cases in Saumya, "Bigamous Marriages by Hindu Men: Myths and Realities," in Jaising, *Justice*, pp. 27–33. Sometimes the first marriage is shown to be invalid, sometimes the second. The risk of invalidation deters prosecution by first wives, and also makes the task of gathering the requisite evidence of bigamy far more difficult.

11   The recognition of ex-wives as included relations under Section 125 was itself controversial in 1973. When the amendment was discussed in the Lok Sabha, members of the Muslim League objected, claiming violations of free exercise. Initially the government denied that there was any religious issue: the purpose of the amendment was simply humanitarian. Later, however, the government changed its stand, adding yet a further amendment to exclude divorced Muslim women from the purview of the new amendment. Nonetheless, Muslim women continued to bring petitions to the courts, and the Supreme Court explicitly pronounced, in two prominent judgments, that they were entitled to do so: the purpose of the law was to help destitute women, and the text had to be interpreted in accordance with this social purpose. See *Bai Tahira v. Ali Hussain*, 1979 (2) Supreme Court Reporter, 75, and AIR 1980 Supreme Court 1930. Thus the conflict between the Supreme Court and the Muslim leadership was of long standing.

12   *Mohammed Ahmed Khan v. Shah Bano Begum & Others* SCR (1985). This famous case has been discussed in many places. The central documents are assembled in Asghar Ali Engineer (ed.), *The Shah Bano Controversy* (Delhi:

Ajanta Publishers, 1987). See also Veena Das, *Critical Events* (Delhi: Oxford University Press, 1992), Chapter 4; Kavita R. Khory, "The Shah Bano Case: Some Political Implications," in Robert Baird (ed.), *Religion and Law in Independent India* (Delhi: Manohar, 1993), pp. 121–37; Amartya Sen, "Secularism and Its Discontents," in *Unravelling the Nation*, ed. Kaushik Basu and Sanjay Subrahmanyam, 1995; Parashar, pp. 173–89 (an unusually comprehensive account of different attitudes within the Islamic community); Zoya Hasan, "Minority Identity, State Policy and the Political Process," in Hasan (ed.), *Forging*, pp. 59–73; Danial Latifi, "After Shah Bano," in Jaising (ed.), *Justice*, pp. 213–15, and "Women, Family Law, and Social Changes," pp. 216–22 (criticizing Muslims who opposed the Supreme Court decision). On general issues about the Indian legal system and its history, see also John H. Mansfield, "The Personal Laws or a Uniform Civil Code?" in Baird (ed.), *Religion and Law*; Tahir Mahmood, *Muslim Personal Law, Role of the State in the Indian Subcontinent* (Nagpur, second edn. 1983).

13 Secular humanist feminism is a very common position among feminists; in American philosophy, it is perhaps the most common position. But today's secular philosophers rarely follow the example of Bertrand Russell, attacking religion explicitly. Instead, they tend to ignore it, and thus secular humanists in philosophy rarely write about religion. Many major works of feminist political philosophy include no discussion of religion at all: to cite just two examples, Alison Jaggar's *Feminist Politics and Human Nature* (Totowa, NJ: Rowman and Littlefield, 1988) and Catharine MacKinnon's *Toward a Feminist Theory of the State* (Cambridge, MA: Harvard University Press, 1989). The two best recent anthologies of feminist social-political thought devote no space to religion, although they discuss many topics only contingently linked to feminism, such as environmentalism and vegetarianism: Alison Jaggar's *Living With Contradictions: Controversies in Feminist Social Ethics* (Boulder, CO: Westview, 1994) and Diana Meyer's *Feminist Social*

Thought: A Reader (New York: Routledge, 1997). In law, feminists more frequently take on religion, because it is a part of their material: thus one striking representative of the secular humanist position I have in mind here is Mary Becker's fine article "The Politics of Women's Wrongs and the Bill of 'Rights': A Bicentennial Perspective," *The University of Chicago Law Review* 59 (1992), pp. 453–517. I shall use this article as my central example of the position criticized, in part because I admire it. It is not a perfect example, because the article ends by proposing less radical change in current policies than its argument would suggest – largely, but not wholly, for practical political reasons.

A perspective closely related to Becker's is developed by Susan Okin in "Is Multiculturalism Bad for Women?", first published in *The Boston Review*, October/November 1997: 25–28, and now in *Is Multiculturalism Bad for Women?* ed. J. Cohen, M. Howard, and M. Nussbaum (Priceton: Princeton University Press, 1999), pp. 7–26: see my response in the same volume, "A Plea for Difficulty," pp. 105–14. Okin's position is more nuanced than Becker's; insofar as she focuses on cases of genuinely egregious violation of woman's capabilities, our practical conclusions are not very dissimilar.

14 Becker does note that "all people need sources of authority outside government" (486), and considers this a reason not to muzzle religion too much. But all her other general statements about religion are strongly negative: "religion perpetuates and reinforces women's subordination, and religious freedom impedes reform" (459); "[r]eligions . . . contribute to women's subordinate status, not only within religious communities' hierarchies, but also in the broader culture" (460); "[a]ll mainstream religious traditions in the United States replace the wonder of women's reproductive power with stories of creation by a male god" (461); "[r]eligion encourages women to live with the status quo rather than destabilizing it by insisting on equality." Okin has a more subtle position, contrasting "progressive, reformed version" of various major

religions with their "more orthodox or fundamentalist versions," but even this begs many questions. Reform Jews typically understand the core of Judaism as a set of timeless moral ideas that are imperfectly captured in biblical and legal texts: thus they do not concede that their version is less "orthodox" than that of the people who call themselves "orthodox," and they understand the term "reform" to mean not that they advocate a religion "reformed" from the original Judaism, but rather that they advocate a reform of defective historical practices in the direction of a full realization of Judaism. Nor, of course, do Roman Catholics and mainstream Protestants concede that "fundamentalist" versions are more original or authentic or that their own positions are "reformed" from an original authentic position.

15 The comprehensive liberalism of Joseph Raz in *The Morality of Freedom* (Oxford: Clarendon Press, 1986) appears to have similar consequences: religious liberty within limits set by a shared comprehensive public view of autonomy. Unlike Mill, Raz discusses religion only briefly (pp. 251–2), and only to advocate religious liberty. Okin discusses her views on this question in *Is Multiculturalism Bad for Women?*, pp. 129–30.

16 Examples of this position include Stephen A. and Frédérique Marglin (eds.), *Dominating Knowledge: Development, Culture, and Resistance* (Oxford: Clarendon Press, 1988), esp. essays by the Marglins and A. Nandy; in the American context, Christina Sommers, *Who Stole Feminism?* (New York: Simon and Schuster, 1994); Elizabeth Fox-Genovese, *Feminism is Not the Story of My Life* (New York: Doubleday, 1996).

17 Such as the Marglins and Ashis Nandy. This group is known for its nostalgic treatment of child temple prostitution: see F. Marglin, *Wives of the God-King: The Rituals of the Devadasis of Puri* (Delhi: Oxford University Press, 1985), and for ambiguous statements about the positive value of *sati*, see Ashis Nandy, article on the Roop Kanwar *sati* in *Mainstream*, February 1988, reprinted in M. R. Anand (ed.), *Sati* (Delhi: B.R. Publishing, 1989). For a different view of *devadasis*, see

Gail Omvedt, "*Devadasi* Custom and the Fight Against It," *Manushi* 4 (Nov.–Dec. 1983), pp. 16–19. For critique of Nandy's position on *sati*, see Sanjukta Gupta and Richard Gombrich, "Another View of Widow-Burning and Womanliness in Indian Public Culture," *Journal of Commonwealth and Comparative Politics* 22 (1984): 262–74, and Imrana Qadeer and Zoya Hasan, "Deadly Politics of the State and Its Apologists," *Economic and Political Weekly* 22 (1987), pp. 1946–49. For further discussion of laws forbidding the glorification of sati, see my "Religion and Women's Human Rights" (note 1).

18 This is in essence the position of Judith C. Miles, "Beyond *Bob Jones*: Toward the Elimination of Governmental Subsidy of Discrimination by Religious Institutions," *Harvard Women's Law Journal* 8 (1985), pp. 31–58. Miles, on sex-equality grounds, favors ending all tax benefits and other related benefits (postage, etc.) to religious institutions, not only to those that have discriminatory practices. Becker sympathizes with this approach, but in the end does not favor it: she would ban tax exemptions and postal subsidies only for those religions that close leadership positions to women.

19 The Chief Justice was not a total secular humanist, however: although he advocated getting rid of religious courts of law, he did not advocate abolishing special constitutional protections for religion.

20 See, for example, Kalima Rose, *Where Women are Leaders*, pp. 83–4, where the story of Draupadi's prayer to Krishna is used to illustrate an episode in Ela Bhatt's life. Bhatt told me in conversation that at the death of her father, a prominent Brahmin judge, her family (in a step unusual for her caste) granted her wish to perform the religious death ceremonies, which are traditionally assigned to a male.

21 I comment on the difficulties this presents for the defense of my balancing test later, in section IV.

22 Maritain, "Truth and Human Fellowship," in *On the Uses of Philosophy: Three Essays* (Princeton: Princeton University Press, 1961), p. 24.

23 Becker states that "Jewish marriage and divorce law do not treat women and men as equals" (464) and that "for purposes of the minyan . . . , [a woman] does not count at all" (464) – ignoring the fact that both of these features have been challenged since the early nineteenth century, and a vast majority of American congregations have rejected such practices. Similarly, Becker ascribes to Judaism as a whole the prayer in which a man thanks God that he was not born a woman (464): this again was rejected by many early in the nineteenth century, and is relatively rare by now. Again, she claims that "the Jewish faith relegates women to serving others, rather than recognizing them as creatures with important spiritual lives" (464) – inaccurate concerning a tradition three out of whose four major branches in the US treat women as full equals in all liturgical and political as well as spiritual matters; the fourth (Orthodox) certainly would also reject this characterization, holding that women have very important spiritual lives, only in a different style from that of males. (Becker's presentation is sometimes hard to follow because she alternates between claims about what "Orthodox" women do and claims about "Judaism" and "the Jewish faith," making no distinction.) Similarly one-sided is Becker's claim that "the Christian valuation of suffering encourages women to accept abuse" (465), and that the Christian view of women's sexuality is consistently negative (466–7). Okin stresses internal diversity, though she understands the more egalitarian versions of Judaism to be "reformed" versions of the tradition rather than its authentic form, a highly controversial (and to my mind mistaken) claim.

24 See the remarks on Becker in the previous note. Okin is generally less polemical, but she simply asserts that God in Christian, Jewish, and Islamic traditions is male; again, this claim would be rejected by large numbers of believers in all these traditions (and not only the most evidently liberal), who would insist that a transcendent being is correctly understood to be entirely beyond gender, and that mythic personifications of God as male are not at the core of the religious conception.

25 This is true even of small communities relatively separate from mainstream culture, which have often been portrayed, nostalgically, as zones of homogeneity and harmony. For a fascinating account of internal diversity and conflict in one such religious tradition, see Fred Kniss, *Disquiet in the Land: Cultural Conflict in American Mennonite Communities* (New Brunswick, NJ: Rutgers University Press, 1997).

26 See my "Judaism and the Love of Reason," forthcoming in Marya Bower and Ruth Groenhout (eds.), *Among Sophia's Daughters: Reflections on Philosophy, Feminism, and Faith* (Indiana University Press).

27 One might reply that Orthodox Jews really do not accept the non-Orthodox as Jews, so in calling their view false I am simply taking one side in this debate. Here I can make two replies. First, it is simply dishonest to refuse to recognize the historical reality of the evolution of Judaism *in some way*, whether by treating the other branches as separate religions, analogous to Christianity, or by recognizing them as Jews. What is objectionable about the Israeli situation is that neither course has been taken, and thus Christians have far more rights than Reform and Conservative Jews. Second, it simply is not true that Orthodox Jews do not and cannot recognize Reform and Conservative Jews as Jews. Very few Orthodox Jews, or even Orthodox rabbis, make such a judgment. I was converted by an Orthodox rabbi, who knew that my practice would not be Orthodox. He gave me some reasons why I should consider Orthodox practice, but he also listened respectfully to my reasons against it; in the end, we agreed to share a core group of commitments, while differing about others. He performed the conversion ceremony, and he maintained vigorously to my fiancé's grandmother that this conversion did in fact make me a Jew. This is a common position. Respect for the Jewishness of other Jews is perfectly compatible with a personal commitment to the idea that Orthodoxy is the only fully correct way of being a Jew: indeed, a common US position resembles the sort of political consensus that members of different

comprehensive views are imagined as forming within Rawlsian political liberalism. Thus, for example, the director of the University of Chicago Hillel, David Rosenberg, is an Orthodox rabbi; qua rabbi, he believes that his type of Jewish practice is best; nonetheless, as he has prominently stated, qua director of Hillel, he is committed to recognizing, respecting, and working with Jewish individuals and groups of all types *as Jews*, including the gay and lesbian Jewish students and many others. He has made a point of this political stance, which clearly involves more than a mere modus vivendi. For valuable discussions of feminism in the Jewish tradition, see Judith Plaskow, *Standing Again at Sinai: Judaism from a Feminist Perpective* (San Francisco, CA: Harper San Francisco, 1990); Rachel Adler, *Engendering Judaism: An Inclusive Theology and Ethics* (Philadelphia and Jerusalem: The Jewish Publication Society, 1998).

28 For one clear, balanced, and well-argued treatment of Christian feminism, see Lisa Cahill, *Sex, Gender, and Christian Ethics* (Cambridge: Cambridge University Press, 1996).

An excellent illustration of the point about dynamism can be found in the recent election of Frank Tracy Griswold, bishop of Chicago, to the office of presiding bishop of the Episcopal Church of the United States of America. Griswold (who was a strong defender of women's role in the church long before it was fashionable, when he was a young assistant minister at the Church of the Redeemer in Bryn Mawr, which I attended as a girl) campaigned for office on a long record of support for women in the priesthood, as well as a more cautiously expressed support for the ordination of openly gay priests. His opponent, an African-American, took more conservative stands on both issues. Griswold won: the voting body decided that this was where they wanted the church to go. His opponents currently speak of him as a "heretic" – see "The Bishop Moves Up a Rank," *Chicago Tribune*, December 30, 1997, section 5, pp. 1, 10; but history will likely judge that theirs are the outlier views (as is

currently the case with Roman Catholics who refuse the vernacular Mass and other changes introduced by Vatican II).

29 Here the historical falsity is even more patent, since Hinduism has no conception of heresy, and has always been a loosely organized set of practices exhibiting much regional variation. This was also true of the Hindu legal system – until the British decided to systematize it for the nation as a whole! Contemporary Hindu fundamentalism is a recent social construct that no more represents Hinduism as a whole than the views of Pat Robertson represent Christianity as a whole.

30 A valuable general exposition of Islamic positions on interpretation and change (criticizing Okin's treatment of Islam) is in Azizah Y. al-Hibri, "Is Western Patriarchal Feminism Bad for Third World/Minority Women?" in Is *Multiculturalism Bad for Women?*, pp. 41–6. For the role of ideas of equal nature in the Muslim women's movement, see Barbara Metcalf, "Reading and Writing about Muslim Women in British India," in Hasan (ed.), *Forging*, pp. 1–21. On the construction of "synthetic traditions" that represent themselves as having great antiquity but do not accurately represent a tradition in all its complexity, see Hannah Papanek, "Afterword: Caging the Lion, a Fable for Our Time," in Rokeya Sakhwat Hossain, *Sultana's Dream*, ed. Roushan Jahan (New York: The Feminist Press at the City University of New York, 1988), pp. 58–85, at p. 61, discussing the wide range of Muslim practices regarding *purdah*. On the creative role of powerful women in the formation of Shi'ite Islam in India, see Juan R. I. Cole, "Shi'ite Noblewomen and Religious Innovation in Awadh," in Violette Graf (ed.), *Lucknow: Memories of a City* (Delhi: Oxford University Press, 1997), pp. 83–90. Cole shows that women were so successful in inscribing women's reproductive role into the idea of religious leadership that male leaders had to adopt a female gender model in order to create new rituals. Here is one example from the 1820s – the son of the creative female religious leader Badshah Begum: "On the day of the birth of the Imams he would behave like a woman in childbed

and pretended that he was suffering from the pains of childbirth . . . The selected attendants prepared dishes used by women in childbed and served them to the king."

31 These may, of course, be not at all the same. In quite a few religions, including Judaism, Hinduism, Islam, and Christianity, there is evidence that earlier practices were much less patriarchal than later ones: Draupadi enjoys a status unknown to the laws of Manu, Deborah plays a prophetic role unknown again among Jewish women until recently, and early Christian communities seem to have been more egalitarian than post-Pauline communities. Similarly, many Islamic feminists believe that many, if not most, oppressive patriarchal elements were introduced by the interpretive tradition and have no solid basis in Quran and Hadith.

32 Again, one should not say "oldest" or even "most orthodox" because this begs all kinds of questions about what the tradition really is. The version of Hinduism espoused by the Bharatiya Janata Party (BJP), for example, is quite new. Moreover, many liberal religious thinkers deny that the oldest stratum of the religion is the most important or essential.

33 This is the type of argument that prevailed in *Wisconsin v. Yoder*; it was argued that requiring children to attend school until the age of sixteen would damage the free exercise of adult members by undermining the future of the community itself.

34 Aristotle already makes the distinction between a corporate sense of "all" and a distributive sense at *Politics* 1261b16–27, saying that in Plato's ideal city it may possibly be true that "all" the city, taken as a whole, will use the terms "mine" and "not mine" in the same way, but not in the sense that "each one of them" will use these terms of the same objects.

35 Similar was the resistance to legal adoptions in India on the grounds that Islam does not permit adoption: see details in "Religion and Women's Human Rights."

36 *Wisconsin v. Yoder*.

37 *US v. Seeger* and *Thomas v. Review Board*, to be discussed in note 69.

38 In *Bob Jones University v. United States* 461 U.S. 574, 103 S. Ct. 2017 (1983), the Court upheld the Internal Revenue Service's denial of tax-exempt status to a religiously grounded institution that had a racially discriminatory admissions policy. Although not affiliated with any specific denomination, the school's stated purpose is "to conduct an institution of learning . . . , giving special emphasis to the Christian religion and the ethics revealed in the Holy Scriptures." (2922) The primary focus of the institution was on preventing interracial dating. Until 1973, the institution completely refused to admit black students; from 1971 to 1975 it admitted only black students "married within their race," giving a few exceptions to long-term members of the university staff. Since 1975, unmarried black students had been permitted to enroll, but a disciplinary rule forbade interracial dating and marriage, stating that violators would be expelled. The Court argued that the government's fundamental, overriding interest in eradicating racial discrimination in education substantially outweighs whatever burden denial of tax benefits places on petitioners' exercise of their religious beliefs. "Petitioners' asserted interests cannot be accommodated with that compelling governmental interest, and no less restrictive means are available to achieve the governmental interest." The opinion concludes that a racially discriminatory institution is not a "charitable institution" within the meaning of established Internal Revenue standards. The opinion did not deny that the refusal of tax-exempt status imposed a burden on religiously based conduct (so it did not exactly express the principle of the moral core in my sense), but it did hold that the compelling state interest in eradicating racial discrimination justified the burden. McConnell, in "Free Exercise Revisionism and the *Smith* Decision," *University of Chicago Law Review* 57 (1990), pp. 1109–53, argues that this is a case where government should make an accommodation: if harm is inflicted on non-coreligionists, it is only through the offensive speech of the institution, and this speech is protected by the free speech clause of the First Amendment.

The "direct effects" of the prohibition "are purely internal to the religious group." One difficulty in assessing this argument is that there is no determinate "religious group" in question, since the school is non-denominational; a second difficulty is occasioned by the fact that many of the parties affected would be minors, who may not choose to attend Bob Jones and who cannot easily extricate themselves from the situation if they don't like the practices. (Presumably black parents would choose such a school for a variety of economic and geographical reasons, prominently including the fact that they were themselves employees of the institution; their children might have little say in the matter if they wished to continue their education.) McConnell argues that the harm these practices may impose on outsiders, if the tax exemption were to be granted, would be a form of speech protected by the free speech clause of the First Amendment. This is highly dubious. It is not the institution's speech that is in question – obviously there was never any question of making their expressive conduct illegal – it is, rather, the act of the government in giving that institution a favored status. For the federal government to favor a discriminatory institution by granting it a tax exemption would involve the federal government in supporting or at least countenancing racial discrimination.

39   Thus *sati* would always be suspect, even when practiced entirely within a religious tradition, because its voluntariness is generally suspect. Even a fully consensual case could be made illegal because the state has reason to prevent citizens from forfeiting life and (in certain ways) health, except in special circumstances. Similarly problematic would be refusals to permit women to go out to look for work, where women are not choosing modesty as a norm but are being forced into this practice by economic dependence, intimidation, and so forth. For an interesting development of the distinction between harms to coreligionists and harms to others, see McConnell, "Free Exercise Revisionism," at 1145, urging that governmental interests do not extend to protecting the members of a religious community "from the consequences of their

religious choices." Thus he defends an exemption to minimum wage/maximum hours laws for a sect that urged members to work without wages for the glory of God (*Alamo Foundation v. Secretary of Labor*, 471 US 290 1985). That this practice involves no harm to nonmembers may surely be questioned: on this, see William P. Marshall, "In Defense of *Smith* and Free Exercise Revisionism," *The University of Chicago Law Review* 58 (1991), pp. 308–28, at 314, arguing that business competitors are unfairly disadvantaged by the foundation's reduced labor costs. But we should also ask some questions about the voluntariness of the practice: are members of the foundation, including its dependent and female members, coerced into working without wages? How free are they to leave? I am inclined to think that the potential for exploitation of the powerless is so great that such an exemption should never be granted. McConnell's other central example of an intrareligious practice that should be accommodated is the *Bob Jones* case. Once again, I shall disagree with his conclusion.

40   For Islam, see Abdullahi An-Na'im who distinguishes between two Koranic periods: see his *Toward an Islamic Reformation: Civil Liberties, Human Rights and International Law* (Syracuse, NY: Syracuse University Press, 1990); Azizah Al'Hibri distinguishes between the Koran, which must, she holds, remain uncriticized, and later schools of interpretation. For a valuable discussion of the Koranic sources for *purdah* – where an adjacent verse, rarely mentioned, mandates a symmetrical norm of purity and modesty for men – see Huma Ahmed-Gosh, "Preserving Identity: A Case Study of Palitpur," in Hasan, *Forging*, pp. 169–87; the relevant verses are cited later in note 45.

41   See K. Greenawalt, "Five Questions about Religion Judges Are Afraid to Ask," forthcoming in Nancy Rosenblum (ed.), *Law and Religion: Obligations of Citizenship and Demands of Faith* (Princeton, NJ: Princeton University Press, 1999), for examples of this, and also examples of when judgments have to be made. See also Michael McConnell, "Free Exercise Revisionism."

42   Edict XII.

43 Lincoln, in *The Viking Portable Lincoln* (New York: Viking, 1992), p. 321.

44 "Judge not that we be not judged" is an utterance, I think, of mercy rather than exculpation. Lincoln means not, don't say that this was wrong, but rather, withhold the punitive and vindictive attitude that could all too easily animate people at this time. This reading is borne out by the famous conclusion of the speech ("With malice toward none, with charity toward all"), which renounces malice while remaining firm in the right. Lincoln's point is that "firmness in the right" should not lead us into a vindictive attitude that would impair our ability to join together to "bind up the nation's wounds."

45 Often quoted in defense of the veiling of women is Quran 24.31, "And say to the believing women that they should lower their gaze and guard their modesty; that they should not display their beauty and ornaments except what must ordinarily appear thereof." But immediately preceding is 24.30: "Say to the believing men that they should lower their gaze and guard their modesty; that will make for greater purity for them. And God is well acquainted with all that they do." See Ahmed-Gosh, cited earlier.

46 See Rokeya, *Sultana's Dream and Selections from The Secluded Ones*, ed. Roushan Jahan (New York: Feminist Press of the City University of New York, 1988). Especially in *The Secluded Ones*, Rokehya focuses on the moral harms of *purdah*, pointing to damages to women's health and even lives caused by the extremes to which tradition pushed the norm that they should not be seen by men.

47 The church has a doctrine of "continuing revelation" – God's purposes are revealed to us gradually in the course of history – that was invoked on June 9, 1978, to justify admitting males of African descent to the priesthood.

48 374 US 398 (1963).

49 Both opponents and critics of the *Smith* decision agree, however, that "in practice the Court sided only rarely with the free exercise claimant, despite some very powerful claims" (McConnell, "Free Exercise Revisionism," p. 1110), usually finding either that the free exercise right was not burdened or that the government interest was compelling (see

McConnell, pp. 1110, 1127–8; Marshall, "Free Exercise Revisionism," pp. 310–11). In effect, the test in practice was weaker than the usual understanding of "compelling interest," which would have allowed government to override a religious claim only in unusual circumstances; some type of heightened scrutiny was applied, but the relevant standard was never very clearly articulated. It is also clear that claimants from religions that seem closely related to the culture's predominant religious traditions fared better than claimants from religions that seem bizarre. "Thus," as William Marshall puts it, "Mrs. Sherbert's claim that she is forbidden to work on Saturday is likely to be accepted as legitimate; Mr. Hodges's claim that he must dress like a chicken when going to court is not" (311, citing *State v. Hodges*, 695 SW2d 171(Tenn. 1985), in which the defendant, held in contempt of court, maintained that dressing like a chicken when in court was "his spiritual attire and his religious belief"). On the weakness of pre-RFRA protections of religion, see also C. Eisgruber and L. Sager, "Why the Religious Freedom Restoration Act is Unconstitutional," *NYU Law Review* 69 (1994), pp. 437–52.

50 110 S. Ct. 1595 (1990).

51 This helps to explain the otherwise somewhat surprising political lineup of the Court, as Justice Scalia and other usually religion-sympathetic conservatives supported a striking departure from settled precedent (though not practice, as already discussed) in the direction of narrowing the sphere of religious liberty, while three liberals – Justices Marshall, Brennan, and Blackmun – backed the more traditional religious libertarian course. (Centrist O'Connor agreed with the dissenters to the extent of deploring the sharp theoretical departure from traditional free exercise jurisprudence, though she concurred in the judgment in the particular case.) Scalia's argument is less surprising, however, if one focuses on the issue of institutional competence and the limiting of judicial discretion, which is one of the prominent themes of his jurisprudence.

52 For a detailed description of the litigation, see McConnell, "Free Exercise Revisionism,"

pp. 1111–14. The plaintiffs were Native American employees of a drug rehabilitation clinic who applied for unemployment compensation after being fired for ingesting peyote sacramentally during a ceremony of the Native American Church. The Oregon Supreme Court repeatedly held that the illegality of the sacramental use of peyote was irrelevant to the determination of unemployment compensation: if religiously motivated, the conduct could not be treated as work-related "misconduct" under the First Amendment. Thus it was somewhat surprising that the question of the law's constitutionality came before the Supreme Court in the first place.

53 Twenty-three states, moreover, specifically exempt the religious use of peyote from their drug laws; the federal government not only exempts peyote but licenses its production and importation, and Oregon itself does not enforce its own law.

54 Scalia wrote that such a requirement would produce "a private right to ignore generally applicable laws," thus creating "a constitutional anomaly." The three liberal Justices dissented, arguing that no convincing reason had been given to depart from settled First Amendment jurisprudence. The discussion of precedent in the majority opinion is entirely unconvincing, and has received heavy criticism from all sides. McConnell calls it "troubling, bordering on the shocking" (1120; detailed analysis at 1120–7); Marshall says that the majority's "use of precedent borders on fiction" (309).

55 The majority opinion acknowledges this danger: it speaks of "plac[ing] at a relative disadvantage those religious practices that are not widely engaged in."

56 For documentation, see McConnell, "Institutions and Interpretation: A Critique of *City of Boerne v. Flores*," *Harvard Law Review* 111 (1997), pp. 153–95, at 159.

57 There has been considerable analysis of the debate preceding the passage of RFRA, as to whether it was genuinely deliberative or merely the jockeying of interest groups; I pass over this question, since it is not relevant to my proposal.

58 *City of Boerne v. Flores*, 117 S. Ct. 2157 (1997). The vote was 6–3, and the majority opinion was written by Justice Kennedy. The case concerned a conflict between a Catholic church that wanted to enlarge its building to allow the entire congregation to celebrate Mass at the same time, and the historic landmark preservation laws, which forbade alterations to the building, whose facade was located in a historic district. (The church's plan was to build out from the back wall, leaving the old Spanish-style structure virtually intact, but the city refused to approve any plan of expansion that would require demolition of any part of the church building, whether inside or outside the historic district.) In August 1997, the church and the city came to an agreement that the church may build a new 850-seat sanctuary behind, and partly hidden by, the original building, most of which will be repaired and preserved at church expense; so the church accomplished its primary objective, though at much greater expense.

59 I do not say that nothing other than the central capabilities can ever provide such a compelling interest; I leave that to be hammered out by each legal tradition as it evolves. In the US, an account of these interests was evolving, before the demise of RFRA. See, for example, *Mack v. O'Leary* (80 F. 3d 1175), 1996, offering a generous definition of "substantial burden," but holding that the maintenance of order in federal prisons was a compelling state interest; and *Sasnett v. Sullivan* (91 F. 3d 1018), 1996, holding that restrictions on the wearing of religious jewelry in prisons are not justified by any compelling state interest and are in violation of RFRA.

60 Contrast *Goldman v. Weinberger*, 475 US 503 (1986).

61 See note 54.

62 See *Hunafa v. Murphy*, 907 F 2d 67 (7th Cir. 1990), upholding a Muslim prisoner's right to receive food uncontaminated by pork and remanded for fact-finding on government interest; the court noted that the intervening *Smith* decision may be raised on remand and may change the outcome. For discussion of other relevant pre-Smith cases, see

McConnell, "Free Exercise Revisionism," p. 1142 n. 143.

63 For discussion of the case and McConnell's argument for an accommodation, see note 38.

64 See Becker, "Women's Wrongs," pp. 484–6, arguing that a *Bob Jones* approach to religion (denying state benefits) is probably constitutionally compelled (not merely permissible) in the case of race, and might also be viewed as compelled in the case of sex. Becker supports banning tax exemptions and postal subsidies and the award of government contracts to religious organizations that close leadership positions to women. She would not favor altogether ending those subsidies, or requiring state regulation of religion to eliminate sexism. As will be clear later, I support Becker's position where educational institutions are concerned, but not with regard to the assignment of religious functions.

65 This is the argument made by McConnell in "Free Exercise Revisionism."

66 See Marshall, "Free Exercise Revisionism"; Marshall does not defend the argument in *Smith*, only the result.

67 *Thomas v. Review Board*, 450 US 707, 713 (1981).

68 Marshall, 320. McConnell, while not accepting that particular argument, also draws attention to the balancing effect of the two clauses, arguing that favoring religion in the context of free exercise is not unfair, since religion is disfavored in the context of establishment: see his "A Response to Professor Marshall," *The University of Chicago Law Review* 58 (1991), pp. 329–32. McConnell has in some areas sought to mitigate the unequal treatment of religion under the establishment clause: see his brief in *Rosenberger v. Rector and Visitors of the University of Virginia*, 115 S, Ct. 2510 (1995).

69 *United States v. Seeger*, 380 US 163 (1965). The court explicitly distinguished "religious training and belief" from "essentially political, sociological, or philosophical views." The test proposed was "whether a given belief that is sincere and meaningful occupies a place in the life of its possessor parallel to that filled by the orthodox belief in God of one who clearly qualifies for the exemption." In ascertaining that Seeger's beliefs did indeed play such a role, the Court drew attention to Seeger's "'belief in and devotion to goodness and virtue for their own sakes, and a religious faith in a purely ethical creed.'" Attention was drawn to the systematic nature of his beliefs (and to Seeger's own references to Plato, Aristotle, and Spinoza); to the similarity of his non-theistic ethical creed to aspects of Hinduism, Buddhism, and the Christian theology of Paul Tillich. The Court concluded that if the proposed test is passed by a system of beliefs, it follows that it is not a "merely personal moral code" in the sense already rejected as a legitimate basis for conscientious objection. See also *Thomas v. Review Board*, 450 US 707 (1981): "Courts should not undertake to dissect religious beliefs because the believer admits that he is 'struggling' with his position or because his beliefs are not articulated with the clarity and precision that a more sophisticated person might employ."

70 For a position on "expressive interests" and free speech jurisprudence with which I largely agree, see Joshua Cohen, "Freedom of Expression," *Philosophy and Public Affairs* 22 (1993), pp. 207–63.

71 Papanek, in "Afterword," in Rokeya Hossain, *Sultana's Dream*, pp. 72–6; Papanek had known Hamida Khala for a long time, and the telling of the story of her life, in the late 1970s, took many days.

72 Papanek, p. 77, describing Muslim home workers who send their children as intermediaries to deal with the middlemen who sell their products. See also Cornelia Sorabji, *India Calling* (London; Nisbet, 1934) describing her struggle as India's first female lawyer (and the first woman to be allowed to take a law degree at Oxford), helping women in *purdah* who were being cheated by male relatives and were forbidden to see a lawyer, all lawyers being male. The many attempts on Sorabji's life are evidence of the magnitude of the problem.

73 "Shah Bano's Open Letter to Muslims," published in *Inquilab*, November 3, 1985, and translated into English by A. Karim Shaikh. Reprinted in Engineer (ed.), pp. 211–12. Shah Bano died in Indore in 1992, at the age of eighty-nine.

Chapter 36

Conceptualizing Women's Human Rights*
Carol C. Gould

[Here] I have taken up the project of globalizing democracy and human rights in the important, although limited, sense of conceiving them to apply both more personally and in more plural ways than is customary. The idea of a more embodied politics, the critical analysis of race and racism and their import for democracy, and the analysis of cultural identities and group rights are all aspects of the broad reconceptualization that I believe is required. In this chapter, I turn to the issue of interpreting human rights to make them more relevant to women's experience.

There has already been considerable progress in reformulating human rights along these lines. At both the theoretical level and in more concrete efforts through the Convention on the Elimination of All Forms of Discrimination against Women (CEDAW) and the work of women's nongovernmental organizations (NGOs), as well as in certain legislative and judicial interpretations in various countries, human rights have increasingly been extended to rectifying discrimination against women and promoting women's

health and education needs, and have begun to be put to use to address gender-specific violence against women. Of course, in practice, this effort has only scratched the surface of the very deep structural inequalities and endemic violence often faced by women because of the profound social effects of historically sedimented systems of patriarchal oppression. On the theoretical side, human rights have been criticized as addressed primarily to the state actions that are feared primarily by men (e.g., torture, wrongful imprisonment, etc.) rather than to the wrongs women suffer, which often have their locus in the home and the so-called private sphere.[1] Yet human rights have also been increasingly reinterpreted in ways that show them to be applicable to nonstate actors (such as nongovernmental organizations, corporations, and even individuals) and in particular to the requirements of preventing harms to women outside the more public sphere of government and the economy, as well as within it.[2]

Needless to say, much more remains to be done at both the practical and the theoretical level if human rights are to really be women's rights as well as men's. In this chapter, I deal with some of the still unclear and controversial theoretical issues that arise concerning

* From Carol C. Gould, *Globalizing Democracy and Human Rights* (Cambridge: Cambridge University Press, 2004), pp. 139–55.

the extension of human rights to women. But I do not focus primarily on the interpretation of the existing list of human rights to apply to women's experience. Others have done this and done it quite well. For example, there is Martha Nussbaum's effort to show the applicability of a long list of human rights to eliminate harms against women[3] in addition to the work collected in *Human Rights of Women* and in *Women's Rights, Human Rights*,[4] as well as the more practical efforts of human rights activists in connection with world conferences and the United Nations and in more regional contexts. Rather, my focus is on some difficult issues concerning how to conceive of women's human rights, within the overall framework of democracy and human rights presented in this work, and I draw on both feminist theory and political philosophy to try to make a certain amount of progress about these questions, keeping in mind that they have practical import as well.

Outstanding Theoretical Questions Concerning Women's Rights

The issues can be summarized as follows:

1   What sort of reconstruction of human rights is required if we take seriously women's historic preoccupation with care and with relations and responsibilities toward others, rather than simply focusing on the traditional emphasis on individual rights-claims and correlative duties? Do human rights in their dominant individualist interpretation, based largely on men's experiences in politics and economic life, in fact conflict with these feminist/feminine emphases on care and the relatedness and responsibilities toward those close to us?

2   How should we understand the public–private distinction that historically underlies human rights discourse if these rights are to be effective in addressing such wrongs to women as domestic abuse, wife battering, and even wife murder? The problematic status of privacy is also of interest here: We can be critical of it as a domain in which such gender-specific violence can continue and yet wish to preserve some sense of it, perhaps in a more relational interpretation than it currently has. The traditional understanding of the public sphere as the state, excluding other institutions such as corporations and voluntary associations, and the private sphere understood as independent of power relations in economic and social life, also merits scrutiny in this connection.

3   Whereas the issue of public and private has been interpreted primarily as applying to the domain of civil and political rights,[5] there is also the crucial question of the interconnections between women's rights and social and economic rights, including especially subsistence, health, the right to work, and education. The connections between these and the elimination of harms and even violence toward women need more examination.

4   A long-standing problem, particularly from the standpoint of liberal political and legal theory, concerns how any so-called special or differentiated rights for women can square with the idea of rights for all human beings and the requirement for equal treatment under the law. Do the recognition of rights concerning pregnancy or maternity or, more generally, any special mention of harms to women – for example, of a sexual nature – somehow violate the requirements of universality and equality?

5   Another issue concerns how to achieve intercultural agreement on women's human rights, given the divergent cultural claims concerning how much inequality for women can be tolerated on grounds of tradition, custom, and religion and, more generally,

the question of how the plurality of cultural approaches impacts human rights and their interpretation. I have discussed this issue in regard to cultural relativism versus the universalism of human rights. As I suggested, its feminist import needs further development if we are to avoid these extremes and also avoid essentializing women's experience or reifying the concept of culture.

6   Finally, there is the question of the impact of globalization and also regionalization on women's human rights. Beyond the traditional emphasis on holding states responsible for human rights violations and the more recent effort to have them monitor wrongs by nonstate actors including not only corporations but also private individuals (e.g., men's actions toward women in the home), there is the further question of whether women's human rights would be better implemented if nation-states were deconstructed or diminished in power, or at least if new, more global institutions of justice and even of government came to have more power than they now do.

Clearly, this is too large a list of topics to discuss adequately here. And even though it would be of value, I think, simply to clarify these problems more fully, I do not want to remain at the level of merely programmatic analysis, even if that were to have a heuristic value. Also, I am in agreement with the overall thrust of the theoretical work on women's human rights thus far and do not want to engage in any polemic with it or advocate an entirely new direction. Therefore, I focus here on a number of the most problematic and unresolved issues where I feel considerably more attention is required if progress on women's human rights is to be deep and not only to remain a matter of extending existing rights to women. In part because it deals with a process still very much under way, I must put aside issue 6, concerning globalization, despite its interest and

importance. It can be noted here that there is a divergence among feminist human rights analysts about the role of the nation-state, with some arguing for its continued centrality,[6] and others for a more internationalist perspective.[7] Of the other five issues, which I abbreviate as (1) rights and care, (2) the private–public distinction, (3) women's social and economic rights, (4) the status of differentiated rights for women, and (5) traditional cultures versus women's equality in a human rights framework, I focus primarily on the first two, with some attention to the other three. Still, I believe that it is useful to consider the various outstanding problems together because they are interrelated and because to a degree they can all be approached from a perspective that emphasizes the importance of both human rights and concrete social relationships.

Care and Human Rights

Turning first, then, to the issue of rights and care, we can observe that this primarily ethical concept, which feminist theorists have drawn from women's experiences of nurturance and supportiveness, has already had some impact on political philosophy in connection with democratic community, where, as we have seen, it involves introducing concern for others more explicitly into the political domain.[8] It has also been tied to international affairs by, for example, Fiona Robinson in her book *Globalizing Care.*[9] But this care discussion has as yet had almost no impact on conceptualizing human rights. In fact, most commentators who discuss care regard it as either standing in opposition to rights discourse (e.g., in the original work of Gilligan concerning two alternative modes of moral development[10] and those influenced by her analysis) or as a necessary supplement to a rights perspective, but still of a completely different order. The reason for this stance is that care is thought to be tied to relations with a particularistic set of those close to one, whereas rights – and particularly human rights – are thought to have a more universalistic scope.

Yet I believe that the connection between rights and care is deeper than heretofore supposed. To see this, we have to look at the nature of human rights themselves and consider whether they are correctly characterized as individualistic, as in their standard interpretation. I have argued that this interpretation is partly incorrect and that to take human rights as simply an enunciation of an Enlightenment universalism of such an abstractly individualistic sort is in error. This is so partly in view of the fact that rights always hold as claims on others, or on society as a whole, to do or refrain from doing something. Clearly, without the intersubjective ties among people presupposed here, the very concept of a right as such a claim on others would make no sense. Although Robinson Crusoe probably did have human rights – inasmuch as he was a proper Englishman, with the upbringing that entailed, who simply found himself marooned on an island – we could not say the same for a truly isolated individual, who lacked any culture or social context. Indeed, it is hard even to conceive of such an individual. It is of course true that in recognizing a human being as a bearer of human rights, we are in fact recognizing someone as a person with freedom and dignity, and this is an abstractly universal moment that holds for every human being regardless of his or her concrete differentiation (although it is not entirely a Kantian moment, we might add, because Kant restricted rights-bearers to rational beings, rather than human beings). It must be granted too that the recognition we accord to human beings does not constitute or socially construct them as human but rather is a recognition of what we take to be an intrinsic property of these beings, namely, their humanness (with all the problems of

moral realism or objectivity that this raises). Still, the context of recognition is a fundamentally intersubjective and social one, indeed one of reciprocal recognition, as Hegel argued, and I would propose that this deeply social conception of reciprocity is built into our idea of human rights themselves. They come into being as claims each has on the others and hence exist as rights only in such a social framework of recognition.

Even more suggestively from a distinctively feminist perspective, human rights can be said to emerge from a practical situation of care and concern, in the following sense: If people did not tend to care about the well-being and more generally the needs of others, then the claim that each can make on the others, however valid, would remain a bare one, and people would lack the motivation needed to take these claims of others seriously and structure society in such a way as to attempt to meet them. From this feminist perspective, then, although care may be most familiar to us in our personal relations with family and friends, its conceptual exclusion from the understanding of politics appears to reflect the male-dominated character of traditional political theory and, specifically, social contract theory,[11] in which individuals are understood as separated from each other, or even as antagonistically related to each other, in a state of nature, and thus lacking fundamental caring relations with others; or, to the degree that they are thought to have such relations, especially with their families, the public–private divide excludes these relations in principle from the political domain. Thus, if feminist ethical theorists are right concerning the centrality of care in human experience, we can analogously see that human rights themselves have some basis in the care and concern we feel not only for those close to us but also for all others, even those who are strangers to us. I have attempted to articulate such a universalization of care in connection with the concept of concrete universality.

Furthermore, the equality built into the human rights conception not only is based on an abstract and justice-based judgment concerning humans as fundamentally equal in their abstract humanness, where this is the product of purely rational reflection on our part, but also grows out of a shared feeling of commonality with others, on the grounds of common needs, suffering, and aspirations – in short, as beings like ourselves. Although we do not already know them, in recognizing others as beings with dignity, we also feel a certain empathy with them and conceive of the others in terms of potential encounters we could have with them as sharing fundamental concerns or as standing in possible relations with us. I would propose that the concept of human rights (as well as of rights more generally) has been deprived and reduced because of the effort to separate it from such a context of shared feeling, and to limit it to a purely rational and theoretical judgment. (This does not entail, of course, that reason itself is not also tied to the emotions in some important ways, but to discuss this would surely take us too far afield at this point. It also does not imply, of course, that there are not feelings of enmity and hostility that we feel toward others as well.)

If we look to this arena of care and concern, derived in part from women's experience in childraising and nurturance of others in the home and beyond it, we find also the corollary concept of responsibility. This concept, too, is a useful corrective to the more abstract notion of duty, normally thought to be correlated with a right. Responsibilities are responsibilities for or to someone, and suggest immediately our ties to the others for whom we feel responsible. Women (and men as well) responsible for the well-being of children, and perhaps also elderly relatives, are tied to these others in ways beyond simply recognizing the rights

they have and their abstract duties to fulfill these rights. Likewise, it can be argued at the more global level that an emphasis on shared responsibilities among states – for example, for ecological management – in place of or perhaps in addition to the rights and duties of states might lead to a greater concern for achieving just outcomes in international affairs.[12] Here, the idea of responsibility for others not only suggests that one is required to do some particular act toward another, after which one may be said to have done one's duty, but also it calls for a more continuing concern with taking care of the well-being of others, including a concern with helping to bring about good and just outcomes for them.

Another implication of care for human rights doctrine is the support this concept gives to the rights to means of subsistence, to health care, and to education, inasmuch as these are fundamental to the life and development of persons. Human rights instruments (and even more so the US Constitution) still tend to denigrate these economic and social rights in favor of the civil and political rights, to the degree that they include them at all. An emphasis on the social and political importance of care and nurturance lends weight, then, to a requirement for meeting people's basic needs, if it can be shown that these are aspects of what people owe each other in societies (as discussed earlier) and not only characterize the particularistic obligations or responsibilities that they have to those close to them. Although as individuals we certainly cannot fully care for all equally (and here care differs from the idea of respect, which is susceptible of this equality), nonetheless I have proposed that there is an extensibility of what we might call basic care that can apply universally. We cannot take care of all others, in the sense of directly being responsible for meeting their needs personally (in the way that we can, for example, for our children, or at least try to do so). Nonetheless, we can be jointly responsible for meeting the basic needs of all the others, and this imposes some fundamental human rights obligations on each of us. In this sense, it makes sense to speak of a human right to care, or to be cared for. Yet this does not necessarily mean that we have to add yet another right to the long list of recognized human rights (although there may be arguments for doing this). But it does entail that the caring rights – such as those to means of subsistence or to health care – have a deep basis not only in the respect we have for others but also in the basic care that we collectively must have for them.

The Public–Private Distinction

Turning now to the vexing second issue as it impacts the conception of women's human rights, we can take note of the helpful work done by Hilary Charlesworth, Celina Romany, Rhonda Copelon, and others[13] to criticize the way traditional human rights doctrine has used the public–private distinction to marginalize harms to women by regarding them as pertaining to the private realm and hence outside the purview of human rights, which, it is held, properly pertain to the actions of states. Of course, many wrongs to women are perpetrated by states. Some of these harms are general, whereas others pertain primarily to women – for example, where rape is perpetrated by the police themselves against women held in custody, or various harms to women as refugees or in time of war.[14] Yet the feminist theorists have shown how both the list and the interpretation of human rights, having been drawn up primarily by men, are concerned primarily with public wrongs, at the expense of harms committed against women in domestic or more private domains of family life and interpersonal relations. These feminist authors have made considerable progress in rectifying the imbalance in

human rights theory – for example, by tying rape to torture[15] or by showing how male bias has led to relative inattention in rights doctrines of considerations of bodily integrity so important to women (in reproductive rights, in protection from sexual assaults, and so forth).[16]

In more practical contexts, too, the CEDAW Convention (along with the subsequent Vienna Declaration on the Elimination of Violence against Women) to a degree helps to diminish the public–private distinction (at least in principle) by insisting that discrimination against, and harms to, women cannot be tolerated even where they are carried out by private individuals, and that it falls to states to attempt to eliminate such discrimination and to deal with such harms, whether in the public or the private sphere. Thus, Article Two requires states "to take all appropriate measures to eliminate discrimination against women *by any person, organization or enterprise*" (2e). Accordingly, such wrongs as wife murder, sati, rape, female genital mutilation, forced prostitution, marital rape, woman battering, domestic abuse, and sexual harassment can all in principle be addressed, even though they may not be directly perpetrated by states but rather by private individuals or by economic, cultural, or social institutions. According to CEDAW, it is incumbent on states to put laws in place to eliminate these and other forms of discrimination. This helpful development (although one that is still mostly theoretical at this point inasmuch as it has not been implemented much in practice) has largely proceeded on the grounds offered over the past several decades by feminist theory – namely, that the personal is political, in that power relations of a customary or institutional sort permeate the private sphere, and legitimate oppressive and unequal treatment of women by men, and that these harms should not be beyond the scope of law and jurisprudence.

Yet many difficult issues remain unresolved in this critique of the distinction between public and private, and some of these bear on our understanding of women's human rights themselves. For one thing, privacy on a certain interpretation is appealed to, at least in the United States, as the main ground for preserving women's reproductive rights regarding abortion. Even apart from this, although the "private" sphere of the family clearly should not be an area where gender-specific violence, or indeed any violence, is tolerated (supposedly, but objectionably, on grounds of "family privacy"), still some sense of privacy is surely worth preserving. After all, we quite rightly would object to the state meddling in our choice of partners, our sexual relations, and, in a very different context, in our communications with others through the mails or the Internet, or again, in regard to medical records and the like. Different strategies are possible here for carving out a domain of privacy that merits protection by right. For one thing, much of what is included in the idea of privacy – including the support it provides for abortion rights – can in fact be captured by an idea of autonomy or freedom, from which the requirements of privacy follow. Thus, we can protect individual choice in the cases just specified by seeing it as a matter of (equal) freedom more fundamentally and of privacy by derivation from that. In this case, we would insist it is a matter of freedom to be able to choose sexual partners, have a child, or again, to control information about oneself and so on.

Beyond this, as far as women's privacy is concerned, we would probably benefit from conceiving privacy in more relational ways than on traditional views that emphasize the separateness of persons. Accordingly, what merits protection is not only my private space but also the shared space of those close to me. An important proviso here, though, would be that violence or other serious harms not be tolerated within this space, and that relations within it proceed on the basis of equality[17] or at least the absence of oppression or discrimination. In this way, a conception of privacy can be preserved at the same time that we recognize the need for a certain degree of public scrutiny of "private discrimination."

However, rethinking privacy in these ways is not sufficient. There is a correlative need to reconceptualize the public sphere, as well as to argue that human rights apply to all these contexts and to nonstate actors within them. In this view, "the public" is extended to the institutional domain of economic and social life, in short, to the domain of organizations such as firms and voluntary associations beyond the interpersonal. The distinction then becomes one between the public or institutional, on the one hand, and the private or individual or interpersonal on the other. (One interesting question that remains, though, which I cannot address here, is the status of the family in this division.) It is interesting to observe too that the concept of nonstate actors, widely used in human rights discussion, in fact applies to two rather different sets: private individuals, on the one hand, and economic, social, and cultural entities on the other. Human rights and responsibilities for their implementation properly fall on all of these.

Women's Social and Economic Rights

The public–private distinction and the case of gender-specific harms – such as domestic violence – directed toward women have been treated primarily in connection with civil and political rights. Yet it seems to me that the sharp separation between these and the social and economic rights within human rights theory and practice is unfortunate, not only in a general sense but also in its specific impact on understanding women's human rights. The status of women's social and economic rights is the third issue enumerated earlier, and here I would like to argue that the relative neglect of such crucial economic and social rights of women as those to means of subsistence, health, and education directly contributes to women's oppression as women and even contributes to several of the gender-specific harms cited earlier, First, Amartya Sen and others have shown how the lack of regard for women's right to life or subsistence – whether through selective abortion or infanticide of girl fetuses or babies, or severe malnutrition due to selective inadequate provision for their subsistence needs, together with their lack of access to adequate health care – has led to millions of missing women worldwide.[18] Women's literacy rates and their lack of rights to work in many countries also differentially harm their life chances.

But we can additionally observe that the deprivation of these economic and social rights negatively impacts women's abilities to protect themselves from the harms to their persons customarily treated in the civil or political domain, and also makes it difficult for them to exercise their rights to political participation. Indeed, several of the abuses considered under the heading of gender-specific violence have strong economic components. Examples here include forced prostitution, where girls or women are sold for material motives; dowry killings or beatings, such as in India, which often proceed on crudely economic grounds;[19] and woman battering and domestic abuse, which at the very least reflect a lack of recognition of women's economic equality. (In the United States, these may be perpetrated by men who resent women's work, as well as by those in deficient financial circumstances, although of course not only by them.) Again, in the case of female genital cutting, African feminist activists have proposed that in addition to cultural factors, this practice is tied

to economic advantage through the requirement of protecting or enhancing women's marriageability status, and the material as well as psychological gain that belonging brings.[20] Perhaps even more clearly, many of these abuses can be meliorated only if attention is also given to equalizing women's standing in economic and social matters, including by access to work and the independent income it can provide and by equal access to education and welfare as well as health care and contraception. (Along these lines, Sen has also shown how, in the case of the Kerala province in India, women's social and economic standing, particularly in terms of education, is a central factor in ensuring generally higher levels of well-being for the population.)[21]

It seems apparent, then, that remedying women's oppression requires considerably more attention to their economic and social rights, beyond the often-cited issue of overcoming the public–private distinction. Yet, as Charlesworth has suggested, the prevalence of this distinction itself impacts these economic rights by reinforcing their interpretation as applying to the public, in the sense of institutional, sphere of economic life – as, for example, the well-known requirement of equal pay for equal work – while applying less or not at all to women's economic independence within the family.[22] Clearly, reinterpretations are required if these economic and social rights are to become more fully applicable to women's experience.

On the importance of social and economic rights, women's human rights activists from Africa, Asia, and Latin America have been in considerable agreement. And this striking consonance in views raises the final question of how to deal with the areas of diversity in cultural approaches to rights and to women's oppression. Before turning to that question, I would like to briefly address the fourth issue outlined earlier.

The Status of Differentiated Rights for Women

If we regard some of the human rights as "special" to women or as sex-differentiated, does this violate the universality of human rights or the requirement of equal treatment under the law? The CEDAW Convention in fact skirts this issue by framing its concerns in terms of eliminating discrimination against women, and it therefore specifies certain particular rights by way of assuring women equal treatment. However, the question remains as to whether we should include any sex-specific rights not only as interpretations of human rights but also as rights themselves and, more generally, what the status of such gender-specific rights might be.

If we understand human rights to be based on a mutual recognition of all humans as equally free in a fundamental way, we can observe that this freedom (as positive freedom) entails their rights to the conditions needed for any human activity whatever and also to those necessary for their fuller self-development. The first set of human rights – to the conditions of human agency in general – include the basic rights, especially those of life and liberty, where "life" signifies not only a right not to be killed but also access to means of subsistence as well as rights to health care, basic education, and certain others. The second set of what we might call nonbasic human rights include those to the conditions for the higher development of human agency in differentiated forms.[23] Unfortunately, as I see it, there is no comparable distinction in human rights documents, which instead treat all of the human rights as equally fundamental, from liberty to the right to a paid vacation. In principle, though, I believe that there is a certain distinction to be made; the basic ones are necessarily very general, inasmuch as they are prerequisites for any human activity

whatever, whereas the nonbasic ones are open to more differentiation according to the diversity of human needs and interests, compatible with the equality entailed in the fundamental idea of equal freedom.

Thus, if we are to treat people equally, we must often treat them in differentiated ways, as argued earlier in this part, in view of their different needs and to a degree their different interests. The case of disabled people with special requirements of access and support services is perhaps the most obvious case, as cited previously. But this principle extends far beyond this one instance. Concrete differences between men and women are also among the differences that may need to be recognized. Of course, one can argue that differences between men and women affect not only the nonbasic rights but also the basic rights, in view of the human biological or social requirements of pregnancy and childbirth. I believe that the account I have given can accommodate this, although I do not see that it affects the enunciation of the basic rights themselves, which necessarily remain general. Beyond this, we can observe that all the rights require interpretations, a sort of inevitable casuistry, in which they are interpreted for the concrete social and historical world as it presents itself, and here too differences between people, including sexual difference, sometimes rightly enter. In short, then, I am arguing that the equality entailed by human rights is fully compatible with, and indeed sometimes requires, differential but equivalent treatment, if this equality is to be realized.

Traditional Cultures Versus Women's Equality in a Human Rights Framework

Let us turn finally to the question about the multiplicity of cultures in connection with conceptualizing women's human rights. We can note that the question is how to deal with the Western dominance in human rights discourse – with its commitment in principle to women's equality and the need for nondiscrimination, its strong public–private divide, its priority to the individual, and its preference for first-generation civil and political rights over second- and third-generation economic, social, cultural, and development rights – in relation to the diversity of cultures worldwide, many of which explicitly advocate sex-stratified societies in which men are dominant. The number and scope of the reservations that various states have registered to the CEDAW Convention are testimony to this contested situation. And given that feminists have been among the most sensitive toward recognizing differences among women as relevant to their theories, we may ask again whether this entails the requirement of accepting cultural norms that we may regard as oppressing women, especially when these norms may be endorsed or implemented by women themselves.

We can observe in this context that we need to avoid not only essentializing women's experience or gender norms more generally but also essentializing cultures, regarding them as uniform and as static or unchanging over time. In fact, there is a diversity of perspectives within cultures, and an important issue for women is that of "Who speaks for the culture?"[24] As we know, women have been relatively silenced in many cultures, at least in the public domain. Thus, in most cases, those who articulate and interpret cultural norms have been men. This inegalitarian and undemocratic situation is beginning to be rectified in many countries, where increasingly we find women's social movements gaining new influence, and we can hope to see more women in the role of interpreting cultural doctrines as well. Thus it is unacceptable for states or the men within them to assert the priority of their traditional cultures if they retain for themselves the sole power to interpret them and to speak for these cultures.

If we recognize that not only gender norms but also cultures are constructed and transformed over time by the people within them as well as through interaction more globally, then we can find in this capacity of people to change themselves and their cultures that very agency that is recognized so centrally as the ground for human rights themselves and that bears some relation to the idea of human dignity, also embodied in these rights. Furthermore, the centrality of the social interaction within and across cultures supports the idea that human rights have a basis in these concrete social relations and not only enunciate an abstract human equality and universality; and I proposed earlier that this gives rise to a norm of concrete universality. It is therefore appropriate to see human rights as emerging from these practical contexts and also as properly subject to interpretation according to changing social and historical mores and practices.

Moreover, if we look at the full range of human rights doctrine, as discussed previously there has been a process of intercultural determination of these rights, and this process needs also to be intensified. This is premised not simply on the idea of a global dialogical community (with Habermassian influences), to which some feminists have appealed,[25] but also on the more concrete social interactions that emerge within and across cultures when people are engaged in common projects and joint social movements, and when they come to feel care for those at some distance from themselves. In these more positive manifestations of globalization – to the degree that they can actually come to the fore in the face of nondemocratic forms of global dominance – we can see the basis for a more open and genuinely intercultural constitution of human rights, as well as more diversity in their interpretation. Still, hard questions remain here, and these brief remarks are not intended to put this difficult issue to rest.

It is also worth observing that, when construed in this open way, it is the human rights themselves that can set appropriate limits to the tolerance of diverse cultural practices, including those oppressive to women. Thus when women's rights to freedom from domination and bodily harm are violated within a given culture as part of its tradition, the approach proposed here gives priority to women's equality and bodily integrity, as among the basic human rights, over regard for such cultural differences. While a general right to the preservation and development of cultural differences may be counted among the human rights, it cannot legitimate actions that violate the basic

human rights of others. In short, there is a normative limit to cultural difference: Pernicious differences – those that violate basic human rights – cannot be claimed as a matter of cultural right.[26]

One final proviso is in order and emerges rather directly from the preceding: Obviously, women's human rights are insufficient by themselves to effect full change in the situation of women. Not only rights but also actual social change in oppressive social relations are needed, with the grassroots movements and activism that this entails. And we require not only more theory but also social critique, as well as efforts to connect the human rights principles discussed here to concrete social relations, which necessarily remain both their ground and their reference point.

Notes

1   See, for example, Hilary Charlesworth, "What are 'Women's International Human Rights'?" and Celina Romany, "State Responsibility Goes Private: A Feminist Critique of the Public/Private Distinction in International Human Rights Law," in *Human Rights of Women*, ed. Rebecca J. Cook (Philadelphia, PA: University of Pennsylvania Press, 1994), pp. 58–115; and Donna Sullivan, "The Public/Private Distinction in International Human Rights Law," in *Women's Rights, Human Rights*, eds. Julie Peters and Andrea Wolper (New York: Routledge, 1995), 126–34.

2   See, for example, Rhonda Copelon, "Intimate Terror: Understanding Domestic Violence as Torture," and Rebecca J. Cook, "State Accountability Under the Convention on the Elimination of All Forms of Discrimination Against Women," in *Human Rights of Women*, 116–52 and 228–56; Charlotte Bunch, "Transforming Human Rights from a Feminist Perspective," and Rebecca J. Cook, "International Human Rights and Women's Reproductive Health," in *Women's Rights, Human Rights*, 11–17 and 256–75.

3   Martha Nussbaum, "Religion and Women's Human Rights," in *Sex and Social Justice* (New York: Oxford University Press, 1999), pp. 81–117.

4   See note 1.

5   See, for example, the discussion in Henry Steiner and Philip Alston, *International Human Rights in Context*, 2nd edn. (Oxford: Oxford University Press, 2000), pp. 158–224.

6   See, for example, Cook, "State Accountability under CEDAW."

7   See especially Karen Knop, "Why Rethinking the Sovereign State is Important for Women's International Human Rights Law," in *Human Rights of Women*, 153–64.

8   See, for example, Sara Ruddick, *Maternal Thinking* (Boston: Beacon Press, 1989), Joan Tronto, *Moral Boundaries: A Political Argument for an Ethic of Case* (New York: Routledge, 1993), Virginia Held, *Feminist Morality* (Chicago: University of Chicago Press, 1993), and Jane Mansbridge, "Feminism and Democratic Community," and Carol C. Gould, "Feminism and Democratic

Community Revisited," in *Democratic Community*, eds. John W. Chapman and Ian Shapiro (New York: New York University Press, 1993), pp. 339–413.

9 Fiona Robinson, *Globalizing Care* (Boulder, CO: Westview Press, 1999).

10 Carol Gilligan, "Moral Orientation and Moral Development," in *Women and Moral Theory*, eds. Eva F. Kittay and Diana T. Meyers (Totowa, NJ: Rowman & Littlefield, 1987), pp. 19–33.

11 See Carole Pateman, *The Sexual Contract* (Stanford, CA: Stanford University Press, 1988).

12 See Robert E. Goodin, "International Ethics and the Environmental Crisis," in *Ethics and International Affairs*, 2nd edn, ed. Joel H. Rosenthal (Washington, DC: Georgetown University Press, 1999), pp. 443–6.

13 See notes 1 and 2.

14 In this connection, we can note the Security Council resolution 1325 (2000) concerning the impact of armed conflict on women (and girls) and their role in peacekeeping and peace-building.

15 Copelon, "Intimate Terror: Understanding Domestic Violence as Torture."

16 Helen Bequaert Holmes, "A Feminist Analysis of the United Nations Declaration of Human Rights," in Carol C. Gould (ed.), *Beyond Domination: New Perspectives on Women and Philosophy* (Totowa, NJ: Rowman & Littlefield, 1984), pp. 256–7. See also Charlesworth, "What are 'Women's International Human Rights'?", p. 73.

17 On this issue, see the essays in Susan Okin et al., *Is Multiculturalism Bad for Women?* (Princeton, NJ: Princeton University Press, 1999).

18 Amartya Sen, "Gender Inequality and Theories of Justice," in *Women, Culture, and Development*, eds. Jonathan Glover and Martha Nussbaum (Oxford: Oxford University Press, 1995), p. 259.

19 See Nussbaum, "Religion and Women's Human Rights," pp. 89–90.

20 Nahid Toubia, "Female Genital Mutilation," in *Women's Rights, Human Rights*.

21 For a recent statement, see Amartya Sen, *Development as Freedom* (New York: Alfred A. Knopf, 2000), Chapter 8.

22 Hilary Charlesworth, "Human Rights as Men's Rights," in *Women's Rights, Human Rights*, p. 108.

23 Ibid., especially pp. 202–4.

24 See Arati Rao, "The Politics of Gender and Culture in International Human Rights Discourse," in *Women's Rights, Human Rights*, pp. 167–75.

25 See Seyla Benhabib, "Cultural Complexity, Moral Interdependence, and the Global Dialogical Community," in *Women, Culture, and Development*, pp. 235–55.

26 For further discussion, see Carol C. Gould, "Cultural Justice and the Limits of Difference: Feminist Contributions to Value Inquiry," *Utopia* (Athens), Vol. 21 (July–Aug. 1996): 131–43; and in revised form in *Norms and Values: Essays in Honor of Virginia Held*, eds. J. G. Haber and M. S. Halfon (Lanham, MD: Rowman & Littlefield, 1998), pp. 73–85.

Part XI

International Environmental Justice

Introduction

Perhaps the last frontier of work in global justice has been in the area of international environmental justice. This section highlights only a small part of the exciting research in this field.

Peter Singer has long championed the environmentalist cause. In the first reading (chapter 37), he argues that there is no greater reason in favor of global action than the damaging impact of human activities on our environment. After documenting the evidence of environmental damage, he then considers various arguments that others have put forward as the best frameworks for agreeing a solution to the damage from human-generated climate change. Singer argues that our atmosphere has a limit to how much greenhouse gases it can absorb without suffering damage. Total global emissions must fall within this limit. The task then is to determine how much each society may emit without collectively surpassing the atmosphere's limit. Singer defends the view that states are offered a per capita share of this limit. Moreover, he supports global emissions trading where a state using less than its total share sells its unused share to other states on the grounds that such trade will help facilitate a smooth transition to a more environmentally friendly global order.

The final reading by Simon Caney (chapter 38) considers the plausibility of the "polluter pays" principle. His argument is that human interests are threatened by changes to the earth's climate. In other words, with increasing evidence of global warming, coastal communities come under threat from rising sea levels, droughts become more frequent leading to food shortages, and diseases, such as malaria and cholera, become more widespread. Changes in the earth's climate that increase the likelihood of these threats to human interests are, at least in part, caused by human activity.

One way forward is to endorse the "polluter pays" principle, which says that when any polluter X generates pollution Y that creates harm Z, and so the polluter X must pay reparations to the cost of Z. What is at stake is not the amount of pollution, but the harm created by the amount of pollution. Thus, if one state generates more pollution than another state, then the former need only pay greater reparations if the harm created by the pollution is greater in value than the harm generated by the latter state.

Caney argues that the "polluter pays" principle is unsatisfactory, even if intuitively appealing. First, we know that taken as a whole polluters have contributed to environmental damage. However, we do not know with sufficient precision how much each participating polluter contributes to pollution in each polluting act. We ought not, therefore, to apply the "polluter pays" principle to polluters individually but to the group as a whole. Second, if we decide to enforce the "polluter pays" principle today, then those who generated pollution in the past – and who have created the current environmental crisis – need not pay for the damage they have caused. That is, the damage has been created by the policies of past generations, and it is unfair to simply have the advanced world pay for damage caused by previous generations. In making them pay, the polluter doesn't pay, but the beneficiaries of past polluters pay.

Instead, Caney argues that people have a right against harm generated by climate change. This view does not rest on humans causing the harm. What it does rest on is the following: (a) we can only permissibly emit greenhouse gases within a certain range, (b) we must compensate others if we exceed this range, and (c) the most advantaged states have a duty to create global institutions to discourage non-compliance. Thus, Caney develops a new "hybrid" account where not only do we hold that the polluter should pay, but that the polluter must be held to account – it is crucial that the polluter comply. Moreover, different states are treated differently. That is, the global poor are permitted higher emissions than the global rich because, Caney argues, the least advantaged should not shoulder the burden of repairing environmental damage.

Both Singer's and Caney's accounts are based on the scientific consensus that human societies have contributed to climate change and its harmful effects on the planet. Yet, both diverge on the question of what justice demands in response to these effects. It is clear that issues of international environmental justice are particularly complex. It is hoped that these chapters not only shed light on the nature of this complexity, but that they also inspire readers to further develop this work.

Chapter 37

One Atmosphere
Peter Singer

The Problem

There can be no clearer illustration of the need for human beings to act globally than the issues raised by the impact of human activity on our atmosphere. That we all share the same planet came to our attention in a particularly pressing way in the 1970s when scientists discovered that the use of chlorofluorocarbons (CFCs) threatens the ozone layer shielding the surface of our planet from the full force of the sun's ultraviolet radiation. Damage to that protective shield would cause cancer rates to rise sharply and could have other effects, for example, on the growth of algae. The threat was especially acute to the world's southernmost cities, since a large hole in the ozone was found to be opening up each year over Antarctica, but in the long term, the entire ozone shield was imperiled. Once the science was accepted, concerted international action followed relatively rapidly with the signing of the Montreal Protocol in 1985. The developed countries phased out virtually all use of CFCs by 1999, and the developing countries, given a ten-

year period of grace, are now moving toward the same goal.

Getting rid of CFCs has turned out to be just the curtain raiser: the main event is climate change, or global warming. Without belittling the pioneering achievement of those who brought about the Montreal Protocol, the problem was not so difficult, for CFCs can be replaced in all their uses at relatively little cost, and the solution to the problem is simply to stop producing them. Climate change is a very different matter.

The scientific evidence that human activities are changing the climate of our planet has been studied by a working group of the Intergovernmental Panel on Climate Change, or IPCC, an international scientific body intended to provide policymakers with an authoritative view of climate change and its causes. The group released its *Third Assessment Report* in 2001, building on earlier reports and incorporating new evidence accumulated over the previous five years. The Report is the work of 122 lead authors and 515 contributing authors, and the research on which it was based was reviewed by 337 experts. Like any scientific document it is open to criticism from other scientists, but it reflects a broad consensus of leading scientific opinion and is by far the most

* From Peter Singer, *One World: The Ethics of Globalization*, 2nd edn. (New Haven, CT: Yale University Press, 2002; 2007), pp. 14–50, 205–8 (notes).

authoritative view at present available on what is happening to our climate.

The *Third Assessment Report* finds that our planet has shown clear signs of warming over the past century. The 1990s were the hottest decade, and 1998 the hottest year, recorded over the 140 years for which meteorological records have been kept. As 2001 drew to a close, the World Meteorological Organization announced that it would be second only to 1998 as the hottest year recorded. In fact nine of the ten hottest years during this period have occurred since 1990, and temperatures are now rising at three times the rate of the early 1900s.[1] Sea levels have risen by between 10 and 20 centimeters (4 to 8 inches) over the past century. Since the 1960s snow and ice cover has decreased by about 10 percent, and mountain glaciers are in retreat everywhere except near the poles. In the past three decades the El Niño effect in the southern hemisphere has become more intense, causing greater variation in rainfall. Paralleling these changes is an unprecedented increase in concentrations of carbon dioxide, methane, and nitrous oxide in the atmosphere, produced by human activities such as burning fossil fuels, the clearing of vegetation, and (in the case of methane) cattle and rice production. Not for at least 420,000 years has there been so much carbon dioxide and methane in the atmosphere.

How much of the change in climate has been produced by human activity, and how much can be explained by natural variation? The *Third Assessment Report* finds "new and stronger evidence that most of the warming observed over the last 50 years is attributable to human activities," and, more specifically, to greenhouse gas emissions. The report also finds it "very likely" that most of the rise in sea levels over the past century is due to global warming.[2] Those of us who have no expertise in the scientific aspects of assessing climate change and its causes can scarcely

disregard the views held by the overwhelming majority of those who do possess that expertise. They could be wrong – the great majority of scientists sometimes are – but in view of what is at stake, to rely on that possibility would be a risky strategy.

What will happen if we continue to emit increasing amounts of greenhouse gases and global warming continues to accelerate? The *Third Assessment Report* estimates that between 1990 and 2100, average global temperatures will rise by at least 1.4°C (2.5°F), and perhaps by as much as 5.8°C (10.4°F).[3] Although these average figures may seem quite small – whether tomorrow is going to be 20°C (69°F) or 22°C (72°F) isn't such a big deal – even a 1°C rise in average temperatures would be greater than any change that has occurred in a single century for the past 10,000 years. Moreover, some regional changes will be more extreme and are much more difficult to predict. Northern landmasses, especially North America and Central Asia, will warm more than the oceans or coastal regions. Precipitation will increase overall, but there will be sharp regional variations, with some areas that now receive adequate rainfall becoming arid. There will also be greater year-to-year fluctuations than at present – which means that droughts and floods will increase. The Asian summer monsoon is likely to become less reliable. It is possible that the changes could be enough to reach critical tipping points at which the weather systems alter and the directions of major ocean currents, such as the Gulf Stream, change.

What will the consequences be for humans?

- As oceans become warmer, hurricanes and tropical storms that are now largely confined to the tropics will move farther from the equator, hitting large urban areas that have not been built to cope with them. This is a prospect that is viewed with great concern in the insurance industry, which has already seen the cost of natural disasters rise dramatically in recent decades.[4]

- Tropical diseases will become more widespread.
- Food production will rise in some regions, especially in the high northern latitudes, and fall in others, including sub-Saharan Africa.
- Sea levels will rise by between 9 and 88 centimeters (between 4 and 35 inches).

Rich nations may, at considerable cost, be able to cope with these changes without enormous loss of life. They are in a better position to store food against the possibility of drought, to move people away from flooded areas, to fight the spread of disease-carrying insects and to build seawalls to keep out the rising seas. Poor nations will not be able to do so much. Bangladesh, the world's most densely populated large country, has the world's largest system of deltas and mud-flats, where mighty rivers like the Ganges and the Brahmaputra reach the sea. The soil in these areas is fertile, but the hazards of living on such low-lying land are great. In 1991 a cyclone hit the coast of Bangladesh, coinciding with high tides that left 10 million people homeless and killed 139,000. Most of these people were living on mudflats in the deltas. People continue to live there in large numbers because they have nowhere else to go. But if sea levels continue to rise, many peasant farmers will have no land left. As many as 70 million people could be affected in Bangladesh, and a similar number in China. Millions more Egyptian farmers on the Nile delta also stand to lose their land. On a smaller scale, Pacific island nations that consist of low-lying atolls face even more drastic losses. Kiribati, placed just to the west of the International Date Line, was the first nation to enter the new millennium. Ironically, it may also be the first to leave it, disappearing beneath the waves. High tides are already causing erosion and polluting fragile sources of fresh water, and some uninhabited islands have been submerged.

Global warming would lead to an increase in summer deaths due to heat stress, but these would be offset by a reduced death toll from winter cold. Much more significant than either of these effects, however, would be the spread of tropical diseases, including diseases carried by insects that need warmth to survive. The *Third Assessment Report* considers several attempts to model the spread of diseases like malaria and dengue, but finds that the research methodology is, at this stage, inadequate to provide good estimates of the numbers likely to be affected.[5]

If the Asian monsoon becomes less reliable, hundreds of millions of peasant farmers in India and other countries will go hungry in the years in which the monsoon brings less rain than normal. They have no other way of obtaining the water needed for growing their crops. In general, less reliable rainfall patterns will cause immense hardship among the large proportion of the world's population who must grow their own food if they want to eat.

The consequences for non-human animals and for biodiversity will also be severe. In some regions plant and animal communities will gradually move farther from the equator, or to higher altitudes, following climate patterns. Elsewhere that option will not be available. Australia's unique alpine plants and animals already survive only on the country's highest alpine plains and peaks. If snow ceases to fall on their territory, they will become extinct. Coastal ecosystems will change dramatically, and warmer waters may destroy coral reefs. These predictions look ahead only as far as 2100, but even if greenhouse gas emissions have been stabilized by that time, changes in climate will persist for hundreds, perhaps thousands of years. A small change in average global temperatures could, over the next millennium, lead to the melting of the Greenland ice cap which, added to the partial melting of the West Antarctic ice sheet, could increase sea levels by 6 meters, or nearly 20 feet.[6]

All of this forces us to think differently about our ethics. Our value system evolved in circumstances in which the atmosphere, like the oceans, seemed an unlimited resource, and responsibilities and harms were generally clear and well defined. If someone hit someone else, it was clear who had done what. Now the twin problems of the ozone hole and of climate change have revealed bizarre new ways of killing people. By spraying deodorant at your armpit in your New York apartment, you could, if you use an aerosol spray propelled by CFCs, be contributing to the skin cancer deaths, many years later, of people living in Punta Arenas, Chile. By driving your car, you could be releasing carbon dioxide that is part of a causal chain leading to lethal floods in Bangladesh.[7] How can we adjust our ethics to take account of this new situation?

Rio and Kyoto

That seemingly harmless and trivial human actions can affect people in distant countries is just beginning to make a significant difference to the sovereignty of individual nations. Under existing international law, individuals and companies can sue for damages if they are harmed by pollution coming from another country, but nations cannot take other nations to court. In January 2002, Norway announced that it would push for a binding international "polluter-pays" scheme for countries. The announcement followed evidence that Britain's Sellafield nuclear power plant is emitting radioactive wastes that are reaching the Norwegian coastline. Lobsters and other shellfish in the North Sea and the Irish Sea have high levels of radioactive technetium-99.[8]

The Sellafield case has revealed a gap in environmental legislation on a global basis. Norway is seeking an international convention on environmental pollution, first at the European level, and then, through the United Nations, globally. The principle is one that is difficult to argue against, but if Norway can force Britain to pay for the damage its leaking nuclear plant causes to their coastline, will not nations like Kiribati be able to sue America for allowing large quantities of carbon dioxide to be emitted into the atmosphere, causing rising sea levels to submerge their island homes? Although the link between rising sea levels and a nation's emissions of greenhouse gases is much more difficult to prove than the link between Britain's nuclear power plant and technetium-99 found along the Norwegian coast, it is hard to draw a clear line of principle between the two cases. Yet accepting the right of Kiribati to sue for damages for American greenhouse gas emissions makes us one world in a new and far more sweeping sense than we ever were before. It gives rise to a need for concerted international action.

Climate change entered the international political arena in 1988, when the United Nations Environment Program and the World Meteorological Office jointly set up the Intergovernmental Panel on Climate Change. In 1990 the IPCC reported that the threat of climate change was real, and a global treaty was needed to deal with it. The United Nations General Assembly resolved to proceed with such a treaty. The United Nations Framework Convention on Climate Change was agreed to in 1992, and opened for signature at the Earth Summit, or more formally, the United Nations Conference on Environment and Development, which was held in Rio de Janeiro in the same year. This "framework convention" has been accepted by 181 governments. It is, as its name suggests, no more than a framework for further action, but it calls for greenhouse gases to be stabilized at safe levels, and it says that the parties to the convention should do this "on the basis of equity and in accordance with their common but differentiated responsibilities and respective capabilities." Developed nations should "take the lead in combating climate change and the adverse effects thereof." The developed nations committed themselves to 1990 levels of emissions by the year 2000, but this commitment was not legally binding.[9] For the United States and several other countries, that was just as well, because they came nowhere near meeting it. In the United States, for example, by 2000 carbon dioxide emissions were 14 percent higher than they were in 1990. Nor was the trend improving, for the increase between 1999 and 2000 was 3.1 percent, the biggest one-year increase since the mid 1990s.[10]

The framework convention builds in what is sometimes called "the precautionary principle," calling on the parties to act to avoid the risk of serious and irreversible damage even in the absence of full scientific certainty. The convention also recognizes a "right to sustainable development," asserting that economic development is essential for addressing climate change. Accordingly, the Rio Earth Summit did not set any emissions reduction targets for developing countries to meet.

The framework convention set up a procedure for holding "conferences of the parties" to assess progress. In 1995, this conference decided that more binding targets were needed. The result, after two years of negotiations, was the 1997 Kyoto Protocol, which set targets for 39 developed nations to limit or reduce their greenhouse gas emissions by 2012. The limits and reductions were designed to reduce total emissions from the developed nations to a level at least 5 percent below 1990 levels. The national targets vary, however, with the European Union nations and the United States having targets of 8 percent and 7 percent, respectively, below 1990 levels, and other nations, such as Australia, being allowed to go over their 1990 levels. These targets were arrived at through negotiations with government leaders, and they were not based on any general principles of fairness, nor much else that can be defended on any terms other than the need to get agreement.[11] This was necessary since under the prevailing conception of national sovereignty, countries cannot be bound to meet their targets unless they decide to sign the treaty that commits them to do so. To assist countries in reaching their targets, the Kyoto Protocol accepted the principle of "emissions trading," by which one country can buy emissions credits from another country that can reach its target with something to spare.

The Kyoto conference did not settle the details of how countries could meet their targets, for example, whether they would be allowed credits for planting forests that soak up carbon dioxide from the atmosphere, and how emissions trading was to operate. After a meeting at The Hague failed to reach agreement on these matters, they were resolved at further meetings held in Bonn and Marrakech in July and November 2001, respectively. There, 178 nations reached an historic agreement that makes it possible to put the Kyoto Protocol into effect. American officials, however, were merely watching from the sidelines. The United States was no longer a party to the agreement.

The Kyoto agreement will not solve the problem of the impact of human activity on the world's climate. It will only slow the changes that are now occurring. For that reason, some skeptics have argued that the likely results do not justify the costs of putting the agreement into effect. In an article in *The Economist*, Bjorn Lomborg writes:

> Despite the intuition that something drastic needs to be done about such a costly problem,

economic analyses clearly show that it will be far more expensive to cut carbon-dioxide emissions radically than to pay the costs of adaptation to the increased temperatures.[12]

Lomborg is right to raise the question of costs. It is conceivable, for example, that the resources the world is proposing to put into reducing greenhouse gas emissions could be better spent on increasing assistance to the world's poorest people, to help them develop economically and so cope better with climate change. But how likely is it that the rich nations would spend the money in this manner? Their past record is not encouraging. A comparatively inefficient way of helping the poor may be better than not helping them at all.

Significantly, Lomborg's highly controversial book, *The Skeptical Environmentalist*, offers a more nuanced picture than the bald statement quoted above. Lomborg himself points out that, even in a worst-case scenario in which Kyoto is implemented in an inefficient way, "there is no way that the cost will send us to the poorhouse." Indeed, he says, one could argue that whether we choose to implement the Kyoto Protocol or to go beyond it, and actually stabilize greenhouse gases:

> The total cost of managing global warming *ad infinitum* would be the same as deferring the [economic] growth curve by less than a year. In other words we would have to wait until 2051 to enjoy the prosperity we would otherwise have enjoyed in 2050. And by that time the average citizen of the world will have become twice as wealthy as she is now.[13]

Lomborg does claim that the Kyoto Protocol will lead to a net loss of $150 billion. This estimate assumes that there will be emissions trading within the developed nations, but not among all nations of the world. It also assumes that the developing nations will remain outside the Protocol – in which case the effect of the agreement will be only to delay, by a few years, the predicted changes to the climate. But if the developing nations join in once they see that the developed nations are serious about tackling their emissions, and if there is global emissions trading, then Lomborg's figures show that the Kyoto pact will bring a net benefit of $61 billion.

These estimates all assume that Lomborg's figures are sound – a questionable assumption, for how shall we price the increased deaths from tropical diseases and flooding that global warming will bring? How much should we pay to prevent the extinction of species and entire ecosystems? Even if we could answer these questions, and agree on the figures that Lomborg uses, we would still need to consider his decision to discount all future costs at an annual rate of 5 percent. A discount rate of 5 percent means that we consider losing $100 today to be the equivalent of losing $95 in a year's time, the equivalent of losing $90.25 in two years' time, and so on. Obviously, then, losing something in, say, 40 years' time isn't going to be worth much, and it wouldn't make sense to spend a lot now to make sure that you don't lose it. To be precise, at this discount rate, it would only be worth spending $14.20 today to make sure that you don't lose $100 in 40 years' time. Since the costs of reducing greenhouse gas emissions will come soon, whereas most of the costs of not doing anything to reduce them fall several decades into the future, this makes a huge difference to the cost/benefit equation. Assume that unchecked global warming will lead to rising sea levels, flooding valuable land in 40 years' time. With an annual discount rate of 5 percent, it is worth spending only $14.20 to prevent flooding that will permanently inundate land worth $100. Losses that will occur a century or more hence dwindle to virtually nothing. This is not because of inflation – we are talking about costs expressed in dollars already adjusted for inflation. It is simply discounting the future. Lomborg justifies the use of a discount rate by arguing that if we invest $14.20 today, we can get a (completely safe) return of 5 percent on it, and so it will grow to $100 in 40 years. Though the use of a discount rate is a standard economic practice, the decision about which rate should be used is highly speculative, and assuming different interest rates, or even acknowledging uncertainty about interest rates, would lead to very different cost/benefit ratios.[14] There is also an ethical issue about discounting the future. True, our investments may increase in value over time, and we will become richer, but the price we are prepared to pay to save human lives, or endangered species, may go up just as much. These values are not consumer goods, like TVs or dishwashers, which drop in value in proportion to our earnings. They are things like health, something that the richer we get, the more we are willing to spend to preserve. An ethical, not an economic, justification would be needed for discounting suffering and death, or the extinction of species, simply because these losses will not occur for 40 years. No such justification has been offered.

It is important to see Kyoto not as the solution to the problem of climate change, but as the first step. It is reasonable to raise questions about whether the relatively minor delay in global warming that Kyoto would bring about is worth the cost. But if we see Kyoto as a necessary step for persuading the developing countries that they too should reduce greenhouse gas emissions, we can see why we should support it. Kyoto provides a platform from which a more far-reaching and also more equitable agreement can be reached. Now we need to ask what that agreement would need to be like to satisfy the requirement of equity or fairness.

What Is an Equitable Distribution?

In the second of the three televised debates held during the 2000 US presidential election, the candidates were asked what they would do about global warming. George W. Bush said:

> I'll tell you one thing I'm not going to do is I'm not going to let the United States carry the burden for cleaning up the world's air, like the Kyoto treaty would have done. China and India were exempted from that treaty. I think we need to be more even-handed.

There are various principles of fairness that people often use to judge what is fair or "even-handed." In political philosophy, it is common to follow Robert Nozick in distinguishing between "historical" principles and "time-slice" principles.[15] An historical principle is one that says: we can't decide, merely by looking at the present situation, whether a given distribution of goods is just or unjust. We must also ask how the situation came about; we must know its history. Are the parties entitled, by an originally justifiable acquisition and a chain of legitimate transfers, to the holdings they now have? If so, the present distribution is just. If not, rectification or compensation will be needed to produce a just distribution. In contrast, a time-slice principle looks at the existing distribution at a particular moment and asks if that distribution satisfies some principles of fairness, irrespective of any preceding sequence of events. I shall look at both of these approaches in turn.

A Historical Principle: "The Polluter Pays" or "You Broke It, Now You Fix It"

Imagine that we live in a village in which everyone puts their wastes down a giant sink.

No one quite knows what happens to the wastes after they go down the sink, but since they disappear and have no adverse impact on anyone, no one worries about it. Some people consume a lot, and so have a lot of waste, while others, with more limited means, have barely any, but the capacity of the sink to dispose of our wastes seems so limitless that no one worries about the difference. As long as that situation continues, it is reasonable to believe that, in putting waste down the sink, we are leaving "enough and as good" for others, because no matter how much we put down it, others can also put as much as they want, without the sink overflowing. This phrase "enough and as good" comes from John Locke's justification of private property in his *Second Treatise on Civil Government*, published in 1690. In that work Locke says that "the earth and all that is therein is given to men for the support and comfort of their being." The earth and its contents "belong to mankind in common." How, then, can there be private property? Because our labor is our own, and hence when we mix our own labor with the land and its products, we make them our own. But why does mixing my labor with the common property of all humankind mean that I have gained property in what belongs to all humankind, rather than lost property in my own labor? It has this effect, Locke says, as long as the appropriation of what is held in common does not prevent there being "enough and as good left in common for others."[16] Locke's justification of the acquisition of private property is the classic historical account of how property can be legitimately acquired, and it has served as the starting point for many more recent discussions. Its significance here is that, if it is valid and the sink is, or appears to be, of limitless capacity, it would justify allowing everyone to put what they want down the sink, even if some put much more than others down it.

Now imagine that conditions change, so that the sink's capacity to carry away our wastes is used up to the full, and there is already some unpleasant seepage that seems to be the result of the sink's being used too much. This seepage causes occasional problems. When the weather is warm, it smells. A nearby water hole where our children swim now has algae blooms that make it unusable. Several respected figures in the village warn that unless usage of the sink is cut down, all the village water supplies will be polluted. At this point, when we continue to throw our usual wastes down the sink we are no longer leaving "enough and as good" for others, and hence our right to unchecked waste disposal becomes questionable. For the sink belongs to us all in common, and by using it without restriction now, we are depriving others of their right to use the sink in the same way without bringing about results none of us wants. We have an example of the well-known "tragedy of the commons."[17] The use of the sink is a limited resource that needs to be shared in some equitable way. But how? A problem of distributive justice has arisen.

Think of the atmosphere as a giant global sink into which we can pour our waste gases. Then once we have used up the capacity of the atmosphere to absorb our gases without harmful consequences, it becomes impossible to justify our usage of this asset by the claim that we are leaving "enough and as good" for others. The atmosphere's capacity to absorb our gases has become a finite resource on which various parties have competing claims. The problem is to allocate those claims justly.

Are there any other arguments that justify taking something that has, for all of human history, belonged to human beings in common, and turning it into private property? Locke has a further argument, arguably inconsistent with his first argument, defending the continued unequal distribution of property even when there is no longer "enough and as good" for others. Comparing the situation of American Indians, where there is no private ownership of land, and hence the land is not cultivated, with that of England, where some landowners hold vast estates and many laborers have no land at all, Locke claims that "a king of a large and fruitful territory there [i.e., in America] feeds, lodges, and is clad worse than a day laborer in England."[18] Therefore, he suggests, even the landless laborer is better off because of the private, though unequal, appropriation of the common asset, and hence should consent to it. The factual basis of Locke's comparison between English laborers and American Indians is evidently dubious, as is its failure to consider other, more equitable ways of ensuring that the land is used productively. But even if the argument worked for the landless English laborer, we cannot defend the private appropriation of the global sink in the same way. The landless laborer who no longer has the opportunity to have a share of what was formerly owned in common should not complain, Locke seems to think, because he is better off than he would have been if inegalitarian private property in land had not been recognized. The parallel argument to this in relation to the use of the global sink would be that even the world's poorest people have benefited from the increased productivity that has come from the use of the global sink by the industrialized nations. But the argument does not work, because many of the world's poorest people, whose shares of the atmosphere's capacity have been appropriated by the industrialized nations, are not able to partake in the benefits of this increased productivity in the industrialized nations – they cannot afford to buy its products – and if rising sea levels inundate their farm lands, or cyclones destroy their homes, they will be much worse off than they would otherwise have been.

Apart from John Locke, the thinker most often quoted in justifying the right of the rich to their wealth is probably Adam Smith. Smith argued that the rich did not deprive the poor of their share of the world's wealth, because:

> The rich only select from the heap what is most precious and agreeable. They consume little more than the poor, and in spite of their natural selfishness and rapacity, though they mean only their own conveniency, though the sole end which they propose from the labours of all the thousands whom they employ, be the gratification of their own vain and insatiable desires, they divide with the poor the produce of all their improvements.[19]

How can this be? Because, Smith tells us, it is as if an "invisible hand" brings about a distribution of the necessaries of life that is "nearly the same" as it would have been if the world had been divided up equally among all its inhabitants. By that Smith means that in order to obtain what they want, the rich spread their wealth throughout the entire economy. But while Smith knew that the rich could be selfish and rapacious, he did not imagine that the rich could, far from consuming "little more" than the poor, consume many times as much of a scarce resource as the poor do. The average American, by driving a car, eating a diet rich in the products of industrialized farming, keeping cool in summer and warm in winter, and consuming products at a hitherto unknown rate, uses more than fifteen times as much of the global atmospheric sink as the average Indian. Thus Americans, along with Australians, Canadians, and to a lesser degree Europeans, effectively deprive those living in poor countries of the opportunity to develop along the lines that the rich ones themselves have taken. If the poor were to behave as the rich now do, global warming would accelerate and almost certainly bring widespread catastrophe.

The putatively historical grounds for justifying private property put forward by its most philosophically significant defenders – writing at a time when capitalism was only beginning its rise to dominance over the world's economy – cannot apply to the current use of the atmosphere. Neither Locke nor Smith provides any justification for the rich having more than their fair share of the finite capacity of the global atmospheric sink. In fact, just the contrary is true. Their arguments imply that this appropriation of a resource once common to all humankind is not justifiable. And since the wealth of the developed nations is inextricably tied to their prodigious use of carbon fuels (a use that began more than 200 years ago and continues unchecked today), it is a small step from here to the conclusion that the present global distribution of wealth is the result of the wrongful expropriation by a small fraction of the world's population of a resource that belongs to all human beings in common.

For those whose principles of justice focus on historical processes, a wrongful expropriation is grounds for rectification or compensation. What sort of rectification or compensation should take place in this situation?

One advantage of being married to someone whose hair is a different color or length from your own is that, when a clump of hair blocks the bath outlet, it's easy to tell whose hair it is. "Get your own hair out of the tub" is a fair and reasonable household rule. Can we, in the case of the atmosphere, trace back what share of responsibility for the blockage is due to which nations? It isn't as easy as looking at hair color, but a few years ago researchers measured world carbon emissions from 1950 to 1986 and found that the United States, with about 5 percent of the world's population at that time, was responsible for 30 percent of the cumulative emissions, whereas India, with 17 percent of the world's population, was responsible for less than 2 percent of the emissions.[20] It is as if, in a village of 20 people all using the same bathtub, one person had shed 30 percent of the hair blocking the drain hole and three people had shed virtually no hair at all. (A more accurate model would show that many more than three had shed virtually no hair at all. Indeed, many developing nations have per capita emissions even lower than India's.) In these circumstances, one basis of deciding who pays the bill for the plumber to clear out the drain would be to divide it up proportionally to the amount of hair from each person that has built up over the period that people have been using the tub, and has caused the present blockage.

There is a counterargument to the claim that the United States is responsible for more of the problem, per head of population, than any other country. The argument is that because the United States has planted so many trees in recent decades, it has actually soaked up more carbon dioxide than it has emitted.[21] But there are many problems with this argument. One is that the United States has been able to reforest only because it earlier cut down much of its great forests, thus releasing the carbon into the atmosphere. As this suggests, much depends on the time period over which the calculation is made. If the period includes the era of cutting down the forests, then the United States comes out much worse than if it starts from the time in which the forest had been cut, but no reforestation had taken place. A second problem is that forest regrowth, while undoubtedly desirable, is not a long-term solution to the emissions problem but a temporary and one-shot expedient, locking up carbon only while the trees are growing. Once the forest is mature and an old tree dies and rots for every new tree that grows, the forest no longer soaks up significant amounts of carbon from the atmosphere.[22]

At present rates of emissions – even including emissions that come from changes in land use like clearing forests – contributions of the developing nations to the atmospheric stock of greenhouse gases will not equal the built-up contributions of the developed nations until about 2038. If we adjust this calculation for population – in other words, if we ask when the contributions of the developing nations per person will equal the per person contributions of the developed nations to the atmospheric stock of greenhouse gases – the answer is: not for at least another century.[23]

If the developed nations had had, during the past century, per capita emissions at the level of the developing nations, we would not today be facing a problem of climate change caused by human activity, and we would have an ample window of opportunity to do something about emissions before they reached a level sufficient to cause a problem. So, to put it in terms a child could understand, as far as the atmosphere is concerned, the developed nations broke it. If we believe that people should contribute to fixing something in proportion to their responsibility for breaking it, then the developed nations owe it to the rest of the world to fix the problem with the atmosphere.

Time-Slice Principles

The historical view of fairness just outlined puts a heavy burden on the developed nations. In their defense, it might be argued that at the time when the developed nations put most of their cumulative contributions of greenhouse gases into the atmosphere, they could not know of the limits to the capacity of the atmosphere to absorb those gases. It would therefore be fairer, it may be claimed, to make a fresh start now and set standards that look to the future, rather than to the past.

There can be circumstances in which we are right to wipe the slate clean and start again. A case can be made for doing so with respect to cumulative emissions that occurred before governments could reasonably be expected to know that these emissions might harm people in other countries. (Although, even here, one could argue that ignorance is no excuse and a stricter standard of liability should prevail, especially since the developed nations reaped the benefits of their early industrialization.) At least since 1990, however, when the Intergovernmental Panel on Climate Change published its first report, solid evidence about the hazards associated with emissions has existed.[24] To wipe the slate clean on what happened since 1990 seems unduly favorable to the industrialized nations that have, despite that evidence, continued to emit a disproportionate share of greenhouse gases. Nevertheless, in order to see whether there are widely held principles of justice that do not impose such stringent requirements on the developed nations as the "polluter pays" principle, let us assume that the poor nations generously overlook the past. We would then need to look for a time-slice principle to decide how much each nation should be allowed to emit.

An Equal Share for Everyone

If we begin by asking, "Why should anyone have a greater claim to part of the global atmospheric sink than any other?" then the first, and simplest response is: "No reason at all." In other words, everyone has the same claim to part of the atmospheric sink as everyone else. This kind of equality seems self-evidently fair, at least as a starting point for discussion, and perhaps, if no good reasons can be found for moving from it, as an end point as well.

If we take this view, then we need to ask how much carbon each country would be allowed to emit and compare that with what they are now emitting. The first question is what total level of carbon emission is acceptable. The Kyoto Protocol aimed to achieve a level for developed nations that was 5 percent below 1990 levels. Suppose that we focus on emissions for the entire planet and aim just to stabilize carbon emissions at their present levels. Then the allocation per person conveniently works out at about 1 metric ton per year. This therefore becomes the basic equitable entitlement for every human being on this planet.

Now compare actual per capita emissions for some key nations. The United States currently produces more than 5 tons of carbon per person per year. Japan and Western European nations have per capita emissions that range from 1.6 tons to 4.2 tons, with most below 3 tons. In the developing world, emissions average 0.6 tons per capita, with China at 0.76 and India at 0.29.[25] This means that to reach an "even-handed" per capita annual emission limit of 1 ton of carbon per person, India would be able to increase its carbon emissions to more than three times what they now are. China would be able to increase its emissions by a more modest 33 percent. The United States, on the other hand, would have to reduce its emissions to no more than one-fifth of present levels.

One objection to this approach is that allowing countries to have allocations based on the number of people they have gives them insufficient incentive to do anything about population growth. But if the global population increases, the per capita amount of carbon that each country is allocated will diminish, for the aim is to keep total carbon emissions below a given level. Therefore a nation that increases its population would be imposing additional burdens on other nations. Even nations with zero population growth would have to decrease their carbon outputs to meet the new, reduced per capita allocation.

By setting national allocations that are tied to a specified population, rather than allowing national allocations to rise with an increase in national population, we can meet this objection. We could fix the national allocation on the country's population in a given year, say 1990, or the year that the agreement comes into force. But since different countries have different proportions of young people about to reach reproductive age, this provision might produce greater hardship in those countries that have younger populations than in those that have older populations. To overcome this, the per capita allocation could be based on an estimate of a country's likely population at some given future date. For example, estimated population sizes for the next 50 years, which are already compiled by the United Nations, might be used.[26] Countries would then receive a reward in terms of an increased emission quota per citizen if they achieved a lower population than had been expected, and a penalty in terms of a reduced emission quota per citizen if they exceeded the population forecast – and there would be no impact on other countries.

Aiding the Worst-off

Giving everyone an equal share of a common resource like the capacity of the atmosphere to absorb our emissions is, I have argued, a fair starting point, a position that should prevail unless there are good reasons for moving from it. Are there such reasons? Some of the best-known accounts of fairness take the view that we should seek to improve the prospects of those who are worst off. Some hold that we should assist the worst-off only if their poverty is due to circumstances for which they are not responsible, like the family, or country, into which they were born, or the abilities they have inherited. Others think we should help the worst-off irrespective of how they have come to be so badly off. Among the various accounts that pay special attention to the situation of the worst-off, by far the most widely discussed is that of John Rawls. Rawls holds that, when we distribute goods, we can only justify giving more to those who are already well off if this will improve the position of those who are worst off. Otherwise, we should give only to those who are, in terms of resources, at the lowest level.[27] This approach allows us to depart from equality, but only when doing so helps the worst-off.

Whereas the strict egalitarian is vulnerable to the objection that equality can be achieved by "leveling down," that is, by bringing the rich down to the level of the poor without improving the position of the poor, Rawls's account is immune to this objection. For example, if allowing some entrepreneurs to become very rich will provide them with incentives to work hard and set up industries that provide employment for the worst-off, and there is no other way to provide that employment, then that inequality would be permissible.

That there are today very great differences in wealth and income between people living in different countries is glaringly obvious. It is equally evident that these differences depend largely on the fact that people are born into different circumstances, rather than because they have failed to take advantage of opportunities open to them. Hence if in distributing the atmosphere's capacity to absorb our waste gases without harmful consequences, we were to reject any distribution that fails to improve the situation of those who, through no fault of their own, are at the bottom of the heap, we would not allow the living standard in poor countries to be reduced while rich countries remain much better off.[28] To put this more concretely: if, to meet the limits set for the United States, taxes or other disincentives are used that go no further than providing incentives for

Americans to drive more fuel-efficient cars, it would not be right to set limits on China that prevent the Chinese from driving cars at all.

In accordance with Rawls's principle, the only grounds on which one could argue against rich nations bearing *all* the costs of reducing emissions would be that to do so would make the poor nations even worse off than they would have been if the rich nations were not bearing all the costs. It is possible to interpret President George W. Bush's announcement of his administration's policy on climate change as an attempt to make this case. Bush said that his administration was adopting a "greenhouse gas intensity approach" which seeks to reduce the amount of greenhouse gases the United States emits per unit of economic activity. Although the target figure he mentioned – an 18 percent reduction over the next 10 years – sounds large, if the US economy continues to grow as it has in the past, such a reduction in greenhouse gas intensity will not prevent an *increase* in the total quantity of greenhouse gases that the United States emits. But Bush justified this by saying "economic growth is the solution, not the problem" and "the United States wants to foster economic growth in the developing world, including the world's poorest nations."[29]

Allowing nations to emit in proportion to their economic activity – in effect, in proportion to their Gross Domestic Product – can be seen as encouraging efficiency, in the sense of leading to the lowest possible level of emissions for the amount produced. But it is also compatible with the United States continuing to emit more emissions, because it is producing more goods. That will mean that other nations must emit less, if catastrophic climate change is to be averted. Hence for Bush's "economic growth is the solution, not the problem" defense of a growth in US emissions to succeed as a Rawlsian defense of continued inequality in per

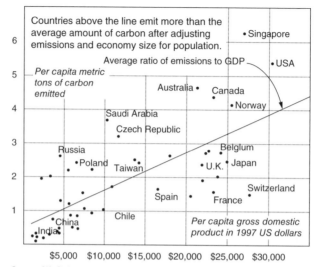

Sources: CIA; Carbon Dioxide Information Analysis Center; James Bronzan,The New York Times

Figure 37.1

capita emissions, it would be necessary to show that United States production not only makes the world as a whole better off, but also makes the poorest nations better off than they would otherwise be.

The major ethical flaw in this argument is that the primary beneficiaries of US production are the residents of the United States itself. The vast majority of the goods and services that the United States produces – 89 percent of them – are consumed in the United States.[30] Even if we focus on the relatively small fraction of goods produced in the United States that are sold abroad, US residents benefit from the employment that is created and, of course, US producers receive payment for the goods they sell abroad. Many residents of other countries, especially the poorest countries, cannot afford to buy goods produced in the United States, and it isn't clear that they benefit from US production.

The factual basis of the argument is also flawed: the United States does not produce more efficiently, in terms of greenhouse gas

emissions, than other nations. Figures published by the US Central Intelligence Agency show that the United States is well above average in the amount of emissions per head it produces in proportion to its per capita GDP (see Figure 37.1). On this basis the United States, Australia, Canada, Saudi Arabia, and Russia are relatively inefficient producers, whereas developing countries like India and China join European nations like Spain, France, and Switzerland in producing a given value of goods per head for a lower than average per capita level of emissions.[31]

Emissions and Gross Domestic Product

Because the efficiency argument fails, we must conclude that a principle that requires us to distribute resources so as to improve the level of the worst-off would still, given the huge resource gap between rich and poor nations, make the rich nations bear all of the costs of the required changes.

The Greatest Happiness Principle

Classical utilitarians would not support any of the principles of fairness discussed so far. They would ask what proposal would lead to the greatest net happiness for all affected – net happiness being what you have left when you deduct the suffering caused from the happiness brought about. An advocate of preference utilitarianism, a more contemporary version of utilitarianism, would instead ask what proposal would lead to the greatest net satisfaction of preferences for all concerned. But in this context, the difference between the two forms of utilitarianism is not very significant. What is much more of a problem, for either of these views, is to indicate how one might do such a calculation. Evidently, there are good utilitarian reasons for capping the emission of greenhouse gases, but what way of doing it will lead to the greatest net benefits?

Perhaps it is because of the difficulty of answering such broad questions about utility that we have other principles, like the ones we have been discussing. They give you easier answers and are more likely to lead to an outcome that approximates the best consequences (or is at least as likely to do so as any calculation we could make without using those principles). The principles discussed above can be justified in utilitarian terms, although each for somewhat different reasons. To go through them in turn:

1. The principle that "the polluter pays," or more generally "you broke it, you fix it," provides a strong incentive to be careful about causing pollution, or breaking things. So if it is upheld as a general rule, there will be less pollution, and people will be more careful in situations where they might break something, all of which will be to the general benefit.
2. The egalitarian principle will not, in general, be what utilitarians with perfect knowledge of all the consequences of their actions would choose. Where there is no other clear criterion for allocating shares, however, it can be an ideal compromise that leads to a peaceful solution, rather than to continued fighting. Arguably, that is the best basis for defending "one person, one vote" as a rule of democracy against claims that those who have more education, or who pay more taxes, or who have served in the military or who believe in the one true God, or who are worse off should have additional votes because of their particular attributes.[32]
3. In practice, utilitarians can often support the principle of distributing resources to those who are worst off, because when you already have a lot, giving you more does not increase your utility as much as when you have only a little. One of the 1.2 billion people in the world living on $1 per day will get much more utility out of an additional $100 than will someone living on $60,000 per year. Similarly, if we have to take $100 from someone, we will cause much less suffering if we take it from the person earning $60,000 than if we take it from the person earning $365 a year. This is known as "diminishing marginal utility." When compared with giving resources to meet someone's core needs, giving further resources "at the margin" to someone else whose core needs have already been satisfied will lead to diminished utility. Hence a utilitarian will generally favor the worst-off when it comes to distributing resources. In contrast to Rawls, however, a utilitarian does not consider this principle to be absolute. The utilitarian always seeks the greatest overall benefit, and it is only a broad rule of thumb that this will generally be obtained by adding to the stock of resources of those who have the least.

The utilitarian would also have to take into account the greater hardship that might be imposed on people living in countries that have difficulty in complying with strict emission standards because their geography or climate compels their citizens to use a greater amount of energy to achieve a given level of comfort than do people living elsewhere. Canadians, for example, could argue that it would simply not be possible to live in many parts of their country without using above average quantities of energy to keep warm. Residents of rich countries might even advance the bolder claim that, since their affluent residents have become used to traveling by car, and keeping their houses cool in warm humid weather, they would suffer more if they have to give up their energy-intensive lifestyle than poorer people will suffer if they never get the chance to experience such comforts.

The utilitarian cannot refuse to consider such claims of hardship, even when they come from those who are already far better off than most of the world's people. As we shall see, however, these claims can be taken into account in a way that is compatible with the general conclusion to which the utilitarian view would otherwise lead: that the United States and other rich nations should bear much more of the burden of reducing greenhouse gas emissions than the poor nations – perhaps even the entire burden.

Fairness: A Proposal

Each of the four principles of fairness I have considered could be defended as the best one to take, or we could take some in combination. I propose, both because of its simplicity, and hence its suitability as a political compromise, and because it seems likely to increase global welfare, that we support the second principle, that of equal per capita future entitlements to a share of the capacity of the atmospheric sink, tied to the current United Nations projection of population growth per country in 2050.

Some will say that this is excessively harsh on industrialized nations like the United States, which will have to cut back the most

on their output of greenhouse gases. But we have now seen that the equal per capita shares principle is much more indulgent to the United States and other developed nations than other principles for which there are strong arguments. If, for example, we combined "the polluter pays" principle with the equal share principle, we would hold that until the excessive amounts of greenhouse gases in the atmosphere that the industrialized nations have put there have been soaked up, the emissions of industrialized nations ought to be held down to much *less* than a per capita equal share. As things stand now, even on an equal per capita share basis, for at least a century the developing nations are going to have to accept lower outputs of greenhouse gases than they would have had to, if the industrialized nations had kept to an equal per capita share in the past. So by saying, "forget about the past, let's start anew," the pure equal per capita share principle is a lot more favorable to the developed countries than an historically based principle would be.

The fact that 178 nations, including every major industrial nation in the world except the United States, have now indicated their intention to ratify the Kyoto Protocol makes the position of the United States particularly odious from an ethical perspective. The claim that the Protocol does not require the developing nations to do their share does not stand up to scrutiny. Americans who think that even the Kyoto Protocol requires America to sacrifice more than it should are really demanding that the poor nations of the world commit themselves to a level that gives them, in perpetuity, lower levels of greenhouse gas production per head of population than the rich nations have. How could that principle be justified? Alternatively, if that is not what the US Government is proposing, what exactly is it proposing?

It is true that there are some circumstances in which we are justified in refusing to contribute if others are not doing their share. If we eat communally and take turns cooking, then I can justifiably feel resentment if there are some who eat but never cook or carry out equivalent tasks for the good of the entire group. But that is not the situation with climate change, in which the behavior of the industrialized nations has been more like that of a person who has left the kitchen tap running but refuses either to turn it off, or to mop up the resulting flood, until you – who spilt an insignificant half-glass of water onto the floor – promise not to spill any more water. Now the other industrialized nations have agreed to turn off the tap (to be strictly accurate, to restrict the flow), leaving the United States, the biggest culprit, alone in its refusal to commit itself to reducing emissions.

Although it is true that the Kyoto Protocol does not initially bind the developing nations, it is generally understood that the developing countries will be brought into the binding section of the agreement after the industrialized nations have begun to move toward their targets. That was the procedure with the successful Montreal Protocol concerning gases that damage the ozone layer, and there is no reason to believe that it will not also happen with the Kyoto Protocol. China, by far the largest greenhouse gas emitter of the developing nations and the only one with the potential to rival the total – not, of course, per capita – emissions of the United States in the foreseeable future, has already, even in the absence of any binding targets, achieved a substantial decline in fossil-fuel CO_2 emissions, thanks to improved efficiency in coal use. Emissions fell from a high of 909 million metric tons of carbon in 1996 to 848 million metric tons of carbon in 1998. Meanwhile US emissions reached an all-time high of 1,906 million metric tons of carbon in 2000, an increase of 2.5 percent over the previous year.[33]

The real objection to allocating the atmosphere's capacity to absorb greenhouse gases to nations on the basis of equal per capita shares is that it would be tremendously dislocating for the industrialized nations to reduce their emissions so much that, within 5, 10, or 15 years, they were not producing more than their share, on a per capita basis, of some acceptable level of greenhouse gases. But fortunately there is a mechanism that, while fully compatible with the equal per capita share principle, can make this transition much easier for the industrialized nations, while at the same time producing great benefits for the developing nations. That mechanism is emissions trading. Emissions trading works on the same simple economic principle of trade in general: if you can buy something from someone else more cheaply than you can produce it yourself, you are better off buying it than making it. In this case, what you can buy will be a transferable quota to produce greenhouse gases, allocated on the basis of an equal per capita share. A country like the United States that is already producing more gases than its share will need its full quota, and then some, but a country like Russia that is below its share will have excess quota that it can sell. If the quota were not transferable, the United States would immediately have to reduce its output to about 20 percent of what it now produces, a political impossibility. In contrast, Russia would have no incentive to maintain its levels of greenhouse gas emissions well below its allowable share. With emissions trading, Russia has an incentive to maximize the amount of quota it can sell, and the United States has, at some cost, an opportunity to acquire the quotas it needs to avoid total disruption of the economy.[34]

Although some may think that emissions trading allows the United States to avoid its burdens too easily, the point is not to punish nations with high emissions, but to produce the best outcome for the atmosphere. Permitting emissions trading gives us a better hope of doing this than prohibiting emissions trading does. The Kyoto Protocol as agreed to in Bonn and Marrakech allows emissions trading between states that have binding quotas. Thus Russia will have quota to sell, but countries like India, Bangladesh, Mozambique, Ethiopia, and many others will not. Emissions trading would be much more effective, and have far better consequences, if all nations were given binding quotas based on their per capita share of the designated total emissions. As we saw earlier in this chapter, even the environmental skeptic Bjorn Lomborg accepts that with global emissions trading, the Kyoto Protocol produces a net economic benefit. Moreover, global emissions trading would give the world's poorest nations something that the rich nations very much want. They would have, at last, something that they can trade in exchange for the resources that will help them to meet their needs. This would be, on most principles of justice or utility, a very good thing indeed. It could also end the argument about making the developing nations part of a binding agreement on emissions, because the developing nations would see that they have a great deal to gain from binding quotas.

Since global emissions trading is both possible and desirable, it also answers two objections to allocating greenhouse gas emissions quotas on the basis of equal per capita shares. First, it answers the objection raised when discussing a utilitarian approach to these problems, that countries like Canada might suffer undue hardship if forced to limit emissions to the same per capita amount as, say, Mexico, because Canadians need to use more energy to survive their winters. But global emissions trading means that Canada would be able to buy the quota it requires from other countries that do not need their full quota. Thus the market would provide a measure of the additional burden put on the world's atmosphere by keeping one's house at a pleasant temperature when it is too cold,

or too hot, outside. Citizens of rich countries could choose to pay that price and keep themselves warm, or cool, as the case may be. They would not, however, be claiming a benefit for themselves that they were not prepared to allow poor countries to have, because the poor countries would benefit by having emission quotas to sell. The claim of undue hardship therefore does not justify allowing rich countries to have a higher per capita emissions quota than poor countries.

Second, global emissions trading answers the objection that equal per capita shares would lead to inefficient production because countries with little industrialization would be able to continue to manufacture goods even though they emit more greenhouse gases per unit of economic activity than highly industrialized nations, while the highly industrialized nations would have to cut back on their manufacturing capacity, even though they produce fewer emissions per unit of economic activity. But as we have seen, the present laissez-faire system allows emitters to reap economic benefits for themselves, while imposing costs on third parties who may or may not share in the benefits of the polluters' high productivity. That is neither a fair nor an efficient outcome. A well-regulated system of per capita entitlements combined with global emissions trading would, by internalizing the true costs of production, lead to a solution that is both fair and efficient.

There are two serious objections, one scientific and one ethical, to global emissions trading. The scientific objection is that we do not have the means to measure emissions accurately for all countries. Hence it would not be possible to know how much quota these countries have to sell, or need to buy. This is something that needs more research, but it should not prove an insuperable obstacle in the long run. As long as estimates are fair, they do not need to be accurate to the last ton of carbon. The ethical objection is that while emissions trading would benefit poor countries if the governments of those countries used it for the benefit of their people, some countries are run by corrupt dictators more interested in increasing their military spending, or adding to their Swiss bank accounts. Emissions trading would simply give them a new way of raising money for these purposes.

The ethical objection is similar to a problem discussed elsewhere and my proposed solution may be clearer after reading that section. It is to refuse to recognize a corrupt dictatorial regime, interested only in self-preservation and self-enrichment, as the legitimate government of the country that has excess quota to sell. In the absence of any legitimate government that can receive payments for quota, the sale of quota could be managed by an international authority answerable to the United Nations. That authority could hold the money it receives in trust until the country has a government able to make a credible claim that the money will be used to benefit the people as a whole.

Down from the Clouds?

To cynical observers of the Washington scene, all this must seem absurdly lacking in political realism. George W. Bush's administration has spurned the Kyoto Protocol, which allows the United States to continue to produce at least four times its per capita share of carbon dioxide. Since 1990 US emission levels have already risen by 14 percent. The half-hearted measures for energy conservation proposed by the Bush administration will, at best, slow that trend. They will not reverse it. So what is the point of discussing proposals that are far *less* likely to be accepted by the US Government than the Kyoto Protocol?

The aim of this chapter is to help us to see that there is no *ethical* basis for the present distribution of the atmosphere's capacity to absorb greenhouse gases without drastic climate change. If the industrialized countries choose to retain this distribution (as the United States does), or to use it as the starting point for a new allocation of the capacity of the global sink (as the countries that accept the Kyoto Protocol do), they are standing simply on their presumed rights as sovereign nations. That claim, and the raw military power these nations yield, makes it impossible for anyone else to impose a more ethically defensible solution on them. If we, as citizens of the industrialized nations, do not understand what would be a fair solution to global warming, then we cannot understand how flagrantly self-serving the position of those opposed to signing even the Kyoto Protocol is. If, on the other hand, we can convey to our fellow citizens a sense of what would be a fair solution to the problem, then it may be possible to change the policies that are now leading the United States to block international cooperation on something that will have an impact on every being on this planet.

Let us consider the implications of this situation a little further. Today the overwhelming majority of nations in the world are united in the view that greenhouse gas emissions should be significantly reduced, and all the major industrial nations but one have committed themselves to doing something about this. That one nation, which happens to be the largest emitter of them all, has refused to commit itself to reducing its emissions. Such a situation gives impetus to the need to think about developing institutions or principles of international law that limit national sovereignty. It should be possible for people whose lands are flooded by sea level rises due to global warming to win damages from nations that emit more than their fair share of greenhouse gases. Another possibility worth considering is sanctions. There have been several occasions on which the United Nations has used sanctions against countries that have been seen as doing something gravely wrong. Arguably the case for sanctions against a nation that is causing harm, often fatal, to the citizens of other countries is even stronger than the case for sanctions against a country like South Africa under apartheid, since that govern-

ment, iniquitous as its policies were, was not a threat to other countries. [. . .] Is it inconceivable that one day a reformed and strengthened United Nations will invoke sanctions against countries that do not play their part in global measures for the protection of the environment?

Notes

1   "This Year was the 2nd Hottest, Confirming a Trend, UN Says," *New York Times*, 19 December 2001, p. A5.

2   J. T. Houghton et al. (eds.), *Climate Change 2001: The Scientific Basis: Contribution of Working Group I to the Third Assessment Report of the Intergovernmental Panel on Climate*, United Nations Environment Program and Intergovernmental Panel on Climate Change (Cambridge University Press, Cambridge, 2001), Summary for Policymakers; available at www.ipcc.ch/pub/tar/wg1/index.htm. See also *Reconciling Observations of Global Temperature Change*, Panel on Reconciling Temperature Observations, National Research Council, National Academy of Sciences, Washington, DC, 2000, available at www.nap.edu/books/0309068916/html. For another example of recent research indicating that anthropogenic climate change is real, see Thomas J. Crowley, "Causes of Climate Change Over the Past 1000 Years," *Science*, 14 July 2000, 289: 270–7.

3   Houghton et al. (eds.), *Climate Change 2001: The Scientific Basis*.

4   Munich Reinsurance, one of the world's largest insurance companies, has estimated that the number of major natural disasters has risen from 16 in the 1960s to 70 in the 1990s. Cited by Christian Aid, Global Advocacy Team Policy Position Paper, *Global Warming: Unnatural Disasters and the World's Poor*, November 2000, www.christianaid.org.uk/indepth/0011glob/globwarm.htm.

5   James McCarthy et al. (eds.), *Climate Change 2001: Impacts, Adaptation, and Vulnerability, Contribution of Working Group II to the Third Assessment Report of the Intergovernmental*

Panel on Climate Change, United Nations Environment Program and Intergovernmental Panel on Climate Change (Cambridge University Press, Cambridge, 2001), ch. 9.7; available at www.ipcc.ch/pub/tar/wg2/index.htm.

6   Houghton et al. (eds.), *Climate Change 2001, The Scientfic Basis*.

7   See Dale Jamieson, "Ethics, Public Policy, and Global Warming," *Science, Technology, and Human Values* 17:2, Spring 1992, pp. 139–53, and "Global Responsibilities: Ethics, Public Health, and Global Environmental Change," *Indiana Journal of Global Legal Studies* 5:1, Fall 1997, pp. 99–119.

8   "Norway Wants Sanctions for Cross Border Polluters," *Reuters News Service*, 1 February 2002, www.planetark.org/dailynewsstory.cfm/newsid/14316/story.htm.

9   *United Nations Framework Convention on Climate Change*, Article 4, section 2, subsections (a) and (b), available at www.unfccc.int/resource/conv/conv.html; *Guide to the Climate Change Negotiation Process*, www.unfccc.int/resource/process/components/reponse/respconv.html.

10   "US Carbon Emissions Jump in 2000," *Los Angeles Times*, 11 November 2001, p. A36, citing figures released by the US Department of Energy's Energy Information Administration on 9 November 2001.

11   Eileen Claussen and Lisa McNeilly, *The Complex Elements of Global Fairness*, Pew Center on Global Climate Change, Washington, DC, 29 October 1998, www.pewclimate.org/projects/pol_equity.cfm.

12   Bjorn Lomborg, "The Truth about the Environment," *The Economist*, 2 August

2001, available at www.economist.com/science/displayStory.cfm?Story_ID=718860&CFID=3046335&CFTOKEN=88404876.

[13] Bjorn Lomborg, *The Skeptical Environmentalist* (Cambridge University Press, Cambridge, 2001), p. 323.

[14] See Richard Newell and William Pizer, *Discounting the Benefits of Future Climate Change Mitigation: How Much Do Uncertain Rates Increase Valuations?* (Pew Center on Global Climate Change, Washington, DC), December 2001. Available at www.pewclimate.org/projects/econ_discounting.cfm.

[15] Robert Nozick, *Anarchy, State and Utopia* (Basic Books, New York, 1974), p. 153.

[16] John Locke, *Second Treatise on Civil Government*, C. B. Macpherson (ed.), Hacket, Indianapolis, 1980, sec. 27, p. 19.

[17] See Garrett Hardin, "The Tragedy of the Commons," *Science*, 162, 1968, pp. 1243–8.

[18] Locke, *Second Treatise on Civil Government*, sec. 41.

[19] Adam Smith, *A Theory of the Moral Sentiments* (Prometheus, Amherst, NY, 2000), IV, i. 10.

[20] Peter Hayes and Kirk Smith (eds.), *The Global Greenhouse Regime: Who Pays?* (Earthscan, London, 1993), ch 2, table 2.4, /80836E00.htm; available at www.unu.edu/unupress/unupbooks/80836e/80836E08.htm.

[21] See S. Fan, M. Gloor, J. Mahlman, S. Pacala, J. Sarmiento, T. Takahashi, and P. Tans, "A Large Terrestrial Carbon Sink in North America Implied by Atmospheric and Oceanic Carbon Dioxide Data and Models," *Science*, 282, 16 October 1998, pp. 442–6.

[22] William Schlesinger and John Lichter, "Limited Carbon Storage in Soil and Litter of Experimental Forest Plots under Increased Atmospheric CO_2," *Nature*, 411, 24 May 2001: 466–9.

[23] Duncan Austin, José Goldemberg, and Gwen Parker, "Contributions to Climate Change: Are Conventional Metrics Misleading the Debate?," World Resource Institute Climate Protection Initiative, Climate Notes, www.igc.org/wri/cpi/notes/metrics.html.

[24] The Intergovernmental Panel on Climate Change, *First Assessment Report* was pub-

lished in three volumes. See especially J. T. Houghton, G. J. Jenkins, and J. J. Ephraums (eds.), *Scientific Assessment of Climate Change – Report of Working Group I* (Cambridge University Press, Cambridge, 1990). For details of the other volumes see www.ipcc.ch/pub/reports.htm.

[25] See C. Marland, T. A. Boden, and R. J. Andres, *Global, Regional, and National Fossil Fuel CO_2 Emissions* (Carbon Dioxide Information Analysis Center, Oak Ridge, Tennessee), available at cdiac.esd.ornl.gov/trends/emis/top96.cap. These are 1996 figures.

[26] Paul Baer et al., "Equity and Greenhouse Gas Responsibility," *Science* 289, 29 September 2000: 2287; Dale Jamieson, "Climate Change and Global Environmental Justice," in P. Edwards and C. Miller (eds.), *Changing the Atmosphere: Expert Knowledge and Global Environmental Governance*, MIT Press (Cambridge, MA: 2001), pp. 287–307.

[27] See John Rawls, *A Theory of Justice*, especially pp. 65–83. For a different way of giving priority to the worst-off, see Derek Parfit, "Equality or Priority?," The Lindley Lecture, University of Kansas, 21 November 1991, reprinted in Matthew Clayton and Andrew Williams (eds.), *The Ideal of Equality* (Macmillan, London, 2000).

[28] This is Rawls's "difference principle," applied without the restriction to national boundaries that are difficult to defend in terms of his own argument.

[29] "President Announces Clear Skies and Global Climate Change Initiative," Office of the Press Secretary, White House, 14 February 2002, www.whitehouse.gov/news/releases/2002/02/20020214–5.html. For amplification of the basis of the administration's policy, see Executive Office of the President, Council of Economic Advisers, 2002 *Economic Report of the President*, US Government Printing Office, Washington, DC, 2002, ch. 6, pp. 244–9, http://w3.access.gpo.gov/eop/.

[30] National Council on Economic Education, "A Case Study: United States International Trade in Goods and Services – May 2001," www.econedlink.org/lessons/index.cfm?lesson=EM196.

31   Andrew Revkin, "Sliced Another Way: Per Capita Emissions," *New York Times,* 17 June 2001, section 4, p. 5.

32   For discussion of equal votes as a compromise, see my *Democracy and Disobedience* (Clarendon Press, Oxford, 1973), pp. 30–41.

33   Energy Information Administration, *Emissions of Greenhouse Gases in the United States 2000,* DOE/EIA-0573 (2000), US Department of Energy, Washington, DC, November 2001, page vii, www.eia.doe.gov/pub/oiaf/1605/cdrom/pdf/ggrpt/057300.pdf.

34   See Jae Edmonds et al., *International Emissions Trading and Global Climate Change: Impacts on the Cost of Greenhouse Gas Mitigation.* A report prepared for the Pew Center on Global Climate Change, December 1999, available at www.pewclimate.org/projects/econ_emissions.cfm.

Chapter 38

Cosmopolitan Justice, Responsibility, and Global Climate Change*
Simon Caney

It's exciting to have a real crisis on your hands when you have spent half your political life dealing with humdrum things like the environment.[1]

The world's climate is undergoing dramatic and rapid changes. Most notably the Earth has been becoming markedly warmer and its weather has, in addition to this, become increasingly unpredictable. These changes have had, and continue to have, important consequences for human life. In this paper I wish to examine what is the fairest way of dealing with the burdens created by global climate change. Who should bear the burdens? Should it be those who caused the problem? Should it be those best able to deal with the problem? Or should it be someone else? In this paper I defend a distinctive cosmopolitan theory of justice, criticize a key principle of international environmental law, and, moreover, challenge the 'common but differentiated responsibility' approach that is affirmed in current international environmental law.

[. . .]

_____
* From _Leiden Journal of International Law_ 18 (2005), pp. 747–72, 774–5.

1   Global Climate Change

Prior to beginning the normative analysis, it is necessary to make three preliminary points.

1   The topic of this paper is one instance of what might be termed 'global environmental justice', by which I mean the global distribution of environmental burdens and benefits. As such, it is worth making some methodological observations about the utility, or otherwise, of applying orthodox theories of distributive justice to climate change. How relevant are the normal theories of justice to this topic? Indeed, are they relevant at all? If they are relevant, in what ways, if any, do they need to be revised or adjusted? To answer this set of questions we may begin by observing that the standard analyses of distributive justice tend to focus on how income and wealth should be distributed among the current members of a state. To construct a theory of global environmental justice requires us to rethink three assumptions underpinning this normal analysis.[2]

First, distributive justice concerns itself with the distribution of burdens and benefits. Now conventional theories of distributive justice tend to focus on benefits such as wealth and income. It is important, then, to ask whether this framework can usefully be extended to include environmental burdens and benefits. In particular, we face the question of how to value the environment. Should it be valued because of its impact on what Rawls terms 'primary goods', by which Rawls means goods such as income, wealth, liberties, opportunities, and the social bases of self-respect?[3] Or should it be valued because of its effects on what Sen and Nussbaum call 'capabilities', where this refers to a person's ability to achieve certain 'functionings'?[4] Here we should be alive to the distinctive aspects of the environment that might mean that its importance (for a theory of justice) cannot be captured by the orthodox liberal discourse of resources, welfare, capabilities, and so on.[5]

Second, whereas conventional theories of distributive justice concern themselves with the distribution of burdens and benefits within a *state*, the issues surrounding climate change require us to examine the *global* distribution of burdens and benefits. An appropriate analysis needs, then, to address whether the kinds of principle that should be adopted at the domestic level should also be adopted at the global level. Perhaps the two are relevantly analogous, in which case the principles that should be implemented at home should also be implemented abroad. Perhaps, however, they are so completely different that we cannot apply principles fit for the domestic realm at the global level.[6] Either way, a theory of justice that is to be applied to global climate change must, of necessity, address the question of whether the global dimensions of the issue make a morally relevant difference.

Third, global environmental justice raises questions of intergenerational justice. This is true in two senses. First, the effects of global climate change will be felt by future people, so that an adequate theory of global environmental justice must provide guidance on what duties to future generations those living at present have. It must consider whether future people have rights, and whether there should be a social discount rate.[7] It must, further, explore whether the principles that apply within a generation will necessarily apply to future generations. Do the principles that apply within one generation differ from those that apply across time into the future? Some, like John Rawls, clearly think that they do, for he holds that the 'difference principle' (that the basic structure should be designed to maximize the condition of the least advantaged) should govern the distribution of resources within one generation but should not be applied intergenerationally. Another principle, that of just savings, determines the obligations persons have to future generations. According to the principle of 'just savings', societies should save enough so that succeeding generations are able to live in a just society. They need not pass on any more than that and certainly need not seek to maximize the condition of the least advantaged persons who will ever live.[8] Second, and furthermore, topics such as climate change require us to explore the moral relevance of decisions taken by previous generations. For example, some of the deleterious effects of industrialization are being felt now. This prompts the question of who should be responsible for dealing with the ill-effects that result from earlier generations. In short, then, a theory of justice that is to apply to global climate change must address the question of how the intergenerational dimensions of the issue make a morally relevant difference.

Drawing on these, then, we can say that an adequate theory of justice in relation to climate change must explain in what ways global climate change affects persons' entitlements and it must do so in a way that (i) is sensitive to the particularities of the environment; (ii) explores the issues that arise from applying principles at the global rather than the domestic level; and (iii) explores the intergenerational dimensions of global climate change.[9]

2 Turning now from methodological considerations to more empirical matters, an adequate analysis of the ethical dimensions of global climate change requires an empirical account of the different ways in which climate change is affecting persons' fundamental interests (by which I mean those interests that a theory of justice should seek to protect). In what follows I shall draw heavily on the findings of the Intergovernmental Panel on Climate Change (IPCC), set up in 1988 by the United Nations Environment Programme (UNEP) and the World Meteorological Organization (WMO).[10] It has now issued three assessment reports – in 1990, 1995 and 2001. For our purposes the key report is *The Third Assessment Report* published in 2001. This includes four volumes – *Climate Change 2001: The Scientific Basis, Climate Change 2001: Impacts, Adaptation and Vulnerability, Climate Change 2001: Mitigation*, and a summary of all three reports, *Climate Change 2001: Synthesis Report*. The findings of the IPCC have, of course, been criticized by a number of people – including, for example, Bjørn Lomborg – and there have, in turn, been replies to those critics.[11] I am not qualified to enter into these debates and so I shall report the IPCC's claims without assuming that those claims are incontestable. The IPCC reports most fully on the impacts of global climate change in its report entitled *Climate Change 2001: Impacts, Adaptation and Vulnerability*. In the latter it claims that global climate change will result, inter alia, in higher sea levels and therefore threaten coastal settlements and small island states. It will also result in higher temperatures and as a consequence will generate drought, crop failure, and heatstroke. The rise in temperature will also lead to an increased incidence of malaria and cholera. To this we should

also add that global climate change will result in greater weather unpredictability. This is, of course, only the briefest of summaries.[12] A fuller account will be introduced later on.

3 Having noted various ways in which climate change has harmful effects, I would now like to clarify what I mean when I refer to 'the burdens of global climate change'. As is commonly recognized, there are two distinct kinds of burden imposed by recent changes to the climate – what I shall term 'mitigation burdens' and 'adaptation burdens'.[13] 'Mitigation burdens', as I am defining that term, are the costs to actors of not engaging in activities that contribute to global climate change. Those who engage in a policy of mitigation bear an opportunity cost: they forego benefits that they could have had if they had engaged in activities which involve the emission of high levels of greenhouse gases (GHGs). To make this concrete, mitigation will involve cutting back on activities like the burning of fossil fuels and, as such, it requires either that persons cut back on their use of cars, electricity, and air flight or that they invest in other kinds of energy resource. Either way, mitigation is, of course, a cost for some.[14] The second kind of burden is what I have termed 'adaptation burdens'. These are the costs to persons of adopting measures which enable them and/or others to cope with the ill-effects of climate change. For there are ways in which people can adapt to some of the predicted outcomes of global climate change. They might, for example, spend more on drugs designed to minimize the spread of cholera and malaria. Or they might spend more on strengthening coastal regions against rising sea levels. These too should obviously count as a burden, for they require resources that could otherwise be spent on other activities.

My focus in this article is on the question 'who should bear the costs caused by climate change?' I shall not explore the difficult question of how much we should seek to mitigate and how much we should seek to adapt. This is, of course, a key question when determining what specific concrete policies should be implemented. It is also the subject of some controversy.[15] However, I wish to set that practical issue aside and simply focus on the more abstract question of who is morally responsible for bearing the burdens of climate change where the latter is silent on the choice between adaptation and mitigation.

2 The 'Polluter Pays' Principle

Let us turn now to a normative analysis of the responsibility of addressing these problems. On whose shoulders should the responsibility rest? Who is duty-bound to bear the burdens of global climate change? One common way of thinking about harms, including both environmental and non-environmental harms, maintains that those who have caused a problem (such as pollution) should foot the bill. In other words the key principle is that 'the polluter should pay'. This principle has considerable intuitive appeal. In everyday situations we frequently think that if someone has produced a harm (they have spilled rubbish on the streets, say) then they should rectify that situation. They as the causers are responsible for the ill-effects.

The 'polluter pays' principle (hereafter PPP) is also one that has been affirmed in a number of international legal agreements.[16] The Organization for Economic Co-operation and Development (OECD), for example, recommended the adoption of the 'polluter pays' principle in Council Recommendations of 26 May 1972 and 14 November 1974.[17] In addition to this, on 21 April 2004 the European Union and Council of Ministers passed a directive affirming the

'polluter pays' principle.[18] The principle has also been recommended by the Commission on Global Governance.[19] In addition to this, a number of academic commentators on the subject have applied this principle to the costs of global climate change. Henry Shue, for example, has drawn on the principle that those who have caused pollution should clear it up, and has argued vigorously that members of industrialized countries have caused global climate change and hence they, and not members of developing countries, should bear the burdens of climate change.[20] Furthermore, others in addition to Shue have argued that this is the right way of thinking about bearing the burdens of global climate change. Eric Neumayer, for instance, argues that the costs of global warming should be determined according to 'historical accountability'.[21] We might further note that the IPCC has addressed the question in *Climate Change 2001: Mitigation.*[22] It sought not to recommend any one course of action but it did cite the 'polluter pays' principle, along with various others, as a possible principle of justice. How appropriate, then, is the 'polluter pays' principle for determining the responsibility to bear the costs of climate change?

Let us begin our analysis by noting two clarificatory points.

First, the principle that the polluter pays usually means literally that if an individual actor, X, performs an action which causes pollution, then that actor should pay for the ill-effects of that action. Let us call this the micro-version. One might, however, reconstruct the PPP to mean also that if actors X, Y, and Z perform actions which together cause pollution, then they should pay for the cost of the ensuing pollution in proportion to the amount of pollution that they have caused. Let us call this the macro-version. This says that polluters (as a class) should pay for the pollution that they (as a class) have caused. So, whereas the micro-version establishes a direct link between an agent's actions and the pollution suffered by others, the macro-version establishes an indirect link between, on the one hand, the actions of a group of people (e.g., emitting carbon dioxide) and, on the other hand, a certain level of pollution.

This distinction is relevant because the micro-version can be applied only when one can identify a specific burden that results from a specific act. It is, however, inapplicable in cases where one cannot trace specific burdens back to earlier individual acts. Now climate change clearly falls into this category. If an industrial plant releases a high level of carbon dioxide into the air we cannot pick out specific individual costs that result from that particular actor and that particular action. The macro-version can, however, accommodate the causation of such effects. Even if one cannot say that A has caused this particular bit of global warming, one can say that this increase in global warming as a whole results from the actions of these actors. Furthermore, note that the macro-version can allow us to ascribe greater responsibilities to some. Even if it does not make sense to say that we can attribute a specifiable bit of global warming to each of them we can still say that those who emit more carbon dioxide than others are more responsible than those others. In principle, then, if one had all the relevant knowledge about agents' GHG emissions it would be possible to make individualistic assessments of just how much each agent owes. In the light of the above, then, we should interpret the PPP (when it is applied to the case of global warming) along the lines suggested by the macro-version.[23]

Second, to apply the 'polluter pays' approach to climate change we need to know 'who is the polluter?' What is the relevant unit of analysis? What kinds of entity are the polluters? Are they individuals, states, or some other entity? Furthermore, which of these entities plays the greatest role? Suppose that the relevant actor is, in fact, states; we then face the empirical question 'which particular states contribute the most?' Our answer to the question 'who pollutes?' is, of course, essential, if we accept the PPP, to enable us to allocate responsibilities and answer the question 'who should pay?'

Many of those who adopt a PPP approach to climate change appear to treat countries as the relevant unit. Shue, for example, makes constant reference to 'countries' and 'states'.[24] Similarly Neumayer refers always to the pollution caused by emitting countries, referring, for example, to 'the Historical Emission Debt (HEDi) of a country'.[25] As he says, his view

> holds countries accountable for the amount of greenhouse gas emissions remaining in the atmosphere emanating from a country's historical emissions. It demands that the major emitters of the past also undertake the major emission reductions in the future as the accumulation of greenhouse gases in the atmosphere is mostly their responsibility and the absorptive capacity of nature is equally allocated to all human beings no matter when or where they live.[26]

In their view, then, the polluters are countries. But is this an appropriate analysis? Consider the following possibilities.

(a) Individuals. First, we might observe that individuals use electricity for heating, cooking, lighting, televisions, and computers, and, of course, they consume fossil fuels by driving cars and by taking aeroplane flights – all of which are responsible for carbon dioxide emissions. The Third Assessment Report of the IPCC, moreover, says in its prescriptions that individuals must change their energy-intensive lifestyles.[27] Should we say, then, that individuals should pay? If so, it would seem that instead of stating simply that each country should

pay its share we should ideally, and in principle, claim that each individual should pay their share.

(b) *Economic corporations.* Perhaps, however, it might be argued that the primary causes of greenhouse gas emissions are those economic corporations which consume vast amounts of fossil fuels and/or bring about deforestation. If this is so, then presumably the primary responsibility should accrue to them.[28]

(c) *States.* Maybe, however, the relevant unit of analysis is the state. As noted above, this is what many commentators on the subject assume. Since they think that states should either cut back on GHG emissions or devote resources to cover the costs of adaptation they must think that states are the primary cause of global climate change.

(d) *International regimes and institutions.* However, it might perhaps be argued that one relevant factor is supra-state institutions and the nature of international law. One might, for example, think, like Thomas Pogge, that the 'explanatory nationalism' adopted by position (c) is untenable, for it fails to recognize the extent to which we are part of a globally interdependent order and that this gives rise to events often seen as domestic in nature.[29] Drawing on this, might one argue that the causes of pollution are not accurately seen as 'countries' or 'states' but rather international institutions or the international system. Perhaps, it might be argued, existing international institutions (such as the World Trade Organization (WTO) and the International Monetary Fund (IMF)), by promoting economic growth, encourage countries to engage in deforestation and the high use of fossil fuels, both activities which lead to climate change.

With this taxonomy in mind, let us make three points. The first is that the likely answer to the question 'who is the polluter?' will involve reference to several different kinds of actor. The aim of the taxonomy above is not to suggest that the appropriate answer lies at one level alone. Second, we should observe that to reach the standard conclusion (namely that certain *countries* should pay) we need to show that options (a), (b), and (d) do not hold. It might, for example, be argued against (d) that international law and regimes do not have any autonomy – they are merely the creations of states and, as such, the relevant level of analysis is the actions of states. And it might be argued against (a) and (b) that it is not possible to ascertain the GHG emissions of individual persons or individual corporations. Given this, we should refer to the GHG emissions of a country as the best approximation available. Alternatively, it might be argued against (a) and (b) that the GHG of individuals or corporations is what has been permitted by the relevant state, so that the latter should be held liable. My aim, here, is not to canvass any of these options, it is simply to point out that the only way to vindicate the conclusion reached by Neumayer, Shue, and others is to establish that the relevant unit of analysis is the state and that the other options collapse into it. Of course, further empirical analysis may reveal that it is simply implausible to hold that states are the appropriate entities and we need a fine-grained analysis which traces the contributions of individuals, corporations, states, and international actors and which accordingly attributes responsibilities to each of these.

Having made these two clarificatory points, let us turn now to consider some of the problems faced by the 'polluter pays' approach to allocating the burdens of climate change.

3 Past Generations

On problem with applying the 'polluter pays' principle to climate change is that much of the damage to the climate was caused by the policies of earlier generations. It is, for example, widely recognized that there have been high levels of carbon dioxide emissions for the last two hundred years, dating back to the Industrial Revolution in western Europe. This poses a simple, if also difficult, problem for the 'polluter pays' principle: who pays when the polluter is no longer alive? And the proposal, made by Neumayer and Shue, that the industrial economies of the first world should pay seems, on the face of it, unfair, for it does not make the actual polluters pay. Their conclusion, then, is not supported by the PPP: indeed it violates the PPP.

This is a powerful objection. However, at least three distinct kinds of response are available to an adherent of the argument under scrutiny.

3.1 The Individualist Position

One reply is given by both Shue and Neumayer. Both raise the problem of past generations but argue that this challenge can be met. In Shue's case, his response is that the current inhabitants of a country are not 'completely unrelated' to previous inhabitants and, as such, they can still bear responsibility for the actions of their ancestors. In particular, says Shue, they enjoy the benefits of the policies adopted by previous generations.[30] As he writes, 'current generations are, and future generations probably will be, continuing beneficiaries of earlier industrial activity'.[31] The same point is made by Neumayer, who writes,

The fundamental counter-argument against not being held accountable for emissions undertaken by past generations is that the current developed countries readily accept the benefits from past emissions in the form of their high standard of living and should therefore not be exempted from being held accountable for the detrimental side-effects with which their living standards were achieved.[32]

Let us call this reply the 'beneficiary pays' principle (BPP). Put more formally, this claims that where A has been made better off by a policy pursued by others, and the pursuit by others of that policy has contributed to the imposition of adverse effects on third parties, then A has an obligation not to pursue that policy itself (mitigation) and/or an obligation to address the harmful effects suffered by the third parties (adaptation).

So if the current inhabitants of industrialized countries have benefited from a policy of fossil-fuel consumption and that policy contributes to a process which harms others, then they are not entitled to consume fossil fuels to the same degree. Their standard of living is higher than it otherwise would have been and they must pay a cost for that.[33]

This line of reasoning has some appeal. Two points, however, should be made about it. First, we should record that the BPP is not a revision of the 'polluter pays' approach, it is an abandonment of it. It would justify imposing a burden on someone who cannot, in any conceivable sense, be said to have brought about an environmental bad but who nonetheless benefits from the policy that caused the environmental bad. In such a case that person is not a polluter but they are a beneficiary. Thus, according to the PPP, they should not be allocated a duty to make a contribution to cover the environmental bad; according to the BPP, however, they should. My second point is that the application of the BPP in this instance is more problematic than it might first seem. The reason for this draws on what Derek Parfit has termed the 'non-identity problem' in his seminal work *Reasons and Persons*. We need therefore to state this problem. In *Reasons and Persons* Parfit drew attention to an important feature of our moral duty to future generations. Parfit begins with the statement that who is born (which particular person) depends on exactly when their parents mated. If someone's parents had mated at a different time, then, of course, a different person would have been born. It follows from this that the policies that persons adopt at one time affect who will be born in the future. So suppose that we build factories now which have no immediate malign effects but which release poisonous fumes in 300 years. Now Parfit's point is this: the policies adopted now led to the birth of different people than would have been born if these policies had not been adopted. The future generations whose lives are threatened by poisonous fumes would not have been born were it not for the factory construction. So they cannot say that they were made worse off or harmed by the policy. The policy, according to Parfit, is bad but it has not made anyone worse off than they would have been if the policy had not been enacted.[34]

Now I think that a very similar point could be made against the use of the 'beneficiary pays' principle by the argument under scrutiny.[35] For it claims that the policies of industrialization benefited people who are currently alive. But in the same way that using up resources did not *harm* future people so industrialization did not make an *improvement* to the standard of living of currently existing people. We cannot say to people, 'You ought to bear the burdens of climate change because without industrialization you would be much worse off than you currently are.' We cannot because without industrialization the 'you' to which the previous sentence refers would not exist. Industrialization has not brought advantages to these people that they would otherwise be without.[36] And since it has not we cannot say to them, 'You should pay for these because your standard of living is higher than it would have been.'[37] For this reason the BPP is unable to show why members of industrialized countries should pay for the costs of the industrialization that was undertaken by previous generations.

3.2   The Collectivist Position

While the first response to the question as to why later generations should pay for the industrializing policies adopted by their ancestors is a rather individualistic one, a second response to the intergenerational challenge affirms a collectivist position.[38] This approach argues that the problem we are addressing arises only if we focus on individual persons. If we focus on individuals then making current individuals pay for pollution that stems from past generations is indeed making someone other than the polluter pay. Suppose, however, that we focus our attention on collective entities like a nation or a state (or an economic corporation). Consider a country such as Britain. It industrialized in the late eighteenth and the nineteenth centuries, thereby contributing to what would become the problem of global warming. Now if we take a collectivist approach we might say that since Britain (the collective) emitted excessive amounts of GHGs during one period in time then Britain (as a collective) may a hundred years later, say, be required to pay for the pollution it has caused, if it has not done so already. To make this collective unit pay *is* to make the polluter pay. So to return to the original objection, one might say that the premise of the objection (namely that the polluter is no longer alive) is incorrect.

Prior to evaluating this argument we should make three observations. First, note that although in this instance I have used an example of a nation as a collective there is no reason to assume that it must take this form. Suppose, for instance, that there is in existence a long-standing corporation. We might argue, in a collectivist vein, that if this entity has emitted high levels of carbon dioxide in the past then it should foot the bill now. The individual decision-makers of the time might be long gone but the corporation persists. Second, we might observe that the collectivist response is also relevant to the preceding discussion of the BPP. My objection to the use of the BPP above was that the acts which led to a higher standard of living (in this case industrialization) did not make the standard of living of currently alive persons higher than it would have been had industrialization never taken place. The collectivist perspective adds a different dimension to this for, as Edward Page has rightly noted, the identities of nations are less changeable over time than those of individuals. Industrialization may have affected which individuals get born: because of it different people are born than would have been born without it. And because of this it is inaccurate to say that currently alive individuals have a higher standard of living than those same individuals would have had if industrialization had never taken place. However, the acts of industrialization did not (let us assume) bring different countries into existence than would otherwise have existed.[39] So to turn to the objection to the BPP: whereas we cannot say that industrialization has bestowed (net) advantages on currently existing individuals that they would otherwise be without, we *can* say that industrialization has bestowed (net) advantages on currently existing countries (such as Britain) that they would otherwise be without. The collectivist response thus enables us to defend the BPP against my Parfit-inspired objection.[40] Third, and finally, we might observe that the collectivist response coheres with the way that some political philosophers have recently argued. For example, in *The Law of Peoples* John Rawls gave two examples which appealed to a similar kind of reasoning in order to rebut a cosmopolitan political morality. In one example Rawls asks us to compare a society which industrializes with one that eschews that path, choosing instead a more pastoral way of life. For his second example Rawls again asks us to compare two societies. One,

by granting women greater reproductive autonomy, results in a more controlled population policy with fewer children being born. The other society, by contrast, does not pursue this kind of population policy. In these scenarios, concludes Rawls, self-governing peoples (liberal or decent) should take responsibility for their policies. So to take the first example, Rawls's view is that justice does not require that the wealthy industrialized society should assist the poorer pastoral society.[41] Similar reasoning is adduced by David Miller, who argues that self-governing nations should be held accountable for their decisions.[42]

Let us now evaluate this collectivist response to the problem of past generations. It is vulnerable to two objections. First, it is not enough to draw attention to the possibility of affirming a collectivist position. We need to ascertain whether we have any reason to prefer a collectivist to an individualist approach. To vindicate the collectivist perspective we need an argument that can show when and why it is accurate to say that a collective caused an environmental bad and hence that that collective must pay. Indeed, we need an argument as to why this description is better than a more individualistic one (individuals a, b, and c polluted, and so individuals a, b, and c should pay). Second, a collectivist approach is vulnerable to a troubling problem. The root problem is that it seems unfair to make individuals pay the costs generated by preceding generations. In taking a collectivist route are we not being unfair to individuals who did not make those decisions and who might have objected violently to those decisions? Can they not reasonably complain that they were not consulted; they did not vote; they disapproved of the policies and, as such, should not be required to pay for decisions that others took. 'Normally', they might add, 'individuals cannot inherit debts from parents or grandparents, so why should this be any different?' For this reason, then, a collectivist response to the problems raised by the excessive GHG emissions of earlier generations is not an attractive position.[43]

3.3   A Third Response

Thus far we have examined two responses to the intergenerational objection. The first contends that people currently living in industrialized countries have benefited from pollution-causing economic growth. The second contends that the relevant causal actors are collectives which still exist today (either corporations or countries or collective units such as 'the industrialized world'). A third response would be to argue that all the burdens of human-induced climate change should be paid for by existing polluters. The suggestion, then, is that current polluters should pay the costs of their pollution and that of previous generations. In this way, it might be said, the mitigation and adaptation costs of climate change are shouldered by the polluters (and not by non-polluters). But this seems unfair: they are paying more than their due. The intuition underlying the PPP (about which more later) is that people should pay for the harm that *they* (not others) have created. It is alien to the spirit of the principle to make people pay for pollution which is not theirs. So even if the proposal does, in one sense, make polluters pay (no non-polluters pay), it does not make sure that the costs of polluters are traced back to the particular polluters and that is what the PPP requires.

The first objection has not challenged the claim that the polluter should pay (except for Shue's revision of the principle). Rather it has shown, first, that proponents of the PPP are not entitled to conclude that current members of industrialized states should pay for the costs of global warming. And, second, it has more generally shown that the PPP cannot say who should bear the costs of

climate change caused by past generations. We might, however, raise questions about the 'polluter pays' principle itself. I now want to consider several challenges to the fundamental principle.

4   Ignorance and Obligation

One doubt about the 'polluter pays' principle is that it is too crude and undiscriminating in its treatment of the relevant duty-bearers. What if someone did not know that performing a certain activity (such as burning fossil fuels) was harmful? And suppose, furthermore, that there was no way in which they could have known that it was harmful. In such a situation their ignorance is excusable and it seems extremely harsh to make them pay for something that they could not have anticipated. This raises a problem for the 'polluter pays' principle in general. It also has considerable relevance for the issue at hand, for it is widely accepted that many who have caused GHG emissions were unaware of the effects of their activities on the earth's atmosphere. Furthermore, their ignorance was not in any way culpable: they could not have been expected to know. This objection, note, applies in different ways to the individualist and collectivist approaches considered earlier. To the collectivist version it says that even if we can deal with past generations because the fossil fuel consumption was due to the past actions of a collective (Britain, say), this collective entity was, until the last two or three decades, excusably ignorant of the effects of fossil fuel consumption. To the individualist version it says that even if we forget about previous generations and focus simply on those currently alive, some of those individuals responsible for high emissions levels were (excusably) unaware of their effects. The objection from ignorance, thus, has more significance for the collectivist than the individualist position. Whereas the individualistic position has to explain how we deal with the GHGs emitted by currently living persons who were in (excusable) ignorance of their effects, the collectivist position has to deal with the GHGs that were emitted by both past and present members of collectives who were in (excusable) ignorance of their effects.

To this argument we might further add that Neumayer's version of the historical approach to climate change is particularly vulnerable. For Neumayer would make current generations of a country pay for all instances where a previous generation of that country emitted more than their equal per capita entitlement.[44] But how could they be expected to know that this was the entitlement? This kind of retrospective justice would seem highly unfair.

Consider now some replies to this line of reasoning. One response to it is that this point no longer has any relevance because it has been known for a considerable period that fossil-fuel consumption and deforestation cause global climate change. This is how Peter Singer, for example, responds; for him the objection of ignorance is inapplicable for post-1990 emissions.[45] Neumayer takes the same tack, but for him the relevant cut-off point is the mid-1980s.[46]

But what of high GHG emissions that took place before 1990 (or the mid-1980s)? This first response leaves pre-1990 pollution uncovered. Individuals before that time caused carbon dioxide emissions which have contributed to global warming and this first response cannot show that pre-1990 polluters should pay for global warming. It therefore leaves some of the burdens of global warming unaddressed. As such it should be supplemented with an account of who should bear the burdens of climate change that result from pre-1990 GHG emissions.

Given this, let us consider a second reply. In his 'Global Environment and International Inequality', Shue argues that it is not

unfair to make those who have emitted high levels of GHGs bear the burden of dealing with climate change, even though at the time they were not aware of the effects of what they were doing. Shue maintains that the objection of ignorance runs together punishment for an action and being held responsible for an action. His suggestion is that it would indeed be unfair to punish someone for actions they could not have known were harmful to others. However, says Shue, it is not unfair to make them pay the costs: after all, they caused the problem.[47]

In reply, it is not clear why we should accord weight to this distinction. If one should not punish ignorant persons causing harm, why is it all right to impose financial burdens on them? More worryingly, Shue's proposal seems unfair on the potential duty-bearers. As Shue himself has noted in another context, we can distinguish between the perspective of rights-bearers and the perspective of duty-bearers.[48] The first approach looks at matters from the point of view of rights-holders and is concerned to ensure that people receive a full protection of their interests. The second approach looks at matters from the point of view of the potential duty-bearers and is concerned to ensure that we do not ask too much of them. Now, utilizing this terminology, I think it is arguable that to make (excusably) ignorant harmers pay is to prioritize the interests of the beneficiaries over those of the ascribed duty-bearers. It is not sensitive to the fact that the alleged duty-bearers could not have been expected to know.[49] Its emphasis is wholly on the interests of the rights-bearers and, as such, does not adequately accommodate the duty-bearer perspective.[50]

Neither of the two replies, then, fully undermines the objection that an unqualified 'polluter pays' principle is unfair on those people who were high emitters of GHGs but who were excusably ignorant of the effects of what they were doing.[51]

5   The Impoverished

Let us turn now to another worry about taking a purely historical approach to distributing environmental responsibilities. The worry is simply that such an approach may be unfair on the impoverished. Consider, for example, a country that has in the recent past caused a great deal of pollution but that remains poor. Since it is poverty-stricken we might argue that it should not have to pay for its pollution. In this kind of situation the 'polluter pays' principle appears unfair, for it asks too much of the poor.

These concerns are powerful, but we must be careful in drawing conclusions here. This argument does not establish that the 'polluter pays' principle should be abandoned. Rather it suggests (if we accept the claim that countries should not be required to pay when they are extremely impoverished) that we should supplement the PPP with an additional (and competing) principle (the poor should not pay). One can, that is, take a pluralist response. In support of this conclusion, consider the following scenario. Suppose that a country that is poor creates considerable pollution. Drawing on the preceding argument we might think that they, the polluters, should not pay. But then suppose that they suddenly become very wealthy (and, for simplicity's sake, do so for reasons absolutely unconnected with their pollution). Since they can now afford to pay for the costs of their pollution we surely think that they should pay and the 'polluter pays' principle (PPP) should now be acted upon because it can, in all fairness, be required of the polluters. Given their new-found wealth they should compensate for the environmental bads they generated. The key point here is that the argument from poverty does not entail that a 'polluter pays' approach should be abandoned. Rather it entails that we should reject a monist, or purist, approach which claims that the responsibility for

addressing environmental harms should only be assigned to those who have caused them, and it argues that the PPP should be supplemented by other principles.

Another point is worth making here, namely that the objection under consideration suggests that an adequate account of people's environmental responsibilities cannot be derived in isolation from an understanding of their 'economic' rights and duties. It illustrates, that is, the case for not adopting an atomistic approach which separates the task of constructing a theory of environmental justice from a theory of economic justice and so on.[52]

6   The Egalitarian Defence

Let us turn now to the rationale often adduced in support of adopting a PPP approach to deal with the intergenerational aspects of global climate change. Those who canvass a 'historical' approach to allocating the responsibilities for addressing climate change often invoke egalitarian principles of justice in support of their position. Shue, for instance, argues that current members of industrialized countries should bear the burdens of climate change on the grounds that

> Once . . . an inequality has been created unilaterally by someone's imposing costs upon other people, we are justified in reversing the inequality by imposing extra burdens upon the producer of the inequality. There are two separate points here. First, we are justified in assigning additional burdens to the party who has been inflicting costs upon us. Second, the minimum extent of the compensatory burden we are justified in assigning is enough to correct the inequality previously unilaterally imposed. The purpose of the extra burden is to restore an equality that was disrupted unilaterally and arbitrarily (or to reduce an inequality that was enlarged unilaterally and arbitrarily).[53]

In a similar vein, Neumayer argues that 'historical accountability is supported by the principle of equality of opportunity'.[54] And Anil Agarwal, Sunita Narain, and Anju Sharma make a similar point:

> some people have used up more than an equitable share of this global resource, and others, less. Through their own industrialization history and current lifestyles that involve very high levels of GHG emissions, industrialized countries have more than used up their share of the absorptive capacity of the atmosphere. In this regard, the global warming problem is their creation, so it is only right that they should take the initial responsibility of reducing emissions while allowing developing countries to achieve at least a basic level of development.[55]

What are we to make of these related lines of reasoning? I should like to make two points in reply. First, the egalitarian argument can work only if we take a collectivist, as opposed to an individualist, approach; second, a collectivist approach is, in this instance, implausible. Consider the first point. The egalitarian argument maintains that countries such as the United States and Britain should pay for the excessive emissions of their ancestors. So the idea is that since the United States, say, used more than its 'fair' share at an earlier period in time it must use less now to even things out. But, this, of course, is taking a collectivist approach. It is claiming that since a collective entity, the United States, emitted more than its fair quota, this same collective entity should emit a reduced quota to make up. The egalitarian argument thus works if we treat communities as the relevant units of analysis. It does not, however, if we focus on the entitlements of individuals. To see this imagine two countries which now have an identical standard of living. Now imagine that one of them, but not the other, emitted excessive amounts of greenhouse gases in the past. It is then proposed that members of the one country should, in virtue of the pollution that took place in the past, make a greater contribution to dealing with global climate change than members of the other country. The first point to note is that this policy is not mandated by a commitment to equality of opportunity. It may be true that some people in the past will have had greater opportunities than some currently living people, but that simply cannot be altered: making their descendants have fewer opportunities will not change that. In fact making their descendants pay for the emissions of previous generations will violate equality, because those individuals will have less than their contemporaries in other countries. So if we take an individualist position, it would be wrong to grant some individuals (those in country A) fewer opportunities than others (those in country B) simply because the people who used to live in country A emitted higher levels of GHGs.

Which position should we take – a collectivist or an individualist one? This leads to my second point. I believe that we should favour the individualist one. To see why consider an example, of two families each with a son. Now suppose that several generations ago one of the families (family A) sent their child to a prestigious and distinguished public school (Eton College, say), whereas family B sent their equivalent child to a quite ordinary school. Now on an individualistic approach, the fact that someone's great-great-great grandfather enjoyed more than fair opportunities does not give us any reason to give them a less than equal opportunity. But the collectivist position is committed to claiming that we should penalize the descendant. It must say that since one *family* had a greater than fair allocation of educational opportunities in the past this must be rectified now by giving it (or, rather, one of its current members) a less than equal opportunity now. But that seems just bizarre and unfair.

In short, then, the egalitarian argument for ascribing responsibilities to current members of industrialized countries is unsuccessful: it could work only if we adopted a collectivist methodology that I have argued is unfair.

7   Incompleteness

Let us turn now to two further general limitations of the 'polluter pays' principle (limitations which also undermine its treatment of global climate change). The first point to be made here is that the 'polluter pays' principle is incomplete, for it requires a background theory of justice and, in particular, an account of persons' entitlements. To see this we should observe that the 'polluter pays' principle maintains that if persons have exceeded their entitlements then they should pay. Given this, to make the claim that someone should pay requires an account of what their entitlement is. In addition to this, to ascertain how much someone should pay also requires a precise account of their entitlements, for we need to know by how much they have exceeded their quota. What we really need, then, is an account of what rights, if any, people have to emit greenhouse gases. Is there no right to emit? Or is there a right to emit a certain fixed amount? In short, then, the 'polluter pays' principle must be located within the context of a general theory of justice and, on its own, it is incomplete.[56]

It is worth recording here that the language used by Shue, Neumayer, and Agarwal, Narain, and Sharma illustrates the point at stake. Shue, for example, argues that those who have 'taken an *unfair* advantage of others by imposing costs upon them without their consent' (my emphasis) should bear the burdens of climate change: his account thus presupposes an understanding of people's 'fair' share.[57] And Neumayer's analysis is predicated on the assumption that each person has an entitlement to an equal per capita allocation of carbon dioxide emissions. He maintains that agents that have exceeded this quota therefore have a responsibility to pay extra later.[58]

Note that this last point is not an objection to the PPP. It is simply pointing out that the PPP requires supplementation.

8   Non-compliance

There is one final query that one might raise about the 'polluter pays' principle (and its application to global climate change). This is that the principle is incomplete in an additional sense. It assigns primary responsibilities – the polluter bears the primary responsibility to bear the burden. Often, however, primary duty-bearers fail to comply with their duties. In such circumstances we might not know who the non-compliers are. Furthermore, even if we do know who they are, we might be unable to make them comply. This prompts the question: what, if anything, should be done if primary duty-bearers do not perform their duties? One option might be to leave the duties unperformed. In the case of global climate change, however, this would be reckless. In light of the havoc it wreaks on people's lives we cannot accept a situation in which there are such widespread and enormously harmful effects on the vulnerable of the world. In the light of this, we have reason to accept a second option, one in which we assign 'secondary' duty-bearers. And the point here is that the PPP is simply unable to provide us with any guidance on this. Since it says only that polluters should pay it cannot tell us who the secondary duty-bearers should be when we are unable to make polluters pay. In this sense, too, it is incomplete.[59]

It may be appropriate to sum up. I have argued that the PPP approach to climate change is inadequate for a number of reasons.

It cannot cope with three kinds of GHG, namely GHGs that were caused by

(i)   earlier generations (*cannot pay*);
(ii) those who are excusably ignorant (*should not be expected to pay*); and
(iii) those who do not comply with their duty not to emit excessive amounts of GHGs (*will not pay*).

Furthermore, the egalitarian argument for the historical application of the 'polluter pays' principle does not work. Finally we have seen two ways in which the historical approach is incomplete: it is silent on what should occur when people do not perform their duty and it needs to be embedded in a theory of justice.

Two other points bear making here. First, it is interesting to return to the methodological preliminaries introduced in section 1, in particular the point that a theory of global environmental justice must be able to cope with the intergenerational dimensions of global environmental problems. For the upshot of the first objection to the PPP (the past generations objection) is that the PPP cannot easily be extended to apply in an intergenerational context. To elaborate further: it is much easier to insist that the polluter should pay when we are dealing with a single generation in which both the polluter and those affected by the pollution are contemporaries. But, as the past generations objection brings out, the principle that the polluter should pay becomes inapplicable when the pollution results from people no longer alive.

Second, although I have argued above that the 'polluter pays' approach is incomplete and unable to deal with various kinds of activity which contribute to global climate change, this, of course, does not entail that it should be rejected outright. In the first instance, it rightly applies to many actors who are currently emitting excessive levels of

GHGs or have, at some stage since 1990, emitted excessive amounts. So even if it should not be applied to the distant past it can apply to the present and near past. Furthermore, even if we reject its application to the past we may still use it for the future. That is, we can inform people of their quota and build institutions that ensure that if people exceed it then they must make compensation.

9   Justice and Rights

Having argued that a purely 'polluter pays' approach is incomplete in a number of ways, we face the question of how it should be supplemented. How should the burden of climate change be distributed?

In this section I wish to outline an alternative way of thinking about global justice and climate change, an account that avoids the weakness of a purely 'polluter pays' approach. The argument begins with the assumption that

(P1)   A person has a right to X when X is a fundamental interest that is weighty enough to generate obligations on others.

This claim draws on Joseph Raz's influential theory of rights. And it follows him in claiming that the role of rights is to protect interests that we prize greatly.[60]

The next step in the argument maintains that

(P2)   Persons have fundamental interests in not suffering from:
(a)   drought and crop failure;
(b)   heatstroke;
(c)   infectious diseases (such as malaria, cholera and dengue);
(d)   flooding and the destruction of homes and infrastructure;
(e)   enforced relocation; and

    (f)   rapid, unpredictable and dramatic changes to their natural, social and economic world.

Yet, as the Third Assessment Report of the IPCC records, all the malign effects listed in (P2) will be generated by climate change. The predicted temperature increases are likely to result in drought and crop failure. They will also lead directly to more deaths through heatstroke. Furthermore, with increased temperatures there is a predicted increase in the spread of malaria, cholera and dengue fever. In addition to this, the increased temperatures are predicted to melt ice formations and thereby contribute to a rise in sea level which will threaten coastal settlements and countries such as Bangladesh which are flat and close to sea level. As well as simply destroying buildings, homes, and infrastructure, a known effect of climate change will be to force some inhabitants of small island states and coastal settlements to relocate. Finally, we should note that the IPCC maintains that global climate change is not simply a matter of global *warming*: it will lead to high levels of unpredictable weather patterns. This jeopardizes a vital interest in stability and being able to make medium- and long-term plans.[61]

    Given this, it follows that there is a strong case for the claim that

    (C)   Persons have the human right not to suffer from the disadvantages generated by global climate change.

Having adduced this argument, note that it (unlike a 'polluter pays' approach) does not necessarily rest on the assumption that climate change is human-induced. Its insistence is that persons' pre-eminent interests be protected and it is not, in itself, concerned with the causes of climate change. Suppose

that climate change is not anthropogenic: this argument would still hold that there is a human right not to suffer from global climate change as long as humans could do something to protect people from the ill-effects of climate change and as long as the duties generated are not excessively onerous. The duties that follow from this right could not, of course, be mitigation-related duties but there could be adaptation-related duties.[62]

    With this account in mind we face two questions: 'who has the duty to bear the burdens of dealing with global climate change?' and 'what are people's entitlements in terms of emitting GHGs?' Let us consider the first question. Drawing on what has been argued so far I would like to propose four different kinds of duty:

    (D1)   All are under a duty not to emit greenhouse gases in excess of their quota.

    (D2)   Those who exceed their quota (and/or have exceeded it since 1990) have a duty to compensate others (through mitigation or adaptation) (a revised version of the 'polluter pays' principle).

But what of GHG emissions arising from (i) previous generations; (ii) excusable ignorance; and (iii) polluters who cannot be made to pay? These, we recall, were the kinds of GHG emission that could not adequately be dealt with by a purely 'polluter pays' approach. My suggestion here is that we accept the following duty:

    (D3)   In the light of (i), (ii), and (iii) the most advantaged have a duty either to reduce their greenhouse gas emissions in proportion to the harm resulting from (i), (ii), and (iii) (mitigation) or to address the ill-effects of climate change resulting from (i), (ii), and (iii) (adaptation) (an ability to pay principle).

These first three principles are, however, inadequate. For we need also to accept that

(D4)   In the light of (iii) the most advantaged have a duty to construct institutions that discourage future non-compliance (an ability to pay principle).[63]

We should not take pollution as a given and then act in a reactive fashion: rather, we should be pro-active and take steps to minimize the likelihood of excessive pollution. And for that reason we should accept (D4). Let us call this the 'hybrid account'.[64]

The key point about this account is that it recognizes that the 'polluter pays' approach needs to be supplemented and it does so by ascribing duties to the most advantaged (an 'ability to pay' approach). The most advantaged can perform the roles attributed to them, and, moreover, it is reasonable to ask them (rather than the needy) to bear this burden since they can bear such burdens more easily. It is true that they may not have caused the problem but this does not mean that they have no duty to help solve this problem. Peter Singer's well-known example of a child drowning in a puddle brings this point out nicely.[65] Suppose that one encounters a child face down in a puddle. The fact that one did not push the child in obviously does not mean that one does not have a duty to aid the child.

It should be noted that this account of persons' duties is incomplete, for we still need to ascertain what counts as a fair quota. As we saw above, it is only with reference to the latter that we can define what counts as *unfair* levels of GHG emissions. It is not possible, in the space available, to answer the question 'what is a fair quota?', but I should

like to suggest that any credible answer to that question must draw on the interest-based account presented above. That is, in ascertaining the appropriate emissions levels we need to balance persons' interests in engaging in activities that involve the emission of GHGs, on the one hand, with persons' interests in not suffering the harms listed in (P2), on the other. We also need to employ a distributive principle. I have argued elsewhere that we have good reason to prioritize the interests of the global poor.[66] For this reason I would suggest, here, that the least advantaged have a right to emit higher GHG emissions than do the more advantaged of the world. As Shue himself argues, it is unfair to make the impoverished shoulder the burden.[67] So my account would entail that the burden of dealing with climate change should rest predominantly with the wealthy of the world, by which I mean affluent persons in the world (not affluent countries).[68]

As such (D1)–(D4) may, in practice, identify as the appropriate bearers of the duty to deal with global climate change many of the same people as a 'polluter pays' approach. It does so, though, for wholly different reasons. We might, speaking loosely, say that the contrast between my hybrid account and a historical approach is that a historical approach is diachronic (concerned with actions over time and who caused the problem), whereas mine has a diachronic element but is also synchronic (concerned with how much people have now and who can bear the sacrifice). It is also important to record that (D1)–(D4) will target different people from a purely 'polluter pays' approach in a number of situations. The two accounts identify the same duty-bearers only in cases where both (i) 'all those who have engaged in activities which cause global climate change are wealthy' and also (ii) 'all those who are wealthy have engaged in activities which cause global climate change'. But these two conditions may not apply. Consider two scenarios: in the first, a unit emits high levels of GHGs but is poor and not able to contribute much to bearing the costs of climate change. In such a case the PPP would ascribe duties to them that my hybrid account would not. Consider now the second scenario: a unit develops in a clean way and becomes wealthy. If we adopt a purely 'polluter pays' approach then this unit should not accrue obligations to bear the costs of global climate change but according to the hybrid account they would.[69] So the hybrid account and the 'polluter pays' account differ in both theory and practice.

Thus far I have introduced the hybrid account and shown how it remedies defects from which the 'polluter pays' approach suffers. Some, however, might object to (D1)–(D4), and to strengthen the hybrid account further I wish to address one objection that might be pressed against it. The objection I have in mind takes issue with (D3) in particular. It runs as follows: (D3) is unfair because it requires those who are advantaged but who have complied with (D1) and (D2) to make up for the failings of those who have not complied with their duties. And, it asks, is this not unfair? Why should those who have been virtuous be required to do yet more (as (D3) would require) because some have failed to live up to their obligations?

Several comments can be made in reply. First, it should be stressed that the hybrid account explicitly seeks to address this concern by insisting, in (D4), that institutions should be designed so as to discourage non-compliance. It aims, therefore, to minimize those demands on people that stem from the non-compliance of others. Second, we might ask the critic what the alternatives are to asking the advantaged to address the climate change caused by non-compliers (as well as that stemming from past generations and excusable ignorance). One option would

be to reject (D3) (and (D4)) and ask the impoverished and needy to pay but, as we have seen, this is unfair. A second option would be to let the harm to the climate that results from the excessive GHG emissions of some go unaddressed. But the problem with this is that the ill-effects that this will have on other people (drought, heatstroke, crop failure, flooding) are so dire that this is unacceptable. Such a position would combine neglect (on the part of those who have exceeded their GHG quota) with indifference (on the part of those who could address the problems resulting from the high GHG emissions of others but choose not to). And if we bear in mind that those who are adversely affected by climate change are frequently poor and disadvantaged,[70] we have yet further reason to think that the advantaged have a duty to bear the burdens of climate change that arise from the non-compliance of others. If the choice is of *either* ascribing duties to the poor and needy *or* allowing serious harm to befall people (many of whom are also poor and needy) *or* ascribing duties to the most advantaged it would seem plausible to go for that third option.[71] One final thought: there is, we can agree, an unfairness involved in asking some to compensate for the shortcomings of others. The question is: how should we best respond to this? My suggestion is that we respond best to this as suggested above, by seeking to minimize those demands and by asking the privileged to bear this extra burden. To this we can add that the virtuous *are* being ill-treated but that the right reaction for them is to take this up with non-compliers (against whom they have just cause for complaint) and not to react by disregarding the legitimate interests of those who would otherwise suffer the dire effects of climate change. For these three reasons, then, (D3) can be defended against this objection.[72]

[. . .]

11   Concluding Remarks

It is time to conclude. Two points in particular are worth stressing – one methodological and the other substantive. The methodological observation takes us to an issue that has run throughout the paper – namely whether we should adopt an individualist methodology or a collectivist one. This issue has cropped up in three different contexts.

First, who are the polluters? If we take an individualist approach then we will say that for some pollution (that of earlier generations) we cannot make the polluter pay, for the individual polluters are dead. If, however, we take a collectivist approach we will say that collective A polluted in an earlier decade (or century) and hence that it should pay for the pollution now.

Second, who has benefited from the use of fossil fuels? Because of the non-identity problem we cannot say to the particular individuals who are alive today, "You enjoy a higher standard of living than you would have done in a world in which industrialization had not occurred." We can, however, make this claim to, and about, collectives.

Third, who is the bearer of the right to emit greenhouse gases (individuals or collectives)? The rationale given by Shue and Neumayer, and by Agarwal, Narain, and Sharma for a historical approach works only if we assume that the answer to this question is "collectives". On an individualist approach, however, the rights-bearers are individuals and it is unjust to impose sacrifices on some current individuals because, and only because, of the excessive emissions of earlier inhabitants of their country.

This paper has argued for an individualist account, but the issue requires a much fuller analysis than has been possible here.

Notes

1   Margaret Thatcher in 1982 during the Falklands War. Quoted in S. Barnes, 'Want to Save the Planet? Then Make Me Your Not So Benevolent Dictator,' *The Times*, 9 April 2005.

2   See, in this context, Rawls's discussion of the 'problems of extension' and in particular, his discussion of the issues surrounding how 'justice as fairness' is extended to deal with the international domain, future generations, duties to the environment, and non-human animals (as well as its extension to the ill): 'The Law of Peoples,' *Collected Papers*, ed. S. Freeman (1999), p. 531 (and, more generally, pp. 531–3). See also J. Rawls, *Political Liberalism* (1993), pp. 20–1.

3   See J. Rawls, *A Theory of Justice* (1999), pp. 54–5, 78–81, 348, and *Justice as Fairness: A Restatement*, ed. E. Kelly (2001), pp. 57–61, 168–76.

4   See M. C. Nussbaum, *Women and Human Development: The Capabilities Approach* (2000), and A. Sen, 'Capability and Well-being,' in M. Nussbaum and A. Sen (eds.), *The Quality of Life* (1993), pp. 30–53. For an excellent analysis of several different accounts of what should be distributed and an assessment of their implications for our evaluation of global climate change see E. Page, *Climate Change, Justice and Future Generations* (2006), ch. 3.

5   In what way might the environment be a distinctive kind of problem? I shall not explore this question fully here, but note that possible answers might be that: (i) some natural resources are non-renewable and hence their consumption is irreversible; (ii) the value of some natural resources cannot adequately be captured in monetary terms; or (iii) many environmental benefits and burdens are essentially public in nature (that is, for a contiguous group of people either all are exposed to an environmental hazard such as air pollution or none are).

6   For more on this, and for my defence of a cosmopolitan approach, see S. Caney, *Justice*

Beyond Borders: A Global Political Theory (2005). See also the defences of a cosmopolitan approach in T. Pogge, 'Recognized and violated by International Law: The Human Rights of the Global Poor', and K.-C. Tan, 'International Toleration: Rawlsian versus Cosmopolitan', both in *Leiden Journal of International Law* 18 (2005).

7 For an analysis of the latter see D. Parfit, *Reasons and Persons* (1986), Appendix F, pp. 480–6.

8 For Rawls's claim that the principles that apply across generations are distinct from those that apply within one generation and for his affirmation of a 'just savings' principle, see J. Rawls, *A Theory of Justice* (1999), pp. 251–8 and Rawls, *Justice as Fairness, supra* note 3, at pp. 159–60. We should also note that Rawls does not simply propose two different principles to govern 'justice to contemporaries' and 'justice to future people'; he also adopts two different methods for deriving these principles. As is well known, his derivation of the principles of justice to govern contemporary members of a society invokes what persons socking to advance their own primary goods would choose in the 'original position'. His derivation of the principles of justice to govern future generations also invokes the original position but, in its last form, stipulates that parties should choose that principle that they would want preceding generations to have honoured. (On the latter see *Justice as Fairness, supra* note 3, at p. 160.) So Rawls treats intergenerational justice very differently from 'justice to contemporaries' – both in the method he employs and in the conclusions he reaches. (Note that Rawls's method for deriving the 'just savings' principle has changed over time: see ibid., at p. 160, n. 39.)

9 See, further, S. Caney, 'Global Distributive Justice and the Environment', in R. Tinnevelt and G. Verschraegen (eds.), *Between Cosmopolitan Ideals and State Sovereignty: Studies on Global Justice*.

10 See the IPCC's website: http://www.ipcc.ch/about/about.htm.

11 B. Lomborg, *The Sceptical Environmentalist: Measuring the Real Stare of the World* (2001),

ch. 24. For one critical response see M. A. Cole, 'Environmental Optimists, Environmental Pessimists and the Real State of the World – An Article Examining *The Sceptical Environmentalist: Measuring the Real State of the World* by Bjørn Lomborg', (2003) *Economic Journal* 113, p. 488, esp. at 373–6.

12 See J. J. McCarthy, O. F. Canziani, N. A. Leary, et al. (eds.), *Climate Change 2001: Impacts, Adaptation and Vulnerability – Contribution of Working Group II to the Third Assessment Report of the Intergovernmental Panel on Climate Change* (2001).

13 The distinction between 'mitigation' and 'adaptation' comes from the IPCC. So, e.g., vol. 2 of the 2001 report of the IPCC focuses on adaptation: see, in particular, B. Smit and O. Pilifosova, 'Adaptation to Climate Change in the Context of Sustainable Development and Equity', in McCarthy et al., *supra note* 12, ch. 18. Vol. 3, by contrast, focuses more on 'mitigation': see B. Metz, O. Davidson, R. Swart, and J. Pan (eds.), *Climate Change 2001: Mitigation – Contribution of Working Group III to the Third Assessment Report of the Intergovernmental Panel on Climate Change* (2001). See also Henry Shue's illuminating analysis of the different ethical questions raised by global climate change: 'Subsistence Emissions and Luxury Emissions,' (1993) 15 *Law and Policy* 40; idem, 'After You: May Action by the Rich be Contingent upon Action by the Poor?' (1994) *Indiana Journal of Global 1 Legal Studies* 344; and idem, 'Avoidable Necessity: Global Warming, International Fairness, and Alternative Energy', in I. Shapiro and J. Wagner deCew (eds.), *Theory and Practice: NOMOS XXXVII* (1995), p. 240.

14 The mitigation costs incurred by an actor A are not restricted to cases where A minimizes A's own GHG emissions. Consider, e.g., the 'Clean Development Mechanism' policy enunciated in Art. 12 of the Kyoto Protocol (http://unfccc.int/resource/docs/convkp/kpeng.html). Under this proposal certain countries (those listed in Annex I) may be given credit for cutting GHG emissions if they support the use of development projects that enable developing countries to develop

in a way which does not emit high levels of GHGs. Since what they do has the effect of lowering GHG emissions and it has a cost for them (the cost of supporting clean development) then, in principle, this cost should be included under the heading of mitigation costs: they are making a sacrifice which enables there to be a reduction in GHG emissions.

[15] See, e.g., Lomborg, *supra* note 11, at, pp. 305–18, esp. 318. Lomborg takes the highly controversial view that it would be more cost effective to focus on 'adaptation' rather than 'mitigation'. For a contrasting view see J. Houghton, *Global Warming: The Complete Briefing* (2004), pp. 242–321 and M. Maslin, *Global Warming: A Very Short Introduction* (2004), pp. 136–43.

[16] For two excellent treatments of the role of the 'polluter pays' principle in international environmental law to which I am much indebted see P. Birnie and A. Boyle, *International Law and the Environment* (2002), pp. 92–5, 383–5; and P. Sands, *Principles of International Environmental Law* (2003), pp. 279–85.

[17] The documents for both Council Recommendations can be found in OECD, *The Polluter Pays Principle: Definition, Analysis, Implementation* (1975).

[18] See Directive 2004/35/CE of the European Parliament and of the Council (passed on 21 April 2004) on environmental liability with regard to the prevention and remedying of environmental damage. The text can be found in the Official Journal of 30 April 2004 (L143) at http://europa.eu.int/eur-lex/pri/en/oj/dat/2004/l_143/l_14320040430en00560075.pdf.

[19] Commission on Global Governance, *Our Global Neighbourhood* (1995), pp. 208, 212.

[20] See H. Shue 'Global Environment and International Inequality', (1999) 75 *International Affairs*, pp. 533–7. Shue writes that his argument is not equivalent to the 'polluter pays' principle because he interprets the PPP to be a 'forward-looking' principle that says that future pollution ought to be paid for by the polluter (at 534). However, I shall interpret the PPP to refer to the view that past, current,

and future pollution ought to be paid for by the polluter. Shue is therefore affirming a 'polluter pays' approach, given the way in which I am defining that term.

[21] See E. Neumayer, 'In Defence of Historical Accountability for Greenhouse Gas Emissions', (2000) 33 *Ecological Economics*, pp. 185–92.

[22] See F. L. Toth and M. Mwandosya, 'Decision-Making Frameworks', in Metz et al., *supra* note 13, ch. 10, s. 10.4.5, 669 (for mention of the 'polluter pays' principle) and 668–73 (for general discussion).

[23] Here it is interesting to note that the European Union's recent directive on environmental liability (2004/35/CE) expressly rejects what I am terming the macro-version of the 'polluter pays' principle and affirms the micro version. See para. 13 and Art. 4 s. 5, available at http://europa.eu.int/eurlex/pri/en/oj/dat/2004/l_143/l_14320040430en00560075.pdf.

[24] See, e.g., Shue, *supra* note 20, at pp. 534, 545. Shue elsewhere refers to 'nations (or other parties)' ('After you', *supra* note 14, at p. 361), but generally assumes that the polluters/payers are nations.

[25] Neumayer, *supra* note 21, at p. 186.

[26] Ibid., at p. 186.

[27] See Toth and Mwandosya, *supra* note 22, at pp. 637–8.

[28] As noted above, Shue maintains that industrialized countries should pay. Notwithstanding this, he also refers to the actions of 'the owners of many coal-burning factories' (*supra* note 20, at p. 535) – a level (b) explanation.

[29] For Pogge's discussion of 'explanatory nationalism' see his *World Poverty and Human Rights: Cosmopolitan Responsibilities and Reforms* (2002), pp. 15, 139–44.

[30] *Supra* note 20, at p. 536.

[31] Ibid., at p. 536; see also 536–7.

[32] *Supra* note 21, at p. 189. I have omitted a footnote (n. 4) which appears after the word 'achieved'.

[33] A similar position is defended by Axel Gosseries in his illuminating and interesting paper, 'Historical Emissions and Free-Riding', (2004) 11 *Ethical Perspectives*, 1, at pp. 36–60.

I came across Gosseries' paper after completing this article and hope to address it more fully subsequently.

34 Parfit, *supra* note 7, ch. 16.

35 This claim about the impossibility of benefiting future people, we should note, has also been made by Thomas Schwartz. In a pioneering paper published in 1978 he presented reasoning like that given in the last paragraph to show that the policies of present generations do not benefit future generations. Schwartz's argument is directed against population policies that are justified on the grounds that they would make future people better off. His argument, though, also tells against claims that current individuals have been made better off by industrialization (and hence that they have a duty to pay for the GHG emissions that were generated by this benefit-producing industrialization). See T. Schwartz, 'Obligations to Posterity', in R. I. Sikora and B. Barry (eds.), *Obligations to Future Generations* (1978), pp. 3–13. I came across Schwartz's paper only when I had finished this article and was making the final revisions. My debt here is to Parfit's work.

36 Here we should note one complication to my argument. In an appendix to *Reasons and Persons* Parfit entertains the possibility that bringing someone into existence can be said to benefit them. He does not commit himself to this view but he does think it is a potentially plausible view. To this extent there is an asymmetry in his treatment of harm to future generations (one cannot harm future people because the dangerous policies affect who is born) and his treatment of benefit to future generations (one can benefit future people by bringing them into existence). See Parfit, *supra* note 7; Appendix G (at 487–90). See, in particular, Parfit's discussion of what he terms 'the two-state requirement', where this states that 'We benefit someone only if we cause him to be better off than he would otherwise at that time have been' (at 487: see further 487–8). I am grateful to Edward Page for bringing this asymmetry to my attention and for a number of very helpful discussions of the issues at stake. I shall not seek to challenge Parfit's arguments to the effect that

bringing people into existence may benefit them (the arguments he musters in Appendix G). I would, however, maintain that to sustain the disanalogous treatment of future harm and future benefit, Parfit needs to confront the possibility that the non-identity problem undermines the claim that we can benefit future people and also needs to explain why that is not correct. Without such an argument, the non-identity problem would (as I have argued in the text) appear to undermine the BPP. Note: Schwartz's account can be contrasted with Parfit's on this point for, unlike Parfit, Schwartz explicitly claims that one cannot either harm or benefit future people: *supra* note 35, at pp. 3–4.

37 We might, of course, say 'you should pay because you are so much better off than others', but this appeals to a quite different principle and will be taken up later in the chapter.

38 A collectivist account is suggested by Edward Page in an ingenious discussion of Parfit's non-identity problem. See E. Page, 'Intergenerational Justice and Climate Change', (1999) 47 *Political Studies* 1, at pp. 61–6. (See also J. Broome, *Counting the Cost of Global Warming* (1992), pp. 34–5.) Page, however, is not addressing the argument I am making. Rather he employs a collectivist approach to rebut Parfit's non-identity problem.

39 Page, *supra* note 38, at pp. 61–6.

40 See also Schwartz's discussion of this position. Schwartz briefly considers the collectivist position described in the text. He rejects it on the grounds that what matters are benefits to individuals; benefits to collectives have no moral weight. *Supra* note 35, at pp. 6–7.

41 See J. Rawls, *The Law of Peoples with 'The Idea of Public Reason Revisited'* (1999), pp. 117–18.

42 D. Miller, 'Justice and Global Inequality', in A. Hurrell and N. Woods (eds.), *Inequality, Globalization, and World Politics* (1999), pp. 193–6.

43 See also Gosseries, *supra* note 33, at pp. 41–2 on this. For a nice discussion of the way in which collectivist approaches are insufficiently sensitive to the entitlements of individuals see K.-C. Tan, *Justice without Borders:*

Cosmopolitanism, Nationalism and Patriotism (2004), pp. 73–4. More generally, see S. Caney, 'Global Equality of Opportunity and the Sovereignty of States', in T. Coates (ed.), *International Justice* (2000), pp. 142–3, for a discussion of the principle at issue.

44 *Supra* note 21, at p. 186.

45 P. Singer, *One World: The Ethics of Globalization* (2002), p. 34.

46 Neumayer, *supra* note 21, at p. 188. Shue also makes this kind of response but does not specify a key date after which one cannot claim excusable ignorance: Shue, *supra* note 20, at p. 536.

47 Shue, *supra* note 20, pp. 535–6. Neumayer makes a similar but distinct reply, arguing that the objection runs together 'blame' and 'accountability'. Blaming those who could not have known of the effects of their actions is unjustified, but they are nonetheless accountable: see *supra* note 21, at p. 188, 189 n. 4.

48 H. Shue, *Basic Rights: Subsistence, Affluence, and US Foreign Policy* (1996), pp. 164–6.

49 A similar position is defended by Gosseries. See his nuanced and persuasive treatment of what he terms 'the ignorance argument', *supra* note 33, at pp. 39–41.

50 This emphasis is evident in Neumayer's discussion: see, e.g., *supra* note 21, at p. 188.

51 We might note a third response. Someone might reply that even though there was not incontrovertible evidence prior to 1990/1985, there was reason to think that GHGs caused global climate change. And drawing on this, they might argue that pre-1990/1985 emitters had a duty to act on the precautionary principle and therefore should have eschewed activities which released high levels of GHGs. Since they did not adopt such a precautionary approach, it might be argued, they should shoulder a proportionate share of the burdens of climate change. The argument then is neither that they did know (response 1) nor that it does not matter that they did not know (response 2): it is that they should have adopted a cautious approach and since they did not they are culpable. How effective this reply is depends on when we think the precautionary principle should be adopted.

52 For further discussion of this methodological point see Caney, *supra* note 9.

53 Shue, *supra* note 20, at pp. 533–4.

54 Neumayer, *supra* note 21, at p. 188.

55 A. Agarwal, S. Narain, and A. Sharma, 'The Global Commons and Environmental Justice – Climate Change,' in *Environmental Justice: International Discourses in Political Economy – Energy and Environmental Policy* (2002), p. 173.

56 My argument, here, is analogous to Rawls's discussion of 'legitimate expectations'. Rawls argues that we cannot define persons' entitlements (their legitimate expectations) until we have identified a valid distributive principle and ascertained what social and political framework would best fulfil that ideal: only when we have the latter can we work out what individual persons are entitled to. In the same spirit, my argument is that we cannot define people's responsibilities until we have identified a valid distributive principle and seen what social and political framework realizes that ideal. See Rawls, *A Theory of Justice*, *supra* note 3, at pp. 88–9, 273–7.

57 *Supra* note 20, at p. 534.

58 *Supra* note 21.

59 The terminology of 'primary' and 'secondary' duty-bearers comes from Shue, *supra* note 48, at p. 59 (see also pp. 57 and 171 for relevant discussion).

60 J. Raz, *The Morality of Freedom* (1986), ch. 7.

61 For a comprehensive account of the effects of climate change and empirical support for the claim that climate change causes phenomena (a) to (f) see McCarthy et al., *supra* note 12. For instance, chapter 9 on human health provides data on the links between climate change and drought (a), heatstroke (b), and malaria, dengue and cholera (c). Chapters 6 and 17 detail the ways in which climate change results in threats to coastal zones and small island states (and thereby results in (d), (e) and (f)).

62 The argument sketched above could be generalized to address other environmental burdens. For an excellent analysis of the human right not to suffer from various environmental harms, the grounds supporting

this right and the correlative duties, see J. Nickel, 'The Human Right to a Safe Environment: Philosophical Perspectives on its Scope and Justification' (1993), 18 *Yale Journal of International Law*, at pp. 281–95. Nickel does not discuss climate change.

63   For an emphasis on constructing fair *institutions* see Shue, *supra* note 48, at pp. 17, 59–60, 159–61, 164–6, 168–9, 173–80, and C. Jones, *Global Justice: Defending Cosmopolitanism* (1999), pp. 66–72, esp. 68–9.

64   For a general discussion of the different kinds of duties generated by human rights see S. Caney, 'Global Poverty and Human Rights: The Case for Positive Duties', in T. Pogge (ed.), *Freedom from Poverty as a Human Right: Who Owes What to the Very Poor?* (2006). For an account that is similar to the hybrid account see Darrel Moellendorf's brief but perceptive discussion in *Cosmopolitan Justice* (2002): 97–100. Like the hybrid account, Moellendorf's account brings together a 'polluter pays' approach with an 'ability to pay' approach. There are, however, several important differences: (i) Moellendorf's view does not take into account excusable ignorance; (ii) he does not address the question of what to do if people do not comply with their duty not to emit excessive GHGs; and (iii) he does not propose a principle akin to (D4).

65   P. Singer, 'Famine, Affluence, and Morality', (1972) 1(3) *Philosophy and Public Affairs*, pp. 229–43. I am grateful to Kok-Chor Tan for advice about how to bring out the normative appeal of (D3) and (D4).

66   Caney, *supra* note 6, at ch. 4.

67   In 'Global Environment and International Inequality', Shue defends not just the 'polluter pays' principle but also an 'ability to pay' principle (*supra* note 20, at pp. 537–40). In addition to this, he argues that there should be a 'guaranteed minimum' threshold below which people should not fall and hence that the very poor should not pay (ibid., at pp. 540–4). Shue's claim is that all three principles yield the same conclusion – affluent countries are responsible for meeting the burdens of climate change (at p. 545). For further discussions where Shue has argued

that the wealthy should bear the mitigation and adaptation costs of climate change and that the poor be given less demanding duties see 'After You: May Action by the Rich be Contingent upon Action by the Poor?', 'Avoidable Necessity: Global Warming, International Fairness, and Alternative Energy', pp. 250–7, and 'Subsistence Emissions and Luxury Emissions', especially pp. 42–3, all *supra* note 13.

68   One common principle suggested is that all persons have an equal per capita right to emit carbon dioxide (see, e.g., R. Attfield, *Environmental Ethics* (2003), 179–80; P. Baer, J. Harte, B. Haya et al., 'Equity and Greenhouse Gas Responsibility' (2000) 289 *Science* 2287; T. Athanasiou and P. Baer, *Dead Heat: Global Justice and Global Warming* (2002), esp. 76–97; Neumayer, *supra* note 21, at pp. 185–92; and S. Bode, 'Equal Emissions Per Capita over Time – A Proposal to Combine *Responsibility* and *Equity of Rights* for Post-2012 GHG Emission Entitlement Allocation,' (2004) 14 *European Environment* pp. 300–16.) For the reason given in the text, however, this seems to me unfair on the poor. (See, too, Shue 'Avoidable Necessity: Global Warming, International Fairness, and Alternative Energy', *supra* note 13, at pp. 250–2, and S. Gardiner, 'Survey Article: Ethics, and Global Climate Change,' (2004) 114 *Ethics*, pp. 584–5).

69   Note that even if (a) and (b) hold and the PPP and the hybrid account identify the same people as duty-bearers, they may well make different demands on different people. They would converge exactly only if (a) and (b) hold, and if (c), there was a perfect positive correlation between how much GHGs persons have emitted, on the one hand, and how much wealth they possess, on the other. Since the PPP allocates duties according to how much GHGs persons have emitted and since the hybrid account allocates duties, in part, according to how much wealth persons have, (c) is necessary to produce total convergence in their ascription of duties.

70   For further on this see the following: J. B. Smith, H.-J. Schellnhuber, and M. M. Q. Mirza, 'Vulnerability to Climate Change

and Reasons for Concern: A Synthesis,' in McCarthy et al., *supra* note 12, esp. at pp. 916, 940–1, 957–8; R. S. J. Tol, T. E. Downing, O. J. Kuik, and J. B. Smith, 'Distributional Aspects of Climate Change Impacts,' (2004) 14(3) *Global Environmental Change*, pp. 259–72; and D. S. G. Thomas and C. Twyman, 'Equity and Justice in Climate Change Adaptation Amongst Natural-Resource-Dependent Societies,' (2005) 15(2) *Global Environmental Change*, pp. 115–24.

[71] For a similar line of reasoning see Moellendorf's persuasive discussion of who should deal with the ill-effects caused by the GHG emissions of earlier generations. Moellendorf convincingly argues that it would be wrong to ask anyone other than the most advantaged to bear the burdens of the GHG emissions of earlier generations. See Moellendorf, *supra* note 64, at p. 100. My claim is that the same reasoning shows that the advantaged should also bear the costs stemming from non-compliance.

[72] As Wouter Werner has noted, the hybrid account may also encounter a problem of non-compliance. What, it might be asked, should happen if some of those designated by (D3) to deal with the problems resulting from some people's non-compliance do not themselves comply with (D3)? Three points can be made in response. First: we should recognize that even if this is a problem for the hybrid account it does not give us reason to reject it but rather to expand on it. The PPP, for example, fares no better: indeed, it fares worse, for the hybrid account, unlike the PPP, at least addresses the issue of non-compliance. Second, if *some* of those designated to perform (D3) fail to do so then one reply is that at least some of their shortfall should be picked up by others of those designated by (D3). The third and final point to make is that there will be limits on this. That is, one can ask only so much of those able to help, though where we draw this line will be a matter of judgement and will depend on, amongst other factors, how much they are able to help and at what cost to themselves. For further pertinent enquiry into persons' moral obligations when others fail to do their duty, see Parfit's pioneering discussion of 'collective consequentialism' (*supra* note 7, at pp. 30–1), and Liam Murphy's extended analysis of this issue in L. Murphy, *Moral Demands in Non-ideal Theory* (2000).

Bibliography

No collection can include all important contributions to its topics. Readers interested in pursuing the topics and arguments of this book further are recommended to turn to any of the following works:

Alexander, Larry, "Justification and Innocent Aggressors," *Wayne Law Review* 33 (1987): 1177–89.

Ali, Suki, Kelly Coate, and Wangui Wa-Goro, eds., *Global Feminist Politics: Identities in a Changing World*. London: Routledge, 2000.

Altman, Andrew and Christopher Heath Wellman, "A Defense of International Criminal Law," *Ethics* 115 (2004): 35–67.

Anand, Ruchi, *International Environmental Justice: A North–South Dimension*. Aldershot: Ashgate, 2004.

Andreou, Chrisoula, "Environmental Damage and the Puzzle of the Self-Torturer," *Philosophy & Public Affairs* 34 (2006): 95–108.

An-Na'im, Abdullahi, *Toward an Islamic Reformation: Civil Liberties, Human Rights, and International Law*. Syracuse, NY: Syracuse University Press, 1990.

Anscombe, G. E. M., *Ethics, Religion, and Politics*, Collected Philosophical Papers, vol. 3. Minneapolis: University of Minnesota Press, 1981.

Anwander, Norbert, "Contributing and Benefiting: Two Grounds for Duties to the Victims of Injustice," *Ethics & International Affairs* 19 (2005): 39–45.

Apel, Karl-Otto, "Kant's 'Toward Perpetual Peace' as Historical Prognosis from the Point of View of Moral Duty," in James Bohman and Matthias Lutz-Bachmann (eds.), *Perpetual Peace: Essays on Kant's Cosmopolitan Ideal*. Cambridge: MIT, 1997, pp. 79–110.

Appiah, Kwame Anthony, *In My Father's House: Africa in the Philosophy of Culture*. Oxford: Oxford University Press, 1992.

——, "Cosmopolitan Patriots," in Martha C. Nussbaum, *For Love of Country: Debating the Limits of Patriotism*, ed. Joshua Cohen. Boston, MA: Beacon Press, 1996, pp. 21–9.

Aquinas, St. Thomas, *Political Writings*, ed. R. W. Dyson. Cambridge: Cambridge University Press, 2002.

Archibungi, Danielle and David Held, eds., *Cosmopolitan Democracy: An Agenda for a New World Order*. Cambridge: Polity, 1995.

Arneson, Richard, "Moral Limits on the Demands of Beneficence?," in Deen K. Chatterjee (ed.), *The Ethics of Assistance: Morality and the Distant Needy*. Cambridge: Cambridge University Press, 2004, pp. 33–58.

——, "Do Patriotic Ties Limit Global Justice Duties?," *Journal of Ethics* 9 (2005): 127–50.

Asoka, *The Edicts of Asoka*, ed. N. A. Nikam and Richard McKeon. Chicago, IL: University of Chicago Press, 1978.

Attfield, Robin and Andrew Belsey, eds., *Philosophy and the Natural Environment*. Cambridge: Cambridge University Press, 1994.

Attfield, Robin and Barry Wilkins, eds., *International Justice and the Third World*. London: Routledge, 1992.

Augustine, St., *The City of God against the Pagans*, ed. R. W. Dyson. Cambridge: Cambridge University Press, 1998.

Balibor, Etienne, "Propositions on Citizenship," *Ethics* 98 (1988): 723–30.

Barber, Benjamin R., "Constitutional Faith," in Martha C. Nussbaum, *For Love of Country: Debating the Limits of Patriotism*, ed. Joshua Cohen. Boston, MA: Beacon Press, 1996, pp. 30–7.

Barnett, Anthony, David Held, and Caspar Henderson, eds., *Debating Globalization*. Cambridge: Polity, 2005.

Barry, Brian, "Do Countries have Moral Obligations?," in S. M. McMurrin (ed.), *The Tanner Lectures on Human Value*, vol. 2. Salt Lake City: University of Utah Press, 1981, pp. 27–44.

——, *Essays in Political Theory*. Oxford: Clarendon Press, 1991.

—— and Matt Matravers, "International Justice," *Routledge Encyclopedia of Philosophy* (http://www.rep.routledge.com/article/S033) (2005).

Bass, Gary J., "*Jus Post Bellum*," *Philosophy & Public Affairs* 32 (2004): 384–412.

Bauer, J. R. and D. A. Bell, eds., *The East Asian Challenge for Human Rights*. Cambridge: Cambridge University Press, 1999.

Baynes, Kenneth, "Communitarian and Cosmopolitan Challenges to Kant's Conception of World Peace", in James Bohman and Matthias Lutz-Bachmann (eds.), *Perpetual Peace: Essays on Kant's Cosmopolitan Ideal*. Cambridge: MIT Press, 1997, pp. 219–34.

Beetham, D., *Democracy and Human Rights*. Cambridge: Polity, 1999.

Beitz, Charles R., "Justice and International Relations," *Philosophy & Public Affairs* 4 (1975): 360–89.

——, "Bounded Morality: Justice and the State in World Politics," *International Organization* 33 (1979): 405–24.

——, "Nonintervention and Communal Integrity," *Philosophy & Public Affairs* 9 (1980): 385–91.

——, "Cosmopolitan Ideals and National Sentiment," *Journal of Philosophy* 80 (1983): 591–600.

——, Marshall Cohen, Thomas Scanlon, and A. John Simmons, eds., *International Ethics*. Princeton, NJ: Princeton University Press, 1985.

——, *Political Theory and International Relations*, 2nd edn. Princeton, NJ: Princeton University Press, 1999.

——, "International Liberalism and Distributive Justice," *World Politics* 51 (1999): 269–96.

——, "Rawls's Law of Peoples," *Ethics* 110 (2000): 669–96.

——, "Does Global Inequality Matter?," *Metaphilosophy* 32 (2001): 95–112.

——, "Human Rights as a Common Concern," *American Political Science Review* 95 (2002): 269–82.

——, "Social and Cosmopolitan Liberalism," *International Affairs* 75 (1999): 515–29.

——, "Human Rights and the Law of Peoples," in Deen K. Chatterjee (ed.), *The Ethics of Assistance: Morality and the Distant Needy*. Cambridge: Cambridge University Press, 1994, 193–214.

——, "Cosmopolitanism and Global Justice," *Journal of Ethics* 9 (2005): 11–27.

Bell, Daniel A. "The East Asian Challenge to Human Rights: Reflections on an East–West Dialogue," *Human Rights Quarterly* 18 (1996): 641–67.

Bentham, Jeremy, "A Plan for an Universal and Perpetual Peace," in *The Works of Jeremy Bentham*, vol. 2, ed. John Bowring. New York: Russell and Russell, 1962, pp. 546–60.

Beran, Harry, "A Liberal Theory of Secession," *Political Studies* 32 (1984): 21–31.

Best, Geoffrey, "Justice, International Relations, and Human Rights," *International Affairs* 71 (1995): 775–800.

Bhagwati, Jagdish, *In Defense of Globalization*. Oxford: Oxford University Press, 2004.

Blake, Michael, "International Criminal Adjudication and the Right to Punish," *Public Affairs Quarterly* 11 (1997): 203–15.

——, "Distributive Justice, State Coercion, and Autonomy," *Philosophy & Public Affairs* 30 (2002): 257–96.

——, "International Justice," *Stanford Encyclopedia of Philosophy* (http://plato.stanford.edu/entries/international-justice/) (2005).

Bohman, James, "The Public Spheres of the World Citizen," in James Bohman and Matthias Lutz-Bachmann (eds.), *Perpetual Peace: Essays on Kant's Cosmopolitan Ideal*. Cambridge, MA: MIT Press, 1997, pp. 179–200.

——, "Republican Cosmopolitanism," *Journal of Political Philosophy* 12 (2004): 336–52.

——, "The Democratic Minimum: Is Democracy a Means to Global Justice?," *Ethics & International Affairs* 19 (2005): 101–16.

Bohman, James and Matthias Lutz-Bachmann, eds., *Perpetual Peace: Essays on Kant's Cosmopolitan Ideal*. Cambridge, MA: MIT Press, 1997.

Bok, Sissela, "From Part to Whole," in Martha C. Nussbaum. *For Love of Country: Debating the Limits of Patriotism*, ed. Joshua Cohen. Boston, MA: Beacon Press, 1996, pp. 38–44.

Bové, José and François, *Food for the Future*. Cambridge: Polity, 2005.

Brock, Gillian, "The Difference Principle, Equality of Opportunity, and Cosmopolitan Justice," *Journal of Moral Philosophy* 2 (2005): 333–51.

——, and Harry Brighouse, eds., *The Philosophy of Cosmopolitanism*. Cambridge: Cambridge University Press, 2005.

——, and Darrel Moellendorf, eds., *Current Debates in Global Justice*. New York: Springer, 2005.

Brooks, Thom, "Cosmopolitanism and Distributing Responsibilities," *Critical Review of International Social and Political Philosophy* 5 (2002): 92–7.

——, "Hegel's Theory of International Politics," *Review of International Studies* 30 (2004): 149–52.

——, and Fabian Freyenhagen, eds., *The Legacy of John Rawls*. London and New York: Continuum, 2005.

——, "Hegel on War" in *Hegel's Political Philosophy: A Systematic Reading of the Philosophy of Right*. Edinburgh: Edinburgh University Press, 2007.

——, "Punishing States that Cause Global Poverty," *William Mitchell Law Review* 33 (2007): 519–32.

——, *Global Justice*. Oxford: Blackwell, forthcoming.

Broome, John, *Counting the Cost of Global Warming*. Isle of Harris: Whitehorse, 1992.

Brown, Chris, *International Relations Theory: New Normative Approaches*. Hemel Hempstead: Harvester Wheatsheaf, 1992.

——, "Universal Human Rights: A Critique," in Tim Dunne and Nicholas J. Wheeler, eds., *Human Rights in Global Politics*. Cambridge: Cambridge University Press, pp. 103–27.

Brown, Peter and Henry Shue, eds., *Boundaries*. Totowa: Rowman & Littlefield, 1981.

Brownlie, Ian, ed., *Basic Documents on Human Rights*, 3rd edn. Oxford: Clarendon Press, 1992.

Brownsword, Roger, ed., *Global Governance and the Quest for Justice: Human Rights*. Oxford: Hart, 2005.

Buchanan, Allen, *Secession: The Morality of Political Divorce from Fort Sumter to Lithuania and Quebec*. Boulder, CO: Westview, 1991.

——, "Theories of Secession," *Philosophy & Public Affairs* 26 (1997): 31–61.

——, "Recognitional Legitimacy," *Philosophy & Public Affairs* 28 (1999): 46–78.

——, "Rawls's Law of Peoples: Rules for a Vanished Westphalian World," *Ethics* 110 (2000): 697–721.

——, *Justice, Legitimacy, and Self-Determination: Moral Foundations for International Law*. Oxford: Oxford University Press, 2003.

——, "Institutionalizing the Just War," *Philosophy & Public Affairs* 34 (2006): 2–38.

Bull, Hedley, "Recapturing the Just War for Political Theory," *World Politics* 31 (1979): 588–99.

Butler, Judith, "Universality in Culture," in Martha C. Nussbaum, *For Love of Country: Debating the Limits of Patriotism*, ed. Joshua Cohen. Boston, MA: Beacon Press, 1996, 45–52.

Cabrera, Luis, *Political Theory of Global Justice: A Cosmopolitan Case for the World State*. London: Routledge, 2004.

Caney, Simon, "Self-Government and Secession: the Case of Nations," *Journal of Political Philosophy* 5 (1997): 351–72.

——, "Nationality, Distributive Justice, and the Use of Force," *Journal of Applied Philosophy* 16 (1999): 123–38.

——, "Global Equality of Opportunity and the Sovereignty of States," in Tony Coates (ed.), *International Justice*. Aldershot: Ashgate, 2000, 130–49.

——, "Human Rights, Compatibility and Diverse Cultures," *Critical Review of International Social and Political Philosophy* 3 (2000): 51–76.

——, "Cosmopolitan Justice and Equalizing Opportunities," *Metaphilosophy* 32 (2001): 113–34.

——, "International Distributive Justice," *Political Studies* 49 (2001): 974–97.

——, "Cosmopolitanism and the Law of Peoples," *Journal of Political Philosophy* 10 (2002): 95–123.

——, *Justice beyond Borders: A Global Political Theory*. Oxford: Oxford University Press, 2004.

——, "Global Poverty, Human Rights and Obligations," in Thomas W. Pogge (ed.), *Global Poverty as a Human Rights Violation*. UNESCO, 2004.

——, "Cosmopolitanism, Democracy, and Distributive Justice," *Canadian Journal of Philosophy* (2004).

——, "Cosmopolitan Justice, Responsibility, and Global Climate Change," *Leiden Journal of International Law* 18 (2005): 747–75.

——, and Peter Jones, eds., *Human Rights and Global Diversity*. London: Frank Cass, 2001.

——, David George, and Peter Jones, eds., *National Rights, International Obligations*. Oxford: Westview, 1996.

Carens, Joseph, "The Rights of Immigrants," in J. Baker (ed.), *Group Rights*. Toronto: University of Toronto Press, 1994, pp. 42–63.

——, "The Integration of Immigrants," *Journal of Moral Philosophy* 2 (2005): 29–46.

Carty, Anthony, "Liberal Economic Rhetoric as an Obstacle to the Democratization of the World Economy," *Ethics* 98 (1988): 742–56.

Chandler, David, "New Rights for Old? Cosmopolitan Citizenship and the Critique of State Sovereignty," *Political Studies* 51 (2003): 332–49.

Chatterjee, Deen K., ed., *The Ethics of Assistance: Morality and the Distant Needy*. Cambridge: Cambridge University Press, 2004.

——, and Don Scheid, eds., *Ethics and Foreign Intervention*. Cambridge: Cambridge University Press, 2003.

Christiano, Thomas, "Secession, Democracy, and Distributive Justice," *Arizona Law Review* 37 (1995): 65–72.

Coady, C. A. J., "The Morality of Terrorism," *Philosophy* 60 (1985): 47–69.

——, "Terrorism, Morality, and Supreme Emergency," *Ethics* 114 (2004): 772–89.

Cochran, Molly, *Normative Theory in International Relations*. Cambridge: Cambridge University Press, 1999.

Cohen, G. A., "Where the Action Is: On the Site of Distributive Justice," *Philosophy & Public Affairs* 26 (1997): 3–30.

——, "Facts and Principles," *Philosophy & Public Affairs* 31 (2003): 211–45.

Cohen, Jean L., "Whose Sovereignty? Empire versus International Law," *Ethics & International Affairs* 18 (2004): 1–24.

Cohen, Joshua and Charles Sabel, "*Extra Rempublicam Nulla Justitia?*," *Philosophy & Public Affairs* 34 (2006): 147–75.

Conroy, John, *Unspeakable Acts, Ordinary People: The Dynamics of Torture*. Berkeley: University of California Press, 2000.

Crocker, David and Toby Linden, eds., *The Ethics of Consumption*. New York: Rowman & Littlefield, 1998.

Cruft, Rowan, "Human Rights and Positive Duties," *Ethics & International Affairs* 19 (2005): 29–37.

Dahl, Robert, "Can International Organizations be Democratic? A Skeptic's View," in Ian Shapiro and Casiano Hacker-Cordon (eds.), *Democracy's Edges*. Cambridge: Cambridge University Press, 1999, pp. 19–36.

De Grieff, Pablo and Ciaran Cronin, eds., *Global Justice and Transnational Politics*. Cambridge, MA: MIT Press, 2002.

de-Shalit, Avner, *The Environment: Between Theory and Practice*. Oxford: Oxford University Press, 2000.

Demartino, George, *Global Economy, Global Justice: Theoretical Objections and Policy Alternatives to Neoliberalism*. London: Routledge, 2000.

Dobson, Andrew, *Justice and the Environment*. Oxford: Oxford University Press, 1998.

——, *Green Political Thought*, 3rd edn. London: Routledge, 2000.

——, *Citizenship and the Environment*. Oxford: Oxford University Press, 2003.

Donnelly, Jack, "The Social Construction of International Human Rights," in Tim Dunne and Nicholas J. Wheeler (eds.), *Human Rights in Global Politics*. Cambridge: Cambridge University Press, 1999.

Dower, Nigel, *World Ethics: The New Agenda*. Edinburgh: Edinburgh University Press, 1998.

Doyle, Michael, *Ways of War and Peace: Realism, Liberalism, and Socialism*. Chicago: Chicago University Press, 1997.

Easterly, William, *The Elusive Quest for Growth: Economists' Adventures and Misadventures in the Tropics*. Cambridge: MIT Press, 2001.

Elshtain, Jean-Bethke, "International Justice as Equal Regard and the Use of Force,", *Ethics & International Affairs* 17 (2003): 63–75.

Erskine, Tony, ed., *Can Institutions Have Responsibilities? Collective Moral Agency and International Relations*. Basingstoke: Palgrave, 2004.

Falk, Richard, "Revisioning Cosmopolitanism," in Martha C. Nussbaum, *For Love of Country: Debating the Limits of Patriotism*, ed. Joshua Cohen. Boston, MA: Beacon Press, 1996, pp. 53–60.

Follesdal, Andreas and Thomas W. Pogge, eds., *Real World Justice: Ground, Principles, Human Rights, and Social Institutions*. Dordrecht: Springer, 2005.

Forsythe, David P., *Human Rights in International Relations*. Cambridge: Cambridge University Press, 2000.

Franceschet, Antonio, *Kant and Liberal Internationalism: Sovereignty, Justice, and Reform*. New York: Palgrave, 2002.

Franck, Thomas, "The Emerging Right to Democratic Governance," *American Journal of International Law* 86 (1992): 46–91.

Frost, Mervyn, *Ethics in International Relations*. Cambridge: Cambridge University Press, 1996.

Fuller, Lisa L., "Poverty Relief, Global Institutions, and the Problem of Compliance," *Journal of Moral Philosophy* 2 (2005): 285–97.

Gardiner, Stephen M., "Ethics and Global Climate Change," *Ethics* 114 (2004): 555–600.

Gauthier, David, "Breaking Up: an Essay on Secession," *Canadian Journal of Philosophy* 24 (1994): 357–72.

George, Robert P., ed., *Natural Law Theory: Contemporary Essays*. Oxford: Oxford University Press, 1992.

Glazer, Nathan, "Limits of Loyalty," in Martha C. Nussbaum, *For Love of Country: Debating the Limits of Patriotism*, ed. Joshua Cohen. Boston, MA: Beacon Press, 1996, pp. 61–5.

Goodin, Robert E., "What is so Special about our Fellow Countrymen?" *Ethics* 98 (1988): 663–86.

——, *Green Political Theory*. Cambridge: Polity, 1992.

Gosseries, Axel, "Historical Emissions and Free-Riding," *Ethical Perspectives* 11 (2004): 36–60.

Gould, Carol C., *Globalizing Democracy and Human Rights*. Cambridge: Cambridge University Press, 2004.

Graham, Gordon, *Ethics and International Relations*. Oxford: Blackwell Publishers, 1997.

Green, Michael, "Social Justice, Voluntarism, and Liberal Nationalism," *Journal of Moral Philosophy* 2 (2005): 265–83.

Green, Thomas Hill, *Lectures on the Principles of Political Obligation*, ed. Paul Harris and John Morrow. Cambridge: Cambridge University Press, 1986.

Gross, Michael L., "Fighting by Other Means in the Mideast: a Critical Analysis of Israel's Assassination Policy," *Political Studies* 51 (2003): 350–68.

Gutmann, Amy, "Democratic Citizenship," in Martha C. Nussbaum, *For Love of Country: Debating the Limits of Patriotism*, ed. Joshua Cohen. Boston, MA: Beacon Press, 1996, pp. 66–71.

Habermas, Jürgen, "Kant's Idea of Perpetual Peace, with the Benefit of Two Hundred Years' Hindsight," in James Bohman and Matthias Lutz-Bachmann (eds.), *Perpetual Peace: Essays on Kant's Cosmopolitan Ideal*. Cambridge, MA: MIT Press, 1997, pp. 113–53.

——, *Inclusion of the Other*. Cambridge, MA: MIT Press, 1998.

——, "On Legitimation through Human Rights," in Pablo De Grieff and Ciaran Cronin (eds.), *Global Justice and Transnational Politics*. Cambridge, MA: MIT Press, 2002, pp. 197–234.

Hayward, Tim, *Ecological Thought: An Introduction*. Cambridge: Polity, 1995.

——, *Political Theory and Ecological Values*. Cambridge: Polity, 1998.

——, *Constitutional Environmental Rights*. Oxford: Oxford University Press, 2005.

——, "Thomas Pogge's Global Resources Dividend: a Critique and an Alternative," *Journal of Moral Philosophy* 2 (2005): 317–32.

Heath, Joseph, "Immigration, Multiculturalism and the Social Contract," *Canadian Journal of Law and Jurisprudence* 10 (1997): 343–61.

Hegel, G. W. F., *Elements of the Philosophy of Right*, ed. Allen W. Wood, trans. H. B. Nisbet. Cambridge: Cambridge University Press, 1991.

Held, David, "Cosmopolitan Democracy and the Global Order: a New Agenda," in James Bohman and Matthias Lutz-Bachmann, eds., *Perpetual Peace: Essays on Kant's Cosmopolitan Ideal*. Cambridge, MA: MIT Press, 1996, pp. 235–51.

——, "The Transformation of Political Community," in Ian Shapiro and Casiano Hacker-Cordon (eds.), *Democracy's Edges*. Cambridge: Cambridge University Press, 1999, pp. 84–111.

——, and Matthias Koenig-Archbungi, eds., *Global Governance and Public Accountability*. Oxford: Blackwell Publishing, 2000.

Hellsten, Sirkku, "Global Justice and the Demand for Global Responsibility," *Journal of Moral Philosophy* 2 (2005): 371–9.

Himmelfarb, Gertrude, "The Illusions of Cosmopolitanism," in Martha C. Nussbaum, *For Love of Country: Debating the Limits of Patriotism*, ed. Joshua Cohen. Boston, MA: Beacon Press, 1996, pp. 72–7.

Hobbes, Thomas, *Leviathan*, ed. Richard Tuck. Cambridge: Cambridge University Press, 1996.

Hohfeld, Wesley, *Fundamental Legal Conceptions as Applied in Judicial Reasoning*. New Haven, CT: Yale University Press, 1919.

Holmes, Stephen and Cass Sunstein, *The Costs of Rights*. New York: W. W. Norton, 1999.

Holzgrefe, J. L. and Robert O. Keohane, eds., *Humanitarian Intervention: Ethical, Legal, and Political Dilemmas*. Cambridge: Cambridge University Press, 2003.

Honneth, Axel, "Is Universalism a Moral Trap? The Presuppositions and Limits of a Politics of Human Rights," in James Bohman and Matthias Lutz-Bachmann (eds.), *Perpetual Peace: Essays on Kant's Cosmopolitan Ideal*. Cambridge, MA: MIT Press, 1997, pp. 155–78.

Hurka, Thomas, "Proportionality in the Morality of War," *Philosophy & Public Affairs* (2005): 34–66.

Hurrell, A. and B. Kingsbury, *The International Politics of the Environment*. Oxford: Oxford University Press, 1992.

Ignatieff, Michael, *Human Rights as Politics and Idolatry*, ed. Amy Guttmann. Princeton, NJ: Princeton University Press, 2001.

Jaggar, Alison, "'Saving Amina': Global Justice for Women and Intercultural Dialogue," *Ethics & International Affairs* 19 (2005): 55–75.

James, Aaron, "Constructing Justice for Existing Practice: Rawls and the Status Quo," *Philosophy & Public Affairs* 33 (2005): 281–316.

Jamieson, Dale, "Global Environmental Justice," *Philosophy* (Supplement) 36 (1994): 199–210.

——, "Ethics and Intentional Climate Change," *Climate Change* 33 (1996): 323–36.

——, "Animal Liberation is an Environmental Ethic," *Environmental Values* 7 (1998): 41–57.

——, "Duties to the Distant: Aid, Assistance, and Intervention in the Developing World," *Journal of Ethics* 9 (2005): 151–70.

Jones, Charles, *Global Justice: Defending Cosmopolitanism*. Oxford: Oxford University Press, 2001.

Jones, Peter, "Group Rights and Group Oppression," *Journal of Political Philosophy* 2 (1994): 353–77.

——, "International Human Rights: Philosophical or Political?," in Simon Caney, David George, and Peter Jones (eds.), *National Rights, International Obligations*. Boulder, CO: Westview, 1996, pp. 183–204.

Julius, A. J., "Basic Structure and the Value of Equality," *Philosophy & Public Affairs* 31 (2003): 321–55.

——, "Nagel's Atlas," *Philosophy & Public Affairs* 34 (2006): 176–92.

Kamm, Frances Myrna, "Justifications for Killing Noncombatants," *Midwest Studies in Philosophy* (2000): 219–28.

——, "Rights," in Jules Coleman and Scott Shapiro (eds.), *Oxford Handbook of Jurisprudence and Philosophy of Law*. Oxford: Oxford University Press, 2002, pp. 476–513.

——, "The New Problem of Distance in Morality," in Deen K. Chatterjee (ed.), *The Ethics of Assistance: Morality and the Distant Needy*. Cambridge: Cambridge University Press, 2004, pp. 59–74.

——, "Failures of Just War Theory: Terror, Harm, and Justice," *Ethics* 114 (2004): 650–92.

——, "Terrorism and Several Moral Distinctions," *Legal Theory* 12 (2006): 19–69.

Kant, Immanuel, *Perpetual Peace*, ed. Lewis White Beck. Indianapolis, IN: Bobbs-Merrill, 1957.

——, *Kant: Political Writings*, 2nd edn., ed. Hans Reiss, trans. H. B. Nisbet. Cambridge: Cambridge University Press, 1991.

Kaplinsky, Raphael, *Globalization, Poverty and Inequality: Between a Rock and Hard Place*. Cambridge: Polity, 2005.

Kelly, Erin, "Human Rights as Foreign Policy Imperatives," in Deen K. Chatterjee (ed.), *The Ethics of Assistance: Morality and the Distant Needy*. Cambridge: Cambridge University Press, 2004, pp. 177–92.

Kramer, Matthew, Nigel Simmonds, and Hillel Steiner, *A Debate over Rights*. Oxford: Oxford University Press, 1998.

Kuper, Andrew, "Rawlsian Global Justice: Beyond the Law of Peoples to a Law of Persons," *Political Theory* 28 (2000): 640–74.

——, "More than Charity: Cosmopolitan Alternatives to the 'Singer Solution'," *Ethics & International Affairs* 16 (2002): 107–20.

——, "Facts, Theories, and Hard Choices: Reply to Peter Singer," *Ethics & International Affairs* 16 (2002): 125–6.

——, *Democracy beyond Borders: Justice and Representation in Global Institutions*. Oxford: Oxford University Press, 2004.

——, ed., *Global Responsibilities: Who Must Deliver on Human Rights?* London: Routledge, 2005.

Kutz, Christopher, "Justice in Reparations: the Cost of Memory and the Value of Talk," *Philosophy & Public Affairs* 32 (2004): 277–312.

——, "The Difference Uniforms Make: Collective Violence in Criminal Law and War," *Philosophy & Public Affairs* 33 (2005): 148–80.

Kymlicka, Will, "Citizenship in an Era of Globalization," in Ian Shapiro and Casiano Hacker-Cordon (eds.), *Democracy's Edges*. Cambridge: Cambridge University Press, 1999, pp. 112–26.

Locke, John, *Two Treatises of Government*, ed. Peter Laslett. Cambridge: Cambridge University Press, 1988.

Lomborg, Bjørn, *The Skeptical Environmentalist: Measuring the Real State of the World*. Cambridge: Cambridge University Press, 2001.

Lu, Catherine, "The One and Many Faces of Cosmopolitanism," *Journal of Political Philosophy* 8 (2000): 244–67.

Luban, David, "Just War and Human Rights," *Philosophy & Public Affairs* 9 (1980): 160–81.

——, "The Romance of the Nation-State," *Philosophy & Public Affairs* 9 (1980): 392–403.

——, "Intervention and Civilization: Some Unhappy Lessons of the Kosovo War," in Pablo De Grieff and Ciaran Cronin (eds.), *Global Justice and Transnational Politics*. Cambridge, MA: MIT Press, 2002, pp. 79–115.

——, "Preventive War," *Philosophy & Public Affairs* 32 (2004): 207–48.

Luper-Foy, Stephen, ed., *Problems of International Justice*. Boulder, CO: Westview Press, 1988.

Lutz-Bachmann, Matthias, "Kant's Idea of Peace and the Philosophical Conception of a World Republic," in James Bohman and Matthias Lutz-Bachmann, eds., *Perpetual Peace: Essays on Kant's Cosmopolitan Ideal*. Cambridge, MA: MIT Press, 1997, pp. 59–77.

MacCormick, Neil, *Legal Right and Social Democracy*. Oxford: Oxford University Press, 1982.

Machiavelli, Niccolo, *The Prince*, ed. Daniel Donno. New York: Bantam, 1966.

Mandle, Jon and Gareth Schott, eds., *Global Justice: An Introduction*. Oxford: Blackwell Publishing, 2006.

Maniates, Michael F., "Individualization: Plant a Tree, Buy a Bike, Save the World?," *Global Environmental Politics* 1 (2001): 31–52.

Mapel, David R., "Coerced Moral Agents? Individual Responsibility for Military Service," *Journal of Political Philosophy* 6 (1998): 171–89.

Margalit, Avishai and Joseph Raz, "National Self-Determination," *Journal of Philosophy* 87 (1990): 439–61.

Marshall, Geoffrey, *Parliamentary Sovereignty and the Commonwealth*. Oxford: Oxford University Press, 1957.

Martin, Rex, *A System of Rights*. Oxford: Clarendon Press, 1993.

Mason, Andrew, "Special Obligations to Compatriots," *Ethics* 107 (1997): 427–47.

Mayer, Ann Elizabeth, *Islam and Human Rights: Tradition and Politics*, 2nd edn. Boulder, CO: Westview Press, 1995.

McCarthy, Thomas, "On the Idea of a Reasonable People," in James Bohman and Matthias Lutz-Bachmann, eds., *Perpetual Peace: Essays on Kant's Cosmopolitan Ideal*. Cambridge, MA: MIT Press, 1997, pp. 201–17.

McConnell, Michael W., "Don't Neglect the Little Platoons," in Martha C. Nussbaum, *For Love of Country: Debating the Limits of Patriotism*, ed. Joshua Cohen. Boston, MA: Beacon Press, 1996, pp. 78–84.

McKim, R. and Jeff McMahan, eds., *The Morality of Nationalism*. Oxford: Oxford University Press, 1997.

McMahan, Jeff, "Innocence, Self-Defense, and Killing in War," *Journal of Political Philosophy* 2 (1994): 193–221.

——, "War as Self-Defense," *Ethics and International Affairs* 18 (2004): 75–80.

——, "The Ethics of Killing in War," *Ethics* 114 (2004): 693–733.

——, "Just Cause for War," *Ethics & International Affairs* 19 (2005): 55–75.

——, *The Ethics of Killing: Self-Defense, War, and Punishment*. Oxford: Oxford University Press, forthcoming.

McPherson, Lionel, "Innocence and Responsibility in War," *Canadian Journal of Philosophy*, forthcoming.

Mill, John Stuart, "A Few Words on Non-Intervention," in *Dissertations and Discussions* (1867), vol. III, pp. 153–78; reprinted in J. S. Mill, *Collected Works of John Stuart Mill*, vol. XXI, ed. John M. Robson. Toronto: University of Toronto Press, 1984, pp. 111–24.

Miller, Christopher, *Environmental Rights: Critical Perspectives*. London: Routledge, 1998.

Miller, David, "The Ethical Significance of Nationality," *Ethics* 98 (1988): 647–62.

——, *On Nationality*. Oxford: Oxford University Press, 1995.

——, *Citizenship and National Identity*. Cambridge: Polity, 2000.

——, "Distributing Responsibilities," *Journal of Political Philosophy* 9 (2001): 453–71.

——, "Cosmopolitanism: a Critique," *Critical Review of International Social and Political Philosophy* 5 (2002): 80–5.

——, "National Responsibility and International Justice," in Deen K. Chatterjee (ed.), *The Ethics of Assistance: Morality and the Distant Needy*. Cambridge: Cambridge University Press, 2004, pp. 123–43.

Miller, Richard, "Beneficence, Duty and Distance," *Philosophy & Public Affairs* 32 (2004).

——, "Cosmopolitan Respect and Patriotic Concern," *Philosophy & Public Affairs* 27 (1998): 202–4.

——, "Moral Closeness and World Community," in Deen K. Chatterjee (ed.), *The Ethics of Assistance: Morality and the Distant Needy*. Cambridge: Cambridge University Press, 2004, pp. 101–22.

Morganthau, Henry, *Politics among Nations*. New York: Alfred A. Knopf, 1985.

Murphy, Liam, "Institutions and the Demands of Justice," *Philosophy & Public Affairs* 27 (1998): 251–91.

——, *Moral Demands in Non-ideal Theory* (Oxford: Oxford University Press, 2003).

Nagel, Thomas, "War and Massacre," *Philosophy & Public Affairs* 1 (1972): 123–44.

——, "The Problem of Global Justice," *Philosophy & Public Affairs* 33 (2005): 113–47.

Nardin, Terry, *Law, Morality, and the Relations between States*. Princeton, NJ: Princeton University Press, 1983.

——, and David R. Mapel, eds., *Traditions of International Ethics*. Cambridge: Cambridge University Press, 1993.

Naticchia, Chris, "The Law of Peoples: the Old and the New," *Journal of Moral Philosophy* 2 (2005): 353–69.

Nickel, James, "The Human Right to a Safe Environment: Philosophical Perspectives on its Scope and Justification," *Yale Journal of International Law* 18 (1993): 281–95.

——, *Making Sense of Human Rights*, 2nd edn. Oxford: Blackwell Publishing, 2007.

Niño, Carlos Santiago, *The Ethics of Human Rights*. Oxford: Clarendon Press, 1991.

Norman, Richard, *Ethics, Killing, and War*. Cambridge: Cambridge University Press, 1995.

Norton, Bryan G., "Environmental Ethics and Weak Anthropocentrism," *Environmental Ethics* 6 (1984): 133–48.

——, *Toward Unity among Environmentalists*. Oxford: Oxford University Press, 1991.

Nussbaum, Martha C., "Kant and Cosmopolitanism," in James Bohman and Matthias Lutz-Bachmann, eds., *Perpetual Peace: Essays on Kant's Cosmopolitan Ideal*. Cambridge, MA: MIT Press, 1997, pp. 25–57.

——, "Human Rights Theory: Capability and Human Rights," *Fordham Law Review* 66 (1997): 273–300.

——, "A Plea for Difficulty," in Susan Moller Okin, *Is Multiculturalism Bad for Women?* ed. Joshua Cohen, Matthew Howard, and Martha C. Nussbaum. Princeton, NJ: Princeton University Press, 1999, pp. 105–14.

——, *Sex and Social Justice*. Oxford: Oxford University Press, 2000.

——, *Women and Human Development: The Capabilities Approach*. Cambridge: Cambridge University Press, 2000.

——, et al. *For Love of Country?* Boston, MA: Beacon Press, 2002.

——, "Capabilities and Human Rights," in Pablo De Grieff and Ciaran Cronin (eds.), *Global Justice and Transnational Politics*. Cambridge, MA: MIT Press, 2002, pp. 117–49.

——, "Capabilities as Fundamental Entitlements: Sen and Social Justice," *Feminist Economics* 9 (2003): 33–59.

——, "Women and Theories of Global Justice: Our Need for New Paradigms," in Deen K. Chatterjee (ed.), *The Ethics of Assistance: Morality and the Distant Needy*. Cambridge: Cambridge University Press, 2004, pp.147–76.

——, *Frontiers of Justice: Disability, Nationality, Species Membership*. Cambridge, MA: Belknap/Harvard University Press, 2006.

——, *The Clash Within: Democracy, Religious Violence, and India's Future*. Cambridge, MA: Belknap/Harvard University Press, 2007.

Nussbaum, Martha C. and Amartya Sen, eds., *The Quality of Life*. Oxford: Oxford University Press, 1993.

Okin, Susan Moller, "*Political Liberalism*, Justice, and Gender," *Ethics* 105 (1994): 23–43.

——, "Feminism and Multiculturalism: Some Tensions," *Ethics* 108 (1998): 661–84.

——, *Is Multiculturalism Bad for Women?*, eds. Joshua Cohen, Matthew Howard, and Martha C. Nussbaum. Princeton, NJ: Princeton University Press, 1999.

O'Flynn, Ian, *Deliberative Democracy and Divided Societies*. New York: Palgrave, 2006.

——, "Divided Societies and Deliberative Democracy," *British Journal of Political Science* 37 (2007): 731–51.

O'Neill, Onora, *Faces of Hunger: An Essay on Poverty, Development, and Justice*. London: George Allen & Unwin, 1986.

——, "Ethical Reasoning and Ideological Pluralism," *Ethics* 98 (1988): 705–22.

——, *Bounds of Justice*. Cambridge: Cambridge University Press, 2000.

——, "Global Justice: Whose Obligations?," in Deen K. Chatterjee (ed.), *The Ethics of Assistance: Morality and the Distant Needy*. Cambridge: Cambridge University Press, 2004, pp. 242–59.

Øverland, Gerhard, "Self-defence among Innocent People," *Journal of Moral Philosophy* 2 (2005): 127–46.

——, "Poverty and the Moral Significance of Contribution," *Journal of Moral Philosophy* 2 (2005): 299–315.

Paehlke, Robert C., *Democracy's Dilemma: Environment, Social Equity, and the Global Economy*. Cambridge, MA: MIT Press, 2003.

Paskins, Barrie, "Torture and Philosophy," *Proceedings of the Aristotelian Society, Supplement* 52 (1978): 165–94.

Patten, Alan, "Liberal Neutrality and Language Policy," *Philosophy & Public Affairs* 31 (2003): 356–86.

——, "Should We Stop Thinking about Poverty in Terms of Helping the Poor?," *Ethics & International Affairs* 19 (2005): 19–27.

Perry, Michael, *The Idea of Human Rights*. Oxford: Oxford University Press, 1998.

Philpott, Daniel, "In Defense of Self-Determination," *Ethics* 105 (1995): 352–85.

Pinsky, Robert, "Eros against Esperanto," in Martha C. Nussbaum, *For Love of Country: Debating the Limits of Patriotism*, ed. Joshua Cohen. Boston, MA: Beacon Press, 1996, pp. 85–90.

Pogge, Thomas W., "Liberalism and Global Justice," *Philosophy & Public Affairs* 15 (1986): 67–81.

——, "Rawls and Global Justice," *Canadian Journal of Philosophy* 18 (1988): 227–56.

——, *Realizing Rawls*. Ithaca, NY: Cornell University Press, 1989.

——, "Cosmopolitanism and Sovereignty," *Ethics* 103 (1992): 48–75.

——, "An Institutional Approach to Humanitarian Intervention," *Public Affairs Quarterly* 6 (1992): 89–103.

——, "An Egalitarian Law of Peoples," *Philosophy & Public Affairs* 23 (1994): 195–224.

——, "On the Site of Distributive Justice: Reflections on Cohen and Murphy," *Philosophy & Public Affairs* 29 (2000): 137–69.

——, "Rawls on International Justice," *Philosophical Quarterly* 51 (2001): 246–53.

——, ed., *Global Justice*. Oxford: Blackwell Publishing, 2001.

——, "Priorities of Global Justice," *Metaphilosophy* 32 (2001): 6–24.

——, *World Poverty and Human Rights*. Cambridge: Polity, 2002.

——, "Cosmopolitanism: a Defence," *Critical Review of International Social and Political Philosophy* 5 (2002): 86–91.

——, "Human Rights and Human Responsibilities," in Pablo De Grieff and Ciaran Cronin (eds.), *Global Justice and Transnational Politics*. Cambridge, MA: MIT Press, 2002, pp. 151–95.

——, "'Assisting' the Global Poor," in Deen K. Chatterjee (ed.), *The Ethics of Assistance: Morality and the Distant Needy*. Cambridge: Cambridge University Press, 2004, pp. 260–88.

——, "World Poverty and Human Rights," *Ethics & International Affairs* 19 (2005): 1–7.

——, "Severe Poverty as a Violation of Negative Duties," *Ethics & International Affairs* 19 (2005): 55–83.

Porter, Gareth, Janet Welsh Brown, and Pamela S. Chasek, eds., *Global Environmental Politics*. Boulder, CO: Westview Press, 2000.

Putnam, Hilary, "Must We Choose Between Patriotism and Universal Reason?," in Martha C. Nussbaum, *For Love of Country: Debating the Limits of Patriotism*, ed. Joshua Cohen. Boston, MA: Beacon Press, 1996, 91–7.

Ramsbotham, Oliver, Tom Woodhouse, and Hugh Miall, *Contemporary Conflict Resolution*, 2nd edn. Cambridge: Polity, 2005.

Ratner, Steven R., "Is International Law Impartial?," *Legal Theory* 11 (2005): 39–74.

Rawls, John, *A Theory of Justice*. Cambridge, MA: Harvard University Press, 1971.

——, *The Law of Peoples*. Cambridge, MA: Harvard University Press, 1999.

Raz, Joseph, *The Morality of Freedom*. Oxford: Oxford University Press, 1986.

Reidy, David A., "Rawls on International Justice: a Defense," *Political Theory* 32 (2004): 291–319.

Ripstein, Arthur, "Beyond the Harm Principle," *Philosophy & Public Affairs* 34 (2006): 215–45.

Risse, Mathias, "How Do We Harm the Global Poor?," *Philosophy & Public Affairs* 33 (2005): 349–76.

——, "Do We Owe the Global Poor Assistance or Rectification?," *Ethics & International Affairs* 19 (2005): 9–18.

——, "What We Owe to the Global Poor," *Journal of Ethics* 9 (2005): 81–117.

Rodin, David, *War and Self-Defense*. Oxford: Clarendon Press, 2002.

——, "Terrorism without Intention," *Ethics* 114 (2004): 752–71.

Sangiovanni, Andrea, "Global Justice, Reciprocity, and the State," *Philosophy & Public Affairs* 35 (2007): 3–39.

Satz, Debra, "What Do We Owe the Global Poor?," *Ethics & International Affairs* 19 (2005): 47–54.

Scanlon, T. M., "Human Rights as a Neutral Concern," in Peter G. Brown and Douglas MacLean (eds.), *Human Rights and US Foreign Policy*. Lexington, MA: Lexington Books, 1979, 83–92.

——, *What We Owe to Each Other*. Cambridge, MA: Harvard University Press, 1998.

——, *The Difficulty of Tolerance: Essays in Political Philosophy*. Cambridge: Cambridge University Press, 2003.

Scarry, Elaine, "The Difficulty of Imaging Other People," in Martha C. Nussbaum, *For Love of Country: Debating the Limits of Patriotism*, ed. Joshua Cohen. Boston, MA: Beacon Press, 1996, 98–110.

Scheffler, Samuel, *Boundaries and Allegiances: Problems of Justice and Responsibility in Liberal Thought*. Oxford: Oxford University Press, 2001.

Sen, Amartya, "Utilitarianism and Welfarism," *Journal of Philosophy* 76 (1979): 463–89.

——, "Rights and Agency," *Philosophy & Public Affairs* 11 (1982): 3–39.

——, "Property and Hunger," *Economics and Philosophy* 4 (1988): 57–68.

——, "Justice: Means versus Freedoms," *Philosophy & Public Affairs* 19 (1990): 111–21.

——, "Humanity and Citizenship," in Martha C. Nussbaum, *For Love of Country: Debating the Limits of Patriotism*, ed. Joshua Cohen. Boston, MA: Beacon Press, 1996, pp. 111–18.

——, *On Economic Inequality*. New York: Clarendon Press, 1997.

——, *Development as Freedom*. New York: Alfred A. Knopf, 1999.

——, "Justice across Borders," in Pablo De Grieff and Ciaran Cronin (eds.), *Global Justice and Transnational Politics*. Cambridge, MA: MIT Press, 2002, pp. 37–51.

——, "Elements of a Theory of Human Rights," *Philosophy & Public Affairs* 32 (2004): 315–56.

——, "Reason, Freedom, and Well-Being," *Utilitas* 18 (2006): 80–96.

Shapiro, Ian and L. Brilmayer, eds., *NOMOS XLI: Global Justice*. New York: New York University Press, 1999.

Sher, George, "Transgenerational Compensation," *Philosophy & Public Affairs* 33 (2005): 181–200.

Shue, Henry, "Torture," *Philosophy & Public Affairs* 7 (1978): 124–43.

——, "Mediating Duties," 98 (1988): 687–704.

——, *Basic Rights: Subsistence, Affluence, and US Foreign Policy*, 2nd edn. Princeton, NJ: Princeton University Press, 1996.

——, "Subsistence Emissions and Luxury Emissions," *Law & Policy* 15 (1993): 39–59.

——, "Thickening Convergence: Human Rights and Cultural Diversity," in Deen K. Chatterjee (ed.), *The Ethics of Assistance: Morality and the Distant Needy*. Cambridge: Cambridge University Press, 2004, pp. 217–41.

Shute, Stephen and Susan Hurley, eds., *On Human Rights: The Oxford Amnesty Lectures 1993*. New York: Basic Books, 1993.

Simon, Robert L., "Justice and the Authority of States," *Monist* 66 (1983): 557–72.

Singer, Peter, "Famine, Affluence, and Morality," *Philosophy & Public Affairs* 1 (1972): 229–43.

——, "Poverty, Facts, and Political Philosophies: Response to 'More than Charity,'" *Ethics & International Affairs* 16 (2002): 121–24.

——, "Achieving the Best Outcome," *Ethics & International Affairs* 16 (2002): 127–8.

——, *One World: The Ethics of Globalization*, 2nd edn. New Haven, CT: Yale University Press, [2002] 2004.

——, "Outsiders: Our Obligations to Those Beyond Our Borders," in Deen K. Chatterjee (ed.), *The Ethics of Assistance: Morality and the Distant Needy*. Cambridge: Cambridge University Press, 2004, pp. 11–32.

Slaughter, Anne-Marie, *A New World Order*. Princeton, NJ: Princeton University Press, 2004.

Smilansky, Saul, "Terrorism, Justification, and Illusion," *Ethics* 114 (2004): 790–805.

Statman, Daniel, "The Morality of Assassination: a Response to Gross," *Political Studies* 51 (2003): 775–9.

——, "Supreme Emergencies Revisited," *Ethics* 117 (2006): 58–79.

Sterba, James P., ed., *Terrorism and International Justice*. Oxford: Oxford University Press, 2003.

Stiglitz, Joseph, *Globalization and Its Discontents*. New York: W. W. Norton, 2002.

Sumner, L. W., *The Moral Foundations of Rights*. Oxford: Oxford University Press, 1987.

Sunstein, Cass R., "Constitutionalism and Secession," *University of Chicago Law Review* 58 (1991): 633–70.

Sussman, David, "What's Wrong with Torture?," *Philosophy & Public Affairs* 33 (2005): 1–33.

Tamir, Yael, *Liberal Nationalism*. Princeton, NJ: Princeton University Press, 1993.

Tan, Kok-Chor, "Liberal Toleration in Rawls's Law of Peoples," *Ethics* 108 (1998): 276–95.

——, *Toleration, Diversity, and Global Justice*. College Park, PA: Penn State University Press, 2000.

——, "Patriotic Obligations," *Monist* 86 (2003): 434–53.

——, *Justice without Borders: Cosmopolitanism, Nationalism and Patriotism*. Cambridge: Cambridge University Press, 2004.

Taylor, Charles, "Why Democracy Needs Patriotism," in Martha C. Nussbaum, *For Love of Country: Debating the Limits of Patriotism*, ed. Joshua Cohen. Boston, MA: Beacon Press, 1996, pp.119–21.

Thomson, Dennis, "Democratic Theory and Global Society," *Journal of Political Philosophy* 7 (1999): 111–25.

Tideman, Nicholas, "Secession as a Human Right," *Journal of Moral Philosophy* 1 (2004): 9–19.

Tobin, James, *Essays in Economics: Theory and Policy*. Cambridge, MA: MIT Press, 1982.

Tuck, Richard, *Natural Rights Theories*. Cambridge: Cambridge University Press, 1976.

——, *The Rights of War and Peace*. Oxford: Oxford University Press, 1999.

Unger, Peter, *Living and Letting Die*. Oxford: Oxford University Press, 1996.

United Nations, *Universal Declaration of Human Rights* (1948).

——, *Declaration of Principles concerning Friendly Relations and Co-operation among States in accordance with the Charter of the United Nations* (1970).

Van den Anker, Christien, *Distributive Justice in a Global Era*. Basingstoke: Palgrave Macmillan, 2005.

Van Gunsteren, Herman R., "Admission to Citizenship," *Ethics* 98 (1988): 731–41.

Vincent, R. J., *Nonintervention and International Order*. Princeton, NJ: Princeton University Press, 1974.

——, *Human Rights and International Relations*. Cambridge: Cambridge University Press, 1986.

Waldron, Jeremy, *Liberal Rights: Collected Papers, 1981–1991*. Cambridge: Cambridge University Press, 1993.

Wall, Steven, "Collective Rights and Individual Autonomy," *Ethics* 117 (2007): 234–64.

Wallerstein, Immanuel, "Neither Patriotism nor Cosmopolitanism," in Martha C. Nussbaum, *For Love of Country: Debating the Limits of Patriotism*, ed. Joshua Cohen. Boston, MA: Beacon Press, 1996, pp. 122–4.

Walz, Kenneth, *Man, the State, and War*. New York: Columbia University Press, [1959] 2001.

Walzer, Michael, "Political Action: the Problem of Dirty Hands," *Philosophy & Public Affairs* 2 (1973): 160–80.

——, "The Moral Standing of States: a Response to Four Critics," *Philosophy & Public Affairs* (1980): 209–29.

——, *Spheres of Justice*. New York: Basic Books, 1983.

——, "The New Tribalism," *Dissent* 39 (1992): 165–9.

——, *Thick and Thin: Moral Argument at Home and Abroad*. Notre Dame: University of Notre Dame Press, 1994.

——, "Spheres of Affection," in Martha C. Nussbaum, *For Love of Country: Debating the Limits of Patriotism*, ed. Joshua Cohen. Boston, MA: Beacon Press, 1996, pp. 125–7.

——, *Just and Unjust Wars*, 3rd edn. New York: Basic Books, [1977] 2000.

——, *Arguing about War*. New Haven, CT: Yale University Press, 2004.

Wapner, Paul and John Willoughby, "The Irony of Environmentalism: the Ecological Futility but Political Necessity of Lifestyle Change," *Ethics & International Affairs* 19 (2005): 77–89.

Wellman, Carl, *A Theory of Rights*. Totowa, NJ: Rowman & Littlefield, 1985.

——, *Real Rights*. Oxford: Oxford University Press, 1995.

——, *An Approach to Rights*. Dordrecht: Kluwer, 1997.

Wellman, Christopher, "A Defense of Secession and Political Self-Determination," *Philosophy & Public Affairs* 24 (1995): 357–72.

Wenar, Leif, "Contractualism and Global Economic Justice," *Metaphilosophy* 32 (2001): 79–94.

——, "The Legitimacy of Peoples," in Pablo De Grieff and Ciaran Cronin (eds.), *Global Politics and Transnational Justice*. Cambridge, MA: MIT Press, 2002, pp. 53–76.

——, "What We Owe to Distant Others," *Politics, Philosophy & Economics* 2 (2003): 283–304.

——, "The Unity of Rawls's Work," *Journal of Moral Philosophy* 1 (2004): 265–75.

——, "The Nature of Rights," *Philosophy & Public Affairs* 33 (2005): 223–52.

——, "Reparations for the Future," *Journal of Social Philosophy* 37 (2006): 396–405.

——, *The Philosophy of Rights*. Oxford: Oxford University Press, forthcoming.

Wendt, Alexander, "Anarchy is What States Make of It: The Social Construction of Power Politics," *International Organization* 46 (1992): 391–425.

Williams, Andrew, "Incentives, Inequality, and Publicity," *Philosophy & Public Affairs* 27 (1998): 225–47.

Zohar, Noam, "Collective War and Individualistic Ethics: Against the Conscription of 'Self-Defense,'" *Political Theory* 21 (1993): 606–22.

Index

Page number in **bold** indicate chapters written by indexed authors.